A COMPANION
TO GREEK LITERATURE

BLACKWELL COMPANIONS TO THE ANCIENT WORLD

This series provides sophisticated and authoritative overviews of periods of ancient history, genres of classical literature, and the most important themes in ancient culture. Each volume comprises approximately twenty-five and forty concise essays written by individual scholars within their area of specialization. The essays are written in a clear, provocative, and lively manner, designed for an international audience of scholars, students, and general readers.

A COMPANION TO GREEK LITERATURE

Edited by

Martin Hose and David Schenker

WILEY Blackwell

Registered Office
John Wiley & Sons, Inc., 111 River Street, Hoboken, NJ 07030, USA

Editorial Office
111 River Street, Hoboken, NJ 07030, USA

For details of our global editorial offices, customer services, and more information about Wiley products visit us at www.wiley.com.

Wiley also publishes its books in a variety of electronic formats and by print-on-demand. Some content that appears in standard print versions of this book may not be available in other formats.

Library of Congress Cataloging-in-Publication Data

A companion to Greek literature / edited by Martin Hose and David Schenker.
     pages   cm – (Blackwell companions to the ancient world)
  Includes bibliographical references and index.
  ISBN 978-1-4443-3942-0 (cloth) 978-1-119-08861-5 (Paperback)
1. Greek literature–History and criticism.   I. Hose, Martin.   II. Schenker, David J.
III. Series: Blackwell companions to the ancient world.
  PA3054.C66 2015
  880.9′001–dc23

                                          2015021582

A catalogue record for this book is available from the British Library.

Cover Design: Wiley
Cover Image: The playwright Menander, detail of fresco from the House of Menander, Pompeii.
© akg-images/De Agostini Picture Library

Set in 9.5/11.5pt Galliard by SPi Global, Pondicherry, India

Printed and bound in Singapore by Markono Print Media Pte Ltd

10 9 8 7 6 5 4 3 2 1

Contents

List of Illustrations

Notes on Contributors

Richard H. Armstrong is Associate Professor of Classical Studies in the Honors College and Department of Modern & Classical Language at the University of Houston. His main interests are in the reception of ancient Greek and Roman literature and translation studies. Besides many book chapters and articles, he is author of *A Compulsion for Antiquity: Freud and the Ancient World* (Cornell University Press, 2005) and *Theory and Theatricality: Classical Drama in the Age of Grand Hysteria* (forthcoming, Oxford University Press).

Markus Asper is Professor of Classics at Humboldt-University at Berlin. He has published on Hellenistic poetry, esp. Callimachus, and ancient Greek literature of science. Among his recent publications are "The Two Cultures of Greek Mathematics" (2009), "Dimensions of Power: Callimachean 'Geopoetics' and the Ptolemaic Empire" (2011) and an edited collection of essays on ancient science writing (*Writing Science. Mathematical and Medical Authorship in Ancient Greece. Science, Technology and Medicine in Ancient Cultures 1*, Berlin 2013).

Nicholas Baechle is Professor of Classical Studies at Hanover College. The focus of his research has been the art language of Greek tragedy. He is the author of *Metrical Constraint and the Interpretation of Style in the Tragic Trimeter* (Lexington Books, 2007). His current area of interest is the evolution and reception of Euripides' poetic style.

Manuel Baumbach is Professor of Classics at the Ruhr-University Bochum. His research focuses on Hellenistic Poetry, the Second Sophistic, the Greek novel and the history of reception. He has published and co-edited books on Lucian, Quintus Smyrnaeus, Posidippus, *Archaic and Classical Greek Epigram* (2010), and *Greek and Latin Epyllion and its Reception* (2012).

Lucio Del Corso is lecturer at the Università di Cassino (Italy), where he teaches papyrology. He has joined several archaeological missions as papyrologist and epigraphist (Tebtynis, Leptis Magna, Antinoupolis). His research topics are Greek papyri and inscriptions, ancient school, and reading and writing practices in the Greek world. He is the author of *La lettura nel mondo ellenistico* (Laterza 2005).

Markus Dubischar is Associate Professor of Classics at Lafayette College; he is the author *of Die Agonszenen bei Euripides: Untersuchungen zu ausgewählten Dramen* (2001), *Auxiliartexte: Studien zur Praxis und Theorie einer Textfunktion im antiken literarischen Feld* (Habilitation, LMU Munich, 2007), and other publications on Greek tragedy and ancient auxiliary texts.

Daniela Dueck is Associate professor at Bar Ilan University in the departments of Classical Studies and History. She is the author of various articles and of *Strabo of Amasia: A Greek Man of Letters in Augustan Rome* (2000); co-editor of *Strabo's Cultural Geography: The Making of a Kolossourgia* (2005); and author of *Geography in Classical Antiquity* (2012). She now runs a research project on geographical fragments preserved in Strabo.

Mike Edwards is Professor of Classics at the University of Roehampton, London. He was formerly Director of the Institute of Classical Studies, University of London. He has published widely on the Attic orators, with commentaries on Antiphon, Andocides and Lysias, as well as a translation of the speeches of Isaeus for the Texas University Press series. He is currently working on an Oxford Classical Text of Isaeus and a commentary on Aeschines, Against Ctesiphon.

Thorsten Fögen is Reader (Associate Professor) at Durham University (UK) and Privatdozent at Humboldt University of Berlin. He is the author of "*Patrii sermonis egestas*": *Einstellungen lateinischer Autoren zu ihrer Muttersprache* (2000) and of *Wissen, Kommunikation und Selbstdarstellung: Zur Struktur und Charakteristik römischer Fachtexte der frühen Kaiserzeit* (2009). He has edited seven volumes, most recently *Tears in the Graeco-Roman World* (Berlin & New York 2009) and *Bodies and Boundaries in Graeco-Roman Antiquity* (Berlin & New York 2009).

Edith Hall is Professor in the Classics Department and Centre for Hellenic Studies at King's College London. She is also co-founder and Consultant Director of the Archive of Performances of Greek and Roman Drama at Oxford University. Her most recent book is *Introducing the Ancient Greeks: From Bronze Age Seafarers to Navigators of the Western Mind* (2014). She is the recipient of the 2015 Erasmus Medal, awarded by the Academy of Europe for an outstanding contribution to international scholarship.

Regina Höschele is Associate Professor at the University of Toronto. Her research focuses on Hellenistic poetry, Greek Imperial literature and ancient erotica; recent publications include two monographs on epigram (*Verrückt nach Frauen: Der Epigrammatiker Rufin* and *Die blütenlesende Muse: Poetik und Textualität antiker Epigrammsammlungen*).

Martin Hose is Professor of Greek Literature at Ludwig-Maximilians-University, Munich, and fellow of the Bavarian Academy. He has published books on Euripides, Greek historiography, Aristotle's fragments, and Synesius.

Jason König is Senior Lecturer in Greek at the University of St Andrews. He works broadly on the Greek literature and culture of the Roman Empire. He is author of *Athletics and Literature in the Roman Empire* (2005) and *Saints and Symposiasts: The Literature of Food and the Symposium in Greco-Roman and Early Christian Culture* (2012), and editor, jointly with Tim Whitmarsh, of *Ordering Knowledge in the Roman Empire* (2007).

David Konstan is Professor of Classics at New York University and Professor Emeritus of Classics and Comparative Literature at Brown University. Among his publications are *Roman Comedy* (1983); *Sexual Symmetry: Love in the Ancient Novel and Related Genres* (1994); *Greek Comedy and Ideology* (1995); *Friendship in the Classical World* (1997); *Pity Transformed* (2001); *The Emotions of the Ancient Greeks: Studies in Aristotle and Classical Literature* (2006); "*A Life Worthy of the Gods*": *The Materialist Psychology of Epicurus* (2008); and *Before Forgiveness: The Origins of a Moral Idea* (2010). He was president of the American Philological Association in 1999, and is a fellow of the American Academy of Arts and Sciences and honorary fellow of the Australian Academy of the Humanities.

Mary Lefkowitz, Andrew W. Mellon Professor in the Humanities, Emerita at Wellesley College is the author of the *Lives of the Greek Poets* (1981, revised edition 2012) and other works about myth and history in ancient Greece.

James McGlew is Professor of Classics at Rutgers New Brunswick. His primary interest is Greek political culture in the Archaic and Classical eras. Author of *Tyranny and Political Culture in Ancient Greece* (1993) and *Citizens on Stage: Comedy and Political Culture in the Athenian Democracy* (2002), he is presently working on equality in democratic Athens.

Anatole Mori is Associate Professor of Classics at the University of Missouri, Columbia. She is the author of *The Politics of Apollonius Rhodius' Argonautica.* Her research interests include Hellenistic literary culture and the construction of gender and genre in Greek poetry.

René Nünlist is Professor of Classics at the University of Cologne and a co-founder of the Basel commentary on the Iliad (2000–). His most recent book is *The Ancient Critic at Work: Terms and Concepts of Literary Criticism in Greek Scholia* (2009, paperback 2011).

Timothy Power is Associate Professor of Classics at Rutgers University, New Brunswick. He is author of *The Culture of Kitharôidia* and is currently writing a book on sound in early Greek literature and society.

Richard Rader is a Visiting Assistant Professor in the department of Classics at the *University of California, Santa Barbara.* He has published a handful of articles on Aeschylus and Greek tragedy and is currently at work on two main projects: a monograph on existential theology in the plays of Aeschylus and a special edition of *Ramus: Critical Studies in Greek and Roman Literature* on new approaches to Greek drama (co-edited with James Collins).

Steve Reece is Professor of Classics at Saint Olaf College in Northfield, Minnesota. He has published a wide variety of articles and book chapters on Homeric studies, New Testament studies, comparative oral traditions, and historical linguistics. He is the author of a book about the rituals of ancient Greek hospitality titled *The Stranger's Welcome* (University of Michigan Press, 1993) and of a

book on early Greek etymology titled *Homer's Winged Words* (E.J. Brill Press, 2009).

Hanna M. Roisman is Arnold Bernhard Professor in Arts and Humanities at Colby College, Maine. In addition to articles and book chapters, she has published, *Loyalty in Early Greek Epic and Tragedy (1984), Nothing Is As It Seems: The Tragedy of the Implicit in Euripides'* Hippolytus (1999), *Sophocles:* Philoctetes (2005), and Sophocles: *Electra* (2008). She is the Editor of the *Encyclopedia of Greek Tragedy* (2014), and co-author of *The Odyssey Re-Formed* (1996), *Euripides:* Alcestis (2003), and Euripides: *Electra* (2010).

Suzanne Saïd is emerita Professor of Classics at Paris X and Columbia University. She has published extensively on Greek literature and reception of antiquity. Her recent books include *Approches de la mythologie grecque* (2008), *Homer and the Odyssey* (2011), and *Le Monde à l'envers: Pouvoir féminin et communauté des femmes en Grèce ancienne* (2013).

David Schenker is Associate Professor of Classical Studies at the University of Missouri. Publications include articles on Aeschylus, Euripides, and Plato.

Jan Stenger is MacDowell Professor of Greek at the University of Glasgow. He is the author of *Poetische Argumentation: Die Funktion der Gnomik in den Epinikien des Bakchylides* (2004) and *Hellenische Identität in der Spätantike* (2009). He is currently working on a monograph about the image of the city in John Chrysostom and on a project on education in late antique Gaza.

Stefan Tilg is Professor of Latin at University of Freiburg, Germany. His main research topics have been Neo-Latin drama and the ancient novel. He is the author of *Chariton of Aphrodisias and the Invention of the Greek Love Novel* (Oxford University Press 2010) and of *Apuleius'* Metamorphoses: *A Study in Roman Fiction* (Oxford University Press 2014).

Antonis Tsakmakis is Associate Professor of Greek at the University of Cyprus. His research topics include Greek Historiography, Ancient

Comedy, the Sophists, Greek Stylistics, the teaching of Greek in Secondary Education. He is author of *Thukydides über die Vergangenheit* (1995), and Co-editor of *Brill's Companion to Thucydides* (2006) and *Thucydides Between History and Literature* (2012).

James Bradley Wells is a poet and classicist who teaches at DePauw University in Greencastle, IN. He is the author of *Pindar's Verbal Art* (2009), a poetry collection, *Bicycle* (2013), and a forthcoming translation of Pindar's victory songs.

Andreas Willi holds the Diebold Chair in Comparative Philology at the University of Oxford. His research focuses on the language/ literature interface in the ancient world, Ancient Greek dialectology and sociolinguistics, and Greek, Latin, and Indo-European historical-comparative grammar; book publications include *The Languages of Aristophanes* (Oxford 2003) and *Sikelismos: Sprache,*

Literatur und Gesellschaft im griechischen Sizilien (Basel 2008).

Emily Wilson is Associate Professor and Graduate Chair in the Department of Classics at the University of Pennsylvania. She has a BA in classics and an M. Phil. in English from Oxford, and did her Ph.D. in Classics and Comparative Literature at Yale. Her publications include *Mocked with Death* (2004), *The Death of Socrates* (2007) and *Six Tragedies of Seneca* (2010), and a forthcoming biography of Seneca.

Victoria Wohl is Professor of Classics at the University of Toronto. She is the author of *Intimate Commerce: Exchange, Gender, and Subjectivity in Greek Tragedy* (Texas University Press, 1998), *Love Among the Ruins: The Erotics of Democracy in Classical Athens* (Princeton University Press, 2003), and *Law's Cosmos: Juridical Discourse in Athenian Forensic Oratory* (Cambridge University Press, 2010).

Abbreviations

1. Abbreviations of Technical Terms and Modern Reference Works & Editions

CEG	Hansen, P.A., ed. 1983–89. *Carmina epigraphica Graeca*, 2 vols. Berlin, New York.
cent.	century
CMG	Acad. Berolinensis, Haunensis, Lipsiensis, eds. 1908 – . *Corpus Medicorum Graecorum*. Berlin.
DK	Diels H., W. Kranz, eds. 1952. *Die Fragmente der Vorsokratiker*. 3 vols. 9th edn. Berlin.
Edelstein–Kidd	Edelstein, L., I. G. Kidd, edd. 1972. *Posidonius. I. The Fragments*. Cambridge.
Erbse	Erbse, H. ed. 1969–1989. *Scholia Graeca in Iliadem (Scholia vetera)*. 7 vols. Berlin.
F	fragmentum/fragment
FGE	Page, D. L. ed. 1981. *Further Greek Epigramms*. Cambridge.
FGrHist	Jacoby, F., ed. 1923–58. *Die Fragmente der griechischen Historiker*. 3 parts with 15 vols. Berlin and Leiden.
GGM	Muller, C., ed. 1855–61. *Geographi Graeci Minores*. 3 vols. Paris.
G-P	Gow, A S.F., D. L. Page, eds. 1965. *The Greek Anthology: Hellenistic Epigrams*. 2 vols. Cambridge.
IEG	West, M.L., ed. 1989–1992. *Iambi et Elegi Graeci ante Alexandrum cantati*. 2 vols. 2nd. edn. Oxford.
IG	Inscriptiones Graecae
KRS	Kirk, G. S., J. E. Raven, M. Schofield, eds. 1982. *The Presocratic Philosophers*. 2nd. edn. Cambridge.
LSJ	Liddell, H. G, R. Scott, eds. 1996. *A Greek–English Lexicon*. Rev. and augm. by H. S. Jones. 9th edn., with a revised supplement. Oxford.
or.	oratio/speech
Paroem. Gr.	Leutsch, E.v., F. G. Schneidewin, eds. 1839–51. *Corpus Paroemiographorum Graecorum*. 2 vols. Göttingen.

PCG	Kassel, R., C. Austin, eds. 1983– . *Poetae Comici Graeci.* Berlin, New York.
Pf	Pfeiffer, R., ed. 1949–52. *Callimachus.* 2 vols. Oxford.
PMG	Page, D., ed. 1962. *Poetae Melici Graeci.* Oxford.
PMGF	Davies. M., ed. 1991. *Poetarum Melicorum Graecorum Fragmenta.* Vol. I. Oxford.
RAC	*Reallexikon für Antike und Christentum.* ed. Th. Klauser et al. Stuttgart 1950–.
RE	*Paulys Realencyclopädie der classischen Altertumswissenschaft.* ed. G. Wissowa, W. Kroll, K. Mittelhaus, K. Ziegler. Stuttgart 1893–1978.
Rose	Rose, V., collegit. 1886. *Aristotelis qui ferebantur librorum fragmenta.* Leipzig.
Σ	Scholion (to)
SH	Lloyd-Jones, H., P. Parsons, eds. 1983. *Supplementum Hellenisticum.* Berlin – New York.
SLG	Page, D., ed. 1974. *Supplementum Lyricis Graecis.* Oxford.
SSR	Giannantoni, G. ed. 1990. *Socratis et Socraticorum Reliquiae.* 4 vols. Naples.
SVF	Ab Arnim, H. ed. 1905–1924. *Stoicorum Veterum Fragmenta.* 4 vols. Leipzig.
T	testimonium/testimony
TrGF	Snell, B. ed. 1986. *Tragicorum Graecorum Fragmenta. Vol. 1. Didascaliae Tragicae. Catalogi Tragicorum et Tragoediarum. Testimonia et Fragmenta Tragicorum Minorum.* 2nd. ed.; Kannicht, R., ed. 1981. *Tragicorum Graecorum Fragmenta. Vol. 2. Fragmenta Adespota.*; Radt, St., ed. 1985. *Tragicorum Graecorum Fragmenta. Vol. 3. Aeschylus.*; Radt. St., ed. 1999. *Tragicorum Graecorum Fragmenta. Vol. 4. Sophocles.* 2nd. ed.; Kannicht, R., ed. 2004. *Tragicorum Graecorum Fragmenta. Vol. 5.1 and Vol. 5.2. Euripides.* Göttingen.
Us.	Usener, H., ed. 1887. *Epicurea.* Leipzig.
V	Voigt, E.-M., ed. 1971. *Sappho et Alcaeus.* Amsterdam.
Walz	Walz, Christian, ed. 1832–36. *Rhetores Graeci.* 9 vols. Stuttgart – Tübingen.
Wehrli	Wehrli, Fritz, ed. & com. 1967–78. *Die Schule des Aristoteles.* 10 Hefte & 2 suppl. 2nd. ed. Basel – Stuttgart.

2.   Abbreviations of Ancient Authors and Works

Aelian
   Tact.   *Tactica*
   Var. Hist.   *Varia historia/Historical miscellany*
Aen. Tact.   Aeneas Tacticus
Aesch.   Aeschylus
   Ag.   *Agamemnon*
   Eum.   *Eumenides*
Alc.   Alcaeus
   Anth. Pal.   *Anthologia Palatina*
Apollonius Citensis
  (Apollonius of Citium)
   De art.   *In Hippocratis De articulis commentarius*
Apoll. Rhod.   Apollonius Rhodius
   Argon.   *Argonautica*
Aratus
   Phaen.   *Phaenomena*
Archil.   Archilochus
Arist.   Aristoteles
   Ath. Pol.   *Athenaion Politeia/Constitution of Athens*
   Gen. an.   *De generatione animalium/*

Gen. corr.	De generatione et corruptione
Hist. an.	Historia animalium
Meteor.	Meteorologica
NE	Ethica Nicomachea
Part. an.	De partibus animalium/
Phys.	Physica/Physics
Poet.	Ars poetica
Pol.	Politica
Rhet.	Rhetorica
Aristid.	Aelius Aristides
Aristoph.	Aristophanes
Ach.	Acharnienses
Av.	Aves/Birds
Eccl.	Ecclesiazusae/Women at the assembly
Equ.	Equites/Knights
Nub.	Nubes/Clouds
Ran.	Ranae/Frogs
Thesm.	Thesmophoriazusae
Vesp.	Vespae/Wasps
Arr.	Arrianus
Epict.	Epicteti dissertationes
Tact.	Tactica
Athen.	Athenaeus
Augustinus	
Con.	Confessiones
Boethius	
De inst. mus.	De institutione musica
Cic.	Cicero
Acad. pr.	
Arch.	Pro Archia poeta
De div.	De divinatione
De fin.	De finibus bonorum et malorum
De nat. deor.	De natura deorum
De off.	De officiis
Inv.	De inventione
Rhet. Her.	(incerti auctoris) Rhetorica ad Herennium
Clem. Al.	Clemens Alexandrinus
Strom.	Stromateis
Demosthenes	
In Phil. I	In Philippum oratio prima (or. 4)
Lept.	Adversus Leptinem (or. 20)
Pro Phorm.	Pro Phormione (or. 36)
Diod. Sic.	Diodorus Siculus
Bibl.	Bibliotheke
Diog. Laer.	Diogenes Laertius
Dion. Hal.	Dionysius Halicarnasseus/Dionysius of Halikarnassos
Ant.	Antiquitates Romanae
De comp. verb.	De compositione verborum
De im.	De imitatione/On imitation

De Thuc.	*De Thucydide*
De vet. orat.	*De oratoribus veteribus*
Pomp. Gem.	*epistula ad Pompeium Geminum*
Eur.	Euripides
Ba.	*Bacchae*
El.	*Electra*
Hcld.	*Heraclidae*
Hipp.	*Hippolytus*
Iph. Aul.	*Iphigenia Aulidensis/Iphigeneia in Aulis*
Med.	*Medea*
Or.	*Orestes*
Suppl.	*Supplices/Hiketides/Suppliant women*
Tro.	*Troades/Trojan women*
Euseb.	Eusebius
Hist. eccl.	*Historia ecclesiastica/Church history*
Gal.	Galen
Ad Thras.	*Ad Thrasybulum liber*
Ars med.	*Ars medica*
Com. Hipp. Ep. III	*In Hippocratis Epidemiarum librum III commentaria III*
De indol.	*De indolentia /*
De puls. diff.	*De pulsuum differentiis libri IV*
In Hipp. Epid. VI comment.	*In Hippocratis Epidemiarum librum sextum commentaria*
Lib. prop.	*De libris propriis*
Hdt.	Herodotus
Heron	
Belop.	*Belopoeica*
Hesiod	
Op.	*Opera et dies/Works and days*
Theog.	*Theogonia/Theogony*
Hippocrates	
De aere	*De aere aquis et locis/Peri aeron hydaton topon/ Airs Waters Places*
De vet. med.	*De vetere medicina/Ancient medicine*
Morb. sacr.	*De morbo sacro*
Homer	
Il.	*Iliad*
Od.	*Odyssey*
Hor.	Horatius
Sat.	*Sermones/Satires*
Ars	*Ars poetica*
Hyginus	
Fab.	*Fabula*
Isid.	Isidorus
Etym.	*Etymologiae*
Isocrates	
Hel.	*Helena*
Pan.	*Panegyricus*
Phil.	*Philippus*

Iustinus
  1. Apol.   *Apologia prima/first apology*
Johannes Lydus
  De mag.   *De magistratibus*
Josephus
  AJ   *Antiquitates Judaicae/Jewish Antiquities*
Juvenal
  Sat.   *Satirae/Satires*
Lib.   Libanius
  Lind. Chron.   *Lindos Chronicle*
Ps.Long.   (Ps.-)Longinus
  De subl.   *De sublimitate/On the sublime*
Luc.   Lucianus
  De merc. cond.   *De mercede conductis/On salaried posts*
  Ind.   *Adversus indoctum/The ignorant book-collector*
  Quomodo hist.   *conscr./Quomodo historia conscribenda sit/How to write history*

Lycurgus
  In Leocr.   *In Leocratem/Against Leocrates*
Lysias
  In Diog.   *In Diogitonem/Against Diogeiton (or. 32)*
Marcellinus
  Vita Thuc.   *Vita Thucydidis*
Mart.   Martialis
Ovid
  Met.   *Metamorphoses*
  Trist.   *Tristiae*
Paus.   Pausanias
Pedianus Dioscurides
  De mat. med.   *De materia medica*
Pers.   Persius
Petr.   Petronius Arbiter
  sat.   *satyricon*
Philon (Mechanicus)
  Belop.   *Belopoeica/On artillery*
Philostratus
  VS   *Vitae sophistarum/Lives of the sophists*
Photius
  Bibl.   *Bibliotheca*
Pindar
  Isth.   *Isthmia/Isthmian ode(s)*
  Nem.   *Nemea/Nemean ode(s)*
  Ol.   *Olympia/Olympian ode(s)*
  Pyth.   *Pythia/Pythian ode(s)*
Plat.   Plato
  Alc.   *Alcibiades*
  Apol.   *Apologia/Apology of Socrates*
  Charm.   *Charmides*
  Conv.   *Convivium/Symposium*
  Euthd.   *Euthydemus*

Euthphr.	*Euthyphro*
Gorg.	*Gorgias*
Hipparch.	*Hipparchus*
Lg.	*Leges/Nomoi*
Parm.	*Parmenides*
Phaed.	*Phaedo*
Phaedr.	*Phaedrus*
Phileb.	*Philebus*
Protag.	*Protagoras*
Rep.	*Res publica/Politeia*
Soph.	*Sophista/Sophistes*
Symp.	*Symposion/Convivium*
Tim.	*Timaeus*

Plinius (maior)/Pliny (the elder)

| *Nat. Hist.* | *Naturalis Historia* |

Plin.   Plinius (minor)/Pliny (the younger)

| *ep.* | *epistulae/letters* |

Plut.   Plutarch

Alc.	*Vita Alcibiadis*
Alex.	*Vita Alexandri*
Amat.	*Amatorius/Erotikos/Dialogue on love*
Ant.	*Vita Antonii*
Cat.	*Vita Catonis*
Conv. sept. sap.	*Convivium septem sapientium/Dinner of the seven wise men*
Crass.	*Vita Crassi*
De gloria Ath.	*De gloria Atheniesium/On the fame of the Athenians*
De mal. Her.	*De malignitate Herodoti/On the malice of Herodotus*
De mus.	*De musica/On music**
De tranq. an.	*De tranquilitate animi/On tranquillity of mind*
Inst. Lac.	*Instituta Laconica/The ancient customs of the Spartans*
Lyc.	*Vita Lycurgi*
Lys.	*Vita Lysandri*
Mar.	*Vita Marii*
Mor.	*Moralia*
Nic.	*Vita Niciae*
QC	*Quaestiones convivales/Sympotic questions*
Quomodo adol.	*Quomodo adolescens poetas audire debeat/How the young man should study poetry*
Sol.	*Vita Solonis*
Them.	*Vita Themistoclis*
Thes.	*Vita Thesei*
Vit. X or.	*Vitae decem oratorum/Lives of the ten orators**

(*: probably not written by Plutarch)

Pol.   Polybius

Porph.   Porphyrius

| *Plot.* | *Vita Plotini* |

Pos.   Posidippus

| *Ep.* | epigramm |

P.Oxy.	
Proclus	
In Eucl.	*In primum Euclidis Elementorum librum commentarii*
Pseudo-Plutarch: see Plutarch	
Ps.Xen.	Pseudo-Xenophon ("The Old Oligarch")
Ath.	*Respublica Atheniensium/On the constitution of Athens*
Quint.	Quintilianus
Inst. orat.	*Institutio oratoria*
Scribonius Largus	
Comp.	*Compositiones*
Seneca	
ep.	*epistula(e)/letter(s)*
Septuaginta	
Gen.	*Genesis*
Sext. Emp.	Sextus Empiricus
Math.	*Adversus Mathematicos/Against the Professors*
Simon.	Simonides
Soph.	Sophocles
Ant.	*Antigone*
El.	*Electra*
O.C.	*Oedipus Coloneus*
O.R.	*Oedipus Rex/King Oedipus*
Phil.	*Philoctetes*
Soz.	Sozomenus
Hist. eccl.	*Historia ecclesiastica/Church history*
Statius	
Theb.	*Thebais*
Strabo	
Geog.	*Geographica/Geography*
Suetonius	
Dom.	*Vita Domitiani*
Testamentum novum	
Acts	*Acta apostolorum/Acts of the apostles*
Col.	*Pauli epistula ad Colossos/Paul's letter to the Colossians*
Theocr.	Theocritus
Id.	*Idyll*
Theophrastus	
Hist. plant.	*Historia plantarum/On plants*
Thgn.	Theognis
Thuc.	Thucydides
Xen.	Xenophon
Cyn.	*Cynegeticus*
De re equ.	*De re equestri/On horsemanship*
HG	*Historia Graeca/Hellenika*
Mem.	*Memorabilia/Apomnemoneumata*
Oec.	*Oeconomicus/*

Introduction: A Companion to Greek Literature

Martin Hose and David Schenker

1. Companion versus History of Literature

It is by no means an undemanding task, in the second decade of the third millennium, to make the corpus of texts known as "Ancient Greek Literature" available to interested readers in an introductory companion volume. The task is demanding not least because the texts constituting "Ancient Greek Literature"[1] still form an integral part of the literary tradition of creative thought, and offer indispensible points of orientation, even in this age of globalization.

Over the past two centuries in the discipline of Classical Studies, works presenting them-selves as literary histories (or as "introductions," a more technical variety), and informed by the current state of research and issues brought to bear upon the text, have attempted to fulfill the task of introducing this body of Greek literature. The genre "history of literature" is, however, in a state of crisis (cf. Wellek 1973; Perkins 1991 and 1992). First, there is an extrinsic crisis: no single scholar can any longer master the entirety of Greek literature and its concomitant scholarship with sufficient depth and thoroughness to write a balanced and informative history. (Significantly, recent literary histories of great scope have been produced only as the collective work of multiple authors.) But far more serious than the extrinsic problem is a problem intrinsic to the form of literary history. As the term "history" indicates, literary history is subject to the demand of presenting a narrative, i.e. a coherent text with a beginning, middle, and end. At the genre's height in the nineteenth century, such a narrative could be easily produced when one – intentionally or unintentionally – constructed literary history as part of the history of a people, or ethnic group, and, influenced by historico-philosophical models conceptualized by the German philosopher Hegel and building on those of Aristotle, one could show how a *Volksgeist* expressed itself in literature. This typically led to narratives that delineated a rise from humble beginnings to a point of consummation (or classicism) and sometimes also discerned a decline and fall. The more deeply literary historiography became aware of its Hegelian intellectual inheritance, the more difficult it became to develop the narrative necessary for a history.

A Companion to Greek Literature, First Edition. Edited by Martin Hose and David Schenker.
© 2016 John Wiley & Sons, Inc. Published 2020 by John Wiley & Sons, Inc.

A second problem also arose as the concept of the "death of the author," evolved by Roland Barthes in 1968, began to take effect upon literary criticism. The author as a historical person was thereby radically negated as an entity and an essential object of literary history, and the author's perspective on aesthetic production was delegitimized. The traditional format, especially that of Greek and Roman literary history, which placed the biography and "being" of the author in the narrative's centre, became obsolete; the alternative concept developed with the "death of the author," i.e. the "birth of the reader," is impractical for Greco-Roman literature, since – in contrast to the literature of modern and contemporary eras (as Hans Robert Jauß conceptualized it in 1970) – the reception of a work by its readers can be ascertained only sporadically. Or, to quote the exquisite imagery of Friedrich Leo (1913, 431): "From the colorful bird which has flown away, there remains in our hand but a feather."

It would seem that the historiography of Greek as well as Roman literature has as yet been unable to recover conceptually from this double crisis.[2] In this situation, the emergent form of the "Companion" offers a new opportunity which has not yet experienced, for better or worse, sustained theoretical reflection or resultant formal constraints. A Companion can, more adequately than the linear, narrative-bound literary history, approach Greek literature from diverse viewpoints with equal stringency and is thereby able to provide internal and external contextualization for this body of literature.

The present volume endeavors to make use of the possibilities offered by the Companion genre and to provide a point of entry into ancient Greek literature.

2.   What is "Greek Literature"?

How does this volume define "Greek literature"? Upon closer consideration, the terms "Greek" and "literature" require clarification. "Greek" might refer to texts composed (a) by Greeks, (b) in the Greek language, or (c) by Greeks in the Greek language. Upon deeper examination option a (together with the closely connected possibility, c) proves to be extremely difficult to apply. A satisfactory definition of what a "Greek" was during the time span from c. 700 BCE to 600 CE appears to be an impossibility, partly because Greek culture itself first found concepts for self-definition in the fifth century BCE, partly because "Greekness" and "Hellenicity" appear as relative or strongly fluctuating categories in light of modern debates on "ethnicity" (cf. Hall 2002 and Dueck, ch. 25 in this volume). It is significant that, for example, Greek culture of the Imperial Period defined "Hellenicity" by the sharing of language and literature (cf. König, ch. 7 in this volume). The term "Greek" therefore lends itself to being understood in the sense of option b, i.e. as texts composed in the Greek language, but here with the recognition that "Greek" synchronically (in view of the diverse Greek dialects) as well as diachronically (in view of its historical linguistic developments, including its "fossilization" as Attic Greek) encompassed a broad spectrum of possibilities (cf. Willi, ch. 29 in this volume).

The term "literature" is no less in need of clarification. At first, the term appears to imply two lines of demarcation. To the extent that it relates to "literacy", it seems to separate from "literature" all that one associates with the realm of orality and oral tradition. To draw such a sharp distinction makes no sense for early Greek literature, in which orality transitions to literacy but important features of orality remain preserved (cf. Reece, ch. 3, and Power, ch. 4 in this volume). Greek "literature" accordingly includes consideration of the "art of words," i.e. works not limited by the conditions denoted by the term "literacy."

Moreover, "literature" designates more than simply "text"; i.e. not everything set down in writing is literature *per se*. In the varieties of philology concerned with modern literature, this distinction has led to literary criticism concentrating above all on texts in the sense of *belles lettres*, and to the compilation of a culture's entire written production (including, e.g., graffiti and so-called functional texts) being viewed as the task of cultural studies (cf. Bal 2002). Notwithstanding the focus on texts belonging to "high literature," the dichotomy has never applied with the same strictness in Classical studies. For good reason: the strict separation of literary and technical texts in contemporary culture is inapplicable to Greco-Roman literature inasmuch as the technical texts of antiquity pose a literary challenge. It is, furthermore, impossible to overlook the fact that Greek literature generated, organized, and recorded knowledge in many and diverse forms (cf. Asper, ch. 26, and Dubischar, ch. 28, in this volume). Among these are technical texts, which must be incorporated into the category of "literature."

Finally, the time frame chosen for this volume requires justification. Considering the purely administrative content of the linear texts of the late second millennium BCE, and the absence of literature in the period between the linear texts and early Greek epic, it may seem only natural that this Companion begins with early epic. The fact that it reaches as far as the sixth century CE, however – a time which may also be considered as "early Byzantine" – demands explanation. This extent is fully legitimate in respect to content: continuities of production and reception are unmistakable in various literary genres such as epic (cf. Cameron 2004) or historiography, in rhetoric (cf. Swain 2004) and in (Neoplatonic) philosophy (cf. Dillon 2004), and can be followed, in spite of the foundation of Constantinople as a new centre of the Greek-speaking world and the establishment of Christianity as imperial religion, well beyond the fourth century (cf. Stenger, ch. 8 in this volume). It is the manifest political and cultural changes of the Eastern Roman Empire during the seventh century which first lastingly transform literary production into a clearly contoured "Byzantine literature." [3]

3. The Concept of this Companion

Greek literature is a corpus of fascinating texts, in which thoughts and concepts of the highest aesthetic order find formulation, ideas which (as mentioned above) can expect to meet with interest even in the twenty-first century. If one presupposes that these texts arose in a context of tradition and challenge which – as shown by the considerable differences between texts of different dates – can be characterized by the term dynamic, then an introduction must be conceptualized in a way that makes the interaction between these factors clear and understandable. This Companion attempts such an approach.

Firstly, as a basis for all following chapters, the material dimension of Greek literature is presented in two stages (Part I, Production and Transmission): Lucio Del Corso illuminates the conditions of writing in Ancient Greece and the production of ancient texts and books (ch. 1), while Richard Armstrong provides an overview of the reception of Greek literature up to the present day (ch. 2).

External factors influencing literary production in the form of cultural or even concrete historical circumstances, challenges, or problems, each of which left behind their distinct signature, are then traced in six chapters (Part II, Greek Literature as a Dynamic System[4]): Steve Reece addresses the dynamic and productive transition from orality to literality (ch. 3), Timothy Power the specific constellations which shaped Archaic literature (ch. 4), James McGlew those of the fifth and fourth century (ch. 5), Anatole Mori the Hellenistic World (ch. 6), Jason König the first centuries of the Imperial Period (ch. 7), and Jan Stenger (ch. 8) the significance of Christianity for Greek literature.

After the wider context of Greek literature has been delineated, the corpus comprising Greek literature is then discussed following its division into "genres" (Part III, Genres). In an order approximately corresponding to that of the literary-historical testimony, Hanna Roisman examines epic (ch. 9), James Wells the poetic forms designated by the term "lyric" (ch. 10), Richard Rader drama (ch. 11), Regina Höschele the epigram and smaller poetic forms (ch. 12), followed by Mike Edwards on oratory (ch. 13), Antonis Tsakmakis on historiography and biography (ch. 14), Martin Hose on forms of philosophical literature (ch. 15), Stefan Tilg on the novel (ch. 16), and Thorsten Fögen on the forms of technical literature (ch. 17).

In a further step, the cast of players important for literature are described (Part IV, The Players). Mary Lefkowitz gives a sketch of the discourses surrounding the authors (ch. 18), René Nünlist considers the recipients (ch. 19), and David Schenker explores individuals who promote or hinder literature (ch. 20). Literature stands in close connection with inner and outer spaces (Part V, Places), which reach from imaginary spaces, handled by Suzanne Saïd (ch. 23), to spaces of production and performance, described by Manuel Baumbach (ch. 22), and actual cities as places of concentrated communication, discussed by Martin Hose (ch. 21).

Literature represents specific knowledge (Part VI, Literature and Knowledge). It is therefore fitting to enquire into the relation of literature and truth to one another (Martin Hose, ch. 24) and to ask how literature contributed to the production of particular forms of self-identity (Daniela Dueck, ch. 25). Literature can, of course, expressly and explicitly "instruct" and thereby convey knowledge (Markus Asper, ch. 26), but it can also do this indirectly (David Konstan, ch. 27). Finally, literature is a medium for bearing complex processes of cultural memory (and forgetting) and for developing a suitable arsenal of forms to this end (Markus Dubischar, ch. 28).

Greek literature had a high aesthetic appeal (Part VII, Literature and Aesthetics), which derives to a considerable degree from the Greek language's possibilities of expression and variety of dialects, as traced by Andreas Willi (ch. 29). There also emerged in Greek literature (especially in poetry) particular methods of intensifying and enriching thoughts and expression, as Nick Baechle analyzes using select examples (ch. 30). Lastly, literature's potential to affect its recipients in various ways is closely connected with the aesthetic dimension; this is discussed by Victoria Wohl (ch. 31).

The relevance which Greek literature continues to hold even in the twenty-first century is founded on the characteristics sketched in chapters 3–31, but it is also the result of a multifaceted reception (Part VIII, The Reception of Greek Literature), which Emily Wilson (ch. 32) and Edith Hall (ch. 33) elucidate with a look at the world of academia and beyond, respectively.

The editors hope that this concept is well suited to a book intended to lend interested readers orientation on their path through Greek literature as a whole, as well as through the individual works. They are well aware that other possibilities for conceptualizing such a book also exist, especially those that work with the vast connective potential of literature, and generate chapters such as "Greek Literature and Religion,"[5] "… and Gender," "… and Politics," "… and Philosophy," and so forth. They have chosen, however, not to develop this in a separate (and, by necessity, large) section on "intersections" since this would have meant a loss of space for the 33 chapters comprising the Companion and at the same time caused additional overlapping – religion and ritual are already handled, for example, in chapters 4, 5, 8, 10, and 11; myth in chapters 4, 9, 10, 11, and 24; gender in chapter 25; politics in chapters 5, 6, 7, 8, and 13; etc. The editors believe that the route they have chosen, namely that of examining Greek literature through a focus on its literary nature, is justified and will prove its worth.

4. Acknowledgments

The editors owe many thanks to Allison Kostka (Wiley-Blackwell) for providing the initiative for this book, her support, her advice and for her unwavering accompaniment of this project; the authors of the chapters, who never lost patience with the editors during the long process of completion, and always met new requests and suggestions with friendliness; and to the assistants to Chair of Greek Philology at the LMU in Munich, Dr Annamaria Peri, Janina Sieber, Markus Hafner, and Julian Schreyer, for their help with the final editing.

NOTES

[1] Several chapters offer a definition of this term; here, at least provisionally, it refers to all texts composed in Greek between the late eighth/early seventh century and the sixth century BCE as part of a continuous and coherent tradition.
[2] For the "rescue" of literary history for more recent literature, see Kablitz 2003. Whitmarsh 2004, 1–17 gives a brilliant short analysis of the problems of "History in Practice," but tries to solve these problems first by "avoiding any grand narrative" (16), and second by avoiding evaluation of literature itself. Instead he refers to literature in its contexts (festival, symposium, theatre, the power of speech, archives) and to conflicts it addresses (cultural identity, gender/power, "sexing the text," slavery). One can ask whether in this approach (the book is part of a series "Cultural History of Literature") a history of literature is transformed into a literal history of culture.
[3] Cf. the overview of Krumbacher 1897, 11–15, which remains instructive in points of literary history.
[4] The term "system" is used in a non-technical sense; it is simply meant to indicate that a fundamental feature of literature is that it reacts, taking on whatever form is appropriate, to the challenges of its time, or rather stands in a "dialogic" relationship with the context in which it was created. There is no intention of assuming system-theoretical models here (Luhmann).
[5] Cf. the instructive contribution by Harrison 2007.

REFERENCES

Bal, M. 2002. *Kulturanalyse*. Frankfurt.
Barthes, R. 1968/1987. "The Death of the Author." In *Image – Music – Text*, 142–48. London. (first edn. 1987).
Cameron, A. 2004. "Poetry and Literary Culture in Late Antiquity." In S. Swain and M. Edwards, eds., *Approaching Late Antiquity. The Transformation from Early to Late Empire*. Oxford, 327–54.
Dillon, J. 2004. "Philosophy as a Profession in Late Antiquity." In Swain and Edwards 2004, 401–18.
Hall, J. M. 2002. *Hellenicity. Between Ethnicity and Culture*. Chicago.
Harrison, Th. 2007. "Greek Religion and Literature." In D. Ogdon (ed.) *A Companion to Greek Religion*, 373–84. Oxford.
Hubbard, Th. K., ed. 2014. *A Companion to Greek and Roman Sexualities*. Oxford.
Jauß, H. R. 1970. *Literaturgeschichte als Provokation*. Frankfurt.
Kablitz, A. 2003. "Literaturwissenschaft als Provokation der Literaturgeschichte." *Poetica* 35: 91–122.
Krumbacher, K. 1897. *Geschichte der byzantinischen Litteratur*. 2 vols. 2nd. edn. Munich.
Leo, F. 1913. *Geschichte der römischen Literatur*. Berlin.
Perkins, D., ed. 1991. *Theoretical Issues of Literary History*. Cambridge, MA
Perkins, D. 1992. *Is Literary History Possible?* Baltimore. MD.
Swain, S. 2004. "Sophists and Emperors: The Case of Libanius." In S. Swain and M. Edwards, eds., *Approaching Late Antiquity. The Transformation from Early to Late Empire*. Oxford, 335–400.
Swain, S. and M. Edwards, eds. 2004. *Approaching Late Antiquity. The Transformation from Early to Late Empire*. Oxford.
Wellek, R. 1973. "The Fall of Literary History." In R. Koselleck, and W.-D. Stempel, eds. *Geschichte – Ereignis und Erzählung*, 426–40. Munich.
Whitmarsh, T. 2004. *Ancient Greek Literature*. Cambridge

PART I

Production and Transmission

CHAPTER 1

Mechanics and Means of Production in Antiquity

Lucio Del Corso

1. Overview

Plato's *Theaetetus*, a philosophical dialogue written during the first half of the fourth century BCE, opens with a scene (142a–143c) which is arguably the oldest example of meta-literature: two characters, Euclides and Terpsion, remember the intense exchanges of ideas which Theaetetus, one of their friends now dying from a battle wound, used to have with Socrates. Before sadness for their friend's fate overtakes them, Euclides tells Terpsion that he has composed a text, comprising a full account of the dialogues of Theaetetus and Socrates, and explains the working method he followed: first he wrote some notes (*hypomnemata*) based on Socrates' reconstruction of his conversations with Theaetetus; later he further developed that text "in tranquility," asking Socrates more than once for explanations of specific topics, and then making the necessary corrections. In this way, Euclides says in conclusion, "I composed almost all the dialogue." The final destination of this process is a *biblion*, a "papyrus roll," which Euclides asks a slave to read aloud, while he and his friend lie on comfortable armchairs. The compositional journey here described is clearly articulated: the literary text is not the consequence of a single or unitary creative action, but rather the result of different phases, each distinguished by a significant interaction between orality and writing. And this interaction between spoken and written word extends long beyond the gestation of the literary works, into their final phases. Plato's dialogues are dotted with reading scenes, always used as a starting point for philosophical reflections, and with references to writing and books,[1] designated variously as *syngramma, biblos, biblion*.

It may seem contradictory to find such a sensibility in Plato: in other passages of his dialogues, the philosopher seems to propose a substantial devaluation of the role of writing as a tool for the preservation and transmission of knowledge; and in a dialogue almost completely devoted to the topic of poetic composition, the *Ion*, the final source of poetic inspiration is divine, and the rhapsode only an instrument for receiving it. But, in fact, Plato's references to the nature of literary creation enlighten rather than contradict each other, and portray the image of a literary civilization where the processes of composition, publication and reception were already articulated in a complex series of events.

A Companion to Greek Literature, First Edition. Edited by Martin Hose and David Schenker.
© 2016 John Wiley & Sons, Inc. Published 2020 by John Wiley & Sons, Inc.

Moving on many centuries, we come to the grey zone of the seventh century, where late antiquity and the Byzantine age overlap. At the end of his *Hodegos*, Anastasius of Sinai,[2] an erudite monk able to defend orthodoxy with a Greek prose worthy of the ancient philosophers, takes leave of the readers begging their pardon "for the many mistakes and repetitions" in his work. Indeed "these dogmas of Christ needed to be sketched out (*proschideusthai*) and corrected (*diorthousai*) and arranged in sections (*stichizesthai*) and then, finally, transcribed in a beautiful script (*kalligrapheisthai*)," but because of a long illness the author could not follow all those steps: "therefore, we composed the treatise in this way, with the fascicule (*tetras*) in front of the sheet of notes (*schedos*). And if, as is possible, we said something which is not appropriate to the correct way of speaking or thinking, we ask you to forgive us: only God is truly firm" (24.120–140 = 320 Uthemann). In Anastasius' apologies – the expression of a civilization substantially different from the age of the *poleis* – the spoken word still plays a role, at least for the completion of the text; and Byzantine culture kept that oral dimension until its twilight (Cavallo 2007). Again striking is the lucid description of a compositional process articulated in very distinct phases (draft version, revised version, final version, editorially arranged and transcribed in calligraphic script), during which the author employed different forms of writing: thus, for Anastasius the *schedos* of the draft is an object different from the *tetras* of the final version, as the *hypomnemata* used by Euclides for the preliminary version of Socrates and Theaetetus' dialogues are different from the *biblion* of the corrected and revised final text. But what exactly was this process of writing, correction and revision? Plato and Anastasius do not give us further details, imagining their public already knew this articulation of the work and the writing materials it was grounded on. But no modern attempt to reconstruct mechanics and means of production of literary texts in the Greek world can leave aside an inquiry in this direction, even if it will be difficult to give univocal answers.

Mechanics similar to those described by Plato or Anastasius can be deduced from many sources, scattered through much of Greek literary history, from the late classical to the beginning of the Byzantine age. But putting the diverse elements into a coherent picture is not an easy task. Greek writers were not much interested in describing the dynamics underlying the compositional process, nor about the tools involved in it. On this point, Latin writers have been much more generous: the epistles of Cicero and Pliny the Younger, Gellius' *Attic Nights*, Quintilian's *Institutio oratoria* (and the list could be much longer) are inexhaustible sources of information about the making of literary texts in ancient Rome (Pecere 2011). For the Greek world, we have nothing comparable. In Greek texts the materiality of the writing processes too often appears to be under a veil; even when an author speaks about his relationship with books and writing, usually he assumes an allusive tone, presuming the knowledge of things or facts we can no longer understand. Because of this behavior, many sources seem ambiguous to modern readers, and have been interpreted sometimes in opposite ways. One way to minimize such difficulties is to check texts against other forms of evidence. Many ancient works of art (from classic Attic vases to imperial sarcophagi) depict scenes with individuals reading or writing on different materials, in open spaces or at home: those objects therefore become precious evidence of Greek intellectual life. Again, significant information can be deduced by the examination of the characteristics of papyri and other writing materials used by the Greeks. But even a combination of such different materials will give us only a partial frame, with few established elements. Iconographic sources could be idealized representations, and above all they are rarely detailed enough; and papyri, for environmental reasons, come only from areas far from the main cultural centers, and are attested only from the beginning of the fourth century BCE, after the end of one of the most productive periods of Greek literature.

Even bearing such limitations in mind, a rapid survey of the extant evidence will allow us to reach a clearer comprehension of literary phenomena. With this in mind, let us return to Plato and Anastasius. As we have seen, the two writers both mention a plurality of different writing items: *biblion, schedos, tetras*, used for revised texts, or more generic *hypomnemata*. Our survey on mechanics and means of production will start from here: the individuation of writing materials and of their functions.

2.   Writing Materials

When Plato wrote the *Theaetetus*, writing was already employed in the Greek world for many public and private purposes, requiring different implements and materials. Texts intended to be exhibited to a large public, to celebrate someone or commemorate some events, were inscribed on marble, stone, bronze or even other metals; such writings were common in the *agora* and along the main streets of Athens and other Greek cities. But literary and iconographic sources show also that, at least since the Classical period, other perishable writing materials were widespread among the upper classes, and were employed for literary texts as well as for many other necessities of daily life. The most common were papyrus and waxed tablets, though it was also possible to write on other objects such as pottery sherds (*ostraka*), leather, lead, or even bones.

2.1.   *Papyrus*

Papyrus was the main writing material employed by the Greeks for a very large part of their history (Lewis 1974). But they did not invent it: papyrus comes from a plant (*Cyperus papyrus*) that flourished along the Nile, in Egypt. The idea to turn this plant into a writing

Figure 1.1   A fragment of a speech written on papyrus for a certain "Appio," dated to the sixth–seventh century CE. Florence, The Biblioteca Medicea Laurenziana, ms PSI XIV 1399. On concession of the MiBACT. Any further reproduction by any means is prohibited.

material which could be assembled in rolls is an Egyptian discovery, whose importance for western civilization can be compared with the developing of geometry and mathematics, or of writing itself (Černy 1952).

The archaeological evidence shows us that by the early third millennium BCE Egyptians understood that a specific variety of the papyrus plant, very widespread along the Nile and in the swamps close to it, could be turned into an easy-to-employ and flexible writing material, and probably after a few decades they started to assemble it in scrolls ("papyrus rolls"), which could contain large amounts of written texts. Papyrus and papyrus rolls, therefore, seem to be as ancient as pharaonic civilization. From at least the second millennium, other populations used papyrus, probably as a consequence of close contacts – both economic and cultural – with Egypt: literary sources such as the "Journey of Wen-Amon" attest that Phoenicians employed papyrus rolls before the twelfth century BCE (Pritchard 1969, 25–29: 28);[3] and even if the most ancient Hebrew and Aramaic papyri are no later than the eighth century BCE, literary and paleographic evidence suggests a much earlier diffusion of such materials.[4] During the first millennium BCE, papyrus became widespread among different civilizations in the Mediterranean area and in the Near East, and finally was employed also by the Greeks to preserve their cultural memories, as a natural consequence of increasing contacts with those populations. We cannot say exactly when the first papyrus rolls arrived in Greece. Most scholars find the sixth century BCE a reasonable date; to the second half of that century belong the most ancient reading scenes depicted in Greek art, on black-figured Attic vases (Immerwahr 1964 and 1973; Del Corso 2003), and literary sources from the beginning of the fifth century contain explicit references to papyrus rolls. Around 570 BCE the opening of the emporium of Naukratis, run and organized by Greek merchants on the Nile Delta, assured to all Greek cities easier access to Egyptian goods and commodities (Boardman 1999, 118–53; Austin 1970). But it is possible that papyrus as a writing material arrived in Greece even earlier. Greeks learned the use of the alphabet from Phoenicians as early as the eighth century BCE,[5] and at that time, as we have seen, Phoenicians normally used papyrus to write. Moreover, contacts between Egypt and Greece are attested even during the dark age following the fall of the Mycenaean kingdoms. The introduction of papyrus to Greece, therefore, could be as ancient as the introduction of alphabetic writing.

In any case, the developing of a bookish mentality was a slow and gradual process, limited only to the literate, in the upper classes of the population. At some point during the Archaic age, important documents and literary texts, even if orally composed and transmitted, began to take definite shape in papyrus rolls or sheets, which sometimes could be stored in public places, such as temples,[6] since proper libraries are not yet attested for that period. This happened not only to short lyric poems or to collections of sympotic texts, such as the elegies forming the Theognidean *corpus*, but also to lengthier poems, such as those ascribed to Homer and Hesiod. A famous literary tradition mentions that the tyrant Pisistratus during the sixth century ordered the whole *Iliad* and *Odyssey* transcribed on papyrus rolls, in order to preserve their integrity.[7] Even if this episode is a tale invented by Hellenistic authors, as many scholars argue (Ferreri 2002), Homeric poetry, along with other crucial works of Greek literature, reached the full status of written text many decades before the Persian wars, and this would have been almost impossible without papyrus rolls.

By the fifth century, writers refer to papyrus as the standard writing material, using the term *biblos/byblos*, together with related forms *biblion/byblion*, or the adjective *biblinos/byblinos* (Del Corso 2003, 8–19). These words denote not just papyrus bookrolls, as is common in later centuries, but more generally any kind of text written on papyrus. Herodotus, e.g., uses *biblos* for any papyrus sheet, such as the letters written by Harpagus to Cyrus, or by Amasis to Polycrates of Samos, or other official messages;[8] even a collection of family documents can be a *biblos*, as we see in Lysias,[9] or a *biblion*, as in Demosthenes.[10] Sometimes comedians refer to reading[11] and like to make jokes using bookrolls;[12] but it is only in Plato's dialogues that the word is exclusively used for bookrolls: we find more than 15 examples of the term with this meaning, referring to philosophical treatises (*Phaed.* 97c), rhetorical works (*Symp.* 177b–c; *Phaedr.* 230d–237a), and poems (*Rep.* 364e–365a).

At the same time, we find more and more references to the use of papyrus for bureaucratic purposes, as in the well-known inscription recording the expenses for the refurbishing of the Erechtheum (IG I³ 476; 408–407 BCE), where the last entries concern the purchase of four writing tablets (*pinakes*) and one blank papyrus roll, probably for accounting. Here the papyrus roll is called *chartes*, a word used also in much later documents for "standard" commercial papyrus rolls.[13]

Our evidence depicts the *biblos* as the repository of written texts in their final shape. In fifth-century sources we find many references to people *reading* their bookrolls, but none to an individual *writing* on them. This status will be characteristic of papyrus rolls for many centuries. In the Classical age, even if the *biblos*, as a material object, was not yet fully defined, its general layout was already set (Del Corso 2003): the text was arranged in many columns, written along the broader side, from left to right; there was no word division and only a few signs were employed to distinguish parts or sections of the text, such as the *paragraphos* – just a short horizontal line – or the *coronis* (an elaborated *paragraphos*, comprising several lines, sometimes joined with other ornamental signs, used to mark the end of a significant section or of the whole text).[14] The writers used a sharp pen (*kalamos*), and a sponge to clear incorrect words or phrases. We do not have a clear idea of the scripts employed in such rolls, but they were likely similar to those we see in some epigraphic texts, such as the thin and square majuscules used in Attic inscriptions recording public expenses or the activities of magistrates. But significant differences probably arose quite soon. The geometric arrangement of writing so characteristic of Attic script – the so called *stoichedon* style – does not seem to fit to bookrolls; and, moreover, during the fifth century a sort of stylistic differentiation among papyrus scripts already had to exist, since Plato (*Lg.* 7.810 a–c) mentions slow, calligraphic scripts as opposed to quickly written scripts.[15]

Our evidence seems to point to a medium very flexible in format and dimension. Confirming this are the two most ancient surviving papyrus bookrolls, even though they date only from around the midpoint of the fourth century BCE:[16] the "Derveni papyrus," found in the necropolis of Derveni (close to the modern Thessaloniki) and containing a commentary to a lost orphic poem,[17] and the "Timotheus papyrus,"[18] found in Abu sir al Malaq (Egypt) and preserving Timotheus' "*nomos*" on the battle of Salamis. The two papyri are almost contemporary – so it is difficult to establish their relative dates – but show striking material differences: not only are the scripts different – more elegant and regular for the Derveni papyrus, quicker and untidier for the Timotheus – but the dimensions of writing columns and of the rolls themselves clearly vary.[19] This may be only partly connected to the characteristics of the transcribed texts: the two rolls reflect a different sensibility about the ultimate role of the book. The columns of the Timotheus papyrus are too broad to be easily read, especially since the words were not divided; the few *paragraphoi* give only a vague idea of the main sections of the poem. Moreover, the roll was assembled specifically to contain only that composition. On the contrary, in the Derveni papyrus the text is arranged to be more easily understood: word-end and column-end always correspond – a useful aid to readers when there is no word division; *paragraphoi* are systematically added to mark sentences and to distinguish verses from their commentary. The Timotheus and the Derveni papyrus, thus, seem to reflect different attitudes toward the book and different bookish mentalities.

These differences arise from a system where the text was conceived first for a specific *performance* or occasion, and not for a public of readers. The duration of the *performance* influenced the length of the composition, and once the occasion was over, the author did not follow any fixed editorial rule to publish his work. He was interested only in preserving the text in its integrity, using the papyrus roll especially for that.

Bookroll formats became more standardized from the Hellenistic age onward, as a consequence of a broader evolution in the attitude toward writing in daily life,[20] and therefore of the birth of new relationships among authors, books, and public, which is now composed not only of "listeners," but more generally of readers. During the Hellenistic age "literary" rolls and "documentary" rolls became clearly distinguished, as reflected lexically: a *biblos* is now the equivalent of Latin *volumen*, or bookroll, and the papyrus rolls or sheets employed for documentary or other daily purposes are generally designated with different words, such as *tomoi*. The new status of the bookroll is clearly reflected in literary sources, especially by poetry, where we find an array of vivid representations of the *biblos*, praised as vehicle of transmission and even source of inspiration for poetry, and sometimes personified and talking to its readers (Bing 1988, 16–48). We can see these changes clearly in Greek papyri found in Egypt. While third-century BCE bookrolls still show a wide variety of formats (Blanchard 1993), from the second century BCE they become more regular: the usual lengths range from 3.50 to 8 meters for poetry rolls, and from 2–2.50 to 15 meters for prose rolls, while the average heights are from 17 to 21 centimeters, even though some rolls are much taller, or even smaller, such as the elegant anthology of epigrammatic poetry Pack² 1598, no more than 5 centimeters tall.[21] A single roll, therefore, kept a single literary work, such as one tragedy, one rhetorical speech, or one book of Homer; the same roll could also collect many short texts of the same author, such as epigrams or lyric compositions, and soon thematic anthologies arose, grouping texts of different authors but similar content. Texts too long to be transcribed in a single bookroll had to be split into different rolls, even if regarded by their author as a single, continuous text.

Such formats reflect a process of emancipating literature from given occasions. Even as performance continues to play a major role in the production of literary texts during all periods of Greek history, starting with the Hellenistic age, writers and poets perceive bookrolls not just as a tool for storing texts, but as the natural vehicle for the diffusion of literary compositions, a vehicle that allowed texts to be read by many more people, and in contexts very different from those they were composed for. At the same time, authors could no longer personally manage the integrity of their works, watching every step of their diffusion, as in the previous age. This factor had a deep impact on the dynamics of publication of literary texts.

During the Imperial age the process of standardizing bookrolls becomes clearer. In a famous passage, the elder Pliny (*Nat. Hist.* 13.74–82) provides us the only extant detailed report on the manufacture of papyrus as writing material in antiquity, describing the Egyptian *ateliers* where papyrus was made as well-organized workshops, following fixed procedures. Pliny lists nine typologies of papyrus sheets, differing in color, smoothness, resistance and dimensions (Lewis 1974, 34–69). Such "commercial" rolls were only a starting point for ancient scribes, who would cut and paste the writing material in response to their needs; so, it is difficult to identify, among extant papyri, rolls which can be linked to Pliny's words. Moreover, we do not know how ancient this working organization was, since something similar already existed under the Ptolemies, and probably even before. Yet Pliny's passage describes a more structured system, and a larger production.

Additionally, in Roman times literary genres were often linked to specific book formats. Technical literature and narratives are often attested on rather tall bookrolls which, even if written by professional hands, exhibit a specific layout, consisting of columns very close to each other, with more lines – and smaller letters – than the average; in these rolls it is easier to find reader-oriented features such as blank spaces, indentation, or lexical signs, whose function was to help readers in understanding and "browsing" the text.[22] On the contrary, masterpieces such as the Homeric poems – the foundation of the whole educational system – were linked to another model of bookroll, more regular in dimensions, layout and scripts (Cavallo and Del Corso 2012).[23] This is obviously a simplistic representation of extremely complex editorial mechanisms. Greek bookrolls, as the evidence from Egypt clearly shows, displayed a wide array of scripts and layouts, keyed to a plurality of practices, and developed to answer to different purposes. The same text could be transcribed by an individual who was learned, though untrained in calligraphic scripts, on a roll made of re-used papyrus sheets, or by an uneducated, professional scribe, on papyrus of the finest quality, thus giving as a result two completely different bookrolls. But in general, the perception of form matching content was so clear in readers' expectations that it also influenced writers' attitudes (Canfora 1995, 11–18).

As a consequence, the social status of bookrolls evolved further: bookrolls are seen as something more than a mere medium for literary texts, and become a real status symbol for Roman élites, sometimes appreciated only for their beauty, precious as jewels,[24] eagerly desired by collectors, either learned lovers of letters – such as Galen, who had in his private library in Rome rare bookrolls written many centuries before[25] – or bored rich people searching for occupations – such as the ignorant book collector satirized by Lucian[26] – or again *parvenus* looking for social legitimation, such as Petronius' Trimalchio, who boasts to have three libraries in his *domus*, but cannot say what is inside them.[27] And the élite proudly show off this status symbol on their tombs and sarcophagi: both cultivated and uneducated – especially in the uncertain years from the Severans on – aspire to be represented in an afterlife where they can wear the philosopher's mantle and grasp a bookroll in their hands (Marrou 1938).

Papyrus bookrolls are still produced during the first centuries of the Byzantine age. The festal letters composed by the patriarchs of Alexandria to announce Easter were written in beautiful calligraphic scripts on papyrus rolls at least until the eighth century CE; and for the same period rolls with pagan literature are also attested. But from the third century CE the codex, the direct ancestor of our book, gradually replaced the roll as the main medium for literature.

2.2.   The Codex

The codex was made of papyrus or parchment sheets folded and bound together, usually under a leather or wood cover. Its origins are even more obscure than the papyrus roll's. As several literary sources attest, by the end of the first century CE in the Roman world it was usual to write on wooden tablets or parchment sheets bound together with strings or similar.[28] The Romans used these first *codices*, in rough and basic forms, from a relatively early period. On the contrary, this technology was unusual to the Greeks, who probably began to use *codices* quite late in their history. The oldest ones found in Egypt are not earlier than the second century CE; moreover, there are no apposite Greek words for it: the codex was referred to using words already employed for other writing technologies, such as *biblos*, *deltos*, or even *membranai*, "leathers," if on parchment; only during the Byzantine age do we find a word which indicates it with a reference to its shape: *teuchos*, which in classical Greek is a "box."

Papyrus codex sheets were cut from blank rolls (Turner 1977), then folded and assembled together in fascicules, in such a way that opening the book there were always two facing pages with fibers in the same direction. The formats varied, but usually papyrus codices were tall and narrow, and had one column of writing on each page, with broad margins around; the largest manuscripts could have two columns. Parchment *codices* looked different from papyrus ones: they were generally square and larger, and even among the most ancient materials it is easier to find exemplars with more than one column per page. From the fourth century CE truly monumental parchment *codices* are attested, such as the so-called "Sinaiticus," where Old and New Testaments are transcribed in wide pages, displaying four columns each.

Whatever the format and material, during late antiquity the codex replaced the roll, becoming the main instrument to preserve and transmit literature. This process, which can be considered one of the most important events in the history of Western culture (Cameron 2011, 455–6), was slow and gradual; it is difficult to trace its steps, and its causes are still debated. We may only say that the transition was completed between the fourth and the fifth century CE, and was the result of multiple factors. "Practical" reasons are always invoked: the codex was cheaper and contained larger amounts of text; moreover, it was easier to read a codex and to find a specific passage in it. In this the codex represented a significant improvement, especially if we consider that during late antiquity there was a diffusion of new texts – including many theological works – and even new literary genres – such as the "encyclopedic" compendia – which expected the reader to identify and focus only on a selected part of the text each time. But other, ideological and socio-cultural factors played a role as well. Christians chose the codex for their Scriptures, and the spread of Christianity implied a wider diffusion of their texts, and of their preferred book form (Roberts and Skeat 1983). On the other hand, Christians were not alone. The codex was largely used by individuals of "middle class" – or of the so-called *media plebs* (Veyne 2000) – who needed specific technical texts (for agriculture, astrology, law, medicine...), but were also accustomed to read some literature for leisure. During late antiquity, as a result of deep transformations in the social structure of the Empire, more and more individuals from such strata became part of the Imperial bureaucracy, changing the composition of local élites. For these new élites the codex was even more natural than the bookroll. The roll thus came to be seen as the technology of traditional culture, patrician and pagan, while the codex appeared as the most suitable medium for the new cultural necessities (Cavallo 2009b).

Rolls and later *codices* were for many centuries the technologies employed by the Greeks to preserve written works in their final (or almost final) shape, such as those kept in private and public libraries, or filed in archives. But daily life also required the production of a number of ephemeral texts, not intended for preservation. For them, sheets or strips of papyrus (or even parchment) could be used, but usually other writing materials were preferred, such as wooden writing tablets, pottery sherds (*ostraka*), lead, gold or even bones.

2.3.   Wax Tablets

Wax tablets (*pinakes*, or more generically *deltoi*) consisted of two (dyptich), or more (polyptich) wooden sheets, whose inner face was carved and filled with a sort of wax. Writing on them was possible with a stylus, pointed at one end while the other was generally broader, like a thin spatula, used to delete portions of text, since the wax could be easily removed. Like other writing materials, tablets are attested for a very long period of time, beginning with use by Babylonians and Hittites during the Bronze Age (Symington 1991; Waal 2011). The wooden dyptich found during the excavations of the shipwreck at Ulu Burun, Turkey (Payton 1991) suggests that the tablet was familiar also in the Aegean world, since at least two members of the crew were Mycenaean (Bachhuber 2006). Those tablets are very similar to the ones used centuries later by Greeks and Romans in shape, dimensions and even the wood they are made of (Warnock and Pendleton 1991, 107). In Greece, writing tablets can be seen for the first time in a famous group of statues of the early sixth BCE, the so called *tamiai* ("treasurers") of the Acropolis of Athens;[29] moreover, from the sixth/fifth centuries BCE we find references to wax tablets in literary sources and vase paintings, and the above-mentioned inscription of the Erechtheum (IG I³ 476) records the purchase of four *pinakes*. Such evidence is now confirmed by the spectacular finds from the tombs in Odos Olgas, Athens, where, as above mentioned, together with the fragments of a papyrus roll, four wax tablets were found, still bearing some lines of a lost poetic composition.[30]

At least since the end of the Archaic period, the use of wax tablets is linked to provisional texts, and to texts that had to be corrected or updated through a period of time, following patterns that remain the same for many centuries (Small 1998). Therefore, tablets were largely employed in documentary practices, especially for lists (of men, places, or goods) or accounts (Arist., *Ath. Pol.* 48), and for the same reason were widely used in schools (Cribiore 1996, 65–9).[31] But wax tablets were also used for more complex texts. During the Hellenistic and Roman ages this is well documented by many pieces of evidence, such as the so-called "Kellis

Figure 1.2 The so-called Sappho Ostrakon. A pottery sherd dated to the second century BCE, a source for Sappho fragment 2V. Florence, The Biblioteca Medicea Laurenziana, ms PSI XIII 1300. On concession of the MiBACT. Any further reproduction by any means is prohibited.

Isocrates," a polyptich found in Kellis (ancient Trimithis), assigned to the third century CE, where someone (a school teacher?) transcribed the *Nicocles*, the *Ad Nicoclem*, and the *Ad Demonicum* (Worp and Rijksbaron 1997). Moreover, since passages could easily be corrected or rewritten on them, *pinakes* were suitable also for literary drafts. In a much disputed passage, Diogenes Laertius (3.37) affirms that when Plato died, his last work, the *Laws*, was still written *en kerois*, "on wax tablets," since the philosopher did not have the time to edit it properly on papyrus, a task taken over, instead, by his pupil Philip of Opus; and other sources mention a wax tablet said to be Plato's, where the opening words of the *Republic* were written several times, arranged in various order (e.g. Dion. Hal., *De comp. verb.* 25; see also Diog. Laer. 3.37, and Quint., *Inst. orat.* 8.6.64). We cannot establish the reliability of such references, even though, for the Imperial age, there are iconographic representations of people taking notes on tablets during the lecture of a philosopher[32] or in similar contexts.

2.4. Metal, Leather, Ostraka

As we have said, since the Archaic age Greeks also wrote on materials not expressly intended for letters. Writing on metals was not uncommon (Jeffery 1990, 55–6). In the Classical period, public texts (such as laws or decrees) were sometimes incised on bronze tablets, and metals were employed also for ritual or magic writings, such as the thin inscribed Orphic gold leaves (Bernabé and Jiménez San Cristóbal 2008), or the lead curse-spells (*defixiones*) found in many cities, from southern Italy to the Black Sea.[33] Lead could also be used for longer texts such as private letters

(Jordan 2000b). Similarly, leather – before the diffusion of parchment – could be used, but it was perceived as foreign or "barbaric"; Ctesias, a fifth-century BCE historian, was struck that the annals of the Persian kings were written on leather,[34] and Herodotus (5.57–9) wonders why the word *diphtherai* (properly "leathers") is sometimes used as synonymous with "bookroll."

The practice of writing on discarded pottery sherds (*ostraka* in Greek), was instead much more common. During the fifth century BCE, *ostraka* were used in Athens especially for a well known judicial procedure, the *ostrakismos*, which required the citizens to write on *ostraka* the names of dangerous individuals who could potentially harm the *polis*.[35] They did this either by inscribing the sherds with a blunt instrument, or writing on them with ink and brush or *kalamos*. Inscribed *ostraka* are by far the majority,[36] but since ink writings survive only under certain circumstances, this practice was probably more widespread than what we see today, and probably not limited to such a specific occasion. Egypt has preserved a much larger number of Greek texts written on pottery, starting with the early Hellenistic age. Most of them are documentary – tax or payment receipts, letters, notes, accounts –, but literary texts are also well represented. Schoolboys could improve their writing skills practicing on *ostraka*, instead of tablets, and teachers sometimes wrote poetry or prose texts on pottery sherds which their students had to transcribe (Cribiore 1996, 63–4). Pottery sherds were a popular writing material because they were abundant and free; it was thus convenient to use them even for official bureaucratic tasks. But outside of school, their literary usages were very limited; the sources make no references to the use of *ostraka* for literary composition.

3.   Writing Practices and Text Composition

This schematic survey points to a conclusion: Greeks had at their disposal a plurality of writing materials and technologies, but they did not use them randomly, or because of external factors (e.g., the scarcity of papyrus). Indeed, the materials had their own specificity and were used for selected purposes. Moreover, at least from the late fifth century BCE the making of complex texts required the joint usage of different materials: one for the draft, another for the definitive, official copy, and this was true both for documents and for literary texts, in prose or poetry. In this process, writers relied mainly on wax tablets or papyrus sheets for the draft, and on papyrus rolls (and then *codices*) for the final version.

Statements like those by Anastasius of Sinai (and more could be quoted) show us that this practice lasted for the entire span of Greek literature: but how ancient was it? We cannot say, nor is this surprising, if we consider the divergences among scholars on the date of the introduction of alphabetic writing to Greece. What we can reasonably suppose is that different techniques of composition coexisted for a long period. Rhapsodes able to improvise epic verses were active for the entire Archaic age[37] and are still attested in Plato's epoch, as with Ion, whose skills are debated in the dialogue named for him (Boyd 1994). The divine inspiration that governed their poetry did not require the use of writing, which would have impeded the kind of performances they were used to. Setting apart the complex cases of the Homeric poems and Hesiod, a different sensibility already arose during the seventh century BCE, when new poetical genres arose which probably required a different compositional attitude. It is difficult to imagine, e.g., that writing did not play a role in developing the complex metrical structures of Alcman's *Partheneion*, or of the compositions meant to boast the virtues of Archilochus' friends. And in the sixth century BCE, the diffusion of literary genres like historiography, whose products were structured as long prose texts – Hecataeus' *Genealogiai* are said to have been in four books – implied the further developing of mechanisms of production based on something more articulated than mere dictation. The perception that composing literary texts was a troublesome matter was common in fifth century BCE Athens, if a comedian as Aristophanes can make jokes about it, as in the *Acharnians* (397 sqq.), where he satirizes Euripides painfully composing a tragedy… reclined on his bed.

To understand the dynamics of creation of a complex literary text we might compare the process for the writing of public documents, which, at least for Athens, can be reconstructed from Aristotle's *Constitution of Athens* and other textual and epigraphic evidence. In Athens, state documents were mostly the results of the following steps: 1. collection of raw materials and basic information; 2. writing of a comprehensive text, with the partial data included – this text was presented to the *boule* or to another appropriate assembly to be discussed and emended; 3. production of the official document, with the addition of a prescript and of the necessary bureaucratic elements (dating formulae, list of the officers in charge, and so on); this text was deposited in an archive and, in some cases, was also inscribed and publicized to all the citizens. For the first step, wax tablets are expressly mentioned as the most suitable material,[38] and the text submitted to the assembly could be on tablets as well; but we may infer that the official copy was often written on papyrus, before being eventually put onto stone.[39] Long literary texts must have followed a similar pattern. Maybe, since the texts were considerably longer, papyrus sheets were employed for the drafts instead of tablets,[40] and the final versions were preserved only in bookrolls: but the overall process must have been quite similar.

Proper descriptions of writers' compositional practices can be found only at the end of the fifth century BCE. They can be read especially in texts from philosophical or rhetorical *milieux*, such as Plato's or Isocrates' schools. The passage of the *Theaetetus*, quoted at the beginning of this chapter, is one of the most detailed: here the genesis of philosophical treatises is described as a dynamic sequence of provisional texts, starting with original notes taken during real dialogues, and slowly tending toward a fixed state, reached by the author working on it again, with a teacher or friends. Such a process is attested, in its main outlines, until late antiquity and beyond, and appears to be common for other kind of texts: historical, medical, scientific, grammatical, rhetorical and so on.

References to preliminary notes can be found in authors varied in interests and date, such as Strabo,[41] Plutarch,[42] Lucian,[43] Aelius Aristides;[44] and we can imagine that this way of composition was later chosen also by Christian intellectuals like Origen and Eusebius – if we consider the length and the accuracy of their impressive works of erudition.[45] Similarly, many authors stress the importance of the phase of correction of provisional texts. This task was sometimes carried over during private readings, as already attested by Isocrates[46] – an author who gives many hints about his attitude toward literary composition (Pinto 2003; Nicolai 2004) – and later by philosophers, such as Theophrastus,[47] historians, such as Polybius,[48] rhetors, such as Libanius,[49] or by a physician–philosopher, such as Galen, who extends similar strategies of composition even to Hippocrates' *Epidemiai*.[50]

Concrete evidence for this method can be found in the large group of Epicurean papyri found, at the beginning of the eighteenth century, in the "Villa dei papiri" in Herculaneum, Italy. The main group of these papyri formed the working library of Philodemus, an Epicurean philosopher who moved from Greece to Italy, where a rich Roman aristocrat, Lucius Calpurnius Piso, probably the owner of the villa (Gigante 1995), sponsored him. Some of Philodemus' papyri – especially the rolls of the *Rhetoric* P. Herc. 1427, 1506, 1674 – are written in an uneven script, with corrections, and show irregular columns and layout; at their end a colophon is added, labeling each as a *hypomnematikon*. If we consider the physical appearance of the rolls, it is likely that the colophon was intended to mark them as provisional texts, made under the supervision of their author, an intermediate step before the definitive, correct edition of the work, which then would have been copied in a calligraphic script by professional hands, well exemplified among the remains of the villa's library.[51]

The rolls of Herculaneum illuminate another characteristic of literary composition: the costs of the production of texts and the relevance of patronage.[52] Philodemus – a secondary character in the history of literature and philosophy – sponsored by Lucius Calpurnius Piso – a Roman patrician but not one of the most powerful men of his times – was aided by a staff of professionals: calligraphers, secretaries, even restorers who cared for his books. Without that team, he could not have composed so many works. But the production of lengthy texts required that kind of organization, the costs of which could be sustained only by the wealthiest members of the élite. So the writer, if not part of the élite himself, needed a sponsor who could cover both his daily expenses and the costs of his research and of the production of his texts. In the history of Greek literature we find only a few organizations that could support writers: the philosophic schools are one example, but they could rely on centuries-old properties and often were originally founded by aristocrats (such as Plato himself). The Hellenistic kings played a key role in literary patronage. The best-known example is the court of the Ptolemies, who founded the Museum, where historians, scientists, poets, and philologists were hosted and had the possibility to have access to the most extensive library in the Greek world (Fraser 1972, 305–35).[53] We must imagine that the Ptolemies also guaranteed them the human resources (and the writing implements) they needed for literary work. But all the Hellenistic monarchs hosted writers, and also, following the Ptolemaic example, managed to create libraries, sometimes impressive, as in Pergamon, assembled with the help of a renowned critic and philologist, Crates of Mallus. In Roman times, the burden of patronage was shared by a plurality of individuals, sometimes occupying key positions in state administration. The examples are many: Scipio Aemilanus, the consul who destroyed Carthage in 146 BCE, was the protector of a circle of Latin and Greek literates, including the philosopher Panaetius and the historian Polybius; later, in the second century CE, the senator Lucius Mestrius Florus sponsored Plutarch, who was also helped by another aristocrat, Quintus Sosius Senecio, friend of Trajan; and still later the influential Julia Domna, wife of Septimius Severus, sponsored an important circle of Greek writers and intellectuals, including Galen and Philostratos. Even Christian intellectuals needed sponsors for their theological researches: Origen wrote his treatises thanks to the financial help of the rich Ambrose, who always supported his efforts; and Eusebius could rely on the help of the emperor Constantinus I himself. Among other forms of patronage, cities, especially in the East, provided honors and benefits – even basic ones, such as free meals, a salary or a house – to writers who praised the community, told its history and myths, or just read compositions that delighted the citizens. Inscriptions scattered everywhere in the Greek world attest this practice over a long period, from early in the Hellenistic age to late antiquity, referring to the occasional composition of texts belonging to many literary genres, including poetry, rhetoric, and history.[54] Unfortunately, the texts written for these purposes are almost completely lost, and the few of them that we may partially reconstruct often survived only because the appreciative citizen audience inscribed them on stone. This is the case, for instance, for the poetic compositions by Isyllus (fourth century BCE), whose verses can be read on a large inscription from Epidaurus (IG IV.1 [ed. min.], 128).[55] This "civic" patronage, due to its local nature, could not assure the preservation of the works which it contributed to produce, but did allow, even in small peripheral cities, the existence of a cultural life, focused on literature and literary texts.

The evidence considered so far is focused on prose texts, but at least from the early Hellenistic age a similar method of composition became characteristic also of poetry. The new poetics codified by the Alexandrians required an attention to formal details, unlike the extemporaneous poetry claimed to be inspired by the gods. So the tablet, the best mechanism for rewriting and correcting, now becomes a symbol of the poet, as the lyre was for the previous age (Bing 1988, 10–48). In the prologue of Callimachus' *Aitia*, the poet, during his investiture by Apollo, has a tablet on his knees (F 1.21–2 Pfeiffer; Fantuzzi and Hunter 2004), and in an epigram by Posidippus even the invoked Muses have a tablet in their hands, although written with gold columns.[56] From this point on, the poet prefers to show himself not as an intermediary between men and gods, but as a seeker of refurbished expressions, chiseling words as a jeweler gold.

Neither the sands of Egypt nor the volcanic muds from Vesuvius have preserved any of the writing tablets used by ancient poets to draft their works. But we can find a slight trace of their literary efforts in a small number of Greek papyri from Egypt, dating from the third century BCE to the sixth CE (Dorandi 1991), where it is possible to read the draft versions of small poetic compositions by the hands of their authors. These autographs share some common characteristics: they show erasures, corrections, substitutions of single words or whole phrases, repetitions, juxtapositions, alternative readings – features not unlike what we find in modern poets' autographs; they are often written on scraps of papyrus previously employed for other texts, such as documents or private letters, because they were not intended for preservation; the handwriting can be more or less cursive, but never calligraphic. Since the composition process could require not just one, but several drafts, we have different typologies of "autographs," reflecting the level of literary elaboration of the text. The most interesting case is that of Dioscorus, a lawyer who lived in Aphrodito (upper Egypt) in the age of Justinian, who wrote metrical *encomia* for the most influential characters of his region.[57] These *encomia* survive among his papers, which contain hundreds of petitions, wills, and contracts. The poems were written on the reverse side or on other blank spaces of the documents (P. Cair. Masp. II 67097 and 67185). Sometimes, several texts were confusedly written one after each other, without any sense of continuity, as in P. Lond. Lit. 100 A–H, whose chaotic layout reflects the juxtaposition of textual segments worked on at different times, as in a poetic sketchbook. But other drafts look quite different, showing a further level of elaboration, probably close to the definitive version. The best example is P. Aphrod. Lit. IV 4, an encomium for a Roman, which shows only minimal corrections and is written in a more carefully executed script. We do not know if Dioscorus had the opportunity to collect his poems in a "book," copied by a professional calligrapher, but his rough drafts provide rather unique evidence of the way ancient poets worked on their texts.

Such mechanics of production, if thoroughly pursued, allowed ancient writers to achieve a certain level of control over the reliability (orthographical, textual, and conceptual) of their texts. But they also had a drawback: they increased the risk that texts could be spread beyond the author's circle without his consent. In general, ancient authors had little opportunity to reclaim ownership of their works: after a text was published – whatever this word meant in ancient times (van Groningen 1963) – even basic information, such as the name of its author, could be easily altered because of the material conditions of transmission, or the malignity of less skilled imitators. It was common that texts belonging to less famous authors were ascribed to those better known, especially for works appealing to a large public, such as speeches, rhetorical works, or even medical treatises. Galen reports that he saw a book in Rome with a treatise falsely ascribed to him.[58] But this problem was much more ancient, evident already in the anthology of lyrics ascribed to Theognis – only partially by the poet – or the *corpus* of juridical speeches of Lysias, which consists mainly of texts not by Lysias (Dover 1968). Drafts were often published without their author's consent, and the author was forced to write apologetic prefaces. Plato already alludes to such a problem in his *Parmenides* (128d–e), but the unauthorized diffusion of works not meant for publication – works in progress or still uncorrected – was a common problem for intellectuals throughout antiquity.[59] Galen wrote two treatises – *On my books* and *On the order of my own books* – to publicize an official list of his authorized works (Mansfeld 1994, 117–47).

Even as the mechanics of text production here summarized were quite common to writers of different epochs, cultural level and talent, there were certainly significant exceptions. Some intellectuals preferred a more direct relationship with writing. A prolific author such as Plotinus is a good example. The philosopher, as his biographer Porphyry relates, composed very quickly; he personally wrote everything he had in mind, in bad handwriting, never reading or polishing the text. Porphyry interprets this prodigious rapidity as a mark of Plotinus' intellectual supremacy; nevertheless, he has to admit that because of this his master's works could seem even more obscure (Porph., *Plot.* 8).

Indeed, the most significant variations in the mechanics of production are closely connected to the role played by the spoken word. The practice of correcting a text after a group reading gave the voice a part in the process of composition, even during the most bookish centuries of Greek literature. The relevance of such readings varied considerably, and had varied influences – difficult to be judged – also on the elaboration of the final texts. But, even during the Imperial age, there were intellectuals and artists who preferred to commit to pure orality. Wandering rhapsodes and poets who performed improvised poems, suited to occasions and local contexts, continued to exist, as epigraphic evidence attests (Pallone 1984). Their contribution to the survival of Greek civilization was very important, even if their works are irremediably lost. And pure orality could also be a choice for intellectuals in the highest cultural circles of their time. Again, good examples can be found in philosophic *milieux*. The stoic Epictetus never wrote a single line of his meditations; what we have from him is a selection of lessons collected and transcribed from notes by his disciple Arrian, who also assembled the *Enchiridion*, a collection of sentiments much appreciated by Romantic poets. And other philosophers shared that choice, including Ammonius, teacher of Plotinus, and even Plotinus himself for the first part of his long career.[60]

The variety of available evidence suggests that the production of a literary text in ancient Greece was a dynamic process, influenced by the contexts of literary communication, the purposes of the message, and the variety of the recipients. This process required the use of different materials and technologies, and developed in the context of a constant interaction between voice and writing. This interaction, therefore, appears not to be limited to selected ways of producing texts – as we have long understood – but, at a deeper level, functions as a structural characteristic of Greek literature, in the prismatic, shining variety of its genres, authors, readers, throughout its long development.

NOTES

[1] See e.g. *Apol.* 26e; *Phaed.* 97c–98b; *Phileb.* 39a; *Symp.* 177b–c; *Phaedr.* 228b; 235d; 243c; 266d; 268c; *Protag.* 329a. Del Corso 2003, 12.

[2] Greek Text in Uthemann 1981.

[3] The author of the tale, describing the many gifts brought to the prince of Byblos Zaker Baal by the priest Wen Amon, mentions, after many other more precious items, 500 rolls of papyrus of the best quality, just before lentils and baskets of fish (Pritchard 1969, 28). However, among extant Phoenician papyri the most ancient can be dated to the seventh century BCE, as e.g. the letter from Arisuth, found in Saqqara (Donner and Röllig 1966–69, nr. 50).

[4] Driver 1976, 79 ff.

[5] For a balanced discussion of this debated topic, see Osborne 1996, 105–12.

[6] Heraclitus' book *On Nature*, e.g., was said to have been deposited by the philosopher in the temple of Artemis at Ephesus (Diog. Laer. 9.6 = Heraclitus DK 22 A 1).

[7] Literary sources are discussed in Skafte Jensen 1980, 128–58 and Ferreri 2002.

[8] Hdt. 1.123; 3.40; 5.14.

[9] *In Diog.* (or. 32), 14.

[10] *Pro Phorm.* (or. 36), 40.

[11] Aristoph., *Ran.* 52–54 (Dionysus, the main character, remembers when he was *alone* reading Euripides' *Andromeda* on a ship).

[12] Aristoph., *Av.* 959–991 (the oracle-sellers appeals to the authority of the roll he grasps in his hands to persuade Peisetairos, the main character, to make different foundation rituals for the city he wants to build); 1035–57 (another character tries to sell Peisetairos laws and decrees from a *biblion*).

[13] Skeat 1982; Capasso 1995, 21–53.

[14] Pfeiffer 1968, 115, 178, 218–20; Turner 1968, 113 with n. 29; cf. Gardthausen 1913, 410–15.

[15] Turner 2009, 8.

[16] Properly, the title of 'oldest Greek papyrus' must be given now to the fragments from the tomb in Daphni, Odos Olgas, Athens, found in 1981 but published (in a provisional way) only in Pöhlmann and West 2012: their archaeological *terminus ante* is 430–420 BCE.

[17] Kouremenos, Parássoglou and Tsantsanoglou 2006.

[18] P. Berol. inv. 9875; Horden 2002, 85–95.

[19] Measures listed in Cavallo and Maehler 2008, nrr. 1 and 2 (with plates and full references).

[20] This change of attitude toward writing and books is stressed also by Harris 1989, 116–46; 329, usually very prudent on the extent of literacy in ancient Greece and Rome.

[21] Cf. Cavallo 1998, 228–42, for the Hellenistic period; Johnson 2004 for the imperial age.

[22] Cavallo 2005, 213–33; Del Corso 2010; see in general also Hägg 1991, 90–101. A different perspective in Stephens 1994.

[23] Good examples are the *Odyssey* roll from Hawara, P. Haw. 24–28, now in Oxford, Bodleian Library, or the "Bankes Homer," P. Lond.Lit. 28, in London, British Library.

[24] Luc., *De merc. cond.* 41 (books with ivory *umbilici*).

[25] *De indol.* 12–15 (Greek text: Boudon-Millot and Jouanna 2010).

[26] Luc., *Ind.*

[27] Petr. 48.

[28] See e.g. Hor., *Sat.* 2.3.1; *Ars* 386 ff.; Quint. 10.3.31; Mart. 1.2.1–4; Pers. 3.10–11.

[29] Athens, *Acropolis Museum* inv. 144, 146, 629. See Payne and Mackworth-Young 1950, 47 (pl. 118.1); Hurwit 1999, 58, with further bibliography.

[30] Pöhlmann and West 2012.

[31] Such continuity can be seen also for the kind of exercises written on the tablets: cf. Turner 1965.

[32] Museo Archeologico Ostiense, inv. 130. Zanker 1995, 260–62, fig. 140.

[33] For a list with full bibliography see Jordan 1985 and 2000a, even if many new *defixiones* have been found in excavations during recent years.

[34] Ctesias, *FGrHist* 688 F 5 = Diod. Sic. 2.32.4.

[35] Lang 1990; Mattingly 1991; Forsdyke 2005.

[36] *Ostraka* written by brush or kalamos: Lang 1990, nrs. 110, 308, 311, 468, 652, 653.

[37] Hunter and Rutherford 2009; West 2010.

[38] See e.g. Arist., *Ath. Pol.* 47.2–3; 49.2; 53.4.

[39] Sickinger 1999; Del Corso 2002. A different perspective in Thomas 1989.

[40] As already supposed by Prentice 1933 for Thucydides. Cf. Dorandi 2007, 13–28.

[41] Strabo, *Geog.* 1.1.23.

[42] *De tranq. an.* 1, 464F.

[43] *Quomodo hist. conscr.*, 48.1.

[44] Aristid., *or.* 24, 2–3 and 8; 26, 25. On the mechanics of composition of rhetorical speeches see Pernot 1993, 423–75.

[45] In general, Grafton and Williams 2006.

[46] See e.g. *Pan.* 200–201 (the author declares that he changed the conclusion of the work after a debate arose while he was reading and correcting it with his students), or *Phil.* 26.

[47] Diog. Laer. 5.37 = Phanias fr. 4 Wehrli.

[48] Pol. 3.32.

[49] Lib., *ep.* 33 and 283. Petit 1956, part. 488–90.

[50] Gal., *In Hipp. Epid. VI comment.* (Greek Text in Wenkebach-Pfaff 1956: *CMG* V 10.2.2), pp. 5; 118; 207. Dorandi 2007, 66–70.

[51] Cavallo 2005, 129–49; Dorandi 2007, 65–81.

[52] Gold 1987; Grafton and Williams 2006, 46–85.

[53] Cf. Schenker, this volume ch. 20, pp. 315–6; Hose ch. 21, pp. 331–4.

[54] Guarducci 1929; Bouvier 1985; Cameron 1995, 47–53.

[55] Kolde 2003.
[56] *Suppl. Hell.* 705.5–6 = 118.5–6 Austin and Bastianini 2002.
[57] Fournet 1999.
[58] *Lib. prop., prooem.*, pp. 8–11 Kühn XIX = 135–6 Boudon-Millot 2007.
[59] See e.g. Diod. Sic. 40.8; Arr., *Epict., praef.* 2–4; Quint., 1, *praef.* 7.
[60] Porph., *Plot.* 3.

REFERENCES

Papyri are quoted following the *Checklist of Editions*: http://library.duke.edu/rubenstein/scriptorium/ papyrus/texts/clist_papyri.html; for inscriptions, the rules of *Supplementum epigraphicum Graecum* are employed.

Atsalos, B. 2001. *La terminologie du livre-manuscrit à l'époque byzantine.* Thessaloniki.

Austin, C. and G. Bastianini. 2002. *Posidippi Pellaei quae supersunt omnia*, Milan.

Austin, M. M. 1970. *Greece and Egypt in the Archaic Age.* Cambridge.

Bachhuber, C. 2006. "Aegean Interest on the Uluburun Ship." *American Journal of Archaeology* 110: 345–63.

Bagnall, R. S., ed. 2009. *Oxford Handbook of Papyrology.* Oxford.

Bagnall, R. S. 2011. *Everyday Writing in the Graeco-Roman East.* Berkeley, CA.

Beck, F. A. G. 1975. *Album of Greek Education.* Sydney.

Bernabé, A. and A. I. Jiménez San Cristóbal. 2008. *Instructions for the Netherworld.* Leiden.

Bing, P. 1988. *The Well-Read Muse.* Göttingen.

Blanchard, A. 1993. "Les papyrus littéraires grecs extraits de cartonnages: études de bibliologie." In M. Maniaci and P. F. Munafò, eds., *Ancient and Medieval Book Materials and Techniques*, Vatican City, 15–40.

Boudon-Millot, V., ed. 2007. *Galien: Introduction Générale: Sur l'ordre de ses propres livres: Sur ses propres livres: Que l'excellent médicin est aussi philosophe.* Paris.

Boudon-Millot, V. and J. Jouanna, eds. 2010. *Galien: Ne pas se chagriner.* Vol. 4. Paris.

Bouvier, H. 1985. "Hommes des lettres dans les inscriptions delphiques." *Zeitschrift für Papyrologie und Epigraphik* 58: 119–35.

Boyd, T. W. 1994. "Where Ion Stood, What Ion Sang." *Harvard Studies in Classical Philology* 96: 109–21.

Bülow-Jacobsen, A. 2009. "Writing Materials in the Ancient World." In R. S. Bagnall, ed., *Oxford Handbook of Papyrology.* Oxford, 3–29.

Cameron, A. 1995. *Callimachus and his Critics.* Princeton.

Cameron, A. 2011. *The Last Pagans of Rome.* Oxford.

Canfora, L. 1995. "Libri e biblioteche." In G. Cambiano, L. Canfora, and D. Lanza, eds., *Lo spazio letterario della Grecia antica*, 2nd edn., Rome, 11–93.

Capasso, M. 1995. *Volumen, Aspetti della tipologia del rotolo librario antico.* Naples.

Cavallo, G. 1998. "Ambizioni universali e isolamento di una cultura." In S. Settis, ed., *I Greci: Storia, arte, cultura e società*, Turin, 215–47.

Cavallo, G. 2005. *Il calamo e il papiro. La scrittura greca dall'età ellenistica ai primi secoli di Bisanzio.* Florence.

Cavallo, G. 2007. *Leggere a Bisanzio.* Milan.

Cavallo, G. 2009a. "Greek and Latin Writing in the Papyri." In R. S. Bagnall, ed., *Oxford Handbook of Papyrology.* Oxford, 101–48.

Cavallo, G. 2009b. "Libro e pubblico alla fine del mondo antico." In G. Cavallo, ed., *Libri, editori e pubblico nel mondo antico.* Rome, 83–132.

Cavallo G., ed. 2009c. *Libri, editori e pubblico nel mondo antico.* Rome.

Černy, J. 1952. *Paper and Books in Ancient Egypt.* London.

Cribiore, R. 1996. *Writing, Teachers, and Students in Graeco-Roman Egypt.* Atlanta, GA.

Del Corso, L. 2002. "I documenti nella Grecia classica tra produzione e conservazione." *Quaderni di storia* 56: 155–89.

Del Corso, L. 2003. "Materiali per una protostoria del libro e delle pratiche di lettura nel mondo greco." *Segno e testo* 1: 5–78.

Del Corso, L. 2005. *La scrittura nel mondo ellenistico*. Rome.

Del Corso, L. 2010. "Il romanzo greco a Ossirinco e i suoi lettori. Osservazioni paleografiche, bibliologiche, storico-culturali." In G. Bastianini and A. Casanova, eds., *I papiri del romanzo antico*, Florence, 247–77.

Donner, H. and W. Röllig. 1966–69. *Kanaanäische und Aramäische Inschriften*, 2nd edn. Wiesbaden.

Dorandi, T. 1991. "Den Autoren über die Schulter geschaut. Arbeitsweise und Autographie bei den antiken Schriftstellern." *Zeitschrift für Papyrologie und Epigraphik* 87: 11–33.

Dorandi, T. 2007. *Nell'officina dei classici. Come lavoravano gli autori antichi*. Rome.

Dover, K. J. 1968. *Lysias and the Corpus Lysiacum*. Berkeley, CA.

Driver, G. R. 1976. *Semitic Writing from Pictograph to Alphabet*. London.

Fantuzzi, M. and R. L. Hunter. 2004. *Tradition and innovation in Hellenistic poetry*. Cambridge.

Ferreri, L. 2002. "La biblioteca del tiranno. Una proposta di interpretazione della cosiddetta redazione pisistratea dei poemi omerici." *Quaderni di storia* 56: 5–47.

Forsdyke, S. 2005. *Exile, Ostracism, and Democracy*. Princeton, NJ.

Fournet, J.-L. 1999. *Hellénisme dans l'Égypte du VIe siècle. La bibliothèque et l'oeuvre de Dioscore d'Aphrodité*. Cairo.

Fraser, P. M. 1972. *Ptolemaic Alexandria*. Oxford.

Gardthausen V. 1913. *Griechische Palaeographie*. Vol. 2, 2nd edn. Leipzig.

Gigante, M. 1995. *Philodemus in Italy. The Books from Herculaneum*. Translated by D. Obbink. Ann Arbor, MI.

Gold, B. K. 1987. *Literary Patronage in Greece and Rome*. Chapel Hill, NC.

Grafton, A. and M. Williams. 2006. *Christianity and the Transformation of the Book*. Cambridge, MA.

Guarducci, M. 1929. *Poeti vaganti e conferenzieri dell'età ellenistica*. Rome.

Harris, W. V. 1989. *Ancient Literacy*. Cambridge, MA.

Horden, J. H. 2002. *The Fragments of Timotheus of Miletus*. Oxford.

Hunter, R. and I. Rutherford, eds. 2009. *Wandering Poets in Ancient Greek Culture: Travel, Locality and Pan-Hellenism*. Cambridge.

Hurwit, J. M. 1999. *The Athenian Acropolis. History, Mythology, and Archaeology from the Neolithic Era to the Present*. Cambridge.

Immerwahr, H. R. 1964. "Book Rolls on Attic Vases." In Ch. Henderson, ed., *Classical, Medieval and Renaissance Studies in Honor of Berthold Louis Ullman*, Vol. 1, Rome, 17–48.

Immerwahr, H. R. 1973. "More Book Rolls on Attic Vases." *Antike Kunst* 16: 143–47.

Jeffery, L. H. 1990. *The Local Scripts of Archaic Greece*. Revised edition with a supplement by A. W. Johnston. Oxford.

Johnson, W. 2004. *Bookrolls and Scribes in Oxyrhynchus*. Toronto.

Johnson, W. 2010. *Readers and Reading Culture in the High Roman Empire*. Oxford.

Jordan, D. R. 1985. "A Survey of Greek Defixiones Not Included in the Special Corpora." *Greek, Roman, and Byzantine Studies* 26: 151–97.

Jordan, D. R. 2000a. "New Greek Curse Tablets (1985–2000)." *Greek, Roman, and Byzantine Studies* 41: 5–46.

Jordan, D. R. 2000b. "A Personal Letter Found in the Athenian Agora." *Hesperia* 69: 91–103.

Kolde, A. 2003. *Politique et religion chez Isyllos d'Epidaure*. Basel.

Kouremenos, T., G. M. Parássoglou, and K. Tsantsanoglou. 2006. *The Derveni Papyrus*. Florence.

Lang, M. L. 1990. *Ostraka*. Princeton, NJ.

Lewis, N. 1974. *Papyrus in Classical Antiquity*. Oxford.

Mansfeld, J. 1994. *Prolegomena: Questions to Be Settled Before the Study of an Author, or a Text*. Leiden.

Marrou, H. 1938. *ΜΟΥΣΙΚΟΣ ΑΝΗΡ: Étude sur les scènes de la vie intellectuelle figurant sur les monuments funéraires romains*. Grenoble.

Mattingly, H. B. 1991. "The Practice of Ostracism at Athens." *Antichthon* 25: 1–26.

Nicolai, R. 2004. *Studi su Isocrate. La comunicazione letteraria nel IV sec. a.C. e i nuovi generi della prosa*. Rome.

Osborne, R. 1996. *Greece in the Making 1200–479 BCE*. London and New York.

Pallone, M. R. 1984. "L'epica agonale in età ellenistica." *Orpheus* 5: 156–66.

Parsons, P. 2007. *City of the Sharp-Nosed Fish. Greek Lives in Roman Egypt*, London.

Payne, H. and Mackworth-Young, G. 1950. *Archaic Marble Sculpture from the Acropolis*. 2nd edn. London.

Payton, R. 1991. "The Ulu Burun Writing-Board Set," *Anatolian Studies* 41, 99–106.

Pecere, O. 2010. *Roma antica e il testo*. Rome.

Pernot, L. 1993. *La rhétorique de l'éloge dans le monde gréco-romain*. Paris.

Petit, P. 1956. "Recherches sur la publication et la diffusion des discours de Libanios." *Historia* 5: 479–509.

Pfeiffer, R. 1968. *History of Classical Scholarship. From the Beginnings to the End of the Hellenistic Age*. Oxford.

Pinto, P. M. 2003. *Per la storia del testo di Isocrate. La testimonianza d'autore*. Bari.

Pöhlmann, W. and M. L. West. 2012. "The Oldest Greek Papyrus and Writing Tablets." *Zeitschrift für Papyrologie und Epigraphik* 180: 1–16.

Pritchard, J. B. 1969. *Ancient Near Eastern Texts Relating to the Old Testament*. 3rd edn. Princeton, NJ.

Roberts, C. H. and T. C. Skeat. 1983. *The Birth of the Codex*. London.

Sickinger, J. P. 1999. *Public Records and Archives in Classical Athens*. Chapel Hill, NC.

Skafte Jensen, M. 1980. *The Homeric Question and the Oral-Formulaic Theory*. Copenhagen.

Small, J. P. 1998. *Wax Tablets of the Mind. Cognitive Studies of Memory and Literacy in Classical Antiquity*. London.

Stephens, S. A. 1994. "Who Read Ancient Novels." In J. Tatum, ed., *The Search for the Ancient Novel*, Baltimore, 405–18.

Symington, D. 1991. "Late Bronze Age Writing-Boards and Their Uses: Textual Evidence from Anatolia and Syria." *Anatolian Studies* 41: 111–23.

Thomas, R. 1989. *Oral Tradition and Written Records in Classical Athens*. Cambridge.

Turner, E. G. 1952. *Athenian Books in the Fifth and Fourth Centuries B.C. An Inaugural Lecture Delivered at University College, London, 22 May 1951*. London.

Turner, E. G. 1965. "Athenians Learn to Write: Plato, *Protagoras* 362d." *Bulletin of the Institute of Classical Studies* 12: 67–69.

Turner, E. G. 1968. *Greek Papyri. An introduction*. Oxford.

Turner, E. G. 1977. *The Typology of the Early Codex*. Philadelphia.

Uthemann, K.-H., ed. 1981. *Anastasius Sinaita: Viae dux* (CCSG 8). Turnhout.

Van Groningen, B. A. 1963. "Ekdosis." *Mnemosyne* 16: 1–17.

Veyne, P. 2000. "La 'plèbe moyenne' sous le haut-empire romain." *Annales. Histoire, Sciences Sociales*, 55, 6: 1169–99.

Waal, W. 2011. "They Wrote on Wood. The Case for a Hieroglyphic Scribal Tradition on Wooden Writing Boards in Hittite Anatolia." *Anatolian Studies* 61: 21–34.

Warnock, P. and M. Pendleton. 1991. "The Wood of the Ulu Burun Diptych." *Anatolian Studies* 41, 107–10.

Wenkebach, E. and F. Pfaff, eds. 1956. *Galeni In Hippocratis Epidemiarum librum VI commentaria I–VI*. Berlin.

West, M. L. 2010. "Rhapsodes at Festivals." *Zeitschrift für Papyrologie und Epigraphik* 173: 1–13.

Worp, K. A. and A. Rijksbaron. 1997. *The Kellis Isokrates Codex*. Oxford.

Zanker, P. 1995. *The Mask of Socrates. The Image of the Intellectual in Antiquity*. Berkeley, CA.

FURTHER READING

For a survey on physical and paleographical characteristics of writing materials see Bülow-Jacobsen 2010 and Cavallo 2010; Parsons 2008, 135–58 starts from papyri to offer a fascinating sketch of ancient book culture; perspectives on the social background of reading and writing (but especially in Roman times) are in Johnson 2010 and Bagnall 2011, this latter offering a rather different perspective from the standard views in Harris 1989. The mechanisms of text production are carefully examined in Dorandi 2007 and Pecere 2010, where most relevant materials are collected. Iconographic evidence may contribute crucially to the reconstruction of cultural practices: see the materials collected in Beck 1975 and Zanker 1995.

CHAPTER 2

A Wound, not a World

Textual Survival and Transmission

Richard H. Armstrong

Pro captu lectoris habent sua fata libelli.
"According to the reader's grasp, books have their destiny."
—(Terentianus Maurus, *De litteris* 1286)

If you open a Greek text today, say a work in the Oxford Classical Text or Teubner series, you are the beneficiary of centuries of effort that have made this text appear before you, imparting a sense of immediate contact with the ancient world. However, there is no unmediated access to this ancient text or the world that produced it, and this awareness is the first step in developing a *philological* consciousness.[1] Countless people have worked hard over centuries to give you this sense of access, i.e. that you have "Homer" or "Sophocles" in your hands. While the emotion of communing directly with antiquity may be sublime, it is in essence an illusion. Grasping this is important, because every reader of an ancient text both benefits and *suffers from* decisions made by a great many other people. Copyists and editors have decided to prefer one version of the text over another – or whether the text will come down to us at all. Outright mistakes were sometimes made by copyists that have led to permanent glitches down the line, which may have been magnified when someone else tried to fix the problem with very little to go on. Occasionally, marginal comments or interlinear glosses have been sucked into the main text and become a permanent addition. In some instances, there might even have been active interventions to make the text say something very different from what it did originally. The *Testimonium Flavianum* is an extreme but instructive case. This is a short passage in Josephus' *Jewish Antiquities* (18.3.3), which contains the only reference to Jesus independent of early Christian writings. Why would its author, a Judean Pharisee of Roman-leaning sympathies, have written positively about Jesus, a Galilean troublemaker, to the extent of calling him the Messiah (*Khristós*) and attesting to his miracles and resurrection? We can easily imagine that Josephus wrote the opposite of this, and that Christian scribes decided to "convert" the text into a friendly witness. But we are stuck with the Greek text as it stands.[2]

So we begin with a simple truth: texts are not organisms and do not reproduce themselves. Their physical survival through centuries of political upheavals, ideological and linguistic

---

A Companion to Greek Literature, First Edition. Edited by Martin Hose and David Schenker.
© 2016 John Wiley & Sons, Inc. Published 2020 by John Wiley & Sons, Inc.

changes, literary fashions, economic catastrophes, floods, fires – not to mention mice and bookworms – is far from guaranteed. Before the age of printing, their survival was tied to a) being valued by someone who would keep them from harm and b) being manually copied by someone educated enough to make appropriate sense and use of them. Generally when we speak of the "survival" of texts as distinct from their transmission, we are talking about their persistence as physical objects. It is rare for complete manuscripts (mss hereafter) to survive intact from earlier than the tenth century CE, though there are exceptions. There are three substantial mss of Vergil from the fifth/sixth centuries CE and fragments of four others, including one as old as the late fourth century CE (Reynolds 1983, 433–4). There are four great uncial mss of the Greek version of the Bible (Septuagint + New Testament) from the fourth and fifth centuries CE (in contrast, the earliest complete ms of the Hebrew Bible, the Codex Leningradensis, dates from 1008 CE). We have over half of an impressive New Testament in the Gothic language, written in gold and silver ink on purple-dyed vellum for Theoderic the Great in the sixth century CE. There are remnants of an *Iliad* ms of the late fifth to early sixth century CE, mostly comprising illustrations cut out from the original book (Bianchi-Bandinelli 1955). Such early mss are more the exception than the rule, and are notably of the *most* valued works from antiquity: Vergil, Homer, and the Bible. Far less care was extended to problematic, pedantic, and polemical works or refuted heresies; and we know of many major works that vanished for no good reason.

Aside from papyrus fragments, most of the textual evidence for ancient works comes from mss later than the tenth century CE. That evidence is as distant from Periclean Athens as our age is from the time of Mohammed. Which is to say, antiquity survives largely as an endeavor of *medieval* civilization – a fact not all classicists readily appreciate, since the general notion of the Classical archive is tied to modern print editions (more on this issue below). A relatively small percentage of Classical scholars today have actually worked directly with a medieval ms or a papyrus fragment. While the age of printing greatly democratized access to ancient texts, it also obscured their material origins by causing scholars to imagine the Classical text as an entity floating somehow above its extant manuscripts. It is therefore quite instructive to take a moment to consider how our knowledge of antiquity is heavily reliant upon the vagaries of material survival. So as a first mental exercise, think this: antiquity is a wound, not a world you can visit. We need to be truly open to feeling the pain of our losses.

1.   The Extent of Our Known Losses

The best way to discuss ancient literature's survival is to contemplate the dark side of the moon first: i.e., what we know for certain did *not* survive, and how this affects our understanding of ancient culture. Perhaps the most dramatic example (no pun intended) is ancient drama, since we can quantify lost plays as units analogous to existing ones, which produces a simple ratio. We have seven of Aeschylus' estimated 70 to 90 plays, and short quotations and fragments of others; seven of Sophocles' 120-plus plays, again with sound bites and bits of others, including extensive fragments of the satyr play *The Trackers* (only made public in 1912); and 18 (19 with the disputed *Rhesus*) of Euripides' estimated 90, with two volumes of intriguing shards (TrGF 5.1–2). The survival rates of complete works for these pillars of Western drama are then roughly: 10 per cent to 7 per cent (Aeschylus), 5.8 per cent (Sophocles), and 20 per cent (Euripides). Compare this to Shakespeare: we have 38 plays in the great folio edition, with perhaps 2 lost; then there are a couple of plays extant of which he was perhaps partial author. Had the Bard's works suffered at the Sophoclean survival rate, we would have instead something like two complete works and one-third of another. Just think of any two Shakespeare plays and imagine trying to create a picture of the Elizabethan stage out of, say, *Titus Andronicus* and *Pericles, Prince of Tyre*. We would *like* to think what remains of the great tragic trinity is their best work, but that is a problematic assumption. We would certainly understand a lot more about the development of myth into drama if we could read Aeschylus' *Laius, Oedipus* and *Sphinx* (the missing parts from the tetralogy that included *Seven Against Thebes*) or Sophocles' *Phaedra* or *Palamedes* (TrGF 4, F 677–93 and F 478–81). We would get more of Aristophanes' jokes if we could read Euripides' *Telephus* or *Andromeda* (TrGF 5.1, 10 and 5.2, 67), and we could understand better that tragedian's capacity for scandal had his *Aeolus* (a play about brother–sister incest – TrGF 5.1, 2) or *Chrysippus* (concerning Laius' pederastic passion for the bastard son of Pelops – TrGF 5.2, 78) come down to us – though the scandal perhaps explains their absence. In sum, more evidence for these authors would doubtless enhance and nuance our understanding of Athenian drama considerably.

What of the other great dramatists of the Classical age? We would certainly like to read more of early tragedy to understand the evolution of the genre, but we have none of Choerilus' alleged 160 plays or of Pratinas' 50, nor are we sure who voted them off the island of posterity. I would love a look at Phrynichus' *Fall of Miletus,* which so upset the Athenians they fined him and outlawed its further production – setting a lasting precedent against tragedies written from contemporary events (Herodotus, *Histories* 6.21). Agathon was a significant enough poet to be portrayed in works by both Plato (*Protagoras* and *Symposium*) and Aristophanes (*Thesmophoriazusae*), and later gossip claimed Euripides wrote the *Chrysippus* out of infatuation for him (Aelian, *Var. Hist.* 2.21); but of his work we have less than 50 lines. While we get by on an appallingly low percentage of known tragedies, we had up to 1912 a *single* satyr play – Euripides' *Cyclops* – to represent that whole genre, one that was a part of every tragedian's output at the dramatic festivals (the normal entry was three tragedies and one satyr play). Now we have a fair amount of one by Sophocles, and much less from two by Aeschylus; this is still far from enough to get a feel for the genre and its relation to comedy and tragedy. Similarly scanty are the remains of the dithyramb, a choral genre that was a major part of several Athenian festivals, with wide participation from among the men and boys of Athens' tribes. It is largely represented by fragments of Pindar, Bacchylides and Timotheus, in spite of centuries of competitive output. Some 20 dithyrambic compositions a year were produced for the City Dionysia alone, not to mention the other festivals in Athens and beyond (Hordern 2002, 22). All of Old Comedy is represented to us by 11 plays of Aristophanes (we know of an additional 32 titles for him); perhaps he was the best choice, but how do we know, really? He falls rather late in the chronology of Old Comedy (he was born between 460 and 450 BCE, while comedy was first entered in the competitions in 488 or 487 BCE), and we have precious little from early comic poets like Chionides and Magnes (Mensching 1964). We could learn much about both comedy and contemporary Athenian politics if we also had at least as many comedies by Eupolis and Cratinus, who along with Aristophanes made up a kind of comic trinity for Horace (*Sat.* 1.4.1). Most of Middle Comedy is in shreds, though we know the names of 50 working poets and Athenaeus attributes more than 800 plays to the period. For New Comedy, we know of nearly 80 playwrights active between 325 and 200 BCE, and 50 working beyond then.

Things are not better if we think of other genres and disciplines. A look at the many names and fragments in Felix Jacoby's *Die Fragmente der griechischen Historiker* can be quite sobering. Hecataeus of Miletus (fl. 500 BCE) was the most important early prose writer in Ionia, but we have only fragments of his writings on geography and mythography. The mythographer and chronicler Hellanicus of Lesbos (c. 480–395 BCE) put a lot of ancient myth and history into an order that was extremely influential in antiquity, but we have little directly from his works.[3] Fifty-three of the 58 books of Theopompus' swollen history of the reign of Philip II of Macedon, published after 324 BCE, survived intact into the ninth century CE; but now it lives in mere snippets in the works of others. We have to write the whole history of Alexander the Great without direct access to any of the contemporary sources: the court history of Callisthenes, the memoirs of Ptolemy, Aristobulus, Nearchus and Onesicritus, or the highly popular and entertaining history of Cleitarchus, full of stories, it seems, culled from surviving veterans. We lack the well-informed and informative histories of the statesman Hieronymus of Cardia (late fourth/early third century BCE), which were an authoritative source for other ancient historians on the period of Alexander's successors in the Hellenistic kingdoms. Nor can we thrill to the gripping but missing *Histories* of Phylarchus (third century BCE), Hieronymus' successor, which Polybius felt came too close to tragedy (Polybius, *Histories* 2.56.6–13). Timaeus of Tauromenium (c. 350–260 BCE) was the most important historian of the western Greek world, who wrote about the colonial history of Magna Graecia, the early Romans, and the Carthaginians; his work lives on in 164 fragments and the background radiation he still projects through Diodorus Siculus' first-century BCE *Bibliothēkē* and the critical animus of Polybius.[4] Similarly, Ephorus of Cyme (c. 405–330 BCE) wrote a 30-book *magnum opus* that Polybius deemed the first universal history and was widely quoted; but we have to get at it mostly by viewing it as an *éminence grise* behind Diodorus. Of Diodorus' own *Bibliothēkē* —which is the most extensively preserved history by a Greek author—we have only 15 of the original 40 books. Historians would doubtless pay a king's ransom for the lost works of Polybius (c. 200–c. 118 BCE), one of the most articulate voices in ancient historiography. Only five of his 40 books of the *Histories* survive intact, with abridgements and excerpts making up the rest of his literary remains. In sum, though harder to calculate, our losses in historiography are clearly vast; Hermann Strasburger ventured a figure of 2.5 per cent for the total of historical works from Classical and Hellenistic antiquity to survive into modern times, or a ratio of 1 : 40 (1977 / 1990, 180–81).

Moving now to philosophy, most of what we know about the pre-Socratics comes from quotations by authors who are trying to refute them. We can be grateful the later philosophers were kind enough to quote their predecessors to some extent, but the bulk of pre-Platonic speculation can be fitted out in a single volume, if one were to dispense with all the apparatus necessary to put the fragments into context.[5] Thus if you want to peek into Parmenides' provocative poem *On Nature,* you'll find only 160 of some estimated 3,000 verses (5 per cent). Only slightly better results await you for Empedocles' *On Nature* and *Purifications,* we have 550 lines out of perhaps 5,000 (11 per cent). Democritus of Abdera, the "laughing philosopher," is credited with 70 book titles by Diogenes Laertius (9.46–9): we have exactly none of these. What we know of the fifth century BCE sophists is largely through Platonic characterization – if not caricature. While we have the flashy *Encomium of Helen* by Gorgias, those wishing to read his *On Nature or the Non-Existent* will have to do with tendentious paraphrases of a much later date. For Protagoras, we don't even have that much, though probably not because of a rampant Athenian book-burning caused by his frank agnosticism, as a later story has it (Diog. Laer. 9.52). Sheer quantity of production was no guarantee of survival to judge from cases like the Stoic philosophers Chrysippus, who reportedly wrote 705 books, routinely cranking out 500 lines a day (Diog. Laer. 7.180–81), and Posidonius, whose work reached far beyond the conventional topics in philosophy to matters ranging from anthropology and geography to seismology and zoology. We know these two thinkers were widely influential, but scholars have to reconstruct their works with considerable effort and much disagreement. Who wouldn't want to read Chrysippus' outrageous interpretation of Zeus and Hera in his lost work *On the Ancient Natural Philosophers,* which used language so indecent it was considered unmentionable by ancient bibliographers (Diog. Laer. 7.187–8)?

Even for well-represented philosophers like Aristotle, there are key parts missing in the extant corpus. Political historians lament the loss of his works on the constitutions of 158 states; though the recovered *Athenian Constitution* may repair that loss for Athens, we clearly have but a tiny fraction of the whole. His *On the Forms* torments us in its absence, since it is a critical discussion of Plato's theories that could reveal a lot about the development of Aristotle's later philosophy.[6] The *Protrepticus* was widely influential in antiquity, moving many to devote themselves to philosophy; how is it this work does not survive, while we still have the pseudo-Aristotelian *Physiognomics*? Cicero's dialogue modeled after the *Protrepticus*, the also lost *Hortensius*, still had the power to turn the young Augustine into a budding philosopher four centuries after it was written (*Conf.* 3.4.7). In fact, we generally lack textual evidence of the elegant Aristotelian dialogues (of which there were something like 18) that Cicero claimed were like a "golden river of discourse" (*flumen orationis aureum, Acad. pr.* 38.119); mostly in the Aristotelian corpus we have revised lecture notes, the style and organization of which leave much to be desired at times. While we do have part of his *Poetics* – arguably one of the most influential aesthetic texts from antiquity and of all time – there appears to be a significant portion missing that treats of comedy, and perhaps discloses the secret of that mysterious term *catharsis*, about which we are too free to speculate in that book's absence.[7]

Our canonical view of Greek literature is the product of such enormous absences. We read Homer with little else to compare it to, since so much of the epic cycle is missing, as is the Hesiodic *Catalogue of Women*. We concentrate heavily on 44 extant plays, but we are unable to reconstruct the complete line-up for a single year of the City Dionysia. We accept Plato's caricatures of the sophists as valid (hence the pejorative meaning of "sophistry" and "sophistic"), and may assume all philosophy is a footnote to him because what came before is so scanty. Our entire view of Greek culture is decidedly skewed toward Athens. We don't get to read the 50 odd plays of Theodectes of Lycia, whose *Lynceus* and *Tydeus* were admired by Aristotle (*Poet.* 1452a27, 1455a9, b29), or the comedies of Epicharmus, who wrote in Sicilian Doric (PCG 1, 9–137). We don't get to read five whole books of Tyrtaeus of Sparta or nine of Sappho of Lesbos, or five of Corinna of Tanagra, as the ancients reportedly did. We sadly lack most of the mimes of Sophron of Syracuse, which, we are told, Plato first brought to Athens and actively imitated in his dialogues, loving them so much he kept a copy under his pillow (Diog. Laer. 3.18). Whether we believe such stories or not, the mimes are a loss (remains in PCG 1, 187–253). We would gain a good deal of information on Athens' famous rival had the works of Sosibius of Sparta (fl. mid-third century BCE) survived. We typically think about the intense production of the poets and scholars of Alexandria only in relation to Roman literature, for which Hellenistic models loomed tremendously large, or in relation to the earlier Greek works they helped to preserve. What remains of the great commentaries of Aristarchus or the alleged 3,500-plus works of Didymus must be gleaned from the scholia in the margins of medieval manuscripts of Homer. Imagine what we would at least know about our losses had Callimachus' vast bibliographical work, the *Pinakes*, survived, which detailed the holdings of the library of Alexandria? The work's full title, *Lists of Those Eminent in All Areas of Learning and Their Writings*, shows the amplitude of his bibliographical ambitions, and its reported 120 bookrolls attest to the scope of his achievement. The fragmentary remains of 58 entries can only serve to torment us about its loss.

We suffer greatly as well from the loss of Greek texts by non-Greek authors, who adopted the literary *koine* to relate important matters to the *oikoumene*, or by Greek authors on non-Greek matters. We have very little of Q. Fabius Pictor, a Roman writing one of the first Roman histories, but in Greek so the civilized world could read it. Lucius Cincius Alimentus also wrote in Greek of his captivity under Hannibal in the Second Punic war – but this eyewitness account is only known indirectly. We have nothing of the works of Silenus of Sicily and Sosylus of Sparta, whose histories of Hannibal's campaigns were heavily pillaged by Polybius and Livy. Hannibal himself was also author of lost works in Greek, we are told—wouldn't those make interesting reading? King Juba II of Numidia wrote extensively in Greek and Latin; his guide to Arabia was a best-seller in Rome, while the Athenians erected a monument in honor of his writings—yet we get few glimpses of this fascinating output, though it percolates Pliny's *Natural History* (Roller 2003). Christian interest has preserved for us the works of Josephus, a Jewish witness to the Roman wars in Judea in the first century CE, but not the vast output of Nicolaus of Damascus (cf. the fragments collected in FGrHist 90), from whom Josephus drew a great deal. This court historian to Herod the Great and biographer of Augustus would hardly be an impartial source, yet his works would certainly fill out the picture of at least the official view of things. And our knowledge of the ancient world might look very different if we had complete copies of Manetho's *Aigyptiaka* and Berossos' *Babyloniaka*, Hellenistic works detailing the histories of Egypt and Babylon written by knowledgeable if fallible men; or Ctesias of Cnidus' *Persika*, written in opposition to Herodotus' *Histories* and still being read by Photius in the ninth century CE, who left us a synopsis (*Bibl.* 72). Imagine what we could learn from the 20 books in Greek about the Etruscans, penned by the future Emperor Claudius, who was among the very last people to know Etruscan (Suetonius, *Divus Claudius* 42.2). How different would later antiquity look to us if we could read all of Arrian's 25-book opus on the Black Sea region, or his full account of the Alans, or his *History of the Parthian Wars* (17 books), or Priscus' history treating extensively of the Huns in the fifth century?

These are examples of our known losses; we should also consider the real possibility of unknown losses (our "unknown unknowns," as Donald Rumsfeld once put it). The texts enumerated here may be just the tip of the iceberg of all that is missing—and I have not even mentioned technical, rhetorical, novelistic, legal, scientific, musical, mathematical, and medical works, or Hellenistic Jewish or early Christian and patristic authors. The contemplation of such deficits is important, as it humbles our attempts to create totalizing reconstructions of antiquity or to effect a mind-meld with an ancient author. It is crucial to distinguish the ontological plenitude known as The Ancient World from the scrappy realities of the ancient archive.

2.   Tales of Survival and Recovery

Only because our losses are so staggering are we greatly advanced by whatever scraps of ancient texts happen to come back to light. Thus, while it is healthy to contemplate seriously the state of our ignorance, it is equally important to be aware that there are still surprises to be had. If we look at antiquity as a whole, we can note with amazement the particular finds that have truly revolutionized our knowledge within the past 120 years: the Amarna letters and Hymn to the Aten (Akkadian and Egyptian texts revealing the lost history of the "heretic Pharaoh" Akhenaten); the Ugaritic texts (Canaanite tablets discovered in 1929, which have contributed substantially to understanding the Old Testament in its ancient context); the Dead Sea Scrolls (texts discovered 1946–1956 that have vastly improved our understanding of Second Temple Judaism and the textual tradition of the Hebrew bible); and the Nag Hammadi library (12 Coptic codices discovered in 1945 that revolutionized the study of gnosticism and early Christianity). We should also note that mere physical discovery only begins a long process that has its dramatic later developments. For example, Linear B, though discovered on artifacts in the late nineteenth century, was not actually deciphered and identified as a syllabary script for an early form of Greek until the 1950s. Or to take another famous example, the papyri found at Herculaneum were "discovered" in the 1750s, but their charred condition left most of them unreadable for decades. Various attempts to unroll them since their discovery often yielded disastrous results, until the introduction of new methods in the mid-1960s and 1970s secured better outcomes; but the process of reading these works remains ongoing, as do the site excavations (Sider 2005).

For all the complications in handling and reading papyri, the gains since the late nineteenth century are still considerable. For Greek literature specifically, we have had significant discoveries for Aeschylus, Alcman, Archilochus, Aristotle, Bacchylides, Callimachus, Empedocles, Epicurus, Euripides, Herodas, Hyperides, Isocrates, Menander, Pindar, Sappho, Simonides, Sophocles and Stesichorus – just to list the better known names. Even recovered copies of things we already have, such as Homer's *Iliad*, can still have great value for understanding ancient textuality, literacy, translation, schooling and even elements of performance. And archaeology has yielded some things beyond canonical authors that were truly unexpected (i.e., among the unknown unknowns), such as the Derveni papyrus. This dates from c. 340 BCE (or even earlier) and is perhaps the oldest surviving ms from Greek antiquity; it was discovered in 1962 and contains an allegorical commentary on an Orphic poem (Betegh 2004, Laks and Most 1997). Another case of unexpected surprise is the Posidippus roll, a papyrus roll of the third–second century BCE comprising 112 poems that surfaced on the market in 1992, which constitutes our first physical example of a book of poems from the ancient world and contains over 600 lines of previously unknown Hellenistic poetry (Gutzwiller 2005; cf. Höschele, ch. 12, pp. 194–6 in this volume).

There is certainly an understandable sense of triumph in recovering great works of the past; it is no small thing to overcome death and oblivion. The case of the comic poet Menander (344 / 3–292/1 BCE) will doubtless remain a prime example of the thrill of cliff-hanging survival. For centuries, one knew that Menander's works were widely influential and imitated by Greek and later Roman authors. Over 900 quotations of various lengths preserved in ancient authors showed the esteem in which he was held, yet not a single play survived intact. But in the twentieth century, archaeological excavations recovered a repurposed codex of Menander (the "Cairo Codex"—used as a jar topper) from a house and another (the "Bodmer Codex") from an abandoned monastery library. Further fragments were recovered from mummy cartonnage, from among the Oxyrhynchus papyri, and, quite recently, from a twice-palimpsested ms in the Vatican (Handley 2011). This means that the casual student of classics today has vastly more Menander to go on than the greatest scholars of the nineteenth century, and is thereby in a position to better understand the post-Classical Greek theater and the Roman stage to boot. Menander now has his own volume in the *Penguin Classics* series, and can be known widely alongside his canonical colleagues. One should never make light of such material advantages, even if what we possess is still a fraction of the whole (Handley 2011, 146 suggests perhaps 5 per cent).

Apart from such spectacular recoveries of major authors, we should also consider the importance of things we learn from less exalted papyrus finds of non-canonical, and unexpected works. The philosophical library uncovered in a villa at Herculaneum has been unkindly described as one filled with the works of "an obscure, verbose, inauthentic Epicurean from Cicero's time" (thus Domenico Comparetti, cited in Sider 2005, 63). Yet from Philodemus' works we learn a good deal about the Epicurean milieu in the Bay of Naples, a background that is quite significant for Roman poets of the generation of Vergil and Horace. As a philosopher–poet, his works reveal attempts made in later Epicureanism to bridge the gap between philosophy and poetry, and some of the poetic theory dealt with in his works clearly has its echoes in the Augustans. Moreover, his philosophical writings teach us many things about some aspects of Epicurus' thought now lost to us – particularly his conception of the gods (Sider 2005, 84–7). He quotes extensively from Epicurus' *On Nature*, a major lost work, portions of which are recoverable from other papyri from the same site. The collection of books taken as a whole provides an interesting picture of the Greco-Roman intellectual life at a crucial moment in Roman culture – and some, like David Sider, hope further excavation may yet reveal still greater treasures, both Greek and Roman (2005, 94–5). It is no longer absurd to hope for such a thing – even if at long odds.

Let us take a closer look at a modest example of what a found text can do to open up our view of antiquity. A papyrus containing a mere 14 lines of text was acquired by the Louvre in 1891, and waited over a century to be published. Annie Bélis first published it in 2004, and M. L. West subsequently published a corrective article on it in 2007 – again we see the long latency between the physical and scholarly phases of "discovery." Two things make it of immediate interest in spite of its brevity. First, it seems to be a scene from the lost *Medea* of Carcinus the Younger (fl. 380–377 BCE), a major figure in his day who composed over 160 plays, one of the highest numbers on record for a tragedian, and is credited with 11 victories in tragic competitions. He was a third-generation tragedian; his grandfather Carcinus the

Elder was victorious at the Dionysia in 446 BCE, and his father Xenocles beat out Euripides in the Dionysia of 415. Yet again, we wonder why this tragic dynasty seems cut out of posterity, particularly since Aristotle refers to Carcinus the Younger several times, and authors like Lysias, Timaeus, Menander and even Athenaeus (late second century CE) quote him – this last author's citation implies Carcinus' works were preserved into the common era. Second, the papyrus has musical notation, precious traces of ancient performance that take the significance of this fragment to a new dimension. From what Bélis and West have reconstructed, this version of the Medea story hinges on an interesting twist: Medea has *not* killed her children, but believes she has sent them away to safety. Yet because she cannot produce them, she is *accused* of having killed them. This is a delicious irony (which West further explores in his article), and a pointed divergence from the Euripidean version that effectively defined Medea as a horrific child-murderer for Western literature. As is often the case, we learn a lot about the creative options poets enjoyed when we have more than one version of a tragic plot. But the musical details are also intriguing: the melody recorded is not contemporary to the text, but one later added for a kind of virtuoso solo recital. This is not, in other words, a text of the whole play, but a *performance* text for a later soloist who, in Imperial times, is bringing out this now classic scene set to new music. So not only does the fragment give us something of intrinsic interest by a reputable post-Classical tragedian, it also gives us a snapshot of the play's *reception* and *re-performance* (see Nervegna 2007). This fragment therefore affords us a view not just of textual survival, but cultural *tradition* – i.e., proof of what at least some ancients valued in their own literature, and how they repurposed it in a later milieu. Carcinus' work clearly had an afterlife, even if it never made it through to the Valhalla of *Penguin Classics*.

3.   Transmission: Copying, Editing, and Textual Criticism

As we have just seen, a papyrus can be discovered and still languish in a drawer (or a cigar box) for decades until a scholar makes it public to the world. This simple fact reveals that mere physical survival means little without the conscious intention of someone *to transmit* this text to a reading public. In the pre-print era, transmission refers to the laborious process of copying out texts by hand; but we have not been in that situation for centuries. We have long since moved from the flux of manuscript culture to the fixity of print, and, save for those texts that come to us directly from the sands of Egypt, such as the Carcinus fragment above, every student of Greek literature should understand the layers of mediation that print culture has created, especially because many of the conventions and limitations of print culture are rapidly changing in the digital age. First, one should know that the advent of printing created a watershed in Western historical consciousness in many ways. The printing of Greek grammars, lexicons, and texts allowed Hellenic culture once again to be a broad possession internationally, this time well north of its homeland in the Mediterranean basin (Geanakoplos 1962; Wilson 1992). However, transforming Greek into an idiom of print culture required the creation of new Greek styles of typography, which gradually left behind the Byzantine manuscript hands and scribal culture (Proctor 1900). A new textual regime also came into play, with standardized accentuation and punctuation, the introduction of line numbers, indexes, and conventions for the layout of poetry and prose. But the precision technology of printing identical copies also brought with it another possibility: the ideal of widely circulating and *constantly improved* texts, i.e. texts that aspire to be much more than a copy of a copy. The cultural shift from "a sequence of corrupted copies to a sequence of improved editions" is a general one affecting all fields of knowledge in the age of printing, when "large-scale data collection did become subject to new forms of feedback which had not been possible in the age of scribes" (Eisenstein 1993, 76–7). The production of such improved editions of ancient texts is known as textual criticism (not to be confused with *literary* criticism, though the two overlap), which reached its greatest development as a field in the nineteenth and twentieth centuries. The development of modern textual criticism was a slow process and it had predecessors going back to the great scholars of Alexandria and Pergamon in antiquity. From the earliest days the desideratum has been to make public the "best text" possible; but just what this entails in terms of both methodology and risk has to be understood in some detail.

We should first distinguish between the words *copy*, *recension*, and *edition* in their technical senses. A copy or transcription is a mechanical attempt to make a new iteration of an original, and we have many late examples of handwritten copies made of much older mss; classed as *recentiores*, these later copies are often assumed to be less interesting than their older originals. A *recension*, however, is a careful collation of available mss copies (and other witnesses, like passages quoted in other works), showing broadly all the evidence for the text in question, known as the textual tradition. A recension's success is clearly reliant on the amount of available evidence – but, paradoxically, can be greatly complicated by a large tradition. Inevitably, such a recension will disclose variant readings, or places where the various mss say different things, and sometimes mss can be classified neatly into groups or families based on these differences (often mistakes they hold in common are the best criteria for classification). Ideally – or rather, *idealistically* – the mss can then be arranged and classified in a genealogical chart known as a stemma, showing which mss are derivative of others (their archetypes), and this stemmatic method would then lead us back to the earliest form of the text (often best represented, one might assume, by the oldest mss) to which we have access. This form of the text might just be late antique or early medieval, and potentially still a good distance from a putative "original" of the fifth century BCE or earlier, depending on the author's date. Most of us can live with that distance, but there are some scholars with unsettling certainty of mind who are convinced they can get us back to a vision of the autograph ms of the ancient author himself. Fundamentally, the classic aspiration of textual criticism is, in the formulation of Paul Maas, "to produce a text as close as possible to the original" (1958, 1). Upon examination of the textual tradition, "if it proves not to give the original, we must try to reconstruct the original by conjecture (*divinatio*) or at least try to isolate the corruption" (Maas 1958, 1).

Thus the traditional textual editor may either be seen as a harmless drudge reporting on the many mss he has either seen in microfilm, examined personally, or learned about from trustworthy persons; or as a daring interventionist and diviner, who makes very real judgments about *emending* or fixing up the text through conjecture. (It is conceivable that he may be both in the course of editing a text over many years.) But to be clear: the textual critic makes use of the *recension* to produce an *edition*, which *he* might feel is the newly restored text of the original author or just the best version possible, but which is always a scholarly construct, a *modern* by-product of an ancient and medieval textual process. Whether or not the modern edition misrepresents "the text" depends entirely on the judgment of the editor and the scholarly community to which he responds – and it may take generations for the jury to render its verdict fully. But the problem is: the modern critical text – through the authority of its editor and availability in libraries and bookstores – displaces the ancient or medieval mss in importance. If you believe the text has been restored or improved, then you will find this unproblematic. But if you are deeply unhappy about the choices the editor made, you will find it vexatious.

The view of stemmatic editing given above is admittedly oversimplified. But at its most extreme, we can see that the stemmatic approach betrays a certain Platonic penchant: one must get through the detritus of the material many (i.e., the various mss) to a noetic union with the immaterial one (the notional archetype, the Urtext, or the autograph ms representing infallibly the author's thought and intentions). The truth is, things are far messier in the typical textual tradition, and they get much worse in cases where we have a great many mss instead of a very few (Homer being a particular case in point). For one thing, medieval Byzantine scholars and scribes did not simply copy from one text mechanically and uncritically. Although every instance of copying from ms to ms could introduce errors (due to ignorance, inattention, or problems with the master copy), it was also an opportunity to collate and correct the new copy from other mss (which the stemmatic enthusiast might impatiently denounce as "horizontal contamination" since he wants things to be neatly arranged in a vertical order of ascending authenticity). We know for a fact that the Byzantine Greeks had access to far more mss than we do, so what they add may be something of great value and antiquity, and not "horizontal" tomfoolery at all. Thus against the initial prejudice in favor of the most ancient mss, Byzantinists have raised the cry *recentiores non deteriores* (more recent copies are not worse ones – Browning 1960). Once one removes the simplistic genealogy of texts from the process, it becomes harder to know what to do with all the discordant readings.

Moreover, the idea of grounding textual criticism on the certitude of an Urtext – stable in meaning, clearly intended by its maker, accessible by hard labor and divination – has been greatly challenged by our evolving sense of ancient textuality's relationship to orality (cf. Reece, ch. 3, pp. 55–6 in this volume), oral poetics, (re)performance (in the cases of epic and drama in particular), multitextuality, and multilocality. In medieval studies, the Platonic stemma lost its attraction long ago in favor of publishing the best ms (*Leithandschrift*) or something more reflective of the typical medieval *reader*, not the demiurgic author (McGann 1992; Cerquiglini 1999; Jeffreys 2008,). Outside of Classical studies, in other words, scholars have opened themselves to the charms of the many over the one, being often more interested in chasing real readerly contexts than notional Urtexts. Pockets of Urtext-hunting textual criticism remain strong in classics – see especially M. L. West's Teubner edition of the *Iliad* (1998–2000) – though as Bolter points out, there remains the irony "that for classical authors the Urtexts are irretrievable, and the texts now established through textual criticism will always be unstable, vacillating among various readings offered by manuscripts and editors" (1993, 161).

But now that the fixity of print is giving way to the new flux and multidirectionality of the digital age, the old print culture consensus may be melting away. For one thing, mss formerly languished in restricted access collections, usually far from the reader of the printed text. The reader had to make do with whatever limited report the editor cared to make of the mss in the apparatus. But now the digitization of major mss, such as those being undertaken by the Homer Multitext Project, effectively – and for the first time, really – democratizes access to the material foundations of ancient texts. While such mss images can be hard to read – one has to have some real paleographical skills – the experience is eye-opening, for the scholar will come to see just how far the print editions are from the textual tradition not only in variant readings, but also in format, orthography, and purpose. Digitization of this textual tradition will also lead to powerful new ways of tracing the complex relationships between texts, doing away with simple Platonic stemmas. And a multitext edition can make available – in ways unthinkable in the fixed medium of print – a wide range of evidence for the text, and not just in the crabbed, apparatus crunching manner of our OCT and Teubner critical texts of yore.

Let us take a concrete example once again in order to understand the kind of problem an editor – and a reader of a critical edition – face. I will use a problem in the text of Homer, since Homeric textual editing presents extremely rich, complex challenges. In the *Iliad*, old Nestor intervenes at a point in book 1 when Achilles and Agamemnon are wrangling shamefully in front of the Greek army. He reminds them of his own past association with other heroes in order to whip them into behaving themselves. Lines 260–61 read in certain manuscripts: ἤδη γάρ ποτ' ἐγὼ καὶ ἀρείοσιν ἠέ περ ὑμῖν / ἀνδράσιν ὡμίλησα ("for back in the day I kept company with men much better than *you*"). Now in line 260 we find other mss reporting ἡμῖν, which changes the meaning to "men much better than *us*." This is a difference of a single letter in the Greek (upsilon vs. eta: which is it?), but the overall change in tone is clear: either Nestor *shames* them by saying his past associates were superior to these two peevish fellows, or *humbles himself* by saying it has been his honor to have consorted with heroes better than himself – and by implication, them too. When confronted by variants, an editor in traditional print editions had to pick *one* and only one for pride of place in the main text, while relegating the other(s) to the marginal existence of the apparatus criticus at the foot of the page. So Thomas Allen's OCT text prints ὑμῖν in the main text, with ἡμῖν reported in *much* smaller print way at the foot of the page, followed by a short and highly abbreviated list of mss that give this variant.

To decide which is better, one has to come up with stories to explain why the variants exist at all, and two easily suggest themselves: either scribes confused the letters eta and upsilon for some reason (making it a problem for the paleographer to explain), or the linguistic shift known as itacism is responsible, whereby the pronunciation of those two formerly distinct vowels became identical, so *us* and *you* sounded alike: /ı: mi:n/. Of the two explanations, the linguistic is more convincing than the paleographical in this case. But explaining *why* variants exist does not help us to decide *which variant* to prefer, so one then must investigate further. The modern editor has help in the case of Homer from his ancient predecessors. We find that this discrepancy has been argued about since the time of the Alexandrian editors, to judge from things reported in the scholia written in the margins of Homeric mss. The first critical editor of Homer was also the first librarian at the great library of Alexandria, Zenodotus of Ephesus (fl. 280 BCE). He appears to have written ὑμῖν in his edition of the text, which was cobbled together from a variety of mss collected at the library from places around the Greek world.[8] (It is possible that Zenodotus, besides making such judgment calls on variants, was the first to divide the *Iliad* and *Odyssey* into 24 books.) In this instance, however, Zenodotus only succeeded in irritating his editorial successor, Aristarchus of Samothrace (c. 220–c. 143 BCE), whose substantial role in shaping Homeric textuality as we encounter it today is being recognized more and more (see especially Nagy 2004). He found Zenodotus' version of line 260 "insolent," (ἐφύβριστος), and argued that by saying "better than *us*" instead, Nestor would be reckoning himself among the lesser men dwarfed by the heroes of yore. Later editors and commentators have agreed with Aristarchus, such as the Byzantine archbishop Eustathius of Thessalonica (c. 1115–1195 / 6 CE), who thought "better than us" was more in keeping with the sentiment "such mortals as we are now" (cf. *Il.* 1.272; Van der Valk 1971, 1:156–7), and G. S. Kirk, who felt Aristarchus might well be right given what follows in the speech (1985, 80). We see "better than us" in certain rather important mss, like the splendid one in Venice known as Venetus A (Dué 2009).

However, other editors side with old Zenodotus, such as Walter Leaf (1852–1927), an assiduous editor of the *Iliad* who quipped that with "better than us" Aristarchus "wished to import into heroic language the conventional mock modesty of the Alexandrian Court. The whole meaning of Nestor's speech is that he himself is the peer of better men than those he is advising" (1900, 1:23). Leaf may have made the assumption here that Aristarchus was a naughty interventionist critic, who willfully "corrected" the text according to his own aesthetic conjectures. Increasingly, however, Gregory Nagy and other scholars are asserting that Aristarchus was not rewriting the text of Homer, but rather putting forward variants that *already* existed in a textual tradition full of such options.[9] But with the traditional editorial mindset, the variants still seem to leave us to decide this as a matter of taste: how tactful can we imagine the indignant Nestor to be here? If textual criticism is "the art and science of balancing historical probabilities," (Kenney 1974, 146), we seem to be at a standstill in a case like this, when ancient variants have equal probabilities. So which one gets to ride in the front seat? Should we flip a coin?

We might well be asking the wrong question here. In fact, Homeric scholarship has recently called into question the posing of such a dilemma, deeming it a pseudo-dilemma. This has to do with a scholarly revolution at both ends. On the one end, Homeric textuality is now being understood very differently by the Oralist school, for whom variation is not a sign of textual *corruption*, but of living variants of an oral poetic tradition (Nagy 2005, 59). Authenticity, in other words, does not lie with the one, the Urtext, but with the many, the real functional variants. Therefore, at the *other* end, i.e. the modern critical text of Homer, we should not work towards a text made up of arbitrary binary choices that yield an apparent "unitext" of a great poet (*unius munus* [...] *maximi poetae*: West 1998, v), but a multitext reflecting a repertory of reported versions, options, *processes*. The fixed regime of print and the paged book could hardly pull this off in any economical manner, but an online multitext edition is currently under development at the Center for Hellenic Studies, fruit of a more radical philology (http://www.homermultitext.org). This is just one example of the great Digital Renaissance under way in our lifetime – and one very good reason for the student of Greek literature today to be very excited about the future of the past. Our voracious technical sophistication may finally help us to get much closer to the manuscript culture of the middle ages and, though in more fragmentary form, the papyrus book roll culture of antiquity. We might even hope, conceptually at least, to glimpse the distant outline of vastly ancient oral traditions from the dawn of Greek civilization. There is much work to be done – and much work to be *undone*. But there has never been a better time to be a scholar and transmitter of Greek literature; the auspices are good for tending the wound that is the ancient archive.

NOTES

[1] I have purposely avoided any attempt here to repeat the standard version of textual survival and transmission surveys. For excellent introductions to the more technical side of these matters, see the Further Reading section, especially Pöhlmann 2009 and Gastgeber 2010 (for a short articles), and Reynolds and Wilson 1991 or Wilamowitz-Moellendorff 1927 / 1982 for a more extensive treatment. Expansive treatments are Pfeiffer 1968 and 1976, and Sandys 1903 / 1998.

[2] For a reconstruction of what Josephus *might* have said, see Robert Eisler's version (1931, 61), printed now in a footnote in the Loeb Josephus, edited by Louis Feldman (*Jewish Antiquities* 18.63, p. 48 note a).

[3] On Hellanicus and the other Atthidographers (historians of Attica), the student now can consult Harding 2008.

[4] Baron 2013 is an elegant monograph dealing at length with how to read a fragmentary Hellenistic historian detached from the animus of Polybius and modern assumptions.

[5] See especially Kahn 2003 on the texts of early philosophy.

[6] For the fragmentary works of Aristotle, see Gigon 1987, selected fragments in Ross 1955 and, e.g., on Aristotle's *On Poets* Janko 2010.

[7] For attempted reconstructions, see Janko 2002 and Watson 2012; see also the discussion in Obbink 2011.

[8] We know this from the A Σ to *Iliad* 1.260; Erbse 1, 1969, 82.

[9] Nagy 2004, 109: "I conclude that it was Aristarchus, not Didymus, who developed a system for the collating of Homeric texts. And it was Aristarchus who led the way in searching for significant variations in the history of Homeric textual tradition."

REFERENCES

Baron, Chr. A. 2013. *Timaeus of Tauromenium and Hellenistic Historiography*. Cambridge.

Bianchi Bandinelli, R. 1955. *Hellenistic–Byzantine Miniatures of the Iliad (Ilias Ambrosiana)*. Olten.

Betegh, G. 2004. *The Derveni Papyrus: Cosmology, Theology, and Interpretation*. Cambridge.

Bolter, J. D. 1993. "Hypertext and the Classical Commentary." In J. Solomon, ed., *Accessing Antiquity: The Computerization of Classical Studies*. Tucson, 157–71.

Browning, R. 1960. "*Recentiores non Deteriores*." *Bulletin of the Institute of Classical Studies* 7: 11–21.

Cerquiglini, B. 1999. *In Praise of the Variant: A Critical History of Philology.* Baltimore, MD.

Dickey, E. 2007. *Ancient Greek Scholarship: A Guide to Finding, Reading, and Understanding Scholia, Commentaries, Lexica, and Grammatical Treatises, from Their Beginnings to the Byzantine Period.* Oxford.

Dué, C., ed. 2009. *Recapturing a Homeric Legacy: Images and Insights from the Venetus A Manuscript of the Iliad.* Cambridge.

Dué, C. and M. Ebbott. 2010. *Iliad 10 and the Poetics of Ambush.* Cambridge, MA.

Eisenstein, E. L. 1993. *The Printing Revolution in Early Modern Europe.* Cambridge.

Eisler, R. 1931. *The Messiah Jesus and John the Baptist according to Flavius Josephus' recently rediscovered Capture of Jerusalem and other Jewish and Christian sources.* London.

Erbse, H. 1969–1988. *Scholia Graeca in Homeri Iliadem (scholia vetera).* 7 vols. Berlin.

Gastgeber, Ch. 2010. "Transmission: History of Greek Literature (500 AD to the Invention of Printing)." In M. Landfester, H. Cancik, and H. Schneider, eds., *Brill's New Pauly, vol. 5, Classical Tradition,* Leiden, 666–72.

Geanakopolos, D. J. 1962. *Greek Scholars in Venice: Studies in the Dissemination of Greek Learning from Byzantium to Western Europe.* Cambridge, MA.

Gigon, O., ed. 1987. *Aristotelis opera. Vol. III. Librorum deperditorum fragmenta,* Berlin.

Gurd, S. 2005. *Iphigenias at Aulis: Textual Multiplicity, Radical Philology.* Ithaca, NY.

Gutzwiller, K., ed. 2005. *The New Posidippus: A Hellenistic Poetry Book.* Oxford.

Handley, E. 2011. "The Rediscovery of Menander." In Obbink and Rutherford 2011, 138–59.

Harding, Ph. 2008. *The Story of Athens: The Fragments of the Local Chronicles of Attika.* New York.

Hordern, J. H. 2002. *The Fragments of Timotheus of Miletus.* Oxford.

Jakoby, F. 1923–58. *Die Fragmente der griechischen Historiker.* Leiden.

Janko, R. 2002. *Aristotle on Comedy : Towards a Reconstruction of Poetics II.* London.

Janko, R., ed. 2010. *Philodemus: On Poems books 3–4, with the Fragments of Aristotle, On Poets.* Oxford.

Jeffreys, M. 2008. "Textual Criticism." In E. Jeffreys, J. Haldon, and R. Cormack, eds., *The Oxford Handbook of Byzantine Studies,* Oxford, 86–94.

Kahn, Ch. H. 2003. "Writing Philosophy: Prose and Poetry from Thales to Plato." In H. Yunis, ed., *Written Texts and the Rise of Literature in Ancient Greece,* Cambridge, 139–61.

Kenney, E. J. 1974. *The Classical Text: Aspects of Editing in the Age of the Printed Book.* Berkeley, CA.

Kirk, G. S. 1985. *The Iliad: A Commentary.* Vol. 1. Cambridge.

Laks, A. and G. W. Most, eds. 1997. *Studies on the Derveni Papyrus.* Oxford.

Leaf, W., ed. 1900. *The Iliad,* 2nd edn. London.

Maas, P. 1958. *Textual Criticism.* Oxford (first edn. 1927).

McGann, J. J. 1992. *A Critique of Modern Textual Criticism.* Charlottesville, VA (first edn. 1982).

Mensching, E. 1964. "Zur Produktivität der Alten Komödie." *Museum Helveticum* 21: 15–49.

Nagy, G. 2004. *Homer's Text and Language.* Urbana, IL.

Nervegna, S. 2007. "Staging Scenes or Plays? Theatrical Revivals of 'Old' Greek Drama in Antiquity." *Zeitschrift für Papyrologie und Epigraphik* 162: 14–42.

Obbink, D. 2011. "Vanishing Conjecture: Lost Books and their Recovery from Aristotle to Eco." In Obbink and Rutherford 2011, 20–47.

Obbink, D. and R. Rutherford, eds. 2011. *Culture in Pieces: Essays on Ancient Texts in Honour of Peter Parsons.* Oxford.

Pfeiffer, R. 1968. *A History of Classical Scholarship from its Beginnings to the End of the Hellenistic Age.* Oxford.

Pfeiffer, R. 1976. *A History of Classical Scholarship from 1300 to 1850.* Oxford.

Pöhlmann, E. 2009. "Textual History." In H. Cancik and H. Schneider, eds., *Brill's New Pauly, vol. 14, Antiquity,* Leiden, 346–58.

Proctor, R. 1900. *The Printing of Greek in the Fifteenth Century.* Oxford.

Reynolds, L. D., ed. 1983. *Texts and Transmission: A Survey of Latin Classics.* Oxford.

Reynolds, L. D. and N. G. Wilson. 1991. *Scribes and Scholars: A Guide to the Transmission of Greek and Latin Literature,* 3rd edn. Oxford.

Roller, D. W. 2003. *The World of Juba II and Kleopatra Selene: Royal Scholarship on Rome's African Frontier.* New York.

Ross, W. D., ed. 1955 *Aristotelis Fragmenta Selecta.* Oxford.

Sandys, J. E. 1998. *A History of Classical Scholarship*. London (first edn. 1903).

Sider, D. 2005. *The Library of The Villa dei Papiri at Herculaneum*. Los Angeles.

Strasburger, H. 1977 / 1990. "Umblick im Trümmerfeld der griechischen Geschichtsschreibung." In W. Schmitthenner and R. Zoepffel, eds., *Studien zur alten Geschichte, vol. 3*, Hildesheim, 167–218.

Van der Valk, M., ed. 1971. *Eustathii Archiepiscopi Thessalonicensis COMMENTARII ad Homeri Iliadem pertinentes*. Leiden.

West, M. L. 2007. "A New Musical Papyrus: Carcinus, 'Medea.'" *Zeitschrift für Papyrologie und Epigraphik* 161:1–10.

West, M. L., ed. 1998. *Homeri Ilias*. Vol. 1 (1–12). Stuttgart.

Wilamowitz-Moellendorff, U. v. 1927 / 1982. *History of Classical Scholarship*. Translated by A. Harris. London (first edn. 1927).

Wilson, N. G. 1992. *From Byzantium to Italy: Greek Studies in the Italian Renaissance*. Baltimore, MD.

FURTHER READING

Transmission

Pöhlmann 2009 is a great place to start to understand fully how texts come to us from antiquity; Reynolds and Wilson 1991 is perhaps still the best and fullest introduction to textual transmission for the undergraduate or graduate. Gastgeber 2010 is a straightforward article on Byzantine transmission of Greek texts.

Dué 2009 offers a very nice illustrated introduction to one of the most important manuscripts of Homer. Dué and Ebbott 2010 is an exemplary edition of a "multitext" of Homer, focused on the most controversial book of the *Iliad* from the editorial perspective. Gurd 2005 gives a provocative examination of textual philology centered on a vexed text of Euripides.

Textual Criticism

Cerquiglini 1999 is a good introduction to a medievalist's view of how textual variation can be seen beyond "corruption" of the text. Jeffreys 2008 offers a short but pugnacious introduction to textual criticism from the Byzantinist's perspective. Eisenstein 1993 is a classic statement of the epistemological shifts afforded by the print revolution. Kenney 1974 is a solid, learned discussion of how printing changed the status of the Classical text. McGann 1982 / 1992 is a short, readable monograph that challenges settled notions of what an editor must accomplish. Dickey 2007 is a very useful guide to help navigate complexities of vital ancillary works.

History of Classical Scholarship

Sandys 1903/1998 is now dated, but still a standard work in multiple volumes; Wilamowitz-Moellendorff 1927/1982 is a briefer monograph on mostly modern Classical scholarship by an icon of Classical studies. Pfeiffer 1968 and Pfeiffer 1976 are standard histories of Classical scholarship that go into considerable detail.

PART II

Greek Literature as a Dynamic System

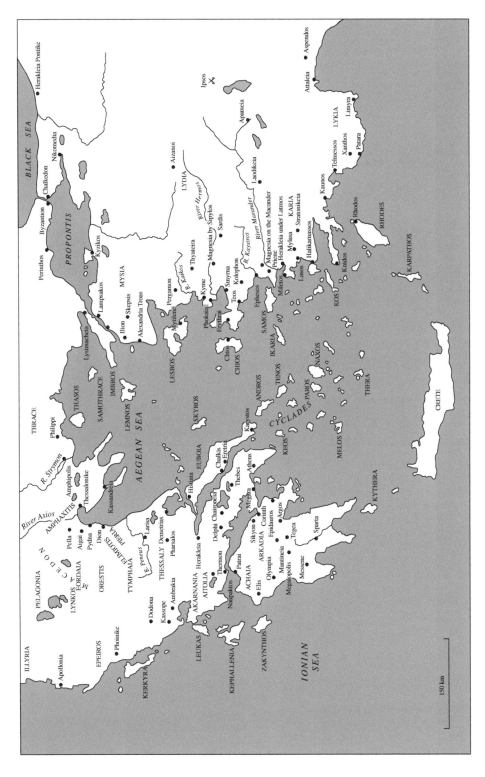

Map 3.1 Greece and Asia Minor.

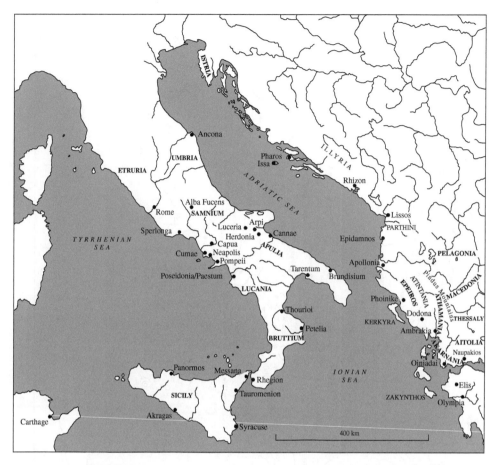

Map 3.2 Italy and the West.

CHAPTER 3

Orality and Literacy

Ancient Greek Literature as Oral Literature

Steve Reece

For most of its history humankind has been illiterate. But this does not mean that humans used to be literarily less sophisticated: they sang hymns to gods, chanted ritual curses, ululated funerary laments, crafted complex genealogies, invented proverbs, fables, and folk-tales, and even composed long heroic epics in demanding metrical forms. All these genres of literature were orally created, orally performed, and orally transmitted to subsequent generations. The inhabitants of the lands that we now know as Greece were no exception. All ancient Greek literature was to some degree oral in nature, and the earliest literature was completely so. Consequently the term "ancient Greek literature" in a literal sense of the words is an oxymoron. For "literature" requires *litterae* "letters": letters written by an author, whether with a reed pen, a printing press, or a keyboard; letters read by a reader, whether on a roll of papyrus, a sheet of paper, or a computer monitor. And these are activities foreign in greater and lesser degrees to the composition, reception, and transmission of much of what we by convention call ancient Greek literature.

A chapter on the orality of ancient Greek literature should properly entail a survey of almost all of ancient Greek literature, and it would require one to proceed accordingly, beginning with Greek epic, which was orally composed, orally performed, and orally transmitted for many generations before anyone felt the need to write it down. We know this for many reasons, most obvious of which is the simple historical reality that during the early stages of Greek epic, between the twelfth and eighth centuries BCE, Greece possessed no writing system. The Cretan syllabic writing system that Greece had used for some centuries before this time was adequate for record-keeping but was not suitable for the recording of Greek epic, even if, as is unlikely, it had crossed anyone's mind to do so; and Greece had not yet adapted the Phoenician writing system that it first used to record various forms of poetry, including epic, and that it still uses today. Greek lyric, both choral and monodic, which was sung to the musical accompaniment of a lyre, had a similar history: the surviving remnants of Greek lyric are from a period well after the first attestation of Greek epic, but lyric reveals, by the great antiquity of its meters, such as the glyconic and pherecratean, that as a genre it actually predates the epic hexameter. Thus, it is no surprise that the Homeric epics themselves mention various types of songs associated with choral lyric: marriage hymns, funeral dirges, harvest songs, the paean, etc. The rise and early stages of lyric, then, like epic, can be placed well back into the pre-literate period of Greek history. Greek iambic verse too must have

A Companion to Greek Literature, First Edition. Edited by Martin Hose and David Schenker.
© 2016 John Wiley & Sons, Inc. Published 2020 by John Wiley & Sons, Inc.

flourished long before its first attestation in writing in the seventh century BCE. Iambic verse was used for ritualized insult and obscenity, activities not prominent in the more heroic epic verse form, yet surely contemporary with it (we get a glimpse of the genre in the episode of Thersites in *Iliad* 2). Greek elegy, though later associated primarily with the silent epigrams inscribed on gravestones, was in its earlier form orally performed to the musical accompaniment of a pipe. Greek drama, too, was fundamentally oral: both tragedies and comedies were composed to be performed orally, with spoken, chanted, and sung parts, and they were intended to be received visually and aurally, by an audience at a particular festival on a particular date. Although scripts were composed before the actual performances, actors were free to manipulate and interpolate, and although these scripts were copied and eventually made their way into collections of texts, and even textbooks, in origin the dramas were intended to be performed but once – to a live audience (cf. Baumbach, this volume, ch. 22, p. 344–52). We could go on: Greek oratory entailed speech before a live audience that was timed by a water clock; Greek philosophy was often presented in the form of an oral dialogue; even the quintessential literary genre of Greek history was designed to be read aloud to an audience of listeners – Herodotus is said to have made a fortune by offering public readings of his work in Athens.

In the late Classical and early Hellenistic periods we can begin to speak more properly of writers and readers of literature (cf. Nünlist, this volume, ch. 19, pp. 296–301), but even then it was normal to read aloud, sometimes privately but usually publicly. Literacy rates remained low throughout Greek history, at least by modern standards, and books lacked the aids to reading that we today take for granted – upper- and lower-case letters, word division, punctuation, sentence and paragraph demarcation, line and page numbers – so the reading of literary works remained the domain of highly trained specialists, and the reception of these works for most people was an aural and communal event. The solitary, silent reading with which we are so familiar today would have struck most ancient Greeks as peculiar, at least in the early period, and someone who conducted himself in such a manner would have been regarded by many as an ἰδιώτης (*idiōtēs* "private person").

Classicists have not always fully appreciated this oral dimension of ancient Greek literature. Being philologists and bibliophiles, we have traditionally regarded textual criticism as the centerpiece of our discipline; we have been *eye* philologists rather than *ear* philologists. More attention to various aspects of historical performance, such as cultural setting and audience reception, has changed the discipline as a whole, and this is nowhere more true than in the study of ancient Greek epic. Our focus in this chapter, then, will be on the ancient epic verse form, not just because it is the earliest attested Greek literature, but also because it illustrates so paradigmatically the fundamentally oral dimension of Greek literature. Moreover, a survey of the history of Greek epic is a case study in how a poem orally performed and aurally received during the earliest period develops over time into an exemplar of a written text, to be dissected and analyzed by teachers and students as a staple of study in the Hellenistic school systems. In short, a survey of the history of Greek epic well illustrates the powerful dynamic between orality and literacy that was at play in all genres of literature throughout Greek history.

1.   Oral Features of Ancient Greek Epic

A century ago it was not uncommon to approach the Homeric epics in much the same manner in which one would approach other great literary epics: Vergil's *Aeneid*, Dante's *Divine Comedy*, Milton's *Paradise Lost*, and even more modern epics such as Tolstoy's *War and Peace*. Critics commonly isolated *exemplum* and *imitatio*, identified textual allusions and verbal irony, and praised Homer's originality and selection of *les mots justes*, as though the individual genius of the author was imprinted on each page of text. Yet, as some realized, even from the earliest period, there was something very different about Homeric epic.

The language (cf. Willi, this volume, ch. 29, pp. 445–7) was very repetitive: ornamental epithets are attached to all the prominent characters ("swift-footed Achilles" occurs 33 times in the *Iliad*; "much-suffering Odysseus" occurs 37 times in the *Odyssey*); half- and whole-line formulae describe the most common actions ("So he spoke, and all of them were stricken with silence" occurs ten times in the *Iliad*, five times in the *Odyssey*; "They put their hands to the good things that lay ready before them" occurs three times in the *Iliad*, 11 times in the *Odyssey*); entire speeches are repeated almost verbatim (Agamemnon's promise of rewards to Achilles in *Iliad* 9.122–57 and again in 9.264–99). Not just words but entire scenes were very stereotypical in nature, with close verbal and structural similarities, especially scenes that narrated frequently occurring activities in the epics: arming for battle (*Il.* 3.328–38, 11.15–46, 16.130–44, 19.364–91); preparation of feasts (*Od.* 1.136–40, 4.52–6; 7.172–6, [10.368–72], 15.135–9, 17.91–5); as well as sacrifice, libation, dressing, bathing, bed-preparation, decision-making, and so forth. Episodes tended to occur as doublets and triplets: e.g. Odysseus' two weeping scenes in Scheria; the suitors' three peltings of Odysseus in his own palace. Likewise, character doublets were very common: e.g., Circe–Calypso; Eurycleia–Eurynome; Melanthius–Melantho.

Similarities in details and sequences of episodes also occurred in larger themes and narrative patterns, such as the combat scenes, in which the following underlying structure can be detected: 1) comrades urge each other on; 2) horses are yoked to chariots; 3) arms and armor are catalogued; 4) the advancing troops are described by a simile; 5) prayers and libations are offered to the gods; 6) genealogies of a pair of combatants are revealed; 7) taunts and counter-taunts are shared by combatants; 8) an individual combat is described, in which warrior A throws a spear at warrior B but misses; B strikes A with his spear, but it glances off; A kills B; 9) B, the defeated warrior, "bites the dust," and his soul goes flying off to Hades; 10) A, the victorious warrior, vaunts over the body of his victim and strips his armor.

Finally, ring composition and other framing devices held the epic narrative together, both on the smaller level of the individual scene and on the larger level of the monumental epic. Simple ring composition involving just a few verses can be observed, for example, at *Iliad* 2.688–94 and 6.269–79. An example of extended ring composition can be observed in Diomedes' speech to Glaucus at *Il.* 6.123–43: A. What mortal man are you? B. Mortals who face me perish. C. But if you are a god … D. I would not fight gods. E. Lycurgus did not live for long after angering the gods. F. [story of Lycurgus]. E. He did not live for long, since he was an enemy to the gods. D. I would not fight gods. C and A. But if you are a mortal … B. Come close and perish. Framing devices hold together larger segments, and even the entire epics: the various adventures of Odysseus' *apologoi* are arranged concentrically around the Hades episode; the entire *Iliad* is symmetrically arranged, with the themes and episodes of Book 24 balancing those of Book 1. The story of the realization of the true causes behind these peculiar features of Homeric style is an interesting and inspiring one, so it is worth telling in some detail.

2.   Oral-Formulaic Theory and Homeric Epic

Homeric studies in the late nineteenth and early twentieth centuries was taken up largely with the "Homeric Question": the who, what, when, where, why, and how of the origin of the Homeric texts. The Unitarians naively effaced many real problems that resided in the Homeric texts in their romantic conviction that there was one poet who created these epics *ex nihilo*. The Analysts vigorously divided the epics up into various lays by different poets plus an array of later interpolations (Poet A, B, C, R, etc.), but they could not agree even among themselves: some offered the view that Homer was the poet at the end of the process who compiled a group of independent earlier lays rather incompetently into one large poem, contributing only the "glue" that kept these individual lays together; others preferred the view that Homer was the poet at the beginning of the process, the brilliant creator of a very ancient short epic to which considerable additions were later made.

Into this quagmire strode Milman Parry, a 21-year old graduate student at the University of California, Berkeley, whose work would eventually render the controversy between Unitarians and Analysts irrelevant. Both were right, and both were wrong. As the Unitarians claimed, a single poet did compose the entire epic, possibly even both epics. But, as the Analysts had realized, this poet was indebted to many earlier poets for his tales and even for the language in which he narrated them. Homer relied upon a long tradition of oral poetry that provided for him the very words (epithets, formulae, type-scenes) that were the building blocks of his epics. First in his master's thesis at Berkeley, then in his doctoral dissertations at the Sorbonne, written under the guidance of the French metrician and linguist Antoine Meillet, Parry proved beyond a shadow of a doubt that Homer's diction was traditional and inherited. This proof was based on his discovery that the system of epithets attached to almost every character and object in the epics was characterized by the features of what he called *complexity* (also *length* and *extension*) and *economy* (also *thrift* and *simplicity*) [the terms most often used today are *scope* and *economy*]. By *complexity* Parry meant that each prominent character and object in Homer had been endowed with an array of epithets so as to be able to fit into any common metrical space: e.g., bucolic diaeresis to line-end; fourth foot male caesura to line-end; third foot male or female caesura to line-end; line-beginning to third foot male or female caesura; full line. Thus every major character could be accommodated effortlessly into a variety of metrical situations. Consider, for example, the common epithets of the hero Hector when in the nominative (subjective) case:

– ◡ ◡ / – ◡ ◡ / – ◡ ◡ / – ◡ ◡ / φαίδιμος Ἕκτωρ (*phaídimos Héktōr*)
– ◡ ◡ / – ◡ ◡ / – ◡ ◡ / – κορυθαίολος Ἕκτωρ (*koruthaíolos Héktōr*)
– ◡ ◡ / – ◡ ◡ / – ◡ μέγας κορυθαίολος Ἕκτωρ (*mégas koruthaíolos Héktōr*)
Ἕκτωρ Πριαμίδης (*Héktōr Priamídēs*) ◡ ◡ / – ◡ ◡ / – ◡ ◡ / – ×
Ἕκτωρ Πριαμίδης βροτολοιγῷ ἶσος Ἄρηϊ (*Héktōr Priamídēs brotoloigói ísos Árēi*)

In Parry's view, the choice of epithets – whether Hector is to be described as "illustrious," "shining-helmed," "great shining-helmed," "son of Priam," or "son of Priam equal to Ares destroyer-of-men" – was determined not so much by the context of the passage as by the requirements of meter.

By *economy* Parry meant that generally only one epithet for a character or object was available to fill each common metrical space: thus Hector is never referred to as φέρτατος Ἕκτωρ (*phér-tatos Héktōr* "pre-eminent Hector"), for example, because the metrically equivalent φαίδιμος Ἕκτωρ (*phaídimos Héktōr* "illustrious Hector") is adequate for the poet's purposes (the metrically equivalent ὄβριμος Ἕκτωρ [*óbrimos Héktōr* "powerful Hector"] is occasionally found, however, because it contributes the added metrical flexibility provided by an epithet that begins with a vowel rather than a consonant). Given a particular metrical space to fill, the poet was not expected to create a new epithet *ex nihilo*; he did not even have to pause to consider a choice between two or more inherited epithets; only one epithet was available for that metrical space.

Admittedly, noun–epithet combinations and formulaic phrases are a feature of many later epics: Vergil's *Aeneas Anchisiades*, Dante's *del magnanimo quell' ombra*; Spencer's *sweet-bleeding myrrh* and *warlike beech*; Milton's *flow'ry dale of Sibma clad with vines*; and even Joyce's *snot-green sea*. Their prevalence is a natural result of trying to imitate an epic style that goes all the way back to Homer. But the imitation is only skin-deep: none of these later "literary" epics has an underlying formulaic system characterized by complexity and economy. In Vergil's *Aeneid*, for example, the hero Aeneas is called both *pius Aeneas* (◡ ◡ / – – / –) and *pater Aeneas* (◡ ◡ / – – / –), metrically equivalent epithets, and therefore uneconomical. Vergil's choice between the two epithets was motivated by the context – whether Aeneas is acting piously or in a fatherly manner – rather than by metrical considerations. Indeed Aeneas is called *bonus* when showing kindness, *magnanimus* when acting bravely, and *heros* when demonstrating heroic qualities. Achieving *le mot juste* was a pressing consideration for Vergil – but not for Homer.

This system of epithets was a component of the more elaborate, and equally systematic, verse-long formulae that are so essential to Homeric diction. For example, the poet relied on the following system of formulae when expressing the action: epithet(s) + man/god/woman/goddess + answered/addressed + him/her/them:

—	– / – ◡◡ / – ◡	◡ / – – / – ◡◡ / – ×
		μέγας κορυθαίολος Ἕκτωρ
		mégas koruthaíolos Héctōr
τὸν		great shining-helmed Hector
tòn		
him	δ᾽ ἠμείβετ᾽ ἔπειτα	Ποσειδάων ἐνοσίχθων
	d᾽ ēmeíbet᾽ épeita	*Poseidáōn enosíkhthōn*
τὴν	then answered	Poseidon the earth-shaker
tḕn		
her	δ᾽ αὖτε προσέειπε	περίφρων Πηνελόπεια
	d᾽ aúte proséeipe	*períphrōn Pēnelópeia*
τοὺς	in turn addressed	prudent Penelope
toùs		
them		θεὰ γλαυκῶπις Ἀθήνη
		theà glaukôpis Athénē
		goddess owl-eyed Athena
		etc.

Elaborate systems such as these suggested to Parry the *traditionality* of Homeric diction: no single poet could have been responsible for such systems; they had been created and nurtured by generations of bards who had passed them down from father to son, from master to student, until they reached Homer in the late eighth century BCE. Virtually every word in the Homeric epics is formulaic and traditional. Very rarely was there a need to turn a new phrase or create a new scene. The poet rather tapped into the vast reservoir of traditional diction that he had inherited.

But proof of Homer's *orality* came unexpectedly when Meillet circumspectly invited Matija Murko, an expert on Yugoslavian heroic poetry from the University of Prague, to attend Parry's defense of his doctoral thesis. Murko pointed out that the orally composed heroic poetry of Yugoslavia had the same type of traditional phraseology, operating in much the same way, as Parry was describing in Homer. Here, in the decasyllabic verse of Serbo-Croatian epic:

1 2	3	4	/	5 6 7 8 9 10
				Miloš čobanine
				Milosh the shepherd
		njemu		nahod Simeune
		to him		*the foundling Simeon*
veli		njojzi		Todore vezire
said		*to her*		*Theodore the high counselor*
		njima		Kraljeviću Marko
		to them		*king's son Marko*
				srpski car-Stjepane
				Serbian emperor Stephen
				etc.

Here, then, was a living oral tradition that could be observed and studied first-hand, a sort of laboratory test of Parry's theories about Homer. This was a project on which Parry was soon to embark: two long trips in the early 1930s through the mountains of Yugoslavia, where he and his assistants, Albert Lord and Nikola Vujnović, recorded over 13,000 songs on 3,500 aluminum disks and transcribed many others. These are the disks and transcriptions that make up the collection that remains one of the crown jewels of Harvard's Widener Library to this day: *The Milman Parry Collection of Oral Literature*. Parry would conclude in his highly analytic way that: a) The diction of Yugoslavian heroic poetry is oral and traditional; b) The diction of Greek epic poetry shows many of the same features that in Yugoslavian poetry are due to that oral and traditional nature; c) Greek epic poetry must be oral and traditional. Thus was born the "oral-formulaic theory," which properly speaking is not merely a theoretical construct but an empirical fact.

The practice of comparing features of different oral traditions opened up an entirely new field of scholarship. Although Parry died tragically at the age of 33, his long-lived apprentice Albert Lord extended the oral-formulaic theory to several other traditions, first to the national European epics, which had for a long time been treated as written texts: the Old French *Chanson de Geste* (including *Roland*), the Medieval German *Nibelungenlied*, the Hispanic *Poema de Mio Cid*, the Old English *Beowulf*; and then old Irish, Arabic, Chinese, Latvian, and Norse traditions. More recently the oral-formulaic theory has been extended to relatively modern traditions: Modern Greek, Turkish, Tunisian, Russian, African, Kurdish, Irish, Native American – to well over 100 independent language groups – and even to such genres as American folk preaching, sports broadcasting, and musical improvisation of various types, such as plainchant, ballad, folksong, blues, jazz, fiddling, and rap.

The result is that Homer's *Iliad* and *Odyssey* have to some extent been disengaged from the genre of monumental literary epics like those of Vergil, Dante, and Milton, and positioned instead within the genre of oral epic traditions in which they more comfortably belong. One can perhaps appreciate the irony in all this: that it was by virtue of very intensive, old-fashioned, text-oriented philology that Classicists began to think of Homer as oral rather than literary.

3.   Internal Evidence for Orality in Homeric Epic

This is something that Classicists should have recognized much earlier. There are many indications within the narratives of the Homeric epics themselves that their composition, performance, and transmission was oral rather than literary in nature. The first indication is that other than the mysterious σήματα λυγρά (*sḗmata lugrá* "baleful signs") in the story of Bellerophon (*Il.* 6.168–70) – a tale drawn wholesale from the Near East, where writing had been known for millennia – the Homeric epics make no reference to writing. This apparent absence of any familiarity with the technology of writing correlates well with what we know archaeologically about the absence of any writing system during the very period in which heroic epic flourished: between the twelfth and the eighth centuries BCE.

Another indication of orality has to do with the portrayal of the bard and his audience within the epic tradition. The *Iliad* and *Odyssey* portray the epic-making process as an oral performance of a song: the picture of the two ἀοιδοί (*aoidoí*, "bards") in the *Odyssey*, Phemius and Demodocus, is of two professionals who sing their songs to the accompaniment of a *cithara* or *phorminx* (lyre-like stringed instruments). Demodocus appears to be attached permanently to the palace of Alcinous on the island of Scheria, while Phemius seems to have taken up temporary residence in Odysseus' palace in Ithaca. They are both honored above all mortals and thought to be divinely inspired because of their ability to sing. They have immense power in being able to immortalize the deeds of men by recalling them in their songs, or contrarily to assure that the deeds of men are forgotten by failing to make mention of them. Both bards are dependent upon the palace for sustenance: they literally "sing for their supper."

Several scenes in the *Odyssey* provide glimpses of the setting and audience of bardic performance. Phemius sings, to the accompaniment of his *cithara*, after the suitors' have feasted at the palace in Ithaca (*Od.* 1.144–55). A "divine singer" plays his *phorminx* during a wedding feast in Sparta, while the people dance and two acrobats revolve around them (*Od.* 4.1–19). Demodocus, the blind bard, who is sitting on a chair in the midst of the feast, is stirred by the Muse to sing and play his *phorminx* after a sacrifice by the Phaeacians (*Od.* 8.40–106). Demodocus sings a final song at Odysseus' request following a feast in Alcinous' palace (*Od.* 8.469–545), after which Odysseus praises the singer with generous words:

> Surely it is a good thing to listen to a singer like this one, whose voice is like the gods; for I think there is no occasion more pleasant than when merriment holds sway over all the people, and those feasting throughout the house sit in order and listen to the singer, and beside them the tables are loaded with bread and meat, and the wine steward draws wine from the mixing bowl and carries it around filling the cups. This is in my opinion the very best of occasions (*Od.* 9.3–11).

Surely this is a portrayal of the status of the bard in Homer's own time. In fact, Homer seems to be drawing a self-portrait here, probably for protreptic purposes. His bards are always presented in a good light: Phemius is one of very few spared Odysseus' vengeance; Demodocus' performance earns him the choicest cut of meat. Homer describes Demodocus as blind: "The Muse gave him both good and evil. She deprived him of his eyes, but she gave him sweet song (*Od.* 8.62–5)." This too may be a self-portrayal. In the "Homeric" *Hymn to Apollo* (169–73) a stranger is imagined asking: "Who is the best of the bards?" The answer: "A blind man who dwells on Chios; his songs are the best." This geographical detail as well may be a self-portrayal by Homer, who in several of the most ancient traditions is said to have come from the island of Chios in Asia Minor.

A third indication of the orality of epic verse within the epics themselves has to do with the perceived status of the Muses in the process of epic verse making. Before beginning any long stretch of song, the poet invokes the divine aid of the Muses, who, as daughters of Memory, enable the poet to remember the details and the overall path of the song. As he begins the monumental task of singing the 12,110 verses of the *Odyssey* Homer invokes a single Muse, a goddess, a daughter of Zeus, asking her to tell the tale of Odysseus' return, and to begin it at some point of her choosing (*Od.* 1.1–10) – she chooses to begin the story at the end, in the tenth year of his return, by means of a clever *hýsteron próteron*. Before beginning the monumental task of singing the 15,693 verses of the *Iliad*, Homer invokes the goddess, i.e., the Muse, to sing the wrath of Achilles (*Il.* 1.1–7); soon thereafter, when he is faced with the daunting task of recalling the long catalogue of Achaean ships that had sailed to Troy, Homer invokes the Muses, the daughters of Zeus, goddesses, who live on Olympus, to help him remember, for they know all things, while men only hear rumor and know nothing (*Il.* 2.484–93). The singer appears helpless without the Muse.

A fourth indication of the orality of epic verse is the acknowledgement within the Homeric epics, which are themselves our earliest surviving literature, that there already existed epic songs of various sorts that were broadly known. The most notorious example is Circe's reminder to Odysseus of the ship Argo "which is on all men's minds" (*Od.* 12.55–72), but there are also references to earlier tales about the Calydonian boar hunt (*Il.* 9.529–99), about the assault of the seven heroes against Thebes and the continuing conflicts in the next generation of these heroes (*Il.* 4.370–410, 5.800–808), and about several other heroes of previous generations, such as Nestor, in his youth (*Il.* 7.132–57, 11.669–760, 23.629–42), Heracles (*Il.* 2.653–70, 5.628–54, 8.362–5, 19.95–133; *Od.* 11.617–26), and Oedipus (*Od.* 11.271–80). Based simply on allusions in the *Iliad* and *Odyssey*, we can infer that Homer was familiar with at least the following epic traditions, and that they may even have been part of his own repertoire: "Jason and the Argonauts," "The Calydonian Boar Hunt," "The Seven against Thebes," "The Epigoni," "The Heraklea," "The Nestorea," and "The Oedipodea," as well as various epics about the Achaean expedition against Troy and its aftermath. And these must be just the tip of the iceberg. To complement these references in the Homeric epics themselves, we have the evidence of a few fragments of later "Cyclic" poems that must be derived ultimately from pre-Homeric forms, we have some later prose summaries of these same Cyclic poems, we have several surviving tragedies, and many more names of tragedies, whose plots were based on pre-Homeric and extra-Homeric epics, and, finally, we have hundreds of depictions of scenes from these epics in the plastic arts, particularly in archaic vase painting. All of these epics, being pre-Homeric, were certainly composed, performed, and transmitted orally, since they flourished during a period when the Greeks had no writing system. In fact many of them failed to survive precisely because they were never written down. This is all a salutary reminder that although from a modern perspective Homer is commonly regarded as the father, the progenitor, of western literature, from an ancient perspective he is the son, the progeny, being the inheritor of a long epic tradition.

4.   From Oral Performance to Written Text

All ancient Greek epic verses that have survived, no matter how oral their background, eventually became written texts; had this not occurred, we would never have known them. When, where, why, and how they became texts are very contentious matters, however, and much ink has been spilt over these questions during the past few generations.

One view is that the epic poets themselves learned how to write and took advantage of this new technology to record their verses in a more fixed and stable medium. Advocates of this view thus account for some of the apparent features of literacy in post-Homeric epic verse, such as Hesiod's *Theogony* and *Works and Days*, as well as the "Homeric" *Hymns*, but they also attribute the extraordinary length, structure, and monumentality of the *Iliad* and *Odyssey* precisely to Homer's ability to write. Some have even suggested that the alphabet was adopted by the Greeks specifically for the purpose of recording the Homeric epics. This view is perhaps motivated by some wishful thinking: it avoids the messiness and complication of other explanations; it offers a romantic notion of an individual poet and his text with which we as literates have become familiar and comfortable; it allows an editor to strive to reconstruct *the* original text of Homer in much the same way as he would *the* original text of Apollonius of Rhodes. But it fails to account for many features in the Homeric texts that indicate that they were not slowly and deliberately written down, with the leisure to reread, reconsider, and revise (see further below). Moreover, it seems most unlikely that it would ever have occurred to a truly orally composing singer to write his songs down as a text. Preservation of the exact words of his songs was never his goal; he could perform these songs again at any time. A written text served him no purpose in performance; on the contrary, he probably performed more freely and comfortably when allowed to sing at his own pace to the accompaniment of his lyre, not with an unwieldy text to encumber him. It must have been someone other than the singer who came up with the idea of recording the songs as written texts.

A second view, the polar opposite of the first, is that the textualization of the Homeric epics was a long and complicated evolutionary process: that the epics remained largely oral, and therefore fluid and unstable, not only among the bards of the earliest period, but also among the rhapsodes of the Archaic period, and even into the Classical and Hellenistic periods in disparate local traditions, well after at least some degree of stabalization was achieved by the textualization of a Panhellenic version at the Panathenaic festival in the late sixth century BCE. The Homeric epics did not become the texts as we (more or less) know them until the Alexandrian librarians of the third and second centuries BCE standardized and canonized them. This view tends to efface Homer's existence as a human being and instead attributes the *Iliad* and *Odyssey* to a mythic figure, a cultural icon, a symbol of oral tradition that we can call, for the sake of shorthand, "Homer." But the epics were actually shaped by generations of mouths *and* hands, slowly crystallized, and not really fixed until the late Classical or even Hellenistic period. This evolutionary view is attractive in many respects, since it offers an explanation for several curious developments relevant to the transmission of the epics: the relative paucity of depictions of Iliadic and Odyssean scenes in the graphic arts during the Archaic period, followed by a surge in popularity of such scenes in the late sixth century BCE (i.e., coincident with a Panathenaic textualization); the sometimes remarkable differences between our inherited texts and the quotations of Homer by Classical authors, the textual versions reported to have existed in the manuscripts available to the Alexandrian editors, and the longer and "eccentric" readings of the Ptolemaic papyri; and the late linguistic forms, especially the "Atticisms" and "hyper-Ionisms" that reside, at least on the veneer, of our inherited texts. But the drawbacks of this view are numerous as well. It fails to account for many important features of the Homeric texts: the overall unity of their narratives; the various types of inconsistencies that remain embedded in their narratives; the absence of multiple versions of the *Iliad* and *Odyssey*; and the fact that the development of the epic art-language appears to have been arrested at a particular moment in time (see further below). As a practical matter the evolutionary view imposes nearly impossible challenges on the modern editor of the Homeric texts, for all textual variants are regarded as *potentially* authentic readings. How is the modern editor to present the fluidity and multiformity of the epic tradition in the form of an edited text that has conventionally placed readings of a supposed original in the favored position above, while demoting supposed variants to the level of the *apparatus criticus* below?

A third view, which falls somewhere in between the other two, though much closer to the first, is that Homer dictated his songs to a learned scribe (or scribes), who recorded the words, probably with a reed pen on papyrus (or perhaps leather). The idea of textualizing the songs did not come from the singer, who, as we have noted, placed no value on written text. It must instead have come from a patron, a sponsor, or a simple admirer, who was familiar with the only mechanism capable of accomplishing this task: oral-dictation. Since the alphabet with which the songs were first textualized originated in Phoenicia, and since the papyrus upon which the text was first transcribed originated in Egypt, and since many components of the songs themselves – the tale-types, themes, and poetic forms – originated in the Levant and Mesopotamia, it does not require too great a leap of faith to suppose that the very idea of writing down the songs originated from someone acquainted with the civilizations of the Near East, where the writing down of epic songs, some even through the process of dictation, and their transmission by means of written text, had been practiced for more than a millennium. Our inherited texts of the *Iliad* and *Odyssey*, in this view, are more or less reliable records – though passed through countless hands over many generations – of what was once an oral-dictated text, i.e., a scribal transcription of a performance orally delivered by a historical Homer in the eighth century.

One obstacle to this view is that the scenario may seem a bit hard to imagine: an oral poet, accustomed to performing his songs to the accompaniment of a lyre to a live audience, is persuaded to perform, or dictate, his songs, probably at a much slower pace than usual, to a scribe, or group of scribes, who record the words of his performance as written text. Yet there are analogues to this process in comparative oral traditions: Parry imagined Homer dictating his songs, while someone else with writing materials wrote them down verse by verse, much as the Serbo-Croatian *guslari* whom he was observing dictated their songs to his assistant Nikola Vujnović (Parry 1971, 451). Albert Lord made further comparisons, and gave the oral-dictation theory a clear and thorough articulation (Lord 1953; 1960, 38–9). The benefits of this view are many: Homer remains a truly oral poet, but at the same time a particular text can be ascribed to him; our inherited texts of the *Iliad* and *Odyssey* can be regarded as vestiges of a real historical performance, delivered at a particular time, in a particular place, by a real living person; several of the most serious obstacles to the other views are obviated, namely that the texts that we have inherited retain several features that seem utterly incompatible with the view of an evolutionary process and, at least in some important respects, with the view of a literate Homer. I wish to highlight four of the most prominent of these features: the unity of the narratives; the various levels of inconcinnities that remain embedded in the narratives; the absence of multiple versions of the *Iliad* and *Odyssey*; and the fixation in time of the epic art-language.

The Unity of the Narratives

The *Iliad* and *Odyssey* are unified narratives whose structures are most clearly observed, whose plots are most intelligently followed, and whose nuances are most pleasurably appreciated, whether by ancient listeners or modern readers, when experienced in their entirety and within a limited time-frame. Episodes are organized in a thoughtful sequence from beginning to end and bound together by a network of interconnected references, by anticipatory and retrospective allusions, by comparative and contrasting parallelisms, and many other similar structuring devices. Neither epic is simply a collection of loosely related episodes – which would be the predictable result of a process of compilation by various hands over a long period, or of a process of gradual accretion within an impersonal oral tradition. Each epic is a work carefully arranged by a personal and inspired singer composing in a performance that was experienced *in toto* on some occasion that provided considerable leisure: a festival, perhaps, or a nobleman's funeral or wedding.

Various Levels of Inconcinnities Embedded in the Narratives

The *Iliad* and *Odyssey* have survived to our day as texts that, even in the forms that have been copied and recopied for many generations, do not have the appearance of having gone through an extensive editorial process – proofreading, correcting, reworking, etc. On the contrary, they retain many features typical of oral composition-in-performance that once uttered could not be retracted. Indeed inconcinnities remain embedded in every level of our inherited texts as vestiges of their origin in oral performance: metrical blunders attributable to the pressures of oral composition-in-performance by a singer who did not go back to his verses after his performance to tidy up the prosodic loose ends (e.g., prosody of *Od.* 7.89); dictional inconcinnities that have resulted from stock formulaic phrases being used in contextually inappropriate circumstances, and whose survival in our texts show that the poet had no opportunity or desire to summon back his words or revise them (e.g., the corpse that "groans heavily" at *Il.* 13.423); small factual errors and larger narrative anomalies that point to a one-time oral-dictation of an epic composition-in-performance that was transmitted thereafter, blemishes and all, with remarkable faithfulness in its textual avatars (e.g., the Trojan soldier Melanippus, who is killed three times over a nine-book stretch of narrative [*Il.* 8.273–7, 15.572–84, 16.692–7]). These are not normal features of deliberately written texts, nor are they conceivable in the evolutionary model; they arise rather from the exigencies of live oral performance which, on the one hand, require that the singer extemporize as he composes during the very act of performance, and, on the other hand, prohibit the singer from retracting or correcting his song once it has left his mouth.

The Absence of Multiple Versions of the Iliad and Odyssey

The evolutionary model, hypothetical in the case of the Homeric epics, has been applied appropriately and productively to the presumed – and in some cases demonstrable – histories of several other oral epic traditions that were eventually fixed in textual forms: e.g., the Sumerian and Akkadian versions of the *Epic of Gilgamesh*, the Sanskrit *Mahabharata* and *Ramayana*, the Persian *Shahnama*. It is instructive, then, to compare the features of the surviving texts of these other epic traditions with those of the Homeric tradition in order to determine if the (hypothetically) similar circumstances during the composition and transmission of these documents have produced similar outcomes. What we discover is that in these other epic traditions there have survived multiple versions that are substantially different from one another, not only in small matters of diction and detail, but also in their essential poetic forms, their larger themes and narrative patterns, their overarching plot structures, and even their total lengths. These multiple versions all have equal claim to authenticity; hence, the search for an archetype is meaningless. In the case of the *Iliad* and *Odyssey*, however, multiple versions have not developed.

While it is true that textual variants occur in quotations of "Homer" by later Classical authors of the fifth and (mostly) fourth centuries BCE, in the reports of the Alexandrian scholars of the third and second century BCE about what they read in earlier editions of Homer, in the readings of the

40 or so surviving remnants of Homeric texts on papyri from the early Ptolemaic period (third–second century BCE), and, though to a much lesser degree, in the 900 or so surviving manuscripts of the post-Aristarchean "vulgate" (i.e., after around 150 BCE), from the perspective of the monumental epics as a whole these variants are comparatively trivial and do not provide the evidence for substantially different versions of the Homeric texts. We have only one version of the *Iliad* and one of the *Odyssey*, with the same characters, the same story, and even the same sequence of episodes – all of which are, moreover, told in a very uniform meter, dialect, diction, and style throughout. There is no evidence that there ever existed any texts of Homer's *Iliad* without a Patroclus, or of Homer's *Odyssey* without a Telemachus. Nor is there any evidence of texts of the *Iliad* and *Odyssey* that were half the size, or twice the size, of our inherited texts. It seems likely, then, that, unlike these other epic traditions, our *Iliad* and *Odyssey* each go back to a single archetype that was fixed in writing and whose text did not thereafter suffer substantial editorial tampering.

The Fixation in Time of the Epic Art-Language

Our inherited texts of the *Iliad* and *Odyssey* reveal a language that was frozen in time, a language that had previously been evolving hand in hand with the vernacular but that had in its eighth-century Ionic form become fixed. There had once existed a vibrant Mycenaean epic tradition, but our inherited texts are not Mycenaean (though there are Mycenaean words and phrases, even poetic formulaic phrases, embedded in them); thereafter there had existed a vibrant Aeolic epic tradition, but our inherited texts are not Aeolic (though Aeolic words and phrases abound, especially ones that provide metrically useful alternatives to the corresponding Ionic forms); thereafter there arose a vibrant Ionic epic tradition, and this is when the linguistic evolution that had so characterized the epic tradition previously was arrested. Though the epics continued to be performed and enjoyed – recited orally and received aurally – the epic *Kunstsprache* "art-language" in which they had for so many generations been composed had become a "dead" language. The language of both the *Iliad* and *Odyssey* attained a high degree of fixation precisely at this period, substantially in the Ionic dialect, and they continued in their later transmission to retain their Ionic forms. This fixation was surely due to textualization. Whether the writing down of these epics enabled them to gain an exceptional status, or whether an exceptional status caused them to be written down, it was textualization, the result of oral-dictation and transcription at a specific time and place (in the case of the *Iliad* and *Odyssey* during the eighth century BCE in Ionia), that assured linguistic fixation. For the epic language did not continue to evolve linguistically – to create innovative forms and formulae – through the seventh, sixth, and fifth centuries, and thereafter, as it had in its more fluid oral form before the eighth century. The so-called "Atticisms" and "hyper-Ionisms" that occur occasionally in our inherited texts are simply a veneer: metrically equivalent modernizations and modifications of an already established text.

5. Homeric Epic as Written Text

We have been following the transformation of the Homeric epics, beginning with their truly oral stage, when they were orally composed, performed, and transmitted by an ἀοιδός (*aoidós* "bard") singing to the accompaniment of his lyre. Thereafter the epics went through a stage during which they were no longer orally composed or transmitted, though they continued to be orally performed by ῥαψῳδοί (*rhapsōidoí*, "song-stitchers") before a live audience, through recitations of memorized texts, albeit with a certain amount of manipulation and extrapolation. The so-called Homeridae, "descendants of Homer," a guild of rhapsodes from Chios from the sixth or possibly seventh century BCE, fall into this category (see Pindar's Nemean 2.1–3 and scholia thereon; also Plato's *Ion* 530d, *Republic* 599e, *Phaedrus* 252b). The third stage was completely textual, when the Homeric epics began to be thought of as collections of papyrus rolls to be bought from a bookseller and perhaps even stored in a library. Athens enjoyed a commercial business in the selling and buying of books by the late fifth century (Eupolis F 327 [PCG]; Plato's *Apology* 26 d–e), and Plato's Academy and Aristotle's Lyceum had actual libraries for research purposes. Yet, even during this stage, the Homeric epics continued to be read aloud, usually in a public forum, as was the common practice with other literary texts as well.

The fascinating history of the Homeric epics did not cease when they became texts (cf. Armstrong, ch. 2, pp. 36–8 in this volume). I wish to conclude with a few words about how these once oral epics became the most literary of literary texts during a particularly bookish period of Greek history: the late Hellenistic period (cf. Nünlist, this volume, ch. 19, pp. 301–7). This was the period of the great scholarly libraries of antiquity: Alexandria, Pergamon, Antioch, etc (cf. Hose, this volume, ch. 21, pp. 331–5). The Homeric texts from around the world were collected, collated, and edited. Each epic was divided into 24 books, and the verses of each book were numbered. The text was weighted down with several types of punctuation marks, along with occasional aspirations and accentuations. Verses were annotated with various critical signs that indicated their perceived textual status. Lexica, glossaries, and commentaries were produced. Scholars debated fine points of textual criticism, word division, and etymology.

The lexical activities of scholars were matched by those of students. Homer's epics had occupied a privileged position in the educational system since the early Classical period (see Plato's *Republic* 376e–98b; Plutarch's *Alcibiades* 7.1). Once students had learned the basics of reading and writing – the alphabet and the syllables – they proceeded at once to Homer, which they read, recited, and memorized. We hear of a certain Nicaratus, who claims that his father made him memorize the entire *Iliad* and *Odyssey* (Xenophon's *Symposium* 3.5). This attention to Homer continued to be the norm during the Hellenistic period, during which time education throughout the eastern Mediterranean world became remarkably homogeneous, composed of a standard ἐγκύκλιος παιδεία (*enkúklios paideía*, "cycle of education") that had Homer as its centerpiece. Lists of Homeric vocabulary were used to learn letters, syllables, and then full words, beginning with monosyllabic words and working up to pentasyllabic words. Homeric verses, especially those of a gnomic nature, were used as models for writing exercises. In the 400 or so school texts that have been discovered among the Egyptian papyri of the Hellenistic and Roman periods are found nearly 100 quotations or citations of Homer. Homer is quoted five times more often than the second most popular author, Euripides, and thirteen times more often than the third most popular author, Menander. Those who continued their education beyond the primary level were expected to know the entirety of the Homeric epics, not simply for their poetic value, but also as a source of mythical, moral, philosophical, geographical, rhetorical, and grammatical information. We cannot help but be struck by a certain irony here: that these truly oral songs that were once composed, performed, and transmitted without the use of writing ended up as Hellenistic school texts that were studied by children to learn their ABC's.

REFERENCES

Arend, W. 1933. *Die typischen Scenen bei Homer*. Berlin.

Cribiore, R. 2001. *Gymnastics of the Mind: Greek Education in Hellenistic and Roman Egypt*. Princeton, NJ.

Fenik, B. 1968. *Typical Battle Scenes in the Iliad: Studies in the Narrative Techniques of Homeric Battle Description*. Wiesbaden.

Foley, J. M. 1990. *Traditional Oral Epic: The Odyssey, Beowulf, and the Serbo-Croatian Return Song*. Berkeley, CA.

Hainsworth, J. B. 1968. *The Flexibility of the Homeric Formula*. Oxford.

Harris, W. V. 1989. *Ancient Literacy*. Cambridge, MA.

Havelock, E. A. 1982. *The Literate Revolution in Greece and its Cultural Consequences*. Princeton, NJ.

Hoekstra, A. 1965. *Homeric Modifications of Formulaic Prototypes: Studies in the Development of Greek Epic Diction*. Amsterdam.

Janko, R. 1990. "The *Iliad* and its Editors: Dictation and Redaction." *Classical Antiquity* 9: 326–34.

Janko, R. 1998. "The Homeric Poems as Oral Dictated Texts." *Classical Quarterly* 48: 1–13.

Kirk, G. S. 1962. *The Songs of Homer*. Cambridge.

Lord, A. B. 1953. "Homer's Originality: Oral Dictated Texts." *Transactions of the American Philological Association* 84: 124–34.

Lord, A. B. 1960. *The Singer of Tales*. Cambridge, MA.

Morgan, T. 1998. *Literate Education in the Hellenistic and Roman Worlds*. Cambridge.

Murray, G. 1911. *The Rise of the Greek Epic*. 2nd edn. Oxford.

Nagy, G. 1996. *Homeric Questions*. Austin, TX.

Ong, W. J. 1982. *Orality and Literacy. The Technologizing of the Word*. London.

Parry, A., ed. 1971. *The Making of Homeric Verse: The Collected Papers of Milman Parry*. Oxford.

Powell, B. B. 1991. *Homer and the Origin of the Greek Alphabet*. Cambridge.

Reece, S. 1993. *The Stranger's Welcome: Oral Theory and the Aesthetics of the Homeric Hospitality Scene*. Ann Arbor, MI.

Reece, S. 2005. "Homer's *Iliad* and *Odyssey*: From Oral Performance to Written Text." In M. Amodio, ed., *New Directions in Oral Theory*, Tempe, AZ, 43–89.

Ruijgh, C. J. 1957. *L' élément achéen dans la langue épique*. Assen.

Ruijgh, C. J. 1985. "Le mycénien et Homère." In A. M. Davies and Y. Duhoux, eds., *Linear B: A 1984 Survey*, Louvain-la-Neuve, 143–90.

Ruijgh, C.J. 1995. "D'Homère aux origines proto-mycéniennes de la tradition épique." In J. P. Crielaard, ed., *Homeric Questions*, Amsterdam, 1–96.

Turner, F. M. 1997. "The Homeric Question." In I. Morris and B. Powell, eds., *A New Companion to Homer*, Leiden, 123–45.

Van Otterlo, W. 1948. *De Ringcompositie als Opbouwprincipe in de Epische Gedicten van Homerus*. Amsterdam.

West, M. L. 1988. "The Rise of Greek Epic." *Journal of Hellenic Studies* 108: 151–72.

West, M. L. 1990. "Archaische Heldendichtung: Singen und Schreiben." In W. Kullmann and M. Reichel, eds., *Der Übergang von der Mündlichkeit zur Literatur bei den Griechen*, Tübingen, 33–50.

FURTHER READING

Ong 1982 and Havelock 1982 offer provocative theories on the consequences of orality and literacy to human consciousness, thought, and culture. Harris 1989 offers a salutary corrective to Classicists and ancient historians who have been guilty of inflating estimates of ancient literacy levels, arguing that Greece remained a predominately oral culture throughout antiquity, with literacy rates generally hovering between 5 and 15 per cent.

On oral-formulaic theory, which is based largely on the systems of epithets and formulae in Homer, Parry's theses and articles, collected by his son in Parry 1971, remain fundamental. Parry's at times rigid views have been softened somewhat by those who have detected more technical flexibility in the systems than he envisaged: e.g., Hoekstra 1965 and Hainsworth 1968. The fundamental work on type-scenes is still Arend 1933: Fenik 1968 applies his work systematically to battle scenes, Reece 1993 to hospitality scenes. The most exhaustive work on ring-composition is van Otterlo 1948. On the extension of oral-formulaic theory to other language groups, i.e., comparative oral traditions, see Lord 1960 and Foley 1990.

For attempts to reconstruct the characteristics of pre-Homeric (oral) epic, see Hoekstra 1965, Ruijgh 1957 and 1985, and West 1988.

On the seminal question of how the oral epics became written texts, West 1990 has argued forcefully for an early written text of Homer; Powell 1991 proposes that the Phoenician writing system was brought to Greece precisely for the purpose of recording the Homeric epics. One may trace the development of the evolutionary model, namely that our inherited texts of Homer are the final product of a long evolution of a fluid oral *and* textual transmission, by following chronologically Murray 1911, Kirk 1962, Foley 1990, and Nagy 1996. The oral dictation model proposed and developed by Parry 1971 and Lord 1953, 1960 has been supported with strong and up-to-date arguments by Janko 1990, 1998 and Ruijgh 1995. Reece 2005 offers an in-depth analysis of these various proposals with extensive bibliography; Turner 1997 provides a general survey of scholarship on the "Homeric Question" from a fairly recent perspective.

Morgan 1998 and Cribiore 2001 present evidence from the Hellenistic and Roman papyri on the centrality of Homer as a text for study in the Hellenistic educational system.

CHAPTER 4

Literature in the Archaic Age

Timothy Power

1. Literature, Lyric, Performance

What was Archaic Greek literature? In the first place, it was mostly poetry. It is true that sixth-century BCE Greece witnessed the emergence of written prose, initially as a vehicle for the sophisticated argumentation of Ionian cosmology. Anaximander of Miletus and Pherecydes of Syros vie for the title of writer of the earliest prose treatise (Purves 2010, 97–110). Neither, however, had a very sizable readership. A presumably wider audience, it has been argued, long knew "oral traditions in prose" (*logoi*) cultivated by "masters of speech" (*logioi*), predecessors of Hecataeus and Herodotus (Nagy 1990, 221–25; cf. Luraghi 2009 for a different view). But the literature of the Archaic period was clearly dominated by poets, most notably the so-called lyric poets. Their distinctive voices, while not as autobiographical as once thought, nevertheless offer a vivid account, both intimate and panoramic, of life in this revolutionary "age of experiment" (Snodgrass 1981).

The lyric poets were not only observers of events around them; they were active, influential participants. In the "song culture" that was Archaic Greece (Herington 1985, 3–4), poetic discourse "belonged to the entire organization of social life" (Ford 1992, 14), playing a structural–functional role in the most important areas of human experience: politics, war, law, morality, religion, education, initiation, selfhood, sexuality and love, loss and grief.

The tag "lyric" has become a scholarly convention, and it remains convenient to use it still (cf. Wells, this volume, ch. 10, pp. 155–7). But it is nonetheless a misnomer, since it covers three distinct, if interactive types of poetry, only one of which regularly involved the lyre in its delivery: melic (subdivided into choral and monodic forms, both usually strophic and sung to the lyre or the *aulos*, a reeded pipe typically played in pairs); elegiac (couplets generally sung solo to the *aulos*); iambic (stichic or epodic verse normally recited without instrumental accompaniment, although more musical settings are not unattested: Rotstein 2010, 229–51).

"Lyric" does have the considerable virtue, however, of reminding us that Archaic poetry was essentially performative. That is, it was typically delivered *viva voce*, in some recognizably musical or near-musical fashion, before audiences assembled on social occasions. Indeed, its existence, in composition, performance, and transmission, was primarily oral and acoustic.

A Companion to Greek Literature, First Edition. Edited by Martin Hose and David Schenker.
© 2016 John Wiley & Sons, Inc. Published 2020 by John Wiley & Sons, Inc.

Transcription tended to be a secondary phenomenon (cf. Ford 2003), and, even where writing was foregrounded, oral performance still played an indispensable role. Thus epigrams (cf. Höschele ch. 12) inscribed on dedicatory and sepulchral monuments were meant to be read aloud by members of the public. In other words, the inscribed texts were scripts for perpetual "live" reperformance, which was integral to the communicative and commemorative function of the poetry (Day 2010, 14–17; cf. Svenbro 1993, 8–63).

2.   Rhapsody and Citharody

Alongside the lyric genres flourished rhapsody and citharody. Rhapsodes recited heroic poetry in dactylic hexameters (cf. Reece, this volume, ch. 3, pp. 47–50), by the later Archaic period most prominently the Panhellenic epics attributed to Homer, the *Iliad* and *Odyssey*, but also a diverse range of material drawn from the Epic Cycle and other, more locally based traditions (Burgess 2004; for the Cycle, see now West 2013). Some also performed Hesiodic wisdom and genealogical poetry (Herington 1985, 167–76). Further, rhapsodes recited preludes, *pro-oimia*, to their epic narratives, in which the Muses and other divinities relevant to the performance occasion were hymnically invoked and their favor requested. A collection of 33 of these, some of them long and complex narratives in their own right, others succinctly functional, has come down to us as the *Homeric Hymns* (Faulkner 2011b; Clay 2011).

Some scholars believe Archaic rhapsodes were largely uncreative performers of scripturally fixed and then rote-memorized texts (e.g. Powell 2007, 40–43). Others view them as creative "recomposers-in-performance" of evolving oral poetic traditions (Nagy 1996; Collins 2004, 167–222). The latter view perhaps better reflects the etymology of the word rhapsode as "one who sews together song(s)." In a hexameter fragment, probably from an early rhapsodic tradition, Homer and Hesiod are themselves depicted as rhapsodes "sewing together song in new hymns" ("Hesiod" F 357 M–W; cf. Pindar *Nem.* 2.1–3). In either case, the fact remains that rhapsodes were as central to Archaic culture as lyric poets, responsible as they were for transmitting and bringing to life in performance a prestigious "poetry of the past" that continued to be politically and ideologically potent in the present (Ford 1992).

It is thus unsurprising that tyrants, who well appreciated how epic poetry could influence collective identity and belief, were intent on controlling rhapsodic performance. During a period of hostilities with Argos, Cleisthenes, tyrant of Sicyon, outlawed rhapsodic contests of Homeric epic on account of its supposedly pro-Argive content (Herodotus 5.67). By contrast, the Peisistratid tyrants of Athens made as centerpiece of their cultural politics the rhapsodic contest of the Panathenaia, where the *Iliad* and *Odyssey* would take canonical form. The latter epic in particular may contain traces of Peisistratean propaganda "sewn in" by compliant rhapsodes (Aloni 2006). The Samian tyrant Polycrates perhaps made a competing bid to control authoritative rhapsodic performance of Homer, one that featured his commissioning of the monumental *Homeric Hymn to Apollo* for the "Delia and Pythia" festival he organized on Delos (Burkert 1979; cf. Aloni 1989). In their patronage of rhapsodes, these tyrants were indeed following a Homeric precedent: the royal possession of bards, whose singing maintained the social order established by the king (Scully 1981).

Citharodic song occupied an important, yet nowadays largely overlooked middle ground between rhapsody and melic. The Archaic citharode was in a sense the direct descendant of the Homeric bard, who sang hymnic and heroic verse to his lyre-like *phorminx* (Gentili 1988, 15). The rhapsodes, mostly of Ionian provenance, would develop this poetic material in a polished hexametrical form suitable for recitation, replacing the *phorminx* with their signature staffs. Citharodes, initially of Aeolian, particularly Lesbian provenance, retained the lyric-epic style of the bards, but greatly elaborated its musical complexity (West 1981, 124–5). They sang heroic narratives, including epic material attributed to Homer ("Plutarch" *De musica* 1132c, 1133c), to the *kithara*, a large "concert" lyre, in compositions called *nomoi*, lengthy showpieces as much for vocal and instrumental prowess as storytelling (Herington 1985, 15–20; Power 2010, 224–314). These *nomoi* were prefaced by *prooimia* analogous to those of the rhapsodes. A few brief dactylic fragments of these survive, attributed to the prototypical citharode Terpander of Antissa, a city on Lesbos (Gostoli 1990). Terpander's speaking name means "he who gives *terpsis* 'musico-poetic pleasure' to men," and, though dated by ancient sources to the early seventh century BCE, he may have been, along the lines of Homer, an idealized figure of legend rather than history, an avatar of the early citharodic tradition, from which our "Terpandrean" fragments may well come (Beecroft 2008).

3.   An Interactive Performance Culture

The melic poet Pindar, however, imagined Terpander to be the inventor of the *skolion*, a type of drinking song quite unlike the virtuosic, epic *nomos* ("Plutarch" *De musica* 1140f), and of the lyre-like instrument that often accompanied it, the *barbitos* (Pindar F 125 S–M). Pindar's claims, while not necessarily historically accurate, nevertheless reflect the reality that rhapsody, citharody, and the various genres of lyric not only shared much the same poetic and musical DNA, but, as co-participants in the living performance culture, remained in dialogue, and sometimes competition, throughout the Archaic and into the Classical period. These relationships could be intertextual in a literary sense, but they were more broadly "interperformative" (cf. Kallio 2011).

The affiliation of lyric monody with citharody is obvious – solo singing to strings – but the latter form also interacted closely with choral melic. Already in the *Odyssey* the proto-citharodic bards Demodocus and Phemius lead choral performances (8.262–5; 23.143–7). Arion of Lesbian Methymna, the "best citharode" of his time (c. 600 BCE) according to Herodotus, was also a pioneering composer of dithyramb (1.23–24), the choral cult song for Dionysus. Herodotus records that Arion left his adopted home of Corinth and the court of its tyrant, Periander, for a tour of Italy and Sicily, where he presumably exhibited his virtuoso citharodic and choral talents. Both may have made an impression on the then-young Sicilian poet Stesichorus, who composed lyric-epic choral songs (works include *Oresteia, Geryoneis*, and *Sack of Troy*) of such length and narrative and dramatic complexity that some scholars insist they must have been performed as citharodic monody. (Cingano 2003, 25–34 effectively defends the traditional view that Stesichorus, "he who sets up the chorus," was predominantly a choral poet; cf. Curtis 2011, 23–37.) Burkert (1987) has proposed that these new choral settings of heroic narrative in turn influenced longer-standing citharodic and rhapsodic performance styles. Decades after Stesichorus, Aeschylus would attempt to emulate citharodic *nomoi* in his *aulos*-accompanied tragic choral odes, which themselves achieved Stesichorean proportions (Aristophanes *Frogs* 1281–1300). Attic tragedians were, as a group, promiscuous borrowers from other genres, both choral and monodic, and tragedy took shape as a complex amalgam of performance elements appropriated from across the spectrum of late Archaic song culture (Herington 1985; Swift 2010).

Other interperformative contacts between Archaic poetic media could be explored, e.g. the rivalry between rhapsodes and citharodes, both performers of epic verse, which may have left textual traces at *Iliad* 2.594–600, where the Muses deprive the lyric singer Thamyris of his "wondrous singing" and "skill in *kithara* playing," thereby rendering him a de facto rhapsode (cf. Wilson 2009, 56–9); the reciprocity between localized choral and Panhellenic rhapsodic traditions, emblematized by the encounter between a prototypical rhapsode-poet, a "blind man who lives on rocky Chios" – probably meant to be Homer himself – and the famous chorus of Delian Maidens at *Homeric Hymn to Apollo* 166–76, where the former proposes that each perpetuate the *kleos* 'fame' of the other, he in performance abroad, they on Delos (Martin 2001, 57–9; Nagy 1996, 56–7); or even the intriguing structural and musical resonances between the "stanzaic" arrangement of elegiac couplets and the strophic form of choral and monodic melic (Faraone 2008).

4. Rhapsodes and Citharodes in Performance

Rhapsodes and citharodes performed solo at the music contests (*mousikoi agones*) attached to the various civic, regional, and Panhellenic festivals that began to proliferate in the Archaic period, often as focal points of the cultural-political agendas of tyrants. Although there is some evidence for amateur rhapsodes and citharodes, they were on the whole itinerant professionals who earned a living from their art, indeed a very good living if successful in the contests and willing to travel afar. Sappho, composing around 600 BCE, acknowledges the famous citharodes of her island, the so-called "Lesbian Singers," as worldly agonists, "outstanding against those of other lands" (F 106 V). One of these citharodes was her contemporary Arion, whose tour of Magna Graecia, which presumably included victories at festivals of prosperous cities, earned him great riches (Herodotus 1.24). Herodotus notably depicts Arion as kind of overseas merchant of song, who even hires a trading ship to take him and his riches back from Italy to Corinth (a *polis* renowned for international commerce; cf. Hornblower 2009, 41). Similarly, the rhapsodic *Works and Days*, in the midst of a discourse on maritime trade, relates how Hesiod, qua paradigmatic itinerant rhapsode, traveled to a song contest at Chalcis, where he won a valuable tripod cauldron that he dedicated to the Heliconian Muses (646–62).

Our textualized representation of the rhapsodic performance tradition preserves no trace of historical rhapsodes as distinct, named individuals. Because rhapsodic poetry was devoted primarily to mythic narrative, the first-person authorial declarations so prominent in lyric poetry were rare. Indeed, there are suggestive ancient and modern comparative indications that even highly creative Archaic rhapsodes made no claims to originality or authorship, deferring instead to tradition and the Muses (Jensen 1980, 62–80). But rhapsodes were skilled, high-visibility performers. How did they present themselves to audiences? It has been argued that they subordinated their own identities to those of idealized composer-performers, viz. Homer and Hesiod, whose personas they mimetically re-enacted in the contest: "[W]hen the rhapsode says 'tell me, Muses' (*Iliad* 2.484) […] this 'I' is not a *representation* of Homer: it *is* Homer" (Nagy 1996, 61). Such impersonation would have been especially apparent in the performance of the *prooimion* to the Hesiodic *Theogony*, where "Hesiod" relates, in the first person, his transformation at the hands of the Muses into a staff-bearing rhapsodic poet (22–35; cf. Martin 2004 on performance of the Hesiodic *Works and Days*). And in the *Homeric Hymn to Apollo*, the reciting rhapsode would have assumed the "I" of the dramatized "Homer" figure, who does not, however, name himself – he is, as it were, the very model of rhapsodic anonymity (cf. Graziosi 2002, 63–4).

Rhapsodes in fact organized themselves (and many were probably born) into clan-like guilds notionally descended from their legendary archetypes, whose "works" they inherited and cultivated as repertoire, and whose biographical lore they authoritatively disseminated (and creatively elaborated: Plato *Rep.* 599e; Isocrates *Hel.* 65). From the island of Chios, there were the Homeridai 'Sons of Homer' (Andersen 2011); from Samos, a rival guild of descendants of Creophylus, legendary rhapsode-poet of a Heraclean epic, *Capture of Oechalia* (Burkert 1972). Likewise, the famous clan (*genos*) of Lesbian citharodes claimed descent from Terpander (Σ Aristophanes *Nub.* 971a).

The picture may be more complicated, however. The collection of *Homeric Hymns* shows that the *prooimion* did allow for prefatory self-referential statements – declarations of intent to sing the forthcoming epic, prayers for victory in the contest – but these were generic, recitable by any performer in the tradition (e.g. 2.495, 21.5, 25.6). Yet the *Hymns*, which are clearly Panhellenically oriented exemplars of the form, may not accurately reflect realities *in situ* of "live" oral performance. Andrew Ford reasonably argues that the *prooimion* presented "an opportunity to lay claim to a large reputation" before a festival audience, and that rhapsodes aggressively asserted their own identities in *prooimia* that "were not included [with the *Hymns*] when performance became text" (Ford 1992, 26–7). The first-person pronouncements of "Hesiod" and "Homer" might thus represent stylized reflections of actual proemial practice as much as scripts to be followed by re-enacting rhapsodes. The citharodic *prooimion* may have presented a similar opportunity, despite the generic tone of our scanty fragments (cf. "Plutarch" *De mus.* 1133c). We need not think, however, that self-promotion and mimetic reenactment were always mutually exclusive: rhapsodes and citharodes may well have made names for themselves by successfully embodying Homer and Terpander in the contests.

Outside of performance proper, individual rhapsodes and citharodes hardly remained anonymous. Around 450 BCE, the rhapsode Terpsicles dedicated a prize tripod inscribed with his name and profession at Dodona (GDI 5786). An inscribed statue base from sixth-century Gela, in Sicily, apparently contains the name Cynaethus, which happens to belong to one of the Chian Homeridai, a rhapsode who supposedly was first to recite Homeric epic in nearby Syracuse (and was said to have composed the *Homeric Hymn to Apollo*; see Burkert 1979, Graziosi 2002, 208–17). Two citharodes, Alkibios and Ophsios, made costly dedications – perhaps statues of themselves or their divine model, Apollo – on the Athenian Acropolis around the end of the sixth century BCE (IG I³.666 and 754; cf. Wilson 2004, 284). They were presumably winners at the Panathenaic festival, which by the late Archaic period had become Greece's premier site for citharody as well as rhapsody (Shapiro 1992), on par with the Panhellenic Pythian *agones* at Delphi and eclipsing the once-prestigious citharodic contest at the Spartan Carneia festival, which Terpander himself had reportedly been first to win (Hellanicus FGrHist 4 F 85).

5.   Sympotic Lyric

Virtually all Archaic lyric was composed for initial performance either in a relatively small, restricted setting, usually indoors, or in a relatively large, inclusive setting, usually outdoors. We can further distinguish these as private and public, though this distinction does not always map easily onto Archaic Greek contexts (cf. Budelmann 2009b, 11–12; Baumbach ch. 22, pp. 345–6 in this volume). The form and content of lyric poetry were intimately bound up with specific performative occasions in one of these broad settings.

The most common restricted-type occasion was the symposium, the wine-drinking party that formed the locus of social and cultural life for the wealth and power elite in the *polis*, a class to which the lyric poets themselves all likely belonged. Here, solo forms – monody, elegy – and iambus, were the rule (with possible exceptions, we shall see). Sympotic lyric tended toward a brevity and musical simplicity, relative at least to citharody and choral melic, which would allow the musically non-professional members of the sympotic group to perform it comfortably for one another over wine. At the level of content, the practices and ambience of the symposium itself impress the poetry performed there with "metasympotic" themes of drinking, friendship, music-making, and, above all, erotic desire, for the symposium could be a space devoted as much to the pleasures (and aestheticized miseries) of Aphrodite as of Dionysus.

The political and moralizing sentiments of sympotic lyric tend also to reflect the elitist, indeed aristocratic ideology of its performers and audience. This seems especially true of lyric monody, which not coincidentally required the greatest musical skill to perform. Amateur yet accomplished lyre singing was the ideal expression of the prestige of aristocratic education and culture, *paideia* (Wilson 2004), and one significantly rooted in the heroic past. Achilles and Patroclus, in a scene that prefigures the performative dynamics of the aristocratic symposium, take turns singing the "glories of men" to the *phorminx* at *Iliad* 9.186–91. Theseus often appears in Archaic vase-paintings holding a lyre, as if the instrument were an essential part of his heroic-aristocratic identity.

Sympotic elegy generally required less musical training and ability – the symposiast had only to sing while an accompanist played the *aulos* – and recited iambus still less. This performative difference from monody may correlate with occasional differences in ideological tonality. For we find in these forms more of what Ian Morris has termed "middling" discourse, language that, while still markedly elitist, nevertheless stakes out a position sympathetic to the universal concerns of the *polis*, in between the competing claims of the aristocracy and the commons, the *demos* (e.g. the elegiac F 5 IEG and the iambic F 37 of Solon of Athens); it can at times also be critical of the aristocratic exceptionalism celebrated in monody (Morris 2000, 161–94, with the important qualifications in Irwin 2005, 58–62).

Such criticism forcefully emerges in the elegies of the poet-philosopher Xenophanes of Colophon. In one, Xenophanes attacks the excesses of Colophonian aristocrats, in particular their civically useless fascination with *habrosyne*, the luxurious lifestyle pursued by the Lydianizing elite (F 3 IEG; cf. Kurke 1992). In another (F 1 IEG), Xenophanes describes an ideal symposium in a way that seems a coded critique of aristocratic sympotic ethics. We are told that symposiasts should not speak of "violent eruptions of *stasis* 'civil strife'" (23), a prohibition perhaps aimed at the stasiotic monodies of Alcaeus of Lesbian Mytilene (cf. Ford 2002, 56), while the decorous, restrained behavior Xenophanes prescribes for drinkers seems a corrective to the convivial and erotic excesses of the Ionian symposium and the exuberant, sometimes publicly disruptive song-and-dance procession, the *komos*, that typically concluded it (cf. Murray 1990b). For Anacreon of Teos, troubador par excellence of the Ionian symposium, the *komos* was a chance to display *habrosyne* in all its proper excess (F 373 PMG); he himself is depicted as a model Lydianizing komast on late Archaic wine vessels (Price 1990).

Importantly, Xenophanes reminds us that the symposium was not a monolithic institution, and that different kinds of sympotic groups called for differently tinged social and cultural perspectives in different poetic forms. For instance, the exhortatory martial elegy of Tyrtaeus, seamlessly merging heroic-aristocratic and civic discourse, was performed at banquets in the campaign tent of the Spartan king and reperformed at the quasi-sympotic military messes at Sparta (Bowie 1990).

But there can be no doubt that the "classic" sympotic configuration was the closed group of around 14 to 30 aristocratic drinkers reclining on couches in the domestic *andron* 'men's quarters'. These were peer companions (*hetairoi*) united by highly exclusionary, even anti-civic values: the essential superiority of aristocratic birth and *paideia* to new money, cultural and political populism (including tyranny), and the prerogatives of citizenship; the fetishization of youthful beauty and the nobility of *amour fou*; self-identification with epic heroes and even gods; the sociocultural cachet of Eastern luxury goods and styles, or *habrosyne* (cf. Kurke 2007, 147–8).

To such a group belongs much of, but not all the elegy attributed to Mimnermus and Theognis, and probably too the martial-exhortatory F 1 IEG of the early elegist Callinus of Ephesus (cf. Irwin 2005, 32–3, 36–7). Mimnermus' sympotic elegy, fixated on youth and *eros* – "What is life, what is pleasure, without golden Aphrodite?" (F 1.1 IEG) – was surely enjoyed and reperformed by the same preening Ionian aristocrats criticized by Xenophanes. Indeed, Mimnermus F 7 IEG reads as a self-validating riposte to such "middling" criticism from the *polis*. "Please yourself.

Of the bitter citizens, some will speak badly of you, others better." The same couplet appears in the corpus of Theognidean elegy (795–6), as do several close variations (e.g. 24–6, 611–14, 797–804; cf. Archilochus F 14 IEG).

What comes down to us as the first book of the *Theognidea* is "songbook" of variously authored Archaic and early Classical elegies. Alongside a core of authentic material by Theognis of Megara are verses elsewhere attributed, with occasional textual variants, to Tyrtaeus, Mimnermus, and Solon, and much that is anonymous. The collected elegies consist largely of paraenetic wisdom, metasympotic discourse, and political commentary, most of it from a decidedly aristocratic perspective, although seemingly more middle-of-the-road sentiments (e.g. 335–6, 823–4) are also present in the mix. The second book of the *Theognidea* is a compilation of mainly pederastic elegies that, as many scholars now believe, a bowdlerizing editor separated out of the first book around 900 CE (West 1974, 43–5; cf. Bowie 2012a, however, who would date the compilation much earlier). The aristocratic character of the symposiasts who would have enjoyed this erotic poetry is neatly summed up in lines 1253–4: "Blessed is he who has beloved *paides* [which can mean either 'boys' or 'sons'], horses of uncloven hoof, hunting dogs, and *xenoi* 'guest-friends' abroad." This couplet, elsewhere attributed to Solon (F 23 IEG), is followed by another couplet that revises the Solonian argument, aligning it still more explicitly with the eroticized ambience of the symposium: "Whoever does not love *paides* [here most definitely 'boys'], horses of uncloven hoof, and dogs, his heart does not enjoy sympotic cheer (*euphrosyne*)" (1255–6). The juxtaposition of the two couplets in the written edition of the *Theognidea* may in fact capture a mode of "literary criticism" that was practiced orally in the Archaic symposium, whereby one symposiast competitively "capped" a poem performed by fellow drinker with a pointed revision (*metapoiesis*) of its contents (Vetta 1980, XXVII–XXXI, 58–62; Collins 2004, 111–34).

Solon's own elegy offers a stylized representation of sympotic *metapoiesis*. In F 20 IEG, he asks that Mimnermus – a poet active several decades before Solon but addressed as if he were physically present – revise the claim made in one of his elegies that it is best to die at 60 (Mimnermus F 6 IEG); Solon thinks 80 a better age to die. Such competing claims about what is best in life are a recurrent theme in lyric, the primary medium for ethical and aesthetic reflection in the Archaic period.

6.   Lesbian Melic

The values of the aristocratic symposium find richest expression in Alcaean monody (cf. Wells ch. 10 of this volume, pp. 160–1). Here there are pederastic themes (F 380, 430, 431 V) and lush evocations of the sympotic environment (e.g. F 140, 362 V) and its lyric music (F 38b, 41 V). Local politics predominate, however, and the main subject is *stasis*: Alcaeus' songs articulate his faction's opposition to popularly elected leaders, above all Pittacus – a tyrant, at least in Alcaeus' opinion (F 348 V) – then emerging from rival factions in Mytilene. Political and cultural elitism combine, however, in what might be called metasympotic invective. F 72 V mocks the barbaric drinking habits of Pittacus' Thracian father. F 70.1–5 V describes a symposium of Pittacus and his *hetairoi* as a gathering of "vain braggarts," surely a negative foil for Alcaeus' own *hetaireia*. The *barbitos* that "plays and feasts" with these vulgarians seems emblematic of Pittacus' lack of musico-poetic sophistication, as well as a reflection of his crowd-pleasing yet corrupt politics (cf. F 70.6–7, 12–13; F 129.20–4 and F 348, with Kurke 1994; Wells, ch. 10 of this volume, p. 161).

In F 298 V Alcaeus deploys myth allegorically, to aggrandize his faction's struggles in Mytilene: a lengthy account of the disastrous rape of Cassandra by the Lesser Ajax, an episode from the Cyclic *Sack of Troy*, serves as epic exemplum for some ruinous trespass of

Pittacus (cf. Hutchinson 2001, 215–27). Other Alcaean accounts of Trojan myth also may have had exemplary or pragmatic force, though we cannot be sure (F 42, 44, 283 V). Personal identification with the heroic past is typical of aristocratic poetry; it is rhetorically essential to encomiastic melic beginning at least with Ibycus, whose praise song for Polycrates of Samos ranks the tyrant's beauty alongside that of epic heroes (S151 PMGF). But Trojan myth had special resonance in Mytilene: Troy was nearby and Lesbos played a significant role in the Epic Cycle. Both Alcaeus and Pittacus participated in a Mytilenean campaign against Athens to retain control of a city near Troy, Sigeion, which seems in part to have been an effort to control the prestigious legacy of the Trojan War (Herodotus 5.94–5; cf. Page 1955, 281; Aloni 1989).

Finally, we may note that Alcaeus' (and Sappho's) treatment of epic material likely represents interperformative engagement with Ionian rhapsodes in Aeolis (cf. Liberman 1999, xiv) as well as with the Lesbian citharodes. So too might Alcaean hymns to Apollo, Hermes, and others (F 307, 308 V; cf. West 2012, 234–5).

Alcaeus' Mytilenean contemporary Sappho also composed monody for an in-group—not a sympotic *hetaireia*, but a circle of aristocratic female companions (*hetairai*, F 160 V), the precise nature and function of which – social, political, sexual, religious – scholars still debate (Greene 1996). That music and poetry were essential to its identity is clear from F 150 V, where Sappho refers to her intimates as *moisopoloi* 'servants of the Muses'. Sapphic monody exhibits much the same formal structures, cultural values, and ideological assumptions as Alcaean lyric, even as its tone, perspectives, and thematic emphases reflect the gender of the poet and her first audience.

It is possible that Sappho composed for female choruses as well (Lardinois 1996; Nagy 2007), though clear evidence for this is elusive. Her poetry contains occasional glimpses of choral performance, e.g. maidens singing at a night-time wedding festivity in F 30.2–5 V, but these do not necessarily indicate the performance mode of Sappho's own songs. However, the recently restored F 58 V, while itself probably monodic, does evoke an especially suggestive choral scenario: in the role of lyric accompanist, Sappho tells a group of girls, almost certainly a chorus, that she is too old to dance with them. Notably, the motif of the aging accompanist appears too in some hexameters of Alcman, which may have formed a solo lyric *prooimion* to a choral song (F 26 PMGF; cf. F 38).

Explicit reference to civil strife is absent from Sappho's poems, but the fractious Mytilenean haut monde is the backdrop for swipes at the musico-poetic accomplishments of rival groups (e.g. F 55 V, Alcaeus F 303A V; Williamson 1995, 86–9). Like Alcaeus, Sappho is drawn to Trojan myth, in particular its female characters, and similarly links it to the here and now. F 44 V recounts the wedding of Andromache and Hector; in F 16.6–16 V a beloved, departed girl, Anactoria, is another Helen; the lacunose F 17 V apparently calls upon Hera to appear "near me" (1), just as the goddess once answered prayers of the Atreidai, when they were waylaid on Lesbos after leaving Troy. In this fragment, not only is the distance between contemporary world and heroic past rhetorically closed, so is the gap between mortal and divine – an eminently aristocratic maneuver (cf. F 1 and 2.13–16 V; cf. Gentili 1988. 83–4).

7. Lydian Glamour

Alcaeus sings of the 2,000 staters his faction received in support from the fabulously wealthy Anatolian kingdom of Lydia (F 69 V). For Sappho, Lydia is home to the rich luxury she prizes (F 58.25 V), but it is less an actual place than a sublime ideal of wealth and beauty, surpassed only by "what one loves" (F 16; cf. 132 V). The "intricately decorated (*poikilan*) headband from [Lydian] Sardis" she evokes at F 98a.10–11 V (cf. F 39) is at once a material status symbol and a metapoetic figure emblematizing the exquisite refinement of Sapphic song, which itself has the potential to become a luxury export (cf. Ferrari 2010). Earlier, the members of Alcman's Spartan chorus had sung, perhaps also with a metapoetic slant, of a "Lydian headband, adornment of violet-eyed girls" (F 1.67–9 PMGF), which was presumably an element of their sumptuous costume. (An ancient biographical tradition made Alcman himself a Lydian émigré to Sparta, though it was probably based on the poet's own mention of a man "from lofty Sardis" (F 16 PMGF), which need not have been self-referential.) In what may be an allusion to one or both of the passages from Sappho and Alcman, the chorus of Pindar's *Nemean* 8 figures its very song as an "intricately crafted, resounding Lydian headband" (15), a vivid materialization of the sonic opulence and refinement – the *poikilia* – of the ode's musical setting.

Indeed, Lydia exerted considerable influence on Archaic song culture as a whole. At the height of its prosperity under Croesus (560–47 BCE), its capital, Sardis, attracted "all the sophisticates of Hellas," including, we are told, Solon (Herodotus 1.29). For long before, however, it had been the focal point of elite Greek aspirations, the home of glamorous tyranny – already "middling" Archilochean iambus significantly *rejects* aristocratic envy of the riches and tyranny of Lydian Gyges (F 19 IEG) – and ground zero of chic *habrosyne*.

The reclining symposium in particular could be called a "Greco-Lydian" institution, as it owes debts to Sardis both real and romantic. It was hearing the *pektis*, a kind of harp, played at "Lydian banquets" that, Pindar claims, inspired Terpander to invent the *barbitos*, the elongated, baritone lyre commonly played in the Archaic symposium (F 125 S–M). As stated earlier, Pindar's scenario is probably imaginary, but it effectively captures the Lydianizing tenor of much sympotic lyric. Harps were likely in vogue among the Assyrianizing elite of seventh-century BCE Sardis, and from there came into the hands of Greek symposiasts and aristocratic women who prized orientalia (Franklin 2007). References to harps, entwined with the language of *eros* and *habrosyne*, stud the poetry of Sappho (F 22.11, 156 V), who according to one tradition invented the *pektis* (Athen. 14.635a), and Anacreon (F 373, 374, 386 PMG), who was also credited with the invention of the *barbitos*. This instrument, while not necessarily derived from Lydia or the harp, was nonetheless associated with the exotic allure of both. To play one was to "play the Lydian," as the sympotic *barbitos*-players wearing Lydian drag on late-sixth-century "Anacreontic vases" from Athens illustrate (Frontisi-Ducroux and Lissarrague 1990).

Pindar's projection of Terpander into Lydia reflects, too, the character of Archaic citharody. Citharodes, outfitted in lavish costume, cultivated their own manner of *habrosyne*, and their art had Lydian overtones. The *kithara* came to be called "Asiatic" because the Lesbian citharodes who developed it lived near – and presumably drew from – Asia, i.e. Lydia (Duris FGrHist 76 F 81; cf. Σ Apollonius of Rhodes 2.777–9). We are told too that the citharodic *nomos* was commonly sung in the Lydian melodic mode (Proclus *ap.* Photius *Bibl.* 320b20–21; cf. Pausanias 9.5.7), in which Pindar himself set some of his choral works (e.g. *Nem.* 4.45, 8.15). Sappho's melodies echoed Sardis as well; she was named the inventor of the Mixolydian mode (Aristoxenus F 81 Wehrli).

8.   The Tyrant's Symposium

Much of the surviving monody of Anacreon and Ibycus was composed for the tyrant's symposium, an affair that shared much of the same elitist cultural ideology with the pure aristocratic symposium – Archaic tyrants were themselves aristocrats – but necessarily had a less partisan political tenor than Alcaeus', and very likely a larger physical setting and a demographically more heterogeneous cohort (cf. Clay 1999, 26–7). These factors affected poetic content as well as form.

Symposia at the Samian court of the tyrant Polycrates, where both Anacreon and Ibycus worked, probably included, alongside poet and tyrant, "blue-blooded aristocrats, prosperous traders and entrepreneurs [...and] other men of more modest means" (Kantzios 2005, 237). The synthetic composition of this drinking group motivated Anacreon's narrowed focus on "common denominator" topics of love and sympotic pleasures and his general, if not complete (e.g. F 353 PMG) avoidance of explicitly political discourse. His elegiac F 2 IEG in fact echoes Xenophanes in criticizing the man who would "speak of strife and tearful war" at symposia; the good symposiast "mixes together the brilliant gifts of Aphrodite and the Muses." The image, evoking the civilized mixing of wine and water, is programmatic for Anacreon's sympotic monody.

Anacreon emulates Lesbian monody's celebration of *habrosyne* with an exuberance fitting the magnificence of his patron – and sympotic *hetairos* – Polycrates (Herodotus 3.121.2). But Anacreontic *habrosyne* is markedly detached from the factional politics of Mytilene; it may rather have served a socially unifying agenda. Lydianizing fashion reached a fever pitch, and had a notably demotic tenor, under Polycrates, who went so far as to recreate on Samos the famous red-light district of Sardis (Clearchus F 44 Wehrli). We hear too that Polycrates won popular favor by lending out sympotic couches and cups to anyone wanting to throw a party (Alexis FGrHist 539 F 2). It seems that hedonistic luxury amounted to an instrument of the tyrant's public policy. And indeed, we might view Anacreon as a kind of minister of Polycratean "party politics," setting an example through his own poetic persona of how best to pursue a (non-partisan) life of erotic and orientalizing sympotic pleasures. In F 388 PMG, an invective song mocking one Artemon, a universally ridiculous *arriviste*, Anacreon offers an instructive example of how *not* to do so (cf. Brown 1983).

After Polycrates' death, Anacreon would play a similar role in Athens, where the Peisistratids summoned him, and where the ceramic record indicates he would spark another Lydianizing craze (Budelmann 2009c, 235–6). The story that Anacreon was transported from Samos to the Peisistratid court in an Athenian penteconter ("Plato" *Hipparchus* 228b–c) may well be apocryphal, but it accurately narrativizes the dynamics of an increasingly cosmopolitan Archaic lyric culture. Anacreon and Ibycus represent a new breed of poet, not a festival agonist like the rhapsodes and citharodes, but similarly itinerant (the citharode/dithyrambic poet Arion's activity at the court of Periander is a significant precedent); a proto-professional freelancer making a Panhellenic reputation abroad, composing and performing not for his own local community, but for various aristocratic and tyrannical houses to which he may or may not have had preexisting ties of *xenia* 'guest-friendship' (cf. Bowie 2009). For tyrants especially, the prestige of lyric poets became an object of geopolitical gamesmanship; enormous energy and resources were put into drawing "star" poets and performers – precious cargo – to their cities and courtly symposia.

Ibycus left his native Rhegium – to which his surviving poetry significantly makes no reference – for Samos, possibly with sojourns en route in Sicily, Sparta, and the court of the Sicyonian tyrant Cleisthenes (Hutchinson 2001, 228–35). The encomium he composed for a young Polycrates is the earliest such praise song recognizably preserved, although fragments suggest he was producing encomiastic poetry for aristocratic patrons before his arrival on Samos (Bowie 2009, 122–7). In the encomium, Ibycus recounts Trojan epic by way of masterful *praeteritio* (S151.1–35 PMGF), passing over its martial themes to a subject more amenable to the erotic ethos of the tyrant's symposium, where this song was probably performed: the beauty of young heroes at Troy (36–45). This in turn leads to praise of Polycrates' beauty, and the remarkable concluding claim: "These [heroes] have a share in beauty forever; you too, Polycrates, will have imperishable *kleos*, in accordance with my song and my *kleos*" (46–48). Poetry's promise to confer immortal renown, *kleos*, because it itself has immortal *kleos*, is rooted in epic, and finds expression elsewhere in lyric (Theognis 237–54; Simonides F 11 IEG). Ibycus personalizes and so strengthens the claim: he is a Panhellenic superstar poet in the making, with his very own *kleos* to share (cf. Sappho F 65.9 V; Nagy 1990, 187–8).

The intertextual challenge posed by Ibycean melic to epic's monopoly on *kleos* might also represent an interperformative challenge to the rhapsodes. Samos and nearby Chios were home to prominent rhapsodic guilds, and rhapsodes, as we saw, would play a significant role in Polycrates' cultural-political agenda. The initial performative status of the encomium is itself debated, however. Most believe it was first performed monodically to the lyre, as we expect from sympotic / erotic song, but some have speculated it was performed chorally, since in form (strophic triads) and content it recalls a slighter version of Stesichorean "choral epic." (Reperformance could, of course, have been monodic.) The typical aristocratic *andron* could not accommodate a chorus of any significant size, but a capacious, grandiose tyrannical symposium was a different story (cf. Cingano 2003, 34–45). An Anacreontic fragment, from a song likely composed for a Polycratean symposium, suggests choral activity there: "I saw Simalus holding the beautiful *pektis* in the chorus" (F 386 PMG).

9.   Choral Melic

Choral melic was, however, typically performed outdoors, before a sizable gathering of people. Most Archaic choruses appeared at festivals, civic, regional, or international in scope, often but not always in the context of an *agon*. They were composed of well-trained yet non-professional singer-dancers, who were in most cases of elite status—public choral performance was a good opportunity for aristocratic families to display their political influence and cultural prestige. Choral melic was "community poetry" par excellence (Stehle 1997, 68–9). Its content –locally and occasionally relevant mythological narrative, hymnic and cultic discourse, gnomic wisdom – accordingly tended to reflect, and indeed articulate, the broad religious, genealogical, and socio-political interests held in common by the festival audience, although those interests were usually refracted through the prism of the elite mentality shared by both the poet and the chorus.

Thus, a Sicilian chorus performing the *Oresteia* of Stesichorus, at what seems to have been a seasonally recurring festival, announces self-referentially, "Songs of the lovely-haired Graces such as these, songs common to the people (*damomata*), must we, devising a Phrygian tune, delicately (*habros*) sing as spring arrives" (F 212 PMGF). As Leslie Kurke observes, Stesichorus "combines the [aristocratic] discourse of *habrosyne* with the claims of the public or common sphere" (2007, 156). We may further note that the chorus' "devising" – through the mediation of the poet – a Phrygian tune is another aristocratic touch, evoking at once elite musical sophistication and privileged access to high-status Anatolian exotica. But unlike in the restricted sympotic context, the chorus promises to publicize such cultural prestige through its *damomata*.

Similarly, in Alcman's *partheneia* 'maiden songs', aristocratic self-regard and civic conscious-ness easily coexist. The chorus of *Partheneion* 1 (cf. Wells ch. 10, pp. 162–3; Willi ch. 29, pp. 449–50 in this volume) celebrates the extraordinary beauty of its chorus leaders, Agido and Hagesichora, and spotlights its own Lydian finery (F 1.64–9 PMGF), while issuing "middling" warnings against excessive ambition (16–17, 36–9; see below). Another, more fragmentary *partheneion* is suffused with dreamy expressions of erotic praise for the ravishing chorus leader, whose "gaze is more melting than sleep and death" (3.61–2). This poetry of "limb-loosening desire" (61), redolent of luxury (71, 77), seems appropriate to the intoxi-cating confines of the symposium or Sappho's sensuous in-group, yet the chorus underlines the entirely public setting of its dance, in the "assembly" (*agon*, 8) and "among the crowd" (*kata straton*, 73). The public dimension is emphasized too by the speaking name assigned to the chorus leader, Astymeloisa, which means "Darling of the City," or, as the chorus glosses it, *melema damoi*, "the people's care." The sentiments of elite chorus and civic audience are thus neatly sutured (cf. Peponi 2007, 356–7).

Choral performance was an occasion for visual delight and musical entertainment – the virtuosic chorus of Delian Maidens was a "great wonder," the enchanting cynosure of Apollo's festival on Delos (*Homeric Hymn to Apollo* 156) – but it also fulfilled deeper cultic and societal functions. Choral song articulated a community's relationship to the gods and the mythical past (cf. *Hymn to Apollo* 158–61) and served to forge and maintain the shared identity of its members (Kowalzig 2007). Claude Calame (2001) argues that Alcmanic *partheneia* were dramatic scripts for Spartan girls' homoerotic initiation rituals prior to marriage. A fundamental sociopolitical function of choruses, virtually transcendent of occasion, was to affirm peace and concord. Their choreographed, collectively voiced displays, which socioeconomically disparate members of the community experienced both as spectators and performers, served as mechanisms and models of *kosmos*, harmonious order both musico-poetic and social, at a time when *stasis* was a constant threat to the *polis* (Nagy 1990, 366–9).

This notion finds rich expression in myth. Toward the end of the *Odyssey*, choral performance significantly occurs at a peak social crisis, immediately after the killing of the suitors. The "sweet song and blameless dance" led by Phemius at once marks Odysseus' restoration of domestic and social order and temporarily diverts the Ithacans who hear the performance from further internecine violence (23.143–52). Pindar imagines the Apollo-led chorus of Muses, in whose performance sound and movement find perfect expression, as the guarantee of universal *kosmos* (*Pythian* 1.1–14). This divine performance must be meant to reflect the pacifying effect of the Pindaric chorus that evokes it. Choral poetry is in fact full of such idealizing "projections" of the actual chorus onto mythical or divine models (e.g. Bacchylides 11.112; 17.101–8, 124–9; cf. Power 2000). Choruses also present themselves as paradigms of social cohesion through direct performative self-references. In a song by Simonides, the chorus describes itself as "sending forth an auspicious cry… from a mind flowing as one (*phrenos homorrotho[u]*)" (F 519 fr. 35.9–10 PMG). The latter phrase neatly expresses "what choral dancing ideally implied: unity of thought" (Stehle 1997, 69).

The mythical narratives of choral song could also work to deter *stasis* by providing examples of its destructive wages. Alcman's maiden chorus recounts the hubristic strife between mythical Spartan dynasts (F 1.1–21 PMGF), strife that is, however, implicitly redeemed in the present by its own graceful, "cosmic" song and dance (Ferrari 2008; cf. Dale 2011, 24–8). Even the Panhellenic myths sung by Stesichorean choruses may have been selected to address local social tensions in Sicily (Burnett 1988).

Related was the belief that choral performance, Apolline paeans in particular, could heal communal sickness. The *Iliad* knows the choral paean as a means of collective catharsis in time of plague (1.472–4; cf. Rutherford 2001, 15, 37). According to one tradition, the paean composer (and proto-lawgiver) Thaletas of Gortyn was summoned by the Delphic oracle from Crete to seventh-century BCE Sparta to cure a plague ("Plutarch" *De mus.* 1146b–c); in another, his songs resolve *stasis* and insure *kosmos* (Plutarch *Lycurgus* 4.2). Similarly, the citharode Terpander was reportedly directed by Delphi to resolve Spartan *stasis* (*De mus.* 1146b). Arion was said to have cured epidemics with his citharodic song (Boethius *De inst. mus.* 1.1).

Such related traditions of musico-poetic catharsis speak to the genetic, interperformative link between choral melic and citharody. It is possible that the tyrant Periander's employment of Arion, citharode and choral dithyrambist, was an attempt to bring the ordering potential of both media to bear on a fractious Corinth. The Peisistratids may have employed the musically versatile Lasus of Hermione for similar ends (Herodotus 7.6), but it would not be until the post-tyrannical democracy that Lasus' institution of annual dithyrambic contests would become a powerful force for social stability in Athens (cf. Wilson 2003, 12–21).

10. Epinician Melic

By the 520s, a new function of choral poetry emerges. Simonides, and very likely Ibycus before him, had begun to marry choral song to the praise of wealthy aristocrats and dynasts, in particular those willing to pay to have their victories in Panhellenic athletic contests poetically celebrated (Rawles 2012). Pindar and Bacchylides would elaborate this practice in the early to middle fifth century, training choruses in cities throughout the Greek world to deliver customized epinician odes in praise of individual victor-patrons. This privatization of the traditionally civic, religious choral medium represents a momentous change. On the one hand, it complemented at the performative level the twin rhetorical goals of most epinician poetry, to glorify the homecoming aristocratic victor as a heroic individual and, simultaneously, to reintegrate him into his community (for which the chorus notionally speaks; cf. Crotty 1982, 104–38; Kurke 1991, 6–7). On the other, privatization likely caused a certain degree of unease. Epinician choruses accordingly worked to create the impression that their performance was communally oriented. For instance, the chorus of Pindar's *Isthmian* 8, composed for the scion of an aristocratic family on the island of Aegina, announces, "Let us sing something sweet for the people" (8). The verb here, *damoomai*, recalls the "people's songs," *damomata*, of Stesichorus' chorus a century earlier (cf. Currie 2005, 18). More generally, epinician poets formulated praise and narrated heroic myths that not only magnified the *kleos* of the victor and his family, but were relevant to the civic community as well.

Although it has been argued that some shorter epinicia were sung at the site of the athletic games immediately after victory (Gelzer 1985, with critique in Eckerman 2012), most odes were surely performed in the victor's city. But where? One possible context is the large-scale, semi-public symposium, as may have been the case with Polycrates' encomium (Clay 1999). Epinician can at least imagine its own monodic *re*performance at the symposium; cf. Pindar *Nemean* 4.13–16, *Pythian* 4.293–9. Some victory odes, however, were probably sung at civic festivals after the victor's homecoming, thereby fusing the epinician chorus directly into the collective social and religious experience of the city. The best candidates for this, however, *Olympian* 3 and *Pythian* 5, were probably not coincidentally commissioned by autocrats (cf. Carey 2007 for an overview of performance scenarios).

The epinician poets composed proper cultic festival songs as well, dithyrambs, paeans, and processional odes, among other genres. Such works were commissioned for choral performance in cities and Panhellenic sanctuaries across Greece, and it is with Simonides, Pindar, and Bacchylides that poetic skill, *sophia*, becomes commodified on an international scale (Gentili 1988, 155–76), and the lyric poet becomes thoroughly professional, capitalizing on the increasingly monetized late Archaic economy. Pindar neatly registers these changes in his second *Isthmian Ode* (ca. 470 BCE), playing off the amateur activity of old-time lyric monodists, who freely composed songs in praise of boys they admired, against the calculating, professional Muse of his own day, who "loves profit" and "works for hire" (*Isth.* 2.1–6).

This distinction, however, is somewhat too pat: Anacreon and Ibycus, the older poets Pindar seems to have in mind, must not have been entirely uninterested in remuneration. Further, Pindar's romanticization of a pre-commercial poetic culture arguably belongs to a more comprehensive rhetorical strategy whereby he at once acknowledges and yet obscures his own status as fee-charging professional (Kurke 1991, 240–56). Unalloyed poetic professionalism, it seems, could be ideologically troubling to Pindar's aristocratic clients, of whom he styled himself a *xenos*, a friend and honored guest, rather than a mere poet-for-hire (e.g. *Nem.* 7.61–3). Some scholars, however, have recently begun to question the consensus view that epinician song-making was in fact a commercial enterprise, arguing instead that epinician poets offered victory songs as uncommissioned gifts, gratis expressions of *xenia* (Pelliccia 2009; Bowie 2012b).

11. Public Elegy and Iambus

Along with choral melic, rhapsody, and citharody, festivals hosted iambic poetry and elegy. Ewen Bowie has convincingly argued that long-form elegy devoted to historical narrative—an intriguing poetic precursor to prose history – and perhaps also mythical accounts was presented at festivals. More specifically, we have evidence suggesting that such elegy featured in musical contests, performed by professional or accomplished amateur aulodes (singers to the *aulos*), agonistic musicians akin to citharodes (Bowie 1986; 2010). Mimnermus composed an elegiac history of Smyrna, presumably separate from his sympotic works and very likely intended for mass consumption. Xenophanes may have composed elegiac *polis* history; Tyrtaeus' *Eunomia* apparently included Spartan history as well. The recently published Simonides F 11 IEG, part of an elegy commemorating the battle of Plataea, seems likely to have had a festival premier (Aloni 2001; cf. Wells ch. 10 in this volume, p. 159). And a still more recent papyrus revelation, a fragment of Archilochus dealing with the mythical king of the Mysians, Telephus (P.Oxy. 4708), may represent the earliest surviving narrative elegy. A festival context for it is certainly possible; the Ephesian philosopher Heraclitus attests to the performance of Archilochus at *agones* in his day, at least, around 500 BCE (DK 22 B 42). As with so much fragmentarily preserved Archaic poetry, however, intermingled interpretive problems bearing upon text, performance, occasion, and genre make certainties impossible (cf. Obbink 2006, and Sider 2006 for broader objections to historical elegy as autonomous genre).

While much of Solon's elegiac poetry must have been intended for the symposium (e.g. F 23–6 IEG), some of his longer political elegies may have been premiered before demotic audiences (West 1974, 12). An anecdotal account reported by Plutarch has Solon surprising Athenians in the agora with an unannounced performance of his 100-line *Salamis* elegy (F 1–3 IEG). While some scholars entirely reject Plutarch's testimony, arguing instead for the poem's initial delivery at a symposium (e.g. Bowie 1986, 19–22), others see in it a credible reflection of more formal delivery at some civic, perhaps festive, gathering (Herington 1985, 34; Stehle 1997, 61). Plato mentions the reperformance of Solonian poetry by Athenian youths at the Apatouria festival in the fifth century BCE (*Timaeus* 21b).

Iambic poetry, much of it (but not all; see Rotstein 2010, 16–57) containing abusive language and earthy, even obscene subject matter, was presumably most at home at drinking parties (cf. Rosen 2003). But longer narrative iambus, such as the Archilochean tetrameters recounting martial exploits (F 88–104, 106–7 IEG), may have been performed by rhapsodes at festivals (Rotstein 2010, 258; 263–66; Stehle 1997, 65).

12. Conclusion

By now it should be clear that the practices and concepts of solitary reading and writing that broadly define modern literary culture are all but foreign to the production and consumption of the poetry and song – lyric in its various monodic and choral forms, rhapsody, and citharody – that by and large constituted Archaic "literature." Although we encounter Archaic poems as purely literary texts, silent and disembodied, we must not forget that most were experienced, audibly and visually, by their original audiences through live performance on socially meaningful occasions. Indeed, performative modality and occasion were prior to and colluded in determining literary-generic elements of textual form and content (cf. Ford 2011, 27–90). We cannot hope to appreciate these elements of any given Archaic poem without trying to recover, from references within the text as well as relevant extra-textual testimony, both literary and archaeological, as much information as we can about both the circumstances of its initial performance and the typical scenarios in which it would have been reperformed.

REFERENCES

Agócs, P., C. Carey, and R. Rawles, eds. 2012. *Reading the Victory Ode*. Cambridge.

Aloni, A. 1989. *L'aedo e i tiranni: Ricerche sull'Inno omerico a Apollo*. Rome.

Aloni, A. 2001. "The Proem of Simonides' Plataea Elegy and the Circumstances of its Performance." In D. Boedeker and D. Sider, eds., *The New Simonides: Contexts of Praise and Desire*, Oxford, 86–105

Aloni, A. 2006. *Da Pilo a Sigeo: Poemi, cantori e scrivani al tempo dei Tiranni*. Alessandria.

Aloni, A. and A. Iannucci. 2007. *L'elegia greca e l'epigramma dalle origini al V secolo*. Florence.

Andersen, Ø. 2011. "Homeridae." In M. Finkelberg, ed., *The Homer Encyclopedia*, 3 vols., Oxford.

Andersen, Ø. and D. T. T. Haug, eds. 2012. *Relative Chronology in Early Greek Epic Poetry*. Cambridge.

Athanassaki, L. and E. L. Bowie, eds. 2011. *Archaic and Classical Choral Song: Performance, Politics, and Dissemination*. Berlin.

Beecroft, A. 2008. "Nine Fragments in Search of an Author: Poetic Lines Attributed to Terpander." *Classical Journal* 103: 225–42.

Bierl, A., A. Lämmle, and K. Wesselmann, eds. 2007. *Literatur und Religion I: Wege zu einer mythisch-rituellen Poetik bei den Griechen*. Berlin.

Boedeker, D. and D. Sider, eds. 2001. *The New Simonides: Contexts of Praise and Desire*. Oxford.

Bowie, E. L. 1986. "Early Greek Elegy, Symposium and Public Festival." *Journal of Hellenic Studies*, 106: 13–35.

Bowie, E. L. 1990. "*Miles Ludens?* The problem of martial exhortation in early Greek elegy." In O. Murray, ed., *Sympotica: A Symposium on the Symposium*, Oxford, 221–9.

Bowie, E. L. 2009. "Wandering Poets, Archaic Style." In R. Hunter and I. Rutherford, eds., *Travelling Poets in Ancient Greek Culture*, Cambridge, 105–36.

Bowie, E. L. 2010. "Historical Narrative in Archaic and Early Classical Greek Elegy." In D. Konstan and A. Raaflaub, eds., *Epic and History*, 145–66.

Bowie, E. L. 2012a. "An Early Chapter in the History of the *Theognidea*." In X. Riu, and J. Pòrtulas, eds., *Approaches to Archaic Greek Poetry*, 121–48.

Bowie, E. L. 2012b. "Epinicians and 'Patrons'." In P. Agócs, C. Carey, and R. Rawles, eds., *Reading the Victory Ode*, Cambridge, 83–92.

Bowra, C. M. 1961. *Greek Lyric Poetry from Alcman to Simonides*. Oxford.

Brown, C. 1983. "From Rags to Riches: Anacreon's Artemon." *Phoenix* 37: 1–15.

Budelmann, F., ed. 2009a. *The Cambridge Companion to Greek Lyric*. Cambridge.

Budelmann, F. 2009b. "Introducing Greek Lyric." In Budelmann 2009a, 1–18.

Budelmann, F. 2009c. "Anacreon and the Anacreonta." In Budelmann 2009a, 227–39.

Burgess, J. 2004. "Performance and the Epic Cycle." *Classical Journal*, 100: 1–23.

Burkert, W. 1972. "Die Leistung eines Kreophylos: Kreophyler, Homeriden und die archaische Heraklesepik." *Museum Helveticum* 29: 74–85.

Burkert, W. 1979. "Kynaithos, Polycrates and the Homeric Hymn to Apollo." In G. W. Bowersock, W. Burkert, and M. C. J. Putnam, eds., *Arktouros: Hellenic Studies presented to B.M.W. Knox on the occasion of his 65th birthday*. Berlin, 53–62.

Burkert, W. 1987. "The Making of Homer in the Sixth Century B.C.: Rhapsodes versus Stesichorus." In M. True, et al., eds., *Papers on the Amasis Painter and His World*, Malibu, CA, 43–62.

Burnett, A. P. 1985. *The Art of Bacchylides*. Cambridge, MA.

Burnett, A. P. 1988. "Jocasta in the West: The Lille Stesichorus." *Classical Antiquity*, 7: 107–54.

Calame, C. 2001. *Choruses of Young Women in Ancient Greece: Their Morphology, Religious Role, and Social Functions*, new and rev. edn. Lanham, MD.

Carey, C. 2007. "Pindar, Place and Performance." In S. Hornblower and C. Morgan, eds., *Pindar's Poetry, Patrons, and Festivals: From Archaic Greece to the Roman Empire*, Oxford, 199–210.

Carey, C. 2009. "Genre, Occasion and Performance." In F. Budelmann, ed., *The Cambridge Companion to Greek Lyric*, Cambridge, 21–38.

Carey, C. 2011. "Alcman: From Laconia to Alexandria." In L. Athanassaki and E. L. Bowie, eds., *Archaic and Classical Choral Song: Performance, Politics, and Dissemination*, Berlin, 437–60.

Cingano, E. 2003. "Entre skolion et enkomion: réflexions sur le <<genre>> et la performance de la lyrique chorale grecque." In J. Jouana and J. Leclant, eds., *La poésie grecque antique: actes du 13e colloque de la villa Kérylos*, Paris, 17–45.

Clay, J. S. 1999. "Pindar's Sympotic *Epinicia*." *Quaderni Urbinati di Cultura Classica* 62: 25–34.

Clay, J. S. 2011. "Homeric Hymns as Genre." In A. Faulkner, ed., *The Homeric Hymns: Interpretative Essays*, Oxford, 232–52.

Collins, B. J., M. Bachvarova, and I. Rutherford, eds. 2007. *Anatolian Interfaces: Hittites, Greeks and Their Neighbors*. Oxford.

Collins, D. 2004. *Master of the Game: Competition and Performance in Greek Poetry.* Washington, DC.

Corner, S. 2010. "Transcendent Drinking: The Symposium at Sea Reconsidered." *Classical Quarterly* 60: 352–80.

Crotty, K. 1982. *Song and Action: The Victory Odes of Pindar.* Baltimore, MD.

Currie, B. 2005. *Pindar and the Cult of the Heroes.* Oxford.

Curtis, P. 2011. *Stesichorus' Geryoneis.* Leiden.

Dale, A. 2011. "Topics in Alcman's *Partheneion*." *Zeitschrift für Papyrologie und Epigraphik* 176: 24–38.

Day, J. 2010. *Archaic Greek Epigram and Dedication: Representation and Reperformance.* Cambridge.

Derda, T., J. Urbanik, and M. Węcowski, eds. 2002. *Euergesias charin: Studies Presented to Benedetto Bravo and Ewa Wipszycka by Their Disciples.* Warsaw.

Eckerman, C. 2012. "Was Epinician Poetry Performed at Panhellenic Sanctuaries?" *Greek, Roman, and Byzantine Studies* 52: 338–60.

Faraone, C. A. 2008. *The Stanzaic Architecture of Early Greek Elegy.* Oxford.

Faulkner, A., ed. 2011a. *The Homeric Hymns: Interpretative Essays.* Oxford.

Faulkner, A. 2011b. "The Collection of *Homeric Hymns*: From the Seventh to the Third Centuries BC." In Faulkner 2011a, 175–205.

Fearn, D. 2007. *Bacchylides: Politics, Performance, Poetic Tradition.* Oxford.

Ferrari, F. 2010. *Sappho's Gift: The Poet and Her Community.* Ann Arbor, MI.

Ferrari, G. 2008. *Alcman and the Cosmos of Sparta.* Chicago.

Finkelberg, M. ed. 2011. *The Homer Encyclopedia.* 3 vols. Oxford.

Ford, A. 1992. *Homer: The Poetry of the Past.* Ithaca, NY.

Ford, A. 2002. *The Origins of Criticism: Literary Culture and Poetic Theory in Classical Greece.* Princeton, NJ.

Ford, A. 2003. "From Letters to Literature: Reading the Song Culture of Ancient Greece." In H. Yunis, ed., *Written Texts and the Rise of Literate Culture in Ancient Greece*, Cambridge, 15–37.

Ford, A. 2011. *Aristotle as Poet: The Song for Hermias and its Contexts.* Oxford.

Franklin, J. 2007. "'A Feast of Music': The Greco-Lydian Musical Movement on the Assyrian Periphery." In B. J.Collins, M. Bachvarova, and I. Rutherford, eds., *Anatolian Interfaces: Hittites, Greeks and Their Neighbors*, Oxford, 193–203.

Franklin, J. 2010. "Remembering Music in Early Greece." In S. Mirelman, ed., *The Historiography of Music in Global Perspective*, Piscataway, NJ, 9–50.

Frontisi-Ducroux, F. and F. Lissarrague, 1990. "From ambiguity to ambivalence: a Dionysiac excursion through the 'Anakreontic' vases." In D. M. Halperin, J. J. Winkler, and F. I. Zeitlin, eds., *Before Sexuality: The Construction of Erotic Experience in the Ancient Greek World*, Princeton, NJ, 211–56.

Gelzer, T. 1985. "*Mousa Authigenes*: Bemerkungen zu einem Typ Pindarischer und Bacchylideischer Epinikien." *Museum Helveticum* 42: 95–120.

Gentili, B. 1988. *Poetry and Its Public in Ancient Greece from Homer to the Fifth Century.* Baltimore.

Gostoli, A. 1990. *Terpandro: Introduzione, testimonianze, testo critico, traduzione e commento.* Rome.

Graziosi, B. 2002. *Inventing Homer: The Early Reception of Epic.* Cambridge.

Greene, E., ed. 1996. *Reading Sappho: Contemporary Approaches.* Berkeley, CA.

Halperin, D. M., J. J. Winkler, and F. I. Zeitlin, eds. 1990. *Before Sexuality: The Construction of Erotic Experience in the Ancient Greek World.* Princeton, NJ.

Herington, C. J. 1985. *Poetry into Drama: Early Tragedy and the Greek Poetic Tradition.* Berkeley, CA.

Hobden, F. 2013. *The Symposion in Ancient Greek Thought and Literature.* Cambridge.

Hornblower, S. 2009. "Greek Lyric and the Politics and Sociologies of Archaic and Classical Greek Communities." In F. Budelmann, ed., *The Cambridge Companion to Greek Lyric*, Cambridge, 39–57.

Hornblower, S. and C. Morgan, eds. 2007. *Pindar's Poetry, Patrons, and Festivals: From Archaic Greece to the Roman Empire.* Oxford.

Hubbard, T. 2011. "The Dissemination of Pindar's Non-Epinician Choral Lyric." In L. Athanassaki and E. L. Bowie, eds., *Archaic and Classical Choral Song: Performance, Politics, and Dissemination*, Berlin, 347–64.

Hunter, R. and I. Rutherford, eds. 2009. *Travelling Poets in Ancient Greek Culture*. Cambridge.

Hutchinson, G. O. 2001. *Greek Lyric Poetry. A Commentary on Selected Larger Pieces*. Oxford.

Irwin, E. 2005. *Solon and Early Greek Poetry: The Politics of Exhortation*. Cambridge.

Jensen, M. S. 1980. *The Homeric Question and the Oral-Formulaic Theory*. Copenhagen.

Jouana, J. and J. Leclant, eds. 2003. *La poésie grecque antique: actes du 13e colloque de la villa Kérylos*. Paris.

Kahn, C. 2003. "Writing Philosophy: Prose and Poetry from Thales to Plato." In H. Yunis, ed., *Written Texts and the Rise of Literate Culture in Ancient Greece*, Cambridge, 139–61.

Kallio, K. 2011. "Interperformative Relationships in Ingrian Oral Poetry." *Oral Tradition* 25: 391–42.

Kantzios, I. 2005. "Tyranny and the Symposium of Anacreon." *Classical Journal* 100: 227–45.

Kirkwood, G. M. 1974. *Early Greek Monody: The History of a Poetic Type*. Ithaca, NY.

Konstan, D. and A. Raaflaub, eds. 2010. *Epic and History*. Oxford.

Kowalzig, B. 2007. *Singing for the Gods: Performances of Myth and Ritual in Archaic and Classical Greece*. Oxford.

Kurke, L. 1991. *The Traffic in Praise: Pindar and the Poetics of Social Economy*. Ithaca, NY.

Kurke, L. 1992. "The politics of ἁβροσύνη in Archaic Greece." *Classical Antiquity* 11: 91–120.

Kurke, L. 1994. "Crisis and Decorum in Sixth-Century Lesbos: Reading Alkaios Otherwise." *Quaderni Urbinati di Cultura Classica* 47: 67–92.

Kurke, L. 1999. *Coins, Bodies, Games, and Gold: The Politics of Meaning in Archaic Greece*. Princeton, NJ.

Kurke, L. 2000. "The Strangeness of "Song Culture": Archaic Greek Poetry." In O. Taplin, ed., *Literature in the Greek & Roman Worlds: A New Perspective*. Oxford, 58–87.

Kurke, L. 2007. "Archaic Greek Poetry." In H. A. Shapiro, ed., *The Cambridge Companion to Archaic Greece*, Cambridge, 141–68.

Lardinois, A. 1996. "Who Sang Sappho's Songs?" In E. Greene, ed., *Reading Sappho: Contemporary Approaches*, Berkeley, CA, 150–72.

Lardinois, A. and L. McClure, eds. 2001. *Making Silence Speak: Women's Voices in Greek Literature and Society*. Princeton.

Liberman, G. 1999. *Alcée. Fragments*. 2 vols. Paris.

Lulli, L. 2011. *Narrare in Distici: L'elegia Greca arcaica e classica di argomento storico-mitico*. Rome.

Luraghi, N. 2009. "The Importance of Being λόγιος." *Classical World* 102: 439–56.

Martin, R. P. 2001. "Just Like a Woman: Enigmas of the Lyric Voice." In A. Lardinois and L. McClure, eds., *Making Silence Speak: Women's Voices in Greek Literature and Society*. Princeton, NJ, 55–74.

Martin, R. P. 2004. "Hesiod and the Didactic Double." *Synthesis* 11: 31–53.

Mirelman, S., ed. 2010. *The Historiography of Music in Global Perspective*. Piscataway, NJ.

Morris, I. 2000. *Archaeology as Cultural History: Words and Things in Iron Age Greece*. Oxford.

Murray, O., ed. 1990a. *Sympotica: A Symposium on the Symposium*. Oxford.

Murray, O. 1990b. "The Affair of the Mysteries: Democracy and the Drinking Group." In Murray, 1990a, 149–61.

Murray, P. and P. Wilson, eds., 2004. *Music and the Muses: The Culture of Mousike in the Classical Athenian City*. Oxford.

Nagy, G. 1990. *Pindar's Homer: The Lyric Possession of an Epic Past*. Baltimore.

Nagy, G. 1996. *Poetry as Performance: Homer and Beyond*. Cambridge.

Nagy, G. 2007. "Did Sappho and Alcaeus Ever Meet? Symmetries of Myth and Ritual in Performing the Songs of Ancient Lesbos." In A. Bierl, A. Lämmle, and K. Wesselmann, eds., *Literatur und Religion I: Wege zu einer mythisch–rituellen Poetik bei den Griechen*, Berlin, 211–69.

Neils, J., ed. 1992. *Goddess and Polis: the Panathenaic Festival in Ancient Athens*. Princeton, NJ.

Obbink, D. 2006. "A New Archilochus Poem." *Zeitschrift für Papyrologie und Epigraphik* 156: 1–9.

Page, D. 1955. *Sappho and Alcaeus*. Oxford.

Pelliccia, H. 2009. "Simonides, Pindar and Bacchylides." In F. Budelmann, ed., *The Cambridge Companion to Greek Lyric*, Cambridge, 240–61.

Peponi, A.-E. 2007. "Sparta's Prima Ballerina: *Choreia* in Alcman's Second *Partheneion* (3 *PMGF*)." *Classical Quarterly* 57: 351–62.

Phillips, D. J. and D. Pritchard, eds. 2003. *Sport and Festival in the Ancient Greek World*. Swansea.

Podlecki, A. J. 1980. "Festivals and Flattery: The Early Greek Tyrants as Patrons of Poetry." *Athenaeum* 68: 371–95.

Powell, B. 2007. *Homer*. Oxford.

Power, T. 2000. "The *Parthenoi* of Bacchylides 13." *Harvard Studies in Classical Philology* 100: 67–81.

Power, T. 2010. *The Culture of Kitharôidia*. Washington, DC.

Price, S. D. 1990. "Anacreontic Vases Reconsidered." *Greek, Roman and Byzantine Studies*, 31:133–75.

Purves, A. C. 2010. *Space and Time in Ancient Greek Narrative*. Cambridge and New York.

Rawles, R. 2012. "Early Epinician: Ibycus and Simonides." In P. Agócs, C. Carey, and R. Rawles, eds., *Reading the Victory Ode*, Cambridge, 3–27.

Riu, X. and J. Pòrtulas, eds. 2012. *Approaches to Archaic Greek Poetry*. Messina.

Rosen, R. 2003. "The Death of Thersites and the Sympotic Performance of Iambic Mockery." *Pallas* 61: 121–36.

Rotstein, A. 2010. *The Idea of Iambos*. Oxford.

Rutherford, I. 2001. *Pindar's Paeans: A Reading of the Fragments with a Survey of the Genre*. Oxford.

Scully, S. 1981. "The Bard as Custodian of Homeric Society: *Odyssey* 3. 263–72." *Quaderni Urbinati di Cultura Classica* 37: 67–83.

Segal, C. 1998. *Aglaia: The Poetry of Alcman, Sappho, Pindar, Bacchylides, and Corinna*. Lanham, MD.

Shapiro, H. A. 1992. "*Mousikoi agones*: Music and Poetry at the Panathenaia." In J. Neils, ed., *Goddess and Polis: the Panathenaic Festival in Ancient Athens*, Princeton, NJ, 53–75.

Shapiro, H. A., ed. 2007. *The Cambridge Companion to Archaic Greece*. Cambridge.

Sider, D. 2006. "The New Simonides and the Question of Historical Elegy." *American Journal of Philology* 127: 327–46.

Snodgrass, A. 1981. *Archaic Greece: The Age of Experiment*. Berkeley, CA.

Stehle, E. 1997. *Performance and Gender in Ancient Greece. Nondramatic Poetry in its Setting*. Princeton, NJ.

Svenbro, J. 1993. *Phrasikleia: An Anthropology of Reading in Ancient Greece*. Ithaca, NY.

Swift, L. 2010. *The Hidden Chorus: Echoes of Genre in Tragic Lyric*. Oxford.

Taplin, O., ed. 2000. *Literature in the Greek & Roman Worlds: A New Perspective*. Oxford.

True, M., et al., eds. 1987. *Papers on the Amasis Painter and His World*. Malibu, CA.

Vetta, M. 1980. *Theognis. Elegiarum Liber Secundus*. Rome.

Watkins, C. 1995. *How to Kill a Dragon: Aspects of Indo-European Poetics*. Oxford.

Węcowski, M. 2002. "Towards a Definition of the Symposion." In T. Derda, J. Urbanik, and M. Węcowski, eds., *Euergesias charin: Studies Presented to Benedetto Bravo and Ewa Wipszycka by Their Disciples*. Warsaw, 337–61.

West, M. L. 1974. *Studies in Greek Elegy and Iambus*. Berlin.

West, M. L. 1981. "The Singing of Homer and the Modes of Early Greek Music." *Journal of Hellenic Studies* 101: 113–29.

West, M. L. 1997. *The East Face of Helicon: West Asiatic Elements in Greek Poetry and Myth*. Oxford.

West, M. L. 2012. "Towards a Chronology of Early Greek Epic." In Ø. Andersen and D.T.T. Haug, eds., *Relative Chronology in Early Greek Epic Poetry*, Cambridge, 224–41.

West, M. L. 2013. *The Epic Cycle: A Commentary on the Lost Troy Epics*. Oxford.

Williamson, M. 1995. *Sappho's Immortal Daughters*. Cambridge, Mass.

Wilson, P. 2003. "The Politics of Dance: Dithyrambic Contest and Social Order in Ancient Greece." In D. J. Phillips and D. Pritchard, eds., *Sport and Festival in the Ancient Greek World*, Swansea, 163–96.

Wilson, P. 2004. "Athenian Strings." In P. Murray and P. Wilson, eds., *Music and the Muses: The Culture of Mousike in the Classical Athenian City*, Oxford, 269–306.

Wilson, P. 2009. "Thamyris the Thracian: the archetypal wandering poet?" In R. Hunter and I. Rutherford, eds., *Travelling Poets in Ancient Greek Culture*, Cambridge, 46–79.

Yunis, H., ed. 2003. *Written Texts and the Rise of Literate Culture in Ancient Greece*. Cambridge.

FURTHER READING

I have tried to include references in this chapter to what are, in my view, the most interesting books and articles on Archaic literary culture produced in the last 25 years or so, with emphasis on recent scholarship in English. Other works, new and old, worth consulting are: Watkins (1995) on Indo-European heritage; West (1997) on Near-Eastern interactions; Murray (1990a), Węcowski (2002), Corner (2010), and Hobden (2013) on the symposium; Bowra (1961), Kirkwood (1974), and Segal (1998) on lyric; Aloni and Iannucci (2007) on elegy, Lulli (2011) on narrative elegy; on tyrants, Podlecki (1980); Burnett (1985) and Fearn (2007) on choral melic; Franklin (2010) on musical culture; Kurke (1999) on ideology; on the reperformance and early written transmission of lyric poetry, Carey (2011), Hubbard (2011); Kahn (2003) on early prose.

CHAPTER 5

Literature in the Classical Age of Greece

James McGlew

What does "Literature in the Classical Age of Greece" mean? It seems appropriate to consider the title assigned to this contribution and its component parts before attempting to define the subject itself. What is literature? What is Greece and what are its proper boundaries? What makes a historical period classical?

Greece certainly offers the least challenge to definition, but is clearly less a geographical designation than a linguistic one (and, by extension, cultural and technological). It encompasses the Greek mainland, Crete and the many Aegean and Ionian Islands, the Greek cities of Asia Minor and the Greek colonies in Italy, Sicily, and on the coasts of the Mediterranean and Black Seas. In the simplest sense, then, Greece means Greek-speaking. Colonies like Cyrene on the coast of Libya had no less claim to be considered Greek than Argos or Athens, despite Cyrene's considerable distance from the mainland. The boundaries of Greek literature match the extent of the Greeks' own movements. Moreover, it was possible, the Greeks themselves believed, to become Greek by learning the Greeks' language: Herodotus explains in detail that the Athenians, who were originally Pelasgian, adopted the language of the sons of Hellen early in their history. Yet, there is also a strong essentializing impulse in the Greeks' own understanding of themselves, their language and culture. Employed as criteria for defining ethnicity, Greek language and culture could sometimes be re-imagined as fundamental and inherent. Greeks of the fifth and fourth century BCE clearly distinguished the periphery and center in cultural terms: some people, they believed, were more Greek than others. No surviving author challenged the significance of the distinction (whether defined in cultural or ethnic terms) between Greek and barbarian in the Classical period. The Athenians, who prided themselves on their racial purity, were particularly hostile to what they perceived as the admixture of barbarian blood; but other Greeks subscribed to this view as well. To be accepted in Athens meant quite a bit outside of Athens, too. Victory for tragedy at the Lenaea at Athens was the culmination of Dionysius the Elder's life; quite literally, in fact, if we can believe the stories his contemporaries told about him: the tyrant, when he heard of his tragedy's success in the bastion of this most Greek of genres, drank himself to death.

As a term, "classical" looks like an imposition of modern terminology on the analysis of fifth- and fourth-century literature and culture.[1] Most evidently what makes "classical" a difficult term is the popular investment placed in it: what is designated "classical" is appreciated as transcending the historical context of its invention, as well as its original use or the interest it originally generated. This use value is greeted by a mixed response. Classicists have worked hard to maintain the currency of Classical literature and culture, but, of course, Classical scholarship itself is not primarily about celebrating Greek literature. To understand Classical texts as scholars is to know what works signify in the context for which they were produced. Classical scholarship is then essentially a kind of archaeological recovery: literary texts become meaningful when viewed in contexts. Yet none of that entirely answers the question whether the surviving records of cultural performances of the fifth and fourth centuries are honored as "classics" by complete accident – in other words, because of the convergence of random conditions and events such as contemporaries' desires to preserve a record of literary (especially dramatic) performances and prose works as well as the relatively low cost of the required technology, or because of factors of a different sort entirely, such as the military and imperialistic success of the Greeks and the perceived need in later periods of European history to appropriate and control Greek fifth- and fourth-century culture. The classicizing tendency of literature shows first traces in Archaic and Classical Greece, although the canon of Archaic and Classical literary works is a later product. Indeed, Greek literature, just because it was largely performative, was fundamentally competitive.

The term "classical" seems more clearly anachronistic when considered primarily as designating a distinct literary style. "Classical" and "archaic" (or for that matter, the more recent term "geometric") migrated to literary studies from nineteenth- and twentieth-century art history. The use of "classical" in this sense reflects an attention to periodization that is not matched in antiquity. Some Greeks, Aristophanes among them, linked style and history, but whether Aristophanes was aiming his comic weapons at tragedy or contemporary forms of education, he treated the link between style and history as evaluative not neutral, as if old and new, past and present were locked in an eternal struggle only thinly veiled by aesthetic matters. Moreover, for Greek works dealing specifically with aesthetics, poetics or the theory of their production (such as Aristotle's *Poetics*), what is now labeled style is regarded as the essential and largely unchanging function of literature (and art generally), rather than the characteristics of any period or the predilections of any particular portion of Greek society. The point can be generalized. While the Greeks of the fifth and fourth century BCE would certainly agree that the historical moments with which we circumscribe the Classical age (Xerxes' expulsion from mainland Greece and Alexander's death) were monumental in Greek political and military history, they would hardly have extended those dates to Greek culture generally. This may reflect a kind of eclectic character of Greek art that is evident, for example, in the very different styles (for us, reflecting different periods) that are merged in the Parthenon frieze. While first-time visitors to the British Museum's exhibit may feel a slight jarring sensation when they see the severe and classical styles intermingled in a single work of art, there is no reason to think that this confluence of styles disturbed the Greeks.[2]

"Literature" too is a difficult term. In addition to the challenge of separating literature from functional writing, the modern concept of literature brings with it a wide array of assumptions, perspectives and principles, many of which are impediments to understanding fifth- and fourth-century BCE analogues. Among the most important: the public and imaginative life of fifth- and fourth-century Greece that is now collected in printed form or arranged in bytes was not "letters" in the post-reformation sense of literature. Of course, most of it (verse and prose) was performative: words themselves capture only a thin record of the original spectacle and reception of Classical Greek literature. But more crucial still, there is little trace in the fifth and fourth century BCE of the private use of literature – as a distinguishing mark of cultural achievement or a potential source of power, enlightenment or consolation – that emerges in late antiquity and has dominated since Luther's translation of the Latin Bible.

What is the aggregate of these reservations and qualifications? Is Classical Greek literature entirely an imposition of modern and contemporary distinctions, perspectives, and values? Is there a justification for a separate treatment of the body of written work that was produced in the period between the expulsion of the Persians and the death of Alexander? A partial answer must be the new critical attitudes (evident in the works themselves as well the audience's social worlds and cultural expectations) that emerge in the late Archaic age. Beginning in the sixth century and increasingly through the fifth and into the fourth, there are new expectations that literature does something more than delighting its audience or helping preserve the memory of remote events. This new critical attitude is most evident in the emergence of prose.

This chapter suggests that the new prose disciplines (philosophy, history, rhetoric, and medicine, among others) reflect the personas, functions, and expectations associated with the rise of prose and give Classical Greek literature an integrity as a distinct field of scholarly interest. Yet much of our anxiety regarding modern assumptions about Classical literature crystallizes around the subject of prose, for the simple reason that prose and the principal prose genres, philosophy, history, and rhetoric, as well as writing itself, the technological innovation on which prose depends, have their roots in the Archaic period. It is obvious, too, that prose stretches the boundaries of literature and literacy: with prose, literature does different things and elicits different expectations than the verse, epic and lyric, of the early Archaic period. Yet if the origins of prose must be located in Archaic Greece, the maturation of the principle prose genres, as forms of discourse making distinctive claims and placing distinctive demands on their audiences, belongs in the Classical age.

Understood primarily as a literary phenomenon, prose is fundamentally significant as distinct from verse. The role that prose writers and their genres give to that distinction varies widely (as we will see), but the variations repeat a single theme. Milesian philosophy, early medical literature, ethnography, and history, all of which begin to appear in the late sixth century BCE, appeal to a literate, intellectually engaged elite; they offer reasoned views and implicitly or explicitly embrace criteria for truth. The genesis of that elite audience (as distinct from an older aristocracy) has occupied scholars for decades and clearly reaches into the social, political, economic, and cultural fabric of Archaic Greece – the importation of an alphabet and the explosion of literacy that this new technology allowed is certainly part of it.[3] Just as certainly the maintenance of that elite was a fundamental part of the cultural life of the Greek cities in which they became prominent. Like prose, the symposium was a social institution that rehearsed conceptions and practices of reciprocity and reflected the features and priorities of a participatory political culture, and, as a crucial part of its function, broke down the walls that separate authors and audience.[4]

This deserves to be considered the primary significance of prose literature when it emerges in the Archaic Greek cities: prose depends on and advertises a distinction between form and meaning, as it effectively bridges the gap between the performer/author and audience. This is in explicit contrast to the performative verse of Archaic Greece (both epic and lyric), which aims to knit form and meaning together in a single inseparable unit that springs (unexplained and unexamined) as the poet's special gift. Put in these material and receptive terms, the contrast which prose writers discovered and exploited seems both flexible and productive. Thus prose might be cast as a reaction against epic poetry's claims to possess a unique access to non-experiential truth, a rejection of the epic's predilection to portray human achievement as a product of heroic virtue, or, more subtly, it might attest to a new sense of the power and responsibilities of the audience and a commitment to the idea that truth (whether historical or philosophical) is a precious but difficult discovery of social man.

In this sense, prose must be considered as a way of thinking and not only as a way of communicating; its emergence reflects changes in the character of its receptive audience as much as the abilities and preferences of its makers. Where does the impetus to write prose come from?

That, at its start in Greek Archaic cultural history, we see the law code as an important early form, as Simon Goldhill notes,[5] suggests that prose reflects and sustains changes in the nature and understanding of truth and social authority and the close link between prose and writing itself. That the early law codes were prose and written seems consonant with their broad dissemination: they were meant for all to see and obey. Knowledge of them did not depend on performers; their interpretation was not left in the hands of poets. (Even Socrates, though he does not believe the many are capable of deciding correct citizen behavior, most certainly does not want such matters decided by self-proclaimed religious experts like Euthyphro.) In fact, just as their publication (inscribed on stone blocks placed in the public area of the city) imply that the citizens who came under their purview have a right to know what the laws say, their prose composition makes transparent the political nature of their invention; that they are the work of men not the utterances of the gods, and that they possess their own power and yet (perhaps as a reflection of that power) can nonetheless be changed. When the Greeks wrote their laws as prose (rather than writing them in verse or leaving them unwritten), they seemed implicitly to acknowledge and even welcome a process of interpretation, as if the precision of prose and even the hardness of the stone on which they are inscribed – the very efforts to make them both specific and universal – announce that they are also conditional and changeable.

Understanding this, the Greeks of the Archaic and Classical period rendered their laws in prose, if they wrote them at all: the differences in the relationship between lawgiving and political decision-making can be read in the tension between written and unwritten law, not between the use of prose and poetry. When they were not written, the decision reflects a profound cultural distrust of the process of interpretation that is inherent in prose. This is the case in the Sparta of Lycurgus, who wanted his laws to remain "inalterable and secure" (Plut. *Lyc.* 13.1).[6]

There are no surviving laws written in verse, yet no less a legal persona than Solon clearly understood (or, perhaps, was later interpreted to understand) the difference between prose and poetry in a legal context. Solon was frustrated by a law that forbade the Athenians even to consider resuming the war with Megara for the possession of the island Salamis. To overcome it, the eventual lawgiver (already the master of his own public persona), appeared at the herald's stone, the paramount place of political speech, transparently as a mad traveler (supported by false reports of his insanity). When a crowd had gathered, he delivered his elegy, "*Salamis*", an impassioned plea to the Athenians to take control of Salamis. In this case, as Solon well knew, poetry gave him a power that prose could not: it allowed him to pretend to a particular kind of identity (he begins a kaleidoscope of identities by proclaiming that he is a herald come from Salamis) – a process of poetic self-invention reforged into a special license for political speech – in effect, an application to speak in a register that was in some sense beyond the strictures of law.[7]

The distinctiveness of prose, in large terms, might be understood as the discovery and the exploration of a gap between form and meaning – in effect, the disrupting of the illusion that is the achievement of successful poetry, that is, a seamless bond between the truths that a text or performance relates and the means of approaching and communicating those truths. For the Greeks, prose literature, far more than the product of stripping poetry of its meter, represents a rejection of poetry's pretense to exist without an active and engaged audience. It incorporates an awareness of context. Prose writers, for the Greeks, lie as freely as poets, and perhaps in more ways. They exaggerate and deceive, they truss up pretty phrases, as Socrates famously complained about his accusers (Plat. *Apol.* 17c), and they lead their listeners astray. But the prose writer is a member of the audience to which he appeals – an equal, with all that that implies. His interests and desires are conspicuous; he takes (or is compelled to take) ownership of what he says. Unlike the epic poet (to whom early prose writers most contrasted themselves), he does not bring (or pretend to bring) other obligations into his performance. In this sense, prose entails and reflects a significant innovation in the persona of the author, whose connection to the material is no longer unquestioned, immediate and absolute, and, more important still, of the audience, which holds a certain power over the author and his material. This is not to say that the relationship between the author and audience is unvarying. In the case of laws, transforming laws into a text is tantamount to creating political space: written law assumes, and helps engender, a political body that obeys laws, punishes those who break them, and is equipped and prepared, if it becomes necessary, to change them. The relationship between author and audience is configured differently and has different significance in different contexts, periods and genres of Classical Greek literature. Form and meaning are constructs; the line between them is not fixed. There is also a fluidity in the relationship of prose and verse, both of which are performed in the Classical period and respond to similar social and political stresses.

The Presocratic philosophers (as they have been labeled since the nineteenth century) offer the earliest image of the emergence of prose as a preferred literary form. The Milesians, standing at the very start of the tradition, eschewed the Hesiodic creation story of a series of cosmological transformations (that is, of being emerging from nothing, an animate cosmos from cold, dormant forces, and, finally, the sovereignty of Zeus out of ceaseless, brutal change). Instead they offered accounts of matter (variously understood) whose transitions and variations do not alter its essential nature. This is no longer a story told by divine informants (the Muses) about divine events through a human mouthpiece. Theory replaces narrative; the author (fully human) and his credentials (his insights, reasoning, evidence, and limitations) mediate between the work and its audience. Thales' inclusion among "the Wise" (Diog. Laer. 1.13.1) as well as the story of his prediction of the total eclipse of 548 BCE, may have helped credential him.[8]

The form of the writing is not allowed to get in the way; the philosopher's prose becomes important not for its art but its (appearance of) artlessness. That Thales according to some (Diog. Laer. 1.23.1) wrote nothing, creates the opposite effect of unwritten laws; the absence of writing on Thales' part takes writing's distinctive power to its logical extreme: opening truth to any and all approximations, effectively magnifying the significance of the process of understanding. From a certain perspective, the prose works of the Milesians (Anaximander, Anaximenes, and Thales, too, if he wrote), just because they are stripped of the art of verse, are nothing if they are not perceived to be true. But the humanness of the undertaking makes the Milesian theories part of a common undertaking, like the different treatments of myths by different vase painters or tragedians. It is this stress on process or inquiry (*historiē*) for which the adoption of prose was a sign and a catalyst (perhaps more even than its nascent rationality) that makes Milesian thought "scientific." And it is to this collective process that authority, when relocated away from a divine source, devolves. To be sure, the rejection of any human access to an unequivocal truth about the physical world was felt as a loss. As Xenophanes (DK 21 B 34) noted in a fragment embraced by later skeptics: if speech should ever stumble upon truth, the achievement itself would nonetheless elude confirmation. Moreover, the commitment to a collective process and the use of prose itself is gradual and inconsistent – Parmenides in the sixth century and Empedocles in the middle of the fifth century (and perhaps Heraclitus whose writings, though prose, were labeled "riddling") were not entirely comfortable trusting their insights and ideas to such processes.[9] If some Presocratics did not entirely swear off the use of verse, its distinctive multivalence, authorial voice and its "finish," if they were reluctant to let their ideas and insights be picked apart, exposed to logical and empirical tests and, in the end, reinterpreted or rejected, there was general agreement that the narrative impulses and theories of the poets of previous generations were inadequate and misleading. Xenophanes' famous complaints (in verse) about the anthropomorphic tendencies of Homer and Hesiod (DK 21 B 11, 14) are seconded by Heraclitus, who (in his distinctively poetic prose) urged that Homer and Archilochus should be thrown out from the competitions and flogged (Diog. Laer. 9.1.10).

Glimmers of the significance of the emergence of prose become clearer when we turn to the genre of history, whose commitment to the new form of writing was yet more complete. History was understood by its practitioners as a process of recovery; whether principally an *epideixis* or a process of research and historical speculation. The truth is difficult to achieve; the author's talents, methods and limitations are on display in his work.

This puts a new light on the historian himself, who presents the past no longer as if he were a simple mouthpiece of the Muses; his person, like the philosopher's, becomes interesting in ways that epic, whose traditional subject matter history assumes, does not recognize. Indeed, Homer's traditional blindness proves his link to the Muses as much as it protects his art from the intrusion of inconvenient scrutiny. So, too, his poet characters. His Demodocus has no need to demonstrate how he knew about Troy when he sings to the Phaeacian elders. The artfulness of his demonstration is very much on display and much praised, but his remoteness from Troy blinds him to personal research and judgment no less effectively than his creator's physical disability. In that respect there is no difference in his treatment, or his audience's appreciation of the truth value, of his two very different subjects, the Achaeans' exploits at Troy and Aphrodite's fling with Ares, except that Odysseus' moans and tears confirm the truth of the former from personal experience. While prose recognizes the difference between prose and poetry; poetry cannot reproduce prose. Yet Homer acknowledges the fixed social boundaries by which the life of the poet is constrained. As a member of his community, the poet is subordinate; the man and his art are separate. Phemius in *Odyssey* 22 is not punished for entertaining the suitors. It is certainly a relief for him to escape the punishment that has just befallen the soothsayer Leiodes, whose claims of innocence Odysseus summarily rejects. The poet can relate monumental achievements and huge wars, but such achievements are beyond his status and he cannot even dare to dream, like Leiodes, that he might one day replace Odysseus in Penelope's bed.[10]

The historian has limits too. He does not claim omniscience. Knowledge of his material is a result of personal acquisition and research. He travels and sees, he hears about things from others, he speculates. Herodotus and Thucydides begin their works with a discussion of their methods, the historian's replacement for the epic invocation of the Muses. Herodotus makes it clear at the outset of his work (1.5) that he will carefully distinguish between what he hears and what he knows; what counts as knowledge, he implies, is not simply personal experience but material that he has filtered through his own sense of historical probability. Thucydides explains the historical composition in fuller terms, but the activity does not seem to differ in basic respects. Historical truth (*akribeia*), Thucydides stresses (1.22.1–2), is difficult to achieve. He has himself heard few of the speeches that indicate the motives of his leading actors; worse still, his memory and those of his sources is less than reliable. His knowledge of events is even less secure. Every experience, even his own, is partial and perspectival. But as great as the challenge, his confidence never wavers; indeed, his credentials as historian seem perfectly suited to fill the gaps of the information available to him. Most importantly these lie in his understanding of human nature (*to anthropinon*: 1.22.4), an acute perception into historical necessity and a commitment to research, all of which allow him to discover historical significance in a mass of information and create what he intends to be a "enduring monument" (*ktēma es aiei*: 1.22.4).[11]

The difference between the historian and the poet becomes an historical *topos* in the fifth century. Thucydides frames his treatment of this difference in broad terms as the distinction between history and myth; *logographoi*, historical prose writers whom Thucydides believes wrote for pleasure not truth (1.21.5), are grouped with the latter. Prose, it seems, provides a necessary platform to communicate historical knowledge, but it is hardly sufficient. Charming verse and riveting narratives, Thucydides suggests in anticipating the complaints of the Platonic Socrates, are equivalent distractions. To group *logographoi* – Herodotus is likely meant to come to mind, who delighted Thucydides' contemporary Athenians reading aloud his accounts of the triumph over the Persians – with the Homeric bards was certainly the worst criticism that Thucydides could level at his predecessors. (Herodotus, of course, like fifth- and fourth-century Attic dramatists, would have rejected Thucydides' distinction between truth and listening pleasure as an unnecessary straitjacket.) In fact, Herodotus fully anticipates Thucydides' attitude toward epic poetry (if not logographers): his opening account of the antecedents of the wars between the Greeks and their eastern neighbors punctures epic storytelling just as it depreciates the events that storytellers told. But there is a new intensity (as well as more targets) in Thucydides. He weighs into the older dispute – largely one-sided – between prose and verse with an acute awareness of a split between words and things and of the power of words both to discover and distort. What is at stake is more than historical preservation, the goal of Herodotus' work (1.1). It is in fact nothing less than the ability of men to recognize (if not actually to change) the events that will build their future.

Greek poets in the late Archaic age were perfectly aware of the ability of their own kind to distort. But they seemed to do so in different ways and for different purposes. Stesichorus, in his *Palinode*, slammed his fellow poets for their treatment of Helen. But he was able to correct their mistakes (and recover his own vision in the bargain: Paus. 3.19.13) without abandoning the tools and authorial posture of the poet. Poetry possesses a seductive power that can and must always be used in the service of truth. To believe Pindar, Homer's *sophia* led him astray in his presentation of Odysseus and Ajax (*Nem.* 7.21–22); this was a serious mistake, but Pindar reserves his real disdain and strongest condemnation for others, like Odysseus and the Achaeans who honor him over Ajax. It may seem paradoxical that Odysseus, of all the heroes at Troy, was closest to poet; Ajax, whose heart and tongue were poorly aligned (*Nem.* 8.24), was the hero whom Pindar most loves. But the paradox is only apparent. Pindar believes in firm social roles. Great deeds were the province of men like Ajax; praise was the work of poets like himself; and the celebration of deeds, once properly adorned by true poets, was the responsibility of the people. Odysseus, who tells his own story and misleads a mass with a blind heart (*Nem.* 7.23–4), undercuts the proper social order. As a result, Ajax, best of the Achaeans after Achilles, is undone by "secret votes" (*Nem.* 8.26) and "hateful deceit" (*Nem.* 8.33).[12]

Serious as he regarded this problem to be, Pindar, like Stesichorus, was convinced that he was properly equipped to fix it. In this, both resemble Xenophanes, who cultivated with his philosophical poetry a contemplative emotional and cognitive state that lent itself to the appreciation of a god untouched by human history or human-like desires, the sort of philosophical position to which Xenophanes himself seems to have subscribed (DK 21 B 23).[13]

The literary criticism of the following generation is far less accommodating to poetry, which, in the course of the fifth century, seems to lose its distinctive claims to be a form of truth. Thucydides certainly takes the more radical line – but so too had Heraclitus, insisting that Homer and Archilochus should be thrown out and flogged (DK 21 B 42) and his complaint that Hesiod was "the teacher of most men" (DK 21 B 57).

And, of course, there was Plato, whose work issued the most damning critique of poetry as a means of discovering truth and who contributed to the literary invention of the dialogue, which should perhaps be considered the most innovative prose genre of the Classical age. Plato was the first to question what actually is stripped from poetry by philosophy and how, once unburdened by its offensive parts, philosophers might come closer to truth. His answers are complicated; his treatment of poetry, however, is relatively straightforward. Socrates in the *Republic* is imagining a city whose founder combed through the available literary arts as if items on a dessert menu; on an emotional diet, they decide that all the offerings are a bit too rich. Plato, early in the *Republic* (373b), lumps poets and painters into a group with (among others) contractors and cosmeticians. They are the city's bloat – frivolous clutter that distracts citizens, leading them and the city away from the necessary and proper goals of civic life. Poets make copies of bad men, copies that seduce their audiences. Mimesis, in Book 10 of the *Republic*, is more complete and annihilating: there is no more of the suggestion that poets might produce good as well as bad copies. As he turns from the effect poetry has on its audience to the nature of copying itself, poetry is redefined as a shadowy lower world of counterfeit copies. The worst of all, Plato's Socrates claims (drawing apparently on both treatments of mimesis), is tragedy, and Homer, whom Plato's Socrates calls "the most poetic and first of tragic poets" (*Rep.* 607a). Whatever its philosophical virtues and vices, Plato's treatment of poetry is significant in literary history as the most complete exploration (before Aristotle) of the extraordinary emotive powers poets wielded over their audiences and for its insistence that, whatever claims they make for themselves, they are responsible to their communities for the use they make of their powers.

Plato's treatment of poetry often strikes his readers as extraordinarily vehement, as if less a critique than an exorcism. Diogenes Laertius' story (3.5) that Plato was an aspiring writer of tragedy when he met Socrates suggests that he was performing the exorcism on himself. Of course, the story may be a fabrication. But if meeting Socrates did not convince Plato that his nascent poetic opus was worthless, it did inspire his greatest contribution to philosophical prose. The Socratic dialogue (or at least Plato's version) answers the question raised by the rejection of writing by Socrates (and perhaps by Thales before him): how can philosophy, when it rejects the strictures, fictions, and lying personas of poetry, discover and communicate philosophical truths?

The dialogue explicitly embraces the fundamental point at the essence of the invention of prose – the awareness of the distinction between form and meaning, or, in this instance, between opinion and truth. The rules imbedded in the Socratic dialogue – particularly the requirements that the interlocutor answer Socrates' questions sincerely and consistently and that the answers alone matter (and whether they can be shown to be true or not), not the authority of the answerer – captures (indeed intensifies) the element of community in the prose treatises of the Milesians. Plato, of course, seems at times to suffer the same ambivalence as some of the Presocratics (Parmenides, for example); moreover, his middle and later work shakes free of the rules (cumbersome for a positive philosophy) of the Socratic dialogue and likewise becomes more accepting of the mythical narratives that are consistently impugned in his Socratic dialogues. This certainly reflects Plato's changing conceptions of what philosophy needs to be able to say. But philosophy, like serious history and scientific inquiry, remains inextricably tied, for him and most Greeks of the Classical age (if not their successors), to prose.

The development of prose, which begins in the Archaic age, is therefore completed in the Classical era with the innovation of the preeminent prose genres, history, philosophical and scientific treatises, rhetoric, and the Socratic dialogue. The transformation in the relationship between the author and audience reflects social and political changes that (however explained) lie at the core of the development of the *polis*: the fundamental literary developments happen in *poleis*. Yet the greatest literary inventions of the age of prose are not prose at all; this honor goes to tragedy and comedy, which emerged in the last decades of the sixth century and the first of the fifth in Athens. We need to consider the emergence of the two in a literary context characterized largely by the dominant position that the prose genres, history, philosophy and natural science, had wrested from poetry for Greek thinking and the nature of individual and civic virtue.

Although there was a flourishing market for written copies of tragedies and comedies in fifth- and fourth-century Greece, and Aristotle (*Poetics* 1452b3–7) thought reading a good tragic story, like Oedipus', stimulated the same emotions to the same degree as experiencing an actual performance,[14] tragedy and comedy were commissioned, written and performed for large citizen audiences at Athens. Moreover, the city paid for these performances through the distinctive use of liturgies – duties placed on the wealthiest Athenians. That rich Athenians saw something of an equivalency in two of the principal fifth-century liturgies – outfitting and maintaining a trireme for the Athenian fleet and supporting a production at the City Dionysia or Lenaea – demonstrates the importance of literary production in fifth-century Athens, as if the citizen who undertook the expense anticipated similar rewards from the two very different activities.[15] (Just as importantly, it suggests that wealth in Athens brought with it the responsibility not only to "give back," but to do so with cultural sophistication and intelligence as well as military and political skills.)

The investment in literary performances at the City Dionysia, Lenaea, and also the Thargelia (though without dramatic works) in fifth-century Athens was huge, but they were also largely Athenian. Tragedy in fifth-century Athens brought myths with their characteristic "momentousness" (*megethos*: Aristotle, *Poetics* 1449b26) to bear in an exploration of the fundamental issues of citizenship (virtue, cooperation, allegiance to community) and a celebration of Athenian democratic life. It is in this sense a creature of Cleisthenic *isonomia*, the creation of a democratic ideology (paradoxically elite in its origins and character) and the beginnings of a political reality of a collective body that seems to have functioned and understood itself as an elite. Like the democracy that hosted it, tragedy merges a profound sense of piety and devotion to tradition with a genuine and penetrating concern for citizen behavior.

Fifth-century Athenian tragedy is not ideologically simple.[16] The surviving works of Athenian tragic poets have relatively little in common with the monumental public art that emerged in Athens in the mid fifth century, and involved an even larger public expense. The Parthenon, for example, awed its spectators, inciting its audience (Athenians and non-Athenians alike) in multiple and complicated ways to an appreciation of a single, overwhelming destiny of Athens; the city is positioned at the center of fundamental cosmological and human events. The works were commissioned by, and certainly appreciated by, the Athenian *demos*, the collective citizen body. It seems less clear that Athenians, when they saw and admired the sculptural art of the Parthenon, however much it aroused their love of Athens, can be understood as performing a specifically democratic act. Tragedy was likewise willing to celebrate Athens in mythological terms. Aeschylus might be understood in his *Persians* to have wanted to comfort his Athenian audience that their victory over Persia was not the product of luck or even of better strategy, leadership, training, not even of courage. What Persia's defeat proves, rather, are the essential and enduring differences between the Athenians and the Persians: the Athenians' victory at Salamis, his audience must exit the theater believing, was no accident. But his play interprets as much as it glorifies Athens. His intense examination of the Persian court (rendered tragic) construes the Athenians' own behavior and identity as the Persian antithesis. *Persians* was the one successful historical tragedy. For Persia, through much of the surviving opus of Aeschylus and his successors, we might easily substitute Thebes. Euripides' plays in the 420s treat the inglorious aftermath of the Trojan War (*Andromache*, *Hecuba* and *Trojan Woman*); they conduct an intense examination of the human costs of warfare without so much as mentioning Athens, whose citizens were then entangled in intense war. This is literature fully engaged in Athenian political culture.

This is clearer still in the case of comedy, which, while eschewing myth, created dramatic structures by drawing for its building material from the hopes and fantasies of common citizens. Comedy makes particular not general points; the misery of war is not a human condition or a consequence of hubris. Rather it is bad when it happens to you and fine for your enemies. Comedy is not for this reason shallow or ephemeral. When the evils of war befall the likes of *Acharnians*' Lamachus, a real political figure and military leader of late fifth-century Athens, they are parodied to embody and animate an abstract principle, and they become entertaining and salutary. And yet for all its engagement in the quotidian social and political world of fifth- and fourth-century Athens, comedy, no more than tragedy, was not simple political speech. The value of Aristophanes' *Knights*, which attacks the Athenian general Cleon with a relentlessness that rivaled Achilles' pursuit of Hector, is hardly vitiated by the Athenians' decision to re-elect him as general a matter of a few weeks after the play's performance. Aristophanic comedy did to Athens' leaders what they refuse to do for themselves: it humanizes them, discovers (or really invents) their weaknesses, puts them on a level plain with the citizens who elect them; in short, it makes them usable.

In effect, then, the fifth- and fourth-century Athenian stage (there is no reason to believe that performative literature outside of Athens was different) was a place for Athenians, as citizens as well as literary artists, to exercise personal responsibility and liability (the personal rewards and risks were obviously great) in contributing to the city's identity and self-reflection. It is possible in this light to argue for a still closer relationship between drama and the new prose disciplines – the influence of medicine and ethnography on tragedy, for example, or Aeschylus' influence on Herodotus.[17]

Yet, tragedy and comedy were Athenian literary arts. The great majority of the audience was Athenian; the mythical material of tragedy and the narrative focus of comedy have a clear Athenian slant. This reflects an important point about literature dominated by the emergence of prose. In general, the Classical age was a period of cultural isolation in the Greek world; the Samian poet Choerilus seems to have wanted to revive epic poetry by writing a Panhellenic treatment of the wars between the Greeks and Persians. If his poem enjoyed popularity for a time, his larger aim was destined to failure. The trend was more to a regionalization of literature, which, rather like many religious cults in fifth-century Greece (e.g. the Eleusinian Mysteries), was "owned" by particular cities. The Greek world, though more populated and prosperous in 450 than 550, was also more isolated. The increasing cultural isolation of a city like Sparta, which seems to have committed few resources to ongoing literary production, is unproblematic for a modern perspective. But Athenians were isolated in their own way too; this is more surprising. To be sure, the picture is hardly simple; and there are important exceptions. Athens exported tragedy and tragedians to Sicily and Macedonia, just as it imported teachers of philosophy and rhetoric, no less than artists and architects, all part of the "good things" (*ta agatha*) that, according to Pericles' "Funeral Oration" (Thuc. 2.38.2) flowed into Athens from all corners of the earth.[18] Yet Herodotus might hope to downgrade the significance of the war between the Achaeans and Trojans and insert the Persian Wars in its place in the collective mind of the Greeks, and Aristophanes in *Acharnians* and *Peace* anticipated a plea common in the generation after Athens' loss to Sparta in 405/4: that the Persians alone were profiting from the internecine warfare of the Greeks. But few in fifth-century Greece easily or voluntarily embraced Panhellenic values. The explosion of literary performance in fifth-century Athens at least cannot be separated from an intensified interest in individual and collective citizen identity.

As important as these new poetic genres are for fifth- and fourth-century BCE Greek literary culture, and as clearly as they reassert the place of verse in Greek performative culture, they are as much products of the flourishing of prose genres as reactions against them. The four surviving writers of Attic drama were all citizens; they offered their works to political equals, they participated in public dialogues and they took serious risks. Their relationship with their audience was based ultimately in shared allegiances, experiences and hopes. To be sure, Greek literature in the fifth century did not entirely lose its national perspective and broader thematic interests (and clearly regains many of them in the Hellenistic period); the Athenians and other Greeks continued to enjoy performances of itinerant singers, the literary descendants of the famous singers like Arion the Methymnian.[19] But if Socrates was right when he tried to compel Agathon and Aristophanes at the end of Plato's *Symposium* (233d) that the same man, employing a single skill, should be able to compose comedy and tragedy, then that man must be a citizen and his distinctive skill, without which he could not even begin to reach his audience, had to be honed from his abilities to persuade and be persuaded by his fellow citizens.

NOTES

[1] See Whitmarsh 2004, 13: "neither the romantic view of periodization nor the post-modern fragmentation of history represents an absolutely true picture of Greek culture." Whitmarsh is addressing the distinction of "Classical" and "post-Classical" literature, but his comments also

fit the distinction between Archaic and Classical, as a distinction between the nascence and apex of the Greek city-state and its cultural production.

[2] There is perhaps a comparable literary example when, at the close of the fifth century, Aeschylus' plays began to be re-performed on the Athenian stage alongside contemporary tragedies.

[3] This was Eric Havelock's thesis a generation ago. For discussions of Havelock's contributions and recent departures from his perspectives and arguments, see the papers collected in Yunis 2003.

[4] See Murray 1990. The symposium was about entertainment, not material instruction; participants took turns singing poetry; prose compositions (such as those offered by Agathon and his friends in Plato's *Symposium*) must have been rare. But these were improvisational performances; everyone participated.

[5] Goldhill 2002, 3. See also Whitmarsh 2004, 106–21 and Kurke 2010. Kurke intriguingly positions the emergence of prose as a crucial element in a cultural revolution that leaves few areas of Greek social and intellectual life untouched.

[6] Spartan law thus becomes a monument that is unthreatened by words, like the virtue of the war dead in Athens, whom an "unwritten monument" in hearts of all men honors (Thuc. 2.43.4).

[7] On the poem and event, see Irwin 2005. Madness, a recurring theme in Solon's poetry, represents an extreme of Solon's poetic self-invention. Solon claims in another elegy that his fellow Athenians doubted his intelligence when he rejected tyranny (Plut. *Sol.* 14; Solon F 33 IEG), and they doubted his sanity, too, when he warned the Athenians about Peisistratus (Diog. Laer. 1.49; cf. Solon F 10 IEG). "Singers (*aoidoi*) tell many lies," Solon brazenly announced in a lost poem (F 29 IEG) – a statement that seems to be considerably richer than a mere accusation leveled at his fellow poets.

[8] Solon, who, as a lawgiver, was likely invested in a similar effort of credentialing (or self-credentialing); his inclusion in the same group of philosophers (Thales, Bias and Myson), tyrants (Cleobulus, Pittacus and Periander) along with his fellow reformer Chilon, may echo this effort.

[9] Heraclitus, though his book enjoyed immense popularity, was called "*ainiktēs*" (and also "*ochloloidoros*," "crowd-reviler") by Timon (Diog. Laer. 9.6.6–7), who chose hexameter for his satirical treatment of philosophers. Among lawgivers, Solon should be compared. His laws, such as they are preserved, were written in prose, but he made full use of the power of verse to explain them and secure for them an authority that they did not in fact possess as a consequence of a political decision made by the Athenian demos. Among later classical literature, Plato's decision to end the *Republic*, his theory of justice as a good independent of the consequences in this world and after, with the myth of Er and the Athenian stranger's insistence on combining laws and preludes (*prooimia*; 722d–723a) also deserve comparison.

[10] Of course, the many-wiled Odysseus is a poet of a different stamp; when he takes a turn to entertain the Phaeacian elders with the account of his trials and adventures, his story unites poet and hero.

[11] In this light, the works of Choerilus of Samos must be counted as one of our greatest losses in Classical literature. Choerilus in one of the few fragments that survive searched for a subject to reinvigorate the fading art of epic. But it was prose history (not Homer) that cast the greatest shadow over Choerilus.

[12] Historians, of course, were understood as capable liars too. Plutarch's *De malignitate Herodoti* chides Herodotus for misrepresentations that are just as serious as those prose authors condemn in poets.

[13] Xenophanes in the *Silloi* (DK 21 B 11) famously accused Homer and Hesiod of misrepresenting the gods and attributing all forms of deceit to them. But this is probably not best understood as a criticism of poetry as a form of knowledge about the world; poets, in this case,

are doing nothing more than all other men. So Xenophanes' provocative claim that "if horses and cattle had hands, ... horses like horses and cattle like cattle would represent their gods and shape their bodies." (DK 21 B 15). While Xenophanes was unhappy with poets, his complaints should be taken as intramural: this is a struggle of elegy (with its considerable satirical powers) against epic and its narrative and descriptive impulses, not between fundamentally different ways or forms of knowing the world.

[14] On the passage, see Ford 2003, 20.

[15] Of course, the actual outlay was not really the same: evidence from Lysias (21.1–3) suggests that outfitting a trireme could cost twice as much as producing tragedy at the City Dionysia.

[16] Cf. on this, Rader, ch. 11, pp. 176–80, and Baechle, ch. 30, pp. 466–71 in this volume.

[17] The question now crystalizes in a debate over tragedy's representation of barbarians. Against J. Hall 2002 who makes tragedy a full partner, along with history and other prose disciplines, in the invention of the barbarian and the solidification of Greek identity, see now, Gruen 2011.

[18] Athens may sometimes have imported tragedies as well. The story that the older Dionysius launched into a fatal celebratory binge when news of his victory at the Lenaea reached him argues for this, even if the story is not quite credible.

[19] See Power 2010. The treatment of these older forms was not at all uncritical. So Power, 500: "Non-elite Athenians accordingly grew more self-confident and expressive in their appreciation and critique of the musicians who performed for them. The connoisseurship (of sorts) displayed by Dicaeopolis, the 'average' citizen hero of Aristophanes' *Acharnians* (produced in 425 BCE), in his withering assessment of the citharodes who competed at the Panathenaic contests of 430 and 426 may represent a relatively recent sociocultural development (13–16), although one that would soon become more common."

REFERENCES

Ford, A. 2002. *The Origins of Criticism: Literary Culture and Poetic Theory in Classical Greece.* Princeton, NJ.

Ford, A. 2003. "From Letters to Literature: Reading the 'Song-Culture' in Classical Greece." In H. Yunis, ed., *Written Texts and the Rise of Literate Culture in Ancient Greece,* Cambridge, 15–37.

Goldhill, S. 2002. *The Invention of Prose.* Oxford.

Gruen, E. S. 2011. *Rethinking the Other in Antiquity.* Princeton.

Hall, J. 2002. *Hellenicity: Between Ethnicity and Culture.* Chicago.

Irwin, E. 2005. *Solon and Early Greek Poetry.* Cambridge.

Konstan, D. 1995. *Greek Comedy and Ideology.* Oxford.

Kurke, L. 2010. *Aesopic Conversations: Popular Tradition, Cultural Dialogue, and the Invention of Greek Prose.* Princeton.

Murray, O., ed. 1990. *Sympotica: A Symposium on the Symposion.* Oxford.

Power, T. 2010. *The Culture of Kitharôidia.* Washington, DC.

Walker, J. 2002. *Rhetoric and Poetics in Antiquity.* Oxford.

Whitmarsh, T. 2004. *Ancient Greek Literature.* Cambridge.

Yunis, H., ed. 2003. *Written Texts and the Rise of Literate Culture in Ancient Greece.* Cambridge.

FURTHER READING

Particularly helpful are the books by Ford 2002, Goldhill 2002, Konstan 1995, Kurke 2010, Walker 2002, and Yunis 2003.

CHAPTER 6

Literature in the Hellenistic World

Anatole Mori

1. Literary Contexts

The Hellenistic period is usually framed by the death of Alexander the Great in 323 BCE and the death of Cleopatra in 30 BCE. These political markers are not arbitrary: the kingdoms of the Successors emerged after Alexander's conquest and ended with the rise of the Roman Empire. Alexander dominated the politics and society of his day, but his exploits may lead us to overlook other, less obvious but no less significant, causes and effects. Our focus on these two dates narrows our perspective, obscuring the many diverse interactions between newer states and older cultures that offer a clearer understanding of how and why the world changed at that time. A more expansive chronological and geographical framework is likely to take us some distance from what is typically expected of an introduction to Hellenistic Greek literature. This chapter attempts to combine an overview of third-century Hellenistic poetry (Section 2: Literary Constructs) with an acknowledgment of the shifting social and political contexts of literary cultures in Syria, Mesopotamia, and Bactria, as well as the more familiar intellectual communities of Egypt, Macedonia, and Pergamon.

Admittedly, the term "*Hellenistic*" reinforces hierarchical notions: it simultaneously places the era below those that were more authentically Hellenic and at the same time obscures the influence of non-Hellenic cultures (North African, Western European, Indian, Persian, and so forth). Antiquity established cultural distinctions that help to reinforce these hierarchies, contrasting, for example, *attikizein*, speaking a (traditional, refined, elegant) Attic dialect, with *hellenizein*, speaking the modified, common *(koine)* dialect spread by Alexander's armies.[1] One hopes to avoid as much as possible relapses into the chauvinistic tendencies to which every age is susceptible, and satisfactory alternatives to "Hellenistic" are hard to imagine and equally liable to fall short in one way or another. In any case, most classicists today would probably not wish to claim that the poetry of classical Athens was somehow "purer" than that of Alexandria, given our familiarity with, for example, the Near Eastern antecedents of Homeric epic.[2] Even so, many still find it difficult to shake the feeling that when we speak of Greek culture, we are talking about the works of the (classical) *poleis* and colonies of the Aegean islands and the Greek mainland rather than those of hybrid kingdoms like Ptolemaic Egypt or the Seleucid Empire, with their diverse territories and (un-Greek) institutions, such as ruler cult.

A Companion to Greek Literature, First Edition. Edited by Martin Hose and David Schenker.
© 2016 John Wiley & Sons, Inc. Published 2020 by John Wiley & Sons, Inc.

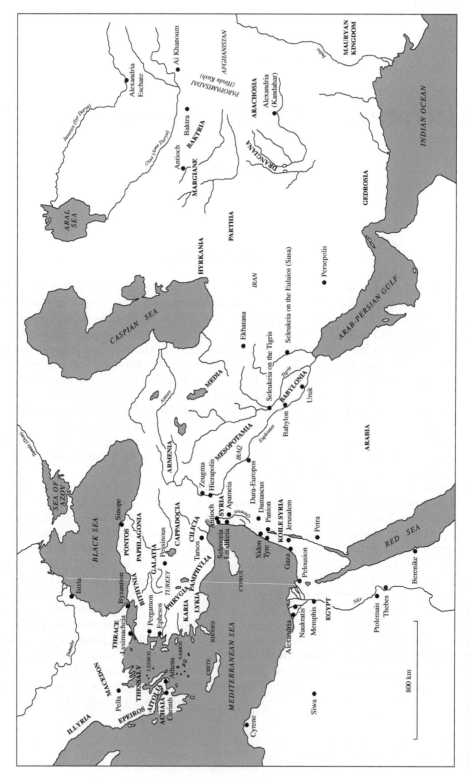

Map 6.1 The Hellenistic World.

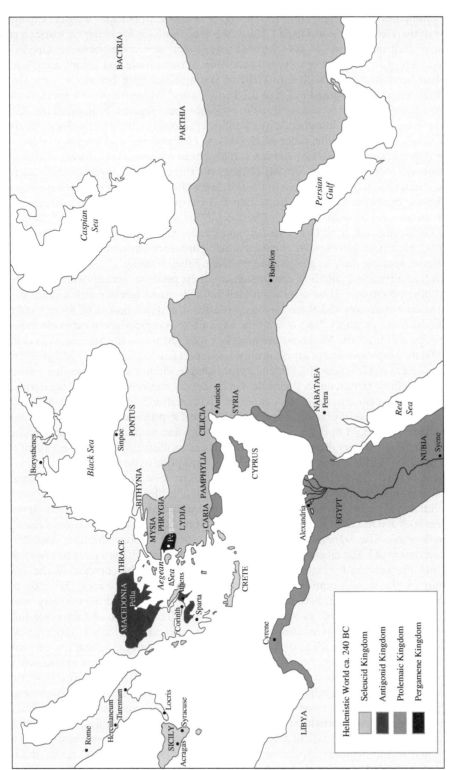

Map 6.2 The Hellenistic kingdoms (c. 240 BCE).

Such sensibilities seem to have come into being, or at least sharper focus, with the expanding horizons of the Hellenistic world itself.[3] This was a time that saw, for better or worse, a rapid diffusion of Hellenic culture. It goes without saying that interactions between Greeks and non-Greeks pre-date the third century BCE, and that through trade and colonization ancient Greeks had been interacting with non-Hellenic communities long before the new Greco-Macedonian kingdoms governed much of the known world. Moreover, Greek speakers (from Macedonia and elsewhere)[4] would continue to influence these regions throughout the Roman and Byzantine eras. The philosopher Sextus Empiricus (second century CE) defined the ability to speak Greek as a fundamental index of Hellenism (*Hellenismos*),[5] and language, along with common customs, kinship, and cult practices, had long been recognized as a marker of Greekness (*to hellenikon*) (Hdt. 8.144). Recent scholarship on the economy, politics, and society of Hellenistic states has accordingly done much to reassess the influence of local communities on the Hellenistic dynasties. Modes of assimilation and interpenetration work in various ways, at different speeds, and in more than one direction. Even as members of other ethnic groups adopted Greek customs, took Greek names, and employed the Greek language (not always voluntarily), Hellenistic Greeks were themselves being influenced by new homelands: adopting their customs, learning their languages, and translating their writings.

Exactly how intentional (and how comprehensive) these processes actually were has attracted much scholarly discussion. How exactly did Hellenistic dynasties interact with local cities and administrations? And how did these interactions affect the development of literary culture? Were the dynamics primarily "top-down," or were there complementary networks exerting influence upwards from the local communities? Are we right to see the Successors as cultural elitists? Did they exploit different ethnic groups by suppressing local traditions and giving preferential treatment to Hellenes? The Ptolemies, for example, did not impose a unified legal code on the diverse ethnic groups under their rule. Greek identity conferred a favored tax status, and onomastic studies demonstrate some degree of Hellenization,[6] although elite Alexandrian Greeks would not necessarily recognize provincial Greco-Egyptians as Hellenes whether or not they could speak Greek.[7] On the other hand, in the third and second centuries several Greeks complained (rightly or not) that they had been assaulted or mistreated simply because of their Hellenic identity: 'Hellene' was usually, but not always, a positive designation.[8]

Relations between Jews and non-Jews were peaceful, at least in third-century Alexandria, where integrationist members of the Jewish community lobbied for the inclusion of their writings in the Great Library.[9] But Jewish social relations varied within Mediterranean society (however one defines it),[10] and reactions to the aggressive imposition of Greek cultural programs elsewhere were not favorable. The *Septuagint*, a Greek translation of the Hebrew scriptures, includes the only extant version of 1 Maccabees (the original Hebrew text is lost).[11] The author of 1 Maccabees (who is not the same as the author of 2 Maccabees) describes the coercion of the Jewish community by the second-century Seleucid ruler Antiochus IV Epiphanes (215–164 BCE). "What happened in Jerusalem between 168 and 164 B.C. went beyond the ordinary internal conflicts of the Seleucid state," as Momigliano observes. "The Temple of Yahwe was turned into a temple of Zeus Olympios, the inhabitants of Jerusalem were called Antiochenes, ... traditional Jewish practices, such as circumcision and observance of the Sabbath, were prohibited."[12] To make matters worse, Antiochus held extravagant parties in the new gymnasium that now abutted the Temple (Athen. 5.195c; 10.439b; 1 Maccabees 20). Herodotus' four criteria of Greek identity were very much on display there, as they would be in any gymnasium, a space where males of all age groups came together not only to exercise, train, and compete, but also to socialize, take part in cult activities, attend lectures, musical and theatrical events, and so on.[13] The Jewish population of Jerusalem accordingly took Antiochus' decadence as normative: as an expression of the depravity typical of Greek life. Some, like Antiochus' agent, the high priest Jason the Oniad, signaled their embrace of *Hellenismos* by frequenting the gymnasium, but many, like the Maccabees, refused and would eventually rebel (2 Maccabees 4.7–15; Josephus, *AJ* 12.5.1).

The situation in Jerusalem was more complicated than this brief discussion suggests, but the point here is simply that Antiochus was an atypical ruler: the majority of Hellenistic kings were less coercive – or at least no more coercive – than their (non-Greek) predecessors. While Hellenistic rulers relied on Greek advisors and sought to preserve Greek culture and customs in these new communities, they made better use of local networks and social structures than was the case in Jerusalem, where Hellenization was decidedly counterproductive, inasmuch as it contributed to a civil war and the resurgence of an independent Jewish state. Political activity within and between Hellenistic states was neither uniform nor systematic; civic groups and institutions were connected via complex networks of peer polities. Peer polity interaction, as Davies writes, amounts to "an untidy set of individual responses to specific situations (whether threats, needs, or opportunities) which were by their nature public and visible to neighbors, were imitated if they were seen to be effective, and therefore came to show certain family resemblances."[14]

The complexity of politics in the Hellenistic period suggests that our consideration of Hellenistic literature should do more than explain who wrote what; as classicists we are liable to characterize Hellenistic literature more narrowly than perhaps we should. Hellenists are traditionally concerned, for the most part, with linguistic practices and the structure and development of Greek literature. The focus of this chapter, too, for a number of reasons, is Greek literature and not that of the Jews (as the preceding paragraphs might suggest). But why is it that we typically locate the literary epicenter of the third-century Greek world in Egypt, rather than Greece, Macedon, or Syria? If all the eastern states had greater resources and were stronger than those of the west, it is reasonable to ask what it was that set Ptolemaic culture apart from that of other urban centers. Was the Great Library of Alexandria[15] an extraordinary response to the Greek diaspora and the loss of traditional performance contexts? Was it a unique expression of the legacy of Aristotelian thought, of Greek *paideia* and the philosophical tradition? Such arguments have been made, and not without reason, but it is easy to forget that Ptolemaic wealth, fondness for spectacle (e.g., the extravagant Grand Procession of Ptolemy II), and emulation of Athenian culture were not atypical for third-century dynasts, and that in many ways, Alexandria was not unique. Hundreds of new Greek-style communities complete with temples, theaters, and gymnasia were founded in Asia during the fourth and third centuries. The archaeological remains of the Greek community of Ai Khanoum, originally one of Alexander's military installations (possibly known in antiquity as Alexandria-on-the-Oxus) in what is now northeastern Afghanistan, show that Greeks maintained their cultural heritage by, among other things, living in a separate district, attending a large theater, and maintaining a gymnasium: "the quintessential public institution of the Greek world."[16] Public buildings in Ai Khanoum included a Mesopotamian-style temple, and a Persian-style administrative center, but Greek influence is clear from the archaeological remains, which include a royal library, a gymnasium and a 5,000-seat Greek theater, the largest in the East.

The Seleucids established many more new cities than the Ptolemies did, but Ptolemy I Soter did found a second Greek capital, Ptolemaïs Hermeiou, in the Thebaid, in order to maintain control over southern Egypt.[17] Although Alexandria remained the center of intellectual life in Egypt long after its holdings are believed to have been lost,[18] Ptolemaïs, together with its neighbor Panopolis, became the center of a new Hellenic literary community in the third – sixth centuries CE, producing a new generation of epic poets including Nonnus, Triphiodorus, and Musaeus.[19] Alexandria, in other words, was not unique as a cultural center, even in Egypt. And while it is true that the Ptolemies promoted scholarship and were the patrons of poets, historians, and intellectuals, the same can be said of the Antigonids in the Macedonian capital of Pella, and the Attalids in the hilltop kingdom of Pergamon.[20] Political rivalries manifested in cultural as well as political and military conflicts. Thus, the conspicuous display of Greek culture was driven in part by inter-state (and inter-city) competition, and this in turn leads us to ask why it is that Alexandria remains uppermost in discussions of Hellenistic literature.

The political advantages, both practical and intangible, of having a reputation for cultural sophistication and for employing musicians, painters, and sculptors, had long been apparent to those in power throughout the Mediterranean world. Some leaders, like Pisistratus of Athens, may or may not legitimately be given the credit for such cultural advancements, but the intentional patronage of others, like Hieron I of Sicily, is well known. The Macedonian kings, dismissed as barbarians by their Greek neighbors to the south, responded by hosting intellectual luminaries: Euripides accepted Archelaus' invitation in the fifth century, and in the third century poets (Antagoras of Rhodes, Alexander the Aetolian), philosophers (Bion of Borysthenes, Menedemus of Eretria), and philosophically inclined poets (Aratus of Soli, Timon of Phlius) spent time at Antigonus Gonatas' court in Pella. Any kingdom with enough coin could become a new cultural center despite any geographical disadvantages. Indeed, actually importing culture may have been less crucial than being known for importing it. Sources report that Zeno turned down a sojourn in Pella (Persaeus went in his stead), and that Theophrastus, Stilpon of Megara, and Cleanthes of Assos all declined invitations to Alexandria.[21] Such refusals have been taken as condemnations of autocratic power (conflicts between kings and intellectuals were not unknown),[22] but an invitation in itself, regardless of acceptance, could indirectly promote a court's cultural sophistication.

That said, some locations are better for cultural preeminence than others. One practical reason for Alexandria's reputation was its foundation on the coast of a comparatively stable region. There would be no significant internal uprisings against the Ptolemies until the end of the third century BCE, and Egypt had always been hard to invade: the shoreline was perilous and the watchtowers in the Delta were well fortified. Memphis, long regarded by Egyptians as the best-situated city in the land (Diod. Sic. 15.43), was 150 miles from the sea, considerably closer than Thebes. But with access to the economic activity of the Mediterranean safeguarded by the Ptolemaic fleet, Alexandria soon supplanted Memphis as Egypt's main port. Alexandria's two large harbors replaced the ancient Egyptian harbor Thonis-Heracleion, and their favorable location west of the Delta was free from the annual silt that choked those nearer the mouths of Nile distributaries. Canals connected the city with the Nile, the best mode of transport for Egypt's other capitals and villages. Accordingly, in its early years Ptolemaic Egypt was more easily managed politically, economically, and socially than the diverse populations of the Seleucid Empire, whose contested borders ranged from Syria to India. While Memphis and Thebes would continue to be important cultural centers, they gradually lost revenue as the good fortune of Egypt increasingly flowed through its new harbors. And we can understand Alexandrian literary culture in much the same way, as a set of works and practices not only engaged with the Greek world, but also nourished and sustained by the riches of the Egyptian cultural climate.

Then, too, the Ptolemies were distinguished not simply by an impulse to promote Greek literary culture, but also by the grand scale that their enterprises attained. Egyptian influence regarding not only the association of divinity with the colossal and monumental but also the veneration of the written word should not be underestimated. The Egyptians first used writing for administrative purposes connected with the royal house and also to preserve important religious performances,[23] a practice that contrasts with those of ancient Greeks, who regulated cult practices by oral transmission rather than by archiving performance texts. Some sacred regulations (*leges sacrae*) were inscribed at Greek cult sites,[24] but, in general, writing played a greater role in Egyptian cult, for it was the responsibility of Egyptian priests (or at least certain classes, since not all were literate) to mark sacred spaces with hieroglyphs. These "divine words" were specifically reserved for such sites, and differed from commonly used Egyptian demotic, the script used in graffiti, narratives,[25] legal contracts, and funerary texts, and for administrative purposes at the local level even in the Ptolemaic period, when it was partially replaced by Greek.

To be sure, Egyptian deities were mostly represented as "preliterate" and thus were not so different (in this regard) from Greek gods.[26] However, as Henrichs comments:

> the representations of divinities in art and literature suggest strongly that Greek gods did not write and were not expected to write. Their apparent indifference to the art of writing sets them apart from the highly literate gods of the Hittite pantheon, and from Thoth, the divine scribe of Egyptian religion.[27]

Nevertheless, the association of writing with divinity was visually represented by sculptures of an ibis-headed Thoth, the scribe of Osiris, and Seshat, the guardian goddess of writing, which stood in Thebes at the entrance to the royal library of the thirteenth-century pharaoh Rameses II. The Egyptian view of Thoth changed over time, but he was primarily thought of as the inventor and lord of "divine words" (hieroglyphs), and associated with the knowledge of creation, the afterlife, magic, divine and human order.

Greek tradition (rightly) attributes the invention of writing to foreign lands, which helps to explain its association (from a Greek perspective) with translation and deception. Plato is said to have studied mathematics in Cyrene and astronomy in Egypt (Diog. Laer. 3.6; Strabo 17.29), and it is tempting to see his characterization of written texts as degraded transcriptions or simulations of reality as, at least in part, a response to Egyptian insistence on the truth-value of hieroglyphs. In any case Herodotus credits Cadmus, the Phoenician founder of Boeotian Thebes, with importing writing to Greece (5.58; cf. *Lind. Chron.* B15 [Higbee 2003]), while the Latin writer Hyginus writes that Mercury, the god of thieves and tradesmen, first brought it from Egypt (*Fab.* 277). Other trickster figures, like Prometheus or Palamedes, are also credited with its invention. As Vasunia observes, "Numerous Greek texts demarcate writing as an area of anxiety, in contrast to the Egyptian traditions surrounding the god Thoth that reflect the vital and cosmic power of writing within the culture."[28] Thoth is not a trickster figure, though Greeks identified him with Hermes. Herodotus regards Thoth's temple in Bubastis as a temple of Hermes (2.138); Diodorus Siculus, whose history preserves much of a fourth-century book on Egypt by the historian Hecataeus of Abdera, reports that it was Thoth who taught the Greeks about *hermeneia*, or "interpretation," meaning the verbal expression of thoughts as well as translation from one language to another (Diod. Sic.1.16).

This sketch of ancient Greek attitudes to writing demonstrates not only regional differences in attitudes to the ethos of writing, but also the potential impact of cultural cross-pollination with Egyptian authors. Egyptian demotic narratives (e.g., the Petese cycle: 70 moralizing tales about good and bad women) were produced in response to Greek writers, such as Herodotus. That literate Greeks were interested in Egyptian theology is clear from Greek epigrams inscribed on four late-second-century BCE stelae from the necropolis of Nag' El Hassaia. The author, Herodes, mentions individuals who are also referred to in Egyptian hieroglyphs on stelae from Edfu.[29] Then, too, histories of Egypt could be written in Greek, as was the fragmentary *Aegyptiaca*, a history of Egypt by an Egyptian priest, Manetho.[30] Some Egyptian authors went so far as to re-imagine the Ptolemaic dynasty as fundamentally Egyptian: *The Tale of Nectanebos' Dream* presents Alexander as the son of an Egyptian pharaoh. In effect, the Hellenic literary culture of Ptolemaic Alexandria was influenced, to some extent, not only by writers of Egyptian tales but also by the country's intellectual climate. The systematic collection of writings in temple libraries was most probably the most significant impetus for the creation of the Alexandrian Library.[31] While the desire to preserve a Hellenic heritage was no doubt integral to the collection and development of Greek literature in non-Greek lands, the literary culture of Alexandria, like that of other Hellenistic capitals, emerged from a confluence of wealth, political stability, and regional traditions in which writing had long played a more central role than it had in Greece.[32]

There are parallels that justify a similar, and possibly more surprising, reappraisal of literary culture in the Seleucid Empire. In 323 BCE Seleucus received Babylon, a rich prize that was crucial for control of the Iranian plateau, but another of Alexander's generals, Antigonus the One-Eyed, inherited a larger swath of western Asian territory. In 315 Antigonus won Babylon as well, but from the perspective of peer polity interaction, Seleucus' subsequent exile in Egypt was well spent, for there he observed Ptolemy's cultural program and cooperative interaction with the temple bureaucracy and other Egyptian institutions.[33] After Antigonus' death in 301, Seleucus came to control much of the former Persian Empire. His destruction of Antigoneia (the only Greek city in Syria at the time) and relocation of its entire population suggest the extent of his hostility to his aggressive predecessor.[34] Seleucus turned out to be much more effective at empire management than Antigonus had been, maintaining royal courts at Babylon and the older Achaemenid capitals (Ecbatana, Susa, and Sardis) while also founding new cities in central Asia and Syria.[35] Within a year Seleucus had secured Syria with four strategically located cities (all named for himself and members of his family): Antioch and Seleucia-in-Pieria to the north; the military installation Apamea-on-the-Orontes and a second port, Laodicia-on-the-Sea, to the south.[36]

In the east the newly founded Seleucia-on-the-Tigris was lost to the Ptolemies in 245. Its central location, not far from Babylon, would have made it a good choice for the principal Seleucid capital.[37] The size of the Greek population of Babylon during the Seleucid dynasty is difficult to estimate (non-Greeks sometimes adopted Greek names), as is the extent to which the city was Hellenized. But the Seleucids were evidently practical with respect to the use of local languages and political hierarchies and institutions, even elevating non-Greeks to key administrative positions.[38] Although they are often thought to have been less energetic with regard to cultivating Greek literary culture in their new capitals than the Ptolemies and Antigonids were,[39] there is some evidence for royal patronage. One of the lost works of Simonides of Magnesia (FGrHist 163) is a poem celebrating the defeat of the Gauls by Seleucus' son (and co-ruler) Antiochus 1 Soter (281–61).[40] Literary culture was also promoted in Antioch, as in Alexandria, through the installation of a library. Casson notes that the library at Antioch "was important enough to entice Euphorion, a distinguished scholar–poet (b. 272 BCE), into accepting Antiochus' offer of the post of director. Nothing else is recorded about it [the library]; apparently it never acquired much of a reputation."[41] The question is: why didn't it? Euphorion's entry in the *Suda*, a Byzantine encyclopedia, notes that he studied with the Theban lyric poet Archeboulus, and enjoyed renown both during and after his lifetime. Only two of his epigrams survive (*Anth. Pal* 6.279, 7.651), but he wrote short epics and a compendium of oracles, and was a notable figure interested, like Callimachus, in allusive narrative and esoteric myths.[42] Literary culture was if anything even more closely tied to political prestige at this time than it had been in previous centuries. Finkelberg observes:

> it would be hard to imagine circumstances under which, say, a Seleucid king might choose to educate his heir by using an edition of Homer imported from the court of his arch-enemy (six wars were waged between Ptolemaic Egypt and Seleucid Syria between 264 and 168 B.C.E.): it is much more likely that he would wish to emphasize his state's cultural self-sufficiency by adopting an edition produced by a Homeric scholar working at his own court or at that of one of his predecessors.[43]

Our current evidence for the resources of the library at Antioch is limited, but we do know that the city itself was a thriving cultural center from the very beginning. Indeed, of Seleucus' four Syrian settlements (called the "Tetrapolis") only Antioch would eventually become a cosmopolis.[44] Sources mention traditional Greek civic institutions such as an agora, gymnasium, and bouleuterion (see Cohen 2006); in the Roman era Antioch became the capital of Syria, and coins from the royal mint bore the honorific title *metropolis* (Cohen 2006). Cicero describes the city as renowned (*celebri*) and filled with learned men and scholarly pursuits (*Arch.* 3.1). It remained a vital urban center of education as a center of the early church in the fourth and fifth centuries CE, a time when much of the western empire went into decline.

There are other good reasons to imagine the literary culture (native as well as Hellenic) of the Seleucid Empire was able to flourish and to rival that of Ptolemaic Egypt. Writing originated in Mesopotamia in approximately 3200 BCE, and written works of one kind or another had flourished there for thousands of years. There is evidence to suggest a minimum ability to read and write among the merchant, elite, and royal classes, although it is true that the literacy rate of the general population, apart from professionally trained scribes, may have been very low (less than 1 percent).[45] The oral Akkadian epic *Gilgamesh* was preserved on twelve tablets housed in Ashurbanipal's royal library in Nineveh.[46] It was performed on special occasions, like the *Enuma Elish*, which celebrated the rise of the god Marduk, and was recited each April in celebration of the New Year. Like the Egyptians, the Babylonians traditionally associated writing with divinity (the goddess Nisaba). Pictograms and then cuneiform clay tablets recorded religious, literary, divinatory, and medical writings in Mesopotamian schools, palaces, and temple libraries.[47] Royal literacy, it is true, was not the norm: "The integration of the highest elite with literacy in Egypt contrasts with the more narrowly scribal use of writing in less monolithic Mesopotamia, whose rulers did not rise through a bureaucracy and were not normally literate."[48] Yet literacy was linked with certain royal figures: some Assyrian kings described themselves as scholars and maintained royal collections, such as Tiglath-Piliser I (twelfth century BCE) and especially the seventh-century BCE ruler Ashurbanipal, whose palace effectively housed the first professional reference library in the Near East.[49] Thus, during the Hellenistic period the Babylonian scribal community viewed the libraries in Antioch and Alexandria as the recipients of a Babylonian tradition.[50]

As we know, things looked different to the Greeks. Of importance is the extent to which Mesopotamian reading practices differed from those of the Greeks. Charpin observes: "there was no 'free' reading: no one is ever depicted reading for pleasure."[51] Differences in audience expectation and in the ethos, function, and style of literature may go some way toward explaining why, for example, Berossus' annalistic *Babyloniaca* failed to attract a wide readership in the Greco-Roman world. Berossus, a third-century Babylonian priest and Chaldaean astrologer, wrote a history of Babylon, one presumably intended not only to correct fifth-century representations by Herodotus and Ctesias (a Greek doctor who lived in the court of Artaxerxes), but also to introduce the guiding principles of Babylonian civilization to Antiochus I.[52] As Kuhrt comments, Berossus' history, like Manetho's history of Egypt, helped the Macedonian rulers to adapt local ideology, generating their own "distinctive political-cultural entities."[53] Yet his history contributed little to the views of the wider classical audience. King lists do not make for lively reading (again, reading pleasure was apparently not a priority) and in any case Berossus' Greek was poor. Thus Berossus' Greek audience, such as it was, largely encountered his history second-hand through other writers: the Stoic Posidonius of Apamea (135–51 BCE), or Alexander Polyhistor (b. 105 BCE).

The limited influence of the *Babyloniaca* among Hellenic readers undoubtedly owes something to its stylistic and thematic differences, but it also owes something to the fortunes of the region. By the second century BCE the Parthians had conquered Babylonia, and Babylon seems to have lost the interest of the Greco-Roman audience.[54] Babylon and Antioch are similar in this regard. The equal of the (continuously inhabited) Alexandria, Rome, and Constantinople, Antioch played an important role until the thirteenth century when the Mamluks destroyed the Christian community; the site was essentially abandoned until the Ottoman foundation of Antakya in 1800.[55] As western heirs to the Greco-Roman classical tradition, then, we are less likely to be familiar with Babylon and Antioch than Alexandria or the hilltop kingdom of Pergamon.

A resourceful Paphlagonian Greek named Philetaerus was the founder of the Pergamene dynasty. Philataerus first served as an officer of Antigonus the One-Eyed, and subsequently maintained the treasury in the fortress of Pergamon for Lysimachus, another of Alexander's Successors. Eventually Philetaerus switched allegiance to the Seleucids and gained control of the citadel. A eunuch as a result of a childhood accident (Strabo, *Geog.* 13.4.1), Philetaerus made his nephew, Attalus, his royal heir. With its cult of Athena, its monumental Altar of Zeus, and its extensive library, Pergamon rivaled the artistic and scholarly activity of its models Athens and Alexandria.[56] Like the Phrygian Philomelids or the Teucrids of Cilicia, the Attalids were dynastic "power holders" who helped stabilize the Seleucid Empire (from which they were independent by 283) before eventually aligning themselves with Rome.[57] For all its glory, our greater familiarity with Pergamon undoubtedly owes a good deal to its inclusion within the Roman Empire (Strabo 13.4.2).

The larger point to be drawn from this discussion is that although institutional libraries, both the collections of written works housed in temples and palaces and the various kinds of readers and writers associated with them, had existed in Asia and northern Africa for centuries before the Hellenistic dynasties, the prominence of literary culture in those realms has often been perceived as a marker of (newly imported) Hellenic sophistication. This is not to say that in Greece there were no public collections or state archives, like those housing the plays of Aeschylus, Sophocles, and Euripides. The sixth-century tyrant Pisistratus was said to have invited Athenians to read works in his personal library (Aulus Gellius 7.17.7), and even if this story is untrue, other individuals, gymnasia, philosophical schools curated library collections that were open to select groups of people.[58] We need to exercise caution, however, regarding what has long been (and continues to be) the dominant view held by classicists: that the *primary* impetus for the installation of public Hellenistic libraries was Greek.[59] So, for example, Demetrius of Phalerum and Strato of Lampsacus, Peripatetic advisors to Ptolemy I Soter, are commonly credited with the foundation of the Library of Alexandria.[60] The fortunes of the Alexandrian Library likewise tend to be romanticized: we hear a variety of explanations for its decline that exaggerate not only its holdings but also the impact of its destruction, whether by political upheaval, cataclysmic disaster, or simply the slow and inevitable deterioration of papyrus in a Mediterranean climate.[61] At the same time we hear little or nothing about either the rise or the fall of the Library of Antioch. Its influence seems to have been underestimated, in part because classicists have been less concerned with Seleucid settlements, which experienced a comparatively high failure rate. Our focus on Ptolemaic Alexandria as well as our gaps in knowledge regarding the literary culture of Hellenistic Antioch may be attributed to accidents of survival and the vagaries of history as well as differences in disciplinary interests.

2.   Literary Constructs

In the Hellenistic period writing played a role in the preservation of what was gradually becoming a literary (rather than oral) tradition, and not just within the ambit of patronage and royal libraries. Production and consumption were not so closely linked, spatially and temporally, as they had been in previous years. If Greek poets were leaving Greece behind, Greek poetry in turn was leaving the poets behind. With the loss of original performance contexts, familiarity with what was increasingly seen as canonical (e.g., Homer) became a more mobile sign of Hellenic identity. The movement from public composition and recitation to (relatively private) reading by no means diminished the appeal of heroic epic – despite the fact that, for the most part, popular culture in antiquity, as Harris points out, "had little to do with reading"

(1989, 126). It is true that literacy rates were never high in antiquity: according to one estimate probably less than ten percent of the male population could read well enough to appreciate literature even in communities with a comparatively high literacy rate (such as fifth-century Athens or second-century CE Rome).[62] But the Greek audience who appreciated and had access to literature most commonly read Homer, to judge from extant literary papyri down through the sixth century CE.[63] Thus the *Iliad* and the *Odyssey* formed the core of Greek *paideia* before and after the Hellenistic period,[64] and these epics continue to be more popular than any other ancient Greek poems down to the present day.

Yet when we refer to Hellenistic literature we are referring not to works that were popular at that time, but rather those that were written then and appreciated by elite and fairly specific communities of writers. Such communities would have included the better known scholar–poets associated with the Alexandrian Library as well as circles of book collectors and "readers with scholarly interests."[65] Contemporary writing included histories (e.g., Polybius) and philosophy (Posidonius); technical writing on medicine, geography (Eratosthenes); or astronomy, mathematics, and engineering (Archimedes, Euclid) as well as paradoxography, discussions of natural wonders and the marvelous.[66] What we most commonly encounter on a reading list of Hellenistic literature, however, are poems: the bucolic poetry of Theocritus, Moschus, and Bion ; epigrams by (among others) Posidippus, Asclepiades, Anyte, and Leonidas;[67] Herodas' mimes; poems by Callimachus in numerous genres (hymn, iambus, elegy, epigram, epic); Aratus' *Phaenomena*; the *Argonautica* by Apollonius of Rhodes;[68] Lycophron's *Alexandra*; with the relatively popular comedies of Menander rounding out the list.

These works all participate to varying degrees in what we refer to as "Hellenistic poetics," meaning not only that the mode of composition had shifted from oral to written, but also that despite generic differences we find commonalities in the selection and treatment of subject matter as well as form and tone. Broadly speaking, Hellenistic poetry avoids linear narrative and plays with character, perspective, and the knowledge of the writer and the reader; it imagines an informed audience, and draws attention to the narrator, his sources, and the various constraints on mortal (and even divine) knowledge. Hellenistic poets were self-conscious about their debts to performance-based genres, primarily epic and lyric and drama, but in their own writings sophistication was tied to reconfiguration rather than close emulation of traditional forms. The blending of generic registers and mixing of elements associated with different traditions is often cited as a common characteristic. The lowborn herdsmen of Theocritus' pastoral *Idylls*, for example, use Homeric dactylic hexameter to celebrate their loves and rivalries; Apollonius infuses his heroic epic with elements drawn from Attic tragedy and Ionian ethnography. Callimachus in particular is known for *polyeideia*, for writing a variety of different types of poems in contrast to earlier figures, like Hesiod, Sappho, Pindar, or Aeschylus, who specialized in one genre.

At the same time, despite or probably because of their distance from the mainland, Hellenistic poets display the same kinds of Hellenocentric biases we associate with earlier periods. As we noted above, in both modern and ancient definitions of Hellenism and Hellenic identity, a single geographical origin (along with language, customs, and kinship) determines linguistic and social affinity. Such definitions are of course complex and vary from place to place, but consider, for example, how Theocritus' character Praxinoa rebukes an Alexandrian stranger for mocking her accent (*Id.* 15.90–93):

> You don't own us! These are *Syracusans* you are ordering about – as Corinthian as Bellerophon I'll have you know. Our accent is pure Peloponnesian, and Dorians, I expect, are allowed to speak like Dorians.[69]

In this passage Praxinoa does not define herself as an Alexandrian or even as a Greek living in Egypt, but as a Syracusan, of Corinthian stock. Praxinoa's self-definition likewise extends to

Theocritus himself, whose employment of what Willi refers to as "generic Doric" throughout the *Idylls* marks him as well as his characters as a Sicilian.[70] For an ancient Greek the line between living in Egypt and actually being Egyptian was thus very clear. It is not surprising that Praxinoa would construct her identity in this way, even though – or perhaps especially because – she was living at not one but two removes from the Peloponnese.[71] Greeks living in Alexandria identified themselves not by their current address but by ancestral linguistic and kinship groups. From their point of view Alexandria was in Egypt (or perhaps beside it), but it was not precisely of it.

One of the main virtues of Alexandria's location was, as we have seen, its proximity to the Nile, but from an ancient Greek perspective Alexandria looked outward to the greater Mediterranean world. In his praise for the Pharos lighthouse, the Macedonian poet Posidippus makes no mention of Egyptians: the lighthouse, he says, was meant to be *Hellenōn sotera*, a savior of the Greeks (*Ep.* 115.1):

> As a saviour of the Greeks, this watchman of Pharos, O lord Proteus,
> Was set up by Sostratus, son of Dexiphanes, from Cnidos.
> For in Egypt there are no look-out posts on a mountain, as in the islands,
> But low lies the breakwater where ships take harbour.
> Therefore this tower, in a straight and upright line,
> Appears to cleave the sky from countless furlongs away,
> During the day, but throughout the night quickly a sailor on the waves
> Will see a great fire blazing from its summit.
> And he may even run to the Bull's horn, and not miss
> Zeus the Saviour, O Proteus, whoever sails this way.
> (tr. Austin and Bastianini 2002)

Egyptians naturally had been sailing along maritime trade routes for thousands of years, but the Greeks saw things differently, and the foundation of the new Greco-Macedonian capital changed the picture. Posidippus picks up the stereotype of Egypt as self-absorbed and inward looking and represents it as a low-lying country lacking in perspicacity and self-definition. The lighthouse, one of the wonders of the world, now connects the land with the heavens (cleaves the sky: *aithera temnein*, Pos. *Ep.* 115.5) and even produces its own astral fire. Callimachus' fragmentary lyric poem, "*The Deification of Arsinoe*" (F 228 Pf), similarly constructs the Pharos as a cosmic hub: the news of the queen's death reaches the gods as the smoke of her funeral pyres rises from the Pharos to the heavens.

Posidippus thus presents the lighthouse as a divine beacon, one intended not to guide Egyptians to their ancestral homeland, but Greeks (and gods) to the harbors of Alexandria, the rising star of a newly Greek world. What attracted many Greeks to Egypt was the splendor of the Ptolemaic kingdom, and the financial opportunities it afforded.[72] The scholar–poets associated with the Great Library were no exception. According to one resilient (although now no longer dominant) view of the period, dependence on royal patronage was detrimental to the native genius of Greek poetry, more properly strengthened by the political struggles and festival competition of the homeland. Hidden away in the recesses of the Great Library, scholar-poets were reduced to petty squabbles and displays of bookish erudition. More recently their work has been recast as an allusive, boldly experimental poetics of exile, rupture, and displacement. Apollonius Rhodius' *Argonautica* is an epic poem that mythologizes Greek contact with foreign lands, providing an origin story for the Greek presence in Asia and Africa as it narrates the voyage of the Argo from Thessaly to the Black Sea, the Adriatic, and the Libyan coast. Set in the generation before the Trojan War, the poem provides an explanatory framework for the events in Homeric epic as well as the contemporary world. Aetiological digressions; inconsistent or even flawed characterization; an intrusive, unreliable narrator; abrupt shifts and breaks in generic style and narrative tone – all of which were viewed by scholars in the recent past as weaknesses and signs of the poem's limitations – are now celebrated as intentional points of discontinuity, as breaks with generic tradition that both respond to and strengthen continuity with it.[73]

It is certainly possible to overstate the extent to which exile and displacement define Hellenistic poetry. Travel was traditionally associated with the life of the ancient singer, or *aoidos*. In the *Odyssey* Eumaeus describes poets as wanderers, as strangers brought to communities for the sake of their specialized knowledge, as skilled workers (*demiourgoi*) like seers, doctors, and shipwrights (*Od.* 17.382–7). Travel is in fact a common feature in biographical stories about later Greek poets, who performed in various festivals, courts, and cities, accompanied patrons, and even carried out diplomatic activities.[74] As itinerant clients of wealthy patrons and monarchs, poets were necessarily mobile, long before the third century and far from the ambit of northern Africa. Apollonius, a native Alexandrian, was himself rumored to have retreated to Rhodes (hence his epithet "Rhodius," "the Rhodian"). The motivation and evidence for his relocation are not secure, but the exile story persists, in part perhaps because traveling was the sort of thing that poets were expected to do, whether from financial necessity or professional obligation.

Yet why, really, would Apollonius have wanted to leave Alexandria?[75] As Gyllis, a character in one of Herodas' mimes observes (1.26–33):

All things – or, if I'm not mistaken, as many things as there are and exist – are in Egypt: fortune, wrestling-schools, power, fine weather, fame, theater, philosophers, gold, young men, a sanctuary of the Theoi Adelphoi, the worthy king, a museum, wine, all good things, as many as one could want – and women, by Persephone, like the stars in looks and number …

Gyllis says she admires Egypt, but her praise is limited to the Greek part of it. What is more, with the exception of the references to the king and the cult of the Theoi Adelphoi, Gyllis' description would fit nearly any prosperous Greek city of the day.[76] Even Ptolemaic ruler cult, a Hellenic graft onto pharaonic stock, could be transplanted from one region to another. What is missing from this catalogue of "all things Egyptian," in other words, are things that actually are Egyptian, such as, for example, mummies, or pyramids, or even the Nile.

By contrast, the history of Egypt by Hecataeus of Abdera, who visited Egypt in the time of Ptolemy I, contains a lengthy discussion of the pyramids (Diod. Sic.1.63–4).[77] Hecataeus did not know Egyptian but sought to correct Herodotus' account by using Egyptian records; his enthusiasm is exceptional for a Greek writer. Hecataeus' discussion of the pyramids, whose grandeur, as he says, would stun onlookers (1.63.3–4), contrasts with the account of Strabo, a first-century BCE Greek writer from Amaseia (a Persian city near the Black Sea that was itself Hellenized in the second century BCE). Strabo is normally grouped with Roman rather than Hellenistic authors, but his treatment of Egypt illustrates the resilience of Greek cultural chauvinism. In his discussion of the pyramids (*Geog.* 17.1.33–5), a metonym for Egypt if ever there was one, Strabo briefly notes that the tombs of kings are exceptional in size and construction. However, the bulk of his discussion suggests that he (like his audience, presumably) was more interested in how the pyramids confirm the wonders of *Greek* life and culture: a love story, a natural marvel, the Trojan War.[78] This is not to say that he had no interest in Egypt, but it does suggest more interest in the links between exotic Egypt and the realities of his own world.[79]

Scholars have accordingly considered the extent to which court poets like Posidippus, Callimachus, Theocritus, and Apollonius drew on Egyptian material. Zanker argues against the claim that the Ptolemies encouraged poets to adopt Egyptian mythology in order to reconcile Greeks to their ideological program: "Would Theocritus [or any of the Alexandrians] be attempting a symbiosis and a harmonization of Greek and Egyptian culture to prove to the Greeks of Alexandria that they need fear no threat to their national identity from Ptolemaic encouragement of Egyptian ritual?" (1989, 84). For one thing, it is unclear whether Greek names or narratives are actually referring to something that is in fact Egyptian. While we do know that Egyptian royal portraits represent Macedonian Ptolemies, it is harder to be sure that Callimachus is in fact repackaging an Egyptian myth in the absence of an explicit assertion. This raises the further complication of motivation: would a Greek audience, even an Alexandrian court audience, necessarily have been expected to appreciate parallels with Egyptian mythological material? Exactly how conversant with the themes of Egyptian pharaonic narratives were Callimachus and his audience? And what would the poet's motivation have been for suppressing explicit references to Egypt – beyond a characteristic literary playfulness?

Explicit references to a properly Egyptian Egypt are not as frequent in Hellenistic literature as one might perhaps expect. In addition to the *Argonautica*, Apollonius, who served as Head Librarian and the royal tutor to Ptolemy III Euergetes, wrote foundation narratives about a number of Greek settlements. Only one passage in the *Argonautica* mentions Egypt, and even there explicit references are downplayed and the focus is on Greek origins and nomenclature. The Colchian Argos tells the Argonauts that Eërie, "Hazy," was the ancient name for Egypt, that Triton was the ancient name for the wide-flowing river (i.e., the Nile) by which all Eërie is watered, and that "a man" (meaning the Egyptian king Sesostris) traveled from Eërie to Europe and Asia and founded many cities (*Argon.* 4.267–76). This last observation alludes to a section in the history of Herodotus, who tells us that the Colchians were descended from Egyptians (2.102–6). Although Apollonius omits this information from Argos' speech, it is likely that a learned audience is being constructed here, one that is sufficiently knowledgeable to recall this connection, and to read Egypt into the poetic figuration of Colchis.

Allusion and selectivity are hallmarks of Hellenistic poetry, yet one may reasonably wonder why Apollonius employs such subtlety with respect to Egypt in particular, not least because much of Book 4 is set in Libya. We find no coy or allusive games in references to Libya, which is mentioned explicitly more than fifteen times. As Stephens has shown, in poetic usage "Libya" figuratively comprised a large swath of African territory that included Alexandria,[80] yet one wonders whether Apollonius is consciously avoiding references to Egypt in order to distance it, figuratively, from the Ptolemaic state. After all, he represents Libya as a harsh land that tests the Greek heroes and nearly destroys them. We hear about the dangers of the Libyan Syrtis Gulf, where the Argo is stranded and two Argonauts die: Canthus, who is killed by Caphaurus, a descendant of Apollo, and Mopsus, bitten by a venomous snake, a descendant of the snakes spawned by drops of blood from Medusa's head. The other Argonauts owe their survival to the intervention of demigods and largely local divinities: the Libyan nymphs, the Hesperides, Poseidon's son Triton, and Zeus' son Heracles (himself an erstwhile Argonaut). Indeed, the only god explicitly angered by the Argonauts during their voyage is Zeus, whose sanction against kin murder is broken by Jason and Medea when they ambush her half-brother. The poem thus attributes the Greek presence in North Africa not to the imperial ambitions of Greeks or Macedonians, but to the vagaries of sea travel and the mandates of fate. Apollonius' Hellenizing inclinations are also apparent here: on the one hand native Libyan gods welcome and aid Greek heroes; on the other, Zeus is angered by the murder of a non-Greek prince (although Apsyrtus does have some standing as the grandson of the god Helius). Apollonius represents the Argonauts, the mythical antecedents of his own (Greco-Macedonian, Alexandrian, royal) audience, as though they have no desire to rule other lands, and he goes so far as to map conquest and imperial pride onto the Egyptian Sesostris and the Colchian king Aietes. His Jason swiftly rejects Hypsipyle's offer of kingship in Lemnos, and his Heracles, who claims that he seeks glory, abruptly drops the quest to search for Hylas. The poem suggests that although Greeks originally had no desire to rule in Africa in general or Egypt in particular, the whole of Libyan territory was already pre-colonized for them by Greek gods and monsters, in the age before the disinterested heroes set in motion Cyrene's foundation.[81]

The aetiological focus of Hellenistic poetry on the origins of Greek cults and practices is well known. Callimachus, born in Cyrene, apparently spent most of his life in North Africa, but his poetry, like that of his contemporary Apollonius, addresses the lives and concerns of the Greeks who lived there. Callimachus commemorates his family, notable citizens of Cyrene, other communal ties, and the kings and queens of a dynasty only two generations old. Like Apollonius he tends not to name Egyptian gods, although he does mention Isis in two epigrams (*Ep.* 57 and 49 Pf). Epigram 49 describes the narrator as scorched in love like the lamps of Isis (l. 4), referring to the Egyptian festival of Isis the Bright, Aset Webenut, called the Lychnapsia in the Greco-Roman period. Lamps and torches were lighted during the night festival, which also involved processions in which the barque of Isis was carried in a larger boat (cf. Hdt. 2.62; Witt 1971, 122). Yet it is telling that Epigram 57 refers not to the temple of Isis, but to the temple of *Inachean* Isis. Isis the daughter of Inachos, forefather of the Argives, literally outshines Isis the sister-wife of Osiris in the midst of an Egyptian festival.[82] The figure is the same, but the patronymic "Inachean," much like Apollonius' use of the name Eërie for Egypt, appropriates it by defining it in Greek terms. Subtext, allusion, and inference are integral to the construction of meaning in Hellenistic poetry, but what Callimachus and Apollonius *do* say explicitly is as expressive as what they do not. Callimachus' pupil, Istrus, also from Cyrene, was interested in Egyptian antiquities "almost uniquely among"[83] the Alexandrians, writing works on Egyptian colonies with Greek mythological origins as well as Greek colonies with Egyptian origins.

The passages we have considered so far show how Egypt and Libya serve as poetic constructs that demonstrate the dynamics of Greek cultural exchange. These poets have less to say about Libya and Egypt and more about Greeks in Libya or the original Greek names for Egyptian gods and landscape features. Their Hellenocentrism and the subtlety of their references come into focus when we think of more explicit acknowledgements of Egyptian society and culture, such as Herodes' epigrams on the stelae from Edfu (noted above), or the prominence of Egyptian sculpture and architecture in Alexandria, particularly in the royal quarter of the city. Images of Egypt were everywhere. The Ptolemies legitimated their rule by adopting Egyptian style and appropriating Egyptian statues and emphasizing the continuity of their rule with that of previous dynasties. This kind of appropriation was in keeping with Egyptian tradition, and they were not the first pharaohs to recycle material from earlier eras.[84] Tradition and ties to the past, in other words, were crucial to the legitimation of the royal house, whether Macedonian or Egyptian.

Questions concerning legitimation and the role of alterity in the formation of cultural identity have been the focus of studies on the Hellenocentric perspective of those Greek intellectuals – poets, historians, and philosophers – who have read Egypt as a kind of primitive society yielding insights into the development of a more sophisticated Greek culture. The tensions between homage to Egypt and an Egyptian mirage, or between the preservation of things Egyptian and their appropriation, or between the assimilation and implicit domination of things Egyptian are never far from a consideration of the nuanced cultural interactions that have been and continue to be intensified, if that is possible, when we consider Ptolemaic Alexandria. As Vasunia has shown, earlier representations of Egypt in works by Aeschylus, Euripides, Herodotus, Plato, and Isocrates constructed it as an other, and its otherness served in turn as a foil for the definition of Greek identity. Yet as we have seen, an interest in Egypt per se, whether it is figured as same or other, seems less pronounced for Greek poets who were born in North Africa but seem, like Theocritus' character Praxinoa, principally concerned with things Greek.

These concerns have generated much work on Egyptian subtexts in recent years. Reed 2000, for example, traces the intrusion of Egyptian ritual codes into the royal celebration of Adonis that is described in Theocritus *Idyll* 15. Some have seen links between the prophecies of Cassandra in Lycophron's *Alexandra* and eastern apocalyptic literature, such as the

Book of Daniel in the Hebrew Bible or the Egyptian "Oracle of the Potter."[85] In "Alibis," an extensive study of the tropes of displacement and dislocation in Callimachus, Selden (1998, 386) sees the duality of the Ptolemaic monarchy reflected in what he sees as Callimachus' equivocations, arguing that in the *Coma Berenices*, "it is Egyptian political ideology and religion that ultimately explain what has transpired as Hellenic history" (1998, 329). Stephens (2003, 9) suggests that for the Alexandrian poets Egypt was losing its otherness: cults like the Apis bull were "incorporated into the allusive matrix of what has become an extended Greco-Egyptian mythological family". On the other hand, Greek stories might well resonate differently in Egypt than they would have on the mainland. In Berenice's vow to dedicate a lock of hair upon the victorious return of her husband Ptolemy III, for example, an Attic audience might hear echoes of Achilles' broken vow to dedicate a lock of hair to the river Spercheios upon his safe return (*Il.* 24.143–51), but an Alexandrian court audience, one that was attuned to the co-presence of Egyptian themes, might also hear the mourning of an Isis who cuts her hair to honor the dead Osiris.[86] On Stephens' view, "The habit of syncretism and allusion to an Egypt already embedded in Greek texts are two means by which poets create a discursive field that can serve to accommodate two different cultural logics. Within this framework a poem that nowhere explicitly names Egypt or an Egyptian idea nonetheless frequently presents a set of incidents that are entirely legible within the framework of Egyptian myth" (2003, 9). From this perspective Egyptian cultural elements are not simply disguised by Greek names but essentially interchangeable with them, privileging neither one side nor the other.

But whether or not we see the resonance of Egyptian and Near Eastern elements, however explicit or embedded they may be, as essential to our understanding of the original significance of Alexandrian poetry for Greek-speaking audiences, it is crucial that we acknowledge the roles played by non-Greek cultures in shaping the institutions that constitute what we think of as the Hellenistic world. Hellenistic literature is not always as Hellenic as we assume, nor is Alexandria, for all its brilliance, unique as we might think. The reputation of Hellenistic literature and also our sense of the prestige of Alexandria have been (and continue to be) shaped by our understanding of a multiplicity of factors. These factors include not only poetic innovation, reception, manuscript tradition, and accidents of survival, but also the reconfiguration of Hellenic identity, the influence of local traditions and political structures, and the competition and peer polity interactions (of various kinds and at various levels) both within and between the Successor states.

NOTES

[1] See Willi, ch. 29, pp. 458 in this volume.

[2] See, e.g., West 2007.

[3] See Dueck, ch. 25, pp. 392 in this volume.

[4] See Hall 2002, 154–6 (with bibliography); Hornblower 2008, 55–8; Worthington 2008, 216–19 on identity and Macedonian as a Greek dialect. In Alexandria Macedonians may have been limited to members of the royal guard; Scheidel 2004, 25, citing Fraser 1972, 1.52–4. Alexander's campaigns greatly reduced the number of Macedonians available for colonizing; see Grainger 1990, 45.

[5] Sext. Emp. *Math.* 1.176: Sextus is here distinguishing a standard based on common idiomatic practice rather than the (improper) use of grammatical analogy (e.g. declensions, based on what ought to follow from the nominative singular).

[6] Clarysse and Thompson 2006, 2.323–8. Manning 2010, 31, observes that the use of ethnic designations in tax collection was a matter of convenience rather than racist policy.

[7] Goudrian 1988, 118–19.

[8] Clarysse and Thompson 2006, 2.142–3.

⁹See Birnbaum 2004, 131–8; Goldstein 2010, 206 with n. 42.

¹⁰See Schwartz 2010.

¹¹On the *Letter of Aristeas*, which claims that Ptolemy Philadelphus arranged for the inclusion of Greek translations of Jewish laws and sacred writings in the Alexandrian library, see Hunter 2011.

¹²Momigliano 1971, 100.

¹³There is, however, no evidence to support the common view that as early as the fourth and third centuries BCE city gymnasia regularly featured libraries: Scholz 2004, 126–7.

¹⁴Davies 2002, 9. See further Ma 2003.

¹⁵See on Alexandria also Hose, ch. 21, 331 in this volume.

¹⁶Mairs 2008, 27–9; Holt 2005, 154–60.

¹⁷Manning 2010, 107–13.

¹⁸The library declined as a center of learning after the reign of Ptolemy VIII (Euergetes II), who banished scholars for favoring his brother Ptolemy VI Philometor. For a clear-eyed assessment of the evidence for the history of the library; see Bagnall 2002.

¹⁹See Cavero 2008.

²⁰On Pergamon see Hose, ch. 21, p. 334 in this volume.

²¹Diog. Laer. 2.115; 5.37; 7.185.

²²The fate of the iambic poet Sotades of Maronea, who condemned the marriage of Ptolemy II to his sister, Arsinoe, is often cited, though see now Carney 2012, 73–74. Other examples include Alexander's execution of the court historian Callisthenes of Olynthus in 327 for conspiracy (see "Callisthenes [1]," Heckel 2006); Antigonus Gonatas' execution of the Atthidographer Philochorus for participating in the Chremonidean war (Philochorus, FGrHist 328 T 1).

²³See Baines 2007, 42.

²⁴Henrichs 2003, 54–7. On *leges sacrae* see, e.g., Petrovic and Petrovic 2006.

²⁵On Egyptian demotic literature, see Dieleman and Moyer 2010; Tait 2013.

²⁶Baines 2007, 88 and 43 n.19.

²⁷Henrichs 2003, 39–40.

²⁸Vasunia 2001, 148–9.

²⁹Yoyotte 1969.

³⁰Dieleman and Moyer 2010; Manning 2013; Dillery 1999.

³¹Ryholt 2013.

³²See Shipley 2000, 242–3; "[…] it may be that what we see as a distinctively Greek creation was a fusion of the philosophical culture of fourth-century Athens with an older way of assembling and controlling the written word" (243).

³³On the construction of the Ptolemaic state, see Manning 2010.

³⁴Cohen 2006, 76–9; Capdetrey 2007, 68–9.

³⁵Seleucid foundations were economically motivated and intended to open up undeveloped land and to create focal points for tax revenues through silver-based exchange. Apherghis 2005, 40.

³⁶Grainger 1990, 47–61; Capdetrey 2007, 67.

³⁷Regarding the date of Seleucia's foundation and its ideological function, see Capdetrey 2007, 52–9.

³⁸On Babylon under the Seleucids, see Sherwin-White 1987.

³⁹Gutzwiller 2007, 9, who points out that we have no evidence for direct Seleucid connection with three Hellenistic authors from Syrian Gadara: the satirist Menippus, the epigrammatist Meleager, and the philosopher Philodemus.

⁴⁰"Simonides." *Suda* Σ 443. See *Suda* On Line. Tr. R. Dyer. 10 June 2000. http://www.stoa. org/sol-entries/sigma/443 (accessed March 29, 2015).

[41] Casson 2001, 48; Fraser 1972, 1.555; Pfeiffer 1968, 122.

[42] "Euphorion." *Suda* E 3801 See *Suda* On Line. Tr. W. Hutton. 10 February 2008. http://www.stoa.org/sol-entries/epsilon/3801 (accessed March 29, 2015). For testimonies and fragments of Euphorion's epic poetry see Page 1941, 488–99 ("Euphorion"); Lightfoot 2009, 189–465.

[43] Finkelberg 2006, 239.

[44] Grainger 1990, 125; on the high failure rate of Seleucid foundations, see p. 81. On Seleucus' possible preference for the Syrian Seleucia as his principal capital (over Antioch), see Cohen 2006, 128–30 n. 3.

[45] Verbrugghe and Wickersham 1996, 19.

[46] Verbrugghe and Wickersham 1996, 20.

[47] Maul 2005, 503–4.

[48] Baines 2007, 83 (citing John A. Brinkman, personal communication).

[49] Casson 2001, 9–15; Charpin 2010, 53–67.

[50] Goldstein 2010; Beaulieu 2006.

[51] Charpin 2010, 67. On reading practices in Greek, see e.g. Ford 2003.

[52] Burstein 1978, 6–7; Kuhrt 1987, 53–6; Haubold et al. 2013.

[53] Kuhrt 1987, 32–56, at 56.

[54] Verbrugghe and Wickersham 32–3.

[55] Grainger 1990, 70–74.

[56] See Gruen 2000.

[57] On relations between the Attalids and the Seleucids, see Chrubasik 2013.

[58] The notion of "public" in this case means an institutional library, somewhere between a private royal library, such as that of Antigonus Gonatas in Pella, and a modern lending library.

[59] E.g., Walbank 1984, 73: "The context [of the libraries at Alexandria, Pella, and Pergamon] was of course entirely Greek, for nothing of this had relevance to the indigenous populations with made up the greater part of the Ptolemaic and Seleucid kingdoms." Parsons 2012, 830 credits Peripatetic influence rather than "the temple and palace libraries of the near east."

[60] Gutzwiller 2007, 19–20.

[61] Bagnall 2002, 358–9.

[62] Harris 1989, 61, 173; see also Hopkins 1991.

[63] See Morgan 2003; Cribiore 1996.

[64] Euripides and Menander were studied (Cribbiore 1996, 46), as were Callimachus' epigrams (Gutzwiller 1998, 183).

[65] Johnson 2010,185.

[66] See Gutzwiller 2007, 131–67.

[67] On epigrams see Höschele, ch. 12, in this volume.

[68] On Apollonius see Roisman, ch. 9, pp. 146–8 in this volume.

[69] *Pace* Praxinoa, Syracusan demographics may in fact have also included Arcadian as well as Corinthian origins; Hornblower 2008, 45–6.

[70] Willi 2012, 284.

[71] See Hornblower 2012.

[72] Both the population and the number of public buildings grew most rapidly during the first century of its existence. Greeks were in the minority in Alexandria: estimates typically suggest less than 10 percent of the population; see now Fischer-Bovet 2011 who estimates only 5 percent. On the layout of the city, see McKenzie 2007.

[73] See Fantuzzi and Hunter 2004, Gutzwiller 2007.

[74] Hunter and Rutherford 2009, 17–18.

[75] That is, if we discount, as most do, the story of the failure of an early version of the epic or his allegedly bitter rivalry with Callimachus. On the quarrel see now Klooster 2011, 121–7.

[76] In terms of scale the Museum was exceptional, but many Greek cities had *museia*: shrines, festivals, and/or schools that honored or were associated with music, poetry, and the arts of the Muses (Fraser 1972, 1.312–14).

[77] On Hecataeus' *Aegyptiaca* see Burstein 1992.

[78] A pharaoh, unnamed by Strabo, honors his wife, Doricha (Rhodopis, Hdt. 2.134–5), by burying her in a tomb; pebbles near the pyramids must be petrified lentils like those found on a plain in Herodotus' home; the nearby Trojan Mountain was named for those left by Menelaus. On Strabo's defense of Homeric geography, in contrast to the criticism of Hellenistic scholars (especially Eratosthenes of Cyrene), see Kim 2010, 47–84.

[79] Vasunia 2001, 20: "The critical reader is compelled to confront the deliberate role of Greeks in defining their object, and to insist that the occultation of this object was carried out in favor of the writers' own interests."

[80] Stephens 2011,190 and 197.

[81] 4.1731–64; cf. 2.500–10 the story of Apollo's relocation of the eponymous nymph Cyrene to Libya.

[82] Another early example of the association between lamps, Hellenization, and Egyptian cult involves the erection of a *lychnaption*, a small classical building (with four Corinthian columns) to house lamplighters, in the temple dromos of the Memphian Sarapeion in Saqqara (Thompson 1988, 28, 212; for the location see the map on p. 23).

[83] Fraser 1972, 1.512, 777–8; 2.737 n. 140.

[84] Der Manuelian 1994, 1: "Over the several millennia of Egyptian history, as ages of unity and prosperity fluctuated with times of instability and decline, archaism was often utilized to reinforce the claims of legitimacy for the aspiring ruler, dynastic house, or even deceased individual desirous of a prosperous afterlife."

[85] West 2000.

[86] Gutzwiller 2007, 192; Nisetich 2001, 287–8.

REFERENCES

Ager, S. and R. Faber, eds. 2013. *Belonging and Isolation in the Hellenistic World*. Phoenix Supplementary Volumes, Vol. 51. Toronto.

Aperghis, G. G. 2005. "City Building and the Seleukid Royal Economy." In Z. H. Archibald, J. K. Davies, and V. Gabrielsen, eds., *Making, Moving, and Managing: The New World of Ancient Economies 323–31 BC*, Oxford, 27–43.

Austin C. and G. Bastianini, eds. 2002. *Posidippi Pellaei quae supersunt omnia*. Milan.

Bagnall, R. 2002. "Alexandria: Library of Dreams," *Proceedings of the American Philosophical Society*, 146: 348–62.

Baines, J. 2007. *Visual and Written Culture in Ancient Egypt*. Oxford.

Beaulieu, P. A. 2006. "De l'Esagil au Mouseion: L'organisation de la recherché scientifique au 4e siècle av. J.-C." In P. Briant and F. Joannès, eds., *La transition entre l'empire achéménide et les royaumes hellénistiques. Persika* 9. Paris. 17–36.

Bilde, P. et al., eds. 1992. *Ethnicity in Hellenistic Egypt*. Aarhus.

Bingen, J. 2007. *Hellenistic Egypt. Monarchy, Society, Economy, Culture*. Berkeley, CA.

Birnbaum, E. 2004. "Portrayals of the Wise and Virtuous in Alexandrian Jewish Works: Jews' Perceptions of Themselves and Others." In W. V. Harris and G. Ruffini, eds., *Ancient Alexandria between Egypt and Greece*, Leiden, 125–60.

Burstein, S., ed. 1978. *The Babyloniaka of Berossus*. 2nd edn. Malibu, CA.

Burstein, S. 1992. "Hecataeus of Abdera's History of Egypt." In J. H. Johnson, ed., *Life in a Multicultural Society: Egypt from Cambyses to Constantine and Beyond*, Chicago, 45–9.

Burstein, S. 2008. "Greek Identity in the Hellenistic Period." In K. Zacharia, ed., *Hellenisms: Culture, Identity, and Ethnicity from Antiquity to Modernity*. Aldershot, 59–77.

Capdetrey, L. 2007. *Le pouvoir Séleucide. Territoire, administration, finance d' un royaume hellénistique* (312–129 avant J.-C.). Rennes.

Carney, E. D. 2013. *Arsinoe of Egypt and Macedon: A Royal Life.* Oxford.

Casson, L. 2001. *Libraries in the Ancient World.* New Haven, CT.

Cavero, L. M. 2008. *Poems in Context: Greek Poetry in the Egyptian Thebiad 200–600 AD.* Berlin.

Charpin, D. 2010, J. M. Todd (tr.) *Reading and Writing in Babylon.* Cambridge, MA.

Chrubasik, B. 2013. "The Attalids and the Seleucid Kings, 281–175 BCE." In P. Thonemann, ed. *Attalid Asia Minor: Money, International Relations, and the State.* Oxford, 83–120.

Clarysse, W. and D. J. Thompson. 2006. *Counting the People in Hellenistic Egypt.* 2 vols. Cambridge.

Cohen, G. 2006. *The Hellenistic Settlements in Syria, the Red Sea Basin, and North Africa.* Berkeley, CA.

Cribb, J. and G. Herrmann, eds. 2007. *After Alexander: Central Asia Before Islam.* Oxford.

Cribiore, R. 1996. *Writing, Students, and Teachers in Graeco-Roman Egypt.* Atlanta, GA.

Davies, J. K. 2002. "The Interpenetration of Hellenistic Sovereignties." In D. Ogden, ed., *The Hellenistic World.* New Perspectives. London, 1–21.

De Breucker, G. 2003. "Berossos and the Mesopotamian Temple as Centre of Knowledge during the Hellenistic Period." In A. A. MacDonald, M. W. Twomey, and G. R. Reinink, eds., *Learned Antiquity. Scholarship and Society in the Near-east the Greco-Roman World, and the Early Medieval West.* Groningen Studies in Cultural Change. Vol. 5. Leuven. 13–23.

Delgado, J. A. Fernández, F. Pordomingo, and A. Stramaglia, eds. 2007. *Escuela y literatura en Grecia Antigua.* Cassino.

Depew, M. and D. Obbink, eds. 2000. *Matrices of Genre. Authors, Canons, and Society.* Cambridge, MA.

Derks, T. and N. Roymans, eds. 2009. *Ethnic Constructs in Antiquity. The Role of Power and Tradition.* Amsterdam.

Der Manuelian, P. 1994. *Living in the Past: Studies in Archaism of the Egyptian Twenty-sixth Dynasty.* New York.

Dieleman, J. and I. S. Moyer. 2010. "Egyptian Literature." In J. J. Clauss and M. Cuypers, eds., *A Companion to Hellenistic Literature.* Oxford, 428–47.

Dillery, J. 1999. "The First Egyptian Narrative History. Manetho and Greek Historiography." *Zeitschrift für Papyrologie und Epigraphik* 127: 93–116.

Fantuzzi, M. and R. Hunter. 2004. *Tradition and Innovation in Hellenistic Poetry.* Cambridge.

Finkelberg, M. 2006. "Regional Texts and the Circulation of Books: The Case of Homer." *Greek, Roman and Byzantine Studies* 46: 231–48.

Fischer-Bovet, C. 2011. "Counting the Greeks in Egypt: Immigration in the First Century of Ptolemaic Rule." In C. Holleran and A. Pudsey, eds., *Demography and the Greco-Roman World. New Insights and Approaches,* Cambridge, 135–54.

Ford, A. 2003. "From Letters to Literature. Reading the 'Song Culture' of Classical Greece." In H. Yunis, ed., *Written Texts and the Rise of Literate Culture in Ancient Greece,* Cambridge, 15–37.

Fraser, P. M. 1972. *Ptolemaic Alexandria.* 3 vols. Oxford.

Gascou, J. 2009. "The Papyrology of the Near East." In R. Bagnall, ed., *The Oxford Handbook of Papyrology.* Oxford, 473–94.

Goldstein, R. 2010. "Late Babylonian Letters on Collecting Tablets and their Hellenistic Background – a Suggestion." *Journal of Near Eastern Studies* 69: 199–207.

Goudriaan, K. 1988. *Ethnicity in Ptolemaic Egypt.* Amsterdam.

Grainger, J. D. 1990. *The Cities of Seleucid Syria.* Oxford.

Gruen, E. S. 2000. "Culture as Policy. The Attalids of Pergamon." In N. T. Grummond and B. S. Ridgway, eds., *From Pergamon to Sperlonga: Sculpture and Context.* Berkeley, CA, 17–31.

Gutzwiller, K. 1998. *Poetic Garlands. Hellenistic Epigrams in Context.* Berkeley, CA.

Gutzwiller, K. 2007. *A Guide to Hellenistic Literature.* Oxford.

Hall, J. M. 2002. *Hellenicity. Between Ethnicity and Culture.* Chicago.

Handis, M. W. 2013. "Myth and History: Galen and the Alexandrian Library." In J. König, K. Oikonomopoulou, and G. Woolf, eds., *Ancient Libraries.* Cambridge, 364–76.

Harder, M. A. 2013. "From Text to Text: The Impact of the Alexandrian Library on the Work of Hellenistic Poets." In J. König, K. Oikonomopoulou, and G. Woolf, eds., *Ancient Libraries.* Cambridge, 96–108.

Harris, W. V. 1989. *Ancient Literacy*. Cambridge, MA.

Harris, W. V. and G. Ruffini, eds. 2004. *Ancient Alexandria between Egypt and Greece*. Leiden.

Haubold, J., G. B. Lanfranchi, R. Rollinger, and J. Steele, eds., 2013. *The World of Berossos*. Wiesbaden.

Heckel, W. 2006. *Who's Who in the Age of Alexander the Great*. Oxford.

Henrichs, A. 2003. "Writing Religion: Inscribed Texts, Ritual Authority, and the Religious Discourse of the Polis." In H. Yunis, ed., *Written Texts and the Rise of Literate Culture in Ancient Greece*, Cambridge, 38–58.

Higbee, C. 2003. *The Lindian Chronicle and the Greek Creation of their Past*. Oxford.

Hoelbl, G. 2001. *A History of the Ptolemaic Empire*. London.

Holt, F. 2005. *Into the Land of Bones: Alexander the Great in Afghanistan*. Berkeley, CA.

Hopkins, K. 1991. "Conquest by Book." In J. H. Humphrey, ed., *Literacy in the Roman World*. Ann Arbor, MI, 133–58.

Hornblower, S. 2008. "Greek Identity in the Archaic and Classical Periods." In K. Zacharia, ed., *Hellenisms. Culture, Identity, and Ethnicity from Antiquity to Modernity*. Aldershot, 37–58.

Hornblower, S. 2012. "Hellenism, Hellenization." In S. Hornblower, A. Spawforth, and E. Eidinow, eds., *The Oxford Classical Dictionary*. Oxford, 656–7.

Hunter, R. 2003. *Theocritus. Encomium of Ptolemy Philadelphus*. Berkeley, CA.

Hunter, R. 2011. "The Letter of Aristeas." In A. Erskine and L. Llewellyn-Jones, eds., *Creating a Hellenistic World*. Swansea, 47–60.

Hunter, R. and I. Rutherford, eds. 2009. *Wandering Poets in Ancient Greek Culture. Travel, Locality, and Pan-Hellenism*. Cambridge.

Jacob, C. 2013. "Fragments of a History of Ancient Libraries." In J. König, K. Oikonomopoulou, and G. Woolf, eds., *Ancient Libraries*. Cambridge, 57–84.

Johnson, W. A. 2010. *Readers and Reading Culture in the High Roman Empire*. Oxford.

Johnson, W. A. 2009 and H. N. Parker, eds. 2009. *Ancient Literacies. The Culture of Reading in Greece and Rome*. Oxford.

Kah, D. and P. Scholz, eds. 2004. *Das hellenistiche Gymnasion*. Berlin.

Kim, L. 2010. *Homer Between History and Fiction in Imperial Greek Literature*. Cambridge.

Klooster, J. 2011. *Poetry as Window and Mirror. Positioning the Poet in Hellenistic Poetry*. Mnemosyne Supplements 330. Leiden.

König, J., K. Oikonomopoulou and G. Woolf, eds. 2013. *Ancient Libraries*. Cambridge.

Kuhrt, A. 1987. "Berossus Babyloniaka and Seleucid Rule in Babylonia." In A. Kuhrt and S. Sherwin-White, 32–56.

Kuhrt, A. and S. Sherwin-White, eds. 1987. *Hellenism in the East*. Berkeley, CA.

Lecuyot, G. 2007. "Ai Khanum Reconstructed." In J. Cribb and G. Herrmann, eds., *After Alexander: Central Asia Before Islam*. Oxford, 155–62.

Leriche, P. 2007. "Bactria, Land of a Thousand Cities." In J. Cribb and G. Herrmann, eds., *After Alexander: Central Asia Before Islam*. Oxford, 121–54.

Lightfoot, J., ed. 2009. *Hellenistic Collection. Philitas. Alexander of Aetolia. Hermesianax. Euphorion. Parthenius*. Cambridge, MA.

Ma, J. 2003. "Peer Polity Interaction in the Hellenistic Age." *Past and Present* 180: 9–39.

Mairs, R. 2008. "Greek Identity and the Settler Community in Hellenistic Bactria and Arachosia." *Migrations and Identities* 1: 19–43.

Manning, J. G. 2010. *The Last Pharaohs: Egypt under the Ptolemies, 305 – 30 BC*. Princeton, NJ.

Manning, J. G. 2013. "Review of K. Ryholt, 2006. *The Petese Stories II*. Copenhagen." *Bibliotheca Orientalis* 70: 57–60.

Maul, S. 2005. "II. Libraries (2) Mesopotamia." In H. Cancik and H. Schneider, eds., *Brill's New Jacoby*. Leiden. 503–4.

McKenzie, J. 2007. *The Architecture of Alexandria and Egypt*. New Haven, CT.

Momigliano, A. 1971. *Alien Wisdom. The Limits of Hellenization*. Cambridge.

Morgan, T. 2003. "Literary Culture in Sixth-Century Egypt." In A. A. Macdonald, M. W. Twomey, and G. J. Reinink, eds., 2003. *Learned Antiquity. Scholarship and Society in the Near-East, the Greco-Roman World, and the Early Medieval West*. Groningen Studies in Cultural Change. Vol. 5. Leuven, 147–61.

Mori, A. 2008. *The Politics of Apollonius Rhodius' Argonautica*. Cambridge.

Moyer, I. 2011. *Egypt and the Limits of Hellenism.* Cambridge.

Nisetich, F. (tr.) 2001. *The Poems of Callimachus.* Oxford.

Page, D. L., ed. 1941. *Select Papyri. Poetry.* Cambridge, MA.

Papaconstantinou, A. ed., 2010. *The Multilingual Experience in Egypt, from the Ptolemies to the Abbasids.* Aldershot.

Parsons, P. J. 2012. "Libraries." In S. Hornblower, A. Spawforth, and E. Eidinow, eds., *The Oxford Classical Dictionary.* Oxford, 830–31.

Petrovic I. and A. Petrovic. 2006. "'Look who is talking now!': Speaker and Communication in Greek Metrical Sacred Regulations." In E. Stavrianopoulou, ed., *Ritual and Communication in the Graeco-Roman World. Kernos* Supplement 16, Liege, 151–80.

Pfeiffer, R. 1968. *History of Classical Scholarship from the Beginning to the End of the Hellenistic Age.* Oxford.

Reed, J. D. 2000. "Arsinoe's Adonis and the Poetics of Ptolemaic Imperialism." *Transactions of the American Philological Association* 130: 319–51.

Robson, E. 2013. "Reading the Libraries of Assyria and Babylonia." In J. König, K. Oikonomopoulou, and G. Woolf, eds., *Ancient Libraries.* Cambridge, 38–56.

Ryholt, K. 2013. "Libraries in Ancient Egypt." In J. König, K. Oikonomopoulou, and G. Woolf, eds., *Ancient Libraries.* Cambridge, 23–37.

Scheidel, W. 2004. "Creating a Metropolis: A Comparative Demographic Perspective." In W. V. Harris and G. Ruffini, eds., *Ancient Alexandria between Egypt and Greece.* Leiden, 1–32.

Scholz, P. 2004. "Elementarunterricht und intellektuelle Bildung im hellenistischen Gymnasion." In D. Kah and P. Scholz, eds., *Das hellenistiche Gymnasion.* Berlin, 103–28.

Schwartz, S. 2010. *Were the Jews a Mediterranean Society? Reciprocity and Solidarity in Ancient Judaism.* Princeton, NJ.

Selden, D. 1998. "Alibis." *Classical Antiquity* 17.2: 289–420.

Sherwin-White, S. 1987. Berossus' *Babyloniaka* and Seleucid Rule in Babylonia." In A. Kuhrt and S. Sherwin-White, eds., *Hellenism in the East.* Berkeley, CA, 32–56.

Shipley, G. 2000. *The Greek World After Alexander 323–30 BC.* London.

Spek, R. J. van der. 1987. "The Babylonian City." In A. Kuhrt and S. Sherwin-White, eds., *Hellenism in the East.* Berkeley, CA, 57–74.

Spek, R. J. van der. 2009. "Multi-ethnicity and ethnic segregation in Hellenistic Babylon." In T. Derks and N. Roymans, eds., *Ethnic Constructs in Antiquity. The Role of Power and Tradition.* Amsterdam, 101–15.

Stephens, S. A. 2003. *Seeing Double: Intercultural Poetics in Ptolemaic Alexandria.* Berkeley, CA.

Stephens, S. A. 2011. "Remapping the Mediterranean: The Argo Adventure in Apollonius and Callimachus." In D. Obbink and R. Rutherford, eds., *Culture in Pieces. Essays on Ancient Texts in Honour of Peter Parsons.* Oxford, 188–207.

Tait, J. 2013. "The Reception of Demotic Narrative." In R. Enmarch and V. M. Lepper, eds., *Ancient Egyptian Literature. Theory and Practice.* Proceedings of the British Academy 188, Oxford, 251–60.

Thompson, D. J. 1989 *Memphis Under the Ptolemies.* Princeton, NJ.

Thompson, D. J. 1992. "Language and Literacy in Early Hellenistic Egypt." In P. Bilde et al., eds., *Ethnicity in Hellenistic Egypt.* Aarhus, 39–52.

Thompson, D. J. 2007. "Education and Culture in Hellenistic Egypt and beyond." In J. A. Fernández Delgado, F. Pordomingo, and A. Stramaglia, eds., *Escuela y literatura en Grecia Antigua.* Cassino, 121–40.

Too, Y. L. 2010. *The Idea of the Library in the Ancient World.* Oxford.

Tovar, S. T. 2010. "Linguistic Identity in Graeco-Roman Egypt." In A. Papaconstantinou, ed., *The Multilingual Experience in Egypt, from the Ptolemies to the Abbasids.* Aldershot, 17–43.

Vasunia, P. 2001. *The Gift of the Nile. Hellenizing Egypt from Aeschylus to Alexander.* Berkeley, CA.

Verbrugge, G. P. and J. M. Wickersham. 1996. *Berossos and Manetho, Introduced and Translated.* Ann Arbor, MI.

Walbank, F. W. 1984, "Monarchies and Monarchic Ideas." In *The Cambridge Ancient History.* Vol. VII.1. Cambridge, 62–100.

West, M. L. 2007. *Indo-European Poetry and Myth.* Oxford.

West, S. 2000. "Lycophron's Alexandra: 'Hindsight as Foresight Makes No Sense?'" In M. Depew and D. Obbink, eds., *Matrices of Genre. Authors, Canons, and Society*. Cambridge, MA, 153–66.

Willi, A. 2012. "'We Speak Peloponnesian: Tradition and Linguistic Identity in Post-Classical Sicilian Literature." In O. Tribulato, ed., *Language and Linguistic Contact in Ancient Sicily*. Cambridge, 265–88.

Witt, R. G. 1971. *Isis in the Greco-Roman World*. Ithaca, NY.

Worthington, I. 2008. *Philip II of Macedonia*. New Haven, CT.

Yoyotte, J. 1969. "Bakthis: religion égyptienne et culture grecque à Edfou." In P. Derchain, ed., *Religions en Égypte hellénistique et romaine*. Paris, 127–41.

Yunis, H., ed. 2003. *Written Texts and the Rise of Literate Culture in Ancient Greece*. Cambridge.

Zadorojnyi, A. V. 2013. "Libraries and *Paideia* in the Second Sophistic." In J. König, K. Oikonomopoulou, and G. Woolf, eds., *Ancient Libraries*. Cambridge, 377–400.

Zanker, G. 1989. "Current Trends in the Study of Hellenic Myth in Early Third-century Alexandrian Poetry: The Case of Theocritus." *Antike und Abendland* 35: 83–103.

FURTHER READING

The bibliography on the politics, society, and literary culture of Greece, Egypt, and the Near East is vast, and I include here only a few suggestions in addition to the works cited in the chapter. Readers interested in Ptolemaic Egypt may also wish to consult Bingen 2007 and Hoelbl 2001. On Greek literary culture in the Hellenistic period, see Burstein 2008, Thompson 1992, and Tovar 2010; for more on Hellenic and Egyptian literary interaction see Hunter 2003, Mori 2008, Moyer 2011, and Stephens 2003. With respect to ancient libraries, Too 2010 offers a good introduction; the chapters by Handis, Harder, Robson, and Zadorojnyi in König 2013 are especially helpful. On Greek identity and ethnic segregation in Asia and Egypt see Derks and Roymans 2009 as well as Kuhrt and Sherwin-White 1987 (Spek's chapters in both of these volumes are instructive); see now also Ager and Faber 2013, *Belonging and Isolation in the Hellenistic World*. Chapters by Lecuyot on Ai Khanoum and Leriche on Bactria in Cribb and Herrmann 2007 are useful; on Berossus and Mesopotamian temples in the Hellenistic period see De Breuker 2003; on Near Eastern papyrology see Gascou 2009.

CHAPTER 7

Greek Literature in the Roman World

Introducing Imperial Greek Literature

Jason König

How did the Greek literature of the Roman Empire relate to its cultural and political context, and to the changes and challenges faced by the Greek-speaking populations of the Roman world?

One immediate problem is the difficulty of deciding where Imperial Greek literature begins and ends. Usually the Imperial period is defined roughly as 31 BCE (the year of Augustus' victory at the Battle of Actium, which set him on the path to being first emperor of Rome) to 312 CE (the conversion of the emperor Constantine to Christianity). However, many of the features we see as central to Imperial Greek literature are visible well outside the chronological boundaries of that period. Some of the most important Greek writers of the reign of Augustus were active well before Actium – for example the historian Diodorus Siculus, who seems to have completed most of his work between about 60 and 30 BCE – and the encounter between Greek intellectuals and Roman patrons in the late Republic made a formative contribution to concerns which were central to Greek literature throughout the following centuries: Greek identity, the Greek past, the relationship between Greece and Rome (e.g., see Schmitz and Wiater 2011). At the other end of the chronological spectrum, the rhetorical works of Libanius and some of his contemporaries from the mid-fourth century have a great deal in common with the sophistic activity which had flourished in the second and early third centuries. Early Christian literature throughout the first four or five centuries CE had a close, albeit highly ambivalent relationship with Greco-Roman traditions (see Stenger, ch. 8, in this volume). Moreover, the Imperial period as defined above is itself very far from uniform. After the reign of Augustus very little Greek literature survives at all before the late first century CE. Nor is there much surviving after the beginning of the so called "third-century crisis" – five decades of military and political upheaval that affected the whole of the empire – in 235 CE.

We can narrow things by focusing in on the remarkable and distinctive intensification of literary activity which took place throughout the long second century, roughly from the work of Dio Chrysostom and Plutarch, whose early writing dates, in both cases, from the 70s and 80s CE, through to the work of Philostratus, some of which was written as late as the 230s. It is a common procedure to treat this sub-period as a more or less coherent unit. It was a time

A Companion to Greek Literature, First Edition. Edited by Martin Hose and David Schenker.
© 2016 John Wiley & Sons, Inc. Published 2020 by John Wiley & Sons, Inc.

of great generic innovation, above all in prose genres. For example it saw the development of the novel form (although our earliest example, Chariton's *Chaireas and Callirhoe*, may have been written earlier, perhaps in the mid first century CE), along with various other examples of experimentation in prose fiction and new approaches to biographical writing. We also see a new scale and a new adventurousness in compilatory styles of writing which included miscellanistic and encyclopaedic compositions as well as more conventional works on technical, scientific and geographical subjects (see König and Whitmarsh 2007; also Morgan 2011 for claims about the importance of the miscellany as one of the most important genres of the Roman Empire). Perhaps most strikingly of all, display oratory gained a new prominence and prestige, and the great Greek orators of the Roman Empire, the sophists, gained fame and fortune for their ability to improvise speeches on themes drawn from classical history.

For reasons of space, most of what I have to say here will focus on that extraordinarily fertile century and a half: I look first at the intellectual culture of the long second century; then at the life of the Greek cities and the way in which that left its mark on the Greek literature of this period; and finally at the impact of Rome and the Roman empire. However, it is important to stress that a full account would have to follow that story much more painstakingly through the century or two before and after. That is an area where much work still remains to be done.

1. Intellectual Culture

The Imperial Greek obsession with the Classical past has not always appealed to modern taste. It had a very bad press in the late nineteenth century and right through the first half of the twentieth century and beyond, associated with derivativeness and nostalgia. In the last few decades we have begun to appreciate the works of this period more on their own terms, and to understand how the Greek authors of the Roman world treated literary creativity as something perfectly compatible with, even dependent upon imitation of the Classical past. They reshaped and defamiliarized their classical models – not least by putting them into prose, in the case of the pre-Imperial poetic heritage – at the same time as celebrating them.

Crucially, this kind of mastery of the literary and linguistic heritage was a powerful instrument of self-presentation for the Greek elites (as Schmitz 1997 has shown). The authors of this period tended to put a great deal of energy into crafting authoritative personas for themselves on paper, and ingenious quotation and adaptation of Classical quotations and Classical models often contributed to that goal, as a way of displaying apparently effortless familiarity with a shared literary archive. Reference to earlier literature was often combined with a sophisticated command of Attic dialect (although some authors went out of their way to reject what they portrayed as excessively pedantic adherence to "Atticism" – Galen and Lucian are the obvious examples, both discussed further below – and in practice Attic dialect seems to have been used in a more relaxed fashion than we sometimes assume: see Kim 2010). Being able to deliver a speech in the language of Demosthenes or to quote ingeniously from Homer when appropriate was a badge of high social status not just in literary writing, but also in the day-to-day life of the Greek elites. Admittedly, not all members of the elite would have attained those skills to the same degree. Most men from educated families would have studied language and literature with a grammarian as well as undergoing some rhetorical training. These highly conservative traditional schooling processes must have brought only a relatively superficial understanding of literary culture for some. Nevertheless, the ideal of a hyper-educated elite was a very powerful one. The experts – the virtuoso sophists who toured around the empire giving display speeches – were iconic representatives of the intelligence and erudition of the educated class as a whole; it was almost as though they displayed those qualities so that other members of the elite would not need to (Schmitz 1997, 63–6).

Perhaps not surprisingly, given the prestige of these skills, their ownership was debated. The intellectual culture of the Roman Empire was highly adversarial. This was a culture where contests in musical and poetic and rhetorical skills were a prominent part of the agonistic festivals that were spread right across the Mediterranean world, most famously at the four-yearly Pythian festival at Delphi but also at hundreds of other smaller events. Those competitive practices were replicated in other kinds of public intellectual display and even within the more private arena of the written text. The most famous and most competitive intellectuals of all were the sophists. The most important evidence for their activity comes from the work of Philostratus, whose work dates from the first half of the third century CE, so rather later than most of the other authors discussed here. He seems to have had a career in sophistic oratory himself, although he also wrote a wide range of non-rhetorical works (including a life of the wonder-working philosopher Apollonius of Tyana, who was active in the late first century CE). His *Lives of the Sophists* (*VS*) gives a lengthy account of his sophistic predecessors and contemporaries from the previous century and a half. Throughout that work he depicts competitiveness almost as a defining feature of sophistic identity (see König 2010). He portrays the sophists denouncing their rivals, taking sides against each other and competing for imperial favor. Often his comments imply something approaching admiration. For example he talks about the quarrel between Favorinus and Polemo as follows: "They may be forgiven for their *philotimia* ("ambition", "ambitious rivalry"), since human nature views ambition as something which never grows old" (*VS* 1.8, 490); and a few lines later of Favorinus: "For those who called Favorinus a sophist precisely this fact – that he had quarreled with a sophist – was sufficient proof, for that spirit of ambition of which I have spoken here is usually directed against rivals from the same profession" (1.8, 491). There are even traces in the work of Philostratus' own involvement in professional rivalry.

There are similar examples from countless other texts and genres. One obvious example is the medical writer Galen. Galen was active in the mid-second century CE. He came from Pergamon in Asia Minor, but much of his career was spent in Rome, where he had links with the imperial family. He was astonishingly prolific: much of his writing does not survive, but what we have fills 22 lengthy volumes in the standard nineteenth-century edition, and covers all branches of ancient medicine, along with a large number of non-medical topics too. He was a hugely influential figure for post-Classical medicine into the seventeenth century and even beyond, but also clearly won great prestige during his own lifetime. One of the ways in which he did so was through repeated disparagement of his intellectual rivals, often in quite unforgiving terms: other doctors who do not match his own intellectual rigor, as he represents it; and representatives of other professions like athletic trainers (see König 2005, 254–300). The latter might seem at first sight like a surprising target, but Galen's concerns make more sense when we see how they are represented as encroaching on Galen's own territory of medical expertise. The ancient world had nothing resembling medical or other scientific qualifications. That was a major factor in the adversarial quality of the intellectual life of the Roman Empire in some disciplines: rhetoric was the most powerful vehicle available for the establishment of authority, and experts often attempted to disparage rivals as a way of proving their own competence (see Barton 1994). Athletics was also an educational rival to other more intellectual pursuits: the gymnasium was one of the major institutions of higher education in the world, used to train young men of the elite as "ephebes," between the ages of 17 and 19 in military and athletic skills. That educational role is presumably another factor in Galen's criticisms, given his desire to stamp out anything that interferes with training of the mind.

In other cases we even see the Imperial Greek elite playing at competition in more relaxed environments. The work of Plutarch is full of examples. Plutarch lived between about 50 and 120 CE, and spent much of his life in the small town of Chaironeia in Boiotia, northwest of Athens. He is best known for his biographical work the *Parallel Lives*, which compares famous Greeks and Romans. But he was above all a philosopher, and he left in addition a vast corpus of broadly philosophical essays known as the *Moralia*. A number of these texts are dialogues set in the present day, with appearances by Plutarch's friends and contemporaries. Between them they give a very vivid glimpse of intellectual life in the late first and early second centuries, and show in particular the importance of competitive debate even in the context of informal social interaction. In his *Sympotic Questions* (*QC*), for example, he recreates a series of nearly 100 dinner-party conversations from across his lifetime. He and his fellow guests playfully debate often quite abstruse topics of literary and scientific interest as if practicing, in a low-key setting, the skills of rhetorical and philosophical argumentation they use with more at stake in other areas of their lives. And a large number of their discussions are set at the Pythian and other festivals: Plutarch hints that the skills he and his fellow guests are displaying are more elevated equivalents of the agonistic skills on display in the festival competitions (see König 2012, 60–89).

Admittedly intellectual rivalry is not presented in an unequivocally positive fashion in these texts – there are plenty of signs of ambivalence. Philostratus includes many examples of competitive behavior which he suggests go beyond what is acceptable (e.g., see *VS* 1.21, 514–15). Galen criticizes the athletic trainers in part precisely because of their excessively combative behavior in debate (e.g., see *Ad Thras.* 46, K 5.895): presumably his point is that their indulgence in disputation lacks the thoughtful, measured quality of his own. Plutarch and his fellow guests make it clear that too much competitiveness and conflict are inappropriate for what he calls the "friend-making" character of the symposium (e.g., see *QC* 1.4, especially the closing statement at 622b). And more generally speaking Plutarch and other philosophically inclined writers (e.g., see Epictetus, *Discourses* 3.25.1–5, with Long 2002, 195–6) tend to stress the importance of competition with the self, rather than glory-seeking competition with others. Some of those views anticipate – although in relatively muted form – the more pronounced wariness of debate and disputation which became increasingly common in early Christian and late antique culture (see Lim 1995).

As these examples suggest, the intellectual relationships of mutual admiration and rivalry, the institutions of education, display and debate, were not just the context for Imperial Greek literature; they were also in some respects its main topic. Some writers, like Plutarch and Philostratus, celebrate intellectual accomplishment, in the works just mentioned. Others, like Galen, take a more sceptical approach. The most famous sceptic of all is the satirical writer, Lucian. We know less about Lucian's life than for many of his contemporaries: for some reason he seems to have been a less prominent figure in the Greek intellectual culture of the Roman world. But from his own work it is clear that he grew up in the city of Samosata in the Roman province of Syria, in what is now southeast Turkey (Greek may not even have been his first language). He is likely to have lived between about 120 and 180 CE. He seems to have had rhetorical aspirations early in his career, but later took a more unconventional course, innovating in a number of different literary forms, most importantly in using the dialogue tradition inherited from Plato for his own distinctively satirical purposes. Lucian is fascinated by the inherent absurdities and contradictions of the Greek literary heritage, which is treated with such reverence by his contemporaries, although he also simultaneously celebrates that heritage through his own ingenious rewriting of it (see Branham 1989). His favorite target is fake intellectuals, especially those who describe themselves as philosophers but without having the necessary integrity and the necessary erudition, and who treat philosophy as a commodity, prizing display and profit above truth and morality (see Whitmarsh 2001, 247–94). In all of this Lucian plays on his position as a cultural outsider: he hints repeatedly that his outsider's gaze gives him a kind of special authority to comment on Greek culture. That pose owes a great deal to motifs of philosophical self-representation. It is quite common for ancient philosophical writers to express concern about the misguided character of contemporary society, and contemporary intellectual culture in particular, and to separate themselves from it. Galen, who saw himself as a doctor as well as a philosopher, is once again a helpful parallel for Lucian: quite frequently he expresses his despair at the intellectual failings of his peers in general terms (e.g., *On the Order of My Own Books* 1, K19.50–52), as well as criticizing named individuals. Lucian is different, however. In many of his works he does indeed take on a philosophical persona as a vehicle for his satire, but he also delights in showing how that persona is just as much at risk of criticism as those he criticizes.

One classic example is his great pair of "anti-biographies" on religious/philosophical charlatans, the *Peregrinus* and the *Alexander*. In both of these works he makes it clear that his own ostensibly respectable narrating persona has a mastery of the techniques of trickery which matches or even surpasses that of his subjects (see König 2006 on the *Peregrinus*). At other times he turns the attention on us as readers. For example his work *On Salaried Posts* (*De merc. cond.*) describes the humiliations experienced by a Greek intellectual employed in a Roman household. Many of Lucian's portrayals of fake philosophers are couched in deliberately non-realistic language drawn from the traditions of comedy and set in the distant past. But this work is set very much in the present day: it punctures the pretensions of the unnamed intellectual in painfully realistic detail. Remarkably, it is in the second person singular and in the present tense. Ostensibly that second-person usage is directed to a specific addressee, who is being invited to imagine the fate which might await him if things go badly, but it is hard to avoid the impression that all of Lucian's readers are being implicated in his criticisms as they read: "The servants stare at you, all the guests watch your every move, nor does the host himself ignore these things, but he has actually instructed some of his servants to watch how you look at his wife or his concubines .... The attendants of the other guests ... mock at your inexperience. As one would expect, you sweat from confusion and you do not dare to drink even when you are thirsty, in case you are viewed as a drunkard" (*De merc. cond.* 15). One of Lucian's great talents, in other words, is to show us how difficult it is to escape from what he represents as the dominant failings of Imperial Greek intellectual culture – ostentation, pretension, fakery, greed, petty rivalry. Even his narrator figures and implied readers are often at risk.

2.　The City

One of the other defining characteristics of the intellectual life of the Roman Empire was its cosmopolitan quality. Philostratus' *Lives of the Sophists* is a case in point. The imaginative geography of this text is fascinating and understudied (but see now Kemezis 2011). The action jumps around between many different parts of the Mediterranean world, in a way which reflects the geographical richness and connectedness of the Roman Empire. In many of his mini-biographies Philostratus records the sophists' close links with several different cities – usually the cities of their birth, and cities they have become particularly associated with as citizens and benefactors later in life. It is also striking, however, that, many of them ultimately take a rather stand-offish stance in relation to the day-to-day political life of these communities, as if their identity as members of a cosmopolitan, empire-wide intellectual elite is what matters to them most of all. Niketes of Smyrna, the first of the Roman-period sophists mentioned by Philostratus (see further in the section following) is a case in point:

> He was thought worthy of great honor by the city of Smyrna, which left nothing unsaid in shouting out its praises of him, viewing him as an amazing man and a great orator. But he seldom came forward to speak in the Assembly, and when the people accused him of being afraid he said, "I fear the people when they are exalting me more than when they abuse me." (*VS* 1.19, 511)

There is accordingly a tendency for the bulk of the action to concentrate in a few locations only – the really big intellectual centers like Athens or Rome or Smyrna. For all the geographical richness of the work, it tends to be quite cursory in its mention of less intellectually prominent cities. Much the same is true in Plutarch's *Sympotic Questions*: the conversations are spread over a very wide range of cities right across the Mediterranean world, sometimes set at symposia associated with sacrificial feasts as part of local festivals, hosted by local civic officials. To that extent the *Sympotic Questions* celebrates the local, civic identities of the Imperial Greek world. It is also striking, however, that these local identities ultimately get only quite cursory attention, in the opening sentences of each chapter: what matters most, in the end, is the atmosphere of harmony and shared intellectual endeavor between members of the educated elite from many different communities, as they launch into erudite conversations on subjects drawn from the pan-Greek heritage.

The Greek authors of the Roman Empire, in other words, often set themselves at one remove from the day-to-day life of the city. Nevertheless civic culture was both a major subject and a major shaping force for Imperial Greek literature. That is perhaps not surprising given the situation on the ground. The cities of the Greek world were for the most part flourishing and wealthy right through the long second century CE, above all in western Asia Minor. Rich benefactors invested vast amounts of money into public buildings, festivals, banquets, gymnasium education and the other public goods that were seen as central to the civilized functioning of any Greek community. The cities had their own active political institutions, and competed among themselves for dominance in their own regions. All of this is attested in the rich epigraphical record, consisting of thousands and thousands of surviving inscriptions, many of which were originally set up to honor benefactors and to preserve the memory of important civic events. Great orators, too, were viewed as prestigious adornments for their home cities. And even if many of them preferred to remove themselves from the day-to-day grind of public life, it is also clear that others found that their rhetorical skills had a very practical usefulness in the institutions of the city, or in representing the interests of the city on embassies.

Perhaps the single most important example is Dio Chrysostom (cf. Edwards ch. 13, 214–5). Dio was an orator and philosopher from the town of Prusa in Bithynia (northwest Turkey). He was roughly contemporary with Plutarch (approximately 40–120 CE). His work too, like most of the authors discussed in this chapter, was remarkably wide-ranging, including speeches of political advice (including a set of four *Kingship Orations*, which may have been addressed to the emperor Trajan), philosophical essays, fictional dialogues, accounts of his travels and works of literary criticism. After what he represents as a period of exile imposed by the emperor Domitian (although the reliability of his account is questioned: Moles 1978), he returned to his home city to play a more active role in civic politics. We have roughly 20 surviving speeches by him addressed to the city of Prusa or to other cities of the Greek world, offering advice on civic harmony and a range of other issues. Even in these political speeches he often takes on a philosophical pose, deploying a distinctly moralizing conception of what is admirable civic practice, and portraying himself as an adviser who sees the right path all the more clearly through having a measure of philosophical detachment. In that sense he has a certain amount in common with Philostratus' sophists, who treat whole cities as their equals or even their inferiors (although they generally lack Dio's philosophical perspective – Dio is included in *Lives of the Sophists* 1.7 in the category of those who are too philosophical to be classed as sophists properly speaking in Philostratus' view, even though they were widely viewed as such). Moreover some of Dio's works offer a distinctively negative impression of city life: the most famous and most complex example is his *Euboian Oration* (*or.* 7), which describes his experience of suffering shipwreck on the island of Euboia, and the hospitality he receives from a rustic hunter and his family. The hunter describes how he has recently visited the city, for only the second time in his life, only to find himself being accused, absurdly, of not paying taxes. His description of the noisy and fickle mob, going through the motions of democratic politics before the eyes of the bewildered hunter, must have been meant as a comical and perhaps slightly depressing take on the institutions of democratic debate that were familiar to Dio's contemporary readers. Moreover, the city, along with its surrounding countryside, is described in a state of physical decline, with sheep and cattle grazing in the *agora* (this passage has in the past been used to support the idea that the populations and economies of the cities of mainland Greece went into decline under Roman rule – that view is now discredited: see Alcock 1993, esp. 29–30 and 85–6 on the *Euboian Oration*). The second half of the work then goes into a diatribe denouncing the kinds of employment which are available in the cities of the Roman Empire for the urban poor. In many of Dio's advice speeches there is similarly strongly worded criticism of the addressees (for example in *Oration* 31 criticizing the people of Rhodes for their habit of engraving new names on old honorific statues; in *Oration* 32, criticizing the people of Alexandria for their disorderly conduct as spectators at theatrical performances and athletic contests; and so on).

However the very fact that Dio puts so much energy into correction of these bad habits suggests that he feels the traditions of civic life are worth fighting for (see Desideri 2000 for the argument that Dio's portrayals of civic life became increasingly positive as his career went on, and that this change coincided with increasingly high valuation of city life by Greek intellectuals more broadly; also Salmeri 2000). All of these speeches reveal an intricate and respectful knowledge of the particular history and circumstances of the city he is addressing. He also returns again and again to an idealized generic view of what an ideal city should have to show for itself. In *or.* 31.102, for example, even as he accuses the Rhodians of not living up to the virtue of their ancestors, he also reminds them in passing that those same ancestors "spent money on all the things you spend it on now – on their festivals, processions, sacrifices, fortifications, jury service, Council." That reminder portrays the landscape of civic practice as a highly traditional, stable phenomenon surviving directly from the classical past into the present (see Ma 2000 on the way in which even the negative portrayal of democracy in action in the *Euboian Oration* implies the continued thriving of traditional democratic institutions in the Roman period). In addition, his speeches conjure up for us a world where cities are measured constantly against each other – the city in the Imperial Greek imagination was never an isolated island, but instead one of a long and glittering chain of comparable communities whose shared values were manifested precisely through their mutual rivalry. It is clear too that Dio himself was closely involved in the intricate details of day-to-day politics within his home city of Prusa, and that he invested a great deal of money and energy in architectural improvements. We know that not just from his own speeches, but also from a pair of letters between Pliny the Younger, as governor of Bithynia, and the emperor Trajan, discussing the problem of how to treat an accusation of misconduct brought against Dio by one of his fellow citizens in relation to one of the building projects he had undertaken on behalf of the city (Pliny, *Letters* 10.81–2).

Plutarch, Dio's near contemporary, is also an important point of reference. As I have already suggested, many of Plutarch's works have an air of timelessness to them, in the sense that they draw heavily on traditional philosophical, literary and historical material. However, his essays of practical philosophical advice are actually very unusual within the philosophical tradition for being so closely engaged with the realities of day-to-day political life, as Lieve Van Hoof has recently shown (Van Hoof 2010): they are generally addressed to named, politically active addressees; they assume that their readers are busy men who have limited time and need a pragmatic summary rather than a professional philosophical treatise; and rather than dismissing worldly concerns with honor Plutarch accommodates them and redirects them. In her reading of Plutarch's *On Exile*, for example, she shows how Plutarch not only sympathizes with worries about the dishonor which results from exile, but also reassures his readers that exile may be a chance to extend and enhance one's honor rather than the opposite; this sets him apart from other philosophical writers on exile who console the reader by arguing that political honor is worthless. One work, *On Precepts of Statescraft*, goes further, offering detailed advice about political conduct aimed at the young man who is about to enter civic life: it has much in common with the work of Dio (see Swain 1996, 162–83; also Jones 1971, 110–21 for Plutarch's political writings more broadly). Plutarch himself must have had considerable experience of local politics, even if he chooses for the most part not to describe his own involvement: he spent most of his career in his small home town of Chaironeia in Boiotia in northern Greece.

Many other texts, too, deal with civic life, even if few of them can match the kind of detailed engagement we find in the work of Dio and in Plutarch's *Precepts*. The genre of the speech in praise of a city is widespread, and we even find instructions for composing this kind of speech in the work of the (third-century) rhetorical writer Menander Rhetor (see Russell and Wilson 1981). Aelius Aristides' speeches in praise of Athens (*Panathenaicus*) and Rome (*On Rome*) are particularly elaborate examples of that genre, as is Favorinus' *Corinthian Oration* (although Favorinus pointedly undermines the encomiastic atmosphere through his criticisms of the Corinthians for taking down the statue they had previously put up in his honor – in that sense he is close to Dio who similarly mixes encomium with criticism).

The historiographical writing of the Roman Empire, too, contributed to civic self-perception, by helping to foster an awareness of the role individual cities had played in the great events of the Greek past. And there was also a long tradition specifically of local history stretching right back to classical Greek culture (see Clarke 2008). One of its most developed and original manifestations is in the *Periegesis* of Pausanias (see Hutton 2005), which describes in astonishing detail the buildings and statues of cities of mainland Greece and the stories lying behind them. Pausanias is of course very different from writers like Dio and Plutarch in his portrayal of civic identity – designedly so – since the identity he is interested in is nearly always focused on the past, and very rarely involves any mention of the contemporaries he meets on his travels or of contemporary political practice. Nevertheless it is worth remembering that the kinds of mythical and historical events he records were themselves actively celebrated in the festivals of these cities, as living parts of their identity in the present day.

Finally the image of the city was important also for the novelistic writing of the Roman period. Most strikingly, even the earliest of the surviving Greek novels (cf. Tilg, ch. 16 in this volume), Chariton's *Chaireas and Callirhoe* (see above for a possible date in the mid-first century), ends with a scene of the hero and heroine being welcomed back by their home city of Syracuse after their travels and tribulations and taking their place as leading members of the civic elite. Chariton's novel is set in the Sicily of the fifth century BCE, but many commentators have assumed nonetheless that this image of final absorption back into the life of the city, with its validation of marriage as an ideal state, would have had appealed directly to the elites of the Roman Empire, who would have viewed the hero and heroine as models for their own lives (see esp. Swain 1996, 101–31; but also more recently Whitmarsh 2011, who stresses the fact that closure is always in tension with open-endedness in the novels). More generally speaking, most of the Greek novels revel in their own geographical richness, whisking us around the Mediterranean world (and even beyond the margins of Greek speaking territory) to glimpse the landscapes of a very wide range of different cities. In that sense, like the *Lives of the Sophists*, and even like some early Christian texts – most obviously the canonical Acts of the Apostles, which charts the journeys of the apostles to an enormous range of cities in quasi-novelistic fashion – they appeal to a sense of geographical fantasy, allowing us to see with our own eyes the glory, or in some cases (like the *Onos* of Pseudo-Lucian, which describes the humiliating adventures of a man who is turned into a donkey and dragged by successive owners through the towns of mainland Greece) the squalor of the cities of the Mediterranean world, each of which had its own distinct identity and history.

3. Rome

How, finally, did Rome (cf. Hose, this volume, ch. 21, pp. 335–7) – the most scrutinized of all the cities of the Roman Empire – influence and shape "Imperial" Greek literature? And how were Romans and their relationship with Greek culture and identity represented by Imperial Greek authors?

There are different ways of answering those questions. Many commentators have stressed the insulation of Greek literature and culture from the realities of the Roman present. For example, the interest in looking back to the pre-Roman past, common in so many different types of Imperial Greek texts, has often been represented as a reaction to the political disempowerment of the Roman present (e.g., Bowie 1974). From a very similar perspective, Simon Swain has mapped out Greek attitudes to Rome in this period at length, right through the long second century, emphasizing the way in which traditional Greek identity tended to be envisaged as something distinct and separable from Roman affiliation (Swain 1996). Others have stressed more the compatibility of Greek identity with Roman citizenship and Roman political involvement, assuming the development of a more and more unified, empire-wide Greco-Roman elite through the second century CE and into the early third (e.g., Bowersock 1969; and more recently Madsen 2009). Tim Whitmarsh (2001) has tried to nuance these approaches by demonstrating that the texts of this period take a very complex, often playful approach to Greek identity and Roman rule, performing and experimenting with different models of what it means to be Greek or Roman, rather than simply defining those terms in clear-cut and monolithic ways.

Those approaches do not always coincide in their interpretations of particular passages or authors, but where they do agree is in the assumption that exploration and celebration of Greek identity was one of the guiding obsessions of Imperial Greek literature, and moreover that it was partly shaped by the encounter with Rome. Some have gone even further in arguing for the influence of Rome on Imperial Greek culture. Most recently, A. J. S. Spawforth (2012) has argued that many features of Greek culture in the Imperial period were in fact due to a deliberate policy of encouraging classicizing images of Greek identity on the part of Augustus and his advisers, with the aim of creating an image of Greek identity compatible with the moral priorities they particularly valued for Roman culture. He argues also that this process was further enhanced by later emperors, Hadrian in particular. On that argument, the idealization of classical Athenian and mainland Greek history and culture, and many other features which we see as archetypally associated with late Greek culture – for example the thriving Greek festival culture of the Roman empire (e.g., see Spawforth 2012, 163–7 on Olympia), or the culture of rhetorical declamation (Spawforth 2012, 73–81) – turn out to have been brought into being at least partly as a consequence of Augustan policy and in response to Roman cultural priorities. Spawforth's argument presents us with a remarkable picture which will no doubt prompt reassessment of much of what we thought we knew about Imperial Greek culture. But even if we choose not to accept his argument in full, it is undeniable that it was Roman rule that made possible much of what is most distinctive in the Greek literature and culture of this period: the cosmopolitan intellectual culture and thriving city life already outlined in this chapter were distinctive consequences of the wealth and interconnectedness of the Roman world. For example, the evidence for Hadrian's financial investment in bolstering Athens' prestige as a cultural center in the second century has long been clear (e.g., see Boatwright 2000, 144–57). Some scholars have suggested that the most important function of sophistic orators was not so much their cultural role but rather their role as ambassadors who would give speeches on behalf of cities before the emperor, and as imperial administrators (see especially Bowersock 1969, and response by Bowie 1982). On that argument, sophistic rhetoric is a good example of the way in which Greek cultural activity could be sustained at least in part by Roman political realities. It is even tempting to feel that the subjection of Greece to Roman rule made it easier to contemplate the Greek world as a unity, with a shared Panhellenic history (Elsner 1992, 17–20 makes that argument for Pausanias, while acknowledging at the same time the way in which Pausanias shuts Rome out of his account of the Greek landscape and Greek history).

When we turn to the texts themselves, we see a very wide spectrum of different possibilities for representing Rome and its relationship with Greek culture. In some cases we even find a range of approaches in tension with each other within a single text. In order to illustrate that point I want to look first, once again, at Philostratus' *Lives of the Sophists*. I aim to show how that text oscillates between, on the one hand, a conception of sophistic oratory as an activity which is intimately and even uncomfortably entwined with Roman rule and Roman emperors, and on the other hand a conception where Rome is utterly and ostentatiously absent. It is perhaps not surprising that modern scholarship has used both of those models, when they are already in tension with each other within one of the most influential of all texts for our understanding of this period (see Kemezis 2011, 17 for a similar point).

Let us look first at the absence of Rome. One striking instance comes in Philostratus' account of the origins of sophistic oratory. He traces it right back to the sophists of the classical period (*VS* 480–82), identifying an "old sophistic", which is described only briefly, and then suggesting that a "second sophistic," associated with distinctive choices of theme and characterization, was founded by the orator Aeschines in the fourth century BCE (that term "Second Sophistic" has often used in modern scholarship, in a misleading extension of Philostratus' usage, as a shorthand for the Greek literature of the long second century CE as a whole). From there Philostratus jumps abruptly forward, by about 400 years, to the career of Niketes of Smyrna, an orator of the mid first century CE (*VS* 1.19, 511–12). In making that move he is not untypical of his contemporaries, who delight in drawing links across the centuries between the present day and the classical past. But it is nevertheless remarkable to see what Philostratus misses out. The background of radical political and cultural change, and the whole complex history of Greek rhetoric and its relationship with growing Roman power in the late Hellenistic and Augustan period, are omitted (barring a couple of cursory mentions – for example Philostratus the Egyptian in 1.5, 486, who is said to have associated with Cleopatra, and Theomnestus of Naucratis in 1.6, 486, who may have been active in Athens in the first century BCE). If Spawforth's account is right (see above), this omission of the formative influence of Augustan Rome on Greek declamatory practices leads to a highly misleading account of where the sophistic declamation of the long second century came from. In the opening sentences of Niketes' life Philostratus acknowledges that the continuity between Niketes and Aeschines four centuries before is not completely smooth – there has been a gap between past and present: "For this man Niketes, having inherited the art of oratory reduced to a meagre state, gave it approaches much more splendid than the ones he himself built for Smyrna." He acknowledges, in other words that Niketes' career is the start of something new, and he hints that it may have taken place in parallel with a new momentum within Greek city life, by his mention of Niketes' civic benefactions. But Rome at first does not seem to be part of the story: this is a purely Greek affair.

Philostratus also repeatedly conjures up the image of an idealized audience of Greeks. For one thing he refers repeatedly to the long-standing traditions of orators speaking to the assembled Greeks at the Olympics and other Panhellenic festivals. Those traditions stretch right back to the Classical period, but Philostratus also gives lots of examples of the sophists of the long second century doing the same thing. For example at 2.27, 618, Philostratus tells us that the sophist Hippodromus "did not neglect attendance at the festivals of the Greeks, but went to them regularly, both in order to declaim and so as not to be forgotten." Not only that, but Philostratus also uses many of the same motifs even outside specific festival settings. His sophists are repeatedly described as speaking to "the Greeks" even when they are not performing at Olympia or Delphi or other equivalent venues. For Philostratus, in other words, one of the defining features of sophistic speech seems to be the fact that it has a notionally festive,

Panhellenic quality. For example, the students and admirers of the sophists are often referred to as "Hellenes" or "Hellenic" or even "Hellas" (i.e. Greece). In 2.10, 587 we hear that the sophist Hadrian of Tyre, holder of the chair of rhetoric in Athens, "whenever he had lectured went home again as an object of envy, escorted by Greeks from everywhere (τοῦ παντάχοθεν Ἑλληνικοῦ)". He wins reverence, too, "by his sharing in Hellenic festivals"; and they (i.e. the Hellenic youth) feel towards him "as sons do to a father who is pleasant and gentle, and who maintains with them the Hellenic dance." Between them these passages give us a remarkable image of the sophist surrounded at all times by an audience which notionally represents the whole of Greece, defined according to traditional festive criteria of the kind that Herodotus refers to in the famous passage in *Histories* 8.144, where the Athenians appeal for unity against the Persian threat by appealing to the shared "shrines and sacrifices" of the Greeks (τὸ Ἑλληνικόν – the same almost untranslatable word used by Philostratus for "Greeks" or "Greek culture" or "Greekness" in the passage just quoted and elsewhere), as well as their shared lifestyle and language and blood.

In other sections of the work, however, we find a very different picture, and the text suggests instead that the Imperial court is the audience that really matters. Often these relationships with Roman power appear quite dysfunctional, as sophists win favor or cause offence in unpredictable ways in the presence of capricious emperors. I suggested a moment ago that Niketes of Smyrna, the first of Philostratus' modern sophists, at first sight stands for an ideal of revived continuity between Greek past and Greek present, and that is indeed the impression we get from the opening page or so of his mini-biography. That impression is abruptly undermined, however, as Rome intrudes in the second half of Philostratus' short account of Niketes' life. There we hear how the emperor Nero summoned him from Smyrna in Asia Minor all the way to Gaul, so that he could defend himself against a vastly disproportionate charge of having insulted a consular official (*VS* 1.19, 512). In that anecdote Philostratus gives us the most vivid illustration imaginable of the way in which the Roman emperors do after all control the sophistic world, at least in some respects. And it is a common pattern in everything that follows that Philostratus will switch from long passages of depoliticized literary analysis, which celebrate the autonomy and antiquity of the sophistic profession, to accounts of the interference of the political sphere, which show that Rome has the power to command and impel the sophists in its own directions, according to its own whims.

Often, of course, we find more harmonious models of the interaction between Greek and Roman. Right back to the late Hellenistic period Greek authors had sought to show the compatibility of Roman rule with Greek culture, often in a rather condescending fashion, for example by stressing the need for Greek knowledge to guide and civilize its Roman conquerors. One of the most famous early examples is Dionysius of Halicarnassus' *Roman Antiquities*, where he argues at length for the Greek origins of Rome and Roman culture (see Tsakmakis, this volume, ch. 14, pp. 226–7). There are many similar examples from later centuries too. For example Aelius Aristides, in his speech *To Rome* already mentioned, praises the city of Rome according to templates derived from traditionally Greek civic encomium, and represents Roman rule as the thing which enables prosperity and cultural flourishing for all inhabitants of the empire (for example see *On Rome* 97–9 for the idea that Roman rule has enabled the flourishing of traditional Greek festival culture; that said, Aristides largely refrains from emphasizing the idea of Greekness in his depiction of the empire's culture, since his key point of praise is the way in which Rome has created a world where distinctions of ethnicity have become almost irrelevant, where all are common citizen: see Richter 2011, 131–4). Plutarch portrays many virtuous and admirable Roman politicians in his *Parallel Lives*, – in fact in many cases they measure up relatively favorably against the famous Greeks with whom they are paired – but he also makes clear the important civilizing influence of Greek education on those Romans who choose to devote themselves to it (see Swain 1990). Similarly in his *Sympotic Questions* he regularly shows us his powerful Roman friends like Sosius Senecio and Mestrius Florus, both of whom held the consulship, taking part as equals in erudite conversation with his fellow guests, but he also makes it clear that they are to be admired here precisely because they are immersing themselves in Greek learning: Greek culture is the dominant force in this relationship. Even in Philostratus' *Lives of the Sophists* we do find ever so often a more positive image of the civilized, mutually respectful relations between Greek learning and Roman power, particularly in the preface (479–80) where Philostratus recalls an earlier conversation about sophistry between himself and his dedicatee, the future emperor Gordian, as if advertising his own ability to transcend the difficulties so many of his sophistic predecessors had in their relations with the imperial family.

Other authors, however, offer a more cynical version of this kind of interconnectedness between Greek and Roman culture. The work of Lucian is an obvious place to look, particularly his text *On Salaried Posts* already mentioned, and another closely related work the *Nigrinus*. In these works Lucian offers a bitter criticism of the Roman patronage system and its corroding effects on the trust and intellectual integrity that should lie at the heart of Greek intellectual and civic life. At the same time, however, he shows us Greek characters who are themselves complicit in their own humiliation, led by their greed into positions almost of servitude. He also stresses how the powerful Roman and the learned Greek are held together by a dynamic relationship of mutual need: each needs the other as a badge of his own status, mired as they are in a world where self-presentation and social position count for everything:

> My view, however, is that the flatterers are more of a disgrace than those who are flattered; in fact the flatterers are almost responsible for the arrogance of the flattered. For when they express admiration for these men's wealth, and praise their gold, and crowd into their gateways early in the morning, and come up to them and address them as if they were masters, what else should we expect them to think? But if by common agreement they were to abstain, even for a little while, from this voluntary slavery, do you not think on the contrary that the rich men would come to the doors of beggars, imploring them not to leave their wealth unviewed and unwitnessed, not to allow the beauty of their tables and the size of their houses to remain pointless and unappreciated. For what they are in love with is not being rich, but being admired for being rich. The truth is, a very beautiful house is of no use to the inhabitant, nor is gold and ivory, unless there is someone to admire them (*Nigrinus* 23).

That image undermines the work done by Plutarch and others in presenting images of civilized harmony between Greece and Rome; it exposes the easy co-operation between Greeks and Romans from the *Sympotic Questions* and other similar works as an elitist fantasy, unconnected with the more squalid reality on the ground. But it is striking that even as it does so it still replicates (albeit in degraded form) those Plutarchan assumptions about the compatibility and interdependence of Greeks and Romans within the Imperial world. Some writers did indeed ignore the Roman present by giving all their attention to the Classical past (and that goes for Lucian himself in much of his work). But we can never look too far in Imperial Greek literature without finding at least some hint of the mutual impact of Roman and Greek culture, and even of their mutual necessity.

REFERENCES

Alcock, S. E. 1993. *Graecia Capta: The Landscapes of Roman Greece*. Cambridge.

Barton, T. 1994. *Power and Knowledge: Astrology, Physiognomics, and Medicine under the Roman Empire*. Ann Arbor, MI.

Boatwright, M. T. 2000. *Hadrian and the Cities of the Roman Empire*. Princeton, NJ.

Bowersock, G. W. 1969. *Greek Sophists in the Roman Empire*. Oxford.

Bowie, E. L. 1974. "Greeks and their Past in the Second Sophistic." In M. I. Finley, ed., *Studies in Ancient Society*, London, 166–209. (Revised version; first published in 1970.)

Bowie, E. L. 1982. "The importance of sophists." *Yale Classical Studies* 27: 29–60.

Branham, R. B. 1989. *Unruly Eloquence: Lucian and the Comedy of Traditions.* Cambridge MA.

Clarke, K. 2008. *Making Time for the Past: Local History and the Polis.* Oxford.

Desideri, P. 2000. "City and Country in Dio." In S. Swain, ed., *Dio Chrysostom: Politics, Letters, and Philosophy.* Oxford, 93–107.

Elsner, J. 1992. "Pausanias: A Greek Pilgrim in the Roman World." *Past and Present* 135: 3–29.

Gleason, M. W. 1995. *Making Men: Sophists and Self-Presentation in Ancient Rome.* Princeton, NJ.

Goldhill, S., ed. 2001. *Being Greek under Rome: Cultural Identity, the Second Sophistic and Development of Empire.* Cambridge.

Hutton, W. 2005. *Describing Greece: Landscape and Literature in the* Periegesis *of Pausanias.* Cambridge.

Jones, C. P. 1971. *Plutarch and Rome.* Oxford.

Jones, C. P. 1978. *The Roman World of Dio Chrysostom.* Cambridge, MA.

Jones, C. P. 1986. *Culture and Society in Lucian.* Cambridge, MA.

Kemezis, A. 2011. "Narrative of Cultural Geography in Philostratus' *Lives of the Sophists.*" In T. Schmidt and P. Fleury, eds., *Perceptions of the Second Sophistic and its Times,* Toronto, 3–22. Toronto.

Kim, L. 2010. "The Literary Heritage as Language: Atticism and the Second Sophistic." In E. J. Bakker, ed., *A Companion to the Ancient Greek Language,* Oxford, 468–82.

König, J. 2005. *Athletics and Literature in the Roman Empire.* Cambridge.

König, J. 2006. "The Cynic and Christian Lives of Lucian's *Peregrinus.*" In B. McGing and J. Mossman, eds., *The Limits of Biography,* Swansea, 227–54.

König, J. 2009. *Greek Literature in the Roman Empire.* London.

König, J. 2010. "Competitiveness and Anti-Competitiveness in Philostratus' *Lives of the Sophists.*" In N. Fisher and H. van Wees, eds., *Competition in the Ancient World,* Swansea, 279–300.

König, J. 2012. *Saints and Symposiasts: The Literature of Food and the Symposium in Greco-Roman and Early Christian Culture.* Cambridge.

König, J. and T. Whitmarsh, eds. 2007. *Ordering Knowledge in the Roman Empire.* Cambridge.

Lim, R. 1995. *Public Disputation, Power, and Social Order in Late Antiquity.* Berkeley, CA.

Long, A. A. 2002. *Epictetus: A Stoic and Socratic Guide to Life.* Oxford.

Ma, J. 2000. "Public Speech and Community in the *Euboicus.*" In S. Swain, ed., *Dio Chrysostom: Politics, Letters, and Philosophy.* Oxford, 108–24.

Madsen, J. M. 2009. *Eager to be Roman: Greek Response to Roman Rule in Pontus and Bithynia.* London.

Moles, J. L. 1978. "The Career and Conversion of Dio Chrysostom." *Journal of Hellenic Studies* 98: 79–100.

Morgan, T. 2011. "Plutarch and Miscellany." In F. Klotz and K. Oikonomopoulou, eds., *The Philosopher's Banquet: Plutarch's* Table Talk *in the Intellectual Culture of the Roman Empire,* Oxford, 49–73.

Richter, D. S. 2011. *Cosmopolis: Imagining Community in Late Classical Athens and the Early Roman Empire.* Oxford.

Russell, D. A. and N. G. Wilson, eds. 1981. *Menander Rhetor.* Oxford.

Salmeri, G. 2000. "Dio, Rome, and the Civic Life of Asia Minor." In S. Swain, ed., *Dio Chrysostom: Politics, Letters, and Philosophy.* Oxford, 53–92.

Schmitz, T. 1997. *Bildung und Macht: Zur sozialen und politischen Funktion der zweiten Sophistik in der griechischen Welt der Kaiserzeit.* Munich.

Schmitz, T. and N. Wiater, eds. 2012. *The Struggle for Identity: Greeks and their Past in the First Century B.C.E.* Stuttgart.

Spawforth, A. J. S. 2012. *Greece and the Augustan Cultural Revolution.* Cambridge.

Swain, S. 1990. "Hellenic Culture and the Roman Heroes of Plutarch." *Journal of Hellenic Studies* 110: 126–45.

Swain, S. 1996. *Hellenism and Empire: Language, Classicism, and Power in the Greek World AD 50–250.* Oxford.

Swain, S. ed. 2000. *Dio Chrysostom: Politics, Letters, and Philosophy.* Oxford.

Van Hoof, L. 2010. *Plutarch's Practical Ethics: The Social Dynamics of Philosophy.* Oxford.

Whitmarsh, T. 2001. *Greek Literature and the Roman Empire: The Politics of Imitation.* Oxford.

Whitmarsh, T. 2005. *The Second Sophistic.* London.

Whitmarsh, T. 2011. *Narrative and Identity in the Ancient Greek Novel: Returning Romance.* Cambridge.

FURTHER READING

Many of the key publications over the last few decades have focused on the theme of identity, and its connection with the classicizing character of Imperial Greek literature. For example, Bowie 1974 has been an influential starting-point for many later studies: he demonstrates the prevalence of classicizing themes within Imperial Greek texts of many different types, and sees this focus on the glorious Greek past as a reaction to political disempowerment; Swain 1996 maps out Greek attitudes to Rome in the literature of the late first to early third centuries CE, and argues for the continuing power of Greek identity as distinguished from Roman; Schmitz 1997 explains the obsession with archaizing *paideia* in Imperial Greek culture by its role as a marker of social distinction; Whitmarsh 2001 stresses the complexity of Imperial Greek representations of identity, as something which is acted out within the experience of writing and reading, rather than something fixed and monolithic (and see Goldhill 2001 for a collection of essays many of which argue along similar lines). Other important works have focused closely on the sophists, and on Philostratus' account of them. For example, Bowersock 1969 has mapped out the role of Greek sophists within the day-to-day life of the Roman world; Gleason 1995 offers a vivid portrait of two of the great sophists of the second century, Polemo and Favorinus, and of their rivalry; Whitmarsh 2005 is a good brief introduction to sophistic oratory in this period. Jones 1971, 1978 and 1986 demonstrates in depth the connections Plutarch, Dio, and Lucian have with the political and cultural figures and events around them. König 2009 is intended to offer basic orientation in the key texts and authors of Imperial Greek literature more broadly defined, including brief discussion of links with early Christian writing in that period. More focused studies on individual authors, texts and themes are far too numerous to list here. The Cambridge University Press monograph series "Greek Culture in the Roman World" covers a very wide range of topics. Schmitz and Wiater 2012 is a collection of essays that offer between them an overview of the Greek literature of the late Hellenistic world, and its connection with themes (especially the theme of identity) which had renewed importance in later centuries.

CHAPTER 8

The Encounter with Christianity

Jan Stenger

1. Two Different Cultures?

The title of this chapter implies three premises, which on closer consideration prove highly problematic. First, the idea of an encounter between Greek literature and Christianity is based on the assumption that it is possible to draw a sharp line between culture and religion as two inherently separated domains. Yet it is open to debate whether any person of Greek antiquity would have perceived religious allegiance in terms that have nothing to do with the culture in which the various cults were practiced. Secondly, to speak of an encounter means to posit an intrinsic opposition, or at least a clear-cut distinction, between two sufficiently independent entities, Greek culture and Christian faith, even if only to argue for an intermixing between them. Such a model imagines Christianity as a distinct cultural tradition seeking to take root in an alien environment. This notion, however, tends to overlook that Christianity originated within Greco-Roman society and grew up in a Hellenized context. In a certain sense, early Christians themselves contributed to this view, since they fashioned themselves as a distinct race, an *ethnos*, thus emphasizing otherness and difference. Thirdly, the title might give the impression that there was a single interaction between two uniform entities, as if it were feasible to discern the one Christian attitude to a monolithic Greek literature. Yet we should consider whether during the course of the Imperial age several encounters of Greek texts and Christian readers and authors took place, reflecting a variety of approaches, individual ideas and mutual influences. Nevertheless, it is legitimate to retain the term "encounter" if we are aware that it has a metaphorical nature and represents a broad spectrum of interactions.

This chapter therefore aims to clarify which effects the encounters of Greek literature with Christianity caused or, more specifically, the ways in which Christians adopted, or rejected, certain kinds of literary forms and conventions, further the extent to which they engaged in the discourse of literature surrounding them. This might lead to a more nuanced description of the relationship, which neither overstates distinctive features nor ignores the common characteristics that existed from the outset. Such an approach may enable us to discern the dynamic processes and the tensions which ultimately resulted in a transformed image of both Greek literature and ancient Christianity.

A Companion to Greek Literature, First Edition. Edited by Martin Hose and David Schenker.
© 2016 John Wiley & Sons, Inc. Published 2020 by John Wiley & Sons, Inc.

2.   Distance and Rejection

From its very beginnings, early Christianity was situated at the crossroads of two venerable and highly developed cultures, Judaism and Hellenism respectively. This combination of different traditions was reflected both in the community's religious practice and its relationship to literature. From its Jewish ancestry, Christianity inherited not only a body of fundamental Scriptures, which transmitted the word of God, to be supplemented in the course of centuries by genuinely Christian writings, but also the reading and exegesis of Scripture as the heart of religious activity. Texts achieved a central place in the communities since they taught the correct belief and the right way of life according to Christ's teaching. Thus, the believers sought authoritative truth in the writings and, simultaneously, guidance on a valuable conduct of life. This emphasis on literature set Christianity apart from Greco-Roman religion, which rested on the observation of obligations owed to the gods, but not on the development of doctrine. It was, however, by the same characteristic that Christianity resembled another important institution of Classical culture, namely the Hellenistic schools. For in the Greek tradition the educational system as dominated by rhetoric and philosophy focused on literature as a means of conveying moral principles and philosophical insight.

Considering the vital importance of texts and the school-like character of early Christianity, it comes as no surprise that its representatives soon devised genres which they considered useful for teaching belief and the Christian life. To preserve and disseminate the deeds and words of Christ, the earliest authors developed a literary form that concentrated on the person of the teacher, depicting Jesus' sayings, his life and his death. These accounts, written down (in chronological order) by Mark, Matthew, Luke and John, bear close similarities to other biographies of antiquity, yet also show significant differences. Whereas previous scholarship emphasized the oral and unliterary nature of the Gospels, more recent analyses have established a high degree of correlation between features of the Gospels and those noted in the Hellenistic *vita*, especially in the Lives of philosophers. Among the similarities are the medium-length size, the chronological structure and the selection of topics and motifs, which indicate a shared family resemblance. The style and the social setting of the Gospels are, however, more popular than most of the Lives. Noting the common features, scholars discuss not only the question of the literary genre of the Gospels but also its possible origins from ancient literary forms. A matter of debate is whether Mark wrote in the genre of the *vita* deliberately or whether he just fell into a natural biographical pattern; generally speaking, the analogies raise the issue of the setting of the Gospel within contemporary culture and of the level of the evangelists' literary awareness. What seems to be clear, though, is that Matthew and Luke attempted to improve Mark's style and to expand and develop his work to bring it into greater conformity with the conventions of the Hellenistic *vita*. This observation might allow the inference that both must have been aware of the similarity between Mark and the Lives, thus being familiar with contemporary literary discourse.

Alongside the Gospels, early Christian teaching was dominated by the form of the letter, which also displays features found in its Classical counterparts. Of the writings contained in our New Testament, the great majority present themselves as letters, the most famous of which are the fourteen traditionally attributed to Paul. In the Hellenistic world, letters were a common instrument of communication for a variety of purposes, ranging from business concerns to literary exchange between intellectuals. This flexible pattern even allowed for giving philosophical exhortation and advice or treating doctrines, whether ethical or cosmological, so that letters might function as short treatises. The integration of these forms into the letter was facilitated by their respective resemblance to modes of oral instruction. Their suitability for various aims made epistles also a valuable tool for the contact between Christian teachers and individuals or, more often, congregations and other groups. Form and function of the letters accordingly are very heterogeneous, and occasionally the pattern of the epistle serves as a frame for works of different genres. As to their relationship to the Hellenistic tradition of letter writing, Christian writers adopted some external features, in particular fixed formulas, which are found at the beginning and the end of the letter. Paul, who with his apostolic letters created the model for the later Christian epistles, took over such generic conventions but modified them significantly to adapt them to Christian needs. For instance, he closes his letters with a blessing in place of the customary "Farewell." Thus, in a similar way as the Gospels, the early letters, though departing from contemporary pagan texts through distinctive features, are after all rooted in the world of Greek literature.

The same consideration holds for a body of writings that is labeled apocryphal. These, although very popular, never found the way into the officially received, authoritative writings during the formative period of the New Testament canon (late second to mid-fourth century). A number of these texts, presented in a narrative mode, deal like the canonical Gospels primarily with the life and teaching of Jesus. Alongside the apocryphal gospels mention must be made especially of a group of works which relate the missionary activities of individual apostles, generally culminating in the apostle's martyrdom. While they invite comparison with the Acts of the Apostles, in that they give historical accounts of the early followers of Jesus, the apocrypha also betray a relationship to a secular genre that one might not expect as a model for religious writings. Although the Acts, stemming from the second and third centuries, convey and commend the beliefs and commitments of popular Christianity, in other words, perform a teaching function, they are meant to entertain and edify their reader even more than to instruct him. The reason for this is that they display characteristics familiar from the ancient novel, which flourished roughly in the same period. The most obvious parallels are the focus on the fate of individuals and the lively depiction of wonders and other unexpected events that advance the action. Despite the affinities with the Hellenistic romances one should note a contrast in style and content. Whereas apocryphal Acts have several narrative elements in common, including the important role of travels and the representation of gender and sexuality, they lack any plot in the strict sense, highlighting instead the works of saving power and showing a vital interest in martyrdom. Therefore, the relationship of the Christian "novelistic" literature to the Hellenistic novels is more complex than recognized by earlier scholarship, which understood the apocryphal *Acts* simply as expressions of Christianity in the form of a Classical genre. More accurately, the texts can be described as an antitype of the novels, inverting and undermining their ideology, thus challenging the traditional values of romantic love and the civic order of the Greek world.

What emerges from our brief overview of three popular forms of writing, Gospels, letters and apocryphal Acts, is that Christian literature shows analogies to various established genres, but does not conform precisely to any of them. Rather, the accounts of the deeds of Jesus and his followers and Paul's epistles make a creative use of generic conventions of contemporary writings, adapting them to the framework of Christian belief and thus transforming them for new purposes. Consequently, although the authors seem to have been acquainted with the conditions of literary production, it remains a controversial issue how close the affinity to Classical culture was and, furthermore, whether it is possible at all to classify Christian writings according to the established matrix of Classical genres. In addition to the coexistence of similarities and divergences or the combination of different generic elements in one single text, it is important to note that there are also works which, only loosely related to Greek parallels, arise from other traditions, most notably the prominent literary type of the apocalypse, a record of visions and revelations. Dealing with ultimate mysteries, the character of the divine realm and the course of cosmic history, the apocalypses stem from Jewish roots, thus entering Greek literature as a new "genre." Accordingly, literary norms as shaped by Classical expectations cannot account for all the features we encounter in Christian texts of the first centuries.

As the early Christians took an ambivalent stance towards the literary discourse of their time, so their attitude to the current cultural code, rhetoric, was informed by ambiguity. In spite of the school-like character of the Church, several of its representatives displayed serious reservations about the shared high culture of the Hellenistic world. Since the original Christians were, as the Bible had documented, people of low origin, unaffected by any higher education, there seemed to be no need to employ the means of Classical rhetoric in preaching; quite the reverse, polished eloquence was often suspected to be opposed to correct belief and simple truth. In a broader perspective, Christian authors expressed a feeling of cultural alienation, claiming that the believers constituted a distinguished community, a "third race", which lived among their fellow citizens as if they were strangers, set apart by purity of life (*Epistle to Diognetus* 5).

Yet at the same time, educated Christians deliberately began to exploit the instruments of Classical learning for their own religious purposes. This is documented by a paschal homily of Melito of Sardis (died c. 180), discovered in the twentieth century, which has fundamentally changed our understanding of the development of early Christian literature. Embellished with chiasms, antitheses, paradoxes, and alliterations, the sermon couches its discussion of Passover in the elaborate, rhythmical prose called "Asiatic," in which contemporary orators of the Second Sophistic, such as Aelius Aristides, dressed their rhetorical displays to enchant a learned audience. From these affinities it can be inferred that already in the Antonine age at least some preachers were willing to adjust their language and literary form to the standards of high culture so that they might also attract the educated, who expected serious thoughts to be expressed in an elaborate manner.

The matter was further complicated by the other branch of Classical education, philosophy, the more so as the schools, also addressing questions of ethics and theology, could be regarded as direct competitors to Christianity. In discussing the encounter with Hellenistic philosophy it has to be borne in mind that also in this domain Judaism had set a precedent, since its theology was from the beginning an object of reflection and investigation and, furthermore, in the Diaspora Judaism itself had been largely Hellenized. In line with this ongoing intercultural exchange, the earliest Christians, living in a Jewish environment, appear to have been markedly influenced by Hellenism. This can be illustrated with the New Testament writings, which occasionally relate explicit encounters between philosophers and Christians. Paul himself not only discussed his faith with the philosophers in Athens (*Acts* 17:18), but also warned against their deceitful teachings (*Col.* 2.8). According to these passages, he perceived the schools as rivals so that he attempted to replace their doctrines with a new "Christian philosophy."

Later on, in the second century, the Apologists more overtly used the intellectual instruments of philosophy in order to present and defend their belief. One of them, Iustinus, or Justin Martyr (died 165), devoted his life to the search for the "true philosophy," which, after an encounter with the philosophical schools, he eventually found in the Christian faith. In his view Christianity was superior to any kind of philosophy because it was proclaimed by the divine *Logos*, whereas the philosophers had only the abstract force of human reason. Consequently, Justin declared that all that is true in philosophy has to be considered the gift of God, thus claiming the insights of the philosophers for the Jewish–Christian tradition. Justin's reinterpretation, then, not only suggested that a thinker like Socrates could be understood as a Christian before Christ, but also argued that Plato's thoughts ultimately derived from the prophets of the Old Testament, as stated in his *First Apology*:

That you may learn that it was from our teachers – we mean the account given through the prophets – that Plato took his statement that God, having converted matter which was shapeless, created the world, hear the very words spoken through Moses, who was the first prophet and of greater antiquity than the Greek writers. (1. *Apol.* 59)

Following this line of argument some authors of the second century began to make a marked distinction between pagan philosophy and Christian faith in that they insisted that all cultural achievements of the Greeks actually belonged to the Jews or to barbarians. According to them, the truth as proclaimed by Scripture and transmitted to Christianity was older than the entire Greek culture.

Altogether, Christian thinking and teaching of the early decades was characterized by ambivalence towards the literature and culture of the surrounding world. On the one hand, the first Christian writers adopted genres and conformed to generic conventions, thereby expounding their message in the linguistic and literary code which was current in their days. To what degree they had received a higher education and had been trained in eloquence is, however, difficult to assess, because a general awareness of literary training permeated much more widely throughout society than just the formal teaching. On the other hand, in spite of the use of rhetorical and philosophical means, the writings of Christian authors reveal unease with, or at times an outright rejection of, the intellectual accomplishments of the Greeks. Thus, in the Christian engagement with Greek literature and learning we observe a variety of attitudes, which reflect not only the individual cultural background of the authors, but also document the possibilities of self-positioning in the interaction between Judaism, Hellenism, and emerging Christianity.

3.   The Correct Use

When we turn to the third century, the relationship between Christianity and Greek literature, though showing obvious continuities, undergoes a significant development, which was to pave the way for a more intimate mutual exchange. While Christian texts gradually entered Greek literary discourse from the fringes in the first two centuries, in the following decades they were becoming altogether more embedded in the cultural and linguistic worlds around them, and their genres reflect that process. As a result, Christian authors were increasingly adopting the techniques of the surrounding educated culture, and operating in a sophisticated literary world.

A striking example of the increasing orientation towards mainstream culture lies in the adoption of the methods of Hellenistic textual and literary criticism in commenting upon the books of Scripture. The outstanding representative of this strategy of appropriation is Origen (c. 185–254), an intellectual and prolific writer, who, after teaching in his home town of Alexandria, moved to Caesarea in Palestine, where he founded a school. Origen employed, for the first time in Christian literature, the traditional forms of Greek scholarship, including critical edition, commentary, and scientific treatise, to display his immense erudition and make it available for future generations. In his commentaries he used the methods and wrote in the terms of the textual criticism and exegetic literature developed by the Alexandrian school of philology for establishing the authenticity of ancient texts and illuminating their meaning. In order to set his interpretation on solid foundations, he conceived and prepared the *Hexapla*, an elaborate instrument for textual criticism of the Hebrew Scriptures. This gigantic scholarly work, which has not come down to us, presented six versions of the *Old Testament* scriptures side by side in parallel columns and was the basis for Origen's exegesis. Although grounded in the philological tradition, the learned activities of Origen differed in crucial ways from those of his pagan colleagues. What made his case peculiar was the nature of the texts on which he applied his interpretative tools. Whereas the Hellenistic grammatical tradition was decidedly Greek, largely ignoring foreign writings and traditions, he focused on a barbarian literature, composed in a non-Greek language, Hebrew. This intercultural synthesis of Greek approaches to learning with non-Greek material is characteristic of Origen's intellect. Hence, in the emergence of a formal biblical scholarship in the third century we encounter the same range of conformity with and departure from Classical patterns as already observed in literary production.

Further, Origen not only practiced biblical scholarship, but also reflected on the hermeneutical principles that guided his activity. His theory presupposes that there are three senses of Scripture: the literal, the moral, and the spiritual. Since alongside passages that are quite straightforward Scripture contains material which cannot be understood literally (e.g. metaphors and impossibilities), the reader is called upon to seek a deeper, hidden meaning in the text. The hermeneutical task is to employ different levels of interpretation corresponding to the three senses. Origen's chief interest was devoted to discerning the hidden, spiritual meaning of Scripture, for which purpose he applied the allegorical method developed in the philosophers' dealings with Homer's poems and especially with their anthropomorphic gods. Following in the footsteps of previous literary critics he conceived an elaborated theory of meaning-production through texts and the recovery of meaning by the interpreter. In doing so, Origen drew attention to the textual and literary dimension of the Bible, thereby aligning Scripture with the works of Hellenic literature.

It comes as no surprise that Christians simultaneously began to express ideas not only on their own writings and the literary forms they used, but also on Classical texts. These two aspects are documented in the work of Origen's teacher, Clement of Alexandria (c. 150–220, cf. Hose, this volume, ch. 21, pp. 334), in particular in his miscellaneous *Stromateis*, literally "patchwork." In this compendium in eight books, in order to prove that Christian thought is congruent with the best of philosophy, Clement assembled and quoted a wide range of Greek sources, mainly criticizing their views. Despite his aim of revealing the superiority of Christianity, his evaluation of Greek culture appears in general more positive than that of other Christians of his time. This attitude reflects Clement's intention to address likewise educated believers and the intelligent pagan (Clem. Al. *Strom.* 7.1.1.1), hence audiences who expected a certain cultural level of an author who wished to be taken seriously.

Moreover, Clement showed himself a conscious writer in that at the beginning of the *Stromateis* he discussed, as pagan authors had done before him, issues of genre and form and, in addition, the relationship between himself and his readers. While the text gives the impression of aimlessness, there is, as Clement claims, an underlying plan, which follows Greek models. He explains further why he has chosen this form and method, namely to conceal the truth from those who are not worthy of it. When elaborating on his teaching methods and the interaction between text and audience, Clement justifies his reception of Hellenic education, as the following passage illustrates:

> Like farmers who irrigate the land before, so we also water with the fresh stream of Greek learning what in it is earthy so that it may receive the spiritual seed thrown into it and may be capable of easily nourishing it. The *Stromateis* will contain the truth mixed together with the doctrines of philosophy, or rather veiled and concealed, as the edible part of the nut by the shell. For, in my opinion, it is fitting that the seeds of truth are kept exclusively for the farmers of faith. (1.1.17.4–18.1)

The opening section of Clement's longest and most important surviving work, as well as further remarks scattered throughout the text, shows us a Christian intellectual who consciously and carefully adopts the contemporary standards of literary discourse for his religious purposes. Fully aware of the conventions of the Classics, he decides to conform to them and to present his thoughts in the stylistic garment of the by then dominant Second Sophistic so that his work is able to participate in the ongoing intellectual debates.

The stance Clement and his disciple Origen took towards high culture also informed their encounter with pagan philosophy, which, as already hinted, was neatly connected to questions of literary presentation. Since the times of the pre-Socratics, philosophers had devised or adapted a variety of types to convey their doctrines to the best possible effect, ranging from didactic poetry to written dialogue to epistle. On this reservoir of philosophical modes of writing Clement and Origen drew as they set out to explain their belief. The former in his *Protrepticus* applied a pattern that philosophers from Socrates on had deployed to encourage readers to adopt their way of life. Yet, now this common genre, used for example by Aristotle and Cicero, served to argue polemically against Greek philosophy, advocating instead Christianity as the true philosophical existence, even though Clement made extensive use in it of Greek literature. Origen's treatise *On First Principles* also bears a close resemblance to a branch of philosophical writing as it closely follows the standard format treating "physics," that is, the relation of God to the created world.

The reception of pagan philosophy by Clement and Origen went, however, far beyond the adaptation of external features of teaching for Christian ends. Rather, they relied heavily on methods of philosophical argument and reasoning established by the Hellenistic schools. Furthermore, the educational programs of both thinkers betray their indebtedness to pagan predecessors, even where they deliberately depart from them. At Alexandria, Origen led his school not so much in the manner of a catechetical institution. Instead he implemented there a complete circle of studies such as was familiar from the traditional education system, yet devoted to a Christian philosophy. The impression of the curriculum as derived from Greek antecedents is at least what Origen's pupil, Gregory Thaumaturgus (c. 213–270) outlines in his farewell address to his teacher. According to him, it comprised a propaedeutic in the dialectics of the Socratic manner, studies in the natural sciences, morals and finally theology, which consisted of two stages, first interpretation and commentary on the most important Greek philosophers, then reading of Scripture, explained by Origen (*In Origenem* 7–15). In adjusting Christian teaching to the classical methods Origen was obviously influenced by the cultural climate of Alexandria, where Greek *paideia* and Jewish tradition had fruitfully combined for a long period.

The impact of philosophical culture was not confined, though, to the external shape of Origen's theological school. Rather, his entire way of thinking owed much to the intellectual environment, in particular to Platonism. It is safe to say that the Platonic tradition provided the intellectual framework for his view on the world and on Christian faith, even to the extent that his critics called into question whether he was a Christian or a Platonist. The pagan philosopher Porphyry has given us a revealing, if tendentious, picture of how Origen dressed his Christianity in a Classical guise:

> But Origen, having been educated as a Greek in Greek literature, rushed headlong into barbarian reck-lessness. And carrying over the skill in learning he hawked it about, living his life as a Christian and against the laws, but in his opinions of the world and of the divine being like a Greek and laying Greek teachings under strange fables. For he was continually studying Plato … (Euseb. *Hist. eccl.* 6.19.7–8)

It should, however, be emphasized here that Origen, though clearly indebted to Plato's thoughts, does not intend to turn Christianity into a philosophical school among others. Quite the reverse, he leaves no doubt that Hellenic philosophy, however precious and useful, has to be purified from its pagan, and therefore dangerous, entailments so that it might serve as propaedeutic studies for Christianity. With Christian religion being the highest form of philosophy, Classical culture is reduced to a subservient role.

The course of the third century witnessed a marked change in the relationship between Christianity and the surrounding literary world. While the earliest Christian authors, though not totally detached from the trends of contemporary culture, had no literary ambitions, later writers such as Clement and Origen not only received a higher education and were "Hellenized" to a certain extent, but also were ready to conform to the conventions of literary discourse. On the one hand, the willingness to adopt the dominant code manifested itself in the intensive use of concrete techniques and methods of literary criticism and philosophy; on the other hand, their writings reflect a sophisticated literary awareness, documented by the deliberate choice of certain genres and by comments on issues of composition and reading. Furthermore, the reception of philosophy, particularly Platonism, resulted in the emergence of an actual Christian philosophy well prepared to enter controversial debates with pagan opponents. Altogether, these developments point to the fact that Christianity embraced the cultural environment to a higher degree than before.

4.   The Decisive Shift

The next stage in the emergence of a Greek Christian literature was reached with the era of the Roman emperor Constantine and the consequences his politics had for late Antique society. After the final attempt to eradicate Christianity at the beginning of the fourth century, the situation was completely reversed when, under Constantine, the Church became tolerated and gained the emperor's patronage. These measures brought about the spread of belief throughout the Empire, involving the gradual Christianization of the imperial aristocracy and eventually the suppression of the traditional cults. Consequently, more members of the well-off families embraced Christian faith, which profoundly influenced the ways in which Christian authors represented doctrines and ideas on religious practice. More precisely, as Christianity permeated the elite, who had been brought up for generations according to the inherited cultural norms, it seemed inevitable to reconsider the value of the literary heritage within the new religious framework and to clarify the stance on education. For similar reasons, the amount of works produced by Christian writers increased considerably, and novel types were devised to address new audiences.

The issue of how to deal with Classical culture remained a cause for misgivings. Inevitably, by virtue of the continuing Christianization of all ranks of society, the believers were faced with serious questions of self-definition and identity, the more so as not every convert adopted the new faith out of religious feelings, let alone was willing to abandon his entrenched habits. In particular those who had grown up in the traditional culture had to reconcile their education with their belief if they did not want to break with their intellectual framework and the entire way of life. This dilemma vexed, for example, the Greek spokesman of the Christian Roman Empire under Constantine, the Church Father Eusebius of Caesarea (c. 260–339). In his constant struggle to defend his religion against learned critics and in his discussion of the three sources of religious identity – Judaism, Hellenism, and Christian tradition – Eusebius seeks to define and negotiate boundaries and to establish a self-definition that might integrate different cultural traits. Even though he stresses the superiority of faith, he refuses to relinquish the best of philosophy and literature to the pagans. In his view, Christian identity lies across ethnic categories so that Hellenic civilization also belongs to the cultural heritage of Christianity (*Praeparatio Evangelica* 1.5.10).

That Classical literature and learning were of vital importance for the self-fashioning of the educated faithful became evident when the last pagan emperor, Julian the "Apostate," himself brought up as a Christian, endeavored to exclude Christians from the whole of Greek culture. In order to deprive them of the advantages of education, in particular of political influence, he issued an edict that tied literature and culture on the one hand and pagan religion on the other hand inextricably together, or rather identified them as one. This measure posed a severe threat to all, such as the Cappadocian bishop Gregory Nazianzen (c. 329–390), who testified by their lives to the synthesis of Greek culture and Christian faith. Thus, the emperor's teaching law reinforced once more the need for Christian intellectuals to define their own position with regard to the Classics. Gregory, a productive author and a skilled rhetorician, launched a harsh attack against Julian's policy, even though only after the emperor's death. In his oration against the Apostate he sarcastically pointed out the absurdity of Julian's conception of education: "Is it only to you that *Hellenizein* belongs? ... Is it only to you that *Attikizein* belongs? ... Is it only to you that poetry belongs?" (*Oration* 4.107–8) Since in Gregory's view culture and literature were disconnected from any religious adherence, no community could lay claim to them. What Gregory in his desire to integrate the heritage of Hellenism into a Christian identity downplayed, however, was that a great deal of the Classical literature put forward ideas which were not easy to reconcile with Christian dogma, a point that Julian had deliberately picked out for his attack.

Not all believers of the Greek-speaking world subscribed to Gregory's appreciation of learning. The fourth century saw the rise to great popularity of the monastic movement, advocating a conduct of life that was markedly different from that of the urban elite. Alongside the spread of monastic culture in the Roman East, a new, popular literary form emerged to become one of the preeminent genres in the following centuries. Hagiography promoted the new role model, depicting the lives of the saints with vivid details, extolling their miracles, and culminating in the death of the saint and his continued activity. The particular shape of the narration was mainly influenced by two factors. First, the Lives of the saints, giving an account of a life from its beginnings to the end, displayed similarities to secular biographies, first and foremost to those of the philosophers. Secondly, however, the nature of the saint's Life was more deeply affected by the evolving cult of the saint or martyr. The most influential exemplar was the *Life of Antony* by his contemporary, the bishop of Alexandria, Athanasius (ca. 298–373). What is worth mentioning is that the author decided to make the lack of schooling a sign of the holiness of the Egyptian monk. Athanasius portrays Antony as uneducated and illiterate, a prophet taught by God alone, yet an accomplished philosopher. The most evident passages on Antony's "natural" wisdom are the stories of his three encounters with pagan philosophers, which reveal that, despite his lack of education, the monk's intelligence surpasses the human and therefore futile logic. In all debates, though, Antony himself argues like a paragon of the traditional schools. Paradoxically, the authors of the *Lives* conformed to pagan literary conventions and methods of classical education, but only to expose secular erudition as unnecessary or even detrimental for Christian faith and conduct. In doing so they again raised the question of how Christian truth, being a revelation handed down to simple fishermen, could meet the standards of the intellectual elite. A rustic, illiterate monk, living in the desert, hardly was a model for urban Christians, not to mention for well-educated bishops.

The ambivalence towards Classical culture was felt and explicitly noticed by such Christian intellectuals who, after having received an education in the schools, came into contact with different forms of Christian existence, especially with monasticism and asceticism. Their conscious and unconscious tensions are evidenced best by the three Cappadocian Fathers, Basil of Caesarea (330–379), his brother Gregory of Nyssa (c. 335–385), and Gregory Nazianzen, as well as by the somewhat younger John Chrysostom (c. 349–407), all born into Christian families. As seen above with Gregory Nazianzen, they exemplified in their own lives that faith and Classical education could come together, but also that this relationship constantly caused qualms. The central problem was of how to deal with literature, which lay at the heart of traditional schooling.

A pragmatic solution to this problem was suggested by Basil's famous *Address to Young Men*. The treatise does not reject pagan literature altogether, but emphasizes the need to distinguish in it what is morally useful and compatible with belief and what is harmful. Thus, the relevance and value of pagan literary works depend on the "correct use" (*chrêsis*) that the reader makes of them guided by Christian morality. By this measure Basil defends the benefits of secular education so that future Church leaders could function as effectively as other educated people. A different answer was given by Chrysostom, who himself turned from pagan to Christian masters, in his treatise *Concerning the Education of Children*. Although he does not deny the advantages of secular schooling for members of the upper classes, he puts reading and discussing the Bible center stage. Chrysostom even gives detailed advice on how to present Biblical narratives so that they are simultaneously attractive reading and edifying to the children. Basil's and Chrysostom's attempts to grapple with the relation of Christianity to pagan literature both document the awareness that the imperial society, though gradually Christianized, could not dispense with Classical literature and learning, unless it were cut off from its cultural heritage. On the other hand, as a consequence of the religious changes, the persistent cultural norms had to be adapted to and integrated into a Christian framework.

Basil's and Chrysostom's reflections on the value of literature bear witness to a phenomenon that can be discerned in the literary production of several late antique Christians. As they considered issues of style and effects on the reader, so they discussed in their own works the genres and stylistic shape they chose, or their ideas of the relation between author and audience. Occasionally, they present themselves not only as self-conscious literati, but also express pride of their literary accomplishments. A case in point is Eusebius who wanted to let his readers know that with his seminal *Church History* he had devised a new genre without any exact predecessor in the history of literature.

> Being the first to enter upon the subject I am attempting to traverse as it were a lonely and unused path. I pray that I may have God as my guide and the power of the Lord as my aid, since I am unable to find even the bare footsteps of those who have traveled the same way before me, except in brief remarks, in which some in one way, others in another, have transmitted to us particular accounts of the times they lived in. (Euseb. *Hist. eccl.* 1.1.3)

This bold claim was justified, since historians of Classical antiquity, for reasons of rhetorical elegance, had avoided incorporating documentary evidence such as letters or edicts in the original into their account. Eusebius, on the contrary, made ample use of direct quotations while dismissing long speeches and the adorned style typical of historiography.

Of particular interest in this respect are the writings of the Cappadocians, which throughout attest to their authors' high erudition. Gregory of Nyssa, himself active as a teacher of rhetoric in his early career, is not only a classicist in style, influenced by the Second Sophistic, and in this comparable to contemporary rhetoricians like Libanius, but also pays much attention to matters of literary form. He explains in his prefaces which genre he is going to use and what the appropriate style or length is in a particular context, or when it may be suitable to combine two genres in a special case. There is always discernable a deliberate planning in his choice of the various forms for different purposes, whether treatise, sermon, dialogue, or letter. Similar observations hold for Gregory Nazianzen, who aspired to create a veritable Christian literature to rival at least the contemporary pagan literature. To this end he embellished his homilies and letters with a vast number of allusions to and quotations of Homer, the tragic poets, Pindar and Plato, as was the practice among erudite writers. In addition, Gregory sought to offer worthwhile products of every type, thereby demonstrating that Christian literature was able to compete with the Classical authors in the whole spectrum of literary activity. Besides his numerous homilies, treatises and letters he left behind a massive body of more than 300 poems close to 18,000 verses, mostly written after his retirement in the 380s. In these poems, which cover a broad range of subjects from autobiography to dogma, Gregory several times points out the choice of verse, for instance by claiming that he employs it for the benefit of the young, in particular those who take pleasure in literature, to furnish them with a kind of sweet medicine (*Poem* 2.1.39.37–41). Furthermore, he demonstrates his poetical skill by making use of a great variety of forms familiar from Classical poetry, including hymns and didactic poems in hexameters, epigrams and occasional poems in elegiacs, and invectives in iambics.

In Synesius of Cyrene (c. 373–414), a further example of the presence of highly educated literary stylists in the episcopate, we see that Christian intellectuals not only had full command of the instruments and registers of Classical literature, but were not even afraid to express thoughts that owed less to Christian faith than to Greek culture. As a member of the provincial elite and a disciple of the Neoplatonist philosopher Hypatia, Synesius agreed to take over the see of his home town only when he was granted permission to retain his philosophical tenets, which notably deviated from Christian dogma. This particular intellectual stance, the syncretism of Neoplatonism, Classical culture, and Christian faith, is clearly documented by his nine hymns, the external features of which (e.g., meter and the Doric dialect) betray in every aspect the poet's great erudition. Never meant to serve in liturgy but purely literary pieces, the hymns speak of the Trinity and of Christ in philosophical terms, not so much in theological ones. Furthermore, Jesus is depicted as a divine hero, a new Hercules, performing similar actions as his mythological counterpart. It is by this intellectual ease of switching between cultural codes and conventions that in the fifth century Nonnus of Panopolis composed epics both of the god Dionysus and of Jesus. His impressive oeuvre consists of a hexameter poem on the life and deeds of the wine-god in 48 books, the largest surviving epic from antiquity, and of a poetical paraphrase of John's Gospel. Nonnus' *Dionysiaca* illustrate best that mythology still was an indispensable component of education and that Christianization did not make any difference in this regard.

In the period commonly referred to as the "Golden Age" of Patristic literature the decisive change took place in the interaction between Christian writing and the surrounding Greek culture. The more Christianity made its way into the heart of Imperial society, the less sustainable became the view that it formed an alternative society with an alternative culture and an alternative literature. Christian authors, although they continued to feel unease with the concomitants of Greek education and literature and, in addition, were highly conscious of these tensions, showed a greater willingness to make the Classical tradition an integral part of their own cultural heritage and a cornerstone of their self-definition. Appreciation of literary accomplishments or philosophical argumentation, it is true, was still far from being taken for granted, but, since Christianity was no longer considered a religion of the lower classes, it was inevitable to address issues of faith and conduct according to the conventions of the current discourse. As Christianity gradually diffused into all areas of life, while the pagan cults ceased, Christian literature eventually became coextensive with Greek literature, capable also of treating purely secular themes or even secularized mythology.

5. Conclusion

After centuries of continued encounter or coexistence of Christianity and Greek literature, the appearance of both was finally transformed, due to the shifting attitudes of the faithful towards the Hellenic world. Roughly speaking, three stages can be distinguished, though they do not strictly succeed one another: rejection, selective use, and coextension. From the outset, Christianity was at the interface of different cultures or cultural environments, moving forward from the periphery of Greek culture to the center. During this process, Christian literature was gradually transformed by its embracing Classical education, while on the other hand it had a strong impact on Greek literature (e.g., genres, themes, social setting, functions) until it superseded, or rather became coextensive with it. Accordingly, this process was not a one-way relationship of Classical influence on Christian writing or vice versa. Rather, it can be regarded as a complex interplay of rejection, appropriation, transformation, enrichment and replacement, a development we may term "osmosis." In the end, Greek literature assumed a different shape or character than it had before its encounter with Christianity. More generally speaking, we can observe how deeply religious (and socio-political) changes affect the system of literature. In conclusion, the framework in which Greek literature was embedded changed by virtue of the rise of Christianity.

REFERENCES

Aune, D. 2003. *The Westminster Dictionary of New Testament and Early Christian Literature and Rhetoric.* Louisville, KY.

Brown, P. 1992. *Power and Persuasion in Late Antiquity: Towards a Christian Empire.* Madison, WI.

Buell, D. K. 1999. *Making Christians: Clement of Alexandria and the Rhetoric of Legitimacy.* Princeton, NJ.

Burridge, R. A. 2004. *What Are the Gospels? A Comparison with Graeco-Roman Biography.* 2nd edn. Grand Rapids, MI.

Cameron, A. 1998. "Education and Literary Culture." In A. Cameron and P. Garnsey, eds., *The Cambridge Ancient History, Vol. XIII: The Late Roman Empire, A.D. 337–425,* Cambridge, 665–707.

Chadwick, H. 2001. *The Church in Ancient Society: From Galilee to Gregory the Great.* Oxford.

Döpp, S. and W. Geerlings, eds. 2000. *Dictionary of Early Christian Literature.* New York.

Edwards, M. J. et al., eds. 1999. *Apologetics in the Roman Empire: Pagans, Jews, and Christians.* Oxford.

Harvey, S. A. and D. G. Hunter, eds. 2008. *The Oxford Handbook of Early Christian Studies.* Oxford.

Heine, R. E. 2010. *Origen: Scholarship in the Service of the Church.* Oxford.

Hock, R. F. et al., eds. 1998. *Ancient Fiction and Early Christian Narrative.* Atlanta, GA.

Moreschini, C., and E. Norelli. 2005. *Early Christian Greek and Latin Literature: A Literary History.* 2 vols. Peabody, MA.

Ridings, D. 1995. *The Attic Moses: The Dependency Theme in Some Early Christian Writers.* Gothenburg.

Schäublin, C. 1974. *Untersuchungen zu Methode und Herkunft der antiochenischen Exegese.* Cologne.

Young, F., L. Ayres, and A. Louth, eds. 2004. *The Cambridge History of Early Christian Literature.* Cambridge.

FURTHER READING

A comprehensive account of Christian Greek literature is given by the collection of Young, Ayres and Louth 2004. Part VI of Harvey and Hunter 2008 provides excellent surveys of recent research on the important Christian literary genres. Basic information on Greek Christian authors and their works can be found in the historical overview of Moreschini and Norelli 2005. Also helpful are the various entries in the lexica of Döpp and Geerlings 2000, and of Aune 2003. For detailed discussion of the relationship between the Gospels and biographical texts see Burridge 2004. The collection of essays in Hock et al. 1998 compares the New Testament writings and the apocryphal Acts with the form and content of ancient fiction. The articles in Edwards et al. 1999 examine the origins and purposes of apologetic literature in the first four centuries. Cameron 1998 is an excellent introduction to the literary culture of late antiquity shared by pagans and Christians, whereas Brown 1992 focuses on the dominance of rhetoric. For the general history of ancient Christianity see Chadwick 2001.

PART III

Genres

CHAPTER 9

Greek Epic

Hanna M. Roisman

In memoriam *of my beloved teacher, Zeev Wolfgang Rubinsohn*

We generally think of an epic poem as a long narrative poem on a serious subject, featuring heroic deeds and involving events significant to a culture or nation. The ancient Greeks, though, defined poems as epics as much by their meter as by their content. Virtually all poems in dactylic hexameter were termed epics.[1] To distinguish epics with different types of contents and purposes, they are classified into sub-genres. This chapter discusses the heroic epic, which relates the deeds of heroes; the didactic epic, which aims at teaching a specific subject matter; and the mock epic, which parodies the heroic epic. More specifically, it discusses the extant epics in each of these sub-genres.[2]

The fundamental differences in the three sub-genres make it difficult to formulate meaningful generalizations about the Greek epic as a whole, as does the very long time span, ranging from Homer, probably in the eighth century BCE, through Nonnus in the fifth century CE (where the discussion in this chapter will end) and beyond. Compounding the difficulty is that most of the ancient Greek epics are lost to us, leaving large gaps in our knowledge. Moreover, since the didactic epics do not have any heroes, only two subjects, as far as I can tell, link them all and allow for a connected discussion of them: the treatment of the gods, and the development of the epic from the poems attributed to Homer and Hesiod, both of whom left an indelible imprint on ancient Greek and Roman literature and well beyond.

In this chapter, I will focus on the latter subject. My aim is not to ferret out the many allusions and parallels to Homer and Hesiod in the other epics. Reams have been written on this subject, discussing in minute detail the adoptions and adaptations by later epic poets of distinctive features of the Homeric language and style and borrowings from Hesiod. What I am interested in conveying is how the Homeric and, to a lesser extent, the Hesiodic, epics served as points of departure for the epic writers that followed them. By "point of departure" I mean both the place at which one starts and the place one leaves. In particular, I will look at the epics' movement away from the Homeric model, as each poet wrote in his own voice about the matters that interested him. The discussions are necessarily brief, and leave out a good deal of information and observations about the Greek epic. The aim is to provide a coherent guide to very disparate works and to arouse interest in them.

A Companion to Greek Literature, First Edition. Edited by Martin Hose and David Schenker.
© 2016 John Wiley & Sons, Inc. Published 2020 by John Wiley & Sons, Inc.

I

Only four epics from the Archaic period have survived more or less intact: Homer's heroic epics *Iliad* (15,778 lines) and *Odyssey* (12,109 lines), believed to have taken their present shape in the eighth century BCE and put into writing by the sixth century, and two didactic epics attributed to Hesiod, born in Ascra in Boeotia, probably no earlier than 750 BCE or later than 720 BCE: *Theogony* (1,022 lines), and *Works and Days* (828 lines).[3]

1. *Iliad* and *Odyssey*

The poet(s) of the *Iliad* and *Odyssey* were consummate storytellers. In both epics, plot, character, and theme converge in a cohesive and compelling whole. The *Iliad*, as announced in line 1, sings the theme of Achilles' wrath (*mēnis*),[4] and the plot focuses on and develops that theme. The poem starts in *medias res*, towards the end of the ten-year-long Trojan War. It deals only with a limited period of time (56 days), which enables the depiction of persons and events in detail and depth. It starts with the poet's plea to the Muse to sing of the wrath of Achilles and its devastation, then quickly moves to the council of the warriors, showing how Agamemnon provokes that anger by appropriating Achilles' concubine *cum* spoil of war Briseis. Most of the *Iliad*'s subsequent events – the foundering of the Greeks as their best fighter nurses his anger; the failed mission to persuade Achilles to rejoin the fighting; the death of Patroclus at the hands of Hector, the Trojans' best warrior; Achilles' rage and remorse, which finally bring him back to the battlefield to avenge Patroclus's death; his furious slaughter of the Trojan warriors, his manhandling of Hector's corpse, and his initial dishonorable refusal to allow him a proper burial – derive from the wrath that drives Achilles and combine to demonstrate the destructive implications of this character trait which, perhaps more than any other, makes for a good fighter and meets the needs of war.

Achilles' absence from most of the fighting enables the Homeric muse to depict with nuance and detail a varied band of warrior-heroes, at once great and flawed, whose special abilities complement one another's. While Achilles is described as the Greeks' best fighter, Odysseus is drawn as their most eloquent, resourceful, and diplomatic (*Il.* 3.216–23; Rutherford 2011). Diomedes displays both the enthusiasm and impulsiveness of youth, Nestor the experience and garrulousness of age, although Agamemnon considers him their best counselor (Roisman 2005; Andersen 2011). Agamemnon shows himself as arrogant and easily deluded, but he is nonetheless the respected leader of the band, with more initiative and determination than Menelaus, who shows a measure of kindness that his brother lacks (Roisman 2011; Van Nortwick 2011). On the Trojan side, Hector's valor and sense of responsibility show up Paris's dandyism, selfishness, and reluctance to exert himself (Griffin 2011b; Schein 2011). Several of the heroes make mistakes that cost the lives of their comrades. All reveal a degree of complexity: the courageous Odysseus runs from battle (*Il.* 8.87–98); the angry Achilles utters some of the most tender and moving lines in the entire epic (e.g., 1.160–68; 9.3217; 16.7–19; 18.98–126). All are compelling, larger-than-life figures.

The action is propelled by the interventions of the gods and by the interactions of the characters, who variously plan and improvise, argue with or support one another, and confront their enemies. Tension – and interest – are generated not only by the graphic descriptions of the battles but also, and even more so, by the conflicts or disagreements among the characters, which arouse in one a desire to hear what they have to say, to know what they think, and to see how they will resolve their clash of wills and respond to the challenges they constantly face. The whole is brought to a satisfying end, both in terms of the plot and the theme, after the funeral games for Patroclus and divine intervention, when Achilles, his anger sated, yields to Priam's pleas to allow Hector a proper burial.

While the *Iliad* supplied later writers with models of the warrior hero, the *Odyssey*, probably composed later than the *Iliad*, provided the model of the daring and resourceful wanderer, the "man of many devices (*polytropos*)," as we are told in the first line, who emerges triumphant from one fantastic adventure after another. Like the *Iliad*, the *Odyssey* focuses only on part of a longer story, forty days in the tenth year of Odysseus's wanderings, shortly before he returns to Ithaca. Its twin strands, man's longing for home and the son's search for his father, are reflected in the interweaving of the stories of Odysseus and Telemachus. The narrative begins simultaneously with Telemachus leaving Ithaca to obtain news of his father and Odysseus's departure from Calypso's island, where he had languished for seven years, and draws to a close with their meeting in Ithaca and their cooperation in slaying the suitors, who have despoiled their home and would deprive Odysseus of his wife and Telemachus of his inheritance. In between, Odysseus's long retrospective narration to the Phaeacians of his adventures leading up to his arrival on their island reveals aspects of his character that warn them not to try to keep him there against his will and persuade them to supply him with the means to return home (Ahl and Roisman 1996, 71–151). Though disparate, the adventures are well connected. Each, more fraught than the previous one, serves as a way-station in Odysseus's journey home and in his struggle with the forces of nature, represented by the sea that constantly tosses him about and by the witches, monsters, and other entities that tempt him, endanger him, and require him to exercise his wits and self control to overcome them.

2. *Theogony* and *Works and Days*

The two earliest didactic epics attributed to Hesiod, the *Theogony*, which tells of the succession of the gods and the battles that led to the pre-eminence of Zeus as the beneficent *cum* punitive ruler of the world, and *Works and Days*, which provides counsel on how to live a just and successful life, resemble the above discussed heroic epics in major ways. They, too, were composed in dactylic hexameter, a meter that apparently lent itself to long narrative recitations. And they, too, start with an invocation to the muses. Yet the famous distinction in the *Theogony* between muses that tell the truth and those that tell lies (26–8) and the poet's statement at the start of *Works and Days* that his purpose is to tell his brother Perses the truth (10) set these epics apart from the heroic epics. Given the lack of elaboration, it is impossible to say with any certainty what the poet meant by truth. It is clear, though, from both poems that he considered myth and fable, and the imaginative descriptions of how they unfolded, within its realm. But the distinction neatly fits the difference between the heroic epic, where telling a compelling story is central, and the didactic epic, where the aim is to convey information. With this distinction, the poet implies that his purpose is to tell the truth, not a well-integrated, riveting story, in which the characters, gods and men alike, move the plot forward.

This does not mean that the didactic epics are without beauty. The muses, as described in *Theogony*, have the double duty of relaying "what will be and what was before" (38) and of doing so harmoniously and melodiously. Far from being a dry succession of "begats," the *Theogony* is filled with lines whose music lifts them off the page. It conveys wonder and awe at the beauty of the world and the power of the deities, for good and for ill. The myriad gods and spirits who populate the universe of the poem imbue it with their vitality, while the gods themselves are brought to life through thumbnail descriptions. For example, in the account of Zeus's birth, the story of how Rhea gets her parents' advice and help in preventing her husband, Kronos, from swallowing the infant Zeus, as he had his other children, is told vividly and succinctly (467–91).

Moreover, the *Theogony* is filled with drama and conflict: Earth and Kronos against Uranus, Rhea and her parents; Earth and Uranus against Kronos and Zeus; the conflict between Prometheus and Zeus; and the ten-year war between the Olympians and Titans, which the

Olympians win with the assistance of the Hundred-Handers whom they had freed of their chains for the purpose. In its vivid descriptions of the battles, Hesiod's poem most resembles the Homeric epics. The resemblance is especially prominent in the second half of the poem, which tells how Zeus defeats his enemies and consolidates his governance. The dialogue in which Zeus asks Obriareus, Cottus, and Gyges to fight on his side (644–63) is reminiscent of dialogues between heroes of the *Iliad*. As in the *Iliad*, each party is presented with dignity, each sets out his position in a logical manner, and the conclusions they reach issue in the next action and beyond. The account of the battle with the Titans, like the battle scenes in the *Iliad*, is filled with the terror and noise of clashing armies, as fighters shout, missiles are hurled, and fires scorch the earth. So is the account of the single combat between Zeus and Typhoeus, the storm god, in which the clash of the "warriors" is rendered as a colossal upheaval of nature.

Nonetheless, the *Theogony* is better in its parts than its whole. The story is secondary. The conflicts that endow it with a measure of tension are inherent in the succession myths on which Hesiod drew (for which see West 1966: 1–16), as is the chronological order which provides the poem with its basic structure; though, in fact, the movement from one episode to the next is sometimes difficult to follow.

Works and Days consists largely of advice on how to lead a just and successful life and focuses on the concerns of ordinary people, farmers and traders and seamen who have to earn their living in uncertain conditions. Neither its contents nor its focus lend themselves to heroic or even dramatic treatment. Nor, as far as Hesiod is concerned, do they require a plot in which the audience, eager to know what will happen, is propelled from one incident to the next. The epic consists largely of disparate elements: an account of the two types of strife, stories of Pandora and the ages of man, the fable of the hawk and the nightingale, an exhortation to justice and to work, advice on being successful, the farmer's calendar and guide for the merchant sailor, and a collection of social and religious counsels. The fact that all the advice is addressed to Perses, Hesiod's brother, provides a loose framework, and the motif of Zeus's justice endows the parts with a certain coherence, as it does the incidents in the *Theogony*. However, Perses is mentioned or addressed only sporadically (10, 27, 286, 299, 397, 611, 641), with large gaps during which the personal advice to him flows into moral generalizations that pertain to all.

There are three stories in the epic – of Prometheus and Pandora, of the four ages of man, and the brief fable of the hawk and the nightingale – wedged between the preceding account of the two types of strife and the moral and practical counsel that take up the last two-thirds of the work. Each story provides a different perspective on, or explanation for, the suffering and injustice that Hesiod sees as the lot of human beings. But they are discrete stories, with no connection other than the theme of human suffering. Any of them could have been cut without being missed or other stories added without disrupting a non-existent flow. The remainder of the poem reads like a how-to book whose moral and practical precepts were rendered in verse because verse was the medium of instruction.

II

The next epics that have come down to us in full are of three different sub-genres. *Phaenomena* or *Visible Signs* or *Appearances* is a didactic epic describing the night sky, written by Aratus, a Greek of Soli in Cilicia, written in the third century BCE. The *Argonautica* by Apollonius Rhodius, is a heroic epic, also written in the third century BCE, telling the story of the Argonauts' pursuit of the golden fleece. *The Battle of the Frogs and Mice* (*Batrachomyomachia*) is a mock epic or "play poem" of unknown authorship and dating. The ancients attributed it to Homer, but modern scholars have dated it anywhere between the sixth and first century BCE (Rotstein 2011). All three poets built upon their predecessors and, in keeping with the fashion of their time, expected their audiences to recognize their allusions and to appreciate the originality of their own renditions (Kidd 1997, 8–10).

3.   Aratus's *Phaenomena*

The best-regarded in a long tradition of astronomical poems that preceded it, and from which Aratus doubtless gleaned both inspiration and artistry, is *Phaenomena* (1,154 lines). Its debts to the language and style of Homer and to themes and stories in Hesiod have been exhaustively noted. But Aratus has essentially left the world of Homer behind and, as scholars have noted, outstripped Hesiod both in his ability to move from point to point in an intelligible and compelling manner and within a cohesive structure, and also in the artistry and sophistication of his style (Lesky 1966, 750–52; Kidd 1997, 5–42).

As befits a pupil of Zeno of Citium (335–263 BCE), Aratus incorporates Stoic thinking into the poem. Scholars point especially to the image of Zeus in the *Hymn to Zeus* by Cleanthes, Zeno's successor as head of the Stoic school in Athens (Kidd 1997, 10–12). Unlike the punitive and angry Hesiodic Zeus, the Stoic Zeus is the life-force of the universe from which we all gather our existence and the rational power that directs everything for the best. Aratus combines the Zeus of the traditional religion with the Stoic one. As Kidd points out (1997, note on line 1) the entire poem displays the presence of Zeus. Zeus is the sky (e.g. 224, 259), the weather god (e.g. 293, 426), the creator of constellations (11, 265), the pervading life force (e.g. 1–4), the benefactor (e.g. 5–10), but also the mythological god (e.g. 31).

To the modern reader, Aratus's subject matter, the array of the heavenly bodies and their impact on climatic and weather conditions on earth, is no more dynamic or compelling than that of Hesiod's *Works and Days*, and we certainly have more accurate information than Aratus provides. Yet *Phaenomena* is a work of extraordinary vitality and excitement. In the first part of the epic, Aratus leads his hearers or readers through the night sky like a tour guide, directing their attention to the various sites, describing and explaining what they see, telling the occasional story, and, above all, sharing with them his wonder at the beauty and power of all that he shows them (e.g. 473). In the *Theogony*, Hesiod had anthropomorphized Night, as he had the other deities. Aratus helps his audience to visualize the constellations by describing them as animals (real or imagined), people, or natural phenomena (e.g. rivers). In doing so, he obviously relied on the names they bore. But he went further, rendering the abstract geographic and mathematical relations among them in pictorial terms and endowing the constellations with motion and will. Thus, the night sky becomes intensely alive. The Bears roll their wagons in opposite directions (26–30) as the Dragon, in between them, reaches over them with the tip of his tail, and a man toiling at some unknown labor has his right foot on the Dragon's head and his arms raised (45–70). Andromeda is threatened by the approach of the great Sea Monster, as the Fish's tail chains converge behind the Monster's back fin (353–66). Examples abound, as the constellations "sweep" across the sky (443).

The tour is a delight and rich with detail. Intermingled with the descriptions of the constellations are climatic, sailing, and agricultural information, along with stories and explanations. We learn about the changes in the position of constellations in different seasons, and when they are and are not visible, their origin and birth, as well as why most of the stars are not named individually (373–6), and a host of other things. The information is provided without a predetermined pattern but always seems pertinent to the stars and constellations being discussed.

The story is also interesting and appealing, brought to life by interjections of the author's voice and concerns. To take only one example of the latter, after pointing out the impossibility of identifying the moving stars, Aratus expresses the hope that he is adequate to expounding the circles of the fixed stars (460–61). The introduction of the authorial voice goes back to the poet's account in the *Theogony* of how he was personally inspired by the Muses (22–5) and to the poet's address to his brother Perses in *Works and Days*. Hesiod, however, remonstrated from a position of superiority and his tone was often sour and censorious. Aratus's voice is amiable, varied, and engaging. Thus, as he moves from describing the sky to explaining how to determine the time of month and to anticipate the weather conditions from the appearance of the sun and moon, his tone shifts appropriately from that of tour guide to that of an eager but gentle instructor who enjoins his students to "take pains to learn" (759), "pay attention" (819, 880), "study" (832, 778), and who cautions them not to neglect signs of a storm (973) or impending fire (983).

4.   Apollonius of Rhodes's *Argonautica*

The legend of the Argonauts' pursuit of the golden fleece is one of the earliest known to the Greeks. In the mythic chronology, it took place a generation before the Trojan War (*Argon.* 1.556–8). Both the *Iliad* and the *Odyssey*, assume their audience's familiarity with it (*Il.* 2.711–15; 7.467–9; *Od.* 10.135–9, 11.252–9; 12.3–4, 59–72).

Apollonius was not only a poet, but, like his teacher and friend the influential poet and literary critic Callimachus, also a learned critic of Greek literature.[5] His *Argonautica* conducts a dialogue with the Homeric epics (Carspecken 1952; Hunter 1993 *passim*).[6] The author's declaration that he will tell the "glorious deeds" (1.1) of men born long ago brings to mind Homer's account of the closely knit band of Argive warriors in the *Iliad*. The Argonauts' adventure-filled sea voyage to bring back the golden fleece recalls Odysseus's perilous voyage back to Ithaca. Like Odysseus, the Argonauts sail from place to place in treacherous seas, encounter a succession of mythical peoples and monsters, and overcome a variety of temptations and dangers before returning home. There are also parallel incidents. Yet even as the *Argonautica* clearly sounds its Homeric legacy, it conscientiously diverges from the Homeric model in its structure, characterization, and realization of its theme.

Structurally, where the Homeric epics are dynamic, the *Argonautica* is linear and static. Both the *Iliad* and *Odyssey* open with conflicts (the *Iliad* with the conflict between Agamemnon and Achilles, the *Odyssey* with the conflict between Telemachus and the suitors) that create interest and propel the action forward. The *Argonautica* opens with a catalogue of the Argonauts. This catalogue harkens back to the catalogue of the ships in the *Iliad*. Both catalogues function to introduce the "armies." However, while Homer places his catalogue in Book 2, after the action has gotten under way, Apollonius places his right at the start of Book 1, thereby starting his story without the tension and excitement that inform the Homeric epics.[7] The catalogue is followed by a series of briefly rendered set scenes—the parting of mother and son, the appointment of Jason to lead the crew, the readying of the ship to sail, and the prophecy of its safe return with the golden fleece – in which everyone says what is required under the circumstances. There are no clashes of will (other than the brief and quickly suppressed outburst of Idas, 1.463–95), or insoluble problems. The narration and dialogues are instrumental, presenting the situation and moving the story from one point to the next. Much of the epic—until Medea enters in Book 3—reads like a series of tableaux.

Jason is cast as an anti-hero. He bears little resemblance to the resourceful, inventive, and ever-ready Odysseus (see also Fantuzzi and Hunter 2004, 107–15, 129), and has nothing of the pride or drive for honor that motivates the warriors of the *Iliad*. His distinguishing features are his beauty and grace, which win him Medea's love (3.443–4, 919–26, 956–61). These qualities link him to Paris, the reprobate dandy of the *Iliad*, whom he resembles not only in his attractiveness to women (e.g. 1.721–68, 3.956–63) but also in his reluctance to put himself at risk. In 3.919–26, the connection is reinforced by the context of Hera's beautifying Jason before his first encounter with Medea, which recalls Aphrodite's luring Helen to Paris' chamber with the statement that he is waiting for her "gleaming in beauty and garments" (*Il.* 3.390–94).[8] It is also reinforced in the account of Jason as he is about to face the bronze-hooved oxen. The description of his gleaming bronze helmet and sword slung over his shoulders (3.1282) recalls the portrayal of Paris striding among the Trojans with his panther skin over his shoulders and his curved bow and sword, as well as the description of his arming before his duel with Menelaus (*Il.* 3.15–18, 334).

At points early in the epic, Jason's lack of the warrior's aggressiveness, his apparent mildness and gentleness, are presented in a favorable light. His readiness to forgive Telamon's insult is attributed to his understanding that Telamon spoke in grief (1.1290–95, 1331–43). His kindness and compassion for the blind Phineus (2.243) are commendable. His decision to ask Aietes for the golden fleece before trying to steal it (3.178–93), and his efforts to calm Aietes' wrath with mild words are evidence of his reason and wisdom (3.382–431).

Yet also from the beginning and increasingly in the course of the narrative, he is shown as lacking in both leadership and courage. He doesn't volunteer to lead the Argonauts, but accepts the post at Heracles' suggestion (1.345–7). In his first act of fighting, he mistakenly kills a friend under the misapprehension that he's an enemy (1.961–1035). He repeatedly leaves others to take the initiative in answering aggression and repelling danger. He accepts Aietes' challenge to yoke his bulls and plow his fields with dragons' teeth because he is cornered and has no choice (3. 422–5). And he carries out the task only when the drugs Medea gives him to make him invincible assure his success. Above all, his characteristic response to adversity is *amēchaniē*. Denoting shiftlessness, helplessness, and despair, it is a term rarely used in the Homeric epics.[9]

Well before the end of the epic it is clear that Jason lacks not only the warrior's stamina, but is also an egotist who exploits Medea's love. His soft-spoken speech (3.975–1007), in which he supplicates, flatters, and promises Medea gratitude in exchange for her help, thereby implying that he will take her with him when he leaves, is consistent with his generally non-aggressive, accommodating tone, but here it smacks of hypocrisy and utilitarianism. The impression becomes certainty with his vague and passionless promise to marry her (3.1120–30) and even more so with his nonchalant readiness to sacrifice her to Apsyrtus and his pursuit of the Colchians in exchange for the golden fleece (4.338–409). Increasingly, the epic of the Argonauts' "glorious deeds" turns into a tale of a man who relies on a woman with magical charms to get him what he wants and who owes his success to his fine looks, good manners, and ability to exploit the feelings of a passionate and initially innocent young girl.

It also becomes the story of Medea, the most, and only, passionate figure in the epic.[10] Torn by her love of Jason and duty to her parents, she is the more compelling figure. Her emotions, considerations, and reactions are described more fully than those of any of the males, with the possible, and only partial, exception of her father.

Jason's passivity and lack of heroism have been noted by generations of scholars (Carspecken 1952, 99–100). It has also been pointed out that the other Argonauts are little better than he (Carspecken 1952, 99–125, *passim*). Some show greater initiative and readiness to face danger. But they, too, are frequently described as afflicted with *amēchaniē*[11] – helpless and despairing – and only a few of them object to Jason's immoral behaviors. The question that arises is why Apollonius chose to create such a weak and tepid hero. This depiction was not necessitated by the legend, which drew Jason as an active hero, though not an admirable one. Pindar's Jason contends with Pelias, his father's half-brother, for rule of his father's land and mobilizes and leads the men who join him on his mission to bring Pelias the golden fleece (*Pyth.* 4). Euripides' Jason is a self-righteous cad and social climber who shamelessly justifies his mistreatment of Medea.

Green (1997, 39), commenting on Apollonius's frequent use of the noun *amēchaniē* for Jason (1.460, 1286; 2.408–11, 23, 885), suggests that it indicates "a pervasive sense of human uncertainty, shiftlessness, and ignorance in the face of the unknown" and argues that it shows "a realistic acceptance of man's limitations." Carspecken (1952, 139) claims that the *Argonautica* "rejects [the Homeric] ideals of physical strength, courage, love, and honor" as unrealistic and inapplicable to its day. Whatever the explanation, it is hard to see how a weak, tepid, and passive hero and his tepid companions can perform "glorious deeds." By the end of the epic, if not much earlier, it is clear that the deeds that are related are not heroic and that the central feature of the heroic epic has been turned on its head.

5.   *Battle of the Frogs and Mice* (*Batrachomyomachia*)

The *Battle of the Frogs and Mice* (303 lines) parodies the *Iliad*.[12] Telling the story of a "clamorous" day war, it brings to bear key conventions of the heroic epic to mock them. The figures who will become the leaders of the two armies, the frog Puff-jaw and the mouse Crumb-snatcher, boastfully introduce themselves by their lineage and key traits. The cause of the war is a foolish and impetuous act—Puff-jaw gives Crumb-snatcher a ride in the sea on his back—analogous to the abduction of Helen – which ends in betrayal (reminiscent of Paris' betrayal of Menelaus) when Puff-jaw dives underwater to escape a water-snake and Crumb-snatcher drowns. As in the *Iliad*, there are councils on two sides, twin scenes of arming, and twin strategy sessions. Zeus calls a council of the gods on Mount Olympus, and there are detailed and bloody battle scenes, in which each blow leads to the next. The poem mocks the values of the Homeric epic and the aggrandizement of war. It also mocks the gods. The council on Mount Olympus ends with Athena's suggestion that the gods amuse themselves by watching the war from heaven, and the poem ends with Hera and Zeus weighing in on opposite sides, and with the victory of the frogs when Zeus sends a contingent of crabs to bite off the tales of the mice. The poem is fun and, in its very act of parody, a tribute to the Homeric model; but it also constitutes a critique of the Homeric values and conventions, which it reduces to absurdity.

III

We now skip several more centuries to the Imperial period, with two epics: Quintus of Symrna's untitled heroic epic of the fourth century CE recounting the events leading up to the fall of Troy and Nonnus of Panopolis's *Dionysiaca*, composed in the fifth century.

6.   Quintus's *The Fall of Troy*

Quintus's epic (14 books, 8,772 lines) has been variously titled *The Fall of Troy*, *The Trojan Epic*, and *Posthomerica*.[13] It draws its material not from Homer's epics, but from three epics of the Epic Cycle (*Aethiopis, Little Iliad,* and *Sack of Ilion*), which covered the Trojan tale from its start to the death of Odysseus.[14] It shares with the *Iliad* a sense of both the glory and abiding sadness of war, and its aspiration to the grandeur of the Homeric epics is evident in the closeness of its language and style to Homer's (James 2004, xxii–xxvii). But like the cyclic epics on which it is based, and which Aristotle faulted for trekking without depth through a succession of events (*Poet.* 1451a16–35, 1452a20–21, 1459a17–59b7), it reads more like a chronicle than a compelling tale in which action is driven by character. Quintus neither achieves nor strives for the integration of character, action, and theme that characterizes the *Iliad* and the *Odyssey*.

His epic plunges into the story without the usual introductory appeal to the muses and without a statement of theme.[15] Like Homer, Quintus restricts his epic to a short time span

(44 days). But while Homer uses the space this gave him to explore the characters of his heroes – Achilles' wrath, Odysseus's resourcefulness – and to show their implications in everything they do, Quintus gives us rather flat and idealized heroes. Over the centuries, generations of poets, especially the tragedians, had fleshed out the heroes of the Trojan War and, in many cases, drew them with a critical eye. Thus, for example, Neoptolemus's cruelty, Odysseus's sleazy scheming, and Philoctetes' self-destructive resentment were highlighted, and the implications of their behavior analyzed. Through selective use of the tradition, Quintus simplified these characters and presented them in an unequivocally positive light (James 2004, xxvi–xxvi, xxviii; 2005, 368). Ignoring Neoptolemus's cruelty, he portrays him solely as the heroic son of a heroic father. In describing his killing of Priam, he doesn't consider the cruelty of the young warrior killing an old man, but rather offers the moral: "The glory of man is never diminished for long/And disgrace can quickly catch one unawares" (13.248–9, tr. James). He depicts Odysseus as unambiguously honorable. Thus, in Book 5, he tells the story of Ajax's suicide after Odysseus is awarded Achilles' armor so as to refute the accusations (made by Menelaus in the text) that Odysseus had obtained the armor dishonestly. In Book 12, he ennobles Odysseus's ploy of the Trojan horse by presenting the attack from the horse as requiring courage and spirit. In Book 9, he downplays Odysseus's betrayal of Philoctetes by framing his abandonment of the injured hero on the deserted island of Lemnos as necessitated by fate, and by depicting Philoctetes as accepting the abandonment without anger or resentment. The idealization of the heroes extends to the collective as well, with the Trojans almost always depicted as fearful and cowering before the superior Achaeans or, alternatively, as foolishly and hubristically over-confident. The result is that instead of a war between two worthy opponents forced into a destructive fight by the selfishness of Paris, which we see in the *Iliad*, we are given a contest between those who are worthy and those who are less so.

It is not only that the heroes are idealized; greater attention is paid to describing the battles than to characterization. For example, Achilles is described as gentle and kind (3.424–6, 550), without ever being shown to be such. Speech is often placed in the mouths of collectives, such as the Argive men, the Danaans, and Trojan people, whereas only specific individuals utter statements in actuality.

Rather than character, what stands out and holds the fourteen books of Quintus's epic together is an ironic perspective: the sense that nothing ever works out as expected. The epic opens with the Trojans, traumatized by Achilles' violence, cowering within the city walls, fearful of venturing outside (1.3–17); but they are killed in the end within the walls. Paris, in contrast, is killed after urging the Trojans to go out and fight rather than retreat behind the walls (2.63–80; 10.235–363). Most of the ironies concern the defeat of hubris or overconfidence, the only character flaw exhibited by virtually all the warriors on both sides. The defeat of the Amazon Queen Penthesileia (who came to fight on the Trojan side) at the hands of Achilles is described as the defeat of a proud and overconfident warrior, an overweening woman, who does not know the limits of her strength or the power of her opponent. But Achilles' own boasting of his strength before he kills her is portentous, and he himself is killed by Apollo for his hubristic defiance (3.40–88, 139–85). All the purported saviors of the Trojans – Penthesileia, Memnon, Eurypylos – boast of their power, promise salvation, are eagerly and hopefully received, only to bring death and destruction on the Trojans and to be killed themselves.

Essentially, character is trumped by two ideas, or ideologies, that Quintus uses his poem to convey. One is the idea, which underpins its ironies, that all is determined by fate. The notion that the war's end is predetermined is also present in the *Iliad*, where the gods are the ultimate arbiters of what befalls the human heroes. The difference is that in Homer, the notion of the gods' power does not undercut the value placed on human deeds and decisions. For Quintus, apparently, it does. If the aim of Homer's muse is to exalt the human warriors, with all their flaws, Quintus's is to show that, for all their greatness, their fate is ultimately determined by the gods, and especially by Zeus. Thus, his epic is filled with statement upon statement of the determinant role of fate or the gods in every incident, and the motives and drives of the characters are secondary in shaping events. Given this outlook, character is of little interest and there is no need to explore or develop it in the poem.

The other idea that undermines characterization is the stoic rejection of passion. The text presents repeated admonitions against strong emotions. Calliope rebukes Thetis for her excessive mourning of Achilles and advises her to accept the Fates (3.630–54). Poseidon commands her to cease her mourning and promises that Achilles will live like a god (3.765–83). Nestor calls upon the Achaeans to stop grieving over Ajax's death and to get on with the practical task of burying him (5.600–611), and urges Podaleirios to temper his grief for his fallen brother (7.37–92). For the reader, such advice undermines the legitimacy of the characters' grief and undercuts its emotional power. So do statements like "a mother/mourns for her son even if he so much as goes out to a feast" (7.389–90), which follows upon Neoptolemus's rejection of his mother's plea that he not join the war after his father's death. Not only grief and yearning, but also anger, are condemned. Achilles, whose heroism must remain unblemished, is not shown as the angry hero of the *Iliad*, and the entire account of Ajax's madness and suicide serves as an object lesson in the disastrous consequences of being carried away by one's anger. For an author who condemns strong passions, there is little point in depicting heroes who embody them. But their passions are precisely what bring characters alive, make them interesting, and enable us to identify with them. Ultimately, Quintus's heroes are not only idealized, but also tepid. Without character depth or development, Quintus's epic resembles a film that offers up a glut of violent scenes for their own sake.

7. Nonnus's *Dionysiaca*

The *Dionysiaca*, the longest poem of Greek antiquity (48 books, 20,426 lines), celebrates the life of the god of wine, who was regarded, along with Heracles, as a great ambassador and representative of international Hellenism (Bowersock 1994, 157). It is a capacious and compendious work, which incorporates the vast lore on Dionysus that was current at the time and a store of mythological detail, much of it not found elsewhere. It encompasses the entire story of Dionysus's life on earth, from several generations before his conception through his apotheosis on Mount Olympus, where he joins his father Zeus. The main adventure it relates, Dionysus's expedition against the Indian king Deriades (13–40), harkens back to the conquests of Alexander the Great (Lesky 1966, 817; Bowersock 1994, 57). In Nonnus's rendition, the expedition was undertaken on Zeus's orders to drive out the impious race of Indians and to teach all the nations his sacred rites and viticulture as a condition for earning his place on Olympus. Dionysus's victory over Deriades in Book 40 is followed by a long and detailed travelogue, recounting his journey to real (e.g., Beroe – Beirut, Tyre; Chuvin 1994, 167–8) and mythological places, in each of which he demonstrates his divine power, whether through fighting or through an act of seduction or rape.

Its narrative is episodic and digressive, its style ornate, full of embellishment and mythological *exempla* (Shorrock 2005, 376–80). Nonnus's verse is exuberant, its energy and movement recalling that of Aratus's astrological epic.

It draws on numerous sources. Homer is the most obvious and most important. Its 48 books, telling first of war and then of Dionysus's journey to join his father on Mount Olympus, parallel the narrative pattern of the *Iliad* and the *Odyssey*, with their 24 books each, telling first of the Trojan War and then of Odysseus's journey home to Ithaca. The invocations to the Muse, the catalogue of forces joining Dionysus's expedition, the battle scenes and funeral games, the gods battling for their favorites on either side, and Hera's deception of Zeus, are among the many echoes of the *Iliad* (Shorrock 2001, 25–111). The epic uses elements of Homeric diction, such as stock epithets and formulae, and recasts and transforms Homeric episodes (see Hopkinson 1994a).

But this sort of engagement is not limited to Homer. The *Dionysiaca* may be viewed as an amalgam of authors and genres. It draws on Hesiod (for its cosmogonies), the Greek tragedians, and erotic elegists, on encomiastic and pastoral poetry, and on foundation stories, Hellenistic astrology, and more (Harries 1994).

Moreover, Nonnus explicitly declares his intention to outdo Homer (Hopkinson 1994a; Shorrock 2005, 381–2). In his first proem (1.34–44), he asks his muse to clothe him in the perfumed garments of Dionysus and to leave Homer the stinking seal skin of Menelaus. He further contrasts his lively and jocular music to the tame sweetness of the reed flute, presumably associated with Homer. In his second proem (25.1–270), in the midst of his account of the Indian War, he asks that he might hold the "inspired spear and shield of father Homer" and hear "the ceaseless call of the skilled trumpet in Homer's verse, that I may destroy what is left of the Indians with my spear of the sprit" (25.265–70, tr. Rouse). In these passages, Nonnus identifies Homer's consummate poetic skills as valuable tools that he will put to use for superior purposes and in a superior way.

Thus, whereas Homer's heroes are mortal and, where they are not assisted by the gods, their exploits confined to a human compass, Nonnus chose as his subject the immortal Dionysus, possessed of the god's protean ability to change shape. Whereas the Homeric epics are tightly structured and their accounts bound within a short space of time, Nonnus's epic is wide in scope and expansive in detail. It incorporates detailed accounts of myths which can stand on their own, tells more about his hero's doings than Homer tells about Achilles and Odysseus, and expands on every incident, every description, and every speech at considerably greater length than similar passages in Homer's poems. There are also more catalogues than in the *Iliad*, longer funeral games, a seemingly endless number of human and non-human warriors, an array of allegorical participants in the fighting, and detailed and erotic descriptions of sexual exploits, which are absent in the *Iliad* and much toned down in the *Odyssey*.

The *Dionysiaca's* supra-Homeric exuberance probably goes a long way to accounting for its great popularity in its day and beyond; the poem continued to be read in Constantinople throughout the Middle Ages. It may also contribute to the difficulties that modern readers, unfamiliar with the mythology, not galvanized by the exploits of the god of wine, and lacking the background to appreciate the poem's variety and virtuosity, experience with the poem. Recent scholars who have sought to revive its reputation have focused on elucidating the poem's episodic and digressive structure, although the chronological order of events is actually not difficult to follow. Thus, Vian (1994), explaining that its structure is obscured by the poem's systematic pursuit of variety, points out unifying motifs and then charts the progress of the Indian War and Dionysus's behavior in it. Shorrock (2001, 10–23; 2005, 376–8) argues that the poem's structure can be viewed as reflecting the intertwined sprigs of the vine and that the poem itself is as intoxicating as wine which alters the reader's perception of 'reality' (Shorrock 2001, 114–16, 207–13).

A more serious obstacle to enjoyment, at least for some readers, may be the poem's characterization. There are no human characters with whom a reader can identify or much care about. The emblematic, primary quality of the many myths the poem relates does not emerge, as they are reduced to stories in an ever-moving adventure. The emotional and psychological potential in the tale of a junior god who seeks acknowledgement of his divinity and reunification with his father is not even hinted at, never mind developed. Dionysus joins Zeus on Olympus only in the last paragraph of the poem, without even a single verbal or non-verbal exchange. This provides a convenient ending to the lengthy tale, but leaves the reader to work out its meaning.

NOTES

[1] Religious and philosophical speculations were also written in dactylic hexameter, as were the relatively short Homeric Hymns. For discussion of the epic genre see Martin 2005; on meter cf. also Reece, ch. 3, pp. 47–50 and Willi, ch. 29, pp. 446–7 in this volume.

[2] The restriction of the discussion to the extant epics excludes the philosophical epics, as well as the short and erudite Hellenistic epics on personal themes by neoterici, such as the Alexandrian Callimachus and Theophrastus (for criticism, see Juvenal *Sat.* 1.1–14). For lack of space, I will not discuss the Homeric Hymns or the Imperial didactic epics: *Halieutica*, an epic in five books on fish and fishing by Oppian of Apamea in Syria (late second century CE), and *Cynegetica* (212–217? CE), an epic in four books on animals and the art of hunting. The mss ascribe *Halieutica* to Oppian of Anazarbus in Cilicia, but the poem's metrics, language and syntax make Oppian of Apamea the more likely author. Nor will I treat the newly discovered Greek poem (1984) of about 360 hexameters *The Vision of Dorotheus* (Kessels and Van der Horst 1987).

[3] For the *Iliad*, see Edwards 2011. For the *Odyssey,* see Griffin (2011a). West claims that the *Theogony* may be the oldest extant Greek poem (1966, 46). For *Works and Days*, see West 1978. For a general discussion of Hesiod see Nelson 2005.

[4] Cf. Konstan, ch. 27, pp. 415–7 in this volume.

[5] For a long time it was believed that Apollonius had fallen out with Callimachus over the latter's objections to poems on a grand scale and preference for small-scale, learned, and recherché poems for the educated. Recently, this assumption has been called into question (Lefkowitz 2012, 113–25). It has been pointed out, for example, that Callimachus's main work, the *Aitia*, is similar in length to Apollonius's *Argonautica* (5,835 lines); that both epics share a distinct aetiological drive (for the difference in perspective between the two, see Köhnken 2010, 136–7), as well as a shared interest in geography and religious practices. It has also been noted that some lines of the *Argonautica* are fashioned on lines of the *Aitia* (noted in the scholia to Apollonius (1.1309). For a general discussion see Nelis 2005; cf. also Mori, ch. 6, pp. 101–2 in this volume.

[6] For a discussion of the literary tastes of the period, see Green 1997, Cameron 1995, Lesky 1966. For Hellenistic epic, see especially Cameron 1995, 263–302, and Ambühl 2010. See also Baechle ch. 30, pp. 463–6 in this volume.

[7] Carspecken 1952, 56–7 suggests that the poet places the catalogue right at the beginning so as to avoid the break in the narrative that its placement in the *Iliad* causes.

[8] Cf. a less explicit attempt of a goddess at rousing the interest of a wife in *Od.* 23.156–63; for *Il.* 6.321–41, and *Argon.* 1.865–74, see Hunter 1993, 49–50 with 33–6.

[9] When it is used, whether in the *Iliad* (8.130, 10.167, 11.310, 13.726, 14.262, 15.14, 19.273) or the *Odyssey* (*Od.* 9.295 cf. 19.363, 560), its connotation is always negative. It is noteworthy that in *Argon.* 3.336 the epithet's gender reference is ambiguous, meaning that it can refer not only to Jason, but also to the "hopeless quest" of the *Argo*.

[10] Cf. Carspecken 1952, 110–11 and Köhnken 2010, 142–3, about the group of Argonauts being the main hero.

[11] E.g., Argus, 2.1140; Jason and his fellow Argonauts 3.423, 432, 504; the entire land of Aeaea 3.893; Peleus 4.880; Ancaeus and the rest of the Argonauts, 4.1259, 1308, 1318; Mopsus, 4.1527.30). The term is also applied to Medea (3.1157 cf. 3.772), just before and after Jason promises her marriage (3.1125–30). The application of the term to Medea is puzzling, considering that she is anything but lacking in energy, purpose, and resourcefulness. The explanation may be that Apollonius is hinting that everyone who becomes involved with Jason becomes infected with the same deficiency that is at the core of his own personality. There is some similarity between Apollonius's linking all those close to Jason by the attribute

of *amēchaniē* and the use of the base *kerd-* to bring together under one descriptor Odysseus, his family, and his close allies in the *Odyssey* (Roisman 1994).

[12]See Sens 2006 for a detailed discussion of the poem's engagement with Homer and Hesiod.

[13]For a full assessment of the *Trojan Epic* see James 2004 and 2005 with bibliography.

[14]For discussion of the Epic Cycle see Burgess 2005.

[15]Combellack 1962, 9–10 suggests that Quintus chose not to invoke the muses so as to present his poem as a direct continuation of the *Iliad*.

REFERENCES

Ahl, F. and Roisman, H. M. 1996. *The Odyssey re-formed*. Ithaca, NY.

Ambühl, A. 2010. "Narrative Hexameter Poetry." In J. J. Clauss and M. Cuypers, eds., *A Companion to Hellenistic Literature*, Oxford, 151–65.

Andersen, Ø. 2011. "Diomedes." In M. Finkelberg, ed., *Homer Encyclopedia*, New York, vol. I, 208–9.

Bowersock, G. 1994. "Dionysus as an Epic Hero." In N. Hopkinson, ed., *Studies in the* Dionysiaca *of Nonnus*, Cambridge, 156–66.

Burgess, J. S. 2005. "The Epic Cycle and Fragments." In J. M. Foley, ed., *A Companion to Ancient Epic*, Oxford, 344–52.

Cameron, A. 1995. *Callimachus and his Critics*. Princeton, NJ.

Carspecken, J. F. 1952. "Apollonius Rhodius and the Homeric Epic." *Yale Classical Studies* 13: 33–143.

Chuvin, P. 1994. "Local Traditions and Classical Mythology in the *Dionysiaca*." In N. Hopkinson, ed., *Studies in the* Dionysiaca *of Nonnus*, Cambridge, 167–82.

Clauss, J. J. and M. Cuypers, eds. 2010. *A Companion to Hellenistic Literature*. Oxford.

Combellack, F. M. 1962. *The War at Troy. What Homer Didn't Tell*. Norman, OK.

Edwards, M. W. 1987. *Homer: Poet of the Iliad*. Baltimore.

Edwards, M. W. 2011. "Iliad." In M. Finkelberg, ed., *Homer Encyclopedia*, New York, vol. II, 397–406.

Fantuzzi, M. and R. Hunter. 2004. *Tradition and Innovation in Hellenistic Poetry*. Cambridge.

Finkelberg, M., ed. 2011. *Homer Encyclopedia*. New York.

Foley, J. M., ed. 2005. *A Companion to Ancient Epic*. Oxford.

Green, P. 1997. *The Argonautika by Apollonios Rhodios*. Berkeley, CA.

Griffin, J. 2011a. "Odyssey." In M. Finkelberg, ed., *Homer Encyclopedia*, New York, vol. II, 588–94.

Griffin, J. 2011b. "Paris." In M. Finkelberg, ed., *Homer Encyclopedia*, New York, vol. II, 627–8.

Harries, B. 1994. "The Pastoral Mode in the *Dionysiaca*." In N. Hopkinson, ed., *Studies in the* Dionysiaca *of Nonnus*, Cambridge, 63–85.

Hopkinson N. 1994a. "Nonnus and Homer." In N. Hopkinson, ed., *Studies in the* Dionysiaca *of Nonnus*, Cambridge, 9–42.

Hopkinson N., ed. 1994. *Studies in the Dionysiaca of Nonnus*. Cambridge.

Hunter, R. 1993. *The* Argonautica *of Apollonius*. Cambridge.

James, A. 2004. *The Trojan Epic: Posthomerica*. Baltimore, MD.

James, A. 2005. "Quintus of Smyrna." In J. J. Clauss and M. Cuypers, eds., *A Companion to Hellenistic Literature*, Oxford, 364–73.

Kessels, A. H. M. and P. W. van der Horst. 1987. "The Vision of Dorotheus." *Vigiliae Christianae* 41: 313–59.

Kidd, D. 1997. *Aratus. Phaenomena*. Cambridge.

Köhnken, A. 2010. "Apollonius' *Argonautica*." In J. J. Clauss and M. Cuypers, eds., *A Companion to Hellenistic Literature*, Oxford, 137–50.

Lefkowitz, M. R. 2012. *The Lives of the Greek Poets*, 2nd edn. Baltimore, MD.

Lesky, A. 1966. *A History of Greek Literature*. New York.

Martin, R. P. 2005. "Epic as Genre." In J. M. Foley, ed., *A Companion to Ancient Epic*, Oxford, 9–19.

Montanari, F. and A. Rengakos, eds. 2006. *La Poésie épique grecque: Métamorphoses d'un genre littéraire*. Vandoevres-Geneva.

Nelis, D. P. 2005. "Apollonius of Rhodes." In J. M. Foley, ed., *A Companion to Ancient Epic*, Oxford, 353–63.

Nelson, S. 2005. "Hesiod." In J. M. Foley, ed., *A Companion to Ancient Epic*, Oxford, 330–43.

Roisman H. M. 1994. "Like Father Like Son: Telemachus' *kerdea*." Rheinisches Museum für Philologie 137: 1–22.

Roisman H. M. 2005. "Nestor the Good Counselor." *Classical Quarterly* 55: 17–38.

Roisman H. M. 2011. "Menelaos." In M. Finkelberg, ed., *Homer Encyclopedia*, New York, vol. II, 506–7.

Rotstein, A. 2011. "Batrachomyomachia." In M. Finkelberg, ed., *Homer Encyclopedia*, New York, vol. I, 124–5.

Rouse, W. H. D. 1940–1942. *Nonnos. Dionysiaca. Mythological Introduction and Notes by H. J. Rose. And notes on Text Criticism by L. R. Lind*. Cambridge, MA.

Rutherford, R. B. 2011. "Odysseus." In M. Finkelberg, ed., *Homer Encyclopedia*, New York, vol. II, 581–3.

Schein, S. L. 2011. "Hector." In M. Finkelberg, ed., *Homer Encyclopedia*, New York, vol. II, 333–4.

Sens, A. 2006. " 'Τίπτε γένος τούμον ζητεῖς;' The *Batrachomyomachia*, Hellenistic Epic Parody and the Homeric Epic." In F. Montanari and A. Rengakos, eds., *La Poésie épique grecque: Métamorphoses d'un genre littéraire*. Vandoevres-Geneva, 215–248.

Shorrock, R. 2001. *The Challenge of Epic: Allusive Engagement in the* Dionysiaca *of Nonnus*. Leiden.

Shorrock, R. 2005. "Nonnus." In J. M. Foley, ed., *A Companion to Ancient Epic*, Oxford, 374–85.

Strauss Clay, J. 2003. *Hesiod's Cosmos*. Cambridge.

Van Nortwick, T. 2011. "Agamemnon." In M. Finkelberg, ed., *Homer Encyclopedia*, New York, vol. I, 14–16.

Vian, F. 1994. "Dionysus in the Indian War: A Contribution to a Study of the Structure of the *Dionysiaca*." In N. Hopkinson, ed., *Studies in the* Dionysiaca *of Nonnus*, Cambridge, 86–98.

West, M. L. 1966. *Theogony*. Oxford.

West, M. L. 1978. *Hesiod: Works & Days*. Oxford.

FURTHER READING

Lesky 1966 is still an excellent comprehensive reference book to all genres of Greek literature. Lefkowitz 2012 is an excellent clearly written source for what we factually know of the Greek poets. *The Homer Encyclopedia*, edited by M. Finkelberg 2011, is the most recent and most comprehensive reference book on Homeric epics and relevant epic works. Edwards1987, 2011 offers a good selection of *Iliad's* books for discussion. J. Strauss Clay 2003 offers an expert discussion of *Theogony* and *Works and Days* with an eye to the overall debate on Hesiod. Green1997 is a comprehensive, accessible, and expertly written commentary on the *Argonautika*. James 2004 is a good place to start one's reading about the *Posthomerica* poem, as is R. Shorrock 2001 on the *Dionysiaca*.

CHAPTER 10

Lyric: Melic, Iambic, Elegiac

James Bradley Wells

To the memory of my teacher John Miles Foley

1. Introduction

"Lyric" is ineffable, perhaps in the sense of being indescribably transcendent or abject verbal art that is poetry or poetical or even poesy, but certainly in the sense of being an underspecified genre rubric. While I will (mostly) spare the reader indulgence in such a typographical convention, any rubric, like "lyric," whose definition risks defaulting to "you know it when you see/hear it," always belongs in danger quotes. A domain so defined is too often the turf of "those with a particular sort of cultural breeding" (Eagleton 1996, viii). If "lyric" is suspect as a critical concept or as an ideological harbinger (Adorno 1974, 45), in the context of classical literature it at best captures what lyric is not: lyric is neither epic nor drama. But some Greek lyric poetries include narrative, and others involve performer(s) and audience in conventional roles sanctioned by tradition. As a lesser member of the *tre corone*, lyric, epic, and drama, lyric is a monolithic and leaky genre rubric based upon a narrow and high conception of genre.[1]

A poem composed by Sappho of Lesbos will serve to illustrate a performance-centered and practice-based approach to genre and voice that accounts for the polymorphic and polyvalent qualities of Greek lyric. Before exploring this approach, I present an overview of the field of Greek lyric poetries.[2]

2. The Field of Greek Lyric

Grouping iambos and elegy with melic poetry under the rubric of lyric poetry has established critical precedents, but the ancient Greek designation for lyric poetry of the Archaic and early Classical periods was *melos* "song" or "melody," rather than "lyric" from *lura* "lyre," and the performer of *melos* was called *melopoios* "song-maker." Alexandrian scholars canonized nine artists (corresponding to the number of Muses) as premier composers of melic poetry: Alcman,

A Companion to Greek Literature, First Edition. Edited by Martin Hose and David Schenker.
© 2016 John Wiley & Sons, Inc. Published 2020 by John Wiley & Sons, Inc.

Alcaeus, Anacreon, Bacchylides, Ibycus, Pindar, Sappho, Simonides, and Stesichorus (Quint. 10.1.61 and Dion. Hal. *De imit.* 2). The earliest attested use of the designation "lyric," circa 100 BCE, applied strictly to melic poets of the Alexandrian canon (*Anth. Pal.* 9.184).[3] In his landmark study *Pindar's Homer*, Gregory Nagy corroborates this "narrow sense" (Budelmann 2009b, 2) of lyric on the basis of historical linguistics and comparative poetics. Nagy contrasts SONG and Speech, where Speech designates ordinary, everyday speech practices and SONG designates special, marked language, such as performed media of communication (Nagy 1990, 17–51). SONG includes *song*, verbal art that is traditionally sung and has musical accompaniment, and *poetry*, whose performance format was recitative. This conception of *poetry* entails a contrast between *poetry* and *song* such that *song* is plus melody and *poetry* is minus melody or reduced melody. *Song* corresponds to *melos*, so that the lyric poetries thus defined are forms of *song* or melic poetry. There are three metrical types of ancient Greek *poetry* (Nagy 1990, 19–20): (1) dactylic hexameter (Homeric epic and hymns, Hesiodic poetry); (2) elegiac distich (dactylic hexameter plus dactylic "pentameter"); (3) iambic trimeter. The "comprehensive sense" of lyric includes *poetry* composed in the Archaic period using these meters (Budelmann 2009b, 2). Critical convention, as well as the facts that melic, iambic, and elegiac poetries share the feature of occasionality and that lyric poetry, according to Roman Jakobson's definition, is "oriented toward the first person" and "intimately linked with the emotive function" of language (Jakobson 1960, 357), license preference for the "comprehensive sense" of lyric in favor of the more rigorous position that *melos* is the exclusive designation for lyric poetry (cf. Kurke 2000, 41 and Harvey 1955, 157). But such preference is a fraught analytical convenience.

Critical convention privileges two generic criteria to map the field of Greek lyric: (1) the formal criterion of metrical design and (2) performance occasion narrowly conceived as private or public.[4] The *agora* or *temenos* "sacred space" was often the site, and a festival often the occasion, for public performances, whose audience included, whether rhetorically or actually, all *polis*-members. I will refer to the private venue as a *hetaireia*, a "group" of *hetairoi*, "male companions," or *hetairai*, "female companions." The *hetaireia* may include family members and close friends who gathered in the home of a host, but the 15 to 30 participants in the *hetaireia* and their ideological cohesion (Kurke 2007, 147) suggest a broader social network than a private group in the sense of being exclusively domestic or intimate (cf. Most 1982, 90). Table 10.1 summarizes major Greek lyric genres and composers whose work survives.

3.   Iambos

Our limited knowledge undermines attempts to generalize about the correspondence between subgenres of iambos and their original context(s) of performance, but one possibility, based in part upon references in iambic poetry to a phallus (Archil. F 66–7 IEG and Hipponax F 78 IEG), is that iambos was "a kind of dramatic monologue performed at public festivals, perhaps originally associated with fertility rituals" (Kurke 2000, 50; cf. Carey 2009b, 151). We find that *iambos* may designate conventional, jocular abuse and sexual humor (cf. Archil. F 42 IEG on fellatio, Semonides F 17 IEG on anal sex, and Hipponax F 70 IEG on an illicit sex act) that occurred in the context of festivals of Demeter and Dionysus (Bowie 2001). Thus in the *Homeric Hymn to Demeter* a figure named Iambe deploys sexual humor to give Demeter a moment of comic relief from her grief over the abduction of Persephone (*Hom. Hymn Dem.* 200–205; cf. Foley 1994, 45–6). This passage locates in the mythological *aition* for the Eleusinian Mysteries the known practice of directing *gephurismoi* "abuse" at participants in the Eleusinian Mysteries.[5] The hymn associates this practice of ritual abuse and sexual humor with the figure of Iambe, whose name becomes eponymous for *gephurismoi* given that such abuse counts as a kind of iambos. Despite the apparent inevitability of defining *iambos*

Table 10.1 Lyric Genres and Lyric Artists

Genre	Composer
Iambos	Archilochus of Paros (seventh century BCE) Semonides of Amorgos (seventh century BCE) Hipponax of Ephesus and Clazomenae (late sixth century BCE) Solon of Athens (fl. 594/3 BCE)
Elegy	Callinus of Ephesus (seventh century BCE) Mimnermus of Smyrna and Colophon (fl. 632–629 BCE) Tyrtaeus of Sparta (seventh century BCE) Theognis of Megara (fl. 640–600 or 550–540 BCE) Solon of Athens (fl. 594/3 BCE) Xenophanes of Colophon (c. 565–470 BCE) Simonides of Ceos (c. 556–468 BCE)
Melic–Monody	Sappho of Mytilene (late seventh/early sixth century BCE) Alcaeus of Mytilene (late seventh/early sixth century BCE) Ibycus of Rhegium (mid-sixth century BCE) Anacreon of Teos (mid-sixth century to early 5th c. BCE)
Melic–Choral	Alcman of Sparta (late seventh century BCE) Stesichorus of Himera, Sicily (632–556 BCE) Simonides of Ceos (ca. 556–468 BCE) Bacchylides of Ceos (ca. 520–450 BCE) Pindar of Thebes (518–438 BCE) Corinna of Tanagra in Boeotia (late archaic, classical, or Hellenistic)

on the basis of meter, "iambic meter got its name from being particularly characteristic of *iamboi*, not vice versa" (West 1974, 22). Where Archilochus claims, "Neither *iamboi* nor delights concern even me" (F 215 IEG), he contrasts *iamboi* with *terpôlai* "delights," suggesting content- or experience-based native conception of *iambos*. Corresponding to Archilochus' *iamboi-terpôlai* contrast, Aristotle (*Poet.* 1448b24–32) links *psogoi* "blame" with the verb *iambizdein*. Further confirming that meter is not a definitive feature of *iambos*, extant iambic poetry in fact includes iambic, trochaic, and epodic (a blend of iambic, trochaic, and dactylic cola) meters (cf. Arist. *Rhet.* 1418b28).

Archilochus is the premier iambic poet.[6] If sexual escapades narrated by a first-person speaker are recurrent in extant iambic poetry (e.g. Archil. F 30–48 IEG), then the "Cologne Epode" of Archilochus (F 196a IEG) is a celebrated case in point (Bowie 2001), as well as an illustration of blame poetics. Ancient sources tell us that Lycambes agreed to a marriage between his daughter Neoboule and Archilochus, but went back on his promise (Archil. F 173 IEG refers to a broken oath). This insult provoked Archilochus to compose poems (F 172–81, 188, and 196a IEG) attacking Lycambes and his daughters. According to legend, Archilochus' attacks were so damning that Lycambes and his daughters committed suicide. This anecdote dramatizes the fact that Archilochus is "a master of blame poetry" (Nagy 1979, 243).

Archilochus's "Cologne Epode," which exemplifies Archilochus's mastery of blame poetics, is a long fragment whose beginning is lost. The extant text begins with the direct discourse of a female figure, who appears on the basis of the content of the fragment itself to be Neoboule's sister. This speaker encourages her addressee, the narrator-performer of events reported in this poem, to pursue Neoboule as a love interest, to which suggestion the narrator-performer responds:

And I answered her, "Daughter of Amphimedo,
a good and ...woman, whom the spoiled earth
now owns, apart from the heavenly act itself,
Aphrodite delights young men in many ways,
any of which will work. You and I, whenever...
grows dark, with god's aid we will make our plans
in quiet. I will obey your commands. Abundant ...
me..., and refuse me nothing, beneath the coping
or behind the gates. I will keep to the grassy garden,
trust me. Let another guy have Neoboule.
She's too long on the vine, twice as old
as you. Her virginal blush and the appeal it used
to have, these have gone to seed. Insatiable...the raving
woman revealed the brunt of her... Give her
to the crows. Let not...this: that I become
a joke to my neighbors for marrying such a woman.
I want you so much more. You are not unfaithful
or duplicitous, but she is too impulsive
and wins the affections of many men. I am afraid
to beget, like a knocked-up dog, blind and early-born
consequences by being too eager." That's what
I said. Then I took the girl and laid her back on
a thick bed of flowers. I covered her with my soft
overcloak. I put my arm under her neck
...relenting...like a fawn... I took her breasts
in my hands. Her young flesh shown, the brink of womanhood.
My caresses covered her entire beautiful body,
and I released my opalescent strength,
my fingers in her strands of auburn hair.
(Archil. 196a, 9–53 IEG)

Blending ribald narrative and blame poetics, the fragment portrays Neoboule as available for a sexual liaison, but the speaker rejects that prospect, preferring instead to seduce Neoboule's sister. Archilochus enacts blame by implicitly condemning Neoboule's qualities as a marriage-eligible woman whose chastity, a high commodity in the cultural poetics of marriage, is compromised. The poem also implies that the same is true of his interlocutor: despite Archilochus's portrayal of events – "coping," "gates," and "grassy garden" appear to be euphemisms for sex acts that do not involve penetration – he nevertheless casts Neoboule's sister as a participant in behavior that compromises her reputation for chastity (Nagy 2007, 223–4). Such poetry may have been humorous and entertaining to some audience, but it must also have served to promote adherence to social norms by deterring behavior that might make one vulnerable to becoming the target of such blame poetry. By implication, the behavior of his daughters impugns Lycambes' social and religious responsibilities as a father, so that he, too, is a target of blame in these verses. On the other hand, humor and entertainment come more to the fore if we see praise as always already implied by blame: to condemn Lycambes and his daughters for sexual impropriety becomes a ludic inversion of blame poetics if such blame implies praise of their actually exemplary conduct.[7]

4. Elegy

The metalanguage for elegy encourages defining the medium in terms of content or meter: *elegos* designates a sung lament, probably in elegiac couplets; *elegeion* designates the elegiac couplet itself; *elegeia* designates a poem or the poetry composed in elegiac couplets.[8] Because the elegiac couplet is one, but not the exclusive, medium for epigram, we would do well to observe that elegiac poetry was composed for performance before an audience in some social event, such as a gathering of *hetairoi*, so that elegy is to be understood as a medium of artistic communication between poet and audience (Aloni 2009, 169–70; cf. Bowie 1986, 27). By contrast, an epigram was inscribed upon a material object, such as a funerary monument or dedication, and was available for the inscribed composition's interlocutors to animate, whether internally or vocally.[9] Erotic and parainetic elegy appears to have been reserved for performance for a *hetaireia* context, such as the symposium, and historical narrative and military exhortation were performed publically for polis-members or on military expedition. Suggestive of its performance in the *hetaireia* context, elegiac poetry regularly features sympotic practices.[10] While Nagy finds that elegy's performance format was recitative, Aloni argues that it was sung, in either case accompanied by the *aulos* (Thgn. 239–43, 531–4, 825, 939–42, and 1055–6), a wind instrument with two pipes joined by a bronze fitting that also served as the mouthpiece, and composed in elegiac distich (Aloni 2009, 170). Other elegiac passages suggest a variety of performance venues: military camp (Archil. F 4 IEG, Thgn. 887–8 and 1043–4), post-symposium nighttime street revelry of the *kômos* (Thgn. 1045–6), in funerary contexts (Simon. F 10–18 IEG).

Simonides' *Plataea elegy* (F 10–18 IEG) exemplifies the potential for composing extended historical narrative in elegiac couplets. We know of narrative elegy, such as Xenophanes' poems on the founding of Colophon (F 3 IEG) and Elea; Solon's lost *Salamis* (F 1–3 IEG) may have been as long as 100 lines (Plut. *Sol.* 8.2); Mimnermus' *Smyrneis* and Simonides' *Plataea elegy*, may have been even longer. Simonides' *Plataea elegy* exemplifies the range of content in elegiac poetry: (1) narration of the battle of Plataea between Panhellenic Greek forces and Persians; (2) celebration of the Greek opposition to the Persians, of Sparta's and its general Pausanias's contribution to that opposition, and of martial virtues; (3) exhortation to emulate the bravery and defense of the homeland exemplified by the Greek forces; and (4) eulogy commemorating the war dead (Rutherford 2001, 41–2).[11]

We see similar features in the poetry of other elegiac poets. Callinus exhorts his addressees to throw off their idleness – an idleness of a particular sort: the word *katakeisthe* (line 1) suggests reclining in a sympotic context (Tedeschi 1978):

> Why are you lying around? When will you have courage
> in your bones, young men? Do you not feel ashamed
> before your neighbors when you are this negligent?
> You suppose that you abide in peaceful
> times, but war has the entire land in its clutches.

> Every Ephesian feels the loss when a man
> of determination dies, a man worthy of
> the half-god heroes when he lived. The people
> look upon him as a fortress. He performs
> the feats of many men though he stands alone.
> (Callinus F 1 IEG, Lines 1–4 and 18–21)

Callinus' exhortation upbraids his addressees for their idleness and celebrates an exemplary person whom the community grieves to lose. This strategy of representing communal grief over the loss of an exemplary citizen as a standard of conduct for Callinus' addressees recalls elegy's eulogistic function. An elegiac poem by Mimnermus similarly exemplifies how elegiac poets address the somber realities of death for parainetic ends:

> Leaves that spring's prolific season brings
> into the world, when leaves burst open under
> the sunlight's power. Like leaves we enjoy youth's blooms

for a stunted hour, unconscious of what good
or bad the gods effect. Ominous Death Spirits
are close by, one of them offering old age's bitter
finish, another, death's ultimatum. Youth's moment
exists as briefly as daylight breaks over the land.
When this moment reaches the end of its course,
to die becomes suddenly better than living on.
The soul's afflictions multiply. Loss of property,
and pain-inflicting poverty follows. Another
person is deprived of children and feeling
this loss more than anything else goes under
the earth, into Hades. Another person has
a fatal illness. No human exists to whom
Zeus does not give a generous portion of misery.
(Mimnermus F 2 IEG)

Elegiac artists also composed erotic poetry. Mimnermus is most well known for poetry that reveled in love and youth, underscoring life's harsher realities by way of contrast with erotic pleasure in the following verses:

What life, what enjoyment exists without golden Aphrodite?
I hope I die when these things no longer matter
to me: one-on-ones in secret, enticing gifts,
the bed. These are youth's blooms. They ravish men
and women alike. When ache-inducing old-age
sets in with its power to make even a beautiful
man an eye-gouging sight, worries break
his mind down, and he does not enjoy beholding
the daylight. He is hateful to boys and useless
to women. God makes old age full of these pains.
(Mimnermus F 1 IEG)

5.   Melos

Alcaeus's poetry[12] sometimes exhibits concerns with sympotic practices and appears to be intended for performance for a *hetaireia*, recalling elegy's non-public performance venue. In other moments Alcaeus' poetry is reminiscent of elegiac narrative and exhortation and of the invective of iambos. Such overlaps in performance venue and poetic strategies across melos, iambos, and elegy presents a case in point for the limitations of the kind of taxonomy represented by Table 10.1. Recalling Callinus F 1 (above), the following passage applies the ship of state metaphor to address social discord and exhort addressees to take action:

This wave approaches in its turn, as we
have seen it do before. It will cause us
the back-breaking work of baling water out
when it fills the ship's... Let's bolster...as fast as we can.
Let's hurry to a safe harbor. Let enervating
fear hold none of us back. We are face to face
with a great... Remember our previous distress,
and at this moment let every one of us be
proven worthy. Never let lack of courage
disgrace our dear parents who lie below the earth.
(Alc. F 6 V)

Although this fragment resembles elegy because of its exhortatory quality, its meters are melic, suggesting sung mode of presentation and lyre-accompaniment. All of Alcaeus' poetry is monodic melic, composed in stanzas of two or four lines, most famously the four-line stanza named for him, the alcaeic.

Alcaeus appears to have been involved in conflict for political leadership at Mytilene. His poetry refers his family's alliance with a figure named Pittacus, who ousted a tyrant Melanchrus (Alc. F 75). When Myrsilus came to power as tyrant of Mytilene, a faction of Mytilenean elites, including Pittacus and Alcaeus (Alc. F 114 and 129), went into exile. Pittacus eventually betrayed his former party and allied with Myrsilus, as we have it from Alcaeus (Alc. F 70 and 129). When Myrsilus died, the community installed Pittacus as ruler to defend against the ongoing resistance to Mytilenean tyranny by Alcaeus and his allies (Alc. F 70 and 348). Against this backdrop, Alcaeus' condemnations (Alc. F 72, 129, 348) of Pittacus' character, appetitive inclinations, and physical appearance that are idiomatic to blame poetics, blurs the line between conventional roles and historical reality: if performer and addressee roles of iambos are conventional, Alcaeus exploits that convention to broadcast his real-time-and-place opposition to Pittacus' regime. This observation bears out when we consider the performance venue for blame poetics: given the relevance of Alcaeus' attacks upon Pittacus for the community, his conception of the *hetaireia* takes the form of a political faction, rather than a group of intimates, as well as those potentially to be won over to that faction (Yatromanolakis 2009a, 207–9). The following fragment exemplifies blame poetics and exhortation:

> ...the people of Lesbos founded... this sanctuary,
> spacious and visible from afar, to be used
> by everyone. They set up altars for
> the blessed immortals. They called Zeus by the name
> of Welcomer, and you, Aeolian, goddess who grants
> us mortals glory, they called Originator of All.
> This third god they named Kemelian – that was Dionysus,
> raw flesh eater. Come, all of you gods, accept
> our prayers. From these toils and heartbreaking exile
> deliver us. Let the punishment of those three gods
> chase down the son of Hyrrhas [i.e. Pittacus], because we one time
> swore... slicing... never to... any of our allies,
> but either to go down dead and cloaked in earth
> at the hands of men who then... against... or to cut
> them down and deliver the people from their misery.
> But beer-gut did not keep his agreement with them.
> Instead he viciously stomped his feet on those oaths
> and gorges himself on our city... lawlessly...
> wrote... gray... Myrsilus...
>
> (Alc. F 129 V)

In this fragment Alcaeus narrates the founding of a sacred precinct on Lesbos, recalling narrative poems about foundations attributed to the elegiac poets Mimnermus, Xenophanes, and Solon, and exhorts addressees to virtuous action, recalling Callinus F 1 (above). The fragment concludes with invective directed against the regular target of Alcaeus' attacks, Pittacus, so that Alcaeus' melic poetry exhibits features of elegy and iambos.

Alcaeus' uses Lesbian vernacular with a blend of Ionic-epic.[13] This reflects a distinguishing feature of monodic melic in contrast with choral melic: whereas monodic melic was composed in local dialects (Lesbian Aeolic in the cases of Sappho and Alcaeus, Ionic vernacular in the case of Anacreon,) for *hetaireia* performance, choral melic was composed using the Doric dialect for public performance. Indicative of this distinction between monodic and choral melic, Alcman's choral melic poetry uses Laconic vernacular, which is broadly Doric, with Ionic epic and Aeolic forms.

Suda reports that Alcman composed *melê* – melic songs – collected by Alexandrian scholars into six books, of which two may have been *partheneia*. The shredded first 35 lines of Alcman's *Louvre Partheneion* (Alcman 1 PMGF)[14] mention such figures as Polydeuces, brother of Castor, the sons of the legendary Spartan king Hippocoon, and the Graces, suggesting mythological content. There were cults at Sparta for Polydeuces and Castor and for the Graces, so that Alcman's home polis provides a basis for linking the song to ritual, an impression confirmed by the 66 mostly complete lines that represent a festival context, possibly the celebration of Orthria (line 62; cf. Krummen 2009, 190–91). Beginning with a gnomic transition (lines 36–9) on the topic of divine punishment and human limitations, the more well-preserved lines of the fragment celebrate two figures, Hagesichora and Agido, and describe the chorus and choral performance. The song may suggest a dawn performance (lines 41–2 and 60–63) and commemorates a (dawn?) goddess called Aotis (line 87), the identity of whom remains disputed.

> The gods' vengeance does exist. Blessed is anyone
> who binds off the day's weft without weeping.
> I though, I sing Agido's light. I look
> upon her as upon the sun, which Agido invokes
> to shine for us as a witness. Our celebrated chorus
> leader prevents me from either praising or blaming
> Agido, for her mere appearance distinguishes
> her, as if someone should put a horse
> in the middle of a cattle herd, a powerful,
> prize-winning horse with thundering hooves,
> one of those horses that belongs in cavernous dreams.
>
> Or do you not see? The racehorse is Enetic,
> but my cousin Hagesichora's hair luminesces
> like unalloyed gold. And the radiance of her face – why
> explain the obvious? This is Hagesichora right here.
> Second in beauty to Agido, she is a Kolaxian
> horse racing against an Ibenian. When we carry
> this robe to Orthria, the Pleiades ascend the divine
> night like dogstar Sirius and bring us battle.
>   (Alcman F 1.36–63 PMGF)

Composed in a first person voice, which intensifies the song's self-reflexive quality, the *Louvre Partheneion* singles out members of the chorus performing the song, dwells upon the physical appearance of those chorus members, and refers to ritual practices, such as bringing a robe (or plow?) to Orthria, that appear to occasion the song (Peponi 2004). The text identifies Hagesichora as *chorostatis* "chorus-leader" (line 84) and emphasizes the beauty of Agido and Hagesichora. Agido is a racehorse out of place in the midst of livestock, a metaphor that verges into another in which Agido and Hagesichora are the two fastest horses, Kolaxian and Ibenian, outpacing other horses – that is to say, excelling the other female chorus members in beauty. Another metaphor expresses the exceptional appearance of Agido and Hagesichora. One is the Pleiades, the other is the star Sirius. These celestial fixtures excel other heavenly bodies in brightness and beauty to the same degree that Agido and Hagesichora excel the other chorus members in beauty. While the first-person voice of the song may indicate that Agido and Hagesichora bring the other chorus members battle in the metaphorical sense of rivaling them in beauty, some argue that the Pleiades may be a chorus.[15] The next lines (64–77) mention other chorus members by name (Nanno (70), Areta (72), Sylakis and Kleësithera (72)). The fineness of their attire – purple garments, golden jewelry, ornamental headbands – and their appearance – the text specifically mentions hair and eyes – displays wealth and prestige. The concluding (extant) lines of the song (78–101) depict festivity and performance, offering praise for gods and singing of the fitness of following the chorus leader's lead. As Krummen observes, "[t]he poem fits into the established system of values of an aristocratic society and a *polis* that regularly reconfirms its history (cf. the myth of the sons of Hippocoon in the first part) and its identity through the celebration of recurring festivals" (2009, 193; cf. Nagy 1996, 57). Such social functions of Alcman's *Louvre Partheneion* are generally consistent with the expectation that the intended audience of choral melic is *polis* members, but also capture the fact that choral song has multiple messages, each addressed to particular constituencies within the *polis*.

In this necessarily selective sampling of iambic, elegiac, and melic poetry, we have seen that even superficial interpretation of Greek lyric requires accounting for praise and blame poetics, occasions for performance, and the ritual and socio-historical contexts in which the poetry is embedded. Although categorization of lyric poetries on the bases of meter and of public versus private original performance has the advantage of simple encapsulation, the taxonomy presented in Table 10.1 is a blunt critical instrument. The extent to which the table captures practices of performance and reperformance and represents how generic conventions, poetic traditions, and occasions for composition shape, and are shaped by, the interaction between performer(s) and audience(s) is too limited to be useful for the interpretation of actual poems.

6.   Rethinking Ancient Greek Lyric

The challenges to establishing taxonomic criteria suitable for a durable and portable definition of lyric genre sometimes lead scholars to question the very concept of genre. Such skepticism reflects less the limitations of genre as a descriptive and analytical vantage point than the fact that, as performed and traditional forms of verbal art, Greek lyric poetries will always be more or less illegible to exegetical, New Critical, and Aristotelian methods of description and classification that reify the text, rather than the performance event, as the object of analysis. The performative turn has made possible important insights into the relationship(s) between textual remains of archaic Greece and the socio-historical contexts in which they are embedded, but an entextualized record of performance is a record of cultural practice in its own right, an instance of culture whose very madeness is expressive and representational.[16]

Greek lyric poetics is sited in the performance arena, whether conceived of as a here-and-now original performance by a song's composer or as a song's reception and transmission through reperformance. Greek lyric poetics is also firmly grounded in a "song culture" saturated with multiple performance occasions and multiple social functions for performed verbal art (Herington 1985). By conceiving of the Greek lyric text as a record of a special kind of speech event, a performance (cf. on this Baumbach ch. 22, pp. 345–6 in this volume), we can better grasp any internal evidence for the framing of the performance arena and gain insight into the role of the audience in performance (Martin 2001).[17] An audience is always already responsive to performance, and the lyric composer is in turn responsive to the anticipated artistic competency and evaluative position of the audience. Far from being "summed up and transcended" in archaic Greek lyric (Fowler 1987, vii), tradition is a crucial resource for an audience, ancient or modern, to evaluate lyric performances and their entextualized records (Nagy 1990, 4, 19, and *passim* and Bauman 2012, 103). Typical occasions for the performance of a given genre of poetry are one dimension of tradition. To give an example relevant to my discussion of Sappho F 31 V below, lament conventionally fits into the matrix of practices associated with death and burial (Alexiou 1974/2002, 3–23) but would be (productively?) out of place in situations where an audience expected performances of mockery or first person narratives of sexual escapades. Some view the occasion–genre link as being so inherently traditional that a composition's genre invokes the occasion conventionally associated with that genre.[18] In addition to typical occasions for performance, traditional structural units of a composition – conveniently illustrated by Homeric phraseological words, typical scenes, and story patterns – "reach out of the immediate instance in which they appear to the fecund totality of the entire tradition, defined synchronically and diachronically, and they bear meanings as wide and deep as the tradition they encode" (Foley 1991, 7). Such reaching-out captures the way in which traditional referentiality works: traditional occasions for performance and the traditional poetics of individual songs enable the audience to evaluate the composer-performer's artistic competence by reference to the shared background knowledge constituted by communally observed artistic conventions (Bauman 1977, 11 and 2012, 99). Performer and audience are interlocutors who share the same knowledge of these conventions, and the performer is bound in a way special to the audience's evaluation of her or his work for its artistic merit. The performer of lyric poetry is as creatively empowered by traditional performance conventions and the enabling dynamics afforded by a responsive audience as the singer of narrative tales. The view of lyric poetry as the poetic product of solipsistic introspection may have more (dubious) validity when it comes to John Keats or Gjertrud Schnackenberg, but in the context of ancient Greece and its traditional art forms, the word is not yet so technologized (cf. Kurke 2000, 41).

In my approach to Greek lyric genre and performance, I follow the example of folklorists and linguistic anthropologists who adopt Mikhail Bakhtin's theory of the utterance to the study of ethnographically derived texts (Bakhtin 1986, 60–102).[19] Bakhtin observes that two or more simple speech genres constitute a complex genre, a theoretical move that enables a kind of multivariate analysis of the elements constituting a complex genre, including performance occasion, participant roles, linguistic register(s), social functions of performance, and the simple speech genres that constitute complex speech genres. One of the constitutive simple speech genres may be so dominant in a given composition that it is definitive of the complex genre. The features of speech genres include the speech subject (who speaks?), the addressee, the speech object (what is the utterance about?), the speech plan (what are the ends or effects of speaking?), the spatial dimension(s) of an utterance (e.g. is the utterance about some "here" or some "there"?), and the temporal dimension of an utterance (e.g. is the utterance about some "now" or some "then," past or future?) (Bakhtin 1986, 60–102; cf. Wells 2009, 61–7).

Deixis provides one basis for identifying these features of simple speech genres and, in broader terms, deictic features of language provide crucial evidence for performance as cultural practice (Levinson 1983, 54–96 and Hanks 1992).[20] Textual artifacts of ancient Greek lyric poetry preserve deictic features of language (pronouns, demonstrative adjectives, adverbs, verb morphology indicating person and number) that point out participants – speech subject, addressee – in the performance event and people or things referred to in a given song – the speech object – and delineate spatial (near, far, in-between) and temporal (past, present, future) dimensions of such pointing-out. Performance events have a contextual ground, the origo, relative to which time, space, participants, and other referents are figured through deixis (Hanks 1992). Deictic features of language point out who or what belongs in the here and now of the performance origo and who or what is there and then (past or future) relative to the performance origo. The textual artifacts of ancient Greek lyric poetry thus preserve deictic features of language that constitute simple speech genres (Bakhtin 1986, 60–102) or registers, complementary terms that emphasize the quality of voice.[21] To identify deictic evidence for speech genres grounds analysis in the performance event, so that we build local knowledge of the means of communicative exchange between composer-performer(s) and audience(s). Another advantage to approaching lyric genre in terms of speech genres: such a methodology foregrounds the performer-audience interaction, analytically siting the lyric *I* in a context in which dialogical dynamics shape its voice(s).

A third advantage to identifying simple speech genres is to discern the individual threads in the fabric of lyric poetry, which proves to be far more multiform than Table 10.1 would suggest.

The selection of simple speech genres and their combination into complex speech genres – and I want to stress that such speech genres, simple and complex, are likely to be canonical within the ambient performance, story, and ritual traditions in which Greek lyric poetries are situated (cf. Martin 1989) – is generic intertextuality, one of three modes of intertextuality explored by folklorist Richard Bauman. Bauman identifies two further modes of intertextuality: reiteration, the re-use of discourse "reported as having been said by another," and parody, the "ludic or inversive transformation of a prior text or genre" (Bauman 2004, 4–10). *Poikilia* is an indigenous metapoetic concept that captures these modes of intertextuality, which saturate iambos, elegy, and melos where the textual remains are sufficiently substantial to evidence them. Focusing on generic intertexuality and parody, I illustrate such poikilian poetics in a premier example of Greek lyric poetry, Sappho F 31 V.[22]

7. "Lyric" Genre

I begin this illustration with a translation of Sappho F 31 V.[23]

A god's equal that man looks
to be to me, the man who sits himself across from you.
Your words breathed into his ear,

4   he is so attentive,
and your perfect laugh – something, I swear,
that traps a frenzied heart in my ribcage.
I take a single look at you, and to speak:

8   this is not possible.
My tongue is useless. A ribbon
of flame undercourses my skin.
My eyes see nothing,

12   ears drum.
Cool perspiration coats my flesh. I tremble,
I tremble and go more bloodless
than field grass. I am on the verge of death,

16   as far as I can tell.
But endure and endure, since even a worker for hire…

(Sappho F 31 V)

One step in the description of lyric genre is to identify a song's complex genre and, by extension, the performance occasion(s) with which that complex genre is conventionally associated, to the extent that extratextual or intratextual evidence makes this possible. In this composition Sappho adapts the traditional lament genre to the context of an erotic relationship.[24] Women conventionally and authoritatively perform lament (Alexiou 1974/2002, 102–3 and 108) as we see, for example, in Homer's *Iliad* where women are represented as the exclusive performers of the genre (Foley 1991, 168). Lament has three features, which occur in an A-B-A pattern: (A) a direct address to the deceased, accompanied by the speaker's accusation that the deceased has left or abandoned the speaker; (B) a narrative recounting the speaker's personal history with the deceased or the expected consequences of the addressee's death for the speaker; (A) a readdress asserts the ultimate intimacy between speaker and deceased (Alexiou 1974/2002, 131–4; cf. Foley 1991, 169–74). Alexiou is unequivocal about the status of lament as a traditional genre: "[w]hile by no means every lament conforms to this pattern, there is a sufficient number of examples, early and late, to establish its traditional basis beyond doubt" (Alexiou 1974/2002, 133). F 31 V appears to conform to this "traditionally sanctioned" form (Foley 1991, 168), cuing an audience to respond to and to evaluate the song as lament at the level of complex genre. But rather than a song addressed to a deceased, F 31 V's addressee is a departed one whom the speaker desires. Thus parody: in an inversive transformation of lament, Sappho deploys a complex genre conventionally associated with a particular occasion, death, for another occasion, love loss. The song's opening address to the departed (lines 1–8) corresponds to the address feature of lament, but in place of an accusation that the deceased addressee has abandoned the mourner, the song's pragmatic mapping *represents* the distance between speaker and addressee. Given a performance context for Sappho's songs, the situational origo is the performer–audience interaction. Relative to that origo, the addressee is distant – *there* relative to the *here* of performance – as indicated by the distal deictic demonstrative *kênos* "that man" (line 1), *plasion* "near" (line 3) to whom Sappho's second person addressee is (cf. Carson 1986, 13 and Rösler 1990). There is poetic tension between the deictically indicated distance between speaker and addressee and their proximity suggested by the song's I–you addressivity. Such tension inheres in the genre of lament where the aggrieved mourns for the loss of an intimate: the nearest of persons occupies death's remotest zone of absence.

Sappho narrates personal consequences (lament feature B) of the loss of the departed addressee (lines 9–16) and captures the physiology of loss and desire, a cartography embossed with intensified resonance when reading 31 V through the lens of lament. Sappho's repurposed version of the narrative feature of lament corresponds to the occasion for its performance: Sappho shapes the effects of the departed's absence as affects resulting from desire's lack of fulfillment. Loss's ultimate effect upon the speaker is that she seems to herself to be dead (lines 15–16), a self-characterization that attributes the lifelessness of the mourned to the mourner. Sappho thus exploits lament's heightened sense of loss to characterize the pain of frustrated eros. The stanzaic structure of F 31 V supports the view that the song is a lament: lament feature A coincides with the first and second stanzas of the poem and lament feature B coincides with the third and fourth stanzas.

The extant text corroborates more than refutes the view that Sappho's F 31 V is a lament adapted to an erotic situation if the last corrupt line of this fragmentary poem is a trace of the readdress feature of lament. *Alla*, "but," marks some shift in the discursive flow from narrative (to readdress?) and *epei*, "since" introduces a clause that would presumably explain that shift. The phrase *pan tolmaton* "each thing must be endured" may resume an I–you mode of communication by virtue of the verbal adjective's imperative function, suggesting a re-address. But it is more secure to say that the addressee is indefinite given the lack of personal reference in the neuter singular phrase *pan tolmaton*. In that case we are witnessing a gnomic generalization: Sappho reworks the expected I–you readdress characteristic of lament to universalize experiences of loss and desire. The immanent art quality of lament enables the composer-performer to so confidently assume the audience's knowledge of lament conventions that she adapts it to embrace the eros experience in addition to the already intensest experiences of death and mourning (cf. Gentili 1988, 84). Such inclusivity of the impersonal construction shapes the occasion of 31 V's performance into a site that includes the audience. This interpretation of the sparest evidence accords with Alexiou's view that "lament was always in some sense collective, and never an exclusively solo performance" (Alexiou 1974/2002, 134).[25]

Acknowledging the limitations of emplotment intended to reconstruct the original context in which the song was embedded (Yatromanolakis 2009a, 206), if F 31 V communicates an adult woman's empathy for younger woman's transition into marriage and adulthood, we can make reasonable interpretations about the song's social import. Given ancient Greek social norms, it is unlikely that a woman would be in such close physical proximity to a man as the pair in the opening lines of the song are depicted as being if the woman were not the man's wife or a *hetaira*. Lament fits the marriage scenario:[26] "[t]he rape of Persephone, for example, by Hades, god of the underworld, sets up a cultural model of marriage as synonymous with sexuality and violence, a kind of death" (Dougherty 1993, 64; cf. Skinner 2005, 105). Add to this André Lardinois's observation that "young Greek women were often imagined as 'dying' the death of a young girl before being reborn as women (and mothers) in marriage" (2001, 82, with documentation). The fact that the ordeal of marriage would have been particular to a young women's experience is my basis for the hypothesis that the addressee of F 31 V is younger than the song's composer–performer.[27] Due to the erotic situation, the composer–performer of F 31 V is more than the Demeter to the Persephone of her addressee. If F 31 V's addressee is a woman transitioning to marriage and adulthood, then the speaker's physiological symptoms represented in the poem may image not only love-sickness, but also embodied recollection of the speaker's own transition into marriage and adulthood. "A god's equal that man looks/to me to be" – perhaps he seems so because of his sexual prerogative in contrast to the speaker's unfulfilled erotic desire, but perhaps, too, because of his social dominance as an adult male in an asymmetrical relationship with his wife (Skinner 2005, 146). Sappho's physiological symptoms may be manifestations of both unfulfilled desire and loss, and this loss may be "personal" and empathetic: that the speaker seems to herself to be dead is a powerful depiction of the older woman's empathy with the addressee's traumatic entry into adulthood through marriage. "But endure and endure" – perhaps Sappho's self-encouragement to bear her love-loss, perhaps Sappho's concession that the ordeal of marriage offers socially prescribed access to female adulthood, perhaps a gesture in which the verbal adjective *pan tolmaton* "each thing is to be endured" has a gnomic connotation that extends the sentiment to her audience – "other women, with whom she shared the experiences of seclusion, disempowerment, and separation" (Kurke 2000, 59) – as a (transgressive (Stehle 2009, 60)) commentary upon undergoing such shared experience (cf. Lardinois 2001, 88). Features of indefiniteness characteristic of the gnomic speech genre de-limit the addressee(s) of *pan tolmaton* "each thing is to be endured," so that the impersonal verbal adjective phrase potentially rings as inclusive of all women who undergo the ordeal of marriage (cf. Foley 1991, 168).

The first person of F 31 V orchestrates the stylistic inflections and, by extension, the audience's evaluative responses to the song's performance in ways that suggest the salience of aspects of Pindar's poetics for lyric poetics generally. Pindar's verbal art is robustly intertextual. His victory song is a complex genre of performance that comprises five speech genres or registers: lyric register (first person statements about the occasion of and for performance), gnomic statement, mythological narrative, *eukhesthai* (the infinitive for "to pray" and "to boast," which captures two functions of this speech genre), and *angelia* "victory announcement" (reports such information as the athletic victor's name, family, achievements, and polis) (Wells 2009, 61–128). Every complex victory song does not include all of these simple speech genres, but no other simple speech genres occur in Pindar's epinician songs, and 19 of Pindar's 45 victory songs exhibit ring-composition structured on the basis of these simple speech genres (Wells 2009, 181 and 193–238).[28] Those fragments of Sappho's corpus sufficiently well preserved to offer evidence for speech genres (e.g. F 1, 2, 5, 16, 17, 31, 44, 81, 94, 111, and 112) also contain only the same simple speech genres as Pindar's *epinikia*, with the exception of *angelia*, which may be particular to *epinikion* as a poetic version of a formal victory announcement, but as narrative about historical (rather than mythological or legendary) events parallels narrative about historical events in other lyric poets.[29] F 31 V's address, lament feature A, is in the *eukhesthai* register by virtue of the dominance of second-person address. The narration of the mourner's personal consequences as a result of loss, lament feature B, is in the lyric register by virtue of its self-reflexive deictic referentiality. The voice of this narrative is first person, not third person. Rather than being self-reflexive by way of referring to or describing poetics or performance as the lyric speech genre does in Pindar, Sappho describes her embodied experience, the physiological symptoms manifest in the composer–performer's body here and now performing before an audience. The possible re-address of F 31 V, tenuously evidenced in the fragmentary last line, may be best described as a hybrid of *eukhesthai* and gnomic registers, the former dominating if the emphasis is on addressivity borne by the imperative function of the verbal adjective, the latter dominating if the generalizing force of the gnomic quality is closer to the communicative surface. Such hybridization of speech genres is a micro-level instance of generic intertextuality.

Given the indexical ground for a performance context, in which the dominantly organizing social interaction is that between performer and audience – this social interaction would be constitutive of the complex speech genre – relational figures emerge. In F 31 V the I–you addressivity of *eukhesthai*, the self-reflexive orientation of the lyric speech genre, the indefinite voice that animates the gnomic register – these various voicings contribute to the polyphony of Sappho's poetry. Pindar applies the term *poikilia* to the art of orchestrating multiple speech genres into an integrated, complex composition and, by implication, orchestrating multiple vocal figures projected against the ground of the performance origo. We should not be surprised to find that Pindar even represents *poikilia* in terms of a weaving metaphor (cf. Nagy 1996, 64–6):

> My mother's mother was Stymphalian, blooming Metopa,
> who bore horse-driving Thebes, whose lovely water
> I drink as I weave [*plekón*]
> a poikilian hymn [*poikilon humnon*] for warriors.
> (Pindar *Ol.* 6.84–7)

The self-reflexive quality of this lyric passage, which refers to the composer and concerns the craft of composition, makes it salient as a metacommunicative assertion that, when it comes to poikilian poetics, the composer–performer's is the dominant voice. Apart from considerations of biography or ideology and in terms of Pindar's own account of his poetics, the lyric voice turns out to be the performing-speaking position of the artist who orchestrates such poikilian poetics. In F 31 V we see *poikilia* in the form of generic intertexuality, and in the decidedly non-ludic "inversive transformation of a prior text or genre" that involves applying lament to a marriage situation, if this interpretation of the situation the song addresses is correct (Bauman 2004, 4–10).

8. Conclusion

With respect to genre, lyric is complex, intertextual, and, minimally, doubly occasional, with original performance and reperformance(s). What we call Greek "lyric" includes too diverse and multiform a field of poetics and poetic practice to allow for an all-encompassing designation or definition of it. There is no evidence for a Grand Theory of Greek "lyric," except, perhaps, from the point of view of "those with a particular sort of cultural breeding." Unlike "lyric," the indigenous metapoetic concept *poikilia* captures the poetics of Greek lyric poetries: in terms of genre, Greek lyric poetry is variegated; in terms of voice, Greek lyric poetry is polyvalent. I do not claim that *poikilia* is exclusively characteristic of Greek lyric poetries; other media possess this quality as well, including epic, dramatic, and prose genres. The point is that *poikilia* as a descriptive and interpretive vantage point corresponds to the poikilian poetics of Greek lyric and makes it possible for us to move beyond analytical accoutrements that can limit our appreciation of such cultural artifacts as extant Greek lyric texts. In order to pursue a philology that captures the *poikilia* of Greek lyric poetry, this chapter models a performance-centered and practice-based approach to genre. Genre is both a salient critical focus in the study of Greek lyric poetry and also an interpretive affordance, especially given the limitations of our decontextualized textual remains. Since participants in the performance event are a feature of genre as I conceive of it, genre affords insight into the dialogical moves through which performers secure a positive evaluation from an audience for their verbal artworks. Voice affords insight into agency, the performer's agency in composition and performance and the audience's agency in the co-creation of the artwork (Bauman 2012, 101). The fact that particular speech genres have sufficiently stable features to be recognizable as such in the poetry of two authors as unalike as Pindar and Sappho – different media, different performance occasions, different socio-historical contexts, and, thus, social functions, for their compositions – may suggest their traditionality. Ring-composition is a recognizably traditional compositional strategy, to be sure, so that Pindar's tendency to use speech genres as building material for ring-composition strongly suggests the traditionality of those speech genres in his epinician compositions. Although similarities between Pindar's speech genres and Sappho's may point the way toward further exploration of the significance of speech genres in ancient Greek lyric poetry, for present purposes I wish to stress that *poikilia* is descriptive of the intertextual dynamics that saturate lyric poetics. In opposition to an intentional philology that obscures difference for the sake of categorization or of staking out ideological ground, I advocate for and, I hope, exemplify a philology intentionally attuned to difference.

NOTES

I wish to thank Martin Hose and David Schenker for their comments on earlier versions and for their diligence in steering this volume to completion.

[1] See Budelmann 2009b, 3, with documentation, Silk 2009, and Brewster 2009, 72–111 on such Romantic conceptions of lyric and the extent of their persistence, as exemplified by subdivisions of areas of specialization within classical philology.

[2] Cf. also Power, ch. 4 in this volume.

[3] For further discussions of lyric versus melos, see Färber 1936, 7–16, Most 1982, 79, and Nagy 1990, 82–3.

[4] Cf. Harvey 1955, Most 1982, Fowler 1987, 86–103, Kurke 2000, 46 and 2007, 145–7.

[5] *Gephurismoi* occurred as the ritual procession from Athens to Eleusis crossed the bridge over the Cephissus River – witness the verb *gephurizdein* "to shout abuse on / from a bridge."

[6] Archilochus also wrote elegiac poetry.

[7] Nagy argues that Lycambes is a stock character (1979, 248–9). This interpretation makes the first scenario – that the blame poetics of Archilochus's "*Cologne Epode*" reinforces social norms – more likely. Such stock characters occur elsewhere: a cook (Semonides F 24 IEG), a poor farmer (Hipponax F 26 IEG), a burglar (Hipponax F 32 IEG). For the view that Lycambes was a historical figure, see Carey (2009b) 153.

[8] Cf. Aloni (2009, 168–9), who further explains, "[n]one of these terms is used self-referentially in the archaic and classical elegies themselves, except in Critias 4.3 IEG, where ἐλεγεῖον has primarily a metrical meaning. It seems impossible to determine the precise relationship between these three terms."

[9] See Day 2010 on the poetics of epigram.

[10] Thgn. 467–96, 503–8, 825–30, 837–40, 1047–8, and 1129–32; Xenophanes F 1 IEG; Simonides F 25 IEG; cf. Carey 2009b, 34–5.

[11] The ancient books into which Tyrtaeus's elegies were collected offer further evidence elegy's range: "exhortations through elegies," "battle songs," "marching songs" (Aloni 2009, 174).

[12] Cf. Power, ch. 4, pp. 64–5 in this volume.

[13] Cf. Willi, ch. 29, pp. 451–2 in this volume.

[14] Cf. on this poem Power, ch. 4, pp. 68, and Willi, ch. 29, pp. 449–50 in this volume.

[15] Whereas Campbell (1982b, 205) more succinctly advocates for the interpretation that the Pleiades are a rival chorus, in his chatty way Hutchinson opposes this view (2001, 90–93).

[16] In performance studies Bauman (1977) is foundational. For a recent overview of approaches to performance, see Bauman 2012.

[17] Throughout I refer to "speech" event, "speech" genre, and "speech" act, stressing the spoken and oral quality of Greek lyric poetries. In doing so I draw from established precedent in folklore, linguistic anthropology, and classical philology, but I do not at all mean to suggest that "speech" is in any way opposed to recitative or sung formats for Greek lyric performance. "Speech" is the most generic term for the mode of communication opposed to writing; my intention is to stress face-to-face oral communication between performer(s) and audience by referring to speech.

[18] Nagy 1994 / 1995 and 2007, Kurke 2000, 46, and Cingano 2003, 22.

[19] The application of Bakhtin's thought to performed media of verbal art is consistent with a long tradition in folklore and linguistic anthropology (Bauman 2000 and 2006).

[20] On applications of pragmatics and, in particular, deixis to the study of archaic Greek poetry, see Rösler 1983 and 1990; Bonifazi 2001, 2004a, b, and c; and Felson 2004a and b; Bakker 2005; and D'Alessio 2009.

[21] I also draw upon the methodological model of linguistic anthropologist William Hanks (1987), who opts for the rubric "discourse genres of practice" in his pragmatic analysis of speech genre and intertextuality.

[22] Reiteration, the reported speech of others, may take the form of direct and indirect discourse in Greek melos, iambos, and elegy, for example in Archil. F 196a IEG (Bowie 2001) and Sappho F 1 V (Nagy 1996, 97–103).

[23] Cf. on this poem Willi, ch. 29, pp. 451–2 in this volume.

[24] Suter 2009 is the inspiration for exploring applications of the ethnography-driven philology I pursued in *Pindar's Verbal Art* to Sappho's poetry. Lardinois summarizes and documents interpretations for and against the view that Sappho F 31 V is a wedding song, observing that the opening line of the poem "recalls the traditional *makarismos* of the groom, and the position of the man and woman, sitting opposite one another, is paralleled by the depiction of other married couples in Greek literature and art" (2001, 90). As I go on to demonstrate below, Sappho F 31 V as lament and as a wedding song are not mutually exclusive interpretations. See also Stehle 1997, 262–318, Calame 2001, 28 and 211, and Dodson-Robinson 2010 on wedding songs in Sappho's corpus.

[25] Arguments in favor of the view that a chorus performed Sappho's songs (Lardinois 1994 and 2001; Calame 2001, 65, 210–14, and 231–3; Nagy 2007, 216) intensify the social group resonance of Sappho F 31 V's performance. For the view that Sappho composed her songs for solo *hetaireia* performance, see Parker 1993. Stehle (1997, 262–318), who distinguishes between Sappho's "wedding songs and other ritual poetry," which were choral, and songs performed for a *hetaireia*, asserts that "the singer of 31 V does not allow room for the listeners' presence in her fiction or insinuate that the group has any function in relationship to her" (1997, 290).

[26] On Sappho F 31 V as a wedding song, see note 24 above.

[27] Compare Lardinois's discussion of Sappho F 114 V, apparently a dialogue between a bride and her now-departing virginity (*parthenia*): "The direct address of the 'deceased' and the accusation that he or she 'left' or 'deserted' the speaker are typical of laments [...] and there is more evidence that brides at their wedding could perform laments for themselves" (2001, 82).

[28] In addition to epinikion, the other genres in which Pindar is known to have composed (hymns, paeans, dithyrambs, prosodia, parthenia, hyporchemata, encomia, and laments) are complex genres. Pindar's songs refer to still other poetic media. *Pyth.* 6 includes traces of *Kheirônos Hupothêkai* "Precepts of Kheiron" and *Isth.* 1 mentions in addition to paean, the *kallinikos* song, Castoreion, didactic poetry, and homecoming invocation (Kurke 1988 and 1990). See also Pindar F 128c.

[29] See Bauman 2000 and 2006 on the differences in chronotope and performance between historical narrative and mythological narrative and Wells 2009, 77–88 for a comparison of historical narrative in *angeliai* "victory announcements" and mythological narrative in Pindar's epinikia.

REFERENCES

Adorno, T. W. 1974. "On Lyric Poetry and Society." In R. Tiedermann, ed., *Notes to Literature Vol. 1.* New York, 37–54.

Agocs, P., C. Carey, and R. Rawles, eds. 2012. *Reading the Victory Ode.* Cambridge.

Alexiou, M. 1974 / 2002. *The Ritual Lament in Greek Tradition.* 2nd edn. Rev. D. Yatromanolakis and P. Roilos. Lanham, MD. (1st edn. 1974).

Aloni, A. 2009. "Elegy: Forms, Functions and Communication." In F. Budelmann, ed., *The Cambridge Companion to Greek Lyric,* Cambridge, 168–88.

Aloni, A. and A. Iannucci. 2007. *L'elegia greca e l'epigramma: Dalle origini al V secolo. Con un'appendice sulla 'nuova' elegia di Archiloco.* Florence.

Athanassaki, L. and E. Bowie, eds. 2011. *Archaic and Classical Choral Song. Performance, Politics and Dissemination.* Berlin.

Bakhtin, M. M. 1986. *Speech Genres and Other Essays.* Edited by C. Emerson and M. Holquist. Austin, TX.

Bakker, E. J. 2005. *Pointing at the Past: From Formula to Performance in Homeric Poetics.* Washington DC.

Battezzato, L. 2009. "Metre and Music." In F. Budelmann, ed., *The Cambridge Companion to Greek Lyric,* Cambridge, 130–146.

Bauman, R. 1977. *Verbal Art as Performance.* Prospect Heights, IL.

Bauman, R. 2000. "Genre." *Journal of Linguistic Anthropology* 9(1–2): 84–87.

Bauman, R. 2004. *A World of Others' Words: Cross-Cultural Perspectives on Intertextuality.* Oxford.

Bauman, R. 2006. "Speech Genres in Cultural Practice." In K. Brown, ed., *Encyclopedia of Language & Linguistics,* 2nd edn., Oxford, vol. 11. 745–58.

Bauman, R. 2012. "Performance." In Bendix and Hasan-Rokem 2012, 94–118.

Bendix, R. F. and G. Hasan-Rokem, eds. 2012. *A Companion to Folklore.* Oxford.

Bierl, A., R. Lämmle, and K. Wesselmann, eds. 2007. *Literatur und Religion 2: Wege zu einer mythisch-rituellen Poetik bei den Griechen.* Berlin.

Blok, J. H. and A. P. M. H. Lardinois, eds. 2006. *Solon of Athens: New Historical and Philological Approaches.* Leiden.

Boedeker, D. and D. Sider. 2001 *The New Simonides.* Oxford.

Bonifazi, A. 2001. *Mescolare un cratere di canti: Pragmatica della poesia epinicia in Pindaro.* Alessandria.

Bonifazi, A. 2004a. "Communication in Pindar's Deictic Acts." *The Poetics of Deixis in Alcman, Pindar, and Other Lyric.* Special issue, *Arethusa* 37(3), 391–414.

Bonifazi, A. 2004b. "Relative Pronouns and Memory: Pindar Beyond Syntax." *Harvard Studies in Classical Philology* 102: 41–68.

Bonifazi, A. 2004c. "ΚΕΙΝΟΣ in Pindar: Between Grammar and Poetic Intention." *Classical Philology* 99: 283–99.

Bowie, E. L. 1986. "Early Greek Elegy, Symposium and Public Festival." *Journal of Hellenic Studies* 106: 13–35.

Bowie, E. L. 2001. "Early Greek Iambic Poetry: The Importance of Narrative." In A. Cavarzere, A. Aloni, and A. Barchiesi, eds. 2001. *Iambic Ideas: Essays on a Poetic Tradition from Archaic Greece to the Late Roman Empire,* Lanham, MD, 1–27.

Boys-Stones, G., B. Graziosa, and P. Vasunia, eds. 2009. *The Oxford Handbook of Hellenic Studies.* Oxford.

Brewster, S. 2009. *Lyric.* London.

Brown, K., ed. 2006. *Encyclopedia of Language & Linguistics,* 2nd edn. Vol. 11. Oxford.

Budelmann, F., ed. 2009a. *The Cambridge Companion to Greek Lyric.* Cambridge.

Budelmann, F. 2009b. "Introducing Greek Lyric." In Budelmann 2009a, 1–18.

172 James Bradley Wells

Calame, C. 2001. *Choruses of Young Women in Ancient Greece: Their Morphology, Religious Role, and Social Functions.* New and rev. edn. Lanham, MD.

Campbell, D. A. 1982a. *Greek Lyric I: Sappho and Alcaeus.* Cambridge, MA.

Campbell, D. A. 1982b. *Greek Lyric Poetry: A Selection of Early Greek Lyric, Elegiac and Iambic Poetry.* Bristol.

Campbell, D. A. 1988. *Greek Lyric II: Anacreon, Anacreonta, Choral Lyric from Olympus to Alcman.* Cambridge, MA.

Campbell, D. A. 1991. *Greek Lyric III: Stesichorus, Ibycus, Simonides, and Others.* Cambridge, MA.

Campbell, D. A. 1992. *Greek Lyric IV: Bacchylides, Corinna, and Others.* Cambridge, MA.

Campbell, D. A. 1993. *Greek Lyric V: The New School of Poetry and Anonymous Songs and Hymns.* Cambridge, MA.

Capra, A. 2009. "Lyric Poetry." In G. Boys-Stones, B. Graziosa, and P. Vasunia, eds. 2009. *The Oxford Handbook of Hellenic Studies,* Oxford, 454–68.

Carey, C. 2009a. "Genre, Occasion and Performance." In F. Budelmann, ed., *The Cambridge Companion to Greek Lyric,* Cambridge, 21–38.

Carey, C. 2009b. "Iambos." In F. Budelmann, ed., *The Cambridge Companion to Greek Lyric,* Cambridge, 149–167.

Carson, A. 1986. *Eros the Bittersweet: An Essay.* Princeton, NJ.

Cavarzere, A., A. Aloni, and A. Barchiesi, eds. 2001. *Iambic Ideas: Essays on a Poetic Tradition from Archaic Greece to the Late Roman Empire.* Lanham, MD.

Cingano, E. 2003. "Entre skolion et enkomion: Réflexions sur le 'genre' et la performance de la lyrique chorale grecque." In J. Jouanna and J. Leclant, *La poésie grecque antique,* Paris, 17–45.

Clay, D. 2004. *Archilochos Heros.* Washington, DC.

D'Alessio, G. B. 2009. "Language and Pragmatics." In F. Budelmann, ed., *The Cambridge Companion to Greek Lyric,* Cambridge, 114–129.

Day, J. W. 2010. *Archaic Greek Epigram and Dedication: Representation and Reperformance.* Cambridge.

Dodson-Robinson, E. 2010. "Helen's 'Judgment of Paris' and Greek Marriage Ritual in Sappho 16." *Arethusa* 43(1): 1–20.

Dougherty, C. 1993. *The Poetics of Colonization: From City to Text in Archaic Greece.* New York.

Duranti, A. and C. Goodwin, eds. 1992. *Rethinking Context: Language as an Interactive Phenomenon.* Cambridge.

Eagleton, T. 1996. *Literary Theory. An Introduction.* 2nd. edn. Minneapolis.

Faraone, C. A. 2008. *The Stanzaic Architecture of Early Greek Elegy.* Oxford.

Färber, H. 1936. *Die Lyrik in der Kunsttheorie der Antike.* Munich.

Felson, N., ed. 2004a. *The Poetics of Deixis in Alcman, Pindar, and Other Lyric.* Special issue, *Arethusa* 37(3).

Felson, N. 2004b. "Introduction." In Felson 2004a, 253–66.

Ferrari, F. 2010. *Sappho's Gift: The Poet and Her Community.* Ann Arbor, MI.

Figueira, T. J. and G. Nagy, eds. 1985. *Theognis of Megara: Poetry and the Polis.* Baltimore.

Foley, J. M. 1991. *Immanent Art. From Structure to Meaning in Traditional Oral Epic.* Bloomington, IN.

Foley, H. P. 1994. *The Homeric Hymn to Demeter: Translation, Commentary, and Interpretive Essays.* Princeton, NJ.

Fowler, R. L. 1987. *The Nature of Early Greek Lyric: Three Preliminary Studies.* Toronto.

Garner, R. S. 2011. *Traditional Elegy: The Interplay of Meter, Tradition, and Context in Early Greek Poetry.* Oxford.

Gentili, B. 1988. *Poetry and Its Public in Ancient Greece: From Homer to the Fifth Century.* Baltimore.

Gerber, D. E. 1999a. *Greek Iambic Poetry: From the Seventh to the Fifth Centuries BC.* Cambridge, MA.

Gerber, D. E. 1999b. *Greek Elegiac Poetry: From the Seventh to the Fifth Centuries BC.* Cambridge, MA.

Hanks, W. F. 1987. "Discourse Genres in a Theory of Practice." *American Ethnologist* 14: 668–92.

Hanks, W. F. 1992. "The Indexical Ground of the Deictic Reference." In A. Duranti and C. Goodwin, eds., *Rethinking Context: Language as an Interactive Phenomenon,* Cambridge, 46–76.

Harvey, A. E. 1955. "The Classification of Greek Lyric Poetry." *Classical Quarterly,* 5: 157–75.

Herington, J. 1985. *Poetry into Drama: Early Tragedy and the Greek Poetic Tradition.* Berkeley, CA.

Hornblower, S. and C. Morgan, eds. 2007. *Pindar's Poetry, Patrons, and Festivals: From Archaic Greece to the Roman Empire.* Oxford.

Hutchinson, G. O. 2001. *Greek Lyric Poetry: A Commentary on Selected Larger Pieces.* Oxford.

Irwin, E. 2005. *Solon and Early Greek Poetry: The Politics of Exhortation*. Cambridge.

Jakobson, R. 1960. "Linguistics and Poetics: Closing Statement." In T. A. Sebeok, ed., *Style in Language*, Cambridge, MA, 350–77.

Jouanna, J. and J. Leclant. 2003. *La poésie grecque antique*. Paris.

Krummen, E. 2009. "Alcman, Stesichorus and Ibycus." In F. Budelmann, ed., *The Cambridge Companion to Greek Lyric*, Cambridge, 189–203.

Kullmann, W. and M. Reichel. 1990. *Der Übergang von der Mündlichkeit zur Literatur bei den Griechen*. Tübingen.

Kurke, L. 1988. "The Poet's Pentathlon: Genre in Pindar's *First Isthmian.*" *Greek, Roman and Byzantine Studies* 29: 97–113.

Kurke, L. 1990. "Pindar's Sixth Pythian and the Tradition of Advice Poetry." *Transactions of the American Philological Association* 120: 85–107.

Kurke, L. 2000. "The Strangeness of 'Song Culture': Archaic Greek Poetry." In O. Taplin, ed., *Literature in the Greek & Roman Worlds: A New Perspective*, Oxford, 58–87.

Kurke, L. 2007. "Archaic Greek Poetry." In H. A. Shapiro, ed., *The Cambridge Companion to Archaic Greece*, 141–68.

Lardinois, A. 1994. "Subject and Circumstance in Sappho's Poetry." *Transactions of the American Philological Association* 124: 57–84.

Lardinois, A. 2001. "Keening Sappho: Female Speech Genres in Sappho's Poetry." In Lardinois and McClure 2001, 75–92.

Lardinois, A. and L. McClure, eds. 2001. *Making Silence Speak: Women's Voices in Greek Literature and Society*. Princeton, NJ.

Levinson, S. C. 1983. *Pragmatics*. Cambridge.

Lowe, N. J. 2007. "Epinikian Eidography." In S. Hornblower and C. Morgan, eds., *Pindar's Poetry, Patrons, and Festivals: From Archaic Greece to the Roman Empire*, Oxford, 167–176.

Luce, J. T., ed. 1982. *Ancient Writers: Greece and Rome*. New York.

Martin, R. P. 1989. *The Language of Heroes: Speech and Performance in the Iliad*. Ithaca, NY.

Martin, R. P. 2001. "Just Like a Woman: Enigmas of the Lyric Voice." In A. Lardinois, and L. McClure, eds., *Making Silence Speak: Women's Voices in Greek Literature and Society*, Princeton, NJ, 55–74.

Most, G. W. 1982. "Greek Lyric Poets." In J. T. Luce, ed. 1982. *Ancient Writers: Greece and Rome*. New York, 75–98.

Nagy, G. 1979. *The Best of the Achaeans: Concepts of the Hero in Archaic Greek Poetry*. Baltimore. (rev. edn. 1999)

Nagy, G. 1990. *Pindar's Homer: The Lyric Possession of an Epic Past*. Baltimore.

Nagy, G. 1994 / 5. "Genre and Occasion." *Mêtis* 9 / 10: 11–25.

Nagy, G. 1996. *Poetry as Performance: Homer and Beyond*. Cambridge.

Nagy, G. 2007. "Did Sappho and Alcaeus Ever Meet? Symmetries of Myth and Ritual in Performing the Songs of Ancient Lesbos." In A. Bierl, R. Lämmle, and K. Wesselmann, eds., *Literatur und Religion 2: Wege zu einer mythisch-rituellen Poetik bei den Griechen*, Berlin, 211–69.

Page, D. 1955. *Sappho and Alcaeus: An Introduction to the Study of Ancient Lesbian Poetry*. Oxford.

Parker, H. 1993. "Sappho Schoolmistress." *Transactions of the American Philological Association* 123: 309–351.

Peponi, A.-E. 2004. "Initiating the Viewer: Deixis and Visual Perception in Alcman's Lyric Drama." *The Poetics of Deixis in Alcman, Pindar, and Other Lyric*. Special issue, *Arethusa* 37(3) 295–316.

Race, W. H. 1997a. *Pindar. Vol. 1: Olympian Odes. Pythian Odes*. Cambridge, MA.

Race, W. H. 1997b. *Pindar. Vol. 2: Nemean Odes. Isthmian Odes. Fragments*. Cambridge, MA.

Rösler, W. 1983. "Über Deixis und einige Aspekte mündlichen und schriftlichen Stils in antiker Lyrik." *Würzburger Jahrbücher für die Altertumswissenschaft* 9: 7–28.

Rösler, W. 1990. "Realitätsbezug und Imagination in Sapphos Gedicht ΦΑΙΝΕΤΑΙ ΜΟΙ ΚΗΝΟΣ." In W. Kullmann, and M. Reichel, *Der Übergang von der Mündlichkeit zur Literatur bei den Griechen*, Tübingen, 271–87.

Rotstein, A. 2010. *The Idea of Iambos*. Oxford.

Rutherford, I. 2001. "The New Simonides: Toward a Commentary." In D. Boedeker and D. Sider, *The New Simonides*, Oxford, 33–54.

Sebeok, T. A., ed. 1960. *Style in Language*. Cambridge, MA.

Shapiro, H. A., ed. 2007. *The Cambridge Companion to Archaic Greece*. Cambridge.

Silk, M. 2009. "Lyric and Lyrics: Perspectives, Ancient and Modern." In F. Budelmann, ed., *The Cambridge Companion to Greek Lyric*, Cambridge, 373–85.

Skinner, M. B. 2005. *Sexuality in Greek and Roman Culture*. Oxford.

Stehle, E. 1997. *Performance and Gender in Ancient Greece. Nondramatic Poetry in its Setting*. Princeton, NJ.

Stehle, E. 2009. "Greek Lyric and Gender." In F. Budelmann, ed., *The Cambridge Companion to Greek Lyric*, Cambridge, 58–71.

Suter, A. 2009. "Lament in Sappho's Poetry." Paper presented at Annual Meeting of the Classical Association of the Atlantic States, October 8–10, 2009.

Taplin, O., ed. 2000. *Literature in the Greek & Roman Worlds: A New Perspective*. Oxford.

Tedeschi, G. 1978. "L'elegia parenetica-guerriera e il simposio: A proposito del fr. 1 W di Callino." Rivista di Studi Classici 26: 203–9.

Thomas, R. 2007. "Fame, Memorial, and Choral Poetry: The Origins of Epinikian Poetry – An Historical Study." In S. Hornblower and C. Morgan, eds., *Pindar's Poetry, Patrons, and Festivals: From Archaic Greece to the Roman Empire*, Oxford, 141–66.

Tiedermann, R, ed. 1974. *Notes to Literature Vol. 1*. New York.

Wells, J. B. 2009. *Pindar's Verbal Art: An Ethnographic Study of Epinician Style*. Washington, D.C.

West, M. L. 1974. *Studies in Greek Elegy and Iambus*. Berlin.

Yatromanolakis, D. 2009a. "Alcaeus and Sappho." In F. Budelmann, ed., *The Cambridge Companion to Greek Lyric*, Cambridge, 204–26.

Yatromanolakis, D. 2009b. "Ancient Greek Popular Song." In F. Budelmann, ed., *The Cambridge Companion to Greek Lyric*, Cambridge, 263–276.

FURTHER READING

Campbell (1982a; 1988; 1991; 1992 and 1993), Gerber (1999a and b), and Race (1997a and b) offer convenient access to Greek texts, based upon major editions, and translations, with ancient testimonia, of virtually all Greek lyric poetry. Campbell 1982b is a popular selection of Greek lyric poetry, with commentary, but it includes no Pindar. Hutchinson 2001 covers selections of melic poetry only. Kurke (2000 and 2007) are good brief introductions to Greek lyric. Capra (2009) is indispensible for understanding the current terrain of Greek lyric scholarship, especially the central role that Italian scholars have played in the formation of the current knowledge-base. Budelmann (2009a) collects essays on the contexts for and themes in Greek lyric poetry, on genres and authors, and on reception. Nagy (1979; 1990 and (1996), Carson (1986), Gentili (1988), Stehle (1997), and Calame (2001) are among the most important books on archaic Greek poetry and poetics available in English. Battezzato's (2009) introduction to Greek lyric meters is superb. A mere sample of noteworthy genre- and author-focused secondary literature includes West (1974), Bowie (2001), Cavarzere, Aloni, and Barchiesi (2001), Carey (2009b), and Rotstein (2010) on iambos; Clay (2004) on Archilochus; West (1974), Bowie (1986), Aloni and Iannucci (2007), Faraone (2008), Aloni (2009), and Garner (2011) on elegy; Irwin (2005) and Blok and Lardinois (2006) on Solon; Boedeker and Sider (2001) on Simonides; Figueira and Nagy (1985) and Martin (2001) on Theognis; Agocs, Carey, and Rawles (2012) on the victory song; Athanassaki and Bowie (2011) on choral song; Page (1955), Parker (1993), Nagy (2007), Yatromanolakis (2009a), and Ferrari (2010) on Sappho and Alcaeus.

CHAPTER 11

The Ethics of Greek Drama

Richard Rader

David Simon, creator of the critically acclaimed television series *The Wire*, knows his Greek tragedy. In a recent interview with *The Believer* magazine he called attention to the model of tragic storytelling that he tried to employ throughout its duration, one he specifically claims to have pilfered from the Greeks:

> Our model is not quite so Shakespearean as other high-end HBO fare. *The Sopranos* and *Deadwood*... offer a good deal of *Macbeth* or *Richard III* or *Hamlet* in their focus on the angst and machinations of the central characters (Tony Soprano, Al Swearengen). Much of our modern theater seems rooted in the Shakespearean discovery of the modern mind. We're stealing instead from an earlier, less-traveled construct – the Greeks – lifting our thematic stance wholesale from Aeschylus, Sophocles, Euripides to create doomed and fated protagonists who confront a rigged game and their own mortality.

More than just a facile acknowledgment of an age-old narrative paradigm, Simon's understanding of the generic distinction between Greek tragedy and the more complex developments of Shakespearean drama illustrates his appreciation of the debt he owes to the Greeks. When he speaks of "doomed and fated protagonists" facing a "rigged game," he invokes not only our critical preoccupation with the superstitious fatalism of particular characters (Oedipus, Orestes, etc.) but also, more importantly, the systems and institutions they invariably butt up against:

> Instead of the old gods, *The Wire* is a Greek tragedy in which the postmodern institutions are the Olympian forces. It's the police department, or the drug economy, or the political structures, or the school administration, or the macroeconomic forces that are throwing the lightning bolts and hitting people in the ass for no decent reason... In this drama, the institutions always prove larger, and those characters with hubris enough to challenge the postmodern construct of American empire are invariably mocked, marginalized, or crushed. Greek tragedy for the new millennium, so to speak.

We might find the one-for-one substitution of "Olympian forces" for "postmodern institutions" a bit heavy-handed, but Simon's insight here is impressive: the protagonists of drama live and act not in a vacuum but in a world defined by institutional structures.

A Companion to Greek Literature, First Edition. Edited by Martin Hose and David Schenker.
© 2016 John Wiley & Sons, Inc. Published 2020 by John Wiley & Sons, Inc.

And the civic ideologies that come to enable, influence, constrict, or destroy inner-city Baltimoreans – in particular the drug economy, law enforcement, and public education – are not so radically different from those that came to define Athenians of the fifth century. Their art, and in particular their drama, would necessarily reflect that.[1]

Simon's comparison of *The Wire* to Greek tragedy did not go unnoticed. Slavoj Žižek, no stranger to the topic either of tragedy or popular culture, weighed in on Simon's characterization in a lecture recently at the Birkbeck Institute for the Humanities at the University of London. The triumph of the show, he claims, is not what he labels its "object realism," its depiction of the "real miserable life of drug-addicted people in Baltimore" (a feature he identifies with naturalism), but rather its "subject realism": It is "as if a community … in this case the community of people of Baltimore wanted to stage their own collective self-representation … Greek tragedy … was, you know, a collective event of a polis, a city staging its own self-representation, experiencing its own being, its antagonisms and so on." For Žižek the communal self-representation on display in the series makes it more fundamentally realist and thus brings it closer to the world of Greek tragedy than its sublimated Olympian forces. Like Simon, though, Žižek's classification of tragedy as a "collective event of a polis," one that dramatizes a city's being and its antagonisms, sounds as if it was ripped from the pages of J. P. Vernant, Simon Goldhill and Froma Zeitlin, the architects essentially of what we now call cultural poetics. The subtle "you know" thrown into the middle (as well as the "and so on" at the end) gives his claim the air of orthodoxy: everybody already knows what Greek tragedy is about.[2]

What are we to make of all this? When the creator of one of contemporary television's most celebrated shows and the most famous living Marxist/psychoanalytic philosopher both speak of *The Wire* as *polis*-centered, we may find ourselves equally put off by the pat invocation of one particular (albeit important) interpretation of tragedy and genuinely surprised how much cultural poetics as a form of criticism has infiltrated our own culture and poetics. In the case of *The Wire*, as well as in the case of Simon's follow-up (and current) hit *Treme*, it is very much and very obviously true that the cities in which the shows' drama takes place, Baltimore and post-Katrina New Orleans respectively, are integrally related to the drama itself. These shows, in other words, are just as much about the cities as they are about any of their individual characters, and though we might imagine that such shows could probably be staged in other cities with somewhat minor changes, much of their appeal would be lost. These characters are specifically Baltimoreans, and imagined as real Baltimoreans, whose lives play out in the city itself.

But what about Athens? Do we all already know what Greek drama is about? Whether the focus is tragedy or comedy, is drama about the city of Athens in the same way as *The Wire* is about Baltimore? Simon and Žižek are not specialists in the drama of the ancient world, to be sure, and would likely acknowledge if pressed that their views come off as slightly canned and monolithic. Their views, however, reveal the extent to which our popular conception of Greek drama equates it almost reflexively with the concerns of fifth-century Athenian civic life.[3] This we might say reflects the triumph of the cultural poetics revolution inaugurated by Jack Winkler and Froma Zeitlin, who dropped a bomb on the study of drama with the publication of *Nothing to Do with Dionysos?* in 1990. The virtue of Winkler and Zeitlin's project, with powerful and by now classic contributions by Goldhill, Nicole Loraux, Josiah Ober and Barry Strauss (including seminal essays by the editors themselves), was its shift away from the narrow formalist historicism of prior scholarship, with its focus on allusions within plays to properly historical events, persons and trends, and toward "the entire social context of the [dramatic] festivals" (1990, 3). Accordingly, practitioners were to consider "how individual plays or groups of dramas directly or indirectly pertained to the concerns of the body politic, which were reflected or deflected in the complex conventions of the stage" (1990, 4). Greek drama on this view was an ideologically embedded and constitutive element of a society in constant negotiation with itself. It would now be a window into the socio-cultural pulse of fifth-century Athens, symptomatizing, antagonizing and, if nothing else, putting on view the historical, religious and political worlds of the city and its citizens.[4]

This understanding of drama, I think, resonates beautifully with what Simon and Žižek claim for *The Wire*, even if only a few of our extant dramas actually take place in the city of Athens itself.[5] Corinth, Argos, Thebes: as Froma Zeitlin (1990) famously claimed, these places served as theoretical screens upon which Athenians projected their darkest fantasies, fears and desires (murder, incest, rape, empire, etc.). Tragedy, in particular, staged a primal game of self–other, a pre-Freudian *fort-da*; it was a venue for Athenians to explore beyond the pleasure principle without the mess of self-doubt, self-recrimination or self-knowledge (or the discovery of a nefarious death drive). The bad stuff only happens *over there*. All the same, projection, repression and denial notwithstanding, the issues acted out in drama always ultimately redounded to the city of Athens itself: staged alongside the presentation of war orphans, tributes to the empire and religious rituals in the Great Dionysia (or Lenaea), drama played its discrete but essential part in offering Athenians an opportunity for ideological self-fashioning.[6]

This is all fine and good, and common sense alone suggests that art goes hand-in-hand with culture and history. But the ease of moving between the world within a play and the world without can be deceptive. Indeed one sticky problem among several with this understanding is that very few (if any) of the characters of tragedy especially bear any relation to "real" people (and again this marks tragedy's difference from comedy).[7] The Eteocleses and Aegeuses and Ismenes might well strike us as staid and normal, and thus capable of bearing our identifications without too much anxiety, but what of figures like Oedipus, Medea, Clytemnestra, and Prometheus? All of their grandiose monstrosities are difficult to fit within the parameters of civic ideology. Their behavior – their very being – is excessive, not necessarily to the point of incomprehensibility but certainly enough to test our faith in their humanity – to say nothing of their citizenship.[8] Why would an Aeschylus, Sophocles, or Euripides (leaving aside the scores of other dramatists whose works have vanished[9]) invest so much artistic energy and creativity in characters who act nothing like our friends, neighbors, and loved-ones? To what extent then does it matter that *Oedipus Tyrannus* was produced near the start of both the Peloponnesian War and a devastating plague, when its eponymous hero discovers he has sired children with his mother, then tries to kill her and, when she foils his attempt with a dreadful suicide, then commits an atrocious and unnecessary act of self-mutilation?[10] What can we glean about Athens from a play like this? Can we really determine whether Sophocles was pro- or anti-Pericles?

It is certainly worth wondering what the play's production might have meant in or for its proper moment, how it was shaped by or responded to its socio-cultural and historical context; it is also worth wondering what an audience might have been thinking in that first revelatory moment of performance (and here for the sake of uncomfortable shorthand let's assume an "audience" can "think" or "experience" as a collective). But anything more than wonder is misguided. This is because the quixotic pursuit of an original audience and the context of an original historical moment brings at least two unwelcome results: guaranteed obsolescence on the part of the play itself and, perhaps more problematically for us, the death of criticism. As to the former: allusions to contemporaneous issues, especially political issues, fix a production to one particular historical date and thus run the risk of leaving it there stranded and mired as new political issues inevitably evolve. In this regard, a play could come to look a lot like an episode of *Saturday Night Live*, which thrives on topicality but for that very reason is passé as soon as the credits roll.[11] Will Ferrell's impressions of George W. Bush from 2000 to 2008, for example, remain hilarious to this day, but their age shows and many of their references have since become footnotes in our cultural and political history. And the further we go back – and the further we move forward – the more the footnotes pile up. Thus in the case of the Greeks and their drama the problems are especially pronounced. Even among professional classicists, how many of us could properly identify the myriad allusions Aristophanes makes to contemporaneous politicians and political affairs, or poets and cultural tastemakers, let alone the plain old everyday frauds, narcissists, and idiots ridiculed in the course of the play? How many of us (again, even professional classicists) have dutifully consulted the commentary of, say, Dover's edition of *Frogs* to identify an obscure name with the distinction of being the butt of a sexual joke – only to have missed the joke entirely? (How many of us simply haven't bothered?) Or, by the time the joke registers, have realized the play has since launched six more, all of which we're also unfamiliar with? This isn't to say comedy can't be riotously funny, only that its formal parameters and tics, in particular its mining of popular political culture, is entirely and necessarily lost on us.[12]

As to the second unwelcome consequence mentioned above, the death of criticism: Perhaps we forget that if a work of art's singular purpose, or the singular reaction it was supposed to elicit in the singular moment of its performance, were discovered (assuming, again uncomfortably, it was supposed to elicit a singular experience in the first place), we could no longer justify the attention and time required to carefully study (and teach) it. We would no longer need to produce innovative scholarship on plays, which would no longer be innovative anyway but rather symptomatic of a refusal to recognize their established truths, and it would be pointless to creatively or interpretively stage new productions. We'd all essentially be out of a job (and could join in Žižek's choral refrain of "Greek tragedy … was, you know, a collective event of a polis."). Fortunately this has yet to happen, and surely one of the reasons we have been spared this fate is because of those excessive characters, whose dramatic lives have a disjointed relationship to every world in which they are staged, who are both of and beyond the cultural and temporal horizons of a proper performance. Seneca did not compose a *Thyestes* because its Greek precedents reflected the reforms of Ephialtes or the evolution of democratic institutions, but because he saw something enduring, something sickening and memorable and thought-provoking, in the plays of the canonical tragedians. And while much in politics may disgust or provoke, nothing in it endures. Perhaps we ought to give Seneca credit for intentionally turning drama into literature, and perhaps for that reason we ought to give the canonical tragedians credit for providing the blueprints. We keep producing innovative studies and critically acclaimed performances because there is always more to say, always another angle or approach.[13]

Obviously – and thankfully – we're still reading and performing Greek drama (and performing little if any Seneca), which would suggest that there's something bigger, something deeper in it that has sustained its popularity and meaningfulness through the years. We may not be able to identify this element with any precision (though I will venture a guess below), which may well be its saving grace, but I believe we can say with some confidence that the past, present or future moment of performance has little to do with it.[14] In fact one of our biggest and most frustrating obstacles to understanding Greek drama remains our paltry evidence for performance and re-performance.[15] Apart from the accidents of transmission and the summary judgments of intellectuals, critics and collectors (like those in Hellenistic Alexandria or later in Byzantium), I suspect part of the reason for this lack of evidence has to do with the inevitable transience of any performance. Productions come and go. Occasionally a performance sticks: apparently Socrates not so fondly remembered a parodic and (to him) destructive portrayal of his character in Aristophanes' *Clouds* nearly 25 years prior to his trial. Perhaps it makes sense for Socrates, the object of the play's humor, to remember. But 25 years is a long time and so it's worth wondering (again, just wondering) how likely it was that any one of the jurors of his trial remembered that same play – if the juror even attended that year's festival and saw the original or the version we have (remember: *Clouds* was revised), or paid attention during its performance, or understood it, or disagreed with it.[16] Socrates obviously disagreed with the "message" of the play (or so it seems), but are we to assume that he thought none of the many other tens of thousands of people in attendance also happened to disagree?[17] On this first reading Socrates (or Plato) seems to intimate that drama, if not at least the cultural or civic experience of the theater, plays such a meaningful role in the life of the city that it sears its imprint in the mind of every citizen like a computer log, and does so moreover in the exact same way with the exact same impression.

If we accept this reading, then perhaps Plato was right in his notorious condemnation of poetry, not so much in his particular conception of ethical inculcation but because he understood that the ethical aspect of drama was its salient feature. Apparently people do remember, ergo we have to censor. In any event it's interesting that what Socrates remembered was not the year deliberative democratic citizens suffered in the throes of the Archidamian period of the war but rather the so-called mischaracterization of his life and work. He recalled the damage it could potentially do to fans of and converts to his new philosophy, the damage it (apparently) eventually did do to him. What seems to have been lost on Socrates is that this very damage – from origins in duplicity to ends in mother-buggering – was already staged in the play itself in the characters of Strepsiades and Pheidippides: This is what happens to you – ethically – when you apprentice with a fraud, a huckster of grandiloquent vanities, a sophist, when you erroneously presume that apprenticing with a master entails automatic ascendance to mastery (and the swindling of your debtors), and ultimately when you are led to the false conclusion that mastery of any art or skill entails knowledge of the good and true.[18] It's hard to believe Socrates missed the joke – that the detractors and opportunists trying to exploit a bastardized version of his thought were Aristophanes' real targets – but even if his misinterpretation was sincere, it still reveals the ethical power (and thus danger) of poetry. That power played a part in killing him.

Aristophanes anticipated all this, whatever his personal feelings were for the real Socrates. And instead of composing a literal *apologia* on his behalf he presciently wrote a play that not only lampoons the silly fixations of philosophers and the irrational cathexes of their critics but also, more importantly, foresees the violence a society as democratic as Athens of the late fifth century is willing to exercise against one of its own quirky creations. The gleeful destruction of Socrates' Thinkery at the close of *Clouds* eerily prefigures the actions of Meletus, Anytus, and Lycon. It would be hard to say which of these two historical documents, Aristophanes' play or Plato's defense, has had a more profound effect on our continuing memory of Socrates, but it is surely easy to discern which has the most currency. Apart from the classroom or the continuing influence of Socratic dialectic, Plato's text has little public visibility.[19] *Clouds*, on the other hand, is a reliable and consistent choice for re-production even to this day.[20] This is in no way to claim that this state of affairs is a *good thing*, only that the ethics of drama has the potential to reach far more people. And Aristophanes, I like to believe, understood that – so did Socrates and Plato ultimately.

So what accounts for the survival of Greek drama, and what accounts for our continued fascination? In a word: ethics. In his treatment of tragedy in the *Poetics* Aristotle defined *ethos* as the wellspring of a character's actions (*praxis*). He famously subordinated *ethos* to *praxis*, however, claiming that action manifested character (and not that character influenced action). This might seem a rather subtle distinction, but whether or not it makes sense to us nowadays, it shifts the focus away from psychology to ethics. For example, when Agamemnon gives in to his wife Clytaemestra and treads upon the tapestries she has laid before him (Aesch. *Ag.* 944–57), we no longer need to ask whether he was simply tired of her nagging. The issue is rather one of decision and consequence: whatever reason he chooses to do it, the result is that he walks to his death.

But the ethical and the psychological, at least as Aristotle distinguished between them, are never so far apart in tragedy. Though we may not have exclusive insight into the minds of tragic protagonists, tragedy in particular illustrates well the ambiguities and dilemmas of decision-making, showing the inextricable, at times inscrutable, link between thought and action. As performative poetry, moreover, drama literally stages "things being done," a generic feature that reveals its revolutionary difference from epic or the novel. In these latter a narrator, omniscient or not, provides insight for us: context, motivation, desire, fear, ambivalence, hypocrisy – in the presence of a narrator these things are radically available to us in ways we perhaps forget. In drama, on the other hand, we have no direct access to these things except as they are acted out in deliberations or decisions. Drama thus starts with inaccessibility: Who is this person? What is she thinking? Why is she doing that? This inaccessibility, though, because it is fundamental to drama's very formal existence, is an obstacle, *not a hindrance*. It enables scrutiny, gives way to insight. Drama, in other words, asks us to figure things (and people) out, to put the pieces together ourselves, to determine whether we have enough to put it together and figure it all out. No matter how much knowledge we or the original (or any) audience has of these characters and their canonical myths, drama requires engagement.[21] And the reflective relationship between audience and actor, reader and character, is an ethical one – drama presupposes ethics.[22]

Nowhere is this more apparent than in Agamemnon's decision early in his eponymous play to sacrifice his daughter Iphigeneia. Marooned at Aulis with the entire Greek force, Agamemnon is presented with a dire situation. After seeing an eagle attack a pregnant hare, the seer Calchas announces that the goddess Artemis demands the blood of a virgin. Agamemnon, understandably stricken, is faced with a dilemma: Do I commit a serious sin by sacrificing my daughter, or do I risk disappointing my army thirsting for Trojan blood? "Which of these choices," he ponders, "comes without awful consequences?" (Aesch. *Ag.* 211) Ultimately and tragically, as we know, Agamemnon chooses his mission over his daughter's life. The description of the sacrifice by the chorus is terrifying[23]: Agamemnon has Iphigeneia bound and gagged, the latter specifically for fear she will call a curse upon him, then kills her. This, of course, drives his wife Clytemnestra to murder him in vengeance upon his return.

The question that always comes to my mind is: Why would Agamemnon need to fear his daughter's curse if her sacrifice is divinely mandated?[24] That's a hedge, and that hedge means something: Agamemnon isn't sure. How does he know that Calchas has interpreted the omen of the eagle correctly (and is it even possible to understand the signs of the gods clearly)? Human sacrifice is anathema, so how can he be sure that the injunction is binding? The play here is notoriously silent. But this is exactly what Aeschylus means to show: the *lack* of understanding that underwrites Agamemnon's decision. The textual and hermeneutic indirection of this episode is a precise illustration of all ethical action. All Agamemnon is left with is a decision, one that reflects no more than his isolation in a world that refuses to give him straight answers. Aeschylus thus means to show us not that Agamemnon's hand was forced, but *how* he confronts maddening undecideability, *how* he resolves his dilemma. Simply put, he gambles: Before slicing into his daughter's throat he says only, "May it turn out well" (*Ag.* 217). This gamble, this distance between thought and action, is tragedy's ethical insight.

Greek tragedy, I would say, is obsessed with this kind of crisis ethics. That may sound unnecessarily provocative, but one of the fundamental truths of tragedy is that we make decisions for reasons which may not be entirely clear to us, and we do so without knowing all the consequences ahead of time. Gods have infinite freedom and knowledge, but we cannot see from their eyes. This distinction is what makes us elementally human. So this "blind" matrix of causes and effects, which surrounds every decision we take, constitutes an ethics: How do we choose a course of action? What desires or ambitions underwrite that choice? What are the potential costs? Who lives and who dies? These are the questions of tragedy. The answers reached by characters, and their subsequent decisions, are ultimately the cause of tragedy.

Consider Oedipus, the most famously ill-fated man in Greek tragedy. Sophocles' *Oedipus Tyrannus* is the paradigmatic expression of man's struggle with the limits of human knowledge. The horror of Oedipus's revelations, so ambitiously and devastatingly structured by Sophocles, gives the lie to our attempts to overcome, let alone understand, the workings of god and fate. We try but we inevitably fail. We are intimately familiar with this reading of *Oedipus*, too familiar perhaps.[25] But is it also possible that the play has an ethical dimension, that it dramatizes the tragedy of human decision-making, not divine conspiracy?

When Creon returns from Delphi with an answer to the plague wrecking the city[26], he cryptically tells Oedipus the Thebans must "cast out the pollution in the city" (*O.R.* 97–8). Are these the words of the oracle? If so they are both frustratingly vague and typical: prophecies from oracles are like dreams for Freud, condensed and displaced, expressed in verse, never transparent. They speak a kind of truth beyond human comprehension and leave us grasping at meaning. And uncertainty leads to tragedy. Oedipus, however, isn't one for riddles – he's the problem-solver extraordinaire. So he presses Creon for more and learns that the former king Laius was murdered and his murderer is in Thebes. Did Creon hear this too from the oracle, or is he drawing the connections himself? If this comes verbatim, why didn't he simply start with it? If it doesn't, why would he assume the "pollution" was Laius' murder and not, say, Laius's own transgression against the gods?[27] Already there is mystery and lots of room for mistake. By the time the seer Tiresias arrives to set in train Oedipus' revelations, Oedipus is already trying to figure out what now seems a problem of his own making, not fate's.[28]

Sophocles wants us to see these gaps, these assumptions, these potential mistakes. Consider the final exposition of his past. Oedipus is an uncanny stranger in Thebes, an immigrant from Corinth. There, after being taunted about his birthright, he visits Delphi to find out whether Polybus and Merope are his real parents. The oracle famously responds that he will kill his father and marry his mother. Aghast, Oedipus flees, unknowingly returning to his origin. We call this dramatic irony, and the play, structured as a series of memories, indulges that retrospective vantage. But because of that irony we risk being as impetuous as Oedipus was at the oracle. Oedipus makes two mistakes: First, he consults the oracle expecting to hear that Polybus and Merope are his real parents. In other words, he expects to find out what (he thinks) he already knows. Oracles, however, do not confirm knowledge; their truth has yet to be realized. Second, and somewhat strangely given his inquisitive nature, Oedipus fails to ask any further questions (like: what could *that* mean?). He may not get the clarification he seeks but he is not limited in the number of times he can ask.[29] Instead he runs and never looks back. These are mistakes that reflect not divine malice but rather a lack of full knowledge. Oedipus is human.

So Oedipus returns home when he thinks he has escaped it. He kills his father, he marries his mother and the traumatic truth comes to light. The bloody punishment he inflicts upon himself at the end is a horrific symbol not only of his blindness but of human blindness in general: We make decisions without ultimately knowing the consequences, and presumption and ambiguity can lead to suffering. All decisions are based on this lack. And all of Oedipus' decisions are his own; Apollo never claims responsibility. For Sophocles, or for us, to intimate as much would be to fall prey to the very same mistakes and the very same misunderstanding that bring Oedipus to his knees. This, Sophocles teaches us, is tragic humanism and Oedipus (like Agamemnon and so many others) learns it the hard way.

If the answers to the ethical questions underlying drama are paramount for the action of a play, as I suggested above, then tragedy in these instances seems to be occasioned by a toxic "knowingness," a presumption of understanding by characters that goes hand-in-hand with their generic lack of understanding. As Jonathan Lear has noted,

> the determination to know can be used to obscure any possibility of finding out... But there is a sickness in this "knowingness": reason is being used to jump ahead to a conclusion, as though there is too much anxiety involved in simply asking a question and waiting for the world to answer. (1998, 192, 191)

Knowingness destroys self and other.

In this vein it is worth dwelling on the family of Oedipus, since it offered to the tragedians a dense nexus of issues, psychological and ethical especially, for exploring the consequences of knowingness. Even Aeschylus' *Seven against Thebes*, for all its idiosyncrasies, reflects this ethical concern. The third and only surviving piece of a Labdacid trilogy, the play offers us a fascinating and disturbing portrait of a man in thrall to his family's history. Critical interest in the play ebbs and flows (while artistic and dramaturgical interest has nearly flatlined), but it is fairly safe to say that *Seven* is the ugly duckling of Aeschylus' oeuvre. *Persians* has the distinction, for better or worse, of being the one historical tragedy we have (and contains one of the most spectacular set pieces in the conjuration of the dead Darius); *Suppliants* speaks to a tangle of political, ethnic and sexual issues; *Prometheus Bound*, though considered of dubious authorship, represented for the Romantics the epitome of intellectual symbolism; and the *Oresteia* is, well, the *Oresteia*.[30] *Seven* occupies an intriguing place in the corpus for good reason: debate has raged about its internal consistency, its ending is surely spurious and its central episode offers a hermeneutic performance of shield-reading – shields which the audience cannot see.[31] This is a far cry dramatically and dramaturgically from pus-oozing and acid-breathing Furies causing spontaneous abortions.[32]

And yet it has survived to us. One explanation for this has to do with the play's connection to the Oedipus saga and to the Thebes-related canon of myths (told in the nearly vanished *Oidipodeia* and *Thebaid* of the epic cycle). A few decades later Sophocles would immortalize the story of Oedipus, and a century later Aristotle would brand it the best drama.[33] The first two plays in the trilogy, *Laius* and *Oedipus* (both lost but for a handful of teasing fragments), seem to have set up the theme of inherited guilt and intergenerational curse, though even this is a desperate conjecture. We are simply left grasping at phantoms. Whatever information we can glean from a play's title – and apparently that little can be deceptive – it is intriguing that *Seven* is not called *Eteocles* (or *Eteocles and Polynices*) given the two precedents, which might suggest that its relationship to the two previous plays may not be what we think it is.[34]

Very little in the play speaks directly to political concerns of the time, and apart from Thebes's place in the Athenian imaginary – as imagined by cultural poetics – very few critics seek to identify proper historical allusions in it anymore.[35] The principal critical fixation of the last half century has been the deterministic force of the curse of the Labdacid line on Eteocles as a free-willing agent. Does he have any choice in the mutually fratricidal combat he will eventually engage in with his brother? Critics, even those who are open-minded about the so-called anachronism of invoking free will in the ancient world[36], seem to have settled on the same answer: No. Or rather: Yes… possibly, but his decision is circumscribed and the outcome is rigged (what critics call "double motivation"), which is essentially the same thing as saying he doesn't have a choice. The play, however, gives the lie to this fatalism.

Consider the exchange between Eteocles and the chorus after he hears that Polynices is stationed behind the seventh gate. Eteocles is not at first as fatalistic as he ends up being. After initially exclaiming, "Now indeed my father's curses come to pass!" (656), he immediately follows with the calm assertion "It would be unseemly of me to make a scene weeping, and I don't want to create even more reasons to lament" (657–8). Although he raises the possibility that his meeting with Polynices is predetermined, he nevertheless maintains a sense of control and balance: "I have faith that Justice is on my side and I will stand against him myself" (672–3). Eteocles takes responsibility for the decision to face his brother, a move underscored by the combination of a middle-voice verb (*xystēstomai*) and an intensifying pronoun (*autos*). He makes this decision looking toward an open future, not an inexorable past. But Eteocles does eventually give in to his fatalism. In his exchange with the chorus he claims things like, "A god surely presses this thing on" (689), "My father's hateful, dreadful curse clings to me" (695–6), and "Oedipus' curse made the spirit rage" (709). It is the chorus of Theban women, the very ones he had just excoriated for their frightened superstition, that tries (and fails) to convince him otherwise: he could give offerings to the gods to avert this outcome (700–701), the malign spirit inflaming his passion could change its mind and come with "gentler breath" (705–8), or he could simply not go (714). The women very clearly believe Eteocles has a choice; that he refuses to listen to them ("You cannot escape god-given misfortunes," 719) does not prove he's right (or that we're right in affirming his refusal to listen). It shows only that his obtuse fatalism runs deep, all the way down to death in fact. And when the chorus launches upon his departure into the history of the Labdacid blight (720–91), this too does not prove that the curse has come to fruition in the conflict between Eteocles and Polynices. Rather the only way they can make sense, retrospectively, of his stolid inflexibility, his outrageous and bullying behavior towards them in particular, is to say the *Geschlechterfluch* (generational curse) must be responsible.[37] It's a rationalization that mistakenly – and tragically – validates the deterministic outlook.

Everyone in the play, it appears, comes to this same conclusion. Likewise for the critical tradition. That in itself would be compelling if it weren't for the fact that *Seven* is a *tragedy*. Eteocles gets himself and several of his comrades killed – unnecessarily – and brings his city to the brink of destruction; Polynices and most of his comrades die gruesome deaths[38]; what remains of the family is left in the hands of Creon, whose unceremonious and tone-deaf first move is to criminalize Polynices and lionize Eteocles (who may have been responsible for the civil war in the first place[39]); the two young daughters of Oedipus, Antigone and Ismene, are thrust into a nightmare of a political and familial situation, one of whom immediately becomes a subversive; and we for our part are happy to conclude with Eteocles that fate sure is a bitch. Here Aeschylus is brilliant in diagnosing our complacency: We are the fatalists, not him. We are the ones who masochistically desire the dooming influence of curse and Erinys, not him. We ultimately are the Eteocleses (and Oedipuses and Laiuses and Oresteses), the kind of people who could visit pain and sorrow upon our families, friends and fellow citizens all the while claiming – just *knowing* – we had no choice.[40] Aeschylus simultaneously exposes and skewers our knowingness.

In short it strikes me as odd that Aeschylus would stage a play whose take-away is that we're all doomed in some way or other and there's nothing we can do about it. Surely there were people in *Seven*'s original audience, as well as in subsequent audiences (whether dramatic, philosophical or literary critical), who left comfortably or uncomfortably with that message – just as there are today. But by the same token there surely must have been others who felt that Eteocles' fixation on the fatal machinery of his life was itself a bit myopic, that his perspective was not just the truth and may well have enabled and facilitated the hellish experience they just witnessed. (Some might even have put the big picture together that Thebes suffered generation after generation because of the respective myopic fixations of its Labdacid leaders, not because the gods had it out for them.) This was in fact the very opinion of the chorus of the play. It's right there in the text. So what then does it mean that we continue to take Eteocles' word for the truth of the matter and ignore the chorus' countervailing perspective? There is probably any number of reasons for that preference, and ultimately only our therapists can really account for them. But it is worth thinking about since it reveals the extent to which our own desires and identifications are invested in the characters of drama. We must always be wary of the fine line between a conjecture and a projection.[41]

We might speculate that Aristophanes was riffing on this investment and dramatic polyvalence in *Frogs*, where the Aeschylus we meet in the underworld, a rather self-important prig, asserts that his *Seven*, because it was "full of war" (*Areōs meston*, 1021), made every one of its spectators desire to be a warrior (*daïos*, 1022). It's up for debate whether that's a good thing – evident in Dionysus' ridiculous retort that the play made Thebans, Athens' enemies, more valiant in war too (1023–4) – but Aeschylus here inserts himself into a distinguished line of poets (Orpheus, Musaeus, Hesiod, Homer) notable for inculcating virtue, in particular martial valor (1025–42). Aeschylus comes away, of course, with the victory in the competition with Euripides – and how not when the latter is depicted as a petulant and prurient populist more concerned with Phaedras and Stheneboeas than Patrocluses and Teucers (1040–44)? Dionysus may have originally come to Hades to bring Euripides back because he was his favorite (48–70), but he is a buffoon like the rest and, for better or worse, changes his mind in favor of Aeschylus.

But why would the Athenians want this bloviating relic back? (Why for that matter would they want the other bloviating hipster back?) How would an old-school conservative dead now some 50 years have any idea how to "save the city"? With a play like *Seven*? It cannot have been lost on many of the spectators of *Frogs* that the contest between these two caricatures of characters, a contest being judged by an idiotic avatar of the festival's patron deity, was taking place in the underworld! Perhaps ultimately that was Aristophanes' metacomedic point: You can't have either of them back, and fantasizing about a past that probably never existed is as effective as attempting a *katabasis*. Wasting your time adjudicating between the dead distracts from the important work of really figuring out how to save the city.[42] I suspect Aristophanes was staking a quiet claim for his own art's salvific potential: tragedy kills, comedy resurrects.[43]

Like Plato after him Aristophanes grasped the ethical import of tragedy, but instead of censorship he recognized the value of inversion. Or so it may seem: ironically or not, *Frogs* offers in its reanimated tragedian and in itself a booster shot to the Athenian immune system[44], but *Clouds* became the symptom of an autoimmune disorder. Aristophanes may have killed Socrates, and in saving Aeschylus he may well also have killed tragedy. But in so doing he kept drama alive far more effectively than Dionysus could have imagined. Perhaps one day we will meet him in Hades – no doubt occupying the Chair of Poetry – and can thank him for it. In the meantime our gratitude will have to consist in searching out those questions beneath drama that animate and reanimate it for us perennially. It's a task with a history as long as the plays themselves, one that has kept them alive to the present day – long beyond the confines of fifth-century Athens. No reason to stop now.

NOTES

[1] The entirety of Simon's interview can be found at: http://www.believermag.com/issues/200708/?read=interview_simon (accessed March 30, 2015).
[2] The entirety of Žižek's speech can be found at: http://backdoorbroadcasting.net/2012/02/slavoj-zizek-the-wire-or-the-clash-of-civilisations-in-one-country/ (accessed March 30, 2015). Frederic Jameson, another titan of contemporary Marxism, has also published an essay recently on realism and utopia in *The Wire* (2010).
[3] If not Athenian civic life, then with chthonic and demonic forces, the numinous and fatal: Simon continues, "The modern mind – particularly those of us in the West – finds [...] fatalism ancient and discomfiting, I think. We are a pretty self-actualized, self-worshipping crowd of postmoderns and the idea that for all of our wherewithal and discretionary income and leisure, we're still fated by indifferent gods, feels to us antiquated and superstitious. We don't accept our gods on such terms anymore; by and large, with the exception of the fundamentalists among us, we don't even grant Yahweh himself that kind of unbridled, interventionist authority." Cf. the perceptive introduction of Eagleton 2003, 1–22 on tragedy as a "cultural signifier, a theodicy" (17) for the modern world.
[4] Cf. on this McGlew, ch. 5, pp. **xx13–15** in this volume.
[5] Here is where tragedy is fundamentally different from comedy and where our lack of historical tragedy is truly remarkable – cf. Castellani 1986, Rosenbloom 1993, 2006, 11–38, Garvie 2009, x. On Phrynichus' fate and further career see Wise 2008, 392–3.
[6] Cf. Goldhill 1990; 2000, Debnar 2007 and Wilson 2009; *contra* see Heath 1987; 2006 Griffin 1998 Rhodes 2003, Carter 2004; 2007.
[7] Agathon, the most highly regarded non-surviving tragedian of antiquity, apparently tried to introduce characters and stories that were neither mythical nor historical (Aristot. *Poet.* 9,

1451b 21). One wonders whether these characters were unpopular for being purely fictional (i.e. non-mythical) or non-heroic.

[8]See, e.g., Edith Hall on *Trachiniae*: "It is through [the play's] stress on the importance of deliberation that it reveals its intimate relationship with the workings of Athenian democracy, where the citizen-audience of drama was also the community's executive body" (2009, 69; cf. also 90–96).

[9]See Cropp 2007 for a survey of the tragic material we no longer have, as collected in the *Tragicorum Graecorum Fragmenta* (Göttingen, 1974–2004).

[10]Dating the play securely is hopeless. Müller (1984) believed that political motives were behind *OT*'s second-place finish and thus suggested a date of 433.

[11]And technically already passé by the time it airs: it is a parody of events already past.

[12]Cf. Crane (1997, 201–2) on comedy's interest in the local as opposed to tragedy's and lyric's interest in the Panhellenic:

> Panhellenic poetry filters out the local and the particular; its achievement was to create a common mythological and poetic space that Hellenes who hated one another could nonetheless share. The in-jokes about Cleonymos, Theoros, Amynias, Nikostratos, and the like transgress against a decorum of reference, for only the labors of scholiasts and prosopographers can render these allusions comprehensible, and none can fully resuscitate their initial punch… [Aristophanes] is… uncompromising to his audience…for he sets the burden of understanding firmly on the shoulders of his audience… Aristophanes challenges those in his audience to be Athenian, completely immersed in the concerns of their city, its ambitions and its fears.

[13]Like that of Will Power (2006), who staged a recent production of *Seven against Thebes*, "The Seven," in hip-hop dress – see Dunning 2006 and Torrance 2007, 128. Even the United States Department of Defense recently allocated money for Theater of War to stage readings of Sophocles' *Ajax* and *Philoctetes* for its veterans who have returned from Iraq and Afghanistan – see Healy 2009.

[14]Likewise the relationship of the dramatic festival to a play cannot be reduced simply to base and superstructure: see Crane 1997, 224 n.14, with reference to Longo 1990.

[15]See Csapo and Slater 1995, Csapo 2010, Ley 2007.

[16]It's likely that Socrates/Plato is responding to a contemporary – an enemy perhaps? – who has found in Aristophanes an aptly negative image of Socrates to latch onto. Though this enemy also seems to assume that everyone remembers, that everyone remembers in the same way, and that no one has changed his or her mind (or simply forgotten) in the time since. Alternatively, one could argue that Socrates/Plato alludes to Aristophanes in a parodic way, i.e. that the audience would be familiar with the conventions of comedy and thus be sympathetic to Socrates' plight (and antipathetic to his accusers). But whether we view the allusions as sincere or parodic, it seems obvious that Socrates felt they would have some traction with his audience.

[17]Possibly the 220 members of the assembly who voted for his acquittal also disagreed.

[18]This after all was Socrates' principal criticism of the poets, craftsmen and politicians in the *Apology*, that their discrete knowledge led them to believe they understood the most important things (*Apol.* 21b –22e).

[19]See Jonathan Lear's scathing review of Alain de Botton's *The Consolations of Philosophy* (2000) in the *New York Times* (May 14, 2000).

[20]According to the Oxford Archive of Performances of Greek and Roman Drama (OAPGRD), between 2000 and 2009 alone 15 different productions were staged, one of which, *Socrates on Trial* (UBC 2008), incorporated elements from Plato's *Apology*, *Crito* and *Phaedo*.

[21]Cf. Aristotle, *Poet.* 9, 1451b24–6 with Antiphanes, *Poetry* F 189 PCG.

[22] Nussbaum (1986) and Williams (1993) remain the best studies of ethics in Greek tragedy, though both analyses presume a deterministic framework in the works of the tragedians.

[23] It is important to keep in mind that this episode is part of the chorus's reflections on the war ten years after the sacrifice has taken place, not in the moment, thus illustrating the distinction and tension between momentarity and memory. And at the end of their ode the chorus shamelessly admits that they were not at Aulis in the first place (*Ag.* 248). Or were they but did not watch the actual sacrifice? Or did they but, as *out' ennepō* might suggest, now refuse to relive it? The question remains.

[24] And is he so simple-minded, for that matter, that he thinks the gods can't read or hear the curse emanating from Iphigeneia's incredulous face and hot streaming tears? Would they fail to act or intervene because of a (human) linguistic discrimination? Fletcher 2012, 35–69 offers the most recent reading of performative utterance (*horkos* in particular) in the play but, like other practitioners of speech-act theory, applies it too literally.

[25] See the introduction of Dawe 2006, esp. pp. 5–6.

[26] Some preliminary questions: Why is the plague happening now? Could it have started earlier and simply gone unnoticed? In that case what took the Thebans so long to recognize it? What was the Sphinx doing in Thebes? Consider the perceptive remarks of Zak (1995, 293 n.7):

> That the Sphinx is not merely the monster the Thebans take her for is confirmed by the symbolic fact that, unlike them, for her the well-being of individuals and of cities (no one can pass into or out of the city without coming to terms with her riddle) are inseparably tied to the philosophical and theological identification of the nature of man and the implications and consequences of that recognition. This is a lesson the Thebans never take to heart. From their reaction to her visitation of their city we see that they assume they must concentrate exclusively upon the pragmatics of individual and collective self-protection if they are to preserve themselves and their city, but in fact her advent may be a terrifying reminder that questions of the present and future welfare of the cities of men cannot be dissociated in that way from anterior questions about man's essence and capacities... There is nothing shortsighted about this divinely sent messenger to men: she comes to warn the Thebans that the destruction of men and the cities of men await all those, like themselves, who look to what "lies before" their feet (who look externally) so as not to trip instead of looking to their feet for the answer to man's power and his weakness, his vision and blindness, and hence his need to seek all the help he can get because he is not free to stop "taking steps" to enact his destiny. Instead of prematurely attempting to rid the city of her terrors, the Thebans should have taken her question (and therefore Oedipus as emblematic man) more to their hearts. The opposite of their countrymen's deceitful creation, the Trojan horse, this odd, terrifying beast comes bearing genuine gifts.

[27] Recall he was warned not to have children but did anyway; the child, Oedipus, was exposed unsuccessfully.

[28] Tiresias says nothing about Apollo, only directly answers the question Oedipus asks him: "Know who killed Laius?" "Yeah, you." It doesn't take a prophet or a divine intervention to figure out that this man some 18 years his wife's junior – who arrived and slid onto the throne around the time the former king went missing, who suffered a convenient amnesia of the king-like figure he happened to murder until he picks up on a one-off comment by Jocasta (that Laius was killed at the meeting of three roads) – is the child of Jocasta and Laius. See the brilliant readings of Ahl 1991 and Heiden 2005.

[29] Croesus notoriously made a similar mistake with the Pythian oracle, choosing to hear only what he wanted. As Herodotus reports, when he charged the oracle with deception (about which great empire he would destroy if he made war upon the Persians), the priestess told him he simply failed to ask for clarification (1.91.4)

[30] To get a sense of the contrasting popularities of these plays, consider that the OAPGRD turns up 737 results related to *Agamemnon* and a paltry 52 for *Seven*. See Torrance 2007, 108–29, esp. 125–8 for discussion of the play's reception and reproduction.

[31] See Torrance 2007, 9–22 for a recent survey of the critical landscape; cf. Hutchinson 1985, xvii–xl for a fuller scholarly treatment.

[32] This memorably disgusting anecdote comes from the *Life of Aeschylus*.

[33] At which point, we might speculate, Aeschylus's version, and later Euripides' version, became redundant. Perhaps it's worth remembering that *OR* was defeated by Philocles, of whom but a few fragments survive.

[34] On the evidence that the Thebans are only ever called "Cadmeans" in the play, Sommerstein 2010, 15, 25 argues that titles were not affixed to individual plays until many years after their performance in a trilogy. It is worth asking to what extent our impressions of the first two plays are retrospective assumptions based on our interpretations of the third.

[35] Cf. Post 1950, Podlecki 1966, 27–41, Cameron 1971, 14, 56–7, Petre 1971, Thalmann 1978, 62–78.

[36] See most recently Michael Frede 2011, who examines only philosophical doctrines starting with Aristotle.

[37] Cf. Käppel 1998, 9–20, Föllinger 2003; 2009, Sewell-Rutter 2007, 136–71, Bees 2009, 73–110.

[38] Tydeus, one of the fiercest of the Argive attackers, even ate the brains of Melanippus (Statius, *Theb.* 8.751ff., Apollodorus 3.6.8)!

[39] So Euripides' *Phoenician Women*, but cf. Berman 2007, 50, 26 with n.1.

[40] See Lear 1998, 199 on pity and the audience's perspective:

> We can feel compassion for Oedipus because he is so human: we can see ourselves reflected in his puffed-up self-importance. But pity also requires a sense of distance. We can see the absurdity in Oedipus' movement of thought, in a way which he cannot... When we pity Oedipus, we can indulge the illusion that we know how things *really* are. It is *Oedipus*, not we, who is stuck with the partial and distorted perspective. Being in the audience, it is as though we are looking on the world from an absolute perspective.

[41] Lear 1998, 199 continues insightfully:

> Then comes the second punch. There comes a moment when we recognize that our pity rests on illusion, the illusion that we know absolutely. But we don't. On this occasion we may well be right that Oedipus is making some disastrous mistakes in his thinking and in his emotional life, but overall we are not fundamentally better off than he is. We each must rely on our own sense of what is reasonable and unreasonable .... We have to give up the illusion of an absolutely independent perspective from which to check how well our reasoning is going – and this should encourage a certain humility. The luxurious sense of distance required for pity vanishes. And fear becomes real. Precisely because of our humility, we too may bring down catastrophe.

[42] See Porter 2005 on this "fantasy of classicism" both displayed and undercut by *Frogs*.

[43] See Heiden 1991.

[44] For this he was handsomely rewarded with both first prize in the competition and a sacred olive wreath equal in honor to a gold crown, the latter of which came with the promise of a re-performance.

REFERENCES

Ahl, F. 1991. *Sophocles' Oedipus: Evidence and Self-Conviction*. Ithaca, NY.

Bees, R. 2009. *Aischylos. Interpretationen zum Verständnis seiner Theologie*. Munich.

Berman, D. 2007. *Myth and Culture in Aeschylus'* Seven against Thebes. Rome.

Bosher, K., ed. 2012. *Theater Outside Athens: Drama in Greek Sicily and South Italy*. Cambridge.

Botton, A. de 2000. *The Consolations of Philosophy*. London.

Burian, P. (2014) *A Companion to Aeschylus*. Oxford.

Cameron, H. D. 1971. *Studies on the Seven Against Thebes of Aeschylus*. The Hague.

Carter, D. 2004. "Was Attic Tragedy Democratic?" *Polis* 21: 1–25.

Carter, D. 2007. *The Politics of Greek Tragedy*. Exeter.

Castellani, V. 1986. "Clio vs. Melpomene; Or, Why so Little Historical Drama from Classical Athens." *Themes in Drama* 8: 1–16.

Crane, G. 1997. "Oikos and Agora: Mapping the Polis in Aristophanes' *Wasps*." In G. Dobrov, ed., *The City as Comedy: Society and Representation in Athenian Drama*, Chapel Hill, NC, 198–229.

Cropp, M. 2007. "Lost Tragedies: A Survey." In J. Gregory, ed., *A Companion to Greek Tragedy*, Oxford, 271–92.

Csapo, E. 2010. *Actors and Icons of the Ancient Theater*. Oxford.

Csapo, E. and W. J. Slater. 1995. *The Context of Athenian Drama*. Ann Arbor, MI.

Dawe, R., ed. 2006. *Sophocles: Oedipus Rex*, 2nd. edn. Cambridge.

Debnar, P. 2007. "Fifth-Century Athenian History and Tragedy." In J. Gregory, ed., *A Companion to Greek Tragedy*, Oxford, 3–22.

Dobrov, G. 2010. *Brill's Companion to the Study of Greek Comedy*. Leiden.

Dunning, J. 2006. "He's Taking Aeschylus Hip-Hop." *New York Times* February 10.

Eagleton, T. 2003. *Sweet Violence: The Idea of the Tragic*. Oxford.

Fletcher, J. 2012. *Performing Oaths in Classical Greek Drama*. Cambridge.

Föllinger, S. 2003. *Genosdependenzen: Studien zur Arbeit am Mythos bei Aischylos*. Göttingen.

Föllinger, S. 2009. *Aischylos: Meister der griechischen Tragödie*. Munich.

Frede, M. 2011. *A Free Will: Origins of the Notion in Ancient Thought*. Berkeley, CA.

Garvie, A. F. 2009. *Aeschylus. Persae*. Oxford.

Goldhill, S. 1990. "The Great Dionysia and Civic Ideology." In J. Winkler and F. Zeitlin, eds., *Nothing to Do with Dionysos? Athenian Drama in its Social Context*, Princeton, NJ, 97–129.

Goldhill, S. 2000. "Civic Ideology and the Problem of Difference: the Politics of Aeschylean Tragedy, Once Again." *Journal of Hellenic Studies* 120: 34–56.

Goldhill, S. 2007. *How to Stage Greek Tragedy Today*. Chicago.

Griffin, J. 1998. "The Social Function of Attic Tragedy." *Classical Quarterly* 48: 39–61.

Griffith, M. 2005. "Satyrs, citizens, and self-presentation." In G. Harrison, ed., *Satyr Drama: Tragedy at Play*, Swansea, 161–99.

Griffith, M. 2010 "Satyr-play and tragedy face to face, East to West." In O. Taplin and R. Wyles, eds., *The Pronomos Vase and its context*, Oxford, 47–63.

Hall, E. 2009. "Deianeira deliberates: precipitate decision-making and *Trachiniae*." In S. Goldhill and E. Hall, eds., *Sophocles and the Greek Tragic Tradition*, Cambridge, 69–96.

Hall, E. 2010. *Greek Tragedy: Suffering Under the Sun*. Oxford.

Halleran, M. 1985. *Stagecraft in Euripides*. London.

Healy, P. 2009. "The Anguish of War for Today's Soldiers, Explored by Sophocles." *New York Times* November 11.

Heath, M. 1987. *The Poetics of Greek Tragedy*. Stanford, CA.

Heath, M. 2006. "The 'Social Function' of Tragedy: Clarifications and Questions." In F. Cairns and V. Liapis, eds., *Dionysalexandros: Essays on Aeschylus and his Fellows Tragedians in Honour of Alexander F. Garvie*, Swansea, 253–81.

Heiden, B. 1991. "Tragedy and Comedy in the *Frogs* of Aristophanes." *Ramus* 20: 95–111.

Heiden, B. 2005. "Eavesdropping on Apollo: Sophocles' *Oedipus the King*." *Literary Imagination* 7: 233–57.

Hutchinson, G. O. 1985. *Aeschylus: Septem Contra Thebas*. Oxford.

Käppel, L. 1998. *Die Konstruktion der Handlung in der* Orestie *des Aischylos. Die Makrostruktur des 'Plot' als Sinnträger in der Darstellung des Geschlechterfluchs*. Munich.

Lear, J. 1998. *Open Minded: Working out the Logic of the Soul*. Cambridge, MA.

Lear, J. 2000. "The Socratic Method." *New York Times* May 14.

Ley, G. 2007. *The Theatricality of Greek Tragedy: Playing Space and Chorus*. Chicago.

Lloyd, M. 2007. *Aeschylus*. Oxford.

Mitchell-Boyask, R. (2012) *A Companion to Euripides*. Oxford.

Müller, C. 1984. *Zur Datierung des sophokleischen Ödipus*. Wiesbaden.

Nussbaum, M. 1986. *The Fragility of Goodness: Luck and Ethics in Greek Tragedy and Philosophy*. Cambridge.

Ormond, K. 2012. *A Companion to Sophocles*. Oxford.

Petre, Z. 1971. "Thèmes Dominants et Attitudes Politiques dans *Les Sept contre Thèbes* d'Eschyle." *Studii Classice* 13: 15–28.

Podlecki, A. J. 1966. *The Political Background of Aeschylean Tragedy*. Ann Arbor, MI.

Podlecki, A. J. 2005. "Aischylos Satyrikos." In G. Harrison, ed., *Satyr Drama: Tragedy at Play*, Swansea, 1–38.

Porter, J. 2005. "Feeling Classical: Classicism and Ancient Literary Classicism." In J. Porter, ed., *Classical Pasts: The Classical Traditions of Greece and Rome*. Princeton, NJ, 301–52.

Post, L. A. 1950. "The Seven Against Thebes as Propaganda for Pericles." *Classical Weekly* 44: 49–52.

Rabinowitz, N. 2008. *Greek Tragedy*. Oxford.

Rehm, R. 2002. *The Play of Space: Spatial Transformation in Greek Tragedy*. Princeton, NJ.

Rhodes, P. J. 2003. "Nothing to Do with Democracy: Athenian Drama and the *Polis*." *Journal of Hellenic Studies* 123: 104–19.

Rosenbloom, D. 1993. "Shouting 'Fire' in a Crowded Theater: Phrynichos' *Capture of Miletus* and the Politics of Fear in Early Greek Tragedy." *Philologus* 137: 159–96.

Rosenbloom, D. 2006. *Aeschylus: Persians*. London.

Scodel, R. 2010. *An Introduction to Greek Tragedy*. Cambridge.

Sewell-Rutter, N. J. 2007. *Guilt by Descent: Moral Inheritance and Decision Making in Greek Tragedy*. Oxford.

Sommerstein, A. 2010. *The Tangled Ways of Zeus: and other studies in and around Greek tragedy*. Oxford.

Storey, I. and A. Allan. 2005. *A Guide to Ancient Greek Drama*. Oxford.

Taplin, O. 1977. *The Stagecraft of Aeschylus*. Oxford.

Taplin, O. 1978. *Greek Tragedy in Action*. Berkeley, CA.

Thalmann, W. 1978. *Dramatic Art in Aeschylus's* Seven Against Thebes. New Haven, CT.

Torrance, I. 2007. *Aeschylus: Seven against Thebes*. London.

Wiles, D. 1997. *Tragedy in Athens: Performance Space and Theatrical Meaning*. Cambridge.

Williams, B. 1993. *Shame and Necessity*. Berkeley, CA.

Wilson, P. 2009. "Tragic Honours and Democracy: Neglected Evidence for the Politics of the Athenian Dionysia." *Classical Quarterly* 59: 8–29.

Wise, J. 2008. "Tragedy as 'An Augury of a Happy Life'." *Arethusa* 41: 381–410.

Zak, W. 1995. *The Polis and the Divine Order:* The Oresteia, Sophocles, *and the Defense of Democracy*. Lewisburg, PA.

Zeitlin, F. 1990. "Thebes: Theater of Self and Society in Athenian Drama." In J. Winkler and F. Zeitlin, eds., *Nothing to Do with Dionysos? Athenian Drama in its Social Context*, Princeton, NJ, 130–67.

FURTHER READING

A number of good overviews of Greek tragedy have appeared recently, all pitched at the general reader: Rabinowitz (2008), Hall (2010), Scodel (2010). Wiley-Blackwell has been responsible for the publication of a number of companions covering nearly all bases of the topics on hand: Storey and Allan (2005) on Greek drama in general; Gregory (2007) on Greek tragedy; Ormond (2012) on Sophocles; Mitchell-Boyask (2012) on Euripides; Burian (2014) on Aeschylus. For comedy see Dobrov's companion with Brill (2010). Michael Lloyd (2007) has collected several of the most important articles on Aeschylus, offering translations of several from their original languages.

Technical aspects of the production of Greek drama are ably covered by Csapo and Slater (1995), Goldhill (2007), and Csapo (2010), and classics by Taplin (1977, 1978) and Halleran (1985) remain useful. Slightly more theoretical approaches to theatrical space can be found in Wiles (1997) and Rehm (2002).

In regard to topics I didn't have space to address: Griffith (2005, 2010) has written typically erudite pieces on satyr-drama, the former of which is published in a recent reappraisal of the topic edited by Harrison (2005). Podlecki's (2005) contribution to this collection, a review of Aeschylus' satyr plays, is also a highlight. Fascinating new work on theater outside Athens, in particular in Sicily and south Italy, is being produced by Bosher (2012), literally and figuratively expanding the borders of what we understand about Greek drama in non-Athenian contexts.

CHAPTER 12

Epigram and Minor Genres

Regina Höschele

1. Introduction

Of all ancient poetic genres epigram is the only one that was from its very start – as early as the eighth century BCE – conceived for readerly reception, not oral performance. As the name itself implies, *epi-grammata* were originally designed to be "written upon" objects (on the history of the term, cf. Puelma 1996): carved on tombstones they served to commemorate the dead; engraved on votive offerings they recorded the name of the dedicator, the deity and, possibly, the dedication's purpose (on the re-performance of the dedicatory ritual through the act of reading, cf. Day 2010; on Archaic/Classical epigram, cf. Baumbach, Petrovic, and Petrovic 2010).[1] Whereas early epigrams were primarily written in hexameters – the use of epic diction served, *inter alia*, to bestow Homeric κλέος on the deceased – the elegiac distich soon became the standard metrical form (other meters, such as iamb and trochee, do occur, but rarely). Although the majority of verse inscriptions are extremely formulaic, the strategies by which epigraphic poems seek to attract attention and convey their message – e.g. by featuring speaking objects (Burzachechi 1962), addressing the passer-by or engaging their reader in a dialogue – can be rather subtle (on "epigraphic performance", cf. Day 2007).

The genre seems to have gained particular prominence in the wake of the Persian Wars, as the Greeks commemorated the victory over their dreaded foe on public monuments (for Persian War epigrams, cf. Higbie 2010). In his *Histories* Herodotus (7.228) quotes what may well be called Antiquity's most renowned text, an epigram in honor of the 300 Spartans who fell at the Battle of Thermopylae in 480 BCE (*Anth. Pal.* 7.249):

Ὦ ξεῖν' ἀγγέλλειν Λακεδαιμονίοις, ὅτι τῇδε
 κείμεθα τοῖς κείνων ῥήμασι πειθόμενοι.

O stranger, bear this message to the Lacedaemonians that we lie here obedient to their orders.

The fact that Herodotus, in the same passage, mentions Simonides (c. 556–468 BCE) as the author of another epitaph may have caused this and further epigrams to be attributed to the Cean poet, under whose name a collection of poems gathered from stone or literary sources

A Companion to Greek Literature, First Edition. Edited by Martin Hose and David Schenker.
© 2016 John Wiley & Sons, Inc. Published 2020 by John Wiley & Sons, Inc.

started to circulate some time in the fourth or third century BCE. The so-called *Sylloge Simonidea*, to which poems of later periods were successively added, constitutes an important forerunner of literary epigram books (Petrovic 2007: 99–109; Sider 2007 plausibly speculates that its core might go back to Simonides himself, who could have used a "sample book" for potential clients).

In the Hellenistic Age, epigram underwent a major transformation, moving from stone to papyrus and turning from anonymous sub-literary *Gebrauchspoesie*, i.e. poetry with a purely pragmatic function, into a highly sophisticated and self-conscious literary genre (actual inscriptions did, of course, continue to be chiseled on stone). Book epigrams regularly play with epigraphic conventions and experiment with the various speech acts of their inscriptional predecessors, drawing the reader's attention, again and again, to their invented nature (Meyer 2005, Tueller 2008). When Leonidas of Tarentum (early third century BCE), for instance, has a man whose corpse was lost at sea refer to his tombstone as a "liar" (ψεύστης ... λίθος, *Anth. Pal.* 7.273.6 = 62.6 G-P), we may take the cenotaph itself as an image for the poem's fictionality: on a metapoetic level, the missing body points to the fact that Kallaischros is, indeed, nothing more than a name (on cenotaphs, cf. Bruss 2005, 97–167). Similarly, Honestus (first century CE) evokes a tomb in search of a corpse lamenting its own uselessness (*Anth. Pal.* 7.274 = 22 G-P):

> I announce the name of Timokles, scanning the salty sea
> in every direction for where his corpse might be.
> Alas, the fish have already eaten him, and I, a superfluous
> stone, bear this inscription engraved on me in vain.

The majority of Greek literary epigrams are preserved in the *Palatine Anthology* (*Anth. Pal.*), a mid-tenth-century codex named after the Bibliotheca Palatina in Heidelberg, where it was discovered around 1600 (on the subsequent history of the codex, cf. Beckby 1965, Vol. 1: 90–98; on its textual history Cameron 1993). This collection largely goes back to an anthology put together by Constantine Cephalas around 900 CE with the help of several ancient anthologies still extant at that time: Meleager's *Stephanos* or *Garland* (c. 100 BCE), the *Garland of* Philip (c. 53 CE) and the *Kyklos* of Agathias (sixth century CE). The so-called *Anthologia Planudea*, assembled in 1299 or 1301 by the Byzantine monk Planudes (on its date, cf. Cameron 1993: 75–7), likewise derives from Cephalas; it comprises fewer poems than the *Anth. Pal.* (about 2,400 vs. 3,700), but 388 epigrams survive exclusively through Planudes and are commonly printed as Book 16 or *Appendix Planudea* of the *Greek Anthology*, a term often used synonymously with *Palatine Anthology*. In addition to these two major compilations, a number of *syllogae minores* have come down to us, some of which also preserve non-Cephalan material (Maltomini 2008).

Book 7 of the *Anth. Pal.* contains hundreds of sepulchral epigrams; some might have been inscribed once, some are made to appear authentic, while others overtly flaunt their artificiality. This long-standing tradition of writing fictional epitaphs is ingeniously mocked by Lucillius, an epigrammatist of the Neronian age (*Anth. Pal.* 11.312; cf. Meyer 2005, 199; Floridi 2010, 11–14; Höschele 2010, 86–8):

> Οὐδενὸς ἐνθάδε νῦν τεθνηκότος, ὦ παροδῖτα,
>   Μάρκος ὁ ποιητὴς ᾠκοδόμηκε τάφον
> καὶ γράψας ἐπίγραμμα μονόστιχον ὧδ᾽ ἐχάραξε·
>   „Κλαύσατε δωδεκέτη Μάξιμον ἐξ Ἐφέσου.“
> οὐδὲ γὰρ εἶδον ἐγώ τινα Μάξιμον· εἰς δ᾽ ἐπίδειξιν
>   ποιητοῦ κλαίειν τοῖς παριοῦσι λέγω.

For no one's corpse, O traveler, did Marcus the poet build here a tomb and, having written an epigram of one line, he engraved it thus: "Bewail 12-year old Maximus from Ephesus". Well, I did not see any Maximus – it is to demonstrate the poet's talent that I bid the passers-by to weep.

The fictitiousness of the situation is exposed already by the poem's incipit, which subverts a common epigraphic formula by using the genitive of οὐδείς instead of the deceased's name: this tomb belongs to "nobody." Hoping to achieve the highest possible degree of authenticity, a poet named Marcus was not content to compose an epitymbion for the written page, but went so far as to erect a real monument on which to inscribe his one-liner. By denying the very existence of a corpse, this "cenotaph" clearly outdoes earlier instances. Indeed the tomb itself reveals that it tells passers-by to weep merely for "epideictic" purposes (v. 5).

Its words here are ambiguous, since κλαίειν λέγω may be understood not only as an exhortation to grieve, but also as the idiom "to hell with you" (LSJ s.v. κλαίω I.2): instead of wishing the passer-by farewell (χαίρειν λέγω), the epitaph quite literally sends its readers off wailing (Floridi 2010, 11 n. 1). It is thus not the *mors immatura* of a 12-year-old boy that brings tears to our eyes, but the poor quality of Marcus's verse (v. 4): his line might work well enough on a real grave (though single pentameters are extremely rare), but in its utter conventionality it hardly serves to advertise the literary genius of our would-be *epigrammatopoios*. The brevity of the quoted epitaph, moreover, stands in ironic contrast to the name of the deceased: little Maximus is mourned in a poem of minimal dimension! One might say that the text stages a "relapidarisation" of the genre, a reversal of epigram's detachment from its original medium – and yet the monument built by Marcus only exists on papyrus, the τάφος, whose material reality is essential to the poem's joke, turns out to be imaginary after all.

2.   From Stone to Book

The (partial) dissociation of epigram from its lapidary context led to multiple semantic shifts, in particular with regard to *deictica*, which are a typical feature of inscriptional verse. If we stand in front of a tomb or votive offering, the reference of local adverbs such as ἐνθάδε or demonstrative pronouns such as τόδε is immediately manifest; if we encounter the same words on the written page, it is up to our imagination to picture the locale or object in question. In the terminology of Karl Bühler, the genre's detachment from stone involved a transformation of the poems' *demonstratio ad oculos* to a *Deixis am Phantasma* (Meyer 2005, 17–20; Höschele 2010, 93–9). In many cases the reader is invited to supplement information not explicitly given in the narrow confines of the text – a process which Peter Bing has famously dubbed *Ergänzungsspiel*. Let us take a quick look at one of the examples discussed in his article, Callimachus *Anth. Pal.* 6.347 = 21 G-P (Bing 1995, 119–22):

Ἄρτεμι, τὶν τόδ' ἄγαλμα Φιληρατὶς εἴσατο τῆδε·
ἀλλὰ σὺ μὲν δέξαι, πότνια, τὴν δὲ σάου.

Artemis, for you Phileratis has set up this gift here. But you, lady, receive it, and keep her safe.

The epigram as such is unremarkable, its content and phrasing appear strictly conventional, and we might wonder what, if anything, distinguishes it as Callimachean. It is indeed possible that the poem was originally inscribed, but in the context of a book it becomes intriguing precisely through what it leaves unsaid: it offers us a brief glimpse of a woman praying to Artemis for salvation, but neither does it detail the circumstances of her dedication (could Phileratis be pregnant?) nor does it tell us what she is offering to the goddess. To quote Bing (1995, 121):

Set in the scroll of Callimachus's epigrams, or in an anthology, the couplet becomes – self-consciously, I believe – "dislocated," or better "unmoored"; τόδ'and τῇδε float free, a provocation to imaginative play. Where is this place? What was this ἄγαλμα?

A text's reader is, of course, always involved in the constitution of meaning, no matter the genre. But as Hunter (1992, 114) observes with regard to epigram,

> Perhaps no literary genre makes such a direct appeal to the reader's powers of intellectual reconstruction, to the *need* to interpret, as does that of epigram; the demand for concision makes 'narrative silences' an almost constitutive part of the genre. In these circumstances, the refusal to speculate amounts to no less than a refusal to read.

Our hermeneutic work, however, does not end with the individual poem. For just as readers of inscribed epigram interpret a poem as part of its physical setting (whether a necropolis, a shrine, or the marketplace), so the readers of literary epigram are invited to interpret a given poem in the context of neighboring texts in the very different confines of the scroll.

3. The Textuality of Epigram Books

In particular, these readers are faced with a crucial question: in what relation does the individual poem stand to the context in which it is transmitted, and what are the dynamics involved in reading epigram collections? For a long time, scholars tended to examine epigrams in isolation. At first glance, this approach seems to be supported by the fact that epigrams are texts of "maximal closure" (Herrnstein Smith 1968, 197), i.e. texts so stringently structured and so effectively concluded that any addition would only reduce their poetic impact. They are, in a manner of speaking, self-sufficient and meant to work on their own. In the medium of the book, however, the semantic potential of individual epigrams can be significantly modified and enhanced by surrounding poems, and this textual interaction seems to have played an integral role in the design of epigrammatic *libelli* (following Argentieri 1998, I use this term with reference to a purposeful arrangement of epigrams by a single author, as opposed to a *sylloge* or mere compilation of texts by one or more epigrammatists).

Unfortunately, Greek epigrams largely come down to us outside of their original contexts, in later anthologies. However, Kathryn Gutzwiller (1998) persuasively argued that Hellenistic epigrammatists composed artfully arranged books, traces of which can still be found in the *Palatine Anthology* – a hypothesis which I have sought to further corroborate, also with regard to the works of later epigrammatists (Höschele 2010). Given the state of transmission, we cannot say much about the dynamics triggered by a sequential reading of the poems in their original order, but it is still possible to reflect upon intratextual relations between epigrams, to discern programmatic poems, which are likely to have occupied a prominent position, and to examine the coherence given to a book by the poet's construction of a specific authorial *persona*.

Even if the texts themselves present us with various speakers, "the reader may nevertheless fashion a poetic creator responsible for the overall design; the presence of that persona is revealed, amid the multiplicity of voices, through thematic repetition, formal cohesiveness, and uniformity of subject matter and tone" (Gutzwiller 1998, 11). A major part of the epigrams by Leonidas of Tarentum, for instance, pose as epitaphs and dedications "commissioned" by low-class characters such as farmers, fishermen or weavers, while the author features himself as a poor exiled wanderer (*Anth. Pal.* 7.715, 6.300), a man chasing mice away from his hut, as they try to steal his meager crumbs (*Anth. Pal.* 6.302). These statements ought not to be taken at face value: Leonidas clearly modeled his *persona* to fit the humble subject matter of his collection, and it is likely that these "autobiographical" poems served a programmatic function as prologues or epilogues to a *libellus* (Gutzwiller 1998, 107–11).

Not all scholars agree, of course, on the significance of the book as a medium for epigrams. Reviving a theory first put forth by Reitzenstein (1893), Alan Cameron (1995, 71–103), for instance, considers the symposium to be the genre's primary setting and even claims that epigrams offering variations on a theme originated as *ex tempore* compositions at the same parties (*contra* Cameron cf. Bing 2000). In their brevity epigrams, no doubt, lend themselves to such improvisation. Cicero, in fact, attests to the improvisatory skills of the second-century epigrammatist Antipater of Sidon (*de oratore* 3.194) and his own contemporary Licinius Archias of Antioch, who is praised for his masterful variations (Cic. *Arch.* 8.18). But even if epigrammatists composed some of their poems for separate occasions, these same poets clearly understood and exploited the semantic impact of the *libellus* on its individual components. For they saw that poems can be made to interact with neighboring texts, when set in a purposeful arrangement, regardless of their origin (on poetry books and epigrammatic *libelli*, cf. Höschele 2010, 10–37).

4. The Traveling Reader

As I have argued elsewhere (Höschele 2007 and 2010, 100–146), the widespread poetological metaphor which equates writing and reading with traveling gains special significance in the case of epigram books, evoking as it does the setting and reception of inscriptional verse: the reader, as a figurative wayfarer, follows in the footsteps of the passer-by traditionally addressed by epitaphs. Epigrams arranged on a two-dimensional scroll can evoke the idea of a three-dimensional space, through which we move in the course of our reading. Two poems by Dioscurides (late third century BCE) may illustrate this point: the first (*Anth. Pal.* 7.37 = 22 G-P) is spoken by a satyr standing on the tomb of Sophocles, while the second (*Anth. Pal.* 7.707 = 23 G-P) features as its speaker another satyr, who praises the Hellenistic poet Sositheus for his revival of satyr drama. Linked by verbal and thematic parallels, the two epigrams are clearly conceived as companion pieces (Höschele 2010, 130–34); most striking, however, is the explicit reference of the second satyr to his "brother" as the guardian of Sophocles' tomb (*Anth. Pal.* 7.707.1–3):

Κἠγὼ Σωσιθέου κομέω νέκυν, ὅσσον ἐν ἄστει/ἄλλος ἀπ' αὐθαίμων ἡμετέρων Σοφοκλῆν, / Σκίρτος ὁ πυρρογένειος

I too, the red-bearded Skirtos, am guarding a corpse, that of Sositheus, just like one of my brothers is guarding Sophocles in the city.

While the incipit of *Anth. Pal.* 7.707 suggests a pairing of the two inscriptions in close physical proximity, what follows paradoxically undermines this impression by locating the tombs in two separate places. We are thus invited to envision a wayfarer coming from Athens and encountering Sositheus's monument somewhere along the road; the distance traveled corresponds to the reader's movement from one poem to the other within the literary landscape of the book: as Bing (1988/2009, 40) remarks, "[t]heir sequential connection – κἠγὼ, "I too" (v. 1) – is that between neighboring texts *on the page*."

5. The New Posidippus

Sequences of funerary, dedicatory or ekphrastic epigrams may thus evoke the grouping of inscriptional verse, be it in a cemetery, a temple or an art gallery. The Milan Posidippus papyrus (P.Mil.Vogl. VIII 309) is a case in point. Published in 2001 by Bastianini and Gallazzi, this sensational find preserves over 100 epigrams – all but two previously unknown – by Posidippus of Pella (first half third century BCE). These grant us a unique glimpse into the workings of an early Greek epigram *libellus* (cf. Acosta-Hughes, Kosmetatou, and Baumbach 2004; Gutzwiller 2005). Not all agree on the nature of this collection: while the *communis opinio* regards Posidippus as its author, some deny that all poems are by him. And while several scholars argue (convincingly in my view) that the arrangement is an artful one, going back to the author himself, others prefer to ascribe it to a later editor. It came, at any rate, as a great surprise that the collection is divided into thematically arranged sections, each headed by a title. Whereas some of the categories, such as *anathematika* or *epitumbia*, are conventional, others appear – at least from a modern perspective – rather exotic (e.g. *lithika* on gem stones, *oionoskopika* on omens, or *iamatika* on healing miracles). The focus on pseudo-inscriptional epigram types and Ptolemaic themes casts our image of the poet, so far known primarily as a composer of amatory epigram, in a new light. This serves to remind us that the *Stephanos* or *Garland* (c. 100 BCE), in which Meleager of Gadara interwove his own compositions with poems of his predecessors (including Posidippus), reflects the aesthetic and thematic preferences of its editor and does not permit us to form a comprehensive picture of any given author, let alone the genre as a whole (on Meleager's anthology, cf. Gutzwiller 1998, 276–322).

One of the most tightly structured sections in the *New Posidippus* is that of the *andriantopoiika* (62–70 Austin-Bastianini; cf. Gutzwiller 2002), which describes a series of bronze statues. Leading our way through this fictional gallery, Posidippus not only functions as an exegete of sorts (Männlein-Robert 2007, 53–81), but also offers an intriguing reflection on contemporary aesthetics together with an implicit metapoetic manifesto. A brief summary cannot do justice to the complexity of these issues, but let us note that each of the sculptures, which range from the Archaic/Classical period to the Hellenistic era, may be said to embody one of two stylistic qualities, σεμνότης ("majesty") and λεπτότης ("fineness"), around which an intense debate had arisen among Hellenistic poets. As Prioux's excellent 2007 study shows, Posidippus does not oppose grandeur in the same manner as Callimachus, and his *andriantopoiika* advocate the possibility of a co-existence between the two styles in ancient and modern art (Prioux 2008, 200–252).

The metapoetic dimension of this assemblage of statuary is best demonstrated by Posidippus's ecphrasis of a tiny chariot fashioned by the sixth-century sculptor Theodorus of Samos (67 A-B²):

c. 14].. [..]. ἄντυγος ἐγγύθεν ἄθρει
  τῆς Θεοδωρείης χειρὸς ὅσος κάματος·
ὄψει γὰρ ζυγόδεσμα καὶ ἡνία καὶ τροχὸν ἵππων
  ἄξονά θ' [ἡνιό]χου τ' ὄμμα καὶ ἄκρα χερῶν·
ὄψει δ' εὖ [*c.* 12]... εος, ἀλλ' ἐπὶ τῷδε
  ἑζομέν[ην ἂν ἴσην ἅρματι] μυῖαν ἴδοις.

[... ... ...] of the chariot, observe at close quarters how hard Theodorus's hand has worked. For you will see the yoke-band, the reins, the ring on the bit of the horses, the axle, as well as the [driver's] eye and the tip of his fingers. And you will see full well [the pole, as thin as a hair], and sitting on it you might see a fly [of the size of the chariot]. (transl. Austin-Bastianini)

In directing our gaze to the delicacy and tininess of Theodorus's piece – a chariot as small as a fly –, Posidippus invites us to associate the miniature's artistry with that of his epigrams (for a similar metapoetic reading of the *lithika*, cf. Prioux 2008, 173–7 and Höschele 2010, 163–70). That the description serves as a medium for Posidippus's poetic self-reflexion is suggested not least of all by the fact that the chariot itself formed part of a self-portrait by Theodorus (Angiò 2001; Sens 2005, 222–4; Prioux 2008, 208 and 249): as Pliny the Elder reports (*Nat.*

Hist. 34.83), the sculptor had fashioned an image of himself, holding a file in his right hand and a *quadriga*-cum-charioteer between three fingers of his left. Even though Posidippus does not explicitly evoke this portrait, the mention of Theodorus's hand, which at first appears to stand metonymically for his craftsmanship, can, I submit, also be understood as a concrete reference to the sculpted hand, which bore the chariot. A similar ambiguity underlies the expression ὅσος κάματος (v. 2), which may denote not only the greatness of Theodorus's labor, but also – ironically – the "magnitude" of its (minuscule) product (Sens 2005, 224). By highlighting the fingertips of the charioteer, Posidippus, moreover, adds a further level of reflexivity: the gesture of the ἡνίοχος holding the reins replicates that of the artist holding the chariot between his fingers, while the emphasis on the figure's gaze calls to mind the viewing eyes of the spectator (note the verbs of "seeing" in vv. 1, 3, 5, 6).

It hardly is a coincidence that the ecphrasis of this Archaic artifice – despite its age a perfect embodiment of λεπτότης – is followed by a description of the Colossus of Rhodes, the gigantic masterpiece of the Hellenistic artist Chares of Lindos (68 A-B). A connection between the two poems is created especially by the parallel ways in which Posidippus underlines the respective size of each sculpture: while Theodorus's chariot is so small that a fly would cover it (67.6 A-B), the image of Helios matches the earth in its grandeur (γᾶς μεγ[έθει παρ]ισ[ῶ]ν, 68.6 A-B). Far more could be said about the links between the two epigrams and their interaction with further texts in the collection. But since these poems have received plenty of critical attention in recent years, let us turn to another, less studied, group of texts to discuss epigrammatic concatenation and a sequential reading's resultant dynamics.

6.   A Sequential Reading of Lucillius *Anth. Pal.* 11.75–7

The example I would like to consider is a series of Lucillius's epigrams targeting boxers. Though modern conceptions link epigram most closely with mockery and witty points, the sub-genre of skoptic, i.e. satiric, epigram fully emerged only in the first century CE (it was the reception of Martial, not that of Greek authors, which shaped the later epigrammatic tradition). Following Cameron (1995), Gideon Nisbet has argued that the main function of satirical epigrams was to serve as entertainment at dinner parties. According to him, the books in which the poems circulated had no literary purpose, but were designed purely for "use at symposia, where antidotes to seriousness are in demand, and where the skoptic poets had found the perfect gap in the market" (2003, 35). However, one should not dismiss the semantic potential of the book so easily, especially in view of the preface to Lucillius's βιβλίον δεύτερον (*Anth. Pal.* 9.572), which proves the existence of at least two authorially edited *libelli* (against Nisbet, cf. also Gutzwiller BMCR 2005.01.19 and Floridi 2010, 34–7).

Most skoptic epigrams are contained in Book 11 of the *Anth. Pal.*; scholars have conjectured that they came to Cephalas via the *Anthologion* of Diogenianus, whom the *Suda* dates to Hadrian's reign (cf. Cameron 1993, 84–90). Whether this was the case or not (note that the *Suda* says nothing about the epigram types assembled by Diogenianus), it is my contention that some sequences still reflect the poems' original arrangement. The three epigrams quoted below, for instance, which introduce the series labeled εἰς πύκτας (*Anth. Pal.* 11.75–81), were in all likelihood conceived for a linear reading (*Anth. Pal.* 11.75–7; similarly Floridi 2010, 22–30 on Lucillius's epigrams about stolen statues):

Οὗτος ὁ νῦν τοιοῦτος Ὀλυμπικὸς εἶχε, Σεβαστέ,
    ῥῖνα, γένειον, ὀφρῦν, ὠτάρια, βλέφαρα·
εἶτ' ἀπογραψάμενος πύκτης ἀπολώλεκε πάντα,
    ὥστ' ἐκ τῶν πατρικῶν μηδὲ λαβεῖν τὸ μέρος·

εἰκόνιον γὰρ ἀδελφὸς ἔχων προενήνοχεν αὐτοῦ,
    καὶ κέκριτ' ἀλλότριος μηδὲν ὅμοιον ἔχων.

Olympicus here, who now looks like this, used to have, Augustus, a nose, a chin, brows, ears and eyelids. But then he enrolled as a boxer and lost everything, so that he did not even get his share of the paternal heritage. For his brother, having a portrait of him, brought it forth [in court], and Olympicus, bearing no similarity to it, was judged to be a stranger.

Ῥύγχος ἔχων τοιοῦτον, Ὀλυμπικέ, μήτ' ἐπὶ κρήνην
    ἔλθῃς, μήτ' ἐνόρα πρός τι διαυγὲς ὕδωρ.
καὶ σὺ γὰρ ὡς Νάρκισσος ἰδὼν τὸ πρόσωπον ἐναργὲς
    τεθνήξῃ μισῶν σαυτὸν ἕως θανάτου.

With such a snout, Olympicus, don't go to any spring and don't look into translucent water. For if you see your face clearly, you will die like Narcissus – hating yourself to death.

Εἰκοσέτους σωθέντος Ὀδυσσέος εἰς τὰ πατρῷα
    ἔγνω τὴν μορφὴν Ἄργος ἰδὼν ὁ κύων·
ἀλλὰ σὺ πυκτεύσας, Στρατοφῶν, ἐπὶ τέσσαρας ὥρας
    οὐ κυσὶν ἄγνωστος, τῇ δὲ πόλει γέγονας.
ἢν ἐθέλῃς τὸ πρόσωπον ἰδεῖν ἐς ἔσοπτρον ἑαυτοῦ,
    «Οὐκ εἰμὶ Στρατοφῶον», αὐτὸς ἐρεῖς ὀμόσας.

When Odysseus, in the 20th year, returned home safely, Argus the dog recognized his appearance upon seeing him. You, however, Stratophon, after four hours of boxing, have become unrecognizable not to dogs, but to your city. If you want to look at your face in a mirror, you yourself will swear: "I am not Stratophon."

The first and third epigrams are centered around the motif of a boxer disfigured beyond recognition. On its own the second poem might appear to mock a man for his innate ugliness. However, given its placement in the series and the fact that its addressee bears the same name ("Olympicus") as the subject of the preceding poem, a name evocative of athletic contests, it is reasonable to assume that the butt of its joke is likewise a boxer with a mutilated face (Robert 1968, 202 n. 2). As I will argue, the poem is, indeed, intimately linked with the two surrounding texts, and its position in the midst of this triad is anything but coincidental. But let us, first of all, examine the individual epigrams.

In his discussion of Lucillius's poems on athletes, Louis Robert (1968) illustrated how the poet parodies the language of inscriptions commemorating athletic victories. Overall one might say that, while *anathematika* and *epitumbia* seek to praise their subjects, skoptic epigram subverts the genre's honorific function by pouring ridicule on its victims and exposing their vices (cf. the excellent introduction to Floridi's 2014 commentary). The beginning of *Anth. Pal.* 11.75, with its use of the formula οὖτος ὁ (often found in epitaphs) and the verb εἶχε, suggests that the poem is about to list the victories of Olympicus (for ἔχω = "to win," cf. Robert 1968, 190–93). Lucillius's address to the emperor (Σεβαστέ) might confirm this impression by evoking an agonistic setting with Nero as presider (Robert 1968, 208–9). The second line, however, records neither games nor disciplines, in which our athlete was victorious, but the facial features he once had – before *losing* (ἀπολώλεκε, v. 3) all of them in boxing matches. In the end, Olympicus, bearing no visible resemblance to his own image, even lost his share of the paternal inheritance, because he was judged (κέκριτ', v. 6) at court (and not at a contest) to be a stranger. The idea that Olympicus's appearance does not match his pictorial representation plays on a *topos* of ekphrastic epigrams, which regularly praise the lifelikeness of art works by pointing out that they look exactly like their subject – in this case the portrait looks more like Olympicus than he does himself!

The third poem of the series, *Anth. Pal.* 11.77, presents a variation of the motif by imagining a boxer, who has become completely unrecognizable after a single fight, as unidentifiable even to himself. Though his match lasted an epic four hours, its duration cannot compete with the long absence of Odysseus, who was identified by his dog after 20 years abroad. By evoking the Odyssean anagnorisis scene, Lucillius creates, I submit, an implicit link to the failed recognition of Olympicus in *Anth. Pal.* 11.75: while the boxer cannot prove his identity and therefore loses what would rightfully be his, the Homeric hero managed to re-assert himself as rightful ruler. Not only is this parallel highlighted through the verbal echo of πατρικῶν (*Anth. Pal.* 11.75.4) in πατρῷα (*Anth. Pal.* 11.77.1), but the idea of Stratophon swearing an oath (ὀμόσας, *Anth. Pal.* 11.77.6) concerning his identity also looks back to the legal setting in the last couplet of *Anth. Pal.* 11.75.

The motif of the mirror, a glance into which would make Stratophon question his own sense of self, connects the epigram in turn with the middle poem, *Anth. Pal.* 11.76, where Olympicus is featured as an anti-Narcissus of sorts (note, too, that the confrontation of the two boxers with their respective mirror image varies the motif of the εἰκόνιον presented by Olympicus's brother in *Anth. Pal.* 11.75). In both cases, the addressee is warned of the danger inherent in seeing the reflection of his πρόσωπον (*Anth. Pal.* 11.76.5 and 77.5): death on the one hand, loss of identity on the other. By characterizing Olympicus's face as an animal-like ῥύγχος (*Anth. Pal.* 11.76.1), Lucillius underlines his lack of human features. Retrospectively, this word choice gains further meaning, as it prepares the ground for the appearance of a real dog, Odysseus's Argus, in *Anth. Pal.* 11.77. The joke of the epigram is relatively simple: Olympicus has been so disfigured that he would die out of self-hate (not self-love), were he to behold himself like Narcissus (as Robert 1968, 202 n. 2 remarks, the conclusion ἕως θανάτου adds an "agonistic" touch by recalling the expression "fighting a combat *to the death*").

But there is more to it than that. Through his evocation of the Narcissus myth, Lucillius, I believe, implicitly alludes to the motif of (non-)recognition, which stands at the center of the other two epigrams. For did the seer Tiresias not prophesy that Narcissus would live to old age – as long as he did not know himself (cf. Ovid *Met.* 3.348: *si se non noverit*[3])? When the youth realizes that he is looking at and pining for his own reflection, he vanishes from unfulfilled desire. Narcissus's self-recognition and its fatal consequences thus stand in telling contrast to the scenes of failed recognition in *Anth. Pal.* 11.75 and 77, where the inability of others to identify Stratophon is accompanied by his own lack of self-recognition. The subtle manner in which *Anth. Pal.* 11.76 is thus interwoven with its surrounding texts – not through overt parallels, but through an implicit mythological reference only perceptible to a reader familiar with the tale of Narcissus – strongly suggests that the poem was conceived for this position. Critics might object that epigrams dealing with the same subject matter are bound to exhibit certain similarities and that verbal echoes are only to be expected. But I hope to have shown how a linear reading can reveal connections that go beyond the purely accidental, how epigrams may enter into a meaningful dialogue with neighboring texts.

7. "The Sting of Love": Variations on a Theme

Another form of textual dialogue is that between epigrams by different authors offering variations on a theme. *Variatio* is an essential feature of the genre, a widespread practice in Hellenistic and later epigram (Ludwig 1968; Tarán 1979), which may be said to have its roots in the grouping of inscriptional poems on the same monuments (for a comparison of epigraphic and literary *variatio*, cf. Fantuzzi 2010). By juxtaposing original and variation(s), Meleager visualized their intertextual relation, making the literary context, which normally has to be supplied through the reader's poetic memory, physically present (cf. Gutzwiller 1998, 227). In many cases he also inscribed himself into the tradition and laid the foundation for future imitations. In what follows I would like to consider one of Meleager's poems on love's bitter-sweetness vis-à-vis two later rewritings. Amatory epigram as such established itself in the early Hellenistic period; appropriating themes previously treated in lyric and elegiac poetry, it paradoxically casts private oral speech "in a form that descends from the public, written speech of inscription" (Gutzwiller 2007, 314). It is, moreover, worthy of note that epigram was to become *the* medium for Greek erotic poetry, having *inter alia* a profound impact on Latin love elegy (Keith 2010).

In *Anth. Pal.* 5.163 (= 50 G-P), Meleager addresses a bee grazing his beloved's skin:

Ἀνθοδίαιτε μέλισσα, τί μοι χροὸς Ἡλιοδώρας
    ψαύεις ἐκπρολιποῦσ' εἰαρινὰς κάλυκας;
ἦ σύ γε μηνύεις ὅτι καὶ γλυκὺ καὶ δυσοΐστου⁴
    πικρὸν ἀεὶ κραδίᾳ κέντρον Ἔρωτος ἔχει;
ναὶ δοκέω τοῦτ' εἶπας· ἰὼ φιλέραστε, παλίμπους
    στεῖχε· πάλαι τὴν σὴν οἴδαμεν ἀγγελίην.

Flower-dwelling bee, why have you left the blossoms of Spring and are touching the skin of my Heliodora? Are you suggesting that she has the sting of cruel-darted Eros, which is both sweet and always bitter to the heart? Yes, I think that's what you mean. Alas, friend of lovers, away with you! I/we have known your message for a long time.

The epigram intriguingly stages its own interpretation by having the speaker analyze the symbolic meaning of the bee, which he views as an emblem of love's bitter-sweetness, a notion going back to Sappho's description of Eros as a "bittersweet unconquerable creeping thing" (γλυκύπικρον ἀμάχανον ὄρπετον, F 130.2 V). Meleager tells the insect to fly away, since he has known its message for a long time – presumably due to his personal experiences with Heliodora. But could one not also take the last line as a comment on the long tradition of the image? Could Meleager not be suggesting on a metapoetic level that *we*, i.e. the poet and his readers (note the plural οἴδαμεν), know all too well what the bee stands for, because we have encountered this and similar metaphors many times before in poetry? If so, then his rejection of the insect can be understood as a self-ironic dismissal of his poem's subject matter – it's almost as though the "bee topos" had forced itself on him and he was now saying with Sappho μήτε μοι μέλι μήτε μέλισσα ("neither honey nor bee for me", F 146 V). Since flowers are a common image for poetry – an image that Meleager himself prominently exploits in the preface to his *Stephanos* (*Anth. Pal.* 4.1 = 1 G-P) –, his question to the "flower-dwelling" bee as to why she has left her usual blossoms to approach Heliodora may thus also be read as: "why has this commonplace infiltrated my poetry?" Given the flowery nature of his anthology, the poet should, of course, not be surprised by the bee's arrival (for the garland imagery and Heliodora's metapoetic function, cf. Höschele 2010, 171–229).

Meleager, at any rate, innovated the conventional image by characterizing the sting of love as simultaneously sweet and bitter (one would expect the sweetness to be associated with the bee's honey, not its κέντρον). In his version, Marcus Argentarius, an epigrammatist of the early Imperial age, returns to the usual dichotomy, while giving another amusing twist to the image (*Anth. Pal.* 5.32 = 2 G-P):

Ποιεῖς πάντα, Μέλισσα, φιλανθέος ἔργα μελίσσης·
    οἶδα καὶ ἐς κραδίην τοῦτο, γύναι, τίθεμαι·
καὶ μέλι μὲν στάζεις ὑπὸ χείλεσιν ἡδὺ φιλεῦσα,
    ἢν δ' αἰτῇς, κέντρῳ τύμμα φέρεις ἄδικον.

You, Melissa, do all the works of the flower-loving bee. I know this and am putting it, lady, into my heart. You drip honey from your lips in giving sweet kisses, but when you ask <for money>, you inflict an unjust wound with your sting.

On a first reading the vocative Μέλισσα, occupying the same *sedes* as in Meleager, looks like an address to the bee (with everything written in majuscules, such a misunderstanding could easily occur), but by the last word of the line it is clear that the poet is addressing a girl with striking similarities to her namesake. Like his predecessor, Argentarius knows (οἶδα ~ οἴδαμεν) about the metaphorical significance of the bee, which he sees reflected in Melissa's nature. After describing her kisses as honey-sweet, he, however, attributes love's bitterness not to the usual emotional pangs, but to the sting of the girl asking for money (αἰτῇς). As so many of Argentarius's darlings, Melissa belongs to the demi-monde of courtesans, where love is inevitably tied to monetary transactions – not unfittingly for a poet called "banker" (Argentarius puns on his cognomen in *Anth. Pal.* 5.16, where he tries to hunt down a girl with silver, ἀργυρέους, coins). In this context it is tempting to understand "all the works" (πάντα ἔργα) done by Melissa as a reference to her sexual availability, her willingness to perform all conceivable *figurae Veneris* for adequate compensation. (Could, moreover, one of Bee's specialties be fellatio and the honey dripping from her lips a result of her oral services?) These sexual innuendos might, in fact, have inspired the following epigram by Cillactor (around 100 CE; *Anth. Pal.* 5.29):

Ἁδὺ τὸ βινεῖν ἐστι. Τίς οὐ λέγει; ἀλλ᾽ ὅταν αἰτῇ
    χαλκόν, πικρότερον γίνεται ἐλλεβόρου.

It is sweet to fuck. Who would deny it? But when she asks for money, it becomes more bitter than hellebore.

The image of the bee is also clearly sexualized in an epigram by Strato (*Anth. Pal.* 12.249), who authored a collection of pederastic poems later named Παιδικὴ Μοῦσα (first/second century CE; cf. Floridi 2007; Höschele 2010, 230–71):

Βουποίητε μέλισσα, πόθεν μέλι τοὐμὸν ἰδοῦσα
    παιδὸς ἐφ᾽ ὑαλέην ὄψιν ὑπερπέτασαι;
οὐ παύσῃ βομβεῦσα καὶ ἀνθολόγοισι θέλουσα
    ποσσὶν ἐφάψασθαι χρωτὸς ἀκηροτάτου;
ἔρρ᾽ ἐπὶ σοὺς μελίπαιδας ὅποι ποτέ, δραπέτι, σίμβλους,
    μή σε δάκω· κἠγὼ κέντρον ἔρωτος ἔχω.

Bull-born bee, whence did you notice my honey and are flying around the crystal-like face of my boy? Won't you stop buzzing about and wanting to touch his skin, which is of the greatest purity, with your flower-collecting feet? Away with you, you runaway, and back to your hives full of honey-boys, lest I bite you. For I too have the sting of love.

Once more the vocative μέλισσα precedes the feminine caesura, while the epithet βουποίητε varies Meleager's ἀνθοδίαιτε with a nod to Argentarius's ποιεῖς. Like Meleager, Strato is none too pleased to see a bee touch his darling's skin (ἐφάψασθαι χρωτὸς ~ χροὸς ψαύεις). But instead of engaging with its symbolic meaning, the epigram re-interprets the opposition of μέλι and κέντρον in concrete sexual terms: while dubbing the boy his "honey", the poet threatens the insect (ἔρρ᾽ ~ παλίμπους στεῖχε) with a phallic gesture by asserting that he too possesses the "erotic prick". That Strato modeled his epigram on Meleager is clear. But beyond the imitation of certain expressions and the poem's general theme, he also seems to have picked up on its metapoetic message. For we may, I believe, understand Strato's initial question about the bee's origin (πόθεν) as an implicit reference to his literary source: isn't the obvious answer that the bee has come from Meleager's *Stephanos*? This metapoetic reading is supported by the characterization of the bee's feet as "flower-collecting" or "anthologizing" (ἀνθολόγοισι), which may function as a sort of Alexandrian "footnote" by pointing directly to Meleager's anthology (for a metapoetic reading, see also Gutzwiller in Floridi 2007, XII). Strato thus mimics not only Meleager's evocation of the bee motif, but also his ennui in the face of such a commonplace, and he amusingly makes his own dismissal more forceful by threatening the insect with sexual violence.

8. Technopaegnia

In addition to being highly self-conscious and allusive, epigram lends itself to any number of literary and formal games. Consider, for instance, the isopsephic epigrams of Leonides of Alexandria (first century CE), where the numerical value of the letters in one line or couplet equals that of the other (Luz 2010, 254–70). The *Anth. Pal.* transmits numerous riddles or γρῖφοι, as well as six pattern poems also known to us through the bucolic tradition (Strodel 2002; Männlein-Robert 2007, 140–54; Luz 2010, 327–53; Kwapisz 2013) and commonly referred to as *technopaegnia* (note, though, that this usage of the term is modern): three of the texts (*Axe, Wings, Egg*) are attributed to Simias of Rhodes (early third century BCE), one (*Syrinx*) to Theocritus, while Dosiadas and Besantion are each credited with an *Altar*-poem. Written in lyric-iambic meters with lines of varying length, *technopaegnia* literally *represent* their respective subject matter by visualizing it through the arrangement of their words on the written page. While the poems were hardly designed for inscription, they do recall early epigraphic practices, where an object's shape determined the layout of the poem engraved upon it. Thus we may, for instance, picture the words of Simias' *Wing*-poem as inscribed on the wings of an Eros statue (*Anth. Pal.* 15.24 cf. Luz 2010, 333–5 with further references).

Wing
λεῦσσέ με τὸν Γᾶς τε βαθυστέρνου ἄνακτ' Ἀκμονίδαν τ' ἄλλυδις ἑδράσαντα·
μηδὲ τρέσῃς, εἰ τόσος ὢν δάσκια βέβριθα λάχνα γένεια.
τᾶμος ἐγὼ γὰρ γενόμαν, ἁνίκ' ἔκραιν' Ἀνάγκα,
πάντα δὲ τᾶς εἶκε φραδαῖσι λυγραῖς
ἑρπετά, πάνθ' ὅσ' ἕρπει
δι' αἴθρας.
Χάους δέ,
οὔτι γε Κύπριδος παῖς
ὠκυπέτας οὐδ' Ἄρεος καλεῦμαι·
οὔτι γὰρ ἔκρανα βίᾳ, πραϋνόῳ δὲ πειθοῖ·
εἶκε δέ μοι Γαῖα Θαλάσσας τε μυχοὶ χάλκεος Οὐρανός τε·
τῶν δ' ἐγὼ ἐκνοσφισάμαν ὠγύγιον σκᾶπτρον, ἔκρινον δὲ θεοῖς θέμιστας.

Behold me, the lord of broad-chested Earth, who placed Acmon's son [Ouranos] elsewhere, and don't be scared, if, small as I am, my chin is densely covered with down.
For I was born back when Necessity held sway
and all bowed to her baleful rules, everything
creeping and everything crawling
through the aether.
Of Chaos,
not of Cypris
and Ares I call myself a swift-winged son.
For I rule not through force, but through gentle-minded persuasion.
But Earth, the Sea's corners and brazen Ouranos bowed to me.
From them I took away the ancient scepter, and I determined laws for the gods.

The confines of this essay do not permit me to discuss this text in more detail. But let me point out in conclusion that we might see a reflection of Eros' birth from Chaos in the generative power of the poem, which creates *ex nihilo* an image of his wings through the *kosmos* of its words, its ἔπεα πτερόεντα (and is it not striking that the text's center, the point of least spatial extension from which the wings emerge, comprises the word Χάους?).

It is not hard to see why playful little poems such as epigrams and *technopaegnia* used to be dismissed as trivial and unworthy of scholarly attention. Luckily, though, the tide has changed, and recent years have seen a great number of important publications on Greek epigram. So far, however, the focus has primarily been on Hellenistic authors, and scholars have yet to mine the *Palatine Anthology* for the epigrammatic production of later ages with all its precious gems.[5]

NOTES

[1] Kaibel's 1878 edition is still a crucial source for stone epigrams; Friedländer and Hoffleit 1948/1987 offer a collection of inscribed verse arranged by meter; the standard edition for *carmina epigraphica* from the eighth to the fourth century BCE is Hansen 1983–1989; metrical inscriptions preserved in literary sources are collected in Preger 1891/1977; Peek 1955/1988 presents funerary epigrams arranged by type; stone epigrams from the Greek East are edited in Merkelbach and Stauber 1998–2002.

[2] The text is quoted after Austin and Bastianini 2002; for a very useful online edition, which is periodically updated, cf. the website of the Center of Hellenic Studies: http://chs.harvard.edu/CHS/article/display/1343. Accessed April 6, 2015.

[3] As Floridi 2014 *ad loc.* observes, Lucillius probably knew the Narcissus myth through Ovid's *Metamorphoses*.

[4] For a discussion of this reading and other emendations, cf. Gutzwiller (forthcoming), *ad loc.*

[5] I would like to thank Peter Bing, Lucia Floridi and Niklas Holzberg for their generous comments on this piece.

REFERENCES

Acosta-Hughes, B., E. Kosmetatou, and M. Baumbach, eds. 2004. *Labored in Papyrus Leaves: Perspectives on an Epigram Collection Attributed to Posidippus (P.Mil.Vogl. VIII 309)*. Cambridge, MA.

Angiò, F. 2001. "Posidippo di Pella, *P. Mil. Vogl.* VIII, 309, col. X, l. 38–col. XI, ll. 1–5 e Plinio il Vecchio (*Nat. Hist.* XXXIV, 83)." *APapyrol* 13: 91–101.

Argentieri, L. 1998. "Epigramma e libro: morfologia delle raccolte epigrammatiche premeleagree." *Zeitschrift für Papyrologie und Epigraphik* 121: 1–20.

Austin, C. and G. Bastianini, eds. 2002. *Posidippi Pellaei quae supersunt*. Milan.

Bastianini, G. and C. Gallazzi, eds. 2001. *Posidippo di Pella: Epigrammi (P.Mil. Vogl. VIII 309)*. Milan.

Baumbach, M., A. Petrovic, and I. Petrovic, eds. 2010. *Archaic and Classical Greek Epigram*. Cambridge.

Beckby, H. 1965–1967. *Anthologia Graeca: Griechisch-Deutsch*. 4 vols. 2nd edn. Munich.

Bing, P. 1988/2009. *The Well-Read Muse: Present and Past in Callimachus and the Hellenistic Poets*. Ann Arbor, MI (first edn. 1988).

Bing, P. 1995. "Ergänzungsspiel in the Epigrams of Callimachus." *Antike und Abendland* 41: 115–31.

Bing, P. 2000. "Text or Performance/Text and Performance: Alan Cameron's *Callimachus and his Critics*." In R. Pretagostini, ed., *La letteratura ellenistica: Problemi e prospettive di ricerca*, Rome, 139–148.

Bing, P. 2009. *The Scroll and the Marble: Studies in Reading and Reception in Hellenistic Poetry*. Ann Arbor, MI.

Bing, P. and S. Bruss, eds. 2007. *Brill's Companion to Hellenistic Epigram*. Leiden.

Bruss, J. S. 2005. *Hidden Presences: Monuments, Gravesites, and Corpses in Greek Funerary Epigram*. Leuven.

Burzachechi, M. 1962. "Oggetti parlanti nelle epigrafi greche." *Epigraphica* 24: 3–54.

Cameron, A. 1993. *The Greek Anthology from Meleager to Planudes*. Oxford.

Cameron, A. 1995. *Callimachus and His Critics*. Princeton, NJ.

Day, J. W. 2007. "Poems on Stone: The Inscribed Antecedents of Hellenistic Epigram." In P. Bing and S. Bruss, eds., *Brill's Companion to Hellenistic Epigram*. Leiden, 29–47.

Day, J. W. 2010. *Archaic Greek Epigram and Dedication: Representation and Reperformance*. Cambridge.

Fantuzzi, M. and R. Hunter. 2004. *Tradition and Innovation in Hellenistic Poetry*. Cambridge.

Fantuzzi, M. 2010. "Typologies of variation on a theme in archaic and classical metrical inscriptions." In M. Baumbach, A. Petrovic, and I. Petrovic, eds., *Archaic and Classical Greek Epigram*. Cambridge, 289–310.

Floridi, L. 2007. *Stratone di Sardi, Epigrammi: Testo critico, traduzione e commento*. Alessandria.

Floridi, L. 2010. "Rivisitazione delle convenzioni epigrammatiche nel sottogenere scoptico." *Materiali e discussioni per l'analisi dei testi classici* 65: 9–42.

Floridi, L. 2014. *Lucillio, Epigrammi: Introduzione, traduzione, testo critico e commento*. Berlin.

Friedländer, P. and H. B. Hoffleit. 1948/1987. *Epigrammata: Greek Inscriptions in Verse, from the Beginnings to the Persian Wars*. Chicago (first edn. 1948).

Gow, A. S. F. and D. L. Page. 1965. *The Greek Anthology: Hellenistic Epigrams*. 2 vols. Cambridge.

Gow, A. S. F. and D. L. Page. 1968. *The Greek Anthology: The Garland of Philip and Some Contemporary Epigrams*. 2 vols. Cambridge.

Gutzwiller, K. J. 1998. *Poetic Garlands: Hellenistic Epigrams in Context*. Berkeley, CA.

Gutzwiller, K. J. 2002. "Posidippus on Statuary." In G. Bastianini and A. Casanova, eds., *Il papiro di Posidippo un anno doppo*, Florence, 41–60.

Gutzwiller, K. J., ed. 2005. *The New Posidippus: A Hellenistic Poetry Book*. Oxford.

Gutzwiller, K. J. 2007. "The Paradox of Amatory Epigram." In P. Bing and S. Bruss, eds., *Brill's Companion to Hellenistic Epigram*, Leiden, 313–32.

Gutzwiller, K. J. forthcoming. *Critical edition and commentary of Meleager's epigrams*. Oxford.

Hansen, P. A. 1983–1989. *Carmina Epigraphica Graeca*. 2 vols. Berlin.

Harder, M. A., R. F. Regtuit, and G. C. Wakker, eds. 2002. *Hellenistic Epigrams*. Leuven.

Herrnstein Smith, B. 1968. *Poetic Closure: A Study of How Poems End*. Chicago.

Higbie, C. 2010. "Epigrams on the Persian Wars: Monuments, Memory and Politics." In M. Baumbach, A. Petrovic, and I. Petrovic, eds., *Archaic and Classical Greek Epigram*, Cambridge, 183–201.

Holzberg, N. 2002. *Martial und das antike Epigramm*. Darmstadt.

Höschele, R. 2007. "The Traveling Reader: Journeys through Ancient Epigram Books." *Transactions of the American Philological Association* 137: 333–69.

Höschele, R. 2010. *Die blütenlesende Muse: Poetik und Textualität antiker Epigrammsammlungen*. Tübingen.

Hunter, R. 1992. "Callimachus and Heraclitus." *Materiali e discussioni per l'analisi dei testi classici* 28: 113–23.

Kaibel, G. 1878. *Epigrammata Graeca ex lapidibus conlecta*. Berlin.

Keith, A., ed. 2010. *Latin Elegy and Hellenistic Epigram: A Tale of Two Genres at Rome*. Cambridge.

Kwapisz, J. 2013. *The Greek Figure Poems*. Leuven.

Ludwig, W. 1968. "Die Kunst der Variation im hellenistischen Liebesepigramm." In A. E. Raubitschek et al., eds., *L'Épigramme Grecque. Sept exposés suivis de discussions*, Vandœuvres-Geneva, 299–348.

Luz, C. 2010. *Technopaegnia: Formspiele in der griechischen Dichtung*. Leiden.

Maltomini, F. 2008. *Tradizione antologica dell' epigramma greco: le sillogi minori di età bizantina e umanistica*. Rome.

Männlein-Robert, I. 2007. *Stimme, Schrift und Bild: Zum Verhältnis der Künste in der hellenistischen Dichtung*. Heidelberg.

Merkelbach, R. and J. Stauber. 1998–2002. *Steinepigramme aus dem griechischen Osten*. 4 vols. Stuttgart, Munich, and Leipzig.

Meyer, D. 2005. *Inszeniertes Lesevergnügen: Das inschriftliche Epigramm und seine Rezeption bei Kallimachos*. Stuttgart.

Nisbet, G. 2003. *Greek Epigram in the Roman Empire: Martial's Forgotten Rivals*. Oxford.

Peek, W. 1955/1988. *Griechische Vers-Inschriften: 1. Grab-Epigramme*. Chicago (first edn. 1955).

Petrovic, A. 2007. *Kommentar zu den simonideischen Versinschriften*. Leiden.

Preger, T. 1891/1977 *Inscriptiones Graecae metricae ex scriptoribus praeter Anthologiam collectae*. Chicago (first edn. 1891).

Prioux, É. 2007. *Regards Alexandrins: Histoire et théorie des arts dans l'épigramme hellénistique*. Leuven.

Prioux, É. 2008. *Petits musées en vers: Épigramme et discours sur les collections antiques*. Paris.

Puelma, M. 1996. "Ἐπίγραμμα – epigramma. Aspekte einer Wortgeschichte." *Museum Helveticum* 53: 123–39.

Reitzenstein, R. 1893. *Epigramm und Skolion: Ein Beitrag zur Geschichte der alexandrinischen Dichtung.* Giessen.

Robert, L. 1968. "Les épigrammes satiriques de Lucillius sur les athlètes: Parodie et réalités." In A. E. Raubitschek et al., eds., *L'Épigramme Grecque. Sept exposés suivis de discussions,* Vandœuvres-Geneva, 181–295.

Sens, A. 2005. "The Art of Poetry and the Poetry of Art. The Unity and Poetics of Posidippus' Statue Poems." In K. J. Gutzwiller, ed., *The New Posidippus: A Hellenistic Poetry Book,* Oxford, 206–25.

Sider, D. 2007. "*Sylloge Simonidea.*" In P. Bing and S. Bruss, eds., *Brill's Companion to Hellenistic Epigram,* Leiden, 113–30.

Strodel, S. 2002. *Zur Überlieferung und zum Verständnis der hellenistischen Technopaignien.* Frankfurt.

Tarán, S. 1979. *The Art of Variation in the Hellenistic Epigram.* Leiden.

Tueller, M. A. 2008. *Look Who's Talking: Innovations in Voice and Identity in Hellenistic Epigram.* Leuven.

FURTHER READINGS

Gow and Page (1965 and 1968) provide ready access to a selection of epigrams available at the time of publication. Bing 2009 contains several articles on epigram (both reprinted and new); Bing and Bruss 2007; Fantuzzi and Hunter 2004 contains an excellent chapter on epigram (pp. 283–349); Harder, Regtuit, and Wakker 2002; Holzberg 2002; An extensive online bibliography on ancient epigram can be found at Holzberg, N.: http://www.niklasholzberg.com/Homepage/Bibliographien.html (accessed March 31, 2015).

CHAPTER 13

Oratory

Practice and Theory

Mike Edwards

Public speaking may be approached from two angles, the actual practice of eloquence, or "oratory," and the theory of how to perform it, or "rhetoric." In many ways this is a false division, *orator* merely being the Latin equivalent of the Greek *rhetor*, and the term "rhetoric" is frequently used to cover both aspects, often with a pejorative connotation (cf. "empty rhetoric"). Nevertheless, the division offers a practical way of approaching a vast topic that lay at the very heart of Greek life.

1. The Early Development of Oratory and Rhetoric

The reader of Greek literature, from Homer onwards, cannot fail to be struck by the frequency with which narrative alternates with direct speech. Almost half of the Homeric epics take the form of speeches, and the ability to speak persuasively was a vital part of the hero's make-up. Phoenix memorably reminds Achilles that he instructed him to be a "speaker of words and a doer of deeds" (*Iliad* 9.443) – in that order.

Aristotle in the *Rhetoric* (1.3) divides oratory into three categories: forensic (law-court oratory), deliberative (political), and epideictic (display). All three are already found in Homer, with assemblies, the trial scene depicted on the Shield of Achilles (*Iliad* 18.497–508), and the funeral orations delivered by Andromache, Hecuba, and Helen over Hector (*Iliad* 24.723–76) – a prominent role rarely afforded to women in the classical period. Since Homer was the fount of all knowledge, it was natural to assume the existence of a "Homeric rhetoric," and later rhetoricians trawled the epics for examples to illustrate their rules (cf. the lost second-century CE treatise *On Rhetoric According to Homer* by the Stoic grammarian Telephus of Pergamon: Suda T 495; *Prolegomena ton staseon* vol. 7, p. 5 Walz). But modern scholars are skeptical about the existence of any developed theory of persuasion at this early stage.

The same applies to the three centuries succeeding Homer, but if instruction in rhetoric remained rudimentary, the practice of speaking flourished. Hesiod comments on the Muses pouring sweet dew on a king's tongue, giving him the ability to speak persuasively in settling

A Companion to Greek Literature, First Edition. Edited by Martin Hose and David Schenker.
© 2016 John Wiley & Sons, Inc. Published 2020 by John Wiley & Sons, Inc.

disputes (*Theogony* 83–7), and there is another legal contest in the *Homeric Hymn to Hermes* (ll. 324–96), after Hermes steals Apollo's cattle. Two major factors in the sixth century contributed significantly to the subsequent flowering of oratory, namely the introduction of prose literature and the development of the city-state (*polis*). Most of the evidence comes from Athens, where the idea of free speech (*isegoria*) flourished. The lawgiver Solon retained the verse form of elegy for the dissemination of his political speeches, and tragedy kept up the poetic momentum in the fifth century, most notably in the trial of Orestes in Aeschylus's *Eumenides* of 458 (ll. 566–753). But it was Herodotus's *Histories* that pointed the way forward, with their numerous deliberative speeches and other debates, including an imaginary discussion in Persia of the best form of constitution (3.80–82). It is highly likely that Herodotus was influenced by a new development in the second half of the fifth century, the advent of the Sophists, but they themselves were preceded in rhetorical thinking by two shadowy figures from Sicily.

For in the desire to attribute the invention of rhetorical theory to a founding father, a separate tradition developed that rhetoric was invented in the first half of the fifth century by Corax of Syracuse and his pupil Tisias. The pair appear in the context of discussions of probability-theory in both Plato (*Phaedrus* 267a, 273a–274a) and Aristotle (*Rhetoric* 2.24.11) – though the fact that Plato attributes the same example of probability to Tisias as Aristotle to Corax is a good indicator of the confusion that already surrounded them in the fourth century. Some scholars have even doubted the existence of Corax.

One of the apocryphal tales attributed to them was that they took each other to court over Tisias's non-payment of Corax's fee for teaching him, which was to be paid if Tisias won his first case. Corax argued that if he won the case he should receive the fee, but that if he lost he should receive it also, because it would demonstrate that he had taught Tisias effectively; while Tisias argued that if he won the case he did not have to pay the fee, and if he lost he did not have to pay it, because he had not won his first case (cf. Sextus Empiricus, *Against the Professors* 2.97–9). A similar story was told of the sophist Protagoras of Abdera and his pupil Euathlus, and this kind of clever intellectual gymnastics links rhetoric and sophistic thinking. For Protagoras there are two contradictory arguments about everything, and it is possible for an orator "to make the weaker case the stronger" (DK 80 A 20–21), hence he wrote *Antilogies* (contradictory arguments), similar to the surviving *Dissoi Logoi* (*Double Arguments*). It was a key part of the sophists' role to teach their pupils how to argue on both sides of a case. They also carried out research: Protagoras was interested in the correct use of language, Prodicus of Ceos in synonyms, Hippias of Elis in rhythm. But it was another sophist who took argumentation to new levels, the Sicilian Gorgias of Leontini.

Gorgias came to Athens on an embassy in 427 and amazed the assembly with his method of speaking. In a long career he taught all over Greece, charging high fees, and Diodorus (12.53) calls him "the first man to devise rules of rhetoric," in another version of the "founding father" tradition. Evidence of Gorgias's skill in argumentation is provided by the *Praise of Helen*, where he justifies Helen's conduct by the alternative propositions that she was obeying the gods, was taken to Troy by force, was persuaded by speech (*logos*), or was overcome by love. Gorgias's parting remark, "I wanted to write the speech as an encomium of Helen and an amusement (*paignion*) for myself" (§ 21), might be taken to indicate a lack of seriousness, but his examination of the powers of *logos* suggests otherwise. The theme of defending the apparently indefensible continues in the *Defense of Palamedes*, an imaginary trial speech against Odysseus's accusation that Palamedes had conspired with the Trojans. Finally, a fragment of Gorgias's *Funeral Oration* falls within the epideictic *epitaphios* genre.

Gorgias's writing is highly artificial. Critics noted the poetic nature of his style, with plenty of metaphors such as "vultures, living tombs" (Pseudo-Longinus, *On the Sublime* 3.2). Word jingles (*paranomasiai*) abound, with assonance, alliteration, and rhyme (*homoioteleuton*), and in his sentence structure there are parallelisms (*isokola*) and antitheses. Together, these so-called "Gorgianic figures" would have a profound influence on later style, though most authors would use them rather more sparingly.

It is hard to exaggerate the impact of the sophists on the literature of the second half of the fifth century. As well as Herodotus, their influence on Euripides and Aristophanes is clear; while Thucydides in his *History* often adopts the sophistic method of presenting speeches in antilogies, as in the Mytilenean Debate (3.38.7), where Cleon criticizes the Athenians for behaving in the assembly as if they were listening to sophistic displays. But it was in the forensic field that the sophistic influence was particularly strong. Plato (*Phaedrus* 266d-267d) gives a list of sophists who were theorizing on courtroom oratory, and the two strands of theory and practice come together in the person of Antiphon of Rhamnus.

2.　The Canon of Ten Attic Orators

Antiphon (*c.* 480–411BCE) was the first member of the Canon of Ten Attic Orators (see below). Executed for his part in the oligarchic revolution in 411, he is described by Thucydides (8.68.1) as being extremely able but suspect to the people because of a reputation for cleverness. Consequently, Antiphon devoted himself to writing speeches for others: again on the "founding father" theme, he was regarded in antiquity as the first professional speechwriter (*logographos*, cf. Pseudo-Plutarch, *Vit. X or.: Life of Antiphon* 832c–d). Three speeches from homicide trials survive under his name, written in the grand style, full of antitheses, that is familiar from Thucydides, whose teacher Antiphon was supposed to be. He also taught rhetoric, as is evidenced by the *Tetralogies*, three sets of imaginary homicide speeches, two on each side as in a real trial (on the assumption that these are genuine works of Antiphon). There is, besides, a fragmentary treatise *On Truth*, attributed to Antiphon the Sophist, and (again assuming they were the same person) this is consistent with the range of activities performed by Protagoras and Gorgias.

With Antiphon we enter roughly a century of well-documented oratory at Athens, primarily in the forensic sphere. Litigants were expected to deliver their own speeches before juries that regularly numbered 200 or more in private suits, and in public cases 500 or more. The parties were allocated a fixed amount of time, measured by a water-clock (*klepsydra*). A litigant might share his allocation of time with a relative or friend who could speak on his behalf as an advocate (*synegoros*). Those who could afford the fees might secure the services of a logographer, a professional speechwriter like Antiphon, who would provide them with a text to learn for recital in court. Evidently, in a legal system where there were no trained judges to guide the juries on matters of law or precedent, far less to maintain silence in court, the ability to speak well in noisy conditions was vital in persuading juries, which had no opportunity to deliberate before they voted.

At some point a list was compiled of those who were regarded as the ten best orators of the fifth and fourth centuries. This canon may have been the work of Alexandrian scholars in the third or second century, but it is uncertain when the list of names we know was finalized. Caecilius of Caleacte wrote a lost treatise in the first century *On the Style of the Ten Orators*, but it is only with the *Lives of the Ten Orators*, wrongly attributed to Plutarch, that we have certain evidence for what became the established membership. Over 100 speeches survive, though included in the corpus are some that were clearly written by others (see below).

The second member of the canon, the aristocratic Andocides (c. 440–c. 390), displays a native talent for speaking that is at times rather uncontrolled. His amateur status perhaps makes his membership of the list slightly surprising, and the second-century CE Athenian sophist Herodes Atticus supposedly replied to an audience who were acclaiming him as one of the Ten

"I am certainly better than Andocides" (Philostratus, *VS* 564–5). Andocides is infamous for his role in two religious scandals of 415, the mutilation of the Herms and profanation of the Mysteries, which forced him into exile. On the second of two unsuccessful attempts to return he delivered *On his Return*, where he shows little contrition, and it was not until the amnesty of 403 that Andocides was finally allowed to resume his citizenship in Athens. He was then prosecuted for impiety in 399, when he delivered *On the Mysteries*, a long but carefully constructed defense which is notable rhetorically for its abuse of his opponents (*diabole*). His free-flowing narrative style, with frequent parentheses and anacoluthon, gives the speech a natural feel, as if unprepared. Andocides was acquitted and served in 392/1 on an embassy to Sparta, but his *On the Peace with the Spartans* failed to persuade the assembly and he again left Athens, disappearing from the historical record. The preserved Andocidean corpus contains a fourth speech, *Against Alcibiades*, which is one of several attacks on the Athenian fifth-century general and his family (cf. Lysias *or.* 14, *or.* 15; Isocrates *or.* 16). Purporting to be a speech delivered at a vote of ostracism in 417, the speech is undoubtedly a later rhetorical exercise.

A speech *Against Andocides* in the Lysiac corpus is also widely accepted as not being a genuine speech by Lysias, but in this instance is usually accepted as being one of those delivered at the *Mysteries* trial. There are several others in the corpus of 34 preserved Lysiac speeches whose authenticity has been questioned, but there are more than enough genuine speeches to enable an informed assessment of the third member of the canon. Lysias (in the tradition 459/8–c. 380) was a Syracusan metic, who moved in the highest Athenian circles (he appears in Plato's *Phaedrus*). His logographic activities were prompted by the loss of the family's wealth in the Peloponnesian War. He briefly enjoyed Athenian citizenship as a result of Thrasybulus's decree honoring those who had helped restore the democracy, and it may have been then that he delivered in person his prosecution of Eratosthenes, one of the Thirty Tyrants, for murdering his brother, Polemarchus. Debarred as a metic from a political career, he concentrated on writing speeches for clients to deliver in court in both public and private cases. The latter include one of Lysias's finest speeches, *On the Killing of Eratosthenes* (who was possibly related to the tyrant). Here Lysias defends a client who has killed his wife's lover but has been accused of entrapment, so breaking the law on justifiable homicide. Another is a prosecution speech, *Against Diogeiton*, which is remarkable for its representation of Diogeiton's own daughter speaking out against him – as a woman, she would have been unable to appear in person as a witness.

Of the corpus of 425 speeches that were extant at the time of the pseudo-Plutarchan *Life* (836a), critics like Dionysius and Caecilius adjudged 192 spurious. The desire to pass off works as being composed by Lysias reflects his position as one of the foremost Attic orators. This status was due to his style, which was recognized for its pure, everyday language. Lysias was thus a leading representative of "Atticism," the stylistic model that many critics in late Republican Rome advocated over the more florid "Asianist" style. Lysias's speeches are clearly arranged, regularly in the fourfold division of proem (introduction), narrative of events, proofs and epilogue (summary of the speech and concluding remarks). For Dionysius it was in his vivid and concise narratives that Lysias excelled as "unquestionably the best of all the orators" (Dion. Hal. *Lysias* 18). These are a key part of his persuasive technique – they carry the reader away with them, just as they must have carried away the original juries. Further, Lysias's speeches have the quality of charm (*charis*), in which none of his successors excelled him (*Lysias* 10); and Dionysius also praises his ability at characterization (*ethopoiia*), by which he means a general portrayal of character, though scholars have rightly detected elements of individual characterization in various speeches. Lysias, according to the *Life* (836a), only lost two cases: true or not, few orators surpassed him.

Isocrates (436–338) was another member of the canon who did not speak in public, in his case due to a weak voice and lack of confidence. Impoverished, like Lysias, by the Peloponnesian

War, Isocrates started as a logographer. Six forensic speeches (of 21 extant speeches/tracts plus nine letters) survive, among which his *On the Team of Horses*, composed for the son of Alcibiades, is rightly renowned. But Isocrates quickly became disillusioned with speechwriting and around 390 opened a school of rhetoric in Athens for the sons of the wealthy. He now began writing rhetorical tracts to serve as core texts for his curriculum, including *Against the Sophists*, where he sets out his own rhetorical agenda, and *Helen* and *Busiris*, where he demonstrates his skill at argument on well-worn themes concerning legendary characters – he was taught by Gorgias, whose influence on his style and method is clear enough. For about ten years he worked on the *Panegyricus*, which advocates a unified Greek crusade against the Persians (another by then conventional theme, following works by Gorgias and Lysias), written in a complex, periodic style with abundant use of "Gorgianic figures." Isocrates goes to great lengths to avoid hiatus (the clashing of vowels in successive syllables) and pays close attention to rhythm, with combinations of the trochee (long vowel followed by short) and iambus (short followed by long). Published in 380, the *Panegyricus* established Isocrates as a key figure in Athenian intellectual circles.

Further, Isocrates positioned himself as a Panhellenic advisor, writing tracts during the 360s concerning Cyprus (*To Nicocles, Nicocles, Evagoras*), Boeotia (*Plataicus*), and the Peloponnese (*Archidamus*). These contain a number of interesting rhetorical advances, including the use of imaginary speech in character (prosopopoeia at the end of *Archidamus*) and a prose encomium of a living person, Evagoras. After Athens' failure in the Social War (357–355), he temporarily favored a Common Peace (*On the Peace*) and recommended a return to the ancestral constitution (*Areopagiticus*); then in the *Antidosis* of 353 Isocrates used the imaginary setting of an Athenian legal procedure to defend his life's activities in an early example of autobiography, where he details his educational system. This followed his defeat in an actual antidosis (an exchange of property), and his involvement in this process indicates the financial success of his school. By the 340s Isocrates was openly advocating the cause of Philip II of Macedon, as the one person capable of uniting the Greeks against Persia. Arguably his most important work, the *Philip* was published in 346, but Isocrates was to be disappointed by Philip's reaction. Disillusioned, he embarked on the *Panathenaicus*, which he was still writing in 339, two or so years short of his centenary. Here Isocrates again presents an *apologia* for his life, combined with a biased comparison of Athens with Sparta. After further unsuccessful appeals to Philip, Isocrates starved himself to death in 338.

The fifth member of the canon, Isaeus (c. 420–340s), was probably from Chalcis on Euboea, and so was another metic, like Lysias. A pupil of Isocrates and a professional logographer, he may have written a rhetorical treatise as well. Eleven speeches survive concerning inheritance cases, plus an extended fragment of a speech on citizenship quoted by Dionysius. The intricacies of the inheritance cases and the complex ways in which he deals with them suggest that Isaeus was an expert in this area of law. His clever argumentation led Dionysius to compare him unfavorably with Lysias (e.g. Dion. Hal. *Isaeus* 3–4), but at the same time this cleverness had a power (*deinotes*) which would be the mark of the greatest orator, Demosthenes, whose teacher Isaeus was thought to be.

The preeminence of Demosthenes (384–322) is reflected not only in the size of the corpus that has come down to us under his name – 60 speeches, an *Erotic Essay*, *Letters* and a collection of *Proems* – but also by the fact that a number of these works are spurious or of doubtful authenticity: as with Lysias, their preservation is due to their inclusion under his name. Demosthenes began by successfully prosecuting his former guardians for dissipating his inheritance, but not all the sums involved were recovered, and he went on to pursue a lucrative career as a speechwriter. At the same time he overcame physical deficiencies, for example by practicing speaking with pebbles in his mouth (Plutarch, *Demosthenes* 11.1), thereby improving his delivery of the speeches that would eventually see him established as the leading political speaker in Athens. Demosthenes' forensic speeches cover a vast array of subjects: the *Against Conon*, an assault case that allows comparison with Lysias's *Against Simon*, reveals a mixture of Lysianic charm and Demosthenic forcefulness that makes it one of his finest.

From 355/4 Demosthenes embarked on his political career through involvement in high-profile public suits, delivering the *Against Leptines* in 355. Most of his early attempts to influence Athenian policy were unsuccessful, including the *First Philippic* (351), when he had come to realize the threat posed by Philip of Macedon. Again, his proposal in the three *Olynthiacs* (349–348) to support that city fully against Philip was not heeded: Olynthus fell, and the Athenians were forced to conclude the Peace of Philocrates in 346. Although of necessity he supported the peace at the time, Demosthenes fell out with one of his fellow ambassadors, Aeschines, and quickly disowned the agreement. The pair had already been at odds during their service on the Council in 347/6, and now through his associate Timarchus Demosthenes attempted to prosecute Aeschines for taking bribes from Philip. Aeschines countered with a successful prosecution of Timarchus for addressing the assembly when debarred by immorality. In 343 Demosthenes tried again, and again Aeschines was successful, if narrowly. Aeschines (c. 397–c. 322) was another member of the canon, and his speeches *Against Timarchus* and *On the Embassy* survive, along with Demosthenes' prosecution speech *On the False Embassy*. Demosthenes continued to advocate resistance to Philip, most notably in the *Third Philippic* (341), which is arguably the finest political speech from antiquity, but the defeat at Chaeronea (338) was a turning point in Greek history. Chosen to deliver what is a model *Funeral Oration* in honor of the fallen, Demosthenes was himself honored by the proposal of Ctesiphon to grant him a gold crown for his services to Athens. However, Aeschines immediately lodged a suit against Ctesiphon for making an illegal proposal. Delaying the trial until what seemed the appropriate moment, Aeschines finally brought the prosecution in 330 with the last of his three speeches that survive, *Against Ctesiphon*, but Demosthenes' reply in *On the Crown*, acting as an advocate for Ctesiphon, won such an overwhelming victory that Aeschines was forced into exile at Rhodes, where he taught rhetoric and was remembered as the founder of the Second Sophistic (see below). Aeschines' rhetorical powers, like his political judgment, have been overshadowed by the dominance of Demosthenes, but the three speeches demonstrate his own high level of rhetorical ability. On the written page he displays wit and a generally simple vocabulary, with extensive argumentation supplemented by quotations from poetry; in delivery he was renowned for his strong voice and rejection of extravagant gestures. Like Andocides, he was not a professional speechwriter, and his at times unpolished style meant that he was ranked less highly by ancient critics than he might have been. Demosthenes' *On the Crown*, on the other hand, is generally acknowledged to be the finest speech of any ancient orator, a masterpiece that defends his political career as a devoted servant of the Athenian democracy. The two pairs of speeches concerning the embassy and crown offer us a rare glimpse of how both parties presented their cases, though we must remember that the speeches were edited for publication. Most of Demosthenes' later speeches do not survive, including his unsuccessful defense in a corruption trial connected with Alexander the Great's fugitive treasurer Harpalus (324/3). When Greece's revolt after Alexander's death failed at Crannon in 322, Demosthenes fled and, so the story goes, committed suicide by drinking poison from his pen.

The remaining members of the canon were contemporaries of Demosthenes. Hyperides, his supporter (389–322), was indeed rated second only to him. After studying under Isocrates and beginning a career as a logographer, Hyperides opened his political career in 363/2 with a prosecution of the prominent politician Aristophon. In 343 he successfully prosecuted Philocrates for his leading role in the peace with Philip, and he remained a prominent anti-Macedonian after Chaeronea. In 324/3 he led the attack on Demosthenes in the Harpalus affair, and he was selected to deliver the *Funeral Oration* of 323, parts of which survive. After the Greek defeat in the Lamian War Hyperides was executed by Antipater, who supposedly ordered that his tongue be cut out. Seventy-seven speeches under his name were known to later critics, who judged 50 genuine. These were lost until papyrus fragments of six speeches were discovered between 1847 and 1892, including parts of the speech against Demosthenes. More recently, fragments of his speeches *Against Timandrus* and *Against Diondas* have been discovered in the Archimedes Palimpsest. Like Lysias, Hyperides uses everyday language, while *On the Sublime* praises his wit, suavity and persuasiveness (chapter 34). Biting sarcasm was evidently matched to a native talent for inventiveness, which supposedly saw him defend the courtesan Phryne by bringing her into court and getting her to show the jurors her breasts.

Lycurgus (c. 390–c. 325/4) ran Athens' finances for 12 years after Chaeronea. He notably oversaw the rebuilding of the theatre of Dionysus, which was complemented by a new, official version of the plays of the three great tragedians, and the completion of a new arsenal. An anti-Macedonian, in 331/0 he prosecuted for treachery one Leocrates, who had left Athens between 338 and 332, and only narrowly lost. Lycurgus also attacked a number of individuals for corrupt practices, but ironically was himself condemned for leaving a deficit in the treasury: his sons, imprisoned because they were unable to repay the inherited debt, were released after an appeal by Demosthenes. Fifteen speeches of Lycurgus were judged genuine by Caecilius, but only the *Against Leocrates* survives. Though influenced stylistically by Isocrates, the frequent hiatuses in his writing reflect that Lycurgus was, like Aeschines, more concerned with what he was saying than with the style in which he said it, and he, too, quoted extensively from poetry.

Finally, the Corinthian Dinarchus (c. 360–c. 290) studied rhetoric at Athens under Theophrastus and became the leading logographer after the deaths of Demosthenes and Hyperides, particularly during the rule of his patron Demetrius of Phalerum. When Athens was liberated by Demetrius Poliorcetes in 307/6 Dinarchus moved to Chalcis; returning in 292, he lived with a friend, Proxenus, but his last recorded act was a prosecution of Proxenus for misappropriating his money. Dionysius judged 60 of the 87 speeches of Dinarchus known to him as genuine, of which only three survive (*Against Demosthenes, Against Aristogeiton* and *Against Philocles*), all concerned with the Harpalus affair. Despite his logographic success and Dionysius's essay, Dinarchus has found few admirers – he was dubbed 'a small-beer Demosthenes' by Hermogenes (*On Ideas* 2.11), and he makes excessive use of invective.

Outside the canon, we have two speeches by the founder of the Cynic school of philosophy, Antisthenes (c. 445–365), who composed antithetical claims to the armor of Achilles by Ajax and Odysseus; the *On the Authors of Written Speeches or On the Sophists* and the accusation of Palamedes by Odysseus written in the first half of the fourth century by Alcidamas; and some speeches preserved in the Demosthenic corpus by Apollodorus (notably 59, *Against Neaera*) and Hegesippus. The apologies (defense speeches) of Socrates composed by Plato and Xenophon also merit mention here.

3. Rhetorical Theory of the Classical Period

Rhetorical theory developed alongside the practice of the canonical orators. Supplementing model speeches for imitation and collections of proems and epilogues, "arts" of rhetoric (*technai*) offered instruction on how to compose a speech. All are now lost, except for two treatises written in the second half of the fourth century. These offer comprehensive courses in rhetoric as it was understood at the time, focusing on the discovery (or "invention") of arguments, arrangement and style. The *Rhetoric to Alexander*, perhaps written by Anaximenes of Lampsacus, divides rhetorical discourse into seven categories (or "species"), six of which are opposites: exhortation and dissuasion, praise and blame, prosecution and defense, and investigation. Topics and arguments for each category are followed by an analysis of the means of persuasion common to them all, and the treatise ends with the speech structure appropriate for each of the categories. But by far the more influential of the two treatises has been Aristotle's *Rhetoric*. In Book 1, after defining his subject (as "the faculty of finding out in any given case the available means of persuasion," *Rhetoric* 1.2) Aristotle discusses the three genres of oratory – deliberative, judicial, and epideictic, each of which (as in the *Rhetoric to Alexander*) has two opposing sides – and the "topics" and arguments appropriate to each. These are logical and objective; in Book 2 he treats subjective and moral proofs, including how the orator should present his own character (*ethos*), the kinds of emotion (*pathos*) that can be aroused in the audience, and the logical proofs that are common to the three genres: "commonplaces," enthymemes (deductive reasoning through rhetorical syllogisms), and examples (inductive reasoning). Book 3 is devoted to style (including the periodic sentence, metaphor, and prose rhythm) and the four parts of the speech.

Although little-read before the first century, the *Rhetoric* acquired increasing influence through the Peripatetic school of Aristotle's successors. Rhetoric itself, however, had many detractors in the classical period, none greater than Plato. As an opponent of democracy, Plato had no time for the oratory of the assembly or the law-courts which had condemned his master Socrates. The sophists are unmasked as purveyors of false wisdom in works such as the *Protagoras* and *Sophist*, and his opposition to rhetoric is developed in a series of dialogues, the *Gorgias, Menexenus, Symposium*, and *Phaedrus*. For Plato, rhetoric as practiced in Athens is not an art, merely an imitation of an art, and far worse is not concerned with justice but with the imposition of the speaker's own will. A philosophic rhetoric would always aim at the truth and justice, and Plato indicates that such a true rhetoric is possible via philosophical discourse.

4.   Oratory and Rhetoric in the Hellenistic Period

Greek oratory reached its peak during the fourth century, and arguably Aristotle's *Rhetoric* was never surpassed as a rhetorical manual. However, the absence of speeches from the Hellenistic period (323–27) and the lack of rhetorical treatises before the first century do not mean that this was a period devoid of either interest or importance. Indeed, a vast amount of systematizing went on, and numerous treatises were written on invention, style, argumentation, delivery, and memory, the "five parts" of rhetoric. Lost works on style (*lexis*) include those of Aristotle's successor Theophrastus, who enumerated the four stylistic "virtues" (*aretai*) of correctness, clarity, appropriateness, and ornamentation. In due course, these virtues were contrasted with the new and elaborate Asiatic style, whose creation was attributed to Hegesias of Magnesia in the third century. The concept of the three genres of style – the grand, middle, and plain – is first found in the Latin treatise of the first century BCE, the *Rhetoric to Herennius* (4.11ff.), but goes back much earlier. Demetrius's *On Style* adds a fourth genre, "forceful" (*deinos*), and if this is a work from the Hellenistic period (though this is much debated) it is the only surviving Greek treatise of that time, along with what remains of Philodemus (see below). Also to be mentioned here is the theory of tropes and figures, known from the *On Tropes* attributed to Tryphon in the first century CE and from Latin sources. Building on Aristotle's discussion of metaphor at *Rhetoric* 3.2–4 (cf. *Poetics* 21) and influenced by Stoic concepts of grammar, the theory developed of deviations from "natural" usage in single words (trope, such as metonymy) and several words (figure). In line with the schematizing tendency of the period, figures were then subdivided into figures of thought (*schemata dianoias*) and of diction (*lexeos*). The theory of argumentation was developed in the second century by Hermagoras of Temnos, who saw that most legal cases depend on rational inquiry, which in turn is facilitated by establishing the "question at issue" (*stasis*). Theophrastus wrote a treatise *On Delivery*, as did Athenaeus in the second century, the results of which are again evident in the *Rhetoric to*

Herennius, and in the rhetorical works of Cicero. Finally, theories of memory, attributed to the sixth-/fifth-century poet Simonides, were developed by Charmadas and Metrodorus of Skepsis in the second/first century. Once more, the earliest preserved discussion is in the *Rhetoric to Herennius* (3.28–40).

The status of rhetoric as an "art" remained controversial in the philosophical schools of the Hellenistic period. The Stoics, who contended that only the Stoic wise man could be the perfect orator, favored a concise style, adding "succinctness" (*suntomia*) to the list of virtues. The Academy adopted a more favorable stance towards rhetoric under Philon of Larissa (159/8–84/3), who taught Cicero. Finally, the Epicurean Philodemus of Gadara (c. 110–40) held meetings at Herculaneum in the so-called Villa of the Papyri, and his polemical *On Rhetoric* survives. Hostile to deliberative and judicial rhetoric, Philodemus grants the status of an "art" to the type of sophistic, epideictic rhetoric that was in his view practiced by Isocrates.

Oratory also flourished in the Hellenistic period, though in different circumstances from before. There was still political activity in the assemblies, elections and interstate negotiations, even if it was now dominated by the aristocracies, and disputes in the law-courts continued. From sources such as Polybius and Livy we know the names of numerous orators, and synopses of speeches made by and in response to ambassadors are preserved on inscriptions. Again, while the schools taught declamation (see below), prominent figures gave public lectures in the gymnasia, and a new type of encomium in praise of a god who has performed a miracle cure is attested in numerous inscriptions and papyri.

5.   Oratory and Rhetoric in the Roman Empire

Criticisms abounded of the decline of oratory and rhetoric after the change in Rome from Republic to Empire at the end of the first century BCE, notably in Tacitus's *Dialogue* (36–41). There were, however, numerous positive developments under the Empire (see König, ch. 7 in this volume). Literary criticism in connection with oratory made great advances under Dionysius of Halicarnassus, who came to Rome in 30 BCE. Seven of his *Critical Essays* concern the Attic orators (*Prologue to the Attic Orators, Lysias, Isocrates, Isaeus, Demosthenes, Letter to Ammaeus* on Demosthenes and Aristotle, and *Dinarchus*; essays on Aeschines and Hyperides do not survive); these promote Atticism, the "imitation" (*mimesis*) of the writing styles of classical Athens, though not uncritically. Demosthenes was the supreme model, and in his analysis of "composition" Dionysius investigated the order of words and flow of sounds that in Demosthenes produced a "middle" style (between "elevated" and "simple") as well as a "middle" harmony (between "austere" and "elegant"). Dionysius's friend Caecilius wrote *On the Style of the Ten Orators* and may have been responsible for settling the membership of the canon (see above). The first-century CE work *On the Sublime*, usually attributed to "Pseudo-Longinus", discusses how to achieve sublimity, or literary excellence, by imitation of classical models, especially Homer, Plato and, of course, Demosthenes.

A second development came in what we would call higher education, where the study of rhetoric was key. Taught by the rhetor, it comprised two stages. After learning grammar at school, students now embarked on "preparatory exercises" (*progymnasmata*). This was nothing new, but the exercises, moving from fable to composing a legal proposal, were now carefully ordered. Information on their content comes from Latin sources (especially Quintilian and Suetonius), but also in Greek from the *Progymnasmata* of Aelius Theon (first century CE) and Pseudo-Hermogenes (second century CE). Students progressed to "declamation" (*melete*), the composition of a fictitious speech. This type of exercise was centuries old (cf. Gorgias's *Palamedes*), but became especially popular at the end of the Republic, the Romans dividing declamation into *controversiae* (judicial speeches) and *suasoriae* (deliberative speeches). Sources include in Latin Seneca the Elder (c. 50 BCE–c. 40 CE) and in Greek Aelius Aristides (second century CE). Eleven of Aristides' twelve preserved *suasoriae*, written in an Atticizing style, are set in classical Greece (e.g. the *Sicilian Orations*, for and against sending reinforcements to the Athenian expedition). Other declamations are found in Lucian, Lesbonax, Polemon, and Hadrian of Tyre, illustrating that declamation was far more than a student exercise: speeches were composed by professors who performed them in public to large crowds and so became celebrities.

Quintilian's *Institutio Oratoria* is one of the most important manuals of rhetoric, but Greek theory also flourished under the Empire. General courses, like that of Apsines (third century), were supplemented by treatises on specific aspects of the subject, such as those by the second-century rhetorician Hermogenes on argumentation (*On Issues*) and style (*On Ideas*). The latter, with its seven types of "forms of style," greatly advances the theories of the Hellenistic period, offering a thorough, systematic approach to the topic. Epideictic rhetoric was not neglected, as is evidenced by the two third-century treatises ascribed to Menander Rhetor.

Epideictic, indeed, came into its own during the Empire, with the prosperity that accompanied the *pax Romana*. Opportunities for speeches praising the "virtues" (*aretai*) of the subject were now legion, whether of the gods, countries or individuals. Examples include the "imperial oration" (*basilikos logos*) in praise of the emperor and the "panegyric" (*paneguris*) at a religious festival, but also private addresses, such as the "birthday oration" (*genethliakos logos*). This does not mean, however, that the two other types of oratory disappeared. There was ample scope in the provinces for Greek orators to speak in courtrooms and before governors, and debates in assemblies were conducted on matters such as the imperial cult or interstate relations. A notable set of speeches that survives is the *Bithynian Orations* of Dio of Prusa (c. 40–after 110 CE; cf. König, ch. 7, pp. 117–8 in this volume).

Dio brings together the two strands of oratory and rhetoric as a member of what Philostratus calls the "Second Sophistic" (*VS* 481, 507). After discussing eight "philosopher sophists" (Dio included) and nine sophists of the fifth to fourth centuries, the "First Sophistic," to whom he adds Aeschines as the founder of the Second Sophistic, Philostratus gives biographies of 40 sophists amongst many more from Imperial times. Few of their works survive, but they include those by Polemon, Hermogenes, and Aelius Aristides. Mostly of aristocratic birth, these sophists were public figures who served on embassies and were prominent in their local communities (Herodes Atticus was the leading figure in Athens). Eighty surviving speeches are attributed to Dio, among which are four discourses *On Kingship* addressed to the emperor Trajan. Two others whose works survive are the multitalented Lucian of Samosata (c. 120–180), author of numerous encomia, and Cassius Longinus (c. 213–272/3), tutor of the philosopher Porphyry executed by the emperor Aurelian; his *Rhetoric* reveals a conventional work on the five parts.

Eventually oratory and rhetoric came into the orbit of Christianity (cf. Stenger, ch. 8, pp. 133–6 in this volume). After initial resistance, increasingly during the second and third centuries Christian apologists such as Tatian in Greek and Tertullian in Latin came to adopt pagan rhetorical methods. In the mode of the times, Gregory Thaumaturgus wrote the Christian epideictic *Thanksgiving to Origen* in 238. After Christianity became the official religion of Rome in the fourth century, Greco-Roman rhetoric combined with the Church Fathers in what is sometimes termed the "Third Sophistic." This was the period of Libanius (314–c. 393), 64 of whose speeches survive, many addressed to emperors and officials, including his funeral oration on the emperor Julian. Another figure is the highly influential author of *progymnasmata*, Aphthonius. Greek Christian rhetoricians include Eusebius of Caesarea, Gregory of Nazianzus and, perhaps most notably of all, Libanius's pupil John Chrysostom (c. 354–407). The centrality of Greek rhetoric to so many aspects of life – education, politics, the law, literature and now religious homilies – ensured its survival into the Middle Ages and beyond.

REFERENCES

Anderson, G. 1986. *Philostratus.* London.

Anderson, G. 1993. *The Second Sophistic.* London.

Carey, C. 1989. *Lysias: Selected Speeches.* Cambridge.

Carey, C. 1992. *Greek Orators VI: Apollodorus Against Neaira.* Warminster.

Carey, C. 2011. *Trials from Classical Athens.* London.

Carey, C. and R. A. Reid. 1985. *Demosthenes: Selected Private Speeches.* Cambridge.

Carey, C., M. Edwards, Z. Farkas, J. Herrman, L. Horváth, G. Mayer, T. Mészáros, P. J. Rhodes, and N. Tchernetska. 2008. "Fragments of Hyperides' *Against Diondas* from the Archimedes Palimpsest." *Zeitschrift fur Papyrologie und Epigraphik* 165: 1-19.

Cole, T. 1991. *The Origins of Rhetoric in Ancient Greece.* Baltimore.

Edwards, M. J. 1994. *The Attic Orators.* Bristol.

Edwards, M. J. 1995. *Greek Orators IV: Andocides.* Warminster.

Edwards, M. J. 1999. *Lysias: Five Speeches.* London.

Edwards, M. J. and S. Usher. 1985. *Greek Orators I: Antiphon and Lysias.* Warminster.

Furley, W. D. 1996. *Andocides and the Herms.* London.

Gagarin, M. 1997. *Antiphon: The Speeches.* Cambridge.

Gagarin, M. and P. Woodruff. 1995. *Early Greek Political Thought from Homer to the Sophists.* Cambridge.

Gunderson, E. 2009. *The Cambridge Companion to Ancient Rhetoric.* Cambridge.

Harris, E. M. 1995. *Aeschines and Athenian Politics.* Oxford.

Heath, M. 1995. *Hermogenes On Issues.* Oxford.

Kennedy, G. A. 1963. *The Art of Persuasion in Greece.* Princeton, NJ.

Kennedy, G. A. 1972. *The Art of Rhetoric in the Roman World, 300 B.C.-A.D. 300.* Princeton, NJ.

Kennedy, G. A. 1983. *Greek Rhetoric Under Christian Emperors.* Princeton,NJ.

Kennedy, G. A. 1991. *Aristotle: On Rhetoric. A Theory of Civic Discourse.* Oxford.

Kennedy, G. A. 1994. *A New History of Classical Rhetoric.* Princeton, NJ.

Kennedy, G. A. 2003. *Progymnasmata: Greek Textbooks of Prose Composition and Rhetoric.* Atlanta, GA.

Kerferd, G. B. 1981. *The Sophistic Movement.* Cambridge.

Kremmydas, C. 2012. *Commentary on Demosthenes Against Leptines.* Oxford.

Kremmydas, C. and K. Tempest, eds. 2013. *Hellenistic Oratory: Continuity and Change.* Oxford.

Loraux, N. 1986. *The Invention of Athens: The Funeral Oration in the Classical City.* Cambridge, MA.

MacDowell, D. M. 1962. *Andokides: On the Mysteries.* Oxford.

MacDowell, D. M. 1990. *Demosthenes: Against Meidias.* Oxford.

MacDowell, D. M. 2009. *Demosthenes the Orator.* Oxford.

Missiou, A. 1992. *The Subversive Oratory of Andokides.* Cambridge.

Pernot, L. 2005. *Rhetoric in Antiquity.* Washington, DC.

Petrie, A. 1922. *Lycurgus: The Speech Against Leocrates.* Cambridge.

Porter, S. E., ed. 1997. *Handbook of Classical Rhetoric in the Hellenistic Period 330 B.C.–A.D. 400.* Leiden.

Russell, D. A. 1983. *Greek Declamation.* Cambridge.

Russell, D. A. 1992. *Dio Chrysostom: Orations VII, XII, XXXVI.* Cambridge.

Russell, D. A. and M. Winterbottom. 1972. *Ancient Literary Criticism: The Principal Texts in New Translations.* Oxford.

Schiappa, E. 1999. *The Beginnings of Rhetorical Theory in Classical Greece.* New Haven, CT.

Sloane, T. O., ed. 2001. *Encyclopedia of Rhetoric.* Oxford.

Swain, S., ed. 2000. *Dio Chrysostom.* Oxford.

Todd, S. C. 2007. *A Commentary on Lysias: Speeches 1–11.* Oxford.

Too, Y. L. 1995. *The Rhetoric of Identity in Isocrates.* Cambridge.

Too, Y. L. 2008. *A Commentary on Isocrates' Antidosis.* Oxford.

Usher, S. 1993. *Greek Orators V: Demosthenes De Corona.* Warminster.

Usher, S. 1999. *Greek Oratory: Tradition and Originality.* Oxford.

Wardy, R. 1996. *The Birth of Rhetoric.* London.

Whitehead, D. 2000. *Hyperides: The Forensic Speeches.* Oxford.

Winter, B. W. 1997. *Philo and Paul Among the Sophists.* Cambridge.

Worthington, I. 1992. *A Historical Commentary on Dinarchus.* Ann Arbor, MI.
Worthington, I., ed. 1994. *Persuasion: Greek Rhetoric in Action.* London.
Worthington, I., ed. 2010. *A Companion to Greek Rhetoric.* Oxford.
Wyse, W. 1904. *The Speeches of Isaeus.* Cambridge.
Yunis, H. 2001. *Demosthenes:* On the Crown. Cambridge.
Yunis, H. 2011. *Plato: Phaedrus.* Cambridge.

FURTHER READING

Translations of the Attic Orators are available in the Loeb and Texas University Press (ed. M. Gagarin) series; see also Carey 2011 for a varied collection of some of the most famous speeches. A selection of commentaries on individual speeches is given below, though some assume a knowledge of Greek. Other useful collections are Gagarin and Woodruff 1995 for the early material, and Russell and Winterbottom 1972 for later texts. Translations of many of the later authors are most readily available in the French Budé series, but the *progymnasmata* have been translated into English by Kennedy (2003). There are a number of general studies of Greek oratory and rhetoric, including Kennedy 1963, 1983, 1994; Edwards 1994; Usher 1999; and Pernot 2005. On early rhetoric see Cole 1991 and Schiappa 1999, though their theories remain controversial (see Pernot 2005, 21–3); also Wardy 1996. For an introduction to the sophists see Kerferd 1981. The Hellenistic period has not generally been well served until recent years, mostly because of the loss of so much primary material – for example, no rhetorical manual survives between Aristotle's *Rhetoric* (or the *Rhetoric to Alexander*) and the Latin *Rhetoric to Herennius*, unless Demetrius is dated in this period. But this situation is changing: see the extensive edited collection of Porter 1997, and now that of Kremmydas and Tempest 2013. The study of Greek oratory and rhetoric after the Roman conquest is inevitably tied up with that of their Latin counterparts, and works on Roman rhetoric may be consulted for Greek, especially Kennedy 1972. But there are numerous volumes devoted to studies of the later Greek rhetoricians, such as Heath 1995 and Swain 2000. The standard overview of Greek declamation is that of Russell 1983, while for a general introduction to the Second Sophistic see Anderson 1993.

The following are valuable resources: Wyse 1904; Petrie 1922; MacDowell 1962, 1990, 2009; Carey and Reid 1985; Edwards and Usher 1985; Anderson 1986; Loraux 1986; Carey 1989, 1992; Kennedy 1991; Missiou 1992; Worthington 1992, 1994, 2010; Russell 1992; Usher 1993; Edwards 1995, 1999; Harris 1995; Too 1995, 2008; Furley 1996; Gagarin 1997; Winter 1997; Whitehead 2000; Sloane 2001; Yunis 2001, 2011; Todd 2007; Carey et al. 2008; Gunderson 2009; Kremmydas 2012.

CHAPTER 14

Historiography and Biography

Antonis Tsakmakis

1. Historiography

1.1. *The Heritage of Ionia*

"History is like the weather", writes Beat Näf (2010, 9). It owes its existence to the flow of time – to changes between various moments in time; but there can be no such notion as "history" (or "weather"), unless somebody perceives the changes and develops an interest in them. Historical writing aims at offering insights into the past, in order to make it meaningful for a community of people. In classical antiquity the past "was not interesting in and of itself …, their culture did not comprise a widespread, broad, and comprehensive interest in history *as such*" (Raaflaub 2012, 15). While "[w]e live in a civilization that too often either ignores the past, or takes it for granted" (Tucker 2009, 6), the term *historia* was used by Herodotus (*Proem*) to denote "knowledge derived from enquiry" – to satisfy a desire to learn more, both about the past and the world around us.

Long before the Greeks wrote about the past (and the present), the Ancient Near East knew written presentations of "recent events from immediately accessible sources which aimed to offer accountability and memorialize the events for future generations," as well as accounts of the "remote past for the purpose of explaining and understanding the present in terms of origins and primary causes" (Van Seters 2000, 2433). They all promoted the construction of collective memory, under the influence of centralized political structures. On the contrary, among Mycenaean documents in Linear B we find no royal genealogies, no chronicles or annals, just as we have no monumental architecture and no written dedications of temples from Greece in this period. Public records appeared after the introduction of the Phoenician alphabet, but the Greek city-states preferred to enshrine their heroes in epic narrative rather than display their accomplishments on inscriptions; also elegy and other types of poetry could deal with historical events using forms which were already used to convey memory. Poetic expression was an appropriate means to relate experience of the past, to construct continuities of values, or to create and confirm identities. The earliest treatments of the great battles against the Persians were in verse (from Simonides, Aeschylus, and Phrynichus), not in prose (Bowie 2001; Grethlein 2010).

A Companion to Greek Literature, First Edition. Edited by Martin Hose and David Schenker.
© 2016 John Wiley & Sons, Inc. Published 2020 by John Wiley & Sons, Inc.

At the end of the sixth century the study of the physical world provided the subject for the first Greek prose works in Ionia. Besides natural philosophy, descriptions of the earth emerged, with its various countries, their inhabitants, culture, legends and history. Rationalism and the primacy of experience and observation over traditional beliefs, two fundamental principles of Ionian science and physical philosophy, were applied not only to the study of the world, but also to stories about the past. We notice both qualities at work in the extant fragments of Hecataeus (c. 500 BCE), author of a *Circuit of the Earth* and a work on mythical genealogies. Talking about Aegyptus's children he remarks (FGrHist 1 F 19): "they were fifty, according to Hesiod, but in my opinion, hardly twenty." How did Hecataeus know better? He obviously relied on everyday experience (or "scientific" knowledge?) about the number of children a woman could bear in her life. And the projection of his own experiences and the neglect of cultural variables such as the possibility of polygamy mark the limit of his approach. He also reviews the tradition about Cerberus, by suggesting that it was a serpent, so poisonous that everyone bitten by it had to die – hence the name "Dog of Hades" (F 27): Hecataeus's interpretation of language usage (a form of human behavior) reveals his conviction that traditional beliefs should be subject to the same epistemological tenets as firsthand knowledge of the world.

This all-embracing ambition of Ionian prose to delve critically into various areas of the physical and cultural environment led to the emergence of various literary sub-genres, which only vaguely can be distinguished from each other in terms of form, content, methodology, and social function: "Generic fluidity was built into the historiographical tradition from the start" (Clarke 1999, 3).

We have lost almost all the Greek literary production on myths and genealogy, travel literature and geography, local history and chronology, ethnography and the history of institutions, memoir literature, and intellectual history; only works on political and military history, or biographies (mostly of political and military leaders) survive intact or in part. The loss is enormous: merely listing the names of lost authors and works known to us would require more than the full length of this chapter. Fragments are not always representative, but reflect the priorities and citing practices of our intermediate sources. Most writers did not name their sources (but many eagerly accused others of plagiarism: e.g. FGrHist 65 T 1b). Disagreement among other authors is a main reason of citation (cf. FGrHist 4 F 18 etc.): we are informed by a scholiast about no less than eight different opinions that seek to explain the term "Phoenician letters" (e.g. FGrHist 10 F 9) – aetiology is a standard practice of antiquarian research. Evidence on names or rare terms is another reason we possess bits from lost works.

The edition of Greek historical fragments, divided into six classifications, was designed by Felix Jacoby, who admirably accomplished the first three parts during his lifetime (Jacoby 1909); the project is now being continued (Schepens 1997) and made available online with *Brill's New Jacoby*.

1.2. Explaining the Polis, Empire, and Defeat

Classical Historiography: Setting the Standards

The Classical period (cf. McGlew, ch. 5 in this volume) bequeathed to posterity the complete works of three historians belonging to consecutive generations and variously connected with Athens. They set the standards for the development of the genre, with their focus on great wars and political history, and found imitators in the Roman period (as Lucian ironically notes, *Quomodo hist. conscr.* 2). Herodotus's work on the Persian Wars (490–479 BCE) was written in Ionian dialect (he came from Dorian/Carian Halicarnassus) and was presented in various places in oral performances in the third quarter of the fifth century (Thomas 2000, 213–85), including at Athens (cf. also Lefkowitz, ch. 18, pp. 289–90 in this volume). Thucydides' incomplete account of the Peloponnesian War (431–404BCE; the account is interrupted in 411, probably due to the historian's death soon after 400) was written to be studied, i.e. recited, in close, interested groups (Morrison 2007, 172–5). Xenophon's *Greek History* tells the story from the end of Thucydides' narrative to the Battle of Mantinea (362BCE). Written in installments in the first half of the fourth century, it is only one among various works of his on several subjects, including the economy, Spartan education, and Socrates (his *Anabasis* is also an account of military incidents, in which the author is a protagonist). Although Xenophon belongs to the first generation of the great stylists in Attic prose, he lived most of his life outside Athens and found himself more in harmony with the Spartan mentality. At least two other continuations of Thucydides are lost: by Theopompus of Chios (probably the most detailed account, ending in 394), and Cratippus; the *Hellenica Oxyrhynchia* are fragments of a work by an unknown author who also relates the same period, following Thucydides' system of dating, by dividing the year in summer and winter. The habit to start where others had stopped becomes frequent in ancient historiography after Xenophon, who ends (*HG* 7.5.27) with the words: "perhaps someone else will have a care for the events that followed after these."

The three surviving historians of the classical period belonged to local elites and had political or military experience (on the social position of historians and their relation to political power see Meissner 1992). Only Herodotus wrote on events prior to his life, based on information mostly collected *in situ*. He is aware of the value of autopsy (Schepens 1980) and also uses documentary evidence, especially inscriptions (Fabiani 2003); indication of and occasional judgment on his sources is part of his implicit argumentative strategy (Thomas 2000). He naturally draws mostly on oral traditions of various provenience and character; their classification and their adaptation to the overall design of his work remains a topic of inquiry (Murray 2001; Luraghi 2005). The exposition of the prehistory of the conflict between the Greeks and the barbarians (including the rise of the Persian Empire and detailed presentations of the peoples conquered by it) is longer than the description of the war itself and preserves rich material on various aspects of Archaic culture, both Greek and eastern. Herodotus presents himself as a "traveler" in a world which he conceives as a unity, or a whole where order prevails – very much in the tradition of Presocratic philosophers (Sandywell 1996) and the tragedians, especially Aeschylus and Sophocles, whom he obviously knows.

The Athenian Thucydides (cf. Lefkowitz, ch. 18, pp. 290–1 in this volume) wrote contemporary history while in exile (after a military failure), but his opening section, the *Archaeology*, applies current theories of progress and power politics to the past. Thucydides sticks to political and military topics; decision-making is important: he illuminates the factors that determine the behavior of persons, groups, and political entities. His careful methodological expressions seem to promise more authentic material than he really does provide (1.22); we find no traces of his sources in the narrative, apart from the sections dealing with the past. The only contemporary documents we come across are treaties, unevenly distributed in specific parts of the work, so that they have raised suspicion that the part in which they surface are unfinished. The speeches of his protagonists (so impressive, that they became a staple of historiography in his wake) are profoundly Thucydidean. Having eliminated any metaphysical agency from the workings of history, Thucydides makes all his persons think, act, and speak in conformity with current doctrines on society, politics, economy, and history – and use the repertoire of contemporary rhetoric. It is, perhaps, for that reason that the speakers seem static and do not appear as individuals in their own right (Marincola 2001, 146). As was also the case with Herodotus, his narrative follows pre-conceived interpretative patterns of shaping reality (Herodotus: Fowler 1996; Thucydides: Raaflaub 2012). The establishment of truth is equally presented as a challenging technical procedure; Thucydides' description of his method owes much to the language of proof in forensic rhetoric (Tsakmakis 1998).

With Xenophon the need to record history appears self-evident. The scope of his work expands beyond the limits of a single war to cover developments in Greece in a continuous narrative (the end point was probably necessitated by his old age). But he is neither, like Herodotus and Ionian prose writers, digressing to illustrate the culture and traditions of peoples, nor, like Thucydides, joining a dialogue with political theorists. He shares common interests with authors of technical treatises on various topics: he is more interested in military tactics, effective management of state affairs and sound political practices. In consonance with his contemporary Isocrates, he is in quest of an ideal leader who could unite Greece.

The radical change in Greek inter-state affairs after the appearance of the influential figure of Philip in the middle of the fourth century is reflected in Theopompus's shift of focus from Greek history in his own *Hellenica* to a central hero in his next work (also lost) entitled *Philippica* (which, however, "included genealogy, ethnography, geography, mythology, and war monograph;" Flower 1994, 153).

Historians from the Classical period are very often well informed in what they report, but also leave a lot to be desired. The design of their works reveals a literary self-consciousness (evident in skillful narrative sections, in the coherence of the content, and culminating in internal responses: see e.g. on Herodotus Rengakos 2011, 355–62; on Thucydides Hunter 1973; on Xenophon's sacrificing historical exhaustiveness for literary completion Lévy 1990; also Grey 1989. A literary character is already claimed for the earliest "historical" sub-genre, the periplous-literature, from its very beginnings: González Ponce 2008). While the authors selectively highlight topics in the service of textual aesthetics, they are constantly concerned with the indication of causality, responsibility and merit. The ideas of exhaustive completeness and systematic balance of focus are unknown in classical historiography. The ideal of truth (which in Hesiod qualified the non-fictional character of a story) develops in Thucydides as the avoidance of factual error; impartiality is primarily felt as the historians' need to sufficiently justify their own positions; explanation results from theories that don't need to be proved further. Historians do not suppress their judgment, which can be explicit or implicit: modern standards of scientific writing were not expected from writers in antiquity. The eclipse of the author, wherever it occurs, is a narrative or rhetorical strategy, not an academic requirement.

Quite inversely, accumulation of information and chronological arrangement prevails over narrative artfulness in works of local history. Their origins remain disputed (especially the question of priority regarding Herodotus), as is their relation to works on the history of a foreign people. While the first authors in this field are difficult to date, we are better informed about Ctesias of Cnidus who wrote on Persian history at the beginning of the fourth century. The earliest form (*horography*: a term used e.g. by Charon [FGrHist 262 T 1] for a local chronicle of his birthplace Lampsacus) probably presented more similarities to oriental annals and chronicles than other historiographical sub-genres, yet served the particular interests of communities. Partly supported by antiquarian research usually associated with sophistic encyclopedism, local histories in the last decades of the fifth century collected tales and documentary material more systematically and incorporated information on various topics. Although local historians usually seem to continue, not to compete with their "colleagues" (Gabba 1982), the eminence of Athens proved a challenge for Athenians and non-Athenians to produce works on Athenian history in the fourth and first half of the third century. The so-called *Atthides* were not uniform in character and goals (Harding 1994, 2007 and Rhodes 1990, who refute Jacoby's, 1949, view that Atthidographers had primarily political concerns; further Nicolai 2010): the earliest attested is by Hellanicus of Lesbos, a prolific writer of the late fifth century, who wrote treatises on various topics and places. Thucydides criticizes him for his brevity on the fifth century; others, like the Athenian Androtion, extensively covered recent and contemporary history. Philochoros, the last and most influential Atthidographer, published amply on Athenian subjects. *Atthides* were used as a source for the Aristotelian *Constitution of the Athenians*, but a close rapport between local history and literature on *politeiai* (whose character ranges from historical to theoretical) cannot be traced (Schepens and Bollansé 1994; Camassa 2010).

Also remarkable is the tradition of regional histories of Sicily, which tried to avoid parochialism and to present Sicily within the wider spectrum of Greek history. Building on this tradition, Timaeus of Tauromenium wrote in the first half of the third century a sizeable, comprehensive history of Western Greece up to 264, starting with the Return of the Heraclidae to stress the Greek origins of the Sicilians. His other work, on chronology, established the method of dating by Olympiads and the practice of synchronism. That Timaeus's narrative ends before the outbreak of the war between Carthage and Rome (whose past he was the first to include in a work on Greek history) is probably a sign that he realized the importance of this struggle for the future of the Greeks (Walbank 1989/90).

A new type of historical writing, the so-called universal history, is announced in the middle of the fourth century with Ephoros of Cyme (a pupil of Isocrates, together with Theopompus, according to ancient sources, which, however, may be biographical fiction inspired by the Panhellenic perspective of his work; see Schwartz 1907; Flower 1994). He wrote the history of the whole world, dedicating separate books to various areas. His moralizing evaluation of central historical figures (a trait he shares with Theopompus) is in alignment with the growing importance of powerful personalities in his time and with an ongoing interest in character in philosophical discourse.

Hellenistic Historiography: One World

No complete historical treatise survives from the three centuries between Chaeroneia and Actium (338–31) – an interval of dramatic political developments, also marked by overwhelming progress in the organization of research and intellectual activity, thanks to libraries, antiquarian and encyclopedic projects (following the lead of Aristotle and his students) and state archives. Alexander and his successors systematically applied practices of documentation and kept official archives with royal correspondence, court-diaries and reports of any kind. These could be helpful to those who had access to them, provided that documents were not falsified (a non-negligible *caveat* from the fourth century onwards). Several historians were personally involved in administration and military command or stood close to the kings; they were present at important moments, or could testify to the king's character, motives, and plans, and could report on private incidents. Alexander's conquest of Asia was recorded by numerous historians who had taken part in the campaign in various capacities (official historian: Callisthenes; admiral: Nearchus; captain: Onesicritus; engineer: Aristobulus; member of the military staff: Ptolemy – later King of Egypt; administrative officers: Ephippus, Chares, and others), which is also reflected in the thematic emphasis of their works; these historians reacted variously to the emergence of Hellenistic monarchy which surpassed the expectations of fourth century pro-monarchy theorists; also controversial were the policies of empire and the adoption of non-Greek traditions. Since the dates of composition of their works vary considerably (from the time of events: Callisthenes, executed in 327, to four decades after the death of Alexander: Aristobulus) their views on Alexander are influenced not only by their ideology, their philosophical preferences, their personal interests and the part they played in the events, but also by their experiences with monarchy after Alexander's death. Alexander's military genius is generally acknowledged, but his personality is variously evaluated in moral and political terms: Ephippus has him governed by passions. Onesicritus presents a philosopher at arms. Aristobulus emphasizes his mission as civilizer. Ptolemy significantly omits negative details. Callisthenes rejected the adopting of non-Greek customs as a tool to integrate diverse ethnic communities into the empire, while Ptolemy and Aristobulus attempted to reconcile Alexander's policy with Greek tradition, and Marsyas gave a more Macedonian colored version. Still, the earliest surviving accounts (Diodorus's Book 17; Plutarch's *Life of Alexander*, Quintus Curtius Rufus's Latin *History of Alexander the Great*) rather follow the so-called vulgate tradition, which owes much to a historian, Cleitarchus, who wrote from second-hand sources.

Hieronymus of Cardia, who wrote the history of the period after Alexander's death, seems to have been the most reliable of the lost Hellenistic historians before Polybius. From his fragments (and Diodorus's account of the period, which largely relies on his work) it appears that he provided accurate and detailed information, used documents and that he had a sense for strategic, social and political problems (Hornblower 1981).

With Polybius from Megalopolis (born around 200) we observe the authentic response of a member of the Greek elite to the next enormous turn in Greek history, the Roman conquest. His family was politically active in the Achaean League. After his deportation to Rome he was associated with the family of Aemilius Paullus and accompanied Scipio Aemilianus in his campaigns; later he served as a diplomat and was again involved in local politics in his home town. He had the opportunity to talk to many protagonists of earlier events and visit sites of historical importance. His statements on method are in agreement with this profile: he regards political and military experience, together with topographical knowledge through autopsy, as indispensable both for the accurate account of the present and for the understanding of the past. He uses sources on earlier events with care, being aware of their bias. He criticizes historians who work in libraries, mainly Timaeus, whom he treated as an antagonist (the entire book 12 is directed against him: on the design of the work see Foulon 2001). He frequently interrupts his narrative with statements on methodology, comments on other historians, and evaluation of events and historical personalities. Polybius praises the *pragmatike historia*, the history of actions (that is, political and military deeds of nations and men in power), as opposed to a history concerned with genealogy or with migrations of people, foundations of cities and links of kinship (9.2.1). The subject of his work is the rise of Roman power from the First Punic War (264 BCE) to the Fall of Carthage (146). His prefatory unit (*prokataskeue*), a review of the past in the tradition of Herodotus and Thucydides, does not contain anything but factual information on the prehistory of his main subject (nonetheless, he is selective, especially on Greek history, Zecchini 2007; on his uneven treatment of documents from various areas see Prandi 2003). The force that moves history is *Tyche*, Fortune, and she is made responsible for Rome's sensational superiority – together with the supremacy of Rome's *mixed* (i.e. balanced) constitution and political institutions (Book 6 is devoted to the discussion of constitutions; see Walbank 1998). His history is universal in geographical scope, but restricted in time, due to its single thematic axis, namely Roman military expansion. Polybius's ambition is to provide his readers with a *synopsis* of history (1.4.1), a view that seizes the totality; thanks to Rome, world history eventually appeared as an organic unit (*somatoeides*, 1.3.4). Polybius's narrative sometimes focuses on the participants' point of view or raises the readers' emotions (Davidson 1991; Marincola 2001, 124–8), in a manner which supports the educative purpose of the work. It assimilates first-hand experience, as the reader becomes (as close as possible to) a spectator or an eyewitness. However, he is critical of pathetic excess; his comments against Phylarchus have contributed to the postulation of a "school" of "tragic historiography" with Phylarchus and Duris as its main representatives, but its existence has been refuted by Fromentin (2001b). For an independent appraisal of Duris, see Knoepfler (2001); Consolo Langher (2001) discusses Aristotelian influence on Duris.

A century later, Diodorus of Sicily, the writer of a truly universal history (a history of mankind from the beginnings to Julius Caesar), praises his own type of historiographical activity as "free of dangers" (an obvious response to Polybius). Diodorus enjoyed the facilities of libraries in Rome to compile his *Historical Library,* the most original and ambitious aspect of which is its design. He starts with the origins of life (in Egypt, for which he was largely following the work of Hecataeus of Abdera), devotes the next books to old oriental empires, and proceeds to Greek and Roman history. For each book he uses different sources, a reason for the unevenness in treatment and quality, as well as for some inconsistencies. Following the logic of a reference work, each book has its own preface to be used separately. In contemporary stoic fashion he declares in his general preface the kinship of men and the unity of the world, driven by Divine Providence into a common "life," as in one city. However, in his narrative Diodorus is not concerned with interpretation and explanation (Guelfucci 2001).

Between Myth and Political Theory. Making History Meaningful

Writers of history show themselves fully aware of both the apparent incompatibility between myth and history and of the challenge to demarcate the territory of each. Mythical material is all but banned from historical writing before the appearance of Christian, ecclesiastic history. Only contemporary history was in essence indifferent to it. Nonetheless, Thucydides did not question the historicity of Minos and Agamemnon even as he chastised poetry as a medium for its distortions and incredible assertions. Similarly, Plutarch is confident that he can give to the story of Theseus "the shape of history," if he "sorts out" elements which "escape our knowledge," i.e., look unlikely and unfounded in terms of verisimilitude (*Thes.* 1). Myth is not equated with "fiction," unless the whole *hypothesis* (the subject-matter) is invented: this is the case, according to Diodorus, with the *mythologia* about the Underworld (1.2.2). In their treatment of myths, historians applied various strategies of rationalization: they disclaimed responsibility for certain details, thus implying skepticism; they dismissed or replaced supernatural elements (Diodorus even regarding some major Gods as personified natural forces, while still accepting mythical facts as true); they applied their judgment to set apart the unacceptable from what they could validate; or they historicized myths, linking them with other traditions in a temporal and causal manner. In Hellenistic times mythical material is commonly used as an argument, incorporated into historical reconstructions or serving etiological assumptions – or the creation of myth itself is explained (Saïd 2007).

Local history and (truly) universal history were unthinkable without myth. Myth satisfied their need for completeness, providing access to origins (an obsession of the Greeks) and ultimate causes; accordingly, myth never ceased to be an authoritative vehicle of truth and political symbolism. Indeed, myth could be an ideal material for the construction of meaningful stories, and in this capacity it was tolerated or exploited by historians. Tragedy made the most of myth in this respect: Aristotle acknowledges this, when he labels tragedy as "more philosophical" than history, because it deals with the *whole* (*Poet.* 1451b5).

But myth only retells beginnings. Historiography is written from the end, and it is the end that gives shape to history. Herodotus's Solon refuses to pass judgment on a person before his end (1.32). Once historiography had established its epistemological status as research backwards within a documented and "accessible" human past, it had to develop its own ways to make this past intelligible. From Herodotus onward, events become meaningful through adequate selection, disposition and narrative presentation, as well as through moral, political or historical evaluation. Herodotus presents to his audience an epic exposition of the Persian Wars that at the same time indicates the ultimate reason for what happened. This reason is identified thanks to a theory of history which permeates the work but is already announced at the very beginning. The story of Croesus, which opens the historical narrative, includes entirely fictional units even as it provides the keys for a reading of the whole work; thus, it takes over – *mutatis mutandis* – a traditional function of myth: to reveal the truth despite fictitiousness. The various explanations proposed for Croesus's fall create a polyphonic universe and simultaneously demonstrate an analytical outlook, without attempting a final synthesis: they vary from moral/ psychological factors (Croesus's greed and his failure to decode an ambiguous oracle) to political reasoning and metaphysical schemes of interpretation (retribution for crimes committed by Gyges, the founder of the dynasty). But all ultimately cohere with the ideological framework of the archaic city-state, which is applied to both the microcosm of the individual and to the macrocosm of historical processes: excess and transgression of boundaries lead to failure.

In Herodotus's world, spatial rather than temporal categories support the construction of historical normativity: Xerxes is punished for his neglect of physical limits. "Traveling" through the world corroborates this realization through illustration of cultural differences. It is acquaintance with place that opens up a temporal perspective to the historian: small cities have been great in the past and *vice versa* – because fortune is unstable. Nonetheless, an attempt at historical periodization is discernible: significant changes can be the result of political reforms. Athens became strong because of the introduction of *isegorie*, the common right to speak publicly, i.e. political participation. Greek freedom is opposed to oriental despotism. The debate (in Greek "fashion") of the Persian princes about the best constitution (3.80–82), only confirms the geographical, cultural and political dichotomy, since monarchy is preferred to oligarchy and democracy. If myth reconciles Greek historiography with unexplorable beginnings, the quest for the ideal form of government opens up possibilities of comprehending the present and mastering the future.

Contrary to Herodotus's predominantly spatial organization of the universe, Thucydides' world is traveling in time. Thucydides' accounts of the past, the *Archaeology* and the *Pentekontaetia* (1.1–23 and 89–117), are introduced as historical arguments: they illustrate processes which generate and explain the new conflict but – unlike the story of Croesus – they don't anticipate the end; still, knowledge of geographical and historical facts about Sicily (6.1–6) could have prevented the Athenians from a wrong decision. Thucydides' intellectualism drives him to reduce causality to ultimate explanations – and merely to imply sophisticated instructions for the future, which are difficult to disclose. The historian asserts that he foresaw the importance of his war (1.1.1) based on his knowledge of the past, and expects his readers to imitate him, using his work which will inform them about their past. Unlike Herodotus, Thucydides is not investing hopes in political systems, which do not hamper human greed and short-sightedness. His praise of leaders under three different constitutions (the tyrants: 6.54.5; oligarchy: 8.97.2; Pericles as a leader of the *demos*: 2.65) indicates that he values a man's ability to optimize the functionality of any system as more essential.

Xenophon silently adopts his predecessor's anti-mythical standards (he significantly resorts elsewhere – in his *Cyropaedia* – to fiction in order to sketch his political utopia). He waits till the epilogue to indicate his reservations for Thucydides' self-confidence: everybody's expectations before Mantinea were disproved (a subversion of Thucydides' opening); confusion prevailed: *akrisia. Krisis* is the term used by Thucydides to indicate the termination of the Persian Wars: rapid *krisis* of this conflict proved, in his opinion, its inferiority to the Peloponnesian War (1.23.1) – an argument to exalt the importance of *his* war (and *his* work). Xenophon had already questioned Thucydides' demarcation of his subject matter by continuing his work beyond the end of the Peloponnesian War. Now he shows that Thucydides' war never ended; hence it cannot be surveyed as a whole from a detached perspective. Furthermore, it is not guaranteed that the polis (the context of Thucydides' political analysis) survived the consequences of the war. Xenophon shares with Herodotus the belief in the possibilities created by a good constitution, which is, however, monarchic – not by conviction, but by historical necessity (his treatment of Jason of Pherai in the 6th Book of the *Hellenica* shows that he regards a monarchy in Greece as a serious possibility, though he was well aware of the importance of the new phenomenon of confederations; Bearzot 2004) –, and he shares with Thucydides the quest for gifted personalities (but he is not looking for a copy of Thucydides' idealized Pericles, whose authority relied on the people, but for a defender of traditional aristocratic values, endowed with practical intelligence). In the same way that Xenophon's *Hellenica* lacks a preface, it also lacks an introductory narrative to provide keys, symbols or paradigms applicable to the whole of history. Instead, we find in the last part of the work a surprising anticipation of events to happen after the termination of the narrative. The history of Jason's successors, the Thessalian tyrants who are trapped in an almost "mythical" cycle of blood, is highly suggestive about the dangers of tyranny (*HG* 6.4.33–7); at the same time, allusions to the story of Gyges (the spouse of a ruler initiates a conspiracy to assassinate him in bed because of his lack of temperance) imply that Xenophon regards himself not only as a continuator of Thucydides but also of Herodotus (Tsakmakis, forthcoming).

If "the Hellenistic age was … in essence the poisoned imperial legacy of an inordinately ambitious, largely apolitical, military genius to posterity" (Green 1989, 182; but see Schepens 1998 on Alexander's political self-consciousness), it is not surprising that the classical historians found no real interlocutors before the rise of Rome (Polybius, 8.11.3, criticizes Theopompus for focusing on a single protagonist in his *Philippica*). Unlike their predecessors, the historians of Alexander could not occupy themselves with the quest for an ideal/better constitution, but had only to pass judgment on the unpredictable, rapid transformations of the political life of the Greeks, which culminated in the emergence of Hellenistic monarchy.

Greek Historians of Rome were confronted with the challenge to explain defeat, to make current political realities intelligible, to confront Greek and Roman identities. Introducing Rome to a Greek audience, Polybius uses traditional stereotypes of Greek and barbarian character to represent Roman virtues and vices respectively (Champion 2004). At the same time he establishes for his Roman readers a perception of and a discourse on Rome that was indebted to the Greek tradition. Accordingly, Polybius picks up the quest for an appropriate form of government. From his praise for the Roman constitution, it follows that the Greeks were defeated not by a superior people, but by a better political system – which is described in terms of a Greek *politeia*. He is explicit in determining the aims of historiography: political education and training to endure the changes of *Tyche* (1.1.2). F. Hartog (2010) has recently argued that the vision of totality stressed by Polybius, and his assumption of a unique, superior historical agent operating beyond the world of contingency, such as *Tyche*, is a response to Aristotle's reservations about historiography. Polybian historiography presents itself as superior to tragedy, because it not only reveals the general mechanics behind the lives of human societies, but also draws upon a subject that is not invented, but true.

Polybius's preoccupation with truth privileges explicitness and "clarity" (*enargeia*) over literary perfection. The ambition to capture the world as a whole is assisted by geography. The historian recreates landscapes to assist the reader to experience what he has not seen (Clarke 1999, 90–91). One of his continuators in the first century CE, Strabo, wrote beside his *History* a *Geography* of the (Augustan) world (the other is Posidonius, who wrote from the perspective of stoic philosophy). Polybius's universal conception of history still is bound to an *apodictic* goal, which serves the understanding of the present (but collapse is inherent in the idea of a "cycle" applied to every constitution; cf. Pelling 2007, 247–8). Diodorus will consequently extend his world history to the ultimate beginnings. For Polybius, the geographical expansion of Roman dominion proves its difference from older empires and is used as an argument for its longevity (but not its eternity; see Baronowski 2011, 153–63). From his own perspective, Diodorus places Rome within a broad framework, which encompasses a succession of empires and inevitably suggests the transience of Rome's power (Sheridan 2010). However, despite his philosophical considerations in the Preface of the work, his practice does not reveal philosophical concerns.

1.3. Imperial Rome: The Form is the Message

Under monarchic regimes (unbiased) writing of contemporary history is rare; in imperial Rome (cf. König, ch. 7, pp. 120–3 in this volume) panegyrists take the cue from the Hellenistic court historians. At the dawn of the new era we come across Nicolaus of Damascus, who wrote a biography of Augustus while he was still in office, also using material from Augustus's *res gestae*. A unique case of contemporary history written in Greek towards the end of the first century CE is the *Judean War* by the Jewish priest and general Josephus (Chapman 2009), who, enjoying the protection of Vespasian and Titus, wrote works in Attic Greek addressed mainly to a Jewish audience, partly to defend his views on the events – he had disagreed with the revolt against Rome–partly to restore Jewish pride after the defeat and to merge Jewish and Greco-Roman traditions.

Dionysius of Halicarnassus is the first Greek historian who also writes extensively on style, which goes to show how rhetoric is now the dominant formative influence on the genre. While his historical work contains several statements on the usefulness of history, his rhetorical treatises are concerned with matters of style, choice of theme (he prefers Herodotus to Thucydides because he believes that only glorious deeds of the past deserve to be remembered) and disposition of material. Dionysius, the main representative of classicism in Rome, promotes a prose style that is very close to Isocrates', but he is also concerned with the restoration of traditional Greek values, which he also projects onto the Roman past (Wiater 2011). His *Roman Archaeology*, published in 7 BCE, is the first complete history of Rome in Greek from the beginnings to 264 (where Polybius begins); Dionysius expounds on the close affinities between Roman and Greek culture, but he also asserts that the founders of Rome were of Greek origin. Dionysius's *interpretatio greca* of Roman history suggests that the Greeks had not been defeated by a foreign people; on the other hand, the Romans were encouraged to regard Greek culture as their own (Fromentin 2001a). Dionysius's discourse creates the illusion that Rome has always been an extension of the glorious Greek past. The revival of the classical attic style was not merely an aesthetic predilection; it invites the reader to read his account against a Greek subtext that implicitly provides the heuristic tools for the analysis of Rome's past and present.

For Dionysius, historiography was a form of rhetoric that endeavored to influence political life in the present. Eventually, the access of the bilingual Roman elites to Greek history was realized through rhetoric. Greek historians were read in schools of rhetoric both as models of style, and as a repository of case studies that were essential for the practice of students. Imitation of Greek originals was the art of Arrian, a governor of Bithynia, who wrote both local history of his country and political/military history of the past (the two historiographical forms revived in the Antonine period and cultivated continuously till the end of the sixth century; for an overview see Hose 1998). His two extant works make use of the linguistic form of different models. His *Anabasis of Alexander* is a successful imitation of Xenophon's prose style, while his *Indica* (which partly depends on the work of Nearchus) imitates Herodotus. In the *Anabasis* he shows himself in full command of the language and narrative strategies of his classical prototype. A good example is the expression he uses to describe the Taulantians' reaction to Alexander's maneuvers during one of his first military operations: οἱ δὲ πάλαι μὲν ἐθαύμαζον τὴν ὀξύτητα ὁρῶντες καὶ τὸν κόσμον τῶν δρωμένων (1.6.3: "the enemy long marveled both at the quickness and the discipline of the action"). While the narrator renders the point of view of Alexander's enemies, the abstract nouns (ὀξύτητα, κόσμον) express the author's evaluation, in the manner of Xenophon. The same holds for the xenophontic ἐθαύμαζον, which (together with κόσμος) makes Alexander appear as a genuine successor of Xenophon's heroes, Socrates, Agesilaus, even Xenophon himself in the *Anabasis* etc., thereby contributing to the full acclimatization of Alexander in the world of classical texts. (Elsewhere Arrian suggests parallels between Alexander and Achilles, following Callisthenes, as well as between Homer and himself. Callisthenes was known to Arrian's principal sources, Ptolemy and Aristobulus.) It is unlikely that such expressions derive from Arrian's Hellenistic sources: the motif of ὀξύτης (acuteness) has been prepared a few lines earlier (1.6.1) by Alexander's expression "ὀξέως δεχομένους", a verbatim reminiscence of Thucydides 2.11.9 (Archidamos's speech during his first invasion into Attica, at the very beginning of the Peloponnesian War).

Thanks to his attic Greek, Arrian can claim a position at the side of canonical historians, and Alexander's exploits can now appear as one of the most glorious periods in Greek history. Arrian's work reflects a Greek self-confidence that is characteristic of the Antonine era. Also characteristic of this period is the design of Appian's historiographical project, a comprehensive history of the Roman world in separate sections, according to a principle that contrasts with Polybius's chronological arrangement (Olympiads). The focus moves from Rome to the provinces, as the history of Rome occupies a distinct set of books, while the history of each province is the theme of independent books, in the order they came under Roman rule (a principle reminiscent of Herodotus). As a consequence, Romans are not the sole protagonists; on the contrary, Appian renders the perspective of both the victorious and the defeated side (Goukowsky 2001a, XXXVII–XLIV; 2001b, LIX–LXVI). Appian is a gifted writer (especially good at drawing characters), whose style and narrative techniques deserve systematic study. As a lawyer educated in Alexandria he might have studied with the famous teacher of rhetoric Theon, whose precepts he seems to be following in some parts of his work (Goukowsky 2001a, XXIII–XXX).

For Greek historians of the third century CE who are fully integrated into the social and political life of the empire, the writing of Roman histories that end up in the present (or very close to it) is part of the construction of their own past. The most important Greek source on the late Republic and the first two centuries of the principate is the *Roman History* of Arrian's countryman and biographer Dio Cassius (early third century). A member of the senatorial class (he became consul), he draws on both Greek and Roman traditions. His approach is realistic, and, despite the limitations of his sources on earlier periods, he is not an uncritical compiler. He is interested in the development of Roman political institutions (Hinard 2005). His style, distinct elements of his thought (cf. Hose 1994, 356–451), and the frequency of long political speeches reveal that Thucydides has been a major source of inspiration for Dio. The speeches of Maecenas and Agrippa, who make suggestions on the optimal form of government Augustus should adopt (Book 52), pick up a standard topic of Greek historiography, especially alluding to Herodotus's Persian debate on the constitutions. Maecenas's speech (whose proposals persuade the new leader) anticipates not only the policy of Augustus but also later ideas that are projected on the early principate (Kuhlmann 2010). The Thucydidean allusions in Dio's historiography create a feeling of cultural and ideological continuity, despite the historical transformations that are fully acknowledged and are also reflected in the language and style of the text.

An otherwise unknown Herodian is the writer of a history of the years 180–238, i.e. of the period after Marcus Aurelius, who appears as an ideal ruler and serves as a foil for the evaluation of his successors. The principle of idealization of a leader is a *topos* in classical historiography (Thucydides' Pericles is the most illustrious example), but here the characterization is not following contemporary political and historical theories, but rules developed by rhetors. Herodian's prosopographic details throughout his work depend largely on *topoi* found in Menander Rhetor's precepts about the so-called *basilikos logos* (Zimmermann 1999, 24–8). The author's critical point of view reflects the ongoing disappointment of Greek (and Roman) elites for the militarization of political life, the anarchy, the decline of the senatorial class, etc. Although Herodian illustrates the crisis of the empire in political terms, modern historians such as Rostovzeff have found in his work valuable indications to support their own conclusions about the economic and social aspects of the crisis (Canfora 1990). Herodian is an able writer and among his historiographical prototypes, Thucydides is clearly his preferred interlocutor. However, the similarities between the two are only superficial. Despite his conventional claims in the preface, Herodian is not an accurate historian; on the contrary his narrative follows principles that resemble the techniques of the novel, of biography and popular literature.

1.4. Conclusion

Greek historiography is impressive with regard to the variety of its sub-genres and subject matters, the number of authors, the texts produced, and the range of erudition included in them. Its importance is not exhausted in the value of the historical data it contains. It eloquently mirrors both the history and the intellectual history of Greece. It proved extremely receptive to a wide variety of stimuli: aesthetic and intellectual developments, changing political conditions, scientific and scholarly advances, and the shifting social needs and educational priorities from the archaic polis to the late Roman Empire, from the initial stages of Greek prose to the emergence of Christian literature. Its all-embracing scope requires a broad definition: for the Greeks, historiography is research and reflection about the human past and present, as it is manifested in human activity and character (see also the following section on biography).

Greek historiography established its literary claims from its very beginnings. Historiography is in dialogue with all literary genres that serve as sources of inspiration for its methods of documentation, representation, and argumentation. It variously exploits and expands theoretical positions and literary traditions in order to crystallize its techniques of highlighting and explaining human activity, memorable deeds, and significant events. Similarly, it describes individuals, communities, social and political processes, intellectual movements and ideas according to the insights of philosophy, psychology, medicine and physical science that prevail at each epoch.

The impact of historiography is equally incalculable. Greek communities consciously used their past as part of their self-definition. By offering authoritative, but also innovative and negotiable versions of the past, the works of historians (designed to be useful and attractive at the same time, regularly claiming to contain true and important information) were instrumental in the perception and construction of reality in the Greek world. For the Greeks, the past is ideally expressed as a meaningful and coherent narrative that transmits knowledge based on methodically collected evidence, open to rational interpretation, and compatible with the intellectual categories which enable them to tackle moral, political, and metaphysical questions. The Greeks seek to reconstruct the past in order to make it meaningful, they try to understand the present through the past; they also justify their claims for the future by referring to the past (contrast these properties with the Roman's fascination with *exempla*: Roller 2009). Accordingly, Greek historiography is negotiating positions between creative imagination and accurate, critical reasoning, between the real and the ideal, between the local and the ecumenical, between experience or verisimilitude and the truth of poetic or mythical imagery, between the power of rulers and the power of the word.

2. Biography

Personal achievement is an inherently attractive topic. In specific epochs or environments, people are exceptionally fascinated by power or intellectual authority. Biography presents available information on the life of outstanding individuals in a selective way that satisfies curiosity or constructs the subject as a moral exemplum. Philosophers and holy men (and women), poets and orators, political and military leaders belong to the common subjects of biography, particularly interesting for, e.g., philosophical circles, students of rhetoric, the Christian communities or the educated elite of imperial Rome, whose members were well aware how much depended on the decisions of a single man.

The boundaries between history and biography are fluid. Some properties of biography cited as setting biography apart from historiography are not unknown to other types of historical writing (Schepens 2007). These include: a restricted topic which requires selection of material; the focus on character; the presentation of actions as manifestations of ethical qualities and philosophical disposition; and assumptions about the utility of biography (education of the reader). Distinctions advocated in antiquity are not more satisfactory. When Plutarch (*Alex.* 1) appeals to the reader's indulgence if he omits many of Alexander's deeds, pointing out that "I am not writing history, but biography; for, great actions do not always reveal the virtues and vices of men ...", his statement has to be regarded as an attempt to negotiate the value of his current choice. Elsewhere, in his treatise *On the malice of Herodotus*, Plutarch demands from historians the application of moral criteria on the selection and presentation of events, undermining again the distinction between historiography and biography: for Plutarch history and biography have for the most part similar functions. Polybius, who asserts (10.21) that he would have illustrated the personality of Philopoemen, if he had not written his biography before, obviously regards them as complementary. Finally, the biographies of thinkers, writers, religious heroes etc. belong instead to intellectual history, which was distinct in antiquity, and, at times, more interesting to scholars or Christians than political history.

Birth, family, education, private incidents (including gossip), career and accomplishments, last words and death, catalogue of works, in some cases will and posthumous arrangements, belong to the expected ingredients of a biography, regularly spiced with anecdotes, doxography, quotes of apothegms, letters, and documentary material; on occasion, judgments on style are passed on orators and other authors. The arrangement of material is loose, but everything is consistent with the person's character (for historical figures), doctrine (for philosophers and heroes of religious faith), work (for poets). This is in alignment with the belief that philosophy is a "way of life" (Hadot 1995) and with the conviction that poetry reflects the *ethos* of its author. A *Life* can reveal admiration or disapproval, but ambiguity is also possible. Death notices are especially open to interpretation, because a person's death figures as a symbol for his life – while death is not under his control, it reveals how others, including supernatural agents, assess the life. The use of reliable historical material is not the rule. Personal acquaintance and testimony make Porphyry's *Life of Plotinus* (about 300 CE) an incomparable example of genuine information. On the contrary, miraculous elements are amply attested in Philostratus's *Life of Apollonius* (third century CE). And with Athanasius's *Life of Antony* (end of fourth century CE), the new type of Christian Hagiography, which will soon develop stereotypical traits, is announced. Freedom and flexibility, the mixture of seriousness and playfulness, of well documented and unbelievable matters, of high and low motives often make Bakhtin's notion of the *seriocomical* applicable to biography (Bakhtin 1984, 101ff.) – affinities between Hellenistic biography and Socratic dialogue (another seriocomical genre) have already been registered by Erler (2007); even if Socrates is unlikely to have influenced the emergence of biography, as Dihle (1987) assumed, the Platonic dialogues appear like tesserae from the mosaic of Socrates' life.

Biographical structures and material are also found in encomia on deceased statesmen – Isocrates' *Euagoras* (after 373) or Xenophon's *Agesilaus* (after 359) are characteristic examples. Oral traditions about important figures were preserved within their families and among followers (or enemies). Thucydides' account of Themistocles' exile and death (1.135–8; cf. 1.90–92) obviously relies on such sources. Stories about legendary figures took the form of fictional biographies, preserved in later, written versions (e.g. the *Vita Aesopi*, the pseudo-Herodotean *Vita Homeri* etc.); in oriental monarchies available historical accounts unsurprisingly followed a biographical pattern focusing on kings, a fact reflected in Herodotus's narrative of earlier Persian history, (reigns of Cyrus and Kambyses) – the pattern is discernible in Xenophon's *Cyropaedeia*, too, a romanesque *Herrscherspiegel* (Reichel 2007). However, we should not automatically assume that any of the above antecedents inspired or influenced later biography, for all their manifest interest in biographical patterning and detail.

Aristoxenos of Taras, a pupil of Aristotle, can be regarded as the first biographer: he wrote *Lives* of Socrates, Plato, Pythagoras and Archytas after the middle of the fourth century. Henceforth, the genre flourished through Hellenistic times, by authors who were moving between philosophical schools and libraries, especially in Athens and Alexandria. Most prominent, among others, are Hermippos (third century), who worked in Alexandria at the side of Callimachus and was extremely productive as a biographer, and Satyros (second century), in whose fragmentary, dialogic *Life of Euripides* (in which one interlocutor is a woman) the biographical interpretation of tragedy as practiced by comedy is exposed rather than adopted (Knöbl 2010). Biographies of literary authors were placed before text editions of their work and those of philosophers were studied in schools. Nevertheless, most of Hellenistic biography "was not an esoteric genre written for in-house consumption. It was aimed at a general audience of educated people" (Fortenbaugh 2007, 50–51). Hellenistic biography exploited a large amount of erudition, but we have to wait until Diogenes Laertius's *Lives of Philosophers* (third century CE) for a complete surviving sample.

The approach of ἦθος as portrayed in Hellenistic biography has always been regarded as a Peripatetic element. The frequency of anecdotes in Aristotle suggests that the philosopher assigned to them a certain value (Fortenbaugh 2007). Through allegory they referred to the *katholou*, the universal, a property he missed in the contingency described by historiography of the Thucydidean type.

Judging from the testimonies, political biographies were less common (though not unknown) till Roman times. Plutarch's (45–125 CE) pairs of *Lives* of Greek and Roman statesmen are the earliest surviving Greek biographies. They range from Theseus to Antonius (from his *Lives* of Roman Emperors and from his other biographies, only few survive). Plutarch is using and citing multiple sources, but his interest in history is inseparable from his pedagogical aims. This is reflected in the comparison, *syncrisis,* which follows each pair. History is a means for the paradigmatic illustration of virtue (preponderantly) and vice; laymen but also political leaders should profit and improve themselves. The common perspective adopted on the Greek and the Roman past fosters the conciliation of both cultures and a convergence of both traditions. The comparative perspective is fruitful not only for a *syncrisis* of individuals but also for historical reflections.

REFERENCES

Bakhtin, M. 1984. *Problems of Dostoevsky's Poetics*, edited by C. Emerson. Minneapolis.

Baronowski, D. W. 2011. *Polybius and Roman Imperialism*. London.

Bearzot C. 2004. *Federalismo e autonomia nelle Elleniche di Senofonte*. Milano.

Bearzot C., and F. Landucci, eds. 2010. *Storie di Atene, Storia dei Greci: Studi e ricerche di attidografia*. Milano.

Birgalias, N., K. Buraselis, P. Cartledge, A. Gartziou-Tatti, and M. Dimopoulou, eds. 2013. *War, Peace and the Panhellenic Games*. Athens.

Bowie, E. L. 2001. "Ancestors of Historiography in Early Greek Elegiac and Iambic Poetry?" In N. Luraghi, ed., *The Historian's Craft in the Age of Herodotus*, Oxford, 45–66.

Camassa, G. 2010. "L'attidografia nella storia degli studi." In C. Bearzot and F. Landucci, eds., *Storie di Atene, Storia dei Greci: Studi e ricerche di attidografia*, Milano, 29–51.

Canfora, L. 1990. "Postface." In D. Roques, ed. and trans., *Hérodien, Histoire des empereures romains*, Postface de L. Canfora, Paris, 301–13.

Cawkwell, G. 1966. "Introduction." In *Xenophon: A History of My Times*, London, 7–46.

Champion, C. B. 2004. *Cultural Politics in Polybius's Histories*. Berkeley, CA.

Chapman, H. 2009. "Josephus." In A. Feldherr, ed., *The Cambridge Companion to the Roman Historians*, Cambridge, 319–31.

Clarke, K. 1999. *Between Geography and History. Hellenistic Constructions of the Roman World*. Oxford.

Clarke, K. 2008. *Making Time for the Past: Local History and the Polis*. Oxford.

Connor, W. R. 1984. *Thucydides*. Princeton, NJ.

Consolo Langher, S. N. 2001. "Moduli storiografici di età ellenistica. Verismo, interessi etnografici e connotazioni economico-sociali nella storiografia 'mimetica'." In S. Bianchetti, E. Galvagno, A. Magnelli, G. Marasco, G. Mariotta, and I. Mastrorosa, eds., *Poikilma: Studi in Onore di Michele R. Cataudella. In Occasione del 60° Compleanno*, La Spezia, 309–22.

Davidson, J. 1991. "The gaze in Polybius's Histories." *Journal of Roman Studies* 81: 10–24.

Dihle, A. 1987. *Die Entstehung der historischen Biographie*. Heidelberg.

Duff, T. 1999. *Plutarch's Lives: Exploring Virtue and Vice*. Oxford.

Erler, M. 2007. "Biographische Elemente bei Platon und in hellenistischer Philosophie." In Erler and Schorn 2007, 11–24.

Erler, M. and S. Schorn, eds. 2007. *Die griechische Biographie in hellenistischer Zeit. Akten des internationalen Kongresses vom 26–29. Juli 2006 in Würzburg*. Berlin.

Fabiani, R. 2003. "Epigrafi in Erodoto." In A. M. Biraschi, P. Desideri, S. Roda, and G. Zecchini, eds., *L'uso dei documenti nella storiografia antica*, Perugia, 163–85.

Flower, M. A. 1994. *Theopompus of Chios: History and Rhetoric in the Fourth Century BC*. Oxford.

Fornara, C. W. 1983. *The Nature of History in Ancient Greece and Rome*. Berkeley, CA.

Fortenbaugh, W. W., 2007. "Biography and the Aristotelian Peripatos." In M. Erler and S. Schorn, eds., *Die griechische Biographie in hellenistischer Zeit. Akten des internationalen Kongresses vom 26–29. Juli 2006 in Würzburg*, Berlin, 45–78.

Foulon, E. 2001. "Polybe et l'histoire universelle." In J. Leclant and F. Chamoux, eds., *Histoire et Historiographie dans l' Antiquité. Actes du 11e colloque de la Villa Kérylos à Beaulieu-sur-Mer les 13 & 14 octobre 2000*, Paris, 45–82.

Fromentin, V. 2001a. "Denys d'Halicarnasse, Historien grec de Rome." In J. Leclant and F. Chamoux, eds., *Histoire et Historiographie dans l' Antiquité. Actes du 11e colloque de la Villa Kérylos à Beaulieu-sur-Mer les 13 & 14 octobre 2000*, Paris, 123–42.

Fromentin, V. 2001b. "L'histoire tragique a-t-elle existé?" In A. Billault and C. Mauduit, *Lectures antiques de la tragédie grecque. Actes de la table ronde du 25 novembre 1999 (Collection du Centre des études et de recherches sur l'occident romain de l'université Lyon 3. Nouvelle série*, 22), Lyon, 77–92.

Fowler, R. 1996. "Herodotos and his Contemporaries." *Journal of Hellenic Studies* 116: 62–87.

Gabba, E. 1982. "Riflessioni sulla 'storiografia locale' antica (fino al II secolo d.C.)." In C. Violante, ed. *La storia locale: Temi, fonte, e metodi della ricerca*, Bologna, 33–9.

Goldmann, B. 1988. *Einheitlichkeit und Eigenständigkeit der Historia Romana des Appian*. Hildesheim and New York.

González Ponce, F. J. 2008. *Periplógrafos griegos I. Épocas Arcaica y Clásica 1: Periplo de Hanón y autores de los siglos VI h V a.C.* Zaragoza.

Goukowsky, P. 2001a. "Un 'compilateur' témoin de son temps: Appien d'Alexandrie et la révolte Juive de 117 ap. J.-C." In J. Leclant and F. Chamoux, eds., *Histoire et Historiographie dans l' Antiquité. Actes du 11e colloque de la Villa Kérylos à Beaulieu-sur-Mer les 13 & 14 octobre 2000*, Paris, 167–203.

Goukowsky, P. 2001b. *Appien, Histoire Romain*. Tome IV. Livre VIII. Paris.

Goukowsky, P. 2001c. *Appien, Histoire Romain*. Tome VII. Livre XII. Paris.

Gould, J. 1989. *Herodotus*. London.

Green, P. 1989. "After Alexander: Some Historiographical Approaches to the Hellenistic Age." In P. Green. *Classical Bearings. Interpreting Ancient History and Culture*, London, 165–92.

Grethlein, J. 2010. *The Greeks and their Past: Poetry, Oratory and History in the fifth century BCE*. Cambridge.

Grey, V. 1989. *The Character of Xenophon's Hellenica*. London.

Guelfucci, M.-R. 2001. "De Polybe à Diodore: Les Leçons de l'histoire." In J. Leclant and F. Chamoux, eds., *Histoire et Historiographie dans l' Antiquité. Actes du 11e colloque de la Villa Kérylos à Beaulieu-sur-Mer les 13 & 14 octobre 2000*, Paris, 83–101.

Hadot, P. 1995. *Qu'est-ce que la philosophie antique?* Paris.

Harding, P. 1994. *Androtion and the Atthis: the Fragments. Translated with Introduction and Commentary*, New York.

Harding, P. 2007. "Local History and Atthidography." In Marincola 2007, 180–88.

Hartog, F. 2010. "Polybius and the First Universal History." In P. Liddel and A. Fear, eds., *Historiae Mundi. Studies in Universal History*, London, 30–40.

Hinard, F. 2005. "Dion Cassius et les institutions de la république romaine." In L. Troiani and G. Zecchini, eds., *La cultura storica nei primi due secoli dell' impero romano*, Roma, 261–81.

Hornblower, J. 1981. *Hieronymus of Cardia*. Oxford.

Hornblower, S. 1994. "Introduction." In S. Hornblower, ed., *Greek Historiography*, Oxford, 1–72.

Hose, M. 1994. *Erneuerung der Vergangenheit: Die Historiker im Imperium Romanum von Florus bis Cassius Dio*. Stuttgart.

Hose, M. 1998 "Zwischen Tradition und Wandel: Die griechische Historiographie zwischen dem Hellenismus und Byzanz." *Plekos*, 1. http://www.plekos.uni-muenchen.de/98,99/ahose.html (accessed April 1, 2015).

Hunter, V. 1973. *Thucydides: The Artful Reporter*. Toronto.

Jacoby, F. 1909. "Über die Entwicklung der griechischen Historiographie und den Plan einer neuen Sammlung der griechischen Historikerfragmente." *Klio* 9: 80–123.

Jacoby, F. 1923– (repr. 1957–). *Die Fragmente der griechischen Historiker & Die Fragmente der griechischen Historiker continued* (by various authors). Leiden (first volumes originally Berlin).

Jacoby, F. 1949. *Atthis: The Local Chronicles of Ancient Athens*. Oxford.

Knöbl, R. 2010. "Talking about Euripides: Paramimesis and Satyrus's *Bios Euripidou*." In P. Borghart and K. de Temmerman, eds., *Biography and Fictionality in the Greek Literary Tradition. (Phrasis. Studies in Language and Literature* 51.1: 37–58.)

Knoepfler, D. 2001. "Trois historiens hellénistiques." In J. Leclant and F. Chamoux, eds., *Histoire et Historiographie dans l' Antiquité. Actes du 11e colloque de la Villa Kérylos à Beaulieu-sur-Mer les 13 & 14 octobre 2000*, Paris, 25–44.

Kuhlmann, P. 2010. "Die Maecenas-Rede bei Cassius Dio: Anachronismen und intertextuelle Bezüge." In D. Pausch, ed., *Stimmen der Geschichte. Funktionen von Reden in der antiken Historiographie*. Berlin, 109–21.

Leclant J. and F. Chamoux. 2001. *Histoire et Historiographie dans l' Antiquité. Actes du 11e colloque de la Villa Kérylos à Beaulieu-sur-Mer les 13 & 14 octobre 2000*. Paris.

Lévy, E. 1990. "L'art de la deformation historique dans les *Hélleniques* de Xénophon." In H. Verdin, G. Schepens, and E. de Keyser, eds., *Purposes of History*, Leuven, 125–57.

Luce, T. J. 1997. *The Greek Historians*. London.

Luraghi, N., ed. 2001. *The Historian's Craft in the Age of Herodotus*. Oxford.

Luraghi, N. 2005. "Le Storie prima delle *Storie*. Prospettive di ricerca." In M. Giangiulio, ed., *Erodoto e il 'Modello Erodoteo': Formazione e trasmissione delle tradizioni storiche in Grecia*, Trento, 61–90.

Marincola, J. 2001. *Greek Historians*. Oxford.

Marincola, J., ed. 2007. *A Companion to Greek and Roman Historiography*, 2 vols. Oxford.

Meissner, B. 1992. *Historiker zwischen Polis und Königshof*. Göttingen.

Meister, K. 1990. *Die griechische Geschichtsschreibung: Von den Anfängen bis zum Ende des Hellenismus*. Stuttgart.

Momigliano, A. 1971. *The Development of Greek Biography*. Cambridge, MA.

Morrison, J. V. 2007. *Reading Thucydides*. Columbus, OH.

Murray, O. 2001. "Herodotus and Oral History." In N. Luraghi, ed., *The Historian's Craft in the Age of Herodotus*, Oxford, 16–44.

Näf, B. 2010. *Antike Geschichtsschreibung: Form – Leistung – Wirkung*. Stuttgart.

Nicolai, R. 2010. "L'attidografia come genere letterario." In C. Bearzot and F. Landucci, eds., *Storie di Atene, Storia dei Greci: Studi e ricerche di attidografia*, Milano, 3–27.

Pelling, C. B. R. 2002. *Plutarch and History*. Swansea.

Pelling, C. B. R. 2007. "The Greek Historians of Rome." In J. Marincola, ed., *A Companion to Greek and Roman Historiography*, Oxford, 244–58.

Prandi, L. 2003. "Tre riflessioni sull'uso dei documenti scritti in Polibio." In A. M. Biraschi, P. Desideri, S. Roda, and G. Zecchini, eds., *L'uso dei documenti nella storiografia antica*, Perugia, 373–90.

Raaflaub, K. A. 2012. "*Ktema es aiei*. Thucydides' Concept of 'Learning through History' and its Realization in his Work." In A. Tsakmakis and M. Tamiolaki, eds., *Thucydides between History and Literature*, Berlin, 3–21.

Reichel, M. 2007. "Xenophon als Biograph." In M. Erler and S. Schorn, eds., *Die griechische Biographie in hellenistischer Zeit. Akten des internationalen Kongresses vom 26–29. Juli 2006 in Würzburg*, Berlin, 25–44.

Rengakos, A. 2011. "Herodot." In B. Zimmermann, ed., *Handbuch der griechischen Literatur der Antike. 1. Band: Die Literatur der archaischen und klassischen Zeit*, München, 338–80.

Rhodes, P. J. 1990. "The Atthidographers." In H. Verdin, G. Schepens, and E. de Keyser, eds., *Purposes of History*, Leuven, 73–81.

Roller, M. 2009. "The exemplary past in Roman historiography and culture." In A. Feldherr, ed., *The Cambridge Companion to the Roman Historians*, Cambridge, 214–30.

Roques, D., ed. and trans. *Hérodien, Histoire des empereures romains*. Paris.

Saïd, S. 2007. "Myth and Historiography." In J. Marincola, ed., *A Companion to Greek and Roman Historiography*, Oxford, 76–88.

Sandywell, B. 1996. *Presocratic Reflexivity: The Construction of Philosophical Discourse c. 600–450 BC*. London.

Schepens, G. 1980. *L' 'autopsie' dans la méthode des historiens grecs du Ve siècle avant J.-C.* Brussel.

Schepens, G. 1997. "Jacoby's FGrHist: Problems, Methods, Prospects." In G. W. Most, ed., *Collecting Fragments*, Göttingen, 144–72.

Schepens, G. 1998. "Das Alexanderbild in den Historikerfragmenten." In W. Schuller, ed., *Politische Theorie und Praxis im Altertum*, Darmstadt, 85–99.

Schepens G. 2007. "Zum Verhältnis von Biographie und Geschichtsschreibung in hellenistischer Zeit." In M. Erler and S. Schorn, eds., *Die griechische Biographie in hellenistischer Zeit. Akten des internationalen Kongresses vom 26–29. Juli 2006 in Würzburg*, Berlin, 335–62.

Schepens, G. and J. Bollansé. 1994. "Frammenti di *politeiai, nomoi,* e *nomima*. Prolegomeni ad una nuova edizione." In S. Cataldi, ed., *Poleis e Politeiai*, Alessandria, 250–85.

Schwartz, E. 1907. "Ephoros." *RE VI.1, 1–16 (Griechische Geschichtsschreiber.* Leipzig 1959, 3–26).

Van Seters, J. 2000. "The Historiography of the Ancient Near East." In J. M. Sasson, ed., *Civilizations of the Ancient Near East*, New York, 2433–44.

Sheridan, B. 2010. "Diodorus's reading of Polybius's universalism." In P. Liddel and A. Fear, eds., *Historiae Mundi: Studies in Universal History*, London, 41–55.

Sonnabend, H. 2002. *Geschichte der antiken Biographie: Von Isokrates bis zur Historia Augusta*. Stuttgart.

Stadter, P. A. 1980. *Arrian of Nicomedia*. Chapel Hill, NC.

Stadter, P. A. 1992. *Plutarch and the Historical Tradition*. London.

Thomas, R. 2000. *Herodotus in Context*. Cambridge.

Tsakmakis A. 1998. "Von der Rhetorik zur Geschichtsschreibung. Das *Methodenkapitel* des Thukydides (I 22, 1–3)." *Rheinische Museum für Philologie* 141: 239–55.

Tsakmakis A. forthcoming. "Between Thucydides and the Future. Narrative Prolepsis and Xenophon's Concept of Historiography." In A. Lianeri et al., eds., *Knowing Future Time in Greek Historiography*, Berlin.

Tsakmakis A. 2013. "ΑΠΟΛΛΩΝ ΤΥΡΑΝΝΟΚΤΟΝΟΣ. Η μοιραία δελφική πανήγυρις του Ιάσονα του Φεραίου στα *Ελληνικά* του Ξενοφώντα." In N. Birgalias, K. Buraselis, P. Cartledge, A. Gartziou-Tatti, and M. Dimopoulou, eds., *War, Peace and the Panhellenic Games*, Athens.

Tucker, A., ed. 2009. *A Companion to the Philosophy of History and Historiography*. Oxford.

Walbank, F. W. 1972. *Polybius*. Berkeley, CA.

Walbank, F. W. 1989/1990. "Timaeus's views on the past." *SCI* 10: 41–54 (=Walbank 2002, 165–77).

Walbank F. W. 1998. "A Greek looks at Rome: Polybius VI revisited." *Scripta Classica Israelica* 17: 45–59 (= Walbank 2002, 277–92).

Walbank, F. W. 2002. *Polybius, Rome and the Hellenistic World: Essays and Reflections*. Cambridge.

Wiater, N. 2011. *The Ideology of Classicism: Language, History, and Identity in Dionysius of Halicarnassus*. Berlin.

Zecchini, G. 2007. "Polibio e la storia non contemporanea." In P. Desideri, S. Roda, and A. M. Biraschi, eds., *Costruzione e uso del passato storico nella cultura antica*, Alessandria, 213–23.

Zimmermann, M. 1999. *Kaiser und Ereignis: Studien zum Geschichtswerk Herodians*. München.

FURTHER READING

In addition to the literature cited, the reader can find general discussions in Fornara 1983, Meister 1990, Luce 1997. Hornblower 1994 provides a concise review of the history of Greek historiography. For readable introductions to, or recent overviews of, the work of surviving historians, see on Herodotus: Gould

1989; on Thucydides: Connor 1984; on Xenophon: Cawkwell 1966; on Polybius: Walbank 1972 and 2002; on Appian Goldmann 1988 and Goukowsky 2001c; on Arrian: Stadter 1980. On other historians, readers can profit from the introductions (especially the most recent general introductions) to the Budé editions. For more literature on individual topics and authors, the reader is referred to the suggestions in Marincola 2007. For most fragmentary preserved authors Jacoby 1923– (and including the *New Brill Jacoby*) is indispensable.

On biography, a good presentation of the material is Momigliano 1971, but it is speculative on the beginnings of biography; on the historical context of ancient biography see Sonnabend 2002; for more suggestions see the bibliography in Erler and Schorn 2007; on Plutarch: Stadter 1992, Duff 1999, Pelling 2002.

CHAPTER 15

Philosophical Writing

Treatise, Dialogue, Diatribe, Epistle

Martin Hose

What we call "Greek philosophy" in the modern sense[1] is a movement of thought that begins in the Archaic period and continues through the whole history of Greek culture. It can be defined as a "purely theoretical activity" aimed at "Erkenntnis," discovering knowledge (Zeller 1919, 7), or in most cases, to be more precise, at discovering knowledge or understanding of the world and human existence.

Philosophical writing, one could insist, for that reason requires literary forms that are apt to guide the reader (or hearer) to just such a *discovery* of knowledge. Without doubt these forms belong in essence to the repertoire of literary writing styles that store knowledge (this is how Asper rightly talks below of "philosophy" in his discussion of "Explicit Knowledge," ch. 26, pp. 406–8 in this volume), but equally we may follow Heraclitus (DK 22 B 40) in seeing a difference between philosophy and other areas of scientific or scholarly writing in the fact that philosophical literature does not aim to pass on *polymathia*: rather, in philosophy the transmission of knowledge should result in discovering it for oneself.

If we review, even superficially, the great corpus of Greek philosophical (prose) writing that runs from the Presocratics to the texts of the so-called Neoplatonists in late antiquity, we can observe that there are certain shared basic structural features and clearly recognizable basic types of writing,[2] which seem to derive from a pre-literary practice of philosophical teaching. Philosophical writing, so it seems, is in principle the translation into written form of two modes of oral[3] philosophical practice. Thus, it reflects either (monologic) instruction or (dialogic) debate. This difference provides this chapter with its structure. It will first treat the forms of monologic instruction (Section 1), then the dialogic debates (Section 2) and finally special forms of philosophical writing (Section 3). The focus is in each case on early forms and types, in order to trace more closely the genesis of each literary form. It will not address philosophical didactic poetry, i.e. the works of Parmenides and Empedocles, as they will be discussed by Markus Asper (ch. 26, pp. 406–7 in this volume).

A Companion to Greek Literature, First Edition. Edited by Martin Hose and David Schenker.
© 2016 John Wiley & Sons, Inc. Published 2020 by John Wiley & Sons, Inc.

1. Monologic Instruction

1.1. *The Apophthegm as Philosophy in Brief*

In Greek literature there is a wide spectrum of forms in which the figure of an authoritative teacher presents philosophical insights, a spectrum that ranges from laconic sayings to extensive treatises. Already in ancient Greek literary histories this spectrum had been translated into a diachronic perspective and the short, apophthegm-like form was placed at the chronological start of philosophical instruction. Thus for example Aristotle (F 13 Rose) had seen the proverb as the remains of an early form of philosophy, and in Plato's *Protagoras* Socrates constructs a philosophy of the Spartans which is specifically understood as being pithy, proverbial wisdom and which is said to have had an influence on the sages of Archaic Greece:

> Well, there are some, both at present and of old, who recognized that Spartanizing is much more a love of wisdom than a love of physical exercise, knowing that the ability to utter such remarks belongs to a perfectly educated man. Among these were Thales of Miletus, and Pittacus of Mytilene, and Bias of Priene, and our own Solon, and Cleobulus of Lindus, and Myson of Chenae, and the seventh of them was said to be Chilon of Sparta. They all emulated and admired and were students of Spartan education, one could tell their wisdom was of this sort by the brief but memorable remarks they each uttered when they met and jointly gave the first fruits of their wisdom to Apollo in his shrine at Delphi, writing what is on every man's lips: Know thyself, and Nothing too much. Why do I say this? Because this was the manner of philosophy among the ancients, a kind of laconic brevity. (Plato, *Prot.* 342e–43b, transl. Allen 1996)

Perhaps taking its cue from this (so Fehling 1985), but perhaps also drawing on older traditions that are reflected, for example, in Herodotus (1.29; so Burkert 1962, 153), the idea arose that there was an important preliminary stage in Greek philosophy, the so-called Seven Sages with their sayings, about whom anecdotes and stories developed, especially in the imperial period (thus Plut., *Conv. sept. sap.*), which ultimately led to their acceptance into the history of philosophy by Diogenes Laertius (Book 1). For each of these Seven Wise Men (there seems never to have been a fixed canon of seven names, but the names Thales, Solon, Chilon and Pittacus are included fairly consistently) one or more[4] apodictic sentences or sayings are transmitted as the core message of their wisdom, for example for Solon the famous μηδὲν ἄγαν, "Nothing too much." The "wisdom" of these sayings[5] was evidently to be worked out by the hearers themselves as a discovery, as is suggested by the Platonic Socrates in the passage cited above.

1.2. *Heraclitus's Obscurity*

Viewed typologically, Heraclitus of Ephesus (see Kahn 1979) is closest to the sayings of the Seven Sages. Around 500 BCE he drew up his philosophical doctrine of the unity of opposites,[6] to which he gave fixed form in the "modern" medium of the book: this book (its title *Peri physeos*, *On Nature*, which is also the title of other books by the Presocratics, was probably given to it later, to sum up the book's aim of providing a comprehensive explanation of the world) is said to have been deposited by the author in the temple of Artemis in Ephesus as a kind of offering (Diog. Laer. 9.6 = DK 22 A 1.6). On the one hand he showed by this that this book had a special value (because it was worthy of dedication to the goddess), and on the other hand it ensured that his work gained a special protection. This last aim seems to have succeeded. For unlike other early Presocratic writings, Heraclitus's text circulated through copies (starting from this "master copy" in Ephesus?) with such an influence that even after his death it gave rise to a school, the "Heracliteans," and well into the high empire it was still available as an object of reception and interpretation (no less than eight commentators on the text are known by name, Diog. Laer. 9.15; on the history of its reception, Mouraviev 1999–2003).

The book's success can be linked to qualities that can be seen in its fragments, namely the pithy, apodictic art of formulating thoughts and the intellectual superiority that the author clearly claims for himself. The apodictic form has led to uncertainty among scholars on whether Heraclitus himself originally designed the work as a book, or whether it was not rather a later collection of the philosopher's orally transmitted sayings (thus Kirk 1954) which an editor arranged under the three rubrics recorded at Diog. Laer. 9.5, "On the Universe," "Politics," and "Theology." However, this hypothesis is countered by the observation that Fragment B 48, which refers to how the different accentuation of the letter-sequence BIOS produces the different meanings "life" or "bow," would clearly only be comprehensible to a reader. It is therefore probable that Heraclitus himself was addressing readers through this book (Kahn 1979, 7; Hölscher 1985).

The apodictic language and the intellectual ambition, or authority, of Heraclitus's book is shown in concise form in a fragment which probably opened the text:

> Of the Logos which is as I describe it[7] men always prove to be uncomprehending, both before they have heard it and when once they have heard it. For although all things happen according to this Logos men are like people of no experience, even when they experience such words and deeds as I explain [...]. (B 1, transl. KRS)

The first-person speaker of this text repeatedly claims to understand the nature of the world better than all other people (including traditional authorities like Homer, Hesiod or Pythagoras, see B 40, B 56, 57, B 81, B 106), and this understanding is announced solemnly in brief, striking sentences like "War is father of all and king of all, and some he shows as gods, others as men; some he makes slaves, others free." (B 53, transl. KRS).

A claim of authority, brevity and, further, the alternation between clarity (which does frequently recur in the fragments) and obscurity (which in the reception of the work earned Heraclitus the nickname of "the Obscure," for example in Cicero, *De div.* 2,133: *valde Heraclitus obscurus*, or led him to be presented as psychologically disturbed, thus Theophrastus, DK 22 A 1.6) evidently provoked readers in the ancient world to exert themselves more intensively to understand the text. This is expressed pointedly in an anecdote transmitted by Diog. Laer. 2.22 (= DK 22 A 4): Socrates is said to have remarked to Euripides about Heraclitus's book, "The part I understand is excellent, and so too is, I dare say, the part I do not understand; but it needs a Delian diver to get to the bottom of it." Heraclitus had evidently succeeded in motivating his readers to plunge into the depths of his thought like Delian divers in order to understand it.

1.3. Anaximander: Cosmogony in Juridical Language

The sayings of the Seven Sages and the book of Heraclitus tried to prompt the hearers or readers through brachylogies (so implicitly borrowing the style of oracles) to engage in active effort to grasp their intellectual discoveries, but in Anaximander (about half a century[8] earlier than Heraclitus) there was a different kind of attempt to present and communicate to the reader new cosmogonic discoveries in the medium of writing while using the new form, the book. The book of Anaximander (later tradition gave it, too, the title *On Nature*) was not lengthy, if we may credit Diogenes Laertius's remark: "His exposition of his doctrines took summary form" (Diog. Laer. 2.2 = DK 12 A 1.2). "Summary" (*kephalaiodes*) means, so far as we can tell from the fragments and testimonia, that Anaximander formulated the main points of his doctrine in a brief and lapidary fashion (but not as riddles). We owe to the late-Antique Aristotle commentator Simplicius (*In Arist. Phys.* 24,13 = DK 12 B 1) a direct citation, embedded in a review of Anaximander's doctrines:

> Anaximander ... said that the first principle and element of existing things was the *apeiron* [indefinite/infinite], ... And the source of coming-to-be for existing things is that into which destruction, too, happens "according to necessity; for they pay penalty and retribution to each other for their injustice according to the assessment of Time," as he describes it in these rather poetical terms. (transl. KRS)

Remarkable here is Anaximander's vocabulary: penalty, retribution, injustice – he used a metaphorical language (Simplicius – and probably Theophrastus, who is Simplicius's source here – calls these "rather poetical terms"), which drew on the language of law to explain the cosmos. From this it has been inferred (Gagarin 2002, esp. Patzer 2006, 101) that Anaximander made these linguistic borrowings intentionally, in order to lend his hypotheses more plausibility or authority by presenting natural processes as a kind of legal procedure. At the same time, this also involves a strategy of implicit persuasion of the recipient, through the fact that the text is composed in legal language and the reciprocal relations in nature are described as ineluctable; to put it in modern terms, he claims to be formulating "natural laws."

1.4. Alcmaeon of Croton: Philosophy as Elite Instructional Speech

The fragments of Heraclitus and Anaximander articulate an authority, but it is not possible to tell from them either the addressee to whom the voice of the text is speaking, or the social context in which the speech occurs. One possibility is that both Heraclitus's and Anaximander's books were in principle addressed to anyone who was prepared to read the text. The fact that Heraclitus deposited his book in the Temple of Artemis, which was open to the public, argues for this, as does the fact that Anaximander's legal language and metaphors imply a claim to universal validity.

The Pythagorean Alcmaeon of Croton (probably around 500 BCE, see Perilli 2001, Zhmud 2013, 407–12) departs from this model in his book. The first sentence of this work (the title here is *On Nature*) is cited by Diogenes Laertius (8.83 = DK 24 B 1): "These are the words of Alcmaeon of Croton, son of Pirithous, which he spake to Brotinus, Leon and Bathyllus: 'Of things invisible, as of mortal things, only the gods have certain knowledge; but to us, as men, only inference from evidence is possible.'" (transl. Hicks, Loeb).

The text presents itself as the record of a speech of instruction ("which he spake") by Alcmaeon, which was addressed to specific persons (to Brotinus etc.). The voice of the text thus acquires the authority of a teacher, who in the first sentence of his speech immediately sets out his "competence" (and so derives authority also from the content), by making a categorical distinction between divine and human knowledge and, further, sets out the specific condition under which human beings may acquire knowledge ("inference from evidence"/*tekmairesthai*).

It is hardly by chance that it is the text of a Pythagorean (the fragments show that Alcmaeon was addressing physiological problems, which he evidently treated empirically) that provides the first instance of a philosophical text styled as a speech of instruction: after all, it can be seen (despite all the problems of method in getting historically reliable information about Pythagoras and his circle) that Pythagoras transmitted his doctrines only to a special, elite audience,[9] whom he "initiated" into his discoveries like the initiates of a mystery cult and with whom he formed a "secret society" (Riedweg 2005, 98). Alcmaeon's "speech of instruction" seems to have imitated Pythagoras's style of teaching and it seems telling that of the three named "listeners," one at least, Bro(n)tinos, is explicitly attested as a Pythagorean (cf. DK 17).

What is remarkable about Alcmaeon's text, further, is that it presents itself as an introduction, and not just an imitation, of elite Pythagorean instruction, but at the same time becomes for this reason especially valuable for a reader, for what would otherwise be communicated only to "the initiated" can here be read in the medium of the book. This first sentence of the work raises its importance and insinuates that the reader will learn a secret by reading it. Alcmaeon, we may conclude from this, here for the first time (at least as far as we can tell from transmitted works) used the book as a medium for promoting the discovery of philosophical knowledge by deploying it as an instrument to make public something that would otherwise remain secret.

1.5. From the Speech to the Text: The Philosophical Book Becomes a Treatise

It can thus be seen that the philosophical books of the sixth century stand in the tradition of oral instruction. The growing familiarity with the medium of the book, which is evident already with Alcmaeon, led to greater use of the specific possibilities of this medium, especially the opportunity to increase the length and complexity of a presentation. This is clearly the case in the texts of the Eleatic philosophers Zeno and Melissus. Both refer to the didactic poem of Parmenides, from around 500 BCE (on which see Asper, this volume, ch. 26, 406–7), in hexameter form (on which see Most 1999), which permitted him to style his findings as a revelation spoken by a goddess, and who had developed a shrewd new approach in Greek philosophy: he "solved" the problem of the origin and nature of the world through a conceptual-logical approach, by making Being central and ascribing to this Being a series of attributes or signs (*semata*; DK 28 B 8.2–6: ungenerated, imperishable, whole, unique, steadfast, complete, nor was it ever, nor will it be, is now, all together, one, holding together; cf. McKirahan 2008). This Parmenidean ontology clearly made a strong impression on the Greek world (Plato's *Parmenides* is an echo of this), but it is equally clear that it was criticized and contested. This is where Zeno started work. His book (here too the title *On Nature* is given to it) defended Parmenides' positions by demonstrating, with different proofs in each case, that the "signs" necessarily exist (as attested by Aristotle [DK 29 A 25–8] and Simplicius [DK 29 B 2]); as the structure of his argumentation he used the so-called "apagogic" proof, that is, the existence of a sign was demonstrated by the proof that the opposite of the sign in question is impossible (Patzer 2006, 120–25).

This argumentation in formal logic required a substantial level of detail and, as it always proceeded in an analogous fashion, it was hardly attractive as rhetoric. Zeno's book was thus directed at the reader, who could double-check its findings, and not at an audience in search of instruction (who would soon have been exhausted). This book thus presents the first attested argumentative treatise in Greek philosophy.

Melissus of Samos (around the mid-fifth century BCE) presented his reflections on Parmenides' ontology in a book that bore the title *On Nature, or On What Exists* (DK 30 A 4). It is not clear whether this double title goes back to Melissus himself or was subsequently given to the book to characterize its content; we know of the content from, firstly, a series of fragments transmitted by Simplicius (DK 30 B 1–10), and secondly through a list of the contents in the pseudo-Aristotelian treatise *On Melissus, Xenonphanes and Gorgias* (Text in DK 30 A 5). Evidently Melissus deduced essential properties of Being (Being is ungenerated, indestructible etc.), like Zeno, by an apagogic method. It is only in recent times that philosophical research has established more clearly that Melissus also departed from his Eleatic predecessors in innovative ways (see Rapp 2013, 576/77). It is not possible to see whether the text deployed special strategies to make it accessible to the reader; the contents list and fragments give the impression that its argumentation was clearer than that of Zeno and Parmenides but at the same time it lacks the element of the paradox, with which Zeno had worked and which made his text interesting (KRS 1983, 401). It thus cannot be excluded that Melissus wrote the first "boring" philosophical text of Greek literature (this is hinted by remarks of Aristotle, which class Melissus as clumsy and "uneducated," see DK 30 A 7 and A 10, cf. Patzer 2006, 127).

With a contemporary of Melissus, Anaxagoras of Clazomenae, it is clear that the philosophical book had now become a firmly established feature of Greek culture. This is shown already by the well known remark that Plato gives to Socrates (*Apol.* 26d): the books of Anaxagoras could be bought for a drachma in the orchestra (that is, probably, in the Agora). It is unclear whether these were new or second-hand books; in the first case we could make deductions about their length (KRS 1983, 357), but in the second case not (thus, convincingly, Brumbaugh 1991).

This work itself, as Simplicius records (DK 59 B 1), was so long that it took up several book-rolls and consequently was divided externally into several "books." We also owe to Simplicius a direct quotation of the sentence that began the first of these books: "All things were together, infinite in respect of both number and smallness; for the small too was infinite. And while all things were together, none of them were plain because of their smallness […]." (DK 59 B 1, transl. KRS 467). Anaxagoras here distinguishes himself from the Eleatics by developing his idea of the world and its genesis as a universal mixture of elements. What is remarkable is that the text begins with the thesis itself, with no "title sentence" presenting the author nor any localization that would mark the text as a "speech" to an audience or students. Instead the reader is left alone with the idea and its development.

In our transmitted sources, some problems are raised by this work. Diogenes Laertius (1.16) reports that Anaxagoras composed a single book, and Simplicius (see above) cites it by the title *Physica*, *On Nature*. In addition there are ancient sources that seem to have known of other works by Anaxagoras: *On Perspective* (A 39), *On the Squaring of the Circle* (A 38), and *Himas* ("band" or "strap") (A 40). The first two titles have rightly been classed by scholars as pseudo-testimonia (Rechenauer 2013, 745), but the third title seems more reliable, though it could also belong to the *Physica*, as a kind of informative subtitle.[10] The book may have been called "band" (thus A 40) because it binds its reader through problems that are hard to solve. This could be a characterization of the writing style of the *Physica*, as is suggested by the opening sentence that leads immediately into Anaxagoras's central theory. Anaxagoras would thus have found a rhetoric for his treatise that would motivate the reader to pursue advanced reading and thus it would even be deploying the instrument of "suspense" about how Anaxagoras is going to solve the problem that has been posed.

1.6.   *The Division of Philosophy into Treatises: Diogenes of Apollonia and Democritus*

With Anaxagoras we reach the point in literary history at which it is clear that Greek philosophers no longer understand "their" philosophy in such a concentrated or focused way that they could bring it together in a single book. From Anaxagoras's *Physica* in several books it is but a small step to composing several books on different aspects of an intellectual structure. This step is first suggested with Diogenes of Apollonia (DK 64, a summary by Rechenauer 2013a), a younger contemporary of Anaxagoras, and is clearly taken by Democritus.

Diogenes of Apollonia, addressed by Theophrastus as the "youngest" (i.e. last) of the natural philosophers (DK 64 A 5), attempted on the basis of previous theories on the world and its origin (see Diller 1941; a re-evaluation in Laks 1983/2008) to give a central position to air (*aer*) and to demonstrate that this air, in various motions and mixtures, is the basic substance of the universe. However, Diogenes did not limit himself to cosmology: he also treated the genesis of life, including the reproduction of animals and the question of soul and perception, perhaps developing these topics out of his cosmology.

Given this breadth of themes, a remark by Simplicius deserves special note (DK 64 A 4). In the sixth century CE Simplicius still had direct access to Diogenes' work *On Nature*, but in this work, which – under the traditional title – set out a cosmology, he also found references by Diogenes to other books of his with the titles *Meteorology*, *Against the Sophists* (by which is meant, according to Simplicius, the natural philosophers prior to Diogenes) and *On the Nature of Man*. It is less probable that Diogenes was by this referring to particular sections of *On Nature*, as Simplicius would have noticed them in that case. So for Diogenes it can be confirmed that he presented a coherent doctrinal structure in several separate works. The book thus became a tool that divided up a field of knowledge and made its aspects accessible separately.

The first sentence of *On Nature* is preserved. It shows that Diogenes reflected upon the capacities of the book format: "It is my opinion that the author, at the beginning of any account, should make his principle or starting-point indisputable, and his explanation simple and dignified." (DK 64 B 1, trans. KRS 596).

With "It is my opinion" this constructs an authority that asserts its own competence, in a similar way to the first sentence in the book of Hecataeus (FGrHist 1 F 1) and some works of the *Corpus Hippocraticum*. Further, and this, too, is comparable to some Hippocratic works, here a basic and precise demand is made of a scientific treatise: the publication and justification ("indisputable") of the starting-point or principle for the account that follows (Gemelli 2007; Gemelli Marciano 2010, 285/6). And finally two demands are made for the style of the presentation: simplicity and dignity. From a purely rhetorical point of view, these two demands are mutually exclusive, for a text can belong either to the *genus humile* or the *genus grande*, but not both. However, Diogenes is evidently not trying to set up a rhetorical paradox, but rather wants to raise the standing of the text by his demand for dignity, and to guarantee its comprehensibility by the demand for simplicity.[11]

By formulating this so pointedly, Diogenes implicitly promises that his own text will meet these demands. At the same time, he implicitly distances himself from other – rival – texts of the previous Presocratics who – so runs the charge – have not made their principles sufficiently clear *a limine* and which are unclear. This fragment of Diogenes can therefore be read both as polemic against other Presocratic texts and at the same time as promoting himself.

The fact that Diogenes makes special demands for the style of presentation shows that he is thinking in the medium of the book and expects his book to be read, by readers whom he wants to tempt into reading it by its elevated language and to lead to discover knowledge through its simplicity or clarity of argumentation. Only a few years later, in the final quarter of the fifth century BCE, Democritus of Abdera (DK 68, in summary Rechenauer 2013b) made use of the medium of book to a downright excessive degree in order to develop further the atomistic doctrine of Leucippus,[12] but perhaps at the cost of not appearing in person as a teacher, and so failing to achieve public influence. This had consequences: "I came to Athens and no one knew me." is a quotation from Democritus recorded by Diogenes Laertius (9.37).[13] As Diogenes goes on to relate, Democritus had known Socrates, but Socrates had not known him. It should therefore be no surprise that, unlike the great master-thinkers of the fifth century such as Parmenides, Zeno or Gorgias, Democritus plays no role in Plato's dialogues.[14]

In the early Imperial period so many works were in circulation under the name of Democritus that Thrasyllus (who is linked in the tradition to a similar re-organization of Plato's works) divided up the ones that he regarded as authentically by Democritus into a total of 13 tetralogies (Diog. Laer. 9.45–9 = DK 68 A 33), i.e. more than 50 books were attributed to Democritus.

The tetralogies structured this extensive corpus into groups of related content that matched the order of scientific knowledge that had become established since the Hellenistic period: ethics, physics, mathematics, music (in the sense of the Greek *mousikḗ*), "technical" subjects, and a group of *asyntakta*, that is, works that could not be classified (in the sense of "miscellaneous"). Democritus's work reveals that philosophical thought and study was trying to comprehend the cosmos and man's place in it through a large-scale process of differentiation in content. Already in the ancient world this breadth of Democritus's work had been a source of fascination: Democritus was compared admiringly to a pentathlete (Diog. Laer. 9.37).

At the same time, this meant that each individual work by Democritus – in contrast to the Presocratics with "one single book" – offered only a segment of the author's thought, that is, it in each case gave the reader the opportunity for only a "partial" discovery of knowledge. Stylistically Democritus seems to have tried to write texts that were attractive to readers (see Patzer 2006, 149–58), and like Diogenes he deployed a double strategy, as can be seen from ancient critiques of style. Cicero's conclusion (*De div.* 2.133 = DK 68 A 34), *valde Heraclitus obscurus, minime Democritus*, shows that Democritus's arguments tried to create a sense of evidentness, and that this evidentness was increased by Democritus's ability to find the right words and images for his arguments in each case (Cicero speaks expressly of *optima verba* [De div. 2.57 = DK 68 A 158] and *clarissima verborum lumina* [Or. 67 = DK 68 A 34]). This verbal art (which also earned Democritus the ironic praise that he was a circumspect chatterer, a "word herder" [DK 68 A 1.40]), was supplemented by the use of choice, and sometimes rare and poetic, words and phrases, which in the Hellenistic period moved none other than Callimachus to make a collection called "Index of the glosses and phrases of Democritus" (DK 68 A 32).

Democritus's extensive output admittedly would present a problem for the reader interested not just in a particular question that was treated in one of the single works. How could such a reader have understood Democritus's philosophy as a whole and in what order were the books to be read? It is no longer possible to tell whether Democritus's works themselves contained any sort of references to the structure of his philosophy as a whole, or at least of some part of it. Thrasyllus "solved" this problem by composing – in the form of an auxiliary text (see Dubischar, ch. 28 in this volume, pp. 435–7) – an introduction or prolegomena to the corpus (DK 68 A 1.41), which probably amounted to a kind of guide to the philosophy.

1.7.   The Differentiation of Text Functions: Treatise and Protreptikos

With Democritus, a form of philosophical writing had finally become established in which philosophical texts appear as systematic presentations of a problem. What had originally been the imitation of a speech by a teacher (see above on Alcmaeon) became a "treatise," a prose work that presents a subject according to particular principles, which in some circumstances could be specific to each topic.[15] This literary form was evidently apt to inspire authors to be productive. From the fourth century BCE the Greek philosophers are distinguished by publication lists that increasingly make an impression through quantity (Diog. Laer. is a central source for this). Thus from the circle of Theophrastus, a student of Aristotle, 220 titles are attested (Diog. Laer. 5.42–50), for Aristoxenus 453 works (F 1 Wehrli). The Stoics were no less enthusiastic in their output. For the founder of the school, Zeno of Citium, only 19 titles of works are recorded (Diog. Laer. 7.4 = SVF 1 F 41), but there is a dramatic rise in productivity among his successors Cleanthes (57 titles, of which 50 are attested in Diog. Laer. 7.174–5 = SVF 1 F 481) and Chrysippus (Diog. Laer. 7.180–81 = SVF 2 F 1 knows of over 700 works). Epicurus, finally, is explicitly called *polygraphotatos,* "most prolific writer" by Diogenes Laertius (10.26; list of works ibid. 10.27–8).

Admittedly this enormous rise in productivity in philosophical literature was to a large extent feeding on itself. For it increasingly became a distinctive feature of a philosophical treatise that it engaged with previous arguments – which were classed or demonstrated as false or insufficient – from other philosophical texts. Thus, as it were, every single text produced new texts that took up polemics against it, sometimes using direct quotation. Carneades, who was head of the Platonic Academy in Athens in the second century BCE, was thus able to conclude pointedly: "For every subject treated by Epicurus, Chrysippus in his contentiousness must treat at equal length; hence he has frequently repeated himself and set down the first thought that occurred to him, and in his haste has left things unrevised, and he has so many citations that they alone fill his books: nor is this unexampled in Zeno and Aristotle." (Diog. Laert. 10.27, transl. Hicks).

Along with the growing number of books there was also greater differentiation of the purposes that the books fulfilled and, linked to that, a differentiation among the readerships that the books addressed. This double differentiation is clearest in the Aristotelian corpus. Three contents lists survive (see Flashar 2004b, 178–9; further Primavesi 2007), naming almost 200 titles in total. These can be divided[16] into a group of works (especially dialogues and propaedeutic works) that spoke to the general educated public and a group of works (the so-called *pragmateiai* or treatises), that were addressed to "specialists." The first group is termed "exoteric" and the second "esoteric" or "acroamatic." It is traditionally assumed that the second group, which by a lucky chance (on which see Primavesi 2007) has been preserved, is composed of transcripts of lectures delivered by Aristotle in his school. Interruptions in the line of thought, repetitions, at times an abbreviated, note-like style, seem to support this. Two things are worth noting, however: the treatises often presuppose knowledge of the exoteric writings on relevant themes and make references to them.[17] Further, the *Nicomachean Ethics* (10.10, 1181b12) close with an explicit advance reference to what is treated in the *Politics* (see Schütrumpf 1989, 182–3). This cross-reference seems odd for a "lecture." When we also consider the fact that everywhere in the treatises we also find passages and sections that seem stylistically polished, it no longer seems certain that these works must, in principle, consist of material by Aristotle that was not designed for publication. Rather, it is possible that they are *hypomnemata* or special works directed to an expert readership (thus Schütrumpf 1989; cf. also Lengen 2002).[18]

From the perspective of the sociology of literature it is important to consider how we should picture such an expert readership. Certainly we may suppose that the members or alumni of the Platonic Academy, then those of the Lyceum and the other Athenian schools of philosophy should first be considered here.[19] That this would indeed amount to sizable numbers of students and alumni is spotlighted by a notice of Diogenes Laertius (5.2.37), who records that Theophrastus had 2,000 students. That such a large expert public – from the entire Greek-speaking world[20] – could come into being is proof of the reputation that the schools had earned. This was of course also thanks to the advantage that in a school important contacts could be made that would be of use to the individual student in later life (see e.g. Trampedach 1994). However, the fact that, for example, both Aristotle and Plato (on whom see below) composed written works for a broader public implies that these books could also serve to promote the school in question.

The Sophists had been more "aggressive" in promoting themselves with model speeches (for example Gorgias' *Helena* and *Palamedes*), and Isocrates had also joined this tradition with his *Helena* and *Busiris.* However, Isocrates, in his so-called Cypriot speeches (*or.* 2, 3, 9) had gone a step further. In *Or.* 2 he addressed the Cypriot ruler Nicocles and explained to him, in the style of a "Mirror of Princes," how useful his model of education was for good government (on which see Eucken 1983, 216–48). These forms of promotion[21] pre-date the (lost) *Protreptikos* (sc. *logos*, i.e. "a promotional speech/text"[22]) of Aristotle.[23] In this text Aristotle addressed Themison, the King of Cyprus, to inspire him to engage in philosophy. From the fragments we can tell that the utility of philosophy for human life was comprehensively presented and philosophy was glossed as the "art of arts and science of sciences" (F 20 Schneeweiß = Ammonius in Isag. Porph. p.6.25 B). With this *Protreptikos* Aristotle created a distinctive literary form that was adopted by many ancient philosophers.[24] However, these *protreptikoi* (attested for, among others, Theophrastus: Diog. Laer. 5.49; Cleanthes: Diog. Laer. 7.91; Epicurus: Diog. Laer. 10.28) are for the most part lost. Nonetheless it is possible to get an impression of the promotional strategies of this literary form from the extant *Protreptikos* of Iamblichus (fourth century CE), who made use of Aristotle's *Protreptikos* (a large number of the relevant fragments of Aristotle come from Iamblichus). A remarkable testimony to the influence of a protreptic work is given by Augustine (*Conf.* 3.4.7), who records – perhaps with considerable literary stylization – that reading Cicero's protreptic work *Hortensius* had changed his life.[25]

Thus by the end of the fourth century BCE a differentiation had become established among the forms of "monologic" philosophical literature, which were now oriented to different readerships, viz. the reader who might yet be won for philosophy, interested educated readers, and philosophically trained readers and the expert public, and this differentiation remained a shaping force until the end of the ancient world. However, from the early fourth century BCE this monologic literature, which mimicked the authoritative voice of the philosopher-author, no longer had a monopoly on the literary transmission of philosophy. For – almost paradoxically – through the inspiration of a philosopher who himself left no written works, an alternative to the monologue appeared which would at once have a powerful influence: the dialogue.

2.   The Dialogue

2.1.   *Sokratikoi Logoi*

Socrates (469–399 BCE) left no written works himself, but he exerted a massive influence both on the development of Greek philosophy and on the development of literature. His particular art of conducting discussions prompted the creation of the literary dialogue, a genre that is a core element of the Western canon.[26] In Athens a circle of young men had gathered around him and were inspired by his manner of dealing with problems in ethics.[27] Plato and Xenophon are undoubtedly the most famous members of this circle but Aeschines, Antisthenes, Aristippus, Eucleides, and Phaedo are all also important, at least for the ancient world, in that Antisthenes marked the start of the Cynic tradition, Aristippus was seen as founder of the Cyrenaic School, Eucleides as founder of the Megarian School, while both Phaedo and Aeschines represent the Elean–Eretrian school (testimonia and fragments in SSR, on which see Döring 1998). In contrast to their master, these students of Socrates made use of the book format, and they too wrote (monologic) treatises. But their distinctive characteristic is that (probably with the exception of Aristippus) they also wrote dialogues,[28] in which their master appeared in discussion with one or more conversation partners. Already in the ancient world this literary form was known as *Sokratikoi Logoi* (e.g. Arist. Poet. 1, 1447b11). Admittedly, this genre itself – reinforced by other images of Socrates such as that drawn by Aristophanes in the *Clouds* – led to such differing pictures of the figure of Socrates that it seems a hopeless task to try to reconstruct out of them the "historical Socrates" (cf. Patzer 2012).

The writings of the Socratics other than Plato and Xenophon survive only in fragments, but we can discern some kind of outline of the form taken by their dialogues. Aeschines (born around 430, died around 356, and so roughly the same age as Plato) wrote, among other things, a dialogue *Alcibiades*, in which evidently Socrates himself recounted his encounter with the young aristocrat Alcibiades and reported his conversations with him in direct speech (SSR VI A 41–53, on which Döring 1998, 204–6). The Socrates of Aeschines, so the text concluded, hoped that he could make the young man better through his love. Diogenes Laertius (2.61) stresses that Aeschines had depicted the particular character of Socrates. In its form the *Alcibiades* seems to have had a kind of narrative introduction, because Socrates reports a conversation that occurred some time previously, in which Socrates must have addressed a listening audience. The ancient world termed this form in Plato "diegematic [i.e. narrative] dialogue" (Diog. Laer. 3.50). Under the name of Aeschines, dialogues of another form were also preserved in the ancient world: Diogenes Laertius (2.60) speaks of dialogues with no beginning, that is, dialogues that begin immediately with the dialogic exchanges themselves. This form, which is also found in Plato, is termed "dramatic dialogue" (Diog. Laer. 3.50). We meet a third form in Xenophon (as a "Socratic" he is admittedly a latecomer and his texts are already reacting to certain works of Plato). Xenophon depicts "his" Socrates in dialogue situations that he expressly draws from his own memory: thus he writes in *Memorabilia* 1.3.1: "so far as I can remember," and there is a similar start to the continuation of the *Memorabilia*, the *Oeconomicus* 1.1: "I once heard how he spoke in dialogue the following about household management." This matches the otherwise odd notice in his *Symposium* (1.1) that Xenophon had been present at the discussions depicted in the *Symposium*. The stress on the participation of the author Xenophon in the dialogues of Socrates is of course a strategy to inscribe into each text the authority of an eye-witness. The stress on the feat of memory that Xenophon thereby undertakes has led scholars to term this dialogue form an "apomnemoneumatic dialogue" (Döring 1998, 180).

Xenophon admittedly takes the *Sokratikoi Logoi* to the borderline of what can be termed a philosophical dialogue. His dialogue scenes sketch less an initially open-ended reflection on basic issues of human existence than a Socrates who – for example in the case of the *Oeconomicus* – passes on plainly useful, "propositional" knowledge. Xenophon can therefore be termed the creator of a new form of dialogue, the "didactic dialogue" (on which see Föllinger 2013, and Fögen, this volume, ch. 17, 275–6), which would go on to be deployed in various spheres of knowledge in the ancient world.

2.2. Plato's Art of Dialogue

Even if the dialogues of other Socratics preceded the Platonic dialogues, already in the ancient world it was incontestable that Plato had developed this form to the point of mastery: "In my opinion Plato, who brought this form of writing to perfection, ought to be adjudged the prize for its invention as well as for its embellishment." writes Diogenes Laertius (3.48, trans. Hicks).

Plato (see overall Görgemanns 1994; Erler 2007) is one of the few ancient authors whose texts survive *in toto*: 43 works are transmitted under his name, 36 of these in a division into tetralogies, which is in turn linked to the name of Thrasyllus (see above on Democritus) but which may be older. Among the 43 transmitted texts there are some that – in some cases already in the ancient world – are considered inauthentic, that is, they have no right to claim Plato as their author. This is true also of the epigrams ascribed to Plato in the *Anthologia Graeca* and the majority of a collection of letters that Plato is supposed to have written (they form the final part of the ninth tetralogy). Among the other 35 works of the tetralogy arrangement there are also some that modern scholars regard as inauthentic or whose authenticity is contested (inauthentic: *Alc. 2, Hipparchus, Amatores, Theages, Minos*; contested: *Alc. 1, Hipp. mai.* and *min., Epinomis*). The fact that, for Plato especially, so many probable *pseudepigrapha* (i.e. works in which the author-name written on the book is a "lie") are preserved reflects the importance of Platonic doctrine (and its reception in "Platonisms") into late antiquity and Byzantine culture.

The works that are certainly authentic are, with one exception, designed as dialogues. The exception is the *Apology*, the defense speech of Socrates in the trial of 399, but composed later by Plato (the precise dating is contested: shortly after 399 or only around 385). The dialogues differ greatly from each other, both in their form and in the degree of their "dialogization." Viewed in the chronology of their composition,[29] they can be divided into three groups: Early Dialogues (*Crito, Protag., Ion, Hippias Maior., Hippias Minor., Euthd., Laches, Charm., Euthphr., Lysis, Rep. I, Gorg., Cratylus, Menexenus*), Middle Dialogues (*Meno, Phaed., Conv.*, these three works are also considered separately as "transitional dialogues"; *Rep., Phaedr., Parm., Theaetetus*) and Late Dialogues (*Soph. Politicus, Phileb., Tim., Critas., Lg.*). This chronological division can be overlaid by a division on the basis of content, which matches the chronological one: thus among the Early Dialogues the group from *Prot.* to *Euthd.* can be characterized as "Sophist dialogues"; *Laches* to *Rep. I* (there are some reasons to believe that this book was composed earlier than the other books of *Rep.*) as "definition dialogues"; from the group of the Middle Dialogues the series from *Meno* to *Phaedr.* as "Idea dialogues" (i.e. the Theory of Ideas, or Forms, is developed in them); *Parm.* to *Phileb.* as "dialogues critical of the Ideas" (in which the Theory of Ideas has a lesser role than terminological differentiations, i.e. diairetic procedures, with the help of which certain knowledge is to be acquired); the last three dialogues, the grand speculative models on cosmogony (so the *Timaeus*), on the ideal state as imagined in earliest times (the *Critias*: here Athens is shown at war with the fictional state Atlantis) and on the ideal constitutional order (the *Laws*, through the example of an imaginary legal code for an imaginary polis-foundation on Crete), mark a return to the Theory of Ideas.

Like the Socratics who preceded him, Plato too begins the series of his dialogues with a character "Socrates" who dominates the dramatized discussions in each case. However, in his later work, this figure increasingly slips into the background: in the *Sophist* the "Eleatic Stranger" (who is close to Parmenides and Zeno) takes on the leading role in the conversation, while in the *Timaeus* and *Critias* (which was probably left unfinished) the speeches by the title figure in each case dominate the discussion and in the *Laws* the characters in the dialogue are the Cretan Cleinias, the Spartan Megillus and an unnamed Athenian Stranger. Furthermore, the kind of discussions that are presented changes in character from the early to the late works: in the early dialogues, especially, lively debates with quick changes between speakers predominate, which imitate in a stylized form[30] an elevated register of spoken language, but the middle and late dialogues increasingly have longer speeches, and not only by Socrates, which ultimately reach the length of veritable lectures (thus e.g. *Timaeus* 27c–92e or *Critias* 108e–121c). In parallel with this there is a shift in the style of the dialogues. In the early dialogues Socrates undertakes to test or refute statements by his conversation-partners (this procedure is conventionally termed *elenchos*),[31] often in the form of a lively conversation which generally ends with the demonstration that what had been thought certain is merely apparent knowledge. In contrast to this, in the late works there are passages that are more strongly expository (and hence have more detailed argumentation), and which, for instance through the development of the Theory of Ideas, aim to lead to new and certain knowledge.

The dialogues display Plato's great literary art of presentation. This begins with the virtuoso treatment of both the dramatic and diegematic dialogue form, which Plato does not merely adopt as found, but rather utilizes (the dramatic form for example in *Euthyphro, Ion, Laches, Phaedrus, Laws*; diegematic form, with Socrates as the narrator who addresses an undefined audience, in *Republic, Lysis, Charmides*) and develops further. Thus the narrative frame of the diegematic dialogue leads into a dialogue and so becomes "dramatic" in the *Protagoras* (an unnamed friend addresses Socrates asking for information) or in the *Phaedo* (Echecrates asks Phaedo for an account of how Socrates died). Further, this frame may be doubled or may even comprise three levels: the *Parmenides* begins diegematically with the narrator Cephalus, who reports to an undefined audience of his meeting with Adeimantus and Glaucon, with whom he sought out Antiphon, who tells them what Pythodorus told him about the meeting of Parmenides and Zeno with Socrates. The introduction to the *Symposium* is similarly complex, beginning dramatically: Apollodorus tells undefined friends of a meeting with an acquaintance who had asked for a report of the dinner long ago at Agathon's house, and which he recounts according to the report of the events that he had heard from Aristodemus.

Further, the dialogues are generally given a specific, historical site for the (of course fictitious) events of the dialogue (see Nails 2002, 308–30): thus the *Symposium* is placed very precisely in February or March 416 BCE (it is "performed" on the occasion of the first victory at the Lenaea of the tragic poet Agathon), and the *Parmenides* takes place in August 450 BCE. Often the date varies in the course of a text: the starting point of the *Republic* is Socrates' visit to the Piraeus on the occasion of a newly organized festival for the goddess Bendis, which would indicate 413/12. Yet in the text there are further allusions to events that would imply "dramatic dates" from 424 to 407 (Nails 324–6). The dating of the *Menexenus* is especially intricate, as it points *prima facie* to 401/400, yet the *epitaphios* that Socrates delivers in the text contains references to the history of Athens down to 387.

Further, the texts give striking characterizations to the principal speakers and sometimes also to the setting in which they act. As a result there are portraits of the important intellectuals of the fifth century, viz. Parmenides, Zeno, Gorgias, Protagoras, Aristophanes (in *Symp.*), but also of the Athenian aristocracy, viz. Callias (in *Protag.*), Nicias (in *Laches*) or Callicles[32] (in *Gorgias*). Plato shows the figures with their characteristics in such a lively way that his sketches have been compared to the dramatic art of Old Comedy and have classed his texts as – also – "social comedies from the period of Periclean culture" (Hoffmann 1950, 23).

The dialogic form itself, as has been repeatedly established by scholarship in various interpretations, is evidently used by Plato as an instrument by which the reader can be led to discover philosophical knowledge. Schleiermacher saw the dialogue as the imitation of a teaching discussion, with the goal of communicating intellectual discovery; Kierkegaard went a step further by viewing the dialogue as a form of philosophical practice that is in principle open, and which was especially well suited to Plato's philosophy. These kinds of interpretations of the dialogic form seem especially apt for understanding the early works, which often lead through lively debates to openly admitted *aporiai* (*Laches, Hippias minor, Euthyphro, Charmides, Euthydemus*: see Erler 1987).

However, within the dialogues Plato needed yet more structural forms designed to guide the reader to intellectual discovery. The use of diairesis as an instrument in the late dialogues has already been noted. This particular form of presentation had developed in the sophistic movement (Prodicus), as was the didactic use of (invented) myths (for example Prodicus's allegory of Hercules at the crossroads, Xen. *Mem.* 2.1.21–34). Plato, too, deployed myths, sometimes to give explanations for origins and beginnings (e.g. in the case of the Prometheus myth, *Prot.* 320c–322e, where Plato may have got the idea from Protagoras himself; in the case of the myth of the birth of Eros, *Symp.* 203b–204c; or of the epochs of the universe, *Statesman* 269c–274e). Even more important as argument are Plato's great eschatological myths which appear at the end of *Gorgias, Phaedo, Republic* and *Phaedrus*. These myths, in a kind of "speech of revelation" (Görgemanns 1994, 69), repeat at more depth in a narrative form, using the language and imagery of myth, what had been said about the soul in a more abstract form in the earlier part of the dialogue. Greek epic uses similes to create spaces of thought and imagination which are parallel to the main narrative, but which make the main narrative easier to understand (see Baechle, ch. 30 in this volume, pp. 464–66). With a similar function Plato, too, deploys similes, which are intended, especially in the *Republic* (6.506d–7.518c), to make clear the Theory of Ideas and the problems of grasping the Ideas: the simile of the sun, the simile of the line and the simile of the cave.

The dialogues of Plato are among the most influential texts in Greek literature. Despite and in part because of their literary qualities, they brought about serious problems, so far as we can tell, for Plato's school after his death. The criticism by Aristotle's student Dicaearchus may seem rather superficial: he claimed that Plato had ruined philosophy because through his dialogues he had prompted countless people to practice philosophy and to do so superficially (PHerc. 1021, I.11–15 [ed. Dorandi 1991, 125, see Burkert 1993/2008, 159–60]). Nonetheless, this criticism is evidence of the effect that Plato's dialogues had on a wider public. Yet it also makes clear that, from the perspective of philosophers who, like the school of Aristotle, worked with "esoteric" writings, Plato's works could seem too accessible and superficial. With regard to the differentiations of philosophical text forms (above, 1.4) that developed in the fourth century, Plato's texts could seem too uniform. Also, determined by the dialogue form, they presented a serious problem: in contrast to, say, Aristotle's treatises, in Plato's work what the author Plato himself found true or false always remains hidden. An authoritative writer's voice is always firmly absent in the dialogues. A philosophically interested reader must therefore apply complex hermeneutic procedures to work out "What Plato Said" (the title of Shorey 1933) and to reconstruct out of the polyphony of voices in the dialogues "The Unity of Plato's Thought" (the title of Shorey 1903). This problem can be traced back to the ancient world. Diogenes Laertius (3.52) solves it in this way: "His [sc. Plato's] own views are expounded by four persons, Socrates, Timaeus, the Athenian Stranger [sc. in the *Laws*], the Eleatic Stranger [sc. in *Sophist* and *Politicus*]." But did, say, the Socrates of the early aporetic dialogues really correspond to Plato's views?

The Academy itself also reacted to these difficulties. It evidently used two strategies to try to compensate for the lack of a *protreptikos* by Plato. (a) Plato had left the *Laws* unfinished; they were completed by Philippus of Opus. Following the *Laws* a treatise was created (perhaps also composed by Philippus), the *Epinomis*.[33] This text was composed in such a way that it could also be read as a *protreptikos* (see Tarán 1975, 142). (b) The orator and philosopher Themistius (fourth century CE) noted in a speech (*or.* 23.295c–d) that Plato's works *Gorgias* and *Apology* had led readers to philosophy, that is, they had a protreptic effect (see Riginos 1976, 184–5). We may suspect that this kind of conversion anecdote chimed with the views of the Academy, as they took the sting out of the lack of protreptic writings as a deficit, by demonstrating that the dialogues themselves could have the same effect. Were these anecdotes perhaps ultimately even put into circulation by the Academy?

The lack of an authoritative voice was explained, in a letter ascribed to Plato (*ep.* 7),[34] as an intentionally adopted concept: in an excursus in that letter (342a–344d) it was shown that grasping the Ideas is only possible by moving up through different degrees and the final, illuminating experience of them will only occur after long discussion in philosophical conversation. For that reason (341b–342a) "Plato" had not composed any works about this. Here the *Letter* picks up the "critique of writing"[35] that Socrates summarizes in the *Phaedrus* (274b–278e): a text can only ever say the same thing, it needs an author to help the reader when there are difficulties in understanding it, for which reason writing and books are not suitable for transmitting intellectual discovery. This critique of writing and the *Seventh Letter*, taken together, can be read as implying that Plato had passed on to his students an "unwritten doctrine" in oral discussions and that this oral discussion was the only proper form of true philosophical learning.[36] This argument gave a plausible explanation for the Academy's lack of any such "esoteric" writings by Plato.

All the same the Academy, too, could not in the long run refrain from deriving from the dialogues doctrines of Plato – *dogmata* – for teaching purposes. We can see what such "extracts" may have looked like from the *Didaskalikos* of Alcinous (or Albinus) in the imperial period, which presents "the" Platonic philosophy in a systematic structure (Summerell and Zimmer 2007).

2.3.   The Dialogue after Plato

As already mentioned above, Aristotle, too, composed dialogues in order to reach a wider public. Diogenes Laertius (5.1), in his list of the writings of Aristotle, gives the titles of 18 dialogues; we can estimate that this would be in length equivalent to around one-third of the length of the Corpus Platonicum, and so approximately 1,000 pages of text in the format of an Oxford Classical Text (see Flashar 2004c). However, the fragments preserve at most 50 pages from them, which can no longer give a true idea of the literary artistry that the ancient world admired in Aristotle.[37] One can speculate that in these dialogues (as already in Plato's later works) positions were developed not in short exchanges but in longer passages of argumentation.[38] Cicero draws attention to two special features: (a) Aristotle appeared in his dialogues as one of the speakers (Cic. *Ad Quintum fratrem* 3.5.1), and (b) the character "Aristotle" led the discussion in these dialogues (Cic. *Ad Atticum* 13.19.4). It is evident that both these characteristics are well suited to avoid the problems that arise (see above) in the Platonic dialogues over the question of what the author's own position is. It is thus not surprising that the future of literature would belong to this Aristotelian model of the dialogue: so far as we can tell from notices in Diogenes Laertius and the few fragments, it seems that he was followed by, among others, Theophrastus and Heraclides Ponticus (whose dialogues, Cicero[39] stresses, had carefully designed historical settings). The dialogues of Cicero himself inscribe themselves into this tradition,[40] and in the early imperial period Plutarch composed numerous works in dialogue form in which he himself also appears as a character (thus in *De E apud Delphos* and the *Quaestiones convivales*). Plutarch departs even further than Aristotle or Cicero from the "Socratic" type of dialogue: the speakers of his dialogues now only make speeches, which are no longer subject to an examination but instead generally serve to make clear different positions on a problem. The dialogue thus increasingly becomes an instrument for the doxographic transmission of knowledge.

3.   Special Forms of Philosophical Writing

So far this chapter has treated monologic and dialogic forms of philosophical literature as ways of writing that are strictly distinct from one another. With regard to the entire philosophical corpus this is a useful distinction, but an artificial one, because, as can be seen from the example of the ever-longer speeches in the late dialogues of Plato or the "monologic" diegematic frames of dialogues, both monologic and dialogic forms repeatedly draw on each other. The combination of monologue and dialogue sometimes even influences the structure of works. Two important examples of this will also be discussed here.

3.1.   The Diatribe

The term "diatribe" – it properly means "pastime" or "entertainment" – is encountered (a) as a term for a literary form in Diogenes Laertius (2.77), who used this term for lectures in popular philosophy by the Cynic Bion of Borysthenes (c. 335–245 BCE); and (b) as a manuscript subscription to the instructional conversations of Epictetus. In the handbook on rhetoric of Hermogenes (*Peri methodou deinotetos* 5) there is even a definition of the term: a diatribe is an "expansion of a short thought of an ethical character."

The term's real career began at the end of the nineteenth century when Wilamowitz discovered (1881, 292–319) in the treatises of the Cynic Teles (third century BCE) particular qualities that he also found in various sermon-like texts of the early and high empire. Out of this he reconstructed a specific type of philosophical instructional speech (or "philosophical sermon") for a wider public, with the special characteristic of turning the presentation into a dialogue. The texts assigned to the genre of diatribe (Wilamowitz did not use the term himself, which was coined by Wendland in 1895) present, to some degree, a *fictus interlocutor*, an opponent invented by the real speaker (or author). This opponent presents in direct speech arguments opposing the presentation of the speaker, with whom the speaker debates – successfully of course. Further, the diatribe is characterized by the use of direct quotations from well known poets such as Homer or Euripides, who are either cited in support or assigned similar adversarial roles to those of the *fictus interlocutor*.

Starting from Wilamowitz and Wendland the idea of a specific genre, the Cynic–Stoic diatribe, initially had a striking career in literary scholarship, which detected a broad reception of the genre in Christian literature (especially in the sermons of, for instance, Gregory of Nazianzus in the fourth century CE) or in Dio Chrysostom and also in Latin literature in the *Satires* of Horace or in Seneca. Admittedly, since the mid-twentieth century more and more doubts have been voiced over whether the diatribe was really a "genre." It has been increasingly recognized that the term diatribe instead captures stylistic qualities, that is, the dialogization of an instructional speech (thus e.g. Stowers 1981). Consequently what remains is the observation that, in a wide range of forms of philosophical instructional speeches in the late Hellenistic and imperial periods, we can trace clear attempts to break up monologue and integrate forms of dialogue.

3.2. The Epistle

The *Protreptikos* of Aristotle (see above) was formally an "Epistle," that is, a letter. In principle the letter is the monologic component of an imaginary dialogue (or at least of a dialogic constellation) between the author and the addressee of the epistle. It contains communications that begin from the author, but which have been shaped by the author to fit the sensibility and knowledge of the recipient. Aristotle's *Protreptikos* thus, as a letter, presupposes that Aristotle assumed Themison would gain by turning to philosophy and that promoting it would therefore make sense from his own (Aristotle's) point of view. At the same time the monologic speech-situation of the epistle, in which the author delivers a speech that is in some measure characterized as one of instruction to the addressee, implies that with the epistle, unlike the dialogue, questions from the addressee in response can only occur in the anticipation of the author.

These conditions of epistolary communication explain why the epistle is especially useful as a form of philosophical writing if the goal is (only) to communicate a doctrine (but not to justify or problematize it). This is the ground for the intensive use of the epistle by Epicurus and the Epicureans. [41] Epicurus's *Epistle to Pythocles* details this function already in the introduction (*ep. Pyth.* 84): Pythocles had asked Epicurus for a short, easily memorable summary of his account of meteorological phenomena, and Epicurus has summarized it in the present epistle (see Erler 1994, 49). When Epicurus calls on his student to memorize his doctrine, the epistle was a tried and tested instrument to assist this effort of memorization. It is also interesting that Epicurus writes not only to specific persons but also to collective addressees: to the *philoi* in Egypt (F 106 Us.), in Asia (F 107 Us.) or in Lampsacus (F 108/9 Us.). This broad circle of addressees suggests that this was an "open" letter-form that aimed also at a general readership, such as was later adopted by early Christianity, especially given that the basic intention there too was to teach (see Hirzel I. 1895, 356).

It can here only be noted that the Stoic *epistulae ad Lucilium* of Seneca are different again from the type of letter deployed by Epicurus.

NOTES

[1] As is well known, in Greek culture itself the term "philosophy" was used very broadly: it can refer to any effort towards education (thus e.g. in Isocrates) and can embrace grammar, music or even geography (so Strabo 1.1.1).

[2] This kind of typological way of viewing philosophical literature has a long tradition: it is found for the first time in Diog. Laer. 1.16, who offers several different possible divisions.

[3] As this chapter concerns literary forms of philosophical practice, it will not address Thales, Pythagoras or Socrates, who did not produce written texts.

[4] Stobaeus 3.1.172 cites a list ascribed to Demetrius of Phalerum, which presents for each of the Seven Sages (in this case Cleobulus, Solon, Chilon, Thales, Pittacus, Bias and Periander) 10–20 memorable sayings (text in DK 10.3).

[5] See on the forms and functions of this kind of proverbial wisdom Jolles 1958, 150–70.

[6] Here and for the other philosophers discussed no treatment is offered of the philosophical content or of specific problems of philosophical interpretation.

[7] Koenen 1993 notes that this refers simultaneously to the Logos as the materially present book as well as to the "eternal" Logos that is described therein.

[8] There is no need to consider here the relation of Anaximander to Pherecydes, as there are some grounds to believe that Pherecydes' book was produced later than that of Anaximander.

[9] There is no contradiction between this and the report that, on the basis of his evidently charismatic appearance, he was also able to win audiences in large numbers (cf. for example the reports in Porphyrius, *Vita Pythagorae* 18; 20, cf. Riedweg 2005, 12–18).

[10] For Philolaus there is a similar problem, as here too Diog. Laer. (8.85 = DK 44 A 1) concludes that Philolaus had only written one book, but at the same time five titles (DK 44 B 1; B 2; B 17; B 21; B 22) are cited for the fragments. See on this Patzer 2006, 141.

[11] The postulate of clarity is also one of the demands made of "technical literature," [see Fögen, this volume ch. 17, pp. 270–1].

[12] Leucippus himself seems to have presented his teaching only in one single book, the *Great World-system*, *megas diakosmos* (DK 68 A 33); it is telling that already in the ancient world this work had been attributed to Democritus. Because it exceeded in size a genuine work of Democritus of the same title, it was distinguished by the addition *megas* (and Democritus's work was then called, by analogy, *mikros diakosmos* – "Small World-system"). There is a similar case in the Corpus Platonicum: *Hippias maior/minor*. See on this Birt 1882, 493/4.

[13] Cf. in contrast Protagoras, Plato, *Protag.* 310b.

[14] This silence on Plato's part was discussed already in the ancient world, see Diog. Laer. 9.40, on which Bollack 1957.

[15] See Asper, ch. 26, pp. 405–6.

[16] Late antique commentators on Aristotle (on whom see Schütrumpf 1989, 187–8), divided the works according to the degree to which the content was general in nature into (a) *merika*, that is, directed to individuals and devised (only) for them; (b) *metaxu*, i.e. documentations, and (c) *katholou*, i.e. for a general public, with here a differentiation between *hypomnemata*, or sketches, and *syntagmata*, fully developed pieces of writing.

[17] There is a list in Bonitz 1870, 104–5.

[18] One may compare the Aristotelian treatises in this respect with the texts of Philodemus found in Herculaneum, which similarly develop Epicurus's doctrines for a specialist readership (Philodemus's school?). In contrast to his epigrams, these writings of Philodemus were evidently not read much outside his immediate circle (or at least not often cited). See on this Burkert 1993/2008, 153.

[19] See on this Scholz 1998.

[20] Not only men: Diog. Laer. 3.1.46 gives a list of students of Plato that includes two women: Lasteneia from Mantinea and Axiothea from Phlius. It is sociologically remarkable, given the restrictions to which women were subjected in Greek culture in their social and legal spaces for action, that this list attests two women who moved specially to Athens for the sake of education.

[21] The "conversion" to philosophy is also a frequent motif in ancient biographical texts about philosophers, see Gigon 1946.

[22] The title itself is also attested for works by Antisthenes (Diog. Laer. 6.1 and 16) and Aristippus (Diog. Laer. 2.85), though it is not clear what was contained in these texts.

[23] The *communis opinio* dates the text to 353–50 BCE; Aristotle would thus be promoting (Plato's) Academy. But there are also opinions (see Schneeweiß 2005, 51–3) that place the text after 335 BCE, i.e. after the founding of the Lyceum. In that case Aristotle would be promoting his own school. It is a telling comment on the text's fragmentary state of preservation that both views are possible on the basis of its known content.

[24] It is not clear whether the "*Protreptika*" attested for Chrysippus (SVF 3.203) and Poseidonius (Diog. Laer. 7.91 and 129) are not perhaps even writings "On *protreptikoi*", that is, they may present reflection on the genre (cf. Poseidonius F 3 Edelstein-Kidd).

[25] A further indication of the importance of this genre is its adoption by other disciplines: thus Galen composed a protreptic promoting the study of medicine, and the *Gymnasticus* of Philostratus (third century CE) also exhibits protreptic characteristics.

[26] See on this the major presentation of Hirzel 1895, and also Hempfer 2002, Goldhill 2008, and most recently Föllinger and Müller 2013.

[27] Plato makes Socrates at *Apol.* 23c/d depict its effect in this respect on young men.

[28] According to Aristotle (F 72 R, cf. also P.Oxy. 3219) the Socratics were not the first to use the dialogue form. He says that they were preceded by Alexamenus of Teos, otherwise entirely unknown to us.

[29] The absolute date at which the chronological series begins is controversial, as it has often been assumed that certain dialogues (e.g. *Ion, Hippias Minor*: Heitsch 2002), were composed within Socrates' lifetime, that is, before 399. Already in the ancient world this had been claimed, e.g., for the *Lysis*: Diog. Laer. 3.35.

[30] The repertoire of tools used for this stylization includes for example the use of non-sequiturs, through which Plato also gives certain thoughts special emphasis. See on this Reinhard 1920, Thesleff 1967.

[31] Structurally the Socratic *elenchos* is close to the particular form of sophistic verbal duel, eristics, which Plato himself performs in the *Euthydemus*.

[32] Unlike in the case of Callias or Nicias, there are no other references to Callicles outside the *Gorgias*. For that reason his historicity is not uncontested in scholarship, on which see Nails 2002, 75–7. It may be noted that (so far) it has not been possible to verify historically dialogue figures such as Timaeus and Philebus.

[33] Here we merely note Brisson 2005, who contests the reasons for denying Plato's authorship of the *Epinomis*.

[34] The debates on the authenticity or otherwise of the *Seventh Letter* are endless. See the overview in Erler 2007, 314–18.

[35] On this too the bibliography has become too large to survey briefly, see as an introduction and summary Görgemanns 1994, 51–5.

[36] The reconstruction of these "unwritten doctrines" (the term is from Aristot. *Phys.* 4.2, 209b15) has therefore been intensively pursued also in modern research on Plato; the starting point is formed by the books of Krämer 1959 and Gaiser 1963.

[37] See the testimonia in Rose 1886, 23–5.

[38] See on this Hirzel 1895, vol. 1, 276–80, who also cites Cicero's comment *flumen orationis aureum fundens Aristoteles* (*Acad. pr.* 119).

[39] Cic. *Ad Att.* 13.19.4; cf. Diog. Laer. 5.89, on which Hirzel 1895, Vol. 1, 321.

[40] Cicero even goes so far as to term his own works *Herakleideion*, see Hirzel 1895, Vol. 1, 547.

[41] See Epicurus's *Epistles* to Herodotus, Pythocles and Menoeceus which according to Diog. Laer. 10.29 summarize the whole of Epicurean doctrine; see further the fragments of epistles F 104-216 Us. There are also (instructional) epistles attested for some of Epicurus's students, Metrodorus, Hermarchus and Philonides.

REFERENCES

Allen, R. E. 1996. *Plato. Ion, Hippias Minor, Laches, Protagoras. Transl. with Comment.* New Haven, CT.

Birt, Th. 1882. *Das antike Buchwesen in seinem Verhältnis zur Literatur.* Berlin.

Blondell, R. 2002. *The Play of Character in Plato's Dialogues.* Cambridge.

Bollack, J. 1957. "Un silence de Platon (Diogène de Laerce IX, 40 = Aristoxène fr. 131 Wehrli)." *Revue de Philologie* 41: 242–6.

Bonitz, H. 1870. *Index Aristotelicus.* Berlin.

Brisson, L. 2005. "Epinomis: authenticity and autorship." In K. Döring, M. Erler, and S. Schorn, eds., *Pseudoplatonica*, Stuttgart, 9–24.

Brumbaugh, R. S. 1991. "The book of Anaxagoras." *Ancient Philosophy* 11: 149–50.

Burkert, W. 1962. *Weisheit und Wissenschaft.* Erlangen.

Burkert, W. 1993/2008. "Platon in Nahaufnahme. Ein Buch aus Herculaneum." In T. A. Szlezák and K.-H. Stanzel, eds., *W. Burkert. Kleine Schriften VIII. Philosophica*, Göttingen (first 1993), 148–66.

Cameron, A. 2014. *Dialoguing in Late Antiquity.* Washington, DC.

Clay, D. 2000. *Platonic Questions: Dialogues with the Silent Philosopher.* University Park, PA.

Diller, H. 1941. "Die philosophiegeschichtliche Stellung des Diogenes von Apollonia." *Hermes* 76: 359–81.

Döring, K. 1998. "Sokrates, die Sokratiker und die von ihnen begründeten Traditionen." In H. Flashar, ed., *Die Philosophie der Antike. Vol. 2/1. Sophistik, Sokrates, Sokratik, Mathematik, Medizin*, Basel, 139–364.

Dorandi, T., ed. 1991. *Filodemo. Storia dei Filosofi [.]. Platone e l'Academia.* Naples.

Erler, M. 1987. *Der Sinn der Aporien in den Dialogen Platons.* Berlin

Erler, M. 1994. "Epikur. Die Schule Epikurs. Lukrez." In H. Flashar, ed., *Die Philosophie der Antike. Vol. 4. Die hellenistische Philosophie*, Basel, 29–490.

Erler, M. 2007. *Die Philosophie der Antike. Vol. 2/2. Platon.* Basel.

Eucken, Chr. 1983. *Isokrates. Seine Positionen in der Auseinandersetzung mit den zeitgenössischen Philosophen.* Berlin.

Fehling, D. 1985. *Die sieben Weisen und die frühgriechische Chronologie.* Bern.

Flashar, H. ed. 1994. *Die Philosophie der Antike. Vol. 4. Die hellenistische Philosophie.* Basel.

Flashar, H. ed. 1998. *Die Philosophie der Antike. Vol. 2/1. Sophistik, Sokrates, Sokratik, Mathematik, Medizin.* Basel.

Flashar, H. ed. 2004a. *Die Philosophie der Antike. Vol. 3. Ältere Akademie, Aristoteles, Peripatos.* 2nd. edn. Basel.

Flashar, H. 2004b. "Aristoteles." In Flashar 2004, 167–492.

Flashar, H. 2004c. "Aristoteles, Über die Philosophie." In A. Bierl, A. Schmitt, and A. Willi, eds., *Antike Literatur in neuer Deutung*, Munich and Leipzig, 257–73.

Flashar, H., D. Bremer, and G. Rechenenauer, eds. 2013. *Die Philosophie der Antike. Vol. 1. Frühgriechische Philosophie.* Basel.

Föllinger, S. 2013. "Charakteristika des Lehrdialogs." In Föllinger and Müller 2013, 23–35.

Föllinger, S., G. M. Müller, eds. 2013. *Der Dialog in der Antike.* Berlin.

Gagarin, M. 2002. "Greek Law and the Presocratics." In V. Caston and D. W. Graham, eds., *Presocratic Philosophy*, Burlington, 19–24.

Gaiser, K. 1963. *Platons ungeschriebene Lehre.* Stuttgart.

Gemelli, L. 2007. "Lire du début. Quelques observations sur les *incipit* des présocratiques." *Philosophie antique* 7: 7–37.

Gemelli Marciano, L. ed. 2010. *Die Vorsokratiker. Vol. III. Auswahl der Fragmente und Zeugnisse, Übersetzung und Erläuterungen.* Mannheim.

Gigon, O. 1946. "Antike Erzählungen über die Berufung zur Philosophie." *Museum Helveticum* 3: 1–21.

Görgemanns, H. 1994. *Platon.* Heidelberg.

Goldhill, S., ed. 2008. *The End of Dialogue in Antiquity.* Cambridge.

Heitsch, E. 2002. "Dialoge Platons vor 399 v. Chr.?" *Nachrichten Gött. Akad., Phil.-hist. Kl. Jg.* 2002.6.

Hempfer, K. W., ed. 2002. *Möglichkeiten des Dialogs. Struktur und Funktion einer literarischen Gattung zwischen Mittelalter und Renaissance.* Stuttgart.

Hicks, R. D., ed. 1925. *Diogenes Laertius. Lives of Eminent Philosophers.* 2 vols. Cambridge, MA.

Hirzel, R. 1895.*Der Dialog. Ein literarhistorischer Versuch.* 2 vols. Leipzig.

Hölscher, U. 1985. "Heraklit zwischen Tradition und Aufklärung." *Antike und Abendland* 31: 1–24.

Hoffmann, E. 1950. *Platon.* Zürich.

Jolles, A. 1958. *Einfache Formen.* 2nd edn. Tübingen.

Kahn, Ch. 1979. *The Art and Thought of Heraclitus. An Edition of the Fragments with Translation and Commentary.* Cambridge.

Kirk, G. S. 1954. *Heraclitus. The Cosmic Fragments.* Cambridge.

Koenen, L. 1993. "Der erste Satz bei Heraklit und Herodot." *Zeitschrift für Papyrologie und Epigraphik* 97: 95–6.

Krämer, H.-J. 1959. *Arete bei Platon und Aristoteles.* Heidelberg.

Laks, A. 1983/2008. *Diogène d' Apollonie: La dernière cosmologie présocratique.* 2nd. edn. St. Augustin (first 1983).

Lengen, R. 2002. *Form und Funktion der aristotelischen Pragmatie.* Stuttgart.

McKirahan, R. 2008. "Signs and Arguments in Parmenides B 8." In P. Curd and D. W. Graham, eds., *The Oxford Handbook of Presocratic Philosophy*, Oxford, 189–229.

Most, G. W. 1999. "The Poetics of Early Greek Philosophy." In A. A. Long, ed., *The Cambridge Companion to Early Greek Philosophy*, Cambridge, 332–62.

Nails, D. 2002. *The People of Plato. A Prosopography of Plato and Other Socratics.* Indianapolis.

Mouraviev, S. ed. 1999–2003. *Héraclite d'Éphèse. La Tradition Antique & Médiévale. A. Témoignages et citations.* 4 vols. St. Augustin.

Patzer, A. 2006. *Wort und Ort. Oralität und Literarizität im sozialen Kontext der frühgriechischen Philosophie.* Freiburg and München.

Patzer, A. 2012. *Studia Socratica. Zwölf Abhandlungen über den historischen Sokrates.* Tübingen.

Perilli, L. 2001. "Alcmeone di Crotone tra filosofia e scienza." *Quaderni Urbinati di Cultura Classica* 69: 55–79.

Primavesi, O. 2007. "Ein Blick in die Stollen von Skepsis: Vier Kapitel zur frühen Überlieferung des Corpus Aristotelicum." *Philologus* 151: 51–77.

Rapp, Chr. 2013. "Melissos aus Samos." In H. Flashar, D. Bremer, and G. Rechenenauer, eds., *Die Philosophie der Antike. Vol. 1. Frühgriechische Philosophie*, Basel, 573–98.

Rechenauer, G. 2013a. "Anaxagoras." In H. Flashar, D. Bremer, and G. Rechenenauer, eds., *Die Philosophie der Antike. Vol. 1. Frühgriechische Philosophie*, Basel, 740–96.

Rechenauer, G. 2013b. "Leukipp und Demokrit." In H. Flashar, D. Bremer, and G. Rechenenauer, eds., *Die Philosophie der Antike. Vol. 1. Frühgriechische Philosophie*, Basel, 833–946.

Reinhard, L. 1920. *Die Anakoluthe bei Platon.* Berlin.

Riedweg, Chr. 2005. *Pythagoras. His Life, Teaching, and Influence.* Ithaca, NY.

Riginos, L. S. 1976. *Platonica. The Anecdotes concerning the life and the writings of Plato.* Leiden.

Rose, V. ed. 1886. *Aristotelis qui ferenbantur librorum fragmenta.* Leipzig.

Rowe, C. J. 2007. *Plato and the Art of Philosophical Writing.* Cambridge.

Schneeweiß, G. 2005. *Aristoteles. Protreptikos. Hinführung zur Philosophie. Rekonstruiert, übersetzt und kommentiert.* Darmstadt.

Scholz, P. 1998. *Der Philosoph und die Politik. Die Ausbildung der philosophischen Lebensform und die Entwicklung des Verhältnisses von Philosophie und Politik im 4. und 3. Jh. v. Chr.* Stuttgart.

Schütrumpf, E. 1989. "Form und Stil Aristotelischer Pragmatien." *Philologus* 133: 177–191.

Shorey, P. 1903. *The Unity of Plato's Thought.* Chicago.

Shorey, P. 1933. *What Plato Said.* Chicago.

Stowers, S. K. 1981. *The Diatribe and Paul's Letter to the Romans.* Ann Arbor, MI.

Summerell, O. F. and T. Zimmer, eds. 2007. *Alkinoos, Didaskalikos. Lehrbuch der Grundsätze Platons.* Berlin.

Tarán, L. 1975. *Academica: Plato, Philip of Opus and the Pseudo-Platonic Epinomis.* Philadelphia.

Thesleff, H. 1967. *Studies in the Styles of Plato.* Helsinki.

Trampedach, K. 1994. *Platon, die Akademie und die zeitgenössische Politik.* Stuttgart.

Voss, B. R. 1970. *Der Dialog in der frühchristlichen Literatur.* München.

Wendland, P. 1895. "Philo und die kynisch-stoische Diatribe." In P. Wendland and O. Kern, eds., *Beiträge zur Geschichte der Griechischen Philosophie und Religion*, Berlin, 3–75.

Wilamowitz-Moellendorff, U. v. 1881. *Antigonos von Karystos.* Berlin.

Zeller, E. 1919. *Die Philosophie der Griechen in ihrer geschichtlichen Entwicklung. Erster Teil. Erste Abteilung.* 6th. edn. Leipzig.

Zhmud, L. 2013. "Pythagoras und die Pythagoreer." In H. Flashar, D. Bremer, and G. Rechenenauer, eds., *Die Philosophie der Antike. Vol. 1. Frühgriechische Philosophie*, Basel, 375–438.

FURTHER READING

Research on Greek philosophy is too large to survey briefly. Accessible routes into it, with generous bibliography, are offered on the Presocratics by Flashar, Bremer, and Rechnauer 2013; on the Sophists and Socratics, Flashar 1998; on Plato, especially, Erler 2007; on the literary form of the Platonic dialogues especially instructive are Clay 2000, Blondell 2002 and Rowe 2007; on Aristotle and the Peripatos, Flashar 2004a; on Hellenistic philosophy, Flashar 1994. Instructive on the social setting of early Greek philosophy is Patzer 2006. Gemelli 2007 provides a new bilingual (Greek–German) edition of the more important Presocratics with an instructive commentary. On the dialogue still fundamental (though outdated in its evaluations) is Hirzel 1895; important new contributions on the dialogue are presented in Föllinger and Müller 2013. On the use of the dialogue in Christian literature see Voss 1970. Goldhill 2008 stated "the end of dialogue in Christian Antiquity" – on this see now Cameron 2014. There are no more recent general accounts of the epistle. On the monologic forms see in this volume Fögen (ch. 17) and Asper (ch. 26).

CHAPTER 16

The Novel

Stefan Tilg

1.   An Un-classical Research Field and a Problem of Terminology

Unlike most other genres discussed in this volume, the Greek novel has emerged as a major field of classical studies only in recent decades. Of course, there were always individual scholars interested in the novel, and following Erwin Rohde's pioneering *Der griechische Roman*, first published in 1876, substantial work on the genre was produced especially (if not only) in continental Europe. But this tradition, like so many others, was almost completely cut off during and after World War II. It was left to a second major book, now by an American, to spark the modern interest for the Greek novel, Edwin P. Perry's *The Ancient Romances* of 1967. From then on, a steadily increasing flow of publications on the Greek novel has come forth. Apart from the fact that studies in the Greek novel still promise comparatively untrodden paths, a number of reasons have raised the genre to its current popularity, for example exciting papyrus finds, a general shift of interest towards later periods of ancient literature (compare the "discovery" of the roughly contemporaneous movement of the "Second Sophistic"), and both narratological and cultural turns in literary criticism. The growing interdisciplinary and comparative approach in the humanities also made classicists more sensitive to a genre which can be compared in many ways with today's major literary genre, the modern novel.

A problem of (English) terminology, however, must be addressed at the outset: while other major European languages have only one, capacious term to refer to longer prose fiction, English normally distinguishes between "novel" (derived from Italian "novella [storia]," "novel story"), and "romance" (derived from Old French "romanz," "narrative in the Romance language" [as opposed to Latin]). "Novel" implies a certain realism and relevance to contemporary everyday life, "romance" improbable characters and exaggerated love stories. Clearly, to a student of English literature, the area in which this distinction was established during the eighteenth century, the Greek novels would rather be romances. On the other hand, the Greek novels were probably part of the normal elite literary culture of antiquity and certainly mattered more to contemporaries than, say, modern Harlequin romances. It is with a view to stressing this

A Companion to Greek Literature, First Edition. Edited by Martin Hose and David Schenker.
© 2016 John Wiley & Sons, Inc. Published 2020 by John Wiley & Sons, Inc.

relevance that classicists today tend to speak of the Greek "novel" rather than the Greek "romance," although both terms can often be found side by side. In fact, the distinction is often enough blurred in English itself, for example when we call Tolkien's romances "fantasy novels" (cf. Trzaskoma 2010, xii). The texts discussed in this chapter can fall under both headings, depending on our perspective and the contexts in which we set them.

2. The Lack of an Ancient Theory and the Question of Genre

The issue over modern terminology would probably not exist if antiquity had created a name for the genre we call the "novel." We would simply use that name, just as we have adopted the terms "epic" and "drama" according to ancient nomenclature. But neither the novelists themselves nor their contemporaries devised a genre tag for our texts. The authors use a number of terms in more or less self-referential ways, for instance *diégema*, "narrative" (part of the title in Chariton) or *historía*, "history" (Longus in his preface, in which he playfully distinguishes his "history of love," *historía érotos*, from traditional history), but none of them becomes standard. Even more strikingly, outside the novels themselves we neither find a related genre theory nor *any* clear reference to our texts. This ancient silence about the novel has long been interpreted as contempt on the part of critics for a trivial and lowly genre, an impression increased by the fact that not a single author of a Greek novel is known otherwise. Recent scholarship, however, has plausibly suggested that the novel, as a "latecomer" to Greek literature, was ignored by literary theory simply because most literary theory was already written by the Imperial period, in which the novel arose (cf. the surveys of the problem by Bowie 1994 and 1996). A further development of the genre system after Alexandrian scholarship was prevented by the classicism of the Second Sophistic, which generally looked at the Attic masters of the fifth and fourth centuries BCE rather than at contemporary literature. And while this speaks to a preference for the old classics in literary theory, it does not necessarily suggest particular disrespect for the novel. The cases of the satirical dialogues of Lucian or the prose hymns of Aelius Aristides could be compared in that they, too, did not receive any attention from literary theory and are practically never cited.

But the silence about the novel raises a further question: if there was no genre tag for our texts, how much of a genre was the novel in antiquity at all? Here we have to distinguish between an idea of genre established by critics and an idea of genre established by literary practice. The first is imposed on the texts at a theoretical level, the second is inherent in the texts through "family resemblances." If only the first idea were valid, we would have to admit that the Greek novel was not a genre at its time and was only labeled as such by modern critics (which could still be reason enough for us to speak of the Greek novel). But this restriction would not do justice to the reality of ancient literature which, like almost all literature, was produced not on the model of some theory but on the model of other literary texts. The fact that certain strains of similar writing were then labeled as this or that by critics was secondary to a sense of belonging to a particular, if flexible and dynamic, framework of generic rules. It is true, however, that the rules of the Greek novel, at least in an inclusive definition, are more malleable than those of other major genres like epic and drama. This is due to the lack of a performative context and the more "open" prose form, which is able to mimic other genres in a number of ways. We are not particularly troubled about the openness of the novel genre in modern times and have learned, rather, to appreciate its wide range as one of its alluring features. As a consequence, we are perfectly used to binomial designations like "historical novel" or "biographical novel" in which a particular species further defines the broad genre "novel" (which to all intents and purposes equals "long prose fiction," especially if we are ready to merge novel and romance). It would have some advantages to apply a similar nomenclature to the Greek novel, but for certain reasons scholars have tended to distinguish a smaller, relatively homogeneous, core of (love) novels from a larger, diffuse, "fringe" of the genre.

3.   The Love Novel and the Importance of the "Big Five"

From its beginning, scholarship on the Greek novel has been under the spell of a body of five fully extant love novels: Chariton's *Callirhoe*, Xenophon's *Ephesiaca*, Achilles Tatius's *Leucippe and Clitophon*, Longus's *Daphnis and Chloe*, and Heliodorus's *Aethiopica*. The titles are not always clear from the transmission and the forms presented here are the conventional ones that are mostly used in scholarship (the same goes for most titles cited in this chapter). Suggestions for alternative titles result in either more homogeneity (cf. Whitmarsh 2005, favoring a generic pattern consisting of a girl's and a boy's name) or more heterogeneity (e.g. Tilg 2010, 214–7, arguing for the addition of "Narratives" [*diegémata*] in Chariton's title: *Narratives about Callirhoe*). As mentioned above, the authors are practically unknown, and we have not received any external information on their works. Nor do the texts themselves give any clear indications as to the time and place of their composition. All this makes dating a very tricky issue. The sequence provided above reflects today's most successful chronological guess, with Chariton falling in the mid-first century, Xenophon in the late first or early second, Achilles and Longus in the second, and Heliodorus in the third or even fourth (always CE).

An impression of the length of their novels may be given on the basis of the English translations collected in Reardon (1989): *Callirhoe* comes out at 103 pages (eight books), the *Ephesiaka* at 41 (five books), *Leucippe and Clitophon* at 113 (eight books), *Daphnis and Chloe* at 63 (four books), and the *Aethiopica* at 239 (ten books). Even considering that the format of Reardon's volume is larger than an average paperback, one can see that the length of at least love novels was shorter than today. Still, they are not only longer than other prose fiction like novellas, but were also published autonomously (while short prose fiction was always part of larger works).

This group of love novels shares some remarkable features in characters, setting and plot: as regards characters, the heroes are an elite couple of teenage boy and girl, with the girl usually cast in the stronger role, as well as receiving more narrative attention and characterization. The sentiment of the romantic couple is pure and idealistic (the odd ironic subversion of the pattern, especially in Achilles Tatius, may be noted), and the focus is on their private life and interests, even if questions of social integration and statehood are a considerable additional issue in authors like Chariton and Heliodorus. The heroes are also examples of piety and often turn to their tutelary gods.

The setting of our texts reflects the wide horizon of the Imperial Greek world. None is set in mainland Greece or centers of classical literature like Attica. Instead, a particular preference can be seen for the Eastern Greek world, Asia Minor, the Levant, and Egypt. But, at least in the early representatives, Chariton and Xenophon, Sicily and Greek colonies in Italy are important, too. Extended excursions to countries beyond the Greek *oikuméne*, especially Persia and (in the *Aethiopica*) Ethiopia, evince a lively interest in foreign cultures.

In terms of plot, we usually see a tripartite structure: 1) an exposition, showing the heroes' mutual falling in love and ending with their violent separation (usually at the hands of pirates or other bandits); 2) a long interval characterized by travels, adventures, and the frustrating search for the lost romantic partner; 3) finally a comparatively short happy ending, in which the lovers find each other again, get married (unless this did not happen at the beginning, as in Chariton and Xenophon), thank the helping gods, are celebrated by the people, and live happily ever after. Longus (cf. also Saïd, ch. 23, pp. 364–5 in this volume) is a notable exception to this plot rule in that he focuses on a slow but steady development of love in the adolescent teenagers instead of action adventures and spatial separation. But by playful allusions to the standard plot (e.g. both Daphnis and Chloe are briefly abducted) even Longus acknowledges his debt to it.

There are a number of further motifs which occur in all or a number of authors and help to create what we could call a web of secondary genre markers, for instance rivals in love, apparent deaths of the heroine, and courtroom scenes (cf. Létoublon 1993). In terms of narrative complexity a certain development can be seen from comparatively simple and linear narratives in the earlier love novels to intricate narrative structures in the later ones (including, e.g. extensive flashbacks, nested narratives, and the restriction of narrative perspective – Achilles Tatius even employs an ego-narrator, similar to the Roman comic novels).

Now, the particular attention given to these texts, sometimes dubbed the "big five" is due to several circumstances: (1) they are fully extant, while many other works of Greek prose fiction are transmitted only in fragments (cf. esp. Stephens and Winkler 1995) or are lost altogether; (2) they are relatively coherent; (3) there is a considerable number of them; (4) they are full-blown fiction as opposed to other novel-like literature which verges on genres like travelogue, historiography, or biography; (5) they appear to have been rather successful and their early examples *may* have, in one way or another, inspired the remarkable surge of prose fiction from the first century CE onwards.

The last point is the most critical for our assessment of the literary-historical significance of the Greek love novel, but at the same time it is the most difficult to prove. After all, there is a chance that our "big five" only look big because some lucky coincidence has preserved them. It is often hard to tell if and how they relate to other kinds of fiction. In any case, to the literary historian's eye, they float in a sea of fragmentary and fully extant texts which suggest a wide range of ancient fiction. I shall attempt to set out these texts in four groups.

4.   Fragmentary Love Novels

First, there is a group of fragmentary texts which seem to belong to the species of the love novel. Prominent examples include *Ninus* (first century CE), a highly fictionalized account of the Assyrian emperor Ninus and his love for Semiramis, in which both are portrayed as teenagers in love; *Metiochus and Parthenope* (cf. esp. Hägg and Utas 2003), another first-century novel, which takes a historical approach similar to Chariton's *Callirhoe* in that both develop their fictional plot within a historical frame; Iamblichus's *Babyloniaca* (second century CE), a somewhat over-the-top romance set in Babylon, which makes ample use of the motif of *doppelgänger* and revels in gruesome elements like crucifixion, cannibalism, and executions. In terms of research, the *Babyloniaca* is also an example for the importance of Byzantine testimonies. In particular, the patriarch Photius (ninth century CE) has provided us in his *Bibliotheca* with a wealth of information about Greek novels like Iamblichus's (cf. *Bibl. cod.* 94) which would otherwise remain very obscure to us.

5.   Family Novels

A second group may be created for texts in which the heroes are not lovers but family (although the family members may pursue their respective love interests individually). The most significant example is Antonius Diogenes' *The Incredible Things beyond Thule*, dating to the late first or second century CE. Today we know about this novel only from a number of fragments and an extensive account in Photius (*Bibl. cod.* 166). In antiquity, however, it seems to have been one of the most popular pieces of prose fiction. Its protagonists are siblings, and as the title already suggests, their adventures, which take us beyond the boundaries of the known world and even to the moon, strain common belief. We could call this a fantastic travel novel.

Another example of a "family novel" may be the Greek original of the anonymous late antique Latin *History of Apollonius, King of Tyre*. I say *may be*, because the question as to whether this text is based on a Greek or rather Latin original from the third century CE is disputed. The story is about the travels and hardships of the fictional king Apollonius and his apparent loss of wife and daughter. At the end, Apollonius is reunited with both (similarly to the lovers in the romantic novels).

Characteristic motifs like travel, shipwreck, or false death establish a close link between these "family novels" and the love novels. Usually the former are seen as dependent on the latter, but the idea cannot be excluded that, for instance, fantastic travel accounts combined with erotic stories in the vein of Antonius Diogenes existed before the first love novels, or that both kinds of novel writing developed from lost common sources. The case of Antonius Diogenes is particularly interesting because he might have written comparatively early (late first or early second century CE) and seems to have far surpassed the early romantic novels in narrative complexity (note, e.g., the famed multiple narrative frame, consisting of no fewer than seven levels of subordination; the encyclopedic character of the novel, discussing, among other things, Pythagorean philosophy; and its impressive length of 24 books, quite obviously in the footsteps of Homer's epics). It is probably false when Photius (*Bibl. cod.* 166.112a1) credits Antonius Diogenes outright as "father" of Greek prose fiction (*plásmata*), but in our picture of the Greek novel, heavily influenced by the "big five," *The Incredible Things beyond Thule* remains a striking anomaly and does not sit well with the idea of a gradual development of narrative techniques from simple beginnings to a complex end.

6.   Lowlife Novels

A third group of texts is characterized by male rogue heroes, coarse eroticism, violent horror, and a comic-satirical outlook on established conventions. All this can be seen in the fragments of Lollianus's *Phoenicica* and the anonymous *Iolaus* fragment (both second century CE). In the *Phoenicica*, for instance, the narrator is among Egyptian robbers eating the heart of a murdered boy to reinforce an oath of loyalty. A following scene of group sex and eerie costume can be read as a gothic literary version of ritual practice. Similarly, the *Iolaus* presents us with a mock ritual of *gálloi*, the castrated worshippers of the goddess Cybele.

It is an open question as to how these texts relate to Petronius's Latin *Satyrica*, which shares with them the main characteristics referred to above and a number of more specific motifs such as the parody of religious cult – the *Iolaus* fragment is even prosimetric, just as the *Satyrica* is throughout. The Greek fragments are later than Petronius (who is usually put in the Neronian period), and it is not completely unthinkable that he was read in the Greek world and set a new trend. A more likely option, however, is that both our extant Greek fragments and Petronius are indebted to preceding strains of lowlife fiction. Perhaps the mother of that kind of writing is the shadowy *Milesiaca* by a certain Aristides (c. 100 BCE; cf. Jensson 2004). Although the work is lost to us, references to it can be found throughout antiquity and even in prominent authors like Ovid (*Trist.* 2.413–20; ibid. 443–4) and Plutarch (*Crass.* 32.2). It would not be surprising if this (in)famous piece of prose fiction, whose raciness is emphasized in virtually all testimonies, had established a whole tradition of Greek and Roman lowlife fiction. Whether it was a collection of novellas set in a loose narrative frame or a more or less coherent, yet episodic, story (as in Petronius) is a matter of dispute in scholarship, with a majority of scholars tending towards the first option.

It is intriguing, however, that the second major Roman novel, Apuleius's *Metamorphoses* refers to the *Milesiaca* as early as its first sentence, in which the author promises a narrative "in that Milesian style" (*sermone isto Milesio*). The picture does not get necessarily clearer, but even more intriguing if we consider that Apuleius's novel is itself a – greatly extended – adaptation of a Greek original, the *Metamorphoseis* of so-called Lucius of Patras. While this text is lost to us (some hints as to its nature can be gathered from Photius, *Bibl. cod.* 129), an abbreviated Greek version (perhaps just an epitome) is transmitted among the works of Lucian (although Lucian might not be its author). The original Greek ass story that can be reconstructed from these sources shares some elementary characteristics with the other texts presented in this group: a male rogue hero (here turned into an ass in the course of the story); coarse sex scenes (here at least one, between a woman and the ass); and an overall comic outlook. Moreover some striking similarities between a robber scene in Apuleius and the fragments of Lollianus have been remarked upon (summarized in Stephens and Winkler 1995, 322–4). If nothing else, this again suggests a certain coherence between our lowlife novels.

It is possible, therefore, to see the remainders of the Greek lowlife novel as part of a larger and relatively autonomous universe of Greek and Latin lowlife fiction. Another account, which has been very successful in Petronius studies, would be that it was precisely the success of the first Greek love novels which prompted a satirical reaction in the shape of lowlife fiction. If we look at Petronius's *Satyrica*, there are certainly a number of motifs which can be read as parodies of related motifs in the love novels: the high social standing of the heroes would be downgraded, the idealistic boy–girl love would turn into predominantly male vulgar sex, the piety of the protagonists into comic subversion of religion. A number of motifs familiar from the romantic novels like shipwrecks and suicide attempts are also prominent in Petronius and could easily be taken as comic allusion to the love novels, especially as in the *Satyrica* they are taken to melodramatic heights. In further consequence, it could be argued that later Greek lowlife novels joined this parodic fashion and thus became a whole species of the novel genre. In this account, then, the lowlife novel would be essentially dependent on the love novel, and the *Milesiaca* would have had far less influence on its development.

7. Fringe Novels

Finally, I come to the fourth and most difficult group. It has been asked whether this group still belongs to the novel genre or, rather, just shares some elements with it. The term "fringe novels," popularized (if not invented) by Niklas Holzberg and inviting to think in categories of center and periphery, is often applied to the texts in question. The web of motifs characteristic of the texts discussed so far is less tightly knit here. What is more, this group is very diverse in itself, and consists of a number of different strands. The main reason why we can group them under a single heading is a common element of fiction. Characteristically, however, the texts concerned consistently pose as something else, for instance travelogues, biography, letters, historiography, or hagiography. Suffice it to adduce selected prominent examples.

The lost utopian travelogue of the Hellenistic writer Euhemerus of Messene is recalled in Diodorus Siculus (5.41–6; 6.1). It describes an (imaginary) journey to an unknown island in the Indian Ocean and the ways of its indigenous society. Particular interest is given to the fact that their gods are deified humans, an idea still known to us under the name of "Euhemerism." In the second century CE, Lucian seems to have parodied imaginary travelogues like this in his programmatically false *True Story*, in which he claims, among other things, to have travelled to the moon and into the belly of a whale. Philostratus's *Life of Apollonius of Tyana* (early third century CE), embroidering the life of the Pythagorean philosopher Apollonius, is an example from the biographical strain, just as is the popular *Alexander Romance* (extant version from the third century CE), which fuses elements of historiography, oral tradition and utopian literature in order to create an exciting story about the life of Alexander the Great.

Collections of fictional letters, dating from the first to second centuries CE, went under the names of Plato, Euripides, Hippocrates, Aeschines, Chion, and Themistocles. Their focus is on the relationships of their supposed writers to political power and the powerful: for instance, of Plato to the tyrant of Syracuse, Dionysius II, or of Plato's lesser known pupil, Chion, to the tyrant Clearchus of Heraclea. Not unlike modern epistolary novels, the narrative perspective in these works is restricted to the letter writer, and any developments surrounding him can only be inferred from his letters.

The so-called *Troy Romances* of so-called Dictys Cretensis and Dares Phrygius (the extant Latin versions are from the fourth/fifth century CE; an earlier Greek version is certain for Dictys and possible for Dares), pretend to give true historical accounts of the events surrounding the Trojan war and the return of the Greek heroes.

Last but not least, Christians soon discovered the potential of prose fiction and used it in a number of apocryphal Acts (most of them extant only in fragments) and in hagiographical writing. A remarkable example is the *Clementine Romance* (extant in a Greek and Latin version from the fourth century CE), the fictional autobiography of Peter's successor on the holy see, pope Clement. It shares some elements with the family novels referred to above, as it starts with the separation of young Clement from his parents and brothers and ends with a happy reunion with them. Other motifs like travel and shipwreck also establish a relatively close link with the novels discussed above.

8. The Elasticity of the Greek Novel

After this brief survey we are in a better position to ask whether the love novel as represented by the "big five" should be seen as the origin and the center of the Greek novel *tout court*. I have already discussed how each of groups 2–4 *may not* hinge on the love novel. It could be added that it is even possible to turn the tables and argue that the love novel is itself a reaction to earlier, perhaps lowlife, kinds of novel writing (cf. e.g. Tilg 2010, 32–6 and 146–55). If the love novel moves out of the center, however, this will affect our whole idea of the Greek novel as a genre. We would certainly include groups 2 and 3 as full-fledged novels, but we might also reconsider our view of the "fringe" texts which mimic other genres. Somewhat confusingly, modern scholarship often addresses them as "romances" anyway (cf. conventional titles like *Alexander Romance*, *Troy Romance*, and *Clementine Romance*).

Should our "novel" tag be elastic enough to accommodate these variegated strains of prose fiction too? From a modern perspective little can be objected to this. Who, for example, would dispute that Marguerite Yourcenar's *Memoirs of Hadrian* is a novel, although it consistently poses as the autobiography of the Emperor Hadrian? We may ask whether the Greeks of the Imperial period were able to adopt a certain "willing suspension of disbelief" or a "contract of fictionality" in the same way as we do, but in the absence of an elaborate ancient theory of fiction and fictionality no conclusive answer to this question can be given. Gorgias's (c. 480–380 BCE) remarks on the aesthetic "deception" (*apáte*) of drama, in which "the deceived is cleverer than the non-deceived" (DK 82 B 23) is at least reminiscent of Coleridge's dictum about the "willing suspension of disbelief." What is more, the theory of late Hellenistic rhetoric about literary narrative (cf. Cic. *Inv.* 1.27; *Rhet. Her.* 1.12–13) clearly shows some awareness of fiction in our sense, especially in the category of *argumentum*, defined as "fictional, yet possible events" (*ficta res, quae tamen fieri potuit*). Ultimately, we also have to acknowledge that the complex ways fiction interacts with reality eludes critics, let alone a larger reading audience, even today, and I doubt if even the most learned reader of the *Memoirs of Hadrian* will be able to completely separate his or her picture of the historical Hadrian from Yourcenar's compelling invention.

9. On the Origin and Significance of the Greek (Love) Novel

I have reserved two big questions for the end: where does the Greek novel come from and what did it mean to people? Given that the genre lacks both performative context and ancient theory, these – often correlated – questions are much more difficult to answer for the novel than, for instance, for epic or drama (although they are not easy there either). On the other hand, considering the elasticity of the genre, it is also hard to give a single answer for all species of the novel. Again a look at our own, extremely diversified, novel genre may be helpful. Who would dare to say how *the* novel matters to *us*? In fact, virtually all considerations of the questions of origin and general significance have revolved around a particular group of texts, the love novel, seen as the center and origin of all ancient novel writing. A critical account of the related theories is therefore all I can give here.

Generally, a shift from mostly literary-historical approaches towards mostly cultural approaches can be observed in modern scholarship. Rohde (1914), for instance, argued that the Greek love novel is a literary cross between fictional travelogue and Hellenistic love poetry, created in the rhetorical milieu of the Second Sophistic. Others traced the love novel back to a range of other genres. In epic poetry, the *Odyssey* certainly deserves pride of place and provides a number of parallels in plot and motifs (e.g. travel, adventures, and final happy reunion of man and wife). Novelists like Chariton and Heliodorus clearly acknowledge their debt to Homer through quotations, extended allusions, and parallels in plot (in Heliodorus, for instance, the heroine is presented as sort of female Odysseus on her *nostos* to Ethiopia). More generally, the novel has often been seen as the natural prose successor of epic, the major narrative form of earlier periods (an idea that can variously be connected with the development of society and literary centers, from a more court-centered, aristocratic, literary culture towards a more open, broader, one). Drama, especially New Comedy, has often been suggested as the origin of the novel because of its freely invented plots and its love stories. Most novelists also make extensive use of dramatic terminology and effect, e.g. when Chariton (5.8.2) comments on a surprising turn of events that "no dramatist (*poietès epì skenés*) ever staged such an astonishing story." But a number of other genres, such as historiography and rhetoric, have also been identified as possible nuclei of the novel. The problem with this approach is that the love novel seems to be indebted to virtually all preceding genres and it is difficult to identify any single one at the cost of others. On the other hand, little would be gained if we included too many genres in the (soon inflationary) equation and proposed that the novel emerged from a combination of epic, drama, historiography, rhetoric, and so on.

This, and a general uneasiness with a purely formal account, has prompted a number of cultural theories about the origin and meaning of the Greek love novel. I only touch on the more or less failed hypotheses of Braun (1938), who suggested that the first novels (including love novels such as *Ninus*) were an outlet of the rising nationalism among non-Greek peoples in the Hellenistic world, and of Kerényi (1927) and Merkelbach (1962), who argue that the love novels have a hidden religious meaning. The dominant idea from Perry (1967) to the 1990s was that the love novel is the genuine literary expression of a pessimistic world view of Hellenistic man, deprived of his traditional life in the polis and thrown into the endless and anonymous expanses of an international *oikuméne*. This sense of forlornness would be reflected in the wandering of the heroes, whereas the happy ending would give the promise of comfort and individual happiness needed for the masses (who are the imagined readership here). Over the last two decades, however, this model has been completely discredited: it has been shown that the novel was a phenomenon of the imperial rather than the Hellenistic period; that polis culture remained central to Greek life; that the alleged pessimism of a whole society is a modern projection; and that the readership of the novels were probably the same elites that read Homer or Thucydides.

To date, no alternative model has found widespread acceptance, but there are two main trends. One is the use of the anthropological model of passage rites to explain the tripartite structure of the love novels. In this model, a pre-liminal phase, introducing the as yet immature heroes, is followed by a liminal phase, characterized by separation from the community and maturation of the heroes' characters, which then leads on to a post-liminal phase including their reintegration into society. The purpose of this "ritual poetics" would be the optimistic celebration of Greek polis life. The second trend partly overlaps with the first and gives it direction: it attempts to read the love novels as expressions of identity of Greek elites under Roman rule. Against this background, the celebration of Greek polis life has been interpreted quite differently, either as veiled protest *against* (e.g. Swain 1996, 101–31, esp. 109 and 130) or as praise *of* Roman rule (e.g. Whitmarsh 2011, 31).

However, even if we leave other strands of novel writing out of the account and focus on the love novel or even the early love novel (represented esp. by Chariton and Xenophon), it may be doubted that a wholesale generic approach could do justice to our individual texts. Although they share a certain matrix, all extant examples have a quite different character: Chariton explores fiction within a historiographical frame, Xenophon is happy with fast-paced adventures, Achilles Tatius at times verges on parody, Longus cross-breeds the novel with the pastoral and Heliodorus uses his epic novel to allude to higher philosophical truths. It would be easy to imagine that an individual author (Xenophon has recently been suggested by O'Sullivan 1995; Chariton by Tilg 2010) at some point hit on a successful literary formula and that others jumped on the bandwagon, not because they or their readers felt that the form carried some well-defined social meaning but because they were eager to bring their own literary variations to it. What is more, if we return to the possibility that the love novel may not have been the center of the novel genre, how much of its alleged cultural significance could it retain?

Perhaps we will have to be content with the observation that the novel (in its broad sense) was a remarkable addition to Greek literature in the Imperial period. Of course, some elementary developments on the literary and culture plane paved its way, for instance the rise of fiction as in New Comedy, the rise of prose in the imperial period, and the "globalization" of the Mediterranean world in Hellenism and the Roman Empire. Once these conditions were met, the novel could have taken its start at any time, from one or many origins. In any case it provided contemporaries with a new, large-scale, means to explore literary ideas and identities in a fictional world, and is a testimony to the vitality and dynamics of later Greek literature – its lasting influence can be seen, e.g., in the European seventeenth-century romances, which were very much under the spell of Heliodorus. How far each of these fictions relates to the culture of its time may be better examined individually than generically.

REFERENCES

Bowie, E. 1994. "The Readership of Greek Novels in the Ancient World." In J. Tatum, ed., *The Search for the Ancient Novel*, Baltimore, 435–59.

Bowie, E. 1996. "The Ancient Readers of the Greek Novels." In G. Schmeling, ed., *The Novel in the Ancient World*, Leiden, 87–106.

Braun, M. 1938. *History and Romance in Graeco-Oriental Literature*. Oxford.

Cueva, E. R. and S. N. Byrne, eds. 2014. *A Companion to the Ancient Novel*. Chichester.

Hägg, T. and B. Utas. 2003. *The Virgin and Her Lover: Fragments of an Ancient Greek Novel and a Persian Epic Poem*. Leiden.

Holzberg, N. 1995. *The Ancient Novel: An Introduction*. London.

Holzberg, N. 2006. *Der antike Roman*. 3rd edn. Darmstadt.

Jensson, G. 2004. *The Recollections of Encolpius: The* Satyrica *of Petronius as Milesian Fiction*. Groningen.

Kerényi, K. 1927. *Die griechisch-orientalische Romanliteratur in religionsgeschichtlicher Beleuchtung: Ein Versuch*. Tübingen.

Létoublon, F. 1993. *Les lieux communs du roman: stéréotypes grecs d'aventure et d'amour.* Leiden.

Merkelbach, R. 1962. *Roman und Mysterium in der Antike.* Munich.

O'Sullivan, J. 1995. *Xenophon of Ephesus: His Compositional Technique and the Birth of the Novel.* Berlin.

Perry, B. E. 1967. *The Ancient Romances: A Literary-Historical Account of Their Origins.* Berkeley, CA.

Plazenet, L. 1997. *L'ébahissement et la délectation: Réception comparée et poétiques du roman grec en France et en Angleterre aux XVIe et XVIIe siècles.* Paris.

Reardon, B. P., ed. 1989. *Collected Ancient Greek Novels.* Berkeley, CA.

Rohde, E. 1914. *Der griechische Roman und seine Vorläufer.* 3rd edn. Leipzig.

Schmeling, G., ed. 1996. *The Novel in the Ancient World,* Leiden.

Schmeling, G., ed. 2003. *The Novel in the Ancient World.* rev. edn. Boston.

Stephens, S. A. and J. J. Winkler. 1995. *Ancient Greek Novels: The Fragments.* Princeton, NJ.

Swain, S. 1996. *Hellenism and Empire: Language, Classicism and Power in the Greek World, AD 50–250.* Oxford.

Tilg, S. 2010. *Chariton of Aphrodisias and the Invention of the Greek Love Novel.* Oxford.

Trzaskoma, S. M. 2010. *Two Novels from Ancient Greece: Chariton's* Callirhoe *and Xenophon of Ephesos'* An Ephesian Story: Anthia and Habrocomes. Indianapolis.

Whitmarsh, T. 2005. "The Greek Novel: Titles and Genre." *American Journal of Phililogy* 126: 587–611.

Whitmarsh, T., ed. 2008. *The Cambridge Companion to the Greek and Roman Novel.* Cambridge.

Whitmarsh, T. 2011. *Narrative and Identity in the Ancient Greek Novel: Returning Romance.* Cambridge.

FURTHER READING

Holzberg 1995 is a good introduction for newcomers to the field, although the English translation, based on the first German edition of 1986, is outdated at times. The 3rd German edition (Holzberg 2006) is more up to date. Schmeling 1996 is the best handbook of the ancient novel and provides reliable and clearly structured articles on most areas. The revised edition (Schmeling 2003) contains a bibliographical supplement. Whitmarsh 2008 is an up-to-date account of social contexts, themes, form, and reception. See now also Cueva and Byrne 2014.

CHAPTER 17

Technical Literature

Thorsten Fögen

1. Introduction

This chapter offers a succinct overview of Greek technical literature. Given the enormous number of texts that fall under this category, the material and ideas that are discussed here represent only a small fraction of what could be said about ancient technical writing. First of all, an attempt is made to define the term "technical literature" and draw attention to the diversity of the large corpus of texts. In the next part, methodological issues are highlighted and some questions are proposed that research on ancient technical literature needs to consider. A synoptic section examines the extent to which ancient technical texts share certain characteristics, in particular with regard to technical terminology, pragmatic and stylistic features, and the role of illustrations. The final section surveys some examples of Greek technical writing: Aristotle and Theophrastus, various medical authors (the *Corpus Hippocraticum* and Galen), Xenophon, and the grammarian Dionysius Thrax.

2. What is "Technical Literature"?

The generic term "technical" is rather unspecific. It is derived from the Greek adjective τεχνικός, which belongs together with the substantive τέχνη, meaning "skill," "craft," "art," or even "cunning"; it has been assumed that τέχνη may be related to the word τέκτων, which normally refers to a craftsman, in particular a carpenter or joiner, and which is probably etymologically connected with the Sanskrit verb *tákṣati* ("fabricate," "elaborate"; cf. the Latin verb *texĕre*: "sew," "weave"). If individuals who practice such a craft or skill follow a certain set of rules or a specific method, knowledge becomes systematic and may constitute a discipline whose principles can be taught and handed down in the form of treatises. Therefore the word τέχνη can also designate a manual that is used for the transmission of learning; adjectives usually specify the type of discipline, e.g. τέχνη γραμματική ("art of grammar") or τέχνη ῥητορική ("art of rhetoric"). It goes without saying

A Companion to Greek Literature, First Edition. Edited by Martin Hose and David Schenker.
© 2016 John Wiley & Sons, Inc. Published 2020 by John Wiley & Sons, Inc.

that there are many disciplines (τέχναι) whose practitioners develop specialist knowledge that has been preserved in the form of written texts, e.g. medicine and pharmacology, mathematics, geography, philosophy, cosmology, astronomy, rhetoric, grammar, architecture, mechanics, warfare, agronomy, or musicology. Unfortunately, many of these ancient treatises have been lost.

Although it seems justified to argue that technical literature transmits knowledge and has a didactic goal, it cannot be denied that different manifestations of this genre exist. This is also suggested by the existence of various terms such as εἰσαγωγή, συναγωγή, ἐγχειρίδιον, ὑπόμνημα, τέχνη, λόγος, πραγματεία, ἐπιτομή, διήγησις or σύνοψις and their Latin equivalents, but the problem is that many of them may be employed for rather diverse types of texts and do not always indicate their specific pragmatic qualities (see van der Eijk 1997, 80, 90). In Graeco-Roman antiquity, the boundaries separating a practical–instructive text (defined primarily on the basis of subject matter) from a literary–aesthetic text (classified primarily on the basis of form) were much more fluid than they are today. This led to a broad spectrum of text types in the technical engagement with a subject, including mere tables of numbers, randomly arranged collections of material that resemble notes or jottings, short and easily intelligible introductions, comprehensive handbooks that endeavor to cover the principles and doctrines of a certain discipline in a systematic and representative way, and highly specialized treatises on particular questions that presuppose a great deal of expertise. Knowledge can also be transmitted in the form of dialogues (e.g. Plato's works and Xenophon's *Oeconomicus*), sometimes embedded in the context of the symposium (e.g. Athenaeus' *Deipnosophistae*), or in the form of letters (see e.g. Epicurus; for letters in medical instruction, see Langslow 2007), or even through didactic poetry that combines instruction with edification.

In order to differentiate between these text types, it may be helpful to rely upon criteria offered by modern pragma- and text linguistics, which analyzes texts within concrete communicative contexts (see e.g. Kalverkämper 1983, Göpferich 1995, Kalverkämper and Baumann 1996, and Wolski 1998). A text is regarded as a complex, thematically and conceptually coherent unit through which a verbal act with a specific communicative meaning is performed. The intention and function of a text is constituted through internal factors, but also through external factors such as addressee, situation, relationship between communicative partners, social background, etc. It is, however, questionable whether such an analytical framework is sufficient to develop a fully coherent classification of text types and their characteristics and functions. One may nonetheless arrive at certain prototypes that are suitable at least for a rough systematization.

The diverse character of the extant prose treatises makes it impossible to maintain that ancient technical texts do not pursue *any* aesthetic or even artistic intentions or that they are always more concerned with content than form. Moreover, they are rarely neutral; indeed, sometimes they can be quite polemical and include attacks on opponents. In many cases, the authors of technical writings seek to insert their presence into their texts; adopting the role of the *je scientifique* ("scientific I"), they are eager to stylize themselves as scholarly as well as moral authorities – a feature that is widespread in other genres, in particular in historiography.

Given the huge amount of variety in ancient technical literature, it seems more appropriate to apply the concept of a generic continuum that takes into account the heterogeneity of the texts subsumed under this heading. Moreover, it must be borne in mind that the character of any given technical text may also be quite heterogeneous in content and style, especially when its author subscribes to the compositional principle of variation (ποικιλία), combining, for example, the exposition of factual knowledge with anecdotal material, moral concerns or socio-political issues.

3. Approaches to Ancient Technical Literature

Although so-called technical writings constitute a considerable portion of the corpus of extant Greek and Latin texts, they are not always given sufficient attention in modern histories of ancient literature, which tend to focus on *belles lettres* represented by genres such as epic, lyric, drama, historiography, or the novel. Given that classical scholars have always published very extensively on ancient technical literature, this may seem very surprising. However, since the *literary* nature of these texts has rarely ever been analyzed more thoroughly, it may become more understandable why overviews and handbooks do not adequately discuss their significance. The vast majority of studies have concentrated on the contents (i.e. the doctrines and ideas) rather than the form of ancient technical texts. In most cases, they have been analyzed for the investigation of scientific knowledge and technologies or for the reconstruction of social and economic conditions in the Graeco-Roman world. In addition, technical literature has been studied for linguistic purposes, with special emphasis on technical terminology. Since the 1990s there has been a constant rise in the number of editions, commentaries, translations and interpretations of ancient technical texts. However, comparative approaches that move beyond the examination of one particular author or discipline are still relatively rare. Only recently have scholars made an attempt to read and understand technical texts as "literature." Many studies that have appeared during the past 20 years have finally moved away from a misguided aesthetic evaluation of technical texts that unjustly tries to weigh them against other genres. Instead, modern approaches explore the specific literary character of technical literature (in particular their narrative and didactic strategies), its social context and its political implications.

Research on ancient technical texts needs to consider the following questions which may, to some extent, also be applied to modern technical literature (see Fögen 2009, 23–4): How is knowledge presented and conveyed? What purpose does technical writing have and who are its intended addressees (novices, laymen, advanced readers, experts)? How extensive are the media for the transmission of knowledge and what are their micro- and macrostructures? What is the function of non-textual elements such as illustrations, formulae, tables etc.? Do certain disciplines have specific traditions of learning and teaching? Do these entail a particular type of rhetoric such as an author's claim of innovation, clarity and intelligibility (σαφήνεια), conciseness (συντομία), usefulness (ὠφέλεια, τὰ χρήσιμα), or concentration on the essential as well as the practical? To what extent do authors use such claims to construct a particularly favorable image of themselves and to disparage writers who work in the same field? What is the role of polemics in ancient technical writing? What is the status of technical writers? Are they real experts whose observations are derived from personal observation (ἐμπειρία and αὐτοψία), or are they armchair scholars who obtain their knowledge from existing books without having acquired practical experience in a certain discipline? Is it justified to apply the term "professionalism" to the ancient world? What constitutes a discipline and how is it perceived by its adherents as well as outsiders? How do technical writers present themselves to their readers? What are the authorities, past and present, to whom they refer? What is the relationship between the writers' self-perception and the actual shape and content of their treatises? For example, do the principles frequently outlined in their prefaces correspond to the rest of the works, or do they just represent topical elements of rhetoric which are seen as indispensable in the context of an introduction that dwells upon methodological issues? Even the title of a technical text may reveal the author's intention or at least a certain program to which he subscribes; he can thus influence the reader's expectations, as is demonstrated by the discussions of titles of technical writings in the prefaces to Pliny the Elder's *Naturalis historia* (praef. 24–7) and Aulus Gellius' *Noctes Atticae* (praef. 4–10).

This admittedly non-exhaustive catalogue of important considerations makes it obvious that the study of technical communication should not ignore its social dimension. Some of the above aspects may be developed further: What is the relationship between a technical writer and society? What kind of status does technical knowledge and its dissemination enjoy among certain social groups? How and under which circumstances do technical texts originate? Which role do dedications (to emperors, politicians, colleagues, friends, interested laymen, etc.) play? Have certain texts been commissioned, for example by their dedicatees? And do such commissions spring from an economic rationale such as the desired improvement of the production of goods or the cultivation of land? Is there a political interest in certain elements of knowledge, for example in the field of warfare and military techniques? How and by whom is knowledge transmitted? Who has access to the media that convey technical information? Are there any elites that generate forms of arcane wisdom reserved for an exclusive minority, in particular in a philosophical or religious setting? Is it possible to observe the development of certain research communities or schools, and how are they related to each other? Ultimately, the aforementioned concerns can be summarized under the more general question of how the social and cultural practices of the Greek and Roman societies are mirrored in technical literature.

For every technical work, the answers may vary considerably; generalizations that are applied to an entire group of texts are rarely helpful. In many cases, it will be impossible to fully reconstruct the social and cultural background of ancient scholarly writings, especially given the difficulty that determining their target audience entails. Nonetheless, a carefully considered methodological framework or at least a set of questions as sketched above will provide valuable guidelines for further enquiries.

4. Some General Characteristics of Ancient Technical Texts

4.1. Technical Terminology

Specialized communication requires specific linguistic tools that scholars have classified under the rubric of technical languages (*Fachsprachen*) and/or special languages (*Sondersprachen*), defined as varieties of a language that are limited in use to certain occupations or professions (group-specific speech forms), but still exhibit a certain overlap with non-technical varieties, in particular with the standard language (see e.g. Cousin 1943, 37–9; Fögen 2009, 13–19, with further references; see also the two-volume handbook edited by Hoffmann, Kalverkämper, and Wiegand 1998–1999). The most conspicuous feature of technical languages is their specific vocabulary, the so-called technical terminology. Terms as part of technical communication within highly developed disciplines tend to be greatly conventionalized and standardized; ideally, they are neutral, unambiguous and monoreferential, so that their meaning within a certain field is independent of any context. However, even technical vocabulary is not completely invariable and may change over time. Technical languages are not exclusively characterized by their specific vocabulary; they also have particular morphological, syntactical and pragmatic structures (see Cousin 1943, 45–52; Thesleff 1966; Fögen 2009, esp. 26–66; Schironi 2010).

Technical terms are frequently discussed by ancient Greek and Roman writers. Early medical writers and Aristotle devote a great deal of attention to terminology (see e.g. Louis 1956 and Lloyd 1983, 152–7; 1987, 183–214; see also Lloyd 2002, 98–125), as do later representatives of other disciplines. There is a clear awareness that all areas of scholarship rely upon terminologies that diverge from everyday speech (see e.g. Galen, *De nominibus medicis* p. 8.13–20 Meyerhof and Schacht; Apollodorus of Damascus p. 138.13–17 W. [= p. 10 Schneider]). The medical writer Rufus of Ephesus emphasizes that a better understanding of a discipline can only be gained through a familiarity with the terminology that it uses (*De nominatione partium hominis* p. 133.1–134.14 Daremberg and Ruelle). Galen, a representative of the same field, devotes a great deal of attention to terminological issues, yet at the same time he repeatedly warns that an obsessive fixation on words may be misguided, as it is likely to lead to unfruitful debates (e.g. *Ad Thras.* 31 [V 864 Kühn], 32 [V 867 Kühn], *Ars med.* 36 [I 405 Kühn], *De optima nostri corporis constitutione* 1 [IV 738–9 Kühn]).

In general, technical terms in ancient texts are easily recognizable for the reader, since they are often accompanied by definitions or certain indicators such as the participle καλούμενος (-η, -ον) or an explanatory relative clause or parenthesis. This proves that many ancient writers feel the need to explain the terms that they use in order to make them as intelligible as possible for their readers. Already in antiquity, there is an awareness of several problems in connection with technical terminology, such as the relationship between technical terms and words occurring in everyday speech, problems with terminological variants, the semantic shift of technical terms, and word-formation through metaphors and metonymy (see Fögen 2009, 39–48).

4.2. Some Pragmatic and Stylistic Features of Ancient Technical Texts

Despite the diversity of ancient technical writings, it is possible to discern some pragmatic and stylistic elements that recur in a sufficiently large number of works. In several instances, technical writers reflect on the specific shape of their treatises, in particular in their prefaces, which may also refer to their target audience. While it cannot be denied that such self-reflexive passages frequently exhibit a topical character and may not always be compatible with the actual nature of the works themselves, they nonetheless indicate which elements and qualities authors regarded as constitutive for a technical text and how they strove to fulfill certain presumed expectations of their readers.

A characteristic feature that is repeatedly emphasized is the careful disposition of the material in which the author of the text claims to have invested a great deal of effort (see e.g. Pedanius Dioscurides, *De mat. med.* praef. 3–5; further Philon, *Belop.* 49 W. [p. 106 Marsden = p. 240 Köchly and Rüstow vol. 1]). In some cases, the systematic arrangement of facts and figures is presented as an advantage over other works whose authors are said to have been less meticulous with regard to structure.

Some writers have attached a table of contents to their treatises to provide their readers with a helpful overview. This is a particularly convenient tool for busy users such as kings or politicians who do not have time to digest the entire work; precisely for that reason, the military writer Aelian, who dedicates his *Tactica* to the emperor Trajan (regn. 98–117 CE), places a table of contents at the outset of his proem (*Tact.* praef. 7, p. 238 Köchly and Rüstow [vol. 2.1]). Several Roman technical authors such as Scribonius Largus (*Comp.* praef. 15, p. 6–16 Sconocchia) and Pliny the Elder (*Nat. hist.* praef. 21–3; with the table of contents following right after the preface) use similar strategies for analogous purposes (see Fögen 2009, 211–14).

The postulate of systematicity is frequently connected with that of linguistic clarity and non-ambiguity (σαφήνεια), as can be seen from writers such as Hippocrates (*De vet. med.* 1–2, esp. 2.3 [I 570–74 Littré]), Heron (*Belop.* 73–4 W. [p. 18 Marsden = p. 202 Köchly and Rüstow vol. 1]), Arrian (*Tact.* 1) or Galen (*De puls. diff.* 4.3 [VIII 723–4 Kühn = Herophilus F 150 von Staden]), to name but a few. The precise definition of perspicuity can be gleaned from rhetorical texts. Quintilian, the Roman professor of oratory writing in the first century CE, recommends the following strategies (*Inst. orat.* 8.2): Words ought to be used in a way that does not deviate from their original or principal meaning. Elements that are not part of common usage, such as archaisms, neologisms, and regionalisms, should be rejected. In addition, an unclear syntactical structure, extremely lengthy sentences, hyperbata or long parentheses ought to be avoided, as they are likely to create ambiguity. The precision of a technical text may also be increased by the insertion of illustrations or graphic sketches, as will be discussed in the subsequent section. The decision to write intelligibly may be induced by a certain type of readership, in particular in cases where very little or no prior disciplinary knowledge can be presupposed.

Apart from systematicity and clarity, ancient technical writers regularly ponder the adequate scope and size of their works. While such factors undoubtedly depend on several criteria, in particular the target audience, authors are typically eager to limit their exposition to the essential and refrain from including superfluous elements. Hippocrates is an early example of this method (see e.g. *De aere aquis locis* 12.1–2 [II 52 Littré = CMG I.1.2 p. 54.4–8]), *Morb. sacr.* 1 [VI 354 Littré]). Several centuries later, Athenaeus Mechanicus, an engineer living in the first or second century CE, polemicizes against verbosity and pleads for a concentration on the most important facts (p. 3.1–7.6 W. [= p. 8–12 Schneider]). In some texts, conciseness is achieved through the avoidance of repetition; for that purpose, cross-references to other chapters of the same work or to different treatises are a useful means (see e.g. Aeneas Tacticus 7.4, 8.5, 21.1–2, 40.8). However, brevity (συντομία) is a virtue that has its limits. Less well-educated readers will be lost if a text is too condensed and does not provide enough explanations; moreover, extreme succinctness may jeopardize the comprehensiveness and representativeness of a work. For that reason, the medical writer Apollonius of Citium is keen to achieve a reasonable balance in his commentary on the Hippocratic text *De articulis*, as he repeatedly underscores (*De art.* 3 [CMG XI 1.1 p. 66.23–5, p. 86.6–7 and p. 96.4–6]); at the same time, he wants his text to be exhaustive (*De art.* 1 [p. 10.14–15], 2 [p. 50.9–11, p. 62.3–7], 3 [p. 64.10–17, p. 104.9–14]). That the pragmatic and stylistic appropriateness or suitability of a technical text is largely determined by its users is often acknowledged, in particular by writers who have produced vastly different works for the needs of distinct groups of readers. For example, in his short overview *On My Own Books*, Galen illustrates how his writings, depending on their target audience, vary with regard to length, style and theoretical sophistication (*Lib. prop.* praef. [XIX 10–11 Kühn], 2 [XIX 22–3 Kühn] and 5 [XIX 33 Kühn], further *De ordine librorum suorum* 1 [XIX 49 Kühn] and *De pulsibus ad tirones* 1 [VIII 453 Kühn]).

From such testimonies one may get the impression that the bulk of technical texts can be associated with what ancient rhetorical theory referred to as the "simple style" (see Lausberg [3]1990, esp. 519–25). While it may be true that the majority of technical authors focus on instruction and factual information and do not deal with any sublime themes, it is misguided to believe that they all completely dispense with any stylistic pretensions. Above all, prefaces are a suitable place for a writer's self-presentation, which is accomplished to a large extent through stylistic choices. However, elements of an elevated style may also be discerned beyond introductions that are supposed to catch the reader's attention. The narrow boundaries of a simple style may be transcended in the form of exempla, illustrations, excursuses, tales, or anecdotes (sometimes of a historical, biographical, or autobiographical nature) that are inserted into the didactic narrative; sometimes texts are interspersed with single lines or longer stretches of verses that are adduced to support an argument through poetic authorities (especially Homer). A more refined style and the inclusion of poetry in technical prose may also be interpreted as mechanisms to create aesthetic pleasure for the audience, in particular for its more learned members, who would presumably appreciate such techniques. At the same time, the avoidance of stylistic dryness and of an unadorned rendering of bare facts may be motivated by a paedagogical impetus: readers who enjoy a certain text will be more receptive to the ideas suggested in it and memorize them more easily.

4.3. The Role of Illustrations

Despite substantial efforts to ensure the intelligibility of a technical text, words alone may not always guarantee absolute clarity, in particular in areas such as mechanics, mathematics, astronomy, biology, medicine, or warfare, which necessitate the description of complex machinery, bodily organs, or geometrical figures. In such cases verbal exposition is sometimes supplemented with illustrations to avoid misunderstandings on the part of the reader. As the reproduction of such illustrations tended to be rather demanding for the copyists of manuscripts and required a certain degree of expertise, numerous illustrations occurring in ancient technical texts have not been preserved in their original configuration. However, it can be gathered from the textual references to figures, diagrams or other sketches as well as from legends that they were a relatively widespread phenomenon in ancient technical writing (for details, see Stückelberger 1994).

An early example of the integration of pictorial representations in technical texts is Aristotle's lost work *De dissectionibus* (Περὶ ἀνατομῶν), presumably an illustrated anatomical atlas, as is suggested by some references in his *Historia animalium* and *De partibus animalium* (e.g. *Hist. an.* I 17 497a30–33, III 1 511a12–14, IV 1 525a8–9; see Stückelberger 1994: 74–8). In a passage in *De partibus animalium*, Aristotle accentuates the different purposes of verbal and pictorial descriptions (*Part. an.* IV 5 679b34–680a3); yet as the *Historia animalium* proves, they can be combined: in the sections on testicles, spermatic cords and bladders (*Hist. an.* IV 1 510a29–35) as well as on the development of the cuttlefish (*Hist. an.* V 18 550a25–7), graphic sketches are accompanied by descriptive legends.

In his work *De articulis* (Περὶ ἄρθρων), a commentary on the eponymous Hippocratic treatise on the surgical treatment of dislocations, the medical writer Apollonius of Citium (first century CE) attaches great importance to intelligibility and therefore recurrently adds illustrations to his text (*De art.* 1 [CMG XI 1.1 p. 14.7–11]; on methodological issues see also *De art.* 2 [p. 38.1–17]). Apollonius uses this method because he considers the occasionally unclear style of the Hippocratic text to be problematic (*De art.* 3 [CMG XI 1.1 p. 112.7–11]; similarly *De art.* 2 [CMG XI 1.1 p. 38.18–21 and ff.]). In his opinion, medical expertise requires practical knowledge, gained through direct personal experience, which makes it easier to visualize the precise meaning of medical texts. With his illustrations, he intends to contribute to a better understanding of how to treat dislocations in the right way.

Immediate transparency was also the motive for writers of other disciplines to incorporate graphic elements. In some treatises on warfare and military machinery the use of sketches is portrayed as an innovation, for example in Aelian's *Tactica* from the early second century CE (*Tact.* 18.1 [p. 334 Köchly and Rüstow vol. 2.1]). In the preface to his *Belopoiika* Heron of Alexandria (presumably first century CE) explicitly states that he writes for experts as well as laymen (*Belop.* 73–4 W. [p. 18 Marsden = p. 202 Köchly & Rüstow vol. 1]; see also Athenaeus Mechanicus p. 39.7–9 W. [= p. 36 Schneider]); it is thus evident that the function of his illustrations is to enable the latter in particular to gain a better understanding of the subject matter. Testimonies such as this one prove once again that it was one of the objectives of technical authors to use a variety of strategies in order to guarantee σαφήνεια of their texts and thus reach as many readers as possible.

5. Some Examples of Greek Technical Writing

5.1. Aristotle and Theophrastus

Among Greek technical authors, Aristotle (384–322 BCE) is undoubtedly among the most widely read. He produced innumerable works on nearly every branch of learning (see, for example, the extensive list of titles in Diogenes Laertius 5.22–7) and has thus rightly been regarded as a true polymath. The sheer size of his work and in particular the amount of data assembled in his biological and historical writings would suggest that he must have had research assistants who compiled information for him through journeys of enquiry, excerpting previous writers' books, or other forms of investigation. Aristotle's extant works, however heterogeneous they may be, often resemble collections of material, scripts or notes of lectures; since their initial use seems to have been restricted to the members of the Peripatos, they usually presuppose a certain familiarity with the topics discussed. For obvious reasons, the authorial persona is far less present than in the works of later writers, and consequently the endeavor for a more elaborate or pleasing style is limited or even non-existent. The scientific character of Aristotle's works is constituted in various ways: he takes a serious interest in the history of the problems that he explores and thus renders comprehensible the basis of his own analysis. He subscribes to the principle of empiricism (see e.g. Lloyd 1970, 99–124; 1979, esp. 200–225) and does not ignore the research of previous scholars. The development of a systematic terminology is apparent, although the technical vocabulary that he coins frequently reveals a proximity to common usage (see e.g. Louis 1956 and Lloyd 1983, 152–7; 1987: 183–214). It is therefore no exaggeration to regard Aristotle as the founding father of modern science and scholarship. At the same time, it must not be overlooked that Aristotle also composed literary texts for a larger audience, predominantly in the form of dialogues. The loss of these exoteric works leaves us with an incomplete picture of a multifaceted authorial personality.

Aristotle's most influential pupil was Theophrastus of Eresus (371–287 BCE) who succeeded him as director of the Peripatos after his death. According to Diogenes Laertius (5.42–50), he was also extremely prolific, but unfortunately the vast majority of his works have not been preserved in their entirety. However, from the extant texts, in particular from the treatises on the natural sciences, it is possible to classify Theophrastus as a writer who, like his master, is indebted not only to systematicity and the judicious use of categories, but also to an empirical approach. As he postulates, the description of plants must be based upon personal observation (θεωρία; see e.g. *Hist. plant.* 1.1.1 and 1.14.4). Although Theophrastus follows Aristotle in many respects, he is by no means uncritical of his doctrines (see e.g. Lloyd 1973, 8–15; 1987: 148–55).

5.2. *Medical Writers: the Corpus Hippocraticum and Galen*

Among ancient technical texts, medical and pharmacological treatises constitute a remarkably large corpus. Perhaps the most famous representatives of this field are Hippocrates (fifth century BCE) and Galen (129–199 CE). Over 60 works written in Ionic dialect have been transmitted as the so-called *Corpus Hippocraticum*, although it is unclear which of them are by the historical Hippocrates. This collection comprises quite heterogeneous treatises written over a period of roughly 500 years, the most recent of which might not have been composed until the first century CE (see e.g. Lloyd 1970, 50–65; see also Thesleff 1966, 107–12; van der Eijk 1997). The prognostics, based upon the careful observation of symptoms and the progression of a disease, as well as the study of individual cases of a certain illness and its different manifestations, can be classified as a specific element of Hippocratic medicine (see Fögen 2005c, esp. 291–3, with further references).

However, ancient medical texts do not restrict themselves to the description of symptoms or case studies; they may also consider how the environment influences the physical and mental wellbeing of people, as is demonstrated, for example, by the short Hippocratic treatise *On Airs, Waters and Places*, probably written during the late fifth century BCE (on this text cf. Asper, ch. 26, p. 404 in this volume). With its 24 chapters, it is addressed to the travelling expert who continually needs to evaluate the specific nature of the places that he visits in order to successfully practice as a healer. A careful assessment of the topography, the climate, the quality of waters and earth as well as the living and eating habits of the citizens of a particular region will lead to insights into the typical local diseases and their treatment (see *De aere aquis et locis* 1–2 [II 12–14 Littré]). Familiarity with the analytical principles of geography, climatology, hydrology, astronomy and dietetics are thus prerequisites for a successful practitioner of medicine.

It is interesting to note that the second half of the text (§§ 12–24) transcends the boundaries of medicine and moves into the sphere of anthropology and ethnography when it declares that climate and environment have a significant impact on the physiognomy, intellect and character of the inhabitants of a specific territory. For example, Asia, with its cultivated land and ideal climate, epitomizes the perfect balance of extremes (ἰσομοιρίη) and thus generates a human race that is "gentler and better-tempered" (*De aere aquis et locis* 12 [II 52–4 Littré]); at the same time, it does not foster bravery, courage, toughness, or industriousness, although the lack of such virtues may to some extent be rooted in Asia's monarchical system (*De aere aquis et locis* 12 [II 54–6 Littré] and 16 [II 62–4 Littré]). The ideas outlined in this treatise must be seen as the expression of certain tendencies that do not claim any absolute validity. A contrast is made not only between Asians and Europeans, but also between members of each group, again due to environmental and climatic factors (see esp. *De aere aquis et locis* 24 [II 86–92 Littré]). This treatise is an early example of how scientific observations may be expounded alongside other agendas such as ethical and political issues. Although the text does not enthusiastically sing the praises of Athenian democracy and its constitution based upon the principle of liberty, it is hard to overlook that it evokes a rather negative image of Asian monarchy.

Ancient medical texts also contain a great deal of information on the medical profession. As the success of doctors was determined by their reputation, they were eager to create a positive image of themselves. It is therefore not surprising that some treatises deal with their outward appearance and conduct (see Fögen 2005c, esp. 289–91). For example, the Hippocratic work *The Doctor* is addressed to young surgeons at the beginning of their medical studies and advises them on how to present themselves correctly towards their patients. In addition to a healthy appearance and a well-balanced temperament, the medical practitioner ought to be morally impeccable (see esp. *De medico* 1 [IX 204–5 Littré]). In the treatise *On Decent Behavior*, the author recommends that medical expertise should be combined with wisdom (σοφίη), dignity, restraint, and decent behavior, qualities that are likely to establish a solid reputation (*De decenti habitu* 3). Such remarks exhibit not only the existence of social expectations and the requirement to comply with them, but also the competition between doctors that compelled them to promote themselves as scholarly experts as well as morally upright citizens (see e.g. Lloyd 1979, 86–98).

How far self-advertisement may proceed and how rhetoric is instrumentalized for that purpose can be observed in the sizeable oeuvre of Galen of Pergamon, court physician of the emperor Marcus Aurelius (for some sophisticated readings, see Asper 2007, esp. 304–11 and 323–67; see also Lloyd 1973, 136–53, further Meißner 1999, 226–45). No other medical writer talks as extensively about his life and activities as he does. With his fierce polemics, he often criticizes the general medical standards of his own time and tries to distinguish himself from other specialists by postulating that medicine and philosophy must be closely related; in particular in his concise outline *The Best Doctor is also a Philosopher* (Ὅτι ὁ ἄριστος ἰατρὸς καὶ φιλόσοφος), he emphasizes the importance of endowing the medical practitioner with systematic training in areas such as physics and logic as well as with a firm moral foundation (see Fögen 2009, 115–17, with further references). He is indeed so famous that inauthentic or unauthorized works are published under his name, which induces him to catalogue his own writings (*Lib. prop.* praef. [XIX 8–10 Kühn]). However, Galen is not really an exception: well-calculated self-presentation as a result of the agonal structure of many professions is a feature that can be observed throughout ancient technical writing (see Fögen 2009, passim).

5.3. *Xenophon*

Xenophon (c. 430–after 355 BCE) is normally identified with historical works such as the *Anabasis*, *Hellenica* and *Cyrupaedia* or his Socratic writings such as the *Memorabilia*, *Apologia* and *Symposium*, but less so with technical treatises, although he published several of them: the *Cynegeticus* on hunting, the *Ways and Means* (Πόροι) on economic issues, two essays *On the Cavalry Commander* (Ἱππαρχικός) and *On Horsemanship* (Περὶ ἱππικῆς); even his *Oeconomicus*, one of his Socratic texts that deals with agriculture, can be classified as technical.

The *Oeconomicus*, "the earliest extensive eulogy of rural life in Greek prose" (Pomeroy 1994, 254), is a dialogic text about the principles of estate management. Socrates recounts to Critobulus how the estate owner Ischomachus described to him his daily life and duties. In the fifth chapter, agriculture is praised for its essential social function and its usefulness (*Oec.* 5.1–2; see also 15.4). Its high value is attributed to the fact that it teaches justice (δικαιοσύνη) and social competence (*Oec.* 5.12–14, 6.10). Socrates goes so far as to regard agriculture as the "mother and nurse of the other arts" (*Oec.* 5.17). It is repeatedly emphasized in the text that agricultural expertise can be acquired effortlessly by observing and imitating the practices of other workers (*Oec.* 6.9, 15.4, 15.10; see also 16.1–5, 18.9–10 and 19.17–19). Personal experience is crucial for success in this field, while the value of theoretical knowledge based upon the study of books is rejected (*Oec.* 16.1; compare later approaches such as the Roman writer Columella's in his *De re rustica*, for which see Fögen 2009, 152–200). Some scholars have argued that the dialogic form of the *Oeconomicus* is a mere ornament and that the invocation of the figure of Socrates, who was not known for his interest in economic issues, is an irritating choice. However, such opinions ignore the didactic function of the dialogue, which enables Xenophon to introduce a setting that presents Socrates as a teacher, asked by Critobulus for training in a discipline that he has not yet mastered. The oral character of his instruction signals how skills in the field of agriculture ought to be passed on, and thus nicely reflects the criticism brought forward against purely theoretical knowledge developed in books. Socrates can be interpreted as a mediator between a real expert (Ischomachus) and a disciple (Critobulus). Since Critobulus was not present at the debate between Socrates and Ischomachus, Socrates explains to him what he has learned from Ischomachus and thus assumes the role of an indirect or auxiliary adviser (for details, see Föllinger 2005, 223–6).

The *Cynegeticus*, whose authenticity has occasionally been questioned for stylistic reasons, is introduced by a rather long mythological section on the origins of hunting and the use of hunting dogs (*Cyn.* 1), which gives the author an opportunity to display a rhetorical proficiency that serves to ennoble the discipline dealt with in this work. However, as is typical of many ancient technical treatises, what follows after the proem is written in a far less elaborate style. In addition to the explanations of hunting techniques as well as the selection and training of suitable hunting dogs, which constitute the major part of the text (*Cyn.* 2–11), Xenophon also points out the various benefits to be derived from this activity (*Cyn.* 12, but see already *Cyn.* 1.18): it strengthens one's health, offers a most appropriate preparation for military duties, and provides sound moral guidance, in particular for those who want to acquire virtue (ἀρετή) and become good citizens – advantages that all serve as clear indicators of the usefulness of this treatise (see also *Cyn.* 13.7). Xenophon's encomium on the merits of an honorable way of life induces him to conclude his treatise in a more elevated style, and he thus correlates this section with the introduction. In the very final chapter (*Cyn.* 13), which may, however, be a spurious addition, he even eloquently defends the educational value of hunting and censures the teaching methods of the sophists – further testimony of the ubiquity of polemics in ancient technical literature.

In comparison with the *Cynegeticus* the proem to the work *On Horsemanship* (Περὶ ἱππικῆς/ *De re equestri*, written shortly after 365 BCE; see Althoff 2005) is not only much more condensed but also less artistic. Right at the beginning, Xenophon underscores his personal experience (ἐμπειρία) in this field and delineates the target audience of his little book, namely "his younger friends" who are to be envisaged as amateurs or non-specialists (ἰδιῶται) as opposed to the professional cavalry commander (see *De re equ.* 2.5, 12.14), the addressee of the Ἱππαρχικός; hence the relationship between Xenophon and his audience is that of a teacher and his pupils, a constellation familiar from didactic poetry. He also mentions Simon of Athens, who already produced a work on horsemanship (of which no more than a short fragment of a few pages in a modern edition has survived), pays tribute to his authority, and promises to cover all aspects that Simon omitted; this statement thus skilfully combines the expression of an appropriate amount of respect for a predecessor with the pretension to surpass the achievement of an earlier expert, a feature that is quite prevalent in ancient technical literature (see Fögen 2009, esp. 27–34). As Althoff (2005, esp. 244, 246–7) has shown, the tone of Περὶ ἱππικῆς is more formal and distanced than that of the Ἱππαρχικός, motivated perhaps by the fact that Xenophon's work on horsemanship was meant to reach a wider circle of readers, which made the use of the rather personal second person singular less suitable.

The example of Xenophon demonstrates that a single author is capable of writing technical treatises of a rather different nature. While this may be explained by a certain desire for variety, it seems more convincing to argue that the style and form of a technical work are determined by a variety of parameters, in particular by its didactic purpose and its audience. An author's decision to give his text a specific structure is certainly not a matter of chance.

5.4. *Dionysius Thrax*

The *Τέχνη γραμματική* of Dionysius Thrax, as we have it today, is a short grammatical treatise of no more than 20 paragraphs that refrains from any stylistic pretensions (for an edition, translation and commentary see Lallot 1998; see also the English translation by Kemp 1987 and the volume edited by Law and Sluiter 1998; cf. Nünlist, ch. 19, pp. 297–8 in this volume). Dionysius was a pupil of the Alexandrian scholar Aristarchus of Samothrace (c. 216–144 BCE), which places him in the second half of the second century BCE. The author of the *Τέχνη γραμματική* nowhere refers to himself, which, among other things, has led some scholars to believe that the work is spurious and belongs to a later period. The author's identity and literary agenda are not even revealed in the succinct preface, which begins straightaway with a definition of grammar ("the empirical knowledge of the general usages of poets and prose writers") and then lists its six different domains, thereby summing up the typical tasks of Alexandrian philologists of the third and second centuries BCE, who engaged in particular in the editing and exegesis of texts of earlier Greek authors, in particular Homer: the reading of texts with correct pronunciation (ἀνάγνωσις ἐντριβὴς κατὰ προσῳδίαν), explanation of poetic tropes (ἐξήγησις κατὰ τοὺς ἐνυπάρχοντας ποιητικοὺς τρόπους), elucidation of obscure words and of stories (γλωσσῶν τε καὶ ἱστοριῶν πρόχειρος ἀπόδοσις), reconstruction of etymologies (ἐτυμολογίας εὕρεσις), discovery of regular patterns (ἀναλογίας ἐκλογισμός), and a critical assessment of poetic works (κρίσις ποιημάτων). However, the actual *Τέχνη γραμματική* covers only very little of these areas: after four extremely short sections on reading (§ 2), accentuation and punctuation (§§ 3–4) and rhapsody (§ 5), the main focus is on letters and syllables (§§ 6–10) and the eight traditional parts of speech (§§ 11–20: noun, verb, participle, article, pronoun, preposition, adverb, and conjunction). As is so often the case in ancient grammatical handbooks, syntax is largely ignored.

Given the nature of the work, the absence of the "scientific I" or of a direct address to the reader is not astonishing: Fuhrmann (1960, 29–34, 145–55) has categorized the *Τέχνη γραμματική* as belonging to the type of "systematic treatise" with common features of rigorous organization, definition and classification. With its clear focus on the systematization of grammatical terms and their exemplification, it was presumably written for users who had already gained a substantial degree of familiarity with the principles of linguistics and simply required an overview that they would consult as a concise compendium. It was not conceived of as an introduction to Greek for foreign learners who had little to no previous experience with the language. On the contrary, the treatise offers a synthesis of the system of the Greek language and explains how the words of a given text ought to be described and classified.

6. Conclusion

This survey, which for reasons of space could only give a very cursory treatment of technical writing and its practitioners, has devoted special attention to some recurrent features that characterize this type of literature despite its remarkable diversity. Of particular importance is the question of how the utilitarian presentation of factual information is combined with other purposes. Technical texts were not written in a vacuum or neutral climate; they frequently expose an explicit or implicit social, political or ethical agenda that can be related to the historical circumstances in which they originate. For that reason, the analysis of how technical authors perceive and present themselves as well as their discipline to their readers, how they construct authority and value systems, and how knowledge and power are linked must be viewed as a fruitful approach to a complex range of documents (see e.g. van der Eijk 1997, 120; Fögen 2009, passim). Hence, the study of ancient technical literature, if done properly, is much more than a narrowly focused history of ideas or scholarship; instead, it can serve as a fruitful enquiry into the cultural and social practices of the Graeco-Roman world.

There has been a welcome increase in scholarship on ancient technical literature in recent years, and a range of editions, commentaries, translations, edited collections, and case studies have done much to illuminate the formal characteristics, literary strategies and communicative idiosyncrasies of the genre. Yet despite several groundbreaking publications it is hard to ignore the fact that a lot more work has to be done. Numerous technical texts are not yet accessible in critical editions that satisfy modern standards, to say nothing about translations. Furthermore, it is impossible to treat Greek and Latin technical writers separately; regardless of some divergences, they share a great many common attributes, the comparative analysis of which will contribute to a better understanding of what constitutes and characterizes ancient technical writing. Another worthwhile task, however arduous and challenging it might be, is the contrasting of Graeco-Roman science and scholarship with other research cultures, for example the Chinese (see e.g. Lloyd 1996 and 2002). Finally, given the strong influence that Graeco-Roman antiquity has had on later periods, a stronger collaboration between classicists and modern philologists who engage in the study of contemporary scientific literature and specialized communication seems equally desirable.

REFERENCES

Althoff, J. 2005. "Form und Funktion der beiden hippologischen Schriften Xenophons *Hipparchicus* und *De re equestri* (mit einem Blick auf Simon von Athen)." In T. Fögen, ed., *Antike Fachtexte – Ancient Technical Texts*, Berlin, 235–52.

Asper, M. 2007. *Griechische Wissenschaftstexte. Formen, Funktionen, Differenzierungsgeschichten*. Stuttgart.

Cousin, J. 1943. "Les langues spéciales." In *Mémorial des Études Latines. Offert par la Société des Études Latines à son fondateur Jules Marouzeau*, Paris, 37–54.

Eijk, P. J. van der. 1997. "Towards a rhetoric of ancient scientific discourse. Some formal characteristics of Greek medical and philosophical texts (Hippocratic Corpus, Aristotle)." In E. J. Bakker, ed., *Grammar as Interpretation. Greek Literature in Its Linguistic Context*, Leiden, 77–129.

Fögen, T. 2005a. "Antike Fachtexte als Forschungsgegenstand." In Fögen 2005b, 1–20.

Fögen, T., ed. 2005b. *Antike Fachtexte – Ancient Technical Texts*. Berlin.

Fögen, T. 2005c. "The role of verbal and non-verbal communication in ancient medical discourse." In S. Kiss, L. Mondin, and G. Salvi, eds., *Latin et langues romanes. Études de linguistique offertes à József Herman à l'occasion de son 80ème anniversaire*, Tübingen, 287–300.

Fögen, T. 2009. *Wissen, Kommunikation und Selbstdarstellung. Zur Struktur und Charakteristik römischer Fachtexte der frühen Kaiserzeit*. Munich.

Föllinger, S. 2005. "Dialogische Elemente in der antiken Fachliteratur." In T. Fögen, ed., *Antike Fachtexte – Ancient Technical Texts*, Berlin, 221–34.

Fuhrmann, M. 1960. *Das systematische Lehrbuch. Ein Beitrag zur Geschichte der Wissenschaften in der Antike*. Göttingen.

Göpferich, S. 1995. *Textsorten in Naturwissenschaften und Technik. Pragmatische Typologie – Kontrastierung – Translation*. Tübingen.

Hoffmann, L., H. Kalverkämper, and H. E. Wiegand, eds. 1998–1999. *Fachsprachen. Ein internationales Handbuch zur Fachsprachenforschung und Terminologiewissenschaft*. Berlin.

Horster, M. and C. Reitz, eds. 2003. *Antike Fachschriftsteller. Literarischer Diskurs und sozialer Kontext*. Stuttgart.

Kalverkämper, H. 1983. "Gattungen, Textsorten, Fachsprachen. Textpragmatische Überlegungen zur Klassifikation." In E. W. B. Hess-Lüttich, ed., *Textproduktion und Textrezeption*, Tübingen, 91–103.

Kalverkämper, H. and K.-D. Baumann, eds. 1996. *Fachliche Textsorten. Komponenten, Relationen, Strategien*. Tübingen.

Kemp, A. 1987. "The *Tekhnē grammatikē* of Dionysius Thrax translated into English." In D. J. Taylor, ed., *The History of Linguistics in the Classical Period*, Amsterdam, 169–89.

Kullmann, W. and J. Althoff, eds. 1993. *Vermittlung und Tradierung von Wissen in der griechischen Kultur*. Tübingen.

Kullmann, W., J. Althoff, and M. Asper, eds. 1998. *Gattungen wissenschaftlicher Literatur in der Antike*. Tübingen.

Lallot, J. 1998. *La grammaire de Denys le Thrace. Traduite et annotée*. 2nd edn. Paris.

Langslow, D. R. 2007. "The *Epistula* in ancient scientific and technical literature, with special reference to medicine." In R. Morello and A. D. Morrison, eds., *Ancient Letters. Classical and Late Antique Epistolography*, Oxford, 211–34.

Lausberg, H. 1990. *Handbuch der literarischen Rhetorik*. 3rd edn. Stuttgart.

Law, V. and I. Sluiter, eds. 1998. *Dionysius Thrax and the Technē grammatikē*. 2nd edn. Münster.

Lloyd, G. E. R. 1970. *Early Greek Science. Thales to Aristotle*. London.

Lloyd, G. E. R. 1973. *Greek Science after Aristotle*. New York.

Lloyd, G. E. R. 1979. *Magic, Reason, and Experience. Studies in the Origins and Development of Greek Science*. London.

Lloyd, G. E. R. 1983. *Science, Folklore and Ideology. Studies in the Life Sciences in Ancient Greece*. Cambridge.

Lloyd, G. E. R. 1987. *The Revolutions of Wisdom. Studies in the Claims and Practice of Ancient Greek Science*. Berkeley, CA.

Lloyd, G. E. R. 1996. *Adversaries and Authorities. Investigations into Ancient Greek and Chinese Science*. Cambridge.

Lloyd, G. E. R. 2002. *The Ambitions of Curiosity. Understanding the World in Ancient Greece and China*. Cambridge.

Louis, P. 1956. "Observations sur le vocabulaire technique d'Aristote." In *Mélanges de philosophie grecque offerts à Mgr. Diès*, Paris, 141–9.

Meißner, B. 1999. *Die technologische Fachliteratur der Antike. Struktur, Überlieferung und Wirkung technischen Wissens in der Antike (ca. 400 v. Chr.–ca. 500 n. Chr.)*. Berlin.

Pomeroy, S. B. 1994. *Xenophon: Oeconomicus. A Social and Historical Commentary*. Oxford.

Santini, C., I. Mastrorosa, and A. Zumbo, eds. 2002. *Letteratura scientifica e tecnica di Grecia e Roma*. Rome.

Schironi, F. 2010. "Technical languages. Science and medicine." In E. J. Bakker, ed., *A Companion to the Ancient Greek Language*, Oxford, 338–53.

Stückelberger, A. 1994. *Bild und Wort. Das illustrierte Fachbuch in der antiken Naturwissenschaft, Medizin und Technik*. Mainz.

Thesleff, H. 1966. "Scientific and technical style in early Greek prose." *Arctos* 4: 89–113.

Wolski, W. 1998. "Fachtextsorten und andere Textklassen. Probleme ihrer Bestimmung, Abgrenzung und Einteilung." In L. Hoffmann, H. Kalverkämper, and H. E. Wiegand, eds., *Fachsprachen. Ein internationales Handbuch zur Fachsprachenforschung und Terminologiewissenschaft*, Berlin, 457–68.

FURTHER READING

The monographs by Lloyd (1970, 1973, 1979, 1983, 1987, 1996, 2002), Meißner (1999), and Asper (2007) are extremely valuable and thorough studies of ancient Greek (and Roman) technical literature. Fuhrmann (1960) is an earlier work that takes a special interest in the structural dimension of technical writings, which are subsumed under the category of the "systematic treatise." Among edited volumes, in particular Kullmann and Althoff (eds.) (1993), Kullmann, Althoff and Asper (eds.) (1998), Santini, Mastrorosa and Zumbo (eds.) (2002), Horster and Reitz (eds.) (2003), and Fögen (ed.) (2005b) deserve to be mentioned. A research bibliography which also lists titles dealing with technical languages and didactic poetry can be found in Fögen (2005a). With a particular focus on the period of the early Empire (first century CE), Fögen (2009) examines not only the lexical, morphological, syntactical and pragmatic characteristics of ancient technical writing, but also various forms of self-presentation of the authors of these texts and their specific rhetorical strategies. The social and ethical aspects of ancient scholarship are also explored; this includes questions such as progress of knowledge, openness and secrecy in the distribution of information and expertise, as well as the practical use and the political dimensions of knowledge (including ideologies and value systems).

PART IV

The Players

The Plane

CHAPTER 18

The Creators of Literature

Mary Lefkowitz

1. Introduction

Much as we would like to know about the lives of the creators of ancient Greek literature, we have access to only a small amount of historical information, and only a small proportion of that can aid us in gaining a deeper understanding of the iconic texts that have inspired European writers throughout the centuries. To take just one example: we have virtually no historical data about Homer, the author whose work was best known and most widely read in the ancient Greek world. Even his name, which means "hostage," appears to be a *nom-de-plume*. No ancient source offers any explanation of how he was able to compose the *Iliad* and the *Odyssey*, which are by far the longest ancient narrative poems that have come down to us.

We know only a little more about later writers. Ancient sources provide us with plausible dates for those who lived in the sixth century and after, and often tell us the titles of what they wrote. But we have no continuous or detailed biographies or contemporary physical portraits. There seem to have been no archives that ancient literary biographers could consult, other than public inscriptions, such as the list of victors in the dramatic competitions in Athens. The raw materials that ancient biographers had at their disposal were the writers' own works or comic poetry about them, such as statements in the first person, and it was from these that they extracted such information as they could about authors' lives. To give shape to their narratives, biographers drew on mythic patterns, such as the stories of heroes who died violent deaths in exile; some included incidents of divine favor or intervention, such as portents in a writer's infancy or early youth that indicated that he would later become famous. But even though ancient literary *Lives* are primarily fictional, the very fact that they exist is an indication that writers were highly regarded by their own societies, especially after their deaths, when some were worshiped as heroes (Alcidamas F 3 Muir = Arist. *Rhet.* 1398b).[1] Writers were among the few whose achievements were thought worthy of individual remembrance, along with politicians, kings, and generals.

Given this dearth of factual information about historical literary figures, in this chapter I shall refer to the ancient biographies only selectively. Instead I shall make use such historical

A Companion to Greek Literature, First Edition. Edited by Martin Hose and David Schenker.
© 2016 John Wiley & Sons, Inc. Published 2020 by John Wiley & Sons, Inc.

information as we have to provide an overview of who the authors were and what they were able to achieve, deriving from what they wrote and others wrote about them a sense of their relation to other literary figures and to their audiences.

2.   Archaic Poets

Throughout antiquity the poems of Homer and Hesiod were studied in schools; every educated person knew their works and learned to read by copying out their verses and reciting them. The various accounts of Homer's life try to account for the accessibility of his works, even to uneducated people, by making him a man of the people, educated, but without money, and a native of Asia Minor, because he composed in a dialect like that spoken in that part of the Greek world. Because the *Iliad* describes the tenth year of the Trojan war, and the events of the *Odyssey* take place in the ten years that followed it, biographers claim that Homer lived not long after the fall of Troy and made his living by entertaining and teaching others.[2] Although treated with respect by most people, he also encounters hostility, and dies in isolation while traveling.

Homer's biographers do not try to explain how he was able to compose all the works later attributed to him. They also assume that he composed without the aid of writing. In his biographies he is a rather less fortunate version of the Phaeacians' blind bard Demodocus in the *Odyssey*, who is taught by the Muses (*Od.* 8.63–4). Homer tells us nothing specific about himself because in his epics he uses the first person only to introduce new themes and to acknowledge his debt to the Muses. In a first-person statement in the *Iliad*, he says nothing about himself that might identify him; instead, he gives all the credit for his knowledge to the Muses (*Il.* 2.484–93). Hesiod's name ("he who emits the song") may be a *nom-de-plume* like Homer's.[3] But he says more about himself than Homer does, telling us that his father came from Cyme in Asia Minor to Ascra in Boeotia (*Op.* 633–40) and claiming that he has been cheated by his brother (*Op.* 37–41). He describes how the Muses came to him while he was herding his sheep on Mt. Helicon, gave him a laurel branch and told him to sing of "the family of the blessed ones who live forever" (*Theog.* 22–34). As the daughters of Memory, the Muses were able to teach him all about seafaring, even though he had never made a sea voyage (*Op.* 662). Hesiod also tells us that he won a prize for his singing at funeral games that took place around 700 BCE (*Op.* 654–7). Because biographers had no certain information about the dates of either poet, they supposed that his principal competitor was Homer.[4]

Poets from Homer on faithfully acknowledge the help that they have received from the Muses (*Il.* 2.491–92). Perhaps because they had no means of understanding the nature of the human mind, and for hundreds of years were not even aware of its precise location in the body, poets always speak of inspiration as if it came from outside of themselves, and speak of it as a physical substance, like dew or honey. Biographers later interpreted the poets' metaphorical descriptions as literal portents; it was said of several poets and even of the prose writer Plato (Cic. *De div.* 1.78; Plin. *Nat. Hist.* 11.55) that in their early youth bees had built a honeycomb in their mouths.[5] This strange portent is not inappropriate: the gift of genius is a burden as well as a sign of divine favor, and a reminder that poetry can bring pain as well as pleasure.

The poets who provide specific information about themselves are the authors of shorter occasional poems composed in elegiac or lyric meters. They emerge as personalities because they tell us about events in their lives, and often mention the names of friends and family. Archilochus of Paros (c. 680–640 BCE) was a soldier as well as a poet, and wrote in vivid detail about his exploits, military and sexual, real and imaginary. We have even more information about the opinions of early sixth-century poet and statesman Solon because he was an Athenian, and most of the classical Greek literature that has come down to us was written by residents of that city. After his death Solon was celebrated for his ethical pronouncements, and listed as one of the Seven Wise Men. Solon's poems about political issues were quoted by Aristotle, and he was remembered after his death as a political reformer who gave common people a voice in the governance of the city. But since Solon's poetry is our principal source of information about Solon, we should not assume that he (or any other poet) was always objective about his accomplishments.[6] Poets tell their audiences what they want them to know, which may or may not be a historically accurate description of exactly who they were or what they actually did.

Solon's contemporary, Alcaeus of Lesbos, spoke about local politics in his poetry, and appears to have invented the metaphor of the ship of state (F 6 V). Sappho of Lesbos, who lived around the same time, describes the landscape of her island, and speaks about her love for young girls; later it was thought that she ran a school for young women (S 261A SLG), but the girls she mentions may have been members of a *helikia* or group of ten age-mates, who sang and danced together during their childhood.[7] In the seventh century there were local poets even in Sparta, where in later times entertainment was discouraged. Fragments survive of the mid-seventh-century poet Alcman's *partheneion*, a choral poem sung by girls dancing in honor of a goddess like Artemis in a local festival (F 1 PMGF). Tyrtaeus of Sparta wrote patriotic elegiacs that were said to have been sung by Spartan hoplites as they marched into battle.

Even though they lived in fiercely independent communities, Greeks throughout the Eastern Mediterranean were bound together by language, religion, and culture. Poets could move from one town to another throughout the Greek world, and apparently still be understood, even when they sang in a different dialect. Biographers imagined that Homer was one of these traveling poets, born near Smyrna in Asia Minor, and that he traveled widely in the course of his lifetime. They presumed that he knew about the geography of the island of Ithaca because he had traveled there before his eyesight failed, eventually went to the island of Chios, where later there was a school of Homeridae ("sons of Homer"), and that he died on the island of Ios, where he was said to have been buried. These stories, although essentially fictional, reflect the peripatetic nature of many later poets' lives.

The sixth-century Ibycus of Rhegium in Western Italy ended up at the court of the tyrant Polycrates of Samos, an island near the coast Asia Minor. There he appears to have written poetry that entertained and flattered his host; such poems of praise composed for secular occasions may have been the precursors of the odes commissioned for victors in athletic contests (F 282 PMG). The poet Anacreon went to Polycrates' court after his homeland of Teos in Asia Minor had been attacked by the Persians; he also spent time in Abdera in Thrace and in Athens. Later he was best known for poems about banquets and love affairs; the style and metrical patterns of his poems were widely influential, and imitated well into the Byzantine Era.[8] Xenophanes of Colophon in Asia Minor (570–c. 468 BCE) claimed to have spent most of his life traveling: "seventy years tossed and turned my thoughts around the land of Hellas" (F 7 IEG). His elegiac poems exhorted his listeners to think in new ways, suggesting that people placed too little value on wisdom (F 2 IEG), and pointing out that human beings created the gods that resembled themselves (F 13 IEG).

3. Fifth-century Poets

The increasing prosperity of the fifth century allowed poets to travel even more widely. A wealthy family brought Simonides of Ceos (b. 556 BCE) to Thessaly; he was also invited to Syracuse and other cities in Sicily and Southern Italy to present odes celebrating victories in athletic contests. He wrote a long elegiac poem about the Greek cities that won the second war against Persia (481–79 BCE), comparing them to the Greek heroes who fought at Troy. He was invited to the court of the tyrant Hieron of Syracuse, who commanded the Greek army that defeated the Carthaginians outside of Naples in 480 BCE. Hieron and his brother-in-law, Theron of Acragas, also brought to Sicily the lyric poet Pindar of Thebes (518–446? BCE) to celebrate their victories at Olympia and Delphi. Pindar started to write victory odes in the 490s, and soon became famous throughout mainland Greece and the western Greek colonies. Hieron's victory in the horse race at Olympia in 476 BCE was celebrated both by Pindar (*Ol.* 1) and Simonides' nephew Bacchylides of Ceos (*Ode* 5).[9] The Athenian dramatist Aeschylus (525/4–456/5 B.C.) was also present; his drama *Women of Aetna* (TrGF 3 T 1.9) was performed to celebrate the founding of the city Aetna in 476/5 BCE.[10]

All that remains of Simonides' poetry are fragments quoted by later authors, but 45 of Pindar's victory odes are preserved in their entirety, celebrating the victories at festivals that drew athletes from all over the Greek world. We also have extensive fragments of his paeans, and a papyrus manuscript with 19 of Bacchylides' poems. Both Pindar and Bacchylides drew on the myths related in the *Iliad* and *Odyssey* and other epics that were well known at the time but survive now only in fragments or brief summaries. Simonides and Bacchylides both wrote lucid and exciting narratives, but of the three Pindar was by far the most original, forging new metaphors, changing and rewriting traditional plots, concentrating his narratives on the particular moments that had the greatest relevance to the general observations that he wished to make in his poems. Individuals and cities throughout mainland Greece and Sicily and the Aegean islands commissioned poems from Pindar for a variety of celebrations. He appears to have attended some of these in person; in other cases (e.g., *Ol.* 6, *Pyth.* 3) he may have sent a delegate to perform the ode and/or supervise its performance. Both in style and in character he appears to have been the antithesis of the impoverished and lonely Homer. Pindar boasts of his aristocratic lineage, and in his poems speaks as if he were the social equal of his patrons.

Pindar's victory odes in particular were admired in antiquity and have been ever since, for their exciting language, ingenious narrative, and profound reflections on human experience, although both ancient and modern critics have often found his poetry difficult to understand, because of its allusiveness and rapid shifts of topic. We have no contemporary descriptions of the victory celebrations, other than the odes themselves, but it seems clear that the first-person speaker of the ode is the poet, and that a band of celebrants (*kōmos*) consisting of the victor's age-mates would dance and sing in connection with the ode's performance.[11] The Athenian dramatist Euripides wrote a victory ode (F 755 PMG) for the Athenian politician and general Alcibiades (c. 450–404 BCE), but only a few other examples of the genre have survived. Athletic and singing competitions continued to be held throughout antiquity, but the works of the local poets employed to compose poems for such celebrations have been lost, other than some fragments of long narrative poems by Pindar's younger contemporary Corinna, which were written in Boeotian dialect.[12]

Songs and hymns had always been composed for festivals honoring the gods, among them the so-called Homeric Hymns. The authors of these hymns do not identify themselves, with the exception of the *Hymn to Apollo*, whose author claims to be Homer himself. In this hymn, which clearly was composed after the Homeric epics had become famous, the poet tells his audience that he is a blind man from Chios, whose poems are the best of all (166–76). His recitation may have been accompanied by or paired with a *choros*, a group that celebrates the gods in dance, because he refers to a group of girls on the island of Delos who can sing in any dialect (156–64). The poet Stesichorus of Himera in Sicily (632/29–556/3 BCE) seems to have followed in that same tradition, composing narrative poems, but in lyric meters that were probably accompanied by dance, which may explain why he used the stage name Stesichorus ("he who sets up the dance") rather than his original name of Tisias.[13] In sixth-century Athens long lyric poems known as dithyrambs were presented at festivals of Dionysus; their narratives drew on the same stock of traditional myths as the epic poets had done before them. According to tradition, tragedies were first produced around 530 BCE by a poet who called himself by the *nom-de-plume* Thespis (a name that derives from the Homeric phrase "sacred song," *thespin aoidēn*); who added a prologue and recitative to choral performance (TrGF 1 T 6). In the fifth century the festival of Dionysus at Athens was the setting for a competition involving solo recitations and choral dance, where the soloists did not speak in their own voices but acted the parts of characters in a narrative. These competitions produced the remarkable and powerful literature known as drama, which was literally the portrayal of an "action."

Why these performances should have taken place in honor of Dionysus has been the subject of considerable speculation, both ancient and modern. A possible explanation is that Dionysus is the god of illusion, in whose rituals men and women play particular roles, and nothing is what it seems to be. The distinctive political situation in Athens, where many citizens knew how to speak to large audiences, may have encouraged theatrical performance. Solon in the late seventh century expressed his thoughts in iambic trimeter, a verse pattern which later was employed as the standard recitative meter of drama.[14] He appears to have enhanced his own stature by role playing, consciously associating himself in political contexts with the figure of Odysseus, throwing off his cloak to call attention to himself, and wearing a traveler's felt hat.[15] The tyrant Peisistratus persuaded the citizens that he was favored by the goddess Athena, by arriving in the city accompanied by a tall woman dressed in armor (Hdt. 1.60.4–5).[16]

But in the fifth-century dramas that have come down to us, political issues figure only indirectly, because the primary function of dramatic performance was religious: every surviving drama celebrates the powers of the gods and reminds the audience of the problems caused by human ignorance. All describe the interactions among members of one particular family when confronted by a particular crisis; they portray the gods as distant, and eager to disengage themselves from human suffering, and emphasize the need for support from human friends and family. These themes were already present in Homer: both the *Iliad* and the *Odyssey* illustrate the notion of learning through suffering, a prominent theme in many dramas. In both epics the narrative takes the form of a series of scenes, each containing dialogue, with marked entrances and exits.

The earliest surviving examples of Greek drama, the seven tragedies by Aeschylus, are polished and sophisticated productions, carefully constructed, featuring dialogues between characters separated by formal lyric passages that were sung by a chorus and accompanied by dancing. Aeschylus himself fought in the first Persian war, and in his drama *Persians* (472 BCE) portrays the return of the Persian king Xerxes after his decisive defeat by the Greeks at Salamis in 480/79 BCE. The language of Aeschylus's choral passages bears some stylistic resemblance to Pindar's verse, with striking metaphors and newly coined compound adjectives. Aeschylus wrote at least 70 dramas and five satyr plays (TrGF 3 T 1.13), an immense output more than equal in length to the two Homeric epics.[17] He seems to have preferred to present a series of dramas that dealt in chronological order with aspects of a particular myth. His only surviving trilogy, the *Oresteia*, celebrates not only the power of the gods, but also the role of Athens in cooperating with them in seeing that justice is done. Because Aeschylus's dramas were performed after his death, his work was so well known more than half a century later that Athenian audiences could enjoy Aristophanes' parody of his style in his comedy the *Frogs* (405 BCE). But even though Aristophanes makes fun of Aeschylus for his ponderous vocabulary and rhythmic sonorities, he has the god Dionysus take Aeschylus (rather than Euripides) back to Athens from the world of the dead, because during his lifetime through his dramas Aeschylus had encouraged the important civic virtues. Unfortunately Aeschylus's biographers used Aristophanes' caricature of Aeschylus as the basis for their portrait of the poet and of his style, emphasizing the dignity of his characterizations and lack of excitement in his plots, opinions that do not do justice to the considerable skill with which he builds suspense and delineates character.

Sophocles (496/5–406/5 BCE) was the son of a landowner in Colonus; freed because of his aristocratic background from practical responsibilities, he managed to be both a poet and statesman. When he was fifteen, he was selected to lead the chorus that sang the paean at the sacrifice after the Athenian victory at Salamis (TrGF 4 T 1.2) As the author of perhaps as many as 123 plays, Sophocles was not only the most prolific of all known dramatists (TrGF 4 T 2), but he won more first prizes (20) than any other poet (TrGF 4 T 1.8). In other competitions he won second prize, but never third prize (TrGF 4 T 1.8). He won his first victory in 469/8 BCE when he was 27, defeating Aeschylus (TrGF 4 T 33, 36).[18] In addition to his career as a dramatist, 443/32 B.C. he served as State Treasurer (*Hellanotamias,* TrGF 4 T 18), and was elected to be a general in the war between Athens and Samos in 441/0 BCE (TrGF 4 T 19 =FGrHist 324 F 38); the equanimity of his character may have contributed to his popularity in the contentious political atmosphere of Athens.[19] He appears to have been highly respected by the Athenians until the end of his life. In 411 BCE he was one of the old men appointed to be one of the commissioners (*probouloi*) who decided to put the government of Athens in the hands of the oligarchic Four Hundred (TrGF 4 T 27).

Ancient critics thought that Sophocles learned about tragedy from Aeschylus (TrGF 4 T 1.4), but his surviving dramas have a distinctive style, and his tragic vision concentrates on human beings, emphasizing the powerlessness of human beings fully to grasp the consequences of their actions. In most of his dramas the gods remain at a distance from the human action, though they influence it indirectly; this naturalism was preferred by Aristotle because it allows human beings to appear to determine the outcome of their own actions (*Poet.* 1454b1–6). Sophocles was later thought to be the most Homeric of the tragic poets (TrGF 4 T 1.19–20), but the original comparison may have been meant to indicate how highly he was valued, rather than to suggest that there were close similarities in style or subject matter.[20] Sophocles characterized his own style as "sharp and artificial" (*pikron kai katatechnon,* TrGF 4 T 100). He frequently uses abstract nouns that express the wider significance of any particular idea, and employs periphrastic verbal constructions that keep the actions they describe from being closely fixed in time, and allow the audience to recognize their general significance.[21]

Euripides (480–406/5 BCE) competed against Sophocles during the whole of his dramatic career, but won only five victories (TrGF 5.1 T 3.5; T 1, IB.5), even though with some 92 dramas he was almost as prolific as his rival. Whatever the judges thought, his audiences were enthusiastic about his dramas. After the Athenians suffered a disastrous defeat in Sicily in 415 B.C., the Syracusans were said to have spared the lives of captured Athenian soldiers because they could recite the latest dramas by Euripides (Satyrus F 6 fr. 39 xix Schorn; Plut. *Nic.* 29). Another indication of Euripides' popularity is that the comic poets frequently made fun of him. He was a character in several of Aristophanes' comedies, including the extant comedies *Thesmophoriazusae* and *Frogs,* even though he and Aristophanes were friends and members of the same *thiasos* (IG II² 3.2343).[22] One reason for his popularity may have been his striking realism, for which he was famous; most of his characters are not noble, but rather vulnerable and fallible. Another reason for his continuing success was the clarity of his diction. While his language is certainly never colloquial, his syntax is less intense and contorted than Sophocles', and the choral passages of his dramas less allusive and easier to understand than those of either of his predecessors. He was a master of suspense, and ingenious adaptation of traditional plots. He also has his characters debate current issues, face the same ethical issues that his audience might encounter in their own lives, and employ some of the words and concepts used by contemporary orators and philosophers.

After his death, however, Euripides became a victim of his own popularity and his vivid portrayals of controversial ideas. In the *Frogs* Aristophanes made fun of him for putting immoral characters such as the adulterous Phaedra onstage (1403); he depicts Euripides praying to different gods, which was one of the charges for which Socrates was tried and executed in 399 BCE (*Apol.* 24b–c). But as Athenian audiences certainly knew, Aristophanes and other comic poets represented as Euripides' own opinions speeches that Euripides had put into the mouths of characters in his dramas, and ignored the fact that the outcome of the dramas themselves never deviated from the norms of conventional piety, and allowed the gods to resolve the problems that had been caused by humans during the course of the dramatic action. If the innocent in Euripides' dramas suffer or are punished beyond what they might be thought to deserve, that is characteristic of all Greek literature, starting with the *Iliad*. Nonetheless, ancient and many modern scholars have taken the comic version of Euripides seriously, and supposed that he intended to raise questions about Greek religion, and in his dramas portrayed the gods ironically.

Comedies had been performed at the festival of Dionysus in Athens for a generation before Aristophanes' first comedy was staged in 427. Comedies, like drama, had speakers and choruses; many of Aristophanes' lyric passages are as complex and imaginative as those composed by the great tragic poets. Also like the lyric poets of previous generations, Aristophanes (c. 450– c. 387 BCE) was by no means modest about his achievements. He liked to have his choruses point out how much better he was than his predecessors or his rivals (e.g., *Ach*. 643–52). In the context of comedy one could say almost anything. There seems to have been no censorship or legislation forbidding slander in Athens during the last half of the fifth century. But in later times comic caricatures were nonetheless taken seriously. Plato says that in his *Clouds* Aristophanes led people to believe that Socrates prayed to strange divinities and expressed the unconventional views of philosophers like Anaxagoras (*Apol.* 18b–d, 23d, 26c–d), matters that in reality did not interest Socrates.[23]

4. Prose Writers

At the same time that dramatic poetry had begun to flourish in Athens, authors of narratives and treatises about non-mythological matters began to write in prose, or language in which metrical patterns were used only sparingly, if at all. In earlier centuries speakers, singers, and writers had chosen to convey important messages in poetry, because its rhythms helped audiences commit their words to memory. In the sixth and fifth centuries some of the writers who were later known as philosophers composed in verse, among them Xenophanes, Parmenides, and Empedocles. But Heraclitus of Ephesus in Asia Minor (ca. 500 BCE) wrote in prose, using short sentences, balancing words against each other, and employing the poetic techniques of assonance and alliteration.[24] Like Hesiod and Pindar, he distinguished himself from ordinary people, claiming that he had better understanding and more extensive knowledge than they of the workings of the universe (DK 22 B 1). Unfortunately, surviving quotations provide no sense of the original context and shape of his writings. The first extended prose work that has survived in its entirety is a history of the wars between the Greeks and the peoples of Asia Minor and Persia, written by Herodotus of Halicarnassus in Asia Minor. A Greek whose father had a non-Greek name, Herodotus must have been a wealthy man, because he was able to travel to Egypt and go as far as Elephantine (modern Aswan) at the first cataract of the Nile. He is said to have written his *Histories* while in exile in Samos, and to have died far from the city of his birth in the Athenian colony of Thurii in southern Italy, sometime after 444/3 BCE (*Suda* E 536; Arist. *Rhet*. 3.9 1409a28).

Aristotle characterized Herodotus's style as "strung out" (*Rhet*. 3.9 1409a24–8), but that does not mean that Herodotus did not arrange his words carefully, for dramatic effect or balance his phrasing.[25] His narrative style reflects the influence of Homer, as does his subject matter, the description of hostilities between nations of the East and West. The "I" of the *Histories* speaks with authority about what happened in the past, and puts words into the mouths of the characters in his narrative. Like Homer and other singers, his aim is to record the famous deeds of men.[26] But unlike Homer, he does not describe the action of the gods, not because he sought to deny their existence, but because (unlike the poet who narrates traditional myths) he had no way of knowing precisely what they did in order to determine the course of human action. Nonetheless he shapes his narrative to show that the Persians were defeated by the Greeks because the Persian king Xerxes did not have sufficient respect for the gods.[27]

Herodotus came to Athens before the start of the Peloponnesian War in 430 BCE, and his work may have been intended, at least indirectly, as a warning to the Athenians about the dangers of over-confidence in their own military power.[28] He is said to have read his work out loud to Athenian audiences; it was, in his own words, meant to be a "display" (*epideixis* 1.1.1). Sophocles may have known or at least have heard him, because some passages in his surviving dramas have close analogies in the *Histories*.[29] Certainly one explicit purpose of Herodotus's history was to make his audience reflect on the tragic nature of human experience.[30]

Thucydides of Athens (c. 460–c.400 BCE) wrote a long narrative account of another great war, perhaps the most destructive that the world at that time had ever seen, the generation-long conflict between Athens and Sparta and their allies, known as the Peloponnesian War (431–404 BCE) which ended in the decisive defeat of Athens. His father's name (Olorus) suggests that the family came from Thrace.[31] Thucydides tells us that he served as a general during the war, but went into exile for 20 years because in 424 he lost the city of Amphipolis to the Spartan general Brasidas (5.26.5). But for this defeat he might never have had the time to write his history, nor the ability to consult with representatives from all the parties involved.

Like Herodotus, Thucydides[32] generally relates events in the order in which they occurred, but with a greater precision than his predecessor, in that he assigns them to a year and season dating from the start of the war in 431. In addition he begins his account with an analysis of the events preceding the war, explaining how the Greeks acquired such power as they had in the middle of the fifth century. He is also more explicit than Herodotus in describing his methodology. He says that he tried to reconstruct the events of the war from as many reports and witnesses as he could discover. He says explicitly that he has written the speeches in his history based on what he heard the speakers had said and on what he thinks they ought to have said. He makes it clear that he is not writing for the purpose of entertainment, but rather to create "a possession for all time," a template for all human history (1.22.1–4). His writing style is artificial and consciously constructed, especially in his speeches, as if (like Sophocles) he were always striving to illustrate the general in the particular.[33]

Although Thucydides rarely mentions the gods in the course of his history, we cannot assume that he did not believe in them; if he did not describe their roles in determining the course of the war, it was because he had no way of knowing what their intentions or actions may have been. Whatever his own beliefs, he shared with Homer and Herodotus a tragic view of history. In his narrative he used the format of dramatic dialogue to describe the opposing views of the Athenians and the inhabitants of the island of Melos, describing how the Athenians took the city, killed the men, and enslaved the women and children (5.84–115). He follows this account of the Melians with a vivid description of how during the previous winter the Athenians were deluded into sending an expedition to Sicily, where they were decisively defeated, a loss that led to their ultimate defeat in the war.

The rapid give and take of dramatic dialogues proved to be a useful format for philosophical investigation.[34] It was adopted by Plato (c. 429–347 BCE) and his pupil Aristotle (384–322 BCE) as the medium in which their ideas might most successfully be put forward.[35] Aristotle's dialogues have been lost, but it is easy to see the influence of drama at work in Plato's dialogues, both in his choice of settings for the dialogues, and in his portrayals of different speakers. The principal character in his dialogues is his teacher Socrates, who questions other characters in order to show that they do not understand what they are saying, and who then usually provides the abstract definition of the concept the other interlocutors have failed to understand. In the works of Plato's contemporary Xenophon (born c. 430 BCE) Socrates appears to be much less intimidating, and more willing to offer practical advice.

Although recognized by philosophers as a pioneer in the development of abstract reasoning, Plato was also a gifted and imaginative narrator, who realized that he could use mythical stories as a means of persuasion, especially when more rigorous methods of analysis could become too difficult for some of his interlocutors to follow. For example, he concludes his long dialogue "*On Justice*" (commonly known now as the *Republic*) not with a summary of the ideal state described in that dialogue, but with a mythical narrative describing the rewards promised after death for those who practice justice in life. Some of Plato's myths, when removed from their original contexts, have had a lasting influence on later writers, in particular his description of the legendary civilization of Atlantis.[36]

Plato was a member of an aristocratic Athenian family, who had the leisure time to listen to Socrates, along with other young men from similar backgrounds. Aristotle came to Athens from Stagira in Macedonia when he was seventeen (in 367) and stayed until 348/7, when he went back to Macedonia for five years to serve as a tutor for Alexander. Aristotle returned to Athens in 343, and remained there for another 20 years. During his stays in Athens he would have been able to see Greek dramas performed in the theater of Dionysus, including works by the great fifth-century dramatists. He recorded his ideas about drama and other types of literature in the *Poetics*, which is the first example of what has since been known as literary criticism.

Among the other beneficiaries of Athenian drama were the orators who delivered long speeches in the Athenian assembly or in the law courts. Rhetorical skill was highly valued in Athenian society, and audiences enjoyed listening to a discourse that was well-argued. Orators like Lysias (*floruit* c. 400 BCE) could draw on the narrative techniques that the dramatists used to provide exciting descriptions in messenger speeches of events that took place offstage. Speeches and debates in drama also had a profound influence on the art of persuasion in law-courts and in political gatherings, in methods of delivery and in the practice of drawing on historical or mythological precedent to make an argument. Athenian orators also made constant use of the techniques employed by poets like Pindar in their songs of praise.[37]

5.   Writers in the Hellenistic Era

In the fifth century, tragedies and comedies had both employed choruses that sang and danced during the performances. But after their defeat in the Peloponnesian war the Athenians no longer had money to pay for the training of choruses, so dramas and comedies such as Aristophanes' *Plutos/"Wealth"* (399) were staged without them. Although in the old democracy playwrights were free to make fun of everyone, in the more restricted atmosphere of the fourth century writers avoided political controversy. Without choruses and references to current events, the plays later known as New Comedy had naturalistic settings (no choruses of singing Frogs!), stock characters, and happy endings, along with ingenious plot twists like those found in fifth-century dramas like Euripides' *Helen*. The most influential writer of this type of "New" Comedy was the Athenian poet Menander (344/3–292/1 BCE). One of his plays survives intact, along with extensive fragments of others. His style owes more to Euripides than to the other dramatists. He was celebrated in antiquity for some of the memorable sayings he put into the mouths of his characters, which were put into a special collection of "One-Liners" (*Monostichoi*). His plays were popular wherever Greek was spoken. His works and those of his contemporaries were adapted for Latin-speaking audiences by Plautus (from 205 to 184 BCE) and Terence (in the 160s BCE).

By the end of the fourth century the most innovative Greek literature was being written outside of Athens. Writers from all over the Greek world were able to write elegant epigrams for a wide variety of occasions, for epitaphs, dedications, symposia, and even personal gifts.[38] Many of these short poems were later collected and presented to new audiences.[39] The most important cultural center appears to have been Alexandria in Egypt, founded in 323 and later ruled by Alexander's general Ptolemy and his descendants, who styled themselves as pharaohs. The autocratic political climate encouraged the production of works that lavished praise on the rulers, praise that was not tempered by the restraint expressed by Bacchylides or Pindar, who repeatedly warned the victors they honored about the transience of human achievement. But in other respects Alexandrian poets paid tribute to their predecessors. They preserved not only their memory, but saw to it that their collected works were stored and organized in a library specially built for the purpose. Scholars such as Aristarchus of Samothrace (c. 216–144 BCE) sought to correct the transmitted texts, removing later additions and corruptions from them, most of which were already present in the manuscripts that he worked with. Poets studied the compositions of the old poets assiduously and incorporated allusions to them into their new poetry, along with information about learned geography and mythology. One of the most influential of these learned poets was Theocritus (*floruit* c. 270), who appears to have been a native of Syracuse in Sicily. In some of his *Idylls* ("little pictures": *eidullia*), Theocritus described in highly literate language the lives of herders in pasturelands in landscapes on Sicily and the island of Cos that many people in his audiences had never seen.[40] Such sophisticated poems about the countryside, known as *boukolika*, were imitated by many later writers, most notably Vergil.

Callimachus of Cyrene (*floruit* 285–46 BCE) and his younger contemporary Apollonius of Rhodes also had a lasting influence on later poetry. Callimachus's works are consciously learned, full of allusions to earlier writers, such as Pindar; also in the manner of earlier poets he made programmatic statements about his work, criticizing others for writing at length, praising himself for his short and elegant narratives, distinguishing himself from others by his wit and his surprising shifts of tone and vocabulary. Ancient critics supposed that Callimachus's references to detractors referred to specific individuals, and imagined that he had quarreled with his younger contemporary Apollonius, who was the author a long epic poem, *The Voyage of the Argo* (*Argonautica*). In fact that epic is one-third of the length of the *Odyssey*, and written in a learned and allusive style that Callimachus would have approved of. Like Theocritus and Callimachus, Apollonius wrote about ancient times and lands that his audiences might never have seen, with a nostalgic poignancy and keen awareness of the presence of death and danger. Virgil knew his work well, and incorporates references to it into his *Aeneid*, comparing and contrasting Aeneas with Apollonius's hero Jason. Although Virgil also had the *Odyssey* and then the *Iliad* in mind when he wrote the *Aeneid*, in tone his epic bears a closer resemblance to the *Argonautica* than it does to the Homeric epics.

Hellenistic prose writers produced exciting and intricate narratives influenced by the ingenious plots of the plays of Euripides and Menander, although without their realism. In the second century CE, Longus used a pastoral setting for his *Daphnis and Chloe*.[41] There seems to have been a large market for tales about young couples who are separated from each other, and after many close escapes and journeys to foreign lands, are able to find each other again, as in Xenophon's *Ephesian Tale* and Heliodorus's *Aethiopica*. Audiences also liked the exotic and fantastic, such as the adventures of Lucius, a man who was turned into a jackass, and the satirically mendacious *True History* by the second-century Lucian of Samosata. These so-called novels clearly had an influence on Hellenistic Jewish writers, (e.g. *Joseph and Asenath*), as well as on early Christian writers, such as the author of the Acts of the Apostles.

Although now in universities we give precedence to the study of authors like Homer and the tragedians, had it not been for the dedication of scholars and writers in the Hellenistic era only quotations from those earlier authors might have come down to us. Without the inspiration of Alexandrian poetry, Latin literature in the first century and after might never have developed the elegance and vitality for which it was later celebrated. The work of Hellenistic writers also provided a model for Plutarch (c. 50–120 CE), whose biographies influenced all later biographical writing and who collected and organized an extensive store of information about ancient customs. The only poet for whom he wrote a Life was Solon, but that is what the poets themselves may have preferred; their fame came from what they created, and it is for their works and not the details of their daily lives that they wanted to be remembered.[42]

NOTES

[1] Clay 2004, 63–98.

[2] In Homer both Achilles (*Il.* 9.189) and Odysseus (*Od.* 9.1–11.224) sing without referring to written texts. Messages are delivered orally, though Bellerophontes brings a tablet inscribed with "dire signs" to the king of Lycia (*Il.* 6. 168–9).

[3] Cf. Kivilo 2010, 9–10.

[4] Lefkowitz 2012, 6, 8.

[5] See esp. Riginos 1976, 17–21.

[6] On Solon's self-portrayal, see Irwin 2005, 264–6; Morrison 2007, 52–3; Irwin 2006, 24.

[7] Calame 1997, 210–14.

[8] See esp. Rosenmeyer 1992, 50–73.

[9] Bacchylides (but not Pindar) wrote an ode for Hieron's victory in the chariot race at Olympia in 468.

[10] Aetna erupted in 479 and 475 B.C.; there are descriptions in *Pyth.* 1.22–8 (cf. *Ol.* 4.7–8) and in the drama *Prometheus Bound* 363–9; Griffith 1983, 152.

[11] See esp. Heath 1988, 180–95; Lefkowitz 1991, 191–201; Lefkowitz 1995, 139–50.

[12] On Corinna's date see Stewart 1998, 278–81; Schachter 2005, 280.

[13] On performing Stesichorus's poems, see Lefkowitz 1991, 192–4. Cf. Kivilo 2010, 72, 77–9.

[14] On Solon's influence on drama, see Else 1965, 60–62, Fränkel 1975, 29, Irwin 2005, 274.

[15] Aristotle commented on Solon's resemblance to Odysseus (F 143 Rose= Σ *Il.* 2.183); see esp. Irwin 2005, 136–42.

[16] Irwin 2005, 151–2, 272.

[17] Aeschylus may have written as many as 90 dramas (TrGF 3 T 2).

[18] Another source credits Sophocles with 113 dramas (TrGF 4 T 1. 18); for a list of known titles, see Lloyd-Jones 1996, vol. 3, 4–9. It is impossible now to know which of the two totals is correct, since some plays were known by more than one title. In either case Sophocles wrote more plays than any other poet.

[19] Aristophanes called him "good-natured" (*eukolos, Ran.* 82 = TrGF 4 T 101).

[20] The philosopher Polemon (TrGF 4 T 115) said that Sophocles was the dramatic Homer, and Homer the epic Sophocles.

[21] On the effects of his language, see esp. Long 1968, 161–9; Budelmann 2000, 61–91.

[22] Other members of Aristophanes' *thiasos* included Simon, portrayed in *Nub.* 351 as a harpy and in 399 as a perjurer, and Amphitheos, who is made to boast in *Ach.* 46 that he is immortal, descended from Demeter. See Henderson 1998, 3.

[23] Henderson 1998, 15–23.

[24] Cf. Hose, ch. 15, pp. 236–7 in this volume.

[25] Denniston 1952, 5–8.

[26] Ford 2007, 814–18.

[27] Sewell-Rutter 2007, 1–14.

[28] On the fall of Persia as a model for Athens, see Fornara 1971, 89–91; Romm 1998, 52–3.

[29] E.g., esp. *Ant.* 904–12/Hdt. 3.119.6 and *O.C.* 337–41/Hdt. 2.35.2; How and Wells 1912, vol. I, 7. Sophocles was said to have written an epigram to Herodotus in 441 / 40 BCE, the year of his generalship ('Sophocles' II, 1044–5 FGE).

[30] For the tragic pattern of Greek historical narrative, see Gould 1989, 116–20. Harrison 2000, 62–3; Mikalson 2003, 149–50.

[31] Hanson 1996, ix.

[32] Cf. Tsakmakis, ch. 14, pp. 218–9 in this volume.

[33] Hornblower 2004, 286.

[34] Cf. Hose, ch. 15, pp. 244–5 in this volume.

[35] For the references to Aristotle's dialogues in ancient sources, see Rose 1886, 23–5.

[36] On the myth of Atlantis see esp. Brisson 1998; Nesselrath 2002.

[37] Bundy 1962; 3–4.

[38] An early example is the second-century BCE papyrus collection of epigrams attributed to Posidippus of Pella in Macedon (*floruit* 270–240 BCE), arranged by subject matter; see Gutzwiller 2005, 1–16, and Höschele, ch. 12, pp. 194–6 in this volume.

[39] Ca. 100 BCE the poet Meleager of Gadara in Palestine collected epigrams by famous poets in his *Garland*; Gutzwiller 1998, 276–322.

[40] Cf. Saïd, ch. 22, pp. 362–4 in this volume.

[41] Cf. Tilg, ch. 16, p. 258, and Saïd, ch. 22, pp. 364–5 in this volume.

[42] See (e.g.) Callimachus, *Epigramm* 2 Pf, and in general Nisbet and Hubbard 1978, 335–6.

REFERENCES

Bowie, E. L. 2009. "Wandering Poets, Archaic Style." In R. Hunter and I. Rutherford, eds., *Wandering Poets in Ancient Greek Culture: Travel Locality and Pan-Hellenism*, Cambridge, 105–36.

Brisson, L. 1998. *Plato the Myth Maker*. Chicago.

Budelmann, F. 2000. *The Language Of Sophocles: Communality, Communication, and Involvement*. Cambridge.

Bundy, E. R. 1962. *Studia Pindarica*. Berkeley, CA.

Calame, C. 1997. *Choruses of Young Women in Ancient Greece*. Lanham, MD.

Clay, D. 2004. *Archilochus Heros: The Cult of Poets in the Greek Polis*. Cambridge, MA.

Denniston, J. D. 1952. *Greek Prose Style*. Oxford.

Else, G. F. 1965. *The Origin and Early Form of Greek Tragedy*. Cambridge, MA.

Fairweather, J. A. 1974. "Fiction in the biographies of Ancient Writers." *Ancient Society* 5: 231–75.

Ford, A. 2007. "Herodotus and the Poets." In R. Strassler, ed., *The Landmark Herodotus*, New York, 816–818.

Fornara, C. W. 1971. *Herodotus: An Interpretive Essay*. Oxford.

Fränkel, H. 1975. *Early Greek Poetry and Philosophy*. New York.

Gould, J. 1989. *Herodotus*. New York.

Graziosi, B. 2002. *Inventing Homer: the Early Reception of Epic*. Cambridge.

Griffith, M., ed. 1983. *Aeschylus: Prometheus Bound*. Cambridge.

Gutzwiller, K. J. 1998. *Poetic Garlands*. Berkeley, CA.

Gutzwiller, K. J., ed. 2005. *The New Posidippus: A Hellenistic Poetry Book*. Oxford.

Hanink, J. 2008. "Literary Politics and the Euripidean Vita." *Proceedings of the Cambridge Philological Society* 54: 113–35.

Hanink, J. 2010. "The Classical Tragedians, from Athenian Idols to Wandering Poets." In I. Gildenhard and M. Revermann, eds., *Beyond the Fifth Century*, Berlin 39–67.

Hanson, V. D. 1996. "Introduction." In R. Strassler, ed., *The Landmark Thucydides*, New York, ix–xxiii.

Harrison, T. 2000. *Divinity and History*. Oxford.

Heath, M. 1988. "Receiving the *Komos*: The Context and Performance of the Epinician." *American Journal of Philology* 109: 180–95.

Henderson, J., ed. 1998. *Aristophanes I: Acharnians, Knights*. Cambridge, MA.

Hornblower, S. 2004. *Thucydides and Pindar*. Oxford.

Howe, W. W. and J. Wells. 1912. *A Commentary on Herodotus*. 2 vols. Oxford.

Irwin, E. 2005. *Solon and Early Greek Poetry*. Cambridge.

Irwin, E. 2006. "The Biographies of Poets: The Case of Solon." In B. McGing and J. Mossman, eds., *The Limits of Ancient Biography*, Swansea, 13–30.

Kivilo, M. 2010. *Early Greek Poets' Lives: The Shaping of the Tradition*. Leiden.

Knöbl, R. 2010. "Talking about Euripides: Paramimesis and Satyrus' *Bios Euripidou*." In P. Borghart and K. De Temmerman, eds., *Biography and Fictionality in the Greek Literary Tradition*. Special issue of *Phrasis. Studies in Language and Literature* 51.1, 37–58. Ghent.

Lefkowitz, M. R. 1981. *The Lives of the Greek Poets*. Baltimore.

Lefkowitz, M. R. 1991. *First-Person Fictions: Pindar's Poetic "I."* Oxford.

Lefkowitz, M. R. 1995. "The First Person in Pindar Reconsidered – Again." *Bulletin of the Institute of Classical Studies* 42: 139–50.

Lefkowitz, M. R. 2012. *The Lives of the Greek Poets*, 2nd edn. Baltimore.

Lloyd-Jones, H., ed. 1994–1996. *Sophocles*. Cambridge, MA.

Long, A. A. 1968. *Language and Thought in Sophocles*. London.

Mikalson, J. D. 2003. *Herodotus and Religion in the Persian Wars*. Chapel Hill, NC.

Morrison, A. D. 2007. *The Narrator in Archaic Greek and Hellenistic Poetry*. Cambridge.

Nesselrath, H.-G. 2002. *Platon und die Erfindung von Atlantis*. Munich.

Nisbet, R. G. M. and M. Hubbard. 1978. *A Commentary on Horace: Odes Book II*. Oxford.

Riginos, A. S. 1976. *Platonica: The Anecdotes Concerning the Life and Writings of Plato*. Leiden.

Romm, J. 1998. *Herodotus*. New Haven, CT.

Rose, V., ed. 1886. *Aristotelis Fragmenta*. Leipzig.

Rosenmeyer, P. A. 1992. *The Poetics of Imitation: Anacreon and the Anacreontic Tradition*. Cambridge.

Schachter, A. 2005. "The Singing Contest of Kitairon and Helikon: Korinna, fr. 654 PMG Col. I and ii. 1–11: Content and Context." In A. Kolde, A. Lukinovich, and A.-L. Rey, eds., *Koryphaiōi Andri: Mélanges offerts à André Hurst*, Geneva, 275–83.

Schorn, S. 2004. *Satyros aus Kallatis*. Basel.

Sewell-Rutter, N. 2007. *Guilt by Descent*. Oxford.

Stewart, A. 1998. "Nuggets: Mining the Texts Again." *American Journal of Archaeology* 102: 271–82.

FURTHER READING

For an overview of the unreliability of the biographical tradition, see esp. Fairweather 1974. In *The Lives of the Greek Poets* (1981), I showed that large portions of the biographies of ancient poets were based on their poetry. In the second edition of that book (2012, Baltimore) I also consider how those biographies can be used as a guide to later understanding and reception of the works of the poets, as has been ably demonstrated for the ancient biographies of Homer by Graziosi 2002. For more detailed information on the biographical tradition of Euripides; see especially Schorn 2004, Hanink 2008 and 2010, and also Knöbl 2010. Irwin 2005 shows why Solon may not have been the champion of democracy that he claims to be. Also valuable is a detailed analysis of the formation of the biographies of several archaic poets by Kivilo 2010, and on Simonides, Bowie 2009.

CHAPTER 19

Users of Literature

René Nünlist

1. Hearers and Readers

The two words that, from a modern perspective, might look like a pair of opposing terms were in fact perfectly compatible for the Greeks. From the last decades of the fifth century BCE onwards, the Greeks were both hearers and, at the same time, readers – because they normally read aloud. True, traces of silent reading in antiquity have been discovered, but it is misleading to conclude that "the phenomenon of reading itself is fundamentally the same in modern and in ancient culture" (Gavrilov 1997, 69). At least two basic differences speak against such an equation. Firstly, silent reading did not supersede reading aloud, which remained common practice throughout antiquity. Secondly, the ancients were in the habit of having literature read to them (Busch 2002). The recognition of how important and widespread this habit was exposes as topical an alleged common-sense argument that has been put forward in favor of widespread silent reading: "common sense rebels against the idea that scholarly readers, for example, did not develop a technique of silent, faster reading" (Knox 1968, 421). But a scholarly reader like Pliny the Elder had his lector read to him whenever there was a chance, during meals, when taking a bath, etc. (Plin. *ep.* 3.5; Johnson 2010, 14). Different times have different means to cope with large amounts of text. (Incidentally, in the case of one of the scholarly readers that Knox mentions *exempli gratia*, the great Alexandrian critic Aristarchus, we even know the name of the lector, Poseidonius: Σ A *Il.* 17.75a *Nic.*) While there is no reason to maintain that the Greeks did not or even could not (conceptually) read silently, the fact remains that it was the exception rather than the rule. Even as readers, they did not stop being hearers, which also means that literature was to them a fundamentally acoustic phenomenon. No surprise, then, that the verb *akouó* (lit. "to hear, listen") regularly means "to read" (Schenkeveld 1992). As late an author as Lucian (second century CE) tellingly instructs his addressee to read the historiographers critically by "opening his ears" (*Quomodo hist. conscr.* 7).

The date given above for the transitional period, the last decades of the fifth century BCE, is determined, among other things, by the arrival of what has been called, with a mild anachronism, "book trade" (Turner 1952). Other indicators include the increasing representation of

A Companion to Greek Literature, First Edition. Edited by Martin Hose and David Schenker.
© 2016 John Wiley & Sons, Inc. Published 2020 by John Wiley & Sons, Inc.

bookrolls in visual arts (esp. in school scenes) or the famous passage from Aristophanes' *Frogs* (52–3, 405 BCE) in which Dionysus reports that he read Euripides' *Andromeda* to himself. The combined evidence shows that the book was no longer considered a mere "repository," the main purpose of which was the preservation of the compositions. Instead it became increasingly important for their reception too. (Here and in what follows "reception" designates the act of reading/hearing literature.)

Previously, the reception of literature had been completely aural (i.e. textless). Whether the specific composition had come into existence assisted by the means of writing (a question that remains hotly debated among modern scholars, at least as far as Homeric poetry is concerned), did not matter much from the point of view of reception. Literature was, in any case, being performed in order to be listened to, which is why "early Greek literature" is, strictly speaking, a contradiction in terms. Even poets who no doubt composed their songs with the help of a pen or scribe (e.g. Pindar) make a point of inserting what has been described as the device of feigned orality (e.g. Scodel 1996). It is thus indicative of the expected mode of reception too, difficult as this might be to comprehend for modern readers who struggle with Pindar's odes.

The notion of the book or written text to be read (out) from brought about a change, but it does not mark an actual watershed. The transition appears to have been comparatively slow. It would take another century or so until, in Hellenistic times, the book was finally established as an indispensable component of the "culture industry." Multiple modes of reception coexisted, since, for instance, live performances continued. What is more, from the viewpoint of the receivers, it did not make much of a difference whether a composition was performed or read to them (not least because the latter included dramatic delivery, see below). To have literature read to oneself remained, to repeat, common practice also through the "bookish" Hellenistic era and beyond. It should, however, be added that, still in Hellenistic times, literary texts start toying with their visual side too, for instance, in the form of acrostichs (e.g. Aratus *Phaen.* 783–7) or *carmina figurata* (Luz 2010; cf. Höschele, ch. 12, 201–2 in this volume). Such features were obviously lost on those who did not have visual access to the text.

Needless to say, the above emphasis on the acoustic side of literature is more than a mere technicality. The common practice of listening to literature no doubt enabled ancient audiences to notice, appreciate and evaluate all those phenomena that are much better caught by the ear than by the eye: meter or, in prose, the rhythm of the clausulae, prosody, hiatus and its avoidance, (differences in) dialect, various types of literary rhetoric (alliteration, assonance, anaphora, etc.). This ability was further enhanced by the fact that the Greeks did not simply learn how to read a text, but how to deliver it. The oldest surviving Greek grammar, attributed to Aristarchus's pupil Dionysius Thrax, divides its subject into six parts, of which reading (*anagnôsis*) is the first:

> By reading is meant the faultless pronunciation of the works of poets or prose writers. When reading, proper attention must be given to style of delivery, to the prosodic features (i.e. accents etc.), and to the correct division of the utterance. From the style of delivery we perceive the true value of the piece, from the prosodic features the art of its construction, and from correct division the overall sense. So that we may read tragedy in a heroic style, comedy in a style suited to everyday life, elegy in plaintive tones, epic vigorously, lyric harmoniously, and laments in a subdued and mournful way. Unless the rules are carefully observed, the true value of the poetry is lost, and the reader's whole approach becomes subject to ridicule (Dion. Thrax, ch. 2, trans. Kemp).

The attribution of the grammar to Dionysius is disputed among scholars, but the quotation comes from the opening chapters, which are considered genuine by many: Lallot 2003, 25; cf. Fögen, ch. 17, 276–7 in this volume. Similar instructions can be found elsewhere: e.g. Quintilian 2.5: on Greek schools.

The quoted passage shows that the average Greek reader was able to read out a text and deliver it in a lively style that suited the particular genre and was probably not too different from the performance of a rhapsode, an actor or an epideictic orator. The audience, on the other hand, semi- and illiterate members perhaps included, were accustomed to listening to a performance-like reading of literary texts with accurate word division and correctly pronounced accentuation.

The importance of these factors can explain why an actor's mishap could be turned into a joke. When performing Euripides' *Orestes* (408 BCE), the actor Hegelochus accidentally mispronounced the word *galên'* (with acute accent on the *êta* and elision at the end) as *galên* (with circumflex on the *êta* and simple word end after *nu*). The seemingly trivial error did not go unnoticed because it meant that Orestes, awaking after a fit of madness, said "after the storm waves I once more see *a weasel*" instead of "calm" (*Or.* 279). The mistake was memorable enough for Aristophanes to make fun of it three years later (*Ran.* 303–4), as did other comedians (Sannyrio F 8 PCG, Strattis F 1 and 63 PCG).

This undiminished focus on the acoustic side of literature also helps explain a phenomenon that otherwise might remain curious or downright odd. Literary experiments such as that of the sixth-century poet Lasus of Hermione, who wrote an entire poem without the letter *sigma* because he did not like its sound (F 704 PMG, cf. F trag. adesp. 655 TrGF 2), paved the way for a development that culminated in Hellenistic times in the theories of the so-called "euphonists". As the name indicates, their main concern was the sound of literature, which to them was as important as content or, in the theory's extremest form, even more important than content (Janko 2000; 2011). It is not clear (*pace* Janko 2011, 229) to what extent these theories, especially in their extreme form, were shared by critics and readers outside the circle of euphonists, who were by no means in agreement with each other. The polemic account of Philodemus, to whom we owe our knowledge about the euphonists, may well give a distorted impression of the situation among Hellenistic critics in general, about whose works we know frustratingly little. Be that as it may, the main point to be made here is that euphonic considerations were never far from a Greek reader's mind in general.

The contributions to a summary "genre" such as companions are bound to make generalizations, due, not least, to the limited space. In the present case, this tendency is aggravated by the regrettable but irremediable fact that ancient sources on reading are scarce and often late (i.e. Roman and/or of the Imperial era). Most of the evidence on which accounts of reading in modern times to no small degree rest (cognitive science, empirical studies, contemporary reports, diaries, etc.) is simply not available. As a general rule, the task becomes the more difficult the further back we go in time. For instance, there is no first-hand evidence on who attended Homer's performances or how they reacted to it. Later sources, on the other hand, if they exist at all, can always be liable to anachronistic distortions. If they cannot be checked against other sources, the question arises to what extent their evidence can be deemed trustworthy. The picture becomes slightly clearer for literature that was produced in subsequent centuries (e.g. classical tragedy or comedy), due to the gradual accumulation of relevant source material. There is, however, no linear increase of clarity or the like. The ongoing discussion on who read (or was meant to read) the novel and to what purpose (Bowie 1994, Holzberg 2006, 52–8) shows that even the readership of a, by Greek standards, late genre can completely elude us.

In the absence of "hard facts," the modern scholar must look for alternatives, in spite of their limited explanatory power. The following types of source are worth singling out (the list makes no pretence to completeness): (1) The immanent poetics, that is, the "program" that literary texts proclaim in more or less veiled language (e.g. figuratively, implicitly, allusively), can contain information regarding the envisaged reception (example: the feigned orality device mentioned above). More specifically, (2) the implied reader, that is, a (hypothetical) reconstruction of the receiver that any given text presupposes (example: the implied reader of Hesiod's *Theogony* is expected to share the positive view of Zeus's supremacy). The implied reader is not the same as (3) the narratee, that is, the "person" to whom the relevant composition is "expressly addressed" (e.g. Perses in Hesiod's *Works and Days* or the indeterminate "you" in Homer: *Il.* 4.223, etc.). Neither the implied reader nor the narratee is identical with the historical reader, but the two former can help us picture the latter. (4) Internal audiences: texts sometimes present or tell of situations in which an audience listen to literature (Example: in the *Odyssey* the Phaeacians listen and react to Demodocus's songs). (5) The response of actual readers, either explicitly (e.g. notes, comments, quotations) or implicitly (e.g. allusions). Oftentimes these readers are themselves authors (example: Simonides approvingly quotes Homer's simile of the leaves: F 19 IEG).

Meticulous collection of the relevant data and careful analysis form the basis of the attempt to reconstruct the actual, historical, contemporary readers, which, needless to say, must be done separately for each text (and is thus impossible in the present context). We should, however, remain aware of the fact that, in spite of our efforts, such a reconstruction will always be hypothetical and no more than an approximation. The wide range of answers that are given in modern scholarship to fundamental questions such as "which part of the Athenian population attended dramatic performances?" (e.g. Goldhill 1997) or "did the audience understand a play like Aristophanes' *Birds* as a concealed warning?" (e.g. Sommerstein 1987, 3–5) perfectly illustrate the difficulty of the task and the ultimate uncertainty of the proposed results.

It is also important to keep in mind that several of the sources mentioned above are liable to bias and distortion, which cautions against uncritically taking them at face value. As a general rule, authors will be reluctant to presuppose or describe an audience that is hostile, bored or stupid, unless, of course, this is the very point, for instance, in comedy or satire. Likewise, the alleged hostility of the audience can be a rhetorical device to make the author's task appear even more difficult (e.g. in Dio Chrysostom's *Trojan Oration* [*or.* 11]). Rhetoric also seems to be at stake when authors contrast two types of audience, as, for example, Thucydides does in the famous chapter on method.

> And it may well be that my history will seem less easy to read because of the absence in it of the romantic element. It will be enough for me, however, if these words of mine are judged useful by those who want to understand clearly the events which happened in the past and which (human nature being what it is) will, at some time or other and in much the same ways, be repeated in the future. My work is not a piece of writing designed to meet the taste of an immediate public, but was done to last for ever (1.22, trans. Warner).

This passage is generally taken as an indication that Thucydides is writing for critical readers and thus a small elite audience (e.g. Yunis 2003b). This may well be right, but are we truly to believe that other readers, when reaching the quoted passage, muttered "Oh, this is not meant for me" and put down the bookroll or walked away from the reading? Is the less sophisticated audience not always that of the others and thus a foil (e.g. Pind. *Ol.* 2.83–6)? A similar reservation may well apply to other texts which are often said to have a decidedly elitist outlook and to strive for the cohesion of a limited group (e.g. the "ivory tower" of learned Hellenistic poets such as Callimachus: see most recently Strootman 2010, 44–5).

Put more generally, one wonders whether the body of ancient readers was indeed substantially more uniform than that of their modern counterparts. At the very least, there must have been various degrees of, to name only two, proficiency and sophistication. (Less experienced readers were not automatically excluded due to the reading habits described above.) Once again we classicists are trapped by the fact that we almost never get to hear the voice of the non-elite members of Greek society, at least not directly. Moreover, even one and the same individual could easily adopt different "reception attitudes" depending on the specific occasion or purpose (slow *vs.* fast reading, intensive *vs.* extensive, once *vs.* several times, alone *vs.* in a group, private *vs.* public, naive *vs.* critical, earnestly *vs.* for entertainment, and so on).

In our attempt to get a hold on the historical reader of a text, we had better not confuse him with the ideal reader. The fact, for instance, that such a critical spirit as Thucydides had no doubts about the historicity of the Trojan war is a healthy reminder. At any rate, it would be rash *a priori* to assume that alternatives or exceptions did not exist (as we saw above in the case of silent reading).

These qualifications notwithstanding, it is possible to determine some general trends, for instance, regarding the purpose of reading literature. "Poets aim either to do good or to give pleasure" (*aut prodesse volunt aut delectare poetae*). Horace's famous line (*Ars poetica* 333) presents in a nutshell the two poles of a spectrum that occurs with regular frequency in one form or the other. "Instruction and entertainment" encompasses a good number of the answers that in the course of time were given to the implicit question "why read literature?". The Homeric epics already make it clear that one of the bard's main tasks was "to entertain" (*terpein*, e.g. *Od.* 17.385). And the "happiness" or "joy" (*euphrosunê*) that host and guests alike feel during a felicitous dinner party depends to no small degree on the performance of poetry (*Od.* 9.3–10). Hesiod's poetry has an unmistakably didactic agenda (cf. Heraclitus DK 22 B 57), the Presocratic philosopher Xenophanes of Colophon declared "from the beginning all mortals have learned from Homer" (DK 21 B 10), and so on. What type of "instruction" or "entertainment" exactly is meant and how these goals are achieved in each case varies, of course, a great deal depending on whom we take as our witness. Whether it is Gorgias, Plato or Aristotle who speaks of the "pleasure" of poetry makes a big difference. The picture gets even more complicated when these witnesses are asked whether or not a particular text has achieved its goals. For Pindar (*Isth.* 3/4.55–7) and Aristophanes' "Aeschylus" (*Ran.* 1034) Homer and his poetry were "divine" (*theios*), for Heraclitus (DK 22 B 42) he deserved the whip; but such differences are only to be expected. What is, perhaps, more surprising from today's perspective is the extent to which Greek readers actually agree on the basic principle that instruction and entertainment are in fact desirable goals of literature. The latter is mostly unproblematic for modern readers too, but they are less likely to welcome instruction as an unquestionable goal, certainly not with the moral undertones that Greeks are accustomed to giving it. "It is a utilitarian view of literature ... which predominated in antiquity" (Hunter 2009, 8). Such a view is bound to have many modern readers raise their eyebrows because they tend to think of literature in non-utilitarian terms.

Another aspect that is worth considering is the physical appearance of books. There was an unmistakable attempt to produce "editions" of literary texts that were aesthetically appealing (e.g. neat scripts, wide margins), even including features that, in a way, made them less user-friendly. A good example is the so-called *scriptio continua*, that is, the absence of word division, which required readers to learn how to recognize where words ended in order to deliver the text properly (see above). The scarcity of other lectional signs (accents, breathings, "quotation marks," or, in dramatic texts and dialogues, identification of speakers, etc.) was probably meant to contribute to the same aesthetic goal (Johnson 2010, 17–22). The drawn picture represents the appearance of literary texts from Hellenistic times onwards. The period that pre-dates the oldest preserved papyri is more difficult to assess because artistic representations (e.g. on vases) are not sufficiently reliable as a guide (esp. for specific details such as script, margins, etc., which are likely to have been influenced by the needs and technical possibilities of the artist). It is, however, unlikely that pre-Hellenistic books looked substantially different. The combined evidence points to an object of considerable prestige – and cost. Socrates' often-quoted dig at Anaxagoras that his works can be bought at the price of one drachma (Plat. *Apol.* 26e) does not testify to the existence of books that were really cheap. At the time, one drachma was a full day's wage for a skilled worker, who could not count on getting hired every day. Jurors – with the same problem – received three obols (= half a drachma) per day. One wonders how many of them, if any, will have been ready to spend that money on a book, even if its price was comparatively low (cf. Hose, ch. 15, pp. 239–40 in this volume). When the chorus of Aristophanes' *Frogs* praises the audience that they are on top of things because "every one of them has a book" (1114), this must be comic exaggeration (Sommerstein 1996, 256, with the then appropriate analogy "They're all on the Internet").

The passage is also instructive because the possession of books is seen as a mark of excellence and intelligence. Some 170 lines earlier in the play (*Ran.* 943), Aristophanes, with his usual versatility, exploited the same phenomenon for what by now has become the stereotype of the bookworm who is out of touch with reality (cf. also F 506 PCG). The target is Euripides, who not only owned many books (*Ran.* 1409) but also had a chorus express the wish that old age might give them the peace and leisure to read books (Eur. F 369.6 TrGF 5, Sommerstein 1996, 239).

It is no coincidence that the first part of this chapter contains several references to Aristophanes' *Frogs*. This play is rightly considered a comparatively early and important witness of ancient literary criticism (most recently Halliwell 2012), a topic to which we now turn.

2. Scholars and Interpreters: Ancient Literary Criticism

Scholars are, needless to say, a particular type of reader, but what makes a scholar a scholar? "Scholarship is the art of understanding, explaining, and restoring the literary tradition." This often-quoted definition, which is the opening sentence of Pfeiffer's masterly *History of Classical Scholarship* (1968, 3), would in this truncated form be of limited value because the three goals are as old as literature itself. In fact, Pfeiffer shows this himself in the first part of his book. The question is rather, as his second sentence indicates, when and, perhaps more importantly, how scholarship became "a separate intellectual discipline." Pfeiffer himself famously put the decisive step between Aristotle and the Hellenistic scholar-poets because, to his mind, the latter had a decidedly anti-Aristotelian agenda. Instead of rehearsing his argument and the reaction it provoked, it will perhaps be better to describe the factors that enable scholarship and enhance the possibilities of those who intend to pursue it.

Scholars must be well-read because this will help them "understand, explain, and restore" the text under consideration. Each new reading will gain from all previous readings. This process is, in principle, unlimited because reading appears to be one of those activities that do not wear off by excessive "use". From their early schooldays onwards, Greeks were accustomed to learning large chunks of poetry by heart. Future scholars will have laid in school the basis on which they built in their subsequent careers by steadily expanding the repertoire of familiar texts. In an age that has unlimited access to internet-based search engines, it is important to remind ourselves that ancient scholars were equipped with a prodigious memory. This is another way of saying that even the scholars who worked at the famous library in Alexandria with its thousands of bookrolls (the exact number is disputed: Stephens 2010, 55), regularly relied on their memories. An anecdote about Aristophanes of Byzantium (T 17 in Slater 1986; Pfeiffer 1968, 191), whether apocryphal or not, nicely catches the spirit. His stupendous memory enabled him to convict contestants at a public literary competition of plagiarism. He then went to the library and proved his allegation by opening countless books. Remembering and looking up go hand in hand and reinforce each other.

The anecdote also testifies to the obvious importance of a big library or, put differently, easy access to large numbers of books. Apart from the well-known Hellenistic libraries in Alexandria or Pergamon, it is also worth remembering that Aristotle was not only the owner of the largest library of the time, but also earned himself the nickname "reader" (*anagnôstês*) among his peers in Plato's Academy (Blum 1977, 45 = 1991, 22), which, under these particular circumstances, points to a truly voracious reader (on Euripides' books see above).

The anecdote about Aristophanes of Byzantium is indicative not only of the possibility but also the urge to prove one's point and document it. (This is the scholarly side of what students of Hellenistic poetry have dubbed the "Alexandrian footnote": Hinds 1998, 1–5.) Scholarship has a lot to do with *Wissenschaftlichkeit*: scholars strive for a type of research that is rooted in sound methodology. They attempt to catch all the relevant examples (or at least a representatively large sample). They try to discern a general rule or pattern in the data and cope with apparent or real exceptions. They do so by digging deep into a large body of material, both immediately relevant and more off the beaten track or even arcane (e.g. unique mythological variants or obscure customs in remote places). Eventually, scholars present their findings in a way that is meant to prove their point and at the same time enables their readers (or hearers) to follow the argument. These in turn either agree or object and try to substantiate their counter-argument, which can lead to a scholarly debate (polemics play a more than marginal role in scholarship). Taken together, we get a list of catchwords such as systematic approach, professionalism, verifiability, scholarly exchange with colleagues, generous resources, long hours of work, etc.

While it would be absurd to deny that any of this existed in pre-Hellenistic times (scholarship is not the kind of activity that is suddenly "discovered," for specific examples see below), it is true that the Ptolemies created research conditions in Alexandria that were far superior even to those in the former center of the intellectual world, Athens. In their large-scale attempt to collect and restore the entire Greek heritage, the Ptolemies were willing to spend a fortune in order to bring to Alexandria both the relevant materials and the "international" experts who were best suited to do the job, which in turn attracted other intelligent people. They thus created an environment that was particularly amenable to all kinds of intellectual activity, which led to masses of tangible results (primary texts [old and new] and secondary literature; much to our chagrin, most of them are lost today). The truism "size matters" plays a role here because the Alexandrian scholars had an unprecedented number of texts at their disposal, which at the same time forced them to find means to cope with it. Some of their "inventions" should probably be read against this backdrop. A good example is Callimachus's *Pinakes* ("tables"). Even though it may have served as a kind of library catalogue too, the *Pinakes* aspired to much more. The entire body of Greek literature was registered and divided into classes. Several of them were identical with established literary genres such as epic, tragedy or comedy. Some categories (esp. lyric) were divided into sub-genres. Callimachus's concern for useability transpires from the fact that the sequence of authors within each unit was alphabetical. From today's perspective, this is an obvious choice, but we must bear in mind that alphabetization was a relatively new thing and far from being "obvious." (The first librarian and Homeric scholar Zenodotus has a fair chance of being the "inventor" of alphabetization. In any case his glossary was arranged alphabetically: Pfeiffer 1968, 115.) Each entry also contained biographical information on the specific author, followed by an alphabetical (?) list of his or her works. The list indicated cases of doubtful authenticity and works that were no longer extant. A quotation of the opening line (*incipit*) helped identify the work in addition to its title(s), which could be more recent and thus not necessarily "authentic." The entry also gave the work's length (in number of lines, i.e. cost). The *Pinakes* was not a complete novelty in that it took some of its principles from the lists of the victors in dramatic competitions which Aristotle had compiled (*didaskaliai*; Blum 1977 = 1991).

The goal of restoring the entire Greek heritage created a need not simply for texts but, more specifically, for good, reliable texts. The Hellenistic scholars, though clearly not the first generation of editors, also began refining the business of editing texts. This said, the similarities between ancient and modern principles of textual criticism should perhaps not be exaggerated.

In recent years, doubts have been raised (e.g. West 2001, 33–45) whether, for example, ancient textual critics truly made a systematic collation (i.e. comparison) of different manuscripts in the style developed in the nineteenth century. Still, the systematization and professionalization that are so typical of this era had an impact on textual criticism too, in that scholars were keen to avoid what they considered random editorial decisions and replace them by principles that were sound and led to verifiable results.

Literary texts in general and the Homeric epics in particular were omnipresent in Greek society. (The widespread comparison of Homer as the "bible of the Greeks" is valid as long as we keep in mind that Homer is not a religious text.) The intervening years had, however, left their mark, in that Homeric Greek became increasingly difficult to understand due to archaic words (semantics), obsolete forms (morphology), ambiguous passages, unfamiliar concepts, etc. Problems like these must have arisen at an early stage. The early reciters of epic poetry, the rhapsodes (not to be confused with the original singers who practiced "composition-in-performance"), regularly supported their performance by means of additional comments and explanations. These will have contained the seeds of literary criticism. The Sophists were by no means indifferent to literature. Protagoras, for example, discussed questions of narrative composition (DK 80 A 30 = Σ pap. *Il.* 21.240, p. 101 Erbse). Texts such as Aristotle's *Homeric Problems* (fragments only) indicate that a kind of special literature had begun developing in the form of monographs (*sungrammata*) that were devoted to particular problems of literary criticism. The difference in Hellenistic times is again more one of degree than kind, in that both the number of such monographs and the specialization of their topics grew noticeably. Things are different with another scholarly format that is still common today and in all likelihood represents a Hellenistic innovation: the running commentary, which explains the text line by line. Word lists that follow the sequence of the text may well have existed before, but running commentaries, which are a much more comprehensive and sophisticated aid to the reader, are not attested before Hellenistic times.

In spite of the professionalization that has been described above as characteristic of Hellenistic scholarship, the specific domain of literary criticism never became recognized as a field of its own. Nor were there attempts to delimit or define the task of a literary critic. Instead the subject that we call "literary criticism" remained, in antiquity, located in a largely undefined grey zone that overlaps with grammar, rhetoric, philosophy, and education. "Ancient literary criticism" is in essence a modern construct, which does not mean that it is a phantom. It does mean, however, that a clear delimitation must not be expected, not least because the persons concerned will not assist us.

As a final step it will be useful to review some of the more important findings and tenets of ancient literary criticism, adding to what has already been said above. For the sake of clarity, each item in the subsequent list is put in the form of a catchy phrase which is then explained and illustrated. These phrases almost never have an immediate equivalent in the relevant ancient sources. Their purpose is to bring out the gist of the matter without, however, forcing the ancient witnesses into saying things they did not actually say, if only indirectly. Moreover, it will be obvious that no individual scholar would have subscribed to all these tenets. The idea is to give an impression of the spectrum of questions that ancient literary critics found worth addressing. My discussions are kept very brief because this in turn allows to show the wide range of topics, which is another aspect of scholarship. The list gives preference to general topics and does not include questions that refer to an individual poet or genre.

Literature (or, more generally, art) is a separate entity with its own principles and rules: credit for this insight must go to Aristotle and his defense of art against Plato's fundamental objections in the *Republic*. Aristotle responded "by holding that the content and meaning of mimetic works cannot justifiably be tested against any fixed criterion of truth or reality" (Halliwell

1989, 153), as Plato had done. Instead, art must be measured by its own standards (*Poet.* 1460b8–15). Aristotle thus made a claim on a large scale that on a slightly smaller scale came to be known as "poetic licence" (*poiêtikê areskeia* or *exousia*), which also helped defend literary texts against petty objections.

Literature is a historical phenomenon and must be read and interpreted accordingly: the age of texts like the Homeric epics posed several problems for later generations of readers (see above). One was that the epics presented a bygone world. As Aristotle (F 166 Rose) recognized, apparent oddities, for example, in the behavior of Homeric characters could be explained by means of the assumption that they reflected a habit that was no longer common. This interpretative principle (which was later called "solution from the <then> habit": *lusis ek tou ethous*) was generalized by Aristarchus in the sense that readers of a historical text must always beware of distortions caused by anachronistic assumptions and unjustified equations (Schmidt 1976). Texts must be read against the backdrop of the period that produced them.

Literature causes emotions: starting with the oldest extant sources (cf. above on *terpein* in Homer), the effect of literature is time and again described as a causation of emotions, which cover a broad range: pleasure, amusement, entertainment, joy, anxiety, fear, agony, suspense, sympathy, pity, anger, surprise, confusion, alarm, passion, etc. No less importantly, the causation of emotions is seen as a fundamental goal or effect of literature. It is again Aristotle who contributes (at least) two crucial building blocks. Firstly, in his much-debated definition of tragic poetry (*Poet.* 1449b24–8) the causation of emotions and their subsequent "cleansing" (*katharsis*) is the undisputed linchpin, even though modern scholarship widely disagrees on the exact details of this process. Secondly, book 2 of his *Rhetoric* (chs. 2–11) contains the earliest systematic treatment of human psychology, because speakers (and thus, by extension, authors) must be intimately familiar with the emotions that they intend to cause.

Literature has an educative function: a clear reflection of this tenet (cf. also above) can be seen in the dominant role that literature played in school. Greek pupils read (or better, learned by heart and recited) literary texts, Homer in particular. Not only was he regarded by many as the "first discoverer" (*prôtos heuretês*) of countless things but also as the source of all wisdom (Hillgruber 1994, 5–35). To read literature was thus considered an important propaedeutic step towards studying philosophy. More generally, education was to a large degree seen as determined by what people had read in school and later. This fundamental position helps explain why literature was so ferociously attacked by critics (e.g. Xenophanes, Heraclitus, Plato) who felt that it had failed to set a suitable model (for Aristotle's reply see above). The idea of a model also played a role in that literary texts were meant to help readers develop their own literary skills by imitating the great masters of literature.

Literature should meet certain standards of appropriateness: the concept of appropriateness (e.g. *to prepon*, on which see Pohlenz 1965) regularly surfaces in ancient literary criticism. It is, however, important to bear in mind that appropriateness is not *a priori* a moral category. It can have undertones that are clearly moralizing, but when, for example, Aristotle demands that the depiction of characters be appropriate (*Poet.* 1454a22–4), the main idea is that characters ought to speak and act in a way that is appropriate to their age, gender, social class, etc. Consequently, when scholars criticize a passage for its lack of propriety, we should not automatically assume that their qualms are ethically motivated.

"A speech <situation> consists of three things: a speaker (ho legôn) and a subject on which he speaks (peri hou legei) and someone addressed (pros hon [sc. legei]; Arist. Rhet. 1358a37–b1, trans. Kennedy; author's emphasis)": Aristotle's succinct definition aptly captures the fundamentals of the communication process that was to have such a long and successful history, for instance, in linguistics and speech act theory: sender, receiver, message. In doing so, he

also identified the main actor of the present chapter. While it is correct to say that pre-twentieth century criticism tends to pay more attention to the author than the reader, there are some important exceptions. For instance, Aristotle's pupil Theophrastus (F 696 Fortenbaugh) persuasively described the workings of the reader's cooperation, which in a way adumbrates reader response theory. And Plutarch (*Quomodo adol.*) explored the activity of the reader and advocated, among other things, a form of reading against the grain (Konstan 2004).

The life of an author is reflected in his work: this widespread notion receives jocular expression in Aristophanes' *Acharnians* (410–13), where it is suggested that "Euripides" likes to bring on stage crippled heroes in rags because he himself shuns exercise and wears rags (cf. *Thesm.* 149–67). Comparable to Seneca's winged word *talis oratio qualis vita* (*ep.* 114.1), the concept underlies numerous critical observations – often with moralizing undertones (Russell 1981/1995, 162–4). At the same time it helps explain why the primary source of ancient biographies is often nothing more than that author's oeuvre.

Sound matters: following up on what has been said above on euphonist theory, the point can be added that arguments from euphony are very common. For instance, Aristarchus rejected Zenodotus's text in *Iliad* 6.34 because it was "cacophonous" (*kakophônos*, Σ A *Il.* 6.34 Ariston.). Moreover, the meticulous analysis of individual sounds fills a considerable section of *On Composition* by Dionysius of Halicarnassus, who also continued one of the euphonists' favored testing methods, the transposition of words.

Literature regularly uses rhetorical tropes and figures: the fundamental insight (e.g. Arist. *Poet.* 1457b1ff.) that language can either be "plain" (*kurios*) or "figurative" (*metaphorikos* and cognates) laid the basis for what was to become an elaborate and, at times, confusingly detailed analysis of rhetorical tropes and figures. Rhetorically interested critics mined the masterpieces of Greek literature for relevant passages in order to use them as illustrating examples in their handbooks. Likewise, commentaries on literary texts would regularly identify and describe their rhetorical features.

Authors strive for variety: Homer's Menelaos already gives expression to the widespread notion that too much of the same ends in "surfeit" (*koros*, *Il.* 13.636). Literature was not exempt (Pind. *Pyth.* 8.29–32, *Nem.* 10.19–20). The concept "variety" (*poikilia*) firmly belonged to the arsenal of ancient critics. The presence of monotony was criticized, authors were praised for its avoidance, often including a description of how exactly this was achieved. A particular challenge for critics was to account for the fact that Homeric poetry contains so many repeated phrases and entire lines and nevertheless possesses "variety."

The literary field can be divided into different genres: the distinction of different genres must have begun at an early stage. Audiences are likely to have felt (or heard) intuitively that there is a generic difference between, say, Stesichorus and Sappho. Plato (*Laws* 700b) gives a remarkably long list of lyric genres: prayers, hymns, dirges, paeans, etc. The focus of Aristotle in his *Poetics* is more on tragedy and epic, but it contains a clear definition of what a tragedy actually is and achieves. Moreover, he has genres develop into others (e.g. heroic poetry into tragedy and iambic poetry into comedy: 1449a2–6), which, among other things, adumbrates literary history (already operative in *Frogs*). The Hellenistic scholars characteristically attempted to carve up the entire literary field into different genres and to assign each text to the appropriate category, not least for editorial reasons. On occasion, this would lead to disputes, for instance, whether Bacchylides' *Cassandra* (F **23 Maehler, with schol.) was a paean (Callimachus) or a dithyramb (Aristarchus).

Literature is a combination of tradition and innovation: authors do not operate in an isolated void but are themselves recipients of a tradition that they may either adopt or modify. Thus the question "what is old (i.e. traditional) here and what is new?" is regularly asked. Interestingly, this may include Homer, who, in spite of his perceived position at the beginning of Greek literature, can nevertheless be seen as the recipient of a tradition (e.g. Σ A *Il.* 11.430*b* Ariston., on the characterization of Odysseus). His treatment of a particular scene can, in turn, influence his successors, which is the basis for the numerous notes on literary dependence (e.g. Σ AT *Il.* 22.210*a Ariston.*).

Interpretation must be text immanent: this tenet is arguably Aristarchus's best-known contribution to the field of literary criticism. It is usually referred to in the form "to elucidate Homer from Homer" (*Homêron ex Homêrou saphênizein*), which aptly expresses the spirit, if perhaps not the letter, of Aristarchus's principle (on which see Montanari 1997, 285–6, with lit.). In answering the questions that a text poses, readers should first and above all resort to that text itself because each text is its best interpreter. The same principle also allowed Aristarchus, for example, to caution against the method of supplementing allegedly "incomplete" mythical accounts by resorting to other sources (e.g. the famous absence of the horse Pegasus from Homer's version of the Bellerophon myth: Σ A *Il.* 6.183*a Ariston.*). It is worth emphasizing that Aristarchus did not apply the principle of "elucidating Homer from Homer" in a dogmatic way but with a healthy sense of proportion that is typical of him (Nünlist forthcoming).

The different voices in a text must be kept separate: Aristotle (F 146 Rose) recognized that alleged contradictions in a text end in smoke when the relevant passages are spoken by different characters. This insight became the basis for what was later called *lusis ek tou prosôpou* ("solution from the character [speaking]"). The concept, if not the term, played an important role for Aristarchus, whose concern for possible anachronisms (see above) made him keep a strict distinction between Homer's voice and that of his characters. Thus he was able to identify a number of remarkable differences between the two narrative levels (Nünlist 2009, 116–19).

A narrative's temporal structure is not identical with that of the underlying story: the distinction, in narratological terms, between *récit* ("plot") and *histoire* ("story") is implicitly present in the *Poetics* of Aristotle, whose term *muthos* clearly represents the plot with its non-chronological structure (the chronological summary of the *Odyssey* is called *logos*. 1455b17). He thus laid the basis for subsequent scholars who would describe the non-chronological structure, among other things, by identifying cases of prolepsis (e.g. *proanaphônêsis*) and analepsis (no standard term and paraphrased instead).

Literary texts can have multiple meanings: the term *huponoia* (lit. "undersense", i.e. "deeper sense," e.g. Plat. *Rep.* 378d) expresses in a colorful way that, underneath the surface meaning, there may be a second meaning that waits to be uncovered by critical readers. The search for a second, deeper sense that was probably the most common among ancient critics is allegorical interpretation. Even though allegorical interpretation need not have originated as a form of defense, in actual practice it could be used to this purpose, for instance, in order to defend Homer for what some critics felt was an inappropriate or even blasphemous depiction of the gods (Konstan 2005).

There is a difference between poetry and prose: the well-known distinction that depends on whether or not the text is in meter is at least as old as Gorgias (DK 82 B 11.9). It incurred the vigorous criticism of Aristotle (*Poet.* 1447b13–23), who argued in favor of a distinction along different lines, replacing the criterion meter by *mimêsis.* In this case, his efforts turned out to be futile. The prose/poetry distinction was to have a very long life. In a related matter, ancient critics generally showed more interest in poetry than prose.

Literature requires close reading: the relevance of this principle for ancient scholars can mostly be deduced from the fact that they time and again propose subtle interpretations that owe their existence to a close reading of the text. It comes thus as a welcome confirmation when Aristarchus expresses the explicit recommendation that "one must look intently (*atenisteon*) at the particular circumstances" of the passage under consideration (Σ A *Il.* 14.84*a Ariston.*). Likewise, Dionysius of Halicarnassus (*De im.* p. 213.17 U.-R.) speaks of "attentive reading" (*epimelês anagnôsis*).

Plots should be well-motivated:

> and these elements (sc. reversal and recognition) should emerge from the very structure of the plot [and not from outside], so that they ensue from the preceding events by necessity or probability; as it makes a great difference whether things happen because of, or only after, their antecedents (Arist. *Poet.* 1452a18–21, trans. Halliwell).

Aristotle's notion that each event should not simply be preceded but actually motivated by a previous event met with approval among subsequent critics, who repeatedly comment on how the event *X* motivates the event *Y*. Taken together, these notes testify to a special interest in plots that are well-motivated and thus coherent. The quotation also documents the widespread concern for plausibility.

As a linear form of art, literature must present simultaneous events one by one: Aristotle (*Poet.* 1459b22–8) saw that narrative texts such as the Homeric epics do contain simultaneous events (contrary to a view sometimes expressed in modern scholarship). Aristarchus (Σ pap. *Il.* 2.788, p. 169 Erbse) spelt out the underlying assumption that this cannot be a literal simultaneity because, as a linear form of art, narrative must present the relevant events sequentially one by one. The implicit contrast is likely to be non-linear forms of art such as painting (Lundon 2002), a contrast that was later fully developed by Lessing in his *Laokoon* (1766).

REFERENCES

Abbenes, J. G. J., S. R. Slings, and I. Sluiter, eds. 1995. *Greek Literary Theory After Aristotle*. Amsterdam.

Atkins, J. W. H. 1934. *Literary Criticism in Antiquity*. 2 vols. London.

Blum, R. 1977. *Kallimachos und die Literaturverzeichnung bei den Griechen: Untersuchungen zur Geschichte der Biobibliographie*. Frankfurt (English translation Madison, WI, 1991).

Bowie, E. 1994. "The Readership of Greek Novels in the Ancient World." In J. Tatum, ed., *The Search for the Ancient Novel*, Baltimore, 435–59.

Busch, S. 2002. "Lautes und leises Lesen in der Antike." *Rheinisches Museum für Philologie* 145: 1–45.

Cavallo, G. and R. Chartier, eds. 1999. *A History of Reading in the West: Studies in Print Culture and the History of the Book*. Boston (Italian translation Rome 1995, French translation Paris 1997).

Clauss, J. J. and M. Cuypers, eds. 2010. *A Companion to Hellenistic Literature*. Oxford.

Del Corso, L. 2005. *La lettura nel mondo ellenistico*. Rome.

Dickey, E. 2007. *Ancient Greek Scholarship: A Guide to Finding, Reading, and Understanding Scholia, Commentaries, Lexica, and Grammatical Treatises, from their Beginnings to the Byzantine Period*. Oxford.

Easterling, P. E., ed. 1997. *The Cambridge Companion to Greek Tragedy*. Cambridge.

Fantuzzi, M. and R. Hunter. 2004. *Tradition and Innovation in Hellenistic Poetry*. Cambridge.

Ford, A. 2002. *The Origins of Criticism: Literary Culture and Poetic Theory in Classical Greece*. Princeton, NJ.

Fraser, P. M. 1972. *Ptolemaic Alexandria*. 3 vols. Oxford.

Gavrilov, A. K. 1997. "Techniques of Reading in Classical Antiquity." *Classical Quarterly* 47: 56–73.

Goldhill, S. 1997. "The Audience of Athenian Tragedy." In P. E. Easterling, ed., *The Cambridge Companion to Greek Tragedy*, Cambridge, 54–68.

Grube, G. M. A. 1965. *The Greek and Roman Critics*. Toronto.

Gutzwiller, K. J. 2010. "Literary Criticism." In J. J. Clauss and M. Cuypers, eds., *A Companion to Hellenistic Literature*. Oxford, 337–65.

Halliwell, S. 1989. "Aristotle's Poetics." In G. A. Kennedy, ed., *The Cambridge History of Literary Criticism: Vol. 1: Classical Criticism*, Cambridge. 149–183.

Halliwell, S. 2012. *Between Ecstasy and Truth: Interpretations of Greek Poetics from Homer to Longinus*. Oxford.

Harriott, R. 1969. *Poetry and Criticism before Plato*. London.

Harris, W. V. 1989. *Ancient Literacy*. Cambridge, MA.

Hillgruber, M. 1994. *Die pseudoplutarchische Schrift De Homero*. Vol. 1. Stuttgart and Leipzig.

Hinds, S. 1998. *Allusion and Intertext: Dynamics of Appropriation in Roman Poetry*. Cambridge.

Holzberg, N. 2006. *Der antike Roman: Eine Einführung*. 3rd edn. Darmstadt.

Hunter, R. 2009. *Critical Moments in Classical Literature: Studies in the Ancient View of Literature and Its Uses*. Cambridge.

Jacob, C. and F. de Polignac, eds. 1992. *Alexandrie IIIe siècle av. J.-C.: Tous les savoirs du monde ou le rêve d'universalité des Ptolémées*. Paris.

Janko, R., ed. 2000. *Philodemus. On Poems Book 1*. Oxford.

Janko, R., ed. 2011. *Philodemus. On Poems Books 3–4*. Oxford.

Johnson, W. A. 2010. *Readers and Reading Culture in the High Roman Empire: A Study of Elite Communities*. Oxford.

Johnson, W. A. and H. N. Parker, eds. 2009. *Ancient Literacies: The Culture of Reading in Greece and Rome*. Oxford.

de Jonge, C. C. 2008. *Between Grammar and Rhetoric: Dionysius of Halicarnassus on Language, Linguistics and Literature*. Leiden.

Kennedy, G. A., ed. 1989. *The Cambridge History of Literary Criticism: Vol. 1: Classical Criticism*. Cambridge.

Knox, B. M. W. 1968. "Silent Reading in Antiquity." *Greek, Roman and Byzantine Studies* 9: 421–35.

Konstan, D. 2004. "'The Birth of the Reader': Plutarch as a Literary Critic." *Scholia* 13: 3–27.

Konstan, D. 2005. "Introduction." In D. A. Russell and D. Konstan, eds., *Heraclitus: Homeric Problems*. Atlanta, GA, xi–xxx.

Lallot, J. 2003. *La grammaire de Denys le Thrace*. 2nd edn. Paris.

Lanata, G. 1963. *Poetica pre-platonica: Testimonianze e frammenti*. Florence.

Ledbetter, G. M. 2003. *Poetics before Plato: Interpretation and Authority in Early Greek Theories of Poetry*. Princeton, NJ.

Lundon, J. 2002. "Aristotle, Aristarchus and Zielinski on the Narration of Simultaneous Events in Homeric Epos." In *Praktika. Proceedings of the 11th International Congress of Classical Studies (Kavala 24–30 August 1999)*, Vol. 2. Athens, 581–91.

Luz, C. 2010. *Technopaignia: Formspiele in der griechischen Dichtung*. Leiden.

Manguel, A. 1996. *A History of Reading*. London.

Meijering, R. 1987. *Literary and Rhetorical Theories in Greek Scholia*. Groningen.

Montanari, F., ed. 1994. *La philologie grecque à l'époque hellénistique et romaine*. Geneva.

Montanari, F. 1997. "The Fragments of Hellenistic Scholarship." In G. W. Most, ed., *Collecting Fragments – Fragmente sammeln*, Göttingen, 273–88.

Montanari, F. and L. Pagani, eds. 2011. *From Scholars to Scholia: Chapters in the History of Ancient Greek Scholarship*. Berlin.

Most, G. W., ed. 1997. *Collecting Fragments – Fragmente sammeln*. Göttingen.

Nünlist, R. 1998. *Poetologische Bildersprache in der frühgriechischen Dichtung*. Stuttgart.

Nünlist, R. 2009. *The Ancient Critic at Work: Terms and Concepts of Literary Criticism in Greek Scholia*. Cambridge.

Nünlist, R. forthcoming. "What does Ὅμηρον ἐξ Ὁμήρου σαφηνίζειν actually mean?" *Hermes* 143.

Olson, D. R. and N. Torrance, eds. 2009. *The Cambridge Handbook of Literacy*. Cambridge.

O'Sullivan, N. 1992. *Alcidamas, Aristophanes and the Beginnings of Greek Stylistic Theory*. Stuttgart.

Pfeiffer, R. 1968. *History of Classical Scholarship: From the Beginnings to the End of the Hellenistic Age*. Oxford.

Pohlenz, M. 1965. "*To prepon*. Ein Beitrag zur Geschichte des griechischen Geistes." In H. Dörrie, ed., *Max Pohlenz. Kleine Schriften*, Vol. 1, Hildesheim, 100-139.

Radermacher, L., ed. 1951. *Artium Scriptores: Reste der voraristotelischen Poetik*. Vienna.

Russell, D. A. 1981/1995. *Criticism in Antiquity*. London (first edn. 1981).

Russell, D. A. and D. Konstan, eds. 2005. *Heraclitus: Homeric Problems*. Atlanta, GA.

Russell, D.A. and M. Winterbottom. 1972. *Ancient Literary Criticism: The Principal Texts in New Translation*. Oxford.

Schenkeveld, D. M. 1992. "Prose Usages of *akouein* 'to read'." *Classical Quarterly* 42: 129–141.

Schmidt, M. 1976. *Die Erklärungen zum Weltbild Homers und zur Kultur der Heroenzeit in den bT-Scholien zur Ilias*. Munich.

Scodel, R. 1996. "Self-correction, Spontaneity, and Orality in Archaic Poetry." In J. Worthington, ed., *Voice into Text: Orality and Literacy in Ancient Greece*, Leiden, 59–79.

Slater, W. J., ed. 1986. *Aristophanis Byzantii Fragmenta*. Berlin.

Sommerstein, A. H., ed. 1987. *The Comedies of Aristophanes. Vol. 6: Birds*. Warminster.

Sommerstein, A. H., ed. 1996. *The Comedies of Aristophanes. Vol. 9: Frogs*. Warminster.

Stephens, S. 2010. "Ptolemaic Alexandria." In J. J. Clauss and M. Cuypers, eds., *A Companion to Hellenistic Literature*. Oxford, 46–61.

Strootman, R. 2010. "Literature and the Kings." In J. J. Clauss and M. Cuypers, eds., *A Companion to Hellenistic Literature*. Oxford, 30–45.

Tatum, J., ed. 1994. *The Search for the Ancient Novel*. Baltimore.

Thomas, R. 1989. *Oral Tradition and Written Record in Classical Athens*. Cambridge.

Thomas, R. 1992. *Literacy and Orality in Ancient Greece*. Cambridge.

Thomas, R. 2009. "Writing, Reading, Public and Private 'Literacies'." In W. A. Johnson and H. N. Parker, eds., *Ancient Literacies: The Culture of Reading in Greece and Rome*, Oxford, 13–45.

Turner, E. G. 1952. *Athenian Books in the Fifth and Fourth Centuries*. London.

Werner, S. 2009. "Literacy Studies in Classics: The Last Twenty Years." In W. A. Johnson and H. N. Parker, eds., *Ancient Literacies: The Culture of Reading in Greece and Rome*, Oxford, 333–82.

West, M. L. 2001. *Studies in the Text and Transmission of the Iliad*. Munich.

Worthington, I., ed. 1996. *Voice into Text: Orality and Literacy in Ancient Greece*. Leiden.

Yunis, H., ed. 2003a. *Written Texts and the Rise of Literate Culture in Ancient Greece*. Cambridge.

Yunis, H. 2003b. "Writing for Reading: Thucydides, Plato, and the Emergence of the Critical Reader." In Yunis 2003a, 189–212.

FURTHER READING

The bibliography on (ancient) reading is enormous. The following titles can serve as a starting-point (incl. relevant bibliography): the recent collection of essays by Johnson and Parker 2009 (incl. the Bibliographical Essay by Werner 2009, focusing on the last 20 years, with an extensive bibliography on pp. 352–82), Del Corso 2005, Johnson 2010. General histories of reading such as Cavallo and Chartier 1999 tend to treat antiquity *en passant*. Manguel's popular book *A History of Reading* (1996), though inspiring, is unreliable as far as antiquity is concerned. For the cognitive side of reading see the collection of essays by Olson and Torrance 2009. On ancient literacy see Harris 1989, Thomas 1989, 1992, 2009.

On Ptolemaic Alexandria see Pfeiffer 1968, Fraser 1972, Jacob and de Polignac 1992, Stephens 2010; on Callimachus's *Pinakes* specifically see Pfeiffer (1968, 127–34), Blum 1977 (readers are advised to use the German original; the English translation (1991) is marred by numerous errors and oddly curtails the footnotes).

On the prehistory of scholarship and literary criticism see Radermacher 1951 (collection of fragments of pre-Aristotelian poetics), Lanata 1963 (annotated edition of fragments of pre-Platonic poetics), Pfeiffer 1968 (part one), Harriott 1969, O'Sullivan 1992, Nünlist 1998, Ford 2002, Ledbetter 2003. On (the history of) scholarship itself see Pfeiffer 1968 (Part 2), Montanari 1994, Dickey 2007, Montanari and Pagani 2011. On ancient literary criticism specifically see Atkins 1934, Grube 1965, Russell 1981/1995, Meijering 1987, Kennedy 1989, Abbenes, Slings, and Sluiter 1995, Fantuzzi and Hunter (2004, 449–61), de Jonge 2008, Hunter 2009, Nünlist 2009, Gutzwiller 2010, Halliwell 2012. These works will also point the way to secondary literature on individual critics and topics mentioned in this chapter. The Greekless reader will find a collection of relevant texts on literary criticism in English translation in Russell and Winterbottom 1972.

CHAPTER 20

Sponsors and Enemies of Literature

David Schenker

Phemius, many other charming tales you know,
The deeds of gods and heroes, and what the poets tell.
Sit nearby and sing one of those, while these men
Drink their wine in silence. But stop singing that song
Of grief, the one that always wears away my heart....
(*Od.* 1.337–41)

Penelope, responding here to the palace bard Phemius, gives us an early glimpse of what we might call Greek literary criticism, and also offers insight into the status of poets and poetry in Homer's world. How did the poets make a living? Under what constraints did they operate? Who would support or oppose literature, and why? What were the mechanisms for doing that? This survey addresses those questions, beginning with Homer, then moving chronologically from the Archaic age to the Classical, Hellenistic, and (briefly) Imperial and early Christian periods, necessarily leaving much out, with a focus first on some of the most prominent forms of patronage of literature and then on opposition to it.

Where there is patronage, it necessarily derives from (at least) two conditions: an economic structure whereby certain individuals or groups have the wherewithal to serve as patrons, and, second, a recognition that literature is worth supporting, for whatever reason. Archaic age tyrants and Hellenistic monarchs are the most obvious examples of patrons, but other members of the elite supported literature in all periods, and in some cases – most notably (but not exclusively) in Classical Athens – support was civic rather than individual, deriving from the *demos* or some part of it. Opposition, too, depends on the assumption that literature has some value, that it is worth arguing against or suppressing. Since sources for this opposition are largely literary, we find not so much a wholesale attack on the idea of literature, coming from some external source, but rather a jockeying for position within the literary world: lyric poets complaining about epic; philosophers finding fault with poets; Christian writers trying to displace or coopt their pagan forebears.

A Companion to Greek Literature, First Edition. Edited by Martin Hose and David Schenker.
© 2016 John Wiley & Sons, Inc. Published 2020 by John Wiley & Sons, Inc.

1. Homeric Song and Singers in Homer

A wide variety of songs and singers flourishes throughout Homer's epics (Herington 1985; Segal 1994), but most pertinent to discussions of patronage are the two professional poets in Homer's *Odyssey*: Phemius in Odysseus's palace on Ithaca and Demodocus in Alcinous's palace among the Phaeacians. These are characters in an epic landscape, filling roles within a particular narrative, and it is admittedly a leap of faith to move from them to real-world poets. But, even so, they provide some of our best evidence for the place of the poet and poetry in the pre-Archaic Greek world (Segal, 1994, Raaflaub 1998).[1] Both Phemius and Demodocus appear as fixtures in their respective palaces, house bards rather than itinerants. Phemius is recognized (at a moment critical to his own survival) as the suitors' regular entertainer (22.330–53); and the Phaeacians treat Demodocus as a reliable retainer, to be called on as needed for a song or accompaniment to dance (8.43–5, 254–5).

Demodocus occupies a central seat among the Phaeacian nobility (8.65–70, 470–73) and is served food and drink with the others. But he also sings for tips – he is pleased, at any rate, when Odysseus, before requesting a song, passes the singer a choice piece of pork (8.474–84). These singers are at the beck and call of the powers in the palaces – Demodocus sings and plays when told (8.254–5) and Phemius's life is spared since he sang for the suitors only under compulsion (22. 330–81) – but they do retain a certain independence of action. Telemachus answers Penelope's rebuke of Phemius (quoted above) by arguing that singers have free rein in their choice of subject, possibly governed by divine influence, and led by the tastes of their audience, who always want to hear the newest song (1.346–52). Both Alcinous, king of the Phaeacians, and the visiting Odysseus recognize that Demodocus is inspired by the gods (8.43–5, 487–98), and the narrator concurs (8.62–5, 499). So inspired, Demodocus can sing whenever the spirit moves him (8.45); but he still performs on command, and twice we see him stop his song when asked (8.98–9, 537–8). In many respects, then, these bards occupy a middling status within the Homeric epics – and perhaps, by extrapolation, in the Homeric world: mingling with the elite, yet serving them, guided both by the gods and by the demands of their masters.[2]

What do the singers offer in return for this support and status? Most valuable to the Homeric heroes is *kleos*, the glory and renown that lives on long after the span of a single human life, and a bard can ensure that with immortalizing song. But it is only in the Archaic period, when the poet himself explains this contribution, that the terms of this exchange become explicit. The Homeric heroes speak often about being motivated by their desire to win *kleos*, (as, e.g., Sarpedon at *Iliad* 12.310 and Hector at *Iliad* 22.305); but the role of the poet in that process gets less attention. Achilles, whiling away the time in his tent, sings of the glorious deeds of men (*klea andron* 9.189), and Helen worries that she and Paris will be the subject of less flattering song in ages to come (6.358). Demodocus's Trojan War songs do offer a measure of *kleos* for Odysseus, at least after he reveals his identity, but the professional singers within *The Odyssey* most explicitly offer something different: entertainment. Phemius plays for the suitors' applause (1.351); the Phaeacians express nothing but pleasure in the songs of Demodocus (8.91, 8.368); and Odysseus, mournful as he hears the Trojan War recollections (8.92), joins in their enjoyment of the Ares, Aphrodite, and Hephaestus song. When songs cease to give pleasure, they are interrupted, by the grieving Penelope and by the thoughtful host Alcinous, who stops Demodocus when he sees his guest crying.

Might the singers also offer in return some form of political or social support? If, like Phemius and Demodocus, actual singers depended upon the elite for their performance context and even their livelihood, it is not unreasonable to expect that singers and their songs would value the hierarchy and undergird the authority of those at the top. And it is true that the epics, as we have them, take for granted a differentiation between classes, with different roles and rewards for each (Morris 1986; Tandy 1997, 190–93).[3] On the other hand, the homely details of the similes throughout the epics, the description of, e.g., Eumaius's hut, and the absence of realism in the portrayal of elite palace life all call into question a necessarily aristocratic performance context for the epics, and suggest that the apparently aristocratic cast of the epics might be no more than "poetic exaggeration" (Dalby 1995). Similar questions about the social and political function of literature arise in the Archaic and Classical periods, where evidence is more plentiful, but conclusions remain mixed.

2.   Archaic Age Patronage

The song culture underlying the Homeric epics continued to flourish from the seventh through the fifth centuries. Examples survive from this period of a great variety of song: elegiac and iambic, choral and monodic, intended for a public or a private audience, deriving from all across the Greek world (cf. Power, ch. 4, and Wells, ch. 10, in this volume). For much of this poetry, we have little reliable information about context, and can only guess about sponsorship or patronage of it, if that sort of support was needed at all. Sappho and Alcaeus of Lesbos, for example, and the Athenian Solon, are poets who seem to have been sufficiently wealthy to compose independent of patronage. But even as early as Archilochus, writing in the mid-seventh century, we find explicit references to the poet's livelihood and the complex relationship between poetry and its patrons. Archilochus presents himself as a soldier–poet (F 1 IEG) who claims to reject (F 19 IEG) the riches of Gyges, the tyrant of Lydia (c. 687–52). Other poets were more willing to accept riches, from wealthy individuals, families, religious and civic groups, and, not least, from tyrants. The rise of tyranny – often with concomitant public works and cultural programs – along with the development of coinage created a fertile environment for patronage in the sixth century. (See Baumbach ch. 22, pp. 348–9, and Power ch. 4, pp. 66–8, in this volume, on archaic tyranny and patronage.) Herodotus's story about Arion (1.23–4) gives us one of the earliest references to a tyrant's support of literature. While most memorable in that story is the dolphin ride that saves Arion from certain drowning, the story begins and ends in the court of Periander, tyrant of Corinth (627–585), where Arion, according to this account, invented the dithyramb and gained widespread fame for his performances. Arion took that fame on tour to Italy, and got so rich that his would-be conveyors back to Greece decided to rob him and throw him overboard. Also from Herodotus (3.121) we learn that Polycrates, the tyrant of Samos from 538–522, hosted the poet Anacreon, whose verses, according to Strabo (14.638), were full of Polycrates. Other sources place the poet Ibycus with Polycrates as well, and one fragment attributed to Ibycus makes explicit one of the basic motives of patronage, the one so often in the background in Homer: "You, too, Polycrates, will have undying fame, as song and my fame can give it" (F 282a.47–8 PMG).

Anacreon left Samos with the fall of Polycrates' tyranny and next appears in Athens along with the poet Simonides (556–468), both of them brought there by Hipparchus, one of the sons of Peisistratus and tyrant circa 528–514. While Aristotle (*Ath. Pol.* 18) attributes the presence of these poets in Athens to the fun-loving nature of Hipparchus (as opposed to the more statesman-like behavior of his brother Hippias), the pseudo-Platonic *Hipparchus* (228b–c) more charitably claims that Hipparchus's motive in sponsoring the poets was to educate and improve the citizens. In the same passage of the *Hipparchus*, we hear that Hipparchus persuaded Simonides to stay in the city "with large fees and gifts." That comment is just one of many in the ancient record that mark Simonides, noted as the first of the poets to take money for his compositions, as being more generally driven by greed (in, e.g., scholion to Pindar, *Isthmian* 2; Aristophanes, *Peace* 695–9; Athenaeus 14.656de). But one of the stories about Simonides (Cicero, *De oratore* 2.86.351–3) focuses rather on the stinginess of his patron, Scopas of Thessaly, where Simonides traveled after the fall of the Peisistratids. In that account, Scopas paid only half an agreed fee for a commissioned poem, complaining that Simonides had sung as much about the Dioscuri as about himself, and suggested he ask those gods for the other half. Later, as Simonides dined with Scopas, an urgent message came, calling Simonides out of the dining hall to meet two young men. As soon as the poet was outside, the roof caved in, killing the stingy patron and his relatives. While we might (with Quintilian *Inst. orat.* 11.2.11–16) question this story, as well as the many about Simonides' greed, they do point to complications inherent in the poet–patron relationship, particularly related to payment.

So far, we are working almost exclusively from testimonia about the relation between poet and patron in his period. Only with Pindar (522–443) and his contemporary Bacchylides, the nephew of Simonides, do we have an extant body of explicitly commissioned poetry, in particular their *epinikia*, poems written to commemorate an athletic victory. From the 17 books of poems credited in antiquity to Pindar, composed for a wide variety of occasions, four books of *epinikia* survive (a total of 45 poems). For Bacchylides, thanks almost entirely to the discovery of a papyrus in 1896, we have a corpus of fragmentary poems that includes 14 *epinikia*. These poems are sufficiently particular that we can tell who commissioned them: in many cases tyrants, not least the Sicilians Hiero of Syracuse, in power 478–67, and Theron of Acragas (488–73); but also wealthy individuals from around the Greek world (Morgan 2007). Both poets refer to their role in celebrating great deeds, and suggest the benefits, for both poet and patron, of the patronage relationship.

For the poet, there is repute and the chance to have a chorus perform a piece of work. Pindar's *Olympian* 1 concludes with the wish that the singer might join future victors (i.e., compose more such songs in the future) and be renowned for his wisdom throughout Greece. That might be enough for the economically self-sufficient, but there's also the matter of pay; economic references are not uncommon in Pindar's poems. *Isthmian* 2 begins with a look back at the good old days, before the Muse was a lover of gain (*philokerdos*) or working for hire, and poets composed freely, singing for any boy who caught their fancy. All of that, Pindar complains, has been replaced by an emphasis on money. A scholiast identifies those early poets as Alcaeus, Ibycus, and Anacreon, and commentators have read this section of the poem variously as a rebuke to Simonides and others who are *philokerdos*, or else as a hint from Pindar that he, too, expects payment (Kurke 1991, 240–56). In either case, payment for poetry is now explicit. Similar in effect is *Pythian* 11.41–2, where the Muse is said to have entered a contract: her silver voice for payment (*misthos*). Bacchylides *Ode* 3, with its focus on the wealth of Hiero, and the proper use of that wealth, more subtly comments on the poet's financial expectations.[4]

But, at least as the poets describe it, the transaction was not entirely financial. Both Pindar and Bacchylides speak of themselves as a *xenos* of their honoree, a social equal connected by ties of hospitality, and the poem itself as the gift offered in expectation of (or response to) a gift of equal value (Kurke 1991, 135–59). References to *xenia* and *charis* are abundant (as in Pindar *Olympian* 1.103, *Pythian* 3.69–72 and 10.64–66, *Nemean* 7.61, and *Isthmian* 6.18; and in Bacchylides 5.12, 13.225–7), and soften the image of the poet as mercenary tradesman or the Muse as a lover of gain. We might recall, in this context, the somewhat ambivalent place of the Homeric bard: at the beck and call of his master, but singing at will and divinely inspired.

And what does the patron get from the deal? The poems themselves suggest, from the poets' perspective of course, that they convey *kleos*, fame lasting even beyond death (as at *Isthmian* 1.67; *Nemean* 4.82–5 and 7.17–24; *Pythian* 3. 107–15). The *epinikia* record specific victories, with the name of the winner and his contest, and, in most cases, mythological comparisons magnify that praise. The poem spreads fame geographically as well. At the start of *Nemean* 5, Pindar compares his poetry to another sort of memorial, the commemorative statue: while the statue stands in one place, his song travels throughout Greece spreading the news of Pytheas's victory (R. Smith 2007, and compare *Isthmian* 2.45–9). Some have argued that the *epinikia* go beyond celebrating the individual aristocratic honoree, and offer support for his entire class, its culture and values – particularly as that class came into conflict with new democratic tendencies (but see Thomas 2007 *contra*). Even as the poems mark the individual as extraordinary, the ethical positions they express are conservative and cautionary, foregrounding moderation, human limitations and dependence on the gods (Race 1997, 1.3–4). Emphasis on these traditional values was one way that the poem could focus on the single grand individual and at the same time integrate that individual back into the traditions and fabric of the polis.

3. Classical Athens: Civic Patronage

Post-Peisistratid Athens, without tyranny, is also largely without the sort of individual patronage that kept Pindar and Bacchylides busy well into the fifth century. Outside Athens, opportunities for that sort of support continued, and even attracted Athenian poets away from home. Aeschylus spent time in Sicily with Hiero, and composed a drama for him, *Aitnaiai*, in honor of the founding of Aitna; Euripides ended his life in the court of Archelaus of Macedon (413–399) where he composed *Archelaus* and *Bacchae*; and the playwright Agathon also worked and died in Archelaus's court (Duncan 2011).

It was a different form of patronage that allowed playwrights, both tragic and comic, to flourish in Athens in the fifth century (cf. Hose, ch. 21, pp. 329–31 in this volume). As the populace, the *demos*, took political power from the few (or the single ruler), so the support for drama, the most visible form of literature in fifth-century Athens, became a public activity. Put differently, the Athenian democracy found a way to integrate large-scale individual expenditure on poetry into a civic context (Kallet 2003). The mechanism for that was one part of a system called the liturgy (*leitourgia*) that required, by law, large donations to the state from wealthy individuals. It was a sort of income tax, directed toward the funding of important state projects, such as the outfitting of a trireme or, more pertinent to this discussion, the training and maintenance of the chorus for a dramatic performance, the *choregia*.[5] While other cities also institutionalized private funding for public drama, only in Athens was there legal coercion (Wilson 2000; 2011). Months before a festival, one of the archons selected from among the wealthiest Athenians the several *choregoi* for the dithyrambic and dramatic competitions. The cost for those chosen was considerable, set at 3,000 drachmas for a tragic *choregos* in 410 (Lysias *or.* 21.1), a demand on private resources that some thought went too far (Ps.Xen. *Ath.* 1.13; Plut. *De gloria Ath.* 349a). There was the training space to rent, food for all the *choreutai* while they trained, and – an expense easily measured and judged by the audience – the *choregos* provided costumes, masks and, at least in one case, gold crowns for the 50 *choreutai* in a dithyramb (Aristoph. *Ach.* 1150ff; Demosthenes, *Meidias* 22). Finally, for the victor in a competition, there was the cost of the choregic monument. What began as a base for displaying the bronze tripod that went to the victorious chorus became, in fifth-century practice, an often monumental memorial to the wealth and generosity of the *choregos* himself.

What the *choregos* gets in return for this lavish expenditure is a vehicle for displaying his *megaloprepeia*, his large-scale civic generosity (Wilson 2000, 141). After the fact, service as a *choregos* became a mark of standing and goodwill toward the state, even a useful form of character reference in a court case (Wilson 2000, 172–84). Also, though, in the egalitarian climate of the Athenian democracy, the *choregos* could go too far. Plutarch mentions the choregic activities of both Themistocles (*Them.* 5) and Alcibiades (*Alc.* 16) in the context of their excessive ambition and suspiciously tyrannical tendencies.

And what influence might the *choregos* have on the content of the play itself? We know, for example, that a young Pericles was *choregos* for Aeschylus's *Persians* in 472, and some have found a (possibly) pro-Periclean cast to the play, noting its emphasis on the accomplishments of Pericles' father Xanthippus or Pericles' political predecessor Themistocles. Working against such readings is the nature of the process by which archons matched a poet and *choregos* (Garvie 2009). To the extent that we can reconstruct that process, it was largely mechanical, rather than driven by ideology (Aristot. *Ath. Pol.* 63; Wilson 2000, 51–7). More productive for readings of the plays, especially tragedies, is the idea that civic funding (even if through the agency of an individual) produced plays that engaged in some way with the values and ideals of the state.[6]

4. Hellenistic Patronage

The political changes following the conquests and death of Alexander brought with them a change in patterns of patronage. Civic support of literature did continue in this period (Hunter 2003, 26–7), but evidence points to the increasing importance of Hellenistic monarchs, in roles much like those played by archaic tyrants before them. Literary output was prodigious in much of the newly expanded Greek world, but particularly noteworthy was the activity surrounding the Ptolemies in Egypt throughout much of the third century BCE (Strootman 2010; Erskine 2010, 23 on literature in the Antigonid and Seleucid courts; see Mori, ch. 6, and Hose, ch. 21, pp. 331–35 in this volume). Ptolemy I Soter (ruled 303–285) and Ptolemy II Philadelphus (285–46) founded and supported the library at Alexandria, intended as a repository of all the literature produced up to that point, as well as the attached museum, a locus for scholarly editing and response to that literature. All of this literary activity is often seen as an attempt to keep alive, and spread even further, the Greek legacy of Alexander even as that legacy was transplanted into North Africa (Erskine 1995).

Callimachus (c. 310–240 BCE) was one of those who worked at the library (perhaps as chief librarian), and he repaid that support by praising the Ptolemies in several of his poems, with varying degrees of explicitness. Zeus watches over all kings, we learn in his *Hymn to Zeus*, but bestows special favor on our lord, who surpasses all others by far, accomplishing rapidly all that he plans (85–90). In his *Hymn to Delos*, Apollo from the womb steers Leto away from Cos, since that island is fated as the birthplace of another god, a Macedonian whose rule will spread to the edges of the earth (160–70). Most explicit is his praise of Berenice, wife of Ptolemy III Euergetes (ruled 246–21), in the fragmentary *Lock of Berenice*, an ingeniously roundabout celebration of Ptolemy's victory in the Syrian Wars (247–6 BCE) and the loyalty of his wife Berenice, who dedicated a lock of her hair in honor of his safe return (Gutzwiller 1992).

Further clues about Hellenistic patronage come from the idylls of Callimachus's contemporary, Theocritus – only clues, since what we have are his requests for and comments about patronage, with no evidence about how (or if) his literary efforts were in fact supported.[7] In *Idyll* 16, written for Hiero II, tyrant of Syracuse, Theocritus alludes explicitly to Homer and Simonides, and nods to Pindar throughout, thereby placing himself squarely within the framework of the archaic system of patronage (Klooster 2011, 54–60; Acosta-Hughes 2010, 179–86; Hunter 1996, 77–109). He reminds Hiero that the tyrants of Thessaly, despite all their wealth, would have been completely forgotten were it not for the poems of Simonides (34–47). And the heroes of Troy would have no glory without the work of Homer (48–57). Theocritus also retains the archaic language of gift exchange, referring to his poems as *charites*, favors he is willing to give those who support him, and he speaks of Hiero bestowing honor on those who sing praises (22–33); but references to money are explicit as well (16–17).

We do not know if this nuanced appeal to Hiero was successful or not, but we do know that in (at least) two poems Theocritus turned his immortalizing praise to another powerful figure, Ptolemy II Philadelphus. *Idyll* 14 is the lament of one Aischinas to his friend Thyonichus about the sorrow of lost love, and the possibility of finding a remedy in the life of a soldier. Thyonichus suggests that Aischinas enlist with Ptolemy, and in the final 15 lines of the poem praises Ptolemy as the best paymaster, most generous of kings, and – perhaps more relevant for a poet than a soldier – he is a lover of the muses (61). But, warns Thyonichus (revealing the need for subtlety in this patronage game), one should not make demands on Ptolemy on every occasion (64). Less subtle is *Idyll* 17, from first to last an encomium of Ptolemy, hymnic in form, that, from the human excellence ascribed to him at the end of Idyll 14, raises him right up to the level of the gods. Among Ptolemy's many accomplishments is his proper use of wealth. He is generous to the gods, to his friends, and, pointedly, to all skilled at singing in the competitions (112–14). In response to this generosity, the intermediaries of the muses sing of Ptolemy himself, thereby ensuring his immortality (115–17). The themes here are familiar, not only from similar Hellenistic examples, but from the archaic models Theocritus is so clearly emulating.

Another poet who draws heavily on archaic forebears is Posidippus, also working in the third century in Alexandria. (cf. Höschele, ch. 12, pp. 194–6, in this volume.) One of the titled sections of his recently discovered poetry book contains 18 epigrams on horse-racing, seven of those commemorating the victories of Ptolemaic kings and queens. Celebration of equestrian victories serves as a platform for praising the royal family more generally, and suggests – though, again, evidence is sketchy – that Posidippus was among those supported in his efforts by the Ptolemies. This is a different sort of *epinikion*, and performance context has changed, but echoes of Pindar ring throughout (Fantuzzi 2005).

5.   Patronage for Greeks in Rome

The forms of literary patronage for Romans in Rome were tied closely to changing social and political systems, and lie beyond the scope of this survey (Gold 1987; White, 1993). Complex in different ways was the Roman reception and support of Greek literature (cf. König, ch. 7, pp. 120–3, Hose, ch. 21, pp. 335–7, in this volume), not least since Romans so often appreciated Greek cultural contributions only in the context of Roman legal and military superiority (as, famously, in Horace *Epistles* 2.1.156–7 and Vergil, *Aeneid* 6.847–53; with cautions from Whitmarsh 2001, 9–20). Evidence for early Roman patronage of Greeks comes from Cicero's speech delivered in 62 BCE in defense of the Greek poet Archias (Gold 1987, 73–86; and also 87–107 on the relationship between Pompey and Theophanes). Cicero discusses Archias's several Roman patrons, and offers proof (against charges to the contrary) that Archias really deserved Roman citizenship in exchange for his literary work. Much of the speech focuses on the many and various benefits of that work: the pleasures to be derived from poetry (*Arch.* 12, 16); the moral value of the good examples included (14); and, taking pride of place, the celebration of Roman military and political exploits, including some of Cicero's own (21, 28–9). For these many contributions to the glory of Rome, Cicero argues, Archias had clearly earned that most valuable of prizes: Roman citizenship.

The resurgence of Greek literature in the late first through third centuries CE, the so-called Second Sophistic, grew out of the stability and wealth of the Roman Empire of that period and the flourishing of the Greek world in particular. The philhellenism of Trajan and Hadrian was most visible, especially in Athens (Whitmarsh 2001, 15–16), but epigraphic evidence reveals that wealthy individuals were reliving the *choregia* in a way, performing acts of euergetism throughout the empire, funding buildings and cultural activities for entire communities (König, ch. 7, pp. 120–1). For patronage of individual authors, however, the evidence is relatively slim, at least in part since the most notable Greek writers in this period were already Roman citizens and financially independent. Plutarch, Dio Chrysostom, and Aelius Aristides, for example, came from wealthy families, while other prominent figures, such as Lucian, supported themselves with their oratorical skills (Swain 1996, for brief biographies).

The advent of Christianity brought new responses to the place of Greek literature in society, responses that, at least initially, were largely negative. Thus, they are best understood in the context not of patronage, but of the long tradition of opposition to literature, to which we now turn.

6.   Opposition

Penelope's reaction to the Trojan War songs, our early example of opposition quoted at the beginning of this chapter, is atypical in its motives, finding fault with a song since it fails to please. We do have one similar example, the response of the Athenians to Phrynichus's tragedy *The Capture of Miletus* from the late 490s, just after the actual fall of Miletus during the Ionian revolt. Herodotus (6.21) tells us that the audience started crying, the playwright was fined for reminding them of their misfortunes, and the play was banned from future production. A more common charge against literature was that its content was not just unpleasant, containing reminders of misfortune past or present, but misguided and even harmful to its audience. Xenophanes of Colophon (fl. second half of sixth century) found fault with Homer and Hesiod for attributing to the gods "everything shameful and blameworthy among men, stealing, committing adultery, and deceiving each other" (DK 21 B 11; cf. Hose, ch. 24, p. 377, in this volume). Late in the fifth century, Aristophanes' *Frogs* staged a comic contest between his caricatures of "Euripides" and "Aeschylus" that included, inter alia, a debate about whose plays were better (or worse) for Athens.[8] (See Wohl, ch. 31, pp. 477–8, in this volume.)

But the most sustained treatment of the potentially damaging effects of literature appears in the dialogues of Plato. Comments on literature in various forms come up throughout the dialogues, but most direct – and most widely debated – are the passages in *Republic*, Books 2–3 (376e–398b) and 10 (595a–608b).[9] In Books 2 and 3 Socrates discusses with Glaucon and Adeimantus the proper education in poetry for the leadership class, the guardians, of his imagined state. They conclude (with Xenophanes above) that poets tell damning tales about the gods and heroes, tales most likely untrue, and even if they are true, tales that ought to be censored. For example, since the gods are good, it cannot be the case that they dispense both evil and good, as the famous passage at *Iliad* 24.527 suggests. That is simply a mistake by Homer (379d). And Hesiod's account of Cronus castrating Uranus, even if true, might give an impressionable youth the idea that he has license to "inflict every kind of punishment on an unjust father." (378a–b). There is thus a need to establish which sorts of stories, in effect what sort of literature, is acceptable. No one will be allowed to say, in prose or verse, that gods can be the cause of anything bad (380b), or that they deceive humans, either in speaking or in taking on different forms (382e).

Particularly dangerous is mimetic poetry, that is (for the purposes of Book 3), poetry delivered not in the voice of the poet but through the speech of characters within the poem (393–4). The danger lies in performance, in the need to adapt the voice and manner to all the characters within the poem. Socrates has nothing but praise for someone who can assimilate himself to a wide variety of characters, including, e.g., women, slaves, cowards, and madmen – but he has no place for such a person in his city. Allowed to remain in the city are only those whose poetry involves the imitation of what is good, noble, and, according to standards Socrates sets out, useful for the running of the state (398a–b).

The speakers return to poetry in Book 10, where considerations about mimesis take a different turn, and entail even further strictures against poetry. The argument here is that all poetry, whether in the voice of the poet or his characters, is essentially imitative. The visual arts provide an analogy: a painting of a bed is an imitation of a physical bed, and that physical bed is just one of many manifestations of the idea of a bed, from which all particular examples take their form. Poetry likewise imitates events in this world, events that are only reflections of an ideal. Poetry is thus an imitation of an imitation of the ideal, standing at three removes from what really matters (596–8). Since it stands so far from the ideal truth itself, poetry appeals to the lower nature of humans, weakening the rational part of the soul by encouraging attention to phantoms (603–5). The conclusion, then, is that poetry, except for hymns of praise, is to be banished from the state (607).

These are striking claims, as revolutionary (and as unlikely of implementation) as Socrates' suggestions about arranged marriage and eugenics in Book 5. What makes the claims about poetry especially puzzling is the regular and repeated reference to poets in the works of Plato – and not just to dismiss them, as in the passages from *Republic*. Perhaps even more striking is Plato's own use of what we might call poetic, or at least literary, modes of argumentation. Most fundamental in this respect is the fact that the dialogues themselves are mimetic, delivered not in the voice of their author, but always through others (and many of those others would not likely be included among those Socrates considers "noble and good"). In addition, several dialogues turn to patently literary modes at key moments, resorting to a myth or story instead of logical argumentation. The *Republic* itself concludes with the tale of Er (614–21), a *muthos* about the afterlife that, Socrates concludes, will save us if we believe it. Equally central and memorable are the stories about the soul in *Phaedo* (109–15) and *Phaedrus* (246–56).

Plato, thus, offers strong opposition to literature and at the same time makes use of literature throughout his corpus, an apparent contradiction that has aroused considerable debate (Destrée and Herrmann 2011). All agree, though, that underlying both opposition and use is Plato's recognition of the power and prominence of poetry in fifth- and fourth-century life. When, for example, in the *Apology* Socrates looks for someone wiser than himself, the poets are among those questioned (*Apol.* 22). The sophist Protagoras, according to Plato, based his considerable reputation on his knowledge and criticism of poetry (*Protag.* 339). What Socrates was doing in the *Apology*, and what Plato is doing throughout his corpus, is offering a replacement for that recognized force in society, often by using its own tools. The "ancient quarrel" between poetry and philosophy which Socrates refers to in *Republic* 19 (607) seems, in fact, a quarrel that Plato has invented, an opportunity for him to set up a worthy successor to the (supposed) wisdom and authority of poetry (Asmis 1992). And he does not hesitate to use the powerful tools of poetry toward his own ends.

7.   Responses to Plato

Plato's pronouncements on poetry cast a long shadow over the reception and criticism of literature in antiquity, and beyond. His student, Aristotle, famously hit back on the subject of *mimesis*, and the effects of mimetic literature on its audience. Imitation, he argues in the *Poetics*, is both natural and pleasant. It is one of the distinguishing features of humans that we learn from imitations or representations; and we take pleasure in successful imitations of even the most unpleasant things (1448b). He agrees with Plato that engagement in mimetic literature arouses the emotions, particularly pity and fear, but where Plato sees that emotional engagement as corrupting the rational faculties, Aristotle emphasizes its positive cleansing influence (1449b, 1453b).

Some four centuries later, Plutarch (c. 46–120 CE) addresses Plato's concerns even more directly, as in his treatise on *How the Young Man Should Study Poetry* (Hunter and Russell 2011). Yes, Plutarch acknowledges, poetry is mimetic and full of lies – and he even quotes many of the same passages (as in section 2) that Socrates held up for censure in *Republic*; but the trained student, he argues, can recognize and avoid those pitfalls and still benefit from the poetry. Strict censorship of poetry or attempts to prohibit it entirely are not only impossible to enforce, but also harmful in denying students one fruitful avenue toward what is truly beneficial, the study of philosophy. Plutarch appropriately reinforces his point with literary references, as in Section 1: rather than stopping our students' ears with wax, we should build on the delight they take in poetry, and train them to exercise judgment and reason in avoiding its seductive dangers.

With the onset of Christianity, the entire corpus of Greek literature receives much the same treatment that Plato gave Homer and others. [10] Those attempting to spread the new doctrine recognized the power of pagan literature, and, at least initially, railed against it. Clement of Alexandria (c. 150–220, or 211) begins his *Exhortation to the Greeks* (*Protrepticus*) with a litany of Greek singers, Arion, Amphion, Orpheus, and their mythical accomplishments, only to relegate them all to the mountaintops whence they came. Singers like those, he argues, were responsible for turning people away from truth, the truth toward which Clement now exhorts them (*Protrepticus* 1). In the process, though, Clement himself reveals his deep knowledge of both the content and the rhetorical strategies of Greek literature. Clement's student Origen (c. 185–254) turned his classical training in a less polemical direction, adapting the literary critical methods developed by Hellenistic Greeks to exegesis of the Hebrew Scriptures.

The fourth-century Cappadocian fathers (Basil of Caesarea, Gregory of Nyssa, and Gregory of Nazianzus) were all trained in Classical literature and recognized the continuing power and popularity of the works of the pagan Greeks. Some few examples reveal their tendency to use those works toward their own ends, rather than simply censoring them. Basil of Caesarea's (330–379) treatise, *Address to Young Men on the Right Use of Greek Literature*, owes much both to Plato and to Plutarch's *How the Young Man Should Study Poetry*. Chock full of references to Hesiod, Homer, Plato, and others, the treatise completely censors only those passages that portray base conduct – and the dangers of the Sirens seal this argument, as in Plutarch. For the rest, the young man, like a bee, should visit only those flowers that promise nourishment, and take from them just what he needs, leaving the showy exterior for those interested only in pleasure or enjoyment. Gregory of Nazianzus (c. 329–390) modeled his *Oration* 4 Against Julian on Demosthenes' *Philippics* and began by evoking Pindaric *encomium* (4.12). The form of the speech, as well as its learned content, thereby establishes Gregory as a credible opponent, and gives him the authority to ridicule the pagan authors that underpinned Julian's self-profession as philosopher king (Elm 2012, 341). Gregory's sophisticated arguments against the Hellenism of Julian served not only to discredit the former emperor, but also to reveal the importance of Greek learning to those who would defend and comprehend Christian doctrine (Elm 2012, 350). Gregory's project, then, is a call for mastering and even championing Greek literature as a necessary tool for the repudiation of the pagan context and content of that literature (Kaldellis 2007, 163). We are a long way indeed from valuing (or censoring) literature for its entertainment value, or relying on it for self-promotion, whether personal or civic. But what has not changed since Penelope chided Phemius is the recognition that literature is too important to ignore.

NOTES

[1] This is to join with those (like Hunter 1996, 93–4) who discount the witness of the so-called Herodotean Vita of Homer, and its picture of the itinerant bard.

[2] Segal 1994, 146, recognizes this uncertain position of the bard, and emphasizes differences between the social positions of Phemius and Demodocus. In a "touch of brilliant self-advertisement," he suggests, "in the happiest society the bard gets the highest honor."(p. 146) A passing remark by the swineherd Eumaeus suggests that not all bards are even as lucky as Phemius. He classes "inspired singers," along with prophets, healers, and skilled workers, in a special class of itinerant *demiourgoi* who, unlike most who show up on the palace doorstep, are always welcome guests (17.380–86). Also different is the self-presentation of the poet Hesiod, whose works are

roughly contemporaneous with the Homeric epics. He presents himself as an inspired shepherd (*Theog.* 22–9) concerned about his inheritance (*Op.* 35–9), who once sailed to Euboea for the funeral games of Amphidamas, and won a tripod in a singing competition (*Op.* 654–9).

[3] One critical tradition argues, more particularly, that support for the Aeneidai, a ruling family in the Troad, motivates the Aeneas prophecies in *Iliad* 20 and the *Homeric Hymn to Aphrodite*. For a recent and reasonable review of the evidence, see Faulkner 2008, 3–18.

[4] Specific information about the amount paid for a poem is scarce and unreliable: one scholion to *Pythian* 1, prompted by the opening of the poem, says Pindar was promised a golden kithara in payment; another, on *Nemean* 5, says that Pindar asked for and received 3,000 drachma for his efforts (Race 1997, vol. 1, 10).

[5] The movement from individual to public influence takes another step with the abolition of the *choregia* by Demetrius of Phalerum around 310; after that date, inscriptions list only the *demos* as the *choregos* (Wilson 2000, 270–76).

[6] In this volume, see Wohl, ch 31, on the political function of tragedy, and Rader, ch. 11, who recognizes that function, even as he proposes an alternative to the political readings.

[7] See Hunter 2003, 29–31, for a survey of possible patrons of Theocritus.

[8] The line between opposition to literature and literary criticism is thin here, as often. Especially in the Hellenistic period, the movement toward separating aesthetic from moral judgments about poetry begins to clarify that distinction. See Nünlist, ch. 19 in this volume, and Gutzwiller 2010.

[9] Murray 1996 usefully collects and comments on these texts, along with *Ion*. These are by no means the only Platonic comments on literature, widely conceived, but the most explicit and sustained.

[10] See Stenger, ch.8, pp. 134–6 in this volume, and Johnson 2012 for full treatment of the complex interactions between early Christians and the Greek literary tradition. For the Jewish response, and the characteristic adaptation of Greek literary forms and ideas, see the articles on Philo of Alexandria collected in Kamesar 2009.

REFERENCES

Acosta-Hughes, B. 2010. *Arion's Lyre: Archaic Lyric Into Hellenistic Poetry*. Princeton, NJ.

Asmis, E. 1992. "Plato on Poetic Creativity." In R. Kraut, ed., *The Cambridge Companion to Plato*. Cambridge, 338–64.

Carter, D. M., ed. 2011. *Why Athens? A Reappraisal of Tragic Politics*. Oxford.

Clauss, J. J. and M. Cuypers, eds. 2010. *A Companion to Hellenistic Literature*. Oxford.

Dalby, A. 1995. "The Iliad, the Odyssey, and their Audiences." *Classical Quarterly* 45: 269–79.

Destrée, P. and F.-G. Herrmann, eds. 2011. *Plato and the Poets. Mnemosyne* Supplement 328. Leiden.

Duncan, A. 2011. "Nothing to Do With Athens? Tragedians at the Courts of Tyrants." In D. M. Carter, ed., *Why Athens? A Reappraisal of Tragic Politics*, Oxford, 69–84.

Elm, S. 2012. *Sons of Hellenism, Fathers of the Church: Emperor Julian, Gregory of Nazianzus, and the Vision of Rome*. Berkeley, CA.

Erskine, A. 1995. "Culture and Power in Ptolemaic Egypt: The Museum and Library of Alexandria." *Greece & Rome* 42.1: 38–48.

Erskine, A. 2010. "From Alexander to Augustus." In J. J. Clauss and M. Cuypers, eds., *A Companion to Hellenistic Literature*, Oxford, 17–29.

Fantuzzi, M. 2005. "Posidippus at Court: The Contribution of the Hippika of P. Mil. Vogl. VIII 309 to the Ideology of Ptolemaic Kingship." In K. Gutzwiller, ed., *The New Posidippus: A Hellenistic Poetry Book*, Oxford, 249–68.

Faulkner, A., ed. 2008. *The Homeric Hymn to Aphrodite: Introduction, Text, and Commentary*. Oxford.

Garvie, A.F., ed. 2009. *Aeschylus: Persae with Introduction and Commentary*. Oxford.

Gold, B.K. 1987. *Literary Patronage in Greece and Rome*. Chapel Hill, NC.

Gutzwiller, K. 1992. "Callimachus' Lock of Berenice: Fantasy, Romance, and Propaganda." *American Journal of Philology* 113: 359–85.

Gutzwiller, K. 2010. "Literary Criticism." In J. J. Clauss and M. Cuypers, eds., *A Companion to Hellenistic Literature*, Oxford, 337–65.

Herington, J. 1985. *Poetry Into Drama: Early Tragedy and the Greek Poetic Tradition.* Berkeley, CA.

Hunter, R. 1996. *Theocritus and the Archaeology of Greek Poetry.* Cambridge.

Hunter, R. 2003. *Theocritus: Encomium of Ptolemy Philadelphus.* Berkeley, CA.

Hunter, R. and D. Russell, eds. 2011. *Plutarch: How To Study Poetry.* Cambridge.

Johnson, A. 2012. "Hellenism and its Discontents." In S. F. Johnson, ed., *The Oxford Handbook of Late Antiquity*, Oxford, 437–66.

Kaldellis, A. 2007. *Hellenism in Byzantium: The Transformation of Greek Identity and the Reception of the Classical Tradition.* Cambridge.

Kallett, L. 2003. "Demos Tyrannos: Wealth, Power, and Economic Patronage." In K. Morgan, ed., *Popular Tyranny*, Austin, TX, 117–53.

Kamesar, A., ed. 2009. *The Cambridge Companion to Philo.* Cambridge.

Klooster, J. 2011. *Poetry as Window and Mirror: Positioning the Poet in Hellenistic Poetry.* Leiden.

Kurke, L. 1991. *The Traffic in Praise: Pindar and the Poetics of Social Economy.* Ithaca, NY.

Morgan, C. 2007. "Debating Patronage: The Cases of Argos and Corinth." In S. Hornblower, and C. Morgan, eds., *Pindar's Poetry, Patrons, and Festivals: From Archaic Greece to the Roman Empire*, Oxford, 214–63.

Morris, I. 1986. "The Use and Abuse of Homer." *Classical Antiquity* 5: 81–138.

Murray, P., ed. 1996. *Plato: On Poetry.* Cambridge.

Raaflaub, K. 1998. "A Historian's Headache: How to Read 'Homeric Society'." In N. Fisher and H. van Wees, eds., *Archaic Greece: New Approaches and New Evidence*, London, 169–93.

Race, W. H., ed. 1997. *Pindar.* 2 vols. Cambridge, MA.

Segal, C. 1994. *Singers, Heroes, and Gods in the* Odyssey. Ithaca, NY.

Smith, R. R. R. 2007. "Pindar, Athletics, and the Early Greek Statue Habit." In S. Hornblower, and C. Morgan, eds., *Pindar's Poetry, Patrons, and Festivals: From Archaic Greece to the Roman Empire*, Oxford, 83–139.

Strootman R. 2010. "Literature and the Kings." In J. J. Clauss and M. Cuypers, eds., *A Companion to Hellenistic Literature*, Oxford, 30–45.

Swain, S. 1996. *Hellenism and Empire: Language, Classicism, and Power in the Greek World AD 50–250.* Oxford.

Tandy, D. 1997. *Warriors Into Traders.* Berkeley, CA.

Thomas, R. 2007. "Fame, Memorial, and Choral Poetry: The Origins of Epinikion Poetry – A Historical Study." In S. Hornblower, and C. Morgan, eds., *Pindar's Poetry, Patrons, and Festivals: From Archaic Greece to the Roman Empire*, Oxford, 141–66.

White, P. 1993. *Promised Verse: Poets in the Society of Augustan Rome.* Cambridge, MA.

Whitmarsh, T. 2001. *Greek Literature and the Roman Empire: The Politics of Imitation.* Oxford.

Wilson, P. 2000. *The Athenian Institution of the* Khoregia: *The Chorus, the City and the Stage.* Cambridge.

Wilson, P. 2011. "The Glue of Democracy? Tragedy, Structure, and Finance." In D. M. Carter, ed., *Why Athens? A Reappraisal of Tragic Politics*, Oxford, 19–43.

FURTHER READING

Gold (1987) provides an overview of most periods, both Greek and Roman, that is still useful. On patronage systems in Pindar, and lyric more broadly, Kurke (1991) has been influential, and see also the excellent collection of articles in Hornblower and Morgan (2007). Wilson (2000) gives a detailed account of all aspects of the Athenian *choregia*. Hunter (1996 and 2003) builds a broad treatment of Hellenistic patronage on his detailed studies of Theocritus. Destrée and Herrmann (2011) collect a variety of viewpoints on Plato and poetry, with full bibliography. See Whitmarsh (2001) for Greek literature in the Imperial period and Stenger, ch. 8 in this volume, on the interface between Greek literature and Christianity.

PART V

The Places

CHAPTER 21

Places of Production

Martin Hose

A striking spatial sociology characterizes Greek literature. On the one hand, it is shaped by poets and literary figures who are not tied to a particular place. Ancient Greek histories of literature saw Homer as a travelling singer,[1] and "wandering poets" remain characteristic of the profession of poet in Greek literature from the Archaic period to late Antiquity.[2] For prose writers, too, a life of traveling from place to place was not unusual. Herodotus is said to have read his texts in public in Athens, Thurii and Olympia[3] and the so-called sophists such as Gorgias delivered their lectures in many different cities. In the Imperial period and in late Antiquity, too, the "virtuoso orator" who travelled from place to place is a prominent phenomenon of Greek literature's sociology.[4]

On the other hand, these wandering producers stand in contrast to another characteristic feature of Greek literature, namely the fact that certain places drew in literary figures or developed their own distinctive literary culture. The history of Greek literature could be written as a history of places of production, beginning in the Archaic period with Sparta and Miletus, moving through Classical Athens, Hellenistic Alexandria and Pergamon, and on to Rome and Constantinople in the Imperial period and late Antiquity.[5] This chapter offers a sketch of this "spatial view of literature."

Urban centers will always offer better opportunities for developing any kind of culture. People and ideas flow into these centers and meet there, and the mere spatial presence together of different ideas and mentalities creates a constellation in which ideas can be discussed – whether in rivalry or collaboration – and thus altered or improved. A concentration of people means a concentration of talents, and creates competition between them. And a concentration of people also means that different interests come into contact, including interest in different forms of culture. An urban space is therefore an ideal laboratory for literature. All these general points apply to Greek literature, but it is necessary to add some specifications. For, at least in the Archaic and Classical periods, literature as a phenomenon in Greece is tied to opportunities for performance. Places that offered a rich festival culture and a correspondingly large number of opportunities for performance could make attractive offers to local poets to persuade them to demonstrate their skills, but could also attract poets from elsewhere. The *agon* as

A Companion to Greek Literature, First Edition. Edited by Martin Hose and David Schenker.
© 2016 John Wiley & Sons, Inc. Published 2020 by John Wiley & Sons, Inc.

a performance form, which could include musical–poetic performances, automatically resulted in an improvement in the quality of the poetry presented.

1. Sparta

Was Sparta an important location for literature? At first glance, it may seem odd to name Sparta alongside Athens and Alexandria, for there is a widely held view, which goes back to Greek literature itself, that Sparta was a crude warrior state in which every institution of social life was designed for the benefit of the Spartiates' military prowess and the oppression of the helots. This image of Sparta has been changed by the research of the past 30 years. However, it must be admitted straight away that the same recent research has increasingly cast doubt on all our hitherto trusted data on early Spartan history. The Dorian invasion and the return of the Heraclids now appear to be the expression of "intentional history," that is, a history that takes account of the ideas of the people who composed it. The wars, too, that Sparta supposedly waged against Messenia – up to four are mentioned in the ancient sources – are becoming ever harder to pin down chronologically. And finally the idea that, in an existential crisis during one of these wars (the second one?) in the seventh or sixth century, Sparta was transformed from a culturally flourishing Archaic community into a warrior state (with an iron currency) cannot be reconciled with the archaeological evidence of the early fifth century.

If we jettison the traditional Spartan image and look with an open mind at the culture of Archaic Sparta, a range of testimonia and texts give a picture of an impressively varied and productive site in the Greek Archaic world, and one that can certainly be ranked as an early cultural center.

A work "On Music," attributed to Plutarch, reports that in Sparta a first school of lyric poetry was founded by Terpander, and a second one by Thaletas of Gortyn, Xenodamus of Cythera, Xenocritus of Locri, Plymnestus of Colophon and Sacadas of Argos, at whose initiative the festival of the Gymnopaedia was founded (*De mus.* 1134b = Thaletas Test. 7 Campbell). With the exception of Terpander, the poets cited in this report are known to us as little more than names. However, it is remarkable that they all – including Terpander, who is said to have been a native of the island of Lesbos – come from outside Sparta (from Crete, from Asia Minor, etc) and yet they are linked to the Spartan festival, the Gymnopaedia. According to the ancient chronology, this festival was founded in 668 BCE. If we take pseudo-Plutarch's report seriously (and there is no reason not to), this means that a Spartan festival of the seventh century attracted poets from all around the Greek world. This appeal, we may conclude, probably rested on generous arrangements for the festival, both in the importance it was accorded in civic life and in providing prestigious prizes for the poets who contributed to it.

The Gymnopaedia mentioned by Ps.-Plutarch were a festival centered on competitions – *agones* – e.g. between choirs of older men, adults or boys. Comparable competitions were offered at other festivals, for example the Carneia, an annual festival sacred to Apollo; every fifth year it was conducted with special lavishness, including musical–poetic *agones*. The Hyacinthia, another festival devoted to Apollo, also featured musical–poetic *agones*.[6]

These three festivals formed a cycle of summer festivities from July to September. Their expansion to include musical–poetic *agones* can be detected from the early seventh century: the Carneia are said to have had this type of content since the 20th Olympiad, i.e. 676/3 BCE, the Gymnopaedia since a victory by Sparta at Thyrea in 546.[7] This development of Spartan festival culture went hand in hand with the increase in the power of its state in the Peloponnese. It is not yet clear whether that was the only ground for the prosperity of the state and the festivals, or if Sparta was also an important economic and cultural stage on the route from east to west, as the archaeological evidence increasingly suggests.

Musical–poetic *agones* mean competition, and competition means rivalry and leads participants to strive to outdo each other. Though it is not possible to reconstruct the concrete organization of the competitions in Sparta, reports mention that choruses competed with each other, though foreign poets did not (thus Alcman F 10(a) PMGF). Nonetheless, the poets' music and poetry was subject to state supervision and had to observe certain rules, as is shown by an anecdote reported by Plutarch (*Inst. Lac.* 17, 238c): to punish Terpander for breaking a rule, the ephors nailed his lyre to a wall.

This "agonistic" context of poetry is reflected in the scattered testimonia and fragments of poets and musicians who were active in Sparta. Terpander is cited as the originator of some striking innovations, namely the seven-stringed lyre, certain lyric forms like the *nomos* (a song sung to the *cithara*) and new scales and rhythms.[8] We may surmise that the victories he won at the Carneia were due to innovations like this.

We can get a faint impression of Sparta's innovative force in poetry and music from the fragments of the two best-preserved Spartan poets, Alcman and Tyrtaeus. Even in antiquity it was debated whether Alcman was a native Spartan or had emigrated there from Lydia, but the choral songs he created around the mid-seventh century came to have almost canonical status in Sparta.[9] A large fragment of a *partheneion* (a song for a choir of girls) has been preserved on papyrus and there are other smaller fragments; they reveal the poet's pride in his artistic skill. F 14a PMGF runs: "Come Muse, clear-voiced Muse of many songs, singer always, begin a new song for girls to sing." This is evidently the proem, invoking the Muses, of a *partheneion*, in which Alcman gives special weight to the aspect of the "new." At the same time, it can be seen from what remains of Alcman's poems that they track a development from simple songs accompanying cult activities – in the case of the *partheneia* these are cult practices by girls, perhaps with an initiatory context – through to demanding and highly artificial works of verbal art with complex meters. This development is a clear expression of Sparta's achievement as a site of literature in the seventh century.

Tyrtaeus offers a comparable picture. He created elegies that were performed at symposia, probably at the end of the seventh century. The fragments of his elegies reflect situations in male-military or civic life: several fragments and testimonia attest a major elegy called *Eunomia* which, with glances to Spartan history, sets out the right behavior according to the Spartan constitution (F 1–8 IEG; cf. Andrewes 1938). Famous (and infamous) is a fragment that presents a poetic paraenesis by a military leader exhorting his troops to courage on the battlefield: "It is a fine thing for a brave man to die when he has fallen among the front ranks ..." (F 10 IEG, transl. Gerber). The elegies of Tyrtaeus build on an existing poetic genre, developing approaches that had been begun, for example, in the earlier elegies of Callinus.

It is not clear how long this "artistic Sparta" maintained its cultural dynamism (see above). The state probably hardened its line definitively in the year 464, when an earthquake and a simultaneous helot revolt presented a radical threat to its existence.

2. Miletus

In contrast to Sparta, the end of Miletus's era as one of the Greek world's innovative cultural centers can be dated precisely: in 494 BCE Persian troops destroyed the city, which had led the revolt against the Great King, and so destroyed an intellectual laboratory that had begun to shape a new understanding of the world. In Sparta culture had blossomed on the basis of festivals, that is, by the will of the state which organized them (however that occurred in practice). In Miletus, on the other hand, the conditions needed for thinkers like Thales or Hecataeus seem to have been provided by what modern sociology of knowledge calls a "constellation." One element of this was the city's distinctive location on an Aegean peninsula sheltered from unfavorable winds and near the valley of the river Maeander, an important trade route from Anatolia to the coast. Miletus was thus a key point in the traffic between East and West. It had a tradition of settlement that went back to the fourth millennium BCE, in which Anatolian, Minoan, Mycenaean and ultimately "Ionian" levels were overlaid. According to tradition, Archaic–Ionian Miletus was the metropolis of over 90 colonies on the Propontis and the Black Sea coast.[10] This is evidence that the city was capable of enormous logistical feats. Knowledge of suitable sites for city foundations must have reached Miletus and been evaluated there; and as the colonies remained linked to Miletus through their cultic ties to the mother city, more knowledge was continually flowing in from them. Miletus was also in close contact with the other cities of Ionia that founded colonies, contact that had a formal structure in a joint assembly, the Panionion, which united the cities in a federation. In the sixth century Miletus was thus the central point in a massive Archaic "knowledge network." The objects of knowledge were the newly explored regions of the Black Sea and the lands along the trade routes to the East and into the Levant as far as Egypt. These had different cultural traditions and peculiarities of fauna and flora, and they also had different celestial constellations from those in the heavens over Miletus. At the same time Miletus came into contact with the ancient learned cultures of the Orient and Egypt and had to face internal and external challenges and tensions (Herodotus 5.28/9 and the various texts quoted in Athenaeus 12.523f–524c refer to social problems and difficulties with neighbors typical for Archaic poleis, which finally led to a *tyrannis*.[11])

It was in this constellation that some members of the Milesian upper class evidently undertook not only to "store up" the knowledge flowing into Miletus, but also to order it. Thales, Anaximander and Anaximenes – scholars group them as "the Milesians" among the so-called Presocratic philosophers – developed hypotheses about the structure of the world, though it is unclear if this happened in an institutional context (e.g. a "school") or if the ideas of these master-thinkers developed through unregulated connections with each other. It seems possible that Anaximander was so close to Thales that we may reasonably describe him as his student, but Anaximenes was significantly later than Anaximander (at least according to the chronology of Apollodorus).[12]

Thales and Anaximander, at least, made public appearances. Herodotus (1.74) reports that Thales predicted the eclipse of 585 to the Ionians and it has been plausibly conjectured that he did so at the meeting of the Panionion. Anaximander is said to have led the expedition from Miletus that founded the colony of Apollonia Pontica (thus Aelian *Var. Hist.* 3.17). These are hints that these Milesian "masterminds" played an active part in the politics of their city; their distinctive discoveries were thus not only owed to the favorable constellation in the city, but were intended to influence it in turn.

This is true also of the fourth important Milesian, Hecataeus; Heraclitus criticizes him in a famous fragment (DK 22 B 40) for his polymathy, which gives us a hint of the kind of constellation that existed in Miletus. Like the Milesian philosophers, Hecataeus[13] attempted to order the information that flowed his way: he compiled the diverse geographical data available to him into a description of the world (as known to him). This work, *Ges Periodos* (*Journey Round the World*), stood in the tradition of the ancient *periplous* genre, which was designed to assist sea travel by giving a description of the world from the point of view of a seafarer, but Hecataeus went so far beyond this tradition that it has even been suspected that he made a map of the world. In addition to this ordering of geography, Hecataeus also attempted to form a coherent system out of the various traditions of Greek mythology. The result was a major work, *Genealogiai*, which organized myths according to the genealogies of the heroes and also criticized some myths on rational grounds. Hecataeus is usually regarded as a "proto-historian," but it is clear that historiography and philosophy have a shared basis in the special constellation of Miletus.

Like Thales, Hecataeus too seems to have been a *Homo politicus.* Herodotus tells (5.36) that he was present when the council of Miletus decided in favor of revolt. He advised against it, based on his knowledge of the size of the Persian Empire, but his advice was in vain: in Hecataeus we meet world history's first ignored political adviser. Catastrophe followed, and Miletus was destroyed. The city itself was soon resettled (and even better than before, thanks to the brilliant design of the urban planner Hippodamus), but it never again achieved the intellectual significance it had held in the sixth century. A last flicker of its former glory is found in a peculiar literary form, the "Milesian Tale," a kind of novella that was picked up, for example, by Petronius (*sat.* 85–7 and 111/2) in the stories about the Ephebe of Pergamon and the Widow of Ephesus (cf. Rawson 1979).

3. Athens

The destruction of Miletus assisted the rise of Athens as a cultural center. After the overthrow of the tyranny at Athens in 510 BCE a development had begun that led in stages to a – by ancient standards – unusually broad participation of citizens in the administration of their city, which we conventionally call "democracy." Athens' double victory over the Persians in 490 and 480/79 gave the city a leading role in the eastern Greek world, after Sparta had withdrawn from the struggle. The successful expansion of the navy that was begun after Marathon and which had brought victory at Salamis secured the city's hegemonic position in a Delian–Attic maritime league, which by the second half of the second century could appear like a tyranny. The importance of the navy also raised the standing of social groups that had not previously participated in the polis, but which got full voting rights in the so-called "Thetic democracy." In this way Athens after the Persian Wars became the center of a political and economic structure that has sometimes been called the "Athenian empire." The city became rich through trade and the tribute of the cities of the League, and was itself marked by an internal dynamism that kept its elites in constant flux and gave political power to broad strata of the population. As with Miletus, in Athens, too, we can speak of a constellation especially favorable to "literature." On the one hand, the political dynamics leading to the emergence and establishment of democracy produced rapid developments in the field of oratory. In the assembly, intensely heated political debates were held; in the court, defendant and prosecutor pleaded their cases before a jury; as part of the public festivals, official speeches were delivered time and again in honor of the city and its citizens, such as at the state funerals for Athenian war dead. In turn, the high frequency of occasions for giving speeches improved the quality of oratory considerably, and, at the same time, the abundance of such occasions enabled the systematization of oratory and development of rhetorical theories. A sophisticated system had thus evolved by the fourth century BCE which differentiated between political (*symboleutic*), juristic (*dicanic*), and festival (*panegyric*) oration and offered formulae for each of these oratorical forms (see Edwards, ch. 13 in this volume).

On the other hand the same political dynamism led to a repurposing of festivals like the Panathenaea or especially the Dionysia, in which the polis celebrated Athens itself and so reaffirmed the new order (on this as a whole, see Pickard-Cambridge 1968; Baumbach, ch. 22, pp. 346–7 in this volume). Already, under the tyrants the festival of Dionysus had been organized as a lavish event with a new form of choral performance (probably in 534), but now it was turned into a central site in the creation of a political identity.[14]

The innovation introduced in 534 by a brilliant artist, Thespis, was to set a speaker opposite a chorus, which made possible a kind of plot. It quickly developed further, thanks to the agonal structure of the festival in the fifth century, and tragedy was born. Under its influence, a high-spirited cult play was developed into an analogous form, comedy, which became part of the

Dionysia from 486. From 509 dithyrambic choirs also took part in an *agon*. A further festival, the Lenaea, was officially expanded in 440 BCE to include competitions in tragedy and comedy.

The performances every year at the Dionysia and Lenaea alone involved ten dithyrambs for adult male choirs, ten dithyrambs for choirs of boys, three satyr plays, 13 tragedies (three trilogies at the Dionysia, two dilogies at the Lenaea) and ten comedies (five per festival), all of them new works, because the re-staging of existing plays was only permitted from 386 BCE onwards. It has been calculated that around 1100 Athenians took part as *choreutes* at these two festivals every year. There was thus an enormous demand for suitable texts: the 20 dithyrambs needed annually at the Dionysia drew in poets from all over the Greek world,[15] and poets like Ion of Chios[16] made themselves available for tragedy, too. (Comedy, in contrast, was closely tied to internal Athenian affairs and so required knowledge that was generally only available to Athenians.)

As in the case of Sparta, in Athens, too, the competitive context of the performances led to enormous pressure to innovate, as documented in the changes in tragedy from Aeschylus's *Persians* (472 BCE) to the last plays of Sophocles (*O.C.*) and Euripides (*Ba.* and *Iph. Aul.*). These continuous innovations extended from formal characteristics of tragedy, the so-called "structural elements" (*Bauformen*), through adaptations of other art forms, such as choral lyric in the choral songs of tragedy, to intellectual developments[17] that were intensified by the so-called sophistic movement. In contrast to Sparta, Athens was not just a laboratory for the arts, but also for ideas about human life, society, and the gods. The democracy obliged the old elites to defend their interests in a public assembly (or in front of large juries of ordinary citizens), and political and social success was tied to the ability to speak in public. Various Greek intellectuals, whom we term "sophists," responded to this need by coming to Athens and offering training in return for money. Plato's *Protagoras* gives a literary presentation of a meeting of famous sophists in the house of the Athenian aristocrat Callias, and from this we may infer that in Athens of the later fifth century "modern" teachings were circulating not just in rhetoric but also in questions of intellectual principles.

Athens attracted visits from artists and intellectuals from the entire Greek world. We know or infer visits by Ion of Chios (see above),[18] Herodotus, Parmenides and Zeno of Elea[19] and Democritus.[20] The ideas that reached Athens in this way were not always perceived as a gain in Athens itself, but could be seen as a threat, as is shown, for example, by the (admittedly problematic) reports of court cases against thinkers like Anaxagoras (Mansfeld 1979/80).

The intense intellectual exchanges that arose in this way made possible a kind of "self-observation" within this exchange, or, to put it differently, not only were poetry and philosophy "produced," but there was also reflection on this production and it was contemplated as a historical phenomenon: early forms of "intellectual history" or "theory of science"[21] had begun. An important condition for this was a development in media: the growth of writing and book culture can be traced throughout the Greek world, but in Athens it gained greater dynamism from the so-called Cleisthenic reforms that followed the overthrow of the tyranny, as their structures, linked to the democracy, required the ability to read and write (Missiou 2011). By the end of the fifth century, books were an upmarket, but nonetheless everyday phenomenon.[22] The existence of books meant the permanent simultaneous presence of old and new poetry, old and new philosophy. This led to comparison and reflection on a body of material that was no longer limited, as it was in a festival *agon*, to what had just been heard: now "old" and "new" could be set in indirect competition. Books also removed the limits on the amount of knowledge that could be collected and applied in the present moment. In the Archaic period "wisdom" had been linked to lived experience (as embodied by Nestor in the *Iliad*, for example), but now the experiences preserved in books could be passed on independently of the people who had experienced them.[23] Thus Thucydides (1.22.4) valued his historical work as a *ktema es aei*, the sophist Hippias (DK 86 A 12, B 6, B 4) compiled a collection (*synagoge*) of the great and important thoughts of poets and prose writers, and reflection on poetry prompted the first attempts at a theory of poetry (Gorgias, *Helen* § 9; Aristophanes, *Frogs*, and Sophocles' book on the chorus: Suda Σ 815).

In the second half of the Peloponnesian War the material basis of Athenian culture changed, but, perhaps, so did its intellectual climate. In Thucydides' history it had still been possible to claim that a special delight in experimentation was a characteristic of Athens at the start of the war (thus in the speech of the Corinthians at 1.70), but the trial of Socrates in 399 reveals a more conservative attitude in the city. The fifth- and fourth-century innovations became institutions: at the Dionysia from 386 "old" comedies became an official part of the *agon*, and in the final third of the fourth century the theater itself was rebuilt in stone.[24] Athenian drama became an institution with a history, and one worth studying, as is shown by Aristotle's *Poetics*. The revolutionary thought of the sophists, which had encouraged Athenian aristocrats like Alcibiades or – in Plato's *Gorgias* – Callicles to pursue an amoral political course, was transformed by Gorgias's student Isocrates into a formal education. In 390, Isocrates founded a proper school, which produced important Athenian politicians and intellectuals: Lycurgus, Isaeus, the historians Ephorus and Theopompus, and even Demosthenes are said to have attended it. Philosophical thought about the basis of the world and human society also settled into an institutional context when Plato, to rival Isocrates, opened his school, the Academy, in 387.

As an organizational form, the philosophical school created a new kind of constellation, in which problems could be thought through with great intensity and whole systems could be worked out discursively. The Academy created the prototype of an institution that could suffer breakaways (e.g. the foundation of the Lyceum by Aristotle in 335) and could set up branches in other locations (this is evident for Alexandria at least). At the end of the fourth century there were four schools: as well as the Academy and "Peripatos," Epicurus's "Kepos" (founded after 305) and Zeno's "Stoa" (founded around 300), attracted significant numbers of students:[25] Epicurus is said to have had 200, and Theophrastus, Aristotle's successor, 2,000 (Diog. Laert. 5.37). If we also consider the rhetorical training offered in Athens inspired by Isocrates, it is clear that Athens had been transformed into a "college town." This change began in the Hellenistic period and later even brought Romans like Cicero (cf. *De fin.* 5.1) and Horace to Athens. It was anchored institutionally in 176 CE, when the emperor Marcus Aurelius set up a paid professorial chair for each of the four major philosophical schools (Cassius Dio 71.32.1; Hadot 2003). Thus the famous phrase that Thucydides (2.41.1) gives to Pericles in the "Epitaphios" became literally true: Athens had become the school (*paideusis*) of all Greece (and beyond).[26]

4. Alexandria

When Alexander the Great founded a city west of the Canopic branch of the Nile in 332/1 – like the other 20 or so cities that he founded, as far as the Hindu Kush, it bore his name "Alexandria" – he could not know that in the modern period this city would become identified with a certain type of literary culture. "Alexandrian" has come to term a literary style in which a *poeta doctus* creates the most refined poetry, characterized by concentrated form and choice expression, associated with the highest standards of erudition and produced for a no less sophisticated readership. That this arose in Alexandria, set up in 331 on the site of a small Egyptian village, is due to a series of fortunate circumstances beginning in the aftermath of Alexander's death in 323. Ptolemy had been appointed satrap of Egypt at the time of Alexander's death and, through smart and energetic maneuvering, he emerged from the struggles between the Diadochoi as king of a rich and stable land, Egypt. He transferred the capital from ancient

Memphis to Alexander's new foundation and, thanks to the wealth of the land of the Nile, he equipped the city lavishly. It appears to have been a magnet not just for Egyptians but also for Greeks, Jews and Orientals. A massive lighthouse on the island of Pharos secured access to the city's commercial harbor by day and night; it was completed around 280 BCE and came to be regarded as one of the wonders of the ancient world.[27] A brilliant court life arose, such as had been a feature of Greek tradition since Polycrates and other tyrants, and all forms of monarchical pomp were pursued. The Ptolemies founded lavish festivals such as the Ptolemaea, founded by Ptolemy II in honor of his father, who died in 279/8; every four years they took place with great pomp. Envoys from the entire Greek world participated. The brilliance of this festival is vividly related in a description by the Hellenistic historian Callixinus (FGrHist 627, F 2, cited in Athenaeus 5,196–203).[28] Another festival was the Dionysia, which inspired an Alexandrian tradition of tragic poetry. Its poets were soon arranged into their own canon of seven "stars," the Pleiad (Sifakis 1967). The Ptolemies competed regularly in the Panhellenic games in the contests traditionally important to monarchs, namely horse and chariot racing, and they had their victories celebrated by poets.[29]

Among the institutions founded by Ptolemy I and his namesakes who succeeded him was a grandly conceived sanctuary to the Muses, the "Mouseion"; scholars were invited from around the Greek world to become members of this cult community. It is likely that this was intended as a way to organize the education of the sons of the Greek elite, on the pattern of the Macedonian court. However, perhaps modeled on the Athenian philosophical schools, a kind of ancient "Institute for Advanced Study" came into being, which profited from a second measure undertaken by the Ptolemies, namely their efforts to collect in Alexandria all the knowledge of the Greek world (and elsewhere, as we can infer). Two anecdotes vividly reveal how intense these efforts were: ships entering Alexandria were regularly searched for books and a copy was made if any were found that were not already held in the royal collections. Also, Ptolemy III is said to have brought to Alexandria from Athens the precious official copy of the tragic poets, which had to be followed by re-stagings of their works. The king had to leave a massive deposit in Athens as surety (15 talents of silver), but the Ptolemies kept the original, sent back a copy – and abandoned their deposit.[30] The giant collections of books gathered in Alexandria were housed in two large libraries (though unfortunately the indications in the ancient and medieval sources are not very clear on the point), one in the area of the royal palace, which is said to have held the massive number of 500,000 (or even 700,000) book rolls, and a smaller one outside the palace, in the area of the sanctuary of Serapis, with 400,000 volumes (Pfeiffer 1968, 98–102). (Whereas the large library was probably designed to impress simply through its size and holdings, but not through elegant reading rooms, the Serapeion library was evidently open to the public).[31] All these figures are, of course, problematic (as is the question of what damage was done to the libraries by the fire started by Julius Caesar in Alexandria in 48 BCE; cf. Hatzimichali 2013). Nevertheless, these libraries were key parts of the distinctive Alexandrian constellation. They made available in a single place (almost) all the authors of Greek literature whose texts had ever been set down in writing. A massive quantity of ideas, histories and data was present, which it was necessary to survey and set in order, if it was to be used. This task was taken up by the "librarians" of Alexandria. In contrast to other libraries, in which important work was generally carried out by an anonymous army of industrious scholars, the names of the first seven "library directors" of Alexandria have been preserved, giving us a hint of the epochal significance of their achievement: Zenodotus, Apollonius of Rhodes, Eratosthenes, Aristophanes of Byzantium, Apollonius the Eidograph, Aristarchus, and Cydas.[32] We also know of other staff, the most famous of whom is certainly Callimachus.

The surveying and ordering of the masses of text had two long-term consequences for the whole production of Greek literature. Firstly, the presence of many copies of the same text in Alexandria meant that, when they differed from each other, the question arose of what the author had actually written: this was the birth of systematic textual criticism. This came to be of immense significance in the subsequent transmission of works, especially those whose transmission showed wide variations, such as the Homeric epics or the Attic dramas, which were altered by actors' interpolations. Secondly, the ordering of the texts required "cataloguing," i.e., first a suitable description of each book and then a systematic order. This was done by Callimachus, who drew up a massive catalogue (*Pinakes*, "boards") in 120 books (Blum 1991).

However, the staff in the library did not just undertake primary philological research. They were also intellectuals (and belonged to the Mouseion) and they themselves composed poetry, among other things. Their constant work with books deepened the tendency, already present in Hellenistic poetry, to reflect in their poetry the relatively new medium of the book and the literary traditions in which they situated themselves (Bing 1988).

Library, Mouseion, and court were all linked: the staff of the Mouseion and the library composed court poetry, educated the Ptolemaic princes and lived off subventions from the court. This constellation, too, had an influence on the poetry, which, being produced in the environment of the Mouseion and the library, was able to develop a high level of erudition and make great demands of its readers (Fantuzzi and Hunter 2004).

This constellation drew scholars and poets to Ptolemaic Alexandria in search of patronage (thus e.g. Theocritus, *Idyll* 17), but the close ties to the court could also be repellent: a famous fragment preserves the mockery of Timon of Phleius, who speaks of a "(bird-)cage of the Muses," in which book-obsessives sit and constantly fight among themselves (SH 786, cf. Kerkhecker 1997).

The decline of the Ptolemaic kingdom, which ultimately led to the annexation of Egypt by the Roman empire, reduced Alexandria to the status of a large multicultural city with good research facilities,[33] thanks to the libraries that remained available in the city through to late antiquity.[34]

The city of Alexandria had a large Jewish community with its own forms of organization; it even received (at an unknown date) the status of a *politeuma*, i.e. partial autonomy. Nonetheless, this community, like other communities in the diaspora, faced the issue of acculturation to the Greek culture around it. In this constellation, Jewish texts were translated into Greek, which is how the *Septuaginta* was created,[35] and Jewish content was set in Greek literary forms, such as the epic fragments of Theodotus (SH 757–64) and Philo (SH 681–6), which drew on the *Septuaginta*, and the *Moses Drama* by Ezekiel (Jacobson 1983). Hellenistic Jewish culture also adopted Alexandrian philology (Honigmann 2003) and its interpretative methods. The extensive oeuvre of Philo of Alexandria in the early first century CE is a high-point of this productive engagement (summary in Borgen 1997): he commented allegorically on Genesis and composed biographies of Moses and Abraham on the Greek model. At the same time he is an important witness to a problem that arose from Alexandria's character as a large ancient city in which various ethnicities and religions lived together and in which minorities might be exposed to repression. This happened to the Jews in 38 CE, when they were the target of pogrom-like persecutions which were tolerated or even supported by the Roman governor Flaccus (Smallwood 1976, 235–50). In the works *In Flaccum* and *Legatio ad Gaium*, Philo wrote about this and about the embassy that he undertook on behalf of the Jewish community to the emperor Caligula to ask for help.

That Alexandria remained a city of scholarship in the following centuries can be seen from its results: around 150 CE the brilliant mathematician Ptolemy, with his *Mathematiké syntaxis* (later called "*Almagest*") produced a large, influential astronomical handbook that placed the earth at the center of the cosmos – the "Ptolemaic Model" of the universe (see Hübner 2000 with further bibliography) that persisted into the early modern period.[36] With the same mathematical precision, he compiled a geography in which all the places on earth known to him were listed with their longitude and latitude.[37]

Early Christianity, too, developed its own tradition of learning in Alexandria, where it could rely on a large community. At the end of the second century Clement (of Alexandria) argued philosophically and eruditely for the intellectual superiority of Christianity over pagan culture. In his works, especially the *Stromateis* ("patchwork carpets"), he quotes from an incredible number of pagan texts, including many tragedies that are today lost (cf. Stenger, ch. 8, pp. 131–2 in this volume). The necessary condition for these quotations was access to such rare books – a sign of life from the cities' libraries and their active use. At the start of the third century, Platonism was given a decisive new impulse by a philosophy teacher in the city, Ammonius Saccas, leading to Neoplatonism (through Ammonius's student Plotinus).

Alexandria remained an intellectually important city after the victory of Christianity. The Christian Arius, presbyter at a church in Alexandria, devised a model of the relation between God the Father and God the Son that was oriented towards philosophical ideas; under the slogan "Arianism" it was one of the ideas immediately subjected to vehement attack by the Alexandrian bishop Athanasius. Traces of the Mouseion are, finally, to be found in the figure of its last attested member, the philosopher and mathematician Theon, who edited Euclid's *Elements* and described the eclipse of the sun of 16 June 364 and that of the moon of 26 November of the same year.[38] An ever more rigid Christianization of Alexandria's culture led (probably in 391) to the destruction of the Serapeion and its library. Another victim of this fundamentalism was Theon's daughter Hypatia (Deakin 2007), whose philosophical and mathematical teaching had attracted students like Synesius of Cyrene to Alexandria until the end of the fourth century. In 415 fanatical Christians murdered Hypatia in a church, and so set a bloody end to the history of the intellectual center Alexandria.

5. Pergamon

Pergamon's rise as an intellectual metropolis in the Hellenistic and Imperial periods is above all the result of the diplomatic skill and prudence of the Attalids, a family with roots in Paphlagonia, a region on the Black Sea Coast that the Greeks tended to view as barbarian. That was the home of Philetaerus, a military man in the service of Lysimachus. In 302 BCE he was given command of the fortress of Pergamon and Lysimachus's silver treasure which was sequestered there. By switching sides to the Seleucids, Philetaerus managed to make political space for himself, and in 260 his nephew and successor Eumenes made himself completely independent. The Attalids successfully established this new realm as a mid-sized power between the Macedonian and Seleucid empires. They pursued a clever political course that played on the conflicting interests of these empires and later also of the power of Rome. Among their political tools was a public image that presented Pergamon as the protector and supporter of Greek power in Asia Minor and Greece. Protection was certainly necessary, as Celtic tribes ("Galatians") had migrated from the Balkans into Asia Minor in the year 280 and plundered and ravaged the country. The Attalids defeated them several times and used these successes for their public image in various ways. Eumenes' son Attalus (I) declared himself king after a victory over the Galatians and adopted the name *Soter* ("savior"). The Attalids publicized their new role in the Greek world through generous benefactions and dedications of magnificent statues. Attalus I had equestrian statues of himself and his most senior officer Epigenes set up in the sanctuary of Apollo in Delos, and through similar dedications the Attalids were present in other Greek sanctuaries too. As the intellectual center of Greek culture, Athens was given special attention. Attalus II donated a grand colonnade at the Agora (a reconstruction of this stands near the site of the ancient agora), and we can trace an attempt by the Attalids to interpret Pergamon's struggle against the Galatians as a parallel to Athens' struggle against the Persians and so to "inherit" in the Hellenistic period the role that Athens had played for Classical Greece.

Pergamon itself was developed to match this notion, as it was transformed from a fortress into a royal residence. Eumenes II (the son of Attalus I) set up a massive altar with a frieze depicting a gigantomachy, a symbol of the victory of (Greek) culture over barbarism.[39] In antiquity it was regarded as one of the wonders of the world;[40] in the *Book of Revelations* (2.13) it is described as "Satan's throne." As in Alexandria, a large library was built, which was to demonstrate the city's wealth and to rival Alexandria; in the mid-first century BCE it is said to have held 200,000 volumes.[41] Intellectuals were tempted into the city to fill the library with intellectual life.[42] Admittedly, it is scholars and scientists rather than poets[43] who are attested at Pergamon, men such as the mathematician Apollonius of Perge, the natural scientist Biton or the travel writer Polemon of Ilium. Philological work was given a distinctive cast by Crates of Mallus. He was an important interpreter of Homer – in contrast to Alexandrian Homeric studies, which concentrated on questions of textual criticism, he seems to have interpreted the text of Homer allegorically.[44] We may ask if this kind of philology was especially apt in a city that, in an "allegorical" interpretation of its own identity, wanted to be understood as a new Athens.

With the death of Attalus III in 133 BCE Pergamon's brilliant years came to an end. In accordance with the King's testament, the kingdom and its riches passed to Rome. Internal uprisings, the Mithridatic wars and finally the Roman civil wars threatened to ruin it. However, once the Roman Empire had been consolidated under Octavian/Augustus, and especially with the reorganization of the tax system, Pergamon recovered over the course of the first century CE. In the second century, promoted by Trajan and Hadrian, it again achieved intellectual importance: in the late first century, there was a major rise in popularity of the cult of Asclepius that is attested in a sanctuary west of the city from the fourth century BCE which was also supported by the Attalids. It became almost proverbial to talk of Asclepius (Edelstein 1945/1998) as "the Pergamene god" (*Pergamenus deus*: Martial 9.16.2). The sanctuary was expanded into a major healing center with infrastructure to match (Hoffmann 1998), in which priests, representing "temple medicine," and doctors, as representatives of "secular medicine," jointly tended the sick. The city's colonnades, theater and large library were frequented by celebrities of the Roman empire, who sought out this "Magic Mountain" to find a cure for real and imagined illnesses. This ancient spa (or "Zauberberg") is at the intellectual heart of the *Sacred Tales* of Aelius Aristides, who spent the years 145 to 147 there, receiving a complex treatment for an exceptionally difficult and numerous set of symptoms. According to the *Sacred Tales*, while he was there he composed a number of poems and orations,[45] including his "Defense of Rhetoric against Plato" (or. 2). Pergamon and the Asclepieion were also where Galen (probably born in 129 or 131 in Pergamon) completed his medical training between 158 and 161, through which he became one of the most important doctors of the pre-modern world (see Hankinson 2008, cf. Fögen, ch. 17, p. 274 in this volume).

The victory of Christianity marked the end of the sanctuary, and Pergamon itself lost its importance in late antiquity. A plague of the mid-sixth century decimated the population. Towards the end of the seventh century, the city again became a fortress, which was to defend the surrounding territory from Arab attack, but in one of these attacks in 715 it was destroyed.

6. Rome

Rome (see König, ch. 7, pp. 120–3 in this volume) is in many respects an important site for Greek literature. Rome reveals the influence of Greek culture in its reception of Greek literature (Hose 1999b): the very start of "Roman" literary history, the *Odusia* of Livius Andronicus, written around the mid-third century, is a translation of Greek literature, and this pattern is continued in early Roman drama. And Roman historiography begins, with Fabius Pictor and

Cincius Alimentus, in Greek. As Rome intervened ever more strongly in the Greek Mediterranean from the second century on, the presence of Greek culture in Rome became ever more intensive. Greek diplomats arrived on embassies, such as the famous "philosophers' embassy" in 155 BCE,[46] when Athens sent the scholarchs of the Academy (Carneades), the Peripatus (Critolaus) and the Stoa (Diogenes of Seleucia) to Rome to make the Athenian case in an internal Greek dispute (Plut. *Cat.* 22/23). Greek private tutors were also present in aristocratic families and, from the second half of the second century BCE on, Greek intellectuals show up repeatedly in the circle of friends (or *cohors amicorum*) of Roman aristocrats, either in Rome or while the latter were in the Greek world (Bowersock 1965, 124): examples are Panaetius with Scipio, Poseidonius or Theophanes of Mytilene with Pompey, Antiochus of Ascalon with Lucullus, and Philodemus with Calpurnius Piso. Some of these Greeks wrote historical works (or in the case of the poet Archias, panegyric poetry) treating the achievements of their Roman patrons and so guaranteeing their patronage.

However, Greek literature's place in Rome was not always won by mutual consent. Rome proceeded violently: Polybius, for example, was brought to Italy as a hostage; and we may surmise that many of the Greek tutors were intellectuals whom Rome had turned into slaves. There is a similar picture in material culture: after Sulla conquered Athens in the First Mithridatic War in 86 BCE, he had the important book collection of the collector Apellicon (which included the famous library of Aristotle) transported to Rome as booty.[47] Evidently for Romans, as for Hellenistic monarchs, possession of large collections of books had become a status symbol.[48]

Rome thus offered both books and high-spending patrons, at the time, at the end of the first century BCE, when the Hellenistic kingdoms collapsed and the cities of Greece became impoverished. It is thus hardly surprising that from now on many Greek intellectuals moved (or got themselves invited) to Rome, so that they could offer their services, show off their skills and, as teachers, pass them on to interested Roman aristocrats, for whom Greek education was a source of prestige. The late Republic saw the historian Diodorus move there from Sicily, the grammarian Philoxenus and the rhetor Apollodorus from Pergamon, and the rhetor Theodorus from Gadara (Kennedy 1972, 337–42). Augustan Rome (Bowersock 1965, 124) drew the historians Timagenes, Dionysius of Halicarnassus, Nicolaus of Damascus, and Strabo (whose massive geography survives),[49] poets like the epigrammatists Crinagoras, Antipater of Thessalonica, and Diodorus of Sardis, as well as Parthenius, who composed a collection of love stories, the *Erotika pathemata*, for his powerful friend Cornelius Gallus to use in his elegies. Dionysius of Halicarnassus, Caecilius of Caleacte (or, probably a little later, "Pseudo-Longinus," the author of a treatise on the sublime) and others taught young Roman aristocrats the Greek language and Greek literature.[50] Both Diodorus (1.4.2/3) and Strabo (14.5.15) explicitly note that this made Rome the center of Greek literature in their day.

This was a necessary condition for one of the most important shifts in direction in Greek literary culture of the Imperial period: in and with Rome (cf. Dion. Hal. *De vet. orat.* 3), probably through the literary critics and teachers gathered there, a paradigm of the best Greek style – Atticism – came to be applied to the entire Greek-speaking world. (It is not clear if this Atticism was "invented" in Rome or if it merely received decisive weight from the teaching of Greek tutors to Roman aristocrats, cf. Dihle 1977, Gelzer 1978, Hose 1999a for further references.) Atticism in rhetoric meant an orientation towards the stylistic ideals of Isocrates and Demosthenes (in contrast to the more lush style of rhetoric that is associated with the term "Asianism" and which was taught well into the first century BCE in the Greek east). It also meant an orientation towards the speech and dialect of the Attic "classics" like Aristophanes, Xenophon, and Plato. Throughout the whole of Greek culture down to the fall of Constantinople in 1453, a key mark of education would now be mastery of Attic in the form in which it was spoken and written in the fifth and fourth centuries.

Rome remained a site of Greek literature in the Imperial period: as the Greek east became ever more strongly part of the *imperium Romanum* and ever more Greeks entered Roman service and ultimately, as senators, joined the empire's elite, the capital of the *imperium* became ever more bilingual (cf. Dihle 1989). Famous representatives of the "Second Sophistic" made public appearances in Rome, such as Aelius Aristides, who in 143 CE delivered his "Speech on Rome," a grand panegyric of the city, before the emperor (cf. Oliver 1953). There is evidence of continuous Greek philosophical activity in the city from Philodemus in the first century BCE, through Epictetus (end of the first century CE) and on to Plotinus, who began to teach in Rome in 244 CE.[51] Major works on the history of Rome were written by Appian and Cassius Dio in the second and third centuries. Even the lowbrow literature of Greece was centered on Rome: the *Deipnosophistae* (*The Learned Banqueters*) of Athenaeus, for instance. He composed this massive work at the end of the second century, probably using the huge library of the wealthy politician Larensis, in whose house he also sets the scene of the banquet attended by a Greco-Roman intellectual elite. To round things off, so it seems, the emperor himself made a contribution to Greek literature, with Marcus Aurelius's – admittedly peculiar – work, the *Meditations*.

From the fourth century onwards, west and east grew apart and knowledge of Greek shrank in the west. Greek intellectuals still came to Rome, but now they wrote in Latin, like Ammianus Marcellinus, with his great history, and Claudian, who wrote panegyric and invective poetry with a political message. A new city had taken Rome's place as the center of Greek literature: Constantinople.

7. Constantinople

It cannot be said when exactly Constantine took the decision to refound the city of Byzantium on the Bosporus as "Constantinople" (in this he was joining a tradition of Roman emperors who had refounded cities under new names). What is clear is that the building work began in 324, and on the 11th of May 330, upon completion of the walls, this "new" city was dedicated. There is no indication that Constantine had intended that the new city named after him would replace Rome: it is only through panegyric texts and Christian historiography that Constantinople became the "New Rome" (Dölger 1937 remains important on this). However Constantine's activities did create a major Greek city that soon flourished and in which, unlike fourth-century Rome with its strong pagan traditions, the Christian church could achieve a dominant position. It was this position that in 381 made it possible for the bishop of Constantinople to be raised to Patriarch of the East (Soz. *Hist. eccl.* 7.9.3). The dynamism of the growing city and the political direction of the *imperium Romanum* under Constantine's successors turned Constantinople into the new capital of the empire and of the administration of its eastern half. As in Hellenistic Alexandria, in Constantinople a large "imperial" library (see Wendel 1954, 246) was part of the facilities of the new imperial residence: Constantius II had it constructed in 356. Julian the Apostate left it his large private collection of books and donated an annex building, and in 372 the emperor Valens ruled that seven *antiquarii* (copyists of old texts – four Greek and three Latin) were to work for the library. It has been suspected that papyrus rolls were systematically transferred to codex form in the imperial library. In 475 it burnt down and with it 120,000 volumes. It was rebuilt, but in 726 – with 36,500 volumes – it burnt down again.

Attached to the library was a kind of imperial university, teaching grammar, rhetoric and philosophy, and from 425 also law, after a reorganization by Theodosius II, who made Constantinople the official capital. The structure of the teaching staff was also fixed: there were to be 31 professorial positions: three rhetors and ten grammarians for Latin, five rhetors and ten grammarians for Greek, one professor of philosophy and two of law (*Codex Theodosianus* 14.9.3, cf. Liebeschuetz 1991, 872).

In addition to the library and university there were also church and private libraries, as well as teachers not paid by the state. All this, together with the imperial court and the patriarchate,[52] gave the city a powerful intellectual influence,[53] but due to the great weight of the schools and the backward-looking work of the libraries, this influence was extremely conservative and focused on preservation and tradition. For example, the goal of the extensive rhetorical and philosophical work of Themistius (c. 317–88) was to comment on Aristotle; Themistius was the most important orator of his day and, as a pagan, he was even able to mediate between the Arian/homoean Christians and the orthodox.[54] Among the grammarians, Priscian (end of the fifth century) stands out: his monumental *Institutio de arte grammatica* offers a synthesis of Greek and Roman grammar (Kaster 1988, 346–8). Around the mid-sixth century, the civil servant John Lydus (Kaster 1988, 306–9) composed antiquarian writings on the Roman months (*De mensibus*), Roman administration (*De magistratibus*) and on omens (*De ostentis*): these books show that the learning nurtured in the libraries of Constantinople was committed to Justinian's idea that the new Constantinople would continue the tradition of Rome.

In ecclesiastical politics, a defense of Nicene orthodoxy was expected, and important theologians like Gregor of Nazianzus (bishop in 380/1) and John Chrysostom (bishop in 397–403/4) both failed in the attempt.

Poetry too appeared in the new city. For the most part it is lost, but from scattered reports about poets we can see that they produced panegyrics for emperors and high officials in large quantity.[55] An unusual feature, which is at the same time an expression of the cultural turn to the past, are the poems composed by the empress Eudocia (c. 405–460): she wrote *centos*, that is, she made new poems that told bible stories out of a patchwork of lines from Homer's *Iliad* and *Odyssey* (see Usher 1998).

Thus Constantinople became a great center in which the tradition of Greek literature from Homer on was "preserved" – in more than one sense.

NOTES

[1] This is expressed pithily in the Imperial-period treatise "*The Contest of Homer and Hesiod*" (text in West 2003, 318–53), on which see Lefkowitz 1981, 18–20.

[2] Hunter and Rutherford 2009. For late antiquity Cameron 1965 remains important.

[3] E.g. "Marcellinus," *Vita Thucydidis* § 54, on the visits, which individually are not beyond doubt; on the phenomenon as a whole see Jacoby 1913, 224–47.

[4] E.g. Libanius's account of his journey from Athens to Antioch, *or.* 1 § 29.

[5] A more detailed account would need to extend the list to include cities like Thebes, Syracuse, Antioch,and (in late antiquity) Gaza, places like Olympia or Delphi at which musical–poetic contests took place in the context of the Greek games, or scholarly centers like Cos (medicine: Hippocrates) or Beirut (legal studies).

[6] On all this, see Nilsson 1906.

[7] Athenaeus 14, 635e/f and 15, 678b/c, citing the Hellenistic scholar Sosibius (FGrHist 595, F 3 and 5).

[8] See the testimonia collected by Campbell 1988, 303–13, no. 11–23.

[9] Cf. Power, ch. 4, p. 68, and Wells, ch. 10, pp. 162–3 in this volume.

[10] Thus Pliny, *Nat. Hist.* 5.112. Cf. also Ehrhardt 1983.

[11] Cf. Robertson 1987; Faraguna 1995.

[12] See, most recently, Schirren and Rechenauer 2013, 182–6.

[13] All important reports about Hecataeus and the fragments of his work are in FGrHist, in which Hecataeus is historian No. 1.

[14] The question of whether and to what extent the poetry performed at these festivals may have constituted political teaching to the Athenians has been the subject of intense discussion since the pioneer work by Meier 1988; see on this, e.g., Carter 2011.

[15] Essential on this is Zimmermann 2008, esp. 36–41; and, further, most recently Kowalzig andWilson 2013.

[16] On the unusual circumstances in the case of Ion, see Stevens 2007.

[17] That in tragedy the whole cosmos of "older" Greek theological and anthropological views is put up for debate, is almost self-evident. See on this recently Cairns 2013.

[18] FGrHist 392 F 13, 14, 15: these fragments attest visits to Athens by Ion.

[19] This is suggested by Plato's dialogue *Parmenides.*

[20] Diog. Laert. 9,36 (= DK 68 B 116) even attests that Democritus was astonished that no-one recognized him in Athens: "I came to Athens and no-one knew me."

[21] This is not to contest that before the fifth century and the constellation in Athens there were already approaches towards literary criticism; archaic poetry contains many reflections on literary critical issues, such as the question of what is good poetry, but as an independent discursive phenomenon, literary criticism first appears in Athens of the fifth century. See Ford 2002, 188–208.

[22] A market for books in Athens is attested e.g. by Eupolis F 327 PCG (probably the earliest attestation) and Plato, *Apol.* 26d; see Turner 1952, 21.

[23] Xenophon ascribes such a hope to the book collector Euthydemus (*Mem.* 4,2).

[24] On the changes in the drama, see Easterling 1997; further, Gildenhard and Revermann 2010.

[25] This explains Athens' interest in exerting an appropriate influence on the persons appointed as heads of the schools, as shown *inter alia* by the law of Sophocles of 306 (or 305) (Diog. Laert. 5.38), according to which only a person explicitly approved by the Council or People could become head.

[26] Cf. Isocrates *or.* 4.50; instructive is Cicero, *De off.* 1,1ff.: a record by a father who is concerned that his son in Athens is not studying properly.

[27] An epigram of Poseidippos (in G-P No. XI) celebrates this building.

[28] See Rice 1983. Callixinus (F 1) also provides a description of an extremely large and luxurious ceremonial ship of Ptolemy IV.

[29] This has been documented again by the new Poseidippus papyrus.

[30] Both anecdotes are reported by Galen, *Com. Hipp. Ep. III*, II.4; see Pfeiffer 1968, 82.

[31] This is suggested by a report in Aphthonius's *Progymnasmata* 12 (p. 48 Spengel; translation in Kennedy 2003, 119).

[32] This list can be drawn up from P.Oxyrh. 1241 and a scholion in a Plautus codex, see in general Pfeiffer 1968, 100.

[33] Thus the Mouseion and the salaries of the scholars working at it probably continued, as shown by a report by Cassius Dio (77.7.3) who explicitly notes that Caracalla stopped the salaries.

[34] Cf. e.g. that report that even Domitian had copies of books lost in Rome made in Alexandria (Suetonius, *Dom.* 20).

[35] It is telling that in the so-called *Letter of Aristeas* the legend is that this translation was produced by 72 Jewish translators at the request of Ptolemy II. See in general Hadas 1951.

[36] Hübner 2000 with further bibliography.

[37] This work is of great importance for historical geography; see the monumental edition and explanatory notes by Stückelberger and Graßhoff 2006, and Stückelberger and Mittenhuber 2009.

[38] Thus Theon in his commentary on the Almagest of Ptolemy, Book 6 (ed. Basle 1538, p. 332 and 319). On this see http://eclipse.gsfc.nasa.gov/eclipse.html.

[39] It is now in Berlin in the Pergamon-Museum.

[40] Lucius Ampelius, in his *Liber memorialis* 8.14, reckons it one of the "miracula mundi."

[41] Thus Plut. *Ant.* 58,9. Where this library was located now seems even less certain, as the localization in the sanctuary of Athena Polias has become doubtful, see Coqueuniot 2013.

[42] Material on this in Susemihl 1891 and 1892.

[43] Attested are Musaeus (Suda M 1296, cf. Susemihl 1891, 406) and Leschides (Suda Λ 311).

[44] Collection of fragments in Mette 1936 and 1952, and Broggiato 2001. See also Nagy 1998.

[45] *Or.* 28 u. 30, on the poems, see *Hieroi logoi* 4,31; 4,38–47. In general see Luchner 2004, 260–64.

[46] Similarly Poseidonius 87 BCE, see Plut. *Mar.* 45.

[47] Strabo p. 609, 16–22C. See, most recently, Tutrone 2013.

[48] This development may have been begun by Aemilius Paullus on his victory over the Macedonians, as can be inferred from Isid. *Etym.* 6,5,1 (Affleck 2013, 124–6). Cicero, *De fin.* 3,7 implies such a library belonged to Lucullus who, like Sulla, collected books.

[49] Cf. Tsakmakis, ch. 15, 225–6 and esp. on Strabo see Dueck, ch. 25, 392–6 in this volume. It seems likely that the exceptional learning that marks e.g. Dion. Hal. *Ant.*, or the quantity of information in Diod. Sic. *Bibl.*, is owed to the excellent libraries in Rome, on which see Hogg 2013 and Diod. Sic. 1.4.2/3.

[50] See for example the addressees of Dion. Hal.'s essays in literary criticism: Q. Aelius Tubero (*De Thuc.*); Metilius Rufus (*De comp. verb.*); Cn. Pompeius Geminus (*Pomp. Gem.*). Ps.-Longinus addresses *De subl.* to a Postumius Terentianus.

[51] In this, as also in the Greek East, "teaching" or "school" is to be understood as a very elastic form of instruction, see Fuhrer 2012.

[52] On the late antique churches built in Constantinople, see Mathews 1971.

[53] It is telling that Libanius (*ep.* 368,1) complains that this is drawing teachers away from Antioch to Constantinople. See on this Kaster (1988) 126/7. Similarly, Johannes Lydus (*De mag.* 3,26) felt its pull in the year 511. It is interesting that, as shown by the case of Synesius, that even a (long) visit by a provincial to the court could produce literature, as with Synesius's *Aigyptioi Logoi* (*De providentia*). See on this Cameron and Long 1993.

[54] See in general on rhetoric in Constantinople, Kennedy 1983, 163–7; on the "Christianization" of rhetoric, Cameron 1991 is instructive.

[55] The evidence for Constantinople is roughly similar to what can be judged of the poetry in late antique Egypt; see Cameron 2004.

REFERENCES

Affleck, M. 2013. "Priests, patrons and playwrights. Libraries in Rome before 168 BC." In J. König, K. Oikonomopoulou, and G. Woolf, eds., *Ancient Libraries*, Cambridge, 124–36.

Allen, R. E. 1983. *The Attalid Kingdom*, Oxford.

Andrewes, A. 1938. "Eunomia." *Classical Quarterly*, 32: 89–102.

Bagnall, R.S. 2002. "Alexandria: Library of dreams." *Proceedings of the American Philological Society*, 146: 348–62.

Berger, A. 2006. "Konstantinopel." *Reallexikon für Antike und Christentum*, 21: 435–83.

Bing, P. 1988. *The Well-Read Muse*. Göttingen.

Blum, R. 1991. *Kallimachos: The Alexandrian Library and the Origins of Bibliography*. Madison, WI.

Borgen, P. 1997. *Philo of Alexandria. An Exegete for his Times*. Leiden.

Bowersock. G.W. 1965. *Augustus and the Greek World*. Oxford.

Broggiato, M. ed. 2001. *Cratete di Mallo, I Frammenti*. La Spezia.

Burkert, W. 2013. "Die frühgriechische Philososphie und der Orient." In H. Flashar, D. Bremer, and G. Rechnauer, eds., *Die Philosophie der Antike. Vol. 1. Frühgriechische Philosophie*, Basel, 97–125.

Cairns, D., ed. 2013. *Tragedy and Archaic Greek Thought*. Swansea.

Calame, C. 1997. *Choruses of Young Women in Ancient Greece*. Lanham, MD.

Cameron, Al. 1965. "Wandering Poets." *Historia*, 14: 470–509.

Cameron, Al. 2004. "Poetry and Literary Culture in Late Antiquity." In S. Swain and M. Edwards, *Approaching Late Antiquity*, Oxford, 327–54.

Cameron, Al., and J. Long, 1993. *Barbarians and Politics at the Court of Arcadius*. Berkeley, CA.

Cameron, Av. 1991. *Christianity and the Rhetoric of Empire. The Development of Christian Discourse*. Berkeley, CA.

Campbell, D. A., ed. & transl. 1988. *Greek Lyric II*. Cambridge, MA.

Carter, D. M., ed. 2011. *Why Athens? A Reappraisal of Tragic Politics*. Oxford.

Coqueugniot, G. 2013. "Where was the royal library of Pergamum?" In J. König, K. Oikonomopoulou, and G. Woolf, eds., *Ancient Libraries*, Cambridge, 109–23.

Deakin, M. A. B. 2007. *Hypatia of Alexandria, Mathematician and Martyr*. Amherst, MA.

Dihle, A. 1977. "Der Beginn des Attizismus." *Antike und Abendland*, 23: 162–77.

Dihle, A. 1989. *Die griechische und lateinische Literatur der Kaiserzeit*. Munich.

Dölger, F 1937. "Rom in der Gedankenwelt der Byzantiner." *Zeitschrift für Kirchengeschichte*, 56: 1–42.

Easterling, P. E. 1997."From Repertoire to Canon." In P. E. Easterling, ed., *The Cambridge Companion to Greek Tragedy*, Cambridge, 211–27.

Edelstein, E. J., and L. Edelstein. 1945/1998. *Asclepius. Collection and Interpretation of the Testimonies*. With a New Introduction by G. B. Ferngren, Baltimore.

Ehrhardt, N. 1983. *Milet und seine Kolonien. Vergleichende Untersuchung der kultischen und politischen Einrichtungen*. Frankfurt.

Fantuzzi, M. and R. Hunter. 2004. *Tradition and Innovation in Hellenistic Poetry*. Cambridge.

Faraguna, M. 1995. "Note di storia milesia arcaica: i Γέργιθες e la στάσις di VI secolo." *Studi micenei ed egeo-anatolici* 36: 37–89.

Ford, A. 2002. *The Origins of Criticism: Literary Culture and Poetic Theory in Classical Greece*. Princeton, NJ.

Fraser, P.M. 1972. *Ptolemaic Alexandria*. 3 Vols. Oxford.

Fritz, K. von. 1978. "Der gemeinsame Ursprung der Geschichtswissenschaft und exakten Wissenschaften bei den Griechen." In K. von Fritz, ed., *Schriften zur griechischen Logik*. Vol. 1, Stuttgart, 23–49.

Fuhrer, T. 2012. "Philosophische Schulen und ihre Kommunikationsräume im spätrepublikanischen und kaiserzeitlichen Rom." In F. Mundt, ed., *Kommunikationsräume im kaiserzeitlichen Rom*, Berlin, 241–52.

Gelzer, T. 1978. "Klassizismus, Attizismus und Asianismus." In H. Flashar, ed., *Le classicisme à Rome*, Vandoeuvres-Geneva, 1–55.

Gildenhard, I., and M. Revermann, eds. 2010. *Beyond the Fifth Century*. Berlin.

Gorman, V. B. 2001. *Miletos, the Ornament of Ionia – a History of the City to 400 B.C.E.* Ann Arbor, MI.

Grig, L., and G. Kelly, eds. 2012. *Two Romes. Rome and Constantinople in Late Antiquity*. Oxford.

Habicht, C. 1988. *Hellenistic Athens and her Philosophers*. Princeton, NJ.

Habicht, C. 1997. *Athens from Alexander to Antony*. Cambridge, MA.

Hadas, M. 1951. *Aristeas to Philocrates (Letter of Aristeas)*. New York.

Hadot, I. 2003 "Der philosophische Unterrichtsbetrieb in der römischen Kaiserzeit." *Rheinisches Museum für Philologie*, 146: 49–71.

Hankinson, R. J. 2008. "The man and his work." In R. J. Hankinson, *The Cambridge Companion to Galen*, Cambridge, 1–33.

Hatzimichali, M. 2013. "Ashes to ashes? The library of Alexandria after 48 BC." In J. König, K. Oikonomopoulou, and G. Woolf, eds., *Ancient Libraries*, Cambridge, 167–82.

Hodkinson, S. 1998. "Lakonian artistic production and the problem of Spartan austerity" In N. Fisher, and H. van Wees, eds., *Archaic Greece*, London, 93–117.

Hoffmann, A. 1998. "The Roman Remodeling of the Asclepieion." In H. Koester, ed., *Pergamum. Citadel of the Gods*, Harrisburg, PA, 41–62.

Hogg, D. 2013. "Libraries in a Greek working life. Dionysius of Halicarnassus, a case study in Rome." In J. König, K. Oikonomopoulou, and G. Woolf, eds., *Ancient Libraries*, Cambridge, 137–51.

Honigman, S. 2003. *The Septuagint and Homeric Scholarship in Alexandria*. London.

Hose, M. 1999a. "Die zweite Begegnung Roms mit den Griechen. Oder: Zu den politischen Ursachen des Attizismus." In G. Vogt-Spira and B. Rommel, eds., *Rezeption und Identität. Die kulturelle Auseinandersetzung Roms mit Griechenland als europäisches Paradigma*, Stuttgart, 274–88.

Hose, M. 1999b. "Postcolonial Theory and Greek Literature in Rome." *Greek, Roman and Byzantine Studies* 40: 303–26.

Hübner, W. 2000. "The Ptolemaic View of the Universe." *Greek, Roman and Byzantine Studies*, 41: 59–93.

Hunter, R., Rutherford, I., eds. 2009. *Wandering Poets in Ancient Greek Culture: Travel, Locality and Pan-Hellenism*. Cambridge.

Jacobson, H. 1983. *The Exagoge of Ezekiel*. Cambridge.

Jacoby, F. 1913. "Herodotos." *Real-Encyclopädie der classischen Altertumswissenschaft* Suppl. II: 205–520.

Kaster, R. A. 1988. *Guardians of Language: The Grammarian and Society in Late Antiquity*. Berkeley, CA.

Kennedy, G. 1972. *The Art of Rhetoric in the Roman World*. Princeton, NJ.

Kennedy, G. 1983. *The Art of Rhetoric under Christian Emperors*. Princeton, NJ.

Kennedy, G.A., transl. 2003. *Progymnasmata. Greek Textbooks of Prose Composition and Rhetoric*. Atlanta, GA.

Kerkhecker, A. 1997. "Μουσέων ἐν ταλάρῳ – Dichter und Dichtung am Ptolemäerhof." *Antike und Abendland*, 43: 124–44.

Koester, H. ed. 1998. *Pergamum. Citadel of the Gods*. Harrisburg, PA.

Kowalzig, B., and P. Wilson, eds. 2013. *Dithyramb in Context*. Oxford.

Lefkowitz, M. 1981. *The Lives of the Greek Poets*. London.

Liebeschuetz, W. 1991. "Hochschule." In *Reallexikon für Antike und Christentum*, 15: 858–911.

Luchner, K. 2004. *Philiatroi. Studien zum Thema der Krankheit in der griechischen Literatur der Kaiserzeit*. Göttingen.

MacLeod, R. ed. 2000. *The Library of Alexandria. Centre of Learning in the Ancient World*. London.

Mansfeld, J. 1979/80. "The chronology of Anaxagoras' Athenian period and the date of his trial." *Mnemosyne*, 32: 39–69 and 33: 17–95.

Mathews, T. F. 1971. *The early churches of Constantinople*. University Park, PA.

Meier, C. 1988. *Die politische Kunst der griechischen Tragödie*. Munich.

Meier, C. 1998. *Athens. A Portrait of the City in its Golden Age*. New York.

Mette, H. J. 1936. *Sphairopoiia. Untersuchungen zur Kosmologie des Krates von Pergamum*. Munich.

Mette, H. J. 1952. *Parateresis. Untersuchungen zur Sprachtheorie des Krates von Pergamum*. Halle.

Missiou, A. 2011. *Literacy and Democracy in Fifth-Century Athens*. Cambridge.

Mundt, F. eds. 2012. *Kommunikationsräume im kaiserzeitlichen Rom*, Berlin.

Nafissi, M. 2009. "Sparta." In K. A. Raaflaub, and H. van Wees, *A Companion to Archaic Greece*, Oxford, 117–137.

Nagy, G. 1998 "The library of Pergamum as a classical model." In H. Koester, *Pergamum. Citadel of the Gods*, Harrisburg, PA, 185–232.

Nilsson, M. P. 1906. *Die griechischen Feste von religiöser Bedeutung mit Ausschluß der Attischen*. Leipzig.

Oliver, J. H. 1953. "The Ruling Power. A study of the Roman Empire in the second century after Christ through the Roman Oration of Aelius Aristides." *Transactions of the American Philosophical Society*, 43.4: 871–1003.

Pfeiffer, R. 1968. *History of Classical Scholarship. From the Beginnings to the End of the Hellenistic Age*. Oxford.

Pickard-Cambridge, A. 1968. *The Dramatic Festivals of Athens*. 2nd. edn. Oxford.

Radt, W. 2011. *Pergamum. Geschichte und Bauten einer antiken Metropole*. Darmstadt.

Rawson E. 1979. "L. Cornelius Sisenna and the Early First Century" *Classical Quarterly*, 29: 327–46.

Rice, E.E. 1983. *The Grand Procession of Ptolemy Philadelphus*. Oxford.

Robertson, N. 1987. "Government and Society at Miletus, 525–442 BC." *Phoenix* 41: 356–98.

Schirren, T., and G. Rechenauer, 2013. "Biographie." In H. Flashar, D. Bremer, and G. Rechnauer, eds., *Die Philosophie der Antike. Vol. 1. Frühgriechische Philosophie*, Basel, 175–214.

Sifakis, G. M. 1967. *Studies in the History of Hellenistic Drama*. London.

Sly, D.I. 1996. *Philo's Alexandria*. London.

Smallwood, E. M. 1976. *The Jews under Roman Rule*. Leiden.

Stevens, A. 2007. "Ion of Chios: Tragedy as Commodity of the Athenian Exchange." In V. Jennings, and A. Katsaros, eds., *The World of Ion of Chios*, Leiden, 243–65.

Stückelberger, A., and F. Graßhoff, eds. 2006. A. *Ptolemaios. Handbuch der Geographie*. 2 vols. Basel.

Stückelberger, A., and F. Mittenhuber, eds. 2009. *Ptolemaios. Handbuch der Geographie. Ergänzungsband*. Basel.

Susemihl, F. 1891, 1892. *Geschichte der griechischen Literatur in der Alexandrinerzeit*. 2 vols. Leipzig.

Thonemann, P. ed. 2013. *Attalid Asia Minor*. Oxford.

Turner, E. 1952. *Athenian Books in the 5th and 4th century*. Oxford.

Tutrone, F. 2013. "Libraries and intellectual debate in the late Republic." In J. König, K. Oikonomopoulou, and G. Woolf, eds., *Ancient Libraries*, Cambridge, 152–66.

Usher, M. D. 1998. *Homeric Stitchings. The Homeric Centos of the Empress Eudocia*. Lanham.

Wendel, C. 1954. "Bibliothek." In *Reallexikon für Antike und Christentum*, 2: 231–74.

West, M. L., ed. & transl. 2003. *Homeric Hymns, Homeric Apocrypha, Lives of Homer*. Cambridge, MA.

Wilson, N. G. 1983. *Scholars of Byzantium*, London.

Zimmermann, B. 2008. *Dithyrambos. Geschichte eine Gattung*. 2nd. edn. Berlin.

FURTHER READING

Sparta: see Nafissi 2009, Hodkinson 1998, and (on choruses) Calame 1997.

Miletus: Erhard 1983, Gorman 2001, Greaves 2002. Burkert 2013 provides an overview on the intellectual relations between Ionia and the East; cf. von Fritz 1978.

Athens: Meier 1998 on Classical Athens; Habicht 1988 and 1997 on post-Classical Athens.

Alexandria: fundamental, Fraser 1972; on the library, see MacLeod 2000 and Bagnall 2002; on post-Hellenistic Alexandria, Sly 1996.

Pergamon: overviews are given by Allen 1983, Koester 1998, Radt 2011, and Thonemann 2013.

Rome: Rome and the Greek World, see especially Bowersock, 1965; on literature, Dihle 1989; on spaces, Mundt 2012.

Constantinople: an excellent overview is given by Berger 2006; on Constantinople and Rome, see Grig and Kelly 2012, on scholarship in Constantinople, see Wilson 1983.

CHAPTER 22

Places of Presentation

Manuel Baumbach

Places of presentation were most important in the production and reception of Ancient Greek literature. In Archaic times almost all poetry (with the exception of epigram) was composed for oral performance, and specific places of presentation were established for different literary genres. Despite growing literacy from the fifth century BCE onwards, oral presentation was also widespread throughout Antiquity with regard to prose texts: we hear that Herodotus presented his *Histories* in public (Marcellinus, *Vit.Thuc.* § 54), some of the dialogues of the second-century CE satirist Lucian might have been composed for public performances, and the Greek novel seems to have been read to a wider audience in Imperial times (see Hägg 1994). Places of presentation were the first "setting in life" (*Sitz im Leben*) of large parts of Greek literature, and they influenced both its production and reception by opening space and setting a frame for literary presentation. Poets, who composed their works for specific occasions at specific places, had to take into account the expectations of their historical audience as well as the demands of the places of presentation. New places inspired new forms of literature, and new rites at established places fostered generic innovations. At the same time, by way of selecting and combining, literature can shape, encode and use actual places of presentation to create new fictitious ones. Thus we have to differentiate between places of presentation described in literature – which might not reflect reality but enact fiction – and the information about places of presentation, which can be taken from art, archaeological remains and non-literary texts (like scholia or inscriptions).

The following overview focuses on oral presentation in public places. Public is taken in the widest sense of the word, starting from a small group gathering in the private sphere of a symposium and ending with the Panhellenic audience at Olympia. At the same time literature was present and presented in the private sphere of individuals from Archaic times onwards, but we cannot single out important places of presentation or find links between specific places and the kind of literature presented. On the contrary, the range of examples is wide: in the *Iliad* (9.185–91) Achilles is singing the "glorious deeds of men" (*klea andron*) in his tent; in Aristophanes' *Frogs* (52–3) Dionysos is reading the *Andromeda* of Euripides on a ship; and on a Red-figure cup of the Antiphon painter a single young man is depicted in the middle of

A Companion to Greek Literature, First Edition. Edited by Martin Hose and David Schenker.
© 2016 John Wiley & Sons, Inc. Published 2020 by John Wiley & Sons, Inc.

nowhere singing "this young man is beautiful" (*ho pais kalos*; cf. Lissarrague 1990,133–4). Thus, literature in its oral (and written) form can be found at almost all places and presented by every kind of person regardless of his/her age, gender or social status – at least within the realms of literature. Apart from many examples of educated people reciting both prose and poetry – such as Phaedrus's performance of a speech of Lysias on Eros in Plato (*Phaedr.* 230e–234c) – we hear of shepherds who compose their own hexametrical verses (Theocr. *Id.* 5) or recite songs (Theocr. *Id.* 10.51); the peasant Trygaios recalls to his daughters a fable of Aesop in Aristophanes' *Pax* 129); and Lucian tells us about the inhabitants of Abdera, who were suffering from a fever that made them "mad with tragedy; … they mostly sang solos from Euripides' *Andromeda*, rendering Perseus's speech in song." (Luc. *Quomodo hist. conscr.*, § 1; trans. Kilburn). Although these fictitious performances of literature do not mirror reality, they reflect upon the usage of literature in the social sphere and discuss possible ways and limits of its reception. If we take into account the widespread ancient practice of reading aloud and look at the many places of presentation, which fostered the view of the "song culture" (Herington 1985, 39) in the Archaic period, we can, however, assume that larger parts of the ancient population had access to literature at least on a small scale.

1. Dais

The earliest place of presentation mentioned in Archaic literature is the Homeric *dais*, a common meal (*Il.* 9.487), to which one is invited, cf. *Il.* 4.343 and *Il.* 1.424 (gods). The *dais* is an early form of the Classical symposium (cf. Latacz 1990, 359–61). It took place in a palace, and the seating was probably in a hierarchical order (cf. Dentzer 1982, 444–5) reflecting the social hierarchies of the invited, mostly aristocratic participants (cf. Clay 2004, 38–9). In Homer there are only a few hints at the exact course of events or possible rites of a *dais*. After the meal (cf. *Od.* 8.72) music, dance and song played an important role (cf. *Od.* 9.2–11 and 21.428–30) and might have been the highlight of the *dais* (τὰ γάρ τ' ἀναθήματα δαιτός, *Od.* 1.152). Aiming at the delight of the participants (cf. *Od.* 8.347), the singers could present both actual topics and historical deeds, either by improvisation or by alteration of orally transmitted poetry. The literature performed was primarily epic, as can be seen from the songs of the two *aoidoi* Phemias and Demodokos in the *Odyssey* (cf. Segal 1992; De Jong 2001, 191).

2. Symposium

"To pour hymns like wine from left to right for you and us." These verses from an elegy of Dionysius Chalcus quoted by Athenaeus (15.669a; trans. Olson) are characteristic not only for the typical drinking rites in a symposium but for the presence of song / literature at this specific place. In contrast to the Homeric *dais* with its epic performances, the symposium is the place of the presentation of Greek lyric (cf. Rösler 1990 and Lissarrague 1990, 123ff. with examples of lyrical performance on symposia on vase paintings). Regardless of a more pragmatic (cf. Rösler 1980) or literary reading (cf. Latacz 1986; Schmitz 2002), lyric in almost all monodic forms is performed primarily in and for sympotic contexts. The symposium took place in the men's room (*andron*) of mostly aristocratic citizens or rulers and was organized along fixed rules (cf. Murray 1990 for an overview of form and function of the symposium). After the common meal and prayers with libation (cf. Athen. 11.462c–f) a symposiarch organized the drinking session, which was characterized by table-talk (cf. Plato's and Xenophon's *Symposia*), play, dance, music and song. With regard to the latter, the contents of the lyric often depended on the interest and configuration of the (male) addressees. It could be a group of like-minded young aristocrats (*hetairia*) with political aims, a gathering of friends (cf. Plat., *Symp*.) or representatives of a court (see below: court). As a consequence we find lyrical poetry with political themes, cultural reflections, individual praise, elegiac and sympotic topics (*skolia*). The kind of presentation could vary: apart from a monodic performance of a singer or a recitation we often find hints at improvisations of the participants, so that literary production and reception fall together. A driving force for the vast production and the high quality (cf. Latacz 1990, 245) of lyrical poetry in the Archaic period was the agonal and alternating singing, probably according to the arrangement of the seating. As Pindar's *Epinikia* show, choral lyric, which was composed for a wider audience (cf. Most 1982), could also be presented in the symposium (*Ol*. 1, *Nem*. 9, *Isth*. 6). A specific place of presentation is occupied by the *komos*, a choral song often performed after the end of a symposium by a number of drunken men roaming through the streets. The *komos* marks the transition from a more private to a public place of presenting lyric. Its themes circled around love and wine and it ended up in yet another semi-public presentation of lyric, the *paraclausithyron* in front of the house of the beloved (cf. Plut. *Amat*. 8, 753b, Cummings 1996 and Copley 1956 for the Roman reception).

3. Festival

The most important places of presentation were religious festivals, from which many poetic genres such as *drama, hymn, threnos, epithalamia* or *epinikia* took their origin, or in which they were later embedded (*epos, paian* or the prose form of *panegyric* speech). The festival context explains not only the strong presence of gods and myth in these poetic genres but also much about form and function. Literature presented at festivals is shaped by the needs and expectations of the participants, the form/kind of festival (*eortai, hierai hemerai, thysiai*), the moment of presentation (procession, *agon*, ritual) and – especially in the Hellenistic period – the intention of the organizers. Depending on the importance of the festival, the presentation of literature could be highly prestigious, reach a wide audience, and significantly boost the reception of the work. The number of festivals steadily increased from Archaic to Hellenistic times, when they reached a peak in frequency, probably due to growing secularization (cf. Chaniotis 1995, 162–3). Festivals, and the literature presented as part of them, thus affected the public life of a polis year round (cf. Burkert 1987). Athens, for example, held as many as 122–144 festivals each year in the Classical period (cf. Cartledge 1985, 99), so many that Demosthenes even accused the Athenians of putting more effort into organizing festivals than into preparations for war (*In Phil*. I [*or*. 4] 26; 35).

Literature presented at festivals had many different addressees: gods, heroes, kings and officials, polis inhabitants and strangers/visitors, people familiar with the cult/festival and newcomers, youth and sometimes also slaves. This literature, then, became a crucial part of the cultural and collective identity of a polis or cult community (cf. Nilsson 1957 for an overview of religious festivals outside Athens with their literary performances). Apart from the mediation and reflection of cult aspects, its functions were the memory of cultural traditions, the representation of the polis, the transmission of political ideas, the creation of social identity, and last but not least the entertainment of the participants. In this regard, in some festivals the *agon* was established as a mode of presentation, so that different poets and singers competed against each other; a growing specialization of the arts and literature can be observed along with an increasing number of *agones* in Hellenistic times (cf. Chaniotis 1990).

The most important festivals in Athens were the Great Dionysia and the Panathenaia (cf. Schenker, ch. 20, pp. **314–5**, and Hose, ch. 21, pp. **329–31** in this volume). The latter was held each year in autumn and every four years (the Great Panathenaia) as a Panhellenic festival. Beginning in the second half of the sixth century BCE, rhapsodes competed in musical *agones* at the Panathenaia, reciting from Homer's *Iliad* (cf. Kotsidou 1991). The recitations were opened by short monodic (hexametrical) hymns, i.e. *prooimia* (Pindar, *Nemea* 2,3), with the pledge for inspiration (cf. the short Homeric Hymns). The Great Dionysia (Pickard Cambridge 1988, 57–125) was the place of origin and presentation both of ancient Greek drama, in all three of its subgenres: tragedy, comedy and satyr play; and also of the dithyramb. Both genres were presented in the form of a musical *agon*. The dithyramb was a cult song for Dionysus organized by each of the ten Athenian tribes and performed as choral lyric; apart from fragments, only six dithyrambs of the fifth-century BCE poet Bacchylides have survived. In the dramatic *agones*, three tragedians competed, each with three tragedies and one satyr play; and five comic playwrights, each with a single comedy, competed in the comic contest (Latacz 1993, 45). Only plays by the three canonical tragedians Aeschylus, Sophocles, and Euripides, and two writers of comedy, Aristophanes (old and middle comedy) and Menander (new comedy), have been preserved.

The actual place of the presentation and performance of both drama and dithyramb was the theater of Dionysus in Athens, which dates back to the late sixth century BCE and hosted up to 17,000 spectators (Plato's account of 30,000 spectators, *Symp.* 175 E, is much too high). The whole city, including slaves, women (Seidensticker 2010, 32–37), and foreigners were allowed to take part. Before the building of the theater, contests in the *Dionysia* and also the *Lenaia*, another festival of Dionysos with dramatic *agones* on a smaller scale, were held in the market-place (*agora*) and a dancing area (*orchestra*). The Rural Dionysia, a festival organized by the demes, also occasionally involved dramatic performances (Pickard-Cambridge 1988, 45).

The presentation of literature in theater as a place of performance shows that literature was staged together with dance and music – two aspects that have been widely lost in the course of tradition. For many works presented in the sixth and fifth century on stage in Athens the first performance also was the last, as plays were only rarely performed more than once (see e.g. Aristophanes, *Ran.*). Outside Athens, however, and from the fourth century onwards, the circulation of written copies and the activity of organized guilds of artists (*technitai*) allowed for the performance of both old and new plays all over Greece (Pickard-Cambridge 1988, 279–305) either in theaters or on transportable wooden stages (*ikria*).

The genre of *epinikion* is closely linked to the four Panhellenic games, in Olympia, Delphi, Nemea, and on the Isthmus of Corinth. *Epinikia* were songs, either monodic or choral (Heath and Lefkowitz 1991), written for the winners of horse races, athletic and musical contests. They were performed both immediately after the end of the festival at the place of the contest and at the home of the winner, either in a procession (Pindar, *Ol.* 9, *Pyth.* 6; 10) or at a symposium (cf. Athanassaki 2009, 266–73). Thus, *epinikia* could have been composed for a double audience (cf. Gelzer 1985) and their early commitment to written form allowed for performance at different places and times. The contents of *epinikia* were linked to the place of performance by praise of the actual victory as well as the deity worshiped at the festival. In addition, the place of origin of the winner, which is also the second place of performance, often influences the choice and presentation of myth in *epinikia*. The function of these songs is to preserve the memory of the victory (Pindar, *Pyth.* 3.114–15) and for that purpose – according to Pindar, *Nemea* 3.7 – the *epinikion* is the best means. Given the large and diverse audience at the Panhellenic games, it is not surprising that many additional performances of different literary forms, ranging from poetry to prose, took place there. Herodotus is said to have read from his *Histories* at the Olympic games (Lucian, *Herodotus* 1) and the sophist Gorgias delivered speeches at the Pythian and Olympic games (Philostratus, *VS* 1.9). Authors thus seem to have used popular places to present and spread their works regardless of their connection to the festival.

Most forms of choral song, which took its origin from cult rituals (Burkert 1985, 162) were presented at religious festivals, either at the holy place (*temenos*) of the worshiped god or during the processions leading to the temple. Some cults even had specialized groups of singers, who carefully prepared choral performances. Pindar wrote cult songs for the *daphnephorika* at Thebes and we know of the Milesian *molpoi* of Apollo Delphinios (Burkert 1985, 161). Although the tendency to perform new poetry at religious festivals was strong, there is evidence for the performance of older songs as well, especially at festivals of local gods, for whom songs with important aetiological significance could be performed repeatedly. This also applies to songs that contain specific historical evidence that was important for the cult-community (cf. Isocrates, *Pan.* 4.158). Some cult songs like the *Delphic Paian* of Philodamos (fourth century BCE) were memorialized in inscriptions in the *temenos*, which shows their importance and indicates a repetitive performance at a specific place.

Religious festivals in a broader sense include the celebrations of death, which were performed both by the public as well as in private, with variation both in the places of performance and the literature presented. Whereas in Archaic times we find public funerals for soldiers, aristocrats, and rulers with song contests of *aoidoi* (cf. Hesiod *Op.* 645–61), from the Classical period onward the prose funeral speech, *epitaphios logos* (cf. Prinz 1997), was established as a kind of epideictic speech in Athens (Demosthenes, *Lept.* [or. 20] 141). It was held in public on the agora and in connection with the erection of a public grave (*demosion sema*) and probably the *telos* at the end of the rite (cf. Binder, Korenjak, and Noack 2007, 2). The earliest transmitted example is the funeral speech of Pericles in Thucydides' *Histories* (2.34–46), which was held for the dead in the first year of the Peloponnesian War. Pericles' *epitaphios logos* functions as a literary *lieu de mémoire* for the Athenian polis and it stresses the collective identity of the Athenians. Menander Rhetor notes that in Athens there was a yearly public funeral speech (2.11), which might have taken place in the theater; against this background Socrates recites Aspasia's fictitious funeral speech in Plato's *Menexenus* (cf. Cicero *Orator* 151). Apart from this, the most popular song of lament was the *threnos*, a choral song composed primarily for private ceremonies held at the tombs of the deceased.

Choral wedding songs (*hymenaios/epithalamion*) were performed either in public at the weddings themselves, during the processions accompanying the bride (*Il.* 18.491–6), or at the symposium held in the husband's house after the wedding. While most of these songs were standardized, individually composed songs can be traced back to aristocratic families (cf. Contiades-Tsitsoni 1990). Literary scenes of choral dance as well as many vase paintings without specific context probably resemble different forms of private festivals like weddings or *komoi*, such as the choral song on Achilles' shield in *Iliad* 18.604ff.

Starting in the fifth century BCE with Isocrates, the *panegyric* became an established form of epideictic speech at various official festivals, mostly to entertain the audience. One final case of the presentation of literature at festivals: performances at the local cults of the poet heroes, which were spread all over Greece, located mostly at the place of birth (or death) of a poet (cf. Clay 2004, 5). A key element of these cults was the performance of "memories in verse and prose" (Arist. *Rhet.* 1.5, 1361a34–6) and most likely, literature of the worshiped poet was presented at these occasions.

4. Court

When Pindar praises the victory of Hieron in the Olympian Horse race of 476 BCE, he visualizes himself as a frequent guest at the "friendly table" of the Syracusan ruler (*Ol.* 1,13–17). This indicates a strong connection between the presentation of literature and the court, places we can observe from the palace complexes (*ta basileia, aule*) of the Archaic rulers to those of the Hellenistic emperors. From Ibycus (sixth century BCE) onwards we hear of poets traveling through Greece in order to present their works at courts (cf. the story of the contest of Hesiod and Homer at the court of Paneides which goes back to the sophist Alcidamas in the fourth century BCE, see West 1967); and some poets like Anacreon were even employed by a ruler at a royal court. As the court was not only the place for discussion and decision-making (cf. Elias 1969) but also for self-presentation and propaganda, the presence of a poet added to the reputation of a court, allowed it to solidify its ethical values, glorious past or political agenda in poetry, and spread those values inside and outside the reign. In this regard, literature presented at a court is in close dialogue with its beliefs and intentions and could strengthen the loyalty amongst the elites. However, the court as place of presentation does not necessarily influence the literature presented: poets could present works there that were written for different occasions; they could try to distance themselves from the court by way of irony or parody; or present work which does not show any connection with the agenda of a court.

The productive connection between courts and literature can be best seen from the Court Societies of the Hellenistic period (cf. Herman 1997 and Weber 1993, Schenker, ch. 20, pp. 315–6 in this volume). In the three main Diadochic states of the Seleucids, Antigonids, and Ptolemies, cultural centers were established in competition with the existing ones at Athens or Pergamon in order to claim cultural predominance within the Greek world. These centers were ideal for the production as well as presentation of literature, thanks in part to the huge libraries established there and the many poets employed to work in an academic setting such as the Museum in Alexandria. Literary activity took place within a closed circle of mostly aristocratic members of the court, to which poets also belonged. The proximity fostered productive literary competition with their colleagues as well as with the literary tradition. From this environment came new literary forms, such as bucolic, epyllion, different epigrammatic subgenres (cf. Posidippus, see Höschele, ch. 12, pp. 194–6 in this volume) or the Greek novel. Although the prestige of the court, the cultural center and its immediate audience affected the production of literature to a certain degree, the oral presentation of the work in Hellenistic times was always accompanied by the published work, so that the book emerged as the most important 'place' of presentation and allowed literature to travel quickly through the Greek speaking world and find multiple venues for performance, both private and public, in a short period of time.

5. School

The presentation of literature at schools was twofold. On the one hand, we have reception of literature selected and presented by a teacher in order to educate his pupils according to the norms of a state or city. Plato, for instance, tried to define a negative canon of literature in his *Republic*, what should not be used in education; and the Alexandrian philologists helped to establish literary canons (cf. Most 1990) used at Hellenistic schools. On the other hand, we find teachers who present their own literature directly to the pupils. Somewhere in between are travelling sophists giving guest lectures or rhapsodes. However, defining the school as a place of presentation of literature remains difficult, as we do not find a homogeneous or organized school system in the Greek world. After the private organization of education in the Archaic period, where we can even speak of a school with regard to Sappho's poetry which was addressed to "educate" young woman before marriage, single *poleis* established their own school systems from Classical times onwards (Marrou 1956). In the early fifth century we find record of financial contributions from states to schools, hints at specific types of schools (*didaskaleion*, Thucydides 7.29), and an increasing number of vase paintings with school scenes. As for the type of literature presented at schools, choral songs that expressed appropriate ethical values (Theognis, Alcman, Solon) were part of the general education (Marrou 1956, 51–104), and "poetry of (morally) good poets" (cf. Plat. *Protag.* 325e2–326a3) was memorized and recited by the school children at the Hellenistic *gymnasion* (cf. Kah and Scholz 2004). Since, especially in Hellenistic times, many well-educated teachers and scholars gave lectures in the *gymnasia* for the *ephebeia*, schools became important places not only for presentation but also for preservation of literature, as many *gymnasia* included libraries at that time (cf. Scholz 2004, 125–8). Furthermore, speeches and philosophical works became important in the course of higher education that, at least at Athens, was primarily offered by rhetorical and philosophical schools. The leading philosophers or sophists of these schools taught, in many cases, their own works, thereby combining the place of presentation and the literature itself into a kind of self-representation. In Hellenistic times when education was built upon growing literacy (Arist. *Pol.* 8.3, 1338a15–17) more literature was edited and thus became available at schools (cf. Nilsson 1957).

6. Literature Presented in Public Space

The most effective and lasting way to present literature in public space was the inscription. Depending on the material and the inscribed objects, inscriptions could preserve literature through time, they could leave the place of their first presentation by being taken from stone to book, enter new contexts and spread far beyond their original location (cf. Baumbach 2000). From Archaic times onwards poetic inscriptions in epigram form were used to preserve the memory of a deceased (grave epigram) or of a person who dedicated a valuable votive (dedicatory epigram). There are epigrams for winners (cf. Ebert 1972) and honorary inscriptions, so that literature in this form was presented almost everywhere. We find poetic epigrams on cups and vases for usage both private (cf. the "Nestor cup," c. 715 BCE) and public (cf. the "Dipylon jug," c. 740 BCE). Epigrams were inscribed on stelai, temple walls, different kinds of monuments, artifacts (such as the chest of Kypselos), statues, or on single stones (cf. Baumbach, Petrovic, and Petrovic 2010). Grave epigrams often took the form of "speaking monuments" (cf. Wachter 2010); they directly addressed the passer-by and asked him or her to stop, read the message aloud and keep the memory alive. A good example of the public dimension and function of epigram is the hero cult of the Archaic poet Archilochus on Paros and the Mnesiepes inscription dating back to the first half of the third century BCE (Clay 2004, 9–24). The inscription is presented as a papyrus (Kontoleon 1952, 36), suggesting that the art of public inscription in Hellenistic times tried to imitate the more private medium of presentation and reception of literature in the form of a book-roll. The addressees of this publication were the participants and visitors of the cult, to whom not only information about the cult hero and the characteristics of the cult were given, but also pieces of poetry themselves: Mnesiepes quotes Archilochus's own poetry several times and thus guarantees for his words a constant and lasting present(ation).

REFERENCES

Athanassaki, L. 2009. "Narratology, Deixis, and the Performance of Choral Lyrik." In J. Grethlein and A. Rengakos, eds., *Narratology and Interpretation*, Berlin, 241–73.

Baumbach, M. 2000. "'Wanderer, kommst Du nach Sparta. …': Zur Rezeption eines Simonides-Epigramms." *Poetica* 32: 1–22.

Baumbach, M., A. Petrovic, and I. Petrovic, eds. 2010. *Archaic and Classical Greek Epigram*, Cambridge.

Binder, V., M. Korenjak, and B. Noack, eds. 2007. *Epitaphien. Tod, Totenrede, Rhetorik*. Rahden.

Burkert, W. 1985. *Greek Religion: Archaic and Classical*. Cambridge, MA.

Burkert, W. 1987. "Die antike Stadt als Festgemeinschaft." In P. Hugger and W. Burkert, eds., *Stadt und Fest*. Unterägeri.

Cartledge, P. A. 1985. "The Greek Religious Festivals." In P.E. Easterling and J.V. Muir, eds., *Greek Religion and Society*, Cambridge, 98–127, 223–6.

Chaniotis, A. 1990. "Zur Frage der Spezialisierung im griechischen Theater des Hellenismus und der Kaiserzeit." *Ktéma* 15: 89–108.

Chaniotis, A. 1995. "Sich selbst feiern? Städtische Feste des Hellenismus im Spannungsfeld von Religion und Politik." In M. Wörrle and P. Zanker, eds., *Stadtbild und Bürgerbild im Hellenismus*, Munich, 147–72.

Clay, D. 2004. *Archilochos Heros: The Cult of Poets in the Greek Polis*. Cambridge, MA.

Contiades-Tsitsoni, E. 1990. *Hymenaios und Epithalamion: das Hochzeitslied in der frühgriechischen Lyrik*. Stuttgart.

Copley, F. O. 1956. *Exclusus Amator: A Study in Latin Love Poetry*. Madison, WI.

Cummings, M. S. 1996. "Observations on the development and code of pre-elegiac paraklausithuron." Ph.D. dissertation. University of Ottawa.

De Jong, I. J. F. 2001. *A Narratological Commentory on the Odyssee*. Cambridge.

Dentzer, J.-M. 1982. *Le motif du banquet couché dans le proche-orient et le monde grec au VIIe siècle au IVe avant J.-C.* Paris.

Ebert, J. 1972. *Griechische Epigramme auf Sieger an gymnischen und hippischen Agonen*. Berlin.

Elias, N. 1969. *Die höfische Gesellschaft*. Darmstadt.

Gelzer, T. 1985. "Mousa Authigenes. Bemerkungen zu einem Typ Pindarischer und Bacchylideischer Epinikien." *Museum Helveticum* 42: 95–120.

Hägg, T. 1994. "Orality, Literacy, and the 'Readership' of the Early Greek Novel." In R. Eriksen, ed., *Contexts of Pre-Novel Narrative: the European Tradition*, Berlin, 47–81.

Heath, M. and M.R. Lefkowitz. 1991. "Epinikian Performance". *Classical Philology* 86: 173–91.

Herington, J. 1985. *Poetry into Drama*. Berkeley, CA.

Herman, G. 1997. "The Court Society of the Hellenistic Age." In P. Cartledge, P. Garnsey, and E.S. Gruen, eds., *Hellenistic Constructs: Essays in Culture, History, and Historiography*, Berkeley, CA, 199–224.

Kah, D. and P. Scholz, eds. 2004. *Das hellenistische Gymnasium*. Berlin.

Kontoleon, N.M. 1952. "Νέαι ἐπιγραφαὶ περὶ τοῦ ᾽Αρχιλόχου ἐκ Πάρου." *Archaiologike Ephemeris* 1952: 32–95.

Kotsidou, H. 1991. *Die musischen Agone der Panathenäen in archaischer und klassischer Zeit*. München.

Latacz, J. 1986. "Zu den 'pragmatischen' Tendenzen der gegenwärtigen gräzistischen Lyrik-Interpretation." *Würzburger Jahrbücher* 12: 35–56.

Latacz, J. 1990. "Die Funktion des Symposions für die entstehende griechische Literatur." In W. Kullmann and M. Reichel, eds., *Der Übergang von der Mündlichkeit zur Literatur bei den Griechen*, Tübingen, 227–64.

Latacz, J. 1993. *Einführung in die griechische Tragödie*. Göttingen.

Lissarrague, F. 1990. *The Aesthetics of the Greek Banquet. Images of Wine and Ritual*. Princeton, NJ.

Marrou, H. I. 1956. *A History of Education in Antiquity*. New York.

Most, G. W. 1982. "Greek Lyric Poets." In T. J. Luce, ed., *Ancient Writers: Greece and Rome*, Vol. 1, New York, 75–98.

Most, G. W. 1990. "Canon Fathers: Literacy, Morality, Power." *Arion* 3.1: 35–60.

Murray, O., ed. 1990. *Sympotica: A Symposium on the Symposion*. Oxford.

Nilsson, M. P. 1957. *Griechische Feste von religiöser Bedeutung mit Ausschluss der attischen*. Darmstadt.

Pickard-Cambridge, A. 1988. *The Dramatic Festivals of Athens*. 2nd edn. Oxford.

Prinz, K. 1997. *Epitaphios logos: Struktur, Funktion und Bedeutung der Bestattungsreden im Athen des 5. und 4. Jahrhunderts*. Frankfurt-Main.

Rösler, W. 1980. *Dichter und Gruppe: Eine Untersuchung zu den Bedingungen und zur historischen Funktion früher griechischer Lyrik am Beispiel Alkaios*. München.

Rösler, W. 1990. "*Mnemosyne* in the *Symposion*." In O. Murray, ed., *Sympotica: A Symposium on the Symposion*. Oxford, 230–37.

Schmitz, T. A. 2002. "Die 'pragmatische' Deutung der frühgriechischen Lyryik: Eine Überprüfung anhand von Sapphos Abschiedsliedern frg. 94 und 96." In J. P. Schwindt, ed., *Klassische Philologie inter disciplinas*, Heidelberg, 51–72.

Scholz, P. 2004. "Elementarunterricht und intellektuelle Bildung im hellenistischen Gymnasium." In D. Kah and P. Scholz, eds., *Das hellenistische Gymnasium*. Berlin, 103–28.

Segal, C. 1992. "Bard and Audience in Homer." In R. Lamberton and J. J. Keanley, eds., *Homer's Ancient Readers: The Hermeneutics of Greek Epic's Earliest Exegetes*, Princeton, NJ, 3–29.

Seidensticker, B. 2010. *Das antike Theater*. München.

Wachter, R. 2010. "The origin of epigrams on 'speaking objects'." In M. Baumbach, A. Petrovic, and I. Petrovic, eds., *Archaic and Classical Greek Epigram*, Cambridge, 250–60.

Weber, G. 1993. *Dichtung und höfische Gesellschaft. Die Rezeption von Zeitgeschichte am Hof der ersten drei Ptolemäer.* Stuttgart.

West, M.L. 1967. "The Contest of Homer and Hesiod." *Classical Quarterly* 17: 433–50.

FURTHER READING

On performance of choral lyric: Athanassaki 2009; Heath and Lefkowitz 1991 provide an overview on Epinician performances. On the symposion, see Latacz 1990 and Murray 1990.

CHAPTER 23

Topos and Topoi

Suzanne Saïd

The study of place/*topos* and commonplaces/*topoi* was initiated in 1948 by E. Curtius in the chapter "The Ideal Landscape" in his *European Literature and the Latin Middle Ages*, followed by two major German publications, by G. Schönbeck, *Der Locus amoenus von Homer bis Horaz* (1962) and W. Elliger, *Die Darstellung der Landschaft in der griechischen Dichtung* (1975), and two influential papers, "Landscape in Greek Poetry" by A. Parry, (1987), and "City Settings in Greek Poetry" by P. E. Easterling, (1989). In the last 20 years many books, colloquia, and collections of papers have been devoted to the representation of space in the ancient world,[1] including the volume on *Space in Ancient Greek Literature* edited by I. J. F. de Jong (2012).

In this chapter I will explore some imaginary presentations of the various kinds of space in poetry and prose: the urban center (πόλις/πτόλις, πτολίεθρον, ἄστυ), its hinterland (agricultural farmland and pastures), and wilderness. I'll begin with Homeric epic, "an authoritative source of the material for Greek mental map-making" (Easterling 1989, 4). I will move to tragedy, concentrating on the plays set at Troy and Athens, in order to compare them with Homeric Troy and Aristophanic Athens, and conclude with three famous descriptions of the *locus amoenus*, in Plato's *Phaedrus*, Theocritus's *Idylls* and Longus's *Daphnis and Chloe*.

1. Iliad

1.1. The Shield

Let us start with the ecphrasis[2] of Achilles' shield (*Il*.18.483–607), and its two beautiful cities that juxtapose opposite aspects of the Homeric world, peace and war, town and countryside, "though in inverse proportion to the rest of the *Iliad*" (Taplin 1980, 12).

The description of the town at peace places side by side the private (a marriage celebration with brides "led from their chambers" and women standing "in their porches," *Il*. 18.492; 497) and the public (a settlement of a law case in the *agora* by elders sitting on smooth stones, *Il*. 18.497; 503–4); while the description of the city under siege is limited to the rampart on which wives and children stand (*Il*. 18.514–15).

A Companion to Greek Literature, First Edition. Edited by Martin Hose and David Schenker.
© 2016 John Wiley & Sons, Inc. Published 2020 by John Wiley & Sons, Inc.

The countryside receives more attention. The description of the farmland, with scenes of plowing and reaping like those found in similes,[3] is complemented by the description of a royal estate "with a thriving vineyard loaded with lovely golden clusters, and the grapes upon it were darkened" (*Il.* 18.561–2). There are also three scenes depicting herding. In the first a successful ambush is set amid typical bucolic scenery: "in a river where there was a watering place for animals, two shepherds came along with their flocks, playing happily on pipes," before being killed (*Il.* 18.520–26). The second pastoral scene associates beauty (the cattle made of gold and tin) with realistic details (they come from the dung of the farmyard), and portrays two marauding lions catching a bull despite the efforts of herdsmen and dogs (*Il.* 18.573–87) – a favorite topic of lion similes (Lonsdale 1990, 41–2). The third, "a pasture large and in a lovely valley for the glimmering sheep flocks, with dwelling places upon it and covered shelters and sheepfolds" (*Il.* 18.587–9), is the only one which excludes violence.

But the shield does not reflect every aspect of the Iliadic world. It totally excludes mountains, forests, and woods. In the similes, these places, inhabited by wild beasts and visited by hunters, woodcutters, or by shepherds trying to catch an escaped bull,[4] are the site of violent phenomena with rivers in spate, raging torrents, ferocious gales, snowstorms, and fires.[5]

1.2.   *The Setting of the Action*

"The principal narrative of the *Iliad* is tightly concentrated; … the action takes place in a small part of the Troad" (Buxton 2004, 149) including the "city of Priam," the Achaean camp, and the plain between them. These settings are usually presented through scattered references; full descriptions are rare and reserved for places of critical narrative significance.

Ilium is first described through epithets emphasizing its sacredness,[6] its greatness,[7] its wealth (*Il.* 10.315; 18.289), its beauty (*Il.*18.512; 21.121), and the number of its inhabitants.[8] Its territory, Τροίη, is characterized by its fertile soil[9] and its good horses (*Il.* 5.551; 16.576). As expected in a heroic world larger than life, the Homeric *polis par excellence*, "is bigger and better and more beautiful than any polis can have been in the late Bronze Age and the so-called Dark Centuries" (Hansen 2005, 16).

The town itself receives only a piecemeal description (Easterling 1989, 6–7). Given the status of the wall as a fundamental marker of the city and the action of the *Iliad*, pride of place is given to the citadel, which is "steep" (*Il.* 15. 71: αἰπύ; 9.419, 686; 13.773; 15.215, 257, 558; 17.328: αἰπεινή), "windswept" (*Il.* 8.499: ἠνεμόεσσαν) and "set on the brow of a hill (*Il.* 22.411: ὀφρυόεσσα), and to its ramparts with their towers and gates.

The acropolis, Pergamon, is occupied by the temples of Athena and Apollo.[10] Since the meetings of the Trojans take place before the doors of Priam (*Il.* 2.788; 7.345–6), it is obvious that the *agora* is located there. Its most important building, "the beautiful palace of Priam" is given a long description in book 6.242–50, a book which is set entirely within the acropolis.

Close to the Achaean ships, there is the Greek camp, which is "a mirror image of Troy" (Haubold 2005, 35). Here also, the emphasis is on the walls surrounded by a deep ditch and a palisade (*Il.* 7.436–41). There is also an *agora* located close to the ships and the barracks of their leader, Agamemnon (*Il.* 7.382–3). The private space consists in the kings' lodgings, conspicuous among them the tent of Achilles. Its construction, described in book 24.448–56, sets the scene for the entrance of Priam and the main action of Book 24.

The fights take place in the plain between the walls of Ilion and the Greek camp. Its landmarks, such as graves[11] and trees,[12] help to locate the action. But there is obviously "an emotional significance" (Griffin 1980, 112) in certain descriptions, such as the mention, during the struggle between Achilles and Hector (*Il.* 22.147–56), of "the sweet-running well springs of Skamandros" and "the fair washing places of stone where the wives of the

Trojans and their fair daughters used to wash their shining garments, in earlier days, in peace, before the sons of the Achaeans came."

1.3. Utopian Places

In contrast with the "miserable mortals," the "blissful gods" live on "radiant Olympus" (*Il.* 13.243). There, Zeus has a palace with golden floor and shining doors (*Il.* 4.1–4; 14.168) and Hephaistos has a house "indestructible, bright as stars, conspicuous among the gods, made of bronze" (*Il.* 18.370–71). When Zeus and Hera made love, "the earth beneath them sent up new growing grass, dewy clover, crocus and hyacinth, so thick and soft it lifted their bodies from the ground" (*Il.* 14.347–9).

2. Odyssey

The landscapes of the *Odyssey* are more diverse since the action is set not only in Ithaca, but also with Telemachus at Pylos and Sparta, and with Odysseus in mythical places such as Calypso's island and Scheria.

2.1. Ithaca

Ithaca, which is defined by its mountain, "the tall, leaf-trembling and conspicuous Neritos" (*Od.* 9.21–2) differs from Troy. It is not a "sacred city," and its epithets as well as its descriptions oscillate between negative and positive. It is rocky, rough, craggy, and surrounded by the sea,[13] but also sunny.[14] According to Telemachus, it is a place only "suited for raising goats," however "it is lovelier than a place for rearing horses."[15] For Odysseus, it is "rugged but a good nurse of men," and "sweeter to look at than any other place."[16] He is echoed by Athena who introduces the island to Odysseus by saying:

> this is a rugged country and not for the driving of horses, but neither is it so unpleasant, though not widely shaped; for there is abundant grain for bread grown there; it produces wine, and there is always rain and the dew to make it fertile; it is good to feed goats and cattle, and timber is there of all sorts, and watering places good through all seasons (*Od.* 13.242–7).

The urban center includes a meeting place which is the setting of various assemblies in books 2, 16, and 24. Its most important building is Odysseus's palace, which is conspicuous,[17] beautiful,[18] lofty,[19] large,[20] and with a high roof.[21] However, it is modest compared to Menelaus's palace, which is praised by Telemachus in superlative terms (*Od.* 4.71–5).

Much more attention is paid to the farmland, which is the setting of the action in books 14–16 and 24: The farmstead of Eumaeus, located "in the remote part of the countryside" (*Od.* 24.150), is reached from the harbor by a rough path among forests (*Od.* 14.1–2). But the house itself is given some kind of epic grandeur. It has a porch (*Od.* 14.5) and its courtyard, "large and beautiful," is "surrounded by a stone wall with wood copings" (*Od.* 14.5–7), a modest adaptation of the copings of the palaces of Alcinous and Odysseus (*Od.* 7.87: Alcinous and 17.267: Odysseus). Laertes' farm, located "away in the countryside" (*Od.* 1.90), but closer to the city, is beautifully cultivated (*Od.* 24.205–6; 336), with a large number of fruit trees producing pears, apples and figs, and a vineyard with all kinds of grapes (*Od.* 23.139, 359; 24.336–44).

Two places in the countryside are also given special attention. First the cave of the Nymphs is carefully placed at the junction between the mythical world of Odysseus's travels and the real world of Ithaca, a status symbolized by its two entrances, one for the men and the other for the gods. It is described twice, by the narrator and by Athena (*Od.* 13.102–12, 346–50), as a typical *locus amoenus* with "an olive tree with spreading leaves ... nearby a cave that is shaded and pleasant, and sacred to the Nymphs ... waters forever flowing." Second, the fountain where Odysseus and Eumaeus meet Melanthios on their way to the palace:

> They arrived at the fountain sweet-running and made of stone, and there the townspeople went for their water. Ithakos had made this, and Neritos and Polyktor, and around it was a grove of black poplars, trees that grow by water, all in a circle, and there was cold water pouring down from the rock above. Over it had been built an altar of the nymphs, and there all the wayfarers made their sacrifice. (*Od.* 17.205–11)

But this idyllic setting strongly contrasts with the exchange of insults and curses which follows (*Od.* 17.212–53).

2.2.   *Utopian Places*

The 'real' world of Ithaca contrasts with mythical places, such as Mount Olympus and the Elysian Fields, where the gods and some heroes lead a pleasant and easy life (*Od.* 6.42–6; 4.563–8).

The island of Calypso, far from gods and men, is first portrayed as a place of delight: around the wide cave of the goddess is a luxuriant grove with alder, black poplar, and fragrant cypress, teeming with all kinds of birds and a vine that ripened with grape clusters, four fountains and soft meadows with parsley and violets (*Od.* 5.63–73). But it is also the place where Odysseus is endlessly weeping for a way home.

Similar contrasts exist in some settings of the *Apologoi*. The place where the Cyclops feeds on human flesh is "overgrown with laurels" (9.182–3) and set in a land reminiscent of golden age with its "crops all growing with no sowing and plowing, wheat, barley and grapes that yield wine from ample clusters swelled by the showers of Zeus" (*Od.* 9.109–11). And the "flowery meadow" of the Sirens is close to a "beach piled with boneheaps of men now rotted away" (*Od.* 12.45–6; 159).

The last stop on Odysseus's journey, Scheria, lovely and fertile (*Od.* 7.18, 79 and 5.34), "far away from the men who eat bread" (*Od.* 6.8), functions as a transition between the mythical universe of Odysseus's adventures and the real world of Ithaca, and combines various aspects of Homeric landscape. Far from the city, there is dense woodland that affords Odysseus a natural shelter (*Od.* 5.475–81), and washing places with abundant water (*Od.* 6.40; 85–7). Closer to the town, Odysseus finds "a glorious grove of poplars sacred to Athena near the road, and a spring runs there, and there is a meadow about it, and there is [Alcinous's] estate and his flowering orchard" (*Od.* 6.291–6).

Introduced by the narrator in book 6.3–10, the town is described first by Nausicaa in book 6.262–7 and again by the narrator in book 7.43–45, 84–102, 112–33. It has "walls long and lofty fitted with stakes, a wonder to look at" (*Od.* 7.44–5), a "fair temple of Poseidon in a place of assembly fitted with stones dragged from the quarries" (*Od.* 6.266–7) and "polished stone seats" (*Od.* 8.6). Its main building is the "lofty palace of the king." Like Menelaus's house, it is "as shining as the sun and the moon" (*Od.* 7.84 = 4.45) and built with bronze, gold and silver (*Od.* 7.86–91). Its marvelous orchard (*Od.* 7.112–32) full of trees and vines bearing fruit throughout the year contrasts with the 'real' garden of Laertes, which gives fruit only in season and requires hard work (*Od.* 24.205–7, 244–7).

3.   Tragic Troy

There are only two surviving plays set at Troy, both located in the gap between the *Iliad* and the *Odyssey*: Sophocles' *Ajax* and Euripides' *Trojan Women*.

The action of *Ajax* takes place after the Judgment of the Arms and concentrates exclusively on the Greeks and their camp. The scenic space is defined by Ajax's barracks, identified with the wooden stage building at the back of the orchestra. It is supposed to be close to the ships, at the last position along the shore (*Ajax* 3–4; 218; 796: σκηνή; 190–91; 1407: κλισίαι), which is exactly the place assigned to *Ajax* in the *Iliad* (*Il.* 8.223–6). Its interior, first described by Athena and Tecmessa (*Ajax* 62–5; 218–20; 233–5), is made visible to the audience when Ajax, surrounded by the cattle he had killed, is rolled out on the *ekkuklema* (*Ajax* 346–7). The camp also includes, in the extra-scenic space, the barracks of the two commanders with its gates (*Ajax* 49) and, close to it, an agora where the Achaeans gather to revile Teucer (*Ajax* 721–2; 749–50).

The plain that extends beyond the camp is the setting of major events. First the meadow (*Ajax* 143–4; 603) where *Ajax* slaughtered the cattle before the beginning of the play and, second, "the baths and the meadows by the shore," "the untrodden place" where the hero plans to go and wash himself (*Ajax* 654–5; 657) and bury Hector's sword, and where the chorus and Tecmessa discover his body.

Allusions to precise buildings are exceptional. At 467, the wall which protects the Trojans (ἔρυμα Τρώων), appears once as a possible setting of Ajax's heroic death, whereas the ditch and the fence surrounding the Greek camp remind Agamemnon of the feat of Ajax who then saved the Greeks (*Ajax* 1273–9, see also *Il.* 15.415–18).

The Trojan landscape is usually described with vague and general terms (significantly, the only descriptive epithet attached to Troy is at 1190, τὰν εὐρώδη Τροῖαν, "vast") and mostly used to convey some information about the feelings of the speaker. Ajax complains that "the surging straits of the sea, the caves by the shore and the pastures of the coast" have long detained him about Troy (*Ajax* 412–15; cf. 419–20). He opposes the victorious campaign of his father Telamon who came back from the land of Ida having won the first prize for valor and his own status in the same place, deprived of his honor by the Argives (*Ajax* 434–40) and hated by Troy and by these plains (*Ajax* 459). His final address to "the streams and rivers of this place here and the plains of Troy" (*Ajax* 862–3), is but a way of emphasizing his isolation. For Teucer, surrounded by the hostile Greek army, and for the chorus who endured ceaseless torments there, Troy is also "a miserable place" (*Ajax* 600–603, 1021–2, 1185–90, 1210: λυγρᾶς … Τροίας).

Euripides' *Trojan Women* is focused on the fate of the women, whose barracks is represented by the *skene* (*Tro.* 32–3 ὑπὸ στέγαις / ταῖσδ', 871 δόμοις γὰρ τοῖσδ' ἐν αἰχμαλωτικοῖς). In this play Euripides turns upside down the Homeric image of Troy and uses the Trojan landscape to convey a sense of total disaster (see Poole 1976). What was once a large city (μεγαλόπολις) has become a non city (ἄπολις; *Tro.* 1292–3; see Croally 1994, 192–4). Right from the beginning, Poseidon describes a city smoldering and sacked (*Tro.* 8–9) and the final 50 lines are full of references to the disappearance of the city, razed to the ground with fire. Allusions to Troy's famous rivers, Scamander (*Tro.* 29; 374–5; 1151–2), and the 'fair flowing' Simois (*Tro.* 810; see *Il.* 6.34) are all associated with death and mourning. Like the similes of the countryside in the *Iliad*, the beautiful description of Troy's surroundings with "the ivy covered glades of Mount Ida, their rivers with melting snow, … the abode which is holy and filled with light" (*Tro.* 1067–70) conjures up an image of rest and peace which intensifies the horror of the city's destruction. The splendid walls built by Poseidon and Apollo, "made of polished stones" and "worked by rule" (*Tro.* 4–6; 46; 814) are always associated with destruction and death: they were already once destroyed by Heracles (*Tro.* 814–16; 819–21) and are used before their second and complete demolition as a place from which to throw Astyanax (*Tro.* 725; 783–5; 1120–22; 1134; 1173–4). The sacred groves are desolate and the gods' shrines are running with blood (*Tro.* 15–16; 562–3). The altar of Zeus has been the setting of Priam's murder (*Tro.* 16–17), the temple of Athena has been outraged by the rape of Cassandra (*Tro.* 67–70), and Polyxena was slaughtered at the tomb of Achilles (*Tro.* 39–40; 622–3). The houses, once visited by divine love (*Tro.* 841–5), where joyful celebrations took place (*Tro.* 544–50; 602–3; 745–6), are overrun by fire (*Tro.* 1300). "The fresh bathing places and the racecourses where once Ganymede exercised are gone" (*Tro.* 833–5).

4.   Tragic Athens

"The well built city of Athens, realm of high hearted Erechtheus" which was named only once in the *Iliad* together with the rich shrine of Athena (*Il.* 2.546–9) is used as a setting for four suppliant plays: Aeschylus's *Eumenides*, Euripides' *Heraclidae* and *Suppliant Women* and Sophocles' *Oedipus at Colonus*.

In *Eumenides*, from line 235, when the action moves from Delphi to Athens, the scenic space is "the city of Pallas" (*Eum.* 19; 772; 1017), successively assimilated to the Acropolis and the temple of Athena with its ancient statue of the goddess (*Eum.* 80; 242; 259), and to the Areopagus. This hill served, in the time of Theseus, as a campsite for the Amazons when they invaded Attica (*Eum.* 685–7), and is used as an indirect way of reminding the audience of one of most celebrated exploits of mythical Athens. In *Eumenides* it becomes the setting of the law court established by Athena to decide the case opposing Orestes and the Erinyes. At the end of the play, the Erinyes are offered by Athena "a place to settle in the recesses of this just land, sitting on gleaming thrones hard by the hearths" (*Eum.* 805–7). This place, which was in fact on the Areopagus (Paus. 1.28.6) is said to be close to the house of Erechtheus that is the temple of Athena Polias (*Eum.* 854–5). This is a slight liberty with topography, but a significant way of translating in geographical terms the reconciliation between the Olympians and the chthonian gods and the close association of the Areopagus with the *Semnai*.

The action of the *Heraclidae* takes place in the Tetrapolis of Marathon (*Hcld.* 32–4; 80–81),[22] at the border of Attica (*Hcld.* 37–8). The scenic space includes an altar of Zeus, as demonstrated by the deictics (*Hcld.* 121; 243–4; 249) and, in the background, a temple represented by the *skene* (*Hcld.* 42). But Marathon is consistently blurred with Athens in such a way that the play seems to take place not in Marathon but in Athens. If the location of the palace of Demophon (*Hcld.* 340; 343; 347) is left unclear, there are many reasons to think, with V. J. Rosivach (1978), that the altar of Zeus *Agoraios* is here purposely confused with the altar of Zeus *Eleutherios* in the Athenian agora. Offstage, the only place of interest is the temple of Athena at Pallene which Eurystheus passes in his chariot in retreat (*Hcld.* 849–50) and which will become the place of his tomb (*Hcld.* 1030–31).

The *Suppliant Women* is set at Eleusis (*Suppl.* 1–2),[23] in the precinct of the temple and the holy hearths of Kore and Demeter (*Suppl.* 30; 33–4; 63–4; 271; 290; 938). The scenic space also includes the cliff hanging over the sanctuary where Evadne appears at the end of the play before leaping into the funeral pyre of her husband (*Suppl.* 1016). The extra-scenic space comprises the funeral pyre of Capaneus and his tomb (*Suppl.* 937–8; 980–83); further away the sacred well of Callichoros (*Suppl.* 359; see Paus. 1.38.6); and, close by, the place where the knife of the sacrifice associated with the oath sworn by Adrastus is to be buried, "near the seven pyres" of the Argive leaders and "beside the triple crossroads of the goddess, hard by the turning to the Isthmus" (*Suppl.* 1205–7; 1211–12; cf. Paus. 1.39.1). There is also, in Athens, the royal palace of Aethra, Aegeus and Theseus (*Suppl.* 29; 360; 1197). Altogether, "local allusions … in the *Supplices* are virtually limited to the prologue and Athena's final speech" (Krummen 1993, 203).

In *Oedipus at Colonus*, "the details of the Athenian landscape strategically transformed and transferred onto stage" (Rodighiero 2012, 57), are given much attention, as demonstrated recently by many scholars.[24]

The scenic space is described in the prologue by Antigone at lines 16–18: "this place is sacred, one can easily guess, with the laurel, the olive and the vine growing everywhere, and inside it many feathered nightingales make their music." It is also untouched by civilization: the rock where Oedipus sits is "unhewn" and "ignores the axe" (*O.C.* 19; 101). An anonymous inhabitant of Colonus complements this description by stressing that this ground "cannot be trodden without pollution [...]. [It is] inviolable and uninhabited. For it belongs to the dread goddesses, daughters of Earth and Darkness [...]. August Poseidon holds it and the fire-bearing god, the Titan Prometheus, is also here, and the spot where you are treading is called the Brazen-footed threshold of this land, the bulwark of Athens" (*O.C.* 37; 39–40; 54–8). This is a "localist reworking of the established literary motif" (Rodighiero 2012, 61) that made Athens into "the bulwark of Hellas."[25] The chorus of Colonan elders echoes these themes in the parodos (*O.C.* 124–8).

The first stasimon, with its famous praise of "the choicest rural dwelling, white Colonus" (*O.C.* 669–70) enriches the description of the grove and transforms it into an ideal *locus amoenus* with a fine climate (like Olympus, Colonus is "never vexed by the sun or by the wind of many winters," *O.C.* 678–9, see *Od.* 6.43–4), lush vegetation and abundant waters (*O.C.* 672–5; 681–91), and is inhabited by Dionysus, the Chorus of the Muses and Aphrodite of the golden reins (*O.C.* 678–80; 691–4).

Major events of the play are also set offstage: the altar of Poseidon, where Theseus performed a sacrifice (888–9) and Polyneices sat as suppliant (1156–9), is "located among the high rocks" (*O.C.* 1493); Oedipus's daughters were kidnapped by Creon and rescued by Theseus at "the pasture west of Oea's snow white rock" (*O.C.* 1059–61); and the messenger describes the place of Oedipus's passing at Colonus (1590–1603) with a mixture of mythical allusions (its bronze threshold, recalling the bronze-footed threshold of the prologue, explicitly associated with Theseus and Peirithous's descent into the underworld) and geographical precision ("the Thorician rock" and "the hill of verdant Demeter that was in view"[26]).

The prominence given to Colonus at the expense of Athens is made possible by a series of geographical displacements. In the prologue Colonus annexes the Areopagus with the sanctuary of the *Semnai*, and the Academy with Prometheus's altar.[27] The first stasimon includes both the Academy, through allusions to the gods who had a temple or an altar there[28] and to the waters of the Cephisus, which was flowing nearby (*O.C.* 685–91; see Wycherly 1978, 222), and also the Acropolis with its "unconquerable and self-renewing olive tree, a terror to the spears of enemies" (*O.C.* 698–9). This latter is an obvious allusion to the miraculous rebirth of the sacred tree after the burning of the Acropolis by Xerxes but also to Archidamus's sparing of the sacred olives when he invaded Attica.[29] The location at Colonus of the disappearance of Oedipus and the pact between Theseus and Peirithous may be Sophoclean innovations as well, as a comparison with Pausanias suggests.[30]

To conclude, in Greek tragedy, imaginary Athens is not "a representation of a particular historical setting or cult," but "a complex association of the myths, institutions and places of Attica ... which demands interpretation in its own terms" (Easterling 2007, 134).

5. Comic Athens

"Comedy [...] celebrates its local, Athenian nature more concretely and pervasively than the most patriotic surviving tragedies" (Crane 1997, 201).[31] Most of the surviving Aristophanic comedies are indeed located in Athens and the exceptions either start from Athens (*Birds*) or return to it at the end (*Frogs*).

The Aristophanic stage is characterized by its fluidity and its interlacing of various spaces: in *Acharnians*, the action is located first at the theater, then at the Pnyx; it moves to the countryside with the house of Dikaiopolis, before returning to the city with the house of Euripides and the parabasis which addresses the audience; and the conclusion is again set in the countryside with the houses of Dikaiopolis and Lamachos (Lanza 2000).

Comic Athens is a multifaceted reality. It oscillates between praise and parody, countryside and town, private and public, reality and myth.

In *Clouds* (300–310), Athens is celebrated as "the rich land of Pallas and a place of valiant men," famous for its mysteries and its festivals. At the end of *Knights* (1323) ancient Athens is portrayed again as "the splendid place, the violet-wreathed, the much envied." But in *Acharnians* Aristophanes makes fun of these inflated Pindaric praises.[32]

From *Acharnians* (425 BCE) to *Peace* (421 BCE), we are offered two opposite views of countryside, a familiar reality for fifth-century Athenians, as demonstrated by the numerous agricultural metaphors and similes.[33] On the one hand, the farmland is devastated by war, emptied of its inhabitants, with its vines trampled (*Ach.* 183; 232; 512; 986–7), its fig-trees cut, its wheat and wine jars broken, and its cattle raided (*Pax* 628–31; 703; 1022–3). On the other, with the return of Peace and her companions, *Opora* (Harvest) and *Theoria* (Festival), a land of Cockaigne, where one enjoys "the life of the farmer, unwashed, unswept, litter-jumbled, bursting with honeybees, bloated with sheep and olives" (*Nub.* 43–5; cf. *Equ.* 805–7), with its smells (*Pax* 525–6; 530–32, *Nub.* 50–52), tastes (e.g. *Pax* 1127–70)[34] and simple pleasures. But in *Birds* (414 BCE) or in *Frogs* (405 BCE), the attractive life in the country becomes an escapist dream enjoyed only by flying birds, or frogs and initiates in the flowery marshes or meadows of the underworld.[35]

In the city, public spaces are perverted. The Prytaneum was the place where ambassadors, public benefactors and victors of major athletic contests were honored and entertained at public expense. But it is only in the Underworld that this privilege is granted to the best artist (*Ran.* 762–70). In Aristophanes' Athens it is usually conferred to swindlers, demagogues or oracle-mongers,[36] and denied to the comic poet Cratinus despite his many victories (*Equ.* 535–6). The same goes for the Pnyx, where the people's meetings always go wrong. In *Acharnians* the assembly, at first unattended, is finally adjourned without any result. In *Knights, Demos*, the People, when sitting on the Pnyx is said to behave like an idiot (*Equ.* 751–5). In *Wasps* (31–6) this point is made graphically in a dream portraying the assembly as a meeting of sheep harangued by a voracious whale.

The fundamental distinction between private and public spaces is often blurred (Auger 1997, 362–9). In *Acharnians* and *Wasps* a private space is transformed before our eyes into a public and civic space: the public market is moved in front of Dikaiopolis's house (*Ach.* 719–29) and Bdelycleon's home is changed into a law court with the help of various domestic implements (*Vesp.* 853–5; 857–9). Conversely, in *Women at the Assembly* the law courts and the porticoes are transformed into men's quarters where public meals will be served, the speaker's platform is used to store mixing bowls and water jugs, and the agora is made into a kitchen by the utensils brought onstage (*Eccl.* 675–8; 728–45).

Real and mythical realms are amalgamated in the *Frogs*. The road from Athens to Hades is supposed to have, like any ordinary road, bakeries, whorehouses, rest areas, and inns (*Ran.* 109–14). It has even been suggested that in depicting the journey of Dionysus, Aristophanes kept close to facts of Athenian topography with the Herakleion at Kynosarges and the sanctuary of Dionysus in the marshes at Agrai.[37]

6. The Setting of Plato's *Phaedrus*

Phaedrus, a dialogue between Socrates and Phaedrus, is unusual for the choice and presentation of its scenery. It is the only Platonic dialogue in which Socrates is "out of place":[38] the man who never set a foot beyond the city walls[39] goes to the countryside in order to engage in philosophical conversation. In contrast with other Platonic dialogues where elaborate settings are usually described by a narrator, "Our only access to the background against which Socrates and Phaedrus walk and speak is through their comments on it" (Ferrari 1990, 2–3). The spatial indications sprinkled over the text are meant to reveal the characters of the speakers and orient the reader to the dialogue's major philosophical concerns.[40]

Phaedrus, who comes from listening to Lysias and is going for a walk outside the city walls for the sake of health (*Phaedr.* 227a), is looking for a place where he can recite Lysias's speech in comfort. Since he is barefoot, he chooses to walk right in the stream – which is "easiest and pleasant especially at this hour and season" (*Phaedr.* 229a) – toward "a very tall plane tree" since "it is shady with a light breeze, there is grass on which to sit or better to lie down" and a stream with "lovely, pure and clear water" (*Phaedr.* 229a–b). It is fitting scenery, therefore, for Nymphs and a likely spot for the rape of Oreithuia by Boreas. But Socrates quickly dismisses the mythical aspects of the setting, since he is interested only in the question of the truth and refuses to endorse any clever interpretation of myths.

While Socrates is initially concerned only with the quietness (ἐν ἡσυχίᾳ) provided by such a setting (*Phaedr.* 229a), he surprisingly bursts into extravagant praise of the scenery:

> By Hera it really is a beautiful resting place (καλή γε ἡ καταγωγή). The plane tree is tall and very broad; the chaste tree lofty and wonderfully shady (τὸ σύσκιον πάγκαλον), and since it is in full bloom, the whole place is filled with its fragrance. From under the plane tree the loveliest (χαριεστάτη) spring runs with very cool water, as our feet can testify. The place appears to be dedicated to Achelous and some of the Nymphs, if we can judge from the statues and votive offerings. Feel the freshness of the air and how pretty and pleasant it is (ὡς ἀγαπητὸν καὶ σφόδρα ἡδύ); how it echoes with the summery, clear song of the cicadas' chorus! The most exquisite thing of all (πάντων δὲ κομψότατον), of course, is the grassy slope: it rises so gently that you can rest your head perfectly (παγκάλως) when you lie down on it. You've really been the most marvelous guide, my dear Phaedrus" (*Phaedr.* 230b–c).

As pointed out by Ferrari (1990, 16), ancient commentators such as Hermias already noted how "Socrates' description of the bower has the air of a formal rhetorical panegyric. Socrates' language is marked not only with elements of a generally sophisticated and elevated style, but by those typical features of rhetorical praise: exhaustiveness and exaggeration." Is this a mere caricature of sophistic panegyrics? In some way it is. But I would like to point out some significant differences. The mention of the symbolic chaste tree, the appeal to smell (the fragrance of the chaste tree) and sounds (the sweet song of the cicadas) instead of sight, and the emphasis on the sacred character of the place (the statues and votive offerings to Achelous and some of the Nymphs) suggest that the enthusiasm inspired by the material beauty of the landscape is, for the philosopher, only a reminder of the true beauty that the souls once perceived when they saw "the plain where truth stands" and "the pasture [which] has the grass that is the right food for the best part of the soul" (*Phaedr.* 248b–c).

Also orienting our interpretation in the same direction is the reappearance of the setting at the transitional point of the dialogue, when the subject shifts from eros to rhetoric. Socrates describes the origin of the cicadas (*Phaedr.* 258e–259d) in order to keep the interlocutors talking, instead of nodding off in the midday heat.

To conclude, Plato's displacement of Socrates in a *locus amoenus* close to a spring sacred to the Nymphs is not "un décor occasionnel" (Motte 1963, 465), but a way to introduce us to a different Socrates, a man possessed by the Nymphs, inspired by divine madness and reminded of a transcendent reality by what he sees here (*Phaedr.* 249e–250a).

7.   Bucolic Landscape in Theocritus's *Idylls*

Theocritus's bucolic *Idylls* are not read today as "a plain image of the way of life amongst the peasants of his country," as Lady Montagu read them, but as "a representation of the poet's literary imagination"[41] and a combination of reality and myth.[42] The hexameter, which had been regularly associated with high topics and heroic or divine characters, is used by Theocritus to create an alternative to Homeric poetry while drawing heavily on it and the literary tradition it inaugurated.[43]

Indeed, the *Idylls* provide an impressive number of references to fauna, geographic particulars and, "in the small compass of about 1,200 lines Theocritus mentions nearly twice as many plants as Homer does in the whole of *Iliad* and *Odyssey*" (Lindsell 1937, 78). The inhabitants of the *Idylls* are humble characters, such as shepherds, herdsmen or reapers, whose rusticity and coarseness are especially emphasized in *Idyll* 5.

But some details are clearly contrary to real facts, as in several examples from *Idyll* 7: cicadas, that sing only in the sun, sing in the shade (*Id.* 7.138–9); the final concert includes birds that, according to ornithologists, never sing during this period (*Id.* 7.140–41; cf. Arnott 1984, 335–6); and trees that grow only in woods are put together with pear, apple, and plum trees that are found only in orchards (*Id.* 7.135–6; 144–6). In the same *Idyll* "the main function of the place names... is not topographical but literary: they create a map of past poetry by associating locations with authors who lived in them or wrote about them" (Krevans 1983, 20).

In the 'mythical' *Idylls* 11, 13, and 22, heroes are set out of place, in a bucolic surrounding. In *Idyll* 11 the realistic description of the ugliness of the Cyclops (*Id.* 11.30–33) contrasts with an alluring evocation of his environment. The Homeric description of his cave (cf. *Od.* 9.182–3) combines with an ironical echo of the Homeric Cyclops' praise of Odysseus's wine as comparable to ambrosia and nectar (cf. *Od.* 9.359):

> "Here there are bays, and here slender cypresses, here is somber ivy, and here the vine's sweet fruit.
> Here there is ice-cold water which dense-wooded Etna sends from its white snow – a drink fit for
> the gods (ποτὸν ἀμβρόσιον)." (*Id.* 11.45–8).

In *Idyll* 13, the Argonauts are set "in a meadow with mighty store of litter for their couches, where they cut sharp sedges and thick galingale " (*Id.* 13.34–5); Hylas meets the dreadful Nymphs in "a spring in a hollow" surrounded with "abundant reeds, fresh green maidenhair and dark blue celandine, carpets of wild celery and creeping dogstooth grass" (*Id.* 13.39–42); and Heracles rampages "through untrodden thorn brakes" (*Id.* 13.64). In *Idyll* 12 the Dioscuri find the awesome spectacle of the giant Amycus in a place similar to Calypso's cave in the *Odyssey,* with an "ever flowing spring brimming with pure water," tall trees and "fragrant flowers" (*Id.* 22.32–43).

The scenery is presented in various ways: scattered details about the actual setting given in dialogues or monologues; full descriptions made by fictional characters or set into songs within the poems; *ecphraseis* or similes.

An illustration of these various presentations is to be found in *Idyll* 1. The dialogue between Thyrsis and an anonymous goatherd first sets the scene of their encounter with a range of deictics, leaving open the choice between two possibilities, the one offered by Thyrsis: "There is sweet music in that pine tree's whisper, goatherd, there by the spring... Come and sit here ...where tamarisks grow and the land slopes away from this mound" (*Id.* 1.1–2; 12–13); and the other by his interlocutor: "Let's sit here under this elm, facing Priapus's image and the spring, there by the oaks and that shepherds' seat" (*Id.* 1.21–3). Thyrsis complements this geographical precision when he introduces himself as "Thyrsis of Etna" (*Id.* 1.65). The landscape appears also through a simile: "Shepherd, your song is sweeter than the water tumbling there from the rock above" (*Id.* 1.7–8). Following that is the bucolic ecphrasis of a κισσύβιον (1.27, cf. *Od.* 9.346), a wooden bowl, which replaces the epic ecphrasis of Achilles' shield. Its three scenes are framed not by a cosmic vision of the world encircled by Ocean but by a floral motif more adapted to the genre: "at his lips winds an ivy pattern, ivy dotted with golden clusters" (*Id.* 1.29–30). In the first scene, a woman is standing between two men without any indication of location (*Id.* 1.32–8). "Next to them an old fisherman standing on a jagged rock" (*Id.* 1.39–40) and "not far from this sea-beaten old man there is a vineyard heavily laden with dark ripe grape-clusters" with a boy "perched on a dry stone wall" (*Id.* 1.45–7). The song of Thyrsis also alludes to places familiar to the Nymphs: "the lovely valleys of Peneus or Pindus" (*Id.* 1.66–7; 69; 72; 77), the mountains and the woods inhabited by wild beasts (*Id.* 1.71–2; 115), and the thickets, woods and groves once haunted by Daphnis, as well as the rivers where he watered his herds (*Id.* 1.116–18). In this song, Hermes is coming "from the mountain" (*Id.* 1.77), Cypris is dismissed to Anchises and Mount Ida where "oaks and galingale grow and the bees hum melodiously about their hives" (*Id.* 105–7). Pan is set far away in Arcadia "in the high mountains of Lycaeus" or in "great Maenalus and the peak of Helice, and that lofty tomb of the son of Lycaon a wonder even to the gods" (*Id.* 1.123–6).

As in Homeric similes, mountains where "thorns and brambles grow everywhere" (*Id.* 4.57), "wild forest" (*Id.* 22.36) and woods, remain a dangerous space. But real shepherds also visit them, pasturing their sheep (*Id.* 3.1–2) or bringing down an escaped bull (*Id.* 4.35–6; cf. *Il.* 13.571–72). There the goatherd Lycidas composed his poems and his fellow poet Simichidas was taught by the Nymphs (*Id.* 7.51, 91–2).

In the *Idylls* the countryside is not only a landscape, but an environment where characters enjoy sensuous pleasures, as demonstrated by the frequency of adjectives such as pleasant (ἁδύς), tender (μαλακός), soft (ἁπαλός), and sweet (γλυκύς). Except for *Idyll* 4 and its caricatured realism, unpleasant elements such as thorns and brambles or painful work are eliminated or set in a distance.

Sometimes the description is reduced to a single detail, a spring or a pine (*Id.* 3). In contrast, in *Idyll* 5, it is doubled when Lacon first invites Comatas to sit with him: "Come and sit here in this grove, under this olive tree…; here water drips cool, there is grass for our couch and grasshoppers sing" (31–4); and Comatas then proposes a far more pleasant setting: "Over here galingale grows, and oaks, and here bees hum with sweet music about their hives. Here two springs give chill water, and birds chirp on trees. The shade too is deeper, and cone-showers drop from the pine overhead" (45–9).

Idyll 7, which recaps all the major themes of the bucolic poems (Payne 2006, 116), transforms a real place set on the island of Cos into a bucolic fiction echoing the cave of Calypso or the garden of Alcinous. It emphasizes the happy satisfaction of the characters who "sank down with pleasure on deep-piled couches of sweet rushes and vine leaves freshly stripped from the bush" (132–4), their enjoyment of the breeze ("many poplars and elms were swaying over our heads," 135–6) and the shade (139), and above all the music of the landscape with the murmur of the water, the chatter of the cicadas, the muttering of the tree-frogs, the song of larks and finches, the moaning of the dove and the humming of the bees (136–42). There is also an appeal to smell: "everything was very fragrant of the rich harvest, fragrant of the fruit" (143). Following this is a picture of an ideal world of plenty: "Pears rolled in abundance by our feet and apples by our sides/young trees hung down to the ground, laden with plums" (144–6) – a paradoxical echo of the description, in the *Odyssey*, of Tantalus's punishment: "at his feet black earth which a god dried away" and "above his head, trees with lofty branches pouring fruits, pears, pomegranates and apples with shining fruits, sweet figs and abundant olives" he could not reach (*Od.* 11.588–90). In the conclusion of *Idyll* 7, taste is not forgotten, with the mention of the wine: "and the four-year seal was removed from the top of their wine jars" (147). But this wine is sublimated through a comparison with its mythical predecessors, the wine that "the old man Chiron set before Heracles in the rocky cave of Pholos" and "the nectar which persuaded the shepherd by the Anapus, Polyphemus to dance about the sheepfold with his feet" (148–53).

8.   The Pastoral Romance of Longus

Longus's pastoral romance (cf. Elliger 1975, 402–16; Tilg, ch. 16, p. 258, in this volume), probably to be dated to the second half of the second century (Morgan 2004, 2), has been justly defined as a "hybrid between the conventional novel (albeit eccentrically modified) and a setting derived substantially from Theocritean pastoral" (Morgan and Harrison 2008, 220). The prologue gives us some guidance for the interpretation of the novel. It is not a direct representation of reality, but an ecphrasis of a painting admired in Lesbos by the narrator, explained to him by an exegete, with a response to it in writing.[44] It is informed by the perspective of the narrator, a visitor from the city (he came there for hunting) whose rhetoric and learnedness contrasts with the naivety of the heroes. The prologue introduces the central themes of the novel: city and countryside, nature and art (τέχνη), eros and mimesis. It also suggests the superiority of art over nature. Indeed, the setting of the paintings, "a grove (ἄλσος) with many trees and flowers irrigated by running waters" was beautiful (καλόν). But the picture (γραφὴ) was more delightful (τερπνοτέρα) still, combining outstanding technique with amorous adventure" (Prologue 1.1). The reader will discover only at the end of the novel that these paintings were dedicated to the Nymphs by the two heroes (4.39.2).

The contrast between town and countryside, mostly implicit in Theocritus's *Idylls*, is made explicit right from the beginning by Longus, who opens his novel with a panoramic view of "a city on Lesbos called Mytilene, of great size and beauty" (1.1.1) followed by a presentation of "the country estate (ἀγρός) of a wealthy man, a most beautiful possession" including "a mountain where wild animals lived, plains where corn grew, slopes planted with vineyards and pastures where flocks grazed and the sea lapped on the soft sand of an expanse of beach." These several aspects of the estate, which is the setting of nearly all the novel, are not given equal attention. The farmland, fields and vineyards appear only occasionally in books 1, 2 and 4[45] with the description of the summer (1.23.1) and in book 4 when the owner Dionysophanes comes to visit his estate (4.13.4). The focus is on the uncultivated space, the pastures where Daphnis and Chloe graze their flocks and the hill (ὄρος), forest (ὕλη) and woods (δρυμός) nearby.

In the novel, forests are usually a place for hunting (2.13.4), inhabited by wolves (1.11.1), and by a wood dove whose singing gives Daphnis an opportunity to recount an etiological myth, maybe inspired by the story of the origin of the cicadas in *Phaedrus*.[46] They are also, as in some Homeric similes, visited by shepherds herding their cows or cutting foliage to feed their kids.[47] In book 3.15–20 they become the setting of Lykainion and Daphnis's love affair. The scenery of the two most important events set there – the discovery of the two heroes by Lamon and Dryas and the attempt of Dorcon to rape Chloe – is given a detailed presentation. The place where Daphnis is found is a mixture of wilderness, "an oak-spinney, a bramble thicket and ivy creeping" and *locus amoenus*: "there was soft grass where the baby lay" (1.1.2). The cave of the Nymphs, referred to often[48] and the setting of some major episodes later on – the dream of Lamon and Dryas, the bath of Daphnis, the oath of Chloe, the pastoral feast offered by Dionysophanes to the villagers[49] – is more fully described, with an emphasis on its size and shape, the water bubbling and "the velvety meadow of lush soft grass" (1.4.1–3). It looks back to book 13 of the *Odyssey*, but significantly introduces art into a natural landscape by replacing the stone-looms of the Nymphs with their statues. In contrast, the description of the place where Dorcon, attempting to rape Chloe, conceals himself in the guise of a wolf – a disguise inspired by the passage of Plato's *Phaedrus* where Socrates compares the sexual appetite to that of wolves for lambs (Morgan 2004, 168) – is a reflection of the wilderness of his character: "the spring was in a deep hollow and the whole area around it was covered with fierce thorns, stunted juniper bushes and thistles" (1.20.3).

The pastures (νομή) where the two heroes graze their flocks are often named, but never described. They are marked only by two trees, the usual oak (δρῦς or φηγός) where they sit[50] and the pine (πίτυς) close to the statue of Pan.[51]

The description of the landscape is usually replaced in the novel by a description of the seasons, a "theme privileged by rhetoricians,"[52] that "articulates the seasonal progression of the narrative ... and proleptically mirrors the affective development of the heroes" (Morgan 2012, 547). I quote only the first one: "It was the start of the spring. The flowers were all abloom in hedgerow, meadow, and mountain. Now there was buzzing of bees, music of songbirds, skipping of newborn sheep. The lambs skipped on the mountains, the bees buzzed in the meadows, the birds filled the thickets with their song" (1.9.1). Morgan's commentary accurately points out its rhetorical character: "the arrangement is elaborately artificial and based on rhetorical principles: the landscape is divided into three elements, each associated with a different species of local fauna,... every motif of this description has its original in literary pastoral" (Morgan 2012, 541).

The two major descriptions of landscape are devoted to a garden (κῆπος) of Philetas and a park (παράδεισος) of Dionysophanes. This choice is in itself significant. Whereas the bucolic poet proposes an idealized portrait of the countryside at large, Longus privileges two spaces that combine nature and art in various proportions. With the garden of Philetas, a creation of human labor (2.3.3), the emphasis is put on the fertilization by nature (Zeitlin 1990, 444–7). If its flowers and trees are so beautiful it is because, as Eros, the powerful principle that underlies all creation, says, "they are watered with the water I have washed in" (2.3.3–5.5). In contrast, the park of Dionysophanes is tended by Lamon who "cleaned the springs so that the water in them would be clean, and removed the dung from the yard so its smell would not offend, and tidied the park so it would look beautiful" (4.1.2). This demonstrates the primacy of art, even if the park includes wild trees and, next to flowers made by art, some which the earth bore. It is protected by a wall and organized according to a precise pattern. The wild trees are planted in such a way that "their natural growth seemed the product of art." Occupying an elevated situation, it offers to its owners "a fine view over the plain... and a fine view over the sea" like the pleasing prospects enjoyed by eighteenth-century English lords[53] and was made to give pleasure all the year round: "There was shade in summer, in spring flowers, in autumn grapes to pick, and fruit in every season" (4.2.6). Like the cave of the prologue, it has at its very center a temple with paintings on Dionysiac themes. It perfectly encapsulates the specificity of a novel where the real harvest of the grapes is replaced by its image, with only the prime bunches left on the stem for the pleasure of the visitors from the city.[54]

NOTES

[1] E.g Hansen 2005, Pouderon 2005, Rosen-Sluiter 2006.

[2] On ecphrasis see Baechle, ch. 30 in this volume.

[3] *Il.*18.541–8 and *Il.* 10.352–3, 13.703–7, plowing; and 18.550–56 and *Il.*11.67–9, reaping.

[4] *Il.* 10.60–62; 12.146–50; 13.471–5, 17.133–6; 18.318–22; 21.485–6, hunters; 11.86–9; 16.663–4, woodcutters; 13.5171–2, shepherds.

[5] *Il.* 16.765–9, tempests; 4.452–5, torrents; 12.278–83, floods; 2.455–6, 11.155–7, 14.396–7, 15.605–6, 20.490–92, fires. See Buxton 1992.

[6] ἱρή 46 occurrences, see Scully 1990, 23–8.

[7] *Il.* 2.332, 803; 7.296; 9.136, 278; 16.448; 17.160; 21.309; 22.21, 251.

[8] *Il.*1.64; 2.133; 5.489; 9.402; 13.380, 815.

[9] *Il.* 3.74, 257; 6.315; 9.239; 16.461; 18.67; 23.215; 24.86.

[10] *Il.* 6.87–9, 269(= 6.279), 6.297, Athéna; 5.445–6, Apollo.

[11] *Il.* 2.793, 811–814; 10.415; 11.166–7, 371–2; 24.389.

[12] *Il.* 6.433–4, 11.167, 22.145, the fig tree; and 6.237, 9.354, the oak tree.

[13] Κραναή, *Od.* 1,247; 15.510; παιπαλόεσσα, *Od.* 11.480; τρηχείη, *Od.* 9.27, 10.417, 463, 13.242; ἀμφίαλος: *Od.* 1.386, 395, 401, 2.293, 21.252.

[14] εὐδείελος: *Od.* 2.167, 9.21, 13.212, 234, 325, 14.344, 19.132.

[15] *Od.* 4.606: αἰγίβοτος, καὶ μᾶλλον ἐπήρατος ἱπποβότοιο.

[16] *Od.*9.27–28: οὔ τι ἐγώ γε / ἧς γαίης δύναμαι γλυκερώτερον ἄλλο ἰδέσθαι.

[17] *Od.* 17. 265: ῥεῖα δ' ἀρίγνωτ' ἐστὶ καὶ ἐν πολλοῖσιν ἰδέσθαι.

[18] καλός: *Od.*16.109, 20.319, 122, 22.495.

[19] ὑψηλός: *Od.* 1.126.

[20] μέγα: *Od.* 7.225, 23.145, 151.

[21] ὑψερεφές: *Od.* 4.757, 7.225, 19.526; ὑψορόφος: 5.42, 115, 7.77.

[22] See Chalkia 1986, 142–9.

[23] See Chalkia 1986, 166–9.

[24] See Krummen 1993, 193–203, Edmunds 1996, Easterling 2006, Rodighiero 2012, and Saïd 2012.

[25] Pindar F 76 M: Ἑλλάδος ἔρεισμα, κλειναὶ ʼΑθᾶναι.

[26] Pausanias saw the temple of Verdant Demeter on his way to the Acropolis (1.22.3) and the Thorician rock has been identified by the *scholium ad OC* 1595 with a deme of the tribe Acamantis.

[27] *O.C.* 39–40, 55–6 . Paus. 1.28.6 and 1.30.2.

[28] *O.C.* 678–80: Dionysos (see Paus.1.29.2); and 691–3: the Muses (see Paus. 1.30.1–2).

[29] Hdt. 8.55, Philochorus FGrHist 328 F 125 and Androtion FGrHist 324 F 39.

[30] Pausanias locates the monument of Oedipus close to the Areopagus and the temple of the *Semnai* (1.28.6–7) and the pact of Theseus and Peirithous on the Acropolis (1.18.4).

[31] See also Saïd 2000.

[32] *Ach.* 673–40 a parody of Pindar F 76 M.

[33] Taillardat 1965, 100–101, 351–2, 418–22.

[34] See Saïd 2000, 199–200.

[35] *Av.* 229–246, *Ran.* 326, 351, 373–4, 448–9.

[36] *Ach.* 124–5: Pseudartabas; *Equ.* 709, 763–6, 1403–4: Cleon; *Pax* 1083: Hierocles.

[37] *Ran.* 137–163. Contra Dover 1993, 61–2.

[38] *Phaedr.*230c Σὺ δέ γε, ὦ θαυμάσιε, ἀτοπώτατός τις φαίνῃ.

[39] *Phaedr.* 230d. Excepting the *Republic*, set in the Piraeus, all Socratic dialogues take place in Athens.

[40] See Motte 1963, Ferrari 1990,1–36, Görgemans 1993.

[41] Payne 2007, 150. See Schönbeck 1962, 112–31, Elliger 1975, 318–64, Segal 1981. 84–234, Pearce 1988, Saïd 1997, Fantuzzi and Hunter 2004, 133–90, Pretagostini 2006, Klooster 2012.

[42] Segal 1981, 210–34: "Landscape into myth."

[43] See Krevans 1983, Pearce 1988 and Griffin 1992.

[44] Prologue 1.3: θαυμάσαντα πόθος ἔσχεν ἀντιγράψαι τῇ γραφῇ.

[45] 1.19,1, 23.1; 2.1.3–4; 4.5.2, 13.4.

[46] 1.27.1–4; Hunter 1983, 56–7.

[47] 1. 27.1; 2.20.2; 2.5.3.

[48] 2.23.2; 4.30.3, 35.4

[49] 1.7.2; 2.39.2; 3.10.3; 4.38.1; 4.39.2.

[50] 1.12.5, 13,4; 2.1.1, 21.3, 30.2, 38.3; 3.12.2, 16.1; 4.15.2

[51] 1.31.3; 2.23.4, 24.2, 39.1; 3.12.2, 24.2

[52] See references in Morgan 2004, 156.

[53] See Williams 1973: ch.12 "Pleasing prospects," 120–26.

[54] 4.5.2: ὡς εἴη καὶ τοῖς ἐκ τῆς πόλεως ἐλθοῦσιν ἐν εἰκόνι καὶ ἡδονῇ γενέσθαι τρυγητοῦ.

REFERENCES

Arnott, W. G. 1984. "Lycidas and double perspective." *Estudios Classicos* 26: 335–6.

Auger, D. 1997. "Figures et representations de la cité et du politique sur la scène d'Aristophane." In P. Thiercy, P. and M. Menu, eds., *Aristophane, la Scène et la Cité*, Bari, 361–77.

Buxton, R. 1992. "Imaginary Greek Mountains." *Journal of Hellenic Studies* 112: 1–15.

Buxton, R. 2004. "Similes and other likenesses." In R. Fowler, ed., *The Cambridge Companion to Homer*, Cambridge, 139–55.

Chalkia, I. 1986. *Lieux et espace dans la tragédie d'Euripide*. Thessaloniki.

Crane, G. 1997. "Oikos and Agora: Mapping the polis in the *Wasps*." In G. W. Dobrov, ed., *The City as Comedy: Society and its representation in Athenian Drama*, Chapel Hill, NC, 198–229.

Croally, N. T. 1994. *Euripidean polemic: The* Trojan Women *and the function of tragedy*. Cambridge.

Curtius, E. R. 1953. *European Literature and the Latin Middle Ages*. Princeton, NJ.

Cusset, C., J.-C. Carrière, M.-H. Garelli-François, and C. Orfanos, eds. 2000. *Où courir? Organisation et symbolique de l'espace dans la comedie antique*. Toulouse.

Cusset, C. 2005. "Fonctions du décor bucolique dans les 'pastorales' de Longus." In B. Pouderon, ed., *Décors et paysages de l'ancien roman des origines à Byzance: Actes du 2e colloque de Tours 24–26 Octobre 2002*, Lyon, 163–78.

De Jong, I., ed. 2012. *Space in Ancient Greek Literature*. Leiden.

Dover, K. 1993. *Aristophanes' Frogs*. Oxford.

Easterling, P. E. 1989. "City Settings in Greek Tragedy." *Proceedings of the Classical Association* 86: 5–17.

Easterling, P. E. 2005. "The Image of the *Polis* in Greek Tragedy." In M. H. Hansen, ed., *The Imaginary Polis*, Copenhagen, 49–72.

Easterling, P. E. 2007. "The Death of Oedipus and What happened Next." In D. Cairns and V. Liapis, eds., *Dionysalexandros: Essays on Aeschylus and his Fellow Tragedians in Honour of A.F. Garvie*, Swansea, 133–50.

Edmunds, L. 1996. *Theatrical Space and Historical Place in Sophocles' Oedipus at Colonus*. Lanham, MD.

Elliger, W. 1975. *Die Darstellung der Landschaft in der griechischen Dichtung*. Berlin.

Fantuzzi, M. and R. Hunter. 2004. *Tradition and Innovation in Hellenistic Poetry*. Cambridge.

Fantuzzi, M. and T. Papanghelis, eds. 2006. *Brill's Companion to Greek and Latin Pastoral*. Leiden.

Ferrari, G. F. R. 1990. *Listening to the cicadas: A study of Plato's Phaedrus*. Cambridge.

Görgemanns, H. 1993. "Zur Deutung der Szene am Illissos in Platons Phaedrus." In G. W. Most, H. Petersmann, and A. M. Ritter, eds., *Philanthropia kai Eusebeia. Festschrift für A. Dihle zum 70 Geburtstag*, Göttingen, 122–47.

Griffin, J. 1980. *Homer on Life and Death*. Oxford.

Griffin, J. 1992. "Theocritus, the *Iliad* and the East." *American Journal of Philology* 113: 189–211.

Gutzwiller, K. 2006. "The Herdsman in Greek Thought." In M. Fantuzzi and T. Papanghelis, eds., *Brill's Companion to Greek and Latin Pastoral*, Leiden, 1–23.

Hansen, M. H., ed. 2005. *The Imaginary Polis*. Copenhagen.

Haubold, J. 2005. "The Homeric Polis." In Hansen 2005, 25–48.

Hölkeskamp, K. J. 2002. "Ptolis and agore: Homer and the archaeology of the city-state." In F. Montanari, ed., *Omero tremila anni dopo*, Rome, 297–342.

Klooster, J. J. H. 2012. "Theocritus." In I. de Jong, ed., *Space in Ancient Greek Literature*, Leiden, 99–120.

Krevans, N. 1983. "Geography and the Literary Tradition in Theocritus." *Transactions of the American Philological Association* 113: 201–20.

Krummen, E. 1993. "Athens and Attica: *polis* and countryside in tragedy." In A, H. Sommerstein, S. Halliwell, J. Henderson, and B. Zimmermann, eds., *Tragedy, Comedy and the Polis*. Bari, 191–217.

Lanza, D. 2000. "Entrelacement des espaces chez Aristophane (l'exemple des Acharniens)." In Cusset et al., eds., *Où courir? Organisation et symbolique de l'espace dans la comedie antique*. Toulouse, 133–9.

Lembach, K. 1970. *Die Pflanzen bei Theokrit*. Heidelberg.

Lindsell, A. 1937. "Was Theocritus a Botanist?" *Greece & Rome*, 6: 78–93.

Lonsdale, S. H. 1990. *Creatures of Speech. Lion, Herding and Hunting similes in the Iliad*. Stuttgart.

Markantonatos, A. and B. Zimmermann, eds. 2012. *Crisis on Stage. Tragedy and Comedy in late Fifth Century Athens*. Berlin and Boston.

Morgan, J. R. 2004. *Longus: Daphnis and Chloe*. Oxford.

Morgan, J. R. and S. Harrison. 2008. "Intertextuality." In T. Whitmarsh, ed., *The Greek and Roman Novel*, Cambridge, 218–36.

Morgan, J. R. 2012. "Longus." In I. de Jong, ed., *Space in Ancient Greek Literature*, 537–55.

Motte, A. 1963. "Le pré sacré de Pan et des Nymphes." *L'Antiquité classique* 32: 460–76.

Parry, A. 1989. "Landscape in Greek Poetry." In A. Parry, with P. H. J. Lloyd-Jones, *The Language of Achilles and Other Papers*, Oxford, 8–35.

Payne, M. 2007. *Theocritus and the Invention of Fiction*. Cambridge.

Pearce, T. E. V. 1988. "The Function of the *locus amoenus* in Theocritus' Seventh Poem." *Rheinisches Museum* 131: 276–304.

Poole, A. 1976. "Total Disaster: Euripides' *Trojan Women*." *Arion* 3: 257–87.

Perutelli, A. 1976. "Natura Selvatica e Genere Bucolico." *Annali della Scuola Normale Superiore di Pisa* 5: 763–75.

Pouderon, B. , ed. 2005. *Lieux, décors et paysages de l'ancien roman des origines à Byzance*. Lyon.

Pretagostini, R. 2006. "How bucolic are Theocritus' pastoral singers?" In M. Fantuzzi and T. Papanghelis, eds., *Brill's Companion to Greek and Latin Pastoral*, Leiden, 57–73.

Rodighiero, A. 2012. "The Sense of Place: *Oedipus at Colonus*, 'Political' Geography and the Defence of a Way of Life." In A. Markantonatos and B. Zimmermann, eds., *Crisis on Stage : Tragedy and Comedy in Late Fifth-Century Athens*, Berlin, 55–80.

Rosen, R. and I. Sluiter, eds. 2006. *City, Countryside, and the Spatial Organization of Value in Classical Antiquity*. Leiden.

Rosivach, V. J. 1978. "The altar of Zeus Agoraios in the *Heraclidae*." *Past and Present* 33: 32–47.

Saïd, S. 1997. "Le paysage des *Idylles* bucoliques." In M. Collot, ed., *Les enjeux du paysage*, Brussels, 13–31.

Saïd, S. 2000. "La campagne d'Aristophane." In Cusset et al., eds., *Où courir? Organisation et symbolique de l'espace dans la comedie antique*. Toulouse, 191–206.

Saïd, S. 2012. "Athens and Athenian Space in *Oedipus at Colonus*." In A. Markantonatos and B. Zimmermann, eds., *Crisis on Stage: Tragedy and Comedy in Late Fifth-Century Athens*, Berlin, 81–100.

Schönbeck, G. 1962. *Der Locus Amoenus von Homer bis Horaz*. Heidelberg.

Scully, S. 1990. *Homer and the Sacred City*. Ithaca, NY.

Segal C. 1981. *Poetry and Myth in Ancient pastoral: Essays on Theocritus and Virgil*. Princeton, NJ.

Taplin, O. 1980. "The Shield of Achilleus within the *Iliad*." *Greece & Rome* 27: 1–21.

Sommerstein, A. H., S. Halliwell, J. Henderson, and B. Zimmermann, eds. 1993: *Tragedy, Comedy and the Polis*. Bari.

Taillardat, J. 1965. *Les images d'Aristophane*. Paris.

Thiercy, P. and M. Menu, eds. 1997. *Aristophane, la Scène et la Cité*. Bari.

Whitmarsh, T., ed. 2008. *The Greek and Roman Novel*. Cambridge.

Wycherley, R. E. 1978. *The stones of Athens*. Princeton, NJ.

Williams, R. 1973. *The Country and the City*. New York.

Zeitlin, F. I. 1990. "The poetics of eros: Nature, Art and Imitation in Longus's Daphnis and Chloe." In D. M. Halperin, J. J. Winkler, and F. I. Zeitlin, eds., *Before Sexuality. The Construction of Erotic Experience in the Ancient Greek World*, Princeton, NJ, 17–464.

FURTHER READING

Chalkia 1986 is a thorough study of space in Euripides' tragedies. De Jong 2012 is a useful but uneven collection of papers on space in Greek literature. Elliger 1975 is a good survey of landscape in Greek poetry. In Hansen 2005 see in particular the papers of Johannes Haubold, " The Homeric Polis," pp. 25–48; and Patricia E. Easterling, "The image of the polis in Greek tragedy," pp.49–72. Krevans 1983 is a landmark paper on Theocritus's *Idylls*. Schönbeck 1962 presents a good survey of the *locus amoenus* in Greek and Latin literature.

PART VI

Literature and Knowledge

CHAPTER 24

Literature and Truth

Martin Hose

"Truth" is a concept with wide philosophical and moral implications. It forms a category by which statements can be classed relative to their referentiality. For what we conventionally call "literature," the concept seems unusable, insofar as there is conventionally a reflected agreement between a literary text and its reader that what is depicted in the text is presented in such a way that it (merely) gives the impression of having happened. Literature thus works in a mode of a kind that may pointedly be characterized as an "as if" mode. The relation between the text (or author) and the readers who accept such an "as if" mode is termed "fictionality," and fictionality is thus part of the modern conception of literature.

It is different with texts that claim to possess a reference to reality[1] and to depict it: a medical treatise, a geographical study or a grammar textbook raise the expectation in a reader that the authors have presented their objects – naturally insofar as their competence permits – in accordance with the existing state of knowledge. These kinds of texts are conventionally classed as "non-fiction" or "factual," and it is possible to make a judgment about them in the categories of "correct" and "true" or "false" and "untrue/lies" (in the latter case authorial intention would be assumed). A necessary precondition for a classification of this kind is the assumption that the statements made by the text can be checked (and, tied to this, that the author has undertaken such a process of checking as part of the composition of the text). In this basic distinction between fictional and non-fictional texts, however, a further differentiation needs to be introduced, for we should not assume that the type of reading behavior that forms the pact between text and reader is unchanging. Reading habits may (1) change over time as the reader's horizons of understanding change; and they may (2) be pursued at the same time by different groups in different ways. This problem becomes especially prominent in the case of religious texts. The groups that share the religion in question will class texts of this type as a revelation or as "sacred texts" and so will read them as non-fiction, while other groups, for whom the religion expressed in the texts is not binding, tend to read the same texts as fiction. This kind of varied reading behavior may be present "synchronically," i.e. when both "believers" and "non-believers" are reading the text in the same period, or it may be present diachronically, when belief in that religion as a whole has disappeared and only "non-believing" readers exist.

A Companion to Greek Literature, First Edition. Edited by Martin Hose and David Schenker.
© 2016 John Wiley & Sons, Inc. Published 2020 by John Wiley & Sons, Inc.

Greek literature has an interesting relation to the division into fictional and factual texts and to the dimension of fictionality. On the one hand, it is not yet clear at what point in Greek cultural history one may assume fictionality as an element in the Greeks' engagement with texts; on the other hand, in Greek culture the category of "myth" appears as a type of discourse that cannot be related to the dichotomy of fiction vs. facts. Whether and to what extent the question of fictionality is interrelated with this question has not yet been definitively determined. The close connection between myth and the question of fictionality is demonstrated concisely in one of the earliest Greek texts, Hesiod's *Theogony*.[2] There the poet, in depicting how the Muses initiated him as a poet (22–34),[3] has these goddesses themselves announce:

> Field-dwelling shepherds, ignoble disgraces, mere bellies:/ we know how to say many false things (*pseudea*) similar to genuine ones,/ but we know, when we wish, how to proclaim true things (*alethea*)." (26–28, transl. Most 2006[4])

In this passage – one of the most frequently discussed in Greek poetry[5] – it may be noted first that "truth" is named as a central characteristic of poetry, and this is done from a position depicted as self-evidently authoritative (it is the Muses who speak, i.e. the central sources of poetic inspiration as commonly understood in the archaic period). However, and the Muses state this explicitly, this is to cite only *one* of the possibilities of poetry. For if the Muses wish it, poetry can express "many false things, similar to genuine ones." Literature, we may conclude from this, is for Hesiod either factual/referential or "false" / "lies." To judge from this passage, the specific capacity of literature to model the beautiful, the interesting, the significant as a fictive world in the mode of "as if," was unknown to early Greek critical reflection on literature, as no particular concept had been found for it. It is even barred as a possible way of thinking about the issue by the use of the term *pseudos*, which holds a broad spectrum of meanings that ranges from an ontological dimension (*pseudos* as simple opposition to "true") through to an essentially moral classification (*pseudos* as "lie").

To what does this statement of the Muses apply? Unless we wish to read this short speech as a definition of poetry according to which it always contains both truth and falsehood,[6] then it must characterize two essentially different kinds of poetry; in that case, on the basis of the context, Hesiodic poetry (whether it is defined as didactic poetry or as *Sachepos*, "factual epic") must be what is characterized by the epithet "true." A large number of scholars have – quite logically – taken the other type of poetry, classed as *pseudos*, to be the Homeric poems (e.g. Kannicht 1980/1996, Puelma 1989). Hesiod would thus be criticizing or at least relativizing the use of the Muses in Homeric epic, and doing so through the Muses themselves, who function as Hesiod's spokespersons, for example in *Iliad* 2.484–7:

> Tell me now, you Muses who have dwellings on Olympus – for you are goddesses and are present and know all things, but we hear only a rumor and know nothing – who were the leaders and lords of the Danaans. (transl. Murray/Wyatt 1999)

In the catalogue of the Greek troops at Troy that follows, the Muses would thus have let the poet/*aoidos* recite inaccurate information, especially as the poet himself admits at *Il.* 2. 486 that he has no knowledge of his own. Nonetheless, it would be too simplistic to read Hesiod's Speech of the Muses as a criticism of Homeric (fictional) epic on account of its fictional character, in contrast to Hesiodic (factual) epic. For: "no Greek ever regarded the Homeric epics as substantially fiction." (West 1966, 46). Further, Hesiod himself in the *Theogony* recounts combats between gods in the mode of heroic epic, and so in principle he too would be exposed to similar criticism.

We may conclude from this that the term *pseudos* here addresses not the "what" but the "how" of epic poetry. This is astonishing, as it is precisely this "what" that – already in later Greek literary criticism – is conventionally termed "myth."

The word *mythos*, in one of its primary senses in Archaic literature, means "(solemn) word," "(elevated) speech," and, derived from this, "tale" or "story." It can be used as a synonym of *logos*. It is only in the fifth century that an opposition develops between *mythos*, which at that time starts to be used for a poetic narrative with no claim to truth, and *logos*, a report that is reliable in the historical sense.[7] In a further step *mythos* comes to be used for the plot of an epic or a tragedy (Arist. *Poet.* 1449b5), and finally in the systematic analysis of rhetorical theory a distinction is made over the degree of facticity of a "narrative" (*dihegesis/narratio*), namely between "historia" (Latin: *res vera*), "plasma" (Lat.: *res ficta* or *argumentum*) and "mythos" (Lat.: *res fabulosa* or *fabula*). Through this last development, myth is defined as a narrative of things that could not happen (as opposed to "plasma": things that could have happened but did not).[8] Through this definition of rhetorical terms, the material of epic and tragedy could be classed as myths, because they contain narratives about events that involve gods (as in the *Iliad*), fabulous creatures (such as the Cyclops in the *Odyssey*, the sphinx and its riddles in Sophocles' *Oedipus Rex* etc.) or heroes with fabulous qualities (like Heracles). All the same, the historical significance of these myths remained uncontested in Greek culture. The factual existence of, e.g., the Trojan War or Heracles as basic data of Greek history was never doubted; and to that extent the Homeric epics, for example, were reckoned in their basic content as "true."

The term myth acquired a new quality from the eighteenth century onwards (on this see Graf 1992). Starting with the German philologist Christian Gottlob Heyne (1729–1812), a "science of myth" developed, which has attempted, in repeated, novel approaches, to find in myth – the epics, tragedies and songs of the ancient poets were regarded as concretizations of the more general, authorless story on which each was based – the prehistoric forms and stages of human thought, whether it be that in myth developments in religious thought, fundamental cultural transitions (such as the process by which the human race became sedentary through agriculture) or historical memories are stored and worked through, or whether it be that myth records structures of an ancient (symbolic) type of thought. All these approaches to explaining myth have been repeatedly abandoned or presented anew in modified form. At the start of the twenty-first century it may be observed that this struggle to understand "myth" as a phenomenon has sparked important impulses for the development of the study of religion and culture. Admittedly, there is at present no clear consensus to which all would subscribe: there are broad definitions (myth as "traditional tale" [Kirk 1970]), but also more complex interpretations, such as that of Burkert (1979, 1998). Beginning from the comparative study of folktales, Burkert relates myths, like folktales, to particular narrative types, and sees in them programs of action which correspond to elementary cultural or biological human relationships. He regards myth and ritual as parallel: rituals are communications in the form of action, which help to shape or manage elemental human situations (such as killing and danger); myths name this kind of situation through language. Ritual, in its mode of action – which admittedly also only acts in play or in the mode of "as if" – can only take the situations up to a certain point, but myth, through the medium of language, in the form of "as if," can allow the situation to become "mythic reality" (Burkert 1997, 39–45).

If we return from the problem of "myth" as a category to the issue of the relation between literature and truth, we may note that a series of modern approaches to myth have not seen it as a purely fictional occurrence, but have wanted to find in it a dimension of meaning of some kind, whether that be understood as cultic, linguistic–structural, historical or otherwise. From this position, one may speak of the "truth of myth."

Burkert's approach yields a new perspective on the question of the fictionality of at least those parts of Archaic literature that represent myths. For if the myths address elemental human situations in a comparable way to rituals, i.e. what in ritual is a threatening gesture or erotic hint is represented in stories as murder and love, then at the level of linguistic action there is an "as if" present which does not tie the meaning of what is represented to the condition of having actually taken place. The "truth" of myth would, on this approach, lie in its "anthropological content," that is, in the fact that the narrated stories of myth allow people to develop and try out patterns of behavior which are comprehensible to them and which help them to deal with their world. If the meaning and function of myth in Archaic Greek culture is defined in this way, it becomes striking that the patterns of the myths are evidently tied to a specific cast of characters, who are not interchangeable and are firmly tied to specific elements of the action. The name Oedipus, for example, implies parricide and incest.[9] On the other hand, it was evidently possible to extend the fixed sequence of actions externally or internally, that is, to expand the known story either by adding stories set before or after the known events, or to make changes within the story by adding new episodes or characters. The *Iliad* shows this in miniature. In Book 24 Priam visits Achilles by night in the Greek camp to receive the body of his son Hector for burial. In a moving scene, Achilles grants that the following morning Priam may return to Troy with Hector. Achilles even gives the enemy hospitality and invites him to eat with him. For this he must overcome Priam's mourning, the rules of which include fasting. He attempts this in an unusual speech (24.599–620), in which he uses Niobe as a "mythological exemplum": she too ate, even though she was mourning her six daughters and six sons, all killed by Apollo and Artemis. Niobe eating is a moment in this myth that is not attested elsewhere, and it may be supposed that the poet of the *Iliad* invented it especially for this situation in the tent of Achilles (Willcock 1964). It is worth noting that the *Iliad* at once acknowledges the "truth" of this new invention: Achilles' mythological argument is successful and Priam allows himself to be persuaded to eat (24.627).

This passage expresses immanently in the text how an extension to a traditional myth functions: it requires a certain plausibility (Niobe's eating is not implausible, given the length of her mourning period) to persuade the addressee (here Priam). As regards the external framework of communication, that is, the relation between the *Iliad* text, the poet and the recipient/reader, this means that the recipient of the *Iliad* must be inclined to accept the extensions or modifications made by the poet of the *Iliad* to the Trojan myth, that is, to accept them as "true."

Admittedly the Niobe paradigm also demonstrates that this kind of truth was presented not as ontological but as persuasive: the recipient must be ready to be convinced. From this it may be inferred that this type of persuasive truth was only ever accepted if it met with a corresponding receptivity on the part of the recipient. To put it in more abstract terms: it was dependent on the horizon of the recipient. Such a horizon was of course neither synchronically nor diachronically unitary. There was no such thing as "the" Archaic, Classical or Hellenistic Greek. Rather, we should assume a broad palette of different horizons, which differed according to the social and geographical location of the recipient and which also shifted over the course of Greek cultural history.

An essential characteristic of Greek literary history, which has not yet been satisfactorily studied, is what we may term "the struggle for the truth."[10] If we work with the dichotomy formulated by Hesiod between "truth" and "lies," which until Aristotle offers no place for the fictional as a distinct category, then every text or poet whose "truth" is no longer accepted, due to changing thought-worlds and experiences, could be accused of lying. It is evident that this fate can only be suffered by those texts which remained present in Greek culture over a long period, that is, texts that were transmitted through the medium of writing.[11] The Homeric epics[12] and Hesiod (by processes that are either unknown or the subject of scholarly controversy)[13] achieved a canonical status early in Greek culture,[14] so they were the principal fields (at least among those identifiable today) in which the struggle for the "truth" occurred. In the fifth century a famous dictum of Herodotus pointedly summarizes the significance of these poets: "For it was they (sc. Homer and Hesiod) who made the theogony for the Greeks and gave the gods eponyms, and defined their offices and skills, and showed their forms." (2.53). It is at precisely this moment that the questioning of the "truth" of these poems begins. Already at the end of the sixth century Xenophanes of Colophon makes the following accusation: "Homer and Hesiod have attributed to the gods/ all sorts of things which are matters of reproach and censure among men:/ theft, adultery, and mutual deceit." (DK 21 B 11, transl. Lesher 1992). Even though this famous fragment does not include the word "lie," the flow of the text makes clear that this is what Xenophanes is implying about the gods represented by Homer and Hesiod. The "truth" of the eighth century thus no longer convinces someone like Xenophanes.[15] The reasons for this may be seen in the creation of new discourses that are conventionally known by the modern term "Presocratic." However, these new thought-worlds are themselves characterized by such major differences from each other that already in the ancient world it was possible to speak of three different philosophical schools: the Ionian (represented by Thales), the Italian (Pythagoras) and the Eleatic (Xenophanes).[16] "A" new truth, which simply superseded the old one, was thus not able to come into existence, not least because the new philosophical truths on offer each contested the others' validity. The concept of truth itself was a matter of controversy in this diversification of discourse: was it applicable solely in the context of logic (the ontology of Parmenides can be interpreted in this way), or must it remain indissolubly dependent on the thinking subject (as Protagoras' statement that "Man is the measure of all things" can be understood)?[17]

A new dimension of experience opened up in Greek culture through intensified contact with other countries and peoples, a result of, among other things, the foundation of colonies abroad. From this, bodies of geographical and "historical" knowledge arose which founded new forms of literature in the medium of writing, such as geographic and ethnographic literature and ultimately the various stages of historiography. Here too the "ancient truths" were put to the test, for which different types of trial were applied. Thus at the start of the fifth century, in his criticism of the tradition Hecataeus of Miletus, the *archegetes* of historiography, was working with the criterion of "common sense" and of one's own judgment: "Hecataeus of Miletus recounts (*mytheitai!*) the following: I write this as it seems true to me. For the stories (*logoi*) of the Greeks are many and laughable, as it seems to me." (FGrHist 1 F 1). Herodotus, the "Father of History," on the other hand, ostentatiously declined to establish the truth and instead set himself the task of collecting the various traditions (*legein ta legomena*, 7.152.3); Thucydides at the end of the fifth century developed a specific critical method of establishing "exactly" (*akribes*) what had happened (1.22) and assessed the "ancient" truths by the measure of probability (*eikos*).

The possibility of checking or testing thus became the central measure of truth, and no longer the authority of the person who announced it. Myth as elevated speech (a mode in which, as seen above, someone like Hecataeus still claimed to speak) had thus lost its universal significance as (sole) guarantor of truth. At around the same time as these new philosophical and historiographical discourses and their "new" rules, specialist sciences developed, especially medicine,[18] the methodologies of which were also based on the principle of testing. Consequently, this pluralization of discourses and the establishment of the criterion of testing has been interpreted as characteristic of a major development in intellectual history, "from mythos to logos" or "from myth to reason" (thus Nestle 1940). This is too schematic,[19] however, as the history of Greek literature continued to be shaped by working with myth.

One may even say that the competition between truths unleashed a force that was productive for those forms of literature that worked with myth. On the one hand myth was rescued "from the outside": an attempt was made to save its truth-claim by a special kind of hermeneutics, the allegorical interpretation. Theagenes of Rhegion, a contemporary of Xenophanes, seems to have been the first to re-interpret the stories of the gods in Homer that had raised objections (such as the so-called theomachy in *Iliad* 23), defending their truth-content on the basis of a "secret meaning" (*hyponoia*) contained in the narrative.[20] This gave rise to a tradition of interpretation that lasted throughout the history of the ancient world. Ironically, this tradition not only asserted the validity of Homer and Hesiod, but used their authority ever more intensively to support the allegorizing intepreter's own specific doctrine, claiming that Homer had already formulated what that doctrine claimed. This was pursued with particular vigor by the Stoics (see Steinmetz 1986; Long 1992). For example, Cicero writes pointedly (*De nat. deor.* 1.41) of the Stoic philosopher Chrysippus that the latter had interpreted the depiction of the gods in the early Greek epics allegorically, "in order that even the most ancient poets ... might seem to have been Stoics." From the imperial period (see Dawson 1992) this type of Stoic allegory is preserved in the *Compendium of the Tradition of Greek Theology* of Cornutus (see Most 1989) and the *Homeric Allegories* of Heraclitus. From a systematic perspective, allegorical interpretation was an attempt to assign to poetry an unambiguously factual dimension;[21] however, a specific truth of poetry cannot be reached through this form of hermeneutics.

Other ways of defending the meaning of poetry against the charge of lying were pursued by the poets themselves. Various strategies can be identified in the poetry of the fifth century. First, there is a clear tendency towards continuous modernization: the characters in the songs of poets like Pindar or Bacchylides, like those in the dramas of the tragedians, think, feel and act in the way that the fifth century considered plausible for human thinking, feeling and acting. Even though the terms used for mental or psychological activity in early epic (Jahn 1987; Clarke 1999) such as *nóos* or *thymós* reappear frequently, their meaning has nonetheless narrowed and shifted (Pellicia 1995). At the same time, mental or psychological processes are presented with much more nuance and tension. The result is that recipients of literature in the fifth century encounter in contemporary poetry mythical figures whose character does not seem outdated or incomprehensible. This continuous modernization becomes a feature of working with myth throughout the rest of Greek literary history and ensures that the processes of myth, which in principle belong to a remote period of time, remained continuously up to date and valid.

It must have been harder to deal with the Homeric–Hesiodic gods. The essential problem had been identified by Xenophanes. To solve it, the following procedures were deployed:

One strategy was to "correct" the myth explicitly, that is, to set up against a problematic "old truth" a new, convincing one: Pindar, for instance, offers in *Olympian* 1.30ff a sanitized version of Tantalus's meal (through which the old version is nonetheless visible).

A second strategy is to reduce the remarkable similarity between gods and men by creating a great distance – compared to that in Homer's account – between god and man. The gods and their behavior become sublime and unfathomable: this is how they appear in Aeschylus.[22] Or else the problematic gods of Homer become "invisible" and the antics criticized by Xenophanes are simply not mentioned: Sophocles in his tragedies gives the gods only a schematic presence on the stage, making them all the more powerful as forces to which humans are exposed.[23]

A third strategy attacks the problem directly, and openly exposes the difficulties created by the traditional myth. Euripides pursues this strategy extensively in his tragedies and "modernizes" the gods in his dramas just as he does the human figures: Aphrodite in *Hippolytus* or Hera in *Heracles furens* appear simply spiteful; Apollo's order to Orestes to murder his mother is presented as a plan that does not follow through and deal with the problems it raises (*El.* 1245/46). The plays themselves sometimes address the topic of the incommensurability of the "Homeric" gods, who act like humans, with the expectations placed on them (cf. *Hipp.* 120), or old myths are explicitly doubted (*El.* 737/38).[24] Consequently, the Euripidean dramas yield a new truth not about the gods, but instead about people. In this tendency, these texts converge with the more progressive intellectual positions that spread in the second half of the fifth century, such as Protagoras's skepticism about the possibility of making reliable statements about the gods (DK 80 B 4), and the claim that

"Man is the measure of all things" (DK 80 B 1). Euripides' plays thus do not represent the death of tragedy, as Friedrich Nietzsche (in *The Birth of Tragedy*) believed, but are rather attempts to assert the truth of myth (at least insofar as they deal with humans).

In sum, this type of continuous modernization allowed poetry not only to succeed in establishing a canon of poets and texts, but also to maintain its standing, for a broad educated section of Greek public life, as an authority that voiced valid truths and wisdom. Plato, for instance, continually has the characters in his dialogues cite poets to begin or support their arguments.[25] Aristotle says in the *Metaphysics* (1, 995a7/8) that there are people who will only accept an argument if it is demonstrated by quotations from the poets (cf. Halliwell 2000).

In the discourses of the sophistic movement in the fifth century, two tendencies develop forcefully in the struggle for the truth of myth. On the one hand, myth is used for teaching purposes (which presupposes a didactic truth at least). Xenophanes had already insisted on the didactic function of early epic: "From the beginning, all have learned from Homer" (DK 21 B 10).[26] This became more concrete among the sophists, in that they employed myth extensively for didactic purposes. However, the allegorical method of interpretation seems to be a necessary condition for this: Prodicus, for example, interpreted gods like Demeter or Dionysus as symbols for bread or wine (DK 84 B 5), and so behind the myth he created, of Hercules at the crossroads (DK 84 B 2), lies a symbolic meaning by which people are called to decide in favor of virtue. Gorgias, on the other hand, used myth as a repertoire of topics with which to demonstrate his rhetorical art (DK 82 B 11: *Encomium of Helen*; B 11a: *Defense of Palamedes*). This sophistic tradition is the background (cf. Reinhardt 1927/1966, 219–27) to Plato's lavish use of myths (of his own invention); their role – generally speaking – is that positions which are developed by Socrates or other characters like Protagoras or Critias in the dialogues can be confirmed in the medium of myth (see Janka and Schäfer 2002, Partenie 2009).

The second tendency is to regard myth and the poetry that conveys it as the bearer of an ancient, primitive truth. Drawing on the past was a characteristic of Greek culture, as it was of the other cultures of the ancient world: the present was generally judged to be of lesser value than a (largely imaginary) past.[27] The evidently greater age of, for instance, Egyptian culture therefore *per se* commanded the respect of the Greeks, as especially Herodotus shows (Book 2; see Burkert 2003, 79–106). It was thus easy to regard older Greek poetry, too, as the bearer of a higher wisdom (and truth) than the present. First steps towards this position were formulated by the sophist Hippias in the introduction to his *Synagoge* (see Patzer 1986), an encyclopaedic compilation (DK 86 B 6). He there declares that his doctrines offer a kind of synthesis of the wisdom of Orpheus, Musaeus, Hesiod, Homer and other poets, as well as Greek and "barbaric" prose authors. Beginning from here, a line can be drawn to Aristotle, who in the *Metaphysics* (12, 1074b1ff) describes myth as the presentation form (*schéma*) of the "ancients": they used it to transmit their discoveries about the nature of the gods, and at the same time they found it an apt form for communicating to the "many" and for turning knowledge into laws. In this way Aristotle explains his own acknowledgement of the "truth" of poetry; however, this truth continues to be factual, as it refers to physical–philosophical "facts." Myth is understood merely as a kind of archaic form of these truths. From here it is only a short step to assume generally that the older a text is, the closer it is to the truth or to wisdom, whether truth is here understood as *logos* revealed in the world, or whether the interest is in its closeness to a divine revelation (see Baltes 1999/2005). Consequently, Homer, Hesiod and the mythical singers Orpheus, Musaeus and Linus, who were regarded as even older, were understood as transmitters of wisdom that rivaled the Egyptian or "Chaldaic" (i.e. Babylonian) doctrines. Aristotle himself (in a fragment [F 53 Rose] of the lost *Protrepticus*, cf. Baltes 1999/2005, 17), however, seemed to regard these barbarian wisdom traditions as philosophy that was not yet completed – for him the completion was to come from Greek thought.

This figure of thought, of granting a special importance to age, was adopted by Jewish and then by early Christian thought and was used as an "argument from age":[28] insofar as Moses (and so the *Pentateuch*) was dated prior to the Trojan War in the chronologies current in the ancient world, he ranked as older than Homer. Jewish literature (including the Prophets) could thus be understood as a source for Greek authors down to Plato (who could have got to know it on his journeys to the Orient);[29] Greek literature had thus gained access to the Judaeo-Christian revelation (which explained their convergence in certain views), but had in part misunderstood it (which explained the divergences).[30] Judaeo-Christian literature was thus proved to be of greater value than Greek literature – that is, from this perspective, literature was assessed under the aspect of its (here, too, factual) truth-content. Within this principle of deep respect for the ancient, which is characteristic of the entire ancient world, Plato, and after him Platonism, holds a specially marked position.[31] In Plato's dialogue *Ion*, the divine inspiration of the poet (in the example of the rhapsode Ion) is acknowledged, but for Plato this does not lead to a specific truth of poetry. On the contrary: like every art, poetry is, as a form of mimesis, just as inferior to reality ontologically as reality is inferior to the world of ideas.[32] Further, Plato repeats (in *Rep.* 2 and 3) the essential criticisms of Xenophanes' polemic against Homer and Hesiod: "Hesiod and Homer and the other poets … composed false stories [*muthous pseudeis*], which they told people and are still telling them." (*Rep.* 3, 377d4–6, transl. Gill). From this follow both the famous rejection of Homer's poetry and the demand for poetry that is limited by censorship in Plato's *Republic*. Plato, too, is thus a long way from recognizing a fictional dimension of poetry.[33] This shaped the attitude of Platonism as a whole. Plutarch made the point sharply (*De gloria Ath.* 348a):

> A myth aims at being a false tale [*pseudes*], resembling a true one;[34] wherefore it is far removed from actual events, if a tale [*logos*] is but a picture and an image of actuality, and a myth is but a picture and image of a tale. (transl. Babbitt 1936).[35]

If we summarize our findings so far about the discourse on the truth of poetry, what is glaringly clear is an insistence on the factual dimension of literature. Attempts to develop a concept of fictionality have not been found. They do exist, however. The most famous attempt at such a concept is found in chapter 9 of Aristotle's *Poetics*. There it is said:

> It will be clear from what I have said [sc. in ch. 7 and 8 on the form of a tragedy] that it is not the poet's function to describe what has actually happened, but the kinds of thing that might happen, that is, that could happen because they are, in the circumstances, either probable or necessary. The difference between the historian and the poet … is that the one [sc. the historian] tells of what has happened, the other of the kinds of things that might happen. For this reason poetry is something more philosophical and more worthy of serious attention than history; for while poetry is concerned with universal truths, history treats of particular facts. (transl. Dorsch)

The distinction made here by Aristotle between poetry and historiography may at first seem illuminating. However, it does not reflect the theory or practice of literature in the ancient world. For with few exceptions ancient historical writing did not tend to report "what really happened," but began in the fourth century to aim systematically at emotional effects like those of tragedy; in addition, ancient historians collected an ever larger arsenal of *topoi* that they could deploy, for example, in accounts of battles or descriptions of cities and countries. Further, they often pursued polemics against each other and accused each other of "lying" (see Wiseman 1993). For example, Herodotus was explicitly called *pseustes* by Ctesias, a rival writing at the start of the fourth century (FGrHist 688 T 8).[36] Similarly, poetry (and the non-factual forms of prose) did not gain much by Aristotle's license (which was admittedly in part directed at Plato's rejection of poetry). For, unlike in the system of rhetoric mentioned above, which recognized fictional narratives through the category of *plasma*, Greek literary criticism evidently remained stuck in the binary opposition of "truth–lies." A distinct category for the fictive cannot be found in it. Paradoxically, this lack, too, released productive literary forces. For, if we look closely, we see that the concept of the lie already had its own special charm early in Greek literature. The speech of the Muses in Hesiod's *Theogony* cited above is an important piece of evidence for this. For the Muses do not seem to regard it as an offense that they sometimes lie, but rather present this skill, even as a divine capacity of their inspiration. Accordingly, countless Greek texts present lying speeches as a special skill of characters in the text (cf. Bowie 1993; Fuchs 1993). Already in the *Iliad* none other than Zeus himself sends Agamemnon a "false dream," which misleads the military commander into giving a deceptive speech to his army (which, as is well known, fails, *Il.* 2.111). The *Odyssey* is riddled with numerous deceptive speeches by the eponymous hero, with which he tries to deceive, among others, the goddess Athena (*Od.* 13. 256–86). The goddess naturally sees through the lie, but instead of being outraged she smiles and strokes Odysseus's hand (*Od.* 13.287/88). She thus explicitly recognizes lying as a (positive) intellectual ability in her protégé. In tragedy, numerous plays (Soph. *Ajax* and *El.*, Eur. *Med.*) work with the instrument of the lying speech, and so it is certainly not chance that the sophist and rhetor Gorgias attempts to appreciate the lie from the point of view of reception aesthetics – that is, the deception of the audience becomes a positive dimension. Gorgias, as Plutarch writes in *De gloria Athen.* (ch. 5, 348c = Gorgias VS 82 B 23) in the context of an appreciation of Athenian drama as "deception," had said, "For he who deceives is more honest than he who does not deceive, and he who is deceived is wiser than he who is not deceived ...." (transl. Babbitt 1936). *In nuce* this presents a sketch – in the vocabulary of lies and deception – of the mechanism of a pact (cf. above) between the producer (= the deceiver) and the recipient (= the deceived) of literature. Gorgias is thus making the attempt, in the face of the lack of terminology and of a concept of fictionality, to use the conceptual schemes available in his culture, namely truth and lies, to define fictional communication: as voluntary and transparent lying in which the recipient willingly allows the deception. Fictional communication is described with the term "lie" continually in Greek literature; there seems to have been a special charm in using the charge of moral misbehavior that always clung to the term *pseudos* to characterize fictionality as a paradox: Lucian, for instance, in *Philopseudes* (ch. 1) ironically problematizes the "remarkable pleasure people take in mendacious subjects."[37]

The lie as mode of communication develops its own grammar as a literary procedure in the course of Greek literary history (though this has not yet been fully researched).[38] Its elements include – paradoxically – the promise to speak the truth or, put more abstractly, an apparatus of authentification. "Lying tales" refer to their fictional status via their assurances that they are telling the truth, or by generous citation of sources and witnesses.[39] If Plato sometimes gives his dialogues a concrete setting and cites his informants for what is recounted, in the imperial period this becomes an indication of the fictive quality of the discussion in question: "The philosophers thus lie about everything" concludes Athenaeus (5, 216c), pointedly referring to this dialogue framework. The Greek novel, too, sometimes makes use of the potential of this kind of authentification,[40] and Lucian sketches in the introduction (ch. 1) to his "True Stories" (according to the author they can only be called this, because they admit from the start that they are lies) the dazzling play of texts that will sometimes arise as they deceive the reader with assurances of their truth (see Moellendorff 2000). In summary it can be concluded that the speech of the Muses in Hesiod's *Theogony*, with its dichotomy of truth and lies, which is intended to characterize poetry (and literature as a whole), is even of symbolic significance for the whole of Greek literary history. As has been shown above, the "truth" of poetry is a problem that commands intense engagement from literary criticism and philosophy, and the concept of the lie as opposed to truth is used in long stretches of Greek literary history – from a modern perspective reductively – to describe and problematize everything in poetry or literature that cannot be classed as true in an ontological sense. The lie, we may conclude, is a central category of Greek literary aesthetics.

NOTES

[1] In the context of the topics sketched here, this term is used for the sake of simplicity, as a cypher for the entire sphere of the non-fictional. The problem that "reality" is tied to "perception of reality" and this, at the level of e.g. physiology, philosophy of perception, etc., implicates a range of highly specialized debates, can be noted here only in passing; it is equally important not to forget that, as a form of perception, "reality" is constituted in the narrative mode.

[2] If we follow West and Burkert, who see Hesiod's poems as older than the Homeric ones, this would in fact be the oldest extant text in Greek literature.

[3] On this Kambylis 1965; cf. Nagy 1989, 31–3.

[4] West 1988 translates *pseudea* as "lies," *alethea* as "reality"!

[5] See most recently Stroh 1976, Kannicht 1980 / 1996, Rösler 1980, Puelma 1989.

[6] Thus Stroh 1976 – but this interpretation has been rejected in all other studies.

[7] This use is first found in a poet, Pindar, *Ol.* 1.29 and *Nem.* 7.23.

[8] This schema is found in Sextus Empiricus, *Adversus mathematicos* 1.263; there are parallels in Roman literature in *Rhet. Her.* 1.12 and Cicero, *Inv.* 1.27.

[9] This is formulated concisely about tragedy in the fourth century, in Antiphanes' comedy *Poiesis* (F 189 PCG): "For if I say Oedipus, the rest is known: the father Laius, the mother Jocasta, the daughters, what kind of children, what he suffered, what he did" (V. 5–8). Corresponding to this, Aristotle (*Poet.* 1453a36–39) gives an example of departing from the myth depicted by tragedy, namely if Orestes did not kill Aegisthus but instead made friends with him.

[10] In what follows I concentrate on the issue of stabilizing myth's claim to truth. I leave undiscussed (although it would also merit investigation) the field in which later Greek thought may have incorrectly regarded statements in early poetry as factual. An example of this is Critias's criticism (DK 88 B 44) of the first-person statements in the poetry of Archilochus, which Critias (mis)interprets as biographical information.

[11] That there was also a high level of "synchronic" presence of poetry in the archaic and classical periods can here only be noted in passing. This is summarized by the pointed characterization of the early Greek world as a "song culture" by Herington 1985.

[12] A detailed history of the influence of the Homeric epics in the ancient world is much needed. First attempts can be found for example by Mehmel 1954, Lamberton and Keaney 1992, and Lamberton 1997.

[13] How we are to understand "the making of Homer" depends on the question of when a text of the *Iliad* or *Odyssey* came into existence: did it essentially exist already in the early seventh century (thus the basic assumption of the Neoanalytic school), did it first come into being in the sixth century in rivalry with the choral lyricists (thus Burkert 1987/2001), or should we think of a text that remained in a state of flux into the Hellenistic period (cf. Nagy 2003)?

[14] Xenophanes, Frg. 9 Diehl appears to name Homer explicitly as universal teacher.

[15] Xenophanes was not alone in his criticism: Heraclitus criticized Homer and Archilochus (DK 22 B 42) and Hesiod (B 40) in similar terms. Solon put it pithily: "Singers tell many lies" (F 29 IEG) – this even became a proverb.

[16] Thus Clem. Al., *Strom.* I 14.62–64. This is preceded by, for instance, Plato, *Sophist* 242c–e. See on this Sassi 2011.

[17] See Heitsch 1979, 42–63.

[18] Lloyd (1987) adopts the pointed title "The Revolutions of Wisdom."

[19] In general, see Buxton 1999a, Most 1999.

[20] See Pfeiffer 1968, 9–11, Richardson 1992.

[21] On the differing classifications of myth in Cornutus and Heraclitus, see Dawson 1992, 39.

[22] Thus emphatically, for instance, in the famous hymn to Zeus in Aesch. *Ag.* 160ff (it is striking that this does not involve any new theological concept, and Aeschylus retains the essential characteristics of traditional religiosity. See Lloyd-Jones 1956/1990.

[23] This is shown concisely in *O.C.* 1623–30, in which the god appears only as an invisible voice, which, further, is reported by a messenger.

[24] On this see also Stinton 1976.

[25] For this, see the "Index of Quotations" in Brandwood 1976, 991–1003.

[26] Plato's dialogues repeatedly show that this position was still valid in the late fifth and fourth centuries, for example when in the *Charmides* (163b) Critias says he learned something from Hesiod.

[27] This appears already, and archetypically, in Nestor's stories in the *Iliad*.

[28] Out of the large scholarly literature on this topic, see Gnilka 2005.

[29] The characterization of Plato as the "Attic Moses" was coined by Numenius (apud Clem. Al., *Strom.* 1.150.4). On this topic as a whole see Ridings 1995.

[30] Borrowing from a phrase in John's Gospel (10.8: "All that ever came before me are thieves and robbers") Clem. Al. (*Strom.* 1.87.2) classed the relation between Jewish and Greek literature as "the thefts of the Greeks."

[31] On this, see the summary by Ferrari 1989.

[32] An example of this is, for instance, the Simile of the Cave, *Rep.* 7, 514a–518b; it is argued in detail by Socrates in *Rep.* 10.

[33] On this the basic treatment is Gill 1993.

[34] On "likeness" and "likelihood" in Plato see now Bryan 2012.

[35] On the relation of Logos and Mythos in Plato, see Halliwell 2000.

[36] Criticism of Herodotus went so far that in the Imperial period the philologist Aelius Harpocration wrote a special treatise with the title *On the lies in Herodotus' Histories.* Plutarch's work *De malignitate Herodoti* belongs to the same tradition.

[37] Similarly Strabo, *Geog.* 1.2.9, who assumes that Homer used lies to make his epics more appealing, or Plutarch, *Quomodo adul.* ch. 2, 16a.

[38] Cf. Weinrich (1966); also Hose (1996).

[39] Factual texts use exactly the same strategies to prove their "truth." A precondition for a satisfactory interpretation of these strategies is thus necessarily a kind of *a priori* expectation on the part of the reader, which is different according to whether one is faced with, e.g., Thucydides as opposed to Lucian.

[40] Cf. e.g. Antonius Diogenes' novel *The Wonders Beyond Thule* (extant only in the summary in Photius, *Bibl.* 166), on which see Morgan (1993), Fuchs (1993), 209; cf. Tilg in this volume 259–60.

REFERENCES

Babbitt, F.C., ed. 1936. *Plutarch's Moralia.* Vol. 4. Cambridge, MA.

Baltes, M. 1999/2005. "Der Platonismus und die Weisheit der Barbaren." In M. Baltes, ed., *ΕΠΙΝΟΗΜΑΤΑ. Kl. Schriften zur antiken Philosophie und Homerischen Dichtung,* Munich (first edn. 1999), 1–26.

Bowie, E. L. 1993. "Lies, Fiction and Slander in Early Greek Poetry." In Chr. Gill and T. P. Wiseman, eds., *Lies and Fiction in the Ancient World,* Exeter, 1–37.

Brandwood, L. 1976. *A Word Index to Plato.* Leeds.

Bryan, J. 2012. *Likeness and Likelihood in the Presocratics and Plato.* Cambridge.

Burkert, W. 1979. *Structure and History in Greek Mythology and Ritual.* Berkeley, CA.

Burkert, W. 1987/2001. "The Making of Homer in the Sixth Century B.C.: Rhapsodes versus Stesichoros." In W. Burkert, ed., *Kleine Schriften I. Homerica,* Göttingen (first edn. 1987), 198–217.

Burkert, W. 1997. Homo necans. *Interpretationen altgriechischer Opferriten und Mythen,* 2nd edn. Berlin.

Burkert, W. 2003. *Die Griechen und der Orient*. Munich.

Buxton, R. 1999. "Introduction." In R. Buxton, ed., *From Myth to Reason? Studies in the Development of Greek Thought*, Oxford, 1–21.

Clarke, M. 1999. *Flesh and Spirit in the Songs of Homer*. Oxford.

Dawson, D. 1992. *Allegorical Readers and Cultural Revision in Ancient Alexandria*. Berkeley, CA.

Dorsch, T. S. 1965. *Aristotle Horace Longinus, Classical Literary Criticism*. Harmondsworth.

Ferrari, G. R. F. 1989. "Plato and poetry." In G. Kennedy, ed., *The Cambridge History of Literary Criticism. Vol. 1. Classical Criticism*, Cambridge, 92–148.

Fuchs, E. 1993. *Pseudologia. Formen und Funktionen fiktionaler Trugrede in der griechischen Literatur der Antike*. Heidelberg.

Gill, Chr. 1993. "Plato on Falsehood – not Fiction." In Chr. Gill and T. P. Wiseman, eds., *Lies and Fiction in the Ancient World*, Exeter, 38–87.

Gnilka, Chr. 2005. "Wahrheit und Ähnlichkeit." In R. v. Haehling, ed., *Griechische Mythologie und frühes Christentum*, Darmstadt, 194–226.

Graf, F. 1992. *Greek Mythology: An Introduction*. Baltimore.

Halliwell, St. 2000. "The Subjection of Muthos to Logos: Plato's Citations of the Poets." *Classical Quarterly* 50: 94–112.

Herington, J. 1985. *Poetry into Drama*. Berkeley, CA.

Heitsch , E. 1979. *Parmenides und die Anfänge der Erkenntniskritik und Logik*. Donauwörth.

Hose, M. 1996. "Fiktionalität und Lüge. Über einen Unterschied zwischen römischer und griechischer Terminologie." *Poetica* 28: 257–74.

Jahn, Th. 1987. *Zum Wortfeld "Seele-Geist" in der Sprache Homers*. Heidelberg.

Janka, M. and Ch. Schäfer, eds. 2002. *Platon als Mythologe*. Darmstadt.

Kambylis, A. 1965. *Die Dichterweihe und ihre Symbolik*. Heidelberg.

Kannicht, R. 1980/1996. "Der alte Streit zwischen Philosophie und Dichtung." In R. Kannicht, ed., *Paradeigmata. Aufsätze zur griechischen Literatur*, Heidelberg (first edn. 1980), 183–223.

Kirk, G. S. 1970. *Myth. Its Meaning and Function in Ancient and Other Cultures*. Berkeley, CA.

Lamberton, R. 1997. "Homer in Antiquity." In I. Morris and B. Powell, eds., *A New Companion to Homer*, Leiden, 33–54.

Lesher, J. E., ed. 1992. *Xenophanes of Colophon: Fragments*. Toronto.

Lloyd, G. E. R. 1987. *The Revolutions of Wisdom. Studies in the Claims and Practice of Ancient Greek Science*. Berkeley, CA.

Lloyd-Jones, H. 1956/1990. "Zeus in Aeschylus." In H. Lloyd-Jones, ed., *Greek Epic, Lyric, and Tragedy*, Oxford (first edn. 1956), 239–61.

Long, A. A. 1992. "Stoic Readings of Homer." In R. Lamberton and J. J. Keaney, eds., *Homer's Ancient Readers*, Princeton, NJ, 41–66.

Mehmel, F. 1954. "Homer und die Griechen." *Antike und Abendland* 4: 16–41.

Moellendorff, P. v. 2000. *Auf der Suche nach der verlogenen Wahrheit. Lukians Wahre Geschichten*. Tübingen.

Morgan, J. R. 1993. "Make-believe and Make Believe: The Fictionality of the Greek Novels." In Chr. Gill and T. P. Wiseman, eds., *Lies and Fiction in the Ancient World, Exeter*, 175–229. Exeter.

Most, G. W. 1989. "Cornutus and Stoic Allegoresis: A Preliminary Report." *Aufstieg und Niedergang der romischen Welt* 2.36.3: 2014–65.

Most, G. W. 1999. "From Logos to Mythos." In R. Buxton, ed., *From Myth to Reason? Studies in the Development of Greek Thought*, Oxford, 25–47.

Most, G.W., ed. 2006. *Hesiod. Theogony, Works and Days, Testimonia*. Cambridge, MA.

Murray, A. T. and W. F. Wyatt, ed. 1999. *Homer. Iliad*. Cambridge, MA.

Nagy, G. 1989. "Early Greek views of poets and poetry." In G. Kennedy, ed., *The Cambridge History of Literary Criticism. Vol. 1. Classical Criticism*, Cambridge, 1–77.

Nagy, G. 2003. "Rev. of West, Studies in the Text and the Transmission of the Iliad." *Gnomon* 75: 481–501.

Nestle, W. 1940. *Vom Mythos zum Logos. Die Selbstentfaltung des griechischen Denkens von Homer bis auf die Sophistik und Sokrates*. Stuttgart.

Partenie, C., ed. 2009. *Plato's Myths*. Cambridge.

Patzer, A. 1986. *Der Sophist Hippias als Philosophiehistoriker.* Freiburg.

Pellicia, H. 1995. *Mind, Body, and Speech in Homer and Pindar.* Göttingen.

Pfeiffer, R. 1968. *History of Classical Scholarship from the Beginnings to the End of the Hellenistic Age.* Oxford.

Puelma, M. 1989. "Der Dichter und die Wahrheit in der griechischen Poetik von Homer bis Aristoteles." *Museum Helveticum* 46: 65–100.

Reinhardt, K. 1927/1966. "Platons Mythen." In K. Reinhardt, ed., *Vermächtnis der Antike*, Göttingen (first edn. 1927), 219–95.

Ridings, D. 1995. *The Attic Moses. The Dependency Theme in Some Early Christian Writers.* Göteborg.

Rösler, W. 1980. "Die Entdeckung der Fiktionalität in der Antike." *Poetica* 12: 283–317.

Sassi, M. M. 2011."Ionian Philosophy and Italic Philosophy: From Diogenes Laertius to Diels." In O. Primavesi and K. Luchner, eds., *The Presocratics from the Latin Middle Ages to Hermann Diels*, Stuttgart, 19–44.

Steinmetz, P. 1986. "Allegorische Deutung und allegorische Dichtung in der alten Stoa." *Rheinische Museum für Philologie* 129: 18–30.

Stinton, T. 1976. "'Si credere dignum est': Some Expressions of Disbelief in Euripides and Others" *Proceedings of the Cambridge Philological Society* 22: 60–89.

Stroh, W. 1978.: "Hesiods lügende Musen." In H. Görgemanns and E. A. Schmidt, eds., *Studien zum antiken Epos*, Meisenheim, 85–112.

Weinrich, H. 1966. *Linguistik der Lüge.* Heidelberg.

West, M. L., ed. 1966. *Hesiod, Theogony.* Oxford.

West, M. L. 1988. *Hesiod, Theogony and Works and Days.* Oxford.

Willcock, M. 1964. "Mythological Paradeigma in the Iliad." *Classical Quarterly* 14: 141–54.

Wiseman, T. P. 1993. "Lying Historians: Seven Types of Mendacity." In Chr. Gill and T. P. Wiseman, eds., *Lies and Fiction in the Ancient World*, Exeter, 122–46.

FURTHER READING

On "mythos" see especially Burkert 1979, on truth and lies see Gill and Wiseman 1993, Fuchs 1993; on fiction and fictionality Rösler 1980 and Hose 1996.

CHAPTER 25

Knowledge of Self

Daniela Dueck

Hermippus in his *Lives* refers to Thales the story which is told by some of Socrates,
namely, that he used to say there were three blessings for which he was grateful to Fortune:
"first, that I was born a human being and not a beast;
next, a man and not a woman;
thirdly, a Greek and not a barbarian"

(Diog. Laer. 1.33)[1]

1.   Literature's Power to Define Borderlines

Every text has a context. This context relies on the time and place in which the text is shaped, and specifically on the personality of its author. Literature is thus an expression of human "self," its author's "self." Even when a literary work does not refer to any personal experience of its author and avoids using the grammatical first person, that is, even when the author's presence is seemingly missing, still, no literary composition is completely objective or sterile of its author's metaphoric fingerprints. Choice of theme and genre, vocabulary, inclusion and exclusion of certain details – all these components reveal the personality of the author. Literature, then, may function as a primary vehicle to mold a concept of self-awareness both for the author and for his audience.

Literature is essentially exclusive: the very existence of literary texts defines a borderline between readers and the analphabetic. In the Greek world this borderline corresponded with other social distinctions because generally only free wealthy males, a minority, could afford to be fully educated.[2] Greek literature was thus created in a society which communicated mainly orally, but some works, known today as written texts, were still available to illiterate persons. Dramatic plays – tragedies and comedies; political and forensic speeches delivered in popular assemblies and law courts; and even the stories of the Homeric epics, could reach the masses orally and through visual channels such as vase paintings. Therefore, explicit or implicit messages related to an individual or a collective "self" could theoretically reach a wide public.

A Companion to Greek Literature, First Edition. Edited by Martin Hose and David Schenker.
© 2016 John Wiley & Sons, Inc. Published 2020 by John Wiley & Sons, Inc.

2.   Defining the "Self": "Self" and Other

Identity is significantly shaped through encounters between the "self" and the "other," whether individuals or communities. The definition of one's "self," in all its levels, is often based on a simple, sensual perception. Distinctions may be based on sight (size, shape, color), hearing (language, intonation, song), touch (softness, roughness), smell and taste. Initial impressions and basic dichotomies are sometimes supplemented by imagination to add details which are not grasped by the senses; thus stereotypes emerge. Self-definition of nations and communities (and perhaps also of individuals) is based on a comparison or contrast with other groups and, through these mental activities, a clearer and more solid social cohesion is created. Along the positive definition of "who we are" there is often the negative one of "who we are not." The Greeks often used analogy and polarity in their intellectual perception of the universe.[3] Accordingly, humans were deemed different from gods but also from animals; men were different from women; adults were unlike children; and Greeks were different from non-Greeks. Common to all definitions was their constant measuring rod: adult free male human. Limited space and thematic considerations cannot allow here a full discussion of each level in the Greek definition of "self." Therefore, this chapter expands on Greek self definition in opposition to foreign identities, but first offers a brief outline of other aspects of the theme.

3.   Humans and Gods[4]

The Greeks commonly grasped their gods as anthropomorphic, looking like humans and behaving like them. Gods were old (Zeus) or young (Hermes), smart (Athena) or silly (Dionysus), beautiful (Aphrodite) or crippled (Hephaestus), just like humans, and they quarreled, loved, got jealous and drunk like men. Homeric polytheism portrayed a family of individual deities which reflected the basic social unit and implied an inner hierarchy: Zeus the father, Hera his wife, and his sons and daughters, sometimes obedient, more often rebellious and deceitful.

Xenophanes, the Presocratic philosopher (c. 570–474 BCE), realized the cultural relativism of the image of the gods as a reflector of "self" and commented that these gods were created by humans mirroring themselves:[5]

> "If cows and horses or lions had hands or could draw with their hands and make things as men can, horses would have drawn horse-like gods, cows cow-like gods and each species would have made the gods' bodies just like their own. Ethiopians say that their gods are flat-nosed and black, and Thracians that theirs have blue eyes and red hair." (Xenophanes DK 21 B 15–16)[6]

Boundaries between humans and gods were defined through several constant and essential differences: humans ate bread and drank wine but gods ate ambrosia and drank nectar; humans had blood flowing in their veins, gods had ichor; humans held incest taboos, gods did not; humans aged and weakened, gods were ever-young and strong; humans eventually died, gods were immortal.[7]

Occasionally, humans were presented as overshadowing gods. Prometheus, a hero acting on behalf of humans, tricked Zeus to choose attractive but inedible sacrificial meat and stole fire to hand it over to mankind. These actions required strengthening of the borderline between man and god, between ruler and subject: men thus earned troublesome women, personified in Pandora, and Prometheus was chained to a remote rock, where an eagle devoured his liver.[8] The Greek idea of "*hybris*" – extreme pride and arrogance causing men to overestimate their capabilities and forget their human limitations – suggested that humans trying to act like gods should be treated as sinners, and tradition promised that they were bound to fall:[9] "for the god suffers pride in none but himself" (Hdt. 7.10ε).

Narrower circles, specifically philosophers, challenged the anthropomorphic notion and offered an alternative, rationalistic concept of gods.[10] The Presocratics were first to emphasize both the physical and the intellectual differences between gods and humans:

> He [god] is not equipped with a human head on a body, nor from his back do two arms grow like branches. He has no feet, no swift knees, no hairy genital organs. He is mind, holy and ineffable, and only mind, which drafts through the universe with its swift thoughts. (Empedocles, DK 31 B 134).[11]

The philosophers tried to explain the world in terms of intelligible principles and therefore depersonalized gods but did not reject divinity altogether. The philosophic distinction between humans and gods suggested a spiritual god and not an anthropomorphic king with his family. The earlier conceptual hierarchy within the assembly of gods reduced to a specification of one god who towers above the others. These theoretical trends paved the road for eventual monotheism.[12] Even in such more spiritual concepts of the divine, kinship between men and deities was implied: "Man is the only one of the animals known to us who has something of the divine in him, or if there are others, he has most" (Arist. *Part. an.* 656 a 8–9),[13] and parallel to this, the concept of man "in the image of God (κατ' εἴκονα θεοῦ)" (*Gen.* 1.27) became prevalent. Stoic teachings, which prevailed throughout Roman antiquity, developed the biological conception of God as a kind of heat or seed from which things grow and identified Him with *pneuma* or breath. In this way they in fact further separated the realms of humans and gods by grasping God as more akin to natural elements than to man.[14]

4.   Humans and Beasts[15]

Living closely with animals, both domestic and wild, the Greeks realized that beasts had a personality. Through personification, they attributed stereotypic character traits to specific animals. In Aesop's fables, for instance, the borderline between humans and animals was blurred: animals spoke, thought, competed, and laughed.[16] At the same time, humans were sometimes compared to animals, as Aristotle shows: "There was a physiognomist who in his lectures used to show how all people's faces could be reduced to those of two or three animals" (Arist. *Gen. An.* 769b21–2).

In real life the basic distinction between animals and men was language, and deeper differences were associated with reason, understanding and rationality:[17]

> "[Alcmaeon] says that man differs from the other creatures in that he alone has understanding, while the other creatures have perception but do not have understanding." (DK 24 B 1a).

Later, Aristotle emphasized the reason–emotion dichotomy as a measure of distinction between men and beasts:

> Being alive seems to be shared even by plants, but we are seeking that which is unique [to man]. Now, we must put aside life functions of nutrition and growth. Some sort of sentient life would follow next. This too seems to be common to a horse and to a cow and to every beast. There remains, then, one practical life of him who possesses reason. (Arist. *NE* 1097b33–1098a4; cf. Arist. *Pol.* 1254a)

The Greek concept of animals was thus anthropocentric: animals were constantly compared to men, who were in turn defined as animals but such that think, laugh and feel.[18] The Stoics grasped this mental hierarchy as a scale in which humans held an intermediate status between beasts and gods.[19]

5. Humans and Monsters[20]

Monsters in Greek mythology, and specifically hybrid creatures that were half human, half animal – centaurs, the Minotaur, Medusa – were usually described as supernatural creatures friendly, or, more often, hostile, to humans. They appeared in literature as deformed not only in body but also in soul and behaving wildly and "unsociably": the Centaurs were traditionally the savage element as opposed to the cultured Lapiths; the Minotaur was a cannibal who devoured Athenian young people; and Medusa gazed at creatures and turned them into stone. Aristotle explained monsters as failures of nature:[21]

> There are failures even in the arts… so that analogous failures in nature may evidently be anticipated as possible… monstrosities will be like failures of purpose in nature. (*Phys.* 2.8, 199a33–b5)

A constant element in the literary depiction of some monsters was their location outside or far from the known, almost domestic sphere.[22] Thus, centaurs and satyrs lived in the wild forests; the Gorgons lived by the edges of the known world; Triton and the Nereids lived in the sea. In this way they were also geographically tagged as outsiders and the normal, standard, tamed "self" remained unthreatened.

6. Men and Women[23]

Although there were exceptions, such as the poems of Sappho of Lesbos, the female voice was practically unheard in Greek antiquity. Teiresias, the mythic prophet, was according to tradition the only man who turned into a woman and therefore could report his experience, but this myth was also created, delivered and written by male authors.[24] Women characters in Greek literature thus reflected male misunderstandings and prejudices. It is, therefore, almost impossible to reconstruct Greek female definition of "self"; we may rather discuss masculine ideas of women which shed light on the self-definition of their male authors.

Greek texts noted the natural and physical differences between men and women: the male body was the model of perfection whereas women were inherently weaker and psychologically frail. The Aristotelian definition clearly suggests that the male is the standard for the essence of human beings: "A woman is, as it were, an infertile male. She is female, in fact, on account of a kind of inadequacy" (Arist. *Gen. An.* 728a). At the same time, some authors proposed the "one-sex" model of the human body. Menstrual blood, for instance, was deemed the same sort of substance as semen, but less pure and concentrated. Accordingly, women were no different from men physically, but were constitutionally inferior and excluded from any form of economic and political power.

Women were associated with danger, strangeness and inferiority, both mental and physical. Laws and customs were meant to curtail their freedom and men acted as guardians of women's chastity. Athenian women, for instance, were associated with hidden interiors while male citizens were associated with the outdoor world (Xen. *Oec.* 7.30). Adolescent girls were "fillies" who needed to be tamed or yoked by marriage (Anacreon F 417 PMG). Once women were married, their assigned role was to give birth to legitimate heirs.

The social role of the sexes was clear cut, as Euripides noted: "I would rather stand three times in the line of battle than give birth to a single child" (Eur. *Med.* 250–51).

The definition of the orthodox social "self" of women, that is, of "ordinary" as opposed to "anomalous" women, was frequently expressed in Greek literature in the negative. Strong, active, brave and eloquent women represented exceptional and frequently threatening situations. Goddesses, for instance, were strong, wise, beautiful females who enchanted men, or were portrayed as gender bending characters. Athena blended in her literary character masculine and feminine attributes: she was a virgin, a warrior maiden, not dominated by a male other than her father; Artemis was also a virgin engaged in the traditionally masculine hunting; Hera, who represented the stereotype of a married woman, was portrayed as a typical nagging and jealous wife. The behavior of the goddesses was however unthreatening because the clear boundary between humans and gods (above) hindered women from any attempt at imitating a goddess. Similarly, Aristophanes in his *Ecclesiazusae* and *Lysistrata* portrayed rebellious women, smarter than men, who initiated social and political changes in the Athenian polis. But both he and his theater audience knew that this was a joke, thus unthreatening to traditional order.

The Amazons were another literary motif which portrayed strong and independent women who lived in an autonomous and self-governed society.[25] This myth involved in some of its versions details which blurred the supposed similarity between Amazons and ordinary women and turned them into freaks: according to one line of tradition, in order to facilitate the use of bows and arrows the Amazons cut their right breast – a symbol of femininity – and thus became, in Greek male eyes, mutilated women and, in fact, unreal ones. Moreover, in Greek literary tradition, Amazons were usually located in the fringes of the known world together with other oddities and monstrosities (see above).

All three examples – goddesses, Amazons, women in comedy – were super-natural, extraordinary, outside the usual social and geographical framework. In this sense it was easier for a male audience to deal with these phenomena; the message in these images strengthened the boundaries between what was appropriate and what was not.

7.   Greeks and Barbarians[26]

Classical literature abounds with descriptions of foreign nations and strange people. This is hardly surprising: any society relates, in one way or another, to encounters with other societies. But the specific way in which any culture refers to "others" is bound to reveal much of its own idea of a collective "self." Greek allusions to foreigners appear in various literary genres and contexts: poetry, philosophy, historiography, oratory and geography. These ethnographic discussions could be short allusions within a broader context, extensive digressions, or entire works – all devoted to the presentation of foreign nations and regions. Greek literature did not include ethnography or geography as a well-defined intellectual field with literary or scientific conventions. However, descriptions of previously unknown people were typically constructed and included usual topics such as character traits, physical appearance, dress and eating customs, sexual behavior, marriage norms, attitude towards the dead and other social rules.[27]

In the *Odyssey* Odysseus lands on the island of the one-eyed Cyclopes:

> Thence we sailed on, grieved at heart, and we came
> to the land of the Cyclopes, an overweening and lawless folk,
> who, trusting in the immortal gods,
> plant nothing with their hands nor plow;
> but all these things spring up for them without sowing or plowing,

wheat, and barley, and vines, which bear the rich clusters of wine,
and the rain of Zeus gives them increase.
Neither assemblies for council have they, nor appointed laws,
but they dwell on the peaks of lofty mountains
in hollow caves, and each one is lawgiver
to his children and his wives, and they reck nothing one of another. (*Od.* 9.105–15)

A significant part of the characterization of the Cyclopes is presented in the negative: they do not cultivate the land, they do not apply laws and justice, and they do not care about anyone but themselves. Their dwelling is distant and inaccessible and they behave antisocially and selfishly. The description thus reflects a clear dichotomy between a political community united within a *polis*, and an apolitical or prepolitical group, i.e. one that has not adopted social norms related to the Greek *polis* such as organized institutions and a well-ordered juristic system.[28]

This political gap featured also in descriptions of prepolitical, tribal communities both in earlier periods and in secluded regions in Greece.[29] A mental opposition thus suggested that there were within the Greek world and simultaneously *poleis* running a typical agricultural way of life and nomadic, non agricultural communities. In the Homeric epic this opposition is one of the earliest measures to assess savagery vs. culture, insiders vs. outsiders, self vs. other.

The massive Mediterranean colonization, beginning in the eighth century BCE, caused the Greeks to first encounter "others." These interactions raised an awareness of the primary difference between the two groups, i.e. language, and the Greek need for self-definition produced the term "*barbaroi*" as opposed to "*Hellenes*." Thucydides (1.3) specifically indicates that earlier there was no awareness, and therefore no definition, of a collective "self" manifested in generalizing denominations. He supports this claim by the absence of the name *barbaroi* from the Homeric epics and by the limited ethnic application of *Hellenes* by the poet. Already in Antiquity it was suggested that the origin of the word *barbaros* and its derivatives was onomatopoeic because the Greeks heard in foreign languages mostly "bar-bar-bar." The word and its derivatives were applied to all non-Greek humans, near or far, civilized or savage.

Solon's reform in Athens (594 BCE), which prohibited the enslavement of Athenian citizens, caused relatively large numbers of non-Greek, foreign slaves to arrive at the *polis*. This situation increased the mental difference between Greek–Athenian–free persons and foreign–*barbaros*–enslaved ones. About a century later, the Persian threat to invade the Greek world resulted in the formation of a Greek coalition of defensive forces to protect the Greek homeland. This unity produced all-Greek awareness and sharpened up the distinction between Greek inherent freedom and the "barbarian" tendency to slavery:

> It is right, mother, that Hellenes should rule barbarians, but not barbarians Hellenes,
> those being slaves, while these are free
> (Eur. *Iph. Aul.* 1400–1401).

The Hellene–*barbaros* opposition functioned as a deliberate strategy to perpetuate the distinction between the two groups. The Greeks entrenched within the walls of these characterizations as part of a conscious wish to separate themselves from others and to nurture pride in their origins and customs. In this mental dichotomy the Greeks placed themselves in a superior position.[30] They emphasized their common language despite the fact that there were various dialects; their common ancestry despite the political division; and their unique religious rites. These unique traits were demonstrated in Panhellenic gatherings such as the Olympic Games, which were exclusively Greek:

> When Alexander chose to contend and entered the lists for that purpose, the Greeks who were to run against him wanted to bar him from the race, saying that the contest should be for Greeks and not for foreigners. Alexander, however, proving himself to be an Argive, was judged to be a Greek. He accordingly competed in the furlong race and tied for first place. (Hdt. 5.22).

The clear opposition within the Greek mind between Hellenes and "barbarians" produced also a concept of an inherent and constant confrontation between the two groups. Plato said the Greek race (*Hellenikon genos*) was by nature an enemy of the barbarians (*Rep.* 5, 470C) and the Athenian orator, Isocrates, reinforced the dichotomy by expressing a total hatred towards barbarians and declaring that they deserve to be mere house-slaves (*Or.* 4.157–9; 181).

Herodotus offered a milder view in his open-mindedness towards life-styles of foreigners. Despite the sharp distinctions he draws between Greek and barbaric customs,[31] he demonstrated an unprejudiced and genuine interest in other ways of life, and recognized, after Pindar, that "custom is lord of all" (3.38), emphasizing that all think their own customs are the best. The attitude of Antiphon the sophist (480–411 BCE) to this issue was even more inclusive and cosmopolitan. He, too, lived at a time when the sharp contrast between Greeks and barbarians took shape, but he maintained that:

> By nature we all equally, both barbarians and Greeks, have an entirely similar origin: for it is fitting to fulfill the natural satisfactions which are necessary to all men ... and in all this none of us is different either as barbarian or as Greek; for we all breathe into the air with mouth and nostrils ....
> (DK 87 B 44 b col. 2)

In 323 BCE, upon his sudden death, Alexander the Great left his successors a world wider than ever, geographically and culturally. The new horizons confronted the Greeks, both physically and through written impressions, with foreign nations previously unknown to them (cf. Mori, ch. 6 in this volume); with exotic and remote landscapes; with rare animals and strange plants. But Hellenistic literature, as opposed to earlier literary expressions, suggested more complex cultural situations in which the traditional dichotomy between Greeks and barbarians was less distinct.[32]

Milder notions appear already in Aristotle's comments on the complex human nature. He based his ideas on the dichotomy between nature (*physis*) and law (*nomos*):

> In some cases things are marked out from the moment of birth to rule or to be ruled... It is manifest therefore that there are cases of people of whom some are freemen and the others slaves by nature, and for these slavery is an institution both expedient and just. But at the same time it is not difficult to see that those who assert the opposite are also right in a manner. The fact is that the terms "slavery" and "slave" are ambiguous; for there is also such a thing as a slave or a man that is in slavery by law, for the law is a sort of agreement under which the things conquered in war are said to belong to their conquerors. Now this conventional right is arraigned by many jurists... for they are compelled to say that there exist certain persons who are essentially slaves everywhere and certain others who are so nowhere. And the same applies also about nobility: our nobles consider themselves noble not only in their own country but everywhere, but they think that barbarian noblemen are only noble in their own country – which implies that there are two kinds of nobility and of freedom, one absolute and the other relative. (*Pol.* 1254a – 1255a)

Aristotle suggests here that some people are enslaved by nature and some by consent, that is by law. He also raises the idea of the ethnic superiority and high descent (*eugeneia*) of the Greeks, which is inherent in any Greek anywhere, whereas among "barbarians" it depends on their location. Essential is, first, the insinuation that the right to enslave is not absolute or universal, and, second, the Greek concept of relative pedigree and freedom, i.e., such that it may be rated on a mental scale.

One of the most detailed expressions of the Hellenistic attitude towards the complexity of human culture is the *Geography*, Strabo of Amasia's comprehensive work.[33] Born in 64 BCE at

Pontus, Asia Minor, Strabo was educated in Hellenistic values in a world in which Rome became the dominant power. After engaging in historiographical writing, he wrote, in the first century CE, a work aimed at surveying all that was known at the time about the inhabited world. According to the best tradition of Greek descriptive geography and by summarizing earlier geographical traditions, Strabo included in this survey numerous details from a variety of fields related to the diverse regions of the world: botany, zoology, topography, as well as history, mythology, and ethnography. The *Geography* is thus abundant with numerous details taken from tens of sources, partly lost, and it offers not only its author's views but also notions which prevailed through generations of Greek geographical writing. As we shall see, Strabo specifically reflects the Hellenistic scholarly and political atmosphere, by frequently citing central authorities of the age, such as Ephorus, Eratosthenes, Polybius, Posidonius, and the Homeric commentators.

Strabo raises again the discussion about the early Greek distinction between Greeks and Barbarians:

> Those, therefore, they called barbarians in the special sense of the term, at first derisively, meaning that they pronounced words thickly or harshly; and then we misused the word as a general ethnic term, thus making a logical distinction between the Greeks and all other races. The fact is, however, that through our long acquaintance and intercourse with the barbarians this effect was at last seen to be the result, not of a thick pronunciation or any natural defect in the vocal organs, but of the peculiarities of their several languages. And there appeared another faulty and barbarian-like pronunciation in our language, whenever any person speaking Greek did not pronounce it correctly, but pronounced the words like barbarians who are only beginning to learn Greek and are unable to speak it accurately, as is also the case with us in speaking their languages. (*Geog.* 14.2.28).

Accordingly, the term "*barbaros*" stemmed from linguistic distinction of the clumsy pronunciation of Greek by non-Greeks. Strabo's words, however, are sympathetic with the "barbarians": he emphasizes that their failure to speak Greek did not originate in a physical or cognitive deficiency. Moreover, he introduces cultural relativism: according to the same criterion, Greeks are also speaking "barbarian" when they pronounce foreign languages.[34]

While the term "*barbaros*" emerged from a linguistic criterion for cultural definition, Greek literature offered additional criteria which were based on other cultural attributes such as life-style, customs, and temperament. A close tie between cultural traits and geographical position was expressed through the Hippocratic notion of the influence of environmental and climatic conditions on the character and appearance of human beings:[35]

> The nations inhabiting the cold places and those of Europe are full of spirit but somewhat deficient in intelligence and skill, so that they continue comparatively free, but lacking in political organization and capacity to rule their neighbors. The peoples of Asia on the other hand are intelligent and skillful in temperament, but lack spirit, so that they are in continuous subjection and slavery. But the Greek race participates in both characters, just as it occupies the middle position geographically, for it is both spirited and intelligent; hence it continues to be free and to have very good political institutions, and to be capable of ruling all mankind if it attains constitutional unity. (Arist. *Pol.* 1327b)

The link between location and character suggests environmental determinism. Accordingly, specific dwelling places would necessarily grow people with determined cultural tendencies such as the ability to rule. Significant is the status of the Greeks within this idea: their personality is also an outcome of their geographical location; because they dwell in the center of the world, they have the best character traits and are therefore superior human beings.

Strabo incorporated in his survey a similar idea suggesting that the world divided into parts not only geographically (i.e. the then-known three continents, Europe, Asia and Africa), but also according to an implied scale of human existence:

> We will commence with Europe, both because its figure is more varied, and also because it is the quarter most favorable to the mental and social ennoblement of man, and produces a greater portion of comforts than the other continents... the whole of Europe is habitable with the exception of a small part, which cannot be dwelt in, on account of the severity of the cold .... The wintry and mountainous parts of the habitable earth would seem to afford by nature but a miserable means of existence; nevertheless, by good management, places scarcely inhabited by any but robbers, may be got into condition. Thus the Greeks, though dwelling amidst rocks and mountains, live in comfort, owing to their economy in government and the arts, and all the other appliances of life. Thus, too, the Romans, after subduing numerous nations who were leading a savage life, either induced by the rockiness of their countries, or want of ports, or severity of the cold, or for other reasons scarcely habitable, have taught the arts of commerce to many who were formerly in total ignorance, and spread civilization amongst the most savage. (*Geog.* 2.5.26)

Strabo here suggests topographical and physical causes for human savagery: mountains, rocks and cold climate hinder habitation and therefore create sparse and secluded communities. The emergence of savage societies is thus based in environmental conditions. It is implied, however, that this environmental determinism is not absolute and hermetic: it is possible to break it with well-established legal and political systems. The case of the Greeks proves this assumption: they succeeded in overcoming rough physical conditions and developing admirable culture and government. Since Strabo lived in an age when the Roman state became the largest and most powerful ever, he also emphasizes the civilizing ramifications of Roman conquest: wild nations became civilized.[36] The basic dichotomy between Greeks vs. Barbarians was thus modified and moderated.

When discussing the meaning of the term "*barbaros*" Strabo goes back to an earlier notion of Eratosthenes:

> He [Eratosthenes] says that it would be better to make such divisions according to good qualities and bad qualities; for not only are many of the Greeks bad, but many of the Barbarians are refined – Indians and Arians, for example, and, further, Romans and Carthaginians, who carry on their governments so admirably. (*Geog.* 1.4.9)

This is a new concept: no more distinction between Greeks and barbarians based on a cultural–linguistic criterion, but a division of mankind according to virtue (*arete*) or the lack of it. This idea implies that there are good and bad barbarians, and therefore, evidently, good and bad Greeks. The standard of evaluation is moral but closely relates to the application of law, government, education and oratory. Beside this model there is another tone within Strabo's survey:

> Our mode of life has spread its change for the worse to almost all peoples, introducing amongst them luxury and sensual pleasures and, to satisfy these vices, base artifices that lead to innumerable acts of greed. So then, much wickedness of this sort has fallen on the barbarian peoples also ... as the result of taking up a seafaring life they not only have become morally worse, indulging in the practice of piracy and of slaying strangers, but also, because of their intercourse with many peoples, have partaken of the luxury and the peddling habits of those peoples. (*Geog.* 7.3.7)

The barbarians then are not morally inferior; on the contrary: there are barbarians known in the Greek world for their integrity and innocence. But "our," i.e. the Greeks' and the Romans', lifestyle has corrupted them and introduced to them, together with extended sea-manship and better communication, bad moral traits. Another aspect which further modified the original dichotomy was the idea of progress which suggested that in earlier times the Greeks were also uncivilized, for instance in Thucydides:[37]

> In ancient times all Hellenes carried weapons because their homes were undefended and intercourse was unsafe; like the Barbarians they went armed in their everyday life. And the continuance of the custom in certain parts of the country indicates that it once prevailed everywhere. The Athenians were the first who laid aside arms and adopted an easier and more luxurious way of life .... On the other hand, the simple dress which is now common was first worn at Sparta .... The Lacedaemonians too were the first who in their athletic exercises stripped naked ... athletes formerly, even when they were contending at Olympia, wore girdles about their loins, a practice which lasted until quite lately, and still prevails among Barbarians, especially those of Asia .... And many other customs which are now confined to the Barbarians might be shown to have existed formerly in Hellas. (Thuc. 1.6.1–6)

Thus, in the past the Greeks ran a lifestyle similar to the barbarian one, but they changed and, as hinted, progressed while the barbarians kept behaving in the same way up to Thucydides' time. The Greeks were formerly "barbarians," therefore the distinction between the two groups is a matter of *nomos* i.e. law or custom, and not of *physis*, i.e., not an inherent and deterministic issue. Such a notion, which enfolds an alternative of change, is certainly more open than the hermetic–dichotomic one, and allows the mental idea of a scale.

Strabo adds another civilizing criterion:

> The Ethiopians at present lead for the most part a wandering life, and are destitute of the means of subsistence, on account of the barrenness of the soil, the disadvantages of climate, and their great distance from us. Now the contrary is the case with the Egyptians in all these respects. For they have lived from the first under a regular form of government, they were a people of civilized manners, and were settled in a well-known country. (*Geog.* 17.1.3)

The civilizing criterion is thus the degree of physical proximity to civilization, represented in this excerpt in the word "us." This word probably refers primarily to the Greeks who saw themselves culturally superior even in a world politically dominated by Rome. At the same time, it might indicate the Romans as well. Accordingly, the degree of civilization is directly correlated to the distance from or proximity to the cultural center. The Strabonian quotation offers a three-part division from center to periphery: "us," the Egyptians, the Ethiopians.

Simultaneously, Strabo emphasizes in his *Geography* again and again the cultural superiority of the Greeks over the Romans. The Romans are indeed the unchallenged political rulers of the world but at the same time they are described as brutish and violent persons who do not have even minimal appreciation of art and science. Strabo alludes to their plunder of artifacts from the Greek world in the east, and does not mention Roman scholars and intellectuals, while there are numerous lists of Greek men of letters according to their places of activity.[38] Accordingly, within the distinction between Greeks and barbarians and the Greek definition of "self," the Romans are indeed closer to the Greeks but still stand one level beneath them.

But there were also changes:

> Later on, beginning from the time of the Trojan War, the Greeks had taken away from the earlier inhabitants much of the interior country also, and indeed had increased in power to such an extent that they called this part of Italy, together with Sicily, Magna Graecia. But today all parts of it, except Taras, Rhegium, and Neapolis, have become completely barbarized. (*Geog.* 6.1.2)

The change in southern Italy is viewed as a process of "barbarization" caused by Roman occupation, meaning that the Romans are "barbarians" compared with earlier Greek settlers. To emphasize this Strabo mentions three Greek enclaves – Taras, Rhegium and Neapolis – which did not experience this change and kept their traditions and cultural character.

Cultural relativism and specific worldviews determine another definition of savagery in Strabo:

> Their [the Britons'] manners are in part like those of the Celts, though in part more simple and more barbarous; insomuch that some of them, though possessing plenty of milk, have not skill enough to make cheese, and are totally unacquainted with horticulture and other matters of husbandry. (*Geog.* 4.5.2)

In the eyes of Strabo (or his source) the criterion for civilization is the ability, or lack of it, to make cheese and till the land. Important here is the use of the comparative mode: the manners of the Britons are more barbarous (*barbarotera*), and this hints at an idea of a scale of barbarism. Additionally, there is a terminology indicating "half-barbarian." Demetrius of Scepsis (third century BCE) was a well-known Hellenistic commentator of the Homeric epics. He was a native of Scepsis, not far from the ancient site of Troy, and therefore added to his discussions geographical and topographical insights based on his personal experience. Strabo quotes his comments on one of the settlements in Asia Minor:

> Gargara was founded by the Assians; but it was not well peopled, for the kings brought into it colonists from Miletopolis when they devastated that city, so that instead of Aeolians, according to Demetrius of Scepsis, the inhabitants of Gargara became semi-barbarians. (*Geog.* 13.1.58 = Demetrius F 36 Gaede)

The settlers, who arrived from Miletopolis in western Asia Minor, were Greek and not barbarians, but their geographical position turned them into half-barbarians. Is it not then, at least theoretically, possible to be – almost quantitatively – more or less Greek or barbarian?

Finally, the complexity of the concept is again explained by Ephorus of Cyme (fourth century BCE) whose historiographical work survives only partially:

> Ephorus said that this peninsula [the Troad] was inhabited by sixteen tribes, of which three were Hellenic and the rest barbarian, except those that were mixed .... And who are the "mixed" tribes? ... even if they had become mixed, still the predominant element has made them either Hellenes or barbarians; and I know nothing of a third tribe of people that is "mixed." (*Geog.* 14.5.23, 25 = *FGrHist* 70 F 162)

Ephorus conceived of races mixed from Greeks and Barbarians, but Strabo did not recognize such a distinction and kept the traditional dichotomy: Greek or Barbarian. We may, however, safely assume that an alternative idea to the dichotomy *barbaroi*–Hellenes emerged and prevailed in the Hellenistic age. Even if we cannot, for lack of evidence, estimate how widespread these alternative suggestions were, Strabo being Strabo, represented a sort of mainstream or at least non-esoteric ideas. In later Greek texts, at the time of the Roman Empire, late antiquity and early Christianity, the terms related to barbarians straightforwardly implied their uncultured manners and their savagery.[39]

8.   Conclusion

Greek literature was generally written by free, rich, educated males mostly for their peers. It therefore reflected their concepts and their identity. Engagements with any creature that was unlike them – beasts, women, foreigners – reinforced the image of their "self." Specifically, in the Archaic Age the encounters of Greeks with foreign peoples produced a dichotomized and unequivocal definition of Hellenic vs. barbaric culture. The linguistic criterion, which was supposedly not judgmental, was the primary means to assess who was a "kin" and who was a "stranger." This initial distinction crystallized into a more complex concept which included also lifestyle and customs. These components became part of somewhat stereotypical definitions of the "barbaric" person. In the Hellenistic Age, as a result of both philosophic discussions and closer interaction with others, it was realized that the situation was more complex. This process considerably weakened the hermetic ethnographic determinism, and created mental scales stretching between several pairs of ends: Greek–barbarian; civilized–savage; center–periphery; present–past; law, order, and government–political chaos; peace–war, robbery; abundance–poverty. In this way, a composite view of the world was created and global population was arranged within these frameworks.

NOTES

[1] Unless otherwise indicated, translations of Greek texts are slightly modified versions of the *Loeb Classical Library* series.

[2] On Greek literacy, see Harris 1989; Thomas 1992; Svenbro 1993; Robb 1994; Worthington 1996; Watson 2001; Worthington and Foley 2002; Yunis 2003; Mackay 2008; Johnson and Parker 2009.

[3] Lloyd 1966.

[4] Freeman 1970; Clay 1983.

[5] Specifically Homer and Hesiod were crowned as the "creators" of gods: Xenophanes DK 21 B 11; Hdt. 2.53.2.

[6] Translated by Waterfield 2000.

[7] Most heroes had mixed divine and human parentage and were therefore often exceptionally powerful, but the boundary of immortality was never crossed. For linguistic borderlines between gods and men see Gera 2003, 49–54.

[8] Hesiod, *Theogony*, 507–70; *Works and Days*, 47–105; Aeschylus, *Prometheus Bound*; Dougherty 2006, esp. 31–43.

[9] Fisher 1992. Greek tragedy emphasized this lesson: Xerxes in Aeschylus's *Persians;* Sophocles' *King Oedipus;* Euripides' *Trojan Women.*

[10] Jaeger 1947.

[11] Translated by Waterfield 2000.

[12] West 1999.

[13] And also in Plat. *Protag.* 322A; Arist. *Part. an.* 686 a27. See Renehan 1981, 251–2.

[14] Algra 2003, 170–78; Sellars 2006, 91–5.

[15] On this theme, see Dierauer 1977; Sorabji 1993; Kalof 2007; Newmyer 2011.

[16] Kurke 2011.

[17] Gera 2003, 11, 57, 207.

[18] Renehan 1981, 239–51.

[19] Wildberger 2008, 47–70.

[20] Atherton 1998; Murgatroyd 2007.

[21] Yartz 1997.

[22] Romm 1992, 77–81; cf. Evans 1999.

[23] Fantham (1994); Blundell (1998).

[24] For this myth see Brisson 1976; Loraux 1997.

[25] Hardwick 1990; Blok 1995.

[26] Fundamental modern literature on this theme with specific emphasis on literature: Long 1986; E.M. Hall 1989; J.M. Hall 1997; Cartledge 2001; Malkin 2001; Harrison 2002; Isaac 2004; Mitchell 2007.

[27] On geographical and ethnographic writing, see: van Paasen 1957; Pédech 1976; Prontera 1983; Rawson 1985; Jacob 1991; Dench 2007; Dueck 2012.

[28] The Homeric opposite of the Cyclopes were the ideal–utopic Phaeacians, see Dougherty 2001, 122–130; Gera 2003, 4–7.

[29] E.g. in Aristotle *Pol.* 1.1.7, 1252b23–4.

[30] Some "barbarians" however were admired for their antiquity or wisdom, e.g. Egyptians, Indians and Babylonians (Strabo 1.4.9; 17.1.3). Herodotus even gained the unflattering nickname *philobarbaros* (lover of barbarians) (Plut. *De mal. Her.* 12 [*Mor.* 857a]). On the attitude of Greeks towards specific nations, see Isaac 2004, 253–491.

[31] For instance the gap between the worldviews of Croesus and Solon (1.29–33); the "opposite" behavior of the Egyptians (2.35–6); the dialogue between Demaratus and Xerxes on Spartan values (7.102–4). And see Hartog 1988.

[32] On the new spirit of Hellenistic geography, see Fraser 1972; Geus 2003.

[33] Clarke 1999, 193–336; Dueck 2000.

[34] On the linguistic aspect see also Gera 2003; Munson 2005.

[35] See the Hippocratic work *Airs, waters, places,* especially ch. 12–14.

[36] Strabo's ideas of civilization: Thollard 1987; van der Vliet 2003; Almagor 2005.

[37] On the Greek idea of progress, see Dodds 1973.

[38] On these lists, see Engels 2005.

[39] Mathisen and Shanzer 2005.

REFERENCES

Algra, K. 2003. "Stoic Theology." In B. Inwood, ed., *The Cambridge Companion to the Stoics,* Cambridge, 153–78.

Almagor, E. 2005. "Who is a Barbarian? The Barbarians in the Ethnological and Cultural Taxonomies of Strabo." In D. Dueck, H. Lindsay, and S. Pothecary, eds., *Strabo's Cultural Geography: The Making of a Kolossourgia,* Cambridge, 42–65.

Atherton, C., ed. 1998. *Monsters and Monstrosity in Greek and Roman Culture.* Bari.

Blok, J. H. 1995. *The Early Amazons. Modern and Ancient Perspectives on a Persistent Myth.* Leiden.

Blundell, S. 1998. *Women in Classical Athens.* London.

Brisson, L. 1976. *Le mythe de Tirésias: essai d'analyse structural.* Leiden.

Cartledge, P. 1993. *The Greeks: A Portrait of Self and Others.* Oxford.

Cartledge, P. 2001. "Greeks and 'Barbarians.'" In A. F. Christidis, ed., *A History of Ancient Greek from the Beginnings to Late Antiquity,* Cambridge, 307–13.

Clarke, K. 1999. *Between Geography and History: Hellenistic Constructions of the Roman World.* Oxford.

Clay, J. S. 1983. *The Wrath of Athena: Gods and men in the Odyssey.* Princeton, NJ.

Cohen, B., ed. 2000. *Not the Classical Ideal: Athens and the Construction of the Other in Greek Art.* Leiden.

Dench, E. 2007. "History and Ethnography." In J. Marincola, ed., *A Companion to Greek and Roman Historiography,* Vol. 2, Oxford, 493–503.

Dierauer, U. 1977. *Tier und Mensch im Denken der Antike: Studien zur Tierpsychologie, Anthropologie und Ethik.* Amsterdam.

Dodds, E. R. 1973. *The Ancient Concept of Progress and Other Essays on Greek Literature and Belief.* Oxford.

Dougherty, C. 2001. *The Raft of Odysseus: The Ethnographic Imagination of Homer's Odyssey.* Oxford.

Dougherty, C. 2006. *Prometheus.* London.

Dueck, D. 2000. *Strabo of Amasia. A Greek Man of Letters in Augustan Rome.* London.

Dueck, D. 2012. *Geography in Classical Antiquity.* Cambridge.

Engels, J. 2005. "Andres Endoxoi or 'Men of High Reputation' in Strabo's Geography." In D. Dueck, H. Lindsay, and S. Pothecary, eds., *Strabo's Cultural Geography: The Making of a Kolossourgia,* Cambridge, 129–43.

Evans, R. 1999. "Ethnography's Freak Show: The Grotesques at the Edges of the Roman earth." *Ramus* 28: 54–73.

Fantham, E. 1994. *Women in the Classical World: Image and Text.* New York.

Fisher, N. 1992. *Hybris: A Study in the Values of Honour and Shame in Ancient Greece.* Warminster.

Foxhall, L. and J. Salmon. 1998. *Thinking Men: Masculinity and Its Self-representation in the Classical Tradition.* London.

Fraser, P. M. 1972. *Ptolemaic Alexandria*, Vol. 1, Oxford, esp. pp. 520–53.

Freeman, K. 1952/1970. *God, Man, and State: Greek Concepts.* Westport, CT (first edn. 1952).

Gera, D. L. 2003. *Ancient Greek Ideas on Speech, Language, and Civilization.* Oxford.

Geus, K. 2003. "Space and Geography." In A. Erskine, ed., *A Companion to the Hellenistic World*, Oxford, 232–45.

Gruen, E. S. 2011. *Rethinking the Other in Antiquity.* Princeton, NJ.

Hall, E. M. 1989. *Inventing the Barbarian: Greek Self-definition through Tragedy.* Oxford.

Hall, J. M. 1997. *Ethnic Identity in Greek Antiquity.* Cambridge.

Hardwick, L. 1990. "Ancient Amazons: Heroes, Outsiders or Women?" *Greece &Rome* 37: 14–36.

Harris, W. V. 1989. *Ancient Literacy.* Cambridge, MA.

Harrison, T., ed. 2002. *Greeks and Barbarians.* Edinburgh.

Hartog, F. 1988. *The Mirror of Herodotus: The Representation of the Other in the Writing of History.* Berkeley, CA.

Isaac, B. 2004. *The Invention of Racism in Classical Antiquity.* Princeton, NJ.

Jacob, C. 1991. *Géographie et ethnographie en Grèce ancienne.* Paris.

Johnson, W. A. and H. N. Parker, eds. 2009. *Ancient Literacies: The Culture of Reading in Greece and Rome.* Oxford.

Kalof, L., ed. 2007. *A Cultural History of Animals in Antiquity.* Oxford.

Kurke, L. 2011. *Aesopic Conversations: Popular Tradition, Cultural Dialogue, and the Invention of Greek Prose.* Princeton, NJ.

Lape, S. 2010. *Race and Citizen Identity in Classical Athenian Democracy.* Cambridge.

Lardinois, A. and L. McClure, eds. 2001. *Making Silence Speak: Women's Voices in Greek Literature and Society.* Princeton, NJ.

Lloyd, G. E. R. 1966. *Polarity and Analogy. Two Types of Argumentation in Early Greek Thought.* Cambridge.

Long, T. 1986. *Barbarians in Greek Comedy.* Carbondale, IL.

Loraux, N. 1997. *The Experiences of Tiresias: The Feminine and the Greek Man.* Princeton, NJ.

Mackay, E. A. 2008. *Orality, Literacy, Memory in the Ancient Greek and Roman World.* Leiden.

Malkin, I., ed. 2001. *Ancient Perceptions of Greek Ethnicity.* Washington, DC.

Mathisen, R. W. and D. Shanzer, eds. 2011. *Romans, Barbarians, and the Transformation of the Roman World: Cultural Interaction and the Creation of Identity in Late Antiquity.* Farnham.

Mitchell, L. G. 2007. *Panhellenism and the Barbarian in Archaic and Classical Greece.* Swansea.

Munson, R. V. 2005. *Black Doves Speak: Herodotus and the Languages of Barbarians.* Washington, DC.

Murgatroyd, P. 2007. *Mythical Monsters in Classical Literature.* London.

Newmyer, S. T. 2011. *Animals in Greek and Roman Thought, A Sourcebook.* London.

Paasen, C. van. 1957. *The Classical Tradition of Geography.* Groningen.

Pédech, P. 1976. *La Géographie des Grecs.* Paris.

Prontera, P., ed. 1983. *Geografia e geografi nel mondo antico: guida storica e critica.* Bari.

Rawson, E. 1985. *Intellectual Life in the Late Roman Republic.* London, esp. pp. 250–66.

Robb, K. 1994. *Literacy and Paideia in Ancient Greece.* Oxford.

Romm, J. S. 1992. *The Edges of the Earth in Ancient Thought: Geography, Exploration and Fiction.* Princeton, NJ.

Sellars, J. 2006. *Stoicism.* Chesham.

Sorabji, R. 1993. *Animal Minds and Human Morals: The Origins of the Western Debate.* New York.

Svenbro, J. 1993. *Phrasikleia: An Anthropology of Reading in Ancient Greece.* Ithaca, NY.

Thollard, P. 1987. *Barbarie et civilisation chez Strabon:* Étude critique des livres III et IV de la *Géographie.* Paris.

Thomas, R. 1992. *Literacy and Orality in Ancient Greece.* Cambridge.

Vliet, E. C. L. van der. 2003. "The Romans and Us: Strabo's *Geography* and the Construction of Ethnicity." *Mnemosyne* 56: 257–72.

Waterfield, R. 2000. *The First Philosophers: The Presocratics and the Sophists.* Oxford.

Watson, J., ed. 2001. *Speaking Volumes: Orality and Literacy in the Greek and Roman World.* Leiden.

Wildberger, J. 2008. "Beast or god? the intermediate Status of Humans and the Physical Basis of the Stoic *scala naturae*." In A. Alexandridis et al., eds., *Mensch und Tier in der Antike: Grenzziehung und Grenzüberschreitung*, Wiesbaden, 47–70.

Worthington, I. 1996. *Voice into Text: Orality and Literacy in Ancient Greece*. Leiden.

Worthington, I. and J. M. Foley, eds. 2002. *Epea and Grammata: Oral and Written Communication in Ancient Greece*. Leiden.

Yartz, F. J. 1997. "Aristotle on Monsters." *Ancient World* 28: 67–72.

Yunis, H., ed. 2003. *Written Texts and the Rise of Literate Culture in Ancient Greece*. Cambridge.

FURTHER READING

For further reading see Cartledge 1993; Cohen 2000; Foxhall and Salmon 1998; Gruen 2011; Lape 2010; Lardinois and McClure 2001.

CHAPTER 26

Explicit Knowledge

Markus Asper

As a concept, explicit knowledge emerged by contrast, when Polanyi discovered and described what he called "tacit knowing".[1] At least since the Socratic question whether something is *didakton* (teachable), and thus explicable, explicit knowledge tends to be over-privileged in philosophical, sociological, and historical discourse. Therefore, Polanyi's shift towards implicit forms of knowledge had a great deal of attraction. Nonetheless, it might be incautious to take for granted the very explicitness of explicit knowledge or the forms it can assume. Storing and transmitting knowledge is a challenge for all societies, ancient or modern, but they have found different ways to deal with it. This article will present an outline of the fields and forms of explicit knowledge in Greek literature, as having a specific context in place and time.

1.   Archaic Didactic Poetry

Mycenaean court administration had, by the twelfth century BCE, developed effective means of storing data in writing, as the extant corpus of Linear-B texts shows.[2] Beyond these collections of mere numbers, places and personal names, however, explicit knowledge does not appear anywhere in these texts. The earliest extant didactic poems, by Hesiod, belong in the eighth century. Therefore, as is the case with epic, we need to assume an oral prehistory for didactic poetry. Since both epic and most of didactic poetry are hexametric, the two genres might have had considerable overlap, certainly with respect to language, to some extent also with regard to content (a ps.-Hesiodic poem, *The Shield of Heracles*, and fragments of a Hesiodic song about seers, the *Melampodia*, bridge the two genres). Naturally, the genre's emergence is impossible to determine with respect to time and place; in its Hesiodic form it shows a mixture of epichoric and diachronic linguistic varieties similar to Homeric epic. Hesiod himself is associated with Euboea and Boeotia. Formally, this genre of didactic poetry is exclusively Greek, but it must have, in its earlier stages of development, just as mainstream Greek culture of the time, been open to acculturation from the East, which is proven by a great number of parallels, especially with the moral teachings of so-called wisdom literature.[3]

A Companion to Greek Literature, First Edition. Edited by Martin Hose and David Schenker.
© 2016 John Wiley & Sons, Inc. Published 2020 by John Wiley & Sons, Inc.

The two didactic poems by Hesiod, the *Theogony* and the *Works and Days*, present knowledge as answering to the two most fundamental questions: "Where do we come from/Where do we belong?" and "What do we have to do, and why?" The first is addressed by way of genealogy and in a continuous basic narrative, the second by assorted advice, arranged according to a rather loose structure and fitted into a pseudo-biographical frame. Both modes are flexible enough to assimilate short narrative digressions (e.g. the myth of Prometheus in *Theogony* or of the five ages in *Works*).

The genealogical mode starts with cosmology, understood as procreation of somehow anthropomorphic entities (Chaos brings forth Night, Night gives birth to Day, etc.), proceeds in time, and ends with the heroic ancestors of Hesiod's audience. Hesiod covered this stretch with his *Theogony*, which ends with the just reign of Zeus established and defended, carried forth by his poems on the genealogies of heroes, arranged according to their female ancestors (thus titled "Catalogue of Women"). The poet, just like the poet of heroic epic, relies on the Muses as daughters of Zeus and Mnemosyne (personified memory) who guarantee that his knowledge is authoritative. Not least due to its stringent narrative structure, the genealogical mode provides the basic framework for cosmology for a long time to come.[4]

The advisory mode's paradigm is Hesiod's *Works and Days*, motivated by a biographical setting: when Hesiod and his brother Perses went to court over their father's inheritance, Perses bribed the judges and therefore got the better part. With his didactic poem, Hesiod wants to show both him and the judges what is right. Just like Near Eastern parallels,[5] the advisory mode provides merely a unifying perspective that can bring together rather heterogeneous forms of explicit knowledge such as aetiological myth (the myth of the ages), fable (the fable of the hawk and the nightingale), moral exhortation and advice on agriculture (what to do when). Far from being a dry list of agricultural knowledge, Hesiod's *Works and Days* attempts to sketch out a mortal world, as opposed to Zeus's reign as it was depicted in the *Theogony*. Taken together, both didactic poems ambitiously give a diptych-like outline of the whole cosmos (Clay 2003).

Similar to Homeric epic, Hesiodic didactic poetry is, to us, the tip of an iceberg of lost didactic texts. There was more wisdom poetry (attested is a ps.-Hesiodic *Counsel of Cheiron*), and perhaps star lore (*Astronomia*). Early sages such as Thales and Pythagoras, although they, according to some, intentionally avoided committing anything to writing, were nonetheless credited with didactic–poetic texts, probably spurious. There must have been several Orphic theogonies, the scarce remaining fragments of which point to a post-Hesiodic date (e.g., a remarkable parody in Aristophanes' *Birds*).[6] For mnemonic reasons, geographical knowledge might have led to early poetic *periplus* texts, perhaps iambic, which described nautical routes by providing lists of what the traveler would have seen on the shore, augmented by information about harbors, distances, etc. These texts are attested from the sixth century onwards (Scylax of Caryanda, Hanno the Carthaginian),[7] but it seems that the geographical concept of text organization is already implicit in the Iliadic catalogue of ships.

Didactic poetry did not vanish with the rise of prose in the sixth century. Some of the Presocratic philosophers preferred didactic poetry well until the latter part of the fifth century (Parmenides, Empedocles, see Section 2.2 "Philosophy"). Not only did poetry come with a certain built-in authority, granted by supernatural sources of inspiration: one could also perform it to a big audience, presumably in public competitions, and it was much easier to commit to memory. The latter features must have been advantageous in a culture which had no institutionalized book-trade. Even when that had happened, early Hellenistic culture developed a sort of second-grade didactic poetry (Aratus, Nicander; see Section 2.3 "Hellenistic and later Didactic Poetry") of which late Republican Roman poets and audiences were so fond that Roman didactic poetry (Lucretius, Vergil's *Georgics*, Ovid's *Metamorphoses*) referred to these

Hellenistic poems as their starting-points, not to Hesiod. In pharmacology, iambic didactic poems were, for purely practical reasons, still written in the first century CE (see Section 2.3).

2. The Career of Prose

In Greek oral society, there was, beside the two obvious options of didactic poetry composed and performed by professionals and oral instruction of varying forms (apprenticeship), a third way of transmitting explicit knowledge: short prescriptions of a traditional, proverb-like status, such as "Know thyself!" or gnomic statements such as "The middle is best." Such pre-theoretic traditional lore was ascribed to a group of half-fictitious men in seventh-century Greece, the so-called "Seven Sages," although both the group and the body of sayings ascribed to it are probably younger than at least the core of the sayings transmitted.[8] Somehow affiliated are traditions of fable, that is, sketches that lead up to prescriptive statements, a sort of popular "ethics," which goes under the name of Aesop (Kurke 2011, esp. 241–4). Apart from such ethical lore, prose becomes visible to us at first in contexts of monumental writing, most notably of law and dedication (Asper 2007a, 75–84). When visualization comes into play, prose is without alternative. With some probability, there must have been a form of more or less ephemeral prose in connection with explicit technical knowledge, especially when numbers and diagrams were concerned, that is, in early large-scale architecture. Probably, the earliest attested literary prose (Pherecydes of Syrus, Anaximander, and Hecataeus of Miletus) emerges around 500 BCE together with schematized visualizations of space, that is, maps and models. Another genre that depends on prose as its vehicle is the commentary, attested in Greek literature since at least the late fourth century by the famous specimen of a philosophical commentary to an Orphic cosmogony (the so-called Derveni Papyrus).[9] During the fifth century, new forms of knowledge-transmitting prose develop rapidly: by the end of the century at the latest, expert knowledge has developed specific forms of prose writing in almost all fields, most significantly in medicine and mathematics.

2.1. *Expert Culture and the Systematic Treatise*

Large bodies of explicit knowledge need material and conventional forms of storage and retrieval (see on this also Fögen, ch. 17 in this volume). Such textual conventions emerge in expert cultures, often in contexts of professional knowledge transfer.[10] Didactic poetry, while traditionally apt for some fields of knowledge,[11] did not provide convenient structures for others. Between c. 500 and 400 BCE, some expert cultures in Greece, e.g. medicine and mathematics, proceeded from oral instruction and, perhaps, live performance, to written accounts of explicit knowledge. Two hundred years later, by 200 BCE, this is true for nearly all expert cultures, professional or not. Across the range of knowledge concerned, the unifying feature of these accounts is "systematicity," i.e., a desire to identify conceptual structures and patterns in the body of knowledge concerned and to use these patterns in order to provide texts that formally mirror the knowledge which they are meant to convey. Lacking ancient terms that cover the whole range of these texts, one might call them simply "systematic treatises."[12] (In what follows I concentrate first on medicine, mathematics, and the so-called sophists. Philosophy will be discussed below.)

Since the earliest times, medical experts were visible in Greek intellectual culture (cf. Machaon in the *Iliad* and *Odyssey* 4.228–32 on experts).[13] In medicine, the number of extant fifth- and fourth-century texts is highest, traditionally associated with Hippocrates of Cos and a medical institution on that island. The so-called *Hippocratic Corpus* contains about

50 texts of varying length, covering almost every aspect of ancient medicine. Some of them contain textual conventions that are even older, especially in what is called "nosology" (e.g., *De morbis* II, *De mulierum affectibus*). At this earlier, pre-Hippocratic, stage medical writing apparently consisted of long lists of standardized paragraphs, collecting, e.g., diseases or recipes. In the most famous of the later fifth-century Hippocratic texts (such as *De morbo sacro*, *De aere aquis et locis*, *On Ancient Medicine*, and *Epidemics I* and *III*) explicit knowledge comes as description of medical phenomena along the lines of traditional patterns (e.g., *de capite ad calcem*, case histories), speculative explanation of these phenomena, and polemics against competing individuals, schools, or even fields. Throughout these texts, authors are more interested in *understanding* the phenomena discussed than in how to treat them. Those texts that are written with a perspective on theory, such as the case histories in *Epidemics*, do not even mention a treating authority at all. Where the focus of the text is explanation, it often assumes a deductive form, that is, observed data is explained by speculative derivation from assumedly self-evident assumptions, such as the axiomatically constructed four elements "wet, dry, cold, hot" or the four humors. As theorists of nature (*physis*), medical theorists both adopted the theories of Presocratic speculation and contributed to it (e.g. the Pythagorean physicist Alcmaeon of Croton). That there were more such medical systems than we know of, is guaranteed by doxographical accounts of medical theories otherwise lost (e.g. in the *Anonymus Londiniensis*). Among the many different forms medical writing can assume (van der Eijk 1997), perhaps most remarkable is the so-called *epideixis*, a personal, often polemical, essay, apparently publicly delivered, that argues in the face of strong opponents for a daring thesis. That is, the *epideixis* is the foremost textual vehicle of competition. This format, typical examples of which are *De morbo sacro* or *De flatibus*, is very close to sophistic practice, and possibly points to an overlap of the two fields. Since Hippocratic medicine became canonical early on, probably in Hellenistic times, its basic assumptions and procedures (humoral pathology, speculative deductive explanation, a focus on anatomy, a personal, competitive voice, strong polemics) became the hallmark of Greek "rational" medicine until Roman imperial times, most notably in the huge oeuvre of Galen (second century CE) who managed, by the overwhelming quantity, explanative quality, and range of his production, to eclipse almost all medical writing before and after himself except for "Hippocrates" and late antique digests of earlier medical literature (see Dubischar, ch. 28 in this volume). Galen was read and used in universities in Europe until the nineteenth century, which explains why Greek "rational" medicine exerted such a strong influence upon modern medical and scientific method and discourse.

Besides "rational medicine," the Greek invention that most heavily influenced modern presentation of explicit knowledge is Greek axiomatic mathematics, which soon became the hallmark of theoretical rigor. Greek theoretical mathematics presents theorems in propositional form, which are then proven by deduction from axiomatic truths and definitions. Euclid's *Elements* and Archimedes' treatises, both dating from the early third century BCE, provide paradigms of the genre (in Euclid's work, earlier mathematics is somehow digested). Mathematical argument in this vein proceeds in thoroughly standardized forms of terminology, syntax, and even proof-structure. Unlike most other forms of Greek theoretical discourse, mathematical text is completely impersonal (apart from the occasional introductory letter). Thus, mathematical argument stands out in comparison to mathematical traditions of other cultures. Nonetheless, it must have emerged from a background of practitioners' knowledge by the end of the fifth century BCE (Asper 2009). Traditionally, the emergence is ascribed to foundational figures such as Thales of Miletus (c. 580 BCE) or Pythagoras of Samos (c. 530 BCE), to both of whom late antique mathematical doxographers such as Proclus and Eutocius assign the discovery of important theorems. Recently, historians of mathematics have been more reserved (e.g., Netz 1999, 272–4). The earliest person to whom we can attach the production of such texts with some certainty is Hippocrates of Chios (c. 420 BCE), who, first among many others, tried to solve the problem of how to "square" the circle, probably in Athens.[14] The pre-Euclidean history of the discourse is difficult to reconstruct; at least, Eudemus of Rhodes' *History of Geometry*, which treated the field down to his own time, the late fourth century BCE, in Peripatetic manner, survives in abridgements (Zhmud 2006, 166–213). Based on him, Proclus gives a list of whom he saw as predecessors of Euclid with respect to unifying theoretical geometry.

At some point in fourth-century Athens, Greek theoretical mathematics came in close contact with Plato's group who, perhaps under contemporary Pythagorean influence (Archytas of Tarentum), emphatically claimed axiomatic–deductive mathematics as paradigmatic knowledge. Later doxographical accounts of early Greek mathematics operate, thus, almost always under Platonic–Aristotelian influence; that is, they attempt to cleanse theoretical mathematics from all practical concerns.[15] As far as one can gather from Hellenistic mathematics, from which survive, besides Euclid and Archimedes, mainly Apollonius of Perga's books on conic sections, Greek theoretical mathematics insisted right from the beginning on being fundamentally different from all application (see the remarks on Archimedes in Plutarch's *Life of Marcellus* 14.8), perhaps in an attempt to appear to the reader as socially superior to professional calculators and surveyors.

Apart from the apparent focus on geometry that characterizes most of Greek theoretical mathematics (the major exception being the third-century CE algebraist Diophantus of Alexandria), the notions of logical rigor, defined entities, axioms, deductive argument, and evident truth are essentially the same in today's mathematics; in addition, the lettered diagram and the proposition serve as the primary units of mathematical argument, then as now.

As with medicine, mathematics became canonized in later Hellenistic times. What survive today are the classics, and then doxographical accounts, either from Pappus's *Collection*, a mathematical encyclopedia of the fourth century CE, or doxography embedded in commentaries upon either Euclid (by Proclus, fourth century CE) or Archimedes (by Eutocius, seventh century CE). In terms of knowledge-presentation, Euclid-style mathematics appears as "super-explicit." It is clearly the ambition of mathematical writers in this tradition to spell out, define, and guarantee as true *all* knowledge the proof depends upon. Only mathematical logic itself is taken for granted and thus remains implicit. Therefore, mathematical discourse has found ways to guarantee the truth of its results, thereby becoming a paradigm of truth-focused argument until today (see on philosophy below, pp. 407–8), a dynamics that actually unfolded without real input by the mathematicians themselves who kept clear of philosophical and, especially, epistemological or ontological discussion.[16]

While these two discourses remained almost exclusive to their respective groups of experts and thus formed fields vaguely similar to modern disciplines, with the so-called "Sophistic movement" discussion of explicit knowledge reached a new intensity, the repercussions of which are still ubiquitous in the Socratics and later fourth-century philosophy. Part of the sophists' challenge of established expert culture was apparently the claim that knowledge by itself is something that structurally transcends disciplinary or professional boundaries and is, thus, by itself a rewarding object of study. The Socratic question whether excellence (*arētē*, often translated as "virtue") is *didakton* ("teachable") mentioned above,[17] deeply concerned Sophistic practice. Besides their focus on successful rhetoric and self-representation, the major sophists also developed new tools or made systematic enquiry into existing ones with respect to language and logic.[18] They also developed at least three new literary formats in order to store and communicate explicit knowledge: the "problem," the doxographical "collection" (*synagōgē*) meant for internal use (reference), and the *tekhnē* ("art," handbook, systematic treatise) for external use. The first collects answers to notorious questions (Ps.-Aristotle's or Alexander of Aphrodisias's *Problēmata* provide good examples), both given in standardized, syllogism-focused form. The second one, the invention of which is credited to Hippias, probably collected sayings or opinions of great writers of the past, arranged according to topics. The third one gives a systematic abridgement of a field of knowledge, with a focus on its conceptual structure (notions, definitions, basic argument). The collection became a standard text format, beginning in the fourth-century Peripatos, then down to late antiquity that produced a great number of such "collections." It is tempting to assume that also the main Peripatetic genre of lasting impact, the *pragmateia*, with its subtle rhetoric and its favored structures (doxography, definition, interplay of induction and deduction) is somehow influenced by Sophistic texts.[19]

These different forms of systematic treatises spread the concept of "systematicity" as a general feature of explicit, decontextualized knowledge and as an approved way of transmission. In the fourth and third centuries BCE, more and more fields of knowledge became explicit in such written form, e.g., to indicate the range of such differentiation, horsemanship (Simon's *Hippikē*), knowledge about machines (Ps.-Aristotle's *Problēmata mēchanika*), architecture (Philon and Ctesibius, early Hellenistic engineers quoted by Vitruvius), and grammar (Dionysius Thrax). In imperial times, the systematic treatise provided, besides the commentary, the standard form of treating fundamental subjects within the philosophical and rhetorical schools, especially introductions and full-blown monographs. "Systematicity," perhaps a Sophistic discovery, transformed the way in which knowledge could become explicit.

2.2. *"Philosophy"*

It may have become clear by now that the modern way to conceptualize ancient fields of knowledge as strictly separated disciplines often leads into anachronism. The three groups discussed above must certainly have had some overlap: there was probably a sophistic strain within Hippocratic medicine, some sophists attempted to set themselves up as mathematicians (notoriously Hippias),[20] etc. The same is true for "philosophy": since philosophy is a category invented and applied retrospectively in Aristotle's *Metaphysics* A to his predecessors back to Thales for certain reasons (Frede 2008), one should not expect to find any specific way of knowledge being or becoming explicit in what we would nowadays call "philosophy." Three phenomena need to be addressed, I think: first, the occasional option of didactic poetry; second, the impact of mathematics on philosophy; third, the dialogue.

Didactic poetry has a rather strange history in Greek literature, which may or may not correspond to its taxonomical shifts:[21] after it had made a strong early appearance with Hesiod and ps.-Hesiod in archaic times, it seemingly vanished more or less until it was re-animated in the third century BCE as part of what one might call a "Hesiodic turn." The only exceptions are two famous didactic–poetic texts by the Presocratic philosopher–poets Parmenides of Elea (first half of fifth century BCE) and Empedocles of Acragas (mid-fifth century BCE). Perhaps they were preceded by Xenophanes (second half of sixth century BCE), a wandering rhapsode who, besides many more traditional topics, also produced hexametric verses about nature's material essence (according to him, earth and water), the material of the stars, and theology. While Milesian and Heraclitean philosophy in the East developed the new genre of the speculative prose treatise, these three Westerners favored old-style epic-didactic meter, for unclear reasons. To some extent, they might have seen some overlap with Hesiod (e.g., divine authority, or the didactic persona as presented in the *Work and Days*, or the overarching narrative temporality of coming-to-be as in the *Theogony*). Perhaps, channels of distribution and opportunities of performance also had a certain impact: in early fifth-century culture, didactic poetry, presumably performed in public competitions, would have reached a much greater audience than prose that depended on written communication.[22]

Parmenides chose to present his two-fold argument as the speech of a goddess to whose realm the first-person narrator mystically ascends. The goddess announces that she will teach the "well-rounded immovable heart of truth" and the mortals' opinions in which there is no true reliability (F 288.30–32 KRS). He seems to say that we can only discern what is real; what is not, cannot be discerned. Thus, being (real) and discerning are the same (DK 28 B 6.1). The goddess now elucidates this claim which implies that motion, change, coming-to-be and passing-away, and time do not exist, although we perceive them. After that, she then seems to give a cosmogonic treatment of what mortals think exists (*doxai broteiai*, B 8.50 ff.): consisting of the two primal elements, light and night, it begins from the stars and, perhaps, ends with embryology, in typical Milesian fashion. The latter might be the best approximation to how one can explain the physical world, by including our perception; the former indicates what is logically, and thus completely, reliable (but non-empirical) – which, however, does not permit any explanation of the world around us. Therefore, both "ways" are to be taken seriously. Their relation is, however, one of epistemic status: the first is certain, the second short of certainty, but reasonable; the first criticizes rigorously what his predecessors and competitors have done; the second does precisely the same, but better. Even these few fragments of Parmenides show how already in late archaic culture explicit knowledge is the product of criticism of former opinions and deductive reasoning that, largely independent of conventional language, can rise to extreme abstraction. Parmenides' strange and beautiful poem typically represents Greek explicit knowledge of nature in that it not only aims at explaining reality, but even discusses the epistemic status of such explanation.

Compared to Parmenides, Empedocles' two didactic poems (*Purifications* and *On Nature*) were more traditional in character: *Purifications* discussed the incarnations of a narrator's soul and the principle of reincarnation in general, presumably close to "Orphic" teachings with some Pythagorean impact. The mode of discourse is reminiscent, to us, of the myth of Er which concludes Plato's *Republic. On Nature* provided a cosmology based on four elements and the two principles of mixture ("love") and separation ("strife"), the ever-shifting relation of which determines cosmological narrative history. The latter poem has unfairly been criticized by Aristotle;[23] modern appreciation, however, has conceded that Empedocles is a masterful composer of, e.g., metaphor and simile. He probably adapts these tools that were so well known from epic and lyric tradition to the newly emerging speculative discourse on nature. In addition, he occasionally attempts to quantify the ratio of the elements in "chemical" compounds, thus trying to be as precise as possible (F 374 KRS). Although the surviving fragments seem to be wildly poetic in many ways, Empedocles' intention would qualify for the label "scientific": e.g., he discusses the workings of our sensory organs and even provides us, within the frame of his cosmological narrative, with a pre-Darwinian account of how functional animals emerged (F 375 f. KRS). Both Parmenides and Empedocles provide vivid examples for how knowledge on nature or philosophical argument in general became explicit. Nonetheless, they did not have followers in that respect (Parmenides' defenders, most famously Zeno of Elea, chose the prose treatise as their medium and attempted to free their presentations from poetic elements as far as they could).

Even before theoretical mathematics emerged, practical mathematical knowledge[24] had a certain impact on philosophical knowledge becoming explicit, largely by the cognitive function of numbers, already in Anaximander.[25] In the competitive climate of Archaic and Classical upper-class culture, monumental writing became a vehicle of authority and representation quite early.[26] A similar desire fueled the intention to be right on controversial issues, be it competitive oratory in various political institutions or writing texts that were meant to last, whether history or nature's explanation was their focus. The vivid polemics the reader encounters in some early writers, most notably in Hecataeus and Heraclitus, does not point to an author's cantankerous character, but to the competitiveness of the field. In such a climate, logical procedures that made one's own logos invincible must have been adopted eagerly, which is true also for medicine. Deductive argument that proceeds in truth-preserving ways from premises generally agreed upon, in order to then reach a clear conclusion, appears as such a procedure.

Mathematics did not invent such argumentative structures, which must have been used, in a non-formalized way, in many situations of debate (for example, *modus tollens* and *reductio ad absurdum*). Once axiomatic-deductive mathematics existed in a formalized way, however, it naturally provided a model of epistemological certainty to the philosophers, from Plato and Aristotle, who adapted the method and its implications to fit their own purposes, down to Galen.[27] Already in late fifth-century texts, however, one can see how thinkers play with adapting the model of mathematical argument to other fields, notably medicine and speculative physics.[28] The lettered diagram as a device that helps to make arguments and texts function across distances of time and space is one of the tools of mathematics that perhaps has had, until today, the greatest career in theory and science. This career starts, as far as we can see, with Aristotle's fondness of diagrammatical argument in many areas, most conspicuously in his analysis of logic. It is also Aristotle who provides the first consistent theory of how explicit knowledge should be gained and epistemologically guaranteed (*Second Analytics*) and how its arguments should be structured (*Prior Analytics*), in both areas starting from and generalizing mathematical arguments of his day.[29]

I conclude my account with dialogue (cf. Hose ch. 15, pp. 244–9 in this volume): Plato's extant works are enigmatic on so many counts that I almost hesitate to add them here as an instance of explicit philosophical knowledge. Throughout Plato's dialogues, however, runs a discourse on the different epistemological forms of knowledge.[30] Mimetic dialogue in Platonic style (*Sōkratikoi logoi*) is, nonetheless, one of the farthest-reaching literary inventions among Greek philosophers, with both a theoretical and a practical reception that begins with Aristotle (cf. *Poet.* on Platonic dialogue, his own dialogues) and continues to our day. The form emerged among Socrates' early followers quite soon after his death.[31] Interlocutors with differing degrees of authority discuss general questions, often concerned with forms of knowledge and practical virtue. Usually, one of the interlocutors is Socrates, who demonstrates to the internal audience of the dialogue that both conventional wisdom and the self-proclaimed authority of experts are ill-founded.[32] Many dialogues give, at least in certain stretches, a realistic account of Socrates' dialectic method and of knowledge-focused dialogue in general. Plato has taken pains to hide his own intentions in adopting this multifaceted genre; certainly, however, the form eases the reader's transition from being unaware of any problem to awareness, by identification with the interlocutors. Thus, the form has been adopted not only in almost all areas, schools and topics of ancient philosophy, it also has, in a stripped-down form, become a very popular form of presenting technical explicit knowledge in later antiquity, the Middle Ages and modern times until the twenty-first century.[33]

2.3. *Hellenistic and Later Didactic Poetry*

After Empedocles, didactic poetry did not die out, as one might have expected: instead, it completely changed its character in the early third century BCE,[34] turning from a knowledge-focused first-order discourse into something else that integrated tradition-focused second-order discourse, early Hellenistic aesthetics, prose sources, and a certain pleasure in describing nature through intermediary texts. Paradigms are Aratus' *Phaenomena* (early third century BCE), a stoically tinted poem on the order of the universe, mostly on astronomy and weather-signs, and Nicander's two intricate poems on poisonous animals (late third century BCE). Both rely on prose sources for what they have to say, and have, to a degree unknown in earlier didactic poetry, spent much energy on the aesthetic side of knowledge-presentation, that is, on philological research. Both are exponents of third-century Alexandrian aesthetics and, thus, became wildly popular among Roman intellectuals in the late republic and early empire: e.g., Lucretius, Cicero, Vergil, and Ovid, all of whom produced, in different ways, didactic poetry in this

Alexandrian manner, that is, self-referential, saturated with philological knowledge, projecting an elusive poetic voice, on the verge of being court-poetry, difficult and beautiful.[35] On the Greek side, this tradition leads to fantastic poems such as Oppian's *On Fishing* (*Halieutika*); on the Latin side, a strong tradition emerges that, like Plato-inspired dialogue, was still written in modern times, e.g. de Polignac's *Anti-Lucretius* (1744). Besides these highbrow poets, there existed also "real" didactic poetry, that is, poems devoted to primary knowledge-transmission, mostly in iambs, devoid of purely literary ambition: from Hellenistic times, the most important was Apollodorus of Athens' *Chronica*, a chronology of Greek history and famous persons.[36] The only complete work still extant is the geographical periplus-poem by Ps.-Scymnus, written in Hellenistic times.[37] Unlikely as it may seem to us, didactic poetry was firmly established in pharmacology, because meter made it easier to control the correct transmission of numbers and measures: preserved by Galen, Servilius Damocrates' iambic pharmacology survives in about 1600 verses.[38]

2.4. Historiography

Explicit knowledge of a shared past, even if it results from construction, is crucial for any sense of community.[39] Thus, one finds knowledge of the past to be an essential ingredient of many ancient Greek genres: among others, epic, epinician poetry, elegy, tragedy, epideictic oratory, against all of which the new genre of historiography had to compete.[40] Nonetheless, historiography turned out to be the most popular field to engage in as a writer of non-fiction: from Hecataeus of Miletus to sixth-century CE writers such as Procopius of Caesarea, more than 1,000 authors are attested. Less than one-fortieth remains.[41] As a consequence, I can only hint at some basic notions here that are typical for Greek historical discourse (see Tsakmakis ch. 14 in this volume).

Genealogy is the mode which communicates explicit knowledge of the past that affects the present directly (heroic epic, on the other hand, treats a past that affects the present only indirectly or even implicitly), by legitimating certain claims to autochthony or political power in a certain region, by providing aetiological explanation to identity-related concerns, and by bridging the gap from historical times to the present. Presumably, genealogical lore that focused on names and successions was part of the oral history[42] of all communities and major clans (compare, e.g., the exchange of Glaucon and Diomedes in *Iliad* book 6). Besides the fragmentary poems by Hesiod, however, such knowledge has not been preserved from early times. Historiography proper apparently began by systematizing and decontextualizing conventional local genealogy.

This beginning is associated with Hecataeus of Miletus's *Genealogiai* (FGrHist 1) in the late sixth century BCE. He was the first to define historiography as a realm of truth as opposed to mere *mythoi* ("stories"), a boundary that is invoked again and again by historiographers and that may thus be taken to *constitute* historiography. Most historiographers present themselves as avid seekers of truth, very often by comparing different versions of oral history or by rationalist criticism of commonly accepted accounts of the past.[43] Sources in the modern sense (inscriptions, archives, etc.) play a surprisingly small role. Similar to early philosophy and medicine, second-order discourse, including polemics against competitors, makes up for a large part of the historian's toolbox.[44]

Explicit knowledge about the past comes in the form of narrative that contains fictitious elements. Such narrative often consists of a chronological and a causal perspective, the two of which often intersect or coalesce. The search for causes motivates the narrative on several levels and often overrides sheer chronology. As in heroic epic, an overarching narrative often contains second-level narratives, e.g., the so-called "short stories" in Herodotus, many of which provide comments upon the meaning of the overarching narrative.[45] Also as in epic, verbatim speeches are a standard device in historiography, which thus crosses over into the realms of fiction.

At prominent points in his work, the historiographer usually declares certain intentions: to save impressive deeds for eternal memory (Herodotus of Halicarnassus), to discern patterns in history that will or may repeat in the reader's future (Thucydides of Athens), to provide moral instruction by reading of great men's lives (Polybius of Apamea). Unlike the rhetoric of modern historiography à la Ranke, the historiographer thus acknowledges the past's impact on his own times. Even in "objective" historiography (an anachronistic label designed for Thucydides), the historiographical narrative still has a certain agenda, which is not taken to compromise the historian's task. Fourth-century dramatic and rhetorical historiography add aesthetic concerns.[46] In the third century BCE the emerging genre of biography further blends facts and fiction, occasionally crossing the line to the novel.[47]

2.5. *Christian Knowledge*

In principle, Christian explicit knowledge adopts all existing pagan forms (see Stenger Ch. 8 in this volume). Christian writers produce works transmitting Christian knowledge in the forms of didactic poetry, the systematic treatise, even mathematics-driven logic (Monarchians).[48] Most influential are the Pagan tools that Christian institutionalized teaching inherits from imperial pagan institutions, foremost, a broad range of commentary. Philological and interpretive tools are largely similar to what Alexandrians applied to Homer and other classics. From a purely formal point of view, as being based on the exegesis of a canonic text, Christian intellectual culture neatly fitted into pagan cultures of canonized traditions.[49]

3. The Aesthetic Presentation of Explicit Knowledge

Perhaps most remarkable in Greek practices of exchanging and transmitting explicit knowledge by way of texts is the great range of forms and devices based on writing that emerged in the process. Many of these are still in use, e.g., the lexicon, the commentary, systematic treatises, the letter, the edition, mathematical text as a mixture of language and diagram, the recipe. Some have had their successes but are now rarely adopted, e.g., literary dialogue as a means of scientific discussion. Others, such as visualization by diagram, are still in full swing.

Across the board, there is a clear desire to produce knowledge-transmitting texts that respond to certain standards that are not only cognitive–epistemic, but also aesthetic: all Socratics and many Peripatetics have produced mimetic dialogue, for example, even when the topics covered were quite distant from even a highbrow colloquial register.[50] Mathematicians have forced their creativity into the straightjacket of impersonal Euclid-type discourse, generalizing expression as far as possible. Nonetheless, Archimedes finds a way to provoke and surprise his readers even under such formal constraints.[51] Medical writing has, almost from the beginning, featured a strong rhetorical component, perhaps due to severe competition among practitioners. Medical rhetoric reaches its most versatile state with Galen who, far from being the "blatherskite" Wilamowitz held him to be,[52] frequently mixes in little parodic sketches, philological acumen, autobiographical constructions, anecdotes and case narratives, beautiful metaphors, and sometimes even Doyle-like detective stories.[53]

Even the "scientific I," that is, the persona-like center of authority in a given text who presents explicit knowledge and with whom the reader can either identify or rebel against, has, in all its different varieties,[54] been outlined by ancient Greek rational-practice writers, philosophical, medical, and mathematical. Objectivity as a concept itself can be ascribed to the texts of Greek science, and certainly its rhetorical employment.[55] As modern writers of explicit knowledge, no matter in what discipline, it is still very difficult for us not to be indebted to ancient Greek theorists.

NOTES

[1] Polanyi 1966/2009, 1–26 mentions Plato's dialogues when trying to explain his concept. For the current discussion of tacit and explicit knowledge see Collins 2010, esp. 157–71.

[2] Texts collected in Ventris and Chadwick 1973.

[3] See the summarizing account of West 1997, esp. 276–333.

[4] There is some discussion of whether the *Theogony* is didactic poetry at all (see Fuhrer 2008a, 1040).

[5] See West 1978 in his commentary, 3–15.

[6] On Orphic theogonies see Betegh 2004, 224–77; 349–72.

[7] For *periploi* from the seventh and sixth century, see Avienus, *De ora maritima* (partially based on an archaic *periplus*); Ps.-Scylax (FGrHist 709), Hanno the Carthaginian (GGM 1.1.14)

[8] Texts in Zeller and Althoff 2006; Kurke 2011, 30–33 and throughout.

[9] For commentary-writing in ancient Greece see v. Staden 2002.

[10] "Expert culture," as used in this contribution, does not necessarily imply professionalism, but some degree of institutionalization which creates a certain consensus among the communicants concerning who is allowed to speak with authority in their field and who is not. Compare Most 1999, 335–6.

[11] I hesitate to use the term "discipline" with its modern institutional overtones, despite Lloyd 2009a.

[12] First comprehensively studied by Fuhrmann 1960. See Fuhrer 2008a, 1026 f., for a list of Greek terms subsumable under "systematic treatise." The problem somehow mirrors the fuzziness of the concept of "didactic poetry."

[13] See Arnott 2004, esp. 155–9.

[14] Text and testimonia discussed by Netz 2004.

[15] See, e.g., Aristoxenos, *On Arithmetics* Fr. 23 Wehrli = DK 58 B 2.

[16] According to the mathematician Amphinomus the discussion of fundamentals is not the business of the mathematician (quoted by Proclus, *In Eucl.* 202.9–12 Fr.).

[17] Polanyi's concept of tacit knowing was developed as a reply to Plato's *Meno* (Polanyi 1966/2009, 28–31).

[18] Mostly Prodicus, see fragments DK 84 A 13–20.

[19] Which is definitely the case for Aristotle's *Rhetoric*.

[20] For Hippias, Protagoras and Bryson as challenging the mathematicians of their day, see Asper 2003, 22–6.

[21] See Fuhrer 2008a, 1035–42. For the verdict of Empedocles by Aristotle, see *Poet.* 1, 1447b17–20.

[22] Most 1999, 335; 350; Asper 2007a, 98–100.

[23] In addition to n. 21, see *Meteor.* II 3, 35 a24–8; *Gen. corr.* II 6, 333b22–334a9.

[24] For which see my summary in Asper 2009, 108–14.

[25] DK 12 A 11, A 21. As far as one can tell, in early Pythagoreanism mathematical structures of argument or mathematical examples did not play any significant role.

[26] On competition, see Asper 2007b, 35–42, 382. On monumental writing see Asper 2007a, 75–6.

[27] E.g., Plato in *Rep.* VI–VII, Aristotle in *Posterior Analytics*, Galen's musings on geometry and medicine in *On Affections and Errors of the Soul* (V 67 ff. Kühn).

[28] For mathematics as a structural model, see the discussion of *hypothesis* in the Hippocratic *De vet. med.* I.1 (I p. 570 Littré = p. 118 Jouanna); compare Diogenes of Apollonia F 596 KRS.

[29] See Detel 1993, 189–90.

[30] Wieland 1982 remains the most influential study of the problem.

[31] Aristotle identifies an otherwise unknown Alexamenos of Teos as the inventor of the genre (*Poet.* 1, 1447b11 in connection with *De Poetis* F 15 ed. O. Gigon). Kahn 1996 provides a great introduction to the topic.

[32] In a nutshell, the typical structure of such a Socratic dialogue is given in Socrates' brief interrogation of the *pais* in Plato's *Meno* 82 A8–85 B7.

[33] For antiquity, see Asper 2007b, 245–62.

[34] Between Empedocles (d. c. 435 BCE) and Aratus (c. 300 BCE) the only didactic poem of which fragments are extant is Archestratus's culinary poem *Hedypatheia*, which foreshadows many elements of Hellenistic didactic poems, but might have been pervaded by a satirical spirit. Translation by Wilkins and Hill 2011.

[35] For a general account of Hellenistic and later didactic poetry see Effe 1977 and Volk 2002.

[36] Fragments in FGrHist 244.

[37] Text in GGM 1, 196–237.

[38] On Damocrates, see Vogt 2005.

[39] See, e.g., Halbwachs 1959 and Assmann 2011.

[40] For these struggles, see Grethlein 2010.

[41] Calculated on the basis of Jacoby numbers. For a sketch, see Strasburger 1977.

[42] The basic comparative account of oral history is Vansina 1985; for Greek historiography see Murray 2001a and 2001b.

[43] E.g., Herodotus 2.112–20 (Helen–logos); Thucydides 6.54–9 (Athenian traditions of tyrannicide).

[44] Thucydides 1.22 is a good example.

[45] Gray 2002. Cf. Griffiths 2006.

[46] Ephorus of Cyme (FGrHist 70, fourth century BCE) and Duris of Samos (FGrHist 76, early third century BCE) are the main players in these two historiographical groups.

[47] Already Xenophon's *Education of Cyrus* contains a great deal of fiction, as does other biographical literature such as Ps.-Callisthenes' *Life of Alexander* or Philostratus's *Life of Apollonius of Tyana*. In addition, several epistolary novels about historical persons have survived, centered around the lives of, e.g., Plato, Hippocrates, and Euripides (see Holzberg 2006, 30–32).

[48] For the sect of the Monarchians who applied Aristotelian–Galenian logic to Christian dogma, see Nutton 1984, esp. 316 f.

[49] For which see the sketch of Netz 1998.

[50] For example, Plato's *Cratylus* or *Parmenides*, Aristotle's *On Poets* (F 14–22 ed. O. Gigon).

[51] See Netz 2010, 66–114.

[52] Wilamowitz 1886, 112 with n. 12 ("unerträglicher Seichbeutel").

[53] See Asper 2010, 99–106.

[54] For medicine, see v. Staden 1994.

[55] See Asper 2007b, 125–35 on impersonality.

REFERENCES

Arnott, R. 2004. "Minoan and Mycenaean Medicine and Its Near Eastern Contacts." In H. F. J. Horstmanshoff and M. Stol, eds., *Magic and Rationality in Ancient Near Eastern and Graeco-Roman Medicine*, Leiden, 153–73.

Asper, M. 2003 "Mathematik, Milieu, Text." *Sudhoffs Archiv* 87: 1–31.

Asper, M. 2007a. "Medienwechsel und kultureller Kontext. Die Entstehung der griechischen Sachprosa." In J. Althoff, ed., *Philosophie und Dichtung im antiken Griechenland*, Stuttgart, 67–102.

Asper, M. 2007b. *Griechische Wissenschaftstexte. Formen, Funktionen, Differenzierungsgeschichten*. Stuttgart.

Asper, M. 2009."The Two Cultures of Mathematics in Ancient Greece." In E. Robson and J. Stedall, eds., *The Oxford Handbook of the History of Mathematics*, Oxford, 107–32.

Asper, M. 2011. "'Frame Tales' in Ancient Greek Science Writing." In H.-H. Pohl and G. Wöhrle, eds., *Form und Gehalt in Texten der griechischen und der chinesischen Philosophie*, Stuttgart, 91–112.

Assmann, J. 2011. *Cultural Memory and Early Civilization. Writing, Remembrance and Political Imagination*. Cambridge.

Betegh, G. 2004. *The Derveni Papyrus. Cosmology, Theology and Interpretation*. Cambridge.

Clay, J. S. 2003. *Hesiod's Cosmos*. Cambridge.

Collins, H. M. 2010. *Tacit and Explicit Knowledge*. Chicago.

Cuomo, S. 2001. *Ancient Mathematics*. London.

Cuomo, S. 2007. *Technology and Culture in Greek and Roman Antiquity*. Cambridge.

Detel, W. 1993. *Aristoteles. Analytica Posteriora*, Vol. 1, 189–90. Berlin.

Effe, B. 1977. *Dichtung und Lehre. Untersuchungen zur Typologie des antiken Lehrgedichts*. Munich.

Eijk, P. J. van der. 1997. "Towards a Rhetoric of Ancient Scientific Discourse ..." In E. J. Bakker, ed., *Grammar as Interpretation. Greek Literature in its Linguistic Context*, Leiden, 77–129.

Feldherr, A. and G. Hardy, eds. 2011. *The Oxford History of Historical Writing*. Vol. 1. Oxford.

Frede, M. 2008. "Aristotle's Account of the Origins of Philosophy." In P. Curd and D. W. Graham, eds., *The Oxford Handbook of Presocratic Philosophy*, Oxford, 501–29.

Fuhrer, T. 2008a. "Lehrbuch." *Reallexikon für Antike und Christentum* 22: 1025–34.

Fuhrer, T. 2008b. "Lehrgedicht." *Reallexikon für Antike und Christentum* 22: 1034–79, 1089–90.

Fuhrmann, M. 1960. *Das systematische Lehrbuch. Ein Beitrag zur Geschichte der Wissenschaften in der Antike*. Göttingen.

Gray, V. 2002. "Short Stories in Herodotus' *Histories*." In E. J. Bakker et al., eds., *Brill's Companion to Herodotus*, Leiden, 291–317.

Grethlein, J. 2010. *The Greeks and Their Past. Poetry, Oratory and History in the Fifth Century* BCE. Cambridge.

Griffiths, A. 2006. "Stories and Storytelling in the *Histories*." In C. Dewald and J. Marincola, eds., *The Cambridge Companion to Herodotus*, Cambridge, 130–44.

Halbwachs, M. 1959. *Le mémoire collective*. Paris.

Holzberg, N. 2006. *Der antike Roman*. 3rd edn. Darmstadt.

Kahn, C. H. 1996. *Plato and the Socratic Dialogue. The Philosophical Use of a Literary Form*. Cambridge.

Kahn, C. H. 2003. "Writing Philosophy. Prose and Poetry from Thales to Plato." In H. Yunis, ed., *Written Texts and the Rise of Literate Culture in Ancient Greece*, Cambridge, 139–61.

Kurke, L. 2011. *Aesopic Conversations. Popular Tradition, Cultural Dialogue, and the Invention of Greek Prose*. Princeton, NJ.

Lloyd, G. E. R. 2009a. *Disciplines in the Making. Cross-Cultural Perspectives on Elites, Learning, and Innovation*. Oxford.

Lloyd, G. E. R. 2009b. "What was Mathematics in the Ancient World? Greek and Chinese Perspectives." In E. Robson and J. Stedall, eds., *The Oxford Handbook of the History of Mathematics*, Oxford, 7–26.

Most, G. W. 1999. "The Poetics of Early Greek Philosophy." In A. A. Long, ed., *The Cambridge Companion to Early Greek Philosophy*, Cambridge, 332–62.

Murray, O. 2001a. "Herodotus and Oral History." 16–44.

Murray, O. 2001b. "Herodotus and Oral History Reconsidered." In N. Luraghi, ed., *The Historian's Craft in the Age of Herodotus*, Oxford, 314–25.

Netz, R. 1998. "Deuteronomic **Texts**: Late Antiquity and the History of Mathematics." *Revue d'histoire des mathématiques* 4: 261–88.

Netz, R. 1999. *The Shaping of Deduction in Greek Mathematics. A Study in Cognitive History*. Cambridge.

Netz, R. 2004. "Eudemus of Rhodes, Hippocrates of Chios and the Earliest Form of a Greek Mathematical Text." *Centaurus* 46: 243–86.

Netz, R. 2010. *Ludic Proof. Greek Mathematics and the Alexandrian Aesthetic*. Cambridge.

Nutton, V. 1984. "Galen in the Eyes of His Contemporaries." *Bulletin of the History of Medicine* 58: 315–24.

Nutton, V. 2004. *Ancient Medicine*. London.

Polanyi, M. 1966/2009. *The Tacit Dimension*. Chicago (first edn. 1966).

Staden, H. von 1994. "Author and Authority. Celsus and the Construction of a Scientific Self." In M. E. Vázquez Buján, ed., *Tradición e innovación de la medicina latina*, Santiago, 103–17.

Staden, H. von 2002. "'A Woman Does Not Become Ambidextrous.' Galen and the Culture of Scientific Commentary." In R. K. Gibson and C. S. Kraus, eds., *The Classical Commentary. History, Practices, Theory*, Leiden, 109–39.

Strasburger, H. 1977. "Umblick im Trümmerfeld der griechischen Geschichtsschreibung." In *Historiographia Antiqua. Festschrift W. Peremans*, Leuven, 3–52.

Vansina, J. 1985. *Oral Tradition as History*. Madison, WI.

Ventris, M. and J. Chadwick. 1973. *Documents in Mycenaean Greek*. 2nd edn. Cambridge.

Vogt, S. 2005. "… er schrieb in Versen, und er tat recht daran: Lehrdichtung im Urteil Galens." In T. Fögen, ed., *Antike Fachtexte/Ancient Technical Texts*, Berlin, 51–78.

Volk, K. 2002. *The Poetics of Latin Didactic: Lucretius, Vergil, Ovid, Manilius*. Oxford.

West, M. L. 1997. *The East Face of Helicon. West Asiatic Elements in Greek Poetry and Myth*. Oxford.

Wieland, W. 1982. *Platon und die Formen des Wissens*. Göttingen.

Wilamowitz-Moellendorff, U. von. 1886. *Isyllos von Epidaurus*, Berlin.

Wilkins, J. and S. Hill 1994/2011. *Archestratus: Fragments from the Life of Luxury. Revised Edition*. Totnes (first 1994).

Zeller, D. and J. Althoff 2006. *Die Sprüche der Sieben Weisen*. Darmstadt.

Zhmud, L. 2006. *The Origin of the History of Science in Classical Antiquity*. Berlin.

FURTHER READING

Lloyd 2009a gives a great overview of Greek "science" and philosophy. For mathematics, an introduction is provided by Lloyd 2009b. For an accessible discussion of Greek mathematics *in toto*, see Cuomo's excellent *Ancient Mathematics* (2001). The two monographs by Netz (1999, 2010) provide stimulating analyses of the field. On Greek technology, see Cuomo 2007. Philosophical writing is the object of Kahn 2003. For medicine, there is Nutton's introduction (Nutton 2004). The novel reader interested in historiography will find up-to-date introductory essays to the major ancient Greek historiographers in Feldherr and Hardy 2011, esp. 97–243.

CHAPTER 27

Implicit Knowledge

David Konstan

We open a translation of Homer's *Iliad* – to begin at the beginning – and prepare to read an epic centered on the wrath (or perhaps it is the anger) of Achilles. But do we know what "wrath" (the Greek word here is *mênis*) meant to the ancient Greeks, whether in Homer's own time or later? We are aware that some things are lost in translation: not just sound and rhythm, but also nuances of meaning. Nor does the problem arise only with translations. If someone who reads classical Greek has been taught that the word *mênis* means "wrath," he or she may unconsciously assimilate the significance of the Greek word to its equivalent in English (or whatever the target language may be), without considering whether the two terms are really identical in meaning. Of course, translators must use their own language, and trust that the finer overtones will emerge from a reading of the work as a whole: we see how an angry Achilles behaves and thereby learn something of what anger was like for him, or for Homer. Still, ancient Greeks will have brought to bear subtly different expectations as they read or listened to their literature, to the extent that their language reflected or encoded values, emotions, or practices that were specific to their culture. For even the way emotions are conceived and experienced may differ from one society to another, as scholars in various fields have come recently to recognize. This implicit knowledge – the tacit understandings that conditioned the way ancient Greeks comprehended and appreciated their texts – is the subject of this chapter.

I begin with anger and the *Iliad*, before discussing several other Greek concepts that, despite fundamental similarities that cut across the language divide, nevertheless diverge in important ways from their nearest English counterparts, including such ideas as friendship, beauty, love, and pity, and habits of reading generally. In each case, I illustrate how a nearer approximation to the Greek idea may affect our understanding of a classical Greek work.

The first word of the *Iliad* – *mênis* – is not the usual Greek term for anger; as scholars have observed, it is particularly associated with divine rage: hence the use of the more elevated term "wrath" in many renderings of the epic (cf. Considine 1986). This gives us some insight into the way Achilles' character and actions are to be judged, but the linguistic question goes deeper. Let us leap three or four centuries forward, to Aristotle's discussion of anger (along with other emotions) in the second book of his *Rhetoric*. Aristotle offers some startling observations. For example, he writes that "it is impossible to be afraid of and angry with someone at

---

A Companion to Greek Literature, First Edition. Edited by Martin Hose and David Schenker.
© 2016 John Wiley & Sons, Inc. Published 2020 by John Wiley & Sons, Inc.

the same time" (2.3, 1380a33), though he allows that we do not like those who intimidate us (2.4, 1381b33). Again, Aristotle claims that we do not get angry at people who fear us; and he says further that we are not angry, or at all events are less angry, with people who have offended us in anger (2.3, 1380a34–5). We may begin to suspect that anger for Aristotle – or rather *orgê*, the term that he employs – may not correspond exactly to our sense of that emotion.

Aristotle's comments do, however, follow plausibly from his definition of *orgê*: "Let *orgê* be a desire, accompanied by pain, for a perceived revenge, on account of a perceived slight on the part of people who are not fit to slight one or one's own" (2.2, 1378a31–3). Aristotle reasons that people who fear us are afraid to offend us (2.3, 1380a22–4); their fear is incompatible with contempt, and hence they cannot slight us (note that slights, according to Aristotle, are the primary, if not the only, cause of anger). Since anger, moreover, is directed toward revenge, it can only arise, Aristotle argues, where revenge is possible. As he puts is: "No one gets angry at someone when it is impossible to achieve revenge, and with those who are far superior in power than themselves people get angry either not at all or less so" (2.2, 1370b13–15). As for those who are angry at us, it is they who are victims of a slight on our part, and so they are not in a position to put us down; as Aristotle says, "no one who is angry offers a slight" (2.2, 1380a6). For Aristotle, the idea of *orgê* is closely bound up with relations of status and honor: we get angry because someone has belittled us, and we either take vengeance or, if we are incapable of doing so, we swallow our pride together with our irritation (we can imagine that slaves were obliged to accept a master's insults in this way, or at least to feign such resignation). Recall that anger, according to Aristotle, is a response to an affront "on the part of people who are not fit to slight" us or our dear ones. Social roles of superiority and inferiority are built into the definition (for fuller discussion, see Konstan 2006: 41–76; on ancient anger more generally, Harris 2001; Braund and Most 2004).

How might Aristotle's conception of anger influence our reading of the *Iliad*? First, we must enter a word of caution: the term that Aristotle subjects to analysis, namely *orgê*, does not occur in Homer; the most common word in epic within this general semantic domain is rather *kholos*, which is related to the word meaning "bile." The sense of anger may have changed over time, even within ancient Greece. Yet Aristotle cites the *Iliad* in the course of his discussion, and he was both intimately familiar with the poem (he edited a version while he was tutoring Alexander the Great) and far closer to Homer's world than we are. What is more, his account fits the case of Achilles very well. Agamemnon insulted Achilles by depriving him of his war prize; as Achilles complains to his mother, the sea nymph Thetis, "wide-ruling Agamemnon has dishonored me" (1.356), and again, "he failed to honor the best of the Achaeans" (1.244). To Agamemnon's face he declares: "Call me a coward, a no-account, if I ever again submit to anything you say" (1.293–4), thereby revealing that he, at least, is not afraid of the leader of the Greek expedition to Troy, and so is in a position to respond angrily to a slight. Later, when Agamemnon sends an embassy to Achilles' tent in an attempt to placate him, Achilles asserts: "My heart swells with anger when I recall those things, how Agamemnon treated me shamefully before the Achaeans as if I were some vagabond without honor" (9.646–8). There is the tacit implication that if Achilles really were a vagabond, there would be no place for anger against so powerful a king (indeed, the priest Chryses, who is violently threatened by Agamemnon when he offers a ransom for the return of his daughter, skulks away with no display of ire, and must appeal to Apollo to avenge him). Honor and status are at the heart of these exchanges. Of course, it is possible that Achilles has overreacted to the offense; but the important thing is that, if Aristotle is at all a reliable guide, what is at stake in the poem is not anger management, as though the *Iliad* were an object lesson in the need to restrain rage, but rather an exploration of natural emotional reactions in a situation where power relations are in a tense equilibrium – and later Greek audiences would have been sensitive to this aspect, as Aristotle's discussion makes clear.

Three-quarters of the way through the *Iliad*, Achilles gives over his anger against Achilles, and directs his fury at Hector, the Trojan warrior who killed Achilles' beloved friend, Patroclus, in battle. It is tempting to see this final portion of the poem as a continuation of Achilles' anger, with simply a displacement of its object (cf. Taplin 1992, 193–202). Such a reading lends an apparent unity to the epic as a whole, with a consistent focus on the passion announced in the first verse. But is it the case that, in slaying Patroclus, Hector has belittled Achilles in a way comparable to Agamemnon's overt humiliation of his greatest warrior? Is Achilles' honor really in question here, or is his quest for vengeance motivated by something else, for example the raw pain at having lost his comrade in arms, and perhaps too a sense of guilt for having sent him out to ward off the Trojan attack while he himself stayed away from the fray? And if this is the case, can we still speak of anger as the passion that moves Achilles? These are delicate issues, and one hesitates to pronounce on them. But I may quote an ancient commentator, whose judgment survives in the marginal notes or scholia to some of the manuscripts of the *Iliad*. A propos the verses in which Achilles declares that, despite the way Agamemnon angered him, he will repress his rage and go forth to fight Hector, this critic remarks: "of the two emotions besetting Achilles' soul, anger [*orgé*] and grief [*lupé*], one wins out .... For the emotion involving Patroclus is strongest of all, and so it is necessary to abandon his wrath [*ménis*] and avenge himself on his enemies" (scholia bT, on *Il.* 18.112–13). An ancient Greek reader, then, recognized a shift from one emotion to another where we might be inclined to see a single, continuous passion at work. This is not to say that the scholiast is necessarily right, but to suggest that taking account of classical perceptions may well affect our interpretation of the epic.

There are many texts that would repay attention to Aristotle's account of anger – examples include Sophocles' *Ajax*, Euripides' *Medea*, and Menander's *Samian Woman* – but I turn now to another idea that informed Greek responses to literature, namely that of beauty. The very question of whether there was a term in ancient Greek signifying beauty in the modern acceptation of that word is vexed. The adjective that is most commonly taken to mean "beautiful" is *kalós*, and *to kalón*, the nominalization of the adjective formed by attaching the definite article (*to*) to the neuter gender, is often rendered as "beauty." Indeed, an entire dialogue by Plato – the *Hippias Maior* – devoted to the notion of *to kalón* is generally assumed to be about beauty. Yet an eminent student of classical philosophy observes in connection with this very dialogue that "there is a deep history of uncertainty about how properly to translate *kalon*." These ambiguities so perplex him, he writes, as to "leave me with the urge, an urge that I will of course resist, to say that the Greeks had no concept of *beauty*. But this much is right: the concept of *beauty* is sufficiently different from that of the *kalon* to make the urge understandable" (Kosman 2010, 346). Perhaps, then, we ought to be on guard about ascribing to classical Greek literature aesthetic values that the Greeks themselves may not have appreciated in the way we do.

There is, however, a Greek word, almost entirely neglected in modern scholarship, that comes closer to meaning "beauty," although it is narrower (rather than broader) in its application than the modern term. The word is *kállos*, a neuter noun spelled with two lambdas and the accent on the first syllable. To take some examples of the use of this noun, in the *Iliad*, the gods are said to have granted Bellerophon *kállos* and "desirable manhood" (6.156); indeed, his host's wife falls passionately in love with him. Paris, too, is beautiful: after Aphrodite has whisked him from the battlefield, she tells Helen that "Paris is in your bedroom and your well-turned bed, glowing in his beauty [*kállos*] and garments" (3.391–2); it was his beauty that caused Helen to run off with him, and the scene of her enamorment is implicitly echoed here in the *Iliad*. Achilles can describe a woman's consummate beauty as rivaling that of Aphrodite (9.389), who is of course the epitome of beauty; Theocritus, writing in the Hellenistic period, describes her as excelling all the goddesses in beauty (17.45). In the Homeric *Hymn to Aphrodite*, Aphrodite falls in love with Anchises, who has his beauty from the gods (5.77), whereas she herself possesses "immortal beauty" (174); Zeus, for his part, seized Ganymede because of his *kállos* (203). The sense of the term *kállos* is beginning to emerge: it typically refers to physical beauty, of the type that can inspire passion or love. What is more, it can be dangerous. In Euripides' *Andromache* (207–8), Andromache tells her tormentor, Hermione: "it is not *kállos*, woman, but virtues that delight one's bedmate." Danae's beauty attracts the erotic attention of Zeus (Euripides F 1132 TrGF), and in Euripides' *Helen*, the heroine laments her fatal beauty. Electra, in Euripides' tragedy by that name, denounces a woman who beautifies herself (*es kállos askei*) as wicked. Xenophon, in the *Memorabilia* (3.11.1), observes that the beauty of the courtesan Theodote was said to over-power reason. Hellenistic epigrams are again revealing. Rufinus (*Anthologia Palatina* 5.70) writes: "You have the *kállos* of Cypris [i.e., Aphrodite], the mouth of Persuasiveness, the body and youth of the Spring Seasons, the voice of Calliope, the mind and modesty of Themis, the arms of Athena." *Kállos* is not the special attribute of Athena or of the Muse (Athena is imposing, but it would be unseemly to call this warlike goddess "pretty"); it pertains above all to Aphrodite (cf. 5.73.5–6, 5.92.1; 5.140). Meleager affirms: "Eros gave Zenophila *kállos*, Cypris gave her sex potions to possess, and the Graces gave her grace" (5.196), and again: "His sweet beauty flashes like lightning; see, he hurls flames with his eyes" (12.110.1–3). Asclepiades writes that he melts like wax near fire when he sees the beauty of Didyme (5.120). The connection between *kállos* and erotic love is abundantly clear. The contrast between the noun and the adjective, moreover, is evident in Theocritus 23.32, where the poet states the commonplace notion that "a boy's beauty [*kállos*] is a fine thing [*kalón*], but it endures a short while."

Ancient Greek, then, did have a word for "beauty," and though it could be applied to natural features such as rivers or man-made objects such as cities, it continued to refer primarily to things that were attractive to the eyes; even when it was used of such abstract items as literary style, it retained a connection with the notion of good physical proportions. Thus Hermogenes, in his treatise *On Style* (second century CE) states:

> In general, beauty [*kállos*] is a symmetry of limbs and parts [*summetria melón kai merón*], along with a good complexion [*eukhroia*], and it is through these that a speech [*logos*] becomes [beautiful].... It is necessary, then, if a speech is to be beautiful [*kalós*], whether it is variegated or uniform, that it have symmetry among these, that is, harmony [*euarmostia*], and that a kind of good complexion bloom upon it, which takes the form of a single quality of character throughout, and which some indeed naturally call the color [*khrôma*] of a speech ....(1.12)

For the Greeks, beauty was but one feature of a work of art, and not necessarily the most impor-tant. Plutarch, in his essay on how to read poems, praises pupils who attend to the moral character (*éthos*) of a work rather than the plot (*historia*) or pretty language (*kállos*), however seductive this might be; only the first kind of student is *philokalos*, a lover of what is noble (30D).

Plato famously ascribed beauty to his ideal forms – those transcendental, immaterial universals that are visible only to the mind's eye (an expression that Plato seems to have coined; cf. *Conv.* 219A, *tês dianoias opsis*; *Rep.* 533D, *to tês psukhês omma*; *Soph.* 254A, *tês psukhês ommata*). If we bear in mind the connotations associated with the word *kállos*, we shall be less surprised to discover that, according to Plato, the soul is drawn to this higher realm of being by *erós*, that is, passionate love (cf. *Phaedr.* 254–5, *Rep.* 403A, 475B, 476B–C, 485A–B, 499B–C). On the other hand, if we take into account only the adjective *kalós*, with its broad gamut of meanings that include "noble," "excellent," and "fine," as well as "beautiful," we risk missing the powerfully erotic dimension not just of Plato's thought, but of the classical Greek appreciation of beauty generally.

Erotic passion is itself a topic that ancient Greeks addressed differently from the way we do. We have seen that it was elicited by beauty, and beauty, or sexual attractiveness, was associated particularly with women or boys (sometimes with effeminate men). There was a close connection between youth and erotic appeal; indeed, those ancient Greeks who wondered about the relationship between Achilles and Patroclus had to decide which of them was older, just in order to classify the pair as lover and beloved (cf. Fantuzzi 2012). Even women, when they were, on occasion, represented as the subjects of sexual desire – that is, as the lover rather than as the loved one – were imagined as being attracted to adolescents, who still retained a girlish look, rather than to adult men of the tough, heroic kind. Women's desire was thus modeled on the pederastic relationship: they were imagined as falling in love in the same way as men (see Konstan 2002). Erotic passion in Greece was generally conceived of as a one-way sentiment, involving a lover or active party, for which the Greek word was *erastés*, and a beloved or *erómenos* (feminine, *erómenê*), who was in the passive role (see Dover 1978: 71–81; Foucault 1978–86; Halperin 1990; Skinner 2005; Davidson 2007: 19: "*Erós* is, with only a few exceptions, utterly one-sided"; for criticism of this view which does not wholly succeed in displacing it, see Hubbard 1998). There was no feminine form of *erastés*: a lover was characteristically male, and so it was all the more natural to render the culturally marginalized conception of a female lover as a distorted type of masculine *erós*. In New Comedy, where love was a principal theme, the only women who are shown as being in love are courtesans; it is not a proper sentiment for a citizen girl.

A Greek approaching one of the ancient novels, such as Longus's *Daphnis and Chloe*, Chariton's *Callirhoe*, or Xenophon's *Ephesian Tale*, written in the first or second century CE, would thus have noticed at once a sharp departure from the classical convention. For here, a young man and woman of like social status fall mutually in love, each attracted by the beauty of the other: they swoon, they take to their bed, and when it comes to lovemaking, Xenophon's protagonists vie with each other to demonstrate their passion. What is more, both the hero and heroine excite the erotic interest of the pirates who capture them: he is young enough to be loved, not just to love (*Ephesian Tale* 2.1). Only five romantic novels of this sort survive, but other such narratives may have circulated orally. We may suppose that the ancient reader had some idea of what to expect from the form of the work: a long prose story involving young lovers who are separated from each other by fortune, maintain their loyalty to one another despite various misadventures and torments, and are finally reunited in the end. One kind of implicit knowledge is simply a sense of genre (for discussion, see Konstan 1994; for a different but complementary view, which treats reciprocal love in the novels as a feature of adolescence, see Lalanne 2006).

As is well known, Aristotle maintained that the proper or typical response to tragedy was a combination of pity and fear, and the view was commonplace (cf. Gorgias *Helen* 9; Plato *Rep.* 606B–C; Isocrates *Pan.* 112, 168). We may imagine that members of the ancient Greek audience had some expectation that they would feel pity for the fortunes of characters on stage. But what did pity, or rather *eleos* (their word), mean to them? Was it comparable to our notion of sympathy or empathy, or did it convey the sense of superiority to the sufferer that has cast the modern idea of pity in a negative light? We may take as a case in point the response to Philoctetes' agony in Sophocles' play: surely he is among the most miserable of all tragic characters, abandoned by the Greek army on the way to Troy because he accidently stepped into a sacred precinct and was bitten in the foot by a poisonous serpent; so terrible were his groans that he was deemed unfit to sail with the rest, and was left to endure, sick and alone, on a deserted island for ten years before his comrades in arms returned to rescue him – not for his sake, but only because it turned out that his bow was needed if Troy was ever to fall. An eminent modern literary critic has written:

> to ask, say, why we feel sympathy for Philoctetes is a pseudo-problem bred by a bogus historicism. We feel sympathy for Philoctetes because he is in agonizing pain from his pus-swollen foot. There is no use in pretending that his foot is a realm of impenetrable otherness which our modern-day notions can grasp only at the cost of brutally colonizing the past. There is nothing hermeneutically opaque about Philoctetes' hobbling and bellowing.

This same critic does allow that classical tragedy is not wholly transparent to us:

> There is, to be sure, a great deal about the art form in which he [that is, Philoctetes] figures which is profoundly obscure to us.

Nevertheless,

> as far as his agony goes, we understand Philoctetes in much the same way as we understand the afflictions of those around us ... . (Eagleton 2003: xii–xiv)

But did the Greeks pity Philoctetes simply because he was in pain? Aristotle explains that pity is "a kind of pain in the case of an apparent destructive or painful harm *in one not deserving to encounter it*, which one might expect oneself, or one of one's own, to suffer, and this when it seems near" (*Rhet*. 2.8, 1385b13–16; my emphasis). This is not the same thing as an instinctive sympathy for someone in pain. Pity for Aristotle – and in this he is in agreement with Greek opinion generally – requires a judgment concerning the desert of the one who is suffering. *Eleos* is a moral response, not an automatic, unreflecting reaction. Was Philoctetes' abandoned unjustly – this is the question that pity invites. When the chorus of Greek sailors first sees the miserable cave in which Philoctetes has dwelled all these years, they exclaim: "I pity him: no human being to care for him, with no companion in sight, miserable, forever alone, he is afflicted by a savage disease and wanders at the mercy of every need that arises" (Soph. *Phil*. 169–75). This is, perhaps, a natural enough sentiment, though they may also be reflecting on the fact that he was suffering through no fault of his own. Later in the play, however, Neoptolemus, who has by this time shifted allegiance from the Greek army and cast his lot with Philoctetes, is provoked by the old man's stubborn refusal to go to Troy, even though his wound can only be cured there, and he exclaims: "it is not just to pardon or to pity those who are involved in self-willed harm, like you" (Soph. *Phil*. 1318–20). Here, then, in the Greek tragedy that most exhibits pity in the characters themselves, we recognize its limitation in the Greek view. If a figure falls as a result of his or her deliberate actions, then pity is not warranted. Of course, it is not always easy to decide questions of responsibility. Should we pity Antigone, or perhaps even Creon? Is Medea to be pitied or condemned? Tragedy does not invite a simple response to such questions. My point is that, in speaking of pity as the emotion elicited by tragedy, Aristotle was not emphasizing the spectacle of pain or suffering as such, but recognizing how the spectators' values are inseparable from the effect of tragedy (cf. Konstan and Kiritsi 2010).

Speaking of Medea, did she murder her children out of jealousy, because Jason was now determined to leave her and marry the Corinthian princess? Some have supposed that she did, whereas others have emphasized her justifiable indignation at Jason's violation of his oaths and neglect of all she had done for him. She made it possible for him to obtain the golden fleece, and now he was allowing her to be sent into exile, alone and unprotected. Perhaps a modern audience is more inclined to see a romantic motive such as jealousy at work, whereas the Greeks would have recognized something more like dishonor, and the desire for revenge this naturally provoked (on Medea's motives, see Boedeker 1991; Mastronarde 2002, 16–22).

A famous poem of Sappho (F 31 V) offers a good illustration of how moderns may infer jealousy where the ancients might have recognized a different motive. Here is the poem (cf. also in this volume Wells ch. 10, pp. 165–8, and Willi ch. 29, pp. 451–2 on the language of this poem), in a nineteenth-century version that nicely reflects the way the poem was (and still is) received (Philips 1893):

Blest as the immortal gods is he,
The youth who fondly sits by thee,
And hears and sees thee, all the while,
Softly speak and sweetly smile.

'Twas this deprived my soul of rest,
And raised such tumults in my breast;
For, while I gazed, in transport tossed,
My breath was gone, my voice was lost;

My bosom glowed; the subtle flame
Ran quick through all my vital frame;
O'er my dim eyes a darkness hung;
My ears with hollow murmurs rung;

In dewy damps my limbs were chilled;
My blood with gentle horrors thrilled:
My feeble pulse forgot to play;
I fainted, sunk, and died away.

Many readers, and the great majority of classical scholars, have interpreted this poem as reflecting Sappho's jealousy, which is inspired by the man who is the rival for her beloved's affection (Catullus's translation of this poem, *carmen* 51, has been similarly understood). The symptoms that Sappho so vividly depicts correspond, it is assumed, to this desperate emotion, and the cause is evidently that another is displacing her in the affections of the woman she adores. Yet, for an ancient reader, those same symptoms were invariably associated not with jealousy but with love itself, or *erós*, which was felt above all as a fire that consumed the self. Seen this way, the man sitting opposite Sappho is not necessarily a rival in love: at all events, he is clearly not possessed by *erós*, since he, unlike Sappho, calmly enjoys the conversation with the other woman. The contrast, in fact, between his cool demeanor and Sappho's own wild passion may be just the point: he is like a god because, in Sappho's view, only a god could sit so close to her beloved and be unaffected by her charms. The point of the comparison is to underscore Sappho's love; jealousy has nothing to do with it (see Furley 2000; Konstan 2006, 219–43). This, then, is another instance in which the ancients brought to their reading an implicit understanding that differs from our own.

The ancient Greeks placed a very high value on friendship, and their expectations of friends and the grief upon losing a friend may sometimes surprise the modern reader. Achilles, in the *Iliad*, exclaims that Patroclus was dearer to him than anyone else, even his father. In Euripides' *Orestes*, the title character affirms the superiority of friendship to all ties of kinship: "it is better to have an outsider as a friend, if he bound to you by character, than ten thousand blood relations" (805–6). Orestes had earlier expressed the view that "friends who are not friends in a crisis are so in name, not in reality" (454–5), and he condemns the hesitation of his uncle, Menelaus, to help him as typical of "what bad friends do for friends" (748). But neither tragedy nor comedy took a great interest, it would appear, in the behavior of bad or false friends; at all events, among the Greek tragedies of which we know or can reconstruct the plot, a majority are based on conflicts within the family (one thinks of the house of Atreus, or of Oedipus), but there seems to be none in which there is a murder or even a falling out between friends. An intimate friend – and this is what the Greek *philos* usually means, as opposed to a mere acquaintance – was, in Aristotle's famous phrase, another self, and this would seem to be the conception that is implicit in Greek literary representations of friendship (see Konstan 2009 for discussion).

The comic essayist Lucian portrays a contest between a Greek and a Scythian over which race values friendship more highly (*Toxaris or On Friendship*). One of the tales recounted by the Scythian describes how a man who was lodging in a foreign town, along with his friend (who had been wounded) and his wife and two children (one still an infant), chose to rescue the friend when the house caught fire and bade his wife look after herself and the children as well as she could. When reproached for this behavior, he replied: "I can beget other children easily enough," said he: "nor was it certain how these would turn out: but it would be long before I got such another friend as Gyndanes; of his affection I have been abundantly satisfied by experience" (trans. Fowler and Fowler 1905). The story makes it clear that there was more than one point of view on whether the Scythian made the right choice; in any case, it is meant to be amusing, and can be taken with a grain of salt. But we ought not to underestimate how strong the bond of friendship might be. Ancient critics, as we have seen, sometimes interpreted Achilles' deep attachment to Patroclus as a sign of pederastic *erós* (in whichever direction); but others saw it simply as friendship (*philia*, or the bond between *philoi*), a different sentiment but no less intense for that.

The right to free expression is fundamental in modern democracies, and in classical Athens, too, citizens of all classes were understood to enjoy the privilege of stating their views openly. In a seminal article, Arnaldo Momigliano wrote: "In the second part of the fifth century and during the greater part of the fourth century every Athenian citizen had the right to speak [in the assembly] unless he disqualified himself by certain specified crimes." This freedom was, according to Momigliano "an Athenian fifth-century idea," and the term that best expressed it was *parrhēsia*: "*Parrhēsia* represented democracy from the point of view of equality of rights" (Momigliano 1973, 259). After the democratic *polis* gave way to Hellenistic kingdoms, however, things changed. The royal courts were hierarchical, and the freedom to speak about matters of policy was by no means guaranteed. The king might consult a council of his friends or advisors, but their liberty to express their views was a privilege, not a right, and there was always the risk that too much frankness might offend the ruler. In this context, candor required courage and flattery was often the safer, if not the nobler, course. In the words of Momigliano (p. 260), after the Athenian democracy yielded to autocracy, "*parrhesia* as a private virtue replaced *parrhesia* as a political right."

There is, however, a danger in projecting back upon ancient democratic institutions a modern notion such as rights. It is true that under the Hellenistic monarchies and the Roman Empire, political writers cautioned against the kind of candor that might smack of insolence. Plutarch, in his treatise on how to distinguish a friend from a flatterer, warns that one must offer advice graciously, and beware of indulging in blame and abuse as though this were authentic *parrhēsia* (66a; cf. 66e). One must also observe the right moment for criticism; otherwise, one "ruins the utility of frankness" (68c). An aphorism attributed to Democritus (DK 86 B 226) runs: "*parrhēsia* is intrinsic to freedom: the difficulty lies in diagnosing the right moment [*kairos*]." The Epicurean philosopher Philodemus, a contemporary of Cicero, notes in his treatise *On Parrhēsia* that one must be careful when admonishing people of high station, since they "suspect that those who converse with them forthrightly are eager for reputation, so that they may be called frank speakers, and they consider such {conduct} as tending to insolence and their own dishonor" (Col. XXIIIb). Kings in particular "consider reproach to be insubordination. They wish, and believe that it is advantageous, to rule over everything and that everything [depend on] and be subordinated to themselves" (Col. XXIVa; trans. Konstan et al. 1998).

Even in democratic Athens, however, outspokenness could easily slide over into shamelessness. Euripides' *Phoenician Women* relates how, after the death of Oedipus, his two sons, Eteocles and Polynices, agreed that each would rule in alternate years. However, Eteocles, who was first to occupy the throne, refused to step down at the end of his term, and Polynices, who had been living in Argos, decided to reclaim his right by force of arms, at the head of an Argive army. Having been summoned by his mother Jocasta, Polynices sneaks into Thebes to meet with her.

Jocasta begins by asking him: "What is the wretched thing for exiles?" Polynices answers: "One thing above all, that one does not have *parrhêsia*." Jocasta then says: "What you have said – not to utter what one thinks – pertains to a slave." Polynices replies: "It is necessary to bear with the stupidities of those in power." Jocasta says: "This too is painful, to play the fool along with fools." "But one must be servile," Polynices states, "contrary to my nature, for profit's sake" (390–95). These lines have been taken to show how important free speech was for citizens of a democracy, even though the setting is Thebes (an oligarchy at the time the play was produced) and Polynices is not a common citizen but a would-be king. A little later, Polynices defend his attack against his homeland with the support of a foreign army by insisting that he is acting unwillingly, in contrast to his brother (433–4). He begs his mother to mediate between her two sons, and adds: "It is an old story, but I'll say it anyway: money is the most valuable thing for people, and holds the greatest power among them. It is for this I've come here, leading ten thousand spearmen; for no poor man is noble" (438–42). These lines have offended critics of the play for over a century, and are bracketed as an interpolation in the magisterial Oxford Classical Text edition edited by James Diggle (vol. 3, 1994). Donald Mastronarde argued in the same year, however, that rejecting the verses is based on a "misunderstanding of the traditional value-system" (Mastronarde 1994, 271 ad vv. 438–42); as he observes: "For a man of conventional aristocratic thinking, the status of high birth is inseparable from the wealth that maintains one's standing among peers and ability to act independently" (p. 270). Even so, to wage war on one's own city and capture it by force, as Polynices himself affirms (cf. 488–9, where he uses the verb *porthein*, "ravage" or "plunder"), for the sake of money is hardly honorable behavior. But we may also take this blunt declaration as a sign of the candor or *parrhêsia* that Polynices lacked while he was living abroad, and which he feels free to employ when he is alone with his mother. This is the negative side of free speech, which shades into shamelessness and a disregard for popular morality. Immediately after Polynices' revelation of his motives, his brother Eteocles enters and presents his case before Jocasta, in lines that are famous for their unabashed celebration of power: "Mother, I will speak out and conceal nothing. I would travel to where the stars and sun rise and beneath the earth if I could accomplish this one thing, possess Tyranny, the greatest of the gods. I do not wish to yield this advantage to anyone else, but to preserve it for myself: for it is cowardice to settle for less and lose the greater portion" (503–10). The Athenian audience may well have regarded such freedom of speech not as a right but as a mark of intolerable arrogance (see Saxonhouse 2006).

Greek readers, then, brought to a text or performance a certain cultural repertoire of values, emotions, and habitual practices that informed their responses to the work at hand. They would not have reflected on these implicit sensibilities, any more than we do, but we have to make an effort to recover something their way of thinking if we are fully to appreciate their literature. Of course, the Greeks had other kinds of knowledge that escapes us today, for example, of local characters and events such as those satirized in Aristophanes' comedies or lampooned in Archilochus's invectives (if indeed they were always real people). This is the kind of indispensable information that one can find in modern commentaries, to the extent that it can be recovered. The memories of the ancients were also stuffed with snatches of poetry, proverbs, mythological stories, and anecdotes that a writer could count on being known, most of it through oral transmission even in the age of elite literacy. This knowledge permitted a rich texture of allusion and what today is called intertextuality, which again can be retrieved in part by careful scholarship. Hesiod's *Works and Days* is a valuable repository of this kind of proverbial wisdom, as are the various collections of adages that survive from antiquity; these texts, like didactic poetry generally, are foreign to us and their popularity is difficult to comprehend, but we ought to recognize that they were a crucial source of knowledge on which people drew, for the most part implicitly, as the occasion demanded. Approached in this way, they may prove more accessible to us as well.

It would be wrong to think of this storehouse of knowledge as a mere skill at recognition, for it served also as a means of actively engaging with literature: that is to say, readers or spectators had their part to play as well. In his essay on how a youth should listen to poems, Plutarch seeks to protect young students from the potentially harmful contents of traditional poetry such as epic or tragedy, in which heroes do and say things that are contrary to the moral principles that Plutarch endorses, by instilling in them a critical attitude toward the texts they read. One of the strategies he recommends is to quote the poet against himself. Thus, where Homer represents gods fighting and wounding each other, the student is encouraged to cite Homer's own affirmation that "the blessed gods are glad all their days" (*Od.* 6.46), which is, he says, the truer view (*Quomodo adol.* 20F). When Sophocles, or rather a character in a Sophoclean play, asserts, "profit is pleasant, even if it comes from falsehoods" (F 833 TrGF), Plutarch exclaims (21A): "but in fact we heard you say that 'false statements never bear fruit'" (F 834 TrGF). Though Plutarch wrote several centuries after the Classical period, his prescriptions plausibly reflect the way people might have thought about and challenged texts, whether written or oral, based on what they took to be sound precepts. Readers and audiences were expected to render judgments, not just to follow the story line. Comedy and tragedy alike, for example, enjoyed staging set debates, called *agónes*, and spectators were placed in the position of jurors in a courtroom, taking the side of one or another party or even criticizing the poet himself (one thinks of Aristophanes' *Frogs*). Such views might well have been voiced aloud: theater-goers did not necessarily maintain the respectful silence demanded of modern audiences.

We may take as an example of the kind of response expected of readers Thucydides' account of the debate over the fate of Plataea (3.53–67), an ally of Athens which was captured by Sparta and Thebes early in the Peloponnesian War. The Thebans and the Plataeans argue over the fate of the city before a panel of five Spartans who act as jurors (*dikastai*, 3.52.3, 3.68.1), with the Thebans pleading for the total destruction of Plataea. The Plataeans, recalling that the Thebans sided with the invading Persians (also called Medes) during the invasion earlier in the century, accuse them of Medism, a common charge; the Thebans, in turn, charge the Plataeans with "Atticism" (3.64.5), as though loyalty to Athens were a betrayal of a comparable order. The Spartans approve the Thebans' side. Now, an Athenian reader would surely view the case differently, and was no doubt expected to see through and contest the judgment. The reader was expected to decide independently, and even emotional appeals invited careful judgment; we may recall that Aristotle defined the *pathê* or emotions as "all those things on account of which people change and differ in regard to their judgments [*kriseis*]" (*Rhet.* 2.1, 1378a20–23).

The preceding discussion is, of course, merely illustrative of the kinds of implicit understandings that informed ancient Greek responses to literature. A more comprehensive treatment is impossible within a short space, and in a way undesirable, since it might give the impression that we can define the classical conceptions once and for all. Rather, they are the subject of ongoing research, and new nuances are continually coming to the surface – and will continue to do so, as the evolution of our own concepts brings new facets of ancient ideas to light. Inevitably, we bring our own implicit knowledge to the reading of classical texts. But we enrich our reading and our understanding both of ancient Greek culture and, I venture to say, our own when we are alert to the different assumptions the Greeks brought to bear, and attempt to recover their conceptions, to the extent we can, and read their texts as they might have done.

REFERENCES

Boedeker, D. 1991. "Euripides' Medea and the Vanity of *Logoi*." *Classical Philology* 86: 95–112.
Braund, S. and G. W. Most, eds. 2004. *Ancient Anger: Perspectives from Homer to Galen*. Cambridge.
Considine, P. 1986. "The Etymology of MHNIS." In J. H. Betts, J. T. Hooker, and J. R. Green, eds., *Studies in Honour of T.B.L. Webster*, Bristol, 53–64.

Davidson, J. 2007. *The Greeks and Greek Love: A Bold New Exploration of the Ancient World*. New York.

Diggle, J., ed. 1994. *Euripidis Fabulae*. Vol. 3. Oxford.

Dover, K. J. 1978. *Greek Homosexuality*. London.

Dover, K. J. 1994. *Greek Popular Morality in the Time of Plato and Aristotle*. Revised edn. Indianapolis.

Eagleton, T. 2003. *Sweet Violence: The Idea of the Tragic*. Oxford.

Fantuzzi, M. 2012. *Achilles in Love*. Oxford.

Foucault, M. 1978–86. *The History of Sexuality*. 3 vols. New York.

Fowler, H. W. and F. G. Fowler. 1905. *The Works of Lucian of Samosata*. Oxford.

Furley, W. D. 2000. "'Fearless, Bloodless … like the Gods': Sappho 31 and the Rhetoric of Godlike." *Classical Quarterly* 50: 7–15.

Halperin, D. M. 1990. *One Hundred Years of Homosexuality and Other Essays on Greek Love*. New York.

Harris, W. V. 2001. *Restraining Rage: The Ideology of Anger Control in Classical Antiquity*. Cambridge.

Hubbard, T. K. 1998. "Popular Perceptions of Elite Homosexuality in Classical Athens." *Arion* 6: 48–78.

Johnson, W. A. 2012. *Readers and Reading Culture in the High Roman Empire: A Study of Elite Communities*. Oxford.

Konstan, D. 1994. *Sexual Symmetry: Love in the Ancient Novel and Related Genres*. Princeton, NJ.

Konstan, D. 2002. "Women, Boys, and the Paradigm of Athenian Pederasty." *Differences* 13.2: 35–56.

Konstan, D. 2006. *The Emotions of the Ancient Greeks: Studies in Aristotle and Classical Literature*. Toronto.

Konstan, D. 2009. "Friends in Tragedy." In E. Karamalengou and Eu. Makrigianni, eds., Ἀντιφίλησις: *Studies on Classical, Byzantine and Modern Greek Literature and Culture in Honour of John-Theophanes A. Papademetriou*, Stuttgart, 109–15.

Konstan, D. 2014. *Beauty: The Fortunes of an Ancient Greek Idea*. Oxford.

Konstan, D., D. Clay, C. Glad, J. Thom, and J. Ware. 1998. *Philodemus On Frank Criticism: Introduction, Translation and Notes*. Atlanta, GA.

Konstan, D. and S. Kiritsi. 2010. "From Pity to Sympathy: Tragic Emotions across the Ages." *The Athens Dialogues E-Journal* 1 (2010). http://athensdialogues.chs.harvard.edu/cgi-bin/WebObjects/ athensdialogues.woa/wa/dist?dis=46 (accessed April 4, 2015).

Kosman, A. 2010. "Beauty and the Good: Situating the Kalon." *Classical Philology* 105: 341–57.

Lalanne, S. 2006. *Une éducation grecque: rites de passage et construction des genres dans le roman grec ancien*. Paris.

Mastronarde, D. J., ed. 1994. *Euripides: Phoenissae*. Cambridge.

Mastronarde, D. J., ed. 2002. *Euripides Medea*. Cambridge.

Momigliano, A. 1973. "Freedom of Speech in Antiquity." In P. P. Wiener, ed., *Dictionary of the History of Ideas: Studies of Selected Pivotal Ideas*, New York, Vol. 2, 252–63.

Pearson, L. 1962. *Popular Ethics in Ancient Greece*. Stanford, CA.

Philips, A. 1893. "Ode To a Loved One." In W. H. Appleton, *Greek Poets in English Verse*, Cambridge.

Saxonhouse, A. 2006. *Free Speech and Democracy in Ancient Athens*. Cambridge.

Skinner, M. 2005. *Sexuality in Greek and Roman Culture*. Oxford.

Sluiter, I. and R. M. Rosen, eds. 2004. *Free Speech in Classical Antiquity*. Leiden.

Taplin, O. 1992. *Homeric Soundings: The Shaping of the Iliad*. Oxford.

Winkler, J. J. 1990. *Constraints of Desire: The Anthropology of Sex and Gender in Ancient Greece*. New York.

FURTHER READING

Dover 1994 is a path-breaking study of how Greeks typically thought and felt, derived not from the philosophers but from comedy, oratory, inscriptions, and other such sources.

In spite of the focus on imperial Rome, Johnson 2012 is immensely revealing about how the ancients read and what they expected of a text.

Konstan 2006 examines a range of emotions, from anger and love to envy and pity, with an emphasis on how the ancient Greek conceptions differed from modern usage.

Konstan 2014 discusses the Greek idea of beauty as a stimulus to erotic desire and what this means for the appreciation of art, then and now.

Pearson 1962 explores justice, loyalty, and other values from Homer to tragedy and beyond; a highly accessible overview.

Sluiter and Rosen 2004 offers a fine collection of essays investigating the nature and limits of free expression in the classical world, from comic vituperation to Socratic cross-examination.

From dream books to magic formulas and ancient novels, Winkler 1990 explores popular customs and values in a crucial area of life.

CHAPTER 28

Preserved Knowledge
Summaries and Compilations

Markus Dubischar

1. Introduction

In the typologically rich field of literature of knowledge – here taken to be synonymous with "technical literature" in a broad sense (cf. Fögen ch. 17 in this volume), encompassing all fields of science and erudition – summaries and compilations can be singled out as the most derivative text types. Their main and defining function is to preserve information that has already been written down and stored in other, earlier texts. While much ancient technical writing and thought is in some way based on or responds to previous works in the discipline's tradition, no texts are more openly indebted to earlier works and less "original" in their own intellectual substance than summaries and compilations.

This relative lack of creativity and novelty, as if this was by all means a fault or weakness, has long kept these text types at the periphery of scholarship on ancient erudite or scientific writing. When compared to works that spring more directly from original intellectual inquiry and labor (Asper 2007; also Göpferich 1995 and Asper, ch. 26 in this volume), summaries and compilations may appear as less interesting because they contain little that is new. When viewed in connection with other writings that owe their existence to earlier texts, for instance, with commentaries or glossaries (Pfeiffer 1968), summaries and handbooks can seem less illustrious again. Whereas the former enable users to read revered older works in their original form, the latter brutally sacrifice primary texts' integrity in order to selectively repackage their content for easier and more convenient use. In the context of knowledge transmission in ancient Greek culture (Kullmann and Althoff 1993; Kullmann, Althoff, and Asper 1998), the fascinating transition from orality to textuality and the subsequent emergence of richly differentiated genres of technical writing make summaries and compilations appear as negligible epiphenomena. Finally, studies of ways in which ancient technical writers assert their authorial voices (Taub 2009) tend to focus on antiquity's prominent intellectual authorities, while summarizers and compilers are left aside as if they had no voice of their own.

The criteria that marginalize summaries and compilations are of course not altogether unjustifiable. However, they miss the area where the true importance of summaries and compilations

A Companion to Greek Literature, First Edition. Edited by Martin Hose and David Schenker.
© 2016 John Wiley & Sons, Inc. Published 2020 by John Wiley & Sons, Inc.

lies: their communicative function. Only recently have these determinedly derivative text types begun to attract collective and systematic attention as literature of knowledge worth studying in its own right (Horster and Reitz 2010). Continuing this line of inquiry, the present contribution will squarely focus on summaries and compilations, attempting to bring out the vital communicative role that these still under-investigated text types play within the larger field of knowledge literature.

2. Summaries

For essentials about summaries of ancient technical writings, the rich survey by Ilona Opelt (1962) is still valuable. The most common Greek term for a "summary" of a technical primary text is *epitomé*, derived from the verb *epitemnein*, "to cut back" (for summaries of poetic and/ or literary texts, usually called *hypotheseis*, see Rossum-Steenbeek 1998 and Horster and Reitz 2010, 247–392). As part of a title, the word *epitomé* is richly attested from the fourth century BCE through late antiquity and beyond. It denotes a self-standing, drastically shortened version of a primary text in any intellectual discipline. As with most genres of ancient technical writing, however, the classificatory terminology is not always clear-cut and consistent. Other expressions are also occasionally used in titles of summaries, such as *Ta ex …* ("Material taken from …"), *synopsis* ("overview"), *epidromé* ("fast approach," "attack"), *eklogai* ("selections"), *encheiridion* ("handbooklet"), *anakephalaiôsis* ("summary of main points"); in addition (see the preface of Galen's *Synopsis De Pulsibus*), *hypographé* ("sketch") and *hypotypôsis* ("outline").

Opelt's summary documents the ubiquitous use of epitomes in antiquity across centuries and disciplines. Listed are more than 120 attested summaries (Opelt 1962, 946–58) in the fields of historiography, philosophy, zoology, grammar, rhetoric, geography, medicine, law, mythography, antiquarian studies, the art of warfare, architecture, agriculture, paroemiography, and poetry (for summaries by Christian writers see Opelt 1962, 963–6). An overview of surviving ancient Greek epitomes based largely on Opelt's survey with updated (necessarily selective) references, may at this point best serve further research.

History
Anonymous, fragmentary epitome of *Philippika* of Theopompus (P. Ryl. 490) (Gigante 1946).
Anonymous, fragmentary epitome (so-called *Heidelberger Epitome*) of a history of the diadochs (Bauer 1914).
Anonymous, *2 Maccabees*: abridgment of a historiographical work by Jason of Cyrene (Schwartz 2008).

Philosophy
Three self-summaries by Epicurus (Arrighetti 1973): *Letter to Herodotus*: intended as an epitome (35; 83) of Epicurus's work *On Nature* (38 books); *Letter to Pythocles*: intended as an epitome (84; also 116) of Epicurus's teachings on celestial phenomena; *Letter to Menoeceus*: characterized by Diogenes Laertius (28–9) as an epitome of Epicurean ethics.
Diogenes Laertius (third century CE): cites the three mentioned Epicurean letters as an epitome of Epicurus's entire philosophy (Diog. Laer. 10.28–9).
Diogenes of Oenoanda (second century CE), fragmentary *Ethical Epitome* and fragmentary *Epitome on Nature*: summaries of Epicurean ethics and physics (Smith 1993).
Heraclides of Lembus (second century BCE), fragmentary epitomes of a biography of Satyrus, Sotion's *Diadochai*, Hermippus's *On Legislators*, *On the Seven Wise Men*, and *On Pythagoras*, and excerpts from Aristotle's *Politeiai* and *Nomima barbarika* (references in Runia 2002).
Ps.-Plutarch, *Epitome of <Plutarch's> "Comparison between Aristophanes and Menander"* (Di Florio 2008).

Ps.-Plutarch, *Epitome of <Plutarch's> "On the Creation of the Soul in <Plato's> Timaeus"* (Cherniss 1974, 347–65; primary text in Cherniss 1974, 133–345).

Arrian (first/second century CE), *Encheiridion*: a self-summary of his own *Diatribes* (four books), a written account of Epictetus's oral teachings (Boter 2007; on the primary text see Wehner 2000).

Arius Didymus, *Epitome of Stoic Ethics* (Pomeroy 1999).

Grammar

Hephaestion (second century CE), *Encheiridion*: an abridgment of his own 48-book treatise *On Meters*, reached in three successive stages of epitomization of eleven books, three books, and one book (Ophuijsen 1987; Urrea Méndez 2003).

Several epitomes of Aelius Herodianus's (second century CE) *Katholike prosodia* (references in Dickey 2007, 75–6 and 81–2): Ps.-Arcadius of Antioch, *Epitome of [Herodian's] Katholike prosodia*; Ioannes Philoponus of Alexandria (sixth century CE), *Tonika parangelmata*: the surviving text is probably itself an epitome of Philoponus's text; a palimpsest containing parts of books 5–7 of the *Katholike prosodia*; Papyrus *P.Ant.* ii. 67 (fourth century CE) containing a part of book 5 of the *Katholike prosodia*.

Geography

Two works by Marcianus of Heracleia (fourth or fifth century CE): *Epitome of the Periplus of the Inner Sea that Menippus of Pergamon Wrote in Three Books* (Müller 1855a); fragmentary *Epitome of the Eleven Books of Artemidorus of Ephesus's Geography* (Müller 1855b).

Medicine

Galen (second century CE), *Synopsis of his own Treatise "On Pulses"* (Kühn 1825; primary text in 16 books in Kühn 1824/25).

Two self-summaries by Oribasius (fourth century CE) of his *Medical Collections* (originally in 70 books, cf. below "Compilations"): *Synopsis for his Son Eustathius* (nine books) (Raeder 1926); *For Enapius* (four books) (Raeder 1926).

Paroemiography

Zenobius (second century CE), *Epitome of <Lucillus> Tarrhaeus's and Didymus's Proverbs Assembled Alphabetically* (Bühler 1982–1999; Benaissa 2009).

Zoology

Aristophanes of Byzantium (256–180 BCE), epitome of Aristotle's *On Animals*: preserved in excerpts in a florilegium by Emperor Constantine VII Porphyrogenitus (tenth century) (Lambros 1885; cf. Hellmann 2010).

A history of the Greek epitome has yet to be written. It would be a worthwhile but also challenging undertaking. First, epitomes are omnipresent in the field of literature of knowledge. They emerge powerfully in the early Hellenistic age (Opelt 1962, 947, 950, 952; Hellmann 2010, 556), as soon as technical writing has established itself as a prominent field of Greek intellectual and literary culture, and they are used in every later century throughout antiquity, with peaks in the fourth and third centuries BCE (early and middle Hellenism), the second century CE (high Empire), and the fourth century CE (Late Antiquity's "renaissance"). Second, the history of the epitome is complicated by the fact that, due to its derivative nature, this genre does not evolve autonomously. Instead, the production and use of summaries are closely tied to developments in their particular disciplines at any given time.

For instance, authors that have abbreviated their own works (Galdi 1922, 257–71; Opelt 1962, 957) form a group that is impressive both in number and in intellectual rank: the historiographers Philochorus of Athens (fourth/third century BCE, the last and most important atthidographer), Dionysius of Halicarnassus (time of Augustus), and Phlegon of Tralles (second century CE, freedman of Hadrian, author of antiquarian, geographical, and paradoxographical works); the philosophers Theophrastus (fourth/third century BCE), Epicurus (fourth/third century BCE), and Chrysippus (third century BCE, developer of the Stoic orthodox philosophical system); the grammarian Hephaestion of Alexandria (second century CE), the geographers Agatharchides of Cnidus (second century BCE) and Timosthenes of Rhodes (third century BCE, works include an influential *Periplus of Egypt, Asia, Europe, and Libya*); the medical writers Galen (second century CE) and Oribasius (fourth century CE); in addition, Varro (first century BCE) and Lactantius (third/fourth century CE) in Latin.

Thus we see self-epitomizers being active in different disciplines and at different times. The situations and contexts, however, in which they write are remarkably similar. Far from representing disciplines in intellectual decline, these authors are prolific writers who shaped their fields during formative periods of high intellectual and literary productivity and, consequently, high competitiveness. In such an environment, asserting one's voice and competence against rivals and critics was necessary in order to gain and maintain a large following as well as authoritative status (Lloyd 1996). This gives self-epitomes a special strategic purpose which has thus far not received sufficient scholarly attention. More patterns governing the practice of writing summaries can surely be discovered when these texts are studied in close connection with the communicative contexts in which they emerge.

As a highly pragmatic text type, epitomes are motivated and shaped by the purpose they are intended to serve for a specific readership in a specific situation. Their principal function, however, is to reduce the primary material's quantity and, oftentimes, also its complexity. Textual consumption is thus made easier while primary information is preserved to the extent determined by the epitomizer. Surviving prefaces of ancient summaries often provide more insight into their writers' reasons for doing what they are doing and occasionally even general reflections on the practice of epitomization (Opelt 1962, 959–60; Dubischar 2010, 46–50). Typically, epitomizers begin by establishing their primary text's authority on the grounds of its author's competence, the primary text's usefulness, or the treated topic's importance. They then describe why, in their opinion, the adequate reception of the primary material in its original form is, or has become, difficult or impossible: the problems are usually attributed to certain qualities or shortcomings of the primary texts themselves or to habits or dispositions of the (potential) readers. Epitomizers regularly conclude their proems by announcing that the summary at hand is their response to the outlined unsatisfactory situation. A wealth of information about ancient literary and textual practices, which is sometimes overlooked, is contained in these prefaces.

The pragmatism of epitomes also manifests itself in other aspects of the genre's profile: its methods, forms, and the repetitiveness of its process. In addition to case studies of individual texts (e.g., Delattre and Delattre 2009; Smith 1993; several contributions in Horster and Reitz 2010), comparative analyses that cast their nets wider (e.g., Kullmann 1999; Schepens and Schorn 2010; van der Eijk 2010; Hellmann 2010) are very rewarding.

The methods of epitomization are best analyzed when an epitome can still be compared with its primary source (Opelt 1962, 960). The cited studies show that there are no two instances in which the epitomizers follow exactly the same method: different primary texts present different problems, and not all audiences have the same communicative needs. However, the fundamental obstacle to communication that motivates epitomization is the primary material's length. Therefore, a number of similarities in the ways most texts are summarized can be identified (Opelt 1962, 960–62). Epitomes of single primary texts typically reduce their primary material's length by 50 to 90 percent. Reminiscent of cut-and-paste practices in today's electronic text editing, ancient epitomes largely consist of excerpts that have been reworked or edited by the epitomizer (Opelt 1962, 960) so as to form a new coherent whole that meets the intended audience's new communicative needs; occasionally, the excerpted material may for this reason even be rearranged, as in the fascinating case of Aristophanes of Byzantium's epitome of Aristotle's *Historia animalium* and *De partibus animalium* (Kullmann 1999, 186–90; Hellmann 2010, 559–70).

An epitomizer's main task is thus selection as to which passages to retain and which not. In this process, information has primacy over form (as, analogously, plot does in *hypotheseis* of literary texts). Epitomizers are likely to "cut" what in their opinion does not belong to the informational core of the primary text. Elements that are easily lost in this way are elaborate introductions, transitions, digressions, explanations, discussions, and, in historiographical texts, speeches. Obviously, many elements that the primary author once saw as integral to his text are thus discarded. This reflects the epitomizer's firm control over the primary text, which can lead to various kinds of tensions between summaries and their source texts (Opelt 1962, 961–2; Mülke 2008, 95–108; Mülke 2010). The proems by Epicurus (*Letter to Herodotus, Letter to Pythocles*), Galen (*Synopsis of "On Pulses"*), and Oribasius (*Synopsis for Eustathius*) – also, in Latin, by Lactantius (*Epitome divinarum institutionum*) – show that the self-epitomizers understandably are most aware of such tensions, and hence most thoughtful about the practice of epitomization. On the other side of the spectrum are careless or incompetent summarizers who fail even to understand the primary text subjected to their treatment (Ps.-Plutarch, *Epitome of <Plutarch's> "On the Creation of the Soul in <Plato's> Timaeus"*; see also Galen's preface to his *Synopsis of "On Pulses"* on circulating flawed epitomes of his works.)

In addition to methodological pluralism, there are also variations in the forms of epitomization. Sometimes not just one primary text but rather a corpus of texts or, yet more abstractly, a body of knowledge is summarized. The latter generates what has been aptly called an "*epitoma rei tractatae*" ("epitome of a treated subject"; Bott 1920). This type of summary is attested early by the *Epitomē tōn Syngeneiōn* by Andron of Halicarnassus (fourth century BCE) and the *Epitomē mythikē* by Phylarchus of Athens or Naucratis (third century BCE) (Opelt 1962, 955 and 947). On the whole, however, these subject summaries are relatively rare among attested Greek epitomes; they become more common among late-Antique Latin texts and among summaries by Christian writers (Opelt 1962, 953–66). This shift suggests that over time knowledge becomes increasingly objectified and separated from the authoritative figures of the past to whose seminal texts the knowledge ultimately goes back (cf. also Eigler 1999, 286 on "material without authorities" ["*Stoff ohne Herren*"] and "authorities without material" ["*Herren ohne Stoff*"] in formations and conceptualizations of popular philosophical knowledge in late antiquity).

Other formal variations concern the resulting text. The Epicurean tradition especially has brought forth a number of special types. Apparently, the school's quasi-missionary impetus and the nature of Epicurean teachings fostered formal inventiveness. Epicurus's Letters to Herodotus, to Pythocles, and to Menoeceus are epistolary (self-)epitomes, each devoted to a different topic. Later, Diogenes Laertius even regards the three letters as a triad in which the totality of Epicurean philosophy is "epitomized" (Diog. Laer. 10.28). Finally, the Epicurean Inscription is a massive epigraphical composite summary (originally approx. 30,000 words). It consists of purposefully arranged excerpts from different writings of the master, which the aged Diogenes of Oenoanda (second century CE) had inscribed on a stoa wall in his city as a permanently and publicly visible "entire handbook of Epicureanism" (Gordon 1996, 2).

In addition, some summaries, abridging primary texts of monumental sizes, stand out because they are exceptionally long themselves, comprising ten or more books. Attested examples (Opelt 1962, 947–56) are Theophrastus's (or a student's) epitome in ten books of his (or the teacher's) *Nomoi* (24 books), Hephaestion's epitome in 11 books of his *Encheiridion* (48 books), Oribasius's *Synopsis for Eustathius* in nine books of his *Medical Collections* (70 books; see below). Oribasius's *Galen-Epitome*, a summary requested by Emperor Julian of nothing less than Galen's medical writings is lost except for its proem (Photios *Bibl.* cod. 173–4), but must have been such a grand work that its organization of the material could later conveniently serve as the model for the *Medical Collections*. It is no coincidence that Hephaestion's big epitome and Oribasius's *Synopsis for Eustathius* are self-summaries; if Theophrastus is the author of the epitome of his *Nomoi*, it, too, would be a self-epitome. Latin summaries confirm the pattern. Among the three large-scale epitomes written in Latin (Opelt 1962, nos. 71, 85, and 111), two by Varro, a prolific writer and polymath, are also self-epitomes. This too shows that self-epitomizers are influential and productive figures to whom securing a wide readership matters greatly.

Since epitomization essentially means quantitative text reduction, it can be repeated on different levels. Some primary texts are epitomized by different writers, such as Plato's *Republic* by Aristotle and possibly Theophrastus; Aristotle's *Historia animalium*, epitomized by Theophrastus and Aristophanes of Byzantium, or Philochorus's *Atthis*, epitomized by Philochorus himself (fourth century BCE) as well as by Asinius Pollio Trallianus (first century BCE). In other instances, one epitomizer abridges several primary texts, as is attested in historiography for Pamphila (first century CE), in philosophy for Epicurus, Chrysippus (third century BCE), and Heraclides Lembus (second century BCE), in grammar for Iulius Vestinus (second century CE), in geography for Agatharchides of Cnidus (second century BCE), Timosthenes of Rhodes (third century BCE), and Marcianus of Heraclea (fourth or fifth century CE), and in medicine for Galen and Oribasius. Occasionally, even (self-)epitomes are further (self-)epitomized: Hephaestion shortened his metrical *opus magnum* of 48 books first to 11, then to three books, and finally down to one book (Opelt 1962, 953; Ophuijsen 1987, 5–6). In a similar fashion, Galen and Oribasius each produced two short versions of a long work written by themselves. Oribasius abridged the monumental *Medical Collections* (see below) in the *Synopsis for Eustathius* (nine books) and in *For Eunapius* (four books). Although the latter is not declared to be an epitome of the former, or an epitome at all for that matter, the relationship between these two short versions is similar to that of successive auto-epitomization (De Lucia 1999, 475–6). Galen, on the other hand, processed his 16-book work *On Pulses* not only in the already mentioned *Synopsis of "On Pulses"* but also in the isagogic work *On Pulses for Beginners* (Asper 2007, 309–10). These repetitions underscore the pragmatism behind epitomization. Different times, and even different audiences at the same time, require or desire short versions that are tailored to their own particular needs. Galen (preface to *Synopsis of "On Pulses"*) consequently formulates the ideal that every reader should produce his own epitomes, which will then be perfectly suited to his individual abilities and needs; Opelt confirms the existence of such "personal" epitomes (1962, no. 16 and no. 22).

3.   Compilations

Large compilations are the second derivative text type to be discussed in this chapter. While massive compilatory handbooks of various kinds are most characteristic of Byzantine erudition, typological precursors appear in the late Hellenistic and early Imperial periods as well as in late Antiquity. Fewer large derivative compilations, however, are attested or preserved than summaries, not least because abridgments are more easily produced, used, and proliferated than long and thematically wide-ranging derivative compilations. Since they have also been studied less by scholars as a distinct type of ancient knowledge literature, the following observations attempt no more than to stake out the field for much-needed further research.

While summaries preserve knowledge by reducing text quantity, large derivative compilations do the opposite, they lead to textual expansion. They bring together, in a new and extensive text that has to be transparently structured, ample material representing large intellectual fields or entire disciplines. This material was previously dispersed among different primary sources that were shorter, more specialized and, in addition, perhaps not easily available or even unknown to potential readers. The Greek term most frequently used for compilatory works of any kind (see below) is *synagōgē* or, in the plural, *synagōgai*, derived from the verb *synagein* ("to bring together"); *syllogē/-ai* ("collection/-s,") also occurs in a similar sense. In addition, some compilations, one of which will be discussed below, are titled *Bibliothēkē* ("*Library*"), and not infrequently a simple noun in the plural suffices as a title that indicates a compilation's contents (examples below). The term "encyclopedia" also suggests itself in English for some cases, but does not directly reflect ancient terminological usage (Doody 2010, 42–58).

Compilatory writings are typologically even less clearly delineated than epitomes. In fact, quite a few *synagōgai* are not of the long and derivative type that, alone, interests us here. Several compilatory works of the Peripatetic tradition and its continuation in Alexandria gather information from the empirical world around them, such as Aristotle's *Politeiai* ("*Constitutions*"), Callimachus's *Ethnikai onomasiai* (*Local nomenclature*), and many others. These texts, however, do not process other, pre-existing texts of knowledge. They are instead original intellectual contributions that open up and establish new fields of learned inquiry (see also Asper 2007, 57–93). Other compilatory texts do draw their contents from already circulating texts of knowledge, but do so in the pursuit of new and more specialized interests. Paradoxographical writings, for instance, process historiographical, geographical, or ethnographical texts of knowledge; in this sense, they are derivative (Schepens and Delcroix 1996; Pajón Leyra 2011). However, with their exclusive focus on curiosities and *adunata* they break away from their primary texts' purposes and make paradoxography a distinct and autonomous field of (popularized) knowledge. A final delineatory complication is that it is sometimes difficult to distinguish between a compilation and a summary. Compilers, too, have to select from their primary material before they can actually go about compiling it (De Lucia 1999, 475). On the other hand, some summaries, especially the *epitomae rei tractatae*, also cover broad thematic ranges. The difference between the two genres is thus gradual rather than categorical, coming down to a question of the ratio of selected vs. discarded primary material as well as the ratio of the derivative vs. the primary material's quantity.

Despite these typological difficulties, it is helpful to point to some texts that are in fact long and thoroughly derivative compilations. They may be regarded as manifestations of a functionally distinct type of literature of knowledge: Didymus Chalcenterus (first century BCE), many composite commentaries; Diodorus Siculus (first century BCE), *Bibliothēkē* (40 books); Pamphilus (first century CE), *On Glosses and Nouns* (95 books); Oribasius (fourth century CE) *Medical Collections* (70 books).

The Alexandrian scholar Didymus Chalcenterus (first century BCE) lived at a pivotal time, when intellectual productivity in scholarship and science was shifting from Alexandria to Rome, a newly-emerging and very different center of learning (Pfeiffer 1968, 265–79; Pöhlmann 1994, 46–68). Didymus's scholarly writings apparently amounted to some 3,500 or 4,000 books. Of particular interest here are his many commentaries on more than 20 "classical" Greek authors, mostly poets but also prose writers. Essentially derivative and compilatory (Braswell 2011, 197; *pace* Harding 2006, 31–9), these "composite commentaries" (Dickey 2007, 7 *et passim*) largely consisted of material excerpted and compiled from the philological works by the great Aristarchus and his predecessors back to Philitas and Zenodotus, all representatives of the most formative and productive period of Alexandrian philology. Later times took Didymus's output to be so useful and authoritative that some of it has survived through scholia transmission, most famously in the Codex Venetus Ilias A. In addition, a second-century papyrus contains, perhaps in epitomized form, parts of Didymus's commentary to Demosthenes' *Philippika* (Gibson 2002; Harding 2006). This late Alexandrian's ancient nicknames, *Chalcenterus* ("Brazen-guts") and *bibliolathas* ("Book-forgetter"), reverentially poke fun at his industriousness but are not directed against the derivative and "epigonal" nature of his work. It is as a preserver that Didymus has remained a central figure in the history of ancient philology (see Dickey 2007, 342 *s.v.* "Didymus").

Diodorus Siculus (also first century BCE) produced a universal history in 40 books, appropriately titled *Bibliothêkê* ("*Library*"; cf. Pliny, *Nat. Hist.* praef. 24–5). Of the three famous Greek works carrying this title, the *Bibliothêkê* of Diodorus is the most thoroughly derivative. Not only does it process earlier historiographical texts but it also is a historiographical text itself. The *Bibliothêkê*-works, however, of Ps.-Apollodorus and Photius (ninth century) do not have the same genre consistency and are therefore better discussed in other contexts (cf. Rossum-Steenbeek 1998, 25–32, 108–11, and 164–9; Schamp 2010).

Diodorus himself describes the situation that motivated him to write this massive work. Most historiographers, he states, have produced historical monographs on "isolated wars waged by an individual nation or an individual state" (1.3.2), that is, on specialized topics. The few authors that had attempted to write universal histories, from the beginning of times down to their own day, were not successful in Didymus's opinion because of historical inaccuracies and systematic omissions (e.g., of barbarian peoples, early mythological accounts, and events later than the Macedonian period; 1.3.2–3). Thus, the situation is bad for readers interested in a universal history as "both the dates of events and the events themselves lie about scattered in many treatises and diverse authors" (1.3.4; similarly 1.3.8).

Diodorus responds by laboriously composing the *Bibliothêkê*, the work of 30 years (1.4.1). As the title announces, this mega-text is intended to serve as a convenient equivalent to an entire historiographical library. Diodorus strove for comprehensive coverage (1.3.6 and elsewhere) while also following a narrative main thread along which the reported events are organized (1.3.8; Sulimani 2011, 23–4, also 109–62). Evidently, Diodorus felt no need to conceal the derivative and compilatory nature of his work, and the *Bibliothêkê* has in fact been characterized and even criticized as a long string of compiled excerpts and paraphrases rather than a literary work in its own right (Schwartz 1905, 663; but see Sulimani 2011, 3–6). However, that Diodorus responded to a real need among the educated population in the ever-growing Roman Empire for general historical information and orientation is underscored by the fact that shortly later Nicolaus of Damascus, Pompeius Trogus, and Strabo embarked on similar universalist projects (Sulimani 2011, 52–3). Like Didymus's writings, the *Bibliothêkê* was too long to survive intact; only books 1–5 and 11–20 have been directly transmitted. However, the work was regarded as important, in less discerning Christian times at any rate, so that parts of it have also been transmitted as excerpts and summaries (Constantinian Excerpts, *Excerpta Hoescheliana*, and in Photius). Even scholars today who are unimpressed by Diodorus's own intellectual achievements praise him for consistently having chosen first-rate primary authors (Stylianou 1998, 2; cf. Sulimani 2011, 57–108), and are fond of books 11–20, our only surviving continuous account of the years 480 to 302 BCE.

In the early Imperial period (first century CE), the Alexandrian grammarian Pamphilus composed a monumental lexicographical compilation, *On Glosses and Nouns*, consisting of no less than 95 books (Wendel 1949, 337–42). It compiled material from a great number of earlier lexicographical works (by Aristophanes of Byzantium, Theodorus, Apion, Apollodorus of Cyrene, Artemidorus, Didymus Chalcenterus, Diodorus, Heracleon, Iatrocles, and Timachidas of Rhodes). To the onomastic material (i.e., common nouns stemming from theme-specific dictionaries of the *Onomastikon*-type), Pamphilus added glosses (*glôssai*, i.e., rare, special, or difficult words) found in glossographical works (Wendel 1949, 338–9). In each thematic section, Pamphilus conveniently arranged the material alphabetically. Thus uniting the disparate results of earlier, more specialized lexicographical scholarship, the resulting text covered in an almost encyclopedic fashion a wide range of themes related to nature and human life (Degani 1995, 514–15).

Because of its rich content, large thematic scope, and convenient organization, Pamphilus's *On Glosses and Nouns* subsequently became an authoritative text itself (Matthaios 2010, 175–6). Athenaeus frequently uses it; in addition, Iulius Vestinus (second century CE) reduced it in an epitome of perhaps 30 books (*Hellenika onomata*), which was then further abridged and rearranged by Diogenianus of Heracleia (second century CE) in his five-book *Pantodapê lexis*, which served as a source for Hesychius's lexicon (fifth or sixth century; Dickey 2007, 88–90). Thus, the reason why Pamphilus's mega-lexicon itself eventually became obsolete and was hence lost, is not that it was "only" a derivative compilation but rather that, because it was a valuable and authoritative text, it was soon made available in shorter versions.

Oribasius's *Medical Collections* (fourth century BCE) will serve as the final example of an ancient compilation that is derivative in nature, comprehensive in scope, and massive in its dimensions. After Emperor Julian had approved of the *Galen-Epitome*, for which he had earlier asked his learned court physician, he requested that Oribasius undertake an even larger project (4.6–12): to search for (*anazêtein*) and compile (*synagein*) the most important writings of "all the best physicians" in a useful and easily consultable compilation (*synagôgê*). Oribasius obediently produced what in effect is a "medical encyclopedia" (van der Eijk 2010) originally consisting of 70 books, of which slightly more than a third are still preserved (books 1–15, 24–5, 43–50). As Oribasius explains in the preface, the material's organization in the *Medical Collections* follows that of the *Galen-Epitome*, and Galen continues to be a central source author in this new work as well. All in all, however, the *Medical Collections* contains excerpts from over a dozen additional authors that represent the discipline's long and impressive history (De Lucia 1999, 484–5). The books of this mega-compilation are transparently divided into chapters whose headers state the topic and, when a new source is used, the author and the title of the cited primary work.

Meeting the request of a culturally ambitious emperor, Oribasius has no need to apologize for delivering "only" a derivative work. Instead he emphasizes in his preface the quality of the compiled primary authors as well as the intended practical benefits of the *Medical Collections*. Centuries later, Photius, also far from criticizing Oribasius for being unoriginal, praises this monumental work as one of the single most useful works on medical theory and practice because of its size and scope, its methodological conscientiousness, and the quality of the selected primary authors (*Bibl.* 174a12–27). The lasting value of the *Medical Collections* is further documented by the fact that Oribasius himself summarized it twice (*Synopsis for Eustathius* and *For Eunapius*, see above); that both these summaries have survived; that 25 books of the *Medical Collections* have also been directly transmitted; and that these extant books today are an invaluable source of information about the history of medicine and about intellectual culture in late antiquity.

The similarities between these four large derivative compilations, written at different times and in different disciplines, are noteworthy. The mentioned compilers were active in times in which powerful (sophisticated, specialized, autonomous, and literarily productive) intellectual traditions had reached stages that for internal and external reasons had become ripe for comprehensive syntheses on a grand scale. Their writers were specialists who knew their fields: Didymus, Pamphilus, and Oribasius were protagonists in truly professionalized "disciplines" (cf. Stichweh 1994, 17, also 52–5). Finally, the great erudite and scientific ambition and effort that manifest themselves in these monumental works is, paradoxically, also responsible for their partial or complete loss in their original form. They were too long, and their contents were too rich for users in later centuries (see below). The texts did, however, partly survive in shorter form as excerpts, summaries, and fragments, attesting to the value continually recognized in them.

4.   The Communicative Function of Summaries and Compilations

It has now become clear that summaries and large derivative compilations are text types that play an important role within literature of knowledge. They were widely used, are attested in large numbers, and respectably preserved through direct or indirect transmission. Our present knowledge of the histories of many ancient intellectual disciplines owes much to these derivative texts. This success, which is remarkably at odds with the limited esteem sometimes granted to summaries and compilations, calls for an explanation. A brief look at system dynamics that shape developments in intellectual disciplines and in literary fields in general will therefore conclude this contribution.

Intellectual disciplines and literary fields can be viewed as "systems," more precisely, as "social systems" that are constituted by communication (Luhmann 1984/1995). These systems only exist when and where there is communication; they grow or shrink with increases or decreases in communication; they disappear when communication ceases to take place. Communication, however, is never inherently stable or guaranteed. Consequently, the most fundamental purpose (*Sinn*) of any communicative system is continually to generate new communication, more precisely, connecting communication (*Anschlusskommunikation*) that will keep the system operating and "going" (Gätje 2008). Well-functioning systems therefore encourage and favor operations (i.e., communicative contributions) that make future connecting communication likely. Contributions that fail to do so run the risk of becoming communicative dead-ends because they do not help the system prolong and extend its "existence" (through continued communication).

This basic operating principle of "social systems" explains the vital importance of summaries and compilations. Two system dynamics are particularly relevant here. The first concerns trends that can be observed in many intellectual disciplines (fuller treatment in Stichweh 1994, 15–51). "Disciplines" form around particular objects of interest, more precisely, around particular "discipline-constituting" questions that these objects raise (*disziplinkonstituierende Fragestellungen*). However, the reservoir of questions that can reasonably be asked so as to elicit sufficient connecting communication is finite. Consequently, communication that makes up a discipline, and over time the discipline's history, tends to follow a typical if not unavoidable trajectory. Its stages include a transition from periods of high innovation frequency (*Innovationshäufigkeit*) and increased internal differentiation and specialization to a period of saturation (*Sättigungsphase*). At this point, a discipline's communicative demands shift. Continual innovation was earlier a reliable strategy for generating further connecting communication, but phases of saturation call more strongly for consolidation of knowledge. Processes of selection and summation now become critical if the continued operation and, thus, existence of the system is to be secured. Important results, texts, and authors must be identified and established as legitimate, valid, authoritative, perhaps even "canonical" or "classical" sources of knowledge. It is this task that gives the two most clearly derivative text types, summaries and compilations, their greatest importance. For selection, summation, and thus, in the long run, preservation of previously textualized knowledge is what these text types do more effectively than any other.

The second important communicative dynamic concerns literary fields, that is, fields of text-based communication in general. Paradoxically, the communicative strength of writing and texts, their ability to transcend the spatial and temporal boundaries of oral communication through textual permanence, also creates considerable communicative problems (cf. Dubischar 2010, 53–6). Well-developed literary fields, in fact, consist of an unmanageable multitude of mostly de-contextualized and only imperfectly re-contextualizeable texts, which readers, always inclined to engage with what they find meaningful, relevant, and worthwhile, have no obligation to read, pick up, or even to take notice of. The literary space is a mostly unfriendly environment for texts, which constantly compete with other texts to be selected by recipients.

This problem seems to be especially grave in the field of literature of knowledge. The evidence suggests that the "best" and "most valuable" (the most complex, long, profound, rich, specialized, carefully argued, and demanding) texts, while initially powerful and seminal because of these very qualities, are over time at a selection disadvantage. Only few comprehensive and systematized *pragmateiai*, the grand genre of ancient technical writing, have survived (Asper 2007, 323–67; also Fuhrmann 1960). Almost all of Epicurus's immense literary output is lost (but we have his three self-summaries and the *Principal Doctrines*). The original writings of the Alexandrian philologists from Zenodotus to Aristarchus have not come down to us (but we have scholia). Many more examples could be added. These "great" and foundational texts were able to emerge as effective communicative contributions only in especially favorable contexts that provided excellent conditions for both literary production (training and working conditions) and reception (adequately pre-dispositioned audience).

When transferred, however, to a new reception context with a less receptive readership (whether at the same or at a later time), these very texts quickly become ineffective at eliciting sufficient connecting communication. In this situation, summaries and compilations emerge to serve as the system's self-help. They are the textual response to the system's own textual problems (Dubischar 2010, 56–63). Summaries and compilations increase the likelihood for primary texts or their contents, as far as possible, to retain or regain readers even under new conditions. In addition, the derivative text types discussed here always reduce the primary material's intellectual or logistical complexity. Therefore, because they are less complex themselves, the new texts can more easily be recontextualized again, should the reception contexts further change – as they inevitably will at some point. It is therefore helpful for a fuller understanding of the function of summaries and compilations to ask not only why groups sometimes prefer to engage with derivative secondary works – as if that were an exception – but also to investigate when, how long, and under which conditions great, seminal, and foundational primary texts are actually able to dominate their field of discourse in their original form.

Both considerations lead to the same conclusion. Epitomization and compilation are vitally important intellectual and literary activities. They play crucial roles in all areas and strata of erudition and science – whether it be within a school, a discipline, or a society at large. The production of derivative texts is not a deplorable mishap in the ongoing cultivation of knowledge in antiquity (or of any other time). Instead, it follows the communicative system's most fundamental purpose and its internal pull to keep operating in a way that will allow further connecting communication to take place. This makes epitomizers and compilers agents of "system rationality" (*Systemrationalität*; cf. Gansel 2011, 49–51 and 86–94). They do what makes sense at a given time for the communicative system in which they operate. In the functionally differentiated realm of erudite and scientific writing, it is largely these derivative writers who bear the load of knowledge transmission, recontextualization, and preservation. Without their works, any group's *Wissenshaushalt* (the "household" of circulating or at least available knowledge) would be much poorer.

REFERENCES

Asper, M. 2007. *Griechische Wissenschaftstexte: Formen, Funktionen, Differenzierungsgeschichten*. Stuttgart.

Assmann, J. 1992/2011. *Cultural Memory and Early Civilization: Writing, Remembrance, and Political Imagination*. Cambridge (first edn. 1992).

Arrighetti, G. 1973. *Epicuro Opere:* Introduzione, testo critico, traduzione e note. 2nd edn. Turin.

Bauer, A. G. 1914. *Die Heidelberger Epitome: Eine Quelle zur Diadochengeschichte*. Leipzig.

Benaissa, A. 2009. "P.Oxy. 4942: Zenobius, Epitome of Didymus and Lucillus of Tarrhae, Book I 29 4B.48/B(2–4)b." *The Oxyrhynchus Papyri* 73: 71–80.

Blair, A. M. 2010. *Too Much to Know: Managing Scholarly Information Before the Modern Age*. New Haven, CT.

Boter, G., ed. 2007. *Epictetus: Encheiridion*. Berlin.

Bott, G. 1920. *De epitomis antiquis*. Marburg.

Bourdieu, P. 1979/1984. *Distinction: A Social Critique of the Judgment of Taste*. Cambridge, MA (1st edn. 1979).

Braswell, B. K. 2011. "Didymus on Pindar." In S. Matthaios, F. Montanari, and A. Rengakos, eds., *Ancient Scholarship and Grammar*, Berlin, 181–97.

Bühler, W., ed. 1982–1999. *Zenobii Athoi proverbia*. Vols. 1, 4, and 5. Göttingen.

Cherniss, H. F., ed. and transl. 1974. *Plutarch's Moralia*. Vol. 13.1. Cambridge MA.

De Lucia, R. 1999. "Doxographical Hints in Oribasius' Collectiones Medicae." In P. J. van der Eijk, ed., *Ancient Histories of Medicine: Essays in Medical Doxography and Historiography in Classical Antiquity*, Leiden, 473–89.

Degani, E. 1995. "La lessicografia." In G. Cambiano, L. Canfora, and D. Lanza, eds., *Lo spazio letterario della Grecia antica, vol. 2: La ricezione e l'attualizzatione del testo*, Rome, 505–27.

Delattre, D. and J. Delattre. 2009. "Sens et puissance de l'abrégé dans l'enseignement d'Épircure." In F. Toulze-Morisset, ed., *Formes de l'écriture, figures de la pensée dans la culture gréco-romaine*, Villeneuve-d'Ascq, 349–82.

Dickey, E. 2007. *Ancient Greek Scholarship: A Guide to Finding, Reading, and Understanding Scholia, Commentaries, Lexica, and Grammatical Treatises, from their Beginnings to the Byzantine Period*. Oxford.

Doody, A. 2010. *Pliny's Encyclopedia: The Reception of the Natural History*. Cambridge.

Dubischar, M. 2010. "Survival of the Most Condensed? Auxiliary Texts, Communications Theory, and Condensation of Knowledge." In M. Horster and C. Reitz, eds., *Condensing Texts, Condensed Texts*, Stuttgart, 39–67.

Eigler, U. 1999. "Strukturen und Voraussetzungen zum Erhalt von philosophischem Wissen in der Spätantike." In T. Fuhrer and M. Erler, eds., *Zur Rezeption der hellenistischen Philosophie in der Spätantike*, Stuttgart, 279–93.

Di Florio, M, ed. 2008. *Plutarco. Il confronto tra Aristofane e Menandro (compendio): Introduzione, testo critico, traduzione e commento*. Naples.

Fuhrmann, M. 1960. *Das systematische Lehrbuch: Ein Beitrag zur Geschichte der Wissenschaften in der Antike*. Göttingen.

Galdi, M. 1922. *L'epitome nella letteratura latina*. Naples.

Gansel, C. 2011. *Textsortenlinguistik*. Stuttgart.

Gätje, O. 2008. "Die Anschlussfähigkeit sprachlicher Kommunikation in Semiosphären." In C. Gansel, ed., *Textsorten und Systemtheorie*, Göttingen, 203–16.

Gibson, C. A. 2002. *Interpreting a Classic: Demosthenes and his Ancient Commentators*. Berkeley, CA.

Gigante, M. 1946. "Frammenti di un'epitome di *Philippika* (P. Ryl. 490)." *La Parola del Passato* 1: 127–37.

Göpferich, S. 1995. *Textsorten in Naturwissenschaften und Technik: Pragmatische Typologie, Kontrastierung, Translation*. Tübingen.

Gordon, P. 1996. *Epicurus in Lycia: The Second-century World of Diogenes of Oenoanda*. Ann Arbor, MI.

Gurd, S. A. 2012. *Work in Progress: Literary Revision as Social Performance in Ancient Rome*. Oxford.

Harding, P. 2006. *Didymos on Demosthenes*. Oxford.

Hellmann, O. 2010. "Antike Verkürzungen biologischer Texte: Voraussetzungen und Formen." In M. Horster and C. Reitz, eds., *Condensing Texts, Condensed Texts*, Stuttgart, 555–83.

Horster, M. and C. Reitz, eds. 2010. *Condensing Texts, Condensed Texts*. Stuttgart.

Kühn, K. G., ed. 1824. "De pulsibus ad tirones." In *Galeni opera omnia*, vol. 8, 453–492. Leipzig.

Kühn, K. G., ed. 1824/5. "De differentia pulsuum /De causis pulsuum/De dignoscendis pulsibus/De praesagitatione ex pulsibus." In *Galeni opera omnia*, Leipzig, vol. 8, 493, vol. 9, 430.

Kühn, K. G., ed. 1825. "Synopsis librorum suorum sedecim de pulsibus." In *Galeni opera omnia*, vol. 9, 431–549. Leipzig.

Kullmann, W. and J. Althoff, eds. 1993. *Vermittlung und Tradierung von Wissen in der griechischen Kultur*. Tübingen.

Kullmann, W., J. Althoff, and M. Asper, eds. 1998. *Gattungen wissenschaftlicher Literatur in der Antike*. Tübingen.

Kullmann, W. 1999. "Zoologische Sammelwerke in der Antike." In G. Wöhrle, J. Althoff, and S. Amigues, eds., *Geschichte der Mathematik und der Naturwissenschaften in der Antike, Bd. 1: Biologie*, Stuttgart, 181–98.

Lambros, S. P., ed. 1885. *Excerptorum Constantini De natura animalium libri duo. Aristophanis historiae animalium epitome subiunctis Aeliani Timothei aliorumque eclogis*. Berlin.

Lloyd, G. E. R. 1996. *Adversaries and Authorities: Investigations into Ancient Greek and Chinese Science.* Cambridge.

Luhmann, N. 1984/1995. *Social Systems.* Stanford, CA (first in German 1984).

Luhmann, N. 1997/2012. *Theory of Society.* Vol. 1. Stanford, CA (first in German 1997).

Matthaios, S. 2010. "Lexikographen über die Schulter geschaut: Tradition und Traditionsbruch in der griechischen Lexikographie." In M. Horster and C. Reitz, eds., *Condensing Texts, Condensed Texts,* Stuttgart, 165–207.

Müller, K., ed. 1855a. *Marciani Heracleensis ex Ponto epitome peripli maris interni, quem tribus libris scripsit Menippus Pergamenus.* In *Geographi Graeci* Minores, Paris, vol. 1, 563–73.

Müller, K., ed. 1855b. *Marciani Heracleensis undecim Artemidori Ephesii geographiae librorum epitome.* In *Geographi Graeci* Minores, Paris, vol. 1, 574–6.

Mülke, M. 2008. *Der Autor und sein Text: die Verfälschung des Originals im Urteil antiker Autoren.* Berlin.

Mülke, M. 2010. "Die Epitome – das bessere Original?" In M. Horster and C. Reitz, eds., *Condensing Texts, Condensed Texts,* Stuttgart, 69–89.

Opelt, I. 1962. "Epitome." In *Reallexikon für Antike und Christentum* 5: 944–73.

Ophuijsen, J. M. van, ed. 1987. *Hephaestion on Metre: A Translation and Commentary.* Leiden.

Pajón Leyra, I. 2011. *Entre ciencia y maravilla: el género literario de la paradoxografía griega.* Zaragoza.

Pöhlmann, E. 1994. *Einführung in die Überlieferungsgeschichte und in die Textkritik der antiken Literatur, Band 1: Altertum.* Darmstadt.

Pfeiffer, R. 1968. *History of Classical Scholarship from the Beginnings to the End of the Hellenistic Age.* Oxford.

Pomeroy, A. J., ed. and transl. 1999. *Arius Didymus: Epitome of Stoic Ethics.* Atlanta, GA.

Raeder, J., ed. 1926. *Oribasii synopsis ad Eustathium filium* et *Oribasii libri ad Eunapium.* In *Corpus Medicorum Graecorum,* vol. 6.3, 1–313. Leipzig.

Raeder, J., ed. 1928–33. *Oribasii collectionum medicarum reliquiae.* In *Corpus Medicorum Graecorum,* vols. 6.1–2. Leipzig.

Rossum-Steenbeek, M. van. 1998. *Greek Readers' Digests? Studies on a Selection of Subliterary Papyri.* Leiden.

Runia, D. 2002. "Heraclides Lembus." In *Brill's New Pauly* 6: 171.

Schamp, J. "Photios Abréviateur." In M. Horster and C. Reitz, eds., *Condensing Texts – Condensed Texts,* Stuttgart, 649–734.

Schepens, G. and K. Delcroix. 1996. "Ancient Paradoxography: Origin, Evolution, Production, and Reception." In O. Pecere and A. Stramaglia, eds., *La letteratura di consumo nel mondo greco-latin,* Cassino, 375–460.

Schepens, G. and S. Schorn. 2010. "Verkürzungen in und von Historiographie in klassischer und helle-nistischer Zeit." In M. Horster and C. Reitz, eds., *Condensing Texts, Condensed Texts,* Stuttgart, 395–433.

Schulze, G. 1992. *Die Erlebnisgesellschaft: Kultursoziologie der Gegenwart.* Frankfurt.

Schwartz, E. 1905. "Diodorus (38)." *Paulys Realencyclopädie* 5: 663–704.

Schwartz, D. R. 2008. *2 Maccabees.* Berlin.

Smith, M. F. 1993. *Diogenes. The Epicurean Inscription: Edited with Introduction, Translation, and Notes.* Naples.

Stichweh, R. 1994. *Wissenschaft, Universität, Professionen: Soziologische Analysen.* Frankfurt.

Stylianou, P. J. 1998. *A Historical Commentary on Diodorus Siculus Book 15.* Oxford.

Sulimani, I. 2011. *Diodorus' Mythistory and the Pagan Mission: Historiography and Culture-Heroes in the first Pentad of the Bibliotheke.* Leiden.

Taub, L. C. and A. Doody, eds. 2009. *Authorial Voices in Greco-Roman Technical Writing.* Trier.

Urrea Méndez, J., ed. 2003. *El léxico métrico de Hefestión.* Amsterdam.

Van der Eijk 2010. "Principles and Practices of Compilation and Abbreviation in the Medical 'Encyclopaedias' of Late Antiquity." In M. Horster and C. Reitz, eds., *Condensing Texts, Condensed Texts,* Stuttgart, 519–54.

Wehner, B. 2000. *Die Funktion der Dialogstruktur in Epiktets Diatriben.* Stuttgart.

Wendel, C. 1949. "Pamphilos (25)." *Paulys Realencyclopädie* 18.3: 336–49.

FURTHER READING

Assmann 1992/2011 studies how early civilizations shaped and cultivated cultural traditions. Other works by Aleida and Jan Assmann could easily be added. Bourdieu 1979/1984 and Schulze 1992 analyze sociological mechanisms behind formations of and judgments about taste levels and taste types; their results are also applicable to debates about the intellectual value and legitimacy of derivative writings. Niklas Luhmann 1997/2012 recapitulates, less abstractly than Luhmann 1984/1995, the author's concepts of "social systems" and "communication." Gurd 2012 and Mülke 2008 explore literary practices that question the notion of "text" as autonomous and unchanging. Blair 2010 describes learned strategies, some very similar to those discussed in this contribution, of processing information overload in Europe's early modern period.

PART VII

Literature and Aesthetics

CHAPTER 29

The Language of Greek Literature

Andreas Willi

1. Prehistoric Roots

The Greek language is first attested in the administrative documents of the second-millennium "Mycenaean" palace culture on the mainland (Mycenae, Thebes, etc.) and in Crete (Cnossos). Although the syllabic "Linear B" script used there was not – as far as we know – employed for literary purposes, various forms of "oral literature" must have existed already at the time. In fact, some scholars have argued that certain linguistic elements in Homeric poetry constitute a Bronze Age literary inheritance (cf. p. 447). Moreover, non-trivial correspondences between Greek epic and lyric poetry and poetic traditions in other parts of the Indo-European world demonstrate an Indo-European ancestry of heroic song not only in terms of shared themes (ranging from cattle-raids to dragon-slaying), but also phraseology. As early as 1853 Adalbert Kuhn highlighted the etymological and semantic parallelism of the Vedic phrase *śrávo … ákṣitam* "imperishable fame" with the juncture κλέος ἄφθιτον in Homer and subsequent Greek poetry. In isolation this could be a coincidence, but in conjunction with further evidence (e.g. epic [θεοί], δωτῆρες ἐάων "[gods] givers of good things" ~ Vedic sg. *dātā́ vásūnām*, Avestan pl. *vohunąm dātārō*) one cannot but recognize here remnants of an Indo-European *Dichtersprache* (Schmitt 1967).

2. Literature and Dialect(s)

Greek literature in a stricter sense begins with the Homeric epics. The following selective *tour d'horizon* will therefore also start from the language of epic. To put things into context, however, some preliminary remarks are necessary.

Like any natural language, Ancient Greek was not a monolithic block. Its diachronic evolution is richly reflected in the literary and epigraphical sources. Also, a vast array of stylistic varieties, associated with specific genres and/or occasions, is recoverable – although we would still like to know more, especially about subliterary registers hiding behind the filtered literary record. But what is most striking about the diversity of Ancient Greek is its dialectal fragmentation, from the beginnings until well into the Hellenistic and Roman periods. The choice of dialect – more than,

A Companion to Greek Literature, First Edition. Edited by Martin Hose and David Schenker.
© 2016 John Wiley & Sons, Inc. Published 2020 by John Wiley & Sons, Inc.

say, a tendency to archaize or innovate, or to select a higher or lower type of register – is often *the* defining characteristic of a genre's linguistic setup. Hence ancient grammarians typically determined whether a given form in a given text was, for instance, "Doric" or "Aeolic," while showing less interest in its diachronic and diastratic classification. Moreover, their dialectal categories were geared towards literary (especially poetic) analysis: to distinguish, as they did, "Ionic," "Attic," "Doric," "Aeolic," and "Koine" Greek makes sense if one wants to classify the basic language of most literary texts, but not when one is dealing with the more narrowly defined dialects in the epigraphic record ("Laconian," "Corinthian," "Attic," "Syracusan," etc.). In other words, even the more locally rooted poets and writers would usually resort to a supra-regional generic dialect, avoiding the more parochial features of their native lects or resorting to a "foreign" variety altogether, if the target genre's conventions so demanded. Thus, the Boeotian poets Hesiod and Pindar did not write in Boeotian, let alone specifically Ascraean or Theban Boeotian, but in the generic "Ionic" and "Doric" of epic and choral lyric poetry respectively. Excepting a few genres, like comedy, which consciously mimic conversational language (cf. pp. 454–5), literature on its own cannot therefore tell us much about the Greek dialects on the ground. On the contrary, the history of the language(s) of Greek literature always has to be read as a history of *Kunstsprachen*, artificial and artistic languages – however reduced the distance between the written (i.e. read/recited) and the spoken word of everyday life may seem on occasion.

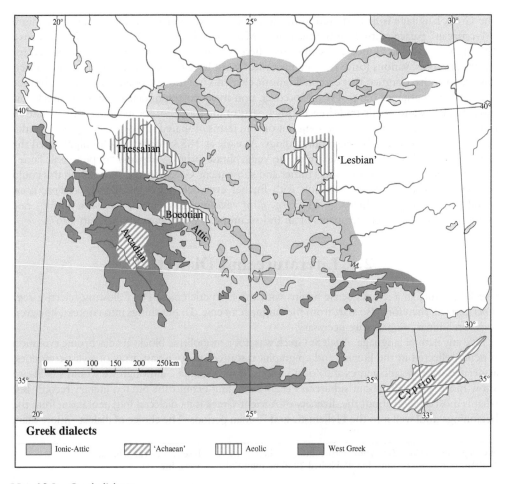

Map 29.1 Greek dialects.

3. The Language of Epic, Elegy, and Epigram

3.1. *Epic Kunstsprache*

The language of epic poetry (Chantraine 1953–58, Risch 1974, Hackstein 2002) is a prime example of a literary *Kunstsprache* (Meister 1921). In Homer we see, side by side, forms from different chronological phases and from at least two distinct dialect areas: Ionic and Aeolic. Furthermore, various elements are unlikely to have belonged to the "real" (spoken) language of any region or period. For illustration, consider *Iliad* 1.1–5:

Μῆνιν ἄειδε, θεά, Πηληϊάδεω Ἀχιλῆος
οὐλομένην, ἣ μυρί᾽ Ἀχαιοῖς ἄλγε᾽ ἔθηκε,
πολλὰς δ᾽ ἰφθίμους ψυχὰς Ἄϊδι προΐαψεν
ἡρώων, αὐτοὺς δὲ ἑλώρια τεῦχε κύνεσσιν
οἰωνοῖσί τε πᾶσι, Διὸς δ᾽ ἐτελείετο βουλή

Sing, goddess, of the wrath of Achilleus son of Peleus, the damned one, which has given countless woes to the Achaeans and hurled many powerful lives into Hades, of heroes: it turned them into prey for dogs, and all the birds, and the will of Zeus was done.

The predominant, or basic, dialect throughout epic is that of (Eastern) Ionia, Homer's alleged home region. A conspicuous phonological feature connecting Ionic with its close relative Attic, and separating them from other dialects including Aeolic, is the change of original */aː/ (ᾱ) into /εː/ (η) (e.g. οὐλομένην, βουλή). Similarly, the genitive ending of Πηληϊάδεω is Ionic, contrasting with both Aeolic -άδᾱ(ο) (as in *Il.* 16.686 Πηληϊάδᾱο) and Attic -άδου. However, θεά in the first line does not follow the ᾱ > η rule just mentioned (Ionic *θεή), nor is a dative plural κύνεσσιν, instead of κυσίν (cf. πᾶσι, not *πάντεσσι), good Ionic: an ending -εσσι instead of -σι in consonant-stem nouns and adjectives is regular only in some non-Ionic dialects, notably Aeolic. Meanwhile, the flexible addition of final -ν to endings like that of the dative plural, or also 3sg. -ε(ν) (cf. προΐαψεν), *is* typical of Ionic, and *not* Aeolic: so κύνεσσιν, being neither Ionic κυσί(ν) nor true Aeolic κύνεσσι, exemplifies the existence of purely artificial forms in Homer.

Turning to the chronological mixture in epic Greek, a famous issue concerns the traces of "digamma" (ϝ) first discovered by Richard Bentley in 1732. In δὲ ἑλώρια the particle δέ is not elided, as would be normal before a vowel (cf. δ᾽ ἰφθίμους). This frequent phenomenon is due to the fact that the word ἑλώρια originally featured an initial consonant */w-/, which was lost in all Greek dialects, though in some – including Ionic – much earlier than in others. Once we notionally re-insert this "digamma" (δὲ [ϝ]ελώρια), elision is justifiably prevented and the line scans as a correct hexameter. However, we cannot re-introduce ϝ in every word where etymological considerations ascertain its prior existence. Sometimes it is the insertion, not the omission, which would lead to (apparent) unmetricality. Thus, in the formula καί μιν φωνήσας [ϝ]έπεα πτερό[ϝ]εντα προσηύδα with masculine φωνήσας a digammatic scansion works well, but in the feminine variant καί μιν φωνήσασ᾽ [†ϝ]έπεα πτερό[ϝ]εντα προσηύδα the retention of ϝ would have wreaked metrical havoc, since φωνήσασα needed a following vowel to be elided. So, although notional ϝ is more often necessary than excluded, singers at the last formative stage of epic language were evidently able to respect *or* disregard it, i.e. to use older and more recent forms next to each other.

Another widespread archaism of epic – and more generally poetic – Greek is the optional omission of the augment in past-tense indicatives. In our excerpt τεῦχε contrasts with ἔθηκε or ἐτελείετο, at least if one resists the temptation of de-augmenting the transmitted text wherever possible (e.g. by emending ἄλγεα θῆκε and δὲ τελείετο). Such a move would be unwise, both because many augments are metrically protected, and because there are observable morphological, syntactic, and semantic tendencies in their use: for example, Homeric aorists with present-tense relevance (~ Engl. "has X-ed") tend to be augmented. Even so, the fact that augmentation is not fully predictable distinguishes the language of epic from any non-literary variety of the Archaic and Classical periods.

3.2.   *Oral Origins and Evolution*

Much of this diachronic and dialectal heterogeneity of epic Greek is due to the genre's oral pre-history. In order to improvise successfully while respecting numerous metrical constraints, bards had to master the technique of formulaic composition, which enabled them to combine truly extemporized passages with prefabricated material (like the speech-introduction formula cited above). Once established in the tradition, such formulae underwent linguistic updating only as long as this did not substantially alter their metrical shape. Meanwhile, the bards' "real" lan-guage was changing also in metrically relevant ways (as with the loss of */w/). Far from being an inconvenience, the resulting competition between metrically different older and younger forms could then facilitate the composition process further (Hoekstra 1965). Epic Greek there-fore developed like an avalanche, taking with it whatever new growth it found along its course.

However, the avalanche model alone does not explain the parallel presence of Aeolic and Ionic elements, and scholarship is more divided in this regard (cf. Willi 2011, with literature: e.g. Wathelet 1970 vs. Miller 1982). According to the "Aeolic phase theory," epic Aeolicisms are a mere by-product of the avalanche's course. Although the last generations of oral poets were Ionians, the epic tradition would have been transferred to Ionia from Aeolic-speaking areas. At the time of the presumed transfer, whatever traditional building block could easily be translated into Ionic was indeed translated: Aeolic forms were retained only where the Ionic equivalent was metrically different. During the preceding Aeolic phase, a line like *Il.* 1.1, for example, would have ended with Πηλῄϊάδἄ' Ἀχιλῆος (with elided Πηλῄϊάδᾱο), but since nothing spoke against a modernization into Ionic Πηλῄϊάδεω Ἀχιλῆος, this is what happened.

By contrast, proponents of the "diffusion theory" look for a continuous epic tradition among the Ionians and their ancestors, perhaps as far back as the Mycenaean period. They stress that many synchronic Aeolicisms are indistinguishable from Proto-Ionic forms. Since Ionic -άδεω, for instance, goes back to *-άδᾱο, a form Πηλῄϊάδᾱο is as "Proto-Ionic" as it is "Aeolic." Wherever this is not the case, as with Aeolic/Homeric infinitives in -εμεν next to Ionic/Homeric -ειν, the Aeolic forms should then be interpreted as mere borrowings, intro-duced in response to linguistic change: thus, a need for -εμεν arose when Proto-Ionic *-εhεν had evolved into *-εεν > -ειν with a different metrical shape.

3.3. *The Hexameter as Witness*

Whichever theory may be correct, the rules of epic meter (cf. Reece, ch. 3, pp. 47–5 in this volume) must have been a determining factor in the selection, retention, and creation of linguistic items. Semantically required forms that did not fit into the hexameter pattern were either substituted by something more suitable, be it an archaism or a borrowing, or adapted to the meter by artificial means. In particular, a Homeric hexameter cannot accommodate words containing a sequence of three short syllables ($\cup \cup \cup$) or a long–short–long sequence ($- \cup -$):

$$- \,\overline{\cup\cup}\, - \,\overline{\cup\cup}\, - \,\overline{\cup\cup}\, - \,\overline{\cup\cup}\, - \,\overline{\cup\cup}\, - \, x$$

Epic language therefore licensed adjustments like the "metrical lengthening" of naturally short syllables (e.g. οὐλομένην for ὀλομένην, the aorist participle of ὄλλυμαι "to be damned") or the manipulation of normal word-formation patterns (e.g. Πηληϊάδεω instead of expected *Πηληΐδεω, with the usual patronymic suffix -ίδης).

And yet, there remain a few Homeric lines which in their transmitted form do not scan as proper hexameters. Given the intrinsic conservatism of oral poetry, it is conceivable that these too are the victims of linguistic change. An eminent case in point is the verse-end formula λιποῦσ᾽ ἀνδροτῆτα καὶ ἥβην "leaving manhood and youth." Here the first syllable of ἀνδροτῆτα must be scanned as short, despite the consonant cluster -νδρ-. This irregularity would disappear if the formula was created when ἀνδροτῆτα was still *anṛtātṃ with vocalic *-ṛ-, hence scanning as ∪ ∪ − ∪· And since the Proto-Greek phoneme *-ṛ- had already developed into -ρο- (*vel sim.*) by the Mycenaean period, a formula presupposing vocalic *-ṛ- might then be taken to imply that hexameter poetry also already existed in pre-Mycenaean times (Mühlestein 1958).

However, this method of dating the beginnings of hexameter epic stands and falls with the premise that the hexameter was structurally immutable – a premise rightly called into question by the "proto-hexameter hypothesis" (Berg 1978). Although the hexameter differs from Greek lyric meter of the Aeolic type (p. 452) in that it has no fixed number of syllables but allows the substitution of one long for a pair of short syllables, this hardly constitutes proof of a pre-Greek (non-Indo-European) Aegean origin (Meillet 1923). Instead, it may represent the outcome of a complex process by which a pair of standard Aeolic-type lines was welded together. If one thus postulates a prehistoric combination of a "glyconic" and a "pherecratean," as shown below, the (hexa)metrically awkward ἀνδροτῆτα formula neatly fills the second part, and restituting vocalic *-ṛ- is no longer necessary; the first two syllables now occupy two slots that are "anceps" (long *or* short) anyway (Tichy 1981):

$$x\ x - \cup \cup - \cup - \mid x\ x - \cup \cup - -$$

In this way, epic meter would gain the same Indo-European ancestry as lyric meter (cf. p. 452), lending additional support to the phraseology-based conclusions mentioned earlier (p. 443) and counterbalancing the potential loss of scansional anomalies as dating criteria for the genre.

3.4. After Homer: Epic and Elegy

At the lower end of the Homeric period, the avalanche petered out fairly quickly. With the advent of writing as a means for textual composition, preservation, and circulation, epic language became less receptive to continuous innovation. The *Odyssey* does seem linguistically more recent than the *Iliad*, and Hesiod and the Homeric hymns more recent than Homer, but such differences are quantitative rather than qualitative (e.g. ϝ less often observed; more genitives in -ου, not -οιο; cf. Janko 1982). Truly non-Homeric features in Hesiod – such as *a*-stem accusative plurals in -ᾰς next to -ᾱς or contracted *a*-stem genitive plurals in -ᾶν next to -άων (and Ionic -έων) – are too marginal to prove the existence of an independent, non-Ionic, epic tradition on the Greek mainland (Pavese 1972). Had there been such a thing, descending directly from an "Aeolic phase," the fundamentally Ionic appearance of Hesiod's language would be surprising. By contrast one easily understands that a Boeotian poet, though steeped in the Ionian tradition, should still occasionally integrate a limited number of convenient local peculiarities.

A comparable situation obtains in what is, formally at least, a sister genre of epic (or more generally, hexametric) poetry: elegy, written in distichs of hexameter + pentameter.

$$- \overline{\cup\cup} - \overline{\cup\cup} - \overline{\cup\cup} - \overline{\cup\cup} - \overline{\cup\cup} - x$$
$$- \overline{\cup\cup} - \overline{\cup\cup} - \mid - \overline{\cup\cup} - \overline{\cup\cup} -$$

The exact origin of the pentameter is again obscure, but, given its structural and typological similarity with the hexameter, some form of genetic relationship is likely. Since the combined distich represents, in any case, a mini-strophe, adherents of the proto-hexameter hypothesis could search for a primeval strophe of four shorter (7–8-syllable) verses behind it.

Even disregarding the metrical connection, the linguistic resemblance of elegy and epic need not surprise. Of course the paraenetic, symposiastic, erotic, or political themes of historical elegy are as distant from each other as Hesiod's didactic poetry is from Homeric narrative, but the genre may have grown from ritual acts of commemoration for the (heroic) dead. However, the language of elegy (West 1974) does differ from that of epic in being slightly less artificial. It may not approximate spoken Ionic as much as iambic language does (p. 453), but Callinus' elegiac register includes, for example, the typically Eastern Ionic forms κοτε and κως, where Homeric epic (and even Archilochus's iambus) regularly show the less geographically restricted ποτε and πως. Similarly, elegiac poets from non-Ionic areas may admit influences from their own cultural backgrounds. When Theognis of Megara uses a short-vowel infinitive φεύγεν "to flee" (Theognis 260 (conjectural)) or Tyrtaeus of Sparta *a*-stem accusative plurals in -ᾰς (cf. p. 447), this echoes not only Hesiod's version of epic Greek but also, more crucially, the Doric of choral lyric (pp. 449–51).

3.5. Epigram

Outside "professional" circles, the language of hexameter/pentameter poetry was watered down even more (Mickey 1981). From the middle of the sixth century, after an initial period where the hexameter dominates, stone epigrams throughout the Greek world are also normally written in distichs. Here, however, phonological and morphological features of the various local dialects intrude constantly, not least in the Archaic age, before processes of literary canonization prevent further erosion. Conversely, patent epicisms like the Aeolic datives in -εσσι or the genitives in -οιο are far less common than in the literary texts. Forms like μνᾶμα and νικάσας (≠ Ionic/epic μνῆμα, νικήσας) are therefore unremarkable in, say, an epigram from Arcadia (CEG 379). More strikingly, though, epigrammatists would not always stop there. Presumably because of the equal prestige of choral lyric poetry, with its conspicuous Doric features, the Euboean (i.e. Ionic-speaking) writer of CEG 108 decided to Doricize the Homeric verse-end ἤματα πάντα into ἄματα πάντα, right next to epic-Ionic forms like μήτηρ (contrast Doric μάτηρ). The linguistic "rules" of the genre thus make room for an almost postmodern "anything goes (as long as it sounds impressive)."

3.6. Later Developments

Despite this undeniable contrast between epigrammatic poetry and dialectally more settled post-Homeric hexameter literature, "epic" language itself never became completely static either. Firstly, authors like Parmenides and Empedocles conveyed their philosophical and scientific ideas in media which resemble those of Homer and Hesiod only at the surface. Their lexicon in particular is often markedly un-Homeric, in terms of constituency (e.g. Parmenides' γέννα "origin," δίζησις "inquiry"), word formation (e.g. Empedocles' nouns in -ωμα, like ῥίζωμα for ῥίζα "root"), and semantics (e.g. ζείδωρος, which Empedocles DK 31 B 151 connects with ζῆν "to live," as "life-giving," while it belongs with ζειαί "wheat" in early epic). Individual experimentation explains many such departures from the epic norm, but some might also originate in nowadays invisible subliterary traditions, of an oracular or Orphic type.

Secondly, significant developments also took place in Hellenistic times, when poets like Callimachus were striving for the "perfect" hexameter. Devising stricter metrical rules – for instance with regard to caesura placement and (avoidance of) vowel elision – they would match this artistry with a correspondingly select vocabulary. Moreover, in their world of generic inter-breeding Callimachus (in his *Hymns* V and VI) and Theocritus (in most of the *Idylls*) chose to cross the language of hexameter poetry with the one great dialect hitherto excluded from it, Doric. In a bucolic context an idealized simple form of language is thereby evoked; but as we read the goatherd's praise of Thyrsis's song in Theocr. 1.7–8, we cannot but also think of *the* counterpart to the resounding stream of Ionic epic – Doric μέλος, to which we turn next:

ἅδιον, ὦ ποιμήν, τὸ τεὸν μέλος ἢ τὸ καταχές
τῆν' ἀπὸ τᾶς πέτρας καταλείβεται ὑψόθεν ὕδωρ.

Sweeter, o shepherd, is your song than how that resounding stream over there tumbles down from the rock up high.

4. The Language of Choral and Monodic Lyric

4.1. *Alcman*

In many ways the meter and language of choral lyric poetry, as we first encounter them in Alcman's Louvre *partheneion* (cf. Wells ch. 10, pp. 162–4 in this volume), are strikingly different from those of epic (Alcman F 1.57–63 PMGF):

Ἀγησιχόρα μὲν αὕτα	x – ‿‿ – ‿ – –
ἁ δὲ δευτέρα πεδ' Ἀγιδὼ τὸ εἶδος	– ‿ – x – ‿ – x – ‿ ‿‿ –
ἵππος Εἰβηνῶι Κολαξαῖος δραμείται.	– ‿ – x – ‿ – x – ‿ – –
ταὶ Πελειάδες γὰρ ἇμιν	– ‿ – x – ‿ – x
ὀρθρίαι φᾶρος φεροίσαις	– ‿ – x – ‿ – –
νύκτα δι' ἀμβροσίαν ἅτε Σείριον	– ‿‿ – ‿‿ – ‿‿ – ‿‿
ἄστρον ἀυειρομέναι μάχονται.	– ‿‿ – ‿‿ – ‿ ‿ –

Hagesichora she is: and she will run second, after Agido, in appearance, a Colaxaean horse to an Ibenian; for the Peleiads, early in the morning, as we carry the dress (plough?) through the immortal night, they fight with us, rising up like the Sirius star.

Within these varied metrical structures, often based on iambic (‿ –), trochaic (– ‿), or dactylic (– ‿‿) rhythms, there is little substitution of long and double-short units. Long stanzas are rhythmically repeated (whence we infer the occasional metrical alternatives indicated in the schema), but overall each composition ends up with its own fingerprint.

Dialectally, Doric is now dominant. Apart from retained ᾱ (e.g. αὕτα, δευτέρα), we notice, for example, the demonstrative pronoun/article ταί (Ion. αἱ), the personal pronoun ἇμιν (Ion. ἡμῖν, Aeol. ἄμμι), or the preposition πεδ(ά) (Ion. μετά). Also, the digamma situation is somewhat different from the one in Homer with its purely prosodic traces of */w/. Not only does the Louvre papyrus once use the actual *letter* ϝ (ϝάνακτα "lord"), it also suggests in several places that the *sound* /w/ was still a reality, at least in certain positions. Thus, in τὸ εἶδος – as in Homer – there is merely the hiatus to indicate the (previous) existence of /w/, but in the participle ἀυειρομέναι (from *ἀϝείρω > αἴρω "to raise") the letter υ represents intervocalic /w/. Elsewhere, though, intervocalic /w/ has disappeared, and we even find subsequent vowel contraction (e.g. φῶς < *φάϝος "light").

Such inconsistency is not restricted to /w/. All the Greek dialects feature "new" long *e*-vowels and *o*-vowels arising from vowel contraction (e.g. inf. **-ehen* > **-een* > Att.-Ion. -ειν = /-ēn/) or consonant-cluster simplification accompanied by "compensatory" vowel lengthening (e.g. acc. pl. **-ons* > Att.-Ion. -ους = /-ōs/); but the timbre of these new long vowels differs from dialect to dialect. Within Doric, one distinguishes "strong" varieties, with open outcomes (inf. -ην = /-ēn/, acc. pl. -ως = /-ōs/; e.g. Laconian), from "mild" ones, with the same close outcomes as in Attic-Ionic (e.g. Corinthian). Unfortunately, our Alcman text eschews classification along these lines. An apparently Mild Doric future δραμεῖται (< **-eetai*), for example, contrasts with a Strong Doric accusative plural ἀρίστως (< **-ons*).

How an editor should deal with an untidy situation like this depends on his/her view of what exactly the transmitted text reflects. Since the Louvre papyrus of Alcman contains certain forms that are peculiar to Laconian (e.g. σιῶν ~ Attic θεῶν "of the gods," with σ- presumably indicating a sound /θ/ like English *th*), some scholars have assumed that the language of Alcman's original must have been close to vernacular seventh-century Laconian (Page 1951). It could well be that the use of /w/ was indeed fluid at the time, as the sound was beginning to be lost. Editorial intervention on the apparently Mild Doric forms of the papyrus (e.g. δραμῆται for transmitted δραμεῖται) would then be necessary, entailing the dismissal of these forms as copying errors due to later scribes who were used to Attic/Koine spellings.

Other forms, however, are neither Laconian nor standard – hence error-inducing – in later times. These, notably the feminine participles in -οισα (e.g. dat. pl. φεροίσαις; contrast Lac. -ωσα, Att. -ουσα) and some short-vowel infinitives (e.g. φαίνεν, even in place of metrically required Lac. φαίνην or Attic/Koine φαίνειν), have given rise to an alternative theory according to which our Alcman text reflects Alexandrian scholarship (Risch 1954). Knowing that Alcman was active in Doric-speaking Sparta, his Alexandrian editors would have assimilated his dialect to Cyrenaean, a Doric variety spoken near Alexandria and featuring both participles in -οισα and infinitives in -εν. To impute such clumsiness and naiveté to ancient scholars is of course disingenuous, and the existence of obvious non-Cyrenaean features in the papyrus also speaks strongly against this view (Cassio 1993).

Finally, a third hypothesis assumes that Alcman's language, no less than that of Homer, started off essentially as a *Kunstsprache* (Hinge 2006). However, within a continuous performance tradition in Sparta itself, Alcman's songs would have been gradually modernized and brought in line with actual Laconian (e.g. σιῶν) – except in the case of features that were unmistakably foreign/poetic (-οισα participles, lack of augment), or where a Laconicization was metrically excluded (e.g. fut. παρήσομες "we will omit," for epichoric παρησοῦμες). In late classical or early Hellenistic times the resulting version was then codified, in the dialectally and chronologically inconsistent shape it had acquired (but with due regard for details, including its Doric accentuation: note e.g. ἀυειρομέναι in the papyrus, against standard -όμεναι).

4.2. Heritage and Inheritance

This last scenario has two advantages. Firstly, it reduces the distance between the language of Alcman's original and other archaic choral lyric. The variety used by Stesichorus of Himera adopts the same *Kunstsprache* elements, including the -οισα and -εν endings discussed, but it is devoid of Laconianisms. Of course this is not to say that the Stesichorean fragments generally resemble those of Alcman. For one thing, Stesichorus – like Ibycus, Simonides, Pindar, and Bacchylides later on – evidences a triadic arrangement with metrically identical ("corresponding") pairs of strophe and antistrophe followed by a metrically distinct epode. For another, Stesichorus's language is rich in epicisms, both formal (e.g. genitives in -οιο) and lexical (epithets, formulae: e.g. F 222(b).209 PMGF ἄναξ ἑκάεργος Ἀπόλλων "Lord Apollo shooting at will").

Although this may have something to do with the prominence of myth, it goes well beyond what we find in mythological passages of Pindar's odes: Stesichorus appears to create consciously a hybrid register for his semi-epic, semi-lyric genre (Willi 2008). By contrast, in later choral lyric a much smoother convergence takes place, as the most distinctive Doric features of choral lyric recede (so that infinitives in -ειν now predominate, the first plural ends in -μεν rather than -μες, or function words such as Doric ὄκα "when," αἰ "if," and ποτί "to" give way to ὅτε, εἰ, and πρός), and less specific poeticisms progress (e.g. unaugmented past-tense forms). This development culminates in the choral songs of Attic tragedy, where "Doric" ᾱ for Attic η is one of the few original traces left, and it reflects the genre's growing internationalization: Simonides, Pindar, and Bacchylides no longer think primarily of local audiences, but operate on a Panhellenic scale – a fact which incidentally explains why the history of their texts should be different from that of Alcman.

Secondly, the non-Laconian elements in Alcman, far from being spurious, may also tell us something about literary (pre)history. Together with a few other features, the participles in -οισα are easiest to interpret as Aeolic. One might thus read them, again, as support for a distinct mainland tradition of Greek poetry (cf. p. 447). However, not all of Alcman's potential Aeolicisms are immediately compatible with this. For example, long *a*-stem datives like ῥοαῖσι "streams" (≠ Dor. ῥοαῖς) can belong to Lesbian Aeolic, but not to Aeolic *tout court*. Hence, it may be relevant that the seventh-century citharode Terpander of Lesbos visited Sparta: the local choral tradition may well have learnt from (poets like) him. In order to explain the *Kunstsprache* part of early choral lyric, all we therefore really need is a culturally influential "school" of poetry in Lesbos. Terpander, of course, is little more than a name to us, and so is Arion of Methymna, but with Sappho and Alcaeus Lesbian lyric, in a monodic guise, becomes a tangible reality.

4.3. The Lesbian Poets

Unlike choral lyric, monodic lyric belongs to restricted settings, to symposia or private ceremonies. As in the case of the epic–elegy–epigram continuum, this difference in destination correlates with a lower degree of linguistic artificiality. The following well-known Sapphic stanza (F 31.1–4 V; cf. Wells this volume, ch. 10, pp. 165–8 and Konstan, this volume, ch. 27, pp. 420–1 on this poem) contains not one linguistic feature which we can confidently exclude from authentic Lesbian Aeolic of *c.* 600 BCE, and many which definitely agree with it (Hamm 1958, Bowie 1981): the lack of initial aspiration and the preservation of ᾱ in ἆδυ (~ ἡδύ), the open long vowel in κῆνος (~ (ἐ)κεῖνος), the geminate -μμ- < *-sm- and the infinitive ending -μεναι in ἔμμεν(αι), the generalizing relative pronoun ὄττις (~ ὅστις), or the "athematic" inflection of the verb φωνέω, i.e. φώνημ⟨μ⟩ι, as in the feminine participle φωνείσας (with diphthongal -εισα < *-ent-ya).

φαίνεταί μοι κῆνος ἴσος θέοισιν	– ∪ – x – ∪ ∪ – ∪ – –
ἔμμεν' ὤνηρ, ὄττις ἐνάντιός τοι	– ∪ – x – ∪ ∪ – ∪ – –
ἰσδάνει καὶ πλάσιον ἆδυ φωνεί-	– ∪ – x – ∪ ∪ – ∪ – –
σας ὐπακούει	– ∪ ∪ – –

That man appears to me to be equal to the gods, the one who sits opposite you and listens as you, close by, speak to him sweetly...

These seem a real person's feelings expressed in a real person's language, faithfully rendering even the "crasis" in ὤνηρ (for ὁ ἀνήρ), a phonetic phenomenon seldom encountered in public poetry. To be sure, Lesbian lyric never excludes pure poeticisms completely, but when they occur, typically as borrowings from epic, they tend to be triggered thematically. Thus, in Sappho's dactylic F 44 V epicisims like ἐνὶ ναυσίν "on the ships" (Lesb. ἐν νάεσσι) or κατὰ πτόλιν "throughout the city" (Lesb. κὰτ/κὰπ πόλιν) fit into the heroic world of Hector and Andromache's wedding, and they match the quasi-epic arrangement of the poem in single lines rather than stanzas. In other words, contemporary Lesbian is the default dialect for Lesbian lyric in a much stricter sense than vernacular Ionic was ever the default variety of epic.

This being fairly obvious, the transmission of Sappho and Alcaeus was spared any but the most superficial normalizing interference. Alexandrian editors carefully preserved or restituted the local dialect features most at risk, trying to ensure an authentic oral rendering. Since, for example, Z was regularly pronounced as a voiced sibilant [z] in Hellenistic times, they adopted spellings like ἰσδάνει (for ἵζάνει, as Sappho would have written herself) to indicate the original sound pattern with [zd]; and since Aeolic barytonesis – whereby words retract the accent as far as the general rules of Greek accentuation allow (e.g. θέοισιν, not θεοῖσιν) – was part of the correct tonal contour in recitation, it too is reflected in the papyri. In due course, this philological interest even led to a renaissance of Lesbian poetry, both in Hellenistic Alexandria (where Theocritus wrote a small number of his *Idylls* in Lesbian dialect and meter) and later in Rome (where Iulia Balbilla, a noblewoman in Emperor Hadrian's entourage, composed elegiac distichs in Lesbian).

4.4. Aeolic Meter

The idea that Sappho and Alcaeus belong to a wider lyric tradition coming to fruition in Lesbos is indirectly borne out also by their "Aeolic" meters. These consist of syllable-counting cola, commonly arranged in stanzas, and often involving an initial sequence of two anceps syllables, the so-called "Aeolic base." Of the many cola types, the glyconic and the pherecratean have already been encountered (p. 447); others include the hagesichorean (x – ∪ ∪ – ∪ – –) and the adonean (– ∪ ∪ – –) occurring in the above "Sapphic stanza" (though the former prefixed by an iambic extension – ∪ –).

Some of these Aeolic lines bear a striking resemblance to similarly structured and strophically arranged Vedic meters. For instance, the glyconic (x x – ∪ ∪ – ∪ –) mirrors the basic colon in Vedic *gāyatrī* stanzas (x x x x ∪ – ∪ –). Moreover, fixed-number seven- or eight-syllable verses are attested in many further Indo-European languages. At least metrically speaking, Aeolic lyric therefore looks like the most archaic manifestation of Greek poetry, its roots possibly extending to Proto-Indo-European itself (Meillet 1923).

4.5. Beyond Lesbos

Given this background it is unsurprising that monodic lyric also existed outside Lesbos. An Ionian singer like Anacreon of Teos *need* not owe his preference for glyconics and similar cola to the Lesbians; there could have been a parallel tradition in Ionia. But in any case, if such a poet was to speak to his audience as naturally as Sappho and Alcaeus did, he could not possibly retain the Lesbian dialect. Hence, Anacreon's lyric provides the Ionic counterpart to the language of Sappho and Alcaeus: not epicizing Ionic (though occasional epicisms are unavoidable), but a variety oriented towards vernacular East Ionic, including phonological parochialisms such as ὄκως and κου for ὄπως and που (cf. p. 448 on Callinus, and subsequently also Ionic, e.g. Herodotean, prose).

Even later, Boeotian too makes a brief appearance in the lyric record, in the fragments of Corinna. Whether these really date from classical times – as suggested by ancient anecdotal evidence – remains controversial, for they could also represent another Hellenistic experiment with "exotic" dialects (cf. pp. 449 and 452 on Theocritus; add Herondas's mimiambs in Ionic). The phonology and orthography of the main witness (*P. Berol.* 284) do not clinch the matter, although they are datable to c. 200 BCE thanks to the spelling conventions adopted (e.g. Φῦβος ~ Φοῖβος, Μώση ~ Μοῦσαι); a previous locally based oral tradition, as with Alcman (p. 450), may seem unlikely in this case, but it cannot be disproved.

5. The Language of Iambus, Comedy, and Tragedy

5.1. *Ionian Iambus*

Private settings, such as aristocratic symposia, provided a typical – though perhaps not the only – performance context also for iambic poetry. Dialectal similarities between Anacreon's lyric and the iambic compositions of East Ionian poets like Archilochus, Semonides, and Hipponax may therefore be expected. Here again, we hear something close to the authentic voice of archaic Ionia, interrupted only rarely by more "literary" elements which may serve parodic purposes. Thus, verbs are almost always augmented, vowels contracted, and crasis forms frequent; both phonology and morphology are thoroughly Ionic (e.g. η < *$\bar{a}$ in words like οἰκίη "house," dat. pl. in -οισι(ν), gen. sg. ἐμεῦ "of me," etc.).

And yet, an iambus could never be mistaken for a lyric song, because of differences in meter and linguistic register. The iambic poets use mostly stichic verses, in which iambic (x – ⌣ –) or trochaic (– ⌣ – x) feet are repeated and resolution of – into ⌣⌣ is legitimate. The iambic trimeter (a) and the trochaic tetrameter (b) are basic, but "limping" ("choliambic") variants ending in x – – – with a long penultimate position also occur:

(a)   x ⌣⌣ ⌣ ⌣⌣ x ⌣⌣ ⌣ ⌣⌣ x – ⌣ –
(b)   ⌣⌣ ⌣ ⌣⌣ x ⌣⌣ ⌣ ⌣⌣ x ⌣⌣ ⌣ ⌣⌣ x – ⌣ –

In terms of register, iambus characteristically pursues its end of personal, social, or political criticism and invective by means of αἰσχρολογία: abusive, vulgar, even obscene vocabulary. Some of this must be drawn from popular speech, just like the odd lexical borrowing from neighboring languages (e.g. Lydian πάλμυς "king, sovereign"). Other ingredients may be invented ad hoc, like Hipponax' adverb πυγιστί formed after adverbs designating a language ("in Pygian") but hinting at πυγή "backside, bottom" and πυγίζειν "to have anal intercourse" (F 92.2 IEG). Similarly, the creation of expressive compounds foreshadows what we later see in Attic comedy: Hipponax, for example, referred to some women as βορβορόπη "dirt-hole" and ἀνασεισίφαλλος "penis-shaker" (F 135 IEG), and the less outspoken Archilochus coined the mock patronymic συκοτραγίδης "Fignibblerson" (F 250 IEG).

5.2. *From Iambus to Early Comedy*

To what extent Ionic ever became a generic default dialect for iambus is difficult to tell because the major representatives of the genre were Ionians anyway. Conceivably the situation was as flexible as in the case of monodic lyric. The Athenian Solon's iambic compositions admittedly show an Ionic guise, but this could be the result of an indirect transmission process in which they were dialectally assimilated to Solon's elegiac verse. A few fragments preserved in a papyrus of the Aristotelian Ἀθηναίων πολιτεία do display Attic forms instead (e.g. ἐλευθέρα for Ion. ἐλευθέρη, ποιούμενος for ποιεύμενος/ποιεόμενος in F 36), but then a contextually conditioned Atticization cannot be ruled out either.

An independent argument in favor of an epichorically-styled iambus outside Ionia may come from comedy, both Doric and Attic. According to Aristotle (*Poet.* 1449b7–9) Crates was the first Athenian comedian to "replace" the ἰαμβικὴ ἰδέα by Sicilian-style plots. By implication Attic comedy must have been iambic in nature before, as indeed intimated by similarities in meter (with trimeters and tetrameters also predominating in comedy) and register. The basic dialect of comedy, however, always mirrored the audience's everyday speech: Attic in Athens, Syracusan Doric in Syracuse (Epicharmus: cf. e.g. F 113.244 PCG ἐπεί νιν φαῦλον εἴμειν κα δοκέω "since I think it might be bad," with νιν ~ αὐτόν, εἴμειν ~ εἶναι, κα ~ ἄν, δοκέω ~ δοκῶ).

Leaving aside their dialectal profile, the scanty fragments of Epicharmus are hard to characterize linguistically (Willi 2008). Occasional vulgarisms and some verbal humor (e.g. F 76, punning on γ' ἔρανον "a party" vs. γέρανον "a crane") are undeniable, and other forms of verbal artistry must have been appreciated as well: otherwise the endless lists of foodstuffs which Athenaeus cites from Epicharmus's *Wedding of Hebe* (Ἥβας γάμος, F 40–62 PCG) would be indigestible. Stylistic parody too must have found its place: Aeschylus was derided for his "continuous" use of the high-flown verb τιμαλφέω "to honor" (F 221 PCG), and the hexametrical F 121 λαοὶ τοξοχίτωνες, ἀκούετε Σειρηνάων "bow-clad people, heed the Sirens" is not only metrically unexpected, but also contains, with Σειρηνάων, a pseudo-epic genitive.

5.3. Attic Comedy

Such parody was to reach its apogee some decades later, in Athens. Aristophanes and his rivals inherited the iambic tradition of λοιδορία "abuse," and they gave it a new home both in comic dialogue and in the marching anapaestic tetrameters of the choral parabasis (⏑⏑ – ⏑⏑ – ⏑⏑ – ⏑⏑ – ⏑⏑ – ⏑⏑ – ⏑⏑ – –). But the preferred way of bringing down the comic target – be it a person or group of people, a social phenomenon, or a literary genre – was now to ridicule it through (hysterically exaggerated) imitation. The conversation between a "normal" Athenian and a tragic poet (Agathon) then sounds as follows (Aristoph. *Thesm.* 149–158):

Ἀγ. χρὴ γὰρ ποιητὴν ἄνδρα πρὸς τὰ δράματα,
ἃ δεῖ ποεῖν, πρὸς ταῦτα τοὺς τρόπους ἔχειν.
αὐτίκα γυναικεῖ' ἢν ποῇ τις δράματα,
μετουσίαν δεῖ τῶν τρόπων τὸ σῶμ' ἔχειν.
Κη. οὐκοῦν κελητίζεις ὅταν Φαίδραν ποῇς;
Ἀγ. ἀνδρεῖα δ' ἢν ποῇ τις, ἐν τῷ σώματι
ἔνεσθ' ὑπάρχον τοῦθ'. ἃ δ' οὐ κεκτήμεθα,
μίμησις ἤδη ταῦτα συνθηρεύεται.
Κη. ὅταν σατύρους τοίνυν ποῇς, καλεῖν ἐμέ,
ἵνα συμποῶ σοὔπισθεν ἐστυκὼς ἐγώ.

Agathon: Onto the plays which he's to make, a poet must direct his ways. Thus, when someone makes women plays, partake in their ways too his body must.

In-Law: So, you enjoy a ride when you write a *Phaedra*?

Agathon: And when someone makes plays of men, inherent bodily this is. Though what we don"t possess, mimesis is what hunts it down.

In-Law: In that case just call me when you write a satyr-play, so I can collaborate from behind, with a stiff one.

Although both characters use the same Attic dialect, the stylistic clash is hilarious. On the one side, Agathon's trimeters show the low rate of long-syllable resolution which is typical of tragic trimeters, in contrast to those of comedy, and his redundant and recherché stateliness is as characteristic of tragedy as it would have been misplaced in a real conversation (e.g. ποιητὴν ἄνδρα for simple ποιητήν, μετουσίαν ἔχειν for μετέχειν, ἔνεσθ' ὑπάρχον for ἔνεστι, συνθηρεύεται for plain παρέχει). On the other side, the In-Law by and large maintains the tragic rhythm (though with help from colloquial crasis in σοὔπισθεν), but slips in vulgar interruptions of an overtly sexual nature (κελητίζεις, ἐστυκώς).

Through such mockery of anything that lies outside linguistic "normality," the language of Attic Old Comedy opposes threats to civic cohesion by elements that are – or could be perceived as – elitist (e.g. epic, tragic, and dithyrambic literature, or also sophistic rhetoric: Willi 2003), alien (e.g. foreign accents and dialects: Colvin 1999), or otherwise disruptive (e.g. oracular superstition). The resulting polyphony thus supports the genre's agenda as much as the poetic language of, say, elegy and choral lyric fulfils an aesthetic role (Willi 2002). But at the same time it opens the door to a new kind of linguistic mimeticism. In Old Comedy, of course, there is no true naturalism as yet, both because comic exaggeration and stereotyping are omnipresent (the historical Agathon hardly talked like Aristophanes' Agathon!) and because humor takes precedence over stylistic consistency. Later on, however, the balance changes. By the time of Menandrean New Comedy, we witness a greater reluctance to disturb linguistic characterization – which now aims at sketching plausible personalities – for the sake of the occasional pun or parody. In that sense, comedy, while retaining its meter, partially (re-)converges with prosaic and largely subliterary mime, from where its Sicilian plot tradition may well have started.

5.4. Tragedy

Since good parody condenses, but contains a kernel of truth, the paratragic verses quoted above (p. 454) have already given a glimpse of tragic language, exemplified further by the following Sophoclean lines (*Ant.* 223–8):

> Φυ.   ἄναξ, ἐρῶ μὲν οὐχ ὅπως τάχους ὕπο
> δύσπνους ἱκάνω κοῦφον ἐξάρας πόδα.
> πολλὰς γὰρ ἔσχον φροντίδων ἐπιστάσεις,
> ὁδοῖς κυκλῶν ἐμαυτὸν εἰς ἀναστροφήν.
> ψυχὴ γὰρ ηὔδα πολλά μοι μυθουμένη,
> "τάλας, τί χωρεῖς οἷ μολὼν δώσεις δίκην

> Guardian: O lord, I will not say that speed-induced I come here, out of breath, and nimbly lifting up my foot; for many were the visitations of my mind, as I was wheeling round myself into my path's return. My soul, indeed, spoke to me much: "You wretch, why walkest thou where you'll be chastised if you go?"

This is again good Attic, as are all spoken passages of tragedy, except that the genre shuns the most parochial dialect features (using e.g. -σσ-/-ρσ- instead of -ττ-/-ρρ- in words like πράσσω "to do" and ἄρσην "male," or restricting the dual number). In comparison with comedy, tragedy also allows more "polymorphy" (Björck 1950), metrically conditioned deviations from the local standard (e.g. Ionicizing ξεῖνος and κούρη for ξένος and κόρη); but comedy, too, occasionally offers non-parodic long datives in -οισι/-αισι next to regular -οις/-αις or first-person plural middle forms in -μεσθα next to -μεθα, and despite its phonological adjustment tragic πράσσω still remains distinct from Ionic πρήσσω. So it is not merely the acceptance of literary alternative forms, or the broader dialectal profile, that separates tragedy from comedy. Even in tragic choruses, Doric features other than the emblematic long ᾱ (p. 451) constitute little more than a superficial veneer (e.g. *a*-stem genitive plurals in -ᾶν, for Att. -ῶν, or pronominal νιν, as also in tragic dialogue).

What truly differentiates the guardian's lines from any speech in comedy is the fact that, for all its funny disruptions, comic discourse always centripetally approaches linguistic realism. By contrast, whether we look at the lexical, phraseological, or syntactic levels, tragedy avoids such realism at any cost. In the excerpt, for example, the replacement of common words by marked poeticisms is prominent (ἄναξ for βασιλεῦ, ηὔδα for ἔλεγε, χωρεῖς for βαδίζεις, μολών for ἐλθών), and other artificialities include prepositional anastrophe (τάχους ὕπο for ὑπὸ τάχους), the omission of definite articles (πόδα, ψυχή), and grammatically unnecessary as well as semantically redundant periphrases (κυκλῶν ἐμαυτὸν εἰς ἀναστροφήν for ἀναστρεφόμενος, ἔσχον φροντίδων ἐπιστάσεις for φροντίδες ἐπέστησαν). That two abstract nouns (ἐπίστασις, ἀναστροφή) are involved in the latter is no coincidence: there is a general tendency to replace concrete lexemes by abstract ones (often in -μα or -σις, e.g. φώνημα "voicing" for φωνή "voice"), and to prefer the non-specific/indefinite to the specific/definite – as if to bear out linguistically Aristotle's view (*Poet.* 1451b6–7) that (notably dramatic) poetry must deal with the general (τὰ καθόλου), not the specific (τὰ καθ᾽ ἕκαστον). Apart from the optional omission of the article, the preference for nominal over verbal types of expression, or the importance of metaphor (Arist. *Poet.* 1459a10), additional elements belonging here are the frequent "poetic plurals" (e.g. δώματα for δῶμα "house"), the use of simplex for compound verbs (e.g. κτείνω "to kill," θνῄσκω "to die" for ἀποκτείνω, ἀποθνῄσκω; the opposite effects tragic redundancy: e.g. εἰσορῶ for ὁρῶ "to see"), or even the remarkable frequency of the less specific subordinators ὅπως/ὡς, literally "how," instead of their standard counterparts final ἵνα "in order that" and declarative ὅτι "that." None of these traits is exclusively tragic, but their dense collocation creates a distinctive register; and this register, however malleable it may prove under the hands of innovators like Euripides (Stevens 1976), keeps as distant from any other high-style poetry as it was removed from the mundane conversations among the audience (cf. Rutherford 2012).

6. The Language of Prose

6.1. Ionic, Attic, Doric

Precisely what such conversations sounded like, we cannot of course know. An approximate rendering exists, at best, in the dialogues of Plato, a known admirer of Sophron's naturalistic mime. The cultivated everyday Attic Plato depicts is one of a whole range of Greek prose languages. In prose as in poetry, dialects, stylistic levels, and degrees of structural complexity varied greatly depending on authors, audiences, and generic purposes (Dover 1997). Compare, for instance, a mythographical fragment of Acusilaus of Argos (FGrHist 2 F 22), one of the earliest prose writers, with a passage from Pericles' funeral speech in Thucydides (2.36.4):

καὶ γίγνεται βασιλεὺς οὗτος Λαπιθέων καὶ τοῖς Κενταύροις πολεμέεσκε. ἔπειτα στήσας ἀκόν[τιον ἐν ἀγορᾶι θεὸν ἐκέλευεν ἀριθμεῖν. θεοῖ]σι δ᾽ οὐκ ἦεν [ἀρεστόν, καὶ] Ζεὺς ἰδὼν αὐτὸν ταῦτα ποιοῦντα ἀπειλεῖ καὶ ἐφορμᾶι τοὺς Κενταύρους, κἀκεῖνοι αὐτὸν κατακόπτουσιν ὄρθιον κατὰ γῆς καὶ ἄνωθεν πέτρην ἐπιτιθεῖσιν σῆμα, καὶ ἀποθνήσκει.

And this one (sc. Kaineus) becomes king of the Lapiths, and he would make war against the Centaurs. Then he set up a spear in the marketplace and gave order to consider it a god. But to the gods it was not pleasing, and Zeus, seeing that he was doing this, threatens him and urges on the Centaurs, and they strike him down, upright underneath the earth, and on top they put a rock as a tombstone, and he dies.

ὧν ἐγὼ τὰ μὲν κατὰ πολέμους ἔργα, οἷς ἕκαστα ἐκτήθη, ἢ εἴ τι αὐτοὶ ἢ οἱ πατέρες ἡμῶν βάρβαρον ἢ Ἕλληνα πολέμιον ἐπιόντα προθύμως ἠμυνάμεθα, μακρηγορεῖν ἐν εἰδόσιν οὐ βουλόμενος, ἐάσω· ἀπὸ δὲ οἵας τε ἐπιτηδεύσεως ἤλθομεν ἐπ᾽ αὐτὰ καὶ μεθ᾽ οἵας πολιτείας καὶ τρόπων ἐξ οἵων μεγάλα ἐγένετο, ταῦτα δηλώσας πρῶτον εἶμι καὶ ἐπὶ τὸν τῶνδε ἔπαινον, νομίζων ἐπί τε τῷ παρόντι οὐκ ἂν ἀπρεπῆ λεχθῆναι αὐτὰ καὶ τὸν πάντα ὅμιλον καὶ ἀστῶν καὶ ξένων ξύμφορον εἶναι ἐπακοῦσαι αὐτῶν.

Since I do not wish to make lengthy speeches before people who know these things, I will omit their deeds in war, by which it all was gained – or also if we ourselves or our fathers readily warded off an attacking enemy, barbarian or Greek: but from what type of enterprise we obtained it all, and under what kind of constitution and through which way of life it then became great, this I will first point out and then move on to the praise of these men, because I think that under the present circumstances it is not unsuitable for these things to be told and it may be useful for the entire crowd of locals and visitors to hear of them.

The Thucydidean passage is written in Attic, whereas Acusilaus used literary Ionic (cf. e.g. the unaugmented uncontracted iterative form πολεμέεσκε, or πέτρην ἐπιτιθεῖσιν vs. Att. πέτραν ἐπιτιθέασι; some Attic features have crept in during the transmission: e.g. word-initial aspiration, Κενταύροις for Κενταύροισι(ν), ποιοῦντα for ποιέοντα/ποιεῦντα). This difference reflects a general change in the history of Greek prose. Since prose writing first flourished among the enlightened intellectual elite of sixth-century Ionia (Miletus), the Ionic dialect was initially adopted also by non-Ionian prosaists, like the Dorian Acusilaus or the Athenian Pherecydes. During the second half of the fifth century, however, Attic prose began to assert itself. The growing cultural and political importance of Athens certainly played a role here, but the emancipation process may have been neither gradual nor restricted to Athens (Willi 2010). Unquestionably some of the earlier Attic prose writers – Antiphon in the *Tetralogies*, Andocides, or Thucydides – seem to be more influenced by Ionic (cf. Dion. Hal. *De Thuc.* 23), or at any rate less outspokenly Attic, than their later colleagues Plato, Xenophon, Lysias. Like the tragedians (p. 455), they would for example avoid the parochial -ττ- in words such as πράσσω/πράττω or use σύν instead of ξύν. However, some other, no less early, Athenian writers (Antiphon the Sophist and the anonymous "Old Oligarch") were not apparently affected by similar hesitations. Thus, the readiness to challenge the Ionic norm – as still observed by, say, the Hippocratic school from Cos or Antiochus of Syracuse – must have varied from the very moment when Attic, and in the colonial West also Doric (Cassio 1989), entered the game. And since challenging norms was high on the agenda of the sophists, this prolific group of internationally mobile prose writers may well be responsible for the resulting dialect competition in classical Greek prose. Eventually, of course, Attic and Attic-based Koine Greek were to win out, but alternative traditions did survive for some time, notably in the West. As late as the third century, Archimedes wrote his mathematical works in Sicilian Doric, and Doric prose was fostered also by the South Italian Pythagoreans (after Philolaus and Archytas), for identitarian reasons as much as out of convenience.

6.2. *Stylistic Elaboration*

In a more central respect too, the colonial West contributed much to the history of Greek prose. The first of our two sample passages, which is not untypical for its age, illustrates well what Aristotle called λέξις εἰρομένη "rambling-on style" (*Rhet.* 1409a24–35). The second, by contrast, shows complex patterns of subordination feeding into multilayered "periods" (λέξις κατεστραμμένη "rounded-off style"). Quite possibly the former is due to texts of this kind originating as lecture notes, which were not to be read as such but elaborated upon during an oral presentation (ἐπίδειξις): the frequency of historical presents also makes this look like a summary more than anything else (γίγνεται, ἀπειλεῖ, ἐφορμᾷ, etc.; cf. Lilja 1968). In any case, the progress from here to Thucydides must be due to stylistic theory, *qua* rhetoric, having become a higher-education subject during the fifth century, first in Sicily (Korax, Teisias) and then, mediated by Gorgias of Leontinoi, in Athens (Denniston 1952). By promoting the so-called "Gorgianic figures" – notably antithesis (ὧν ἐγὼ τὰ μὲν … ἐάσω ~ ἀπὸ δὲ οἵας … εἶμι καὶ ἐπὶ τὸν τῶνδε ἔπαινον), parisosis (νομίζων … λεχθῆναι αὐτά ~ καὶ τὸν πάντα ὅμιλον … ἐπακοῦσαι αὐτῶν), and homoeoteleuton (rhyme: καὶ ἀστῶν καὶ ξένων … ἐπακοῦσαι αὐτῶν), all used to balance out individual clauses in the period – Gorgias ennobled oratory, and through it other prose, into something comparable in status to poetry, *Kunstprosa* (Norden 1898). Such teaching was then continued by Gorgias's pupil Isocrates, whose obsession with euphony not only made him avoid hiatus and consonantal dissonance, but also follow Thrasymachus of Chalcedon, the "inventor" of prose rhythm, in seeking out specific rhythmical patterns. In order to keep prose distinct from poetry, poetic rhythms were proscribed at the end of clauses and periods (e.g. – ∪ ∪ – x, as in a hexameter), and clearly prosaic patterns favored (e.g. – ∪ – x, as often in Antisthenes, or paeonic – ∪ ∪ ∪ and ∪ ∪ ∪ –, as discussed by Arist. *Rhet.* 1409a12–21: note that καὶ ἐπὶ τὸν τῶνδ(ε) ἔπαινον above is analyzable as ∪ ∪ ∪ – | – ∪ – x, although in individual cases coincidence can rarely be ruled out).

6.3.   *Post-Classical Directions*

Subsequently, rhetorical theory developed into an ever more complex system, as distinctions between stylistic levels – including the tripartition into a grand, middle, and plain type (ἁδρὸς vs. μέσος vs. ἰσχνὸς χαρακτήρ) – and their correlation with specific names (e.g. Gorgias vs. Isocrates vs. Lysias) and/or purposes began to be codified. Leaving aside technical prose (Rydbeck 1967), whose authors forsook literary elaboration for maximal precision (with new "technical" vocabulary: e.g. adjectives in -ικός and -ώδης, abstract nouns in -σις and -ία, compounding), any such classification was transferable from oratory to other genres (e.g. "grand" Thucydides vs. "middle" Herodotus vs. "plain" Xenophon for historiography).

At the same time, however, a more narrowly linguistic issue became as important as the ideal selection of lexemes or the weighing of clauses. Starting in the fourth century, the various local dialects were gradually leveled out and eventually, though sometimes only centuries later, replaced by "Koine Greek," an Attic stripped of its more exceptional characteristics (such as the geminates -ρρ- and -ττ- previously mentioned: pp. 455 and 457; cf. Debrunner and Scherer 1969). As the Koine itself evolved further, the gap between it and the dialect of Attic prose around 400 BCE continuously widened. Hence, after Hellenistic and Roman scholars had canonized much of this prose, later writers had to decide whether to follow the classical models or to stay closer to the (educated) spoken Greek of their own time – for instance by abandoning the optative, merging the functions of the aorist and the perfect, substituting preposition-governed substantival infinitives to subordinate clauses, or just regularizing paradigms (e.g. οἴδαμεν/ἐδώκαμεν for ἴσμεν/ἔδομεν). Both were sensible options, and so both were taken. On the one side, intellectuals like Polybius and Plutarch wrote in literary Koine Greek, whereas the Koine used by Hellenistic and Roman novelists or in the *New Testament* catered for less demanding audiences; technical and philosophical writers like Galen or Epictetus occupied some middle ground. On the other side, Dionysius of Halicarnassus was a prominent exponent of a first "Atticist" wave, in the first centuries BCE / CE, holding up the clarity (σαφήνεια) of the major Attic orators against the pomposity of the more recent "Asianic" style (of which less direct evidence survives, although the letters of St Paul may give an idea); later on, in the second and third centuries AD when a second wave led by grammarians and lexicographers such as Phrynichus and Pollux promoted the exclusive use of classical vocabulary, authors like Aelius Aristides, Arrian, or Lucian chose to follow suit (Schmid 1887–97). Admittedly, not all of them showed the same degree of doggedness, but the fundamental divide between an artificially classicizing, purist literary language and a more popular alternative had now become so ingrained that it was to survive until modern times, where the struggle between *katharevousa* and *dimotiki* has only just been overcome. Thus, the linguistic history of Ancient Greek literature both started and ended with a *Kunstsprache* – but as in every good ring composition much intricate action happened in between.

REFERENCES

Adrados, F. R. 2005. *A History of the Greek Language: From its Origins to the Present.* Leiden.

Bakker, E. J., ed. 2010. *A Companion to the Ancient Greek Language.* Oxford.

Berg, N. 1978. "Parergon metricum: der Ursprung des griechischen Hexameters." *Münchener Studien zur Sprachwissenschaft* 37: 11–36.

Björck, G. 1950. *Das Alpha impurum und die tragische Kunstsprache.* Uppsala.

Bowie, A. M. 1981. *The Poetic Dialect of Sappho and Alcaeus.* New York.

Buck, C. D. 1955. *The Greek Dialects: Grammar, Selected Inscriptions, Glossary.* Chicago.

Cassio, A. C. 1989. "Lo sviluppo della prosa dorica e le tradizioni occidentali della retorica greca." In A. C. Cassio, ed., *Tra Sicilia e Magna Grecia: Aspetti di interazione culturale nel IV sec. a. C.*, Rome, 137–57.

Cassio, A. C. 1993. "Alcmane, il dialetto di Cirene e la filologia alessandrina." *Rivista di Filologia* 121: 24–36.

Cassio, A. C., ed. 2008. *Storia delle lingue letterarie greche.* Florence.

Chantraine, P. 1953–58. *Grammaire homérique.* 2 vols. Paris.

Colvin, S. 1999. *Dialect in Aristophanes and the Politics of Language in Ancient Greek Literature.* Oxford.

Colvin, S. 2007. *A Historical Greek Reader: Mycenaean to the Koiné.* Oxford.

Colvin, S. 2014. *A Brief History of Ancient Greek.* Oxford.

Debrunner, A. and A. Scherer. 1969. *Geschichte der griechischen Sprache II: Grundfragen und Grundzüge des nachklassischen Griechisch*, 2nd edn. Berlin.

Denniston, J. D. 1952. *Greek Prose Style.* Oxford.

Dover, K. J. 1997. *The Evolution of Greek Prose Style.* Oxford.

Hackstein, O. 2002. *Die Sprachform der homerischen Epen. Faktoren morphologischer Variabilität in literarischen Frühformen: Traditionen, Sprachwandel, sprachliche Anachronismen.* Wiesbaden.

Hamm, E.-M. 1958. *Grammatik zu Sappho und Alkaios*, 2nd edn. Berlin.

Hiersche, R. 1970. *Grundzüge der griechischen Sprachgeschichte bis zur klassischen Zeit.* Wiesbaden.

Hinge, G. 2006. *Die Sprache Alkmans: Textgeschichte und Sprachgeschichte.* Wiesbaden.

Hoekstra, A. 1965. *Homeric Modifications of Formulaic Prototypes: Studies in the Development of Greek Epic Diction.* Amsterdam.

Horrocks, G. 2010. *Greek: A History of the Language and its Speakers*, 2nd edn. Oxford.

Janko, R. 1982. *Homer, Hesiod, and the Hymns: Diachronic Development in Epic Diction.* Cambridge.

Lilja, S. 1968. *On the Style of the Earliest Greek Prose.* Helsinki.

Meillet, A. 1923. *Les Origines indo-européennes des mètres grecs.* Paris.

Meillet, A. 1975. *Aperçu d'une histoire de la langue grecque*, 8th edn. Paris.

Meister, K. 1921. *Die homerische Kunstsprache.* Leipzig.

Mickey, K. 1981. "Dialect consciousness and literary language: an example from Ancient Greek." *Transactions of the Philological Society* 35–66.

Miller, D. G. 1982. *Homer and the Ionian Epic Tradition.* Innsbruck.

Miller, D. G. 2013. *Ancient Greek Dialects and Early Authors: Introduction to the Dialect Mixture in Homer, with Notes on Lyric and Herodotus.* Berlin.

Mühlestein, H. 1958. "Einige mykenische Wörter." *Museum Helveticum* 15: 222–6.

Norden, E. 1898. *Die antike Kunstprosa vom VI. Jahrhundert v. Chr. bis in die Zeit der Renaissance.* 2 vols. Leipzig.

Page, D. L. 1951. *Alcman: The Partheneion.* Oxford.

Palmer, L. R. 1980. *The Greek Language.* London.

Risch, E. 1954. "Die Sprache Alkmans." *Museum Helveticum* 11: 20–37.

Risch, E. 1974. *Wortbildung der homerischen Sprache*, 2nd edn. Berlin.

Rutherford, R. B. 2012. *Greek Tragic Style: Form, Language and Interpretation*. Cambridge.

Rydbeck, L. 1967. *Fachprosa, vermeintliche Volkssprache und Neues Testament: Zur Beurteilung der sprachlichen Niveauunterschiede im nachklassischen Griechisch*. Uppsala.

Schmid, W. 1887–97. *Der Atticismus in seinen Hauptvertretern von Dionysius von Halikarnass bis auf den zweiten Philostratus*. 5 vols. Stuttgart.

Schmitt, R. 1967. *Dichtung und Dichtersprache in indogermanischer Zeit*. Wiesbaden.

Schmitt, R. 1991. *Einführung in die griechischen Dialekte*. 2nd edn. Darmstadt.

Stevens, Ph. T. 1976. *Colloquial Expressions in Euripides*. Wiesbaden.

Tichy, E. 1981. "Hom. ἀνδροτῆτα und die Vorgeschichte des daktylischen Hexameters." *Glotta* 59: 28–67.

Wathelet, P. 1970. *Les Traits éoliens dans la langue de l'épopée grecque*. Rome.

West, M. L. 1974. *Studies in Greek Elegy and Iambus*. Berlin.

West, M. L. 1982. *Greek Metre*. Oxford.

Willi, A. 2002. "Languages on stage: Aristophanic language, cultural history, and Athenian identity." In A. Willi, ed., *The Language of Greek Comedy*. Oxford, 111–49.

Willi, A. 2003. *The Languages of Aristophanes: Aspects of Linguistic Variation in Classical Attic Greek*. Oxford.

Willi, A. 2008. *Sikelismos: Sprache, Literatur und Gesellschaft im griechischen Sizilien (8.–5. Jh. v. Chr.)*. Basel.

Willi, A. 2010. "Attic as the language of the Classics." In Ch. C. Caragounis, ed., *Greek: A Language in Evolution*. Hildesheim, 101–18.

Willi, A. 2011. "Language, Homeric." In M. Finkelberg, ed., *The Homer Encyclopedia*. Oxford. 2.459–64.

FURTHER READING

All histories of the Greek language (e.g. Hiersche 1970, Meillet 1975, Palmer 1980, Adrados 2005, Horrocks 2010, Colvin 2014; cf. also Miller 2013) include chapters on the literary dialects and registers, but by far the best treatment for each genre, with commented excerpts and ample bibliography, is to be found in Cassio (2008). In English, the relevant chapters in Bakker (2010) provide reliable up-to-date guidance, as does the annotated reader by Colvin (2007). Greek meter is presented clearly and exhaustively by West (1982); for an overview over the Greek dialects and their characteristics Buck (1955) and Schmitt (1991) remain standard.

CHAPTER 30

Poetic Devices in Greek Literature
Pleasure and Creative Appropriation

Nicholas Baechle

αἴνει δὲ παλαιὸν μὲν οἶνον, ἄνθεα δ᾽ ὕμνων νεωτέρων.
(Praise old wine, but fresh blooms of songs.)

Pind. Ol. 9.48–9

Anyone who reads Greek poetry has been pulled up short by the beauty and richness of striking passages – similes in Homer,[1] images in Pindar, metaphors in Aeschylus. But what would count as a successful use of a poetic device for a Greek audience? To begin with, what counts as a device? And how are we, at such a remove historically and culturally, to gauge what success might mean? For the sake of argument: poetic devices call attention to themselves through a deviation from a narrative line – as with ecphrasis or simile – or a perceptible thickening of the poetic quality of the language – as with metaphor or pictorial description – or by both means. And a successful device, as opposed to the inert or merely imitative, is whatever is perceived as such by an audience. This definition of a successful device sounds circular but helps us keep an eye on the complexities of our hermeneutic position. We are more conscious of trying to locate our interpretation within the aesthetic and interpretative horizon of expectation of the original audience, and we are reminded that our own horizon of expectation results from a history of reception (Jauss 1967/1982 and Holub 1989, 57–69). More positively, these definitions focus on the open-ended potential of poetic devices; they allowed the poet the possibility of reorienting his audience's attention to expressive resources allowed by the tradition and to the skill displayed in their creative appropriation. Greek poets were working within a tradition constantly re-elaborating itself and composing for an audience, or for readers, with a cultivated sense of poetic possibility. And since each use of a device was *new*, an audience member or reader was alive to further possibility, a realization of a device that was pleasurable, engaging, even surprising or unsettling.

Given the range of devices available and the nature of the tradition, simultaneously so rich and so fragmented, only a sketch can be attempted here. An extensive taxonomy, as in the rhetorical tradition, is not possible. Nor is it possible to do justice to the history of particular devices. Offered instead are heuristically conceived interpretative discussions of three treatments of ecphrasis, and of other devices bound with them in the same poetic contexts.[2] Three poets, working within diverse cultural horizons, will be considered – the composer of Hesiod's *Shield*, Apollonius Rhodius, and

---

A Companion to Greek Literature, First Edition. Edited by Martin Hose and David Schenker.
© 2016 John Wiley & Sons, Inc. Published 2020 by John Wiley & Sons, Inc.

Euripides – and the focus will be on their responses to and uses of the kind of ecphrasis that begins with Homer's description of Achilles' shield. The aim is to make use of a particularly fruitful example to illustrate a number of the possibilities opened up through the poet's reorientation of the audience's attention. These are both thematic, given that such devices thus become noticeable parts of the poem's workings, and intertextual, given the poet's appropriation of the genre he was working in and his relation to other parts of the tradition. But we cannot forget the novelty of a performance or text, and the sheer pleasure an audience or readers took in poetry as an event unfolding in the moment.

1. The *Shield*: Pleasure and New Realizations of Traditional Devices

The *Shield* is a short epic narrative of Heracles' fight with the robber Cycnus, and with his father Ares, and is dated to the late seventh or early sixth century (Janko 1986, 42–3). It has survived in the manuscript tradition because it was attributed to Hesiod and embedded in his *Catalogue of Women* (Most 2006, lv–lix). As the title indicates, its most prominent feature is an extended ecphrasis describing Heracles' shield, and it has often been seen as the work of a second- or third-rate poet emulating the ecphrasis of *Iliad* 18.[3] But both the limitations of the poet and his obvious efforts to please his audience are in fact valuable. The text allows us to focus on a basic question easily overlooked by modern readers preoccupied with textual interpretation and historical contextualization: how did poetic devices open up a shared and familiar space for enjoyment of the poet's skill and inventiveness?

The description of a shield is an iconic generic device, clearly bounded, which by interrupting the narrative calls attention to the unfolding of inventive description.[4] Moreover, because this form of ecphrasis was both notional and traditional, it invited elaboration.[5] As various critics have noted, in addition to being disproportionately long in relation to the surrounding narrative, this ecphrasis is both longer than Homer's and has a larger number of scenes. Apparently, the realization of the device seemed to the poet to demand excess and expansion – and he delivered. Visible in flashes, however, is a creative response to what we can assume were many previous ecphrastic descriptions:

Ἐν δ’ ἦν ἠυκόμου Δανάης τέκος, ἱππότα Περσεύς,
οὔτ’ ἄρ’ ἐπιψαύων σάκεος ποσὶν οὔθ’ ἑκὰς αὐτοῦ,
θαῦμα μέγα φράσσασθ’, ἐπεὶ οὐδαμῇ ἐστήρικτο
[. . .].
αὐτὸς δὲ σπεύδοντι καὶ ἐρρίγοντι ἐοικὼς
Περσεὺς Δαναΐδης ἐτιταίνετο· ταὶ δὲ μετ’ αὐτὸν
Γοργόνες ἄπλητοί τε καὶ οὐ φαταὶ ἐρρώοντο
ἱέμεναι μαπέειν· ἐπὶ δὲ χλωροῦ ἀδάμαντος
βαινουσέων ἰάχεσκε σάκος μεγάλῳ ὀρυμαγδῷ
ὀξέα καὶ λιγέως· ἐπὶ δὲ ζώνῃσι δράκοντε
δοιὼ ἀπηωρεῦντ’ ἐπικυρτώοντε κάρηνα·
λίχμαζον δ’ ἄρα τώ γε, μένει δ’ ἐχάρασσον ὀδόντας
ἄγρια δερκομένω· ἐπὶ δὲ δεινοῖσι καρήνοις
Γοργείοις ἐδονεῖτο μέγας φόβος ...
(*Aspis* 216–18 and 228–37)

Upon it was fine-haired Danae's son, the horseman Perseus, neither touching the shield with his feet nor far from it – a great wonder to observe, since nowhere was he attached to it ....

Perseus himself, Danae's son, was outstretched, and he looked as though he were hastening and shuddering. The Gorgons, dreadful and unspeakable, were rushing after him, eager to catch him; as they ran on the pallid adamant, the shield resounded sharply and piercingly with a loud noise. At their girdles, two serpents hung down, their heads arching forward; both of them were licking with their tongues, and they ground their teeth with strength, glaring savagely. Upon the terrible heads of the Gorgons rioted great Fear. (trans. Most 2007)

Whatever our judgments as to the success of the intended effects, the poet is clearly composing for an acculturated audience experienced in the oral performance of epic. Ecphrasis lends itself to vivid narrative description, made all the more so by an emphasis on the artfulness that seems to convert the pictorial image into life and movement. This description intensifies such effects to the point of wonder: the pictures jump out of, and even off, a flat visual field, as the first image does. And there is noise as well; the grinding of teeth is heard repeatedly, and here the shield rings with the running of the Gorgons, who have also popped up into a third dimension (cf. Vernant 1997, 391–2).

This must have been fun. How we understand the audience's taste is another matter. Martin (2005) has argued that the poem is a piece of pulp epic, evidence of a trash aesthetic. His interpretation emphasizes its preoccupation with death, gore, and the macabre. (See, especially, lines 144–60 and 248–69.) Others have started from these emphases and interpreted the ecphrasis in relation to the surrounding narrative. The horrors of war are vividly represented on the shield of a hero who defeats not only a violent robber but also War himself. Hence, the value of Heracles' victory can be magnified (Fränkel 1975) or, since it is achieved through warfare, both valorized and subverted (Thalmann 1984). Such thematic reading of ecphrasis seems natural to us; there is a productive tension created by an interplay between the contextual ground and a description that calls attention to itself (Fowler, 1991, 25–28 and 33–35).

This same tension must have been evident to its original audience, in part because the ecphrasis could not but be heard against Homer's. His picture of cosmic order is one in which warfare has a place, but which embraces a much fuller, and ultimately more reassuring, evocation of human life (Elsner 2002, 3–6). As Conte has argued, ancient poetry functioned as and through a repertoire of traditional generic means, including poetic devices like ecphrasis, which opens up the possibility of allusion. However we deal with the theoretical problem of authorial intent,[6] then, the texts assume, and can demonstrate for us, diverse cultural competencies.[7] Even in listening to an unsubtle poet, an ancient audience must have responded in several ways, conceptually distinguishable but experientially implicated with one another.

2. Apollonius and 'Textualized' Epic.
The Play of Tradition and his Readers' Responses

This becomes more evident when we look at the ecphrasis on Jason's cloak in the Lemnian episode of the *Argonautika*.[8] The epic tradition has advanced more than 300 years and become thoroughly textualized, for want of a better word. Poetry, even epic, is usually divorced from public performance. Apollonius is writing for an audience of Hellenistic readers, some of them scholars, steeped in the Homeric text and its conventions; his text will assume similar responses but play in a sophisticated way with generic norms and allusion.[9]

Lemnos is the first stop on the Argonauts' journey, and Jason first finds adventure there. After a recounting of the unfortunate erotic history of the Lemnian women and a description of their initial fear and consternation, the story moves on, by means of messages and deliberation, to an invitation to come to Hypsipyle. Jason puts on his cloak to go:

Αὐτὰρ ὅγ᾽ ἀμφ᾽ ὤμοισι, θεᾶς Ἰτωνίδος ἔργον,
δίπλακα πορφυρέην περονήσατο, τήν οἱ ὄπασσε
Παλλάς, ὅτε πρῶτον δρυόχους ἐπεβάλλετο νηὸς
Ἀργοῦς, καὶ κανόνεσσι δάε ζυγὰ μετρήσασθαι.
τῆς μὲν ῥηίτερόν κεν ἐς ἠέλιον ἀνιόντα
ὄσσε βάλοις ἢ κεῖνο μεταβλέψειας ἔρευθος·
δὴ γάρ τοι μέσση μὲν ἐρευθήεσσα τέτυκτο·
ἄκρα δὲ πορφυρέη πάντη πέλεν, ἐν δ᾽ ἄρ᾽ ἑκάστῳ
τέρματι δαίδαλα πολλὰ διακριδὸν εὖ ἐπέπαστο ...
           (Apoll. Rhod. *Argon.* 1.721–29)

Around his shoulders Jason pinned a double cloak of purple, the work of the Itonian goddess, which Pallas had given to him when first she set up the stocks for the building the *Argo* and issued instructions for measuring the cross-beams with the rule. You could cast your eyes more easily towards the rising sun than gaze upon the brilliant redness of the cloak. Its centre was bright red, the border all the way round purple, and along the full length of the edge had been woven many cunning designs in sequence. (trans. Hunter 1993a)

The panels on the cloak represent diverse mythological scenes. Though modern readers seem agreed that the collection is programmatic and/or thematically proleptic, there is much disagreement about its interpretation.[10] For the Hellenistic reader, encountering this passage for the first time, the startling presentation and contextualization of the ecphrasis would have been a more immediate interpretative provocation. As has often been argued, the choice of object, an overwhelmingly beautiful cloak, calls deliberate attention to the poet's deviation from the obvious model, the ecphrasis of *Iliad* 18, and to the nature of the subsequent interlude with Hypsipyle as a kind of erotic *aristeia* (e.g., Hunter 1993b, 48). This interpretation is based in part on Apollonius' exploitation of conventional elements from arming scenes. The clearest signal, for the kind of reader assumed, would have been the light coming off the cloak. The motif of the gleam of armor and weapons is a sign of heroic strength and of coming success in battle.[11]

That motif is often realized, and foregrounded, through similes invoking fire, stars, etc., both during arming scenes and the hero's *aristeia*. It is most developed during Achilles' arming and long *aristeia* in *Iliad* 19–22.[12] The opening line of the simile concluding this scene, as Jason sets off to meet Hypsipyle, would have been doubly significant:

Βῆ δ᾽ ἴμεναι προτὶ ἄστυ, φαεινῷ ἀστέρι ἶσος,
ὅν ῥά τε νηγατέῃσιν ἐεργόμεναι καλύβῃσιν
νύμφαι θηήσαντο δόμων ὕπερ ἀντέλλοντα,
καί σφισι κυανέοιο δι᾽ αἰθέρος ὄμματα θέλγει
καλὸν ἐρευθόμενος, γάνυται δέ τε ἠιθέοιο
παρθένος ἱμείρουσα μετ᾽ ἀλλοδαποῖσιν ἐόντος
ἀνδράσιν, ᾧ κέν μιν μνηστὴν κομέωσι τοκῆες –
τῷ ἴκελος προπόλοιο κατὰ στίβον ἤιεν ἥρως·
           (Apoll. Rhod. *Argon.* 1.774–81)

He went towards the city like the bright star whose rising is admired by young brides, shut up in their new-built chambers. Its red brilliance through the dark air bewitches their eyes, and the virgin, too, rejoices in her desire for the young man who lives in a distant city, the future husband for whom her parents are keeping her. Like that star did the hero follow behind the messenger. (trans. Hunter 1993a)

First, because of the audience's experience with the use of such similes in two recurrent narrative contexts, their adaptation to an erotic narrative would have been surprising, entertaining, and thought provoking.[13] Second, the simile alludes to Achilles' *aristeia* and in particular to its climax, in *Iliad* 22. When Priam sees Achilles approaching the city (cf. προτὶ ἄστυ, *Il.* 22.21), Achilles is compared to Orion, the Dog Star, a sign of disease and destruction (*Il.* 22.25–31). On the wall, Priam laments, beats his head in grief, and pleads with Hector, stationed at the gates below, to avoid a fatal duel with Achilles. And at the climax of the narrative sequence following, after Hector has run away and then turned to stand his ground, Achilles' spear, which will soon pass through Hector's neck, is described with another star simile (*Il.* 22.317–20), and this time the comparison is to Hesperos, the evening star, as in Apollonius' simile.[14]

Making the connection between Jason and Achilles, then, depends on the reader's assimilation of epic conventions, on perceiving multiple allusions – both indirect, to the shield ecphrasis, and direct, to the star similes – and on a response to the interactions among poetic devices and allusions. How the reader conceives of that connection is an open question. Many modern readers have assumed a contrastive relationship, between a new kind of Apollonian hero, defined by erotic power, persuasion, and diplomacy, and a conventional epic heroism represented by Achilles, defined by strength, courage, and the seemingly less ambiguous problem of facing death in battle.[15] However, this reduces the possibilities opened up here for reading heroism or, better, heroic agency. Barchiesi (2001, 146–47) argues that allusion means two open interpretative fields are brought into relation; comparing A to B demands interpreting the intertext in relation to B, as well as the alluding text in relation to A. Neither Apollonius's version of heroism nor Homer's can be so easily pinned down, even if thinking about Jason means thinking about Achilles' actions and heroism as a field of reference.[16]

Moreover, making sense of the content of the simile, its connection with the ecphrasis, and the choice of a cloak as its subject demands a further intertextual field of reference, Odysseus' dealings with women. The simile hinges on the evening star, associated with love and marriage (Fränkel 1968, 105; Vian 1974, 86). And the women watching the star include both young brides waiting for their husbands and a lone virgin, waiting to be married to a fiancé, when he returns from a foreign land. These are easily connected to the Lemnian women and Hypsipyle. And the simile, taking on an implicit narrative function, conveys their feelings, sentimental and perhaps self-deluding.[17] However, the idea of the virgin waiting for her fiancé to return is puzzling. Jason is coming from foreign parts and will *become* a possible fiancé (in her eyes), but the reference only makes complete sense if Odysseus is brought in via a doubled allusion. As an unmarried daughter of a king receiving a charismatic stranger, whom she will want to marry, Hypsipyle can be likened to Nausicaa. But because of the reference to the cloak, and the particular circumstances of the virgin in the simile, Hypsipyle's emotional vulnerability can also be compared to Penelope's, in the scene in which Odysseus, in disguise, describes the cloak, pin, and tunic that she had given him at parting. He wore a thick, doubled, purple cloak, like Jason's; the artistry of the pin was so lifelike it evoked wonder, which recalls some of the effects in Apollonius's description (esp. *Argon.* 1.763–67); and his tunic was so fine that "many women gazed at it [or him?]" (*Od.* 19.225–35).[18] Odysseus' story praises Penelope's gifts and skill in weaving, but also, implicitly, his effect on women. Further, it demonstrates his abilities in the direction of persuasion and manipulation. All this Penelope confirms, when she bursts into tears of longing and grief. Thus, the simile and the Odyssean templates taken together seem to imply that Hypsipyle will be doubly helpless before Jason, both because of her inexperience and because of his "heroic" amatory powers. But questions are raised both as to the nature of Odysseus' powers and as to the uses that Jason will make of his own.

Thinking about Jason's version of heroic agency, and about what kind of poem we find ourselves in, demands triangulating Apollonius' text with versions of heroism and heroic action from both the *Odyssey* and the *Iliad*. However these questions are considered, it is clear that conspicuous poetic devices, manipulation of epic convention, and complex forms of allusion must have pulled the reader in; the text assumed and provoked several forms of response. And it demonstrates brilliantly the kind of open-ended textual play made possible through skillful generic positioning and appropriation of multiple means provided by the tradition. This is one of the most important aims of the passage as a whole, and the combination of ecphrasis and simile in particular; the readerly possibilities offered by the poem are demonstrated, as are Apollonius' abilities as a poet.

3.   Euripides and the Performance Culture of Athenian Drama

Modern scholars take to this kind of reading like ducks to water. What may be harder to appreciate fully are the analogous forms of communication in the performance culture in which Euripides composed. The audience of Athenian tragedy was intimately acquainted with a repertoire of poetic means, and "intertextual" reference was always possible, even if the culture was still largely oral; the current performance was measured against and connected to a continuing history of experience, and to the larger poetic tradition as well.[19] Simultaneously, everyone concerned was familiar with the methods, technique, and talents of the poet's rivals; in a competitive context, succeeding as a playwright meant calling attention to creative appropriation.[20] In the immediacy of performance, engagement and taking pleasure in the poet's skill and inventiveness went hand in hand. Further, a tragedian was very much aware of operating within a system of distinctive and evolving forms of performance; in the same festival context, the audience could be responding to comedy, satyr play, and dithyramb, each with its own poetic resources and version, or versions, of *Kunstsprache(n)*. In sum, there was a hothouse atmosphere for the exploitation and development of poetic devices of all kinds.

For tragedy, this thesis is hard to substantiate in detail; so much of the production of so many poets has been lost. Moreover, tragedy very seldom makes its competitive dynamics evident. The problem of evidence, of points of reference for assessing the distinctiveness or conventionality of a piece of tragic poetry, always remains. But Old Comedy is vocal about competition and innovation.[21] There is self-assertive and ongoing play with the poet's persona, as well as critical back and forth with rivals. This is easiest to follow in the rivalry staged by Aristophanes and an older competitor, Cratinus. Cratinus was one of the greatest poets of Old Comedy but is presented in Aristophanes' *Knights* as a drunk and a has-been (*Equ.* 526–36) and, by implication, as no longer intimate with the personified – and female – Comedy, whose lover was now Aristophanes (*Equ.* 515–16). Cratinus responded the next year with *Wineflask* (*Pytine*), in part by one-upping Aristophanes' sexual metaphor. A scholion to *Knights* (Σ Aristoph. *Equ.* 400a = Cratinus, *Pytine* test. ii, PCG Vol. IV) tells us that Cratinus was the protagonist and married to Comedy; he is a husband, not just a newly successful lover. But the metaphor is extended. She wants to divorce Cratinus for κάκωσις, maltreatment; seemingly, she is an ἐπίκληρος, an "heiress," and her husband is not doing his legally prescribed sexual duty because he is a drunk and/or old and impotent.[22]

Using this extended metaphor as a premise, Cratinus has constructed a play that makes clearer the comic poet's relation to his audience and the function of comic personae. No longer "performing" for Comedy means not succeeding with comedy's audience. Only in performance, as he engages and gratifies his audience by demonstrating his capabilities as a comedian, can he be successful. Accordingly, Cratinus takes what might be seen as damaging abuse, his drunkenness and/or impotence, and integrates it into an inventive plot that leads, presumably, to his vindication, if not his reformation. And he won, defeating the first version of Aristophanes'

Clouds. The play was thus an ironic demonstration of comedic virility. Moreover, even though he is constructing what might be read at some points as externally referential biography, his comic persona is a function of the ongoing game he is playing with his younger rival, and not easily disentangled from the construction of the play.[23]

The same use of poetic personae bound up with the internal workings of the comedy and of sexual metaphors for poetic inventiveness is evident in *Frogs*. Clearly, the presentation of Euripides' persona has been shaped by a system of oppositions to Aeschylus'.[24] Dionysus has been overcome with longing for Euripides, a "γόνιμον ποιητὴν [. . .] ὅστις ῥῆμα γενναῖον λάκοι" (*Ran.* 96–7), "a potent poet who can utter forth a noble phrase." All the tragedians left in Athens after his death are only capable of "piddling on tragedy" (*Ran.* 95: προσουρήσαντα τῇ τραγῳδίᾳ). Like Cratinus, Euripides is, it seems, a virile poet, which should mean he is capable of inventive diction in a traditional sense, of startling metaphor, striking compounds, etc. Still, Dionysus's samples of Euripidean phrases, like his taste and judgment, are presented as ridiculous.[25] An opposition to the strength and impetus of Aeschylean language is anticipated (esp., *Ran.* 836–39, 853–55, 924–29, 1056–61). But Dionysus' original motivation, his longing for renewed and exciting verbal performance, made intuitive sense to an Athenian audience. And Euripides was capable of giving his audience this kind of pleasure; he is not poetically impotent, though the play forces a contrast between his verbal qualities – especially in sophistically flavored argument, which implies trimeter dialogue – and those of Aeschylus (esp., *Ran.* 771–6, 814–29, 937–43, 1491–8). When the comic focus is on lyric, Euripides is presented as all too capable of pleasing his audience. Aeschylus is now presented as a different kind of contrastive foil; his lyrics are beautiful (*Ran.* 1252–6), but monotonous (1261 ff.). Euripides', on the other hand, are exciting but meretricious. Aeschylus brings on Euripides' Muse to provide a vulgar musical accompaniment to his first sample of Euripidean lyric, and on seeing her Dionysus says: αὕτη ποθ' ἡ Μοῦσ' οὐκ ἐλεσβίαζεν, οὔ. "*This* Muse wasn't a whore in her previous life. Oh, no." (1308).[26] The joke follows up on a reference to the vulgarity of Euripides' musical sources (1301–3), some with erotic associations.[27] And it is extended by Aeschylus at the end of the parody, when he talks about Euripides, "ἀνὰ τὸ δωδεκαμήχανον Κυρήνης μελοποιῶν," "composing lyrics with tricks by the dozen, like Cyrene" (1327–8). Cyrene was a famously versatile prostitute; Euripides is pandering to the taste of the audience, and his lyric is pleasuring them like an inventive sexual performer.

The jokes help in developing a picture of Euripides' performative relationship with his audience, and make up to some extent for our not being able to make comparisons with run-of-the-mill competitors. Euripides must have succeeded as a composer of lyric, with at least a significant part of his audience, partly through creative use of innovations associated with the so-called New Music.[28] He proved himself as a performer, and one capable of conspicuous innovation, which is what allows Aristophanes to skewer him. As usual, Aristophanes seems fascinated, not at all repelled, by Euripides' experimentation with the limits and resources of generic means (Silk 2000, 50–52 and 415–17).

In terms of its discernible poetic flavor, as opposed to its hypothetical musical effect, Aeschylus's pastiche is aimed at the pictorial and picturesque style associated with dithyramb and utilized by Euripides in the later stages of his career.[29] Lyrics like this must have given his audience pleasure. Otherwise, the jokes in *Frogs* are not as funny as they could be, and it is hard to account fully, in a competitive context, for the developments in dithyramb or for its influence on tragic lyric. In fact, we have explicit ancient testimony (Plut. *Lys.* 15.2–3 and *Nic.* 29) as to the popularity of Euripidean lyric in the late fifth century.

This is the kind of lyric we get in the first *stasimon* of the *Electra*,[30] in which Euripides' ecphrasis on Achilles' shield occurs. Particularly in the first strophe and antistrophe, the ode is built up through a series of striking images, often expanded internally by the paratactic accretion of pictorial detail, and making frequent use of descriptive adjectives, some of them novel compounds:[31]

κλειναὶ νᾶες, αἵ ποτ' ἔβατε Τροίαν
τοῖς ἀμετρήτοις ἐρετμοῖς
πέμπουσαι χορεύματα Νηρήιδων,
ἵν' ὁ φίλαυλος ἔπαλλε δελ-   435
φὶς πρώιραις κυανεμβόλοι-
σιν εἱλισσόμενος,
πορεύων τὸν τᾶς Θέτιδος
κοῦφον ἅλμα ποδῶν Ἀχιλῆ
σὺν Ἀγαμέμνονι Τρωίας   440
ἐπὶ Σιμουντίδας ἀκτάς.
Νηρῆιδες δ' Εὐβοῖδας ἄκρας λιποῦσαι
μόχθους ἀσπιστὰς ἀκμόνων
Ἡφαίστου χρυσέων ἔφερον τευχέων,
ἀνά τε Πήλιον ἀνά τ' ἐρυ-   445
μνᾶς Ὄσσας ἱερὰς νάπας
Νυμφαίας σκοπιὰς
†κόρας μάτευσ'† ἔνθα πατὴρ
ἱππότας τρέφεν Ἑλλάδι φῶς
Θέτιδος εἰναλίας γόνον   450
ταχύπορον πόδ' Ἀτρείδαις.
                    (Eur. *El.* 432–51)

Glorious ships, which once went Troyward on those countless oars, convoying the Nereids' dances, as the aulos-loving dolphin leaped and whirled at dark-nosed prows and brought the son of Thetis, Achilles light-springing in his step, with Agamemnon to the shores of Simois by Troy. Nereids coming from Euboean capes bore armourer's labours from Hephaestus' anvil, a golden equipage, up along Pelion, along sheer Ossa's sacred woodland slopes, eyries of the Nymphs, †seeking the maidens† where the old horse-man was nurturing a bright light for Hellas, sea-dwelling Thetis' child, swift runner for the Atreidae. (trans. Cropp 1988)

As the episode ended, the audience's attention shifted to dance and song, and they expected not only greater poetic elevation but also a demonstration of the poet's skill. As with epic ecphrasis, an audience familiar with Euripidean lyric could be pulled in by the unfolding of the pleasures inherent in an expansive description. For modern readers, it has been hard to resist dismissing the description as ornate and simply decorative. It seems elevated but not "heightened" as Silk (2010, 436–37) puts it, that is, noticeably dense in potential meaning, as with metaphor. As Barlow (1971/2008) has argued, Euripides often exploits the possibilities of visual imagery; he has an unusual visual imagination and a talent for building significant pictorial sequences. Nevertheless, he has suffered through comparison with Aeschylus, who has been judged, since the time of the *Frogs*, as more forceful and inventive, especially in regard to metaphor.[32]

Another problem, hard to separate from the first, is the ode's relevance. It has been seen, particularly in the first strophe and antistrophe, as lacking an organic connection to the dramatic context.[33] Even Barlow (1971/2008, 20) takes this view: "The classic case of pictorial irrelevance is in the *Electra* where the chorus describe in highly colourful language the Nereids with Achilles' armour." Panagl (1971, 88–9) provides a nuanced reading that illustrates these problems and their interconnection. The glorification of Achilles in these initial pictures magnifies the stature of Agamemnon by association. (Note *El.* 440 and 451.) But there is an "obvious contradiction, inherent in this ripe expression of choral lyric, the discrepancy between sense and enjoyment, a disproportion between what is understood as essential and proper to content and the attractive details, which pull eye and ear away from dramatic action and unfold in imagination."

His conclusion suggests an interpretative point of departure: we can start from the taste and acculturation of the audience and assume Euripides has calibrated this imagery accordingly, to produce a calculated series of effects. The audience is seduced by sensuous detail. But because of that immediate pleasure, they must be all the more aware of an odd transposition; an epic narrative is being developed in a dithyrambic mode.[34] The listener is carried along through a series of pictures. At times there are holes in the narrative line, as in the antistrophe when the ode moves backwards in time and the Nereids are encountered in mid-progress from Lemnos, where, presumably, they got the arms from Hephaestus, and Thetis (*El.* 442–44), and on their way to Pelion.[35] On the other hand, there are sustained emotional and aesthetic effects, an oddly festive tone and a quasi-processional sense of movement. This suits focalization through the Chorus; they begin the play on their way to participate in a festival procession, as a part of the Argive Heraea.[36] But as the ode moves beyond the ornate and satisfying language of the strophe, the audience may be uncertain as to the narrative's ultimate point, its destination; where is this series of pictures carrying them, as well as Achilles?

The answer is not at all clear. What seems clearer is that the Chorus is, implicitly, embarking on a wishful analogy between an idealized young Achilles and the young Orestes; they have just heard of his possible arrival (*El.* 391–403, esp. 401–3), and they hope he will succeed, even triumph. Just as the tone and feeling of the narrative so far follow from their collective identity, so too the picture of Achilles is colored idiosyncratically, so as to give more substance to that analogy. In the Heraea procession, young men supposed to be of exceptional purity, on the verge of manhood and ready to bear arms, carried a sacred golden shield to the shrine of Hera.[37] Innovations in the narrative make it easier for the analogy to work. The youth of Achilles is emphasized by the connection with Cheiron, "the old horse-man"; Achilles is just leaving his tutelage and will leave from his cave for Troy, not from Phthia. And his status as an *ephebe* is brought out by bringing him his armor at this point in his story.

Obviously, this means Achilles will not be taking the armor given his father by the gods when he married Thetis (*Il.* 17.194–97 and 18.82–85). This further departure from the *Iliad*'s story would not necessarily have struck the audience as surprising. The introduction to the following ecphrasis is surprising, however:

> Ἰλιόθεν δ' ἔκλυόν τινος ἐν λιμέσιν
> Ναυπλίοις βεβῶτος
> τᾶς σᾶς, ὦ Θέτιδος παῖ,
> κλεινᾶς ἀσπίδος ἐν κύκλωι   455
> τοιάδε σήματα †δείματα
> Φρύγια† τετύχθαι·
> (Eur. *El.* 452–57)

From a man of Troy sojourning at Nauplia harbour I heard, O son of Thetis, that on the circle of your famous shield were wrought these emblems, †terrors for the Phrygians† ... (trans. Cropp 1988)

The shield is famous, but in what sense? The famous shield of Achilles is the shield of the *Iliad*, brought to Achilles after the loss of Peleus' armor. The innovative retelling calls attention to the intertext it supplants (Lowenstam 1993, 209). The audience does not have to disbelieve in the premise that for this play this is Achilles' story, but they may feel more strongly that the chorus is presenting an epic story in an oddly un-epic mode.

The substance of the ecphrasis provokes a similar reaction, if the poetic qualities of Homer's ecphrasis are called to mind:

περιδρόμωι μὲν ἴτυος ἕδραι
Περσέα λαιμοτόμαν ὑπὲρ ἁλὸς
ποτανοῖσι πεδίλοις κορυφὰν Γοργόνος ἴσχειν,   460
Διὸς ἀγγέλωι σὺν Ἑρμᾶι,
τῶι Μαίας ἀγροτῆρι κούρωι
ἐν δὲ μέσωι κατέλαμπε σάκει φαέθων
κύκλος ἁλίοιο   465
ἵπποις ἄμ πτεροέσσαις
ἄστρων τ' αἰθέριοι χοροί,
Πλειάδες Ὑάδες, †Ἕκτορος
ὄμμασι† τροπαῖοι·

(Eur. *El.* 458–69)

On the rim's encircling field was Perseus over the sea with flying sandals, holding, throat severed, the Gorgon's head, in company with Zeus's herald Hermes, the rustic child of Maia. On the buckler's centre radiant shone down the circle of the sun on winged horses and constellations dancing in the heavens, Pleiads and Hyads, to turn back †the eyes of Hector† ... (trans. Cropp 1988)

There is no movement into extended narrative through a description of figural representation. Instead the ecphrasis tends towards the emblematic, as if it were restricted by its notional objects, figurative images like archaic shield blazons.[38] The description of Perseus shows him at a familiar moment in the story. But there are no Gorgons, as often in art (Cropp 1988, on 459–62), and no pursuit, as we saw in vivid and extravagant form in the *Shield*, only a frozen moment. In fact, this is the general effect of all the images in this section of the ode (on the helmet and sword, as well as shield); instead of marked expansion and poetic inventiveness, there is a series of compact, conventionally heroic images, the Sphinx, the Chimaera, and an image of horses on the battlefield (*El.* 470–78).

At the same time, the images largely displace their narrative ground. The sole exception is the reference at the end of the shield ecphrasis to the flight and fear of Hector.[39] Because of the images of sun and stars, we are reminded of the epic motif of gleaming weapons, especially as it is used in Book 22, where Hector flees in panic from Achilles (*Il.* 22.131–7). Yet how are we to think about Hector's fear and flight without thinking of Patroclus, which means Achilles' role in his death, his overwhelming grief, his passion for revenge, and its tragic consequences, both for the Trojans and himself?

In sum, Euripides' ecphrasis seems to call attention to its displacement of narrative context through conventional imagery. Yet it calls attention, again, to the *Iliad*'s narrative, which the ode seemed to be setting out to replace. The audience may end up feeling that the ode presents a trite and reductive vision of heroic action, one divorced from the kind of narrative we find in the *Iliad*, where Achilles' triumph comes at a cost, and his choices have tragic consequences. Therefore, when the Chorus, comes back to the dramatic here and now, pointing the moral it seems, the audience may be unsure as to whether they can follow them to this conclusion:

τοιῶνδ' ἄνακτα δοριπόνων
ἔκανεν ἀνδρῶν, Τυνδαρί,   480
σὰ λέχεα, κακόφρον κόρα.
τοιγάρ σοί ποτ' οὐρανίδαι

πέμψουσιν θανάτου δίκαν.
ἔτ' ἔτι φόνιον ὑπὸ δέραν   485
ὄψομαι αἷμα χυθὲν σιδάρωι.
      (Eur. *El.* 479–86)

Such were those spear-toiling men whose lord your union killed, thou evil-minded child of Tyndareus. For that shall the gods in heaven one day send death upon you in retribution. Still, still shall I see beneath your throat the murderous gush of iron-spilled blood. (trans. Cropp 1988)

Exactly what kind of "spear-toiling" men are these? Are they all golden *ephebes* untouched by everything that happened afterwards at Troy? Do such heroes exist?

The problem underlying both the Chorus' wishful analogy and their reductive vision of heroism is, of course, matricide. Of all the kinds of revenge possible, none is more certain of producing a narrative of less-than-heroic action, tragic consequence, and regret. That is the realization the play will produce for not only Electra and Orestes (*El.* 1177–1231) but for the Chorus as well (1172-6). This interpretation of the ode's contextual significance is not surprising.[40] But the innovative means by which Euripides plays with his audience's pre-dispositions and perceptions are, especially since he is competing for their attention and approval. In the first strophe and antistrophe, he seems to be setting them up to react on the basis of, and also against, the pleasure they take in a generic form of poetic expression. And in the shield ecphrasis he plays with the tension between their expectations and a challenging and perhaps unsatisfying realization, in a subtly allusive mode and a reduced and restricted poetic form. He was clearly willing to take risks in exploring the possibilities of his poetic resources.

That makes him typical, or at least exemplary. He allows us to see better the challenge facing any tragic writer in innovative appropriation of those resources. He also reminds us that the Greek poetry remaining to us offers few obvious and unsophisticated performances. The *Shield* is atypical, and therefore a valuable reference point. Mostly, we are stuck with very skillful performers, like Euripides and Apollonius, which means that the use of a poetic device is rarely a matter of simple imitation and emulation; it is inseparable from the interplay of multiple devices, and from the possibilities opened up by the audience's expectations and acculturation.

NOTES

[1] On epic language and epic poetic devices cf. also Reece, ch. 3, 46–7, and Saïd, ch. 23, 353–6 in this volume.

[2] The history of ecphrasis, especially in the later rhetorical tradition, has been intensively discussed. As an introduction, see Hagstrum 1958 and Elsner 2002. For a relatively recent collection of articles with further bibliography, see Bartsch and Elsner 2007.

[3] On this ecphrasis see Saïd, ch. 23, pp. 353–4 in this volume.

[4] Compare, Hamon 1982. His discussion of novelistic description points to this essential connection between a shift from narrative and its forms of expectation to a focus on inventiveness and the unfolding of descriptive language.

[5] For notional ecphrasis, as opposed to description of an actual work of art, see Hollander 1995, 4–5.

[6] See, for example, Hinds 1998, 47–51.

[7] For a concise summary of Conte's theoretical orientation in this regard, see Segal's introduction to Conte 1994 (esp., viii-ix and xii-xiii). Compare Conte 1986, esp. 28–31 and 37–38 and, for a discussion of how these ideas relate to the writing of literary history, Conte, 1999, 1–10.

[8] On Apollonius Rhodius cf. also Mori, ch. 6, pp. 102–3, and Roisman, ch. 9, pp. 146–8 in this volume.

[9] For summary discussion, see Fantuzzi and Hunter 2004, 17–26 and 89–98.

[10] See esp. Fusillo 1985, 300–306 and Hunter 1993b, 57–59.

[11] See Coray 2009, on *Il.* 19.374–81 and Krischer 1971, 36–38.

[12] See Coray 2009 on 19.16–17 and Scott 1974, 66–68 and 113–30.

[13] For the correlation of simile-types and recurrent narrative contexts in oral performance, and the possibility of adaptation to new contexts, see Scott 2009, 17–41. Compare Carspecken 1952, 75 and Effe 2001, 165–66.

[14] Compare Richardson 1993, on *Il.* 22.25–32 and 317–21.

[15] For a summary discussion, see Hunter 1993a, 8–12.

[16] For discussion of the problem of heroism in Apollonius, see Hunter 1988; 1993b, 12–25; and Goldhill 1991, 313–16.

[17] On the narrative function of Apollonius' similes, see Carspecken 1952, 85–88. For the women's feelings, see Fränkel 1968, 105.

[18] Because of these multiple parallels, Hunter 1993b, 52–53, calls this episode the "main situational model" for the scene surrounding the ecphrasis.

[19] Halliwell 2011, 112–113, provides a useful discussion of the forms of verbal analysis implied by the contest of *Frogs*. For a wider-angle view of the audience's various competencies, see Revermann 2006.

[20] For helpful treatments of poetic composition from this point of view, see Griffith 1990, esp. 187–89; Seidensticker 1996/2005, esp. 249–53 and 275–76; and Mastronarde 2000, esp. 23–27.

[21] See, first of all, Sommerstein 1992, 17–22.

[22] See Cratinus F 193, 194, 195, and 199 PCG. For this interpretation of the scholion, see Bakola 2010, 18–20 and 275–78.

[23] See Biles 2011, 29–31 and Rosen 2000.

[24] See Silk 2000, 289-91, who discusses the organization of Aristophanes' plays similarly, and compare Hunter 2009, 36–52.

[25] See Dover 1993, 10–11; Halliwell 2011, 140–43 and 147–48; and Hunter 2009, 131–33.

[26] This translation assumes the line is a statement (not a question), and ironic, and that the primary meaning is a sexual reference to fellatio, not a possible musical reference to Lesbian singers. (Fellatio and prostitution can be treated as synonymous. See, e.g., *Ach.* 523–29, with Olson 2002 on 528-29.) See Dover 1993 and compare Jocelyn 1980, 33 and de Simone 2008, 481–83.

[27] See Dover 1993 and de Simone 2008, 480.

[28] For an interesting discussion of perceptions of and responses to musical innovation in fifth-century Athens, see D'Angour, 2006, 264–76.

[29] For further discussion, see Rau 1967, 127–31.

[30] The play's date is closer to 420 than 415. See Cropp 1988, l-li. But it is not necessarily at the outer limit of the period in which the audience would have been familiar with Euripides' dithyrambic style. See Csapo 2000, 405–15.

[31] See Kranz 1933, 239–44; Panagl 1971, 230–237; and Cropp 1988, 127.

[32] See esp. Barlow 1971/2008, 1-16. For the influence of *Frogs*, see Hunter 2009, 29–36 and 127–34.

[33] Symptomatic, and important for the reception of the play, is Kranz 1933, 251–57. Most recent responses assume an underlying coherence and address the problem of relevance as an interpretative challenge. Though conceptualized in various ways and embedded in varied interpretations of the play, they often assume the presentation of the heroic and mythical world of

the ode is a foil for, or in thematic tension with, a darker and more mundane dramatic world, categorized in one sense or another as realistic. For a discussion of the slipperiness of the term "realism" as applied to Euripides and a sampling of interpretative approaches, see Goff 2000.

[34] Compare, Kranz 1933, 239–44 and 256–57; Panagl 1971, 230–37; and Csapo 2009, 95–96.

[35] The geographical sequence is confusing, but this seems plausible. See Denniston 1939, on lines 442 and 445–46.

[36] Compare Zeitlin 1970 and Cropp 1988, on 173–74.

[37] See Plutarch, *De proverbiis Alexandrinorum* 1.44 (Paroem. Gr. I, 327) and Aen. Tact. 1.17, with Burkert 1983, 163 and Pötscher 1996 / 97, 26–27.

[38] Compare De Romilly 1990, 269–70. On shield blazons, see Spier 1990, 112-15 and 122–24.

[39] The sense seems clear, even if the text is in doubt. See Slings 1997, 149–50.

[40] Compare Hose 1991, 105–6 and Mastronarde 2010, 139–40.

REFERENCES

Bakola, E. 2010. *Cratinus and the Art of Comedy*. Oxford.

Barchiesi, A. 2001. *Speaking Volumes: Narrative and Intertext in Ovid and other Latin poets*. London.

Barlow, S. 1971/2008. *The Imagery of Euripides*, 3rd edn. London.

Bartsch, S. and J. Elsner, eds. 2007. *Classical Philology* 102.1 (Special Issue on Ecphrasis).

Biles, Z. 2011. *Aristophanes and the Poetics of Competition*. Cambridge.

Burkert, W. 1983. Homo necans: *The Anthropology of Ancient Greek Sacrificial Ritual and Myth*. Berkeley, CA.

Carspecken, J. 1952. "Apollonius Rhodius and the Homeric Epic." *Yale Classical Studies* 13: 35–143.

Conte, G.B. 1986. *The Rhetoric of Imitation: Genre and Poetic Memory in Virgil and Other Latin Poets*. Ithaca, NY.

Conte, G.B. 1994. *Genres and Readers: Lucretius, Love Elegy, Pliny's Encyclopedia*. Baltimore.

Conte, G.B. 1999. *Latin Literature. A History*, 2nd edn. Baltimore.

Coray, M. 2009. *Homers Ilias, Gesamtkommentar. Band VI: Neunzehnter Gesang (T). Faszikel 2: Kommentar*. Berlin.

Cropp, M. 1988. *Euripides: Electra*. Oxford.

Cropp, M., K. Lee, and D. Sansone, eds. 2000. *Euripides and Tragic Theatre in the Late Fifth Century*. Champaign, IL. (= *Illinois Classical Studies* 24/25).

Csapo, E. 2000. "Later Euripidean Music." In Cropp, Lee, and Sansone, eds., 399–426.

Csapo, E. 2009. "New Music's Gallery of Images: The 'Dithyrambic' First Stasimon of Euripides' *Electra*." In R. Cousland and J. Hume, eds., *The Play of Texts and Fragments: Essays in Honour of Martin Cropp*, Leiden, 95-109.

D'Angour, A. 2006. "The New Music – So What's New?" In S. Goldhill and R. Osborne, eds., *Rethinking Revolutions Through Ancient Greece*, Cambridge, 264-83.

Denniston, J. 1939. *Euripides: Electra*. Oxford.

Depew, M. and D. Obbink. 2000. *Matrices of Genre: Authors, Canons, and Society*. Cambridge, MA.

de Romilly, J. 1990. "Un bouclier tragique." *In Studi di Filologia Classica in Onore di Giusto Monaco*, Palermo, 265–73.

de Simone, M. 2008. "The 'Lesbian' Muse in Tragedy: Euripides *ΜΕΛΟΠΟΙΟΣ* in Aristoph. *Ra.* 1301-28," *Classical Quarterly* 58: 479–90.

Dover, K. 1993. *Aristophanes: Frogs*. Oxford.

Effe, B. 2001. "The Similes of Apollonius Rhodius. Intertextuality and Epic Innovation." In T. Papanghelis and A. Rengakos, eds., *A Companion to Apollonius Rhodius*, Leiden, 147–69.

Elsner, J. 2002. "The Genres of Ekphrasis." In J. Elsner, ed., *The Verbal and the Visual: Cultures of Ekphrasis in Antiquity* (= *Ramus* 31), 1–18.

Fantuzzi, M. and R. Hunter. 2004. *Tradition and Innovation in Hellenistic Poetry*. Cambridge.

Fowler, D. 1991. "Narrate and Describe: The Problem of Ekphrasis." *Journal of Roman Studies* 81: 25–35.

Fränkel, H. 1968. *Noten zu den Argonautika des Apollonios*. Munich.

Fränkel, H. 1975. *Early Greek Poetry and Philosophy*. New York.

Fusillo, M. 1985. *Il tempo delle Argonautiche: Un'analisi del racconto in Apollonio Rodio*. Rome.

Genette, G. 1982. *Figures of Literary Discourse*. New York.

Goff, B. 2000. "Try to Make it Real Compared to What? Euripides' *Electra* and the Play of Genres." In M. Cropp, K. Lee, and D. Sansone, eds., *Euripides and Tragic Theatre in the Late Fifth Century*. Champaign, IL, 93–105.

Goldhill, S. 1991. *The Poet's Voice: Essays on Poetics and Greek Literature*. Cambridge.

Griffith, M. 1990. "Contest and Contradiction in Early Greek Poetry." In M. Griffith and D. Mastronarde, eds., *Cabinet of the Muses. Essays on Classical and Comparative Literature in Honor of Thomas G. Rosenmeyer*, Atlanta, GA, 185–207.

Hagstrum, J. 1958. *The Sister Arts: the Tradition of Literary Pictorialism and English Poetry from Dryden to Gray*. Chicago.

Halliwell, S. 2011. *Between Ecstasy and Truth. Interpretations of Greek Poetics from Homer to Longinus*. Oxford.

Hamon, P. 1982. "What is a Description?" In T. Todorov, ed., *French Literary Theory Today*, Cambridge, 147–78.

Hinds, S. 1998. *Allusion and Intertext: Dynamics of Appropriation in Roman Poetry*. Cambridge.

Hollander, J. 1995. *The Gazer's Spirit: Poems Speaking to Silent Works of Art*. Chicago.

Holub, R. 1989. *Reception Theory: A Critical Introduction*. London.

Hose, M. 1991. *Studien zum Chor bei Euripides*. Vol. 2. Stuttgart.

Hunter, R. 1988. "'Short on Heroics': Jason in the *Argonautica*." *Classical Quarterly* 38: 436–53.

Hunter, R., transl. 1993a. *Apollonius of Rhodes. Jason and the Golden Fleece*. Oxford.

Hunter, R. 1993b. *The Argonautica of Apollonius: Literary Studies*. Cambridge.

Hunter, R. 2009. *Critical Moments in Classical Literature: Studies in the Ancient View of Literature and its Uses*. Cambridge.

Janko, R. 1986. "The *Shield of Heracles* and the Legend of Cycnus." *Classical Quarterly* 36: 38–59.

Jauss, H.-R. 1967/1982. "Literary History as a Challenge to Literary Theory." In *Toward and Aesthetic of Reception*, 3–45. Minneapolis.

Jocelyn, H. 1980. "A Greek Indecency and its Students: λαικάζειν." *Proceedings of the Cambridge Philological Society* 206: 12–66.

Kranz, W. 1933. *Stasimon. Untersuchungen zu Form und Gehalt der griechischen Tragödie*. Berlin.

Krischer, T. 1971. *Formale Konventionen der homerischen Epik*. Munich.

Lowenstam, S. 1993. "The Arming of Achilleus on Early Greek Vases." *Classical Antiquity* 12: 199–218.

Martin, R. 2005. "Pulp Epic: the *Catalogue* and the *Shield*." In R. Hunter, ed, *The Hesiodic Catalogue of Women: Constructions and Reconstructions*, Cambridge, 153–75.

Mastronarde, D.J. 2000. "Euripidean Tragedy and Genre: the Terminology and its Problems." In M. Cropp, K. Lee, and D. Sansone, eds., *Euripides and Tragic Theatre in the Late Fifth Century*. Champaign, IL, 23–39.

Mastronarde, D.J. 2010. *The Art of Euripides. Dramatic Technique and Social Context*. Cambridge.

Michelini, A. 1987. *Euripides and the Tragic Tradition*. Madison, WI.

Most, G.W. 2000. "Generating Genres: The Idea of the Tragic." In m. Depew and D. Obbink, eds., *Matrices of Genre: Authors, Canons, and Society*. Cambridge, MA, 15–35.

Most, G.W., ed. & transl. 2006. *Hesiod: Theogony, Works and Days, Testimonia*. Cambridge, MA.

Most, G.W., ed. & transl. 2007. *Hesiod: The Shield, Catalogue of Women, Other Fragments*. Cambridge, MA.

Olson, S.D. 2002. *Aristophanes: Acharnians*. Oxford.

Panagl, O. 1971. *Die "dithyrambischen Stasima" des Euripides. Untersuchungen zur Komposition und Erzähltechnik*. Vienna.

Pötscher, W. 1996/97. "Das Hera-Fest im Heraion von Argos (Hdt. 1, 31 und Eur., 169 ff.)." *Acta antiqua Academiae Scientiarum Hungaricae* 37: 25–36.

Rau, P. 1967. *Paratragodia. Untersuchung einer komischen Form des Aristophanes*. Munich.

Revermann, M. 2006. "The Competence of Theatre Audiences in Fifth- and Fourth-Century Athens." *Journal of Hellenic Studies* 126: 99–124.

Richardson, N. 1993. *The Iliad: A Commentary. Volume VI: Books* 21–24. Cambridge.

Rosen, R. 2000. "Cratinus' *Pytine* and the Construction of the Comic Self." In D. Harvey and J. Wilkins, eds., *The Rivals of Aristophanes: Studies in Athenian Old Comedy*, London, 23–39.

Scott, W. 1974. *The Oral Nature of the Homeric Simile.* Leiden.

Scott, W. 2009. *The Artistry of the Homeric Simile.* Lebanon, NH.

Seidensticker, B. 1996/2005. "Die griechische Tragödie als literarischer Wettbewerb." In J. Holzhausen, ed., *Über das Vergnügen an tragischen Gegenständen: Studien zum antiken Drama*, Munich, 246–78.

Silk, M. 2000. *Aristophanes and the Definition of Comedy.* Oxford.

Silk, M. 2010. "The Language of Greek Lyric Poetry." In E. Bakker, ed., *A Companion to the Ancient Greek Language*, Oxford, 424–40.

Slings, S. 1997. "Notes on Euripides' *Electra.*" *Mnemosyne* 50: 131–64.

Sommerstein, A. 1992. "Old Comedians on Old Comedy." In B. Zimmermann, ed., *Antike Dramentheorien und ihre Rezeption*, Stuttgart, 14–33.

Spier, J. 1990. "Emblems in Archaic Greece." *Bulletin of the Institute of Classical Studies* 37: 107–29.

Thalmann, W. 1984. *Conventions of Form and Thought in Early Greek Epic Poetry.* Baltimore.

Tynyanov, Y. 1924/2000. "The Literary Fact." In D. Duff, ed., *Modern Genre Theory*, Harlow, 29–49.

Tynyanov, Y. 1929/1978. " On Literary Evolution." In L. Matjka and K. Pomorska, eds. *Readings in Russion Poetics: Formalist and Structuralist Views* Ann Arbor, MI, 66-78.

Vernant, J.-P. 1997. "Les semblances de Pandora." In F. Blaise, P. Judet de La Combe, and P. Rousseau, eds., *Le métier du mythe. Lectures d' Hésiode*, 381–92.

Vian, F. 1974. *Apollonios de Rhodes: Argonautiques, Tome I, Chants I-II.* Paris.

Zeitlin, F. 1970. "The Argive Festival of Hera and Euripides' *Electra.*" *Transactions and Proceedings of the American Philological Association* 102: 645–69.

FURTHER READING

Work relevant to these questions is extremely varied and in principle inexhaustible. Conte and Jauss, whose thinking provided essential orientation for this discussion, point the way toward further reading in, respectively, the tradition of structuralist poetics (e.g., Genette 1982) and Russian Formalism (e.g., Tynyanov, 1924/2000 and 1929/1978). Their approaches intersect with other forms of theoretical discussion as well, like genre theory. (For classicists, Depew and Obbink 2000 is a good place to start.) But the theoretical framing of a literary-historical approach is only one dimension. Philological work on particular poetic devices, for example the history of discussion of epic simile (e.g., Scott 2009) or of generic styles of poetic language (e.g., Panagl 1971) is indispensable. And inseparable from the philological tradition is the tradition of interpretation of any given text, almost always voluminous, which leads to the history of reception, by now an education in itself. (See, as an illustration, Most 2000 and Michelini 1987, 3–51, on Euripides.)

CHAPTER 31

The Function of Literature

Victoria Wohl

"The function of literature": the very phrase evokes the defensiveness of literature departments struggling to justify their existence to budget-cutting administrators. But the question of literature's function is as old as literature itself. Does literature have a (any) function? Does it have a (single) function? These questions impinge upon the very definition of literature: what (if anything) literature does helps define what (if anything) literature is.[1]

At first glance the issue might seem fairly straightforward for ancient Greece, where literature was composed for and consumed at specific occasions, and its function was tied to that of the occasion, be it to celebrate the victory of an Olympic competitor (as in Pindar's epinicians), to exhort the troops (Tyrtaeus' elegies), or to honor the dead (the funeral oration). Some genres and texts were more closely tied to this functional context than others, of course. We might trace a continuum from an actual funeral dirge (*thrēnos*) to the dramatic dirges sung by characters in tragedy; from a real epitaph like Simonides' for the dead at Marathon to the highly polished epitaphic epigrams of the Hellenistic writers, whose imitation of the form was a literary game unencumbered by actual stone. That continuum is sometimes taken as a historical trajectory, but even as the Greeks came to understand genre in more formal and abstract terms (Ford 2002), their literature never lost its performative function. Attic tragedy, for instance, seems to have originated as a ritual for Dionysus; that function had so faded by the fifth century that it gave rise to the adage, "nothing to do with Dionysus." But that ritual function could always be re-activated as a source of poetic meaning, as in Euripides' *Bacchae*, where pointed metatheatricality collapses the Dionysiac worship within the play, with the play as Dionysiac worship.

But while the performative context might have determined the form of Greek literature (one wouldn't sing a *thrēnos* at a wedding or an *epithalamion* at a funeral) it did not fully determine its meaning.[2] Take as an example these lines of Sappho (F 105a V):

οἶον τὸ γλυκύμαλον ἐρεύθεται ἄκρωι ἐπ᾽ ὕσδωι,
ἄκρον ἐπ᾽ ἀκροτάτωι, λελάθοντο δὲ μαλοδρόπηες,
οὐ μὰν ἐκλελάθοντ᾽, ἀλλ᾽ οὐκ ἐδύναντ᾽ ἐπίκεσθαι

A Companion to Greek Literature, First Edition. Edited by Martin Hose and David Schenker.
© 2016 John Wiley & Sons, Inc. Published 2020 by John Wiley & Sons, Inc.

as the sweetapple reddens on a high branch
   high on the highest branch and the applepickers forgot –
no, not forgot: were unable to reach
(trans. Carson 2002)

For us this fragment appears in isolation as an *objet d'art* (DuBois 1995, 31–54). We can admire its euphony and metrical balance, its use of polyptoton (the repetition of "high") to mimic the sense of distance, the self-correction that produces an impression of spontaneity, as if the poet notices the scene at exactly the same moment as the pickers notice the apple and both simultaneously are reaching for their object and failing to grasp it. But this fragment was probably originally part of an *epithalamion*, a wedding song. Its function would have been to adorn the occasion and honor the bride, whom the simile of the sweet, unreachable apple depicts as both pure and ripe for marriage. This "sweetapple" is about to be plucked, and the function of the song was presumably to celebrate that inevitability. And yet there is an anticipatory sadness to these lines that sits ill with that purpose. The very beauty of the image of this solitary, sweet, reddening apple, sublime in its unreachability, generates regret for its inevitable harvest. These lines pull against the function of the poem as a whole, the celebration of a union that will end this fragile moment of suspension and, plucking the apple, obliterate the simile. This artful image thus complicates the poem's performance of its epithalamic purpose; the poem's aesthetics exceed its function and stand in a certain tension to it. Indeed, we might say that this is precisely what makes these lines literature: their irreducibility to simple functionality.

My chapter fleshes out this hypothesis by looking at the two primary functions of literature as the ancient Greeks saw it: to educate its audience (a social–didactic function) and to entertain them (an emotional–hedonic function). The two are not mutually exclusive, of course, but neither are they always mutually reinforcing. The emotions literature arouses and the pleasure it gives operate independently of its social and ideological aims and can subvert (as well as support) them. This means that while literature clearly did serve important social functions, as we shall see, it can never be reduced to a single function – "*the* function of literature" – or subordinated to a logic of pure functionality, and this is precisely what makes it literature.

1.   To Improve Men in the City

In Aristophanes' *Frogs*, Dionysus goes to the underworld, determined to bring back a "clever poet" (ποιητοῦ δεξιοῦ, 71) "so that the city may be saved to lead its choruses" (1419). In Hades he presides as judge over a contest to determine which tragedian, Aeschylus or Euripides, shall return to the living. This famous competition between the two playwrights is one of our earliest pieces of literary criticism. The two compete on stylistic terms – the metrical intricacies of their lyrics, their choice of diction – but also on the benefit each offers to the city. Aeschylus claims that his magnificent martial verse made the Athenians better warriors, while Euripides' scandalous plots incited them to incest and adultery (1013–88). Euripides counters that his plays, by introducing logic and rhetoric, taught the audience to speak and think and question (950–79). Despite their artistic differences, the two playwrights agree on the essential criteria for a good poet: "artistic skill and advice, and that we improve men in the city" (Δεξιότητος καί νουθεσίας, ὅτι βελτίους τε ποιούμεν τοὺς ἀνθρώπους ἐν ταῖς πόλεσιν, 1009–10). The two have different views on precisely how drama makes citizens better, but they both assume that literature has an ethical, as well as an aesthetic, function and expect it to serve a serious social purpose (Dover 1993, 13–15).

The belief that literature could and should serve a didactic, ethical, or social function had a long and honorable pedigree in Greek tradition, as the character Aeschylus himself points out. From the beginning, he says, the best poets have been "useful" (ὠφέλιμοι, 1031): Orpheus taught the mysteries, Musaeus prophecy and cures for diseases; Hesiod taught till- ing of the soil, and "the divine Homer" marshaling, arming, and military valor (1030–36). Of course, the immediate fungibility of literature's teaching is questionable – could one really win fifth-century battles with tactics learned from Homer?[3] – and in fact it is ques- tioned even in *Frogs*, for when the tragedians are asked to weigh in on the concrete problems facing Athens, the advice they give – in verses culled from their own plays – is ludicrous, impractical, or hopelessly obscure (1420–66). But the assumption of literature's fundamental utility is accepted without debate. As Aeschylus puts it, "Boys have a teacher who instructs them, but adults have poets" (1055–6).

Earlier chapters in this volume have documented the Greeks' use of literature as a source of technical (see Fögen, ch. 17, and Asper, ch. 26 in this volume), historical (see Tsakmakis, ch. 14, and Dubischar, ch. 28 in this volume), or moral knowledge (see Konstan, ch. 27 in this volume). The association of oral poetry with divinely inspired memory and the view of poetic activity not as the creation of original fictions but as the transmission of established truths (cf. Hose, ch. 24 in this volume) vested literature with the authority of tradition, an authority underwritten by the gods themselves (Detienne 1996 [1967], 29–52). Even after this link bet- ween poetry, memory, and truth became attenuated with the spread of writing and the "secu- larization" of poetry, literature retained its authority as a token, if not a source, of truth. The fourth-century orator Lycurgus, for example, quotes extended passages of Homer, Tyrtaeus, and Euripides in his court case against Leocrates (*In Leocr.* §§100–10; cf. 92, 132); these venerable poets testify to the noblest ideals of Greek patriotism and valor, and indict Leocrates by his failure to live up to them. Lycurgus quotes his passages out of context and interprets them simplistically, if not tendentiously. But his interpretation is less telling than the mere gesture of citation: just by quoting these canonical literary authors, Lycurgus lays claim to their prestige.[4] Lycurgus apparently deployed a similar strategy outside the court- room, too: as archon in c. 330 BCE he oversaw the compilation of official texts of the plays of Aeschylus, Sophocles, and Euripides and the reconstruction of the Theater of Dionysus. In using poetry to augment his own political authority, Lycurgus was following a familiar tradition: his Athenian contemporaries may have recalled that the dramatic festival of the City Dionysia was established in the 530s by the tyrant Peisistratus as part of the consolida- tion of his own power.

If literature could bolster the power of a dominant individual, it could also serve the interests of the dominant class. For example, Hesiod's vision of monarchical power, both divine (in the *Theogony*) and human (in *Works and Days*), places the imprimatur of his divinely inspired verse on both the dominant class and the prevailing class structure of his own society. Human kings are legitimated by their connection to the king of the gods, and those who swallow bribes or give crooked judgments delegitimate themselves, not the institution of kingship. Hesiod's verse supports this structure of power in part by mystifying it: the successional struggles of the past are in the past (*Theogony*); in the present era, monarchical power is represented not as won in a struggle against others and at their real expense, but as part of the just order of the cosmos, revealed to the poet on Mount Helikon by the Muses themselves.[5] Similarly, Pindar's highly adorned praise of athletic victors (leavened with discreet warnings against greed and *hybris*) celebrates not only the individual victor and his household but also the elite class to which they belonged, again euphemizing dominance won in a competitive field of intra-elite (and occa- sionally inter-class) rivalry as the natural product of divine ancestry and hereditary virtue, including the virtue of recognizing and rewarding a good poet (e.g. *Pythian* 10.64–72, on which see Rose 1992, 141–84). Indeed, epinician, the genre of praise-poetry Pindar wrote, seems a perfect blend of form and function: the genre's aesthetics, with its intricate mytholog- ical narratives and ornate, gold-encrusted imagery, makes the poem itself a prestige object, a form of symbolic capital for its recipient (Kurke 1991). One can see why the tyrants of archaic Greece collected poets the way modern autocrats do mansions or racing cars.[6]

Thus, if literature served a social purpose, as Aristophanes' underworld-tragedians agree, that purpose was often, in practice, strongly conservative: to "save the city" meant saving the existing social hierarchy and the individuals or groups who enjoyed dominance within it. That is nowhere more obvious than in sympotic literature (cf. Baumbach, this volume ch. 22, pp. 345–6). One thinks of Theognis, denouncing the vulgarity of the *nouveaux-riches* and the evils of social miscegenation in the same finely turned elegiacs in which he lauds the beauty of the boy Kyrnus and vaunts the immortalizing power of his own poetry. The didactic function of poetry here serves an obvious (conservative) social end as Theognis initiates Kyrnus into the values – social, moral, and aesthetic – of his class (e.g. Thgn. 15–18, 27–38, 563–6, and see Cobb-Stevens 1985 and Levine 1985). Plato writes the conservative function of (sympotic) literature into law in the *Laws*: his Athenian proposes the symposium as a school of self-restraint and sympotic music as a means of training the soul in the pleasures of virtue (*Lg.* 652a–55b). The wise legislator will accordingly compel the poets to depict the happiness of the just man and the misery of the unjust (660e–61c), with strict penalties for those who do otherwise (662b). A play on the double meaning of *nomos* – both law and musical mode (800a) – makes the poet into a sort of policeman who upholds the state's laws by strict adherence to the laws of music, including Law #3: "the poet shall not compose anything that goes against the laws of the city and what it defines as just, beautiful and good" (801c–d). The didactic role of literature here reaches a dismal extreme, as both education and literature (not to mention drinking) are reduced to tedious rehearsals of the doxic and the nomic.

Of course not everyone thought the symposium should showcase state-mandated choruses of old men singing morally edifying songs. In the classical period, and particularly in democratic Athens, sympotic poetry was not only a weapon of social conflict but also its object. In Aristophanes' *Clouds* the old father Strepsiades, along with the avatar of traditional education "Just Argument," praises the good old days, when boys learned the old songs by heart and sang them to tunes passed down from their fathers (*Nub.* 966–8). But when Strepsiades asks his son Pheidippides to sing one of the old tunes – Simonides or Aeschylus – at a symposium the young man scorns them as boring and outmoded and instead offers a new musical selection, the scandalous verses of Euripides (1352–79). The play presents this radical new literature (the so-called New Music) as part of the sophistic movement of the late fifth century, which challenged received wisdom and traditional values and which the older generation naturally viewed as the end of civilization. Little wonder that *Clouds* closes with Strepsiades burning down the "Thinkery" where Pheidippides acquired his new literary sensibility.

Pheidippides' revolutionary musical tastes and his father's reaction to them show that if literature often served to consolidate the dominant class and to reproduce its ideology and social dominance, it could also act as a vehicle for ideological critique and challenge to the status quo. Hesiod tells the fable of the hawk and the nightingale (*Works and Days* 202–12): the powerful hawk's threats to the bardic bird are answered by the poem as a whole, as the poet speaks as an advocate for *dikê* (justice) against the *hybris* of crooked kings.[7] Indeed, one might even say that literature emerged in Greece in this opposition between hawk and nightingale, that it was precisely by taking an oppositional stance toward power that poets asserted the autonomy of literature and thus defined it as a discernible domain. One narrative of the "invention" of literature gives a pivotal role to the seventh-century poet Archilochus, master of abusive "blame poetry" and supposedly the first poet to write in his own voice about his own (fictionalized) life experiences (Fränkel 1950, 147–70; cf. Will 1969; Burnet 1983, 6–7, 15–32; Gentili 1988, 179–96). The extant fragments present a persona that is cynical and anti-heroic (e.g., F 5 IEG); rejecting wealth and power (F 19 IEG, F 114 IEG) they identify with an anti-elitist ethos. Likewise, Leslie Kurke has recently argued that Greek prose came into its own as a literary form by appropriating the dissident voice of the slave–provocateur Aesop: both Plato and Herodotus, she argues, incorporated (even as they disavowed) aspects of this abject and subversive tradition in order to define their novel genres of writing and articulate their opposition to the ideologies (philosophical or political) of their day (Kurke 2011, esp. 241–431). We have already seen another example in the "New Music" of which Pheidippides is such a fan in *Clouds*. While it is difficult to reconstruct the positive social or political agenda behind this aesthetic movement, for its critics (including Plato, *Laws* 669b–70b), this voluble, emotional style of song inspired effeminacy and inconstancy at best, anarchy at worst, and represented everything they hated about the radical democracy (Csapo 2004). That this was the first literary movement to generate extensive theorization marks its importance in the evolution of literature as a distinct field; that one of its main theoretical forefathers, Damon of Oa, was ostracized from Athens gives some measure of precisely how radical it seemed (Wallace 2004).

In *Clouds* Euripides is the poster-boy for the New Music. In *Frogs*, too, and in fact throughout Aristophanes, Euripides appears as a subversive figure whose dramas defy Athens' cultural, social, and political *nomoi* (e.g. *Acharnians* 394–556, *Thesmophoriazusai*). There is much in his plays that seems to bear out this characterization. His *Orestes*, for instance, takes on both the literary tradition and the political status quo. The weak and demoralized protagonist seems unable to enact his myth and his vacillation threatens to rewrite the canonical narrative of Aeschylus's *Oresteia*, as well as normative ideals of heroism and elite manliness. The gods are absent and unreliable in this play, and the democratic assembly is a vehicle of corrupt rhetoric and mob violence (Zeitlin 1980, Euben 1986). Such challenges to contemporary Athenian ideals and ideologies are the rule rather than the exception in Euripides' plays and, indeed, in tragedy as a whole. One might think of the way Sophocles' *Antigone* questions the ideology, articulated most forcefully in Pericles' funeral oration in Thucydides, of the primacy of the polis over the individual and family. Or the way his *Philoctetes* suggests that a young soldier may be acting justly by following his own conscience against the explicit order of his military commander. If tragedians are school-masters for grown-ups, what did Sophocles' audience learn from this lesson in insubordination? As Simon Goldhill (1987, 74) remarks, "Rather than simply reflecting the cultural values of a fifth-century audience, …rather than offering simple didactic messages from the city's poets to the citizens, tragedy seems deliberately to problematize, to make difficult the assumption of the values of the civic discourse."

This problematization is all the more radical, as Goldhill emphasizes, when we remember the context of these plays, the City Dionysia (cf. Hose, this volume ch. 21, pp. 329–31). Given the civic importance of this festival and the huge investment of the polis's resources, communal and individual, in the dramatic productions, we might expect the plays themselves to contribute to this magnificent self-display of Athens' power and beneficence. We might thus posit that tragedy functioned as what Louis Althusser (1971) calls an ideological state apparatus, enacting and reproducing the dominant ideology of the democratic state. Tragedy does often present an idealized vision of Athens as the birthplace of law and justice (Aeschylus's *Oresteia*) and champion of suppliants (Euripides' *Heraclidae* and *Supplices*), a place where intractable tragic problems find resolution (see Zeitlin 1990). If ideology in Althusser's model "represents the imaginary relationship of individuals to their real conditions of existence" (1971, 162), then tragedy's frequent depiction of Athens as powerful, just, and eternally democratic helps to solidify that imaginary relationship, binding individuals in the audience to an idealized vision of their polis and erasing or smoothing over any inconsistencies between that ideal and the audience's daily reality.

On the one hand, then, tragedy seems to function institutionally as part of the ideological apparatus of the polis; on the other hand, it often seems, as Goldhill says, "deliberately to problematize" central ideological tenets of that polis. We might explain this apparent contradiction as a peculiarity of Athens' radical democracy: one of the virtues of democracy, after all, is its openness to auto-critique, its invitation of challenge from its own citizens and its willingness to debate even its most basic presuppositions. In this regard, tragedy may be thought to reproduce Athenian democratic ideology precisely by challenging it. The spectral Euripides in *Frogs* suggests as much when he claims that his drama is more democratic (δημοκρατικὸν, 952) than Aeschylus's because it teaches the audience "to think, see, understand, twist things around, to scheme, to suspect wrongs, to consider things from all angles" (957–58). In this same vein, N. T. Croally (1994, 43) offers "a three-word description of tragic didacticism: tragedy questions ideology."

This equivocal ideological lesson is unique neither to tragedy, though, nor to democracy. Instead, it is part of the broader function of literature as a site, as well as an instrument and object, of ideological struggle. As Fredric Jameson (1981) has most famously argued, literature in its very form articulates and thereby mediates antagonisms between opposed class interests, between dominant and dominated factions of society, between traditional and emerging ideologies. These antagonisms, features of every social formation, are articulated within the work of literature merely by virtue of its existing in a certain time and place, and they are irreducible in the work because they are irreducible in its social world (Balibar and Macherey 1981, 88). In tragedy, this ideological complexity is built into the basic formal features of the work. Jean-Pierre Vernant (1988) showed how the ambiguities of tragedy's language crystallized the tensions of its historical moment: the shifting meaning of *dikē* in Sophocles' *Antigone*, for instance, reflects a contest, undecided and undecidable at the time the play was produced, between legal and religious notions of justice. So, too, he argues that the very structure of tragedy, with its dialogue between individual heroic protagonists who speak in the contemporary dialect of fifth-century Athens and a collective chorus singing archaic lyrics, encodes a chiasmic dialectic between a heroic, mythic past and a democratic, civic, present. Tragedy does not take sides in this dialectic (it hardly could) but instead represents it for its audience precisely as a tension. By giving mimetic form to issues that may have been latent or unrecognizable in reality, tragedy brings them to the level of consciousness and makes them available for discussion and debate.

Tragedy perhaps privileges ambiguity more than other literary genres, but a similar process of mediation can be seen even in works that, at first glance, appear fully ideologically overdetermined. Theognis's insistent equation of moral, social, and aesthetic goodness reflects a historical moment when the definition of *to kalon* ("the good") and the title of *hoi kaloi* ("good men") were bitterly contested and the hegemony of the landed birth elite could no longer be taken for granted. In his virulent attack on the new elite Theognis ventriloquizes, despite himself, their political claims: in his poetry, merchants and goatskin-wearing rustics invade the private symposium and mingle with the old elite in a way that would not happen in reality for centuries to come (e.g. Thgn. 53–68, 183–96, 289–92, 667–82). Peter Rose (1992, 141–84) identifies a similar dynamic in Pindar's tenth *Pythian*: this poem, like all Pindar's epinicia, works to naturalize the social prerogatives of its elite recipient as a matter of inherited excellence; its exquisitely self-conscious poetic language serves that end, but also denaturalizes elite hegemony by showing it to be the result of the poet's own labor of praise. The poem's very beauty, as Rose demonstrates, works simultaneously toward two opposing ideological ends (cf. Kurke 1991, 163–262).

These works do more than simply mirror the tensions of their historical and social contexts: merely by presenting them in a specific literary form they also propose imaginary solutions (Jameson 1981, 75–9). In tragedy's dialectic between elite protagonist and collective chorus, it is the former who acts and suffers (and whose action and suffering constitute the drama) but the latter which always survives at the end. Perhaps this is not surprising given tragedy's civic role, but in some cases the text's formal properties work against the ostensible aims of the author: Pindar may deploy his ornate language in order to glorify his aristocratic patron but, as Rose suggests, that same language demands that the elite victor share his honor with the decidedly non-elite poet.

These examples show how the work's aesthetic form exceeds its putative ideological function. This excess means that while literary works can – and, as we have seen, often did – serve didactic or ideological ends, they cannot be reduced to a simple lesson or a single ideology without significant violence to the work. This is precisely what makes literature a potent site of ideological mediation. It may also be what defines it as literature: when Homer is read as a military manual; when tragedy is seen as a mere ideological apparatus of the democracy and Pindar taken as a fawning parasite upon the elite; when poetry becomes a mere moral sampler – in short, when literature is reduced to a single function and hence to mere functionality – it arguably stops being literature.[8]

2. The Longing for a Poet

While Aristophanes' Aeschylus and Euripides agree, as we have seen, that literature should educate and edify, what initially drives Dionysus to Hades is not a scheme to save Athens but his consuming "desire" for a poet (ἵμερος, 59), a longing he compares to a yearning for pea-soup. Dionysus tells us that he was reading Euripides' *Andromeda* when "a sudden longing struck [his] heart" (53–4); a longing not for a woman, not for a boy, not for a man, but for Euripides (πόθος Εὐριπίδου, 66–7). This visceral, quasi-erotic longing, which "devours" Dionysus (δαρδάπτει, 66) points us toward the second function of literature in ancient Greece: to arouse emotion or give pleasure (Heath 1987; cf. Griffin 1998). These two functions, the hedonic and the didactic, were not mutually exclusive, of course: Aristophanes himself took pride in combining them, mixing the ridiculous and the serious (πολλὰ μὲν γελοῖα ... πολλὰ δὲ σπουδαῖα, *Frogs* 389–90) and "teaching what is best" (*Acharnians* 658) by making the audience laugh. But if the two were, ideally, inseparable, they were not always so perfectly aligned. Through the irrational "longings" it arouses, literature works on its audience's unconscious in complex and unpredictable ways. Like its aesthetic form (to which it is obviously connected) the emotional pleasure of a literary work exceeds its conscious function and vitiates all attempts to subordinate the work to a logic of rational utility.

The hedonic view of literature, like the didactic, had a long tradition in Greek thought. The chorus of Hesiod's Muses is beautiful and alluring (χοροὺς ... καλούς ἱμερόεντας, *Theogony* 7–8; cf. 64–5): it evokes precisely the longing (ἵμερος) that Dionysus feels for tragedy. With their lovely (ἐρατὴν, 65), sweet (ἡδεῖα, 40) voices, they delight (τέρπουσι, 37) the mind of Zeus and make mortals forget their cares (55). This same vocabulary of sweetness, loveliness, and delight recurs throughout the archaic and classical periods to characterize poetry (Heath 1987, 5–7). That the same qualities were valued in prose is indicated by Thucydides' contrarian boast that his own history will be "less delightful" (ἀτερπέστερον) to the listener than that of his predecessors but more useful for analyzing historical reality (1.22.4). This vocabulary of aesthetic pleasure overlaps considerably with that of erotic pleasure: Dionysus's "longing" for Euripides is elaborated in Plato, who compares the effect of beautiful literature to a destructive passion that the sensible lover must resist (*Republic* 607e). Thus a Greek might have concurred with Susan Sontag (1966, 14) that to speak of art requires not a hermeneutics but an erotics.[9]

The pleasure of literature's arousal is primarily emotional and linked to what ancient literary theorists termed its *psychagōgia*, literally, "leading of the soul" (Plato *Phaedrus* 261a8, 271c10; Aristotle *Poetics* 1450a33, 1450b17; Isocrates 2.49.6, 9.10.9; Timocles F 6 PCG; Aristoxenos F 123 Wehrli). In the *Odyssey*, bards can delight their listeners but also produce suffering if they sing of subjects that hit too close to home (*Od.* 1.325–53; 8.44–5, 60–96, 367–8, 477–543; 9.2–10): for Penelope, songs of the Greeks' baleful homecoming arouse sorrowful longing for her husband (1.340–44), while the tale of the sack of Troy reduces Odysseus to tears of pity (8.521–31). In that poem a good host will change the song to something more upbeat, but elsewhere it becomes clear that longing and tears are also part of the pleasure of song. Gorgias, the fifth-century sophist and theorist of rhetoric, characterizes *logos* – crafted speech – as a kind of divine incantation that induces pleasure and reduces pain (ἐπῳδαὶ ἐπαγωγοὶ ἡδονῆς, ἀπαγωγοὶ λύπης, *Helen*, DK 82 B 11, § 10, cf. § 8); part of its power, for him, is its ability to arouse "fearful shuddering, tearful pity, and sorrow-loving longing" (φρίκη περίφοβος καὶ ἔλεος πολύδακρυς καὶ πόθος φιλοπενθής, *Helen* § 9). While Gorgias attributes this emotional effect to all language, Aristotle famously postulates that the arousal of pity and fear is the "particular pleasure" of tragedy (ἡδονὴ οἰκεία, *Poetics* 1453b10–15) and the end toward which its reversals and recognitions are best deployed. Perhaps this is why, in Plato's *Minos*, Socrates characterizes tragedy as the genre of poetry "most delightful to the masses and most able to move the soul" (δημοτερπέστατόν τε καὶ ψυχαγωγικώτατον, 321a5).

Of course, from Plato this was a backhanded compliment. For him literature's emotional and hedonic effect makes it powerful, but also morally and socially dangerous. As a mode of mimesis, literature is suspect by nature (and drama especially so, as a purely imitative art-form). Within a metaphysics governed by the Forms, artistic representations are an imitation of an imitation and thus stand at two steps' remove from the truth (*Republic* 595a–603b). In their ignorance, poets often depict things that are untrue, such as gods behaving immorally (377d–82c) or heroes succumbing to despair (387d–88e, 603e–606c), and their audiences believe it due to the inherent charm (κήλησιν) of the poetry (601a–b). This mendacious imitation produces a mimetic effect in its audience. Like Aristophanes' Aeschylus, Plato imagines that if a tragedy imitates good men its audience will become good in imitation of them. But the reverse is also true. Poetic imitation can corrupt even a good man, infecting him with the emotions he sees depicted (605c–606d). When we enjoy a tragic scene of lamentation, to take Plato's example, we give free rein to excessive emotions that in our daily lives we should seek to restrain. The rational part of our soul temporarily lets down its guard, both because the suffering is not our own and because it is pleasurable to watch (606a–b). But that theatrical experience has real-life consequences: simulated emotions become part of our very *physis* (395d2–3) and imitating shameful acts habituates us to accepting or even performing those acts in real life (606b–d). Like associating with bad people, watching morally suspect performances harms the viewer, making him take on the character of what he enjoys on stage (ὁμοιοῦσθαι δήπου ἀνάγκη τὸν χαίροντα ὁποτέροις ἂν χαίρῃ, *Laws* 656b4–5).

Enjoyment is, in fact, key in this process of mimetic degradation. Virtue and vice first enter the soul through pleasure and pain, as Plato explains in the *Laws*, and education is essentially the correct formation of those sensations (653a–c). Poetic pleasure facilitates the surreptitious infiltration of emotions: its aesthetic qualities allow art to permeate the soul (*Republic* 401d5–e1; cf. *Laws* 659d–60a). And while that makes it potentially beneficial it also makes it dangerous, and more dangerous the more "poetic and pleasing" a work is (ποιητικὰ καὶ ἡδέα, *Republic* 387b1–5; cf. 397d–98b). Literature thus occupies the negative pole in the pervasive Platonic dichotomy between the pleasurable and the good: like a pastry-chef in comparison to a doctor, a poet seeks only to gratify his audience not to improve them (*Gorgias* 500a–502c). Literature's pleasure not only stands apart from truth – as it had ever since the Muses warned Hesiod that their songs may or may not be true (*Theogony* 27–8) – but stands against it (cf. Gorgias DK 82 B 23; *Dissoi Logoi* DK 90, 3.25–6; Thucydides 1.22.4; Pindar *Nemean* 7.19–25; Isocrates 2.49).

Small wonder, then, that Plato bans poets from his ideal republic, permitting only hymns to the gods and eulogies of virtuous men, but not the pernicious seductions of "the sweetened Muse" (τὴν ἡδυσμένην Μοῦσαν, *Republic* 607a5). There are, of course, good reasons to be leery of Plato's censorious views on literature and the positivist ontology from which they stem. But one needn't subscribe to his prohibition in order to recognize behind his hostility to literature an astute observation about the potentially disruptive effect of its aesthetic and emotional pleasure: precisely because it works on the psyche, the unconscious, literature's *psychagōgia* will always potentially exceed the conscious rulings of the lawmaker's *logos* and threaten to sabotage his best-laid plans.

Aristotle responds to this same potential threat not by banning poetry but by attempting to harness its *psychagōgia* to rational ethical ends. For him, literature's emotional arousal does not preclude, and ideally stimulates, a cognitive response (*Poetics* 1448b4–19; see Halliwell 2002, 177–206). Since the men and actions literature imitates necessarily have an ethical quality, good or bad, the audience is always making ethical determinations (1448a1–18). In tragedy, these ethical judgments are solicited in part through the arousal of emotion: Aristotle's definition of tragedy unites mimesis of serious actions, "sweetened" language (ἡδυσμένῳ λόγῳ), and the arousal of pity and fear in a way that suggests that the ethical, hedonic, and emotional can ideally work together (1449b24–8). Tragedy's emotional *psychagōgia* (1450a33) helps us to better understand the relationship between action and character and between virtue and happiness (1449b36–50a4, 1450a15–25). Its goal, its "particular pleasure" (ἡδονὴν ... οἰκείαν, 1453b11), is a *katharsis* of pity and fear, not the purgation of those emotions but their clarification, as Stephen Halliwell (1987, 90) explains, "a powerful emotional experience which not only gives our natural feelings of pity and fear full play, but does so in a way which conduces to their rightful functioning as part of our understanding of, and response to, events in the human world."

Aristotle thus purifies literary *hēdonē* of its perverse Platonic associations by yoking it to rationality and its positive social and ethical aims. But in so doing he underestimates the erratic, anomic force of literature's pleasure that so troubled Plato. Operating at the level of the unconscious – emotion, desire, enjoyment – literature's *psychagōgia* cannot be fully subordinated to conscious cognition nor reliably deployed in the service of a rational didactic, social, or ideological functionality.

I close with a brief illustration of this claim, drawn from that supremely psychagogic (*psykhagōgikōtaton*, Plato *Minos* 321a5) genre, tragedy. Euripides' *Ion* tells the story of Ion, the mythical king of Athens and progenitor of its empire. Born from Apollo's rape of the autochthonous Athenian princess Creusa, Ion was exposed as an infant and raised as a temple slave in Delphi. The play dramatizes his emotional reunion with his mother and assumption of his identity as Athenian king and hero. The play is pleasurable, to be sure, perhaps one of Euripides' most pleasurable. But the subject matter makes it hard to take it as merely pleasurable. The play speaks overtly to the Athenian ideologies of autochthony and imperial destiny; but what it says – its political or ideological message – is far from clear. Some scholars see the play as affirming these seminal Athenian beliefs: stressing the "happy ending," in which Athena herself appears ex machina to confirm Ion's divine paternity and proclaim his and his city's future glory, they read *Ion* as a celebration of Athens and its imperial hegemony (e.g. Swift 2008, 80–100; cf. Dougherty 1996). Others view the play as a critique of these same ideologies, an ironic debunking of Athens' myth of origins and a cynical exposé of the violence, xenophobia, and misogyny it entails (Saxonhouse 1986; Hoffer 1996).

What makes such contradictory readings not only possible but, I think, inescapable, is the play's emotional trajectory. The drama is structured by the delayed recognition between mother and son. In the opening scene the two meet and, unaware of the other's identity, confess their longing, Creusa for the child she was forced to abandon, Ion for the mother he never knew. A series of misunderstandings keeps them apart and nearly results in murder, and it is only in the play's final moment that they are joyfully reunited. To the extent that the audience identifies with the characters and shares their desire, they will long for that reunion and greet it when it finally comes as simultaneously natural and miraculous. But the audience's emotional commitment to the happiness of the happy ending also entails a commitment to the Athenian ideologies of autochthony and imperialism this family reunion presages. The play's structure of deferred recognition and the investment it produces in Ion's Athenian identity make it difficult to buy fully into an ironic or negative reading of the play. At the same time, though, the drama's pathos makes it difficult to accept an uncritically positive reading. Late in the play, in despair at the thought that she will never have a child, Creusa denounces the god who raped and abandoned her in one of the most beautiful and emotionally intense monodies in all of Greek tragedy (859–922). Apollo never appears to defend himself against her charges, and her despairing lament, even as it casts into relief the emotional reversal of the happy ending, also reverberates as a minor note of uncertainty within it. The play works to move its audience, to give pleasure by arousing emotions of pity and fear, of longing, frustration, and satisfaction. This emotional *psychagōgia* simultaneously leads toward the ideologically loaded finale and pulls against it. Its multidirectional emotive force makes it impossible to reduce the play to any single ideological function or straightforward lesson, even as the play's insistent engagement with Athenian ideology makes it impossible to read it as just a simple romance of maternal love.

Ion illustrates the ways in which literature's emotional impact and the pleasure it provides complicate its social functionality and resist reduction to a rational logic of utility. This same resistance can be felt even in Aristophanes' *Frogs*, for all its unquestioned assumption that literature should be socially useful. For the literary contest in Hades is not ultimately won on the basis of pedagogical value or social utility, nor for that matter on aesthetic merit, despite the elaborate mechanisms contrived for its quantification. Instead, Dionysus simply follows his heart: "I will choose the one my *psyche* wants," he says (Αἱρήσομαι γὰρ ὅνπερ ἡ ψυχὴ θέλει, *Frogs* 1468). This emotional verdict is never justified; its apparent capriciousness – Dionysus went to Hades longing for Euripides but chooses Aeschylus – is never explained.[10] Literary pleasure, the desire Plato compared to erotic madness, refuses to be subordinated to the utilitarian logic that governs the poetic contest: its *psychagōgia* follows its own path. Whether this erratic passion ultimately supports literature's social function is left an open question: Dionysus does bring back a poet, but it is not obvious that Aeschylus, with his outmoded advice, will actually save the city. With historical hindsight, we know that he did not; nor did Aristophanes, for all that he was awarded a crown for the good counsel he offered in *Frogs* (*Vita Aristophanis*, PCG III.2, p. 2, l. 36–6). But to ask literature to save the city is to demand both too much of it and too little. As the god of tragedy suggests, literature can and should serve a social function, but it cannot be reduced to that function. For the emotional pleasure it produces will always exceed any simple functionality and this, in the end, is what makes it literature.

NOTES

[1] The Greeks had no category of literature as such and their discussions often seem from our perspective either too broad (including music and dance) or too narrow (excluding prose). Cf. Introduction to this volume, pp. 2–3. In speaking of literature's function the question of historical perspective immediately arises: what we consider the function of literature today may not be the same as what the Greeks thought it was. This paper will focus on the latter but doesn't preclude the former: for reasons that will become apparent, Greek literature may well have had functions that were not (and could not be) recognized or articulated at the time.

[2] In fact, the form of the work is not fully determined by its function either: one can think of the Homeric Hymns, which vastly outgrew their original purpose of introducing epics.

[3] Plato asks this question at *Republic* 599d–600a. Cf. Ford 2002, 201–8.

[4] He was not alone in this: compare, for example, Aeschines 1.141–2, 151–3; 3.134–5. Aristotle recommends citing the poets as witnesses: *Rhetoric* 1.15.13.

[5] On literature's mystification of the field of power see Bourdieu 1993, esp. 74–111.

[6] Pindar, Bacchylides, Simonides, and Aeschylus all spent time at the court of Hieron of Syracuse, for instance, and the first three, at least, wrote poems in his honor. See Gentili 1988, 155–76 on the changing economics of poetic production in ancient Greece.

[7] Hesiod does not critique monarchical power *tout court*, as we have seen, but only its corrupt pretenders. If his poetry has a critical function, it is reformist not revolutionary.

[8] Balibar and Macherey 1981, 93–5: literary texts produce their own literariness in the interpretations they generate; "this way a text can very easily stop being literary or become so under new conditions." See also Derrida 1992, 44–8.

[9] Porter 2010, in his emphasis on the sensual basis of Greek aesthetics, perhaps comes closest to providing such an "erotics" of ancient art.

[10] It does not help that the text at the end of the play is troubled: see Dover 1993, 373–6.

REFERENCES

Althusser, L. 1971. "Ideology and Ideological State Apparatuses (Notes towards an Investigation)." In *Lenin and Philosophy and Other Essays*, New York, 127–86.

Balibar, É. and P. Macherey. 1981. "On Literature as an Ideological Form." In R. J. C. Young, ed., *Untying the Text: A Post-Structuralist Reader*, London, 79–99.

Bourdieu, P. 1993. *The Field of Cultural Production*. Ed. by R. Johnson. New York.

Burnett, A.P. 1983. *Three Archaic Poets: Archilochus, Alcaeus, Sappho*. Cambridge, MA.

Carson, A, transl. 2002. *If Not, Winter: Fragments of Sappho*. New York.

Cobb-Stevens, V. 1985. "Opposites, Reversals, and Ambiguities: The Unsettled World of Theognis". In T.J. Figueira, and G. Nagy, eds., *Theognis of Megara: Poetry and the Polis*, Baltimore, 159–75.

Croally, N. T. 1994. *Euripidean Polemic: the Trojan Women and the Function of Tragedy*. Cambridge.

Csapo, E. 2004. "The Politics of the New Music." In P. Murray and P. Wilson, eds., *Music and the Muses: The Culture of Mousike in the Classical Athenian City*, Oxford, 207–48.

Derrida, J. 1992. "This Strange Institution Called Literature: An Interview with Jacques Derrida." In D. Attridge, ed., *Acts of Literature*, New York, 33–75.

Detienne, M. 1996 [1967]. *The Masters of Truth in Archaic Greece*, New York.

Dougherty, C. 1996. "Democratic Contradictions and the Synoptic Illusion of Euripides' *Ion*." In J. Ober and C. Hedrick, eds., *Dēmokratia: A Conversation on Democracies, Ancient and Modern*, Princeton, NJ, 249–70.

Dover, K., ed. 1993. *Aristophanes Frogs*. Oxford.

DuBois, P. 1995. *Sappho Is Burning*. Chicago.

Euben, J.P. 1986. "Political Corruption in Euripides' *Orestes*." In *Greek Tragedy and Political Theory*, Berkeley, CA, 222–51.

Figueira, T.J. and G. Nagy, eds. 1985. *Theognis of Megara: Poetry and the Polis*. Baltimore.

Ford, A. 2002. *The Origins of Criticism: Literary Culture and Poetic Theory in Classical Greece*. Princeton, NJ.

Fränkel, H. 1950. *Dichtung und Philosophie des frühen Griechentums*. Munich.

Gentili, B. 1988. *Poetry and Its Public in Ancient Greece: From Homer to the Fifth Century*. Baltimore.

Goldhill, S. 1987. "The Great Dionysia and Civic Ideology." *Journal of Hellenic Studies* 107: 58–76.

Griffin, J. 1998. "The Social Function of Attic Tragedy." *Classical Quarterly* 48: 39–61.

Halliwell, S., ed. 1987. *The Poetics of Aristotle*. London.

Halliwell, S. 2002. *The Aesthetics of Mimesis: Ancient Texts and Modern Problems*. Princeton, NJ.

Heath, M. 1987. *The Poetics of Greek Tragedy*. London.

Hoffer, S.E. 1996. "Violence, Culture, and the Workings of Ideology in Euripides' *Ion*." *Classical Antiquity* 15: 289–318.

Jameson, F. 1971. *Marxism and Form*. Princeton, NJ.

Jameson, F. 1981. *The Political Unconscious: Narrative as a Socially Symbolic Act*. Ithaca, NY.

Kurke, L. 1991. *The Traffic in Praise: Pindar and the Poetics of Social Economy*. Ithaca, NY.

Kurke, L. 2011. *Aesopic Conversations: Popular Tradition, Cultural Dialogue, and the Invention of Greek Prose*. Princeton, NJ.

Levine, D.B. 1985. *Symposium and the Polis*. In T. J. Figueira, and G. Nagy, eds., *Theognis of Megara: Poetry and the Polis*, Baltimore, 176–96.

Porter, J.I. 2010. *The Origins of Aesthetic Thought in Ancient Greece: Matter, Sensation, and Experience*. Cambridge.

Rose, P.W. 1992. *Sons of the Gods, Children of Earth: Ideology and Literary Form in Ancient Greece*. Ithaca, NY.

Saxonhouse, A. 1986. "Myths and the Origins of Cities: Reflections on the Autochthony Theme in Euripides' *Ion*." In J.P. Euben, ed., *Greek Tragedy and Political Theory*, Berkeley, CA, 252–73.

Sontag, S. 1966. *Against Interpretation and Other Essays*. New York.

Swift, L. 2008. *Euripides: Ion*. London.

Vernant, J.-P. 1988. "Tensions and Ambiguities in Greek Tragedy." In J.-P. Vernant and P. Vidal-Naquet, eds., *Myth and Tragedy in Ancient Greece*, New York, 29–48.

Wallace, R.W. 2004. "Damon of Oa: A Music Theorist Ostracized?" In P. Murray and P. Wilson, eds., *Music and the Muses: The Culture of Mousike in the Classical Athenian City*, Oxford, 249–67.

Will, F. 1969. *Archilochos*. New York.

Zeitlin, F.I. 1980. "The Closet of Masks: Role-Playing and Myth-Making in the *Orestes* of Euripides." *Ramus* 9: 51–77.

Zeitlin, F.I. 1990. "Thebes: Theater of Self and Society in Athenian Drama." In J.J. Winkler and F.I. Zeitlin, eds., *Nothing to Do With Dionysus? Athenian Drama in its Social Context*. Princeton, NJ, 103–67.

FURTHER READING

Bourdieu, P. 1993. *The Field of Cultural Production*. Edited by R. Johnson. New York. Essays by the prominent sociologist on the role of art within the structures of society.

Detienne, M. 1996 [1967]. *The Masters of Truth in Archaic Greece*, New York. Traces the evolution of the concept of truth in ancient Greece.

Ford, A. 2002. *The Origins of Criticism: Literary Culture and Poetic Theory in Classical Greece*. Princeton. A detailed but accessible study of the emergence of literary criticism in ancient Greece.

Halliwell, S. 2002. *The Aesthetics of Mimesis: Ancient Texts and Modern Problems*. Princeton. A broad-ranging analysis of ancient Greek thought on this key concept in Western aesthetics.

Jameson, F. 1981. *The Political Unconscious: Narrative as a Socially Symbolic Act*. Ithaca, NY. One of the most influential works of Marxist literary criticism.

Porter, J. I. 2010. *The Origins of Aesthetic Thought in Ancient Greece: Matter, Sensation, and Experience*. Cambridge. Presents an innovative argument for the materialist foundations of ancient Greek aesthetic thought.

Rose, P. W. 1992. *Sons of the Gods, Children of Earth: Ideology and Literary Form in Ancient Greece*. Ithaca, NY. Examines the ideology of inherited excellence in a variety of Greek literary texts.

FURTHER READING

PART VIII

The Reception of Greek Literature

CHAPTER 32

Trends in Greek Literature in the Contemporary Academy

Emily Wilson

1. Preliminaries

I begin with a few words about the (limited) scope and (partial) narrative of this chapter. My focus is primarily on developments and changes in the academic study of Greek literature in North America over the past generation, with an emphasis on the ways that the field has both been informed by, and has itself informed, developments in literary and cultural theory in this country.[1] I will not have space for a detailed consideration of each stage in modern scholarship on Greek literature even in the US, nor for extensive analysis of the academic situation in Europe and the UK, each of which has a significantly different history and different institutional structure from that of the US. But, since academic trends in one country do not exist in a vacuum, I begin with a brief sketch of the development of ancient Greek scholarship in Germany and Britain. I then move to Greek studies in the US in recent times, pointing out some directions in which the field has moved from the perspective both of undergraduate education and of scholarly analysis, and flagging in particular the mutually productive relationship between Greek literary scholarship and literary theory in the last 30 years or so. I shall argue that the current situation for Greek scholarship and education in Greek literature at all levels is less dire than has often been claimed. Hellenists have never been more fully attuned to the differences between ancient Greek culture and our own, nor more aware of the power of this alien literature to provoke, inspire, irritate and change us.

2. Beginnings: Germany and Britain in the Nineteenth and Early Twentieth Century[2]

It is traditional to begin the story of the professional study of Greek literature with Germany in the time of the Enlightenment. Figures such as J. J. Winckelmann, in the eighteenth century, a representative of the "new German humanism," idolized the Greeks, against the then-much-more-familiar Romans, as the first creators of true beauty in art. Notoriously, German intellectuals

A Companion to Greek Literature, First Edition. Edited by Martin Hose and David Schenker.
© 2016 John Wiley & Sons, Inc. Published 2020 by John Wiley & Sons, Inc.

of this period began to identify themselves with the Greeks. The Romantic notion of Greece as the source of perfect, clean, impersonal beauty, as well as of desires and personal expression (supposedly absent from Roman culture), of ruins, nature, and the sublime, spread in various different ways throughout European and British culture, and was complemented by increasing numbers of elite young men (including, most famously, Goethe), who travelled to Greece itself on the Grand Tour. Greece, as well as Italy – or even more so – had now become an essential element in a gentleman's education, especially in Germany, a nation now "tyrannized" by an obsession with ancient Greece (Butler 1939/2012).

Goethe and other key figures in the "German humanist" movement were interested in Greece primarily for aesthetic reasons and as an inspiration for their own work. The German study of Greek literature was transformed in the nineteenth century with the emergence of scholars who aimed at a far more thoroughly "scientific" study of ancient history and philology. These figures believed in the possibility of eventually creating a totalized vision of all the reality of ancient culture through scientific method: *Altertumswissenschaft*. Philology was no longer seen as a separate pursuit from ancient history, archaeology, or art history; rather, it encompassed all of them. Philipp August Böckh, for example, in a lecture at the opening of the congress of German philologists in 1850, defined the subject as the historical construction of the entire life of the past (Horstmann 1992). Beyond the universities, Greek literature became a cornerstone of secondary-school education in the gymnasia of Germany.

The most famous scholar to emerge from this educational and intellectual model was also the most vehement voice against it: Friedrich Nietzsche, who was educated in "scientific" philology at the University of Bonn, but who became a radical opponent of his contemporaries' approach to the study of Greek literature. Thanks to his supervisor F. W. Ritschl, he was appointed to a professorship at the exceptionally early age of 24 at the University of Basel. But he fell out with the academic establishment of Greek scholars, including Ritschl and Ulrich von Wilamowitz-Moellendorff, one of the foremost philologists of the day, who wrote vehemently against Nietzsche's work (including his first published book, *The Birth of Tragedy*, 1871). Wilamowitz insisted (in "Future Philology!" a review of *The Birth of Tragedy*: Wilamowitz 1872/2000) that Nietzsche's whole methodology was wrong-headed and opposed to truth (see Porter 2000, Most 2003). Nietzsche himself admitted that he had been inspired in his interpretation of Greek tragedy by the music of Richard Wagner and the philosophy of Schopenhauer, which Wilamowitz regarded as an anachronistic and absurd approach. The scholar, he argued, ought to proceed in a spirit of pure truth, rather than importing his own cultural and ideological preoccupations into the study of the past. Nietzsche responded with a series of counter-attacks, which made clear how deep the gulf was between his way of seeing Greek literature and that of the scientific philologists. The Wilamowitz–Nietzsche quarrel has cast a long shadow, and raises issues that continue to surface in the study of Greek literature. For Nietzsche, modern culture was entirely relevant for an investigation of the Greeks; for philologists such as Wilamowitz, it was inadmissible evidence, and could lead to nothing but anachronism.

Moreover, Nietzsche insisted that the earlier generation of German Philhellenes (such as Winckelmann and Goethe) had wholly misunderstood the Greeks; they thought of them as only rational and beautiful, neglecting the central importance of madness and violence and mental sickness in Greek culture and literature (see Porter 2000). Nietzsche's relationship with Greek literature was often polemical and antagonistic. He suggests in *The Birth of Tragedy* that the true Greeks – meaning Aeschylus and Sophocles – were admirable for reasons precisely opposed to those of European Enlightenment admirers of Classical literature (one common bugbear being Goethe, who, Nietzsche insists, "did not understand the Greeks": Nietzsche 1998). They were to be celebrated not for their rationality or their calm, but for their courageous willingness to look directly at the irrational, painful depths of human experience. But here and elsewhere in his work, Nietzsche suggests that certain other figures in Greek literature – including Euripides and, above all, Socrates – barely deserve the name of "Greek"; they tainted Greek profundity with their trivializing rationalism.

Wilamowitz dismissed all this as "infantile," "a pile of rubbish," and scored many hits against Nietzsche's slapdash use of evidence and willingness to extrapolate ideas that contradict or go far beyond the facts. Nietzsche was defended by some in the philological community (such as Rohde), but felt isolated, and conducted an ongoing defense of his own position about how one ought to study ancient, and specifically Greek, literature. One particularly important battle in this war is represented by his "We Philologists" (Nietzsche 1874/1974), in which he insists that the kind of scholars represented by Wilamowitz (not mentioned by name) had fundamentally misunderstood the point of studying ancient literature and culture. They believed that their task was to establish a total reconstruction of the past, from some objective position, disinterestedly – a goal that Nietzsche describes as "anemic." Nietzsche saw the task of the philologist as a dynamic engagement between the past and the present, and of the present by means of the past: "If we make it our task to understand our own age better by means of antiquity, then our task will be an everlasting one." Nietzsche also insisted that "a philologist must first of all be a man," and that the desire to engage with the past itself emerges from the experience of the present: "there are no disinterested philologists." For Nietzsche, the value of studying Greek culture and literature at all, for the "strong" philologist, is in order to "take possession" of the "entire Hellenic mode of thinking"; and he also claims, in a deliberate paradox, that his goal is to establish the "complete enmity between our present 'culture' and antiquity." Contemporary philologists have, he suggests, entirely misunderstood Greek culture; if they were really to understand it, they would "shrink from it, horror-stricken," since, as he says later in the same essay, "a sincere leaning towards antiquity renders one unchristian."

Nietzsche's critique did not, of course, destroy the new science, and the attitudes represented by Wilamowitz continued in the academic study of Greek literature, arguably to this day. But the goals and methods of *Altertumswissenschaft* were, as Hugh Lloyd-Jones has noted, "linked with the German drive towards domination in Europe" (Lloyd-Jones 1982, xviii). Developments within the academy were inevitably intertwined with larger social and political changes. The First World War disrupted the endeavors of German Greek scholars, and in the interwar years, academics had less faith in the positivist models of the past, and many, especially Jewish scholars, came under threat from National Socialism: many important scholars emigrated from Germany to Britain or the US, where their work had a major impact on developments in the field in those countries (Calder 1990). These include Werner Jaeger, who emigrated to the US in 1936 because of his dissatisfaction with Hitler's regime, and took up professorships first at Chicago, and then at Harvard. His three-volume work, *Paedeia*, from 1945, can be seen as a conjunction of the scientific ideal of total knowledge of antiquity with a new ideological urgency: Jaeger saw his evocation of Greek culture as a way to combat the dangers and decadence, as he saw it, of contemporary Europe. Eduard Fraenkel (a Jewish scholar, who had studied with Wilamowitz) and Rudolf Pfeiffer (not himself Jewish, but married to a Jewish woman) were forced to emigrate to England in the 1930s, where they took up positions at Oxford; both these scholars had a huge impact on the British study of Classical, and especially Greek, literature. Fraenkel's seminars on Aeschylus and Horace soon became the stuff of legend, while Pfeiffer's work both on the fragments of Callimachus, and on the history of Classical scholarship in antiquity, demonstrated to English-speaking academics how far a rigorous, Germanic style of scholarship could take one.

The first part of the twentieth century marked the end of Germany as the dominant voice in the academic study of Greek literature, although the influence of the idea of *Altertumswissenschaft* is still discernible to this day. Histories of Greek literature scholarship that emerge from the German tradition tend to present the twentieth century as a period of various kinds of decline from the majestic heights attained by scholars such as Wilamowitz. Joachim Latacz (Latacz 2013) claims that the "present situation of Greek philology, particularly in its European motherlands, is unstable." But narratives from a British or North American perspective tend to give a more mixed picture. We should, then, first have a brief look at the different histories of Hellenic studies in these two countries, before turning to more recent times and to American shores.

In Britain in the nineteenth century, Classical studies, including the study of Greek literature and culture as well as Latin, were closely intertwined with the creation and perpetuation of a social elite. Greek literature was seen to have value in providing aesthetic and moral training for the gentlemen, clergy, and politicians of the future; there was far less expectation that those who studied Greek literature as undergraduates would ever make significant scholarly contributions (Stray 1998). Both at Oxbridge and in the major public secondary schools (such as Eton, Winchester, and Thomas Arnold's Rugby), the study of Greek literature was seen as essential for creating a cultured upper class, and training its members in both morality and aesthetics. Matthew Arnold's famous and hugely influential essay, "Culture and Anarchy" (1869/1998), gives a useful insight into the Victorian perspective on Greek literature. Arnold argues that Hellenic culture is a "study of perfection," and he defines perfection as something spiritual, moral, intellectual, and aesthetic, all at the same time. He suggests, too, that the "immense spiritual significance of the Greeks" lies in their having grasped this idea in its totality: they, more than any other people in world history, were "inspired with this central and happy idea of the essential character of human perfection." The ancient Greeks, for Arnold, as well as their art and their literature, represent the epitome of human perfection, rationality, tranquility, and spiritual enlightenment.

We can see, then, that in Britain, some of the spirit of Goethe's Romantic vision of Greek literature lingered on, untouched by the new science of antiquity which had developed in Germany. This helps explain why there were so few massive scholarly productions in Greek philology from Britain in this period, despite the large numbers of people who studied the literature. The goal of reading Greek literature in Britain was not to advance the cause of scholarly truth, but to improve oneself. The culture has gradually changed, thanks in part to the influence of German immigrant scholars. Nowadays, British academics, under pressure to publish for the dreaded Research Assessment Exercises, complain no less than Americans about the drive to churn out scholarship in quantity rather than quality (contrast Ross 1989).

3. American Hellenic History

Professional Greek studies in the United States developed in ways that, institutionally, were modeled on Germany. The Ph.D. program, involving years of graduate study in seminars followed by the writing of a thesis under the close supervision of a *Doktorvater*, is an adaptation of the German model (see Ross 1989). There have been wonderful productions of American Greek scholarship in very much the German tradition; Smyth's Greek Grammar is only the most prominent example (Smyth 1920/1984). Some institutions in North America have enabled huge philological advances on very much the German model; the *Thesaurus Linguae Graecae*, which in its digitized version aims to preserve and make searchable as much as possible of Greek literature, is one of the most important examples. The *TLG* was founded in 1972 at University of California Irvine, and remains one of the glories of Hellenic studies worldwide.

In terms of human capital, there have been American attempts to create institutional contexts for work by groups of scholars and to enable the free exchange of ideas, although the goal is often less the gathering of information about the ancient world as a totality, than the re-creation and celebration of the Greeks as an ideal. An important such enterprise is the thriving Center for Hellenic Studies in Washington DC, founded in 1962 with an endowment "to rediscover the humanism of the Hellenic Greeks" (Center for Hellenic Studies 2015). American philologists have, by and large, resisted the German scientific method, as well as the German traditions of scholarly co-operation and group-projects, and have moved, increasingly, towards more personal and more literary forms of analysis of Greek literature. It is true, as Ross notes (Ross 1989), that the conjunction of British and German traditions has produced "tensions which have still not been resolved," in the American study of Greek literature. But it is a mistake to whine about this situation; the productive dialogue between scholarly traditions is one reason why the study of Greek literature in the contemporary North American academy is more vibrant and interesting than ever.

Both in America and, to a lesser extent, in Britain and Europe, Greek has shifted from being a subject commonly taught and sometimes learned in secondary school, to being a subject which is often begun only at the undergraduate level; the same is gradually happening for Latin as well, although at a slower rate. At Oxford, for instance, Classics has for over twenty years been available to students who enter with no Greek; the degree is now open to those with neither ancient language ("If you haven't studied Latin, or haven't studied Greek, or haven't studied either, you can at Oxford," the Classics at Oxford website reassures the prospective applicant who is innocent of all Greek or Latin: Classics at Oxford 2015). This model began much earlier in America than in Britain or Germany. Americans have, throughout the twentieth century, been "late-learners," to use Diskin Clay's term (Clay 1989; cf. Calder 1994). As Clay also suggests, there are both advantages and disadvantages to this position. On the one hand, a person who comes to Greek only at the relatively advanced age of 18 or 20 may not be ready to write a critical commentary on a Classical author by the time she is 25 or so. The German modes of Greek philology do not fit well with this model of education. On the other hand, American scholars have been exposed to a wider range of other subjects before they begin their concentrated research in Greek and Latin. They are therefore often better prepared to engage in perceptive literary and cultural criticism, and comparative work, than those who have tunneled down in Greek and only Greek, from earliest youth.

Another major advantage of the new/American system, one that has often not been stressed sufficiently, is that it makes Greek studies open to anybody who can attend college, rather than confining the field to those who have attended the (usually fee-paying, usually all-male) secondary schools which offer training in the language (Calder 1990). This is good not only for social equality (and that is arguably the more important consideration), but also for the discipline itself. There is more diversity of voice in the scholarly conversation nowadays than there once was, and this in itself is part of the explanation for the exciting diversity of approaches visible in contemporary Hellenic studies. A further important development in terms of opening up the discipline to people from all different social groups is the increasing number of post-baccalaureate programs in classics across the US; the first, at the University of Pennsylvania, began in 1984, and serves students who are not yet strong enough in Greek and/or Latin to begin a doctoral program.

Of course, attainment of total social equality within the world of Hellenic studies is still far beyond reach. I note here that in the current volume, there is a wide range of nationalities, but not a wide range of ethnicities (most participants are Caucasian North American or Caucasian European; people of Asian or, even more, African descent are minimally represented in Hellenic studies). Moreover, of the 33 participants, only seven are female – a score of just over one in five. It seems fairly clear that there is a glass ceiling in the academic study of Greek literature, as in many other disciplines. The numbers of men and women enrolled in undergraduate classes, and in graduate programs, seems to be fairly even, but the numbers represented among tenured faculty, and invited to participate in edited volumes, are often not as evenly spread. Women and minorities are often disproportionately represented in adjunct language teaching positions, and are disproportionately likely to move to an administrative or secondary school position after beginning a Ph. D. in Greek literature – for obvious cultural and institutional reasons. This is worth emphasizing, since the situation is unlikely to change without a great deal of effort on the part of both scholars themselves, and institutional administrators.

There is, however, much to celebrate in the current American model. The number of students in the US who learn Greek is relatively small, certainly as compared to Britain or Germany in the late nineteenth century. But those who do study the language have usually chosen to do so, and are highly motivated, in ways that were certainly not the case for every class of little boys marched through Greek grammar in the British public schools or German gymnasia of old. Moreover, an interesting trend since the 1960s is that a significant group of students choose to study Greek rather than Latin – instead of beginning with Latin and moving on to Greek, in the more traditional manner. Greek in the 1960s became fashionable, in a way that Latin was not, and it remains significantly more cool in the eyes of American undergraduates, presumably partly because it is so rarely offered in high schools. Roman Catholic schools have an obvious reason to teach Latin, but little motive to offer Greek; Greek therefore, by default and rather paradoxically, becomes the secular ancient language. Whereas once, "classics" was imagined in the undergraduate mind as a single entity, the two subjects have now become disentangled – a situation that is somewhat advantageous for Greek studies. During the 1980s in particular, students seem to have chosen to study Greek in preference to Latin. But Latin is now again on the rise. The Modern Language Association maintains a list of enrollments in non-English language classes, which goes back to 1958 (although numbers for Greek and Latin only begin in 1968), and includes some illuminating statistics on undergraduate numbers in Greek language classes over the course of that period (Modern Language Association 2013). In 1968, Latin had 34,981 students enrolled across the US, while Greek had 19,285. Greek enrollments rose rapidly, to reach a peak of 25,848 in 1977; Latin enrollments dropped in the same period, and reached a low of 24,391 in 1977. In other words, in the 1970s there were, at least momentarily, more students taking classes in Greek than in Latin. Since that time, the numbers have evened out, and are now back to more or less the same level as they were in 1968: 20,695 took Greek in 2009, and 32,606 took Latin.

Of course, since college enrollments have increased exponentially since the 1960s, these figures represent a huge relative decline in the percentage of college students who are studying either Classical language. But it will not do for either Hellenists or Latinists to bemoan their situation too loudly, since relative to some other national language and literature departments, the Classical languages are still doing very well. For obvious reasons, some languages have increased enrollments enormously in the past forty years: Arabic and Chinese enrollments have both increased thirty-fold. But in the same period, other languages – such as German – have plummeted, again for obvious reasons. The real issue here is not whether classics in general, or Greek in particular, are under threat; both are faring far better than many other small humanities departments. The important question is rather whether humanities disciplines, and especially those with a commitment to history, literature, and language study, can band together to defend the place of the humanities within a broader academic framework where, increasingly, funding and prestige tends to go to the sciences.

In this battle, classics in general, and Greek in particular, have an essential part to play, since they are, especially in the US, so central to the "core" or "canon" of the humanities as it has been imagined and institutionalized in the twentieth century. In the US, in fairly sharp contrast to Britain and Europe, there is a long and vigorous institutional history of teaching Greek texts in translation for undergraduate classes. I might note in passing that my British friends are often astonished to learn how many Americans have read the *Iliad* in translation, a feat which is almost unheard-of in the UK. The Columbia Core, which was founded in 1919, has often been seen as a direct response to US involvement in World War I, providing a justification for American intervention by positing a shared cultural heritage for Europeans and Americans, which centered on the Greeks. Many other Great Books courses, which generally begin with Homer and Greek tragedy, developed at a time – between the wars, during the Great Depression – when many in the US were eagerly looking for a kind of communal, shared cultural point of origin, to unite a fractured world, combat the dangers of nationalism, and provide a kind of value that seemed all the more important in a time of deep economic scarcity. Jaeger's model of "Paedeia" was extremely influential at this time.

The Core itself, and its many cousins, sisters and daughters in other universities across the states, has changed a great deal in the past century, and has opened up to include a far less Eurocentric focus. This has also meant that Greek literature is somewhat less central to the curriculum than it once was – although it remains an essential element in "Literature Humanities," a survey of what are still labeled "the great works of Western literature," beginning with Homer; Greek literature is also perhaps paradoxically, essential to "Contemporary Civilization," a survey of Western political thought which begins with Plato and Aristotle. Columbia is not alone in both attempting to challenge the pre-eminent position of Greek literature in its curriculum, and also continuing to award it a somewhat privileged place in the students' course of study.

To see how radically the study of Greek literature within the Anglo-American academy has changed over the past hundred years or so, a good starting point is to look at a few of the different introductory handbooks on the subject that have appeared in that time. These are often aimed at undergraduates, or graduate students preparing for exams at an early stage of their careers, rather than primarily for scholars at the coalface of research in the subject. But for that very reason, they are particularly useful indicators of assumptions made by contemporary scholars about the state of play in the field at the time.

At the start of the twentieth century, a student or general reader in search of an overview of Greek literature could turn to Alfred and Maurice Croiset's *Histoire de la littérature Grecque*, published in five substantial volumes (Croiset 1898–1929). The authors abridged their work into a single volume, and it was translated into English and published in 1904 (Croiset 1904). Even a quick glance reveals several significant differences between the representation of Greek literature in this work and its presentation in more recent introductions. The most obvious point we can deduce from this publication is that there was in 1904 a real market for a book on Greek literature which runs – in its abridged form! – to 563 pages of close-packed ten-point type. The translator's preface notes the "demand" of "English students" for a "concise, well-written, scholarly manual on the subject" (Croiset 1904: ix.). The Croisets themselves suggest that the readers of their "Manual" will be "students in the secondary schools," and "readers who wish to inform themselves quickly as to the essential facts of Greek literature." In the twentieth century, the average high school student or general reader is not likely to find this book a particularly quick read, and it is highly unlikely that most who are not specializing in the subject or a related field (graduate students in classics or ancient history) would feel the need to devote quite so much time to acquiring a "basic" knowledge of Greek literature.

A related point to note is that the Croiset Manual assumes that the high school or general reader will already know rather a lot about Greek literature. Although all extensive quotations are translated, there are a good sprinkling of terms in untransliterated Greek. There are discussions of technical issues that would be incomprehensible to an uninitiated contemporary reader: for instance, the Greek use of the term "melic" is defined, but "strophe" and "monody" are not, and the discussions of lyric meter would make tough going for a Greek-less reader ("Stesichorus composed long strophes, whose dactylic members, variously combined with epitrites (– u – –), formed large and ample groups," Croiset 1904: 130). This is not stuff that a modern publisher would feel she could lay before the unsuspecting general public.

We can contrast Croiset with the various introductions to Greek literature that have appeared in English in more recent times – including the present volume. Important examples in the genre include Hadas 1950, Lesky 1957/1963, Dover 1980 (intended as a replacement for Bowra 1933), the *Cambridge History of Greek Literature* (Easterling and Knox 1985), Taplin 2000, and Whitmarsh 2004. If we trace these texts in chronological sequence, one important observation is that single-author monumental studies that aim to cover the whole field in the kind of depth and detail intended by Croiset have become a thing of the past. There are two main reasons for the change. The first is that the field of Greek literature has come to seem far bigger and more multifaceted than it did a hundred years ago. For that reason, it now seems unlikely that a single scholar could hope to cover the whole area in a definitive way. Studies that do aim to cover the whole of Greek literature, even schematically – like the Cambridge History, or like the present volume – rely on the perspectives of many different hands. The most successful single-author studies of recent years, such as Tim Whitmarsh's *Ancient Greek Literature* (Whitmarsh 2004), prove the rule. Rather than trying to provide a narrative history of the entire field, as the older studies did, Whitmarsh takes a novel, and deliberately non-chronological approach, dividing the topic into a series of case studies in cultural and literary issues (in sections titled "Concepts," "Contexts," and "Conflicts"). It is characteristic of contemporary approaches to the subject in that there is a great deal of emphasis here on various different performance contexts; Greek literature is no longer seen as existing solely, or even primarily, on the page (a point to which I shall return).

Moreover, Whitmarsh deliberately disrupts the kind of narrative history represented by the older introductions, which tend to march chronologically through a list of individual authors – the literary version of the Great Man model of history. Whitmarsh's interest is less in evoking a series of megalithic individual writers than in contextualizing texts as both the products, and producers, of cultural conflict. Whitmarsh devotes a lot of attention to ideological conflicts, and draws attention to ways in which the Greeks might seem less-than-ideal, from the perspective of modern political ideologies. He invites us to see most of the authors of Greek literature as racist, sexist slave-owners, with strange views about sexuality, by focusing on ethnic identity, representations of women, imaginings of same-sex and irregular sexualities, and on slavery and social status. These topics cannot be found in the earlier overviews I have cited – despite those books' claims to exhaustive treatment. The change is not merely the result of fashion or "political correctness." Rather, there is a new awareness among students of Greek literature that we, at our current moment in cultural history, need not, and in fact cannot, see the Greeks as "perfect." Eliminating this prejudice allows us new room to interrogate the ways in which their culture was both radically different from, and also similar to, our own.

The second main reason why modern overviews of Greek literature tend to be either multi-authored, or else short and deliberately partial, is because the market for these books has changed significantly over the past generation or two. Bowra's already slim 250 pp. volume (Bowra 1933) was replaced by an even slimmer (186 page) book (Dover et al. 1985), which was a collaboration of four different scholars, and which included far more quotation, in translation, than the original – designed to give "tasters" of Greek literature for readers who might never have read even a little bit of Hesiod.

Croiset's assumption of a well-informed "general reader," with a strong urge to acquire even more knowledge, is obviously the outcome of an institutional and social world in which Greek literature had a very different place from that which it has today. Knowledge of Greek literature was once a highly valuable piece of "cultural capital," to borrow a phrase from John Guillory; it allowed its possessor to rise in social rank and to be more impressive to others in society (Guillory 1993, drawing on Bourdieu 1984).

Guillory's central point is that the cultural value given to a particular text in a particular society is not entirely deducible from, or reducible to, the content of that text, or its authorship. Hence, books by and about white men may be read in an institutional context which does, or which does not, favor white men, while conversely, a canon that includes books by and about black women may, or may not, further the political and social interests of black women.

The debate about canon formation is particularly important for classicists, both Latinists and Hellenists, given the central place that "the classics" have had in the academy, and their extraordinarily high cultural capital until a generation or two ago. One of the major trends within the academic discussion of the discipline has been an increasing self-consciousness about questions of canonicity and authority. As we have already seen, the study of Greek literature played an essential role in the formation, self-fashioning and perpetuation of a social elite and of national identity, in both Germany and Britain in the late nineteenth century. The work of the sociologist Christopher Stray has examined the processes by which Classical education developed its peculiar social standing during this period (Stray 1998; Stray and Hardwick 2008). Stray shows how, in the course of that period, the study of Latin and Greek shifted from being a marker of high social class, to a occupying relatively marginalized position in both school and university contexts.

In Britain, Greek and Latin were once essential components not only to socio-cultural capital, but even for an academic career – especially at Oxford and Cambridge. During the nineteenth and twentieth century, students hoping to start working for an undergraduate degree at Oxford had to take an initial examination, known as the "Little Go," which involved questions in Greek, Latin and mathematics. A similar exam was set for second year undergraduates at Cambridge. Both were abolished in 1960. The abolition of these exams corresponded with a general feeling that the educational system of the country was unfairly weighted towards the privileged. In 1944, a tripartite school system had been set up, with an exam to be taken by all children at the age of 11. Those who did best in the exam were channeled into "grammar schools," which taught Latin and Greek, and were supposed to be academically rigorous. Those who did less well were siphoned into either technical schools, or the vaguely named "secondary modern" schools. In conjunction with the Oxbridge entrance exams, which required Latin and Greek, the result of this system was that it was all but impossible for a child from a poor background who had failed the 11-plus exam and thus missed the grammar-school boat, to get into these elite universities. In the 1960s and 1970s, the tripartite school system itself was phased out, and – at the same time as the abolition of the grammar schools – Latin and Greek became less and less commonly taught in state schools.

The inter-relationship of the discipline with social structures and institutions has become a major issue for Hellenists themselves, and is part of the drive behind the increasing interest of classicists in the reception of Greek (and Latin) literature, culture and history. Notably, quite a lot of work in this field has dealt with the problematic legacy of the classics and of the Greeks in particular, including the appropriations of ideas of Greece and Rome by the Nazis and also including colonial and postcolonial receptions (Goldhill 2002, Hardwick and Gillespie 2007).

At the same time, Hellenists have worked hard to maintain and try to increase their market-share within contemporary versions of the Great Western Canon or World Literature courses that are taught across the US. They have also tried to keep general readers informed and engaged with ancient Greek literature. Important interventions in these areas are made by Hellenists who write for the general literary press, such as Daniel Mendelsohn (Mendelsohn 2012). Even more important in keeping Greek literature available and interesting for a wide readership and audience are the new translations of old texts which have appeared in recent years; for instance, the translations of Homer and Greek tragedy by both Robert Fagles and Stanley Lombardo have been big sellers, and have made Greek poetry available to thousands of people who will never have time to learn Greek.

4.   Greek Literary Studies as a Subset of Literary and Cultural Studies

The two terms at stake in the current volume – "Greek" and "literature" – have come to seem increasingly problematic to contemporary Hellenists within the academy. First, scholars today, far more than a generation or two ago, tend to be aware of the fluid boundaries that separate ancient Greek culture from the other cultures of the ancient Mediterranean (Egyptian, Near Eastern, and so on: see West 1999; Bernal 1987–1991; discussion of the controversies surrounding Bernal is in Lefkowitz 1996). Scholars are also conscious that the canon of "Greek literature" can arguably include all kinds of texts that might not seem particularly Greek at all. New studies of ancient ethnography have encouraged a more complex idea of what it meant to be "Greek" in the ancient world (Hall 1997, Gruen 2005, Gruen 2011), while more literary studies have focused on how these texts "invent," and disparage, "the barbarian" (Hall 1991; Vasunia 2001). Moreover, as Hellenists have become more open to post-Classical periods of Greek literature, and also to post-Classical, non-Greek reception, the field of study has expanded temporally as well as spatially. Many contemporary Hellenists study, for instance, the work of writers who were not themselves native Greeks, or who did not live in Greece or under Greek political power (such as Lucian and other writers of the Second Sophistic); or texts that use literary languages rather than pure Attic (is "Homeric Greek" the same as actual Greek? and what justifies an equation of the Achaeans with the Greeks?); or even texts that are obviously neither in Greek nor written by Greeks (such as translations of Greek literature into Latin or modern languages, or the many imitations and allusions, re-readings and misreadings, that form part of the fabric of the "reception" of Greek literature). Charles Martindale (2006) has forcefully argued that reception is, and should be, absolutely central to the discipline of classics, not merely marginalized in the ways that it often has been. The current volume mostly stops at 600 CE; but for some Hellenists today, a text like Derek Walcott's *Omeros* is as much part of their field as the speeches of Demosthenes, or more so (e.g. Hall 2008).

The second term, "literature," is, if anything, even more problematic for contemporary classicists, and in other "literature" departments. The Russian Formalist Roman Jacobson first introduced the term "literariness" (*literaturnost*) back in 1921, to designate the peculiar prop- erties that supposedly distinguish literature as such from other cultural productions. Formalism, in all the literary branches of the academy (including English departments and the other national literatures as well as Classics), conjoined with various forms of structuralism, as well as with the native, Anglo-American ideas of New Criticism, to produce criticism focused on literature "as such," divorced from social and cultural context. Deconstruction, of the type practiced by Jacques Derrida and Paul de Man, was both a natural outgrowth of formalism, and its death-knell. The deconstructionists sought to identify points of self-contradiction in any text they studied, such that the text could be shown to be saying both one thing, and its opposite. The exercise was par- ticularly popular in the 1970's, when conspiracy theories were everywhere, but came to seem increasingly sterile, and perhaps even dangerous. Notoriously, Paul de Man was posthumously "outed" as a Nazi collaborator by a graduate student named Ortwyn de Graef, in 1987. Regardless of whether the ad hominem attack was true or false, the strict focus on literature "in itself" ("*il n'y a pas de hors-texte*," in Derrida's words) had come to seem like a political cop-out.

Moreover, contemporary scholars have become increasingly aware that the boundaries of genre and decorum traditionally drawn between "literature" and other kinds of verbal produc- tion may themselves be the product of a particular time and place – and often indeed of a particular ideological agenda on the part of reader, writer, or both; there is arguably no way to determine a priori what counts as "literature," and what does not. In the world of Greek literary studies, I will give just two examples of how this phenomenon has played out. First, scholars in ancient Greek philosophy, especially Platonists, have become increasingly aware that the institutional and critical divisions between "Greek philosophy" and "Greek literature" are not self-evident. Andrea Nightingale has usefully suggested that Plato's dialogues themselves are deeply concerned to construct an image of "philosophy" which is distinct from, but takes over the cultural place of, oratory in Greek society; the generic borders are a function of the text, not prior to it (Nightingale 1995). Many recent scholars have pointed to the importance of paying close attention to "literary" features of the Platonic dialogue, such as characteriza- tion, setting, tone and point of view (e.g. Blondell 2002). This is a boundary which has not entirely dissolved: departmental divisions between philosophers and literary scholars remain in many institutions, and many Hellenists still see a difference between reading Plato "as literature," and reading him "as philosophy."

My second example is the increasing interest shown by Hellenists in authors who have little or no pretensions to literary merit, and who may not even be authors. A crucial example here is Aesop, an author who exists only as a function of Greek culture, and who was almost entirely neglected until relatively recent times (see Kurke 2011). Contemporary scholars of Greek literature have been deeply influenced by a number of interventions in the field in the mid-twentieth century, which pointed to the Greeks and Greek literature as both less rational, and more alien, than writers like Arnold might have led us to believe. E. R. Dodd's work was influential here (Dodds 1963), as were a number of works by French scholars and theorists of the 1960s and 1970s. It was in this period, in fact, that French theory became a vital influence on American studies of Greek literature. Classic examples here include the work of Jean-Pierre Vernant and Pierre Vidal-Naquet, who (themselves partly inspired by Nietzsche as well as Lévi-Strauss) insisted on a "Dionysiac" reading of Greek literature and culture (Vernant and Vidal-Naquet 1988). Modern scholars are thoroughly liberated from the idea that the Greeks were either more rational or more harmonious, more well-balanced, than ourselves, and this in turn has enabled the field to turn with more precise attention to aspects of Greek "literature" which were neglected when the Greeks were supposed to be the representatives of high culture and of rationalism. Essential examples here include the study of Greek medical writings and other proto-scientific literature – a vast body of texts which are being given far more attention by contemporary scholars than by those of a generation or two ago; and the study of Greek magic (e.g. Holmes 2010, Rihll 1999, Clay 2003, Taub 2008).

The past two decades in the academy have seen the rise to dominance of New Historicism and Cultural Studies, which borrow many of the techniques of the deconstructionists (such as the identification of "fault-lines" or contradictions in a body of material), but apply them to societies rather than to the closed, "literary" world of the text. Theorists such as Hayden White and Michel Foucault have encouraged wariness about "positivist" models of history; we have been urged to see the task of the historian not as an assertion of a series of facts, but as a construction of slippery negotiations of power, both between social groups within the past, and between the scholars of the present and the people of the past. Culture, rather than either literature or history, has become the preferred term for what many scholars say they study.

Another way to trace this narrative is through the so-called "linguistic turn" that humanities disciplines have taken in the course of the twentieth century. The styles of historicism which emerged in the nineteenth century, following Hegel and Marx, tended to involve teleological accounts of the progression from one historical period to another, and a relatively stable idea of how each period could be described by the historian – as a set of events or "facts" about social relationships. The work of the linguist Ferdinand de Saussure in the early twentieth century acted as an influential intervention in many fields of the humanities, in that it suggested that we should shift our attention from the search for "facts," either about language or culture, towards an analysis of the closed systems of arbitrary signs, composed of signifiers and signifieds, which constitute human forms of meaning-making. Similarly, the work of philosophers of language and ethics, in both English and German traditions, drew attention to problems of categorization and individuation, and reminded us that language itself is not merely an instrument for generating meaning, but a complex social and cultural phenomenon, which both forms and is formed by our experience of the world; particularly central thinkers on these issues are Ludwig Wittgenstein and J. Austin (see e.g. Wittgenstein 1953, Austin 1962).

Saussure's model of the linguistic sign within the larger structure of language is defined by difference; that is, "cat" takes its meaning from its differentiation from other signs in the linguistic system of English (rather than, say, from its putative relationship with an external reality). The idea of structural dichotomies that generate cultural meaning became extremely influential in anthropology, for instance in the work of Claude Lévi-Strauss. After Lévi-Strauss, anthropologists such as Clifford Geertz took the discipline in a less abstract direction, arguing that ethnography should not be practiced, and in fact cannot be practiced, by a priori hypotheses or by "plain" observation of "facts," but rather, it is a writerly, textual discipline, which involves, above all, a "thick" description of observed phenomena (Geertz 1977). We make sense of an alien culture, according to Geertz, only when we can describe their ways of seeing and of meaning, in as much detail and as much from the inside as possible.

Each of these trends played a part in generating New Historicism, which emerged both from Geertzian anthropology and from Foucault, and which remains probably the most dominant mode of cultural analysis in the academy. New Historicism relies heavily on the evocative, telling anecdote, which is teased out to provide a "thick" description, and which is used to challenge or question received wisdom about a particular historical period, writer or work of art (Gallagher and Greenblatt 2000).

On one level, then, to say that contemporary Hellenist scholars tend to be interested in Greek literature as a lens into, and as a sub-set of, Greek culture – rather than in Greek literary history as its own closed world – is simply to say that the study of Greek literature is not separate from the trends of the contemporary literary academy as a whole. We would not expect it to be otherwise. The same is true of contemporary Hellenists' awareness of the complexities of national identities, as well as other forms of social identity (political, sexual, physical, intellectual, and so on). Postcolonialism is a major topic in the contemporary academy, including in literature departments; awareness of colonialism and its legacy in more recent periods of history has been part of the inspiration for Hellenists to develop their study of colonialism, multiculturalism, displacement and empire in the Greek world. More broadly, sexuality studies (including queer theory as well as various forms of feminist and gender studies), the study of race and ethnicity, and subalterity (the study of any social group viewed as "other" by the dominant social class) are, for obvious and very good reasons, growing fields in the academy as a whole; again, it is no surprise that Hellenists play a part in the trend.

Each literary and cultural discipline within the humanities has attempted to become more self-conscious over the past generation or so. In a context where the humanities are under increasing threat, both economically and in terms of their status within the social hierarchy of the university, and of society at large, scholars in the humanities have become increasingly aware that they themselves are participating in an enterprise which is not value-neutral, but whose value is not self-evident. Literary "greatness" or "beauty" are no longer terms that most academics feel comfortable in using, at least not in print. Reception studies and studies of changing literary and cultural canons have become essential elements in all contemporary literature departments.

But there is something distinctive in the ways that these trends have affected the study of Greek literature, and I shall suggest that this is due to two distinctive, inter-related features of the Hellenist's field of study. We move on in the final section, then, to consider how the study of Greek literature is distinctive within the broader discourses of the academic humanities, literary studies, and cultural and historical studies.

5. Performance; Canonicity; Theory

The first essential point is that Hellenists have become increasingly conscious of the fact that much of Greek literature, especially but not only our earliest texts (such as Homer and Hesiod), is based on oral composition (see Reece, ch. 3 in this volume). "Literature" (from the Latin litterae, "letters") implies written words on a physical page. Africanists have promoted the alternative term "oralture" to describe verbal artistic creations which exist primarily or exclusively in an oral context. Since the pioneering studies of the Parrys and Alfred Lord in the early twentieth century – which included research into the then-living traditions of oral poetry in the then-Yugoslavia – Hellenists have become increasingly aware that "literature" is a misnomer for many of our Greek "texts," including lyric poems and drama, which were composed for performance with musical accompaniment. Even prose works from ancient Greece are often misread by readers attuned to a primarily literary and literate system of cultural production: oratory was obviously composed for performance and engaged with other performative genres (Duncan 2006), but the same may well have been often true for historical, philosophical, and scientific texts (Havelock 1987; Ong 2002; see also the speculative Charalabopoulos 2011). Orality is different for Hellenists than for many other humanities fields, because scholars have been aware of its importance for several generations, and because Greek literature, at the cusp of orality, is arguably different in this respect from almost any other body of literature. I will return presently to the major implications of an awareness of orality for the contemporary study of Greek literature.

The second major reason why Greek literary scholars have a distinctive place within the dominant trends in the academy towards cultural history, reception studies, consciousness about canonicity, and awareness of the complexities of power relationships, is because Greek literature has traditionally been seen as the first, and greatest, of the European national literatures. The Greeks are, in the words of Bernard Knox (1993), the oldest of the dead white European males (cf. Hall, this volume ch. 33, p. 525). As C. M. Bowra puts it at the start of his introduction to the subject, *Ancient Greek Literature* (Bowra 1933, 9), Greek literature has a "peculiar place" in the history of European literature, in that it is, he claims, both the first such literature, and the most influential, and, most importantly, because of its "perfection": in many genres of literature, Bowra insists, the work of the Greeks has been "held up as a type of perfection and followed as the pattern of what all such work should be."

Contemporary scholars are extremely unlikely to assert, with Bowra, that Greek literature is special for its unique "perfection." Moreover, contemporary scholars are unlikely to adopt the position, also suggested by Bowra, that there was something ethically and intellectually superior about the Greeks themselves, and perhaps metaphysically as well – that, as he puts it, they had "the child's gift of seeing things with absolute clarity and concentration," and that they were somehow more alive than we are ourselves: they were "men" (sic) whose "eyes were open and whose wits were alive" (Bowra 1933, 18). Modern scholars generally believe that the Greeks were no better than ourselves, and in some ways, were perhaps worse; it is salutary to remember that nobody in antiquity really questioned the institution of slavery, and nobody promoted absolute equality for men and women (DuBois 2009). But modern scholars, even those who are most conscious of the imperfection of the Greeks, still have to grapple with the legacy of two thousand years in which the Greeks and their literature were, in some way or other, imagined to be superior, or at least more harmonious, or more perfect, or more truthful, than our own. Here, we must acknowledge ourselves as rather more the heirs of Nietzsche than of Wilamowitz in the study of Greek literature.

But it is only against the background of nineteenth- and early-twentieth-century debates about the cultural meanings of Greek literature that we can understand the distance that Greek literary scholarship has travelled in the last couple of generations. In particular, we must always bear in mind the heavy shadow cast by the question, at stake in so many of the thinkers I have mentioned, of whether the Greeks were more perfect, more rational, or more harmonious than anybody else. The central insight that the fields of linguistics, psychology, anthropology, philosophy, and literary theory have enabled Hellenists to reach is that Greek literature is far less exceptional, and far less "perfect," harmonious or rational, than the Victorian vision suggested.

The peculiar status of Greek literature as "literature," and the peculiar status of ancient Greek literature as the "original" or "primary," most classical of Classics, have meant that recent academic responses to Greek literature are both engaged with broader scholarly trends and also highly specific in their engagement with those trends. Indeed, there are certain ways in which Hellenists are not merely following an academic band-wagon, but rather, leading the way. Ancient Greek literature has proved good to think with for many key thinkers and theorists of the twentieth century, who in turn have proved to be highly influential far beyond departments of Classical studies (see Leonard 2005).

Many of the most important theorists in the past hundred years or so have drawn on Greek literature in their work – beginning with Nietzsche, Marx and Freud. In a further level of disciplinary self-consciousness, Hellenists have studied theorists and philosophers and cultural critics studying Greek literature. It is tempting to assume that Greek literary studies will only take from the wider world of Anglo-American and European intellectual culture. But often the exchange has happened the other way around, and has developed in fertile ways on both sides. One famous example is Derrida's essay on Plato ("Plato's Pharmacy"), which teases out the ambiguities in Plato's usage of the metaphor of writing as a *pharmakon*, to suggest that the Platonic text undermines the dichotomies it seems to establish (such as the contrast between speech and writing, and between philosophy and myth) (see Leonard 2010).

Another famous instance of a theorist who turned his attention to Greek and Roman antiquity is Foucault, whose *History of Sexuality* (especially the second volume) drew heavily from the work of the Greek literature scholar, Kenneth Dover, on "Greek homosexuality" (as Dover called it). It was through his studies of Greek and Roman literature and philosophy, too, that Foucault began to move, in his last works, towards an attempt at reformulations of identity ("the care of the self"). Classical scholars have sometimes criticized Foucault for getting ancient literature wrong, or being unsubtle or derivative in his readings of Greek literary texts; a primary example is Simon Goldhill's book, *Foucault's Virginity*, which argues that Foucault, and classicists influenced by him, have adopted too narrowly ideological a vision of Greek literature (especially the Greek novel). But in the wake of both Dover and Foucault, scholars of Greek literature and culture have continued to debate whether or not our modern categories of sexual orientation have any applicability in the ancient Greek world. Some (like Halperin 1999) have produced arguments in favor of seeing the Greek understanding and experience of sexuality as radically different from our own – a claim which implies that modern categories of "homo-" and "hetero-" sexuality are culturally conditioned, not natural kinds; others (most recently James Davidson) have challenged this view, which is often seen as threatening to the modern quest for gay rights (Davidson 2009). A key element in this debate is the question of whether sexuality, in a Greek cultural context, can be reduced to relationships of power and penetration (the two "p's" being equated by some scholars, such as Dover, but not by others, such as Davidson).

Feminism and gender studies have also had an important influence on readings of Greek literature in recent years, and, conversely, theorists of both gender and identity have made extensive use of Greek literature and Greek myth. For the latter, key instances are Lacan's uses of Plato and of Sophocles' *Antigone*, as well as Judith Butler's reading of *Antigone* (Lacan 1988, Miller 2007, Butler 2000). In the world of Classical scholarship, some feminists have attempted to recover "real" women's voices and lives (Green 2005, Lardinois and McClure 2001). Others have analyzed the stereotypes surrounding the representation of women in Greek culture: a landmark book in this area was Pomeroy 1975. Some scholars have focused on female characters and "female" voices in male-authored works of Greek literature, as, for example, the work of Sheila Murnaghan on Penelope in the *Odyssey* (Murnaghan 1987), and work on female lament in tragedy (Dué 2006); or Kirk Ormand on the complex social and sexual position of female characters in Sophocles (Ormand 1999). Others have unpacked Greek literary representations and constructions of masculinity. Scholars of Greek literature are far more conscious than they were a generation or two ago, that the texts we have are the products of a social elite whose identity was shaped largely by the exclusion of significant groups of people with whom they lived – including both women, slaves, and children (Murnaghan and Joshel 1998). The implications of this realization have only just begun to be analyzed.

There are two further dimensions of contemporary Greek literary studies that must be emphasized: a shift away from the narrow focus on the Classical period, and a shift towards attention to performance contexts and to the languages of the body. As I have already hinted, the field is far less focused on Classical Athens than it was even 20 or 30 years ago. It is noticeable that Dover, West, Griffin, and Bowie's introduction to "Ancient Greek literature" devotes eight out of its ten chapters exclusively to the Archaic and Classical periods; Greek literature 300–50 BCE gets just one short chapter, and "after 50 B.C." gets another. The authors justify this skewing of the material on aesthetic grounds; they claim that "the archaic and classical periods together are the most creative and inventive period" (Dover et al. 1980, 3). Contemporary scholars are far less likely to limit their field of study in this way, partly because we are conscious that taste is historically contingent, and we no longer imagine that aesthetic considerations are the only ones by which to decide which literature might be interesting. The period of the Second Sophistic has inspired numerous recent studies, as has the genre of the Greek novel, which had been rather neglected and sniffily regarded in previous generations.

Contemporary Greek scholars are also much more interested in the whole experience of Greeks living under Roman power, and Greek writers from all parts of the Greek-speaking world: Lucian and Plutarch studies are on the rise (see Goldhill 2002). Greek scholars of the Archaic and Classical periods, too, have become much more aware of the complex systems of exchange and cultural identity suggested by these texts. Bourdieu is, again, an important inspiration here. I have already touched on the importance of post-Classical reception studies for contemporary Hellenists, but it is also worth mentioning that the study of reception of Greek literature, within Greek literature itself, is also a major trend in the field (Grethlein 2010; Graziosi 2007; Lamberton 1997; Garland 2004). Greek literature is no longer imagined to have sprung, fully formed, like Athena from the head of Zeus; rather, scholars have paid increasing attention to the ways that Greek literature itself was shaped and reshaped in the many hundred years of its history, and the ways that later Greek writers meditated on, responded to, or criticized their predecessors. Greek literature, in other words, has a long and diverse history, and a wide and diverse geography. Greek literary scholars today tend to be highly conscious that the Greeks saw themselves as engaged in cultural traditions with a long history (cf. D'Angour 2011).

Secondly, performance and performativity have become key terms in the study of Greek literature. "Performativity" was a buzz-word in the academy in the 1990s, partly in response to Judith Butler's study of gender and sexuality as a social "performance" rather than a biological reality (Butler 1990). But within the world of Greek literary studies, performance has a much longer and broader history. Scholars of Homer are still working to come to grips with the insights of Milman Parry and Alfred Lord, at the start of the twentieth century, about the oral tradition from which these written epics emerged (Nagy 1999). In Greek drama, scholars are increasingly interested in working to reconstruct the performance contexts for these theatrical works of literature (Taplin 1977; Csapo 2010; Revermann 2006). A related thread is the drive to set Greek drama in a broader civic context (Winkler and Zeitlin 1990). Scholars of Greek lyric poetry have become increasingly interested in reconstructing musical and choreographical performance contexts for these texts which we encounter as words on a page (Wilson 2000, etc.). Greek prose literature is often investigated with greater attention to performance contexts and to oral literary traditions. A deepened awareness of ritual practice as an essential feature of Greek experience, including literary experience, has been one of the most important trends in contemporary studies. Performance and orality are essential to our current understanding of Archaic and Classical poetics, criticism, and the authority of literature (Ford 2002). A related trend is an increasing, and increasingly more sophisticated, awareness that Greek literary categories, including genre, do not map onto our own, and can often be understood only through a thick understanding of performance contexts and interacting oral modes (e.g. Swift 2010).

Studies of Greek politics and Greek domestic and sexual relationships (and of the intersections between the worlds of the *polis* and the *oikos*) have built on the realization that we can read Greek myth and culture in structuralist or poststructuralist terms, and that we need not expect the Greeks to "make sense" (e.g. Loraux 2000). Also crucial here is the work of Walter Burkert, a pioneer in the anthropological study of Greek religion (and a German emigré) (e.g. Burkert 1979). Students of Greek philosophy and rhetorical theory, too, have become far more aware of the range of (non-rational, or quasi-rational) ways in which people, including the ancient Greeks, experience and think about the world; this kind of insight has led to a usefully precise new attention to Greek religious practice and its representations in literary texts, and also to reappraisals of what the Greeks themselves thought literature was for (in, for example, Peter Struck's discussions of "symbolic" or allegorical modes of reading in Greek antiquity, Struck 2004).

Much of the most interesting work in Greek literature in recent years has emerged from an awareness that the Greeks were no less engaged in conflicts between diverse social groups than we are ourselves – while, at the same time, people found themselves engaged in complex patterns of social connection and exchange. Most of our extant texts in Greek literature are composed by elite males. Contemporary scholars have done much to elucidate our texts as sites for the construction of elite male identity, and also to think through their representations of marginalized or othered social groups, both within and outside Greek society – including children and old people as well as slaves, women, metics, foreigners, and the poor. "Exchange" itself has been an important term in Greek literary/cultural studies in recent years (Wohl 1998), and at least two influential studies (Kurke 1999, Seaford 2004) have traced a connection between the development of money and other forms of economic exchange in the Greek world, with both cultural and literary developments; these scholars have reminded us that metaphor is another kind of exchange, and the metaphors and imagery in Greek texts should be understood in the context of a spectrum of other types of exchange, including material and economic.

A final point to emphasize about the contemporary preoccupation with reading Greek literature within a "thick" cultural context is that the Greek author is, if not dead, certainly far less staunchly alive than he or she was in the days of Bowra. Bowra insists that even our earliest and most problematic Greek "author," Homer, was indeed an author in very much the same ways that George Eliot was an author: "his name was Homer and he came from the Greek coastland of Asia Minor" (Bowra 1933, 19). Contemporary scholars would hardly make such assertions about Homer "himself," and are also far less likely to be focused so narrowly on Greek literature as the product of an individual's mind and pen. But the concept of the "author-function" (Foucault 1979) has enabled illuminating new studies of Greek literary texts and collections whose authorship is difficult or impossible to reconstruct (such as Aesop, Hesiod, Anacreon and Theognis). Scholars are increasingly open to the possibility that literary texts, even great ones, may be the product of more than one individual; and that the works of Greek literature that we have may have gone through many different mutations before they reach our eyes. Partly inspired by persona theory, Hellenists have become aware of the extent to which the supposed biographical information we are given about ancient Greek authors is often best read as a set of gestures and tropes, rather than fact (Lefkowitz 1991, Lefkowitz 2012; on the first-person tropes of comedy and satire, Rosen 2007).

I have, for most of this essay, focused on the ways that new cultural and intellectual trends in the contemporary academy have enabled new ways of reading the Greek texts that we have. But there are at least two other ways that contemporary studies of Greek literature has opened up in new directions, and is continuing to do so. One is that archaeological finds have unearthed exciting new additions to our existing canon of Greek literature (and the sands of Egypt and elsewhere may continue to add new riches). Among the most famous examples is the so-called New Sappho, published only in 2004; but there are many others, and some of the standard texts of Greek literature (such as Campbell's *Greek Lyric*, Campbell 1967) may well become superseded in the light of new discoveries (see Budelmann 2009). Another exciting new development is the Philodemus Project, which involves the long-awaited decipherment of the texts preserved from the House of Papyri in Pompeii; this is a team-project directed by academics from both UCLA (David Blank) and the UK (Richard Janko and Dirk Obbink), and involving others from Germany and Italy as well as others from the US and UK. This is, in other words, a work of collaborative philology in the mold of the old dreams of *Altertumswissenschaft.*

The second important new direction provided by practical or technical advances is in digital humanities. More and more Greek literature is now available in online databases, such as Perseus; we already have TLG available online. New technology, in Greek studies as elsewhere, may enable new kinds of undergraduate and secondary school teaching (such as the "flipped classroom," in which lectures are experienced at home, and homework is done in class). The old lexica are now available for mobile devices, allowing both students and scholars to search through Liddell while waiting in line or on an airplane (and not miss out on scholarship when the library closes). The new databases also enable us as scholars to ask and answer new kinds of questions about the texts by those oldest of all dead white males. The old German dream of collecting together all possible knowledge of the ancient world is thus closer than it has ever been, thanks to digital technologies; but we can also approach these databases of Greek texts with a different, more critical (more Nietzschean?) spirit.

We study Greek literature as the product of a culture which is shocking as well as partially inspiring, and with an awareness that it is both recognizable and deeply alien. Shelley famously claimed (in the introduction to *Hellas*, 1822, in Shelley 2009: 551) that "We are all Greeks. Our laws, our literature, our religious, our art, have their roots in Greece." Contemporary Hellenic scholars tend to recognize that we are, in essential ways, not Greeks; and that is all the more reason to keep on studying them.

NOTES

[1] The distinctiveness of classical scholarship in the US, in comparison to Britain and Europe, is very well analyzed by Calder 1994. Calder rightly draws attention to various advantages of the American over the European systems, including greater openness to women scholars, and less despotism exercised by older academics over their younger counterparts. For more detailed analysis of the special reception of Greek and Roman myth, literature and history in the US, see Winterer 2004.

[2] For details on the history of classical philology in the twentieth century, see Arighetti 1989. I have been particularly helped by Diskin Clay's account of the history of Greek philology in the North American twentieth-century academy (Clay 1989), and David Ross on the history of Latin philology in the same period (Ross 1989). I have also used Latacz 2013, who focuses primarily on Germany, and again takes a rather dismal view of the current situation. Also useful is Lloyd-Jones 1989, who also evokes the relationship of German philology with British and North American traditions. I have tried to complement these accounts by focusing on more recent trends, by considering how "scholarship," as well as "Greek" and "literature," might be defined more broadly, and by taking a significantly less gloomy line on contemporary Greek scholarship in the US.

REFERENCES

D'Angour, A. 2011. *The Greeks and the New*. Cambridge.

Arighetti, G., D. Fogazza, L. Gamberale, and F. Montanari, eds. 1989. *La Filologia Greca y Latina nel XX secolo*. 3 vols. Pisa.

Arnold, M. 1998. *Culture and Anarchy and other Writings*, edited by Stefan Collini. Cambridge. (*Culture and Anarchy* first edn. 1869).

Austin, J. L. 1962. *How to do Things with Words*. Cambridge, MA.

Bernal, M. 1987–1991. *Black Athena: The Afroasiatic Roots of Classical Civilization*. New Brunswick, NJ.

Blondell, R. 2002. *The Play of Character in Plato's Dialogues*. Cambridge.

Bourdieu, P. 1984. *Distinction: A Social Critique of the Judgment of Taste*. Cambridge.

Bowra, C. M. 1933. *Ancient Greek Literature*. Oxford.

Budelmann, F., ed. 2009. *Cambridge Companion to Greek Lyric*. Cambridge.

Burkert, W. 1979. *Structure and History in Greek mythology and ritual*. Berkeley, CA.

Butler, E. M. 1939/2012. *The Tyranny of Greece over Germany: A Study of the Influence Exercised by Greek Art and Poetry over the Great German Writers of the Eighteenth, Nineteenth and Twentieth Centuries*. Cambridge (first edn. 1939).

Butler, J. 1990. *Gender Trouble: Feminism and the Subversion of Identity*. New York.

Butler, J. 2000. *Antigone's Claim: Kinship between Life and Death*. New York.

Calder, W. M. III, 1994. "Classical Scholarship in the United States: An introductory essay." In W. W. Briggs, ed., *Biographical Dictionary of North American Classicists*, Westport, CT, xix–xxxix.

Calder, W. M. III. 1990. "The Refugee Classical Scholars in the USA: An Evaluation of their Contribution." *Illinois Classical Studies* 17: 153–73.

Campbell, D. A., ed. 1967. *Greek Lyric Poetry: A Selection of Early Greek Lyric, Elegiac and Iambic Poetry*. New York.

Center for Hellenic Studies. 2015. "About the Center." Accessed April 6, 2015 http://chs.harvard.edu/CHS/article/display/5388?menuId=1.

Charalabopoulos, Nikos G. 2011. *Platonic Drama and its Ancient Reception*. Cambridge.

Classics at Oxford, 2015. "Admissions." Accessed April 6, 2015 http://www.classics.ox.ac.uk/Admissions.html

Clay, D. 1989. "Greek Studies." In Arighetti, G., D. Fogazza, L. Gamberale, and F. Montanari, eds., *La Filologia Greca y Latina nel XX secolo*. 3 vols. Pisa, vol. 1, 264–94.

Clay, Jenny Strauss, 2003. *Hesiod's Cosmos*. Cambridge.

Croiset, A. and M. Croiset. 1898–1929. *Histoire de la Litterature Grecque*. Paris.

Croiset, A. and M. Croiset. 1904. *An Abridged History of Greek Literature*. New York.

Csapo, E. 2010. *Actors and Icons of the Ancient Theater*. Oxford.

Davidson, J. 2009. *The Greeks and Greek Love: A Bold New Exploration of the Ancient World*. New York.

Dodds, E. R. 1963. *The Greeks and the Irrational*. Berkeley, CA.

Dover, K. 1989. *Greek Homosexuality*. Boston.

Dover, K., E. L. Bowie, J. Griffin, and M. L. West, eds. 1980. *Ancient Greek Literature*. Oxford.

DuBois, P. 2009. *Slavery: Antiquity and its legacy*. Oxford.

Dué, C. 2006. *The Captive Woman's Lament in Greek tragedy*. Austin, TX.

Duncan, A. 2006. *Performance and Identity in the classical world*. Cambridge.

Easterling, P. E. and B. M. W. Knox, eds. 1985. *The Cambridge History of Classical Literature, I: Greek Literature*. Cambridge.

Ford, A. 2002. *The Origins of Criticism: Literary culture and poetic theory in classical Greece*. Princeton, NJ.

Foucault, M. 1979. "What is an Author?" In *Textual Strategies: Perspectives in Post-Structuralist Criticism*, edited by J. V. Harari. Ithaca, NY. (Delivered as a lecture in 1969.)

Gallagher, C. and S. Greenblatt, eds. 2000. *Practicing New Historicism*. Chicago.

Garland, R. 2004. *Surviving Greek tragedy*. London.

Geertz, C. 1977. *The Interpretation of Cultures: Selected essays*. New York.

Goldhill, S. 2002. *Who Needs Greek? Contests in the Cultural History of Hellenism*. Cambridge.

Graziosi, B. 2002. *Inventing Homer: The Early Reception of epic*. Cambridge.

Greene, E. 2005. *Women Poets in Ancient Greece and Rome*. Norman OK.

Grethlein, J. 2010. *The Greeks and their Past: Poetry, Oratory and History in the Fifth Century BCE.* Cambridge.

Gruen, E. S. 2001. *Rethinking the Other in Antiquity.* Princeton, NJ.

Gruen, E. S. 2005. *Cultural Borrowings and Ethnic Appropriations in Antiquity.* Stuttgart.

Guillory, J. 1993. *Cultural Capital: The Politics of Canon Formation.* Chicago.

Hadas, M. 1950. *A History of Greek Literature.* New York.

Hall, E. 1991. *Inventing the Barbarian.* Oxford.

Hall, E. 2008. *The Return of Ulysses.* Baltimore.

Hall, J. 1997. *Ethnic Identity in Greek Identity.* Cambridge.

Halperin, D. 1990. *One Hundred Years of Homosexuality: And Other Essays on Greek Love.* New York.

Hardwick, L. and C. Gillespie, eds. 2007. *Classics in Post-Colonial Worlds.* Oxford.

Havelock, E. 1987. *The Literate Revolution in Greece and its Cultural Consequences.* Princeton, NJ.

Holmes, B. 2010. *The Symptom and the Subject: The Emergence of the Physical Body in Ancient Greece.* Princeton, NJ.

Horstmann, A. 1992. *Antike Theoria und moderne Wissenschaft: August Boeckhs Konzeption der Philologie.* Frankfurt.

Knox, B. 1993. *The Oldest Dead White European Males: Reflections on the Classics.* New York.

Kurke, L. 1999. *Coins, Bodies, Games and Gold.* Princeton, NJ.

Kurke, L. 2011. *Aesopic Conversations: Popular Tradition, Cultural Dialogue, and the Invention of Greek Prose.* Princeton, NJ.

Lacan, J. 1988. *The Seminar of Jacques Lacan,* edited by J.-A. Miller. New York.

Lamberton, R. and J. J. Keaney, eds. 1992. *Homer's Ancient Readers: the hermeneutics of Greek epic's earliest exegetes.* Princeton, NJ.

Lardinois, A. and L. McClure, eds. 2001. *Making Silence Speak.* Princeton, NJ.

Latacz, J. 2013. "Modern Philology." In *Brill's New Pauly,* online 15/2: 255–78. Accessed March 1 2014.

Lefkowitz, M. R. 1991. *First-person Fictions: Pindar's Poetic "I."* Oxford.

Lefkowitz, M. R. 2012. *The Lives of the Greek Poets.* 2nd edn. Baltimore.

Lefkowitz, M. R., and G. MacLean Rogers, eds. 1996. *Black Athena Revisited.* Chapel Hill, NC.

Leonard, M, ed. 2010. *Derrida and Antiquity.* Oxford.

Leonard, M. 2005. *Athens in Paris: Ancient Greece and the Political in Post-war French Thought.* Oxford.

Lesky, A. 1957/1963. *A History of Greek Literature.* New York (first edn.1957).

Lloyd-Jones, H. 1982. "Introduction." In U. von Wilamowitz-Moellendorff 1921/1982, "Future Philology!" *New Nietzsche Studies* 4: i–xxxii.

Loraux, N. 2000. *Born of the Earth: Myth and politics in Athens.* Ithaca, NY.

Martindale, C. 2006. "Introduction: Thinking Through Reception." In C. Martindale and R. Thomas, eds. *Classics and the Uses of Reception.* New York, 1–13.

Mendelsohn, D. 2012. *Waiting for the Barbarians: Essays from the Classics to Pop Culture.* New York.

Miller, P. A. 1998. "The Classical Roots of Post-Structuralism: Lacan, Derrida and Foucault." *International Journal of the Classical Tradition* 5: 204–25.

Miller, P. A., 2007. "Lacan's Antigone: The Sublime Object and the Ethics of Interpretation." *Phoenix* 61: 1–14.

Modern Language Association. 2013. "Language Enrollment Database." Accessed April 6, 2015 http://www.mla.org/flsurvey_search.

Most, G. 2003. "On the Use and Abuse of Ancient Greece for Life." *HyperNietzsche* 2003.11.09. Accessed April 6, 2015.

Murnaghan, S. 1987. *Disguise and Recognition in the Odyssey.* Princeton, NJ.

Murnaghan, S. and S. Joshel, eds. 1998. *Women and Slaves in Greco-Roman Culture: Differential Equations.* New York.

Nagy, G. 1999. *The Best of the Achaeans: Concepts of the Hero in Archaic Greek Poetry.* Baltimore.

Nietzsche, F. 1874/1974, "Notes for 'We philologists'." *Arion,* n.s. 1, 279–380 (first 1874).

Nietzsche, F. 1998. *Twilight of the Idols.* Oxford.

Nightingale, A. 1995. *Genres in Dialogue: Plato and the Construct of Philosophy.* Cambridge.

Ong, W. J. 2002. *Orality and Literacy: The Technologizing of the Word.* New York.

Ormand, K. 1999. *Exchange and the Maiden: Marriage in Sophoclean tragedy.* Austin, TX.

Pomeroy, S. 1975. *Goddesses, Whores, Wives, and Slaves: Women in Classical Antiquity.* New York.

Porter, J. I., *Nietzsche and the Philology of the Future*, Stanford, CA.

Revermann, M. 2006. *Comic Business: Theatricality, Dramatic Technique, and Performance Contexts of Aristophanic Comedy.* Oxford.

Rihll, T. E. 1999. *Greek Science.* Oxford.

Rosen, R. 2007. *Making Mockery: The poetics of ancient satire.* Oxford.

Ross, D. 1989. "United States: Latin philology." In G. Arighetti, D. Fogazza, L. Gamberale, and F. Montanari, eds., *La Filologia Greca y Latina nel XX secolo.* 3 vols. Pisa vol. 1, 295–394.

Seaford, R. 2004. *Money and the Ancient Greek Mind.* Cambridge.

Shelley, P. B. 2009. *The Major Works,* edited by Z. Leader and M. O' Neill. Oxford.

Smyth, H. W. 1920/1984. *Greek Grammar.* Boston (first edn. 1920).

Stray, C. 1998. *Classics Transformed: Schools, Universities, and Society in England, 1830–1960.* Oxford.

Stray, C. and L. Hardwick, eds. 2008. *Companion to Classical Receptions.* Oxford.

Struck, P. 2004. *Birth of the Symbol: Ancient Readers at the Limits of their Texts.* Princeton, NJ.

Swift, L. 2010. *The Hidden Chorus: Echoes of Genre in Tragic Lyric.* Oxford.

Taplin, O. 1977. *The Stagecraft of Aeschylus: The Dramatic Use of Entrances and Exits in Greek tragedy.* Oxford.

Taub, L. 2008. *Aetna and the Moon: Explaining Nature in ancient Greece and Rome.* Corvallis, OR.

Vasunia, P. 2001. *The Gift of the Nile: Hellenizing Egypt from Aeschylus to Alexandria.* Berkeley, CA.

Vernant, J. P. and P. Vidal-Naquet. 1988. *Myth and Tragedy in Ancient Greece.* New York.

West, M. 1999. *The East Face of Helicon: West Asiatic Elements in Greek Poetry and Myth.* Oxford.

Whitmarsh, T. 2001. *Ancient Greek Literature.* Cambridge.

Wilamowitz-Moellendorff, U. von. 1872/2000. "Future Philology!" *New Nietzsche Studies* 4: 1–33 (first 1872).

FURTHER READING

On the German background, especially Nietzsche, a stimulating starting point is Porter 2002. For surveys of the field of Greek studies, see Latacz 2013 and Calder 1994. On the British institutional history, see Stray 1998. To glimpse some of the changes in the field over the past generation, it is instructive to look at Easterling and Knox 1985, and Whitmarsh 2001.

CHAPTER 33

The Reception of Ancient Greek Literature and Western Identity

Edith Hall

*My heroes are no longer the warriors and kings but the things of peace equal to one another
the drying onions being equal to the tree trunk crossing the marsh.
But no one has so far succeeded in singing an epic of peace.*

These words belong to "Homer," the elderly storyteller in Wim Wenders' 1987 movie, *Der Himmel über Berlin*. As we listen to "Homer's" thoughts on the difficulty of creating art out of the experience of peace, we are shown footage from the end of World War II. Soldiers supervise women trying to identify the corpses of their children after the bombing of Berlin. The camera lingers on a tiny cadaver, with eyes closed and mouth open, screaming noiselessly. The baby lies beneath a high wall scarred with bombardment. Behind this shocking image lurks the original Homeric epic of warriors and kings, the *Iliad*, in book 6 of which we meet the infant Astyanax on the wall of Troy from which he will be thrown.

This pivotal moment in Wenders' film constitutes a "reception" of ancient Greek literature. Regardless of whether all the spectators of the film knew Homer's *Iliad*, we can't dispute the intensity of the relationship between ancient epic poem and screenplay, on which Wenders collaborated with Peter Handke. There is, however, room for debate as to the nature of that relationship. Is Wenders making an admiring statement about Homeric epic as the foundational text in the history of war literature, thus anchoring his own film in a cultural tradition that reaches back to archaic Greece? Or is his stance more critical? Is he resisting Iliadic values, holding the tradition they represent accountable, attributing responsibility for Western civilization's lamentable history of warfare to the values celebrated in the ancient epic? Or perhaps the overriding impulse, rather, is an emotional one, of grave compassion? The humane tone of Wenders' film, with its sympathetic angels supporting humans who suffer in the city kept apart by warring superpowers, places it in a similar category to the *Iliad*. Or, to be precise, it places it in a similar category to the more reflective moments of the *Iliad*, such as the meeting of the two bereaved men from opposing sides, Achilles and Priam, in its last book.

This tone resonates with the humanist reading of the epic proposed in an important essay, Simone Weil's "The Iliad, or the Poem of Force," written in the ominous year of 1939.[1] The same encounter is eloquently retold in David Malouf's delicate novel *Ransom* (2009). While the Western fatalities in Afghanistan rose inexorably during the summer when I wrote this essay, the nature of the *Iliad* as a commemoration of men's death in combat was also refocused by Alice Oswald in her poignant 2011 poem *Memorial*. The psychological disturbance undergone by Iliadic heroes, as discussed by the North American psychiatrist Jonathan Shay's *Achilles in Vietnam: Combat Trauma and the Undoing of Character* (1994), put ancient Greek portraits of traumatized warriors (in Euripides' *Heracles* and Sophocles' *Trachiniae, Ajax* and *Philoctetes* as well as epic) on the contemporary cultural radar.[2]

Yet there is another interpretation of Wenders' filmic sequence. The lines quoted above are preceded by images of "Homer," sitting in a Berlin library. Gazing on a model of the revolving planets, he says that he is speaking "as in the beginning, in my sing-song voice which sustains me, saved by the tale from present troubles." He then reflects that if he abandons storytelling, then humanity will forget its storyteller, and thus also its childhood (*Kindschaft*). This alludes to the way that German Romanticism defined ancient Greece ever since J. J. Winckelmann and Karl Marx. Wenders' "Homer" self-consciously reflects on the role of the maker of art – poet or film director – in the mediation of reality. The artist is somehow protected, by the tale he tells, or retells, from the contingent troubles of his era. He is also the agent and repository of art: storytelling is memory. If humans forget their story-teller, then they lose all recollection of their childhood.

In this mournful cinematic sequence we can identify the presence of at least four modes of "reception" of Greek literature. (1) The archetypal text is authoritative, foundational, generative, and infinitely susceptible to emulation and renewal. (2) The ancient text creates generic expectations and values which, on the contrary, are implicated in the perpetuation of a mindset which produces unnecessary human suffering: it is in the *difference* between the original and the new artefact or "reception" that the importance lies. Either in form or content, it resists or reacts *against* the archetype. (3) The ancient text provides a stance or viewpoint on the world; it is a cultural phenomenon crystallizing an emotionally charged reaction to life; it is the source of a worldview inflected by a particular psychological tone. In this type of "tonal" reception the ancient genre is often replaced by a new medium – cinema or lyric poetry instead of epic, prose fiction instead of drama.[3] (4) The ancient text provides a point of departure for self-conscious thinking about aesthetics – the nature and purpose of art. Such thinking often shows the "receiving" author engaging with an additional ancient text – one of the "classics" of literary criticism which were written in Greek – Aristotle's *Poetics*, or *On the Sublime* attributed to Longinus. These four basic modes of reception – emulative, resistant, tonal, and self-consciously aesthetic – can all be present in the same artwork, interacting with and confirming, or alternatively undermining, one another.

More than 30 major authors of pagan literature survive who wrote in dialects of ancient Greek. In a discussion of their reception in connection with "Western" identity, the problem of the definition of "Western" arises. The concept refers to no intelligible geographical, political, religious, or economic category, was invented in the early nineteenth century by white northern Europeans, has historically both incorporated and excluded several countries (notably Russia, Israel and areas of Latin America), and has posited several different antitypes including the Moslem world, the non-Christian world, "Asia," "the Orient," "primitives," all non-capitalist economies, countries which do not explicitly subscribe to vaguely defined notions of "democracy," "liberty" or "freedom" (Meier 2011), and "the Eastern bloc" or non-NATO members during the Cold War (cf. the excellent survey of this problem by Bavaj 2011).

The second question is which organizational principle to adopt in surveying the reception of ancient Greek literature, even assuming a critical understanding of the term "Western." Each nation has responded differently to the ancient Greeks. The Hellenism of French baroque theater (Racine),[4] and twentieth-century philosophy (Sartre, Foucault, Derrida),[5] is not identical to the Hellenism fused with Slavic Christianity which inspired Catherine the Great to found cities with ancient Greek names, and rediscover the ancient inhabitants of the Crimea – the Amazons, the Tauric Iphigenia, and Mithridates Eupator.[6] In North America, where the model of the Roman Republic dominated the Early Modern reception of antiquity (Onuf and Cole 2011), cultural possession of ancient Greece was acrimoniously contested: in the nineteenth century the model of democratic Athens depicted in Thucydides was claimed by both Basil Gildersleeve, the champion of the Confederate South and founding father of American Classics, and by his opponent Abraham Lincoln.[7] Later, Hellenism was associated with the American Modernists' staking of a claim to a national literature to rival that of the old world, above all in the self-consciously local recontextualization of the *Oresteia* by Eugene O'Neill as *Mourning Becomes Electra* (1931). Yet certain broad aesthetic and intellectual developments – the Nietzschean, Frazerian and Modernist fascination with ancient Greek ritual, for example –have transcended national and ethnic boundaries (see Ackerman 1991).

Even more difficult would be a dissection of "Western" identity in terms of the *multiple* identities of people who have lived in the "West" and responded to ancient Greek literature – "Hebrew" may have signified something contrasting with "Hellene" to many nineteenth- and early twentieth-century Christian "Westerners" who saw themselves as descended from an Aryan, Indo-European *Ur*-community which embraced both Indian and Greek culture but excluded Jews.[8] Yet the "West" has also long been home to Jewish artists and intellectuals whose responses to the ancient Greeks are hardly less valid. Another obvious set of sub-headings would relate to the ancient genres – not only epic but lyric, tragic, comic, rhetorical, historiographical, philosophical, pastoral, epigrammatic, and so on. A fourth would be to use the modern, "receiving" category of genre, medium or discipline, such as opera, ballet, or film,[9] anthropology, philosophy or psychology. A fifth would be to take discrete areas of subject-matter or urgent interest to the third-millennial world – the reception of the myths relating to Troy,[10] or of ancient representations of sex, gender, and sexuality. This would have the advantage of making more room for the presence of the ancient Greeks in contemporary debates, for example those surrounding homosexual rights,[11] or inequities connected with social class (Hall 2008c). But it would reduce the space available for considering the role of other ancient literary texts in earlier periods. Euripides' *Hecuba*, for example, although not often performed today, was a crucial text in the invention of Renaissance revenge tragedy.[12]

Most of the ancient authors who have exerted influence on posterity date to the archaic and classical periods. This lends logic to the simplest solution, which is to discuss their afterlives in the chronological order in which the originals were produced. But I refer intermittently within that framework to the four fundamental types of reaction identified as contributing to the impact of the "Homer" sequence in Wim Wenders' movie: emulation, resistance, adoption of tone, and aesthetic self-consciousness. I have also, unashamedly, indulged my own preferences in terms of the selection of both ancient and modern artworks, since in an essay of this length, on such a vast topic, there is no hope of achieving either comprehensive or balanced coverage.

The chronological framework is further vindicated as organizing principle because reception is cumulative. The reception of ancient Greek literature begins at the point that it is first "received," which means by its first audience member or reader. There is, for example, no instantiation of ancient Greek literature (or Latin, for that matter) which does not "receive," in however subterranean a manner, the poems attributed to Homer. These formed the basis of the education of ancient Mediterranean society from the seventh century BCE; that curriculum was in turn adopted by Western humanists. It does not matter whether Homer is actually read, said John Ruskin, since "All Greek gentlemen were educated under Homer. All Roman gentlemen, by Greek literature. All Italian, and French, and English gentlemen, by Roman literature, and by its principles."[13] Hegel (1837/1923, 5.29) had foreshadowed Ruskin's diagnosis in saying that "Homer is that element in which the Greek world lived, as a human lives in the air." For a thousand years, schoolboys living under the Macedonian or Roman empires, even those whose first languages were Syrian, Nubian, or Gallic, copied out Homeric verses, summarized individual books, and committed swathes of Homeric hexameters to memory (in Xenophon's *Symposium* 3.5 Niceratus says that his upper-class father required him to learn *all* of Homer by heart); they studied them when they were learning to be statesman, soldiers, lawyers, historians, or artists (see Marrou 1956, 162, and Kindstrand 1973).[14] In the case of the *Iliad*, no later author could make a fresh start when shaping a representation of heroes in combat, a funeral, an embassy, gods in colloquy, or a review of an army by people standing on a wall. In the case of the *Odyssey*, the same applies to a representation of a voyage, a metamorphosis, an altercation with savages, an encounter with anyone dead, a father–son relationship, a recognition token, or a reunion between husband and wife.

Reception is a continuous process which began in antiquity and has, with interruptions, continued ever since; our responses to a text are also conditioned by earlier responses. Every new response to a classic text alters the total picture of its influence. Some ancient texts have engendered such definitive receptions, which become "classics" themselves, that they interfere forever with responses to the Greek original: it is difficult to think about the heroine of Euripides' *Iphigenia in Tauris* without interference from Goethe's morally enhanced *Iphigenie auf Tauris* (1786). It is almost impossible to stage Sophocles' *Electra* without acknowledging the tenacity in the public imagination of the psychotic Modernist heroine in the one-act opera *Elektra* by Richard Strauss and Hugo von Hofmannsthal (1909).[15] When a great artwork like the *Odyssey* stimulates the production of others, such as Virgil's *Aeneid*, Monteverdi's *Il ritorno d'Ulisse in patria* (1640), Joyce's *Ulysses* (1922) or Ralph Waldo Ellison's *Invisible Man* (1952),[16] cultural history changes irrevocably. According to T. S. Eliot, collectively such "existing monuments form an ideal order among themselves." But this will always be "modified by the introduction of the new (the really new) work of art among them." Thus Eliot would have seen Derek Walcott's more recent reaction to Homeric epic in *Omeros* (1990) as changing forever how we see its precursors: "for in order to persist after the supervention of novelty, the whole existing order must be, if ever so slightly, altered."[17]

The extent of the cultural penetration of the *Odyssey* is partly a result of its use in books aimed at children. In 1808, William Godwin published Charles and Mary Lamb's *The Adventures of Ulysses*, the first ever children's *Odyssey* and the one which inspired James Joyce. But three years before that commission, Godwin had published his own version of the ancient Greek fables of Aesop, *Fables, Ancient and Modern*. He was motivated by Locke's recommendation in *Some Thoughts Concerning Education* (1693) of Aesop's Fables as "the best, which being stories apt to delight and entertain a child, may yet afford useful reflections to a grown man" (Locke 1705/1968, 259; 256). Indeed, Aesop's *Fables* and the *Odyssey* have been the two ancient texts which have been turned into more children's books – and therefore imbibed at a more impressionable age by a wider public – than any others. They are also the two most susceptible to transformation into other media – there were both Aesop and *Odyssey* animated cartoons by 1950, and they can both be watched on television, listened to on audiobooks, and seen in all kinds of theater.

Most people's access to Aesop's *Fables* is restricted to under a hundred of his short stories or narratives, mostly featuring talking animals and strong moral messages. A few almost always appear in post-Renaissance collections – the mouse and the lion, the fox and the grapes, the tortoise and the hare. Because the fables were retold in Latin by Phaedrus, however, and used in ancient and medieval education, no single canonical text has ever emerged from the confusing manuscript recensions. Yet these simple little tales for children, as they are stereotyped, have been admired by famous thinkers from Democritus, Socrates, Martin Luther, and Jean-Jacques Rousseau to Malcolm X (Hall forthcoming c).[18] Aesop also has a greater claim to be a global cultural property than any other Western classic author. Judging by the inventories of books distributed in the New World by the Spanish in the sixteenth and seventeenth centuries, Aesop has been taken wherever Europeans have gone (Revello 1957, 175).

Most of the fables are set in a rural, peacetime, context, and in antiquity were associated with a lower-class, anti-heroic worldview. In art aiming at a more elevated tone, however, ancient authors used personnel from higher up the social scale, where masculinity was inseparable from militarism. The question of the impossibility of an epic of peace, by Wenders' "Homer," was already asked soon after the *Iliad* emerged. The Greeks had in Hesiod a hexameter poet whose *Works and Days* assembled verses relevant to the everyday concerns of the archaic peasant farmer, but can it be described as an "epic" in the sense meant by Wenders' "Homer"? In an ancient text incorporating lines poem in the same "epic" meter, *The Contest of Homer and Hesiod*, exactly this question is posed. Homer pits exciting verses about weapons and violence against Hesiod's didactic expositions of agricultural lore and folk wisdom. The internal audience think Homer should win, on the aesthetic ground that his poetry excites them and "goes beyond the level of the ordinary," but the wise king bestows the prize on Hesiod, on the moral ground that the poet who invited men to live peacefully should defeat the poet – Homer – who lingered on slaughter (*Contest* § 14, ed. West 2003) The first great reception of this statement of the rival claims of art to engender pleasure and to be useful occurs in the competition between martial and pacific genres of poetry won by the peasant vintner Trygaeus in Aristophanes' comedy *Peace* (421 BCE):[19] this play itself has a fascinating reception culminating in Peter Hacks' adaptation, staged in the GDR (1962), where the ancient Greek classics had a distinctive, politicized reception (Seidensticker 1992 and 2007).

Outside academia, Hesiod's works are not imitated much today, although he is studied as evidence for mythology, farming, and astrology. But his *Theogony* contains nothing less than the founding text of the Western concept of the poet's vocation (22–35; cf. on these lines Hose, ch. 24, pp. 374–5 in this volume): Hesiod says that the Muses once taught him when he was shepherding his lambs in the foothills of Helicon. They complained that shepherds are lowly creatures who only think of their stomachs, while they, the Muses, have superior knowledge:

> We know how to speak about many things which resemble the truth,
> But when we want to we also know how to utter the truth.

Giving Hesiod a laurel branch, they breathed into him a wonderful voice in which "to sing of the future and the past." They ordered him to hymn the immortals, but to address themselves, the Muses, first and last.

This account of Hesiod's realization of his poetic calling is profound. The Muses' description of their capacities reveals an intense self-consciousness, already in the Archaic period, of the nature and function of art. The Muses know that poetry can take people into a mental realm which transcends the material, bodily aspects of existence. They know that it can represent things which are not empirically discernible, and may not be real or have happened at all: on the other hand, poetry can represent absolute truth. Poetry allows the poet to range across time, allowing abstract thought, historical record and prophecy. One function of this gift is to celebrate the immortals, themselves not empirically discernible, and immune to temporal categories as understood by human beings. But the poet must always invoke the Muses who bestowed this gift of transcendence upon him. Hesiod demonstrates that what makes ancient Greek poetry great is not just its power, diversity, beauty, or exciting content. It is its inherently self-reflexive nature – its own awareness of its status as cultural phenomenon, repository of knowledge, and thrilling medium which can both disguise and reveal the truth.

It is impossible to overstate the importance of Hesiod's visitation by the Muses to Western poetry. The episode underpinned the self-conscious programmatic statements of aesthetics in much subsequent Classical literature. Mount Helicon had become the key symbol of poetic inspiration by the Roman Imperial period (Hurst and Schachter 1996), when the tourist Pausanias followed a trail to the Hippocrene fountain and Hesiod's tomb (Pausanias 9.28–37). The encounter on Helicon has been an enduring image for a poet's first awakening to the urge to create poetry, from the anthology of poems in English collected by John Bodenham and first published in 1600 under the title *Englands Helicon*, to poets alive in the third millennium. One of the best is Seamus Heaney's 1966 poem "Personal Helicon." He remembers a moment, as a child, when his senses were transfixed as he witnessed a bucket crash into a well:

> As a child, they could not keep me from wells
> And old pumps with buckets and windlasses.
> I loved the dark drop, the trapped sky, the smells
> Of waterweed, fungus and dank moss.
>
> One, in a brickyard, with a rotted board top.
> I savoured the rich crash when a bucket
> Plummeted down at the end of a rope.
> So deep you saw no reflection in it.[20]

Heaney's "I" here is a direct response to Hesiod's "I," receiving the laurel branch on Helicon. Hesiod's "I" inaugurated a key characteristic of the lyric, elegiac, and iambic poets between Homer and the first surviving Greek tragedy: the strong presence of the authorial persona, an individual subject putting their own stamp on well-known myths, or expressing personal responses to love and politics. It was through thinking about these poets that the ancient Greeks, moreover, invented the self-conscious theorizing of the "I" voice, in Plato's assault on the speciousness of *oratio recta* in his discussion of mimesis in *Republic* (book 2–3).[21] This was followed by Aristotle's perceptive treatment of how assuming another persona can allow an author to express controversial views, as Archilochus (so Aristotle says) used the *ēthos* of Charon the carpenter in order to denounce wealth and tyranny.[22]

The archaic Tyrtaeus's name and martial elegies have been invoked by patriot warriors including the imagined audience of Claude Joseph Rouget de Lisle's lyrics for *Le Marseillaise*, 1792 (Vidal-Naquet 1995, 95; 101).[23] Anacreon's actual poems have been less influential than his reputation as the poet who celebrated parties, drinking, and sex, a reputation apparent in the title *Anacreontea* given to the ancient collection of poems falsely attributed to him, and the label "*Anacreontic*" given to a seven-syllable verse line which he was misunderstood as using by some Early Modern poets. He also appeared as an erotic hero in danced entertainments such as Rameau's *Anacréon*, 1754 (Gillespie 1988, 68–77). Stesichorus has recently attracted a leading author with an interest in the relationship between poetry and subjectivity, since Anne Carson's brilliant "novel in verse," *Autobiography of Red*, is a narrative inspired by the fragmentary *Geryoneis* (Carson 1997; see Hall 2009b).

However, Sappho, as the archetypal female poet, has dominated the reception of Greek lyric (see Michelakis 2009). Her reputation was secured by the admiration later antiquity felt for her poem, "He seems to me to be equal to a god" (F 31 V).[24] Catullus produced his own hetero-sexual version (Catullus 51), and the author of *On the Sublime* (see below) identified it as an example of sublimity in the selection of details which collectively expressed the emotions (Ps.Long., *De subl.* 10). In the Early Modern and eighteenth-century period, Sappho stood not for women poets but for an ecstatic posture in lyric self-expression, which could be shared by the male poet (Maxwell 2001), and in this she exerted an impact on, for example, Tennyson (Reynolds 2001). Victorian, Modernist and subsequent Lesbians have found the poetry of Sappho inspirational;[25] the classically trained poets Josephine Balmer (1992) and Anne Carson (2003) have produced outstanding translations.

The influence of Pindar has been narrow, aesthetic, and felt most in the seventeenth and eighteenth centuries. Curiously, the term "Pindarick" often designated lyrical poetry free of metrical laws (that is, the opposite of the strophic and triadic uniformity which Pindar actually exemplified), or inventive and imaginative, rather than specifically encomiastic (Gillespie 1988, 186–93; Wilson 1989, 26–9). A better understanding of the form and performance context of epinician odes followed the publication, in 1749, of the first major English translation of twelve odes of Pindar, by Gilbert West, especially since it was accompanied by his treatise on the Olympic Games. A Pindaric ode in ancient Greek by Oxford classicist Armand d'Angour was commissioned to celebrate the 2004 Olympics in Athens, where it was performed on August 29.[26]

Some plays by the three great Athenian tragedians have enjoyed, since the late 1960s, a renaissance as performance scripts in the professional theater not only of the West but of the world. Aeschylus's *Oresteia*, Sophocles' Theban plays, *Philoctetes* and *Electra*, Euripides' *Medea*, *Trojan Women*, *Bacchae* and *Iphigenia in Aulis* have all become standard constituents of the performance repertoire, attracting titanic figures in the theater and film industries such as Peter Stein, Peter Hall, Ariane Mnouchine, Fiona Shaw, Tadashi Suzuki, Yukio Ninagawa, and Michael Cacoyannis.[27] The tragedies have been translated or adapted by major poets and writers in several languages, including Heiner Müller, Seamus Heaney and Ted Hughes:[28] Tony Harrison has not only translated the *Oresteia* and other Greek plays, but created a new play about class struggle from the story of the discovery of the papyri containing Sophocles' satyr play *Ichneutae* in his *Trackers of Oxyrhynchus*, 1988 (see Taplin 1991, Hall 2007a). But many scholars regard the moment at which Greek tragedy first achieved cultural prominence as the mid-nineteenth century, when it chimed in tune with the emergent identity of Modernity. Evolutionary biology marked the shift from a belief in a providential *status quo* to a doctrine that humans can only ameliorate suffering, just as in the Greek tragic universe virtue is not necessarily rewarded. After Darwin, the Greeks' pagan, polytheist acceptance of human misery could be mapped onto the modern anti-providential outlook, with its emphasis on random and arbitrary causation. Moreover, Greek tragedy fascinated all three other great architects of the modern Western identity, Marx, Freud, and Nietzsche.

For Marx, the supreme tragedian was Aeschylus, especially the *Prometheus Bound* attributed to him. The technocratic Titan who breaks the chains of subjection to despotism lurks behind the imagery of the *Communist Manifesto* and Marx's pictorial self-representation as editor of the *Rheinische Zeitung*.[29] Yet Aeschylus, the earliest of the tragedians, was the last to become well known, since almost all his plays were not translated into modern languages until the later eighteenth century. Although the subterranean influence of *Agamemnon*, as mediated through the Senecan version, can be felt theatrically between 1600 and the mid-eighteenth century (Ewbank 2005, Hall 2005), the play which drew attention to Aeschylus in the age of the French revolution and the European Abolition debates was *Prometheus Bound*. The possibility that Aeschylus might profitably be translated was entertained after the appearance of Pompignan's French version of 1770 (Macintosh 2008), and the first English rendering of *Prometheus Bound* appeared in 1773. It was followed by J. G. Schlosser's German translation *Prometheus in Fesseln*, Ferenc Verseghy's in Hungarian (1792) and Melchiorre Cesarotti's in Italian (1794). The sudden accessibility of Aeschylus's play explains why Prometheus became a political icon for the Romantics, representing the ultimate triumph of liberty through steadfastness and courage against the evils of tyranny (Curran 1986, Hall 2005).

The line of defiant Prometheuses stretches from Goethe's unfinished "Prometheus" (c. 1773) and Shelley's visionary *Prometheus Unbound* (1820) to Tony Harrison's feature film *Prometheus* (1998), a rewriting of the ancient tragedy as a lament for the death throes of the mining industry in the UK; it takes to unprecedented levels the art of matching tightly edited visual sequences to poetic rhythm (Hall 2002a). The other Aeschylean play which inspired the revolutionaries of the early nineteenth century, including Shelley in his *Hellas* (1821), was *Persians*, in which another, more problematic aspect of the Western identity was rooted: the hardy, freedom-loving, masculine self as defined against the perceived "oriental," decadent, tyrannical "other" – a divisive conceptual scheme which still dogs international relationships. *Persians* relates how the Persian court reacted to the news that its forces had been defeated in 472 BCE by the Greeks at the battle of Salamis near Athens. It is the earliest Western text to assemble many images of Asia as soft, effeminate, despotic, decadent, extravagant, and hierarchical – that is, the opposite of how the "West" has come to define itself (Hall 1989, ch. 2). In the Renaissance *Persians* was rediscovered as a prefiguration of the triumph of Christianity over Islam; during the Greek War of Independence it became a manifesto of Hellenic nationalism. More recently, it has been used by theater directors including Peter Sellars and Claudia Bosse in a resistant manner, to explore the ideological undercurrents of the wars in the Gulf, Iraq, and Afghanistan.[30]

The reception of *Persians* is intertwined with the reception of the accounts of the Persian wars in Herodotus's *Histories* (see below, and Bridges, Hall, and Rhodes 2007), and, to a lesser extent, with the Persian war epigrams of Simonides, which have attracted the attention of contemporary poets.[31] Aeschylus's tragedy is also one the two Greek plays which vie for the title of having been the first to be performed since antiquity. It was recited at an event which equated Achaemenid Persia with the Ottoman Empire, thus reading ancient Asia through a lens triumphally conditioned by Christian views of Islam. This appropriation of ancient Greek literature as the cultural property of the Christian West was to remain unchallenged until postcolonial thinkers investigated the reception and preservation of ancient Greek writings, literary as well as philosophical, in the Arab intellectual tradition.[32] The performance of *Persians* in 1571, in Italian or the Latin version of Saint-Ravy, celebrated the victory of a Western naval alliance, including the Venetians of the Heptanesian islands and led by John of Austria, which had defeated the Ottoman fleet at the Battle of Lepanto,[33] a feat which came to represent the defining moment in the creation of Western liberty.

The tragedy which received a more full performance 14 years later was the version of Sophocles' *Oedipus Tyrannus* staged on March 3, 1585 in Vicenza's Olympic Theater, designed by Palladio himself (see Fiorese 1984).[34] The choice of play was connected with the reception of Aristotle's treatise *Poetics*, which treats Sophocles' Oedipus as the paradigmatic tragic hero. Sixteenth-century Italian intellectuals had expended energy examining Aristotle's prescriptions for drama, including his so-called unities, especially the reference to the action taking place "within a single revolution of the sun" (1449b9–16). Key texts had been Francesco Robertelli's 1548 commentary and Ludovico Castelvetro's *Poetica d'Aristotele vulgarizzata* (1570). Staging the play which Aristotle most admired was intended to test the validity of these "rules"; an adaptation by Giovanni Rucellai of the play which Aristotle discusses with equal enthusiasm, Euripides' *Iphigenia in Tauris*, had probably been performed in the 1520s in Florence.[35]

The impact of the Aristotelian "unity of time" has been immense, but has taken the form of both emulation and resistance. Imitation of temporal unity has produced some of the best crafted plays in the repertoire, for example Racine's *Athalie*, with its compression of retrospective and prospective viewpoints.[36] But the idea of temporal unity has also played a role, through reactions *against* it by authors such as Lope de Vega (Crino 1961), in the development of dramaturgical practice. By the eighteenth century, the experience of Shakespeare in the English tradition and the influence of Lessing on the Continent underlay the debate on the "unity of time" which permeated other media than drama, above all fiction.[37] In the twentieth century, this discussion of time in art informed the experiments of avant-garde directors in the cinema, such as Alain Robbe-Grillet.[38]

Oedipus Tyrannus became a favorite of French Enlightenment writers including Voltaire, who interpreted it as an allegory of the damage a corrupt monarchy can inflict on its subjects (see Macintosh 2009, 73–81). But the thinker who made the word "Oedipal" along with "complex" central to the Western mind was Sigmund Freud. Freud's psychoanalytical reading was partly a response to the actor Jean Mounet-Sully's 1885–6 performance in Lacroix's *L'Oedipe roi* at the Comédie-Française in Paris.[39] When it comes to the theater history of the twentieth century, however, the Sophoclean tragedy that has dominated is *Antigone*. This process began when the philosopher Hegel in his *Phenomenology of Mind* and *Aesthetics* identified the irreconcilable conflict between the institutions of the family and the civic order portrayed in *Antigone* as the quintessential example of the ethical collision he viewed as definitive of tragedy and indeed of the dialectical view of history. As a result, modern-language translations of *Antigone*, performed to music by Mendelssohn, became an international rage in the 1840s.[40] But it was World War II that elicited the two great, politically contrasting adaptations, by the Frenchman Jean Anouilh (1944) and the German Bertolt Brecht (1947, which used as its starting-point Hölderlin's translation). Versions of *Antigone* are now performed more frequently and in more countries of the world than those of any other Greek tragedy.[41]

To Friedrich Nietzsche[42] in section 9 of *The Birth of Tragedy* (1872), Oedipus represents magnificent passivity in the face of Dionysian wisdom, while Prometheus's agency unites the Apollonian and Dionysian (Silk and Stern 1983, 252ff.). But the most significant tragedy for Nietzsche's revolutionary vision of the Greeks, with its emphasis on the demonic, ecstatic and counter-rational in their culture, was Euripides' *Bacchae*. Although Nietzsche claims that *Bacchae* is critical of the Dionysiac, his stress on the threat the Dionysiac presents to reason shows that Euripides' Bacchic drama had informed his vision of tragedy. This emerges from his account of the genre as a vehicle of Dionysian emotional enchantment rooted in the dithyrambic chorus, of the Dionysiac desire "to sink back into the original oneness of nature"; it lies behind his description of the "vision" in which "the chorus beholds its lord and master" and becomes "an attending chorus" (Segal 1983, 102–4).

Euripides took time to establish his post-Renaissance reputation as a master of the genre. Although his capacity to elicit pity brought him admirers during the cult of sentiment in the mid-eighteenth century (Hall and Macintosh 2005, 64–98), the derision of his works in A.W. Schlegel's lectures on drama (1809–11) discouraged imitators. *Medea* was alone in being constantly adapted, a legacy of the French classical line leading via Corneille to Seneca rather than Euripides, but the important feature of Euripides' play, that Medea kills her children in cold blood, was consistently obscured (Hall 2000). It was not until the rediscovery of Greek tragedy as a performance medium that could work in modern-language translations (rather than adaptations), a development delayed until the late nineteenth century, that the theatrical power of Euripidean tragedy was acknowledged. The first use of a Greek tragedy to make a political protest was the 1905 production in London by Granville-Barker of Gilbert Murray's translation of *Trojan Women*, which equated the atrocities committed against the women of Troy by the Greeks with the abuse of Boer women and children by the British in South Africa. Two years later, the same team's *Medea* spoke to the anger of campaigners for women's suffrage, some of whom had been gaoled (Hall and Macintosh 2005, 508–20).

There are three fifth-century dramatists who founded tragedy for the West, but there is only one comic playwright, Aristophanes. This makes him hard to avoid. There is so much self-conscious scrutiny of comic theater in Aristophanes' plays that he can be described as the founding father not only of comedy but of the theory of the Comic (Silk 2000, ch. 2, 7, 8). Intercultural comparisons of forms of comic humor juxtapose non-European models – Japanese Kyogen, contemporary Japanese comic fiction, the masked Yuyachkani festive drama of Peru – first and foremost with Aristophanes. Arab playwrights stress that the pagan ancient Greeks contributed to the cultural base of both the Eastern and Western Mediterranean, and use Aristophanes in discussions of comic dialects and the role of laughter in public life (references in Hall 2007d, 26 n.4). Precedents for every tradition of humor in the West have also, with justification, been identified in Aristophanes: personal and philosophical satire, mimicry, parody, puns, *double entendre*, Saturnalian role inversion, Rabelaisian and Bakhtinian carnival, drag acts and cross-dressing, stand-up, bawd and scatology, slapstick, farce, and knockabout.[43] In addition, Aristophanes is routinely invoked as ancestor in discussions of Shakespearean comedy and romance, W.S. Gilbert's operettas, the grotesque Absurdist theater of Alfred Jarry (especially *Ubu Roi* of 1896), the anti-war comedy of Shaw, Brecht's distancing narrative modes, the Theater of the Absurd of Beckett and Ionesco, the plays of Friedrich Dürrenmatt, and the Surrealism of Spike Milligan and Monty Python (further references in Hall 2007d, 26-7 n.6).

Not that the acknowledged influence of Aristophanes has been confined to entertainments advertising themselves as "comic theater": Aristophanes has been identified behind the birth of Western Literary Criticism, the Western notion of Freedom of Speech, Juvenalian vituperation, Swift's satire, Sterne's novels, eighteenth-century German classicism, humorous journalism, and the genre of the political cartoon. Historians of science fiction claim a genealogy reaching back to the supernatural "journeys to other worlds" undertaken by Aristophanic heroes to Olympus, Cloudcuckooland, or the Underworld; Marcel Duchamp traced the roots of Dada's farcical spirit to Aristophanic scenarios; *Birds, Frogs,* and *Wasps* are invoked in connection with fables of zoomorphism from Apuleius to Kafka and Orwell; *Acharnians, Peace,* and *Lysistrata* are mentioned in connection with musical agitprop and the politicized revue theater of Joan Littlewood, especially *Oh! What a Lovely War* (1963).[44]

In Herodotus and Thucydides, the fifth-century Greek world also produced two models of historiography which have informed all subsequent Western attempts in that genre. Herodotus's *Histories* have become eponymous of a genre and a discipline (Hartog 2000), and the ultimate source for the narrative of the Persian wars, including the last stand of the Spartans at Thermopylae. This has been subject to hundreds of laudatory retellings from antiquity to the ludicrously violent movie directed by Zack Snyder, *300* (2007).[45] The Renaissance Herodotus was, like Xenophon's *Education of Cyrus*, first read as a moralist and mirror of princes; his reliability (at least as an ethnographer) was however taken seriously once Stephanus had in his 1566 *Apologia pro Herodoto* pointed to the similarities between some of his barbarians and the savages in ethnographic reports arriving from the New World. Herodotus's first English-language translation (1584), a version of books I–II attributed to Barnaby Rich, recommends him to the reader as often strange, "but for the most part true." Yet the Early Modern and eighteenth-century Herodotus was turned into a novelist (his 1709 translator, Isaac Littlebury, was inspired by the success previously enjoyed by his translation of Fénelon's rites-of-passage novel *Télémaque*); Herodotus was contrasted by serious thinkers like David Hume with Thucydides, the father of "real" history. The self-contained narratives that Herodotus embedded in his work were ransacked by playwrights and Romantics rediscovering oral traditions, most famously in Schiller's ballad *Der Ring des Polykrates* (1798). The rehabilitation of Herodotus as a serious thinker in the nineteenth century was related to the rise of anthropology and imperial ethnography. By 1874, in his *Social Life of Greece*, the Irish scholar J. P. Mahaffy (no anticolonial thinker), challenged the superiority of Thucydides as historian. In the twentieth century, Arnaldo Momigliano and Isaiah Berlin illustrated the unparalleled achievement of Herodotus in the philosophy as well as the practice of history (Momigliano 1958). This makes it paradoxical that within popular culture, as demonstrated in *300*, the "grand narrative" of the liberty-loving West's defeat of an eternally despotic Oriental foe, a narrative for which Herodotus is indeed partly responsible, remains perniciously seductive (Hall 2006, ch. 7; Hall 2007b).

In the twentieth century, both fifth-century Greek historians have been adopted as forefathers by journalists and news reporters (Kapuściński 2007; Carey 1987); Thucydides has also been used in military training (Rahe 2006). Indeed, in his *History of the Peloponnesian War*, the tragic tone and insistence that causation needs to be understood in terms of human psychological or economic factors, rather than theology, make him sound eerily modern. His greatest impact has been on other historiographers, especially in France and Britain (Archambault 1967;

Hicks 1996), and on political theorists.[46] His emulators have included Machiavelli, Hobbes (whose translation of Thucydides was published in 1628: see Slomp 2000), Max Weber (cf. Hennis 2003), and more recently analysts of the Cold War, who have heard resonances in the opposing portraits Thucydides painted of Athenian and Spartan self-definition and imperial strategy.[47] Although Thucydides' grimness has produced fewer receptions outside serious analytical writing than Herodotus's more variegated style, some passages have affected more literary genres: Pericles' funeral oration has been imitated in countless public speeches, including not only Lincoln's Gettysburg address and the inaugural speech which Ted Sorensen wrote for J. F. Kennedy; Thucydides' description of the plague at Athens underlies Defoe's account of the London plague of 1665 in his *A Journal of the Plague Year* (1722).[48] Thucydides himself appears as a character, alongside Pericles and Sophocles, in Gore Vidal's novel of the fifth-century diplomatic world, *Creation* (1981).

The classical Greeks also invented philosophical prose dialogue. Socrates himself wrote nothing, although his influence, through his students Xenophon and Plato, has been incalculable. But even Xenophon's *Memorabilia of Socrates* has been overshadowed in influence by his account of the retreat of ten thousand Greek soldiers from central Asia in his *Anabasis*. As Rood (2004) has shown, this stirring account of military endurance, culminating in the great cry "The Sea, the sea!" when the "marching army" reaches the southern coast of the Euxine, has contributed to the construction of North American masculinity and military identity. The impact of the Platonic dialogues in terms of Western philosophy can't be discussed here, but a few have developed an afterlife of a more artistic kind. Plato's *Symposium* has inspired paintings and literary discussions of eros;[49] the discussions of poetic inspiration in his *Ion* and *Republic* have fascinated poets including Samuel Taylor Coleridge and novelists including Iris Murdoch (Vigus 2009; Zuba 2009); the prison dialogues *Crito* and *Phaedo* inaugurated a tradition of literary and dramatic scenarios set behind bars; the dialogues which discuss the lost civilization of Atlantis, *Timaeus* and *Critias*, have cast a shadow over the development of utopian and science fiction writing ever since Francis Bacon's 1627 essay *The New Atlantis* (Berneri 1982; Brown 2008).

Formal rhetoric used to be studied more than it is nowadays, and the major speeches of Demosthenes were important models. Translations have been used in propaganda wars since the Elizabethan English attacks on the reputation of Spain (Sullivan 2004). They made an impact in style, tone and content on the British activist and political philosopher John Stuart Mill, as his polemic *On Liberty* reveals. Demosthenes became entangled in World War I when Engelbert Drerup, in *Aus einer alten Advokatenrepublik* (1916), depicted Demosthenes as a career demagogue exploiting common people, like the rhetorically adept British and French politicians David Lloyd-George and Raymond Poincaré (Adams 1963, 149–52).

The surviving texts of Menander's comedies were not discovered until too late to exert an equivalent influence on Western culture as the other great names in ancient Greek literature, although we can feel his submerged influence through his impact on the Roman comic tradition and other Latin genres including love elegy. Moreover, the papyrus finds, especially the *Dyskolos*, have allowed acknowledgement of Menander's claim to be the founder of the European "comedy of manners" (Webster 1959), still a living form in televised situation comedy. The aesthetic influence of Callimachus' lapidary poetry, likewise, has been exerted through his Roman emulators, Catullus, Propertius, and Ovid. The Hellenistic poet with the greatest direct impact on Western culture is Apollonius the Rhodian, whose epic *Argonautica* has made the story of Jason and the golden fleece familiar. Important receptions include Grillparzer's *Das goldene Vließ* (1821), a dramatic trilogy which fuses the *Argonautica* with Euripides' *Medea* in an emotional and atmospheric theatrical experience, and William Morris's lyrical, melancholy narrative poem in rhyming couplets, *The Life and Death of Jason* (1867). Morris, as a visual artist, responded to the ecphrasis and colorful imagery of Apollonius. Two films have ensured that Apollonius's epic has penetrated deep strata of global popular culture. The revolutionary special effects created by animator Ray Harryhausen for *Jason and the Argonauts* (1963, dir. Don Chaffey) turned the ancient epic into a foundational text for innovation in the twentieth century's most important new cultural medium. On the other hand, Pasolini's *Medea* (1969) resists Apollonius's negative portrayal of the Colchians to offer a critique of Western cultural imperialism.

Amongst Theocritus's *Idylls*, the pastoral examples have been much admired, but usually exerted their diffuse influence on the pastoral in the visual arts and opera, as well as in poetry, through or alongside the Latin *Eclogues* of Virgil and Longus's pastoral novel *Daphnis and Chloe*. But of equal significance in the history of poetry has been the aesthetic idiom of Theocritus's *Idylls*, as medium-length poems imitating direct speech, with a paradoxical combination of simplicity, faux-innocence, intimacy, authorial self-consciousness, sophisticated artistry, wistfulness, and nostalgia.[50] This aspect of Theocritus's presence was felt in late eighteenth and especially nineteenth -century poetry. Great "Theocritean" idylls include Leopardi's poems "To Silvia," "The solitary thrush" and "Saturday in the village" (1828–1829), and Tennyson's "English Idylls," especially "The Gardener's Daughter" (1835).

One text in ancient Greek whose role in the creation of Western culture is often underestimated is the treatise *On Sublimity* attributed to "Longinus." After a French translation by Boileau was published in 1674, the text was devoured by European thinkers, craving for insights into art's psychological effects.[51] The quest of "Longinus" for the "sublime" – the moments when literature elevates the hearer to a higher level of consciousness and sensory delight than is possible in ordinary life – was to underpin the project of Romantic art to instate "imagination" at its core, and the invention of philosophical aesthetics by Burke and Kant. But it was also instrumental in encouraging imitation of the ancient Greek classic authors "Longinus" admired – Herodotus, Plato and Demosthenes as well as Homer and Sappho (this volume, chs. 13–14).

"Longinus" may have been Jewish. He finds the sublime not only in Greek literature, but in the first book of Genesis. His date his disputed, but he probably worked in the late first century CE, like the Jewish historiographer Flavius Josephus of Jerusalem. Josephus's literary achievement has begun to be better appreciated (Redondo 2000), along with his importance to Romantic poetry including Coleridge's *The Rime of the Ancient Mariner* (Bilik 1989). Josephus's works *The Jewish War* and *Antiquities of the Jews* have since antiquity provided essential information about religious origins to both Christians and Jews. In the Middle Ages Josephus was consulted as an authority on matters including astronomy, natural history, and chronology, and provided Christian Crusaders with the seminal account, in the legend of Alexander, of Alexander's apocryphal encounter with the High Priest at Jerusalem, for example in Gautier de Chatillon's twelfth-century epic *Alexandreis sive Gesta Alexandri Magni* (Sanford 1935). Indeed, Josephus was often read alongside the ancient *Alexander Romance*, which was one of the Greek texts to exert the widest influence over literature in non-Western languages including Armenian, Georgian, Syriac, and thence Arabic, Persian, Ethiopic, Hebrew, and Turkish (Stoneman 2008). More recently, the authority of Josephus alerted the world to anti-Semitism in Lion Feuchtwanger's trilogy of novels *Der jüdische Krieg* (1932), *Die Söhne* (1935) and *Der Tag wird kommen* (1942).

The contribution made by slightly later imperial Greek literature to the culture of posterity includes romantic fiction, understood as intricate and exciting narratives depicting heterosexual couples kept apart until a climactic reunion. Heliodorus's *Ethiopian Story* and Achilles Tatius's *Leucippe and Clitophon* informed Renaissance and Early Modern experiments in prose fiction;[52] Longus's *Daphnis and Chloe* has been published in more than a staggering 500 editions, was admired by Goethe and illustrated by Marc Chagall.[53] Yet amongst authors writing in Greek under the Roman Empire, Plutarch's biographies and Lucian's humorous sketches have no rivals in the making of Western culture. They both featured on school and university curricula in the Renaissance and Early Modern periods.

Plutarch of Chaeronea in Boeotia was prolific, but it is his *Lives* rather than his ethical treatises (*Moralia*) which have attained the status of all-time classics. Collected biographies of distinguished men have sometimes identified themselves as following his example, as in Thomas Mortimer's *The British Plutarch: being a select collection of the lives at large of the most eminent men, natives of Great Britain and Ireland, from the reign of Henry VIII to George II* (1762). Anecdotes from the *Lives* fed the Renaissance craving for data about ancient education, art, and theater (Hall 2002b). But Plutarch has informed later literature most through the adoption of individual *Lives* in drama and politics. Shakespeare's *Julius Caesar, Antony and Cleopatra,* and *Coriolanus* use Plutarch's biographies of Caesar, Brutus, Marcus Antonius, and Coriolanus, in the English translation by Thomas North of the 1559 French translation by Jacques Amyot, Bishop of Auxerre.[54] In the context of the revolutions in France in 1789 and Haiti in 1791, attention was paid to Plutarch's biographies of heroes claimed by the causes of republicanism and anti-slavery, Cato, Brutus, the Gracchi, and the account of Spartacus's slave revolt in the *Life of Crassus*.[55] The portrait of the Spartan constitution and militaristic way of life in Plutarch's *Life of Lycurgus* has also excited admirers from Machiavelli to the Zack Snyder, director of *300* (2007).[56]

If Plutarch bequeathed to posterity moralizing biography, Lucian's legacy has been a literary stance characterized by satire, rationalism, absurdism, and knowing parody. Lucian was himself much influenced by the scenarios of Aristophanes, the dialectic of Plato, and the scathing ridicule he derived from the (lost) works of Menippus, the Cynic satirist of the third century BCE. Lucian's *True Histories* (a fictional account of a journey to the moon and ancestor of science fiction) and *Dialogues of the Dead* seminally impacted Renaissance authors – More's *Utopia* (1516), Erasmus's *Colloquies* (1518), Rabelais' *Gargantua and Pantagruel* (1532–52), Shakespeare's *Timon of Athens,* Jonson's comedies (Duncan 2010), Swift's *Gulliver's Travels* (1726), and Fielding. Voltaire's *Candide* (1759) and *Conversation between Lucian, Erasmus and Rabelais in the Elysian Fields* (1753) imitate Lucian's elevation of philosophy over ignorance and superstition. The same can be said of Wieland's later works, especially his satire on provincial life in *Die Abderiten, eine sehr wahrscheinliche Geschichte,* 1774 (Robinson 1979). Lucian dropped ambiguous, contradictory clues relating to his own life history, which spawned a specialist genre of biographies. The most important was Dryden's *Life of Lucian,* 1696 (see Richter 2005).

Even my inadequate survey here of some responses to ancient Greek literary authors may have provided some sense of their contribution to Western identity, or at least to the cultural forms, idioms, images, and tones of voice in which that identity has been imagined and articulated. Part of that identity has been derived from Europe's historical role as the center from which world empires have been built and administered; the canon of classical authors was also the basis of the curriculum of the era of Western imperialism from the first Portuguese expeditions to Atlantic islands in the fifteenth century. This association has inevitably elicited a conflicted response amongst communities exploited by Western empires. At one end of the spectrum there has been an angry rejection of the authors who symbolize the European domination of the planet. Aristotle's recommendation that the action of a tragedy take place within a single revolution of the sun has become the target of Postcolonial and African American literary theorists who have launched critiques of Western aesthetic ideals from a politicized perspective. Okur, for example, has shown how the "unity" of African American drama is related to a circular concept of action, rather than the linear one privileged by the European tradition (Okur 1993, esp. 97).

Yet many postcolonial authors have seen their hybrid identities, their cultural bilingualism, as an opportunity. Some stress that ancient Greek literature was one of many literatures the world has known, and indeed was preceded by more ancient texts in Mesopotamian and Egyptian languages. Others draw parallels between the indigenous mythologies of non-Western lands and narratives and those of the ancient Greeks, for example in the Nigerian Wole Soyinka's fusion of the cults of Dionysus and the Yoruba god Ogun in his *Bacchae of Euripides: A Communion Rite* (1973), or Jatinder Verma's *Ramayanan Odyssey* (2001).[57]

There is a new response to the challenge of disentangling the Western classics from the legacy of empire in the strategies of contemporary "transcultural" writers. Acutely aware that the ancient Mediterranean was an ethnic and cultural melting-pot, they argue that the literature it produced has the potential to liberate rather than restrict the contemporary project of a trans-cultural art.[58] Take one recent response to Moschus's epyllion *Europa* (second century BCE), which used elaborate pictorialism to ornament the story of the abduction of Europa by Zeus disguised as a bull. The poet Moniza Alvi, a Briton of Pakistani origins, has transformed Moschus's hexameters into a sequence of free-verse poems, *Europa* (2008), which explores the trauma caused by divisions between men and women, colonizer and colonized. The figure of Europa, torn from her Levantine homeland to be raped in Crete, symbolizes the historical fracture between East and West. Moschus's picture of Europa, her yearning arms stretched towards to the friends from whom the bull had separated her, becomes the figure for Alvi's awareness of her lost language and community:

> Her friends were there – Then they'd gone,
> spirited away like childhood.
> She wrapped their voices
> around her, tucked them under her arm.
> Aloneness – like a thistle on her tongue.

(Alvi 2008, 25)

Europa's Phoenician playmates are both a presence and an absence. Europa takes their voices with her, but the immateriality of her ancestral memories only underlines her cultural isolation.

In rewriting Moschus's *Europa* in her first-person voice, Alvi also challenges the exclusion of female subjectivity from the reception of ancient Greek literature. Until the twentieth century, few women had access to education in the ancient Greek language or literature, although there were always prodigious counter-examples – Anne Dacier (1654–1720, the translator of Homer, Anacreon, Sappho, and Aristophanes); Elizabeth Carter, who produced the definitive eighteenth-century translation of Epictetus; George Eliot, the most intellectual of all the great nineteenth-century novelists in English, who studied Greek tragedy intently.[59] Elizabeth Barrett Browning translated *Prometheus Bound* (1833) and by 1856 had fulfilled her childhood dream of becoming the "feminine of Homer" by making a travelling quest heroine the narrating subject of her verse epic *Aurora Leigh* (Hardwick 2000b and Hurst 2006).

Creative responses to ancient Greek literature by women remained rare until the Modernist period, when Euripides appealed to North Americans including Isadora Duncan (in her chore-ography to *Iphigenia*), "H.D." (Hilda Doolittle), whose translation of choruses from *Iphigenia in Aulis* (1915) and *Hippolytus Temporizes* (1927) show how much her pioneering lapidary "Imagism" owed to Euripidean diction and imagery. In the novelist Willa Cather's masterpiece, *The Professor's House* (1925), Professor Godfrey St. Peter is himself based on her understanding of Euripides as an isolated, depressed, but brilliant intellectual able to analyze but not actively intervene in the unrolling tragedy of human civilization (Hall forthcoming *b*). It became inevitable that feminists would engage with Greek literature once Simone de Beauvoir had pointed in *Le Deuxième Sexe* (1949) to the significance as charter text for patriarchy of Athena's vote for Orestes and Apollo against the claims of Clytemnestra and the Erinyes in Aeschylus's *Eumenides*. In the last three decades, ancient Greek authors have been systematically reap-praised by creative artists as well as academics, who have self-consciously read them "against the grain" to discover how texts created in (and received under) conditions of patriarchy can be recuperated for a more gender-sensitive epoch. Inge Merkel's novel *Eine ganz gewöhnliche Ehe: Odysseus und Penelope* (1987), Ariane Mnouchkine's production of *Iphigenia in Aulis* and the *Oresteia* as *Les Atrides* (1990), and Christa Wolf's *Medea: Stimmen* (1996) are among the most significant examples.[60]

It was partly in response to the feminist reassessment of literature by ancient Greek men that Knox labelled them ODWEMS, the Oldest Dead White European Males.[61] But he was also responding to the allegation that classical culture was hijacked by Western imperialism. Other, less critical labels have long been attached to our dialogue with the Greeks. An antique rhetorician liked the image of Homer "sowing the seeds of art" (Browning 1992, 136). The notion of the Classical "tradition" or "heritage" implies a legacy, passed down generations like the family teaspoons.[62] Judith Kazantzis defines herself more rapaciously as a "pirate," with ancient poetry being "perennially open to plunder."[63] The theater director Peter Sellars sees each classic text as an antique house that can be redecorated in any era's style, while remaining essentially the same.[64] Taplin (1989) proposes the volatile image of "Greek Fire," a substance that burns under water. Greek culture, according to this analogy, is present in invisible yet incendiary forms. For the Prussian scholar Ulrich von Wilamowitz-Moellendorff (1908, 25; cf. Lloyd-Jones 1982, 177–8), the metaphor of necromancy came from the Homeric scene before Odysseus enters the world of the dead: "We know that ghosts cannot speak until they have drunk blood; and the spirits which we evoke demand the blood of our hearts." But for the world citizen for whom the Greeks have stopped belonging exclusively to the West, perhaps the most potent image is Derek Walcott's description, repeated in poems including *Omeros*, of "All that Greek manure under the green bananas."[65] The Greek legacy is left behind – it is excrement – but it has also fertilized his Caribbean imagination. This beautifully captures the paradoxical nature of classical literature to peoples colonized by "Western" powers.

NOTES

[1] Weil's essay was first published in French in 1940. It has been translated and included in many anthologies and in the critical edition of Holoka 2003.

[2] See also Shay 2002; Riley 2004; Crimp 2004; Hall 2008a, ch. 13; Hall 2011a.

[3] On transforming epic into lyric verse, see Murnaghan and Roberts 2002; on the use of ancient Greek tragedy in contemporary fiction, see Hall 2009a.

[4] On which see Mazouer 2010.

[5] On which see Leonard 2005.

[6] Hall 2012a chs. 1 and 8.

[7] See the essays in Hall, Alston, and McConnell 2011, especially those by Monoson, Malamud, and Vandiver and Lupher.

[8] See Prickett 1989; Rajak 1999; Goldhill 2002, 1–3, 36–7, 95–100.

[9] On ancient Greek literature in opera, see Goldhill 2008, Brown and Ograjenšek 2010, Hall 2012a, ch. 8.; in dance, see Hall 2008b and especially Macintosh 2010; in cinema, see McDonald 1983; MacKinnon 1986; Michelakis 2004; Boschi and Bozzato 2005; Winkler 2001.

[10] Individual mythical names supply the organizing principle in the standard work of reference for the reception of classical mythology, Reid 1993. Some Greek mythical figures have elicited a tidal wave of interdisciplinary studies, for example Medea, on whom see e.g. Macintosh, Hall and Taplin 2000; Bätzner, Dreyer, Fischer-Lichte, and Schönhagen 2010; Bartel and Simon 2010.

[11] See Dowling 1994; Verstraete and Provencal 2005; Orrells 2011.

[12] Heath 1987; T. Harrison 2009.

[13] "The Mystery of Life and Its Arts" (1868), first published as Ruskin 1869.

[14] Cf. Nünlist, this volume ch. 19, 304.

[15] Goldhill 2002, 108–77.

[16] On which see Rankine 2006.

[17] "Tradition and the Individual Talent," in Eliot 1975, 38.

[18] Hall forthcoming a.

[19] Richardson 1981; Hall 2006, ch. 11. The contest also informs the competition between Aeschylus and Euripides in Aristophanes' *Frogs*: see Rosen 2004.

[20] Published in Heaney 1990.

[21] Cf. Schenker, this volume ch. 20, 317–8.

[22] *Rhet.* 3.1418b30 = Archilochus F 19 IEG. See also Hdt. 1.12.2; Ford 2002, 147; Hall 2007c.

[23] Vidal-Naquet 1995, 95, 101.

[24] See on this fragment Wells, this volume ch. 10, 165–8, and Willi, this volume ch. 29, 451–2.

[25] Grahn 1985; Prins 1995 and 1999; Williamson 2009; Collecott 1999.

[26] The ode can be accessed at http://www.armand-dangour.com/pindaric-odes/. Accessed April 6, 2015.

[27] The bibliography on the reception of ancient drama in performance is vast. Early, pioneering studies include Solomos 1974, Walton 1984, Smith 1988, McDonald 1992, and Flashar 1991. For more surveys see Hall 2004a, 2010a, ch. 8; and Hall and Harrop 2010; for the history of Greek tragedy on the British stage, Hall and Macintosh 2005; for Greek drama in Africa, Wetmore 2001; for drama of the African diaspora, see Wetmore 2003; Goff and Simpson 2007, Greenwood 2010; for tragedy, Brown and Silverstone 2007; for female roles in modern performances, Dillon and Wilmer 2005; for earlier German performances of the *Oresteia*, see Fischer-Lichte 2004 and 2008. There are also relevant articles in Hardwick and Stray 2008.

[28] On Müller see Lefèvre 2000 and Birringer 1990; on Heaney, Taplin 2004; on Hughes, Hardwick 2009.

[29] Harrison 1998, xvi–xviii; Hall 2011b with fig. 8.9.

[30] See Van Steen 2007; Hall 2004b, 176–83; 2007b; 2010a, 248–32.

[31] See Carson 1999, Don Paterson's poem "The Reading" in Paterson 2003, and Crawford and MacBeath 2011.

[32] Lyons 1982; Badawi 1987; Gutas 1998; Etman 2008.

[33] On the Zante *Persians* see Hall 2007b; on importance in the Renaissance of the Latinized Aeschylus by Jean de Saint-Ravy ("Sanravius"), Ewbank 2005.

[34] See Fiorese 1984.

[35] Rucellai's *Oreste* is printed in Rucellai 1772; see Hall 2012a, ch. 8.

[36] Campbell 1991. The plot of *Athalie* also constitutes a "reception" of Euripides' *Ion*.

[37] See e.g. Laurence Sterne's *Tristram Shandy* (1759) Book 3 ch. 12, Henry Fielding's *Tom Jones* (1749) book 5 ch.1, and Samuel Johnson's crucial argument in *The Rambler* 156 (1751).

[38] Alter 1964, 366. On the impact of Aristotle's temporal "unity," see Hall 2012b.

[39] See Frankland 2000, 30–32, 68, 142–3, 206; Macintosh 2009, 111–12, 130–45, 159–61.

[40] Steiner 1984; Flashar 1991, 60–81; Hall and Macintosh 2005, 316–49.

[41] Hall 2004a, 18–19; Mee and Foley 2011.

[42] Cf. Wilson, this volume ch. 32, 492.

[43] Cartledge 1990, 72–6; further references in Hall 2007d, 26 n. 5.

[44] For Aristophanes in Germany, see Holtermann 2004. Van Steen 2000 traces the history of Aristophanic performance in Greece; Gamel 2002 draws connections between Aristophanic classical scholarship and performance practice.

[45] Bridges, Hall, and Rhodes 2007.

[46] Recent surveys of the influence of Thucydides include Fromentin, Gotteland, and Payen 2010; Iglesias-Zoido 2011.

[47] See Tritle 2006 and the chapter "Kissinger and Thucydides" in Burns 2010.

[48] Rubincam 2004.

[49] See Paz 1995, Wang 1997 and the articles by Lesher, Clay and O'Connor in Lesher, Nails and Frisbee 2006. For Plato's presence in the poetry of C.P. Cavafy, see Zamarou 2005.

[50] Gillespie 1988, 207–14; Kegel-Brinkgreve 1990.

[51] Wood 1972; Hall and Macintosh 2005, 52.

[52] Skretkowicz 2010; Beardon 2011. See also the chapter "Heliodorus and early modern literary culture" in Mentz 2006.

[53] Barber 1989; Hardin 2000. The Chagall lithographs are reproduced in Paul Turner 1994.

[54] Pelling 2011, 64–7; Bajma Griga 2007; the essays by Roe and Braden in Martindale and Taylor 2004. On *Coriolanus*, see Pelling 2002, ch. 18.

[55] On Crassus / Spartacus, see Hunnings 2007. See also Hall, Alston, and McConnell 2011, 3, 66–8, 29, 67, 85 and n.4, 281, 310–11, 359.

[56] Rawson 1969. Thanks to Chris Pelling for helpful advice on the reception of Plutarch.

[57] On Soyinka, see Bishop 1983; on Verma, see McConnell 2010.

[58] See the sensible remarks of Galinsky 1992, 150–52 and the articles collected in Hardwick and Gillespie 2007. On Homer, see also Graziosi and Greenwood 2007 and Hall 2008a, chs. 5–6.

[59] Jenkyns 1980, ch. 6; Easterling 1991; Hall and Macintosh 2005, 331–2.

[60] See especially Komar 2003; Foley 2004; Hall 2005; Hall 2008, ch. 9; Macintosh 2009 181–7.

[61] The title of Knox 1993.

[62] See the titles of Highet 1949 and Bolgar 1954.

[63] Kazantzis 1999, 7. See also Hardwick 2000, 19, on the metaphor of retrieving buried treasure.

[64] Quoted in Lahr 1993.

[65] Walcott 1949, 15; see also Walcott 1990, 271.

REFERENCES

Ackerman, R. 1991. *The Myth and Ritual School: J. G. Frazer and the Cambridge Ritualists.* New York.

Adams, C. D. 1963. *Demosthenes and his Influence.* New York.

Alter, J. V. 1964. "Alain Robbe-Grillet and the 'Cinematographic Style'." *Modern Language Journal* 48: 363–6.

Alvi, M. 2008. *Europa.* Tarset, Northumberland.

Archambault, P. J. 1967. "Thucydides in France: The Notion of 'Justice' in the Memoires of Philippe De Commynes." *Journal of the History of Ideas* 28: 89–98.

Badawi, A. R. 1987. *La transmission de la philosophie grecque au monde arabe.* Paris.

Bajma Griga, S. 2007. *Da Plutarco a Shakespeare.* Turin.

Balmer, J. 1992. *Sappho: Poems and Fragments.* 2nd edn. Newcastle upon Tyne.

Barber, G. 1989. *Daphnis and Chloe: The Markets and Metamorphoses of an Unknown Bestseller.* London.

Bartel, H. and A. Simon, eds. 2010. *Unbinding Medea: Interdisciplinary Approaches to a Classical Myth from Antiquity to the 21st Century.* Oxford.

Bätzner, N., M. Dreyer, E. Fischer-Lichte, and A. Schönhagen, eds. 2010. *Medeamorphosen: Mythos und ästhetische Transformation.* Munich.

Bavaj, R. 2011. "The West: A Conceptual Exploration." Europäische Geschichte Online. Accessed April 6, 2015. http://www.ieg-ego.eu/en/threads/crossroads/political-spaces/political-ideas-of-regional-order/riccardo-bavaj-the-west-a-conceptual-exploration.

Beardon, E. B. 2011. *The Emblematics of the Self: Ekphrasis and Identity in Renaissance Imitations of Greek Romance.* Toronto.

Berneri, M. L. 1982. *Reise durch Utopia; mit Plato, Plutarch, Aristophanes, Morus, Campanella, Andrea, Bacon, Rabelais, de Foigny, Cabet, Bellamy.* Berlin.

Bilik, D. 1989. "Josephus, Mosollamus, and the Ancient Mariner." *Studies in Philology* 86: 87–95.

Birringer, J. 1990. "'Medea': Landscapes beyond History." *New German Critique* 50: 85–112.

Bishop, N. 1983. "A Nigerian Version of a Greek Classic: Soyinka's Transformation of 'The Bacchae'." *Research in African Literatures* 14: 68–80.

Bolgar, R. R. 1954. *The Classical Heritage and its Beneficiaries.* Cambridge

Boschi, A. and A. Bozzato. 2005. *I Greci al cinema.* Bologna.

Bridges, E., E. Hall, and P. J. Rhodes, eds. 2007. *Cultural Responses to the Persian Wars.* Oxford.

Brown, P. and S. Ograjenšek, eds. 2010. *Ancient Drama in Music for the Modern Stage.* Oxford.

Brown, S. A. 2008. "Plato's Stepchildren: Science Fiction and the Classics." In L. Hardwick, L. and C. Stray, eds., *A Companion to Classical Receptions*, Oxford, 415–27.

Brown, S. A. and C. Silverstone, eds. 2007. *Tragedy in Transition.* Oxford.

Browning, R. 1992. "The Byzantines and Homer." In R. Lamberton and J. J. Keaney, eds., *The Hermeneutics of Greek Epic's Earliest Exegetes*, Princeton, NJ, 34–48.

Budelmann, F., ed. 2009. *The Cambridge Companion to Greek Lyric.* Cambridge.

Burns, T., ed. 2006. *Recovering Reason: Essays in Honor of Thomas L. Pangle.* Lanham, MD.

Campbell, J. 1991. "The Unity of Time in 'Athalie'." *Modern Language Review* 86: 573–9.

Carey, J. 1987. *The Faber Book of Reportage.* London.

Carson, A. 1997. *The Autobiography of Red. A Novel In Verse.* New York.

Carson, A. 1999. *Economy of the Unlost: Reading Simonides of Keos with Paul Celan.* Princeton, NJ.

Carson, A. 2003. *If Not, Winter: Fragments of Sappho.* New York.

Cartledge, P. 1990. *Aristophanes and his Theatre of the Absurd.* Bristol.

Clarke, G. W., ed. 1989. *Rediscovering Hellenism: The Hellenic Inheritance and the English Imagination.* Cambridge.

Collecott, D. 1999. *H. D. and Sapphic Modernism, 1910–1950.* Cambridge.

Crawford, R. and N. MacBeath. 2011. *Simonides.* Edinburgh.

Crimp, M. 2004. *Cruel and Tender. After Sophocles' Trachiniae.* London.

Crino, A. M. 1961. "Lope de Vega's exertions for the abolition of the unities in dramatic practice." *Modern Language Notes* 76: 259–61.

Curran, S. 1986. "The Political Prometheus." *Studies in Romanticism* 70: 273–81.

Dillon, J. and S. Wilmer, eds. 2005. *Rebel Women: Staging Ancient Greek Drama Today.* London.

Dowling, L. 1994. *Hellenism and Homosexuality in Victorian Oxford.* Ithaca, NY.

Drerup, E. *Aus einer alten Advokatenrepublik.* Paderborn.

Duncan, D. 2010. *Ben Jonson and the Lucianic Tradition.* Cambridge.

Easterling, P. E. 1991. "George Eliot and Greek tragedy." *Arion* 1–2: 60–74

Eliot, T. S. 1975. *Selected Prose. Edited with an introduction by F. Kermode.* New York.

Etman, A. 2008. "Translation at the Intersection of Traditions: The Arab Reception of the Classics." In L. Hardwick, L. and C. Stray, eds., *A Companion to Classical Receptions*, Oxford, 141–52.

Ewbank, I.-S. 2005. "Striking Too Short at Greeks." In F. Macintosh, P. Michelakis, E. Hall, and O. Taplin, eds., *Agamemnon in Performance: 458 BC to AD 2004*, Oxford, 37–52.

Fiorese, F., ed. 1984. *Edipo tiranno. Orsatto Giustiniani; con la lettera di Filippo Pigafetta che descrive la rappresentazione dell'Edipo re di Sofocle al Teatro Olimpico di Vicenza nel 1585.* Vicenza.

Fischer-Lichte, E. 2004. "Thinking About the Origins of Theatre in the 1970s." In E. Hall, F. Macintosh, and A. Wrigley, eds., *Dionysus since 69: Greek Tragedy at the Dawn of the Third Millennium*, Oxford, 329–60.

Fischer-Lichte, E. 2008. "Resurrecting ancient Greece in Nazi Germany: The *Oresteia* as part of the Olympic Games in 1936." In M. Revermann and P. Wilson, eds., *Performance, Iconography, Reception: Studies in Honour of Oliver Taplin*, Oxford, 481–98.

Flashar, H. 1991. *Inszenierung der Antike*. Munich.

Foley, H. 2004. "Bad Women: Gender Politics in Late Twentieth-century Performance and Revision of Greek Tragedy." In E. Hall, F. Macintosh, and A. Wrigley, eds., *Dionysus since 69: Greek Tragedy at the Dawn of the Third Millennium*, Oxford, 77–111.

Ford, A. 2002. *The Origins of Criticism: Literary Culture and Poetic Theory in Classical Greece*. Princeton, NJ.

Frankland, G. 2000. *Freud's Literary Culture*. Cambridge.

Fromentin, V., S. Gotteland, and P. Payen, eds. 2010. *Ombres de Thucydide*. Bordeaux.

Galinsky, K. 1992. *Classical and Modern Interactions*. Austin TX.

Gamel, M.-K., ed. 2002. *Performing/transforming Aristophanes' Thesmophoriazousai*. Baltimore.

Gillespie, S. 1988. *The Poets on the Classics: an Anthology*. London.

Goff, B. and M. Simpson. 2007. *Crossroads in the Black Aegean: Oedipus, Antigone, and Dramas of the African diaspora*. Oxford.

Goldhill, S. 2002. *Who Needs Greek? Contests in the Cultural History of Hellenism*. Cambridge.

Goldhill, S. 2008. "Wagner's Greeks: The Politics of Hellenism." In M. Revermann and P. Wilson, eds., *Performance, Iconography, Reception: Studies in Honour of Oliver Taplin*, Oxford, 453–80.

Grahn, J. 1985. *The Highest Apple: Sappho and the Lesbian Poetic Tradition*. San Francisco.

Graziosi, B. and E. Greenwood, eds. 2007. *Homer in the Twentieth Century: Between World Literature and the Western Canon*. Oxford.

Greenwood, E. 2010. *Afro-Greeks: Dialogues between Anglophone Caribbean Literature and Classics in the Twentieth Century*. Oxford

Gutas, D. 1998. *Greek Thought, Arab Culture: the Graeco-Arabic Translation Movement in Baghdad and Early 'Abbāsid Society (2nd–4th/8th–10th centuries)*. New York.

Hall, E. 1989. *Inventing the Barbarian: Greek Self-Definition through Tragedy*. Oxford.

Hall, E. 2000. "Medea on the 18th-century London Stage." In E. Hall, F. Macintosh, and O. Taplin, eds., *Medea in Performance 1500–2000.*, Oxford, 49–74.

Hall, E. 2002a. "Tony Harrison's *Prometheus*: A View from the Left." *Arion* 10: 129–40.

Hall, E. 2002b. "The Ancient Actor's Presence since the Renaissance." In P. E. Easterling and E. Hall, eds., *Greek and Roman Actors: Aspects of an Ancient Profession*, Cambridge, 419–34.

Hall, E. 2004a. "Why Greek Tragedy in the Late Twentieth Century?" In E. Hall, F. Macintosh, and A. Wrigley, eds., *Dionysus since 69: Greek Tragedy at the Dawn of the Third Millennium*, Oxford, 1–46.

Hall, E. 2004b. "Aeschylus, Race, Class and War." In E. Hall, F. Macintosh, and A. Wrigley, eds., *Dionysus since 69: Greek Tragedy at the Dawn of the Third Millennium*, Oxford, 169–97.

Hall, E. 2005. "Aeschylus' Clytemnestra *versus* her Senecan Tradition." In F. Macintosh, P. Michelakis, E. Hall, and O. Taplin, eds., *Agamemnon in Performance: 458 BC to AD 2004*, Oxford, 53–75.

Hall, E. 2006. *The Theatrical Cast of Athens. Interactions between Ancient Greek Drama and Society*. Oxford.

Hall, E. 2007a. "Classics, Class and Cloacina: Tony Harrison's Humane Coprology." *Arion* 15: 111–36.

Hall, E. 2007b. "Aeschylus' *Persians* from Xerxes to Saddam Hussein." In E. Bridges, E. Hall, and P. J. Rhodes, eds., *Cultural Responses to the Persian Wars*, Oxford, 167–99.

Hall, E. 2007c. "Subjects, Selves and Survivors." *Helios* 34: 125–59.

Hall, E. 2007d. "Introduction: Aristophanic Laughter across the Centuries." In E. Hall and A. Wrigley, eds., *Aristophanes in Performance*, Oxford, 1–29.

Hall, E. 2008a. *The Return of Ulysses: A Cultural History of Homer's Odyssey*. Baltimore.

Hall, E. 2008b. "Ancient Pantomime and the Rise of Ballet." In E. Hall and R. Wyles, eds., *New Directions in Ancient Pantomime*, Oxford, 363–77.

Hall, E. 2008c. "Putting the Class into Classical Reception." In L.Hardwick,L. and C. Stray, eds., *A Companion to Classical Receptions*, Oxford, 386–407.

Hall, E. 2009a. "Greek Tragedy and the Politics of Subjectivity in Recent Fiction." *Classical Receptions Journal*, 1: 23–42.

Hall, E. 2009b. "The Autobiography of the Western Subject: Carson's Geryon." In S. J. Harrison, ed., *Living Classics: Greece and Rome in Contemporary Poetry in English*, Oxford, 218–37.

Hall, E. 2010a. *Greek Tragedy: Suffering under the Sun*. Oxford.

Hall, E. 2011a. "Ancient Greek Responses to Suffering: Thinking with Philoctetes." In J. Nelis, ed., *Receptions of Antiquity (Festschrift for Freddy Decreus)*, Gent, 161–8.

Hall, E. 2011b. "The Problem with Prometheus: Myth, Abolition, and Radicalism." In E. Hall, R. Alston, and J. McConnell, eds., *Ancient Slavery and Abolition: Hobbes to Hollywood*, Oxford, 209–46.

Hall, E. 2012a. *Adventures with Iphigenia in Tauris: A Cultural History of Euripides' Black Sea Tragedy*. New York.

Hall, E. 2012b. "The Social Significance of the 'Unity of Time'." In M. Zagdoun and F. Malhomme, eds., *Renaissances de la Tragédie. Atti Accademia Pontaniana*, suppl. 60, 145–54.

Hall, E. forthcoming a. "Aesop the Morphing Fabulist." In H. Lovatt and O. Hodkinson, eds., *Changing the Greeks and Romans: Metamorphosing Antiquity for Children*, Cambridge.

Hall, E. forthcoming b. "Greek Tragedy and North American Modernism." In K. Bosher, F. Macintosh, J. McConnell, and P. Rankine, eds., *Greek Drama and the Americas*, Oxford.

Hall, E., R. Alston, and J. McConnell, eds. 2011. *Ancient Slavery and Abolition: Hobbes to Hollywood*. Oxford.

Hall, E. and S. Harrop, eds. 2010. *Theorising Performance: Greek Drama, Cultural History, and Critical Practice*. London.

Hall, E. and F. Macintosh. 2005. *Greek Tragedy and the British Theatre 1660–1914*. Oxford.

Hall, E., F. Macintosh, and O. Taplin, eds. 2000. *Medea in Performance 1500–2000*. Oxford.

Hall, E., F. Macintosh, and A. Wrigley, eds. 2004. *Dionysus since 69: Greek Tragedy at the Dawn of the Third Millennium*. Oxford.

Hall, E. and A. Wrigley, eds. 2007. *Aristophanes in Performance*. Oxford.

Hardin, R. 2000. *Love in a Green Shade: Idyllic Romances Ancient to Modern*. Lincoln, NE.

Hardwick, L. 2000a. *Translating Words, Translating Cultures*. London.

Hardwick, L. 2000b. "Theatres of the Mind: Greek Tragedy in Women's Writing in England in the Nineteenth Century." In L. Hardwick, P. Easterling, N. Lowe, and F. Macintosh, eds., *Theatre: Ancient and Modern*, Milton Keynes, 68–71.

Hardwick, L. 2009. "Can Modern Poets do Classical Drama?" In R. Rees, ed., *Ted Hughes and the Classics*, Oxford, 39–61.

Hardwick, L. and C. Gillespie, eds. 2007. *Classics in Postcolonial Worlds*. Oxford.

Hardwick, L. and C. Stray, eds. 2008. *A Companion to Classical Receptions*. Oxford.

Harrison, S. J., ed. 2009. *Living Classics: Greece and Rome in Contemporary Poetry in English*. Oxford.

Harrison, T. 1998. *Prometheus*. London.

Harrison, T. 2009. "Weeping for Hecuba." In S. J. Harrison, ed., *Living Classics: Greece and Rome in Contemporary Poetry in English*, Oxford, 117–21.

Hartog, F. 2000. "The Invention of History: The Pre-History of a Concept from Homer to Herodotus." *History and Theory* 39: 384–95.

Heaney, S. 1990. *New Selected Poems 1966–1987*. London.

Heath, M. 1987. "Iure principem locum tenet: Euripides' *Hecuba*." *Bulletin of the Institute of Classical Studies* 34: 40–68.

Hegel, G. W. F. 1837/1923. *Vorlesungen über die Philosophie der Weltgeschichte*, edited by G. Lasson. Leipzig (first edn. 1837).

Hennis, W. 2003. *Max Weber und Thukydides: die "hellenische Geisteskultur" und die Ursprünge von Webers politischer Denkart*. Göttingen.

Hicks, P. 1996. *Neoclassical History and English Culture: from Clarendon to Hume*. Basingstoke.

Highet, G. 1949. *The Classical Tradition: Greek and Roman Influences on Western Literature*. Oxford.

Holoka, J., ed. 2003. *Simone Weil's the Iliad or the Poem of Force: A Critical Edition*. Oxford.

Holtermann, M. 2004. *Der deutsche Aristophanes*. Göttingen.

Hunnings, L. 2007. "Spartacus in Nineteenth-century England." In C. Stray, ed., *Rethinking the Classics*, London, 1–19.

Hurst, A. and A. Schachter. 1996. *La montagne des Muses*. Geneva.

Hurst, I. 2006. *Victorian Women and the Classics*. Oxford.

Iglesias-Zoido, J. C. 2011. *El legado de Tucídides en la cultura occidental*. Coimbra.

Jenkyns, R. 1980. *The Victorians and Ancient Greece*. Oxford.

Kapuściński, R. 2007. *Travels with Herodotus*. London.

Kazantzis, J. 1999. *The Odysseus Poems: Fictions on the Odyssey of Homer*. Tregarne, Cornwall.

Kegel-Brinkgreve, E. 1990. *The Echoing Woods: Bucolic and Pastoral from Theocritus to Wordsworth*. Amsterdam.

Kindstrand, J. F. 1973. *Homer in der zweiten Sophistik*. Uppsala.

Knox, B. 1993. *The Oldest Dead White European Males and Other Reflections on the Classics*. New York.

Komar, K. L. 2003. *Reclaiming Klytemnestra: Revenge or Reconciliation*. Urbana, IL.

Lahr, J. 1993. "Inventing the Enemy." *New Yorker*, October 18, 103–6.

Lefèvre, E. 2000. "Sophokles' und Heiner Müllers *Philoktet*." In S. Gödde, ed., *Skenika: Beiträge zum antiken Theater und seiner Rezeption: Festschrift zum 65. Geburtstag von Horst-Dieter Blume*, Darmstadt, 419–38.

Leonard, M. 2005. *Athens in Paris: Ancient Greece and the Political in Post-War French Thought*. Oxford.

Lesher, J. H., D. Nails and C. C. Frisbee, eds. 2006. *Plato's Symposium: Issues in Interpretation and Reception*. Washington, DC.

Lloyd-Jones, H. 1982. *Blood for the Ghosts: Classical Influences in the Nineteenth and Twentieth Centuries*. London.

Locke, J. 1705/1968. *Some Thoughts Concerning Education*, 5th edn., reproduced in *The Educational Writings of John Locke*, edited by J. L. Axtell. Cambridge (first edn. 1705).

Lynch, J. 1986. *Henry Fielding and the Heliodoran Novel: Romance, Epic, and Fielding's new Province of Writing*. Rutherford, NJ.

Lyons, M. C. 1982. *Aristotle's Ars rhetorica: The Arabic version*. 2 vols. Cambridge.

Macintosh, F. 2008. "The 'Rediscovery' of Aeschylus for the Modern Stage." In J. Jouanna, F. Montanari and A.-C. Hernández, eds., *Eschyle. Entretiens Hardt* vol. 55, Vandoeuvres-Geneva, 435–59.

Macintosh, F., E. Hall, and O. Taplin, eds. 2000. *Medea in Performance 1500–2000*. Oxford.

Macintosh, F., P. Michelakis, E. Hall, and O. Taplin, eds. 2005. *Agamemnon in Performance: 458 BC to AD 2004*. Oxford.

MacKinnon, K. 1986. *Greek Tragedy into Film*. London.

Marrou, H.-I. 1956. *A History of Education in Antiquity*. New York.

Martindale, C. and A. B. Taylor. 2004. *Shakespeare and the Classics*. Cambridge.

Maxwell, C. 2001. *The Female Sublime*. Manchester.

Mazouer, C. 2010. *Le théâtre français de l'âge classique. II l'apogée du classicisme*. Paris.

McConnell, J. 2010. "Achieving Presence: Jatinder Verma and the Cross-Cultural Work of Tara Arts." In E. Hall and Phioze Vasunia, eds., *India, Greece and Rome 1757–2007*. BICS supplement 108, London, 143–57.

McDonald, M. 1983. *Euripides in Cinema*. Philadelphia.

McDonald, M. 1992. *Ancient Sun, Modern Light*. New York.

Mee, E. and H. Foley. 2011, ed. *Antigone on the Contemporary World Stage*. Oxford.

Meier, C. 2011. *A Culture of Freedom: Ancient Greece and the Origins of Europe*. Oxford.

Mentz, S. 2006. *Romance for Sale in Early Modern England: The Rise of Prose Fiction*. Aldershot.

Michelakis, P. 2004. "Greek Tragedy in Cinema: Theatre, Politics, History." In E. Hall, F. Macintosh, and A. Wrigley, eds., *Dionysus since 69: Greek Tragedy at the Dawn of the Third Millennium*, Oxford, 199–217.

Michelakis, P. 2009. "Greek Lyric from the Renaissance to the Eighteenth Century." In F. Budelmann, ed., *The Cambridge Companion to Greek Lyric*, Cambridge, 336–51.

Momigliano, A. 1958. "The Place of Herodotus in the History of Historiography." *History* 43: 1–13.

Murnaghan, S. and D. H. Roberts. 2002. "Penelope's Song: The Lyric *Odysseys* of Linda Pastan and Louise Glück." *Classical and Modern Literature* 22: 1–33.

Okur, N. A. 1993. "Afrocentricity as a Generative Idea in the Study of African American Drama." *Journal of Black Studies*, 24: 88–108

Onuf, P. S. and N. P. Cole, eds. 2011. *Thomas Jefferson, the Classical World, and Early America*. Charlottesville, VA.

Orrells, D. 2011. *Classical Culture and Modern Masculinity*. Oxford.

Paterson, D. 2003. *Landing Light*. London.

Paz, O. 1995. *The Double Flame: Love and Eroticism*. New York.

Pelling, C. 2002. *Plutarch and History*. Oxford.

Pelling, C, ed. 2011. *Plutarch, Caesar*. Oxford.

Prickett, S. 1989. "'Hebrew' versus 'Hellene' as a Principle of Literary Criticism." In G. W. Clarke, ed., *Rediscovering Hellenism: The Hellenic Inheritance and the English Imagination*, Cambridge, 137–59.

Prins, Y. 1995. "Sappho Doubled: Michael Field." *Yale Journal of Criticism* 8: 165–86.

Prins, Y. 1999. *Victorian Sappho*. Princeton, NJ.

Rahe, P. A. 2006. "Thucydides as Educator." In W. Murray and R. H. Sinnreich, eds., *The Past as Prologue: the Importance of History to the Military Profession*, Cambridge, 95–110.

Rajak, T. 1999. "Jews and Greeks: The Invention and Exploitation of Polarities in the 19th Century." In M. Bidiss and M. Wyke, eds., *The Uses and Abuses of Antiquity*, Bern, 57–77.

Rankine, P. D. 2006. *Ulysses in Black: Ralph Ellison, Classicism, and African American Literature*. Madison, WI.

Rawson, E. 1969. *The Spartan Tradition in European Thought*. Oxford.

Redondo, J. 2000. "The Greek Literary Language of the Hebrew Historian Josephus." *Hermes* 128: 420–34.

Reid, J. D. 1993. *The Oxford Guide to Classical Mythology in the Arts*. 2 vols. Oxford.

Revello, J. T. 1957. "Sixteenth-Century Reading in the Indies." *The Americas* 14: 175–82.

Revermann, M. and P. Wilson, eds. 2008. *Performance, Iconography, Reception: Studies in Honour of Oliver Taplin*. Oxford.

Reynolds, M. 2001. "Fragments of an Elegy: Tennyson Reading Sappho." *Tennyson Society. Occasional Papers* 11. London.

Richardson, N. J. 1981. "The Contest of Homer and Hesiod and Alcidamas' *Mouseion*." *Classical Quarterly* 31: 1–10.

Richter, D. 2005. "Lives and Afterlives of Lucian of Samosata." *Arion* 13: 75–100.

Riley, K. 2004. "Heracles as Dr Strangelove and G. I. Joe." In E. Hall, F. Macintosh, and A. Wrigley, eds., *Dionysus since 69: Greek Tragedy at the Dawn of the Third Millennium*, Oxford, 113–41.

Robinson, C. 1979. *Lucian and his Influence in Europe*. London.

Rood, T. 2004. *The Sea! The Sea! The Shout of the Ten Thousand in the Modern Imagination*. London.

Rosen, R. 2004. "Aristophanes' *Frogs* and the *Contest of Homer and Hesiod*." *Transactions of the American Philological Association*, 134: 295–322.

Rubincam, C. 2004. "Thucydides and Defoe: Two Plague Narratives." *International Journal of the Classical Tradition* 11: 194–212.

Rucellai, G. 1772. *Le opere di M. Giovanni Rucellai: ora per la prima volta in un volume raccolte, e con somma diligenza ristampate*. Padua.

Ruskin, J. 1869. *The Mystery of Life and its Arts: Being the Third Lecture of Sesame and Lilies*. New York.

Sanford, E. M. 1935. "Propaganda and Censorship in the Transmission of Josephus." *Transactions of the American Philological Association*, 66: 127–45.

Sanravius, J. 1555. *Aeschyli poetae vetustissimi tragoediae sex, quot quidem extant / summa fide ac diligentia è graeco in latinum sermonem, pro utriusq[ue] linguæ tyronibus, ad verbum conuersae*. Basel.

Segal, C. 1983. "Review of *Nietzsche on Tragedy* by M. S. Silk and J. P. Stern." *Journal of Modern History* 55: 102–5.

Seidensticker, B. 1992. "The Political Use of Antiquity in the Literature of the German Democratic Republic." *Illinois Classical Studies* 17: 347–67.

Seidensticker, B. 2007. "'Aristophanes is Back!' Peter Hacks' Adaptation of *Peace*." In E. Hall and A. Wrigley, eds., *Aristophanes in Performance*, Oxford, 194–208.

Shay, J. 2002. *Odysseus in America: Combat Trauma and the Trials of Homecoming*. New York.

Silk, M. S. 2000. *Aristophanes and the Definition of Comedy*. Oxford.

Silk, M. S. and J. P. Stern. 1983. *Nietzsche on Tragedy*. Cambridge.

Skretkowicz, V. 2010. *European Erotic Romance: Philhellene Protestantism, Renaissance Translation and English Literary Politics*. Manchester.

Slomp, G. 2000. *Thomas Hobbes and the Political Philosophy of Glory*. New York.

Smith, B. R. 1988. *Ancient Scripts and Modern Experience on the English Stage, 1500–1700*. Princeton, NJ.

Solomos, A. 1974. *The Living Aristophanes*. Ann Arbor, MI.

Steiner, G. 1984. *Antigones*. Revised edn. Oxford.

Stoneman, R. 2008. *Alexander the Great: A Life in Legend*. New Haven, CT.

Sullivan, R. G. 2004. "Demosthenes' Renaissance Philipics: Thomas Wilson's 1570 Translation as Anti-Spanish Propaganda." *Advances in the History of Rhetoric* 7: 111–37.

Taplin, O. 1989. *Greek Fire*. London.

Taplin, O. 1991. "Satyrs on the Borderline: *Trackers* in the Development of Tony Harrison's Theatre Work." In N. Astley, ed., *Tony Harrison*, Newcastle upon Tyne, 458–64.

Taplin, O. 2004. "Sophocles' *Philoctetes*, Seamus Heaney's, and Some Other Recent Half-rhymes." In E. Hall, F. Macintosh, and A. Wrigley, eds., *Dionysus since 69: Greek Tragedy at the Dawn of the Third Millennium*, Oxford, 145–67.

Taplin, O. 2009. "The Homeric Convergences and Divergences of Seamus Heaney and Michael Longley." In S. J. Harrison, ed., *Living Classics: Greece and Rome in Contemporary Poetry in English*, Oxford, 163–71.

Tritle, L. 2006. "Thucydides and the Cold War." In M. Meckler, ed., *Classical Antiquity and the Politics of America: from George Washington to George W. Bush*, Waco, TX, 127–40.

Turner, P., transl. 1994. *Longus. Daphnis and Chloe, with 42 colour plates after the lithographs by Marc Chagall*. Munich.

Van Steen, G. 2000. *Venom in Verse: Aristophanes in Modern Greece*. Princeton, NJ.

Van Steen, G. 2007. "Enacting History and Patriotic Myth: Aeschylus' *Persians* on the Eve of the Greek War of Independence." In E. Bridges, E. Hall, and P. J. Rhodes, eds., *Cultural Responses to the Persian Wars*, Oxford, 299–329.

Verstraete, B. and V. Provencal, eds. 2005. *Same-sex Desire and Love in Greco-Roman Antiquity and in the Classical Tradition of the West*. Special Issue of *Journal of Homosexuality* 49: 3–4.

Vidal-Naquet, P. 1995. *Politics Ancient and Modern*. Cambridge.

Vigus, J. 2009. *Platonic Coleridge*. Oxford and London.

Walcott, D. 1949. *Epitaph for the Young*. Bridgetown.

Walcott, D. 1990. *Omeros*. London.

Walton, M. 1984. *The Greek Sense of Theatre*. London.

Walton, M. 2006. *Found in Translation: Greek drama in English*. Cambridge.

Wang, J. 1997. *Novelistic Love in the Platonic Tradition: Fielding, Faulkner, and the Postmodernists*. Lanham MD.

Webster, T. B. L. 1959. *The Birth of Modern Comedy of Manners*. Canberra.

West, M. L., ed. and transl. 2003. *Homeric Hymns. Homeric Apocrypha. Lives of Homer*. Cambridge, MA.

Wetmore, K. 2001. *The Athenian Sun in an African Sky*. Jefferson, NC.

Wetmore, K. 2003. *Black Dionysus: Greek Tragedy and African American Theatre*. Jefferson, NC.

Wilamowitz-Moellendorff, U. von. 1908. *Greek Historical Writing, and Apollo. Two Lectures Delivered before the University of Oxford*. Oxford.

Williamson, M. 2009. "Sappho and Pindar in the Nineteenth and Twentieth Centuries." In F. Budelmann, ed., *The Cambridge Companion to Greek Lyric*, Cambridge, 352–70.

Wilson, P. 1989. "'High Pindaricks Upon Stilts': A Case-Study in the Eighteenth-Century Classical Tradition." In G. W. Clarke, ed., *Rediscovering Hellenism: The Hellenic Inheritance and the English Imagination*, Cambridge, 23–41.

Winkler, M, ed. 2001. *Classical Myth and Culture in the Cinema*. 2nd edn. Oxford.

Wood, T. E. B. 1972. *The Word "Sublime" and its Context, 1650–1760*. The Hague.

Zamarou, R. 2005. *Kavaphēs kai Platōn*. Athens.

Zuba, S. 2009. *Iris Murdoch's Contemporary Retrieval of Plato: The Influence of an Ancient Philosopher on a Modern Novelist, with a foreword by W. Desmond*. Lewiston, NY.

Index

The index was compiled by Markus Hafner, Annamaria Peri, Julian Schreyer and Janina Sieber, Munich.

A Companion to Greek Literature, First Edition. Edited by Martin Hose and David Schenker.
© 2016 John Wiley & Sons, Inc. Published 2020 by John Wiley & Sons, Inc.